Goldmine's

PRICE GUIDE

to

·COLLECTIBLE·
·RECORD·
ALBUMS

FOURTH EDITION

Neal Umphred

with special contributors
Norman Feinberg & Gary Johnson

Published by

**krause
publications**

700 E. State Street • Iola, WI 54990-0001

Please call or write for our free catalog of music publications. Our toll-free number to place an order or obtain a free catalog is 800-258-0929 or please use our regular business telephone 715-445-2214 for editorial comment and further information.

Library of Congress Catalog Number: 89-83584
ISBN: 0-87341-325-3

Printed in the United States of America

Table of Contents

An Acknowledging Foreword

First and oh so important: The prices in this book are for Near Mint records. That is: *A nearly mint record comfortably housed in a nearly mint cover*. I stress this because far too many folks out there selling used records haven't the foggiest damn notion of what "Near Mint" means and attempt to palm off inferior merchandise under the self-imposed delusion that they *do* know what they are doing! (Please turn to that portion of the introduction dealing with "Grading Records" and read *exactly* what "Near Mint" means.) When it comes time for pricing their wares, many of these sellers gaze longingly at the NM value listed in the book when they should be staring fixedly at the VG+ column and adjusting their way down. Somehow, a lot of the flak falls on *my* head. And I ain't pickin' on dealers; what the buyer thinks is generally irrelevant to my point here. . .

Not a very friendly opening? Then let's try something from my foreword to *Goldmine's Price Guide To Collectible Jazz Albums*, quoted here for its uplifting qualities *and* the fact that my girlfriend wants to see her name in two books:

"In May of 1993 I sojourned to the mysterious East and did a couple of shows in the New York/New Jersey area. After setting up my table with assorted price guides for sale I was accosted by an irate jazz fan who let me know in less than subtle terms what a disservice I had done the hobby with the preposterously low prices I had assigned the records, more or less across the board. As I attempted to deal with this man's [genuine and heartfelt] criticisms, a second jazz aficionado approached and asked for a word or two with the author.

"Excusing myself from the first person, I then sat back and listened as I was criticized again for the pricing of the jazz book. 'And what, exactly, is your complaint, sir?,' says I. 'Well, they're too damned high! You're pricing the average collector out of the market,' says he. At which point I introduced the two collectors to one another. Accompanying me that day was the inimitable Jan Bittenbender, who was appalled by the directness of the gentlemen's attacks and inquired if this was normal behavior for record collectors. I wasn't sure how to answer. . .

"At another show, a collector approached me and politely inquired as to how I had arrived at a value of $100 for a certain female vocalist's album. 'Why, is it too low?' I asked. 'Oh, no. I would think it's way too high,' he replied. To which I asked my favorite retort: 'And do you have a near mint copy in your collection?' And he assured me that he had scored a virtually unplayed mint copy a couple of years ago [for a fraction of the value listed in my book]. 'I'll give you $100 for it right now,' I said, offering him five twenties. 'I'd never sell it for that!' at which point he paused, then added 'Uh, I see your point.'

"Neither of these accountings are meant to insult the intelligence or the integrity of the individuals involved. Rather, it is an attempt to provide the reader with a glimpse into some of the pitfalls that accompany the issuance of a price guide in any field of collectibles. . ."

Since the publication of these paragraphs, I have witnessed a not too complimentary review of the jazz book by a major dealer who castigated me for the *preposterously low prices assigned to hundreds of collectible jazz albums*. A

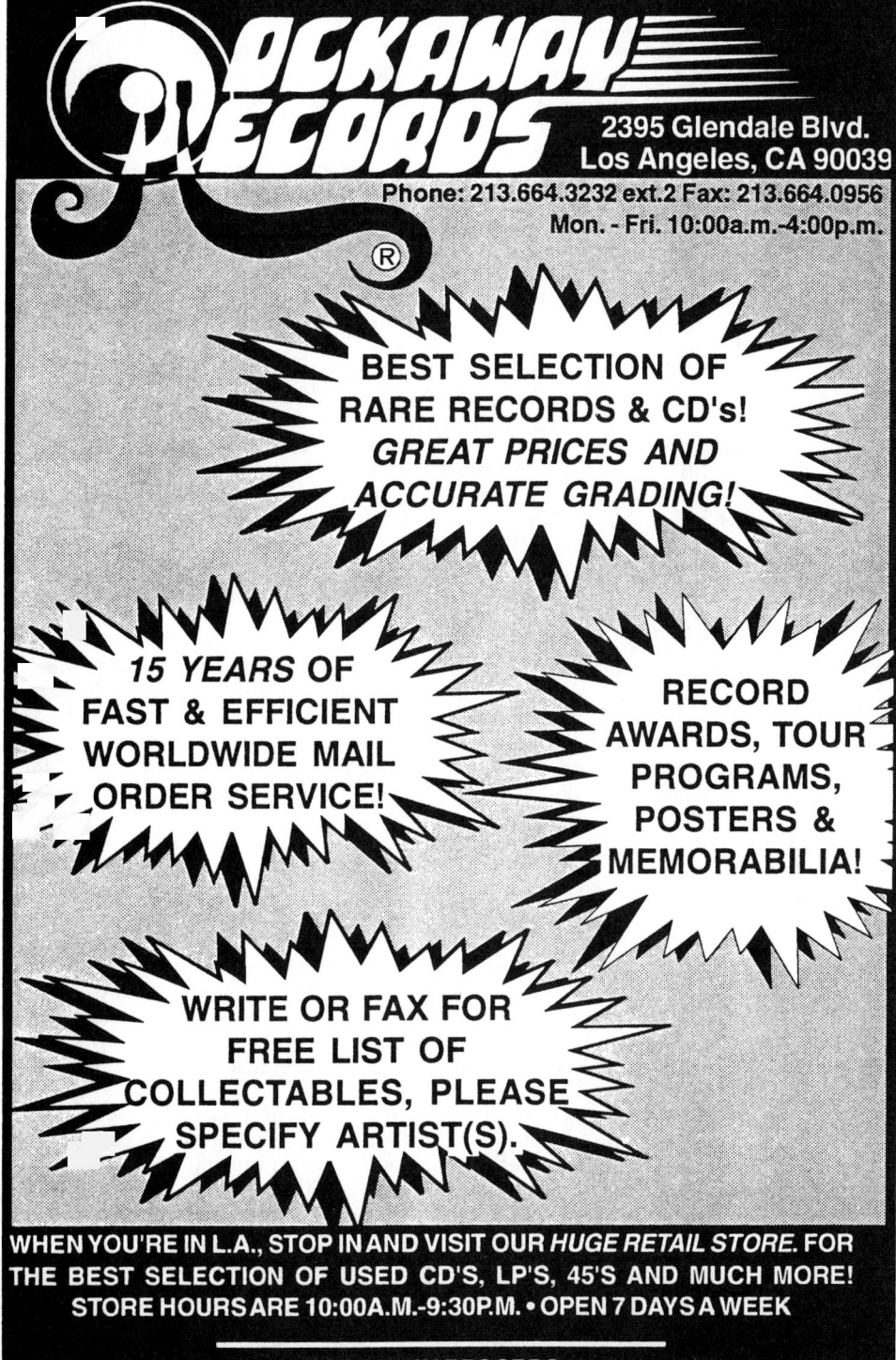

few days after reading this review I received a letter from a collector castigating me for the *preposterously high prices assigned to hundreds of collectible jazz albums.*, claiming that, since the advent of the compact disc, so many vinyl collectors had dumped their LPs on the market that he hasn't had to pay a fraction of the values quoted in my book.

And then there is the *other* side: Probably the single most oft-repeated remark I receive concerning this book went something like "I don't care about the prices; just get the listings right." And, I can assure you, the listings in this edition are far more accurate— if less complete— than those of the previous three. Which brings us to the good news/bad news department: The bad news is that, due to the ever-accumulating data, and the lack of pages (gotta keep these books affordable), I have had to jettison thousands of titles from this edition.

That's right, literally thousands of LPs that were in the third edition are missing from this one (good reason to hang onto your older editions). Titles dropped were those with an established value of $20 or less. That is, I have eliminated most of the "common stuff." Why they were dropped is the good news: I have replaced them *with thousands of new titles* with values in excess of $25. While this steers the book even further from complete discographies (never an intended goal by me but a complaint I hear nonetheless), it does head the book even further towards the goal I have always envisioned and that the book's title makes obvious: a price guide for truly "collectible" albums. This influx of new listings is made possible by the expanding interest in aspects of music that have been all but ignored over the years.

Witness the explosion of interest in, and the consequent rise in values of, "cocktail music" and other "incredibly strange music" of the '50s and early '60s. A few years ago, many of these hotly sought-after artifacts, originally recorded and released to fit comfortably in Ward and June Cleaver's collection for those weekend get-togethers (come to think of it, Martin Denny does whet one's whistle for a modestly dry martini) could be found in dollar bins everywhere. . .

The majority of the photos in this edition were taken by John Christensen of Renton, WA, (who provided the negatives to KP for processing) from his own collection and that of George Bigelow of Everett, WA. Other photos by Ben Brown of Raleigh, NC, and Cristina Taccone of San Francisco, CA . These two brought so many great covers to my place for approval that after shooting eight rolls of film, I wasn't able to get even a tenth of the records from my own collection shot that I had intended for this edition! Should the reader be interested in submitting photos of albums for consideration, please follow this advice: Use a 35 MM camera with 400 ASA (or 27° ISO) black & white film (Tri-X appears to work best) at 1/125th-of-a-second shutter speed (or faster) to prevent blurring.

Shoot the covers from directly above— *not at an angle*— on a pure white backdrop allowing as much of the cover to fill the frame as possible without cutting off the edges of the album. Set at least two table lamps with non-glare bulbs on either side of the cover and, holding the camera with a *masterful* hand or using a tripod, making sure that there is as little glare as possible on the cover. Any and all photos should be addressed to me, Box 40116, Bellevue, WA, USA 98015. For those wishing to contribute corrections, additions or suggestions for future editions, please don't hesitate to write me. While I can't promise that each and every letter will get a personal response in the mail, I do assure you that every bit of data is entered into the computer and given consideration.

There are certain aspects of record collecting that are not dealt with in this—or any other—book. For instance, the original metal stamper for the *Johnny Burnette & The Rock And Roll Trio* album was recently found. While it is unlikely that the finder will part with this artifact, should he *choose* to sell it, such a treasure would no doubt easily fetch five figures! While this is truly a wondrous find, that it qualifies as a legitimate "record collectible" is debatable.

Another situation that needs addressing is the case of "rare" records that no one seems to want. Charlie Essmeier writes "I recently saw a white label promo of *Sam The Sham And The Pharaohs' Second Album.* Does anyone want it? It is undoubtedly a very rare record and I'm sure a white label of *Wooly Bully* would excite people, if I could find one." In my own case, I purchased a small cache of mint records that included a number of such promos, such as Barry Manilow, Yes and The Eagles, among others. I priced them at $10-15 each and took 'em to our shows here in Seattle. I believe I sold one of them in two years. . .

One thing I will not be a part of is placing premium values on albums with holes punched out of them, ridiculously referred to as "promo-holes." it's simply to easy for anyone with a hole-punch to make up all the promos the market will bare. So, in my guides, these are simply cut-outs. This does not include covers where "PROMO" or "FREE" are perforated into the corner. At this point, these aforementioned promos remain, for the most part, uncatalogued.

Which brings us to stock copies that are stamped promo, which are starting to receive attention from starved collectors who have everything else by a favorite artist. While I can't go into all of the details, alums designated promotionally by being stamped having stickers affixed to the cover, etc., are escalating in value, a trend that should continue.

While the counterfeiting of records has existed almost since the first record was manufactured, in the collectibles market of the past thirty or so years, most unauthorized reproductions of rare records have been done on a small scale by collectors for collectors. That is, the repros have rarely been presented as anything but repros. This is not the case with the current mania for RIAA Gold and Platinum Record Awards, where duplicity appears to be as ingrained in many of the suppliers as the desire to hang a cherished Award on the wall is with the buyer. This sorry state of affairs is dealt with in Christopher Chatman's article, "Genuine, Pirate & Fake RIAA Awards," located in this book's appendices.

Acknowledgements

As it has been pointed out to me that it is traditional to do one's acknowledgements in the foreword, I will do just that for the first time. Amassing the data necessary for this and other price guides takes years and, even after thumbing through countless books, magazines, fanzines, discographies, etc., much of the most important information remains elusive. That is because the collectors and dealers privy to this knowledge tend to guard it religiously, often in the belief that ignorance best serves their own needs. And an unwary owner of a truly rare record *can* be duped, especially if the information is either not in the price guide or, perhaps worse, is entered erroneously. My job is not to tout myself as an authority in any given field but, rather, to seek out the truly knowledgeable and convince them to share their information.

As the cover states, both Norman Feinberg and Gary Johnson deserve special accolades. Gary, who with brother Wayne is responsible for the Los Angeles branch of Rockaway Records, has been a constant source of information for so many years I can't remember when I didn't rely on him for advice! He has fed me so many additions and corrections that his input probably permeates every page of this book.

And Norman, who has been keeping collectors *and* dealers awake for years with his ads for New York's Blue Chip Records, stepped forward and willingly addressed the most pressing need of the first two editions of this book: The pre-Beatles rhythm'n blues and rock'n roll albums that constitute the majority of "the rarest and most valuable albums in the world." Norman has been avidly— and intelligently— collecting albums so long that he can remember when it seemed like he was the only person in New York who wasn't after doowop 45s. . .

While I receive a good deal of input from collectors and dealers from many countries— through phone calls, at record shows or shops, mostly through the mail— much of it consists of a single addition, correction (thanks to everyone, and there were *lots* of you, who corrected me on The Weird-Ohs) or a bit of advice. I simply can't acknowledge each and every one in these pages, but I do like to reserve space for those who contribute more than a little, some *quite* a bit more. So, without those folks listed below plus Joanne McConnell and Kinks Kompletist Roger Kulp, whose addresses I lost, this would be a different, and, believe me, a lesser book. . .

Gregg Biggs *CVC Collectables* *Celina, OH*	*Charlie Essmeier* *Retro Records* *Salt Lake City, UT*	*Norman Feinberg* *Blue Chip Records* *South Salem, NY*
Michael & Virginia Hall *Eagle Records* *Topeka, KS*	*Gary Johnson* *Rockaway Records* *Los Angeles, CA*	*Scott* *Saturn Records* *Oakland, CA*
George Bigelow *Everett, WA*	*David Edwards* *Eaton, OH*	*Cliff Morehouse* *North Haven, CT*
Jim Blatt *Vancouver, WA*	*John J. Fitzpatrick* *W. Peabody, MA*	*Lawrence M. Palmer* *Arlington, VA*
Stephen Braitman *San Francisco, CA*	*Joe Goldmark* *San Francisco, CA*	*Jef Michael Piehler* *Burbank, CA*
Vick Brown *Silver Spring, MD*	*Steve Harris* *Panarama City, CA*	*Walter Stempek* *Salem, OR*
John Christensen *Renton, WA*	*Kerry Hopkins* *Falls Church, VA*	*Delano Stewart* *Eastpointe, MI*
G. L. Conley *Joshua Tree, CA*	*Viktor Lindner* *Salzburd, Austria*	*Rod Sweetland* *Sacramento, CA*
John S David *Elmsford, NY*	*Seth A. Mandel* *West Hartford, CT*	*John DeBlaiso* *Renton, WA*

While there are some entertaining books out there that occasionally reach the big book stores, most of the publications of interest to collectors are almost invisible. If I kept repeating the bibliography of source books, eventually it would take up pages. So, for a more complete listing of the volumes used in the compilation of the first three volumes of this book, just refer to those volumes.

While most of the new data in this volume comes from individuals, these books did help: John Storm Roberts' *Black Music Of Two Worlds*, Praeger Publishers, 1972; Tony Rees' *Rare Rock-A Collectors' Guide*, Blandford Press 1985; Kristin Baggelaar and Donald Milton's *Folk Music: More Than A Song*, Thomas Y. Crowell Co., 1976; and Ray M. Lawless' *Folksingers And Folksongs In America,* Duell, Sloan & Pearce, 1960. And, thank the gods for books such as *Incredibly Strange Music,* a series of interviews with people who collect records outside of the norm assembled by V. Vale and Andrea Juno, Re/Search Publications, 1993.

Finally, will every dealer and collector-who-occasionally-sells please Please PLEASE me by putting a stop to the practice of affixing price stickers to the front covers of albums! I know this is stretching things a wee bit, but every time I walk into a store or browse through a show and witness this willful assault upon the integrity of the artifact for sale I wonder if, when selling a used car, this person paints the asking price on the hood. If you can't put the records in protective plastic bags with stickers, why not try removeable labels on the back cover.

Neal Umphred
September 1994

So, Who's Really High Here?

"Yo! Just because one person paid — — — for a record doesn't mean that's what the record's *really* worth. . ." This is the remark I hear most often concerning the [presumed] excessively high values assigned to a record in one of my books. And, for the most part, I agree with the sentiments in this observation. . . most of the time. Not only do I generally *not* consider an extreme price paid for a fairly common record but the reader will note that I tend to take a rather conservative tack (those who know me personally might say I have a jaundiced view) when navigating the values of the more recent "collectibles" or artists. For instance, there was a time not too long ago when anything bearing Debbie Harry's likeness was an instant sale (including bootlegs featuring Ms. Harry's lovely face superimposed upon some rather, er, raunchily posed figures). Or who can forget the great Police vogue that followed? And Springsteen collectors have long paid excessive prices for new promos that have gained little in value since their release.

Certainly I try not to let such phenomenon have an undue effect on the values assigned. But, when the *only* copy of a record that has been offered for sale or auction on the open market for several years sells above and beyond anyone's wildest imaginations, when that sale is the only documented sale of that item in recent memory (and likely to be the only one for some time), then that sale, by definition, *must* have a bearing on the value assigned that record. And four-figure sales for collectible records have become common. So, when the reader pages through this book and succumbs to "sticker shock" when coming upon a truly rare (and desirable) record, please bear in mind. . .

. . .the prices in this book attempt to document what records are worth *on the current collectors market*. What that means to you, the average reader, is that these prices reflect more or less *what you should expect to pay an established dealer to acquire a record that you desire*. Should you, a collector, choose to sell your records, the chances are good that, unless you run an ad in *Goldmine*, *you will not see these prices being paid for your records*. Certainly, if you want to sell them to a dealer, you won't even come close. (Unfortunately, record dealers are not known for paying the most reasonable of rates for their inventory. In fact, if they entered any other business and tried to run it the way they run a record business, they'd be collecting food stamps within the year.)

The price that anyone will buy (or sell) an item for is often linked closely with the geographic and economic environment he or she is living in. A collector in New York City *should expect to pay more* for a given item than a collector from Wilkes-Barre, PA. After all, the Manhattan collector pays more for rent, a slice of pizza, a restaurant dinner, or tickets to the Mets and Yankees, because a New York City resident will be paid commensurately more for his job. Similarly, just as a dealer takes for granted that he or she will pay less for records when stocking his or her shop in Wilkes-Barre, the dealer should also expect to sell them for less *in the same market*.

This book makes no attempt at completeness; rather, the reader will find more than 25,000 listings that cover, more or less, the most collectible records in the most collected genres. While the discographies of many artists are complete, for others they are obviously incomplete. This approach is not meant as an artistic judgement on my behalf but rather an economical one. There *are* going to be instances where the information here is incomplete or wrong; it is almost unimaginable for any book listing tens of thousands of records not to make some errors. These may range in nature from common typographical errors, to transferring erroneous data from a flawed source, to incomplete research (missing catalog numbers, incorrect values assigned to records).

Although the scope of this book is wide ranging in terms of domestic releases, it does not begin to detail the staggering variety of collectible records from around the world. In most countries an album need sell only 100,000 copies to qualify for gold status, one-fifth the minimum for an American release. In effect this means that hit LPs in many countries are "rare" by American standards. The likelihood of their turning up here years later is remote. While those Americans who actively collect foreign records are relatively few, the even smaller amount of the truly rare pieces makes competition intense.

A rare and desirable rock 'n roll album from the '50s from such major markets as Canada, England or France in VG condition will regularly sell for hundreds of dollars, as near mint ones may not exist at this point in time! Imports since 1970 are more common and command reasonable prices. The attraction of these records are self-evident upon examination: In terms of the variety of releases and the quality of both the pressing and the appearance, the United States takes a back seat to many other countries.

It is difficult to view a collection of foreign records and not feel the desire to plunge right into a whole new field of collecting, one that is as rewarding and far more aesthetic than merely collecting domestic releases. Some dealers make a point of keeping large inventories of the more desirable recent releases. At the time, there is no reliable source for pricing and comparative shopping is nearly impossible. If the reader chooses to get into this aspect of the hobby, he or she will have to contact other fans and collectors and learn from scratch.

Page Breakdown

Artists are listed alphabetically using a single artist's last name first while the first important word in a group's name is the basis for their listing. When an artist's name is followed by a slash "/" and another name, it means that the artist has recorded under two similar names. For instance, "CHICAGO/CHICAGO TRANSIT AUTHORITY," tells the reader that albums listed under either of those two names can be found under that one listing.

When two different artists name appear in a heading, such as "BROWN, ROY / WYNONIE HARRIS," where the names are obviously different artists and there is a space to either side of the slash, the reader needs to understand that the album(s) listed there is a compilation of tracks by the artists.

References are kept to a minimum and refer the reader to another artist when the artist or group in question is named in the title of an album or is inseparably linked with the recording. Listing references for artists who appeared on other artist's recording is a book in itself. Should the reader desire one, Terry Hounsome and Tim Chambre's *Rock Record* (Blandford Press, 1987) is recommended, with thousands of listings of who played on what, when, and where!

The records are listed chronologically by label, interrupted by sound-track appearances. I have used fairly standard alphabetization throughout; there should be no real surprises for anyone familiar with an encyclopedia. Necessary notes are usually listed in italics in parentheses below the appropriate section or selections. Following is an example from the Julie London listing:

Label/Catalogue #		Title	Year	VG+	NM
LONDON, JULIE					
Liberty LRP-3006	*(M)*	**Julie Is Her Name**	1956	**20.00**	**50.00**
Liberty LST-7027	*(S)*	**Julie Is Her Name** *(Blue vinyl)*	1958	**40.00**	**100.00**
Liberty LST-7027	*(S)*	**Julie Is Her Name** *(Red vinyl)*	1958	**40.00**	**100.00**
Liberty LST-7027	*(S)*	**Julie Is Her Name**	1958	**16.00**	**40.00**
Liberty LRP-3012	*(M)*	**Lonely Girl**	1956	**20.00**	**50.00**
Liberty LST-7029	*(S)*	**Lonely Girl**	1958	**16.00**	**40.00**
Liberty SL-9002	*(M)*	**Calendar Girl** *(Gatefold cover)*	1956	**40.00**	**100.00**
Liberty LRP-3043	*(M)*	**About The Blues**	1957	**16.00**	**40.00**
Liberty LST-7012	*(S)*	**About The Blues**	1958	**16.00**	**40.00**
Liberty LRP-3060	*(M)*	**Make Love To Me**	1957	**16.00**	**40.00**
— *Liberty mono albums above have green labels; stereo albums have silver on black labels.*—					
Liberty LRP-3291	*(M)*	**Julie's Golden Greats** *(White cover)*	1963	**8.00**	**20.00**
Liberty LST-7291	*(S)*	**Julie's Golden Greats** *(White cover)*	1963	**10.00**	**25.00**
Liberty LRP-3291	*(M)*	**Julie's Golden Greats** *(Black cover)*	1963	**8.00**	**20.00**
Liberty LST-7291	*(S)*	**Julie's Golden Greats** *(Black cover)*	1963	**10.00**	**25.00**
(Liberty 32/7291 is a compilation with one new track.)					
— *Liberty albums above have black labels with a gold & white logo on the side.*—					

The first column indicates the label and catalog number. The second features a key notation for the record's sound: an "M" denotes a monaural record-ing, while an "S" means the record is stereo. An "E" indicates that the stereo effect of the album has been electronically created while a "P" indicates a partially stereo record (while most of the tracks *are* stereo, one or more are either mono or electronic stereo). "Q" indicates quadraphonic.

Finally, "DJ" means that the record is a record issued exclusively for promotional reasons. That is, the title and number and, usually, the specific con-tent, were not made available to the public. This would generally indicate in-store samplers to arouse consumer interest, and radio station specials, such as interviews, live performances or samplers. Promos in the '50s and '60s should be assumed to be mono; those from the '70s on, stereo.

The record's title is the middle column; specific notes short enough to place on the same line follow. In this case, the existence of two different colored vinyl versions of Liberty 7027 are noted. (Ms. London's discography also indi-cates that the stereo versions of her early albums were mixed and released sev-eral years after the initial release of the mono originals.) These are followed by the regular first pressing on black vinyl.

Subsequent releases, also listed, have standard single sleeve covers. This is followed by the year of release. The final two columns, the prices, are for records in the two most "collectible" conditions, very-good-plus (VG+) and near-mint (NM), and are dealt with at length below.

For those artists who achieved a long lasting popularity that saw their recordings repeatedly reissued I have attempted to list brief notations about particular records. *Notes indented beneath an album and enclosed in parenthe-ses refer only to the title under which it is listed*, unless, of course, the note says otherwise. These may refer to that record's particular label or any other aspect

Julie London's discography includes various label changes, colored vinyl, and even a cover variation. While her early albums have long been sought after both for their lovingly exploitational covers and the sultry, close-miked singing within, collectors have awakened to the fact that many of her late '60s albums are very difficult to find.

that requires attention. In the example above, the note "(Liberty 32/7291 is a compilation with one new track.)" refers only to *Julie's Golden Greats*. In this particular note there are two parts, the second referring specifically to the stereo release. (Of course, the parenthetical notes tell the reader that there are two different covers for this album.)

Notes that are centered and open (i.e., lacking parentheses) refer to two or more titles and are almost exclusively dealing with label specifications. These notes always include the qualifier "above" in their statements! As in the case of the above example: "Liberty mono albums above have green labels; stereo albums have silver on black labels." which applies to all of the albums above it.

There are several other parenthetical notes that are used on the same line as the title (space allowing): "No cover" indicates a record issued in a plain, unmarked cardboard sleeve (usually privately printed albums). Most soundtrack albums are listed as "Soundtrack;" in some cases, the abbreviation "Sdtk" was used. Similarly, while it was unnecessary to denote titles by specialist labels (Mobile Fidelity, Nautilus, Direct Disk) as half-speed masters, major labels that dipped into the audiophile field with such product are noted as "Half-speed master" (or simply "Half-speed"). Other peculiarities (colored vinyl, white label promos, etc.) are also noted in parentheses with the title.

Grading the Records

When purchasing a record at a show or through the mail (or even many stores) the buyer does not get to listen to it. For that reason, records are usually graded by visual standards, not aural. Unfortunately, this method relies on the subjectivity of the grader's eyes— or viewpoint— and the fact that records do not always play as good— or bad— as they look. For this reason *records almost always look better when selling than when buying*. Of course, the arguments against play-grading are similar: the subjectivity of the listener is also a factor, a factor that is multiplied by the type of equipment the grader is playing the record on to form his or her judgement. So, for the sake of convenience and necessity, visual grading is the standard by which almost all dealers and collectors work.

When grading a disc, *grade the overall wear of the vinyl*. A record advertised as "NM" or "VG" should tell the prospective buyer the shape of the playable vinyl. Common sense should be used: un-played records that are warped cannot be Mint. When defining the grades, it is difficult to describe several without discussing defects and/or the way the disc plays; these are included to help define the grade, not to cause confusion. Such defects as stickers on the label or tape on the jacket should be addressed separately with abbreviated notations (a list of which can be found in the opposing sidebar, "Record Collecting Abbreviations"). A reliable set of these notations have been developed over the years covering virtually every type of defect that can occur to a record or its cover; a list of most of the more common abbreviations and their meanings follow the grading definitions below.

Visual grading is most important in mail-order transactions where a buyer doesn't see his purchase until his check has cleared the bank. Grading needs to be as accurate as possible. The aim of grading is to make the buyer visualize the record and not be disappointed when that record arrives! A record that is accurately graded should play the same (or better) than the grading.

In-person deals do not require a grade of any sort; if you are holding a record that has obviously been played a hundred times, you don't need a grade to determine whether or not you are going to purchase that disc.

Always grade records under a good, steady light. A 100 watt light bulb in a common desk-lamp will do an adequate job; most major defects will jump out and allow you to make a reasonably accurate assessment. Grading a record using light from the ceiling or from deflected sunlight entering the window will often "hide" paper scuffs, discoloration, groove wear and even some fingerprints. Remember, mistakes in grading are a problem all dealers and collectors are prone to make. Do not condemn a dealer for one mistake; but, when the mistake is the norm, find someone else to buy your records from. . .

Mint. A Mint (M) record should appear to have just left the manufacturer without any handling; that is, it should appear perfect! No scuffs or scratches, blotches or stains, labels or writing, tears or splits; nothing. And age has nothing to do with it; *the same standards for Mint apply to a 10" soundtrack from 1954 as they do to a heavy metal album from 1989!* There are no sliding values for Mint.

A Mint album cover should appear to have never have had a record in it; no ring-wear, dog-eared corners, writing, seam-splits. I define ring-wear as any imprint on the cover from the record that it formerly held. *Any* imprint. To many dealers and collectors the ink has to be worn off for them to recognize ring-wear and grade a cover down. Uh-uh. Mint means perfect and nothing else.

Near Mint. A record that is otherwise Mint but has one or two tiny, inconsequential flaws that do not affect the play is Near Mint (NM) and should command 85-95% of the Mint price. For many, Near Mint and Mint-Minus mean the same thing; for the sake of this article, they are interchangeable. When dealing with a seller that discriminates between the two grades, inquire as to what the dealer means when he calls one record M- and another NM.

Many dealers and collectors take the position that any used (opened) record cannot be verified as Mint so they use M- to describe what appears to be a perfect record that has been opened. Covers should still be close to perfect with minor signs of wear or age just becoming evident: slight ring-wear, minor denting to a corner, or writing on the cover should all be noted properly.

Many records *are available* in Near Mint/Mint condition, although these are generally more recent and the prices are nominal. That is, most dealers set a minimum price on the records they sell in their store, usually dollars ($3.99-4.99), just for normal, everyday, all-too-readily-available records. Whether they are unplayed or "merely" near mint the price will be the same: it wouldn't be worth the dealer's time to stock the single unless that minimum price was met.

Sometimes referred to as "Excellent," a ***Very Good Plus*** (VG+) record has been handled and played either infrequently or very carefully. That is, an item obviously not perfect, but not *too* far from it. On a disc, this could mean that there are light paper scuffs from sliding in and out of a sleeve or the vinyl may have lost some— *not all*— of its original luster. A slight scratch that did not affect play in an otherwise nearly Mint disc would be acceptably VG+ for most collectors; a scratch of any sort that audibly clicked throughout the music would not be acceptable. Always list the flaws in a VG+ record or cover.

As a rule of thumb, a VG+ item is worth 50-60%, of the NM value, although this ratio varies with the rarity of the item. That is, a record that is fairly common in NM/M condition has little real value in VG+ to most collectors; consequently 25-35% may be more appropriate. On the other hand, truly rare records will fetch 75% in VG+. (By rare, I am referring to items in which the supply is merely a fraction of the demand and the record sells for hundreds of dollars. . .) On covers, some wear from storage is acceptable, especially light wear that does not affect the beauty of the artwork. Listing the flaws when selling is safest.

Very Good (VG) records will display visible signs of handling and playing, such as loss of vinyl luster, light surface scratches, groove wear, and spindle trails from countless spins on the turntable. A VG record looks like it will have some audible surface noise when it is played, although any such noise should not overwhelm the musical experience. VG records should appear to have been well-played although well-loved by a responsible owner. Gouges in the plating from slapping the disc down onto the spindle, rips in the label from pulling stickers formerly affixed, etc., are all unacceptable.

As more and more collectors spend more and more money on their acquisitions, the lower limits of acceptability for an item to be admitted into their collection rises. That is, to many collectors, a record in VG condition is not acceptable unless the item is truly rare and virtually unavailable in any other condition! And then, only if the price is scaled appropriately to match the condition. Used but not abused might sum up this grade. A VG record should command approximately 20-30% of the Near Mint price.

This is a difficult grade when discussing paper goods. Like a disc, usually a cover is VG when a variety of problems are evident: ring wear, seam splits, bent corners, loss of gloss, stains, etc. An aggravated combination of two of these problems— never all of them— would likely cause a sleeve to be graded VG.

Good ("G") in record collecting parlance all too often means a beat, trashed, take-it-to-the-flea-market frisbee. Good should mean that the record is well-played with any number of defects that collectors normally shy away from, such as an almost complete loss of surface sheen, aggravating surface noise, etc. Still, the purchaser, knowing full well that he or she is buying a Good record, should be able to take it home, slap it onto the turntable and have a good time listening to it. Records that do not provide this most fundamental requirement are just no good. A Good record should command 10-15% of the Near Mint price.

A Good cover has seen considerable handling over a course of years and displays the obvious signs: ring-wear on the cover; some seam-splitting, particularly along the bottom, which would receive the brunt of the record's sliding in and out; corners may be dog-eared to a light degree; an infatuated owner may have written his or her name somewhere; etc. If a record or cover is beneath your contempt, it is not in "G" condition; look below for the appropriate grade.

Any record or cover that does not qualify for the above "Good" grading should be seen as **Poor** and command 0-5% of the Mint price. Make a friend and give any "P" record away as a freebee to anyone who expresses interest in it. . .

Finally, it should always be borne in mind that visual evidence can be deceiving. A record properly manufactured with a high quality plating may look VG+ and play Near Mint; this is particularly true of records from the '50s through the mid '60s, when print runs were dramatically smaller, vinyl was fresher and more care was paid to the entire procedure. Records from this period are a better investment in VG+ condition than the more recent American product.

In fact, many LPs from the '50s can be purchased in VG condition at reasonable prices and will play far better than the price paid would indicate. A record manufactured from recycled vinyl with poor plating (too many from the past 15 years) may look Mint and play VG. Still, most dealers do not have the time to listen to each item in their inventory, so visual standards remain.

Pricing the Records

If you, as a collector, have spent more than a decade hunting for a key item for your collection, all the while assuming that *you will find it in nice shape at an affordable price* (the goal—and, too often, the delusion—of every collector of anything), at some point the realization that such a goal may not be as attainable as first surmised will probably occur. Which brings me to my redundant but sagely advice: *When you are offered a record for which you have been actively searching for more than five years, do not argue with the price. . . pay it.* The corollary to this bit of wisdom would be: If you don't, you may not see it again for another five years, *and* it will cost even more.

As for the fluctuations in the market, well, for those readers who expect values to rise automatically, the collectibles market is not all that different from the commodities market or the stock exchange, and *everyone* knows the wild fluctuations that occur there. So, while most prices do remain stable, or rise gradually, some rise dramatically while others actually go down. Value is established almost solely by supply and demand: Prices go up when the current demand is greater than the available supply; prices go down when the available supply is greater than the current demand.

Any number of factors can cause prices to rise or decline. The factors that cause the value of a rare, desirable record to rise are obvious. The most dramatic leveller is probably the warehouse find, where boxes of a supposedly rare record turn up in sufficient quantities to meet the immediate demand, driving its value down for the near future. On the most mundane of levels, the value of a fairly common, out of print album can decline when that album is released as a compact disc, although the drop is usually temporary. When the supply dropped on the market in the wake of the record's digitalized debut is exhausted, the record will often return to its earlier value.

So, the dealer should use this guide as just that. . . a guide. Basically, if you only find that this book helps point out the relatively rare pieces from the more common items, *even if you don't believe that you can get those prices in your market,* then the book is of value. Of course, for the collector, what may be of paramount importance is not the prices but the discographies themselves.

I believe that the more accurate, encompassing and detailed this book is the better it serves every one involved. For the dealer who is concerned that he or she may no longer be able to pick up good records for a [pitiful] fraction of their value—and as precarious an existence as wheeling and dealing in collectibles can be, that is certainly a justifiable fear—I maintain that while you will almost certainly find the instances of buying $100 records for a buck are diminished by the existence of this book, that the verification of the true market value of collec-

Record Collecting Abbreviations

Listed here are common abbreviations used in advertising to describe flaws and their locations on a record or cover. Dealers have different ways of using these abbreviations; some capitalize them ("DJ"), some use periods after each letter ("n.a.p.") and some use a slash ("c/o"). Those marked with an asterisk (*) should always be listed when advertising an item for sale or auction.

cc	*cut corner**
co	*cut out**
coh	*cut-out hole**
c-33	*compact-33 1/3 rpm single or EP*
cvr	*cover*
dj	*disc jockey, or promotional, copy*
imp	*import*
ips	*inches per second*
lbl	*label*
lp	*12" 33 1/3 rpm long playing album*
mo	*mono*
nap	*(does) not affect play*
ol	*on label*
org	*original*
pln cvr	*plain paper jacket (no picture or titles)*
promo	*promotional copy*
q	*quadraphonic*
re	*reissue*
reel	*reel to reel tape*
repro	*reproduction, or counterfeit*
2nd pr	*second pressing*
slt wrp	*slight warp**
sm	*saw mark (a cut-out mark)**
sm splt	*seam split**
sol	*sticker on the label**
sr	*slight ring-wear on the front cover**
st	*stereo*
ss	*still sealed*
stkr	*sticker*
10"	*10" 33 1/3 rpm album*
t&ts	*(disc jockey) title & timing strip*
toc	*tape on the cover**
tol	*tape on the label**
ts	*taped seams**
wlp	*white label promo*
wol	*writing on the label**

tible vinyl *by this book* encourages more and more people to spend their hard-earned money on otherwise dubious investments. That is, the advantage you lose in those buys are more than compensated for by being able to service a broader market, a more educated clientele.

Should this sound like a snow job, bear in mind that in virtually every other field of collecting the price guide(s) recognized by the collectors in that field have helped the dealers enormously. One has only to turn his or her attention to what comic books and sports cards have become. Both were once regarded as "lowly" as records—lower, really—and both have left records far behind as a volatile, fluid place of business and, yes, fun.

This book is not billed as the bible for record collectors nor as the blue book of vinyl junkies. *And* it is certainly not the "official" price guide for anything. Nor does this book reflect *my opinions* of what *your records* are worth. The prices here are an attempt *to document what collectible records are worth on the open collectors market*, primarily that market that is reached both nationally and internationally by dealers and collectors through the mail, either through such collectors publications as *Goldmine* or through individual mailing lists that have been assembled over a period of time. That is, that market which is the largest and most eager to purchase really rare records.

The records listed here are taken from a variety of printed sources plus the input of the contributors. This input and a constant scrutiny of the set-sale and auctions placed in the pages of *Goldmine* also played a part in the make-up of this book. I strived for a sense of internal consistency with the pricing so that the book as a whole works as a guideline for each region of the country to use as on outline for their own market. *Every item in this book has been scrutinized by several contributors.* The values that were decided upon represent a ball park value that takes into account each of the prices submitted by those contributors.

This book is not the work of one person; it does not reflect my opinions of what your records are worth. Instead, I solicited the assistance of many collectors and dealers whom I have known for several years, both personally and professionally. Each dealer and collector was requested to provide *current values based on recent sales or purchases*, not transactions from years ago.

The prices quoted are for opened copies in either VG+ or NM condition. I use a scale that evaluates the Very Good Plus, or Excellent, condition record as a sliding percentage of the NM value as little as 40% and as much as 66%. VG prices are, for easy reference, approximately one-half (50%) of the listed VG+ value. The normal rule of thumb for pricing is that the cover makes up 40-50% of the value and the record 50-60%, although there are exceptions to this rule.

For most used records the reader using this guide should start with the first, lower price and work his or her way up to a reasonable estimate. Most used records are not Near Mint and the reader is advised not to delude him/herself that the high price applies to each and every record found.

The prices quoted reflect the market during the period in which this book was assembled; *I cannot guarantee that they will remain the same for any length of time following the publication of this book.* In fact, price guides tend to have a direct—and often immediate—effect on the very market they attempt to chronicle.

The release of the new information from such a book into the general market can influence what collectors collect and, consequently, what prices are paid. Thus, prices listed here may be made obsolete *by their very listing*, especially when the listing offers new information or information that contradicts previously published information.

Okay— We've arrived at a point where my opinion of what your records are worth *does* come into play. . . There are some records that can be found in lesser conditions but are apparently impossible to find in Near Mint. In those cases no figure was assigned to the NM price column but a suggested range was noted parenthetically beneath the title. [Some notes are more detailed, giving a price range for the record in VG, VG+ and NM. This was necessary primarily for '50s R&B albums which may be plentiful in VG, rather rare in VG+ and all but impossible in NM.] This is not to imply that the record is worth either the highest or the lowest value but rather that this range is a reasonable assessment of the transactions over the past and the opinions of the contributors who wheel and deal in the specific area covering the specific title. Using The Beatles as an example:

BEATLES, THE

Vee Jay LP-1062	(M)	**Introducing The Beatles** *("Ad back")*	1963	*See below*
Vee Jay SR-1062	(P)	**Introducing The Beatles** *("Ad back")*	1963	*See below*

(Includes "Love Me Do" and "P.S. I Love You." The back cover has ads for 25 other Vee Jay albums. Mono copies have a suggested Near Mint value of $3,000-4,000; stereo copies have a suggested Near Mint value of $8,000-12,000.)

As noted in the price column, the reader's attention is referred to the note, which gives an estimated NM value for the mono version of the album of $3,000 to $4,000 and $8,000-12,000 for the stereo pressing. What this means for a seller with a near mint stereo copy is that he/she might consider asking $12,000 for the album but should not be upset if "forced" to accept a mere $8,000. Conversely, while a buyer might win this record for as little as $8,000 he should not be surprised to find the bidding escalate to the $12,000 range. The same title in lesser condition should cut the estimated value dramtically, as I use the minimum value in the spread as the base for the calculations. So, a VG+ stereo copy would have a range of approximately $3,500-5,500; a VG copy, $1,500-2,500.

Bear in my that these are my suggestions, not dictates. They also apply to records that meet the standards of grading espoused by this book, sold on the open, competitive market, and, generally, by dealers or collectors with some reputation for accuracy and honesty. Instances where these records sell for less (or more) will occur— do occur. The *average* dealer or collector is often years (at least months) behind the reality of the market when it comes to the specialized knowledge of truly rare records, mainly because they are so rare that few, if anyone, ever sees them for sale at any price.

The more knowledgeable you are, the more useful and informative this book will be, if only that the informed reader will be better able to assimilate the information and make use of it regularly.

Many collectors have expressed concern over the effects the overseas buyer has had on American records. The continued slump in America's ability to cope with honest competition (versus the collusion of the domestic market in general) may have glutted the coffers of the multi-national corporations that bend our elected officials' ears. This slump has also led to a weakened dollar and, thus, the ability of the European and Japanese collector to outbid the American collector. To ignore these events would be both futile and counter-productive. Thus, a reasonably common item that goes for a bigger dollar overseas is not unduly affected because the foreign collectors only purchase a fraction of the copies put up for sale each year!

But a record that turns up infrequently (only a few times a year), and invariably leaves the country to an overseas collector who bids two or three times what American collectors believe the record is "really" worth, then those prices *do* determine the value of those records. I would, in effect, be doing you, the user of this book, a disservice were I to choose any other option. *The average American collector needs to know what he or she should expect to have to bid to win a truly rare and desirable record in an open auction on the open market.* Please bear in mind that many of the records listed here, especially those with three figure values, will sell for considerably more overseas.

And then, of course, there are the budget labels. . . Many labels sprang up over the years that specialized in leasing masters of previously released material, usually of artists who were no longer hot, and all too often issuing albums in the cheapest possible manner: poor mastering, poor pressings on low grade vinyl, etc. These labels include Crown, Diplomat, Grand Prix, Guest Star, Spin-o-rama, Wyncote, and the undisputed king of low budget labels in America, Pickwick. While some of these labels did collect important material— Crown began by issuing great R&B— most of them issued albums of less than collectible consequence. Spingboard seemed to flood the department stores of America with a slew of new titles in the first few years of the '70s, many compiling sides that had not previously appeared on albums and which have become modestly collectible. Needless to say, most of the albums have little value and are almost impossible to sell, even sealed, for more than a few bucks.

Shrinkwrap, Cover Stickers & Bonus Photos

Please note that the prices quoted are for opened copies in either VG+ or NM condition. In many cases collectors are willing to pay a premium for still-sealed copies. Depending on the age and desirability of the record, the premium may be a modest 10% to 100% above the NM price; in the case of certain items, the increase would be greater. Sealed copies of Beatles albums on Capitol are worth three or four times the NM price listed in these pages.

Albums with a sticker on the shrink-wrap advertising an enclosed bonus or calling attention to a hit single generally command a premium above and beyond what plain shrink-wrap would generate. While this could be a modest 10% for common albums or less collectible artists, it can double the price of a rare record or desirable name.

Even more important is the practice of applying stickers directly to the cover. While dozens of Presley albums came with stickers on the shrink wrap, only a few carried a sticker on the cover and each of these is considerably more valuable than its corresponding number without the sticker. The first such album was *A Date With Elvis,* an album prepared while Elvis was in the U.S. Army in 1958-59. Nowhere on this album are the list of song titles and the possibility exists that this was to have been held as Elvis' "new" album should RCA be able to get Elvis into the studio while he was still in the service. The prepared sleeve *was* used for a compilation of earlier, released recordings and RCA applied a red sticker with the song titles directly to the front cover.

A year later the jacket for Elvis' first album of new recordings after leaving the Army was prepared while Elvis was still active. As RCA could not have known the album's contents, *Elvis Is Back!* was prepared without song titles printed on the cover. When Elvis was whisked into RCA's Nashville studios for four days in March and April, 1960, enough material for three singles and an album was completed. When the contents of the LP were decided, RCA again stuck a sticker with the song titles to the cover. (Later pressings of both albums have the contents printed on the cover.)

Capitol also took to applying stickers to covers calling attention to a big hit or something of note on the LP, including several Beach Boys and Kingston Trio albums (although they could not be identified in time for this volume). And, while they certainly require a premium, they are not in the league of the Presley items above. Of a different concern is the recently documented existence of the Beatles' first Apple album, *The Beatles,* with at least two different possible stickers attached to the otherwise blank white covers. One sticker, nine inches in length and a garishly translucent red, noted the album's song titles and other pertinent data. A second sticker, a more modest four inches in length, also exists. Given the nature of the album's pristine graphics, I would assume these stickers were applied to copies sent to radio stations so that programmers would know what they were receiving.

Companies often included a "bonus photo" to special albums or deluxe packagings. This practice became gospel with RCA's release of the [generally go-dawful] Elvis soundtracks of the '60s. These bonuses are noted when known throughout the listings. Should the reader have an album with such a bonus that is not listed, he or she should certainly consider the photo to be a desirable acquisition worth more than the album without such a photo.

In the mid '60s, record companies began printing on the covers of select albums a black circular notification of the title's being awarded a "Gold Record Award Audited And Certified By RIAA." This was, no doubt, meant to impress upon prospective purchasers the fact that so many others had already bought the album that perhaps he or she should also add this to his or her collection. . . For the most part these stickers were added to the album *after it had sold the required amount* (and for more on that, please refer to the article on RIAA Gold & Platinum Records in the appendices of this book).

So, excepting those albums that were certified Gold based on advance orders, it must be assumed that copies of an album bearing this seal are, in fact, technical second pressings and that technical first pressings exist without the seal. The importance of this cannot be underestimated: Finding copies of Ray Charles' classic *Modern Sounds In Country & Western* or any of The Mamas & The Papas' first three albums without this seal can be frustrating. While it was not possible to document the many cases where this seal denotes a second pressing, the reader should be aware of this.

As for still-sealed albums: First, shrink-wrapping albums at the factory was not a common practice until the early to mid-'60s. A label as large as Capitol was using the fact that their albums were "poly-wrapped in the factory" as late as January 1964 as a selling point to the consumer. Should you be offered an album from the '50s or early '60s still sealed in shrink-wrap, think twice. Generally, a dealer cannot be held responsible for what is inside a sealed jacket.

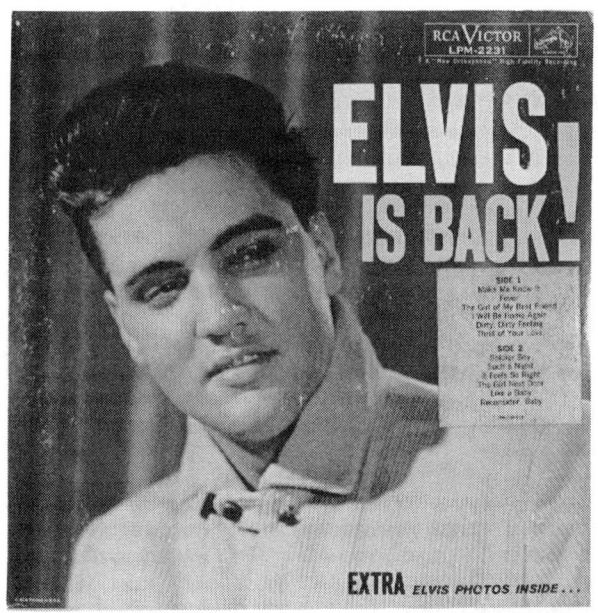

As an example of cover stickers there is probably none better than *Elvis Is Back!*, recorded and released within weeks of Presley's discharge from the U.S. Army in 1960. Since the jacket was printed prior to the recording session (to hasten the process of getting the album on the street), the actual songs that would make up the record were not known, so stickers with the titles were affixed to the front after the fact. Original pressings of the album titled the fourth song on the second side as "The Girl Next Door," which appeared on both the label and the sticker (top). All subsequent pressings title the song "The Girl Next Door Went A' Walking" and a new sticker was made up with the title change (bottom).

For example, during Elvis' career RCA often printed far more covers than records on the initial run (it saved money) and subsequently used the covers until they ran out. It is rather common to find second and third pressing records in first pressing covers. Consequently, Elvis collectors are not as obsessed with sealed copies and would rather see an opened Mint copy than take a chance on a sealed one.

There is also the practice of re-sealing albums. This was done over the years by the record companies and by firms specializing in remainders (I don't remember anyone calling them cut-outs in the '60s). Prior to the sales boom of the mid '70s, the industry had a very loose policy regarding returns; many of us over "thirtysomething" grew up able to test a purchase out on the store's turntable before taking it home. (*And* were often able to return records that we just plain didn't like. Of course, those were pre-corporate days when retail operations were independently owned and operated, and the proprietor knew most of his customers and catered to their needs).

When purchasing a valuable sealed collectible at a shop or show, pay for the record *with the mutual understanding* that you will open it *immediately after purchase, in front of the dealer,* and if the record inside is not what it should be, *you may return it on the spot.* Do not purchase a sealed record, leave, and return later claiming that you got the wrong record or a damaged copy. Naturally, very few dealers will offer a refund in such a case. On a less savory note, there are more than a few dealers and shops that do their own shrink-wrapping.

Two areas where still-sealed albums have enormous consequence: Beatles '60s Capitol albums and audiophile pressings. While any Beatles mono album still-sealed is worth several times the listed Near Mint value, ascertaining exactly which pressing is in a still-sealed stereo cover is another matter. The recommended manner of determining is to hold the sealed album with the open end, or "mouth," of the jacket down and tap the jacket in an attempt to get the record and its attendant inner sleeve to move down towards the mouth so that the sleeve can be viewed (gravity alone will seldom accomplish this). Capitol almost always packaged their '60s LPs in colored paper sleeves (including varying shades of blue, brown, green, red and a sepia-like yellow) that advertised other Capitol albums. So, if one of those colored sleeves is visible, then one can assume with almost complete certainty that the album within is an original, black "rainbow" label pressing.

The continuing of the escalation of the value of sealed half-speeds is dealt with in a separate article in this book, "From Wide-Channel Stereo To Multi-Channel Mono." For the first time, included will be complete listings for each of the most collected audiophile labels and a price guide for factory-sealed copies of each released title. The interested reader/collector is thereby referred to said piece.

From Wide-Channel Stereo
To Multi-Channel Mono

"I'm basically a one-mike mono man. . . I like natural sound. You know, stereo came in and set back the recording business twenty years, I think, with isolation and all that. . . The more mikes you have open and everything, the more distortion there is. [Tape] made it possible to make more dishonest records than there ever had been, through splicing." These quotes come from legendary A&R man, John Hammond (from conversations with Ted Fox, *In The Groove*, St, Martin's, 1986). Mr. Hammond's opinions are striking, powerful and, in many respects, correct (although the "dishonest records" he is referring are almost exclusively heavily spliced classical recordings sold as "live" recitals).

Hammond is not alone in his belief; Berry Gordy, whose creative role in his Motown empire should never be underestimated, is said to have assigned the mono mixdowns to his best engineers, allowing the novices the stereo mixing. That is why so many Motown stereo albums sound washed out compared to their mono counterparts, *especially* the 45 RPM singles. No less an authority than John Lennon maintained that "You haven't heard *Sgt. Pepper* if you haven't heard it in mono." And, of course, the proclivities of such production geniiuses as Phil Spector and Brian Wilson were firmly founded on the joys of monaural sound.

Of course, there are benefits to multi-track recording, especially if you are a fan of the type of albums conceived and recorded in the mid-'60s, when overdubbing allowed creative attempts to capture aspects of the psychedelic experience on tape. But many of the recordings made today would be better off if they were cut "live" in an ambient environment with as few mikes as possible and a sensitive engineer at the board. . . That is not about to happen: For whatever reason, contemporary artists are immersed in technology. (Interestingly, since I first wrote this, things have changed: Many artists and engineers are returning to recording πlive in the studio" as much as possible *and* on analog equipment and tape. Overdubs are being held to a minimum and the final transfer is, of necessity, digital. Mind you, for the most part this is occurring with smaller, independent labels, but it is a positive sign for all concerned with "real" sounding music.)

During the early years of stereo in the States much of the best rock 'n roll, rhythm 'n blues and country 'n western recordings were done under less than state-of-the-art conditions and the technicians involved were far more adept in mixing down to mono than creating a good stereo two-track master for the "wide channel" stereo in vogue at the time. Conversely, by the late '60s the ability, or sensibility, to mix multi-track recordings down to a single mono track had been "lost" by the majority of the engineers and producers of popular recordings.

Original wide-channel stereo recordings made no attempt at reality but went for effect. The placement of individual instruments in the two separate channels made for a more involving listening experience, essentially inviting the brain to participate in completing the mix-down from the widely disparate signals emanating from the two speakers. Collectors of this type of technology pursue the best examples of it, not necessarily concentrating on the particular type of music involved.

Today's technicians have lost the means to mix contemporary multi-tracks (24, 48, 64, ad infinitum) down into the popular stereo of the '60s, known affectionately as "wide channel" stereo due to the distinct placement of the individual sounds in the two channels. Consequently, when a CD version of a popular '50s or '60s multi-track recording is remixed, the listening experience for the older fan can be downright shocking! While the track *may* be cleaned up and the dynamics expanded, the new mix can be disconcertingly different from the original. The wide channel stereo sound is often gone, replaced by the more natural, less affecting mix (often referred to as "multi-channel mono") with which today's engineers are familiar.

Early Stereo 1958-1963

While two track recordings were made through the mid '50s, very few rock, blues or country records were cut that way. Atlantic began issuing stereo albums in 1959 but did not see the majority of their two-channel transfers completed until several years later. James Brown's first stereo outing was 1963's *Jump Around* (King 771) while Chuck Berry didn't see a stereo release until 1964 (*St. Louis To Liverpool*, Chess 1488). This could at least be excused by the fact that they recorded for small, independent labels that catered to a black market, those least likely to have replaced their hi-fi with a stereo..

Even such hit-makers as Ricky Nelson and George Jones were not recorded in stereo by their companies until 1960 (*More Songs By Ricky*, Imperial 12057 and *George Jones Sings Hank Williams*, Mercury 60596). And while Elvis wasn't cut on two-track until '60 (*Elvis Is Back!*, RCA Victor 2231), had his career not been impeded by military service it's *possible* RCA might have seen fit to escort their bread and butter into one of their modern studios. . . (During Elvis' January 1957 session at Radio Recorders in Hollywood, the studio's normal back-up recorder was on the blink, calling for the new-fangled two-track recorder to used instead. These back-up recordings were eventually located and duly issued by RCA as *Stereo '57 (Essential Elvis, Vol. 2)* in 1988. While they are fun to listen to, nobody is going to make any glowing claims for the stereophonic listening experience. . .)

Early albums from these genres in true stereo are rare and highly desirable. The first rock 'n roll LP to contain true stereo recordings appears to have been Duane Eddy's *Have "Twangy" Guitar— Will Travel* (Jamie 3000, 1958). Within a few years, the stereo masters were lost! So, while Eddy's first album has been available in rechanneled stereo for thirty years, the early pressings are among the most sought-after stereo albums of the '50s.

The Teddy Bears Sing! (Imperial 12067, 1959) is a legendary stereo album, long commanding big bucks (although it appears to be cooling off as a high-ticket item among older collectors). Featuring neophyte Phil Spector as one of the Teddys, the clean, wide open sound makes this desirable as a rock 'n roll rarity, as a stereo album and as a Spector artifact. Oddly, Spector would, of course, evolve into the field's first really creative producer in the early '60s, and, as the head of his own label, he mixed everything down to mono, refusing to allow stereo masters out of his office!

Roy Orbison's first two albums for Monument, *Lonely And Blue* (14002, 1961) and *Crying* (14007, 1962), are considered by many to be among the very finest pop/rock stereo albums ever made. In this case, the extraordinary sound,

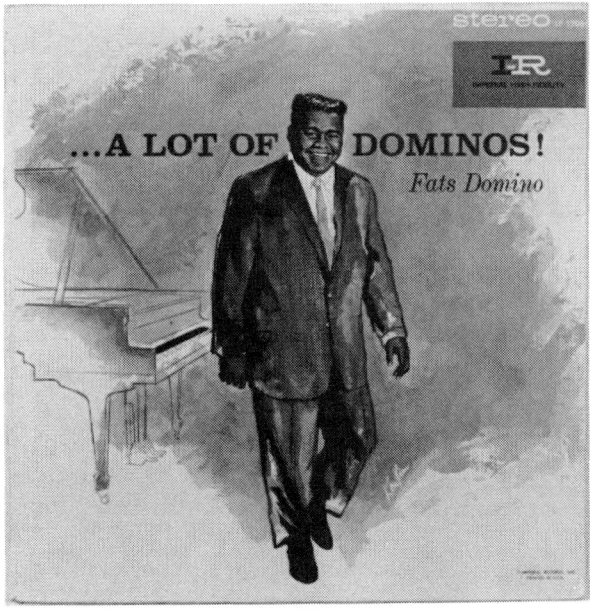

Long collected as one of the earliest stereo pop/rock albums, The Teddy Bears Sing! *features the nascent talents of one Phil Spector as singer, songwriter and arranger, and Carol Kleinbard, who later made a splash during the surf era as Carol Connors. 1961's* A Lot Of Dominos *is one of only two albums issued in stereo during Fats' fifteen-year stay with Imperial.*

impeccably produced by Fred Foster and magically mixed by Bill Porter, and the gorgeous performances more than justify the records' reps. In between these extremes are Fats Domino's two lonely stereo releases for Imperial, *A Lot Of Dominos* (12066, 1960) and *Let The Four Winds Blow* (12073, 1961) both issued on black labels with silver print and among Fats' rarest albums. Two very hot stereo albums with collectors are both of the ever-yummy Shelley Fabares' offerings, *Shelly* and *The Things We Did Last Summer* (Colpix 426 and 431, both from 1962).

Both of Del Shannon's first two albums, *Runaway* (Big Top 3003, 1961) and *Little Town Flirt* (1308, 1963), were issued in stereo, apparently unknown to the artist. The albums were shipped in mono covers, sometimes stamped "Stereo" and sometimes unmarked, saving the company the additional royalty pay-ments the more expensive stereo discs required. *Little Town Flirt* even carries a mono label and must be played to ascertain whether or not it is mono or stereo! While these records are of modest artistic achievement and rudimentary stereo, they continue to escalate in value due not only to their rarity (which existed on the day of their release) but the fact that the stereo master tapes have long since vanished. Also on Big Top is Sammy Turner's *Lavender Blue Moods* (Big Top 1301, 1962), another rare stereo album .

In some cases, economics can affect a record's rarity. Due to the in-credible mix-up that the Chicago-based rhythm 'n blues label Vee Jay went through in the '60s (a time when even having The Beatles *and* The Four Seasons on the label couldn't save them), many of their albums had virtually nonexistent stereo press runs. Gene Chandler's *Duke Of Earl* (Vee Jay 1040, 1962) is virtually impossible to find in stereo. When boxes of supposedly stereo copies of *Duke Of Earl* found their way onto the market in the late '70s, the discs inside proved to be mono, leading many to believe they were reproductions.

Vee Jay's stereo problems didn't end with the Duke. Stereo copies of the label's biggest selling album, *Introducing The Beatles* (1062), are so rare that any version of either the original 1963 pressing with "Love Me Do" and "P.S. I Love You" or the 1964 reissue with "Please Please Me" and "Ask Me Why" is a four figure record in collectible condition. The same holds true for the stereo versions of *The Beatles Vs. The Four Seasons* (30), *The Beatles & Frank Ifield On Stage* (1085), and *Songs, Pictures & Stories Of The Fabulous Beatles* (1092).

And it's not just The Fab Four: When the British Invasion was in full swing, many of the tapes that were sent to the States were dramatically altered by American engineers in anticipation of the expectations of the American mar-ket, often adding over-generous echo and/or reverb to fill in the "hole" left by the cleaner British separation. Most U.S. fans grew up hearing a very different set of recordings than what their cross-Atlantic counterparts were listening to (or, for that matter, what the artists *intended* them to hear). This was so common that an attempt to list the tracks/albums affected would take up pages; suffice to say that virtually everyone suffered under this system.

When imports became common in the early '70s, listeners were often astounded at hearing the differences between the U.K. versions of albums such as *Aftermath* or *Revolver*, where the lack of echo made both Jagger's and Lennon's voices decidedly English, an effect softened by the American tinkering. (The interested Beatles fan should turn to John Christensen's "The Uncommon Stereo Beatles" in the Appendices of this book for more on this topic.)

The joys of two channel listening are not merely confined to rock music fans; to some extent the interest lies in both country and rhythm 'n blues, which is, admittedly, not as strong but has been growing. In the field of classical music, stereo specialists have become so rampant as to all but dominate the field. The pursuit of such proven labels as RCA Victor's "Living Stereo" (with a "shaded dog," of course) and Mercury's "Living Presence" originals has moved whole runs of titles into the $100 to $1,000 range while leaving their mono counterparts as used record store staples.

About the only field where this is not the rule is with jazz collecting, where the serious listener tends to prefer the unencumbered straight to tape mono sound over the often doctored stereo effect. But even here the audiophile is making his/her presence known: Original stereo pressings of Miles Davis' *Kind Of Blue* on Columbia is selling for $150-300 if the data stamped and etched into the trail-off vinyl indicates a primo pressing And, while the older jazz aficionado prefers mono, according to Rockaway's Gary Johnson, he has found that the newer, younger collectors of the musical form founded on the blue note show as much verve for collecting stereo as mono, thus giving the stereo pressings a boost in prestige (and value).

There are often non-annotated differences between the mono and stereo versions of an album. While many, if not most, of the studios recording jazz in the '50s began using two tracks as far back as 1956-57, most of them did so only for the increased latitude it allowed in mixing down to mono. When stereo became a viable commercial medium toward the end of the decade, many companies re-turned to the original multi-track tapes and mixed them for stereo release. Thus hundreds of titles, recorded with only mono in mind, were issued to the new stereo enthusiasts. Many of these contain the most rudimentary form of stereo, with little or none of the stereophonic imaging that makes the enjoyment of stereo essential to most listeners. For that matter alone, aside from having the *original* mix, most jazz collectors prefer the mono over the stereo, even when the stereo is the rarer of the two.

For instance, while Verve cut their artists on two-tracks as early as 1957, they did not see fit to issue any stereo albums until 1960. While original mono releases were issued primarily on the 2000 and 8000 series (with their 4000 series reserved almost exclusively for the work of the protean Miss Ella Fitzger-ald), the stereo series was on the 6000 series. As titles were issued in stereo as Verve saw fit or as the masters were made available to him, they do not run con-currently with the mono counterparts. For instance, Verve 8264, *Ella Fitzgerald At The Opera House,* was issued in mono in 1958 and in stereo in 1960 as 6026. But 6019, *Ella Swings Lightly,* is the stereo version of 4021, issued in 1959. Simi-lar situatiions occurred with Columbia's 8000 and Mercury 60000 series.

More importantly, completely different takes may be used on the mono and the stereo versions, *or* the artist may actually go back into the studio and rerecord the entire album for stereo! For instance, *Ellington Indigos* features two different sets of takes for each cut on the mono (Columbia 1085, 1958) and the stereo (8053, 1959) albums. While this might seem trivial to a non-fan, to an Ellingtonian, this is the same as having two different albums. [To further compli-cate matters, when CBS reissued the album as part of its digitally remastered "Jazz Masterpieces," they used the stereo mixes and included previously unre-leased outtakes. So for the Duke completist, one would need a mono pressing, a stereo pressing *and* the digital stereo pressings!]

When Capitol decided to issue June Christy's first album, *Something Cool*, in stereo in 1960, they whisked the singer and a band back into the studios and recorded the entire album from scratch. And, while almost all collectors prefer the performance on the original, it nonetheless functions as an entirely "new" album for Christy collectors.

On another, related topic, in *Jazz West Coast*, Robert Gordon notes "[Pacific Jazz/World Pacific owner Richard] Bock produced a great many fine albums over the years, but one wishes he could have resisted the urge to splice and otherwise tamper with his tapes, a temptation to which he all too often succumbed." Gordon uses as an example Jim Hall's *Jazz Guitar:* The original sessions (on Pacific Jazz 1227 in 1957) featured a trio with Red Mitchell, bass, and Carl Perkins, piano. When Bock reissued the album in 1963 (Pacific Jazz LP/ST 79), he overdubbed a drum track, making the recording a quartet. Tampering with the integrity of the original recording arouses the ire of most listeners. Of course, collector-wise, it does create a new version to be sought.

While many collectors cringe at early stereo, virtually every record collector enters a paroxysm of rage when electronically rechanneled stereo is brought up. Every effort has been made to identify those albums where the engineers took a mono signal and "created" a stereo effect with the use of boosted trebles/bass, echo, phase, etc. RCA Victor reissued all of Elvis' '50s albums in an "electronically rechanneled for stereo" format in the early '60s. This was acceptable *(sic)* as long as the mono versions of these albums remained in print. But, by 1969 all a person could buy was the horrific fake stereo sound, leaving several generations of fans growing up with a very distorted concept of Elvis' sound.

A more extreme case is that of Brian Wilson and his Beach Boys. Brian was the first of the producer/artists who both performed and had complete control of the studio, including the mixing board. But, as Mr. Wilson is deaf in one ear and can not hear stereophonically, all the group's early albums that appear in "full dimensional stereo" were mixed into two-tracks by Brian's engineer, Chuck Britz. While these are excellent wide channel separations, for the hard-core BW aficionado they are a step removed from the complete aural image intended by the artist. Unfortunately, this point was rendered moot in 1965 when the Beach Boys' albums were issued in "duophonic stereo," Capitol's trademarked fake stereo process that all but ruined the subtleties and nuances of Wilson's extraordinary mono productions.

And, for those aforementioned hardcores: *Pet Sounds*, that ultimate in monophonic listening experience, does exist in its multi-track, unmixed form. Bruce Johnston wistfully recalled spending a night years ago with those tapes mixing a stereo master for the entire album, a master that he knew wouldn't see the light of day For further proof of this pudding, refer to the compact disc of *Stack-O-Tracks*, which contains stereo backing tracks for "Sloop John B," "Wouldn't It Be Nice," "God Only Knows," and "Here Today."

There are several electronically rechanneled albums that command big bucks entirely because of their rarity. Examples include *Presenting Dion And The Belmonts* (Laurie LLPS-2002, 1959), *The Crystals Twist Uptown* (Philles DT-90722), The Knights' *Hot Rod High* (Capitol DT-2189, 1964), The Trashmen's *Surfin' Bird* (Garret GAS-200, 1964), and Otis Redding's *Pain In My Heart* (Atco SD-33-161, 1967).

Late Mono 1967-1970

The practice of issuing new albums in both mono and stereo was phased out of the American market by the late '60s. While the major labels kept their mono stampers going through 1968, the press runs for these were miniscule, with distribution and sales correspondingly low. Just as stereo copies of Elvis' first few albums from 1960 are worth considerably more than the monos, the reverse is true for his albums from this period. The mono version of 1967's *Clambake* (RCA Victor 3893) is currently worth nearly four times the original stereo version. But this pales in comparison to his 1968 albums: *Elvis' Gold Records, Volume 4* (3921) and *Speedway* (3989), are worth 300 times the stereo originals! But this may not be true for smaller, independent labels, who, more wary of the bottom line, began deleting monos from their catalog as early as 1967. There may be considerably more mono titles from 1968 than remain undocumented.

Several West Coast bands have highly collectable mono albums from this period: At one time or another, every member of Jefferson Airplane has expressed disgust with the distracting echo and distortion of the stereo *Surrealistic Pillow* (RCA Victor 3766, 1967). But the mono mix is devoid of most of this echo and a more accurate reflection of the band's intentions (*and* a better listening experience). *The Grateful Dead* (Warner Bros. 1689, 1967) is far more potent a mix than the readily available stereo version and essential for Deadheads.

The Doors (Elektra 4007, 1967) is a must for Morrison aficionados. Seems that when Jim recorded the album's closer, "The End," he was still tingling from the previous night's acid experience (No, dear, there are no such things as "flashbacks") and was a bit more uninhibited than usual. At the song's climax, where he rants "Father, I want to kill you" and the band goes into its raga rave-up, there comes a point where Morrison can be heard chanting "Kill, kill, kill." He followed this with a muttered "Fuck, fuck, fuck," which was buried in the stereo mix but can be discerned on the up-front mono mix.

Sgt. Pepper's Lonely Heart's Club Band (MAL-2653, 1967), while a cornerstone of multi-track recording and *still* a lot of fun to hear on head-phones, has its adherents as a monaural experience. The dub-downs from the multi-tracks to mono were supervised by producer and fifth Beatle George Martin, usually with the group, while the stereo mix-downs were left to the engineer. Unfortunately, by 1967, few of the group's legions of fans were interested in mono, making *Pepper* and *Magical Mystery Tour* (MAL-2835, 1967) among the rarest commercially issued Beatles albums on Capitol.

Some labels continued to release promotional albums in mono after phasing it out commercially. Jimi Hendrix's *Electric Ladyland* (Reprise 6307, 1968) is the not only most valuable mono promo, it is also the hottest and most sought-after of Hendrix's vinyl artifacts. Other collectible promos include The Who's *Magic Bus* (Decca 5064, 1968), which garners some of its value due to the fact that several of the tracks on the stereo versions are messily rechanneled, and 1969's *Tommy* (Decca 7205).

Monomania is not restricted to "important" albums or "major" artists: While earlier albums by The Monkees are garage-sale staples, *The Birds, The Bees & The Monkees* (Colgems 109, 1968) is the rarest commercially issued album by the post-fab four. Both *Steppenwolf* and *Steppenwolf The Second* (Dunhill 50029 and 50037, 1968) are rare and sought after.

In many cases, when purchasing a rare late mono album all one is acquiring is a rarity. By the middle of 1967 many companies simply had their engineers take the two track stereo masters and dub them down into a single track instead of preparing a properly mixed mono master. Because of this, many of these albums are decidedly inferior to their stereo counterparts, producing an unbalanced, muddy sound.

There are many other mono albums from '68 that have not attracted enough attention to be able to make a real statement about them. For instance, based on the existence of the two aforementioned Presley titles, I have assumed that there are a good many RCA titles from this period also issued, especially several noteworthy country/western artists. This includes, but is not restricted to, Dolly Parton's *Just Because I'm A Woman* (3949), Hank Snow's *Hits, Hits And More Hits* (3965), Porter Wagoner's *The Bottom Of The Bottle* (3986) and Porter and Dolly's *Just Between You And Me* (3926). Each of these was assigned a near mint value of $100 in the price guide; assuming they exist, that would seem a conservative estimate of the difficulty a collector would have in finding them. . .

Considering the unlikelihood of the mono mixes of any these LPs making it onto CD (although EMI/Capitol's issuing the Beatles complete catalog in mono *and* stereo is not only not out of the question, it is recommended), it becomes all the more desirable to own and hear the truly classic albums of the '60s the way the bands wanted you to hear them (and none of these LPs have climbed into the stratosphere with Elvis. . . yet.)

After the demise of mono, many of the majors appeared to rethink their position on the practise of "electronically rechanneling" mono masters into a horrid phony stereo. By the '70s archival material was surfacing in original mono for the first time in years. RCA again was notable with Elvis' *Sun Sessions* in 1975, compiling for the first time what many historians consider to be the most important body of rock 'n roll music ever recorded.

Many important albums were issued in mono abroad after the American labels had discontinued the practice. These range from 1968's *The Beatles* and *Beggar's Banquet* (which is far more dynamic and powerful in mono) through 1969's *Let It Bleed, The Kinks Are The Village Green Preservation Society* and several prominent non-Beatles Apple titles. The collector interested in pursuing foreign pressings such as these is advised to expect a precarious but interesting pursuit.

Then there is the quadramania of the early '70s. Quadraphonic (a different signal emanating from four different channels and requiring separate electronic components to decode the signals) pressings are attractive for a variety of reasons, scarcity being the most obvious. But of far more interest is the fact that many quads have radically different, and sometimes superior, mixes to the original stereo. The best known instance is *Sly & The Family Stone's Greatest Hits:* The stereo album contains three singles— "Everybody Is A Star," "Hot Fun In The Summertime," and "Thank You (Falletinme Be Mice Elf Again)"— in fake stereo.

When their engineers mastered the quadraphonic album, they dug up the original multi-tracks and issued all of the tracks in four channel sound, the closest approximation of stereo that collectors have found of the aforementioned trio! Jefferson Airplane's *Volunteers* is also notable for including at least four tracks with alternate takes or mixes. These remained unavailable to the public until the release of the compact disc boxed set *Jefferson Airplane Loves You.*

Two of 1967's more sought-after monaural albums: Surrealistic Pillow *is burdened with some of the most reverberant echo in pop history. While this is still evident on the mono mix, it is noticeably diminished, making the listening experience more rewarding.* The Doors *is also cleaner in mono, but more important is the fact that an important part of the one track's performance that was buried in the stereo mix can be heard on the mono album.*

Record Collecting & The Audiophile

One interesting group of record collectors shuns the emulation of individual artists or styles in favor of the recording's overall sound. These collectors are concerned with an accurate recreation of the musical event as it originally occurred in its natural environment. Many of these listeners place a primary emphasis on "sound field" recordings, those that, by use of the most appropriate equipment in the proper environment, with mikes properly placed and, most importantly, no post-recording manipulation of the signal, come closest to achieving the idealized sound presentation. Needless to say, most of this is not applicable to popular music, where the very opposite is the case: Most pop recordings since the mid-'60s have been recorded in the sterile environment of the studio, often in bits and pieces, with the use of over-dubbing, compression, etc., grossly over-using the medium to manipulate the message.

Originally dubbed "golden ears," these hobbyists emerging from early hi-fi were not simply satisfied with whatever technology was available on a mass-produced basis for a reasonable price. They pursued a more perfect medium through the selection of the correct gear, the placement of speakers, the "tweaking" of each and every facet of their equipment and the environment in which it was enjoyed. Often perceived as obsessed by the more relaxed majority, many of the innovations now taken for granted, both in the hardware (the electronics and other playback equipment) and the software (the records), can be traced directly to the insights and perseverance of these pioneers.

In record collecting, the term "audiophile" is generally applied to those who specialize in high-quality recordings on high-quality vinyl. While every album *could have* been an audiophile pressing, few were and the standard of quality, especially in the amount of pressings done from each stamper to the quality of the vinyl used, dropped during the '70s. It was also quite normal for the major companies to finish up the making of an album—after the recording and post-production technical work is complete—by cutting a master lacquer disc in a matter of hours. From these are produced "mothers" and from them the "stampers" from which the records are actually pressed.

In a high volume business with a name star, the stampers can be used well past the point of their being able to reproduce the extremes in the highs and lows from the master. In fact, the industry's disregard for their customers and, of course, the apparent lack of discrimination *of* their customers, led to enormous quantities of noticeably inferior records flooding the American retail racks. Some sources claim that as much as 75-80% of the press run of Michael Jackson's *Thriller* were shipped defective. . . and the company knew and could not care less!

The vogue for half-speed mastered albums was ushered in by Mobile Fidelity Sound Laboratories at the end of the '70s and lasted, more or less, through the early years of the "digital revolution" of the '80s. As the general level of quality of American manufactured records dropped like a proverbial SAT score, this enterprising company stepped in and leased master tapes from the original companies, manufacturing high quality records with a correspondingly high price. Eventually, several other companies followed suit and a mini-industry serving the perceived needs of a dedicated few blossomed. Mobile Fidelity's "Original Master Recording" series utilized a mastering process whereby the master lacquer was cut at 16 2/3 RPM rather than the industry standard of 33 1/3 (hence, half-speed mastered). This allowed the cutting of the grooves twice as much time to capture each nuance of the analogue recording.

Other steps—special mastering equipment including custom designed cutting heads, amplifiers, etc.—were taken to ensure accuracy but the most important to collectors was the shipping of the stampers to Japan where the albums were pressed on JVC's trademarked "Super Vinyl". This not only ensured a more faithful reproduction of the sound but allowed the user to play the disc repeatedly with less fear of damaging the grooves. Each album was pressed with a maximum number of 5,000 copies from each of the four stampers taken from the "mother," at which point the stampers were destroyed. Thus each disc was a "limited edition" of such noticeably superior quality that left many a listener speechless upon first hearing.

Sheffield Lab, Wilson Audio and Reference Recordings, also specialized in audiophile pressings but their main output was jazz and classical and therefore outside the perimeters of this volume. The Nautilus label half-speed "SuperDiscs" were less successful on the market than MFSL and consequently their titles are a bit harder to find, although the demand is not as great from the collectors. Other collectible audiophile labels exist outside the boundaries of the increasingly xenophobic U.S., such as Cube (Germany), Vertigo (U.K.), CBS (Canada, Germany and Japan), Nimbus (U.K.) and A&M (Canada). These companies' products are often available domestically and sought out by audiophiles.

Among the major labels, CBS poured out a number of their Columbia and Epic catalog in this format, but these were done in relatively small printings, did not fare well on the retail racks and thus, the demand for certain titles is increasing. The actual pressings themselves, from inception through mastering and pressing, were qualitatively far behind the smaller companies, leaving a great deal to be desired. When the relative failure of this line was obvious, rather than simply delete the titles and make them available to cut-out bins nationwide, CBS simply recalled them and recycled the vinyl for future use, making many of the CBS titles difficult indeed to track down. Thus their value as collectibles outstrips their value as vehicles for a truly pleasing listening experience. Collectors are continually discovering "new" CBS titles in this format.

While the prices for audiophile oriented collectibles will continue to rise steadily if not always dramatically. "Don't be fooled by the digital revolution," advises Charlie Essmeier of Retro Records. "The prices of these LPs are continuing to increase. Titles that were common just two years ago are commanding high prices today. Ry Cooder's *Jazz* has turned out to be the most highly sought-after Mobile Fidelity album and perhaps the rarest, as well. I'm also pleased to hear that they plan to release some new vinyl titles in 1993; they obviously feel that the demand is still there. Not that it's news to me: I sell lots of import titles that aren't pressed on vinyl here. And some that are. . . Who can find them?"

Promotional collectibles associated with these labels include test pressings made for each of Mobile Fidelity's "Original Master Recordings." These have plain white labels and were issued in plain cardboard jackets.; early titles have "JVC Sample Record-Not For Sale" printed on them (and possible handwritten information) while later pressings read "MFSL Inc." These generally sell for approximately twice the title's listed Near Mint value. They also manufactured test pressings for each of The Beatles' titles for their "Ultra High Quality Recording" (UHQR) series (the next step up from the "OMR"). Nautilus pressed promo copies of their titles on white labels and issued them in plain cardboard covers with a sticker of a nautilus shell. While these follow the general guidelines for promos, it needs to be pointed out that the promo for John & Yoko's *Double Fantasy* is the rarest and most valuable of the Nautilus promos.

The concerns of the audiophile has spawned several nationally distributed publications, the best known being *Stereo Review* and *Audio*. The more arcane aspects of the hobby has also spawned at least two publications that deal at least peripherally with the concerns of the software (i.e., the recorded medium, either vinyl or CD). Both *The Absolute Sound* and *Stereophile* devote space to reviewing exceptionally well recorded and manufactured music and, while the emphasis is often on the more spectacular classical realms, they do pay some attention to other types of music. (All four of the aforementioned periodicals are available at any well-stocked magazine stand.)

It should be interesting to observe where current standards are heading. CBS has introduced their new series of [higher priced] CDs with superior mixes and sound due to the improved ability of the "bits" that can be sampled. This from an industry that has told us that compact discs were already perfect. . .

There is also the issue of still-sealed copies of audiophile recordings. The demand here, which may be far in excess of that of the mainstream collector, is best placed in context by considering that many audiophiles have cartridges on their tonearms worth more than the average collector's entire sound system. The idea of subjecting said cartridge to the trauma of a worn record makes little sense. Please note that not all audiophiles want sealed copies; many demand opened, examined copies in mint condition; this way any defects originated at the manufacturer's level may be observed by both the seller and the buyer.

While the reader will find the listings of most audiophile pressings throughout the book, the prices quoted there are for open, presumably played copies. The listings here are for factory-sealed copies of the three main "audiophile" labels: Mobile Fidelity, Nautilus and Direct-Disk Labs. While there are other labels, these are the ones that command the most attention and the most money. Regarding the current state of the market, good ol' Charlie noted "It's hard to get a premium for sealed copies of the CBS titles, largely because they have a bad reputation soundwise. Oddly enough, these are the hardest half-speed mastered LPs to find in sealed condition!" Titles with an asterisk (*) were issued as part of a MFSL's boxed sets, which are listed and priced separately.

Price Guide To Still-Sealed "Original Master Recordings"

MFSL 1-001	The Mystic Moods Orchestra, *Emotions*	1979	75.00-100.00
MFSL 1-002	The Mystic Moods Orchestra, *Cosmic Forces*	1979	75.00-100.00
MFSL 1-003	The Mystic Moods Orchestra, *Stormy Weekend*	1979	75.00-100.00
MFSL 1-004	Sound effects, *The Power & The Majesty:*		
	Rain 'n Train Demonstration Disc	1979	75.00-100.00
MFSL 1-005	Supertramp, *Crime Of The Century*	1979	75.00-100.00
MFSL 1-006	John Klemmer, *Touch*	1979	75.00-100.00
MFSL 1-007	Steely Dan, *Katy Lied*	1979	300.00-400.00
MFSL 1-008	Zubin Mehta & The Los Angeles Philharmonic, *Suites From*		
	"Star Wars" and "Close Encounters Of The Third Kind"	1979	300.00-400.00
MFSL 1-009	Al Stewart, *Year Of The Cat*	1979	75.00-100.00
MFSL 1-010	The Crusaders, *Chain Reaction*	1979	75.00-100.00
MFSL 1-011	George Benson, *Breezin'*	1979	50.00-75.00
MFSL 1-012	Fleetwood Mac, *Fleetwood Mac*	1979	75.00-100.00
MFSL 2-013	Little Feat, *Waiting For Columbus* (2 LPs)	1979	150.00-200.00
MFSL 1-014	The Grateful Dead, *American Beauty*	1979	150.00-200.00
MFSL 1-015	Emmylou Harris, *Quarter Moon In A Ten Cent Town*	1979	75.00-100.00
MFSL 1-016	Joe Sample, *Rainbow Seeker*	1979	50.00-75.00
MFSL 1-017	Pink Floyd, *Dark Side Of The Moon*	1979	100.00-150.00
MFSL 1-018	Gordon Lightfoot, *Sundown*	1979	75.00-100.00
MFSL 1-019	Al Jarreau, *All Fly Home*	1979	30.00-50.00
MFSL 1-020	Poco, *Legend*	1979	30.00-50.00

MFSL 1-021	Steve Miller, *Fly Like An Eagle*	1979	**75.00-100.00**
MFSL 1-022	Manhattan Transfer, *Manhattan Transfer Live*	1979	**50.00-75.00**
MFSL 1-023	The Beatles, *Abbey Road*	1979	**100.00-150.00**
MFSL 2-024	Neil Diamond, *Hot August Night* (2 LPs)	1979	**50.00-75.00**
MFSL 1-025	Earl Klugh, *Fingerpaintings*	1979	**75.00-100.00**
MFSL 1-026	Styx, *Grand Illusion*	1979	**50.00-75.00**
MFSL 1-027	Steeleye Span, *All Around My Hat*	1979	**30.00-50.00**
MFSL 1-028	Melissa Manchester, *Melissa*	1979	**25.00-40.00**
MFSL 1-029	Pablo Cruise, *A Place In The Sun*	1979	**25.00-40.00**
MFSL 1-030	Eric Clapton, *Slowhand*	1980	**100.00-150.00**
MFSL 1-031	Emerson, Lake & Palmer, *Pictures At An Exhibition*	1980	**50.00-75.00**
MFSL 1-032	Natalie Cole, *Thankful*	1980	**25.00-40.00**
MFSL 1-033	Steely Dan, *Aja*	1980	**75.00-100.00**
MFSL 1-034	Bob Seger, *Night Moves*	1980	**75.00-100.00**
MFSL 1-035	Cat Stevens, *Tea For The Tillerman*	1980	**75.00-100.00**
MFSL 1-036	The Little River Band, *First Under The Wire*	1980	**25.00-40.00**
MFSL 1-037	Creedence Clearwater Revival, *Cosmo's Factory*	1980	**175.00-225.00**
MFSL 1-038	The Atlanta Rhythm Section, *Champagne Jam*	1980	**50.00-75.00**
MFSL 1-039	The Band, *Music From Big Pink*	1980	**100.00-150.00**
MFSL 1-040	Olivia Newton-John, *Totally Hot!*	1980	**25.00-40.00**
MFSL 1-041	Gino Vannelli, *Powerful People*	1980	**30.00-50.00**
MFSL 1-042	The Moody Blues, *Days Of Future Passed*	1980	**100.00-150.00**
MFSL 1-043	Crystal Gayle, *We Must Believe In Magic*	1980	**20.00-30.00**
MFSL 1-044	Kenny Rogers, *Gambler*	1980	**20.00-30.00**
MFSL 1-045	Supertramp, *Breakfast In America*	1980	**50.00-75.00**
MFSL 1-046	*Title unknown*	1980	*Unreleased*
MFSL 1-047	The Beatles, *Magical Mystery Tour*	1980	**200.00-300.00**
MFSL 1-048	Judy Garland & Liza Minelli, *Live At London Palladium*	1980	**25.00-40.00**
MFSL 1-049	Kenny Rogers, *Greatest Hits*	1980	**25.00-40.00**
MFSL 1-050	Blondie, *Parallel Lines*	1980	**40.00-60.00**
MFSL 1-051	The Doors, *The Doors*	1980	**150.00-200.00**
MFSL 1-052	Foreigner, *Double Vision*	1980	**40.00-60.00**
MFSL 1-053	Herb Alpert, *Rise*	1980	**25.00-40.00**
MFSL 1-054	Rod Stewart, *Blondes Have More Fun*	1980	**30.00-50.00**
MFSL 1-055	Jackson Browne, *The Pretender*	1980	**30.00-50.00**
MFSL 1-056	Country Joe McDonald, *Paradise With An Ocean View*	1980	**30.00-50.00**
MFSL 1-057	Pat Benatar, *In The Heat Of The Night*	1980	**25.00-40.00**
MFSL 1-058	Gerry Rafferty, *City To City*	1980	**50.00-75.00**
MFSL 1-059	Elvis Presley, *From Elvis In Memphis*	1980	**75.00-100.00**
MFSL 1-060	The Rolling Stones, *Sticky Fingers*	1980	**50.00-75.00**
MFSL 1-061	Jethro Tull, *Aqualung*	1980	**200.00-300.00**
MFSL 1-062	Genesis, *Trick Of The Tail*	1981	**100.00-150.00**
MFSL 1-063	Alice Cooper, *Welcome To My Nightmare*	1981	**85.00-125.00**
MFSL 1-064	David Bowie, *The Rise & Fall Of Ziggy Stardust*	1981	**85.00-125.00**
MFSL 1-065	Led Zeppelin, *Led Zeppelin II*	1981	**100.00-150.00**
MFSL 2-066	Cream, *Wheels Of Fire* (2 LPs)	1981	**85.00-125.00**
MFSL 1-067	Queen, *A Night At The Opera*	1981	**175.00-225.00**
MFSL 1-068	Chuck Mangione, *Feels So Good*	1981	**30.00-50.00**
MFSL 1-069	Hall & Oates, *Abandoned Luncheonette*	1981	**30.00-50.00**
MFSL 1-070	The Kinks, *Misfits*	1981	**25.00-40.00**
MFSL 1-071	Neil Diamond, *The Jazz Singer*	1981	**40.00-60.00**
MFSL 2-072	The Beatles, *The Beatles* (2 LPs)	1982	**100.00-150.00**
MFSL 1-073	Kim Carnes, *Mistaken Identity*	1982	**30.00-50.00**
MFSL 1-074	*Title unknown*	1982	*Unreleased*
MFSL 1-075	King Crimson, *In The Court Of The Crimson King*	1982	**100.00-150.00**
MFSL 1-076	Earl Klugh, *Late Night Guitar*	1982	**85.00-125.00**
MFSL 1-077	Yes, *Close To The Edge*	1982	**100.00-150.00**
MFSL 1-078	Quincy Jones, *You've Got It Bad Girl*	1982	**50.00-75.00**
MFSL 1-079	Jim Croce, *You Don't Mess Around With Jim*	1982	**50.00-75.00**
MFSL 1-080	Joe Jackson, *Night And Day*	1982	**30.00-50.00**
MFSL 1-081	Nat King Cole, *Nay King Cole Sings George Shearing Plays*	1982	**100.00-150.00**
MFSL 1-082	Al Stewart, *Time Passages*	1982	**30.00-50.00**
MFSL 1-083	David Bowie, *Let's Dance*	1982	**25.00-40.00**
MFSL 1-084	Alan Parsons Project, *I, Robot*	1982	**40.00-60.00**
MFSL 1-085	Ry Cooder, *Jazz*	1982	**400.00-500.00**
MFSL 1-086	Frank Sinatra, *Nice And Easy*	1982	**25.00-40.00**
MFSL 1-087	The Rolling Stones, *Some Girls*	1982	**85.00-125.00**
MFSL 1-088	Crosby, Stills, Nash & Young, *Deja Vu*	1982	**300.00-400.00**
MFSL 1-089	Rickie Lee Jones, *Rickie Lee Jones*	1982	**300.00-400.00**

MFSL 1-090	The Modern Jazz Quartet, *Live At The Lighthouse*	1982	**30.00-50.00**
MFSL 1-091	Stan Kenton, *Kenton Plays Wagner*	1982	**30.00-50.00**
MFSL 1-092	Jethro Tull, *The Broadsword And The Beast*	1982	**50.00-75.00**
MFSL 1-093	Red Nichols & The 5 Pennies, *At Marineland*	1982	**25.00-40.00**
MFSL 2-094	Lena Horne, *The Lady And Her Music* (2 LPs)	1982	**50.00-75.00**
MFSL 1-095	Andre Previn, *West Side Story*	1982	**25.00-40.00**
MFSL 1-096	The L.A. Jazz Choir, *Listen*	1982	**100.00-150.00**
MFSL 1-097	Barry Manilow, *Barry Manilow I*	1982	**25.00-40.00**
MFSL 1-098	Dionne Warwick, *Hot! Live And Otherwise*	1982	**25.00-40.00**
MFSL 1-099	Renaissance, *Scheherazade*	1982	**100.00-150.00**
MFSL 1-100	The Beatles, *Sgt. Pepper's Lonely Hearts Club Band*	1982	**40.00-60.00**
MFSL 1-101	The Beatles, *Please, Please Me*	1983	**30.00-50.00**
MFSL 1-102	The Beatles, *With The Beatles*	1983	**300.00-400.00**
MFSL 1-103	The Beatles, *A Hard Day's Night*	1983	**30.00-50.00**
MFSL 1-104	The Beatles, *Beatles For Sale*	1983	**30.00-50.00**
MFSL 1-105	The Beatles, *Help!*	1983	**30.00-50.00**
MFSL 1-106	The Beatles, *Rubber Soul*	1983	**50.00-75.00**
MFSL 1-107	The Beatles, *Revolver*	1984	**30.00-50.00**
MFSL 1-108	The Beatles, *Yellow Submarine*	1984	**85.00-125.00**
MFSL 1-109	The Beatles, *Let It Be*	1984	**30.00-50.00**
MFSL 1-110	The Beatles, *The Beatles "Rarities"*	1984	*Unreleased*
MFSL 1-111	Stephane Grapelli & Barney Kessel, *I Remember Django*	1984	**50.00-75.00**
MFSL 1-112	Vince Guaraldi, *Cast Your Fate To The Wind*	1984	**75.00-100.00**
MFSL 1-113	Air Supply, *The One That You Love*	1984	**25.00-40.00**
MFSL 1-114	Bob Dylan, *The Times They Are A-Changin'*	1984	**30.00-50.00**
MFSL 1-115	The Who, *Face Dances*	1984	**25.00-40.00**
MFSL 1-116	The Beach Boys, *Surfer Girl*	1984	**30.00-50.00**
MFSL 1-117	Tony Bennett & Bill Evans, *Tony Bennett / Bill Evans*	1984	**75.00-100.00**
MFSL 1-118	Sergio Mendes, *Sergio Mendes & Brasil '66*	1984	**75.00-100.00**
MFSL 1-119	Fleetwood Mac, *Mirage*	1984	**75.00-100.00**
MFSL 1-120	Donald Fagen, *Nightfly*	1984	**50.00-75.00**
MFSL 1-121	Stevie Nicks, *Bella Donna*	1984	**75.00-100.00**
MFSL 1-122	The Doobie Brothers, *Takin' It To The Streets*	1984	**50.00-75.00**
MFSL 1-123	David Foster, *The Best Of Me*	1984	**25.00-40.00**
MFSL 1-124	Bob James & Earl Klugh, *Two Of A Kind*	1984	**75.00-100.00**
MFSL 1-125	*Title unknown*	1984	*Unreleased*
MFSL 1-126	The Eagles, *Hotel California*	1984	**200.00-300.00**
MFSL 1-127	Bob Seger, *Against The Wind*	1984	**30.00-50.00**
MFSL 2-128	Chicago, *Chicago Transit Authority* (2 LPs)	1984	**75.00-100.00**
MFSL 1-129	Count Basie, *Basie Plays Hefti*	1984	**100.00-150.00**
MFSL 1-130	Frank Sinatra, *Swing Easy / Songs For Young Lovers*	1984	*
MFSL 1-131	Frank Sinatra, *In The Wee Small Hours*	1984	*
MFSL 1-132	Frank Sinatra, *Close To You*	1984	*
MFSL 1-133	Frank Sinatra, *A Swingin' Affair*	1984	*
MFSL 1-134	Frank Sinatra, *Where Are You?*	1984	*
MFSL 1-135	Frank Sinatra, *A Jolly Christmas*	1984	**30.00-50.00**
MFSL 1-136	Frank Sinatra, *Come Fly With Me*	1984	*
MFSL 1-137	Frank Sinatra, *Sings For Only The Lonely*	1984	*
MFSL 1-138	Frank Sinatra, *Come Dance With Me*	1984	*
MFSL 1-139	Frank Sinatra, *Look To Your Heart*	1984	*
MFSL 1-140	Frank Sinatra, *No One Cares*	1984	*
MFSL 1-141	Frank Sinatra, *Sinatra's Swingin' Session*	1984	*
MFSL 1-142	Frank Sinatra, *All The Way*	1984	*
MFSL 1-143	Frank Sinatra, *Come Swing With Me*	1984	*
MFSL 1-144	Journey, *Escape*	1984	**250.00-350.00**
MFSL 1-145	Frank Sinatra, *Sinatra Sings. . . Of Love And Things*	1984	*
MFSL 1-146	Frank Sinatra, *Songs For Swingin' Lovers*	1984	*
MFSL 1-147	Lee Ritenour, *Captain Fingers*	1984	**25.00-40.00**
MFSL 1-148	Jefferson Airplane, *Crown Of Creation*	1984	**25.00-40.00**
MFSL 1-149	Michael McDonald, *If That's What It Takes*	1984	**25.00-40.00**
MFSL 3-150	Soundtrack, *Victory At Sea* (3 LPs)	1984	**150.00-200.00**
MFSL 1-151	The Moody Blues, *Seventh Sojourn*	1984	**100.00-150.00**
MFSL 1-152	Spandau Ballet, *True*	1984	**25.00-40.00**
MFSL 1-153	John Lennon, *Imagine*	1984	**30.00-50.00**
MFSL 1-154	Janis Joplin, *Pearl*	1984	*Unreleased*
MFSL 2-155	Louis Armstrong & Duke Ellington, *The Great Reunion* (2 LPs)	1984	**100.00-150.00**
MFSL 1-156	*Title unknown*	1984	*Unreleased*
MFSL 1-157	The Allman Brothers, *Eat A Peach*	1984	**250.00-350.00**
MFSL 1-158	Linda Ronstadt, *What's New?*	1984	**75.00-100.00**

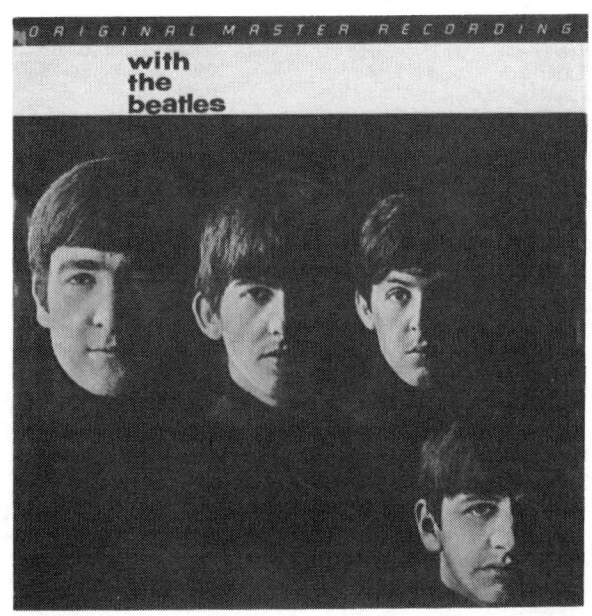

Mobile Fidelity's low print runs, high standards of quality, and the continuing demand for quality pressings make the bulk of their catalog quite collectible to the artist's fans and to audiophiles. The two examples here both fetch three figures: Katy Lied because it sold poorly and is hard to find; With The Beatles because the stamper the company was using cracked during production, halting the sales of the otherwise "best-selling" Beatles.

MFSL 1-159	Earth, Wind & Fire, *That's The Way Of The World*	1984	**30.00-50.00**
MFSL 2-160	Elton John, *Goodbye Yellow Brick Road* (2 LPs)	1984	**50.00-75.00**
MFSL 1-161	The Rolling Stones, *The Rolling Stones*	1984	•
MFSL 1-162	The Rolling Stones, *12 x 5*	1984	•
MFSL 1-163	The Rolling Stones, *Out Of Our Heads*	1984	•
MFSL 1-164	The Rolling Stones, *Aftermath*	1984	•
MFSL 1-165	The Rolling Stones, *Between The Buttons*	1984	•
MFSL 1-166	The Rolling Stones, *Their Satanic Majesties Request*	1984	•
MFSL 1-167	The Rolling Stones, *Beggar's Banquet*	1984	•
MFSL 1-168	The Rolling Stones, *Let It Bleed*	1984	•
MFSL 1-169	The Rolling Stones, *Get Your Ya Ya's Out*	1984	•
MFSL 2-170	The Rolling Stones, *Hot Rocks* (2 LPs)	1984	•
MFSL 1-171	Johnny Mathis, *Heavenly*	1984	**30.00-50.00**
MFSL 1-172	The Grateful Dead, *From The Mars Hotel*	1984	**50.00-75.00**
MFSL 1-173	Simon & Garfunkel, *Bridge Over Troubled Water*	1984	**30.00-50.00**
MFSL 1-174	*Title unknown*	1984	*Unreleased*
MFSL 1-175	Andrew Powell & The Philharmonia Orchestra, *Best Of The Alan Parsons Project*	1984	**25.00-40.00**
MFSL 1-176	Charlie Daniels, *Million Mile Reflections*	1984	**30.00-50.00**
MFSL 1-177	Miles Davis, *Someday My Prince Will Come*	1984	**100.00-150.00**
MFSL 1-178	Mike Bloomfield, Al Kooper, & Steve Stills, *Super Session*	1984	**30.00-50.00**
MFSL 1-179	Gerry Mulligan, *At The Village Vanguard*	1984	**30.00-50.00**
MFSL 1-180	*Title unknown*	1985	*Unreleased*
MFSL 1-181	Huey Lewis & The News, *Sports*	1985	**30.00-50.00**
MFSL 1-182	Duran Duran, *Seven And The Ragged Tiger*	1985	**30.00-50.00**
MFSL 1-183	John Mayall, *Bluesbreakers Featuring Eric Clapton*	1985	**30.00-50.00**
MFSL 1-184	*Title unknown*	1985	*Unreleased*
MFSL 1-185	Sting, *Dream Of The Blue Turtles*	1985	**30.00-50.00**
MFSL 1-186	Blind Faith, *Blind Faith*	1985	**30.00-50.00**
MFSL 1-187	Jethro Tull, *Thick As A Brick*	1985	**30.00-50.00**
MFSL 3-188	Roy Budd & LSO, *Final Frontier* (3 LPs)	1985	**150.00-200.00**
MFSL 3-189	*Title unknown*	1985	*Unreleased*
MFSL 1-190	Pink Floyd, *Meddle*	1985	**50.00-75.00**
MFSL 5-200	Various artists, *Woodstock* (5 LPs)	1985	**200.00-300.00**
BC-1	The Beatles, *The Beatles*	1982	**500.00-750.00**
	(14 album boxed set issued with a "Geodisc" cartridge alignment tool.)		
SC-1	Frank Sinatra, *Frank Sinatra*	1984	**300.00-400.00**
	(16 album boxed set issued with a "Geodisc" cartridge alignment tool.)		
RC-1	The Rolling Stones, *The Rolling Stones*	1984	**300.00-500.00**
	(11 album boxed set issued with a "Geodisc" cartridge alignment tool, a booklet containing full-color reproductions of the Stones' album and a numbered coupon to be mailed in MFSL to receive a "Beggar's Banquet" toilt cover poster.)		

Price Guide To Still-Sealed "Ultra High Quality Recordings"

MFQR 1-005	Supertramp, *Crime Of The Century*	1982	**200.00-300.00**
MFQR 1-017	Pink Floyd, *Dark Side Of The Moon*	1982	**400.00-600.00**
MFQR 1-023	The Beatles, *Abbey Road*	1982	*Unreleased*
MFQR 1-025	Earl Klugh, *Fingerpaintings*	1982	**150.00-200.00**
MFQR 1-035	Cat Stevens, *Tea For The Tillerman*	1982	**150.00-200.00**
MFQR 1-047	The Beatles, *Magical Mystery Tour*	1982	*Unreleased*
MFQR 1-072	The Beatles, *The Beatles* (2 LPs)	1982	*Unreleased*
MFQR 1-084	Alan Parsons Project, *I, Robot*	1982	**100.00-150.00**
MFQR 1-089	Rickie Lee Jones, *Rickie Lee Jones*	1982	*Unreleased*
MFQR 1-100	The Beatles, *Sgt. Pepper's Lonely Hearts Club Band*	1982	**300.00-400.00**
MFQR 1-101	The Beatles, *Please, Please Me*	198?	*Unreleased*
MFQR 1-102	The Beatles, *With The Beatles*	198?	*Unreleased*
MFQR 1-103	The Beatles, *A Hard Day's Night*	198?	*Unreleased*
MFQR 1-104	The Beatles, *Beatles For Sale*	198?	*Unreleased*
MFQR 1-105	The Beatles, *Help!*	198?	*Unreleased*
MFQR 1-106	The Beatles, *Rubber Soul*	198?	*Unreleased*
MFQR 1-107	The Beatles, *Revolver*	198?	*Unreleased*
MFQR 1-108	The Beatles, *Yellow Submarine*	198?	*Unreleased*
MFQR 1-109	The Beatles, *Let It Be*	198?	*Unreleased*
MFQR 1-1507	Lorin Maazel, *Feste Romane*	198?	**75.00-100.00**
MFQR 1-1510	Sir George Solti, *Holst: The Planets*	198?	**100.00-150.00**

Price Guide To Still-Sealed "Super Disks"

SD-16601	Tower Of Power, **Back To Oakland**	*1980*	**25.00-40.00**
SD-16602	*Title unknown*	*1980*	*Unreleased*
SD-16603	Jean Luc Ponty, **Cosmic Messenger**	*1980*	**75.00-100.00**
SD-16604	Van Morrison, **Moondance**	*1980*	**100.00-150.00**
SD-16605	**Blood, Sweat & Tears**	*1980*	**100.00-150.00**
SD-16606	Loggins & Messina, **Full Sail**	*1980*	**40.00-60.00**
SD-16607	Judy Collins, **Judith**	*1980*	**50.00-75.00**
SD-16608	Carly Simon, **Boys In The Trees**	*1980*	**25.00-40.00**
SD-16609	*Title unknown*	*1980*	*Unreleased*
SD-16610	The Who, **Who Are You?**	*1980*	**30.00-50.00**
SD-16611	Michael Franks, **Tiger In The Rain**	*1980*	**50.00-75.00**
SD-16612	Neil Diamond, **12 Greatest Hits**	*1980*	**100.00-150.00**
SD-16613	*Title unknown*	*1980*	*Unreleased*
SD-16614	Elton John, **Goodbye Yellow Brick Road** (2 LPs)	*1980*	**100.00-150.00**
SD-16615	Peter Gabriel, **Peter Gabriel**	*1980*	**150.00-200.00**
SD-16616	B. B. King, **Midnight Believer**	*1980*	**75.00-100.00**
SD-16617	The Outlaws, **The Outlaws**	*1980*	**50.00-75.00**
SD-16618	*Title unknown*	*1980*	*Unreleased*
SD-16619	The Grateful Dead, **Terrapin Station**	*1980*	**250.00-350.00**
SD-16620	The Dixie Dregs, **Dregs Of The Earth**	*1980*	**75.00-100.00**
SD-16621	Jeff Lorber Fusion, **Watersign**	*1980*	**75.00-100.00**
SD-16622	The Brecker Brothers, **Detente**	*1980*	**25.00-40.00**
SD-16623	*Title unknown*	*1980*	*Unreleased*
SD-16624	*Title unknown*	*1980*	*Unreleased*
SD-16625	*Title unknown*	*1980*	*Unreleased*
SD-16626	*Title unknown*	*1980*	*Unreleased*
SD-16627	*Title unknown*	*1980*	*Unreleased*
SD-16628	*Title unknown*	*1980*	*Unreleased*
SD-16629	Derek & The Dominos, **Layla** (2 LPs)	*1980*	**150.00-200.00**
SD-166??	Lou Reed, **The Bells**	*1980*	*Unreleased*

Price Guide To Still-Sealed "SuperDiscs"

NR-1	Randy Sharp, **First In Line** (Styrofoam cover)	*1980*	**50.00-75.00**
NR-1	Randy Sharp, **First In Line** (Standard cover)	*1980*	**30.00-50.00**
NR-2	The Kingston Trio, **Aspen Gold**	*1980*	**50.00-75.00**
NR-3	Heart, **Dreamboat Annie**	*1980*	**100.00-150.00**
NR-4	John Klemmer, **Straight From The Heart**	*1980*	**200.00-300.00**
NR-5	The Doobie Brothers, **The Captain & Me**	*1980*	**100.00-150.00**
NR-6	Pablo Cruise, **Lifeline**	*1980*	**25.00-40.00**
NR-7	Tim Weisberg, **Tip Of The Weisberg**	*1980*	**25.00-40.00**
NR-8	Fleetwood Mac, **Rumours**	*1980*	**50.00-75.00**
NR-9	Spyro Gyra, **Morning Dance**	*1980*	**75.00-100.00**
NR-10	Seals & Crofts, **Summer Breeze**	*1980*	**50.00-75.00**
NR-11	Joni Mitchell, **Court And Spark**	*1980*	**200.00-300.00**
NR-12	Joan Baez, **Diamonds And Rust**	*198?*	**85.00-125.00**
NR-13	Chico Hamilton, **Reaching For The Top**	*198?*	**30.00-50.00**
NR-14	The Cars, **The Cars**	*198?*	**50.00-75.00**
NR-15	Styx, **Pieces Of Eight**	*198?*	**30.00-50.00**
NR-16	Rita Coolidge, **Anytime. . . Anywhere**	*198?*	**30.00-50.00**
NR-17	The Bee Gees, **Spirits Having Flown**	*1981*	**25.00-40.00**
NR-18	The Doobie Brothers, **Minute By Minute**	*198?*	**50.00-75.00**
NR-19	The Police, **Zenyatta Mendatta**	*198?*	**50.00-75.00**
NR-20	Abba, **Arrival**	*198?*	**30.00-50.00**
NR-21	The Moody Blues, **On The Threshold Of A Dream**	*198?*	**200.00-300.00**
NR-22	John Klemmer, **Finesse**	*198?*	**50.00-75.00**
NR-23	Ambrosia, **Life Beyond L.A.**	*198?*	**30.00-50.00**
NR-24	Little Feat, **Time Loves A Hero**	*198?*	**100.00-150.00**
NR-25	The J. Geils Band, **Love Stinks**	*198?*	**30.00-50.00**
NR-26	Linda Ronstadt, **Simple Dreams**	*198?*	**150.00-200.00**
NR-27	Styx, **Cornerstone**	*198?*	**30.00-50.00**
NR-28	Pablo Cruise, **Worlds Away**	*198?*	**25.00-40.00**
NR-29	James Taylor, **Gorilla**	*198?*	**40.00-60.00**
NR-30	The Allman Brothers, **Live At Fillmore East**	*198?*	**200.00-300.00**
NR-31	Air Supply, **Lost In Love**	*198?*	**25.00-40.00**

NR-32	Eric Clapton, *Just One Night*	*198?*	**100.00-150.00**
NR-33	Melissa Manchester, *Don't Cry Out Loud*	*198?*	**25.00-40.00**
NR-34	Al Stewart, *24 Carrots*	*198?*	**30.00-50.00**
NR-35	Gino Vannelli, *Brother To Brother*	*198?*	**25.00-40.00**
NR-36	Crystal Gayle, *When I Dream*	*198?*	**25.00-40.00**
NR-37	Diana Ross, *Diana*	*198?*	**30.00-50.00**
NR-38	The Pretenders, *Pretenders*	*198?*	**30.00-50.00**
NR-39	Grover Washington, Jr., *Winelight*	*198?*	**100.00-150.00**
NR-40	The Police, *Ghost In The Machine*	*1982*	**75.00-100.00**
NR-41	Lee Ritenour, *Rit*	*1982*	**50.00-75.00**
NR-42	The Bee Gees, *Living Eyes*	*1982*	*Unreleased*
NR-43	Elton John, *Greatest Hits*	*1982*	**200.00-300.00**
NR-44	Neil Young, *Harvest*	*1982*	**250.00-350.00**
NR-45	Styx, *Paradise Theatre*	*1982*	**30.00-50.00**
NR-46	Earl Klugh, *Crazy For You*	*1982*	**50.00-75.00**
NR-47	John Lennon & Yoko Ono, *Double Fantasy*	*1982*	**150.00-200.00**
NR-48	*Crosby, Stills & Nash*	*1982*	**300.00-400.00**
NR-49	The Cars, *Candy-O*	*1982*	**50.00-75.00**
NR-50	Victor Feldman, *Secret Of The Andes*	*1982*	**50.00-75.00**
NR-51	Lalo Schifrin, *Ins And Outs*	*1982*	**50.00-75.00**
NR-52	Quincy Jones, *The Dude*	*1982*	**30.00-50.00**
NR-53	John Kay & Steppenwolf, *Wolftracks*	*1982*	**30.00-50.00**
NR-54	Luciano Pavarotti, *Bravo Pavarotti*	*1982*	**25.00-40.00**
NR-55	Al Jarreau, *Breaking Away*	*1982*	**25.00-40.00**
NR-56	Marcel Moise, *Mozart's Gran Partita*	*1982*	*Unreleased*
NR-57	Maynard Ferguson, *Storm*	*1982*	**30.00-50.00**
NR-58	Spirit, *Potatoland*	*1982*	*Unreleased*
NR-59	London Philharmonic, *Tchaikovsky's Sleeping Beauty*	*1982*	*Unreleased*
NR-60	London Philharmonic, *Beethoven's Symphony #2*	*1982*	*Unreleased*
NR-61	London Philharmonic, *Mozart's Symphony #41*	*1982*	*Unreleased*
NR-62	Victor Feldman, *Soft Shoulder*	*1982*	**75.00-100.00**

The World's Most Valuable Album

On May 12, 1963, Bob Dylan was scheduled to appear on Ed Sullivan's Show, guaranteeing him his largest audience outside of the circumscribed world of folk music. Dylan was planning to perform "Talkin' John Birch Blues," a farcical romp from his upcoming album, *The Freewheelin' Bob Dylan*. He had auditioned the song for Sullivan and the show's producer, and both were enthusiastic. Needless to say, Dylan's manager, Albert Grossman, was ebullient at the possibilities such exposure meant. On the eve of the show during a dress rehearsal the editor in charge of CBS-TV programming decided there were problems with the lyrics, which lampooned the absurdities of racism in general and Birchers in particular.

CBS decided that the risk of offending viewers below the Mason-Dixon was too great and Dylan was informed that he would not be singing that particular song. It was suggested he opt for something less topical, perhaps something the audience might already be familiar with, "like a Clancy Brothers tune." Dylan walked out. The stories that circulated in the folk world riled up everybody, all of whom were righteously on the singer's side.

The song had already been recorded and the album, widely anticipated by retailers as a big seller, was ready for shipping. Suddenly, the album was pulled and taken back into the studio. There are two versions of this story: One has Columbia, the recording branch of CBS, taking the logical conclusion (at least, based on the Sullivan decision) that the song was potentially libelous and should not be on the album, thus dictating the change. Another has the vindictive singer claiming that what wasn't good enough for TV couldn't be fit for disc and, at Columbia's expense, he had the record remastered.

Along with the Birch track, also pulled were "Gamblin' Willie's Dead Man's Hand," "Rocks And Gravel," and "Let Me Die In My Footsteps," a powerful condemnation of the bunker mentality then permeating much of America when citizens were being scared into spending a fortune constructing [ultimately useless] underground shelters in case of nuclear war. The three additional tracks, requiring both sides to be remastered, stand as some proof that the album's callback was at least partially instigated by Dylan.

During the pressing of the new version of the album, at least one run using the original stampers was made, although the new labels listing the replacement songs were pressed onto the vinyl, and they were slipped into the second version cover. (Mono copies of this album with the matrix number in the trail-off vinyl that end with a dash and a numeral one ("− 1") followed by a letter indicate the original stamper. Copies with a "2" or above are the later, remastered stampers.) There is no way to know how many of these "mispressings" made it out on the market but there are few known in the hands of collectors and these are always mono copies, or, at least, they were. . ..

In 1990, Los Angeles' Rockaway Records sold a mono copy graded "VG-" for $8,000 to a collector who wasn't about to miss out on a copy in the hopes of eventually finding one in collectable condition. In 1991 a nearly mint mono copy was put up for auction through Yesterday Records of Portland, Oregon, in an open auction in *Goldmine* magazine with a final price in excess of $10,000.

It was assumed that only mono pressings would exist. In fact, in the entry for this album in the first two editions of this book, I noted that "all known copies are mono" and did not even list the possibility of a stereo version. The sale of the near mint copy for five figures and the notation in the book earned the mono version the unofficial title as the "world's most valuable album."

Then, in April 1992 a collector in New York found a stereo copy at a church thrift shop! While the record was well-played, the labels correctly listed the deleted tracks, something none of the monos had done. The record was offered for sale through Greenwich Village's Strider Records, again in the pages of *Goldmine*, and after some furious bidding, the album was eventually sold for more than $10,000 (although it is a given in the field that had the record been in better condition it might have fetched twice that). A second stereo copy was found and sold by a dealer in Californie. It, too, was not in the best of condition but it fetched a similar sum.

While the John Birch song has been a staple of bootlegs since the early '70s where it is generally listed as "Talkin' John Birch Society Blues," on Columbia's three CD boxed set of rare Dylan material, *the bootleg series, volumes 1-3*, it is listed as "Talkin' John Birch Paranoid Blues." It should be noted that the label on the 1963 stereo album lists the song as "Talkin' John Birch Blues."

While all known original mono copies of The Freewheelin' Bob Dylan *with the deleted tracks have later labels listing the replacement songs, the sole stereo copy—found in 1992 in a thrift shop in New York's Greenwich Village—does list the original line-up on the label. Side 1 (shown here) lists "Rocks And Gravel" and "Let Me Die In My Footsteps" as the second and third songs, respectively. Side 2 (not shown) lists "Gamblin' Willie's Dead Man's Hand" and "Talkin' John Birch Blues" as the second and fifth songs. Note that a U.S. copy of the cover with the deleted tracks listed has not been found. CBS of Canada did print such covers, although all copies of the records list and play the replacement tracks. Collectible copies of this Canadian cover are currently worth approximately $100-200.*

The 100 Most Valuable U.S. Albums

Below are the albums with the highest assigned current market values as of late 1994. The criterion for this list is that the item must be a domestically manufactured vinyl album, either commercial or promotional. Acetates, incomplete cover slicks and Compact Discs are ineligible. Titles are listed in descending order of value (naturally). Those with the same value are listed alphabetically by artist; two or more titles by the same artist with the same value are listed chronologically. Values with an asterisk (*) indicate that the value assigned *for this list* is an average taken from the suggested range of Near Mint values in the main listings of the book. That is, a near mint copy of that record could sell for quite a bit less or considerably more than the value listed below.

There are 104 listings from the main body of this edition with a minimum value of $2,000. This is a rather significant step up from last edition's list, where the minimum value was $1,200. In fact, there are enough records listed within the pages of this book with values between $1,500 and $1,800 to extend this list by several pages! While it is fairly obvious that Bob Dylan enjoys the prestige of having both the #1 and the #2 most valuable albums (plus three more listings), it is Liverpool's own Beatles that dominate with 30 listings, almost one-third of the top 100. Most of these are the damnnear-impossible to find Vee Jay stereo releases or the album that is probably the single most sought-after album in the world, the *Yesterday... & Today* "butcher cover."

In contrast, the King, Elvis Presley, places a mere half-dozen titles (plus one various artists comp that owes its exorbitant value to Presley's presence). Of course, each of these Elvis listings are for promotional albums; his regular releases sold far too many copies to ever qualify for this list. . . There are also two-dozen rhythm'n blues or blues and another six rock'n roll albums from the pre-Beatles era; fifteen '60s artifacts, most of which are independent psychedelic pressings; a half-dozen '70s rarities, two by ex-Beatles; a couple of all-but-unknown gospel albums from Berry Gordy's Tamla/Motown enterprise; and such loners as a pair of unreleased albums by Jack Kerouac and Frank Sinatra.

The opinions of several contributors to say what they want about individual titles, hopefully to educate and elucidate the record's value. These opinions remain the exclusive property of the individuals; don't hold me responsible for a statement that is either grossly inaccurate or is the polar opposite of yours, unless, of course, it's mine expressed. These remarks are in quotes and are followed by the initials of the remarker: Norman Feinberg (NF), Gary Johnson (GJ), Ashley Johnson (AJ), Neal Skok (NS) and myself (NU).

---

1. BOB DYLAN

Columbia CS-8786   (S)   **The Freewheelin' Bob Dylan**   1963   **20,000.00+**

(Original stereo pressings contain four songs— "Talking John Birch Blues," "Let Me Die In My Footsteps," "Rocks And Gravel" and "Gamblin' Willie's Dead Man's Hand"— deleted from all subsequent pressings. For more information refer to the article "The World's Most Valuable Album" above. "As two copies in VG have sold for more than $12,000, I must assume that a NM copy would go for a record sum in excess of $20,000." — NU)

2. BOB DYLAN
Columbia CL-1986   (M)   **The Freewheelin' Bob Dylan**   1963   **15,000.00** •
(*This is the mono version of the album above. It is important to note that while the stereo album above lists the deleted tracks on the label, no mono copy containing the deleted tracks have been found with the labels listing those tracks. That is, mono copies of this album have first pressing records with second pressing labels. "While Freewheelin' is a better album with the replacement tracks, it's a shame that 'Footstep' and 'Birch' couldn't have stayed. They would have added to the album's pre-WWIII paranoia. Also, the topicality of this album could easily have fit in the Reagan-Bush years. . ." — NU*)

BILLY WARD & THE DOMINOES
Federal 295-94   (10")   **Billy Ward & His Dominoes**   1955   **15,000.00** •
(*The Dominoes were one of the most important of the early groups, marked by strong leads with great harmonies on influential material. Out of their ranks rose both Clyde McPhatter (and thus, The Drifters) and Jackie Wilson.. "The first R&B group LP. Mint copies are all but non-existent." — NF*)

4. THE BEATLES
Vee Jay SR-1062   (S)   **Introducing The Beatles** (Ad back)   1963   **10,000.00** •
(*First stereo pressing with "Love Me Do" and "P.S. I Love You." The back cover features ads for 25 other Vee Jay albums "Aside from its collectibility, it remains an under-rated rock'n roll album." — NU.*)

THE BEATLES / FRANK IFIELD
Vee Jay LPS-1085   (S)   **On Stage** (Portrait cover)   1964   **10,000.00** •
(*This second pressing cover features a full-color painting of the Fab Four in place of the cartoon of an eccentric British chap on the original. "A not so clever recycling of some of the material on Introducing The Beatles coupled with the very non-Invasionish crooning of Mr. Ifield." — NU*)

IKE & TINA TURNER
Philles PHLPS-4011   (S)   **River Deep-Mountain High**   1966   **10,000.00** •
(*"River Deep-Mountain High" the single, often cited by both fans and critics as one of the genre's greatest achievements, was viewed as an event at the time of its release by both producer Phil Spector, his admirers and his detractors. After it failed to even dent the top 40, Uncle Phil blamed his "enemies" for the failure. And he could be right; it's almost impossible to hear this amazing single and not think "Hit Record!" After AM stations torpedoed the next single, the album was pressed in minute quantities, apparently without Spector's knowledge, to gain access to the stereo-only FM radio stations. No covers are known to have been completed. This was eventually issued by A&M in 1969.*)

7. THE BEATLES
Vee Jay PRO-202   (DJ)   **Hear The Beatles Tell All** (White label promo)   1964   **8,000.00** •
(*Interviews with the Mop Tops from 1964. The album was issued commercially in mono in '64 and in stereo by Vee Jay International in 1979.*)

THE BEATLES
Capitol ST-2553   (S)   **Yesterday And Today** (Butcher cover)   1966   **8,000.00** •
(*Throughout the first few years of the Beatles' American career, Capitol was paring the original EMI/Parlophone albums down from 14 tracks to eleven for U.S. consumption, butchering the group's work and its intent. The left-overs were used to compile "new" albums, none of which, for the most part, have counterparts anywhere else in the world. As a means of protest, this album sported a cover photo of the four Fabs in doctor smocks cheekily handling dismembered baby-doll parts and slabs of raw meat. . . After initial copies were distributed the album was withdrawn and a new cover with a shot off four nattily attired but docile lads posing with a steamer trunk was adapted. Hirelings were paid to remove the original cover and affix the new one but, as they were paid by the piece, many took to merely pasting the second, "trunk" cover over the "butcher cover." Copies of the album with the original cover never having had a second cover pasted on to it are referred to as "first state butchers." Copies with both covers—i.e., the original cover and the second cover pasted on it—are referred to as "second state butchers."*)

CHARLES BROWN
Aladdin 702   (10")   **Mood Music** (Red vinyl)   1952   **8,000.00** •
(*This classic by the legendary Brown—who is still doing personal appearances—is arguably the rarest of the rare Aladdin 10" albums.*)

THE MIDNIGHTERS
Federal 295-90   (10")   **The Midnighters: Their Greatest Hits**   1955   **8,000.00** •
(*The first long-player by this classic R&B ensemble. "New Mint copies of this album are almost non-existent and are seldom for sale. A truly mint copy of this LP has not been available in years." — NF*)

AMOS MILBURN
Aladdin 704   (10")   **Rockin' The Boogie** (Red vinyl)   1954   **8,000.00** •
(*This was Amos' first LP; his last was recorded for Motown and released in 1963.*)

AMOS MILBURN / WYNONIE HARRIS / CROWN PRINCE WATERFORD
Aladdin 703   (10") **Party After Hours** (Red vinyl)   1954   **8,000.00** *
   (This r&b collection features three of Aladdin's favorite artists; while Milburn rated an album of
his own, Aladdin 704, Rockin' The Boogie (also on this list), neither Harris nor Waterford saw their work
on LP other than collections such as this.)

13. THE BEATLES
Apple SO-385   (S) **Hey Jude/The Beatles Again** (Alternate cover)   1970   **7,500.00** *
   (Alternate cover prototypes were designed for this album when it bore the working title "The
Beatles Again." Several graphic variations— including one cover with the front and back cover photos
switched— are known to exist and the suggested value refers to any of the variations. The value is entirely
for the cover, with or without the record inside.)

JACK KEROUAC
Dot DLP-3154   (M) **Poetry For The Beat Generation**   1959   **7,500.00** *
   (Preposterously rare collection withdrawn by Dot and issued on their Hanover subsidiary,
which is also rare. The value assigned is based on the assumption that this album would attract the
attention of literary aficionados as well as record collectors.)

THE ROLLING STONES
London LL-3402   (M) **12 X 5** (Blue vinyl)   1966   **7,500.00** *
   (One copy of The Stones' second American LP was found in 1989 on blue vinyl. Its official
original remains a mystery although the record, graded "Poor" by the seller, immediately sold for
$2,000.)

16. JOHNNY BURNETTE & THE ROCK 'N' ROLL TRIO
Coral CRL-57080   (M) **Johnny Burnette & The Rock 'N' Roll Trio**   1956   **6,000.00** *
   (The "trio" in the title is deceptive: This is really Johnny Burnette with brother Dorsey and
Paul Burlison. Along with RCA Victor LPM-1254, Elvis Presley, this is one of the first— and definitive—
rockabilly albums. "Most copies fall into the VG or less grading, selling for $200-500. Mint copies are
virtually unknown and would command prices in the $10,000 range." — NF)

PRINCE
Warner Bros. 25677   (DJ) **The Black Album** (2 LP promo)   1987   **6,000.00** *
   (This promotional version of Prince's withdrawn [by the artist] album is actually two 12"
records that play at 45 RPM and contains the entirety of the regular album. There are two known copies
in the hands of collectors, one of which, graded VG+, sold for $6,000 during the first weeks of 1993.)

18. FRANK BALLARD
Phillips Inter.1985   (M) **Rhythm-Blues Party**   1962   **5,000.00**
   ("Copies of this album in collectible condition are so rare that delineating a price for condition
is ludicrous. There are probably fewer than ten copies known to exist." — NF)

BOB DYLAN
Columbia PC-33235   (DJ) **Blood On The Tracks** (Original test pressing)   1975   **5,000.00** *
   (Original test pressings— issued in plain cardboard jackets— feature alternate takes of five
songs of "Tangled Up In Blue," "If You See Her Say Hello," "You're A Big Girl Now," "Idiot Wind" and "Lily,
Rosemary And The Jack Of Hearts." A copy graded VG+ fetched $5,000 in 1991. "Another case where
Dylan's instincts are spot on. While the original versions all have something to offer, this is a better
album for the often sloppy but genuinely inspired replacement versions." — NU)

THE FIVE ROYALES
Apollo LP-488   (M) **The Rockin' Five Royales** (Purple & silver label)   1956   **5,000.00** *
   (This purple vinyl original had silver print. Later pressings dropped the [expensive] silver print.
A copy graded VG+ sold for $3,500 in 1993.)

21. BOYD BENNETT
King 395-594   (M) **Boyd Bennett**   1956   **4,500.00** *
   (This is one of the rarest— and most desirable— of all the Kings.)

DAVID BOWIE
RCA Victor CPL1-0576   (S) **Diamond Dogs** (Genitals cover)   1974   **4,500.00** *
   (The cover, a painting of a dog with Bowie's head, clearly shows the canine's genitals. . . at rest.
Prior to release the Bowiedog was effectively neutered by an airbrush. These "dickless" covers are as
common as hen's beaks. The value here is entirely for the cover, with or without the record inside.. "Once
only rumored to exist and then only as a slick not affixed to the cardboard, there are now four known
copies, the two most recent sold for $4,000 and $6,000." — NF)

JOHN LENNON & YOKO ONO
Nautilus NR-47   (S)   **Double Fantasy** *(Alternate cover)*   *1980*   **4,500.00** •
(Alternate cover prototype has bright yellow strokes added to the background and a red heart drawn on Yoko's bosom. There is one known copy and it is not for sale. The estimate is for the cover alone and based wholly on assumption. . .)

REVEREND COLUMBUS MANN
Tamla T-227   (M)   **They Shall Be Mine**   *1962*   **4,500.00** •
(A miniscule printing, possibly done as a personal favor by Berry Gordy for Mann, was distributed in Detroit, probably to the Reverend's flock, and is one of the rarest of all Motown albums.)

BIG JAY McNEELY
Federal 295-96   (10")   **Big Jay McNeely**   *1954*   **4,500.00** •
(Primarily a major R&B session man given a shot at solo success by Federal and King.)

PRINCE
Warner Bros. 25677   (S)   **The Black Album**   *1987*   **4,500.00** •
(This is the version prepared for commercial release in 1987 but pulled by Prince. A sealed copy sold in 1990 for $5,000.)

27. THE BEATLES
Vee Jay SR-1062   (S)   **Introducing The Beatles** *(Blank back)*   *1963*   **4,000.00** •
(First pressing with "Love Me Do" and "P.S. I Love You." The back cover is completely blank, devoid of any printing..)

THE BEATLES / FRANK IFIELD
Vee Jay LP-1085   (M)   **On Stage** *(Portrait cover)*   *1964*   **4,000.00** •
(This second pressing cover features a full-color painting of the Fab Four in place of the cartoon of an eccentric British chap on the original.)

CHARLES BROWN
Aladdin 702   (10")   **Mood Music** *(Black vinyl)*   *1952*   **4,000.00** •
(The original pressing is on red vinyl and twice as valuable as this black vinyl reissue.)

THE CRICKETS
Brunswick BL-54038   (M)   **The Chirping Crickets** *(Yellow label promo)*   *1957*   **4,000.00** •
("Three copies have sold in the past two years in this price range." — NU)

BOB DYLAN
Columbia CL-1986   (DJ)   **The Freewheelin' Bob Dylan** *(White label promo)*   *1963*   **4,000.00** •
(For the story on this title, refer to the first listing of this list. This white label promo plays the second version with "Masters Of War," etc., but the front cover has a DJ title & timing strip listing the deleted tracks, including "Talkin' John Birch Blues.")

THE FENDERMEN
Soma MG-1240   (M)   **Mule Skinner Blues** *(Blue vinyl)*   *1960*   **4,000.00**
(A copy of this album on blue vinyl turned up in 1992 and was promptly sold for $4,000.)

FRANK FROST & THE NIGHTHAWKS
Phillips Inter.1975   (M)   **Hey Boss Man!**   *1961*   **4,000.00**
(Supposedly there were only 500 copies of this LP pressed. In 1975 a noted West Coast collector found 490 odd covers without records. "There are probably less than 10 complete copies in the hands of collectors today." — NF)

SMILEY LEWIS
Imperial LP-9141   (M)   **I Hear You Knocking** *(Green vinyl)*   *1961*   **4,000.00** •
("I wouldn't have believed it existed. . . until I found and sold one." — NF)

PAUL & LINDA McCARTNEY
Apple MAS-3375   (DJ)   **Ram** *(Mono promo)*   *1971*   **4,000.00** •
(The label does not identify this as a promotional release but it clearly states that the album in "Monaural." In most cases it was was shipped to radio stations in the same cover as the regular stereo version, sometimes the two LPs were side by side in the same jacket.)

AMOS MILBURN
Aladdin 704   (10")   **Rockin' The Boogie** *(Black vinyl)*   *1954*   **4,000.00** •
(The original pressing is on red vinyl and twice as valuable as this black vinyl reissue.)

SMILEY LEWIS

I HEAR YOU KNOCKING

If this chart were run like a national top 100 survey, Smiley Lewis' I Hear You Knocking would rate an exploding bullet, but not for just any copy of this fine rhythm'n blues outing. A collector turned up a copy of this album on green vinyl, providing the field with an immediate rarity of note.

AMOS MILBURN / WYNONIE HARRIS / CROWN PRINCE WATERFORD
Aladdin 703   *(10")* **Party After Hours** *(Black vinyl)*   1954 **4,000.00**
   (The original pressing is on red vinyl and twice as valuable as this black vinyl reissue.)

GATEMOUTH MOORE
King 684   *(M)* **Gatemouth Moore Sings The Blues** 1960 **4,000.00**
   (This album, Moore's sole release of the '50s and '60s, has been erroneously titled in previous editions of this book as I'm A Fool To Care. "One of the legendary King albums; only a few have survived the past four decades. A Near Mint copy recently sold for $3,000." — NF)

THE ROLLING STONES
London NPS-3   *(DJ)* **Through The Past, Darkly** *(Picture disc)* 1969 **4,000.00** •
   (Prototypes for a rejected picture disc back in '69. Two variations are known: one has the cover from "High Tide & Green Grass" on both sides the other has "High Tide" backed with Ten Years After's "Sssh." The value is entirely for the record whether or not it includes a cover.)

FRANK SINATRA
Reprise FS-1028 *(S)* **Sinatra-Jobim** *(Test pressing)* 1969 **4,000.00** •
   (This album, a follow-up to 1967's successful "Francis Albert Sinatra And Antonio Carlos Jobim," was cancelled after test pressings were made. I assigned this record the the widest suggested range in the book, $2,000-6,000, due to both the lack of knowledge concerning its rarity and the utter unpredictability of Sinatra collectors. Company notes show that 3,500 copies were manufactured as 8-track tapes and all but three ordered destroyed. . . Issued in a plain cardboard jacket.)

VARIOUS ARTISTS SOUNDTRACK
DCA Productions *(DJ)* **Rock, Rock, Rock** *(With cover)* 1956 **4,000.00** •
   (Publisher's demo disc intended for inclusion in the soundtrack for the movie of the same name. The price here is for the rare version with a printed cover. The album was issued to most stations in a plain jacket and these carry a Near Mint value of $2,000-4,000.)

42. THE BEATLES
Vee Jay LP-1062 *(M)* **Introducing The Beatles** *(Ad back)* 1963 **3,500.00** •
   (First mono pressing with "Love Me Do" and "P.S. I Love You." The back cover features ads for 25 other Vee Jay albums.)

THE BEATLES
Capitol T-2553 *(M)* **Yesterday And Today** *(Butcher cover)* 1966 **3,500.00** •
   (First-state mono "butcher cover." Refer to the first-state stereo butcher "Yesterday And Today," listed above for the full story on this rarity.)

44. THE BACHS
Raio *(No number)* *(S)* **Out Of The Bachs**   1967 **3,000.00**
   (A VG copy sold for $2,000 prior to the discovery of a small cache of sealed copies, three of which have reportedly sold for $5,000 each. "Minor key, haunting and melodic... like an American Zombies if they were in a garage/psych mood." — NS)

THE BEATLES / THE FOUR SEASONS
Vee Jay DXS-30 *(S)* **The Beatles Vs. The Four Seasons** 1964 **3,000.00** •
   (This double-album collects Vee Jay 1062, "Introducing The Beatles," with 1065, "The Golden Hits Of The Four Seasons." It was issued with a fold-open, full-color poster of the Liverpudlians, worth an additional $300 in Near Mint condition. The mono version of this album is worth $500. Beatles collectors seeking to piece together the most perfect set of this album— cover plus the two discs— have driven the value of The Four Seasons album up beyond what a Seasons' collector would normally value the album at!)

THE BEATLES
Apple KAL-1004 *(DJ)* **Yellow Submarine** *(Radio spots)* 1968 **3,000.00** •
   (This album contains a series of brief "spots," or plugs, intended for radio broadcast to promote the animated film. Issued in a plain cardboard jacket.)

ROY BROWN / WYNONIE HARRIS / EDDIE VINSON
King 668   *(M)* **Battle Of The Blues, Volume 4** 1960 **3,000.00** •
   (This various artists compilation features tracks by each of the three R&B giants. "One of the rarest and most sought-after numbers on King.." — NF) 3000-5000

DAMON
Ankh 968   *(S)* **Song Of A Gypsy** *(Gatefold cover)* 1970 **3,000.00**
   (Original versions of this privately pressed psych album have gatefold covers with both an Egyptian ankh and the title embossed on the front. Reissued with a standard single-pocket cover.)

FRACTION
Angelus WR-5005   (S)   **Moon Blood**   197?   **3,000.00**
(This privately pressed psychedelic collectible was issued in a cover with a die-cut "window" to allow the moon on the inner sleeve to show through.)

LLOYD GLENN
Swing Time 1901   (10")   **Lloyd Glenn**   1952   **3,000.00**
("There are probably less than 10 copies in the hands of collectors. One sold for $2,750 in 1991." — NF)

THE GOSPEL STARS
Tamla TM-222   (M)   **The Great Gospel Stars**   1961   **3,000.00** •
("This is by far the rarest LP on any Motown related label; there are only a few copies known to exist. A Mint copy sold for $3,000 in 1991." — NF)

THE INDEX
D. C. *(No number)*   (M)   **The Index**   1968   **3,000.00**
(The price is for original record in an original cover, both featuring "New York Mining Disaster." Most copies have the original record in a second pressing cover which lists "Fire Eyes." "Along with Tom Rapp's Yetti-Men, this is one of the missing links between surf and psych." — NS)

JEFFERSON AIRPLANE
RCA Victor LPM-3584   (M)   **Jefferson Airplane Takes Off!**   1966   **3,000.00** •
(Original mono pressings contain "Runnin' 'Round This World" and alternate takes of both "Go To Her" and "Let Me In," whose lyrics make allusions to sex and LSD. These three were deleted from all subsequent pressings. The latter two were replaced by cleaned up versions while "Runnin'" sat on the shelf until it was gathered onto the "Early Flight" album five years later. Stereo copies with these tracks are not known to exist.)

THE MIDNIGHTERS
Federal 395-541   (M)   **The Midnighters: Their Greatest Hits**   1955   **3,000.00** •
(This is the 12" repackage of the 10" version. "Very rare in collectible condition and generally sold in VG or less for $100-200." — NF)

THE MIDNIGHTERS
Federal 395-581   (M)   **The Midnighters, Volume 2**   1955   **3,000.00** •
(Their second 12" album for Federal. As rare as the first.)

THE MUSIC EMPORIUM
Sentinal 69001   (S)   **The Music Emporium**   1969   **3,000.00**
(Privately pressed psych album is one of the classics of its genre. "Typifies West Coast acid/psych with some nice raga type songs." — NS)

ELVIS PRESLEY
RCA Victor   (S)   **International Hotel Presents Elvis, 1969**   1969   **3,000.00** •
(Complimentary boxed set [supposedly] limited to 2,000 copies presented to the hotel's dinner guests for Elvis' first show of the year. The box contains a letter of introduction and thanks from Elvis, Colonel Parker and RCA, which is essential for completeness and a variety of souvenirs and records generally available elsewhere. More than 95% of the value is for the box alone.)

ELVIS PRESLEY
RCA Victor   (S)   **International Hotel Presents Elvis, 1970**   1970   **3,000.00** •
(Complimentary boxed set [supposedly] limited to 2,000 copies presented to the hotel's dinner guests for Elvis' first show of the year. The box contains a letter of introduction and thanks from Elvis, Colonel Parker and RCA, which is essential for completeness and a variety of souvenirs and records generally available elsewhere. More than 95% of the value is for the box alone.)

ELVIS PRESLEY
RCA Victor VPSX-6089   (Q)   **Aloha From Hawaii Via Satellite** *(Tuna cover)*   1973   **3,000.00** •
(Van Camp, the sponsors of Elvis' 1973 CBS TV Special, acquired stock copies of the album and affixed stickers to the cover with their Chicken Of The Sea tuna maid noting the special. A sheet with a picture of Elvis and a description of the show was included and these LPs were distributed to members of the corporate office.. As the records were available commercially, the value is for the cover alone.)

THE ROLLING STONES
London NP-1   (DJ)   **High Tide & Green Grass** *(Alternate cover)*   1966   **3,000.00** •
(This rejected cover prototype has the same graphics as the released version except title on the front is on two lines [the released version has the title on three lines] and in radically different type. One copy is known to exist. The value is for the cover alone.)

VARIOUS ARTISTS SOUNDTRACK
(No label)   *(DJ)*   **Carnival Rock** *(Soundtrack)*   1956   **3,000.00** •
    (This sampler from the movie of the same name was pressed on red vinyl and shipped to radio stations in a plain cardboard or paper sleeve.)

VARIOUS ARTISTS SOUNDTRACK
Universal Unlimited   *(10")*   **Rock, Pretty Baby** *(Red vinyl)*   1956   **3,000.00** •
    (Promotional radio transcription from the film. Commercially issued by Decca.)

63. **THE BEATLES**
United Arts. UAL-3366 *(DJ)*   **A Hard Day's Night** *(White label promo)*   1964   **2,500.00** •
    (This is the white label promo edition of the commercially released album to the Fab Four's first feature film. Exactly why this promo is so rare is unknown; this movie was heavily promoted by U.A. as producers of both the film and the soundtrack. . .)

THE BEATLES
Capitol ST-2553   *(S)*   **Yesterday And Today** *(2nd state butcher cover)* 1966   **2,500.00** •
    (This is the second-state "butcher cover" with the "trunk" cover pasted over the original "butcher" cover. For the story on this title, refer to the listing for the "first-state stereo" listed above.)

THE FIVE ROYALES
Apollo LP-488   *(M)*   **The Rockin' Five Royales** *(Green label)*   1956   **2,500.00**

LONNIE JOHNSON
King 395-520   *(M)*   **Lonesome Road**   1958   **2,500.00** •
    ("One of the most sought-after LPs on King. Mint copies are impossible to find and would fetch prices in excess of $2,500." — NF)

LITTLE ESTHER
King 622   *(M)*   **Down Memory Lane With Little Esther**   1959   **2,500.00** •
    ("Among the best R&B albums ever made, Little Esther Phillips' masterpiece is high on everyone's want-list. A Mint copy would command a price in the $3,000-4,000 range." — NF)

ELVIS PRESLEY
RCA Victor AFL1-2428 *(S)*   **Moody Blue** *(Purple-on-white "splash" vinyl)*   1977   **2,500.00** •

ELVIS PRESLEY
RCA Victor AFL1-2428 *(S)*   **Moody Blue** *(Red-on-white "splash" vinyl)*   1977   **2,500.00** •

ELVIS PRESLEY
RCA Victor AFL1-2428 *(S)*   **Moody Blue** *(Yellow-on-white "splash" vinyl)*   1977   **2,500.00** •
    ("These three listings are prototype test pressings done under RCA's authorization and then distributed to company execs. these should not be confused with the solid colored vinyl pressings of this album, worth about half of these multi-color pressings. This album— Elvis' last release prior to his death— was mediocre even by the less than inspiring standards he had been setting for himself the previous half-dozen years." — NU)

LULA REED
King 604   *(M)*   **Blue And Moody**   1959   **2,500.00** •
    ("Mint copies of this album are extremely rare commanding prices in excess of $2,000." — NF)

VARIOUS ARTISTS
Aladdin LP-710   *(M)*   **Rock And Roll With Rhythm And Blues**   195?   **2,500.00** •
    (Although this album is part of the Aladdin's 700 series for 10" albums it is 12" only.)

73. **THE BEATLES**
United Arts. Help-Show *(DJ)*   **Help!** *(One-sided, open-end interview)*   1965   **2,400.00** •
    (This one-sided disc, issued in a plain cardboard jacket, should not be confused with the more common [sic] two-sided interview album.)

74. **THE CHAMPS**
Challenge CHL-601   *(M)*   **Go Champs Go** *(Blue vinyl)*   1958   **2,250.00** •
    ("A legendary piece of colored vinyl by the makers of 'Tequila'." — NU)

JIMI HENDRIX EXPERIENCE
Reprise 2R-6307   *(M)*   **Electric Ladyland** *(White label promo mono)*   1968   **2,250.00** •
    ("Probably the rarest and hottest Hendrix collectible around." — GJ)

VARIOUS ARTISTS SOUNDTRACK
Warner Bros. *(No #)*   *(DJ)* **Jamboree** *(Soundtrack)*   1955   **2,250.00** *
    (This soundtrack contains snippets of songs by a potpourri of artists of the time and was shipped out to radio stations. It is one of the rarest albums of the rock 'n roll era and sells for $300-500 in VG or less condition.)

77. THE TOKENS
B.T. Puppy BTPS-10?? *(S)* **Intercourse**   1971   **2,000.00+**
    ("The rarest white vocal group record in the world. There are currently two copies known in the hands of collectors. Guess why it didn't receive a lot of distribution. . ." — NU)

78. THE BEATLES
Vee Jay SR-1062   *(S)* **Introducing The Beatles**   1964   **2,000.00** *
    (Second stereo pressings with "Please Please Me" and "Ask Me Why." There are three known label variations for this title, each with the same approximate value.)

THE BEATLES
Vee Jay VJS-1092   *(S)* **Songs, Pictures And Stories**   1964   **2,000.00** *
    (Issued in a nifty gatefold cover where the front flap is only 8" across. This album contains second pressings of Vee Jay 1062, Introducing The Beatles with "Please Please Me" and "Ask Me Why." There are three label variations for this title, each currently carrying the same approximate value.)

THE BEATLES
Mobile Fid. MFQR-023   *(S)* **Abbey Road** *(UHQR test pressing)*   1982   **2,000.00** *
    (Mobile Fidelity Sound Laboratories made "Ultra High Quality Recording" test pressings for this and each of the Beatles albums below for potential commercial release. Word is that less than a dozen per title were pressed, making these outlandishly rare.)

THE BEATLES
Mobile Fid. MFQR-047   *(P)* **Magical Mystery Tour** *(UHQR test pressing)*   1982   **2,000.00** *

THE BEATLES
Mobile Fid. MFQR-072   *(S)* **The Beatles** *(UHQR test pressing)*   1982   **2,000.00** *

THE BEATLES
Mobile Fid. MFQR-100   *(S)* **Sgt. Pepper** *(UHQR test pressing)*   1982   **2,000.00** *

THE BEATLES
Mobile Fid. MFQR-101   *(P)* **Please Please Me** *(UHQR test pressing)*   1982   **2,000.00** *

THE BEATLES
Mobile Fid. MFQR-102   *(S)* **With The Beatles** *(UHQR test pressing)*   1982   **2,000.00** *

THE BEATLES
Mobile Fid. MFQR-103   *(S)* **A Hard Day's Night** *(UHQR test pressing)*   1982   **2,000.00** *

THE BEATLES
Mobile Fid. MFQR-104   *(S)* **Beatles For Sale** *(UHQR test pressing)*   1982   **2,000.00** *

THE BEATLES
Mobile Fid. MFQR-105   *(S)* **Help!** *(UHQR test pressing)*   1982   **2,000.00** *

THE BEATLES
Mobile Fid. MFQR-106   *(S)* **Rubber Soul** *(UHQR test pressing)*   1982   **2,000.00** *

THE BEATLES
Mobile Fid. MFQR-107   *(S)* **Revolver** *(UHQR test pressing)*   1982   **2,000.00** *

THE BEATLES
Mobile Fid. MFQR-108   *(P)* **Yellow Submarine** *(UHQR test pressing)*   1982   **2,000.00** *

THE BEATLES
Mobile Fid. MFQR-109   *(S)* **Let It Be** *(UHQR test pressing)*   1982   **2,000.00** *

BRIGADE
Band'n Vocal RS-1066   *(S)* **Last Laugh**   1970   **2,000.00** *
    (Privately pressed album from a NW group. "Highly over-rated album with a couple of high points, including a psychedelic Doorsish number." — NS)

JACKSON BROWNE
(No label)   (S)   **"Jackson Browne's First Album"**   1967   **2,000.00** •
(*This double-album is the Holy Grail for Jackson's fan. Actually, this is an untitled publishers demo intended to get other, established artists to record the his songs. None of these recordings have been released to the public. Issued in a plain cardboard jacket.*)

THE CRESTS
Coed LPC-901   (M)   **The Crests Sing All The Biggies** (*Promo*)   1960   **2,000.00** •
(*Red label "Advance Preview" copy of this classic white vocal group.*)

THE FIVE KEYS
Aladdin 806   (M)   **The Best Of The Five Keys** (*Maroon label*)   1956   **2,000.00** •
(*First pressings with a blue label are twice as valuable as this reissue.*)

BUDDY HOLLY
Decca DL-8707   (M)   **That'll Be The Day** (*Black & silver label*)   1958   **2,000.00**
(*This album contains Holly's pre-Cricket recordings for Decca, who had tried— with little real success— to groom the Holly into a country' western singer. "One of the single rarest white rock'n roll albums of the '50s. Even the black "rainbow" label reissues from the '60s are rare." — NU*)

MARIANI
Sonobeat 1001   (M)   **Perpetuum Mobile**   196?   **2,000.00**
(*Impossibly rare small label '60s psych.*)

THE NEW TWEEDY BROTHERS
Ridon 234   (S)   **The New Tweedy Brothers** (*Hexagonal cover*)   196?   **2,000.00**
(*Although they're from Portland they sound more like a Bay Area group with a tremeloed guitar sound ala John Cipollina." — NS*)

THE PENGUINS
Dootone DTL-204   (M)   **Best In Rhythm 'N Blues** (*Red vinyl*)   1957   **2,000.00** •
(*Although this is a various artists album with the second side containing tracks by The Dootones, Meadowlarks and Medallions, as all of side one is by The Penguins this is generally considered their first album by collectors.*)

PHAPHNER
Dragon LP-101   (S)   **Overdrive**   197?   **2,000.00** •
(*"People are finally deciding this privately pressed psych album is a really good record as well as a really rare record. . . after they have all disappeared." — AJ.*)

VARIOUS ARTISTS
RCA Victor SP-33-66   (DJ)   **Christmas Programming From RCA Victor**   1959   **2,000.00** •
(*This seasonal sampler features one Elvis track and is one of the few various artists sampler that seems to whet all Elvis collectors appetites. The nifty paper sleeve with the full-color cartoon drawing of Santa Claus— counterfeits are black & white— also features a photo of the artists included.." — NU*)

VARIOUS ARTISTS SOUNDTRACK
(No label)   (DJ)   **Go, Johnny, Go** (*Soundtrack*)   1959   **2,000.00** •
(*Sent out to radio stations in a plain cardboard jacket. Copies were handed out at the movie's premiere in a deluxe box that also included a a lobby card and a "press pass" to the showing. The box is preposterously rare with no reasonable way to suggest a value.*)

THE WEST COAST POP ART EXPERIMENTAL BAND
Fifo M101   (M)   **West Coast Pop Art Experimental Band**   1966   **2,000.00**
(*A privately pressed psych album from a group that later recorded several fine albums for Reprise. Copies of this album recently turned up without covers and quickly sold out. . .*)

The Big Four-Speed, Duo-Quad, Posi-Traction Sound Of The Cars

While the collecting of records relating to cars and hot rods has been a part of the hobby for decades, for the most part the records collected were vocal songs about the four wheel passion, generally sung by a group. Most of these were a manifestation of the "West Coast Sound" of the '60s originated by Brian Wilson's Beach Boys with a nod to the early Jan & Dean recordings. Yet there is *another* aspect of collecting car records and that is the collecting of albums that deal directly with the world of racing, primarily sound effects and documentaries. These albums are usually collected outside of the mainstream record collecting hobby by men and women who are motor enthusiasts.

While some of these collectors seek only those records that deal with a specific car (say, a '64 Mustang), others collect those records that deal with a *type* of car, such as the 'Cuda, GTO or 'Vette. And, of even more interest, is the fact that the record itself (both its contents and its condition) may be of secondary import. What many of these collectors are looking for is the photo of the car on the cover! The most *common* car collectible is any album that pictures a car on the cover and a collector of a specific type of car might find a need for each and every album with that car pictured.

American's fascination with automobiles was instantaneous with the introduction of the earliest cars; when Henry Ford made cars accessible to almost every working manjack, their popularity increased. Drag racing as we know it today took shape in the years prior to WWII with the formation of the Southern California Timing Association by Art Tilton. After the war, the SCTA under Wally Parks founded the races at the Bonneville Salt Flats that have become synonymous with land speed trials (and accomplishments).

At about this same time the first issues of *Hot Rod* magazine were published under the auspices of Bob Petersen and Bob Lindsay. Within a year, Petersen had formed the Hollywood Associates and held his first custom car show, which introduced to a wider public the imagination of George Barris, who would eventually customize cars for many celebrities, notably Elvis Presley. Barris' creations inspired an entire generation of car customizers. This passion for alteration eventually reached teenagers and led to a boom in the sales of scale-model plastic car kits which led to a plethora of related 'zines.

This reached a peak of sorts with the even smaller slot-car racing phenomenon of the mid-'60s. In 1964 the Ford Motor Company and the Aurora Model Company, also the manufacturer of 1/72 scale slot-cars, held a national contest in which the winner received a college scholarship *and* the first Ford Mustang off the production line. The winner, a high school student from Kingston, PA, chose a fire red convertible; one can only imagine what that car would be worth on the collector's market today. . .

Of course, this passion for wheels manifested itself in popular culture: Hollywood, whose "creators" may understand little that occurs outside of their tinseled town, certainly know how to exploit a fad. From James Dean's love of sports cars and Marlon Brando draped over a motorcycle cycle in *The Wild Ones* through the immensely popular *American Graffiti* of 1973, wheels have played a pivotal role in many a film. The ones of the most interest here are the purely exploitational B-films, where the low budget allowed the cars and tracks almost as much time as the actors. Interestingly, the two earliest of these cult classics predate much of the frenzy normally associated with four wheel frenzy: *The Devil On Wheels* from 1947 and *Hot Rods,* 1950, are years ahead of the pack.

The bulk of these films settle in comfortably with the rest of the explosion of youth-consciousness prodded by rock 'n roll: *Hot Rod Girl* from 1956; *Hot Rod Rumble, Dragstrip Girl,* and *Hot Rod Gang* from 1957; *Hot Car Girl, Dragstrip Riot, Joy Ride,* and *Teenage Thunder* from 1958; *Daddy-O, The Ghost Of Dragstrip Hollow, Road Racers, Speed Crazy,* and an early Roger Corman film, *T-Bird Gang* from 1959. By this time the fad had fizzled, at least for Hollywood, and few films in this vein were forthcoming. Exceptions include 1960's *The Wild Ride,* one of Jack Nicholson's earliest claims to fame; and 1961's *The Choppers.*

Things picked up again briefly in the mid-'60s, which could arguably have had as much to do with the success of Elvis Presley and Ann-Margret in *Viva Las Vegas* (1964) as with the West Coast music scene. *The Lively Set,* also from 1964, featured "Boss Baracuda," written by Terry Melcher and Bobby Darin and performed by The Surfaris. This was followed by 1965's *Daytona Beach Weekend,* 1965; *Hot Rod Hullabaloo* and Elvis' *Spinout,* both 1966; *Hot Rods To Hell* (1967); and Elvis again in *Speedway* (1968), this time with old buddy and occasional temptress Nancy Sinatra. The final film in this run was 1969's *Wild Wheels.*

As a separate subset, there are the biker films of the late '60s (many of which featured the fuzz guitar of Davie Allan and his Arrows, usually with Mike Curb as accomplice, and released as soundtracks on Capitol's Tower and Sidewalk subsidiaries), although the most famous of this type, *Easy Rider,* which is neither a "biker flick" nor is exploitational.

Several television series of the time picked up on the auto scene, the most obvious being *77 Sunset Strip,* whose secondary regular, Kookie, was a hunk who parked cars at the club and drove an asphalt-eater off duty. Played with oleaginous charm by Eddie Byrnes, he hit the top 10 with "Kookie, Kookie, (Lend Me Your Comb)," a novelty duet with Connie Stevens, another TV personality (as Cricket on *Hawaiian Eye*). Less visible as an auto showplace was *Dobie Gillis,* which presented the world with the inimitable Maynard G. Krebs, also featured Barris' XM: SC-210, a chopped and slanted '31 Ford.

As for the music, While there were many artists working in the same genre, basically covering the same scenes, often using the same instruments (and players), the sounds of the records did vary. Three recording artists who also produced were summed up neatly if too simply by Roger Christian when he noted "There all different kinds of producers: Brian [Wilson] in the early days was more into vocals; Jan [Berry] was into tracks, and Gary [Usher] was into both tracks and vocals."

Brian Wilson and The Beach Boys are forever linked in the minds of several generations of fans as the progenitors of surf music. This is not true, as the genre was really an instrumental form; BW basically applied his fascination with Four Freshmen harmonies to basic rock 'n roll chord changes and set lyrics dealing with the waves and beaches and grabbed the bulk of the fame from the sport. Accurate credits here would be to grant Wilson with the creation of a subspecies of the genre, the surf-vocal song. *And,* the group could have justifiably called themselves the Ho-Dads (a term applied to 'rodders by their surfing rivals in Southern California) or the Shut Downs, as their early records were filled with songs about cars, and it is here that the real credit to Wilson can be attributed for "inventing" a genre, the car/hot rod song.

While Wilson composed his first car song, the boss "409," with Gary Usher, he wrote most of his tributes to the internally combustionized mode of transportation with either Roger Christian (the majority of the *Little Deuce Coupe* album and "Don't Worry, Baby") or Mike Love ("Our Car Club," "Fun, Fun, Fun," and "Little Honda"), although the best and most successful song in the genre, "I Get Around," was written by Brian sans partner. Several standouts from this time were co-written by Brian with Christian and Jan Berry and recorded by Berry with partner Dean Torrence, including "Drag City;" one of the true car classics, "Dead Man's Curve;" and "Move Out Little Mustang," recorded under a pseudonym as The Rally Packs. Usher and Christian also teamed up as writing partners, producing several faves in the form, notably "Hot Rod High," written for The Surfaris.

In the wake of The Beach Boys' success, a host of recording artists hopped aboard and cut car songs, many of them West Coasters themselves. This includes the aforementioned Jan & Dean; the "king of the surf guitar," Dick Dale; future Beach Boy Bruce Johnston, who recorded with Terry Melcher as Bruce & Terry, The Rip Chords and The Catalinas; The Surfaris (under the direction of Usher) plus a host of others. As was usual for the questing imagination of Wilson, by the time everyone else was catching up to him, Brian would hang out the laundry on the subject. He'd drop the hammer, put it to the wood and move on to another area, getting a "hole shot" before the industry knew the rules had changed. As a farewell to the genre, Brian included a wonderfully zany medley of "I Get Around"/"Little Deuce Coupe" on 1966's ever-underrated [and personally recommended] *Beach Boys' Party!*

Just as it is impossible to conceive of car songs without Brian Wilson and The Beach Boys, it is almost as difficult to imagine its success without the attention paid the form by Capitol Records. The first real album of car songs was *Shut Down,* from June 1963, which collected tracks from several Capitol artists, including the title tune by The Beach Boys. This was followed in October by *Hot Rod Rally,* another various artists set that introduced the world to Gary Usher's Super Stocks, and The Beach Boys' *Little Deuce Coupe.* At the same time these were being released to the public, other comps were assembled for promotional use and shipped of to radio stations. This includes one of the rarest and most sought-after albums in the genre, *Hot Rod Music On Capitol.* (It should be noted that two staff producers, Nick Venet and Jim Economides, were responsible for many of the auto related recordings of this time.)

Usher's role in the development of the nascent West Coast sound should never be underestimated. As Brain's first song writing partner and as a man with experience in the industry, something BW was sorely lacking, Gary was able to influence Wilson's working patterns. As session player/singer Richie Burns (with The Hondells and The Super Stocks, among other Usher related projects) once noted: "Gary nurtured The Beach Boys; he brought them along, rehearsed with them, and he brought them over to my house in Burbank and they would sit there, like little kids, and say 'Gee, Gary, will we ever be as good as those guys?'"

As a writer, performer and/or producer, Usher was active with The Competitors for Dot, The Hondells for Mercury, The Revells for Reprise (in conjunction with the Revell Model company), The Road Runners for London, and The Surfaris for Decca. In 1964 he "created" both The Silly Surfers and The Weird-Ohs and recorded an album, *Music To Make Models By*, for the Hawk Model Company on the fictitious Hairy Records label. The jacket art was designed to make both sides look like front covers by the two different acts. In a move of admirable chutzpah, Usher signed both artists to Mercury and recorded albums for each: *The Sounds Of The The Silly Surfers* and *The Sounds Of The Weird-Ohs* were issued in 1965.

But his main projects were for Capitol: With Ed "Big Daddy" Roth, a funny car creator and artist noted for his outrageous— and impossible— combination of machines with monsters, including the ever lovable Ratfink, Gary produced three albums as Mr. Gasser & The Weirdos. He also created with albums for The Ghouls, The Kickstands and The Knights. Perhaps his most enduring creation is the three albums he recorded as The Super Stock; in Japan, these are revered almost as highly as Brian Wilson and The Beach Boys. (Capitol has discussed a Gary Usher compact disc release of two or three CDs covering all of the above with unreleased material. It remains in limbo.)

Gary finished the '60s as one of that era's finest and least appreciated producers, who can claim some of the credit for beauty of The Byrds' *Younger Than Yesterday, The Notorious Byrd Brothers* and *Sweetheart Of The Rodeo*. He was also instrumental in the creation of Chad & Jeremy's *Of Cabbages & Kings*, a concept album that cost Columbia a lot of money that sank like a stone, greatly damaging Gary's standing with company executives. . . Like most of the people from this time, his fortunes— and fame— waned in the '70s. Usher's final project before his recent death was the— are you ready?— nurturing and encouragement of an older Brian Wilson into the first steps of his "comeback" album. Unfortunately, like others associated with Brian's recent career, he was unfairly treated by Wilson and his management.

Some overlooked albums from this era include the first two from the T-Bones, a faceless assemblage of LA studio musicians, who would later go gold with "No Matter What Shape (Your Stomach's In)," a popular riff from the then current Alka-Seltzer commercials on television. Both *Boss Drag* and *Boss Drag At The Beach* are hard to find, feature great cover shots of dragsters, and some nifty instrumental versions of popular hits by other artists. And, while most collectors seek out The Tokens' first album on RCA Victor, *The Lion Sleeps Tonight* from 1961, their third long-player, *Wheels*, 1964, is arguably rarer and is fetching increasing sums from auto collectors both for its contents and its packaging. The same is true for another RCA group, The Astronauts, whose 1964 album, *Competition Coupe,*, is also revving up in value.

A variance on the theme of this article are the "low riders." This is a term referring to a form of customizing in which the rear suspension of the car is lowered and the car, generally a classic from the '50s or early '60s, has its rear wheel skirts attached, giving the impression that the riders are really, *really* low to the ground. This form of expression is usually associated with portions of the Hispanic population of Southern California. And, while the individuals garner their moniker from the appearance of their automobiles, the music they prefer— that is, the music that is associated with the low riders— is almost exclusively black, group vocal ("doo wop") music of the '50s. This fascinating subculture is not covered in this article.

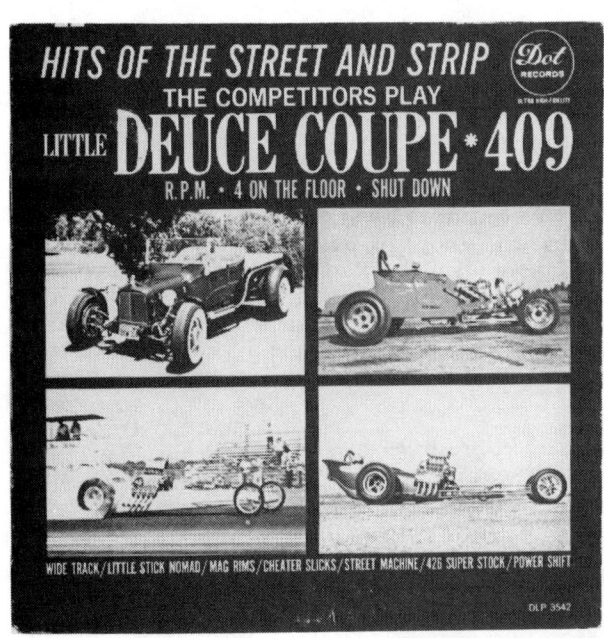

Gary Usher made his first big waves by collaborating with Brian Wilson on some of the Beach Boy's early songs ("409," "The Lonely Sea," and "In My Room" come to mind). He then signed several production deals, primarily with Capitol, where he created (i.e., basically wrote, arranged, produced and usually performed) one successful group, The Superstocks, and several known only to collectors, including The Ghouls, The Kickstands, and The Knights, whose outrageously rare album, Hot Rod High, is pictured here. For Dot he created The Competitors' Hits Of The Street And Strip, another big ticket item. Both of these rarities are also highly sought after by automotive collectors, not only for their great covers but for the auto-oriented songs.

While the impetus of this article is on the ever-growing collectibility of car-related albums, it must be understood that the primary force behind this genre's popularity at the time was the 45 RPM single. Certainly the singles catalogs of of many of the artists listed above require scrutiny by car-song collectors. In his excellent *Surf City/Drag City* book, Rob Burt includes a "Hot Wheels Top Twenty," listed below followed by the year of release and their peak position on *Billboard's* Hot 100 charts (the observant reader will note that Mr. Burt appears to have linked *his* chart positions with those of *Billboard's*). One asterisk (*) indicates that the track is the B-side of a single; two (**) indicates that the track was not issued as a single but charted as an EP track; and three (***) indicates an instrumental, which explains the appearance of The Duals single well in advance of Brian Wilson's efforts. Finally, note that Wilson's name appears on twelve of the nineteen song's writing credits.

1.	The Beach Boys: *I Get Around*	1964	#1	
2.	Jan & Dean: *The Little Old Lady From Pasadena*	1964	#3	
3.	The Rip Chords: *Hey, Little Cobra*	1963	#4	
4.	The Beach Boys: *Fun, Fun, Fun*	1964	#5	
5.	Jan & Dean: *Dead Man's Curve*	1964	#8	
6.	The Hondells: *Little Honda*	1964	#9	
7.	Jan & Dean: *Drag City*	1963	#10	
8.	The Beach Boys: *Little Deuce Coupe*	1963	#15	*
9.	The Beach Boys: *Shut Down*	1963	#23	*
10.	The Beach Boys: *Don't Worry, Baby*	1964	#24	*
11.	The Duals: *Stick Shift*	1961	#21	***
12.	The Rip Chords: *Three Window Coupe*	1964	#25	
13.	Ronny & The Daytonas: *Bucket 'T'*	1964	#54	
14.	The Beach Boys: *Little Honda*	1964	#65	**
15.	The Beach Boys: *409*	1962	#76	*
16.	Jan & Dean: *The Anaheim, Azusa & Cucamonga Sewing Circle, Book Review And Timing Association*	1964	#77	
17.	The Rumblers: *Boss*	1963	#87	***
18.	Bruce & Terry: *Custom Machine*	1964	#85	
19.	The Hondells: *My Buddy Seat*	1964	#87	
20.	Dick Dale: *The Scavenger*	1963	#98	***

While these songs are almost universally known in the hobby, there are a few 45s that need to be singled out, Pat Boone's "Little Honda" being a perfect example. The entire track was cut by Terry Melcher using studio musicians with he and buddy Bruce Johnston emulating the Beach Boys' vocal parts and ol' White Bucks laying the lead on top. Apparently everyone but the decision-makers associated with The Beach Boys knew this was a hit and the competition to get the first one out was intense. Boone's version was beaten to the charts by The Hondells (under Gary Usher) and died a quiet death, only to be resurrected as one of the most collectible car related records of the decade!

Records dealing with the Pontiac GTO are are among the most collectible of the genre. While Ronny & The Daytonas "G.T.O." is probably the most widely known and collected there are a pair of GTO records that are legend in the hobby: "Go, Go, GTO" by Carol & Cheryl, and Paul Revere & The Raiders' "The Judge." Carol & Cheryl are sisters Annette and Cheryl Kleinbard. Annette, who gained her foothold in the recording industry as lead singer for The Teddy Bears ("To Know Him Is To Love Him"), enjoyed success as a songwriter and singer under the name Carol Connors in the '60s. "Go, Go, GTO," is not known to exist as a stock copy, but promotional copies currently command $200-300 in Near Mint condition. Additionally, this single is rumored to have been released credited to The Carmel Sisters. If such a record exists, it is truly rare.

Issued by Columbia Special Products in 1969 as a service to Pontiac and their new model, "The Judge," was a compact-33 mini-LP with the title song and a half-dozen others. The record has a label that resembles the custom hubcap of a Pontiac Rally II and was issued in a picture cover. Easily the rarest Raiders related single, a VG+ copy sold way back in the '80s for $250. The most recent sale, last year, was of a practically mint copy and the purchaser gladly paid $1,000 to add it to his collection, one of the largest Pontiac-related record collections extant. He claims there are only a handful of copies known to exist.

The listings for the movie info in this article was provided by John Black of Backtrack Video & Records, Seattle, WA, and his former partner and confidant, Fred "Mondo Video" Hopkins. The data on the car-sound albums was provided by Jon Hardgrove, proprietor of the Carburetor Shop in Eldon, MO, and a collector of Pontiac GTO memorabilia. Much of the information for this aspect of record collecting is owed to the efforts of Tim Goebel of Tempe, AZ. Finally, any reader who collects these records that can supply appropriate years, corrections, suggestions, missing titles, etc., is encouraged to write Neal Umphred, Box 40116, Bellevue, WA 98015.

Price Guide To Non-Musical Auto Albums

The list below covers those albums devoted more or less to the carriers of the internal combustion engine. The values are averages: Rather than list two specific values, I have opted for a suggested price spread for albums in collectible condition (VG+ to NM) as overall condition of the LP is often of secondary importance to the automotive enthusiast as long as the cover is clean. Each listing is preceded by a parenthetical code that identifies the type of recording the album contains. The key to the abbreviations is:

E.	Sound Effects
G.	Grand Prix / Formula One
H.	Hot Rods, Dragsters & Super Stocks
I.	Indianapolis 500
L.	Land Speed Trials
M.	Miscellaneous Cycles, karts, drag boats, etc
N.	NASCAR Stock cars
P.	Personality Interview or profile
S.	Sports Car Racing

Such specialized notations as "Grand Prix / Formula One," "Indianapolis 500," "NASCAR stock cars," or even "Land speed trials" and "Sports car racing" should be self-explanatory to even a novice. "Hot rods, etc." includes albums devoted to rods, dragsters and super stocks. "Sound effects" denotes albums usually containing sounds of the bash including engines revving, tires peeling, and any other non-abstract aspect of the genre. "Miscellaneous" includes just about any other aspect not covered by the other categories, including 'cycles, karts, and drag boats. Dating these records was a problem.

P.	Allendor USR-8684	(S)	**I've Never Been Scared In A Race Car** (Interview with Richard Petty)	197?	50.00-75.00
P.	Amherst AMH-1003	(M)	**Evel Knievel**	1974	25.00-40.00
S.	Arkay AR-1009	(M)	**Sounds Of Laguna Seca 1957**	1958	25.00-40.00
M.	Associated Four A4-102	(M)	**Race-A-Rama**	196?	40.00-60.00

S.	Audio Fid. DFM-3031	(M)	**Sound Effects: Daytona Speedway**	*1964*	**12.00-20.00**
S.	Audio Fid. DFS-7031	(S)	**Sound Effects: Daytona Speedway**	*1964*	**15.00-25.00**
H.	Audio Fid. DFM-3032	(M)	**The 1964 Winternationals**	*1964*	**15.00-25.00**
H.	Audio Fid. DFS-7032	(S)	**The 1964 Winternationals**	*1964*	**20.00-30.00**
H.	Audio Fid. DFM-3033	(M)	**Drag Race Sound Effects**	*1964*	**15.00-25.00**
H.	Audio Fid. DFS-7033	(S)	**Drag Race Sound Effects**	*1964*	**20.00-30.00**
E.	Audio Fid. DFM-3034	(M)	**Demolition Derby Sound Effects**	*1964*	**12.00-20.00**
E.	Audio Fid. DFMS-7034	(S)	**Demolition Derby Sound Effects**	*1964*	**15.00-25.00**
H.	Audio Fid. DFM-3035	(M)	**Motorcycle Scramble Sound Effects**	*1964*	**12.00-20.00**
H.	Audio Fid. DFS-7035	(S)	**Motorcycle Scramble Sound Effects**	*1964*	**15.00-25.00**
E.	Audio Fid. DFS-5890	(S)	**Sound Effects**	*197?*	**12.00-20.00**
E.	Audio Fid. DFS-7777	(S)	**Sound Effects**	*197?*	**12.00-20.00**
H.	Battle 6130	(M)	**Hot Rod Caravan**	*196?*	**15.00-25.00**
H.	Battle 96130	(S)	**Hot Rod Caravan**	*196?*	**20.00-30.00**
H.	Battle 6131	(M)	**Hot Rods-U.S.A.**	*196?*	**15.00-25.00**
H.	Battle 96131	(S)	**Hot Rods-U.S.A.**	*196?*	**20.00-30.00**
H.	Battle 6132	(M)	**Cement Roasters**	*196?*	**15.00-25.00**
H.	Battle 96132	(S)	**Cement Roasters**	*196?*	**20.00-30.00**
H.	Battle 6133	(M)	**Hot Stuff On The Asphalt**	*196?*	**15.00-25.00**
H.	Battle 96133	(S)	**Hot Stuff On The Asphalt**	*196?*	**20.00-30.00**
H.	Battle 6134	(M)	**Rods And Drags Forever**	*196?*	**15.00-25.00**
H.	Battle 96134	(S)	**Rods And Drags Forever**	*196?*	**20.00-30.00**
H.	Battle 6135	(M)	**Chrome On The Range**	*196?*	**15.00-25.00**
H.	Battle 96135	(S)	**Chrome On The Range**	*196?*	**20.00-30.00**
H.	Battle 6136	(M)	**Dig Out!**	*196?*	**15.00-25.00**
H.	Battle 96136	(S)	**Dig Out!**	*196?*	**20.00-30.00**
G.	Battle 6137	(M)	**Sports Car Caravan**	*196?*	**12.00-20.00**
G.	Battle 96137	(S)	**Sports Car Caravan**	*196?*	**15.00-25.00**
G.	Battle 6138	(M)	**Grand Prix USA**	*196?*	**15.00-25.00**
G.	Battle 96138	(S)	**Grand Prix USA**	*196?*	**20.00-30.00**
S.	Battle 6139	(M)	**Road Racing America**	*196?*	**15.00-25.00**
S.	Battle 96139	(S)	**Road Racing America**	*196?*	**20.00-30.00**
S.	Battle 6140	(M)	**'Sickels Galore!**	*196?*	**15.00-25.00**
S.	Battle 96140	(S)	**'Sickels Galore!**	*196?*	**20.00-30.00**
H.	Bowmar B-573	(M)	**Drag Racing Pix Dix**	*196?*	**25.00-40.00**
H.	Capitol T-2001	(M)	**The Big Sounds Of The Drags**	*1963*	**12.00-20.00**
H.	Capitol ST-2001	(S)	**The Big Sounds Of The Drags**	*1963*	**15.00-25.00**
S.	Capitol T-2004	(M)	**The Big Sounds Of The Sports Cars**	*1963*	**12.00-20.00**
S.	Capitol ST-2004	(S)	**The Big Sounds Of The Sports Cars**	*1963*	**15.00-25.00**
M.	Capitol T-2049	(M)	**The Big Sounds Of The Drag Boats**	*1963*	**15.00-25.00**
M.	Capitol ST-2049	(S)	**The Big Sounds Of The Drag Boats**	*1963*	**20.00-30.00**
H.	Capitol TAO-2145	(M)	**The History Of Drag Racing**	*1964*	**35.00-50.00**
H.	Capitol STAO-2145	(S)	**The History Of Drag Racing**	*1964*	**40.00-60.00**
H.	Capitol T-2146	(M)	**The Big Sounds Of The Drags, Volume 2**	*1964*	**12.00-20.00**
H.	Capitol ST-2146	(S)	**The Big Sounds Of The Drags, Volume 2**	*1964*	**15.00-25.00**
H.	Capitol T-2147	(M)	**The Big Sounds Of The Go-Karts**	*1964*	**15.00-25.00**
H.	Capitol ST-2147	(S)	**The Big Sounds Of The Go-Karts**	*1964*	**20.00-30.00**
L.	Capitol KAO-2175	(M)	**Breedlove 500+**	*1964*	**35.00-50.00**
L.	Capitol SKAO-2175	(S)	**Breedlove 500+**	*1964*	**40.00-60.00**
H.	Dot DLP-3566	(M)	**Drag Strip Sounds**	*1963*	**25.00-40.00**
H.	Dot DLP-25566	(S)	**Drag Strip Sounds**	*1963*	**35.00-50.00**
H.	E.G. Kaiser LP-602	(M)	**AHRA Summer Nationals Drag Sounds**	*196?*	**12.00-20.00**
H.	E.T. LPM-7001	(M)	**Soundsville, Vol. 1**	*196?*	**40.00-60.00**
H.	Fleetwood FLD-1	(M)	**The Sounds Of Auto Racing**	*1963*	**15.00-25.00**
H.	Fleetwood FLD-1S	(S)	**The Sounds Of Auto Racing**	*1963*	**20.00-30.00**
H.	Fleetwood FLP-4001	(M)	**Sounds Of Sanford**	*1963*	**15.00-25.00**
H.	Fleetwood FLP-4001S	(S)	**Sounds Of Sanford**	*1963*	**20.00-30.00**
H.	Fleetwood FLP-4002	(M)	**The 1963 Winternationals**	*1963*	**15.00-25.00**
H.	Fleetwood FLP-4002S	(S)	**The 1963 Winternationals**	*1963*	**20.00-30.00**
H.	Fleetwood FLP-4003	(M)	**AHRA 1963 Winter Championships**	*1963*	**15.00-25.00**
H.	Fleetwood FLP-4003S	(S)	**AHRA 1963 Winter Championships**	*1963*	**20.00-30.00**

H.	Fleetwood FLP-4004	(M)	**Bakersfield '63**	*1963*	**15.00-25.00**
H.	Fleetwood FLP-4004S	(S)	**Bakersfield '63**	*1963*	**20.00-30.00**
H.	Fleetwood FLP-4005	(M)	**1320 Special**	*1963*	**100.00-150.00**
H.	Fleetwood FLP-4005S	(S)	**1320 Special**	*1963*	**150.00-200.00**
N.	Fleetwood FLP-4006	(M)	**Rebel 300**	*1963*	**25.00-40.00**
N.	Fleetwood FLP-4006S	(S)	**Rebel 300**	*1963*	**35.00-50.00**
N.	Fleetwood FLP-4007	(M)	**Indianapolis 500**	*1963*	**15.00-25.00**
N.	Fleetwood FLP-4007S	(S)	**Indianapolis 500**	*1963*	**20.00-30.00**
N.	Fleetwood FLP-4008	(M)	**The World 600**	*1963*	**25.00-40.00**
N.	Fleetwood FLP-4008S	(S)	**The World 600**	*1963*	**35.00-50.00**
N.	Fleetwood FLP-4009	(M)	**Daytona "Firecracker" 400**	*1963*	**25.00-40.00**
N.	Fleetwood FLP-4009S	(S)	**Daytona "Firecracker" 400**	*1963*	**35.00-50.00**
L.	Fleetwood FLP-4010	(M)	**407.45**	*1963*	**35.00-50.00**
L.	Fleetwood FLP-4010S	(S)	**407.45**	*1963*	**40.00-60.00**
H.	Fleetwood FLP-4011	(M)	**The 1963 Nationals**	*1964*	**15.00-25.00**
H.	Fleetwood FLP-4011S	(S)	**The 1963 Nationals**	*1964*	**20.00-30.00**
S.	Fleetwood FLP-4012	(M)	**Road America 500 (SCCA) Elkhart Lake**	*1964*	**15.00-25.00**
S.	Fleetwood FLP-4012S	(S)	**Road America 500 (SCCA) Elkhart Lake**	*1964*	**20.00-30.00**
G.	Fleetwood FLP-4013	(M)	**Grand Prix Of The United States**	*1964*	**25.00-40.00**
G.	Fleetwood FLP-4013S	(S)	**Grand Prix Of The United States**	*1964*	**35.00-50.00**
M.	Fleetwood FLP-4014	(M)	**Drag Boats**	*1964*	**25.00-40.00**
M.	Fleetwood FLP-4014S	(S)	**Drag Boats**	*1964*	**35.00-50.00**
H.	Fleetwood FLP-4016	(M)	**The 1964 Winternationals**	*1964*	**15.00-25.00**
H.	Fleetwood FLP-4016S	(S)	**The 1964 Winternationals**	*1964*	**20.00-30.00**
H.	Fleetwood FLP-4017	(M)	**Bakersfield '64**	*1964*	**25.00-40.00**
H.	Fleetwood FLP-4017S	(S)	**Bakersfield '64**	*1964*	**35.00-50.00**
N.	Fleetwood FLP-4018	(M)	**Daytona 500**	*1964*	**25.00-40.00**
N.	Fleetwood FLP-4018S	(S)	**Daytona 500**	*1964*	**35.00-50.00**
S.	Fleetwood FLP-4019	(M)	**Sebring 1964**	*1964*	**25.00-40.00**
S.	Fleetwood FLP-4019S	(S)	**Sebring 1964**	*1964*	**35.00-50.00**
L.	Fleetwood FMS-1006	(S)	**Great Moments From The Indy 500**	*1974*	**25.00-40.00**
S.	Folkways FX-6140	(M)	**Sports Car Grand Prix Of Watkins Glen**	*1956*	**40.00-60.00**
S.	Fortissimo XK-8003	(S)	**Racing Cars**	*1959*	**50.00-75.00**
			(This unique stereo album plays the grooves from the inside out; i.e., from the label out to the edge!)		
H.	High Perform. HP-8000	(M)	**Hurst Takes You The The '64 Nationals**	*1964*	**25.00-40.00**
H.	High Perform. HPS-8000	(S)	**Hurst Takes You The The '64 Nationals**	*1964*	**35.00-50.00**
G.	High Perform. HP-8001	(M)	**Hurst '64-United States Grand Prix**	*1964*	**25.00-40.00**
G.	High Perform. HPS-8001	(S)	**Hurst '64-United States Grand Prix**	*1964*	**35.00-50.00**
G.	International 56007	(M)	**The Exciting Sounds Of Le Mans**	*1966*	**40.00-60.00**
G.	International 56007S	(S)	**The Exciting Sounds Of Le Mans**	*1966*	**50.00-75.00**
H.	Keystone	(M)	**Sox & Martin's "The Drags"**	*196?*	**50.00-75.00**
H.	Kiderian KPR-3333	(M)	**Sounds Of Drag Racing**	*1974*	**12.00-20.00**
H.	Lesco LE-200	(M)	**Sounds Of The Indy Nationals**	*1967*	**25.00-40.00**
E.	Major LP-1024	(M)	**Sound Effects, Volume 9**	*196?*	**12.00-20.00**
P.	MCA MCKS-506	(S)	**Championship Year**	*1970*	**50.00-75.00**
			(Interview with Jackie Stewart)		
L.	Mercury MG-20315	(M)	**500 Miles To Glory**	*1959*	**35.00-50.00**
L.	Mercury SR-60024	(S)	**500 Miles To Glory**	*1959*	**40.00-60.00**
G.	MGM E-4457	(M)	**The Grand Prix Challenge Of Champions**	*1967*	**15.00-25.00**
G.	MGM SE-4457	(S)	**The Grand Prix Challenge Of Champions**	*1967*	**20.00-30.00**
P.	Mobile Fidelity MF-101	(M)	**Dan Gurney: His World Of Racing**	*1965*	**100.00-150.00**
P.	Mobile Fidelity MFS-101	(S)	**Dan Gurney: His World Of Racing**	*196?*	**150.00-200.00**
M.	Newhall NN-101	(M)	**Motorcycle Man**	*196?*	**12.00-20.00**

H.	Performance PPPS-1001	(M)	13th Annual Winternationals	1973	20.00-30.00
H.	Performance PPPS-1002	(S)	4th Annual Gatornationals	1973	20.00-30.00
H.	Performance PPPS-1003	(M)	9th Annual Springnationals	1973	20.00-30.00
H.	Performance PPPS-1004	(S)	4th Annual Summernationals	1973	20.00-30.00
S.	Pirelli PLP-9	(M)	The Grand Prix Of Gibraltar	196?	12.00-20.00
S.	Riverside RLP-6	(M)	Sounds Of Speed	1960	15.00-25.00
S.	Riverside RS-96	(S)	Sounds Of Speed	1960	20.00-30.00
S.	Riverside RLP-12-833	(M)	The Grand Prix Of Gibraltar	1958	25.00-40.00
S.	Riverside RLP-5001	(M)	Sounds Of Sebring	1957	40.00-60.00
S.	Riverside RLP-5002	(M)	Sports Cars In Hi-Fi	1957	20.00-30.00
S.	Riverside RLP-1101	(S)	Sports Cars In Stereo	1957	20.00-30.00
S.	Riverside RLP-5003	(M)	Pit Stop	1957	20.00-30.00
P.	Riverside RLP-5004	(M)	Britain's Greatest Racing Driver (Interview with Stirling Moss)	1957	75.00-125.00
P.	Riverside RLP-5005	(M)	Around The Racing Circuit With Phil Hill	1957	75.00-125.00
P.	Riverside RLP-5006	(M)	The Career Of A Great American Racing Driver (Interview with Shelby)	1957	200.00-250.00
P.	Riverside RLP-5007	(M)	A Memorial Tribute (For Marquis d'Portago)	1957	75.00-125.00
S.	Riverside RLP-5008	(M)	Sounds Of Sebring 1957	1957	40.00-60.00
S.	Riverside RLP-5010	(M)	Cuban Corners	1958	20.00-30.00
S.	Riverside RLP-5011	(M)	Sounds Of Sebring 1958	1958	20.00-30.00
S.	Riverside RLP-5012	(M)	Mercedes-Benz, The W125 And W163	1959	20.00-30.00
S.	Riverside RLP-5013	(M)	Vintage Sports Cars In Hi-Fi	1959	15.00-25.00
S.	Riverside RLP-1115	(S)	Vintage Sports Cars In Stereo	1959	20.00-30.00
S.	Riverside RLP-5014	(M)	Sounds Of Sebring 1959	1959	20.00-30.00
S.	Riverside RLP-1146	(S)	Sounds Of Sebring 1959	1959	15.00-25.00
S.	Riverside RLP-5015	(M)	Sports Cars At Sebring In Hi-Fi	1960	15.00-25.00
S.	Riverside RLP-1144	(S)	Sports Cars At Sebring In Stereo	1960	20.00-30.00
G.	Riverside RLP-5016	(M)	United States Grand Prix-Sebring 1959	1960	15.00-25.00
G.	Riverside RLP-1165	(S)	United States Grand Prix-Sebring 1959	1960	20.00-30.00
G.	Riverside RLP-5017	(M)	Grand Prix Cars In Action At Sebring	1960	15.00-25.00
G.	Riverside RLP-1166	(S)	Grand Prix Cars In Action At Sebring	1960	20.00-30.00
S.	Riverside RLP-5018	(M)	Sounds Of Sebring 1960	1960	15.00-25.00
S.	Riverside RLP-1173	(S)	Sounds Of Sebring 1960	1960	20.00-30.00
S.	Riverside RLP-5019	(M)	Sing A Song Of Sports Cars	1961	15.00-25.00
S.	Riverside RLP-1181	(S)	Sing A Song Of Sports Cars	1961	20.00-30.00
S.	Riverside RLP-5020	(M)	The Race/Mercedes-Benz 1937-1955	1961	20.00-30.00
G.	Riverside RLP-5021	(M)	The Grand Prix Of The United States	1961	15.00-25.00
G.	Riverside RS-95021	(S)	The Grand Prix Of The United States	1961	20.00-30.00
G.	Riverside RLP-5022	(M)	Farewell To A Formula	1961	15.00-25.00
G.	Riverside RS-95022	(S)	Farewell To A Formula	1961	20.00-30.00
S.	Riverside RLP-5023	(M)	Sounds Of Sebring 1961	1961	15.00-25.00
S.	Riverside RS-95023	(S)	Sounds Of Sebring 1961	1961	20.00-30.00
S.	Riverside RLP-5024	(M)	Sebring Corners	1962	15.00-25.00
S.	Riverside RS-95024	(S)	Sebring Corners	1962	20.00-30.00
S.	Riverside RLP-5025	(M)	Mercedes-Benz 75th Anniversary	1962	75.00-100.00
S.	Riverside RS-95025	(S)	Mercedes-Benz 75th Anniversary	1962	100.00-150.00
S.	Riverside RLP-5027	(M)	Sounds Of Sebring 1962	1962	15.00-25.00
S.	Riverside RS-95027	(S)	Sounds Of Sebring 1962	1962	20.00-30.00
G.	Riverside RLP-5028	(M)	Grand Prix Cars At Watkins Glen 1962	1962	15.00-25.00
G.	Riverside RS-95028	(S)	Grand Prix Cars At Watkins Glen 1962	1962	20.00-30.00
H.	Riverside RLP-5502	(M)	Hot Rods And Dragsters In Hi-Fi	1960	25.00-40.00
H.	Riverside RLP-1154	(S)	Hot Rods And Dragsters In Stereo	1960	35.00-50.00
H.	Riverside RLP-5503	(M)	Hot Rods In Action	1960	25.00-40.00
H.	Riverside RLP-1161	(S)	Hot Rods In Action	1960	35.00-50.00
L.	Riverside RLP-5504	(M)	On The Drag Strip	1960	35.00-50.00
L.	Riverside RLP-1184	(S)	On The Drag Strip	1960	40.00-60.00
L.	Riverside RLP-5506	(M)	Bonneville 1960	1960	75.00-100.00
L.	Riverside RS-95506	(S)	Bonneville 1960	1960	100.00-150.00
M.	Riverside RLP-5507	(M)	Karts In Action	1960	25.00-40.00
M.	Riverside RS-95507	(S)	Karts In Action	1960	35.00-50.00
H.	Riverside RLP-5509	(M)	Hot Rod Heaven/Bakersfield Smoker	1961	15.00-25.00
H.	Riverside RS-95509	(S)	Hot Rod Heaven/Bakersfield Smoker	1961	20.00-30.00
M.	Riverside RLP-5511	(M)	Scramble	1961	15.00-25.00
M.	Riverside RS-59511	(S)	Scramble	1961	20.00-30.00
L.	Riverside RLP-5513	(M)	The Fastest 500	1961	25.00-40.00
L.	Riverside RS-95513	(S)	The Fastest 500	1961	35.00-50.00

Probably the most desirable of the automotive albums is this interview/overview of the career of racing great Carroll Shelby from Riverside's "Sports Car Special" 5000 series.

H	Riverside RLP-5515	(M)	Hot Cars At The Winternationals	1961	15.00-25.00
H	Riverside RS-95515	(S)	Hot Cars At The Winternationals	1961	20.00-30.00
H	Riverside RLP-5516	(M)	Super Stocks	1962	25.00-40.00
H	Riverside RS-95516	(S)	Super Stocks	1962	35.00-50.00
H	Riverside RLP-5517	(M)	Rods 'N' Rails	1962	15.00-25.00
H	Riverside RS-95517	(S)	Rods 'N' Rails	1962	20.00-30.00
H	Riverside RLP-5518	(M)	Hot Rods, Dragsters And Super Stocks	1962	25.00-40.00
H	Riverside RS-95518	(S)	Hot Rods, Dragsters And Super Stocks	1962	35.00-50.00
H	Riverside RLP-5519	(M)	Burning Slicks	1962	15.00-25.00
H	Riverside RS-95519	(S)	Burning Slicks	1962	20.00-30.00
H	Riverside RLP-5544	(M)	On The Drag Strip	1959	15.00-25.00
H	Riverside RLP-1184	(S)	On The Drag Strip	1959	20.00-30.00
S	Riverside RLP-12833	(M)	The Grand Prix Of Gibraltar	1959	75.00-100.00
S	Riverside SDP-33	(M)	The Golden Age Of Sebring	1959	100.00-150.00
S	Riverside SDP-44	(M)	The Wonderful World Of Sports Cars	1959	100.00-150.00
S	Rosemont RPLP-1160	(M)	The Pure Sound Of Speed	1960	50.00-75.00
H	Schofield	(M)	Dragsters And Hot Rods In Action	1960	40.00-60.00
H	Schofield LP-400	(M)	Dragsters And Competition Cars In Action	1960	35.00-50.00
H	Schofield LP-401	(S)	Dragsters And Competition Cars In Action	1960	40.00-60.00
S	Schofield LP-550	(M)	Senior TT: Isle Of Man 1959	1959	20.00-30.00
G	Schofield LP-551	(M)	The Formula One Grand Prix Car	1959	40.00-60.00
S	Schofield LP-552	(M)	1959 Isle Of Man TT	1959	20.00-30.00
G	Schofield LP-553	(M)	The Monaco Grand Prix 1959	1960	40.00-60.00
S	Schofield LP-559	(M)	1960 Isle Of Man TT	1960	20.00-30.00
S	Schofield LP-560	(M)	1961 Isle Of Man TT (Part 1)	1961	20.00-30.00
S	Schofield LP-561	(M)	1961 Isle Of Man TT (Part 2)	1961	20.00-30.00
S	Schofield LP-562	(M)	1962 Isle Of Man TT (Part 1)	1962	20.00-30.00
S	Schofield LP-563	(M)	1962 Isle Of Man TT (Part 2)	1962	20.00-30.00
S	Schofield LP-564	(M)	1963 Isle Of Man TT (Part 1)	1963	20.00-30.00
S	Schofield LP-565	(M)	1963 Isle Of Man TT (Part 2)	1963	20.00-30.00
S	Schofield LP-566	(M)	1964 Isle Of Man TT (Part 1)	1964	20.00-30.00
S	Schofield LP-567	(M)	1964 Isle Of Man TT (Part 2)	1964	20.00-30.00
H	Schofield LP-570	(M)	Dragfest	1965	35.00-50.00
H	Schofield LPS-570	(S)	Dragfest	1965	40.00-60.00
S	Schofield LP-574	(M)	1965 Isle Of Man TT (Part 1)	1965	20.00-30.00
S	Schofield LP-575	(M)	1965 Isle Of Man TT (Part 2)	1965	20.00-30.00
S	Schofield LP-577	(M)	1967 Isle Of Man TT (Part 1)	1967	20.00-30.00
S	Schofield LP-578	(M)	1967 Isle Of Man TT (Part 2)	1967	20.00-30.00
P.	Souvenir S-2692	(M)	George Hurst And Don Garlits Interview	196?	25.00-40.00
P.	SSN NI-676	(S)	One Who Dared (Interview with Gary Irvin)	197?	25.00-40.00
P.	TGR 720	(S)	Meet Richard Petty	197?	12.00-20.00

The Grateful Dead As Album Artists (Collecting Uncle John's Band)

Now synonymous with the halcyon years of the psychedelic '60s and to that period's leftovers (i.e., those of us who hang on to an ever crumbling belief system that is not centered on avaricious ambition), The Grateful Dead have defied all normal showbiz *(sic)* odds for nearly three decades. Rock critics, most of whom seem to have grown up in Detroit or New York and have dedicated their professional careers to the deification of the MC-5 and The Velvet Underground, appear to harbor lifelong grudges against West Coast bands. This has led to the Dead being written off as recording artists, despite the fact that *Anthem Of The Sun* and *Aoxomoxoa* are still, twenty five years later, among the most avante garde of all rock albums; or that *Live/Dead* ranks among the finest live albums in the genre; or that *Workingman's Dead* and *American Beauty* are quintessential classics of the waning days of San Francisco psychedelia merging with the back-to-the-country phenomenon that was to follow. It is almost impossible to imagine such efforts being conceived, let alone attempted, in the current milieu.

Originally performing as The Warlocks, the group came to the attention of both Stanley Augustus Owsley III, manufacturer of the world's most legendary acid during the heyday of consciousness expansion, who became the group's patron and mentor, known affectionately as "Bear." *History Of The Grateful Dead, Volume 1* (Warner Bros. 2721, #60 in '73) was subtitled *Bear's Choice*, as this performance from the Fillmore East during February 1970 was Owsley's selection to inaugurate this series (of which a second volume never followed).

At the same time, they hooked up with Ken Kesey, author of the highly lauded *One Flew Over The Cuckoo's Nest*, who sought bigger game than topping the *New York Times* best-seller list. Accompanying Kesey and his Merry Pranksters in the original Acid Tests, the group rather quickly evolved into The Grateful(ly) Dead, with the "classic" line-up consisting of Jerry Garcia, lead guitar, Bob Weir, rhythm guitar, Phil Lesh, bass, Bill Kreutzmann, drums, and Ron "Pigpen" McKernan, organ. Prior to their corporate debut, a small label, Sound City, issued *The Acid Test*, an LP that contained a collage of sounds and statements from Kesey, a few of which featured the early Dead. This rarity is desirable not only among rock collectors but also with literary collectors.

The group then signed with MGM, who had no idea of how to record the band (not an uncommon problem and one that would plague them throughout their career). While nothing from this period appears to have been completed in the studio, MGM's attempts to capture the group live showed up years later on a pair of albums on their Sunflower subsidiary. *Vintage Dead* (5001, released in 1970 and reaching #127) and *Historic Dead* (5004, climbing to #154 in '71) are poorly recorded and the group certainly doesn't shine. Both albums were quickly deleted. Verve, a subsidiary of MGM, had set aside the catalog number V6-5093 for the Dead in the early '70s but never released it. Whether this was a repackage of the Sunflower albums or additional live recordings from the period is unknown.

Their Warner Bros. debut, *The Grateful Dead* (WS-1689) was recorded in three days and has a crude yet distinct feel, making the album somewhat popular with non-Dead fans who dig the garage sound The LP reached #73 on *Billboard's* charts. Originally issued on the then extant gold label in both mono and stereo, it sold modestly and is hard to find on its original label. It was then reissued on the company's new green label with the Warner/7 Arts "W7" logo. This label lasted a few years and a second green label, this one replacing the "W7" with the more familiar "WB" logo.

After befriending and jamming with Kreutzmann, percussionist extraordinaire Mickey Hart joined in 1967, and the ever underrated keyboardist Tom Constanten, who had impressed the group with his use of prepared tapes, also signed aboard. The Dead's next album, *Anthem Of The Sun* (WS-1749 and #87 in '68) reflect a great many changes: Taking six months to record in the studio and on the road, the band built up a considerable debt (six figures worth) in studio time to Warner Bros. They also emerged as an avante garde group, as the album appeared to be a [labored] attempt to capture some of the psychic and intellectual arabesques that LSD could put an individual through. This album was in contrast to their galvanized, improvised live shows, the foundation for their popularity within the Bay Area. In 1971, Phil Lesh took the multi-track tapes for *Anthem Of The Sun* back into the studio and remixed them. This new version, the original garish purple cover was replaced with an even less attractive white cover. This is one of the more difficult Dead albums to find.

Aoxomoxoa (WS-1790 and #73 in '69) followed in the same vein, although more relaxed and considerably less expensive. This album is also justly noted for its awe-inspiring psychedelic cover by legendary San Francisco poster/comix artist Rick Griffin. The album is worth owning just for the cover!

During the 1969 Christmas season the group finally released an album that captured the essence of their emerging legend. *Live/Dead* (W2S-1830 and #64 in '70) was a double-album, recorded "live" in studio before assembled friends, family and industry people, that showcased both the groups rock'n roll roots with a thundering "Turn On Your Lovelight" and their "out thereness," especially on the lovely "St. Stephen-melting-into-Dark Star." After the LP's release, Constanten retired, devoting his energies to the study of Scientology.

Each of the aforementioned trio of albums were originally issued on WB's green label with the "W7" logo (for the merged "Warner Bros./7 Arts" corporate identity) on top. (Collectors Note: As these initial pressings were followed in 1970 by second pressings on the same green label with the "W7" replaced by the now ever-familiar "WB" logo there is often some confusion by both sellers and buyers alike. The original "W7" pressings are in the hard-to-find category, especially in Near Mint condition, while the "WB" pressings are fairly common.)

Crosby, Still and Nash offered the group a bit of timely, if unlikely, advice and the Dead took the time in 1970 to compose a series of [more or less] psychedelic country tunes that showcased for the first— and only— time, their ensemble vocals. *Workingman's Dead* (WS-1869, #27 in '70) and *American Beauty* (WS-1893, #30 in '71) were enormously successful. The music, which balanced a wondrously fine line between the exciting and the laid-back, attracted a legion of new listeners, many of whom staid on as lifelong fans. These masterpieces were followed by another double live set, *Grateful Dead* (W2S-1935, #25 in '71), which attempted to carry their "new" sound into the arena.

This was followed by a tour of Europe, which basically introduced new members Keith and Donna Godchaux, and their presence can be felt on the live triple album that followed, *Europe '72* (3WX-2668, #24 in '72). Shortly after the LP's release, keyboardist Pigpen died from "hard living." It was these two LPs and their ten sides of live performances that laid the groundwork for the future and remain the basis for their ongoing success.

Both of these, along with *Workingman's Dead* and *American Beauty*, first saw the light of day on the green "WB" label, although none of them has gained status as a truly collectible record. Each of the Dead albums—from the first eponymous album through *Skeletons From The Closet*—remained in print through the CD era and have and undergone numerous label changes, none of which have any real value at this time (this includes first pressings of subsequent Warner Bros. releases).

Three of the members also issued solo albums for Warner Bros. during this period: *Garcia* (BS-2582, #35 in '72) can stand as another Dead album in sound and performance, featuring members of the group on several tracks. Weir's *Ace* (BS-2627, #68 in '72) veers off in directions that would become a part of the Dead's later sound as does Hart's lone solo project, the under-rated *Rolling Thunder* (BS-2635, #190 in '72). Oddly, when *Ace* was reissued (on Warner's "Burbank street" label), they replaced the photo of Weir on the back cover with a new one. This trio of albums went out of print rather quickly.

Each of the Warner Bros. albums, both group and solo, were issued as white label promos to radio stations. The solo albums often contained a sheet of paper with a brief artist bio, notes on the music and times for the LP's individual tracks.

By 1973 the group had fulfilled all of their contractual obligations with Warner Bros., including the reimbursement of the studio bill for *Anthem*. They had also turned in four straight top 40 albums, the last of which, *Europe '72*, had become the group's first RIAA Gold Record. Four other Warner albums would eventually achieve the same status: *The Grateful Dead, Workingman's Dead, American Beauty*, and a "best of" compilation, *Skeleton's From The Closet*, (MS-2764, #75 in '74). Following in the footsteps as such illustrious predecessors as the Beach Boys' aborted Brother Records and the Beatles rotted Apple, in the Dead opted to start their own label, Grateful Dead Records, with a subsidiary, Round Records, for family related projects. This endeavor, which was to end up a failure, did lead to the group's successfully establishing its own publishing company and booking agency, both of which have since served the band and its adherents well since.

The Dead managed to issue four albums on their own label, the first, *Wake Of The Flood* (GD-01, #18 in '73), had an almost jazzy feeling as the group attempted some real improvisation in a studio setting. The jacket featured artwork by San Francisco poster wizard Rick Griffin, the man responsible for the ground-breaking cover gracing *Aoxomoxoa*. First pressings failed to adequately document the roles of various individuals on the back cover, leaving a rather large "empty" space in Griff's artwork. Later covers, pressed in much smaller quantities than the original, rectified this by adding the necessary credits. In a bit of irony, the group had several hundred copies pressed on green vinyl as specials for their fan club. In the wake of local flooding in California, most of these experienced severe water damage. The few that escaped the bath are highly desirable.

In a similar vein was *Grateful Dead From The Mars Hotel* (GD-102, #16 in '74),. Both of these albums sold well straight off, all climbing into *Billboard's* top 20. Unfortunately, while the Dead may have had their own label *and* a certain guaranteed demand for their product, they had no reliable means of distribution by which to get said product to that desiring market. Thus, while the chart positions are admirable, actual sales were disappointing, as the group couldn't capitalize on the initial impetus in the market.

The group then signed a manufacturing and distribution deal with United Artists; copies of the aforementioned pair of albums can be found with U.A. stickers affixed to the shrink-wrap. The first release under the new arrangement was *Blues For Allah* (LA-494, #12 in '75), which many consider their finest album after leaving Warner Bros. In 1975 United Artists gathered together a sampling of their recent output and issued *For Dead Heads* (SP-114) to AM and FM radio stations around the country. While this contains nothing new, it is nonetheless one of the few Dead collectibles of a promotional nature. Their final release under their own imprint was the staggeringly mediocre *Steal Your Face* (LA-620, #56 in '76) yet another double "live" set, this time from Bill Graham's Winterland. The album was issued as an effort to recoup capital lost on the group's first film project.

After moving to Arista in '77, they proceeded to almost destroy what critical foundation they had with a series of increasingly mediocre material and performances. While *Terrapin Station* (7001, #28 in '77) does enjoy its admirers and is the best of the Arista studio albums. Little Feat's Lowell George produced their next outing, *Shakedown Street* (4198, #41 in '78), their weakest studio album until the release of *Go To Heaven* (9508, #23 in '80) which looked like the Dead's concession to *Saturday Night Fever!* In early '79, the Godchauxs and The Dead parted over musical differences; keyboardist Keith was killed in an auto accident shortly afterward. They were replaced by keyboardist Brent Mydland. The Arista albums as a group are the least admired *and* the most readily available of the group's opus and can generally be found in any used record store.

Such is not the case with their next two albums: *Reckoning* (8604, #43 in '81), a double live acoustic set, and *Dead Set* (8606, #29 in '81), a double live electric outing, followed one another and restored the group's critical status, at least among the converted. For some inexplicable reason, *Reckoning* was quickly deleted and replaced by a budget reissue on the Pair label. Arista also pursued radio programmers interest with *Grateful Dead Sampler* (SP-35) and a special edition of *Terrapin* where the individual tracks were "banded for airplay."

When the vogue for audiophile pressings hit its stride in the late '70s, Mobile Fidelity Sound Labs issued both *American Beauty* and *Grateful Dead From The Mars Hotel* as part of their lauded "Original Master Recording" series of half-speed masters (MFSL-1-014 and 172, respectively). Direct Disk's audiophile pressing of *Terrapin Station* (SD-16619) is one of the rarest and most sought-after of the half-speeds.

Of course, in 1987 the Grateful Dead released their first top ten album, *In The Dark* (also receiving their first and only Platinum Record Award) and their first top ten single "Touch Of Grey" These made the group thousands of new devotees. Unfortunately, Mydland's drug abuse would not leave him around to enjoy the Dead's massive commercial success to follow.

MGM & The Mothers Of Invention

While visiting L.A.'s Whiskey A-Go Go in November 1965, MGM staff producer Tom Wilson (a vastly neglected contributor to '60s rock music) witnessed a performance by a motley crew of characters with the longest, most unkempt hair his brown eyes had ever beheld playing some rather far-out rhythm 'n blues. He offered the group a contract with a miniscule $2,500 advance but agreed to a recording budget in excess of $20,000, an almost unheard sum of money in those days prior to *Pet Sounds* and *Sgt. Pepper*. Upon hearing that they had signed a hirsute group called "The Mothers," MGM execs quickly assigned the group to their otherwise almost exclusively jazz Verve subsidiary and tacked "Of Invention" onto their moniker, completely altering its intended [sexual] connotation. Under leader Frank Zappa's direction (and his standout lead guitar), vocalist Ray Collins, drummer Jimmy Carl Black, bassist Roy Estrada and Elliott Ingbar on second guitar entered the studio and, over the next three years, recorded a series of albums that established their place in rock's pantheon and produced a number of notable collectibles. . .

Released in August 1966 to almost universal confusion *and* consternation, *Freak Out* (Verve V/V6-5005) was a bizarre two-record collection of tracks that owed as much to the avante garde-isms of Edgar Varese, Karlheinz Stockhausen and John Cage as it did more acceptable *(sic)* sources such as '50s doowop and '60s social consciousness. With its outlandish sounds, often ludicrous, smarmy vocals that included noises one normally did not associate with creativity, and blending an utter and complete disdain for the obsessions and affectations of the white middling class with a decidedly scatological sense of humor, it sounded to many as a monolithic slab of noise conceived primarily to offend.

Nonetheless, the album stands as an almost visionary success ("It can't happen here") and it did establish Zappa and his Mothers as a force to be reckoned with. One can make a strong argument for *Freak Out* as one of rock's first "concept" albums, a precursor to the headier days fast approaching. After months of Zappa's campaigning in the then burgeoning underground press, it eventually reached *Billboard's* charts in February 1967 (23 weeks on the charts, peaking at #130), accumulating relatively healthy sales [over a period of years] for so daring a project.

As an artifact, the album remains of high interest: The initial pressings had a blurb on the inside cover calling attention to the offer of a free map to "freak out spots" located in the sunny locales of Los Angeles and its environs. The lucky listener had merely to send away and the map would magically appear in his or her mail-box. Exactly how many fans sent off for the map is conjecture. Based on the rarity of the map today, one would conclude not too many young Americans were all that interested in L.A. (at least not when that groovy Mecca of Love, San Francisco, beckoned instead). With subsequent pressings of the album, the blurb and its attendant offer were removed from the cover.

Collectors should note that while it has always been assumed that there was a coupon included with the album to be mailed in, that appears not to have been the case. . . Even more interesting is the fact that Verve had scheduled a single-album version of *Freak Out* and assigned it catalogue number V/V6-5006 before balking, although it was issued in Europe as a single. Should a U.S. copy of this album turn up, even as a test pressing, it would immediately assume a place as the rarest of all Zappa related records.

This was followed by the compositionally denser, collage-like *Absolutely Free* (Verve V/V6-5013), on which Zappa's penchant for hammering his listeners with his not-so-subtle humor reared its soon to be ubiquitous presence. Again, the combination of contemporary classical conceptions with references to the Duke of Earl and "baby love" left most listeners in apoplexy, although it was obvious that something was happening and most folks didn't know what it was. . . the perfect basis for a cult-like following. Oddly, *Absolutely Free* was an even bigger chart success, verging on top 40 respectability through the summer of '67 (22 weeks on the charts, reaching at #41), in some part due to Zappa's insightful promotion of the album through arresting ads in the pages of Marvel and DC comic books (it wasn't too farfetched that if a teenager could identify with Peter Parker or Bruce Banner they could transfer those feelings to other, more musical, freaks). *Free* also solidified their claim as rock's most outrageous group, a claim they shared with fellow iconoclasts The Village Fugs.

For their third long-player the group produced one of the '60s' finest Rock-With-A-Capital-R albums: *We're Only In It For The Money* (Verve V/V6-5045), was a technological marvel, one of the first rock albums recorded on an eight-track machine (creatively engineered by Gary Kellgren). As a conceptual look at the ugly and brutal underside of Leave-It-To-Beaver America, *Money* was also an often silly, often terrifying peek at the hypocrisies [as perceived by Zappa] of the then emerging American pop counter-culture. The liner notes steered the reader to Franz Kafka's *Penal Colony* with references to the reopening of California's concentration camps, then under serious discussion by the enlightened governorship of Ronald Ray-gun. The cover art was an hilarious parody of *Sgt. Pepper's Lonely Heart's Club Band* that so offended one of the Fabs that the label was forced to turn the gatefold cover inside out to avoid legal intervention. This controversy only helped the album reach an amazing #30 on the charts, although it spent only 19 weeks on the charts, less than the previous album. (Shortly after its release, Ian Underwood underwent Motherhood.)

Original pressings included the lines "I will love the police as they kick the shit out of me" in the song "Who Needs The Peace Corps" and "And I still remember Mama with her apron and her pad feeding all the boys at Ed's Cafe" in the song "Let's Make The Water Turn Black." Later pressings have both of these lines pruned from the tapes. While the little bit of scatology in the former may have been deemed offensive, one is hard put to understand the need to erase the latter. And exactly who the editing was done for is a bit of a mystery: The rarity of the edited version of the album indicates that it had little, if any distribution. [A personal aside here: A friend of mine, Robert Evans, was involved in booking rock'n roll shows into Wilkes-Barre, PA, back in the late '60s and early '70s. After staging a triumphant show with The Mothers, he later entertained the group, apparently hitting it off with Zappa, who presented Bob with a copy of the edited album as a gift, telling him how rare the album was *more than twenty years ago!*]

Lumpy Gravy was recorded as a modern classical piece by Zappa with the Abnuceals Emuukha Electric Symphony Orchestra, a large assemblage of studio musicians, and initially for Capitol Records, who were willing to exploit Zappa's reputation by indulging his desire to compose and record a more "classical" album. When MGM cried foul, Capitol dropped the project. After Frank had The Mothers add vocal and instrumental overdubs, the album was released as Verve V6-8741 (the reader should note that Verve reserved its 8000 series for jazz titles; the few pop titles they released in the '60s and '70s were on the 5000 series, where all of the other Mothers albums were released). *Gravy* continued the directions and experimentations of the earlier albums, cementing Zappa's reputation as a [perverted] pop genius.

It was promoted by Zappa as the second part of *We're Only In It For The Money*, hinting that he had even more grand concepts than had been assumed. To his credit, the two albums can be played as a single piece; a clever taper can splice and edit several albums out of the two LPs different tracks and be hard put to tell where the songs originated. And most fans and historians tend to view the two as a conceptual whole when discussing this period of Zappa's work.

In a move that baffled virtually everyone, The Mothers then issued *Cruising With Ruben & The Jets* (Verve V6-5055), a tribute to the doowop music that the members had grown up with that was both unerringly accurate and playfully complex, underpinning the simplistic teenage emotions of the lyrics with allusions to 20th century classicism and modern jazz. (Varese is quoted on the cover.) This album baffled almost everyone, and sold less than zilchteen copies to devoted family members, friends and hardcore fans (actually, it spent a dozen weeks on the charts in early '69, peaking at #110). As Zappa's early excursions into the world of recording came to light, it was evident that he had more than a passing fancy for '50s R&B group vocal records and this album took on new meaning.

A set of three "bonus' paper inserts is associated with this album, each having something to do with the '50s greaser concept of the music. They include "The Story Of Ruben & The Jets," "How To Comb & Set A Jellyroll," and a guide on how to do the "bop." These may have been included with early pressings of the album— unlikely given their extreme rarity— or as part of a promotional package. These may be the ultimate Mothers collectibles, since I know of no one who knows of anyone who has ever seen these gems.

By 1969 Zappa and MGM were at loggerheads: Zappa claimed the label owed the group more royalties and wanted greater freedom in production while the label wanted more saleable product. Zappa fulfilled his contractual obligations by compiling *Mothermania/The Best Of The Mothers* (Verve V6-5068, which spent 9 weeks on the charts during the spring of '69, eventually hitting #151), which deserves a proper place in The Mothers' canon as it is a brilliant selection of material from the first three albums woven together by Zappa into a "new" concept album that stands alongside the earlier releases.

He then broke with MGM and dissolved The Mothers because he was "tired of playing for people who clap for all the wrong reasons," displaying the snotty, condescending attitude that would alienate him from a good many of his former followers (and attract a lot of exactly the sort of audience he was insulting). He then formed Bizarre/Straight Records, signed an artist/production deal with Warner/Reprise, and assembled a new group of more talented but less idiosyncratic Mothers.

MGM followed this upheaval with several "new" albums: *The XXXX Of The Mothers Of Invention* (Verve V6-5074, 1969) was an interesting package. While not up to the level of *Mothermania* as a retrospective, it has a gross cover that sits comfortably alongside his other product from the time and it is hard to find fault with any collection from his Verve days. MGM also compiled two more, lesser sets: *The Mothers Of Invention* (released it on its "Archetypes" series in 1970 as MGM GAS-112) and *The Worst Of The Mothers* (MGM SE-4754, 1971), neither of which have anything but historical importance to archivists.

Zappa's Bizarre/Straight empire never really took off. While he signed and worked with a number of notable artists, including Captain Beefheart's *Trout Mask Replica,* a justly lauded masterwork of demented Delta blues, and a group of wackos called Alice Cooper that dressed in girl's clothing, none of them sold many units (aside from his own work with and without the new Mothers). As for Zappa, while he remained a wondrous composer and his picking got even better, much of his later lyrics seemed to have been based squarely on the most sopho-moric aspects of the Verve endeavors. While this endeared him to one group of [wit impaired] listeners, it tended to make him more of a running joke in the eyes of writers, critics and more discerning fans of the genre. . .

Record Company Label Directory

This section outlines the many graphic changes record companies' labels have undergone through the years and will assist the reader in identifying original albums from later pressings. I have kept the explanations as brief and to the point as possible. The dates and catalog numbers during the label transitions are approximate; you may find that you have pressings of an album on an earlier label than I have listed. I would certainly appreciate having any such errors of this type called to my attention so that future editions can be corrected.

One area that needs a little exposition is that of promotional releases. The most common method of printing promotional records has been to press them with white labels with plain black print, hence the term "white label promo." As these white labels are obvious manifestations of the labels special attention, they are the most popular with collectors. Some labels used their regular label, or a slightly modified version, and had "Audition Copy" or "Promotional Copy" incorporated into the label's typesetting; these are also promos. In this book records with such notices stamped on or with a sticker affixed to the label or cover are not considered promos (although this will change).

Promotional records are usually pressed in small runs on quality vinyl— often at plants that specialize in small print runs— making it a better pressing than the stock copies. Needless to say, they are quite collectible and generally command a premium above the normal value of the record, although the premium may be minimal. To list each and every promo version of the albums in this book would practically double the size of the book. Instead, the reader should assume that a promo of most records exist and, in pricing, that such a promo is worth no less than the value listed for the stock copy and, generally, no more than twice the listed value. Listed exceptions are those albums that are more common than the stock version or those promos that are worth considerably more than the stock or, in a very few cases, where the promo is different or noteworthy.

In a money saving move, many companies dropped the practice of printing special promo records and simply took to designating stock copies as intended for promotional purposes by affixing a disclaimer to the cover usually reading "For Promotional Use Only-Not Intended For Sale." This took the most common form of stamping the disclaimer in [black] ink or embossing it with gold print. For a while in the mid-'60s Columbia affixed a gold "promo" sticker to the cover. Generally, these do not command a great deal of attention from collectors. Certainly a slight premium may be attached to a record so designated, but these disclaimers do not, for the most part, set the hearts of collectors afire.

One exception is Capitol Records, who, during the '60s, often added the word "PROMO" or "FREE" in perforated lettering in the upper right corner. While this is a blatant damage to the artwork, albums so marked do draw collectors' attention and regularly fetch a reasonable premium. Capitol also took to the practice of punching a hole in the corner of the cover and handing these out as promos. *These so-called "promo-holes" are not recognized by this book as worth attention.* Anyone with a hole-punch can construct all of such promos he or she might need to soak gullible collectors. The reader is advised that this position is not generally shared and many collectors seek out these albums, even though they should really be classified as cut-outs.

When large amounts of records were deleted in the mid-'60s, many of which were monos, most companies simply "cut out" the number from their catalogs and sold the remaining copies to wholesalers, where they ended up in "5 & 10s" around the country for 99¢. By the '80s, companies began clipping the corners of deleted titles; this was originally a small clip but grew to the point where huge portions of covers were left lying on the floor after the record was sent out to the distributors. Almost without exception cut-out marks on albums reduce any record's value. The sole exception being Warner Bros. and Reprise, who had the novel idea of placing a small brass rivet in the upper left corner of their cut-outs during the waning '60s. These tend to attract some collectors, who will pay a regular price for such a cut-out.

A&M From 1963 through mid-'73, A&M used a brown label. From then until 1985 the label was a silver gray with a large brown "AM" fading into the background.

ABC-Paramount From 1956 through 1961 (#101-400) a black label was issued with ABC-Paramount on top and "A Product of Am-Par Record Corp" on the bottom. From 1962 through 1966 (#400-560s) the black label reads "A Product of ABC-Paramount Records Inc." During 1966-67, the logo was changed to "abc records" in a box at the top. Throughout these years, mono albums bore an "ABC" prefix; stereo had an "ABCS" prefix. White label promos were issued.

From 1968 to 1974, the label was black with "abc" on top and "New York, NY" on the bottom. Other labels include black with the logo in children's blocks in and purple on gold from 1973 to 1978. In 1979 ABC came under MCA's control.

Ace From inception through the early '60s a black label was issued with "Ace" in silver print on top. This was replaced by a black label with "ACE" in an oval.

Apple From November 1968 through early 1970 the Apple label read "A subsidiary of Capitol Industries, Inc" on the bottom. This was replaced with "Mfd. by Apple Records, Inc" from 1970 until 1974. The final run of albums from 1974-75 included an "All Rights Reserved" disclaimer.

Argo Through 1964 Argo, primarlily a jazz label, used a black label with silver print. During 1965 the company also issued a silver label with black print and a brown label with pink print along with the original label. Throughout these years, mono albums bore an "LP" prefix; stereo albums had an "LPS" prefix. By 1966 Argo albums were released on Cadet, a label that lasted into the '70s.

Arista From 1972 through 1976 (#4000-4105) the label was light blue with "Arista Records" beneath the logo on top. For a few months in late 1976 and early 1977 the blue label read "Arista" beneath the logo on top. This was replaced with a black label (#4110-4205). From 1978 until 1984 the company returned to a blue label with "Arista" on the left side of the logo on top. Beginning in 1985 a black & blue label was used with "Arista" floating above a mountain skyline.

Asylum   For the first few releases (#5051-5066) the label was white with the company's logo in a circle on top. In 1973 the label used a sky with clouds motif (#5067-5099, 1000-1040s). This label was modified slightly in 1975 to include the Warner Bros. logo in the lower right; this label ran through 1984. Note: A solid blue label was used briefly in 1976. In 1985 the label turned black & orange.

Atco   A subsidiary of Atlantic, initial pressings from 1958 through the latter part of 1961 (#101-138) were on a solid yellow label with a harp in the upper left. From 1961 through 1968, mono albums had a gold & gray label with a white stripe through the center with "ATCO" in large print (#139-226). Stereo albums were purple & brown with the white stripe (#139-256).

In 1969, after the demise of mono, all albums returned to a solid yellow with an 1841 Broadway, NYC address printed on the bottom. When Atlantic was sold to the Warner conglomerate, the address was changed to 75 Rockefeller Plaza, NYC. From 1978 through 1984 the company used a solid gray label; since then Atlantic has used a gray label made up of countless tiny "Atco" logos.

Atlantic   From 1950 through mid 1960, mono albums were issued on a black label with silver print (#8000-8040 and 1200-1332). In 1958 select titles were mixed into stereo and issued on a green label, all of which are difficult to find.

A transition label, referred to as the "bullseye label," was in use briefly from approximately 8026-8036: Mono albums had an orange, purple & black fan around the spindle hole with "Atlantic" in an orange & purple band on top. For stereo albums there is a green & blue border around the label; the fan around the hole is also green & blue. There may have been no new titles released on this bullseye label, only reissues of previously issued titles.

From 1960 through late '61 (#8032-8059 and 1333-1378) Atlantic mono LPs were orange & purple while stereo albums were green & blue. Each label had a white band through the center with a white pinwheel— or "fan"— logo in a black box on the right side. From the end of 1961 through '66 (#8060-8125 and 1379-1463) the fan switched to black on white with "Atlantic" running vertically alongside it. From 1966 through 1968 (#8126-8178 and 1464-1499) "Atlantic" ran horizontally beneath the fan. After 1968 the label, now stereo only, switched to a green & orange with the company's 1841 Broadway, NYC address on the bottom.

From 1973 through 1975 a Rockefeller Plaza address appeared at the bottom, and from 1975 through the late '80s "A Warner Communications Company" appeared on the bottom. White label promos were issued from the mid-'60s on.

Bang   From inception through the mid-'70s Bang used a red & white label with a derringer on top. This was replaced in the early '70s with a yellow labl. From 1973 through 1977 a sky with clouds design was employed. This was followed by a light brown label with a red logo on top.

Bearsville   Initial releases had a light brown label with "Distributed by Ampex" on the bottom. From 1971 through the mid-'70s the label read "Distributed by Warner Bros." on the bottom. 1977 until 1981 saw no distribution motto; however, in 1981 a "3300 Warner Blvd" address was added.

Bell   From inception through 1969 a blue label was issued with silver print. The label was silver from 1970 through 1975.

Bethlehem   Throughout the '50s Bethlehem, primarlily a jazz label,mono albums carried a "BCP" prefix and featured a maroon label with silver print with the "Bethlehem" logo in an arc across the top. In the latter years of that decade, the "Bethlehem" logo changed to black letters in a silver box across the top. The stereo albums are identified with an "SBCP" prefix on a blue label. Stereo albums on this label are rare! In the 1960s, after they were acquired by King Records, the new covers and LPs carried King's Cincinnati, Ohio address.

Big Tree   In 1970 the label was red with "Product of Big Tree Enterprises Limited" on the bottom. This was replaced by "Distributed by Ampex" in 1971-72; "Distributed by Bell" in 1972-73; and "Distributed by Atlantic" from 1974-76.

Blue Thumb   The first four LPs had a black label. From the fifth release through approximately the mid-60s the off-white label had a thumb print on top. This was finally replaced with a purple label with the "abc" logo on top in 1974.

Bluesville   Originals on this subsidiary of Prestige have bright blue labels with the logo in block print on top. Second pressings had flat blue labels with the Prestige trident logo on the right side.

BluesWay   During the first year, 1967-68, the label was blue. This was replaced by a black label with a blue perimeter.

Brother   The Beach Boys' label saw one LP issued in 1967, *Smiley Smile*, manufactured by Capitol. The label was resurrected in 1970 under the Warner /Reprise umbrella. During 1970-76 the pale yellow label read "A Subsidiary and Licensee of Warner Bros., Inc" on the bottom. From mid-'76 through 1979 the label read "A Division of Warner Bros. Records, Inc" on the bottom.

Brunswick   From 1950 through the early '60s, Brunswick used a black label with silver print. Yellow label promos were issued. In late 1962 through 1972, the company switched to a black label with a rainbow through the center and "A Division of Decca Records" along the perimeter.

Throughout these years mono albums bore a "BL" prefix, while stereo LPs carried a "BL-7" prefix. Since 1972 a black label was used with the rainbow and "Manufactured by Brunswick Record Corp" along the perimeter.

Buddah   From 1968 until 1973 the multi-color label had a silhouette of a Buddah on the bottom. From 1973 through 1978 an orange label was used with a smiling Buddah on the bottom. This was replaced by a black label with the Arista logo on the bottom.

Cadence   From inception through 1962 a maroon label was used with a silver top. During the company's final year the label was red with a black border.

Cadet   From 1965, when Cadet took over Argo, through 1968, the company used a blue label. In 1969 a blue label fading into white was issued. A pink & yellow label was in effect in the early '70s, replaced briefly by a pink & orange label.

Calendar   During 1967-68 the label was orange with Zodiac figures around the perimeter. During late 1968-69 it was orange with a "K" on top. The label then became Kirshner Records.

Camden   This budget subsidiary of RCA Victor repackaged material from the parent label's catalog, sometimes using obscure 45 and EP tracks. Camden's original label was a pink/purple. From 1958 through 1964, a blue label was used with a purple perimeter. From 1964 until 1968, a blue label was used with a dark blue perimeter fading into light blue.

Throughout this time mono albums bore a "CAL" prefix; stereo titles had a "CAS" prefix. Stereo numbers ending with an "e" denoted reprocessed stereo. From 1969 until 1975 a dark blue label was in effect. In 1976 the entire line was turned over to Pickwick.

Cameo   From 1959-61 the label was orange with a cameo logo on top. From 1961 through the rest of the decade it was a red & black label with the cameo on the right. In the late '60s a purple label was used with the cameo on top.

Capitol   From 1949 through 1953 (#100-344), they basically issued a green label with "Long Playing Microgroove" on the bottom. Ten-inch albums bore an "H" prefix. From 1953 through 1958 (#345-1050s) a turquoise label with "Long Playing" on the bottom was in effect, with a gray or black label also used during this time. The twelve-inch albums generally carried a "T" prefix although certain titles carried a "W." Yellow label promos were issued.

In 1958-59 (#1021-1225) Capitol switched to a black label with a rainbow perimeter and both the Capitol dome logo and "Long Playing High-Fidelity" printed on the left side. From 1959 until 1962 (#1225-1660s), the black/rainbow label had the logo and a silver line on the left. Black label promos were issued with "Not For Sale" on the bottom. The "T" and "W" prefixes were used for monos while an "ST" or "SW" was saved for stereos.

A "DT" or "DW" indicates that the album was electronically rechanneled stereo using Capitol's patented "duo-phonic stereo" process ethod of altering the mono signal beyond recognition. Special releases with gatefold covers received "KAO" or "MAS" prefixes with either an "S" or "D" added for stereo.

From 1962 through 1969 (#1658-2999 and the new series beginning with 100 through the early 200s), Capitol issued a black label with the logo on top, using the "T"/"ST" prefix. Note: On each of these black rainbow labels the copyright data is along the lower perimeter in white print on the black label

After 1969 the situation is rather confusing: A [lime] green label was used from mid-'69 through mid-'72 (#208-11105). A red label with a purple target-like logo on top was used from mid-'72 through mid-'75. Simultaneously, an orange label was used with "Capitol" on the bottom from late 1972 through late 1975. In late 1975 an "Unauthorized duplication" disclaimer was added to the perimeter print on top of the orange label from late 1975 through early 1978. From mid-'78 through 1983 the label was purple.

During this time a variety of prefixes were used, although "ST" remained the primary designation. In 1984 Capitol returned to the classic black rainbow label of the '60s except this time the copyright data was on top in black print in the rainbow. And, the company began manufacturing white label promos.

Capricorn   In 1970 the label was a yellow Atco label with "Capricorn Records Series" on the bottom. In 1971 it was pink. From 1972 through 1974 the label was a plain tan. From 1975 until 1978 it was light brown with a large goat facing right. This was replaced by a light brown label with a [different] goat facing left.

Casablanca   In 1974 the label was blue with "Manufactured and Distributed by Warner Bros. Records, Inc." on the bottom. In 1975 and early 1976 the blue label read "Manufactured and Distributed by Casablanca Records" on the bottom.

From 1976 through 1977 (#7026-7050) the label featured a desert scene with three camels in the foreground. 1976 until 1981 (#7050s-7250s) saw the camels replaced with a film crew and "Manufactured and Distributed by Casablanca Records" on the bottom. Since 1981 the label has read "Manufactured and Distributed by Polygram Records" on the bottom.

Challenge   Through the mid-'60s the label was blue with "Challenge" in an oval on top. During the '60s the label carried a plain "CHALLENGE" logo on top.

Chancellor   Initial releases in 1958-59 had pink labels; after that, black.

Checker   From inception through 1966 (the 1400 series and 2900-2996) the label was black with silver print although some were maroon with silver. In 1966 (#2997-3001) a light blue label was used with checkers on top. From 1967 through the early '70s a blue label that fades into white at the bottom was in effect. Finally, a blue label was used with a purple band through the center.

Chess   Through 1966 (#1400-1490s), Chess used a black label with silver print although some were blue with silver. White label promos from these years are rare. During 1966 they used a black label with a chess piece on top. From 1967 through the early '70s a blue label that fades into white at the bottom was used.

From 1972 until 1977 the label was orange with a blue band through the center. The 50000 and 60000 series used then was under the direction of the GRT Corporation. Later issues were owned by the All Platinum Record Group. The '80s had a blue label with a checker-like effect along the lower perimeter.

Chrysalis   From 1972 until 1976 (#1000-1130s) the label was green. In 1977 a blue label fading up into white was used with an "All Rights Reserved" disclaimer added in 1982.

Clarion   This budget subsidiary of Atlantic/Atco repackaged material from the parent label's catalog.

Colgems   The red & white label in 1966-67 read "TM of Colgems Records" beneath the logo on top. This motto was dropped in 1968.

Colpix From inception through the early '60s the company used a gold label with "Colpix" in large red letters on top. In 1963 a strip of movie film was added. Later pressings were on a blue label. Stereo numbers are decidedly rarer than their mono counterparts.

Columbia From 1949 through 1955 Columbia used a red label with gold print and "Long Playing" on the bottom (#500-650). A variety of prefixes, "CL," "GL" and "ML," were used before the company settled on "CL." From 1955 through 1962 (#650 through the early 1800s) mono albums had red labels with six white-on-black, highly stylized camera "eye"-on-a-tripod logos on each side of the label.

From 1962 through 1965 (#1780-2379) the white-on-black eye logos were replaced with two white eye logos, one on each side of the spindle hole, and read "Guaranteed High Fidelity" on the bottom. From 1965 through 1968 (#2380-2811) the red mono label read "360 Sound Mono" in white on the bottom. Note: Some later pressings from 1967-68 read "Mono" only.

Columbia apparently began manufacturing stereo albums (the 8000 series) in early 1959; the initial 8000 numbers were assigned randomly as mono albums were mixed into stereo and released. By 1960 designating stereo was simple: CS-6800 was added to the mono catalog number to denote stereo. Thus, Columbia CL-2372, The Byrds' *Mr. Tambourine Man,* would be CS-9172!

8000-8579 featured the red label with the six eye logos. From 1962 through 1965 (#8630-9128) stereo labels featured the two white eye logos with "360 Sound Stereo" in black on the bottom. Two arrows, one on each side pointing up, were added to the "360 Sound Stereo" in the last 1/3 of 1963. From 1965 through 1970 (#9130-9999, 1-30, and 30000-30050), stereo labels read "360 Sound Stereo" with the arrows in white at the bottom.

After 1970 the red label reads "Columbia" in gold letters a half-dozen times around the perimeter. The only way to note a first pressings is by the prefix in the catalog number, which have included, but are not limited to, "CS," "C," "G," "KC," and "PC," although some of these prefixes have been used on reissues of earlier titles. Columbia subsidiaries include Epic and Harmony.

Coral From inception through 1963 Coral albums were issued on a maroon label; blue label promos were issued. From 1963 through 1968 a black label was used with a rainbow center and read "A Subsidiary of Decca Records." From 1968 through 1970 "A Subsidiary of MCA" replaced the Decca motto. Throughout these years, mono albums bore a "CRL" prefix; stereo albums, a "CRL-7." Refer to MCA.

Cotillion From 1969 till late 1972 this Atlantic subsidiary used a grey label with an "1841 Broadway" address on the bottom. The address was changed to "75 Rockefeller Plaza" in the mid-'70s. Finally, Cotillion switched to a purple label.

Crown Arising from the ashes of Modern Records, Crown used a black label with silver print through 1960, often reissuing the earlier label's titles. By 1960, Crown specialized in low budget reissues, pressed on the cheapest vinyl available and often with completely misleading credits. Second labels were gray, followed by another black label with the Crown logo in color. When Crown began issuing albums in rechanneled stereo, the sound was among the worse ever developed. Consequently, the fake stereo titles are avoided by all but completists.

88

Curtom From 1968 until 1972 the plain yellow label had a Broadway address on the bottom; 1973 until 1975 saw the address changed to 7th Ave. After the mid-'70s the yellow label sported a psychedelic multi-color top.

Decca From 1949 through 1954 Decca had a black label with gold print. From 1954 through 1960 (early 8000s through #8981) they had a black label with silver print. Pink label promos were issued. From 1960 through 1966 (#4000-4830s), the label was black with a rainbow stripe and reads "Mfrd. by Decca Records."

From 1967 through 1971 "A Division of MCA" was printed beneath the rainbow. White label promos were issued. For approximately one year, 1971-72, "Mfd. by MCA" was added. After that, reissues appeared on the MCA label. Mono albums bore a "DL" prefix; stereo albums with a "DL-7." By 1973 MCA had entirely eaten up the label and its product.

Del-Fi Original label (1201) were blue with a black border containing blue circles. The next label (1202-1246) was basically black with blue/gold diamonds around the border. Reissues from the '80s have a gold label.

Deram From inception through the early '70s the label was basically white with "London" beneath the Deram logo on top. During the '70s the white label had a brown top. The '80s versions read "Manufactured by Phonogram, Inc" on top.

Dolton From 1959 until 1962 the mono 2000 series and the stereo 8000s had a light blue label with a Sunset Blvd. address on the bottom. From late 1962 through late 1965 Dolton used a dark blue label with a fish logo on the left. This was replaced in 1966 by a black label with a "D" logo on the left. By 1967 Dolton was owned by Liberty.

Dore Initial releases in the early '60s were on a light blue label with a feather on top. The '70s version was a dark blue with a larger feather on top. The late '70s saw a black label with a still larger feather.

Dot During 1955-56 (the 3000 series), Dot issued a maroon label with "Gallatin, Tennessee" on the bottom. During late 1956 or early '57 the address was "Hollywood, California." From 1957 through 1967 (#3030-3830s), a black label was used with "Long Play" and "Dot" in script on the top.

In 1968 "A Division of Paramount" appeared on the bottom. Throughout these years, mono albums bore a "DLP" prefix with a 3000 number; stereo albums bore the same "DLP" but were a 25000 series; i.e., the last three digits of the mono and stereos were identical.

From 1968 through 1970 the Paramount mountain logo appeared in a box with the Dot logo at the top of the label. From 1970 through 1974, the Dot logo appeared in a box on top with "A Division of Famous Music Corp" on the bottom. During 1974 until 1978, a purple & yellow label was in effect. After 1978 select Dot titles were reissued on ABC.

Duke From inception through 1961 the label was purple & yellow. During the remainder of the decade the label was orange.

The illustrations above may help to clarify certain differences in Columbia labels: The design used throughout the '50s and into 1962 (illustrated here by Adventures Of The Heart) is often referred to as the "eyes logo" label as it carried three highly stylized, white-on-black camera logos on each side of the spindle hole (a total of six per label). This was modified and the trio of eyes were replaced by a single white-on-red eye logo. During this period, stereo labels were first issued with the "360 Sound" motto in black print on the bottom without an arrow on each side (Bob Dylan), then black with arrows (Another Side Of Bob Dylan), and finally, in white with the arrows (Johnny's Newest Hits). In 1970, the label was altered again, this time with a series of six tiny eye logos interspersed around the label with a half-dozen "Columbias," all in gold print.

Dunhill   From 1965 through 1968 (#50000-50020s) the label was black with "Dunhill" on top with "Distributed by ABC Records" on the bottom. From 50020s - 50031 the label read "A Subsidiary of ABC Records." From 1968 through 1974 (#50032-50170s) both "Dunhill" and the "abc" logo were in a box on top. In 1973 a black label was used that featured children's blocks on top. During its final year, 1974-75, the label was purple. By 1975 Dunhill was a part of ABC.

Elektra   During the '50s a white label was used with an electron logo on top. This was replaced with a grey label a small guitar player on top. From 1961 until 1966 a gold label was used with a large guitar player on top. The gold label was replaced from 1966 until 1969 (#4007-4040s) with a flat brownish label. During 1969-70 the label was red (#4040s-5007). Throughout the rest of the decade the label was multi-colored with a butterfly in the upper right. This was replaced by a red label with a Warner Bros. logo on the bottom. After 1983 the label was black.

EmArcy   From 1954 through 1958 EmArcy, primarily a jazz label, used a blue label with silver print and a drummer at the top. Like other Mercury subsidiaries, an "MG" prefix was used on the mono 36000 series. When titles were released in stereo, an "SR" prefix was used with an 80000 number. In the '60s a gray label was issued. Reissues in the '80s featured a brown & gold label with the drummer. Note: Some titles were reissued on special blue Mercury/EmArcy Jazz labels, often appearing here in stereo for the first time.

End   The label was originally gray with a dog on top that read "Product of End Music, Inc" at the bottom. This was replaced with a gray "dog" label that read "A Division of Roulette Records, Inc" on the bottom. This was replaced in the early '60s with a label that had "End" on end on either side.

Epic   As Columbia's primary subsidiary, from inception through 1962 Epic carried a yellow label with black lines radiating out along the perimeter; stereo issues read "Stereorama" across the top. During 1962-63, a yellow label was used with "Epic" appearing eight times around the perimeter for mono albums; stereos read "Stereo" and "Epic" three times each around the perimeter.

From 1963 through 1965 (#24/26040s-24/26150s) a yellow label was used with "A Product of CBS" on the bottom. From 1965 through 1972 (#24/26150s-31992) the same yellow label deleted the CBS motto was in print. From 1973 until 1978 Epic issued an orange label and replaced that with a black label in 1978.

Initially, mono albums bore an "LG" or "LN" prefix. When titles from the 3000 series were issued in stereo they carried a "BN" prefix and were part of the 500 series. By the '60s, the bulk of the releases were either in the LN-24000 mono series or the BN-26000 stereo series.

Etiquette   Original labels were red with a Tacoma, WA address on the bottom. Reissues have a purple-ish red label but bear a Seattle, WA address and the copyright date along with a 1984 on the bottom.

Excello   The company's original orange label was replaced in the latter '60s with a white label with a colored arrow on top.

Fantasy From inception through the 1960s, mono albums had a red/maroon label. 10" albums bore a number "3" prefix. 12" albums began with 200 and also bore the "3" prefix. When the label added stereo in the early 1960s, they used an 8000 series number; these originals had a blue label with silver print and were pressed on stiff, non-flexible vinyl. White label promos were issued.

Fantasy began pressing its albums on colored vinyl with their 10" series; copies of these albums have been seen on red, blue, green & purple vinyl; some were on rainbow-like pressings of different colors; these are rather rare. With the inception of their 12" line in 1955, all new albums were pressed on red vinyl. This book assumes that *all* of the original mono releases from 1955 through 1957 were pressed on thick, dark red vinyl, often with a mottling effect of the red dye in the vinyl. For a brief period, approximately twelve months during 1957-58, new releases were pressed on black vinyl. By '58 red wax was back. . . Pressings from this point on were still on the thick vinyl but were a lovely, translucent red. In-print titles were pressed on this wax before reverting the black in the early '60s.

When Fantasy began issuing stereo in 1962, these were pressed on the same thick vinyl as the mono only using a translucent blue. These would then revert to modern black vinyl for the duration of the decade.

A popular title could have been pressed first on thick, dark red vinyl then on the thick black vinyl of the '50s with little or no "grooveguard" around the disc's perimeter to keep the stylus from sliding off. Third pressings would be on the thick translucent red vinyl while final mono pressings from the early '60s would have been on thinner, more modern black vinyl with the now familiar grooveguard. Then a blue stereo pressing in 1962 followed by a black vinyl stereo reissue through the rest of the decade.

From 1972 through 1978, Fantasy used a brown label on both their new original releases and their various reissues, including the jazz label, Milestone. Eventually, Fantasy absorbed a number of labels and *their* subsidiaries, including Prestige, New Jazz, Bluesville, Moodsville, Swingville, Riverside, Debut, Milestone, Pablo and Galaxy. Much of this music was reissued as new titles on Milestone in the '70s (often as annotated two-fers) or as part of their Original Jazz Classic series ("OJC" prefix) of reissues in the '80s.

Fire Original labels were white with red print (100-102). Later pressings have red labels with black print.

Gee In the '50s the label was red label; they switched to a gray label in the '60s.

Geffen In the early '80s the cream label had technical information printed around the perimeter. In 1984 the print was not used and in 1985 the label was changed to black.

Gordy A purple label with "Gordy" in yellow script on top was used from 1962 through 1967. After 1967 the purple label had a yellow slash through the middle with the logo on the left side.

Harmony   This budget subsidiary of Columbia repackaged material from the parent label's catalog. Harmony used a maroon label from 1957 through 1959 (#7000-7150). For the next twelve years they issued a black label.

Harvest   A yellow & green label was used from 1969 until 1976. From 1977 until 1985 the label had an EMI Records Ltd. copyright notice on the bottom.

Hi   Hi's first release (12001) had a black label with "Hi" in red print outlined in silver. They then switched to an orange & white label through 1976 (12/32002 through stereo 32089). This was replaced by a plain gray/silver label with "Hi" on the left. A few titles in 1972-73 were issued with a white label with the "Hi" logo on top with the "London" logo beneath it. After 1976 the label was black.

Hickory   Through the early '60s a black label was used with "Hickory" in silver print on top. From 1964 until 1972 a black label with colored stripes on top was in effect, and from 1973 until 1975 the label was brown with the MGM logo on the right. The rest of the '70s saw a purple & yellow label with the "abc" logo on top.

Hifi   "Hifi" is the better known I.D. for Los Angeles' High Fidelity Records.

I.R.S.   From the late '70s through the first years of the '80s the label was white. It was replaced in 1981 by a silver label and, again in 1985 by a goldish label.

Imperial   From 1950 through 1958 (#9000-9040s) Imperial featured a maroon label. From 1958 through 1964 (#9045-9267) they used a black label with stars and colored rays on top. White label promos were issued. A black & pink label was in effect from 1964 through 1966 (#9268-9320s). From 1966 through 1969, a black & green label was used with "Product Of Liberty Records" on the bottom.

Mono albums bore an "LP" prefix and were part of the 9000 series. When stereo was added in the late '50s, these albums carried the same "LP" prefix but were part of the 12000 series. For the first one hundred and seventy-four releases (12000-12173), stereo albums were mixed and released accoring to perceived need. That is, the stereo release numbers do not correspond with the catalog numbers of the original mono albums.

With 12174 on, the mono and stereo catalog numbers coincided (for example, the mono was LP-9174 while the stereo was LP-12174, etc.) Original stereo albums featured a black label with silver print; later pressings had the black label with the stars. After Liberty was purchased by United Artists in 1970, "Liberty/UA, Inc" was added to the label.

Impulse   Originally a subsidiary of ABC, Impulse albums (1-100 and the first few titles on the 9000 series) through 1968 had a glossy orange & brown label; second pressings have identical colors ecept they have a flatter finish. Mono albums bore an "A" prefix while stereos carried an "AS." From 1969 through 1972, the label was red & black; from 1973-74, black; and, from 1974-78, purple & green. Impulse is now a part of the MCA Corporation.

International Artists   Each of this company's original '60s albums were reissued in 1979 with identical covers and labels. The originals are on thick vinyl; reissues are on the thinner vinyl and have "Masterfonics" stamped in the trail-off vinyl.

Island   In 1972-73 the label had a sunray motif with the logo. In 1974 the label featured a stylized figure on water skies. From 1975 until 1978 the label was black. From 1978 until 1981 it was orange & blue. In 1982-83 the label had a purple top with a skyscraper on the left. After 1983 the blue or black label noted the Warner Communication Corporation along the bottom.

Jamie   In 1958 the label was yellow. From 1959 until 1967 it was white & gold and from 1967 through 1970, brown & orange.

Janus   From 1970 until 1976 (the 3000 series and the early 7000s) the label was light brownish gold. In 1977-78 the label was a reddish orange.

Josie   From inception through the early '60s the label was a cream color with blue print. Through the latter '60s and into the '70s the label was light brown.

Jubilee   From inception through 1958 Jubilee used a blue label. From 1958 through 1960, a black label was used with "jubilee" in a silver "sunburst" oval on top. Throughout the '60s, a black label was used with "jubilee" in a multi-colored "sunburst." Mono albums carried a "JGL" prefix; stereos had a "JGS."

Kama Sutra   From 1965 until 1969 (#8000-8070s) the label was yellow. From 1969 until 1972 (#2000-2050s) the label was pink. After 1972 the label had a forest scene on top.

Kapp   From 1956 through 1959 Kapp used a maroon or blue label. A black & blue label with a "K" logo was in effect from 1959 through 1962. A black & blue label with a red major's hat was used from 1962 through 1964. From 1964 through 1971 black label was black with the major's hat on top.

Throughout these years, mono albums bore a "KL" prefix and were part of the 1000 series; white label promos were issued. Stereo albums were designated with a "KS" and a 5000 number. An orange & purple label was used during 1971-73.

King   From inception through most of the 600 series, the label was black with silver lettering and, most importantly, the "KING" logo on top was 2" wide from "K" to "G" in thin print. White label promos from these years are very rare. Covers: Original covers (#500 through approximately 610) have the logo in a box in the upper right with "King" in script and "HiFi" in block print. From 1958-60 (#610-690), the logo was an ellipse with "KING" in block letters. For the last few titles in the 600 series and the first few 700s 1960 through 1962, the logo read "High Fidelity" with "KING" in open block letters.

King 10" albums bore a "295" prefix for the suggested retail price of $2.95. The first 12" albums carried a "395" prefix through 1960.

From late 1960 or early '61 (the early 700s) through 1966 the black crownless label remained except the "KING" logo on top was noticeably larger, with thicker print that made it 3" wide. The few stereo albums released during this time had blue labels. White label promos from these years are rare. Covers: From 1960 through 1962 (early 700s-810), the logo read "High Fidelity" with "KING" in open block letters. From 1963-66, the logo had a crown atop the "KING" in open block letters.

From 1966 through the mid-'70s a blue or black label was used with a crown on top. Covers: From 1966-68 (through the 1040s), the logo had a crown atop "KING" in open block letters. After 1969, the logo was a stylized "K" with "KING" in capital letters as the K's leg. Throughout the rest of the label's run a brownish gold or black label with a "K" logo on top was in service.

Kirshner From 1969 until 1973 the label was the same as the latter Calendar label: Orange with a "K" logo on top. After 1974 it was white with a multi-color top.

Laurie The original label (1002) was gold with black lettering, "Laurie" in a semicircle on top and "Mastersound" around the bottom. After that it gets confusing: The labels of originals and reissues are essentially the same except on the original pressings the dots in the five points of the star are large with plenty of white space. On later pressings the dots are noticeably smaller with considerably less white space.

LeGrand The original '60s releases have a red & gold label without a crown on top. Reissues from the '80s have a crown on top and a white band in the middle.

Liberty From inception through 1960 (#3000-3130s) Liberty boasted an aqua blue, or turquoise, label with silver print. When stereo albums, many of which were reprocessed, were issued on the 7000 series in the late '50s, a black label was used with silver print. Throughout these years, mono albums bore an "LRP" prefix; white label promos were issued. Some titles were issued as part of the 6000 series with an "LRS" prefix. Stereo albums were designated with "LST."

For the first one hundred releases (7000-7099), stereo albums were mixed and released according to perceived need. That is, the stereo release numbers do not correspond with the catalog numbers of the original mono albums. With 7100 on, the mono and stereo catalog numbers coincided (for example, the mono was LRP-3100 while the stereo was LST-7100, etc.)

A black label with a rainbow and a gold logo was used from 1960 through 1966 (#3150-3440 and 13/14000s). From 1966 through 1969 (#3440-7620s and 13/14000s) "Liberty Records, Inc" was added beneath a blue logo. Off-white or cream label promos were issued. After Liberty was sold in 1970, "Liberty/UA, Inc" was added beneath the blue logo. In the '80s a gray label was in use.

London From inception through 1964, mono albums had a red or maroon label with silver print and featured an "ffrr"/ear logo on top. White label promos were issued. When stereo was added, a blue label was issued with "ffss" in a circle on top; all are true stereo. From 1963 through 1965 mono albums had a red/maroon label, and stereo LPs had a blue label with a plain "London" in silver print on top. From 1965 until 1969 "London" appeared in a box on top. After 1969 "London" appeared in blue print in a silver box at the top.

Throughout these years, mono albums bore an "LL" prefix and carried a four digit number. Stereo releases had a "PS" prefix and a three digit number, usually dropping the first number from the mono designation.

Mainstream   Original albums in 1965-66 bore a light, silvery-blue label. White label promos were issued. Later pressings had a "Red Lion Production" in the upper right.

MCA   From 1973 through 1978 (#2000-2300s) a black label was used with a rainbow. A light brown label with a darker perimeter was in used from 1977 until 1979 (the 3000 series and the early 5000s). After 1980 the label showed a blue sky & clouds motif. Note: A blue label with rainbow was used on the MCA reissues.

Mercury   Original albums in 1949 on the 1000 series had a black label with gold print. From the mid-'50s through 1963 (#20000-20700) mono albums had a black label with silver print and a plain logo on top. Mono albums carried an "MG" prefix; yellow label promos were issued. The first stereo albums (the SR-60000 series) appeared in 1957 with a black label with silver print. From 1961-64 (#20600-20900) the label for mono and stereo was black with an oval logo on top.

From 1964 through 1968 (#20900-61190) a red label was used with Mercury's head on top. White label promos were issued. A red label with twelve oval logos around perimeter was used from 1969 through 1973 (#61200-61300s and 600-670s). During 1973-74 (#680-on) Mercury issued a red label with seven oval logos around perimeter. A colored label with a skyscraper was in print from 1974 through 1982 (the 1000 series). After 1982 the label was black with "Marketed by Polygram" on the bottom.

Mercury's budget label was Wing and they distributed several others, primarily the Norman Granz labels, Clef, Down Home, Norgran and Verve through 1960, along with Savoy and Regent.

MGM   Original MGM albums of the '50s (#3000-3770s) have a yellow & black label. From 1960 through 1968 (#3770s-4515) MGM used a black label with a multi-color logo. Yellow & white label promos were issued. Throughout these years, mono albums bore an "E" prefix; stereo albums carried an "SE."

From 1968 through 1976 the label was a blue & gold swirl label with "A Division of Metro-Goldwyn-Mayer" on the bottom. From 1976 on the blue & gold swirl label had a street address on the bottom. Yellow label promos were issued.

MGM's subsidiaries include Metrojazz and later the budget label, Metro. In 1961 they purchased Verve from Norman Granz, altering that label's cataloging system. For more information refer to Verve below.

Minit   Through most of the '60s the label was orange. This was replaced by a black label in the late '60s and early '70s.

Monument   1961-62 releases had a copper & white swirl label. This was replaced in 1962-63 with a white & rainbow swirl label. From 1963 until 1976 a light green label was used with a gold perimeter and a Henderson, Tenn, address on the bottom. From 1966 until 1971 the Tenn. location was dropped. A brownish orange label was used from 1971 until 1976. This was replaced in 1976 with a black label. Finally, a silver label was used in the early '80s.

Motown   Some original labels were white. From 1962 on Motown used a blue label with a map pinpointing Detroit at the top of the label. On original pressings during 1962-63 the map extended from the East Coast to Kansas; there was a W. Grand Blvd. address beneath the map. Original pressings on this lable (600-62?) did not have any yellow in the logo!

These were reissued with yellow added to the logo. From 1963 until 1969 the map was scaled down to extend from Pennsylvania to Indiana, and the W. Grand Blvd. address was printed at the bottom. From 1969 until 1983 "A Product of Motown" appeared on the bottom in lieu of the Detroit address. After 1983 the label notes MCA as the distributor.

Musicor   Initial pressings in 1962 were on a brown label. A black label with "Distributed by United Artists" on the bottom was used from 1962 into 1964. The United Artists reference was dropped from mid-'64 through 1969. During the first half of the '70s the label was orange; later, the label was green & yellow.

Ode   From 1968 until 1970 the label was yellow. During 1970-71 it was white & silver with "Ode 70" in the upper right. From 1971 until 1975 the white & silver label specified "Ode Records Inc." Finally, a light brown label with the Epic logo was in effect from 1975 until 1978.

Paramount   In 1969 the label was gray with "A Division of Paramount Pictures" on the bottom. In the early '70s the gray label read "A Division of Famous Music." A few titles in 1971-72 featured a blue label. Note: This company is not affiliated with ABC-Paramount.

Parkway   In 1960-61 the label was orange with a "harp, horns & score" logo on each side. From 1961 until 1966 the label was orange & yellow with two harps on top. During 1967-68 the label was gold.

Parrot   From 1965 until 1971 the label was black with "Distributed by London Records, Inc" on the bottom. From 1972 until 1974 the black label read "A Product of London Records."

Philips   From inception through 1963 (#001-120s) Philips used a black label with "Chicago 1, Illinois" on the bottom. From 1964 until 1966, the black label had "Vendor: Mercury" on the bottom. From 1966 until 1970, the black label was used with no disclaimers on the bottom. Throughout this time, mono albums bore a "PHM" prefix and were part of the 200-000 series; stereo titles had a "PHS" prefix and were part of the 600-000 series. Gold or white label promos were issued. From 1970 until 1974 a black label was used with "Manufactured and Distributed by Mercury" on the bottom.

Polydor   From 1969 until 1978 the label was red with no street address. From 1978 until 1982 the red label carried a Seventh Ave. address on the bottom.

Prestige: From inception through 1956 (7000-7140), Prestige albums had a black on yellow label with the company's "W. 50th Street, NYC" address on top. From 1957-1964 (7141-7320s), the same black on yellow label featured a "Bergenfield, NJ" address. In 1960 stereo titles were released on a black on silver Bergenfield label carrying a "PRST" prefix.

In 1964-67, titles were issued with a blue label with the company's new trident logo on the right; a few titles were reissued on this label and are rather hard to find. From 1967 through '69, the blue label carried the trident in a circle on top. In 1969-72, the label was purple with the encircled trident on top. After the label was purchased by Fantasy, a green label was used (white label promos were issued). In the '80s, select titles were reissued, often in stereo, with a facsimile of the original yellow label and an OJC ("Original Jazz Classic") prefix.

RCA Victor From 1950 through 1954, RCA Victor albums had a green label. For one year, 1954-55, the company switched to a glossy black label with Nipper the dog on top in outline only. The 10" albums bore an "LPT" or "LPM" prefix and were issued with a 3000 number.

From 1955 through 1963 (LPM 2000-2700s) the classic shiny black label with the full-bodied Nipper on top appeared with "Long 33 1/3 Play" on the bottom. During 1963-64, (LPM 2700s-2999), "Mono" was printed on the bottom, which was ultimately replaced by "Monaural" from 1964 until 1968 (LPM 3000-3900s). Note: Some albums issued in 1966-67 read "Mono Dynagroove."

Stereo albums from 1958 through 1963 (LSP 2000-700s) had a shiny black label with the full-bodied Nipper on top appeared with "Living Stereo" on the bottom. From 1964 through 1968 (LSP 3000-4000s) only "Stereo" appeared on the bottom. Note: Some albums issued in 1966-67 read "Stereo Dynagroove."

From late 1968 through 1971 (LSP 4000-4460s) an orange label was issued on stiff, non-flexible vinyl. Many, if not most, of these were reissued with identical labels on RCA's ridiculously flimsy "dynaflex" vinyl. From 1971 through 1976 (LSP 4460s-1039) the same orange label was in effect but with "dynaflex" printed on the bottom. During 1975-76 the label was a light brown label. In 1976, the label was again black except Nipper was now located in the upper right at approximately 1 or 2 o'clock.

Regent A subsidiary of Savoy, Regent, primarily a jazz label, was distributed by Mercury and carried an "MG" prefix. Original Regent releases used a green label; red labels are reissues.

Reprise Initially Frank Sinatra's pet project, Reprise was incorporated into Warner Bros. within a few years. From inception through 1968, Reprise used a pink, gold, & green label with a large steamboat in the upper left (#6000-6280s). Note: Reprise had a jazz series that was yellow, red, & green with an angel in the upper left in print during the early '60s. From 1968 through 1970, a brown & orange label was used with a smaller steamboat and the "W7" logo on top (#6280s-6400s and 2000-2025). White label promos were issued.

Throughout this time, mono titles on the 6000 series had an "R" prefix; stereo titles were originally issued with an "R6" and then an "RS" prefix. This applied to the 1000 series, basically reserved for Sinatra. Eventually, the mono 1000s had an "F" prefix while the stereos had an "FS." During 1970-76 a brown label was used without the "W7" logo (the early 6400s on). White label promos were issued.

Riverside From inception through 1956 (#100-240s) Riverside, primarlily a jazz label, used a blue on white label. From 1956 through 1963 (#240s-476) the label was blue with a mike & two reels of tape on top. Stereo titles beginning in late

1958 had a black label with the mike & reels logo. For a brief period in 1963-64, mono and stereo labels were blue without the mike & reels logo; this was definitely used on 477 and may have turned up on a few others and some reissues. These labels read "Bill Grauer Productions" on the bottom.

Initially, the mono albums began with 100 and carried an "RLP-12" prefix. Initial stereo releases were on an 1100 series with the new numbers assigned as the remixes for mono titles were made available; i.e., the stereo numbers do not necessarily correspond with their original mono counterparts. When new titles were automatically released in both mono and stereo, the monos retained the three digit figure (the late 200s or early 300s) and the "RLP" prefix. Stereo titles had the same three digit number but bore an "RS-9" prefix.

From 1964 through 1967 (#478-499) the label was turquoise with "Orpheum Prod." on the bottom. After ABC took over distribution of the label in 1967 the earlier material was reissued with black on brown labels. In the mid-'80s select titles were reissued, often in stereo, by Fantasy with a facsimile of the original blue on white label but with an OJC prefix for "Original Jazz Classic."

Roulette   Original issues in 1957-58 (#25000-25050) had black labels. From 1959 through 1962 (#25050-25180 and 52000-52050) a white label was issued with criss-crossed color bars. For a brief period in 1962-63, an orange & pink label was used. After 1963 Roulette used an orange & yellow label with a roulette wheel design. Throughout this time, mono albums bore a "R" prefix; white label promos were issued. Stereo titles had a "SR" prefix. Since 1977, the orange & yellow label with a roulette wheel label shows "Made in USA by Roulette Inc" at the bottom.

RSO   From 1973 until 1981 a light brown label was used with a red cow logo on top. This was replaced by a silver label with a red cow in 1981.

Savoy   All original issues on Savoy, primarlily a jazz label, from 1950 through the '60s had maroon labels. Distributed by Mercury, this label also used an "MG" prefix. Their subsidiary was Regent. When titles were reissued in the '70s a red or brown label was used with "Distributed by Arista" on the bottom.

Scepter   The original label (501) was red with "Scepter" in black script outlined in silver. From 1962 until 1971 the label was orange with an oval-like center. Although a few titles had solid white or red labels. In 1972-73 a multi-color label was in use on general releases with the special "Citation Series" carrying a yellow label. From 1974 until 1976 the label was blue.

Shelter   The first dozen titles in 1971-72 (#8900-8910) had a red label with a Superman-like logo on the left. From 1972 through the latter part of 1973 the red label had a blacked out Superman logo on top. In 1974-75 a gold label was used with "Distributed by MCA Records, Inc" on the bottom. In 1976 a yellowish gold label had "Distributed by ABC Records" on the bottom. From 1977 until 1979 the label had a crescent moon along the left side.

Sire   From 1968 through 1970 a white label was used with both the Sire and London logos on top. Since then, a yellow label was used with a blue or purple stylized "S" on top. During 1970-71 the label read "Distributed by Polydor Records" on the bottom.

Reprise Records, started by and almost solely supported by Frank Sinatra's sales, used a steamboat on their label through the early '70s. Originally a pink, gold and green label with a large steamboat and "reprise:" in a banner (illustrated here by Movin' With Nancy), in 1968 it switched to a brown and orange label with a noticeably smaller boat and both a "W7" and ":r" logo on top (Are You Experienced?). By 1970 the label was brown and the "W7" had been dropped from the top (The Great Lost Kinks Album).

From 1972 until 1974 the label read "Distributed by Famous Music Corp." From 1974 until 1976 it read "Distributed by ABC Records." During the rest of the '70s the label read "Marketed by Warner Bros." In the '80s the Warner motto was joined by a "3300 Warner Blvd" address.

<u>Smash</u> From 1961 through 1968 a flat red label was used with black print. From 1968 until 1971 the red label carried a Mercury logo in an oval on top.

<u>Soul</u> This Motown subsidiary's first releases (701-702) had a white & red label. This was immediately changed to a purple label in late 1965.

<u>Specialty</u> From 1957 through the early '70s the label was gold with a black top. The '80s reissues had a white label with a black top.

<u>Stax</u> From 1962 through 1968 the label on mono albums was blue with a stack of records on top; stereo albums were yellow with the stack. From 1968 until 1971 the yellow label had a finger-snapping logo in a blue box on the left and then in a brown box. Since the mid-'70s the label was purple fading into white.

<u>Sue</u> From 1961 through the mid-'60s the label was orange; later titles and reissues are black.

<u>Sunset</u> This budget subsidiary of Liberty repackaged material from the parent label's catalog. Original releases through 1969 had a black & blue label that read "A Division of Liberty Records" on the bottom. After 1970 the same label read "Liberty/U.A." on the bottom.

<u>Tamla</u> Original labels (220-231?) were white with a black & purple record overlapping the purple globe. There was a brief transition label, similar to the original, except tan & yellow, that may have only been used on a couple of [first?] pressings. These are rarer than their white label counterparts.

During 1961-63 the label was yellow with the overlapping record/globe on top. From 1963 until 1968 the yellow label showed two discs on top, one a record and one with the company imprint. After 1968 the yellow label had a brown top.

<u>Tampa</u>: Original labels through 1957 were black with colored vinyl pressings. As I have not been able to identify all of these, the reader will find one listing for these titles. Later black vinyl pressings have pink labels. Stereo pressings apparently also exist, although, again, information at this time is sketchy.

<u>Threshold</u> From 1970 until 1973 the label was white. This was replaced with a blue label in 1973.

<u>Tower</u> This subsidiary of Capitol used a dull orange label from 1965 until 1968. Several titles were reissued in 1968 on a striped label. Mono albums carried a "T" prefix while stereo LPs were "ST" and rechanneled stereo, "DT."

<u>Track</u> From 1967 until 1971 the label was black; during 1972, it was silver. After 1973 the label was a dark brown.

20th Century Fox   From inception through the early '60s, the label was a light blue with "20th Fox" on top. From the early '60s through the early '70s, a black label was issued. During the '70s the label changed to aquamarine. From 1977 through the '80s, a light brown label was used with spotlights on top.

United Artists   In 1958-59, U.A. used a red & black label. In 1959 mono albums had red labels, while stereos were blue. A black label with a large "UA" logo on top was briefly issued in 1960. From 1960 through 1968 (#3120-6640) the label was black with "United Artists" in a box on top.

From 1968 through 1970 (#6640-6710s) the label was purple & orange. White label promos were issued. Throughout this period, mono albums (the UAL 3000 and 4000 series) and stereos (UAS 6000s and 5000s) had a "UAS" prefix.

During 1970-71 (#6710-6700s and early 5500s and 5200s) the label was black & orange. In 1971-75 (#6780 on and 100-540) the label was a light brown. From 1975 through 1977 (#540-760) "Music & Record Group" was added to the bottom of the brown label. After 1977 a "sun burst" design was used on the label.

Valiant   During the first half of the '60s the label was blue; during the latter half it was red.

Vanguard   From inception through 1963 (the 9000 mono series) Vanguard used a maroon label with silver print and a horseman logo on top. For the first one hundred and forty-one releases (2000-2140), stereo albums were mixed and released according to perceived need. That is, the stereo release numbers do not correspond with the catalog numbers of the original mono albums. With 2141 on, the mono and stereo catalog numbers were the same with a "7" added to the stereo number For example, the mono was VRS-9141 while the stereo was VSD-79141, etc.

Stereo albums (both the 2000 and 79000 series) had a black label with silver print. From 1963 through 1970 the company issued a gold-brown or silvery-gray label with a white horseman logo on the bottom. White label promos were issued. Throughout these years, monos bore a "VRS" prefix while stereos had a "VSD." During the '70s a marble "swirl" effect label was issued.

Vee Jay   From inception through 1959 the first few albums (#1000-1013?) had a maroon label with silver print; the few stereo releases were gray with black print. From 1960 through 1963 a glossy black label was used with a rainbow perimeter and the Vee Jay logo in an oval at the top of the label (#1010s-1070s and the 3000 series). From 1963 through 1965 (#1060-1070s) the glossy black rainbow label featured the logo in brackets. During 1965-66, a flat black label was used with silver print. Throughout these years Vee Jay's basic prefix was the common "LP." White label promos were issued.

When stereos were issued they bore either an "LPS," SR" or "VRS" prefix. Note: Stereo Vee Jay albums are very rare; while this book notes the staggering difference between some monos and stereos, the necessary data is not currently available to note all of these rarities. Thus, when happening across a stereo Vee Jay bear in mind that it may be rarer than the prices in this book indicate. . .

When Vee Jay went bankrupt in 1966, the demand for a lot of their product remained and was met illegally. Many Vee Jay titles remained available throughout the '70s with black labels on pressings that are dramatically inferior to the originals. In fact, they resemble barely professional counterfeits: the covers are photo-reproductions of the originals, and the pressings are abominable, with poor sound and noticeable noise from recycled vinyl. While the most common was *Introducing The Beatles*, poorly reproduced Jimmy Reed albums and several jazz titles proliferated.

During the '70s "VJ International" and a "Vintage Series" appeared. During the '70s and the '80s, a red label with the brackets logo was also used.

<u>Verve</u>   Verve was jazz impressario Norman Granz' flagship label. He began this by consolidating his previous Clef, Down Home, and Norgran labels, and reissuing the bulk of the earlier titles. From 1956 through 1960 Verve used a black label with silver print and "Long Playing Microgroove Verve Records, Inc" on the bottom. Verve titles carried an "MGV" prefix and were issued exclusively in mono. When select titles were remixed in stereo and issued on the 6000 series in late 1959-60, they carried an "MGVS" prefix.

When the label was purchased by MGM in 1960, most of the catalog was reissued with the monos designated with a "V" and the stereos with a "V6." The original 8000 series number was kept for both. The new parent company retained the original black with silver print label but "MGM Records-A Division Of Metro-Goldwyn-Mayer, Inc." was included on the bottom. From 1966 through 1971 MGM's Sunset address is also on the bottom. From 1972 until 1975, a white label was used with blue MGM and Verve logos. White label promos were issued.

<u>Vik</u>   This RCA subsidiary had black labels with a multi-color logo on top.

<u>Virgin</u>   From 1972 until 1975 the label was a full color picture of two young women— one must suppose they are the artist's, ahem, ideal virgins— with "Dist. by Atlantic Recording Corp." on the bottom. From 1975 until 1978 it read "Distributed by CBS Records." After 1978 the label was white.

<u>Volt</u>   From 1967 until 1969 the label was yellow. From 1969 until 1973 it was blue. After 1973 the label was brown.

<u>Wand</u>   Through most of the '60s (#650-690s) the label was white with a black top. From 1970 until 1974 the label had a marble effect. After 1974 the label was a dark orange.

<u>Warner Brothers</u>   From 1958 through 1962 (#1200-1470) Warner Bros. used a gray label with a black & yellow logo on top for mono albums. From 1962 until 1965 (#1470-1620) a gray label was used with a black & white logo on top. During this period stero albums carried a gold label.

From 1966 through 1968 (#1920-1730) both the mono and the stereo releases had a gold label. From 1968 through 1970 a green label was used with the "W7" logo on top. Throughout these years, mono albums carried a "W" prefix; stereos had a "WS" prefix. White label promos were issued.

When Warner Bros. switched their albums over to a lime green label in 1967, they carried their "Warner Bros.-Seven Arts Records" motto along the perimeter at the top with a "W7" logo in a box beneath it, shown above on Live/Dead. By 1970 the same green labels read "Warner Bros. Records" with the "WB" shield logo, illustrated here by Tupelo Honey.

During 1970-72, the "W7" on the green label was changed to a "WB" logo. During 1973-75, the label featured a Burbank street scene. From 1978 through the '80s, a tan label was issued.

White Whale From 1965 until 1970 (#7100-7120s) the label was solid blue; after 1970 it was blue with concentric white circles.

Wing This budget subsidiary of Mercury repackaged material from the parent label's catalog. From inception through the '50s Wing had a blue label with silver print and the "Wing" logo in an oval on top, often with "Jazz" above it. Several titles were issued simultaneously on Mercury and Wing. Throughout the '60s, when Wing was exclusively a budget label, a blue or black label was used with "Mercury" above the "Wing" logo.

Mono albums were on the 12000 series with an "MGW" prefix, while stereo LPs carried an "SRW" prefix on the 16000 series. From 1970 through 1971, a blue label featured both the Wing logo and the oval Mercury logo alongside it on top.

World Pacific: In 1957 Pacific Jazz changed its name to World Pacific; both new titles and older catalog titles were issued on the new imprints. From 1960 until 1965, the Pacific Jazz label was back, starting all over with number "1." From 1965 until 1970, both Pacific Jazz and World Pacific ran, with the later issuing non-jazz material covering the gamut from rock to pop to international. Both companies used a black, orange, & yellow label. During the late '70s and early '80s, the company used a blue & green "waves" design for the label.

In *Jazz West Coast*, Robert Gordon notes "[Owner Richard] Bock produced a great many fine albums over the years, but one wishes he could have resisted the urge to splice and otherwise tamper with his tapes, a temptation to which he all too often succumbed." An example is Jim Hall's *Jazz Guitar:* The original sessions (on Pacific Jazz/World Pacific 1227) featured a trio with Red Mitchell, bass, and Carl Perkins, piano. When Bock reissued the album in 1963 (Pacific Jazz 79), he overdubbed a drum track, making the recording a quartet. Tampering with the integrity of the original recording arouses the ire of most listeners. Of course, collector-wise, it does create a new version to be sought. . .

"X" The RCA subsidiary had white labels with a huge red "X" on top.

A. F. O. EXECUTIVES, THE

A.F.O. LP-0002	(M)	A Compendium	196?	80.00	200.00

AARON, TOSSI

Prestige Inter. PR-13055	(M)	Tossi Aaron Sings Jewish Songs	1962	12.00	30.00

ABBA

Atlantic PR-300	(DJ)	Abba	1978	12.00	30.00
Atlantic PR-432	(DJ)	A Collection Of Hits	1982	12.00	30.00
Atlantic PR-436	(DJ)	The Abba Special (2 LPs)	1983	20.00	50.00

ABBEY TAVERN SINGERS, THE

V.I.P. 402	(M)	We're Off To Dublin In The Green	1966	16.00	40.00
V.I.P. S-402	(S)	We're Off To Dublin In The Green	1966	20.00	50.00

ABBIE-GAYE, KEN & MEL
Abbie-Gaye, Ken Stephens and Mel Johnson.

Trac SA-101-8	(S)	Country Music Jubilee	196?	20.00	50.00

ABBOTT, O. J.
O. J. Abbot was a singer of traditional Irish, British and Canadian lumberjack songs.

Folkways FM-4051	(M)	Irish And British Songs From The Ottawa Valley	1961	10.00	25.00

ABRAHAM, ROGER

Prestige Inter. PR-13034	(M)	Make Me A Pallet On The Floor	1961	12.00	30.00

AC/DC

Atlantic LAAS-001	(DJ)	Live At The Atlantic Studios	1977	12.00	30.00
		(Convincing counterfeits of LAAS-001 exist.)			
Atlantic PR-562	(DJ)	Flick Of The Switch Interview Album	1983	10.00	25.00

ACE, JOHNNY

Duke DLP-70	(10")	Memorial Album For Johnny Ace	1955	500.00	1,200.00
Duke DLP-71	(M)	Memorial Album For Johnny Ace	1956	200.00	400.00
		(First pressings of Ace 71 have purple & yellow labels in a cover that does not have a playing card on the front.)			
Duke DLP-71	(M)	Memorial Album For Johnny Ace	1961	80.00	200.00
		(Second pressings have purple & yellow labels in a cover with a playing card on the front.)			

ACES COMBO, THE

Justice JLP-134	(S)	Introducing The Aces Combo	196?	300.00	500.00

ACUFF, ROY

Columbia HL-9004	(10")	Songs Of The Smokey Mountains	1949	60.00	150.00
Columbia HL-9010	(10")	Old Time Barn Dance	1949	60.00	150.00
Columbia HL-9013	(10")	Songs Of The Saddle	1949	60.00	150.00
Harmony HL-7082	(M)	Great Speckled Bird	1958	10.00	25.00
Capitol T-617	(M)	Songs Of The Smoky Mountains	1955	24.00	60.00
Capitol T-1870	(M)	Songs Of The Smoky Mountains	1963	12.00	30.00
Capitol DT-1870	(E)	Songs Of The Smoky Mountains	1963	8.00	20.00
Capitol T-2103	(M)	The Great Roy Acuff	1964	10.00	25.00
Capitol ST-2103	(S)	The Great Roy Acuff	1964	8.00	20.00
Capitol DT-2103	(E)	The Great Roy Acuff	1964	6.00	15.00
Capitol T-2276	(M)	The Voice Of Country Music	1965	12.00	30.00
Capitol ST-2276	(S)	The Voice Of Country Music	1965	14.00	35.00
MGM E-3707	(M)	Favorite Hymns	1958	30.00	75.00
MGM E-4044	(M)	Hymn Time	1962	12.00	30.00
MGM SE-4044	(E)	Hymn Time	1962	8.00	20.00
Hickory LPM-101	(M)	Once More It's Roy Acuff	1962	12.00	30.00

Label & Catalog #		Title	Year	VG+	NM
Hickory LPM-109	(M)	**The King Of Country Music**	1963	12.00	30.00
Hickory LPM-113	(M)	**Roy Acuff—Star Of The Grand Ole Opry**	1963	12.00	30.00
Hickory LPM-114	(M)	**The World Is His Stage**	1963	12.00	30.00
Hickory LPM-115	(M)	**Roy Acuff Sings American Folk Songs**	1963	12.00	30.00
Hickory LPM-117	(M)	**Hand-Clapping Gospel Songs**	1963	10.00	25.00
Hickory LPM-119	(M)	**Country Music Hall Of Fame**	1964	10.00	25.00
Hickory LPM-125	(M)	**Great Train Songs**	1965	10.00	25.00
Hickory LPS-125	(E)	**Great Train Songs**	1965	6.00	15.00
Hickory DT-90698	(E)	**Great Train Songs** (Capitol Record Club)	1965	10.00	25.00
Elektra EC-10-1-78	(DJ)	**Interview With Roy Acuff**	1978	12.00	30.00

ADAMS, DON
Don Adams is a comedian best known for his role as Maxwell Smart on TV's "Get Smart."

Signature SM-1010	(M)	**Don Adams**	1960	16.00	40.00
Roulette R-25317	(M)	**The Detective**	1966	8.00	20.00
Roulette SR-25317	(S)	**The Detective**	1966	10.00	25.00

ADAMS, EDIE

MGM E-3751	(M)	**Music To Listen To Records To**	1959	20.00	50.00
MGM SE-3751	(S)	**Music To Listen To Records To**	1959	30.00	75.00

ADAMS, FAYE

Warwick W-2031	(M)	**Shake A Hand**	1961	300.00	750.00
Zion 2104	(M)	**Faye Adams Sings The Lord's Prayer**	196?	20.00	50.00

ADAMS, J. T.

Wrangler W-3007	(M)	**J. T. Adams And The Men Of Texas**	196?	8.00	20.00
Wrangler WS-3007	(M)	**J. T. Adams And The Men Of Texas**	196?	10.00	25.00
Wrangler W-3038	(M)	**Voices Skyward**	196?	8.00	20.00
Wrangler WS-3038	(M)	**Voices Skyward**	196?	10.00	25.00
Bluesville BVLP-1077	(M)	**Indiana Avenue Blues**	1964	30.00	75.00
		— Bluesville albums above have bright blue labels with silver print.—			
Bluesville BVLP-1077	(M)	**Indiana Avenue Blues**	196?	12.00	30.00
		— Bluesville albums above have blue labels with a trident logo on the right side.—			

ADAMS, JERRI: *Refer to* GOLDMINE'S PRICE GUIDE TO COLLECTIBLE JAZZ ALBUMS

ADAMS, MIKE, & THE RED JACKETS

Crown CLP-5312	(M)	**Surfer's Beat**	1963	8.00	20.00
Crown CST-312	(S)	**Surfer's Beat**	1963	10.00	25.00
Crown CST-312	(S)	**Surfer's Beat** (Colored vinyl)	1963	20.00	50.00

ADKINS, JACK

Starday SLP-168	(M)	**Jack Adkins**	1962	16.00	40.00

ADRIAN & THE SUNSETS

Sunset 63-601	(M)	**Breakthrough** (Multi-colored vinyl)	1963	80.00	200.00
Sunset 63-601	(M)	**Breakthrough**	1963	40.00	100.00
Sunset SE-63-601	(S)	**Breakthrough** (Multi-colored vinyl)	1963	150.00	300.00
Sunset SE-63-601	(S)	**Breakthrough**	1963	80.00	200.00

ADVENTURERS, THE

Columbia CL-2147	(M)	**Can't Stop Twistin'**	1961	20.00	50.00
Columbia CS-8547	(S)	**Can't Stop Twistin'**	1961	30.00	75.00

AEROSMITH

Columbia KC-32005	(S)	**Aerosmith** (Orange cover)	1973	10.00	25.00
Columbia KCQ-32847	(Q)	**Get Your Wings**	1974	10.00	25.00
Columbia JCQ-33479	(Q)	**Toys In The Attic**	1975	10.00	25.00
Columbia PCQ-34165	(Q)	**Rocks**	1976	10.00	25.00
Columbia A3S-187	(DJ)	**Pure Gold From Rock 'n' Roll's Golden Boys**	1976	20.00	50.00
		(Columbia 187 is a boxed set of the group's first three albums.)			
Columbia (No number)	(DJ)	**The First Decade** (8 LP box)	1982	50.00	125.00
		("The First Decade" is a boxed set of the group's first eight albums.)			

AFFINITY

Paramount PAS-5027	(S)	**Affinity**	1970	10.00	25.00

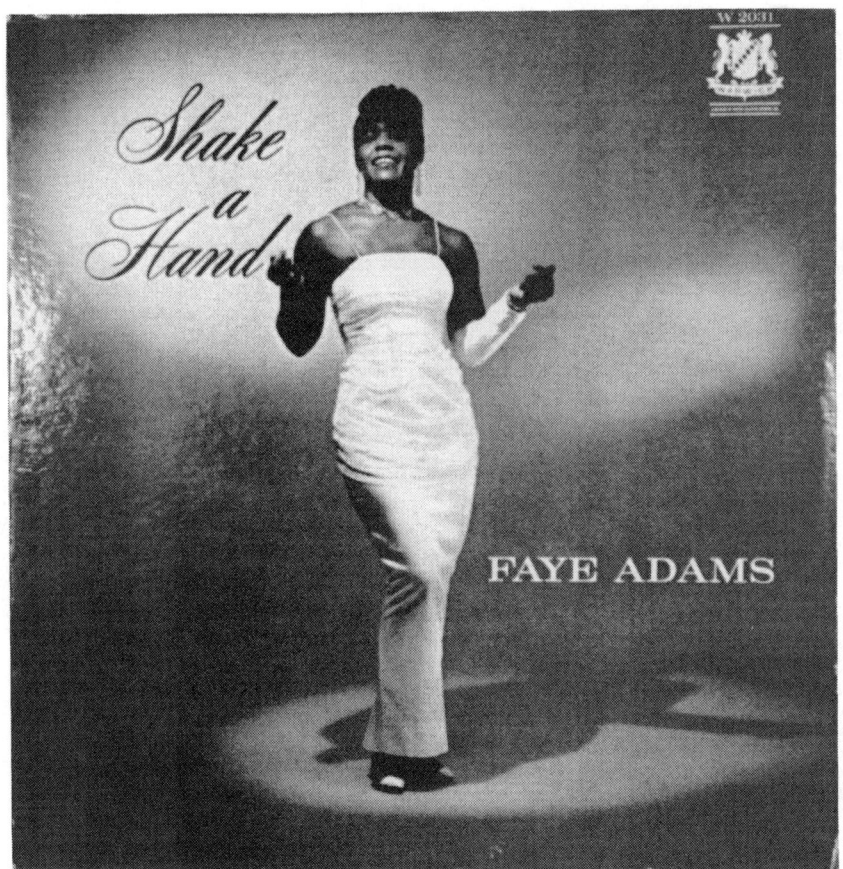

Ms. Faye Adams' claim to fame is her transcendent rhythm'n blues hit, "Shake A Hand," also the title of her highly collectible first album for Warwick. While Warwick was manufacturing stereo albums at this time, there are only mono copies of this title known to exist.

Label & Catalog #		Title	Year	VG+	NM
AFTERGLOW					
M. T. A. 5010	(M)	**Afterglow**	1967	16.00	40.00
AGAPE					
Mark MRS-2170	(S)	**Gospel Hard Rock**	1971	40.00	100.00
Renrut 101	(S)	**Victims Of Tradition**	1973	50.00	125.00
AGBE, NAIF					
Audio Fidelity AFLP-1980	(M)	**El Debke**	1960	8.00	20.00
Audio Fidelity AFSD-5980	(S)	**El Debke**	1960	12.00	30.00
AGE OF REASON, THE					
Georgetown	(M)	**The Age Of Reason**	196?	60.00	150.00
AGGREGATION					
L.H.I. 12008	(S)	**Mind Odyssey**	1967	80.00	200.00

AHBEZ, EDEN
Eden Ahbez's claim to fame is as the composer of Nat Cole's "Nature Boy," a role he took earnestly as this album dsiplays a very pre-hippie consciousness.

Del-Fi DFLP-	(M)	**Eden's Island**	196?	50.00	125.00
AKENS, JEWEL					
Era EL-110	(M)	**The Birds And The Bees**	1965	14.00	35.00
Era ES-110	(S)	**The Birds And The Bees**	1965	20.00	50.00

ALABAMA
Alabama is Jeff Cook, Teddy gentry, Mark herndon and Randy Owen. They originally recorded as Wild Country, under which the L. S. I. albums below were released. After signing with RCA the masters for these albums and the remaining copies were destroyed.

L. S. I. LP-1??	(S)	**Wild Country**	1977	800.00	1,200.00
L. S. I. LP-177	(S)	**Deuces Wild**	1978	800.00	1,200.00
Plantation PLP-44	(S)	**Wild Country**	1981	10.00	25.00
Plantation PLP-44	(S)	**Wild Country** *(Gold vinyl)*	1981	20.00	50.00
		(PLP-44 is a compilation of 45 sides and other odds & ends.)			
ALAIMO, STEVE					
Checker LP-2981	(M)	**Twist With Steve Alaimo**	1961	30.00	75.00
Checker LP-2983	(M)	**Mashed Potatoes**	1962	30.00	75.00
Checker LP-2986	(M)	**Every Day I Have To Cry**	1963	30.00	75.00
Crown CLP-5382	(M)	**Steve Alaimo**	1963	10.00	25.00
Crown CST-382	(E)	**Steve Alaimo**	1963	5.00	12.00
ABC-Paramount ABC-501	(M)	**Starring Steve Alaimo**	1965	12.00	30.00
ABC-Paramount ABCS-501	(S)	**Starring Steve Alaimo**	1965	16.00	40.00
ABC-Paramount ABC-531	(M)	**Where The Action Is**	1965	12.00	30.00
ABC-Paramount ABCS-531	(S)	**Where The Action Is**	1965	16.00	40.00
ABC-Paramount ABC-551	(M)	**Steve Alaimo Sings And Swings**	1966	12.00	30.00
ABC-Paramount ABCS-551	(S)	**Steve Alaimo Sings And Swings**	1966	16.00	40.00
ALBATROSS					
Anvil 8100	(S)	**Albatross**	197?	150.00	300.00
ALBERGHETTI, ANNA MARIA					
Mercury MG-20056	(M)	**Songs By Anna Maria Alberghetti**	1956	12.00	30.00
Capitol T-887	(M)	**I Can't Resist You**	1957	12.00	30.00
Capitol T-1379	(M)	**Warm And Willing**	1963	12.00	30.00
ALBERT, EDDIE					
Kapp KP-1000	(M)	**One God**	1954	12.00	30.00
Kapp KP-1017	(M)	**Eddie Albert And Margo**	1956	12.00	30.00
Kapp KP-1083	(M)	**September Song**	1957	12.00	30.00
ALBERT, EDDIE, & JOANNE GILBERT					
Dot DLP-9009	(M)	**The Nina, The Pinta And The Santa Maria**	1962	10.00	25.00
Dot DLP-25009	(M)	**The Nina, The Pinta And The Santa Maria**	1962	12.00	30.00

Label & Catalog #		Title	Year	VG+	NM

ALBERTS, AL
Alberts was formerly the lead singer of The Four Aces.

Coral CRL-57259	(M)	**A Man Has Got To Sing**	1959	12.00	30.00
Coral CRL-757259	(S)	**A Man Has Got To Sing**	1959	16.00	40.00

ALBRIGHT, LOLA: Refer to GOLDMINE'S PRICE GUIDE TO COLLECTIBLE JAZZ ALBUMS

ALEONG, ALI, & THE NOBLES

Reprise R-6020	(M)	**C'mon Baby, Let's Dance**	1962	10.00	25.00
Reprise R9-6020	(S)	**C'mon Baby, Let's Dance**	1962	12.00	30.00
Reprise R-6011	(M)	**Twistin' The Hits**	1962	10.00	25.00
Reprise R9-6011	(S)	**Twistin' The Hits**	1962	12.00	30.00
Vee Jay LP-1060	(M)	**Come Surf With Me**	1963	14.00	35.00
Vee Jay SR-1060	(S)	**Come Surf With Me**	1963	20.00	50.00

ALEX, BILL

Wrangler W-1008	(M)	**Bill Alex**	1962	8.00	20.00
Wrangler WS-1008	(S)	**Bill Alex**	1962	10.00	25.00

ALEXANDER, ARTHUR

Dot DLP-3434	(M)	**You Better Move On**	1962	40.00	100.00
Dot DLP-25434	(S)	**You Better Move On**	1962	80.00	200.00
Warner Bros. B-2592	(S)	**Arthur Alexander**	1972	10.00	25.00

ALEXANDER'S TIMELESS BLOOZBAND

Smack 1001	(M)	**Alexander's Timeless Bloozband**	1967	60.00	150.00
Uni 73021	(S)	**For Sale**	1968	10.00	25.00

ALEXANDRIA, LOREZ: Refer to GOLDMINE'S PRICE GUIDE TO COLLECTIBLE JAZZ ALBUMS

ALI, MUHAMMED
World boxing champion Muhammed Ali originally recorded as Cassius Clay.

Crimson Dyn. LPN-6020	(S)	**Muhammed Ali**	1976	20.00	50.00
St. John's ALI-1	(S)	**Muhammed Ali Vs. Mr. Tooth Decay**	1976	10.00	25.00

ALKIRE, EDDIE

Full-Tone FM-646	(M)	**Exciting New Colors**	196?	14.00	35.00
Full-Tone FM-647	(M)	**Exotic Steel Guitar**	196?	14.00	35.00
Full-Tone FM-648	(M)	**Steel Guitar Style**	196?	14.00	35.00
Full-Tone FM-649	(M)	**Jazz Steel Guitar**	196?	14.00	35.00

ALL AMERICAN RAMBLERS, THE

Gone G-5006	(M)	**Destination Dixie**	1958	20.00	50.00

ALL STARS, THE

Gramophone 20192	(M)	**Boogie Woogie**	196?	20.00	50.00

ALLAN, CHAD, & THE EXPRESSIONS
Chad Allan was an original member of The Guess Who. Refer to Brave Belt.

Scepter SP-533	(M)	**Shakin' All Over**	1966	16.00	40.00
Scepter SPS-533	(S)	**Shakin' All Over**	1966	16.00	40.00
		("Shakin' All Over," "Clock On The Wall," and			
		"Till We Kissed" are rechanneled.)			

ALLAN, DAVIE/DAVIE ALLAN & THE ARROWS
Davie Allan's fuzzed guitar graced the soundtracks of many B-movies of the late '60s, including many, having not been released on record, that aren't listed below.

Tower T-5002	(M)	**Apache '65**	1965	20.00	50.00
Tower DT-5002	(E)	**Apache '65**	1965	16.00	40.00
Tower T-5043	(M)	**The Wild Angels** *(Soundtrack)*	1966	12.00	30.00
Tower DT-5043	(E)	**The Wild Angels** *(Soundtrack)*	1966	8.00	20.00
Tower T-5056	(M)	**The Wild Angels, Volume 2** *(Soundtrack)*	1967	12.00	30.00
Tower DT-5056	(E)	**The Wild Angels, Volume 2** *(Soundtrack)*	1967	8.00	20.00
Tower T-5074	(M)	**Devil's Angels** *(Soundtrack)*	1967	12.00	30.00
Tower DT-5074	(E)	**Devil's Angels** *(Soundtrack)*	1967	8.00	20.00
Tower T-5078	(M)	**Blues Theme**	1967	20.00	50.00
Tower DT-5078	(E)	**Blues Theme**	1967	16.00	40.00
Tower T-5083	(M)	**Mondo Hollywood** *(Soundtrack)*	1968	12.00	30.00
Tower DT-5083	(E)	**Mondo Hollywood** *(Soundtrack)*	1968	8.00	20.00

Label & Catalog #		Title	Year	VG+	NM
Tower DT-5094	(E)	**Cycledelic Sounds**	1968	20.00	50.00
Tower SKAO-5099	(S)	**Wild In The Streets** (Soundtrack)	1968	12.00	30.00
Tower ST-5124	(E)	**The Hellcats** (Soundtrack)	1968	10.00	25.00
Tower ST-5141	(S)	**Killers Three** (Soundtrack)	1968	10.00	25.00
Sidewalk T-5902	(M)	**Thunder Alley** (Soundtrack)	1967	8.00	20.00
Sidewalk ST-5902	(S)	**Thunder Alley** (Soundtrack)	1967	10.00	25.00
Sidewalk T-5903	(M)	**Teenage Rebellion** (Soundtrack)	1967	12.00	30.00
Sidewalk DT-5903	(E)	**Teenage Rebellion** (Soundtrack)	1967	8.00	20.00
Sidewalk T-5910	(M)	**Glory Stompers** (Soundtrack)	1967	12.00	30.00
Sidewalk DT-5910	(E)	**Glory Stompers** (Soundtrack)	1967	8.00	20.00
Sidewalk DT-5911	(P)	**Mary Jane** (Soundtrack)	1968	10.00	25.00
Sidewalk ST-5914	(S)	**Wild Racers** (Soundtrack)	1968	12.00	30.00

ALLEN, DAVE

Label & Catalog #		Title	Year	VG+	NM
International Art. 11	(S)	**Color Blind**	1969	20.00	50.00
International Art. 11	(S)	**Color Blind**	1979	6.00	15.00

(Reissues of I.A. 11 have "Masterfonics" in the trail-off vinyl.)

ALLEN, DAVID
David Allen is a jazz-based vocalist.

Label & Catalog #		Title	Year	VG+	NM
World Pacific WP-408	(M)	**A Sure Thing**	1957	30.00	75.00
World Pacific ST-1006	(S)	**A Sure Thing**	1958	20.00	50.00
World Pacific WP-1250	(M)	**Let's Face The Music And Dance**	1958	16.00	40.00
World Pacific WP-1295	(M)	**David Allen Sings The Music Of Jerome Kern**	1960	12.00	30.00
World Pacific ST-1295	(S)	**David Allen Sings The Music Of Jerome Kern**	1960	10.00	25.00

(World Pacific 1295 is a reissue of 408/1006.)

Label & Catalog #		Title	Year	VG+	NM
Warner Bros. W-1268	(M)	**I Only Have Eyes For You**	1959	8.00	20.00
Warner Bros. WS-1268	(S)	**I Only Have Eyes For You**	1959	10.00	25.00

ALLEN, LEE

Label & Catalog #		Title	Year	VG+	NM
Ember ELP-200	(M)	**Walkin' With Mr. Lee** (Red label)	1958	200.00	500.00
Ember ELP-200	(M)	**Walkin' With Mr. Lee** ("Logs" logo label)	1959	80.00	200.00
Ember ELP-200	(M)	**Walkin' With Mr. Lee** (Black & red label)	1961	60.00	150.00

ALLEN, LEE
Lee Allen is a bluegrass guitar player and singer. JLP-127 also features Ralph Stanley.

Label & Catalog #		Title	Year	VG+	NM
Jalyn JLP-127	(M)	**Songs Of Love And Tragedy**	196?	10.00	25.00

ALLEN, RAY, & THE UPBEATS

Label & Catalog #		Title	Year	VG+	NM
Blast BLP-6804	(M)	**A Tribute To 6**	1964	50.00	150.00

ALLEN, REX

Label & Catalog #		Title	Year	VG+	NM
Decca DL-8402	(M)	**Under Western Skies**	1956	24.00	60.00
Decca DL-8776	(M)	**Mister Cowboy**	1959	16.00	40.00
Decca DL-78776	(S)	**Mister Cowboy**	1959	24.00	60.00
Hacienda WWLP-101	(M)	**Rex Allen Sings**	1960	80.00	200.00
Buena Vista BV-3307	(M)	**Rex Allen Sings 16 Favorites**	1961	20.00	50.00
Mercury MG-20719	(M)	**Faith Of A Man**	1962	12.00	30.00
Mercury SR-60719	(S)	**Faith Of A Man**	1962	16.00	40.00
Mercury MG-20752	(M)	**Rex Allen Sings And Tells Tales**	1962	12.00	30.00
Mercury SR-60752	(S)	**Rex Allen Sings And Tells Tales**	1962	16.00	40.00

ALLEN, RICHIE/RICHIE ALLEN & THE PACIFIC SURFERS

Label & Catalog #		Title	Year	VG+	NM
Imperial LP-9212	(M)	**Stranger From Durango**	1963	16.00	40.00
Imperial LP-12212	(S)	**Stranger From Durango**	1963	20.00	50.00
Imperial LP-9229	(M)	**The Rising Surf**	1963	20.00	50.00
Imperial LP-12229	(S)	**The Rising Surf**	1963	30.00	75.00
Imperial LP-9243	(M)	**Surfer's Slide**	1963	20.00	50.00
Imperial LP-12243	(S)	**Surfer's Slide**	1963	30.00	75.00

ALLEN, ROSALIE

Label & Catalog #		Title	Year	VG+	NM
Waldorf Music Hall 150	(10")	**Rosalie Allen Sings Country & Western**	1955	40.00	100.00
Grand Award GA-33-330	(M)	**Songs Of The Golden West**	1956	16.00	40.00
RCA Victor LPM-2313	(M)	**Rosalie Allen**	1961	8.00	20.00
RCA Victor LSP-2313	(S)	**Rosalie Allen**	1961	10.00	25.00

ALLEN, ROSALIE / ELTON BRITT

Label & Catalog #		Title	Year	VG+	NM
Waldorf Music Hall 1206	(M)	**Rosalie Allen And Elton Britt**	195?	40.00	100.00
Grand Award GA-33-262	(M)	**Starring Elton Britt And Rosalie Allen**	1955	16.00	40.00

Label & Catalog #		Title	Year	VG+	NM

ALLEN, STEVE
Steve Allen is a composer and pianist who hosted a popular TV show in the '50s.

Decca DL-8151	(M)	Steve Allen's All Star Jazz Concert, Vol. 1	1955	12.00	30.00
Decca DL-8152	(M)	Steve Allen's All Star Jazz Concert, Vol. 2	1955	12.00	30.00
Coral CRL-57004	(M)	Music For Tonight	1955	10.00	25.00
Coral CRL-57015	(M)	Tonight At Midnight	1956	10.00	25.00
Coral CRL-57018	(M)	Jazz For Tonight	1956	12.00	30.00
Coral CRL-57019	(M)	Steve Sings	1956	10.00	25.00
Coral CRL-57028	(M)	Let's Dance	1956	12.00	30.00
Coral CRL-57047	(M)	Allen Plays Allen	1956	10.00	25.00
Coral CRL-57070	(M)	The Steve Allen Show	1957	10.00	25.00
Roulette R-25053	(M)	Steve Allen At The Round Table	1959	10.00	25.00
Roulette SR-25053	(S)	Steve Allen At The Round Table	1959	8.00	20.00
Dot DLP-3194	(M)	...And All That Jazz (With Manny Albam)	1959	10.00	25.00
Dot DLP-25194	(S)	...And All That Jazz (With Manny Albam)	1959	8.00	20.00

ALLEN, TONY, & THE NIGHT OWLS

Crown CLP-5231	(M)	Rock & Roll With Tony Allen	1960	40.00	100.00
Crown CST-249	(S)	Rock & Roll With Tony Allen	1960	60.00	150.00

ALLEN, WOODY

Colpix CP-488	(M)	Woody Allen	1964	10.00	25.00
Colpix SCP-488	(E)	Woody Allen	1964	10.00	25.00
Colpix CP-518	(M)	Woody Allen 2	1965	10.00	25.00
Capitol ST-2986	(S)	The Third Woody Allen Album	1968	10.00	25.00
Garrison Systems 2513/4	(DJ)	"Play It Again, Sam" Open-End Interview	1972	30.00	75.00

ALLEN & ROSSI

Mercury MG-21077	(M)	The Adventures Of Batman & Rubin	1966	12.00	30.00
Mercury SR-61077	(S)	The Adventures Of Batman & Rubin	1966	16.00	40.00
		(Batman & Rubin were created and written by Bob Kane, the creator and original artist of The Batman.)			

ALLISON, GENE

Vee Jay LP-1009	(M)	Gene Allison (Maroon label)	1959	80.00	200.00
Vee Jay LP-1009	(M)	Gene Allison (Black label)	196?	30.00	75.00
Vee Jay SLP-1009	(E)	Gene Allison (Black label)	196?	20.00	50.00

ALLISON, JOHN

Ficker C-10001	(M)	Heroes, Heroines & Mishaps— American Folk Song Series, Vol. 1	1957	16.00	40.00

ALLISON, KEITH
Produced by Gary Usher. Refer to The Falconaires; Paul Revere & The Raiders.

Columbia CL-2641	(M)	Keith Allison In Action	1967	10.00	25.00
Columbia CS-9441	(S)	Keith Allison In Action	1967	12.00	30.00

ALLISON, MOSE: Refer to GOLDMINE'S PRICE GUIDE TO COLLECTIBLE JAZZ ALBUMS

ALLMAN, SHELDON

Hifi R-415	(M)	Folk Songs For The 21st Century	1959	16.00	40.00
Del Fi DFLP-1213	(M)	Sing Along With Drac	1960	16.00	40.00
Del Fi DFST-1213	(S)	Sing Along With Drac	1960	20.00	50.00

ALLMAN BROTHERS BAND, THE
The Allman Brothers feature Duane and Gregg Allman and Dickie Betts.

Capricorn CX4-0102	(Q)	Eat A Peach (2 LPs)	1974	12.00	30.00
Capricorn PRO-545	(DJ)	Duane Allman Dialogs	1972	12.00	30.00
Capricorn CX4-0131	(Q)	Live At Fillmore East (2 LPs)	1974	20.00	50.00
		(CX4-0131 contains alternate takes from the stereo versions.)			
Nautilus NR-30	(S)	Live At Fillmore East (2 LPs)	1981	30.00	90.00
Mobile Fidelity MFSL-157	(S)	Eat A Peach (2 LPs)	1984	50.00	150.00

ALLSUP, TOMMY
Allsup was a member of The Crickets.

Reprise R-6182	(M)	Tommy Allsup Plays The Buddy Holly Songbook	1965	20.00	50.00
Reprise RS-6182	(S)	Tommy Allsup Plays The Buddy Holly Songbook	1965	30.00	75.00

Label & Catalog #		Title	Year	VG+	NM

ALMANAC SINGERS, THE
The Almanac Singerss— Lee Hays, Millard Lampell and Pete Seeger with Woody Guthrie— were a vocal and instrumental group playing traditional American folk music.. Refer to The Weavers.

Folkways FH-5285	(M)	**Talking Union**	195?	16.00	40.00
Mainstream 56005	(M)	**The Soil And The Sea**	1964	12.00	30.00
Mainstream S-6005	(E)	**The Soil And The Sea**	1964	8.00	20.00

ALPAKA, ALFRED
Decca DL-542)	(1")	**My Isle Of Golden Dreams**	195?	14.00	35.00

AMBO, LUCKY
Canatal CTLP-4001	(S)	**Old Time Fiddlin'**	196?	10.00	25.00

AMBOY DUKES, THE
The Amboy Dukes feature Ted Nugent.

Mainstream 56104	(M)	**The Amboy Dukes**	1968	30.00	75.00
Mainstream S-6104	(S)	**The Amboy Dukes**	1968	20.00	50.00
Mainstream S-6112	(S)	**Journey To The Center Of The Mind**	1968	20.00	50.00
Mainstream S-6118	(S)	**Migration**	1968	20.00	50.00
Mainstream S-6125	(S)	**The Best Of The Original Amboy Dukes**	1969	12.00	30.00
Mainstream S-421	(S)	**Ted Nugent & The Amboy Dukes**	197?	12.00	30.00
Mainstream S-2-801	(S)	**Journeys And Migrations** (2 LPs)	1974	12.00	30.00
		(Mainstream 801 repackages 6112 and 6118.)			
Polydor 24-4012	(S)	**Marriage On The Rocks**	1970	10.00	25.00
Polydor 24-4035	(S)	**Survival Of The Fittest**	1970	10.00	25.00

AMBROSE SLADE
Ambrose Slade later achieved success as Slade.

Fontana SRF-67598	(S)	**Ballzy** (White label promo)	1969	20.00	50.00
Fontana SRF-67598	(S)	**Ballzy**	1969	24.00	60.00

AMERICAN BLUES, THE
American Blues features Frank Beard and Dusty Hill, later of ZZ Top.

Karma KLP-1001	(M)	**The American Blues Is Here**	1967	200.00	400.00
Uni 73044	(S)	**The American Blues Do Their Thing**	1969	30.00	75.00

AMERICAN BLUES EXCHANGE, THE
Tayl TLS-1	(M)	**Blueprint**	1969	60.00	150.00

AMERICAN DREAM, THE
Ampex 10101	(S)	**The American Dream**	1970	10.00	25.00

AMERICAN REVOLUTION
Flick Disc FLS-54002	(S)	**American Revolution**	1968	10.00	25.00

AMES BROTHERS, THE
Coral CRL-56014	(10")	**Sing A Song Of Christmas**	1950	20.00	50.00
Coral CRL-56017	(10")	**In The Evening By The Moonlight**	1951	20.00	50.00
Coral CRL-56024	(10")	**Sentimental Me**	1951	20.00	50.00
Coral CRL-56025	(10")	**Hoop-De-Hoo**	1951	20.00	50.00
Coral CRL-56042	(10")	**Sweet Leilani**	1951	20.00	50.00
Coral CRL-56050	(10")	**Favorite Spirituals**	1952	20.00	50.00
Coral CRL-56079	(10")	**Home On The Range**	1952	20.00	50.00
Coral CRL-56080	(10")	**Merry Christmas 1952**	1952	20.00	50.00
Coral CRL-56097	(10")	**Favorite Songs**	1954	20.00	50.00
RCA Victor LPM-3186	(10")	**It Must Be True**	1954	20.00	50.00
Coral CRL-57031	(M)	**Ames Brothers Concert**	1956	12.00	30.00
Coral CRL-57054	(M)	**Love's Old Sweet Song**	1956	12.00	30.00
Coral CRL-57166	(M)	**Sounds Of Christmas Harmony**	1957	12.00	30.00
Coral CRL-57176	(M)	**Love Serenade**	1957	12.00	30.00
Coral CRL-57338	(M)	**Our Golden Favorites**	1960	10.00	25.00
Coral CRL-757338	(S)	**Our Golden Favorites**	1960	12.00	30.00
RCA Victor LPM-1142	(M)	**Exactly Like You**	1956	12.00	30.00
RCA Victor LPM-1157	(M)	**Four Brothers**	1956	12.00	30.00
RCA Victor LPM-1228	(M)	**The Ames Brothers With Hugo Winterhalter**	1956	12.00	30.00
RCA Victor LPM-1487	(M)	**Sweet Seventeen**	1957	12.00	30.00
RCA Victor LPM-1541	(M)	**There'll Always Be A Christmas**	1957	12.00	30.00
RCA Victor LPM-1680	(M)	**Destination Moon**	1958	10.00	25.00
RCA Victor LSP-1680	(S)	**Destination Moon**	1958	12.00	30.00

Label & Catalog #		Title	Year	VG+	NM
RCA Victor LPM-1855	(M)	Smoochin' Time	1958	10.00	25.00
RCA Victor LSP-1855	(S)	Smoochin' Time	1958	12.00	30.00
RCA Victor LPM-1859	(M)	The Best Of The Ames Brothers	1958	10.00	25.00
RCA Victor LSP-1859	(E)	The Best Of The Ames Brothers	1958	8.00	20.00
RCA Victor LPM-1954	(M)	Famous Hits Of Famous Quartets	1959	8.00	20.00
RCA Victor LSP-1954	(S)	Famous Hits Of Famous Quartets	1959	10.00	25.00
RCA Victor LPM-1998	(M)	The Best In The Country	1959	8.00	20.00
RCA Victor LSP-1998	(S)	The Best In The Country	1959	10.00	25.00
RCA Victor LPM-2009	(M)	Words And Music	1959	8.00	20.00
RCA Victor LSP-2009	(S)	Words And Music	1959	10.00	25.00
RCA Victor LPM-2100	(M)	Hello, Amigos	1960	8.00	20.00
RCA Victor LSP-2100	(S)	Hello, Amigos	1960	10.00	25.00
RCA Victor LPM-2182	(M)	The Blend And The Beat	1960	8.00	20.00
RCA Victor LSP-2182	(S)	The Blend And The Beat	1960	10.00	25.00
RCA Victor LPM-2273	(M)	The Best Of The Bands	1960	8.00	20.00
RCA Victor LSP-2273	(S)	The Best Of The Bands	1960	10.00	25.00

— RCA mono albums above have "Long Play" on the bottom of the label; stereo albums have "Living Stereo" on the bottom.—

AMON DUUL/AMON DUUL II

Prophesy PRS-1003	(S)	Amon Duul	1970	10.00	25.00

AMOS, TORI: *Refer to* Y KANT TORI READ

AMULET

Shadow AC-00084	(S)	Amulet	1980	40.00	100.00

ANCIENT GREASE

Mercury SR-61305	(S)	Women And Children First	1970	10.00	25.00

ANDERS & PONCIA
Anders & Poncia also recorded as The Innocence; The Tradewinds.

Warner Bros. WS-1778	(S)	The Anders & Poncia Album	1969	12.00	30.00

ANDERSON, AL
Anderson originally recorded with Wildweeds and later with NRBQ.

Vanguard VSD-79324	(S)	Al Anderson	1972	10.00	25.00
Vanguard VSQ-79324	(Q)	Al Anderson	1973	14.00	35.00

ANDERSON, BILL/BILL ANDERSON & THE PO' BOYS
Refer to The Po' Boys.

Decca DL-4091	(M)	Introducing Bill Anderson, Ernest Ashworth (+ Four More)	1962	8.00	20.00
Decca DL-74091	(S)	Introducing Bill Anderson, Ernest Ashworth (+ Four More)	1962	10.00	25.00

(Technically a various artists album, Decca 4091 nonetheless must be considered Anderson's "first" album.)

Decca DL-4192	(M)	Bill Anderson Sings Country Songs	1962	8.00	20.00
Decca DL-74192	(S)	Bill Anderson Sings Country Songs	1962	10.00	25.00
Decca DL-4427	(M)	Still	1963	8.00	20.00
Decca DL-74427	(S)	Still	1963	10.00	25.00
Decca DL-4499	(M)	Bill Anderson Sings	1964	8.00	20.00
Decca DL-74499	(S)	Bill Anderson Sings	1964	10.00	25.00
Decca DL-4600	(M)	Bill Anderson Showcase	1964	8.00	20.00
Decca DL-74600	(S)	Bill Anderson Showcase	1964	10.00	25.00
Decca DL-4646	(M)	From This Pen	1965	8.00	20.00
Decca DL-74646	(S)	From This Pen	1965	10.00	25.00
Decca DL-4686	(M)	Bright Lights And Country Music	1965	8.00	20.00
Decca DL-74686	(S)	Bright Lights And Country Music	1965	10.00	25.00

— Decca albums above have black labels with "Mfrd by Decca" beneath the rainbow.—

ANDERSON, CASEY

Elektra EKL-192	(M)	Goin' Places	1960	8.00	20.00
Elektra EKS-7192	(S)	Goin' Places	1960	10.00	25.00
Atco 33-149	(M)	The Bag I'm In	1962	8.00	20.00
Atco SD-33-149	(S)	The Bag I'm In	1962	10.00	25.00
Atco 33-166	(M)	More Pretty Girls Than One	1964	8.00	20.00
Atco SD-33-166	(S)	More Pretty Girls Than One	1964	10.00	25.00

Label & Catalog #		Title	Year	VG+	NM
Atco 33-172	(M)	Live At The Ice House	1965	8.00	20.00
Atco SD-33-172	(S)	Live At The Ice House	1965	10.00	25.00
Atco 33-176	(M)	Blues Is A Woman Gone	1965	8.00	20.00
Atco SD-33-176	(S)	Blues Is A Woman Gone	1965	10.00	25.00

ANDERSON, ERNESTINE: *Refer to* GOLDMINE'S PRICE GUIDE TO COLLECTIBLE JAZZ ALBUMS

ANDERSON, IVIE: *Refer to* GOLDMINE'S PRICE GUIDE TO COLLECTIBLE JAZZ ALBUMS

ANDERSON, LIZ
The former Elizabeth Jane Haaby is also the wife of Casey Anderson and the mom of Lynn Anderson.

RCA Victor LPM-3852	(S)	Cookin' Up Hits	1967	10.00	25.00
RCA Victor LSP-3852	(S)	Cookin' Up Hits	1967	6.00	15.00
RCA Victor LPM-3869	(S)	Liz Anderson Sings	1968	12.00	30.00
RCA Victor LSP-3869	(S)	Liz Anderson Sings	1968	6.00	15.00
RCA Victor LPM-3908	(S)	Liz Anderson Sings Her Favorites	1968	12.00	30.00
RCA Victor LSP-3908	(S)	Liz Anderson Sings Her Favorites	1968	6.00	15.00
		—RCA albums above have black labels.—			

ANDERSON, MARGIE

Parade SP-364	(M)	The Blues	196?	16.00	40.00

ANDERSON, MARIAN

RCA Victor LRM-7006	(10")	Eleven Great Spirituals	195?	60.00	150.00
RCA Victor LM-110	(10")	Marian Anderson Sings Spirituals	195?	60.00	150.00
RCA Victor LM-2032	(M)	Marian Anderson Sings Spirituals	195?	40.00	100.00
		(RCA 2032 repackages material from 7006 and 110.)			

ANDERSON, MILDRED

Bluesville BVLP-1004	(M)	Person To Person	1960	20.00	50.00
Bluesville BVLP-1017	(M)	No More In Life	1961	20.00	50.00
		— Bluesville albums above have bright blue labels with silver print.—			
Bluesville BVLP-1004	(M)	Person To Person	1964	10.00	25.00
Bluesville BVLP-1017	(M)	No More In Life	1964	10.00	25.00
		—Bluesville albums above have blue labels with a trident logo on the right side.—			

ANDERSON, PINK
Pink Anderson is a singer and guitar player in the old-time "medicine show" tradition.

Bluesville BVLP-1038	(M)	Carolina Blues Man	1961	40.00	100.00
Bluesville BVLP-1051	(M)	Medicine Show Man	1962	40.00	100.00
Bluesville BVLP-1071	(M)	Ballad And Folk Singer—Volume 3	1963	40.00	100.00
		— Bluesville albums above have bright blue labels with silver print.—			
Bluesville BVLP-1038	(M)	Carolina Blues Man	1964	12.00	30.00
Bluesville BVLP-1051	(M)	Medicine Show Man	1964	12.00	30.00
Bluesville BVLP-1071	(M)	Ballad And Folk Singer—Volume 3	1964	12.00	30.00
		— Bluesville albums above have blue labels with a trident logo on the right side.—			

ANDERSON, PINK / REV. GARY DAVIS

Riverside RLP-12-611	(M)	Carolina Street Ballads / Harlem Street Spirituals	1951	20.00	50.00

ANDREWS, ERNIE: *Refer to* GOLDMINE'S PRICE GUIDE TO COLLECTIBLE JAZZ ALBUMS

ANDREWS, JULIE

RCA Victor LOC-1018	(M)	The Boy Friend *(Original Cast)*	1954	20.00	50.00
Columbia OL-5090	(M)	My Fair Lady *(Original Cast)*	1956	12.00	30.00
Columbia OL-5190	(M)	Cinderella *(Soundtrack)*	1957	12.00	30.00
Angel 65041	(M)	Tell It Again *(With Moondog)*	1957	20.00	50.00
RCA Victor LPM-1403	(M)	The Lass With The Delicate Air	1957	20.00	50.00
		(Some copies of RCA 1403 were issued in a jacket with a pale blue cover and "Julie Andrews" in a drawing of a ovular picture frame.)			
RCA Victor LPM-1403	(M)	The Lass With The Delicate Air	1957	16.00	40.00
RCA Victor LSP-1403	(S)	The Lass With The Delicate Air	1958	30.00	75.00
RCA Victor LPM-1681	(M)	Julie Andrews Sings	1958	12.00	30.00
RCA Victor LSP-1681	(S)	Julie Andrews Sings	1958	20.00	50.00
RCA Victor LOP-1001	(M)	Rose Marie *(Soundtrack)*	1958	8.00	20.00
RCA Victor LSO-1001	(S)	Rose Marie *(Soundtrack)*	1958	12.00	30.00
		—RCA mono albums above have black labels with "Long Play" on the bottom; stereo albums have "Living Stereo" on the bottom.—			

Label & Catalog #		Title	Year	VG+	NM
Columbia OL-5615	(M)	My Fair Lady (Original Cast)	1959	8.00	20.00
Columbia OS-2015	(S)	My Fair Lady (Original Cast)	1959	10.00	25.00
Columbia OL-5620	(M)	Camelot (Original Cast. Gatefold cover)	1960	8.00	20.00
Columbia OS-2031	(S)	Camelot (Original Cast. Gatefold cover)	1960	10.00	25.00
Columbia CL-1712	(M)	Broadway's Fair Julie	1962	8.00	20.00
Columbia CS-8512	(S)	Broadway's Fair Julie	1962	10.00	25.00
Columbia CL-1886	(M)	Don't Go In The Lion's Cage Tonight	1962	8.00	20.00
Columbia CS-8686	(S)	Don't Go In The Lion's Cage Tonight	1962	10.00	25.00
— Columbia albums above have three white "eye" logos on each side of the spindle hole.—					
RCA Victor COM-111	(M)	Mary Poppins (Soundtrack)	1964	6.00	15.00
RCA Victor CSO-111	(S)	Mary Poppins (Soundtrack)	1964	10.00	25.00
— RCA albums above have black labels.—					

ANDREWS, LEE, & THE HEARTS

Lost-Nite LP-101	(M)	Lee Andrews & The Hearts' Biggest Hits (Yellow vinyl)	1964	50.00	125.00
Lost-Nite LP-101	(M)	Lee Andrews & The Hearts' Biggest Hits	1964	20.00	50.00
Lost-Nite LP-113	(M)	Dean Tyler Presents Lee Andrews & The Hearts Live	1965	20.00	50.00

ANDREWS SISTERS, THE
LaVerne, Maxine and Peggy Andrews also recorded with Bing Crosby.

Decca DL-5019	(10")	Merry Christmas	1950	16.00	40.00
Decca DL-5020	(10")	Christmas Greetings	1950	16.00	40.00
Decca DL-5065	(10")	Tropical Songs	1950	16.00	40.00
Decca DL-5120	(10")	The Andrews Sisters	1950	16.00	40.00
Decca DL-5155	(10")	Club 15	1950	16.00	40.00
Decca DL-5264	(10")	Berlin Songs	1950	16.00	40.00
Decca DL-5282	(10")	Christmas Cheer	1950	16.00	40.00
Decca DL-5284	(10")	Mr. Music (Soundtrack)	1951	40.00	100.00
Decca DL-5306	(10")	I Love To Tell The Story	1951	16.00	40.00
Decca DL-5331	(10")	Country Style	1952	16.00	40.00
Decca DL-5423	(10")	My Isle Of Golden Dreams	1952	16.00	40.00
Decca DL-5438	(10")	Sing, Sing, Sing	1953	16.00	40.00
Decca DL-8354	(M)	Jingle Bells	1956	12.00	30.00
Decca DL-8360	(M)	By Popular Demand	1957	12.00	30.00
Decca DL-7019	(M)	Curtain Call	1956	12.00	30.00
Capitol T-790	(M)	The Andrews Sisters In Hi-Fi	1957	12.00	30.00
Capitol T-860	(M)	Fresh And Fancy Free	1957	12.00	30.00
Capitol T-973	(M)	Dancing Twenties	1958	12.00	30.00
— Capitol albums above have turquoise or gray labels.—					

ANGELS, THE

Caprice LP-1001	(M)	And The Angels Sing	1962	30.00	75.00
Caprice SLP-1001	(S)	And The Angels Sing	1962	40.00	100.00
Smash MGS-27039	(M)	My Boyfriend's Back	1963	14.00	35.00
Smash SRS-67039	(S)	My Boyfriend's Back	1963	20.00	50.00
("Til" is rechanneled on this album.)					
Smash MGS-27048	(M)	A Halo To You	1964	12.00	30.00
Smash SRS-67048	(S)	A Halo To You	1964	16.00	40.00
Ascot AM-13009	(M)	The Angels—Twelve Of Their Greatest Hits	1964	10.00	25.00
Ascot ALS-6009	(S)	The Angels—Twelve Of Their Greatest Hits	1964	12.00	30.00
(The Ascot album is a repackage of Caprice 1001.)					

ANIMALS, THE/ERIC BURDON & THE ANIMALS
The original Animals were Eric Burdon, Chas Chandler, Alan Price, John Steel and Hilton Valentine. By early 1966 Price and Steel left, replaced by Dave Rowberry and Barry Jenkins. By the end of 1966 the group split with Burdon and Jenkins forming Eric Burdon & The Animals (MGM 4433 on).

MGM E-4264	(M)	The Animals (Yellow label promo)	1964	60.00	150.00
MGM E-4264	(M)	The Animals	1964	16.00	40.00
MGM SE-4264	(E)	The Animals	1964	12.00	30.00
MGM T-90687	(M)	The Animals (Capitol Record Club)	1965	40.00	100.00
MGM E-4281	(M)	The Animals On Tour (Yellow label promo)	1965	60.00	150.00
MGM E-4281	(M)	The Animals On Tour	1965	16.00	40.00
MGM SE-4281	(E)	The Animals On Tour	1965	12.00	30.00
MGM E-4305	(M)	Animal Tracks (Yellow label promo)	1965	60.00	150.00
MGM E-4305	(M)	Animal Tracks	1965	20.00	50.00
MGM SE-4305	(E)	Animal Tracks	1965	16.00	40.00

Label & Catalog #		Title	Year	VG+	NM
MGM T-90571	(M)	Animal Tracks (Capitol Record Club)	1965	40.00	100.00
MGM E-4324	(M)	The Best Of The Animals (Yellow label)	1966	40.00	100.00
MGM E-4324	(M)	The Best Of The Animals	1966	8.00	20.00
MGM SKAO-90622	(M)	The Best Of The Animals (Capitol Record Club)	1969	10.00	25.00
MGM SE-4324	(P)	The Best Of The Animals	1966	10.00	25.00
ABC-Paramount ABC-536	(M)	The Dangerous Christmas Of Red Riding Hood (Soundtrack)	1965	12.00	30.00
ABC-Paramount ABCS-536	(S)	The Dangerous Christmas Of Red Riding Hood (Soundtrack)	1965	30.00	75.00
MGM E-4384	(M)	Animalization (Yellow label promo)	1966	40.00	100.00
MGM E-4384	(M)	Animalization	1966	10.00	25.00
MGM SE-4384	(S)	Animalization	1966	12.00	30.00
		("Inside Looking Out" is rechanneled on this album.)			
MGM E-4414	(M)	Animalism (Yellow label promo)	1966	40.00	100.00
MGM E-4414	(M)	Animalism	1966	10.00	25.00
MGM SE-4414	(S)	Animalism	1966	12.00	30.00
		("All Night Long" and "The Other Side Of This Life" were arranged by Frank Zappa.)			
MGM E-4433	(M)	Eric Is Here	1967	8.00	20.00
MGM SE-4433	(S)	Eric Is Here	1967	10.00	25.00
MGM E-4454	(M)	Best Of Eric Burdon & The Animals, Vol. 2	1967	8.00	20.00
MGM SE-4454	(P)	Best Of Eric Burdon & The Animals, Vol. 2	1967	10.00	25.00
MGM E-4484	(M)	Winds Of Change	1967	8.00	20.00
MGM SE-4484	(S)	Winds Of Change	1967	10.00	25.00
— MGM albums above have black labels with a multi-color logo on top.—					
MGM E-4537	(M)	The Twain Shall Meet	1968	12.00	30.00
MGM SE-4537	(S)	The Twain Shall Meet	1968	10.00	25.00
MGM E-4553	(M)	Every One Of Us	1968	12.00	30.00
MGM SE-4553	(S)	Every One Of Us	1968	10.00	25.00
MGM SE-4591	(S)	Love Is (2 LPs)	1969	20.00	50.00

ANKA, PAUL

Label & Catalog #		Title	Year	VG+	NM
Riviera 0047	(M)	Paul Anka & Others	1959	60.00	150.00
		(Riviera 0047 is actually a various artists album containing Anka's pre-ABC Paramount sides.)			
ABC-Paramount 240	(M)	Paul Anka	1958	20.00	50.00
ABC-Paramount 296	(M)	My Heart Sings	1959	14.00	35.00
ABC-Paramount S-296	(S)	My Heart Sings	1959	20.00	50.00
ABC-Paramount 323	(M)	Paul Anka Sings His Big 15	1960	20.00	50.00
ABC-Paramount S-323	(E)	Paul Anka Sings His Big 15	1960	16.00	40.00
ABC-Paramount 347	(M)	Paul Anka Swings For Young Lovers	1960	12.00	30.00
ABC-Paramount S-347	(S)	Paul Anka Swings For Young Lovers	1960	16.00	40.00
ABC-Paramount 353	(M)	Anka At The Copa	1960	12.00	30.00
ABC-Paramount S-353	(S)	Anka At The Copa	1960	16.00	40.00
ABC-Paramount 360	(M)	It's Christmas Everywhere	1960	12.00	30.00
ABC-Paramount S-360	(S)	It's Christmas Everywhere	1960	16.00	40.00
ABC-Paramount 371	(M)	Strictly Instrumental	1961	12.00	30.00
ABC-Paramount S-371	(S)	Strictly Instrumental	1961	16.00	40.00
ABC-Paramount 390	(M)	Paul Anka Sings His Big 15, Volume 2	1961	12.00	30.00
ABC-Paramount S-390	(S)	Paul Anka Sings His Big 15, Volume 2	1961	16.00	40.00
ABC-Paramount 409	(M)	Paul Anka Sings His Big 15, Volume 3	1962	12.00	30.00
ABC-Paramount S-409	(S)	Paul Anka Sings His Big 15, Volume 3	1962	16.00	40.00
ABC-Paramount 420	(M)	Diana	1962	12.00	30.00
ABC-Paramount S-420	(S)	Diana	1962	16.00	40.00
RCA Victor LPM-2502	(M)	Young, Alive And In Love!	1962	8.00	20.00
RCA Victor LSP-2502	(S)	Young, Alive And In Love!	1962	12.00	30.00
RCA Victor LPM-2575	(M)	Let's Sit This One Out!	1962	8.00	20.00
RCA Victor LSP-2575	(S)	Let's Sit This One Out!	1962	12.00	30.00
RCA Victor LPM-2614	(M)	Our Man Around The World	1963	8.00	20.00
RCA Victor LSP-2614	(S)	Our Man Around The World	1963	12.00	30.00
RCA Victor LPM-2691	(M)	Paul Anka's 21 Golden Hits	1963	8.00	20.00
RCA Victor LSP-2691	(S)	Paul Anka's 21 Golden Hits	1963	12.00	30.00
— RCA mono albums above have "Long Play" on the bottom of the label; stereo albums have "Living Stereo" on the bottom.—					

Ann-Margret's Songs From The Swinger and Other Swingin' Songs *is often listed as a soundtrack, as it was in the previous editions of this book, but it is, in fact, a collection featuring tunes from the movie among others, as the sub-title makes evident. Nonetheless, it is her rarest album and hunted after by soundtrack aficionados.*

Label & Catalog #		Title	Year	VG+	NM

ANN-MARGRET
Refer to Lee Hazlewood & Ann-Margret.

RCA Victor LPM-2399	(M)	**And Here She Is**	1961	12.00	30.00
RCA Victor LSP-2399	(S)	**And Here She Is**	1961	16.00	40.00
RCA Victor LPM-2453	(M)	**On The Way Up**	1961	12.00	30.00
RCA Victor LSP-2453	(S)	**On The Way Up**	1961	16.00	40.00
Dot DLP-9011	(M)	**State Fair** *(Soundtrack)*	1962	12.00	30.00
Dot DLP-25011	(S)	**State Fair** *(Soundtrack)*	1962	16.00	40.00
RCA Victor LPM-2551	(M)	**The Vivacious One**	1962	12.00	30.00
RCA Victor LSP-2551	(S)	**The Vivacious One**	1962	16.00	40.00
RCA Victor LPM-2659	(M)	**Bachelor's Paradise**	1963	12.00	30.00
RCA Victor LSP-2659	(S)	**Bachelor's Paradise**	1963	16.00	40.00

— RCA mono albums above have "Long Play" on the bottom of the label; stereo albums have "Living Stereo" on the bottom.—

RCA Victor LOC-1081	(M)	**Bye Bye Birdie** *(Soundtrack)*	1963	8.00	20.00
RCA Victor LSO-1081	(S)	**Bye Bye Birdie** *(Soundtrack)*	1963	12.00	30.00

(Original covers for RCA 1081 do not have A-M on the front.)

RCA Victor LOC-1101	(M)	**The Pleasure Seekers** *(Soundtrack)*	1965	16.00	40.00
RCA Victor LSO-1101	(S)	**The Pleasure Seekers** *(Soundtrack)*	1965	20.00	50.00
RCA Victor LPM-3710	(M)	**Songs From "The Swinger"**	1966	24.00	60.00
RCA Victor LSP-3710	(S)	**Songs From "The Swinger"**	1966	30.00	75.00

ANNETTE
Annette's popularity is directly proportional to her development as an original member of TV's eeska-mooska Mouseketeers.

Mickey Mouse MM-24	(M)	**Songs From Annette**	1959	40.00	100.00
Buena Vista BV-3301	(M)	**Annette**	1959	40.00	100.00
Buena Vista BV-3302	(M)	**Annette Sings Anka**	1960	40.00	100.00
Buena Vista BV-3303	(M)	**Hawaiiannette**	1960	30.00	75.00
Buena Vista BV-3304	(M)	**Italiannette**	1960	30.00	75.00
Buena Vista BV-3305	(M)	**Dance Annette**	1961	30.00	75.00
Buena Vista BV-3309	(M)	**The Parent Trap** *(Soundtrack)*	1961	20.00	50.00
Buena Vista STER-3309	(S)	**The Parent Trap** *(Soundtrack)*	1961	30.00	75.00
Buena Vista BV-4022	(M)	**Babes In Toyland** *(Soundtrack)*	1961	20.00	50.00
Buena Vista STER-4022	(S)	**Babes In Toyland** *(Soundtrack)*	1961	30.00	75.00

(Both B.V. 3309 and 4022 also feature Tommy Sands.)

Buena Vista BV-3312	(M)	**The Story Of My Teens**	1962	30.00	75.00
Buena Vista BV-3313	(M)	**Teen Street**	1962	30.00	75.00
Buena Vista BV-3314	(M)	**Muscle Beach Party**	1963	30.00	75.00
Buena Vista STER-3314	(S)	**Muscle Beach Party**	1963	60.00	150.00

(B.V. 3314 features songs from the movie "Muscle Beach Party.")

Buena Vista BV-3316	(M)	**Beach Party**	1963	30.00	75.00
Buena Vista STER-3316	(S)	**Beach Party**	1963	50.00	125.00

(B.V. 3316 features songs from the movie "Beach Party.")

Buena Vista CR2567-70	(DJ)	**Merlin Jones** *(Radio spots & interview)*	1963	100.00	250.00
Buena Vista BV-3320	(M)	**Annette On Campus**	1964	20.00	50.00
Buena Vista STER-3320	(S)	**Annette On Campus**	1964	40.00	100.00
Buena Vista BV-3324	(M)	**Annette At Bikini Beach**	1964	20.00	50.00
Buena Vista STER-3324	(S)	**Annette At Bikini Beach**	1964	40.00	100.00

(B.V. 3324, and BV-3328 below, feature "The Monkey's Uncle," on which The Beach Boys back Annette.)

Buena Vista BV-3325	(M)	**Annette's Pajama Party**	1964	16.00	40.00
Buena Vista STER-3325	(S)	**Annette's Pajama Party**	1964	40.00	100.00
Buena Vista BV-3327	(M)	**Annette Sings Golden Surfin' Hits**	1964	40.00	100.00
Buena Vista STER-3327	(S)	**Annette Sings Golden Surfin' Hits**	1964	60.00	150.00
Buena Vista BV-3328	(M)	**Something Borrowed, Something Blue**	1964	30.00	75.00
Buena Vista STER-3328	(S)	**Something Borrowed, Something Blue**	1964	60.00	150.00

("Ma, He's Makin' Eyes At Me," "Mr. Piano Man," "Crystal Ball," and "Canzoni D'Amore" are rechanneled on this album.)

Disneyland DQ-1245	(M)	**Walt Disney's Wonderful World Of Color**	1964	10.00	25.00
Disneyland DQS-1245	(S)	**Walt Disney's Wonderful World Of Color**	1964	16.00	40.00
Disneyland DQ-1267	(M)	**The Best Of Broadway**	1965	12.00	30.00
Disneyland DQ-1287	(M)	**Tubby The Tuba**	1966	10.00	25.00
Disneyland DQS-1287	(S)	**Tubby The Tuba**	1966	16.00	40.00
Disneyland DQ-1293	(M)	**State And College Songs**	1967	10.00	25.00
Disneyland DQS-1293	(S)	**State And College Songs**	1967	16.00	40.00
Sidewalk T-5902	(M)	**Thunder Alley** *(Soundtrack)*	1967	8.00	20.00
Sidewalk ST-5902	(S)	**Thunder Alley** *(Soundtrack)*	1967	10.00	25.00
Buena Vista BV-4037	(M)	**Annette Funicello**	1972	20.00	50.00

Annette is a very much a product of her time and her albums are collected primarily as artifacts by collectors who came of age in the '50s, when Ms. Funicello grew before our very eyes from a chubby young Mouseketeer into an alluring young lady. While she enjoyed success in a series of beach movies, her career as a recording artist never really struck much gold. The Annette Sings Anka teams her with Anka the composer and accompanist with a nice cover that captures the two teenaged heartthrobs in a relaxed, if posed, mood.

Label & Catalog #		Title	Year	VG+	NM
ANNETTE / TIMOTHY CAREY					
Famous Amer. Stars 1282/3(DJ)		**Head** *(10" interview)*	1968	80.00	200.00
ANNETTE / BOB HOPE					
Backman Products 379	(DJ)	**Celebrity Profiles With Dick Strout**	1965	60.00	150.00
		(10" album on blue vinyl of 5 minutes interviews with each artist.)			
ANNETTE & HAYLEY MILLS					
Buena Vista BV-3508	(M)	**Annette And Hayley** *(Paper sleeve)*	1964	300.00	600.00
ANONYMOUS					
A-Major AMLS-1002	(S)	**Inside The Shadow** *(With booklet)*	1976	100.00	250.00
		(Original pressings of AMLS-1002 have a blue cover.)			
A-Major AMLS-1002	(S)	**Inside The Shadow** *(With booklet)*	1981	20.00	50.00
		(Later pressings have a black on white cover.)			
ANT TRIP CEREMONY					
C. R. C. 2129	(M)	**Twenty-Four Hours**	1967	500.00	750.00
APPEL, DAVE					
Cameo C-1004	(M)	**Alone Together**	1959	12.00	30.00
APPLE CORE					
SSS Inter.	(S)	**Apple Core** *(Blue vinyl)*	197?	10.00	25.00
J. S. R.	(S)	**Behind The Rear**	1979	10.00	25.00
APPLETREE THEATRE					
Verve/Forecast FT-3042	(M)	**Playback**	1968	10.00	25.00
Verve/Forecast FTS-3042	(S)	**Playback**	1968	12.00	30.00
APOSTLES, THE					
M. G. 79909	(M)	**The Apostles On Crusade**	196?	60.00	150.00
APOSTLES, THE					
Sound Recording CO-1245	(M)	**An Hour Of Prayer**	196?	60.00	150.00
AQUATONES, THE					
Fargo 3001	(M)	**The Aquatones Sing**	1964	80.00	200.00
ARCESIA					
Alpha 103	(S)	**Arcesia/Reachin'**	197?	300.00	600.00
ARCHER, FRANCES, & BEVERLY GILE					
Archer and Gile are singers of traditional folk songs from many countries in many languages.					
Disneyland WDL-3006	(M)	**Folk Songs From Far Corners**	195?	16.00	40.00
Disneyland WDL-3023	(M)	**Community Concert**	195?	16.00	40.00
ARCHIES, THE					
The sound of The Archies is a creation of Ron Dante.					
Calendar KES-101	(S)	**The Archies**	1968	10.00	25.00
Calendar *(No number)*	(DJ)	**Everything's Archie Box**	1969	40.00	100.00
		(Promotional boxed set includes a sealed copy of KES-101 with buttons, black & white photos and a press kit.)			
Calendar KES-103	(S)	**Everything's Archie**	1969	10.00	25.00
Kirshner KES-110	(S)	**This Is Love**	1971	10.00	25.00
ARCHITECT					
Architect AR-101	(S)	**Architect**	197?	40.00	100.00
ARDEN, TONI					
Decca DL-8651	(M)	**Miss Toni Arden**	1957	12.00	30.00
Decca DL-8765	(M)	**Sing A Song Of Italy**	1958	10.00	25.00
Decca DL-78765	(S)	**Sing A Song Of Italy**	1958	12.00	30.00
Decca DL-8875	(M)	**Besame**	1959	10.00	25.00
Decca DL-78875	(S)	**Besame**	1959	12.00	30.00
ARGO, ARTHUR					
Arthur Argo is a Scottish songwriter and singer of traditional songs.					
Prestige Int. PRLP-13048	(M)	**Lyrical Erotica, Vol. 2**	1962	12.00	30.00

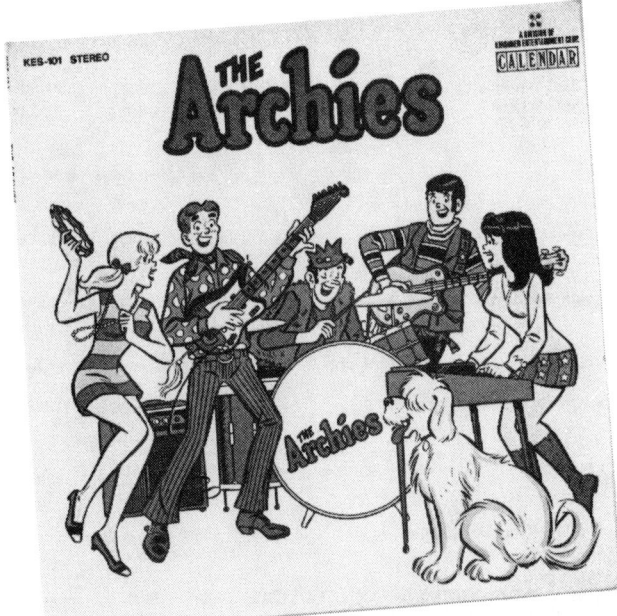

The Archies were a studio creation of Don Kirshner, never one to miss a gimmick, and here it's a good one: A hip cartoon musical group based squarely on the immensely popular and long-lived comic book characters with lead vocals by the versatile Ron Dante. Their music was a bit too cute even for fans of The Monkees (who apparently turned down the chance to record "Sugar Sugar"), whom Kirshner hoped to emulate in terms of success. While the casual collector usually knows the first albums it is their ultimate outing, This Is Love, that is the rarest of their oeuvre.

Label & Catalog #		Title	Year	VG+	NM

ARISTOCATS, THE
| Hifi R-610 | (M) | Boogie And Blues | 1959 | 16.00 | 40.00 |
| Hifi SR-610 | (S) | Boogie And Blues | 1959 | 24.00 | 60.00 |

ARK
| Ark 810-71 | (S) | Voyages | 1978 | 360.00 | 600.00 |

ARKANGEL
| Joyeuse Garde JGR-001 | (S) | Wind Face | 1980 | 12.00 | 30.00 |

ARKANSAS BLUEGRASS BOYS, THE
| Smigar 6275 | (M) | Bluegrass Special | 1962 | 16.00 | 40.00 |

ARKIN, ALAN
Alan Arkin is a folksinger who later recorded with The Babysitters and The Tarriers. He achieved greater fame as a movie actor. Refer to Ed McCurdy.
| Elektra EKL-2 | (10") | Folksongs (& 2 1/2 That Aren't) | 195? | 40.00 | 100.00 |

ARMAGEDDON
| Amos 73075 | (S) | Armageddon | 1969 | 10.00 | 25.00 |

ARMSTRONG, GEORGE & GERRY
Mr and Mrs Armstrong also recorded with The Golden Ring.
| Folkways FA-2335 | (M) | Simple Gifts | 1959 | 10.00 | 25.00 |

ARMSTRONG, LOUIS: *Refer to* **GOLDMINE'S PRICE GUIDE TO COLLECTIBLE JAZZ ALBUMS**

ARNAZ, DESI
| RCA Victor LPM-3096 | (10") | Babalu! | 1954 | 60.00 | 150.00 |

ARNOLD, BILLY BOY
| Prestige PRLP-7389 | (M) | Blues On The South Side | 1965 | 10.00 | 25.00 |
| Prestige PRST-7389 | (S) | Blues On The South Side | 1965 | 12.00 | 30.00 |

— Prestige albums above have blue labels with a trident logo on the right side.—

ARNOLD, EDDY
RCA Victor LPM-3027	(10")	Anytime	1952	40.00	100.00
RCA Victor LPM-3031	(10")	All-Time Hits From The Hills	1952	40.00	100.00
RCA Victor LPM-3117	(10")	All-Time Favorites	1953	40.00	100.00
RCA Victor LPM-3219	(10")	The Chapel On The Hill	1954	40.00	100.00
RCA Victor LPM-3230	(10")	An American Institution (With booklet)	1954	60.00	150.00
RCA Victor LPM-3230	(10")	An American Institution (Without booklet)	1954	40.00	100.00
RCA Victor LPM-1111	(M)	Wanderin' With Eddy Arnold	1955	20.00	50.00
RCA Victor LPM-1223	(M)	All-Time Favorites	1955	20.00	50.00
RCA Victor LPM-1224	(M)	Anytime	1955	20.00	50.00
RCA Victor LPM-1225	(M)	The Chapel On The Hill	1955	20.00	50.00
RCA Victor LPM-1293	(M)	A Dozen Hits	1956	20.00	50.00
RCA Victor LPM-1377	(M)	A Little On The Lonely Side	1956	20.00	50.00
RCA Victor LPM-1484	(M)	When They Were Young	1957	16.00	40.00
RCA Victor LPM-1575	(M)	My Darling, My Darling	1957	16.00	40.00
RCA Victor LPM-1733	(M)	Praise Him, Praise Him	1958	16.00	40.00
RCA Victor LPM-1928	(M)	Have Guitar, Will Travel	1959	12.00	30.00
RCA Victor LSP-1928	(S)	Have Guitar, Will Travel	1959	16.00	40.00
RCA Victor LPM-2036	(M)	Thereby Hangs A Tale	1959	12.00	30.00
RCA Victor LSP-2036	(S)	Thereby Hangs A Tale	1959	16.00	40.00
RCA Victor LPM-2185	(M)	Eddy Arnold Sings Them Again	1960	10.00	25.00
RCA Victor LSP-2185	(S)	Eddy Arnold Sings Them Again	1960	12.00	30.00
RCA Victor LPM-2268	(M)	You Gotta Have Love	1960	10.00	25.00
RCA Victor LSP-2268	(S)	You Gotta Have Love	1960	12.00	30.00
RCA Victor LPM-2337	(M)	Let's Make Memories Tonight	1961	10.00	25.00
RCA Victor LSP-2337	(S)	Let's Make Memories Tonight	1961	12.00	30.00
RCA Victor LPM-2471	(M)	One More Time	1961	10.00	25.00
RCA Victor LSP-2471	(S)	One More Time	1961	12.00	30.00
RCA Victor PRS-346	(DJ)	Christmas With Eddy Arnold	1961	20.00	50.00
RCA Victor LPM-2554	(M)	Christmas With Eddy Arnold	1961	10.00	25.00
RCA Victor LSP-2554	(S)	Christmas With Eddy Arnold	1961	12.00	30.00
RCA Victor LPM-2578	(M)	Cattle Call	1962	10.00	25.00
RCA Victor LSP-2578	(S)	Cattle Call	1962	12.00	30.00

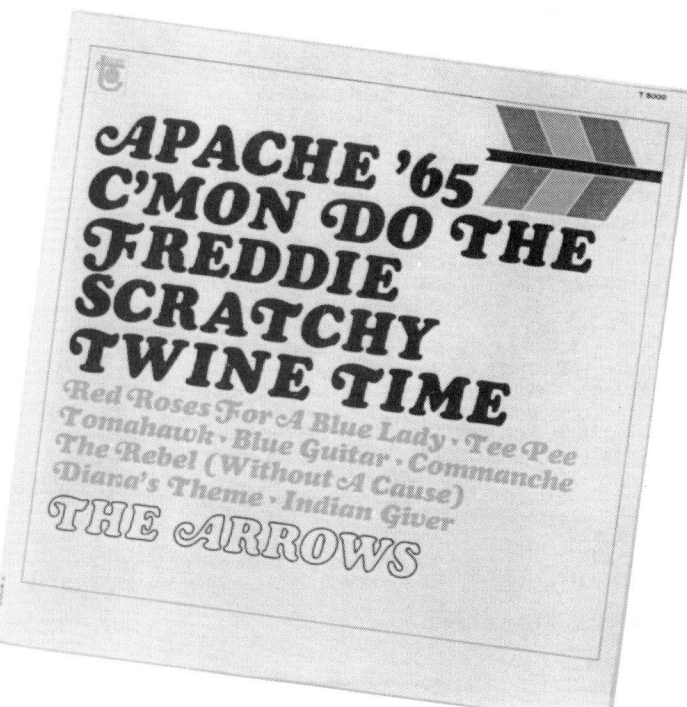

Originally scoring for Tower with the proto-psych "Apache '65," as The Arrows, Davie Allan and band quickly developed into the most sought-after musicians in Hollywood when it came to filling soundtracks for grade-B youth exploitation films, especially if there was a biker theme . . .

Label & Catalog #		Title	Year	VG+	NM
RCA Victor LPM-2596	(M)	**Our Man Down South**	1962	10.00	25.00
RCA Victor LSP-2596	(S)	**Our Man Down South**	1962	12.00	30.00
RCA Victor LPM-2629	(M)	**Faithfully Yours**	1963	10.00	25.00
RCA Victor LSP-2629	(S)	**Faithfully Yours**	1963	12.00	30.00

— RCA mono albums above have "Long Play" on the bottom of the label; stereo albums have "Living Stereo" on the bottom. —

RCA Victor LPM-2811	(M)	**Folk Song Book**	1964	10.00	25.00
RCA Victor LSP-2811	(S)	**Folk Song Book**	1964	10.00	25.00
RCA Victor LPM-2909	(M)	**Sometimes I'm Happy, Sometimes I'm Blue**	1964	8.00	20.00
RCA Victor LSP-2909	(S)	**Sometimes I'm Happy, Sometimes I'm Blue**	1964	10.00	25.00
RCA Victor LPM-2951	(M)	**Pop Hits From The Country Side**	1964	8.00	20.00
RCA Victor LSP-2951	(S)	**Pop Hits From The Country Side**	1964	10.00	25.00

— RCA mono albums above have "Mono" on the bottom of the label; stereo albums have "Stereo" on the bottom. —

RCA Victor LPM-3753	(M)	**Lonely Again**	1967	12.00	30.00
RCA Victor LSP-3753	(S)	**Lonely Again**	1967	8.00	20.00
RCA Victor LPM-3869	(M)	**Turn The World Around**	1967	12.00	30.00
RCA Victor LSP-3869	(S)	**Turn The World Around**	1967	8.00	20.00
RCA Victor LPM-3931	(M)	**The Everlovin' World Of Eddy Arnold**	1968	20.00	50.00
RCA Victor LSP-3931	(S)	**The Everlovin' World Of Eddy Arnold**	1968	8.00	20.00

— RCA mono albums above have "Monaural" on the bottom of the label; stereo albums have "Stereo" on the bottom. —

ARNOLD, KAY

Sims LP-126	(M)	**Kay Arnold Sings Eddy Arnold**	196?	8.00	20.00
Sims LPS-126	(S)	**Kay Arnold Sings Eddy Arnold**	196?	10.00	25.00

ARROWS, THE: *Refer to* DAVIE ALLAN

ART OF LOVIN'

Mainstream S-6113	(S)	**Art Of Lovin'**	1968	10.00	25.00

ARTHUR
Arthur Lee Harper.

LHI 12000	(S)	**Dreams And Images**	1968	16.00	40.00

ARTHUR, GEORGE K.

MGM E-3151	(M)	**Prize Package**	1955	10.00	25.00

ARTISTICS, THE

OKeh OKL-4119	(M)	**Get My Hands On Some Lovin'**	1967	12.00	30.00
OKeh OKS-14119	(S)	**Get My Hands On Some Lovin'**	1967	16.00	40.00
Brunswick BL-54123	(M)	**I'm Gonna Miss You**	1967	8.00	20.00
Brunswick BL-754123	(S)	**I'm Gonna Miss You**	1967	10.00	25.00
Brunswick BL-754139	(S)	**The Articulate Artistics**	1968	10.00	25.00
Brunswick BL-754153	(S)	**What Happened**	1969	10.00	25.00

ARZACHEL

Roulette SR-42036	(S)	**Arzachel**	1969	60.00	150.00

ASHER, JANE

London OSA-1206	(M)	**Alice In Wonderland**	1965	20.00	50.00

ASHER & LITTLE JIMMY

Decca DL-4785	(M)	**Mountain Ballads And Old Hymns**	1966	10.00	25.00
Decca DL-74785	(S)	**Mountain Ballads And Old Hymns**	1966	12.00	30.00

ASHES

Vault 125	(S)	**Ashes**	1968	10.00	25.00

ASHKAN

Sire SES-97017	(S)	**In From The Cold**	1970	16.00	40.00

ASHLEY, CLARENCE "TOM"

Clarence "Tom" Ashley is an oldtime mountain singer and banjo player whose original recordings were instrumental in the development of modern country music. Ashley is accompanied by Doc Watson on both albums. Refer to The Carolina Tar Heels.

Folkways FA-2355	(M)	**Oldtime Music At Clarence Ashley's, Vol. I**	1961	10.00	25.00
Folkways FA-2359	(M)	**Oldtime Music At Clarence Ashley's, Vol. II**	1961	10.00	25.00

Label & Catalog #		Title	Year	VG+	NM
ASHLEY, LEON					
RCA Victor LPM-3900	(M)	**Laura (What's He Got That I Ain't Got?)**	1968	12.00	30.00
RCA Victor LSP-3900	(S)	**Laura (What's He Got That I Ain't Got?)**	1968	6.00	15.00

ASHLEY, TOM: *Refer to* **CLARENCE ASHLEY**

ASHWORTH, ERNEST: *Refer to* **BILL ANDERSON**

ASSOCIATION, THE					
Valiant VLM-5002	(M)	**And Then Along Comes The Association**	1966	8.00	20.00
Valiant VLS-25002	(S)	**And Then Along Comes The Association**	1966	10.00	25.00
Valiant VLM-5004	(M)	**Renaissance**	1966	8.00	20.00
Valiant VLS-25004	(S)	**Renaissance**	1966	10.00	25.00
		(First pressings of "Renaissance" do not mention			
		the single "No Fair At All" on the front cover.)			

ASTAIRE, FRED
Refer to Bing Crosby & Fred Astaire.

Mercury/Clef MGC-1001-4	(M)	**The Fred Astaire Story**	1953		*See below*
		("The Fred Astaire Story" is a limited edition, spiral-bound album of			
		four blue vinyl LPs limited to an edition of 1,384 numbered copies			
		signed by Mr. Astaire. Each album contains 11 pages of photos			
		by Gjon Mili and a folio of drawings by David Stone Martin.			
		Rare with a suggested Near Mint value of $1,000-2,000.)			
Mercury MGC-1001	(M)	**The Fred Astaire Story, Volume 1**	1954	40.00	100.00
Mercury MGC-1002	(M)	**The Fred Astaire Story, Volume 2**	1954	40.00	100.00
Mercury MGC-1003	(M)	**The Fred Astaire Story, Volume 3**	1954	40.00	100.00
Mercury MGC-1004	(M)	**The Fred Astaire Story, Volume 4**	1954	40.00	100.00
Clef MGC-662	(M)	**The Fred Astaire Story, Volume 1**	1955	20.00	50.00
Clef MGC-663	(M)	**The Fred Astaire Story, Volume 2**	1955	20.00	50.00
Clef MGC-664	(M)	**The Fred Astaire Story, Volume 3**	1955	20.00	50.00
Clef MGC-665	(M)	**The Fred Astaire Story, Volume 4**	1955	20.00	50.00
Verve MGV-2010	(M)	**Mr. Top Hat**	1956	20.00	50.00
		(Verve 2010 contains selections from "The Fred Astaire Story.")			
Verve MGV-15001	(M)	**Funny Face** *(Soundtrack)*	1956	20.00	50.00
Verve MGV-2114	(M)	**Easy To Dance With**	1958	20.00	50.00
		—*Verve albums above have "Verve Records, Inc." on the bottom of the label.*—			
MGM E-502	(10")	**Easter Parade** *(Soundtrack)*	1950	40.00	100.00
MGM E-516	(10")	**Three Little Words** *(Soundtrack)*	1950	40.00	100.00
MGM E-3051	(M)	**The Bandwagon** *(Soundtrack)*	1953	20.00	50.00
MGM E-3227	(M)	**Easter Parade** *(Soundtrack)*	1955	30.00	75.00
MGM E-3229	(M)	**Three Little Words /**			
		Good News *(Soundtracks)*	1955	30.00	75.00
MGM E-3413	(M)	**Shoes With Wings**	1956	20.00	50.00
MGM E-3542	(M)	**Silk Stockings** *(Soundtrack)*	1957	20.00	50.00
MGM SE-3542	(S)	**Silk Stockings** *(Soundtrack)*	1957	20.00	50.00
MGM E-3768	(M)	**Three Little Words /**			
		Annie Get Your Gun *(Soundtracks)*	1960	12.00	30.00
		—*MGM albums above have black labels with silver print.*—			
"X" LVA-1001	(M)	**Bandwagon** *(Soundtrack)*	1955	30.00	75.00
RCA Victor LSA-3082	(M)	**Bandwagon** *(Soundtrack)*	195?	20.00	50.00
RCA Victor LPM03155	(M)	**Bandwagon /**			
		The Little Shows *(Soundtracks)*	1953	16.00	40.00
Coral CRL-57008	(M)	**Cavalcade Of Dance**	1955	20.00	50.00
Epic LN-3103	(M)	**Nothing Thrilled Us Half As Much**	1955	20.00	50.00
Epic LN-3137	(M)	**The Best Of Fred Astaire**	1955	20.00	50.00
Chrysler CC-1	(DJ)	**An Evening With Fred Astaire**	1958	30.00	75.00
Chrysler K8OP-1087	(DJ)	**Another Evening With Fred Astaire**	1959	30.00	75.00
Chrysler M80P-1003	(DJ)	**Astaire Time**	1960	30.00	75.00
		(The three Chrysler promotional albums above contain songs			
		and non-musical material from Astaire's television specials)			
Kapp KL-1165	(M)	**Fred Astaire Now**	1959	10.00	25.00
Kapp KS-3165	(S)	**Fred Astaire Now**	1959	14.00	35.00
Lion L-70121	(M)	**Fred Astaire/Sound Tracks**	1959	16.00	40.00
Choreo A-1	(M)	**Three Evenings With Fred Astaire**	1960	20.00	50.00
		(Choreo 1 contain material from Astaire's television specials)			

Label & Catalog #		Title	Year	VG+	NM

ASTRONAUTS, THE
The Astronauts later recorded as Hardwater.

RCA Victor LPM-2760	(M)	**Surfin' With The Astronauts**	1963	20.00	50.00
RCA Victor LSP-2760	(S)	**Surfin' With The Astronauts**	1963	30.00	75.00
RCA Victor LPM-2782	(M)	**Everything Is A-OK**	1964	16.00	40.00
RCA Victor LSP-2782	(S)	**Everything Is A-OK**	1964	20.00	50.00
RCA Victor LPM-2858	(M)	**Competition Coupe**	1964	30.00	75.00
RCA Victor LSP-2858	(S)	**Competition Coupe**	1964	40.00	100.00
RCA Victor LPM-2903	(M)	**The Astronauts Orbit Campus**	1964	12.00	30.00
RCA Victor LSP-2903	(S)	**The Astronauts Orbit Campus**	1964	16.00	40.00
RCA Victor PRM-183	(M)	**Rockin' With The Astronauts** *(Promo)*	1964	12.00	30.00
RCA Victor LPM-3441	(M)	**Wild On The Beach** *(Soundtrack)*	1965	12.00	30.00
RCA Victor LSP-3441	(S)	**Wild On The Beach** *(Soundtrack)*	1965	16.00	40.00
RCA Victor LPM-3307	(M)	**The Astronauts Go Go Go**	1965	12.00	30.00
RCA Victor LSP-3307	(S)	**The Astronauts Go Go Go**	1965	16.00	40.00
RCA Victor LPM-3359	(M)	**Favorites For You From Us**	1965	12.00	30.00
RCA Victor LSP-3359	(S)	**Favorites For You From Us**	1965	16.00	40.00
RCA Victor LPM-3454	(M)	**Down The Line**	1966	12.00	30.00
RCA Victor LSP-3454	(S)	**Down The Line**	1966	16.00	40.00
RCA Victor LPM-3733	(M)	**Travelin' Men**	1967	20.00	50.00
RCA Victor LSP-3733	(S)	**Travelin' Men**	1967	16.00	40.00

ASTRONAUTS, THE / THE LIVERPOOL FIVE

RCA Victor PRS-251	(S)	**Stereo Festival** *(Promo sampler)*	1967	60.00	150.00

ATCHER, BOBBY

Columbia HL-9006	(10")	**Early American Folk Songs**	1949	40.00	100.00
Columbia HL-9013	(10")	**Songs Of The Saddle**	1949	40.00	100.00
Columbia CL-2232	(M)	**The Dean Of Cowboy Singers**	1964	10.00	25.00
Columbia CS-9032	(E)	**The Dean Of Cowboy Singers**	1964	6.00	15.00

ATKINS, CHET
Chet Atkins was the pre-eminent country'n western picker through the '50s and '60s, working with virtually every artist who came through Nashville, including Elvis' sides into the early '60s.. As an RCA A&R man/producer, he was instrumental in developing the laid-back sound associated with Nashville. In 1961 RCA revamped each of Chet's albums released through that year with new cover art, although the original "Long Play" label records were still in use. .Brief notes are used below to assist the reader in identifying which is which. In 1967 RCA reissued each of Chet's '50s albums in electronically reprocessed stereo except 1383, issued in phony stereo in 1962 . Since these are such latter-day reissues with very little interest to all but the completist, they are not listed below. . . Refer to The Atkins String Company; The Country All-Stars; The First Nashville Guitar Quartet; The Nashville String Band; Jerry Reed; The Nashville All-Stars. Note:

RCA Victor LPM-3079	(10")	**Chet Atkins' Gallopin' Guitar**	1952	60.00	150.00
RCA Victor LPM-3169	(10")	**Stringin' Along With Chet Atkins**	1953	50.00	125.00
RCA Victor LPM-1090	(M)	**A Session With Chet Atkins**	1954	24.00	60.00
		(Original covers for LPM-1090 are red)			
RCA Victor LPM-1090	(M)	**A Session With Chet Atkins**	1961	8.00	20.00
		(Later covers feature a woman and guitars.)			
RCA Victor LPM-1197	(M)	**Chet Atkins In Three Dimensions**	1956	20.00	50.00
		(Original pressings for LPM-1197 have a black & white guitar cover.)			
RCA Victor LPM-1197	(M)	**Chet Atkins In Three Dimensions**	1961	8.00	20.00
		(Later pressings feature a red guitar cover.)			
RCA Victor LPM-1236	(M)	**Stringin' Along With Chet Atkins**	1956	20.00	50.00
		(Original covers for LPM-1236 are orange.)			
RCA Victor LPM-1236	(M)	**Stringin' Along With Chet Atkins**	1961	8.00	20.00
		(Later covers are full-color.)			
RCA Victor LPM-1383	(M)	**Finger Style Guitar**	1956	20.00	50.00
		(On original covers for LPM-1383 Chet's face is not visible.)			
RCA Victor LPM-1383	(M)	**Finger Style Guitar**	1961	8.00	20.00
		(On later pressings Chet's face is visible on the cover.)			
RCA Victor LPM-1544	(M)	**Chet Atkins At Home**	1957	20.00	50.00
		(Original covers for LPM-1544 have the title in block letters.)			
RCA Victor LPM-1544	(M)	**Chet Atkins At Home**	1961	8.00	20.00
		(Later covers feature the title in script print.)			
RCA Victor LPM-1577	(M)	**Hi Fi In Focus**	1957	20.00	50.00
		(Original covers for LPM-1577 do not feature guitars.)			
RCA Victor LPM-1577	(M)	**Hi Fi In Focus**	1961	8.00	20.00
		(Later covers have a guitar.)			

Label & Catalog #		Title	Year	VG+	NM
RCA Victor LPM-1993	(M)	**Chet Atkins In Hollywood**	1959	12.00	30.00
RCA Victor LSP-1993	(S)	**Chet Atkins In Hollywood**	1959	20.00	50.00
		(Original covers for RCA 1993 feature a guitar "floating" against a nighttime backdrop.)			
RCA Victor LPM-1993	(M)	**Chet Atkins In Hollywood**	1961	8.00	20.00
RCA Victor LSP-1993	(S)	**Chet Atkins In Hollywood**	1961	12.00	30.00
		(Later covers feature a daytime shot of a guitar hanging around the corner of Hollywood and Vine with a beautiful blonde..)			
RCA Victor LPM-2025	(M)	**Hum & Strum Along** *(With instruction book)*	1959	14.00	35.00
RCA Victor LSP-2025	(S)	**Hum & Strum Along** *(With instruction book)*	1959	20.00	50.00
RCA Victor LPM-2025	(M)	**Hum & Strum Along** *(Without the book)*	1959	10.00	25.00
RCA Victor LSP-2025	(S)	**Hum & Strum Along** *(Without the book)*	1959	16.00	40.00
RCA Victor LPM-2103	(M)	**Mister Guitar**	1959	12.00	30.00
RCA Victor LSP-2103	(S)	**Mister Guitar**	1959	20.00	50.00
		(Original covers for RCA 2103 feature a lone guitar.)			
RCA Victor LPM-2103	(M)	**Mister Guitar**	1961	8.00	20.00
RCA Victor LSP-2103	(S)	**Mister Guitar**	1961	12.00	30.00
		(Later covers feature a guitar accompanied by a woman.)			
RCA Victor LPM-2161	(M)	**Teensville**	1960	12.00	30.00
RCA Victor LSP-2161	(S)	**Teensville**	1960	20.00	50.00
		(On original covers for RCA 2161 the title overlaps the photo.)			
RCA Victor LPM-2161	(M)	**Teensville**	1961	8.00	20.00
RCA Victor LSP-2161	(S)	**Teensville**	1961	12.00	30.00
		(Later covers feature the title in a black strip at the top of the cover.)			
RCA Victor LPM-2175	(M)	**The Other Chet Atkins**	1961	8.00	20.00
RCA Victor LSP-2175	(S)	**The Other Chet Atkins**	1961	12.00	30.00
RCA Victor LPM-2232	(M)	**Chet Atkins' Workshop**	1961	8.00	20.00
RCA Victor LSP-2232	(S)	**Chet Atkins' Workshop**	1961	10.00	25.00
RCA Victor LPM-2346	(M)	**The Most Popular Guitar**	1961	8.00	20.00
RCA Victor LSP-2346	(S)	**The Most Popular Guitar**	1961	10.00	25.00
RCA Victor LPM-2423	(M)	**Christmas With Chet Atkins**	1961	8.00	20.00
RCA Victor LSP-2423	(S)	**Christmas With Chet Atkins**	1961	10.00	25.00
RCA Victor LPM-2450	(M)	**Down Home**	1962	8.00	20.00
RCA Victor LSP-2450	(S)	**Down Home**	1962	10.00	25.00
RCA Victor LPM-2549	(M)	**Caribbean Guitar**	1962	8.00	20.00
RCA Victor LSP-2549	(S)	**Caribbean Guitar**	1962	10.00	25.00
RCA Victor LPM-2601	(M)	**Back Home Hymns**	1962	8.00	20.00
RCA Victor LSP-2601	(S)	**Back Home Hymns**	1962	10.00	25.00
RCA Victor LPM-2616	(M)	**Our Man In Nashville**	1963	8.00	20.00
RCA Victor LSP-2616	(S)	**Our Man In Nashville**	1963	10.00	25.00
RCA Victor LPM-2678	(M)	**Travelin'**	1963	8.00	20.00
RCA Victor LSP-2678	(S)	**Travelin'**	1963	10.00	25.00
RCA Victor LPM-2719	(M)	**Teen Scene**	1963	8.00	20.00
RCA Victor LSP-2719	(S)	**Teen Scene**	1963	10.00	25.00
		— RCA mono albums above have "Long Play" on the bottom of the label; stereo albums have "Living Stereo" on the bottom.—			
RCA Victor LPM-3531	(M)	**Chet Atkins Picks On The Beatles**	1965	10.00	25.00
RCA Victor LSP-3531	(S)	**Chet Atkins Picks On The Beatles**	1965	12.00	30.00
Dolton BLP-16506	(M)	**Play Guitar With Chet Atkins**	1966	10.00	25.00
Dolton BST-17506	(S)	**Play Guitar With Chet Atkins**	1966	12.00	30.00
RCA Victor LSP-3728	(M)	**It's A Guitar World**	1967	12.00	30.00
RCA Victor LSP-3728	(S)	**It's A Guitar World**	1967	5.00	12.00
RCA Victor LSP-3818	(M)	**Chet Atkins Picks The Best**	1967	12.00	30.00
RCA Victor LSP-3818	(S)	**Chet Atkins Picks The Best**	1967	5.00	12.00
RCA Victor LSP-3885	(M)	**Class Guitar**	1967	12.00	30.00
RCA Victor LSP-3885	(S)	**Class Guitar**	1967	5.00	12.00
RCA Victor LSP-3992	(M)	**Solo Flights**	1968	20.00	50.00
RCA Victor LSP-3992	(S)	**Solo Flights**	1968	5.00	12.00
		—RCA Victor albums above have black labels with Nipper on top.—			

ATLANTA RHYTHM SECTION, THE

Mobile Fidelity MFSL-038	(S)	**Champagne Jam**	1980	10.00	30.00

ATTILA
Attila features Billy Joel.

Epic E-30030	(S)	**Attila**	1970	10.00	25.00

Label & Catalog #		Title	Year	VG+	NM
AU-GO-GO SINGERS, THE					
The Au-Go-Gos feature Steve Stills and Rich Furay, later of The Buffalo Springfield.					
Roulette R-25280	(M)	**They Call Us The Au Go-Go Singers**	1964	20.00	50.00
Roulette SR-25280	(S)	**They Call Us The Au Go-Go Singers**	1964	30.00	75.00
AUM					
Sire SES-97007	(S)	**Bluesvibes**	1969	10.00	25.00
Fillmore F-30002	(S)	**Resurrection**	1969	12.00	30.00
AUSTIN, CLAIRE: Refer to GOLDMINE'S PRICE GUIDE TO COLLECTIBLE JAZZ ALBUMS					
AUSTIN, GENE					
RCA Victor LPM-3200	(10")	**My Blue Heaven**	195?	30.00	75.00
"X" LVA-1007	(M)	**Gene Austin Sings All-Time Favorites**	195?	20.00	50.00
Decca DL-8433	(M)	**My Blue Heaven**	1957	20.00	50.00
Dot DLP-3300	(M)	**Great Hits**	1960	8.00	20.00
Dot DLP-25300	(S)	**Great Hits**	1960	12.00	30.00
RCA Victor LPM-2490	(M)	**My Blue Heaven**	1962	8.00	20.00
RCA Victor LSP-2490	(S)	**My Blue Heaven**	1962	10.00	25.00
AUSTIN, GENE, & VERNON DALHART & JIMMIE RODGERS					
RCA Victor LPT-6 (10")	(M)	**Folk Singers**	195?	40.00	100.00
AUSTIN, SIL					
Refer to Red Prysock & Sil Austin.					
Mercury MG-20237	(M)	**Slow Walk Rock**	1957	20.00	50.00
Mercury MG-20320	(M)	**Everything Is Shakin'**	1958	20.00	50.00
Mercury MG-20???	(M)	**Sil Austin Plays Pretty For The People**	1959	12.00	30.00
Mercury SR-60096	(S)	**Sil Austin Plays Pretty For The People**	1959	16.00	40.00
Mercury MG-20546	(M)	**Soft, Plaintive And Moody**	1960	12.00	30.00
Mercury SR-60236	(S)	**Soft, Plaintive And Moody**	1960	16.00	40.00
Mercury MG-20663	(M)	**Golden Saxophone Hits**	1961	10.00	25.00
Mercury SR-60663	(S)	**Golden Saxophone Hits**	1961	12.00	30.00
AUTOSALVAGE					
RCA Victor LPM-3940	(M)	**Autosalvage**	1968	20.00	50.00
RCA Victor LSP-3940	(S)	**Autosalvage**	1968	10.00	25.00
AUTRY, GENE					
Columbia JL-8001	(10")	**Gene Autry At The Rodeo**	1949	60.00	150.00
Columbia JL-8009	(10")	**Stampede**	1949	60.00	150.00
Columbia JL-8012	(10")	**Champion**	1950	60.00	150.00
Columbia HL-9001	(10")	**Western Classics, Volume 1**	1949	60.00	150.00
Columbia HL-9002	(10")	**Western Classics, Volume 2**	1949	60.00	150.00
Columbia CL-6020	(10")	**Easter Favorites**	1949	60.00	150.00
Columbia CL-6137	(10")	**Merry Christmas**	1950	60.00	150.00
Columbia MJV-82	(10")	**The Story Of The Nativity**	1955	40.00	100.00
Columbia MJV-83	(10")	**Little Johnny Pilgrim And Guffy**	1955	40.00	100.00
Columbia MJV-94	(10")	**Rusty, The Rocking Horse**	1955	40.00	100.00
Columbia CL-2547	(10")	**Merry Christmas**	1955	40.00	100.00
Columbia CL-2568	(10")	**Gene Autry Sings Peter Cottontail**	1955	40.00	100.00
		(Columbia 2568 is a reissue of 6020.)			
Columbia CL-677	(M)	**Gene Autry And Champion**	1955	30.00	75.00
Challenge CHL-600	(M)	**Christmas With Gene Autry**	1958	20.00	50.00
Columbia CL-1575	(M)	**Gene Autry's Greatest Hits**	1961	14.00	35.00
Harmony HL-9505	(M)	**Gene Autry And Champion**	1959	16.00	40.00
Harmony HL-9550	(M)	**Christmas Favorites**	1964	12.00	30.00
Harmony HL-9555	(M)	**First Easter Record For Children**	1965	12.00	30.00
Harmony HL-7332	(M)	**Gene Autry's Great Western Hits**	1965	10.00	25.00
Harmony HS-7332	(E)	**Gene Autry's Great Western Hits**	1965	6.00	15.00
Harmony HL-7376	(M)	**Back In The Saddle Again**	1968	10.00	25.00
Harmony HS-7376	(E)	**Back In The Saddle Again**	1968	6.00	15.00
Harmony HL-7399	(M)	**Gene Autry Sings**	1968	10.00	25.00
Harmony HS-7399	(E)	**Gene Autry Sings**	1968	6.00	15.00
RCA Victor LPM-2623	(M)	**Gene Autry's Golden Hits**	1962	10.00	25.00
RCA Victor LSP-2623	(S)	**Gene Autry's Golden Hits**	1962	10.00	25.00
Melody Ranch 101	(M)	**Melody Ranch**	1965	16.00	40.00
Murray Hill 897296	(M)	**Melody Ranch Radio Show** *(4 LP box)*	197?	10.00	25.00

Gene Autry, soon to be former owner of the California Angels, formerly the Los Angeles Angels, made his mark on the world as one of Hollywood's two most famous singing cowboys (the other also finds his way into this book). In a string of western films he chased the bad guys atop his trusty steed, Champion, who, unlike Mr. Ed, doesn't sing so he doesn't have any listings in this book.

Label & Catalog #		Title	Year	VG+	NM
AVALANCHES, THE					
Warner Bros. W-1525	(M)	**Ski Surfin'**	1963	12.00	30.00
Warner Bros. WS-1525	(S)	**Ski Surfin'**	1963	16.00	40.00
AVALON, FRANKIE					
Refer to Fabian / Frankie Avalon.					
Chancellor CHL-5001	(M)	**Frankie Avalon**	1958	30.00	75.00
Chancellor CHL-5002	(M)	**The Young Frankie Avalon**	1959	30.00	75.00
Chancellor CHLS-5002	(S)	**The Young Frankie Avalon**	1959	40.00	100..00
		— Chancellor albums above have pink labels.—			
Chancellor CHL-5001	(M)	**Frankie Avalon**	1960	20.00	50.00
Chancellor CHL-5002	(M)	**The Young Frankie Avalon**	1960	20.00	50.00
Chancellor CHLS-5002	(S)	**The Young Frankie Avalon**	1960	30.00	75.00
Chancellor CHLX-5004	(M)	**Swingin' On A Rainbow**	1960	24.00	60.00
Chancellor CHLXS-5004	(S)	**Swingin' On A Rainbow**	1960	30.00	75.00
Chancellor CHL-69801	(M)	**Young And In Love**	1960	30.00	75.00
		(Boxed set with photos and a 3-D portrait.)			
Chancellor CHL-5011	(M)	**Summer Scene**	1960	16.00	40.00
Chancellor CHLS-5011	(S)	**Summer Scene**	1960	24.00	60.00
Chancellor CHL-5018	(M)	**A Whole Lot Of Frankie**	1961	16.00	40.00
Chancellor CHL-5022	(M)	**And Now About Mr. Avalon**	1961	16.00	40.00
Chancellor CHLS-5022	(S)	**And Now About Mr. Avalon**	1961	20.00	50.00
Chancellor CHL-5025	(M)	**Italiano**	1962	10.00	25.00
Chancellor CHLS-5025	(S)	**Italiano**	1962	16.00	40.00
Chancellor CHL-5027	(M)	**You Are Mine**	1962	10.00	25.00
Chancellor CHLS-5027	(S)	**You Are Mine**	1962	16.00	40.00
Chancellor CHL-5031	(M)	**Frankie Avalon's Christmas Album**	1962	10.00	25.00
Chancellor CHLS-5031	(S)	**Frankie Avalon's Christmas Album**	1962	16.00	40.00
Chancellor CHL-5032	(M)	**Cleopatra Plus 13 Other Great Hits**	1963	10.00	25.00
Chancellor CHLS-5032	(S)	**Cleopatra Plus 13 Other Great Hits**	1963	16.00	40.00
		— Chancellor albums above have black labels.—			
United Arts. UAL-3371	(M)	**Songs From Muscle Beach Party**	1964	8.00	20.00
United Arts. UAS-6371	(S)	**Songs From Muscle Beach Party**	1964	12.00	30.00
United Arts. UAL-3382	(M)	**Frankie Avalon's 15 Greatest Hits**	1964	8.00	20.00
United Arts. UAS-6382	(P)	**Frankie Avalon's 15 Greatest Hits**	1964	10.00	25.00
		(A collection of hits originally issued on Chancellor.)			
United Arts. UAL-4121	(M)	**I'll Take Sweden** *(Soundtrack)*	1965	8.00	20.00
United Arts. UAS-5121	(S)	**I'll Take Sweden** *(Soundtrack)*	1965	10.00	25.00
AVENGERS VI, THE					
Mark-56 Records	(M)	**Real Cool Hits**	1965	100.00	250.00
AVERAGE WHITE BAND, THE					
MCA 345	(S)	**Show Your Hands**	1973	10.00	25.00
AVONS, THE					
Hull HLP-1000	(M)	**The Avons** *(Red label)*	1960	250.00	500.00
AXTON, HOYT					
Horizon WP-1601	(M)	**The Balladeer**	1962	10.00	25.00
Horizon ST-1601	(S)	**The Balladeer**	1962	12.00	30.00
Horizon WP-1613	(M)	**Thunder 'N Lightnin'**	1963	10.00	25.00
Horizon ST-1613	(S)	**Thunder 'N Lightnin'**	1963	12.00	30.00
Horizon WP-1621	(M)	**Saturday's Child**	1963	10.00	25.00
Horizon ST-1621	(S)	**Saturday's Child**	1963	12.00	30.00
Vee Jay LP-1098	(M)	**Hoyt Axton Explodes!**	1964	10.00	25.00
Vee Jay LPS-1098	(E)	**Hoyt Axton Explodes!**	1964	8.00	20.00
Vee Jay LP-1118	(M)	**The Best Of Hoyt Axton**	1964	8.00	20.00
Vee Jay LPS-1118	(S)	**The Best Of Hoyt Axton**	1964	10.00	25.00
Vee Jay LP-1126	(M)	**Greenback Dollar**	1964	8.00	20.00
Vee Jay LPS-1126	(S)	**Greenback Dollar**	1964	12.00	30.00
Vee Jay LP-1127	(M)	**Saturday's Child**	1964	8.00	20.00
Vee Jay LPS-1127	(S)	**Saturday's Child**	1964	12.00	30.00
Vee Jay LP-1128	(M)	**Thunder 'N Lightnin'**	1964	8.00	20.00
Vee Jay LPS-1128	(S)	**Thunder 'N Lightnin'**	1964	12.00	30.00
Surrey S-1005	(M)	**Mr. Greenback Dollar Man**	1965	8.00	20.00
Surrey SS-1005	(S)	**Mr. Greenback Dollar Man**	1965	10.00	25.00
Exodus EX-301	(M)	**Hoyt Axton Sings Bessie Smith**	1966	8.00	20.00
Exodus EXS-301	(S)	**Hoyt Axton Sings Bessie Smith**	1966	10.00	25.00

Label & Catalog #		Title	Year	VG+	NM

AYCOCK, EARL
Mercury MG-20282　　*(M)*　**Earl Aycock**　　1958　10.00　25.00

AZAMA, ETHEL: *Refer to* **GOLDMINE'S PRICE GUIDE TO COLLECTIBLE JAZZ ALBUMS**

AZTECS, THE
World Artists WAM-2001　*(M)*　**Live At The Ad-Lib Club Of London**　1964　20.00　50.00

AZITIS
Elco SC-EC-5555　　*(S)*　**Help!**　　1974　100.00　250.00

B

B. F. TRIKE

Rockadellic	(S)	**B. F. Trike**	1989	30.00	75.00

BABY HUEY

Curtom CRS-8007	(S)	**The Living Legend**	1970	16.00	40.00

BABY RAY

Baby Ray is a pseudonym for Ray Stevens.

Imperial LP-9335	(M)	**Where Soul Lives**	1967	10.00	25.00
Imperial LP-12335	(S)	**Where Soul Lives**	1967	12.00	30.00

BABYSITTERS, THE

The Babysitters—Alan Arkin, Lee Hays and Doris Kaplan—played and sang tradiional folk songs.

Vanguard VRS-9042	(M)	**Folk Songs For Children And Parents**	1958	16.00	40.00
Vanguard VSD-2042	(S)	**Folk Songs For Children And Parents**	1960	16.00	40.00
Vanguard VRS-9053	(M)	**Songs And Fun With The Babysitters**	1959	16.00	40.00
Vanguard VSD-2053	(S)	**Songs And Fun With The Babysitters**	1960	16.00	40.00

BACHELORS, THE

London LL-3353	(M)	**Presenting The Bachelors**	1964	8.00	20.00
London PS-353	(S)	**Presenting The Bachelors**	1964	10.00	25.00
London LL-3393	(M)	**Back Again**	1964	8.00	20.00
London PS-393	(S)	**Back Again**	1964	10.00	25.00
London LL-3418	(M)	**No Arms Can Ever Hold You**	1965	8.00	20.00
London PS-418	(S)	**No Arms Can Ever Hold You**	1965	10.00	25.00
London LL-3435	(M)	**Marie**	1965	8.00	20.00
London PS-435	(S)	**Marie**	1965	10.00	25.00
		(On both PS 435 and 491 below "Marie" is rechanneled.)			
London LL-3460	(M)	**Hits Of The '60s**	1966	8.00	20.00
London PS-460	(S)	**Hits Of The '60s**	1966	10.00	25.00
London LL-3491	(M)	**The Bachelors' Girls**	1966	8.00	20.00
London PS-491	(S)	**The Bachelors' Girls)**	1966	10.00	25.00
London LL-3518	(M	**Golden All-Time Hits**	1967	8.00	20.00
London PS-518	(S)	**Golden All-Time Hits**	1967	10.00	25.00
London PS-528	(S)	**The Bachelors '68**	1968	10.00	25.00

BACHS, THE

Raio *(No number)*	(S)	**Out Of The Bachs**	1967	2,000.00	3,000.00

BADFINGER

Badfinger originally recorded as The Iveys. Refer to George Harrison & Friends.

Commonwealth UN. 6004	(S)	**The Magic Christian** *(Sdtk with Ringo)*	1970	10.00	25.00
Apple ST-3364	(S)	**Magic Christian Music**	1970	12.00	30.00
		(Apple label with "A Subsidiary of Capitol" on the bottom.)			
Apple ST-3364	(S)	**Magic Christian Music**	1970	10.00	25.00
		(Apple label with "Manufactured by Apple" on the bottom.)			
Apple SKAO-3367	(S)	**No Dice**	1970	16.00	40.00
Apple SW-3387	(S)	**Straight Up**	1971	30.00	75.00
Apple SW-3411	(S)	**Ass**	1973	10.00	25.00

BADGE

LPS-1	(S)	**Badge & Co.**	1977	150.00	300.00

BAEZ, JOAN

Joan Baez is the preminent songstress of popular American folk music of the '60s and is often referred to as the "Queen of Folk Music." Her first album appearance was on a compilation, "Folksingers 'Round Harvard Square," on the Veritas label in the Various Artists section of this book.

Vanguard VRS-9078	(M)	**Joan Baez**	1960	8.00	20.00
Vanguard VSD-2077	(S)	**Joan Baez**	1960	10.00	25.00
Vanguard VRS-9094	(M)	**Joan Baez, Vol. 2**	1961	8.00	20.00
Vanguard VSD-2097	(S)	**Joan Baez, Vol. 2**	1961	10.00	25.00

Badfinger originally recorded as The Ivies, releasing an album on The Beatles' Apple Records in Europe and Japan, although it was never distributed in the States. Changing their name, apparently at John Beatle's inspiration, and recording Paul Beatle's "Come And Get It" for inclusion in Ringo Beatle's first feature film, "The Magic Christian," they were a worldwide smash for a cuppla years. This, their third album, Straight Up, was originally to be produced in its entirety by George Beatle, who was repaying them for their services as the backing band for George's concert to aid Bangla Desh. Due to extenuating circumstances, was completed under the direction of Todd Rundgren. The album sold well (Billboard's charts featured it for 32 weeks, peaking at #31),. Copies flooded the nation's cut-out bins for years, as though distributors were experiencing a epidemic. Then, they were gone. This album eventually found a second life in the wake of power-pop mania, with prices for sealed copies fetching three figures, although it has since settled into a more modest place in the collectors market. Oh, and another thing: It's a pretty good little LP, too.

Label & Catalog #		Title	Year	VG+	NM
Vanguard VRS-9112	(M)	Joan Baez In Concert	1962	8.00	20.00
Vanguard VSD-2122	(S)	Joan Baez In Concert	1962	10.00	25.00
Vanguard VRS-9113	(M)	Joan Baez In Concert, Part 2	1963	8.00	20.00
Vanguard VSD-2123	(S)	Joan Baez In Concert, Part 2	1963	10.00	25.00
— Vanguard mono albums above have maroon labels; stereo albums have black labels.—					
A&M SP-8375	(S)	From Every Stage (White label promo)	1976	60.00	150.00
Nautilus NR-12	(S)	Diamonds And Rust	198?	12.00	36.00

BAGDASARIAN, ROSS
Bagdasarian as David Seville was the mastermind behind The Chipmunks.

Liberty LRP-3451	(M)	The Crazy, Mixed-Up World Of Ross Bagdasarian	1966	16.00	40.00
Liberty LST-7451	(S)	The Crazy, Mixed-Up World Of Ross Bagdasarian	1966	20.00	50.00

BAHLU, KAHLI

World Pacific ST-????	(S)	Cosmic Remembrance	1967	30.00	75.00

BAILES BROTHERS, THE
The Bailes Brothers are Homer, Johnny, Kyle and Walter.

Audio Lab AL-1511	(M)	Avenue Of Prayer	1959	80.00	200.00

BAILEY, MILDRED: *Refer to* GOLDMINE'S PRICE GUIDE TO COLLECTIBLE JAZZ ALBUMS

BAILEY, PEARL

Columbia CL-6099	(10")	Pearl Bailey Entertains	1950	20.00	50.00
Coral CRL-56068	(10")	Say Si Si	1953	20.00	50.00
Coral CRL-56078	(10")	I'm With You	1953	20.00	50.00
Columbia ML-4969	(M)	House Of Flowers (Soundtrack)	1954	20.00	50.00
Capitol L-355	(M)	St. Louis Woman (Soundtrack)	1955	40.00	100.00
Mercury MG-20187	(M)	The One And Only Pearl Bailey Sings	1956	16.00	40.00
Mercury MG-20277	(M)	The Intoxicating Pearl Bailey	1957	16.00	40.00
Coral CRL-57037	(M)	Birth Of The Blues	1956	16.00	40.00
Coral CRL-57162	(M)	Cultured Pearl	1957	16.00	40.00
Vocalion VL-3621	(M)	Gems By Pearl Bailey	1958	10.00	25.00
Columbia OL-5410	(M)	Porgy And Bess (Soundtrack)	1959	8.00	20.00
Columbia OS-2016	(S)	Porgy And Bess (Soundtrack)	1959	12.00	30.00
RCA Victor LOC-1090	(M)	Les Poupees De Paris (Soundtrack)	1964	14.00	35.00
RCA Victor LSO-1090	(S)	Les Poupees De Paris (Soundtrack)	1964	20.00	50.00
RCA Victor LOC-1147	(M)	Hello, Dolly (Soundtrack)	1964	8.00	20.00
RCA Victor LSO-1147	(S)	Hello, Dolly (Soundtrack)	1964	10.00	25.00

BAILLARGEON, HELENE
Classically trained Helene Baillargeon is a Canadian singer of traditional folk songs.

Folkways FW-829	(10")	Christmas Songs Of French Canada	195?	20.00	50.00
Folkways FC-7229	(10")	Christmas Songs Of French Canada	195?	20.00	50.00

BAILLARGEON, HELENE, & ALAN MILLS
Refer to Alan Mills.

Folkways FP-918	(10")	Duet Songs Of French Canada	1955	30.00	75.00
Folkways FW-6918	(10")	Duet Songs Of French Canada	1955	30.00	75.00
Folkways FW-6923	(10")	Songs Of Acadia	1955	30.00	75.00

BAIN, BOB

Capitol T-965	(M)	Rockin,' Rollin' And Strollin'	1958	40.00	100.00
Capitol T-1201	(M)	Latin Love	1959	16.00	40.00
Capitol ST-1201	(S)	Latin Love	1959	20.00	50.00
Capitol T-1500	(M)	Guitar De Amor	1961	12.00	30.00
Capitol ST-1500	(S)	Guitar De Amor	1961	16.00	40.00

BAKER, JOSEPHINE

Columbia FL-9532	(10")	Josephine Baker	1951	30.00	75.00
Columbia FL-9533	(10")	Chansons Americaines	1951	30.00	75.00
Columbia ML-2608	(10")	Josephine Baker Sings	1952	30.00	75.00
Columbia ML-2609	(10")	Chansons Americaines	1952	30.00	75.00
Columbia ML-2613	(10")	Encores Americaines	1952	30.00	75.00
Jolly Roger 5015	(10")	Josephine Baker	1951	20.00	50.00
Mercury MG-25105	(10")	The Inimitable Josephine Baker	1952	30.00	75.00
Mercury MG-25151	(10")	Avec Josephine Baker	1952	30.00	75.00

Mickey Baker was a stalwart in the rhythm'n blues scene, providing exciting guitar for hundreds of records. He also teamed up with a young protege, Sylvia Vanderpool, and scored as one of the '50s' more interesting duets, Mickey & Sylvia, scoring the ever-popular "Love Is Strange." After their break-up, Mr. B recorded this excellent album, to negligible sales.

Label & Catalog #		Title	Year	VG+	NM
RCA Victor LPM-2475	(M)	The Fabulous Josephine Baker	1962	12.00	30.00
RCA Victor LSP-2475	(S)	The Fabulous Josephine Baker	1962	16.00	40.00

BAKER, KENNY
Kenny Baker is a bluegrass fiddler associated with Bill Monroe's Blue Grass Boys in the '50s and '60s. Refer to Josh Graves & Kenny Baker.

Camden CAL-131	(M)	Song Hits Through The Yesr	195?	10.00	25.00

BAKER, LAVERN

Atlantic 8002	(M)	LaVern	1956	80.00	200.00
Atlantic 8007	(M)	LaVern Baker	1957	80.00	200.00
Atlantic 1281	(M)	LaVern Baker Sings Bessie Smith	1958	50.00	125.00
Atlantic SD-1281	(S)	LaVern Baker Sings Bessie Smith	1959	60.00	150.00
Atlantic 8030	(M)	Blues Ballads	1959	50.00	125.00
Atlantic 8030	(M)	Blues Ballads (White "bullseye" label)	1959	100.00	250.00
Atlantic 8036	(M)	Precious Memories	1959	50.00	125.00
Atlantic 8036	(M)	Precious Memories (White "bullseye" label)	1959	100.00	250.00
Atlantic SD-8036	(S)	Precious Memories	1959	60.00	150.00
Atlantic SD-8036	(S)	Precious Memories (White "bullseye" label)	1959	150.00	300.00

— Atlantic mono albums above have black labels; stereo albums have green labels.—

Atlantic 8002	(M)	LaVern	1960	12.00	30.00
Atlantic 1281	(M)	LaVern Baker Sings Bessie Smith	1960	12.00	30.00
Atlantic SD-1281	(S)	LaVern Baker Sings Bessie Smith	1960	16.00	40.00
Atlantic 8030	(M)	Blues Ballads	1960	12.00	30.00
Atlantic 8036	(M)	Precious Memories	1960	12.00	30.00
Atlantic SD-8036	(S)	Precious Memories	1960	16.00	40.00
Atlantic 8050	(M)	Saved	1961	30.00	75.00
Atlantic SD-8050	(S)	Saved	1961	40.00	100.00

— Atlantic albums above have muti-colored labels with a white "fan" logo on the right side.—

Atlantic 8071	(M)	See See Rider	1963	20.00	50.00
Atlantic SD-8071	(S)	See See Rider	1963	30.00	75.00
Atlantic 8078	(M)	The Best Of LaVern Baker	1963	60.00	150.00

— Atlantic albums above have muti-colored labels with a black "fan" logo on the right side.—

BAKER, MICKEY
Formerly one half of Mickey & Sylvia. Refer to Champion Jack Dupree; Brother John Sellers.

Atlantic 8035	(M)	Wildest Guitar	1959	60.00	150.00
Atlantic SD-8035	(S)	Wildest Guitar	1959	80.00	200.00

— Atlantic mono albums above have black labels; stereo albums have green labels.—

Atlantic 8035	(M)	Wildest Guitar	196?	14.00	35.00
Atlantic SD-8035	(S)	Wildest Guitar	196?	20.00	50.00

— Atlantic albums above have muti-colored labels with a white "fan" logo on the right side.—

King 839	(M)	But Wild (Black crownless label)	1963	200.00	400.00
King KS-839	(E)	But Wild (Blue label with a crown)	196?	14.00	35.00

BAKER, RONNIE

Warner Bros. W-1212	(M)	Oh, Johnny!	1958	16.00	40.00

BALDRY, LONG JOHN

Ascot ALM-13022	(M)	Long John's Blues	1965	16.00	40.00
Ascot ALS-16022	(E)	Long John's Blues	1965	10.00	25.00

BALLADEERS, THE

Del-Fi DFLP-1204	(M)	Alive-O!	1959	16.00	40.00
Del-Fi DFLPS-1204	(S)	Alive-O!	1959	24.00	60.00

(Stereo copies of Del-Fi 1204 were issued in mono jackets.)

BALLARD, FRANK

Phillips Int. PLP-1985	(M)	Rhythm-Blues Party	1962	2,500.00	5,000.00

BALLARD, HANK
Hank Ballard rose to prominence as the lead singer for the legendary rhythm'n blues vocal group The Midnighters. By the late '50s management had rearranged the group and they recorded their singles as Hank Ballard & The Midnighters. As the titles below indicate, he was more or less sold to the album market as a solo, which is why the classic, early group material is listed under The Midnighters while the later recordings of both Hank with and without The Midnighters is listed here. . .

King 618	(M)	Singin And Swingin'	1959	80.00	200.00
King 674	(M)	The One & Only Hank Ballard (Brown cover)	1960	80.00	200.00
King 674	(M)	The One & Only Hank Ballard (Green cover)	1960	70.00	175.00

Label & Catalog #		Title	Year	VG+	NM
King 700	(M)	Finger Poppin' Time	1960	70.00	175.00
King 740	(M)	Spotlight On Hank Ballard	1961	70.00	175.00
King KS-740	(S)	Spotlight On Hank Ballard	1961	150.00	300.00
King 748	(M)	Let's Go Again	1961	60.00	150.00
King 759	(M)	Sing Along	1961	60.00	150.00
King 781	(M)	The Twistin' Fools	1962	60.00	150.00
King 793	(M)	Jumpin' Hank Ballard	1962	60.00	150.00
King 815	(M)	The 1963 Sound Of Hank Ballard	1963	60.00	150.00
King 867	(M)	Biggest Hits	1963	60.00	150.00
King 896	(M)	A Star In Your Eyes	1964	60.00	150.00
—King albums above have crownless black labels.—					
King 913	(M)	Those Lazy, Lazy Days	1965	30.00	75.00
King 927	(M)	Glad Songs, Sad Songs	1966	30.00	75.00
King 950	(M)	24 Hit Tunes	1966	24.00	60.00
King 981	(M)	24 Great Songs	1968	16.00	40.00
King KSD-1052	(S)	You Keep A Good Man Down	1969	16.00	40.00
		(KSD-1052 was produced by James Brown.)			

BALLARD, KAYE

Label & Catalog #		Title	Year	VG+	NM
MGM E-3704	(M)	The Fanny Brice Story In Song	1959	8.00	20.00
MGM SE-3704	(S)	The Fanny Brice Story In Song	1959	10.00	25.00
United Arts. UAL-3043	(M)	Kaye Ballard Swings	1959	8.00	20.00
United Arts. UAS-6043	(S)	Kaye Ballard Swings	1959	10.00	25.00
United Arts. UAL-3155	(M)	Kaye Ballard Live?	1960	8.00	20.00
United Arts. UAS-6155	(S)	Kaye Ballard Live?	1960	10.00	25.00
United Arts. UAL-3165	(M)	Ha-Ha Boo-Hoo	1960	8.00	20.00
United Arts. UAS-6165	(S)	Ha-Ha Boo-Hoo	1960	10.00	25.00

BANANA SPLITS, THE

Label & Catalog #		Title	Year	VG+	NM
Decca DL-75075	(S)	We're The Banana Splits	1969	70.00	175.00
Rhodes Prod.	(S)	We're The Banana Splits (Picture disc)	1985	16.00	40.00
		(The $40 value is for those copies that do not play Banana Splits music, which is the majority of those manufactured.)			
Rhodes Prod.	(S)	We're The Banana Splits (Picture disc)	1985	80.00	200.00
		(The $200 value is for those copies that do play The Banana Splits.)			

BAND, THE

The Band is Rick Danko, Levon Helm, Garth Hudson, Richard Manuel and Robbie Robertson. Refer to Bob Dylan; John Hammond; Ronnie Hawkins; Steve Miller / Quicksilver Messenger Service / The Band.

Label & Catalog #		Title	Year	VG+	NM
Capitol SKAO-2955	(S)	Music From Big Pink	1968	8.00	20.00
Capitol ST-132	(S)	The Band	1969		See below
		(Should ST-132 esist with black "rainbow" labels it would have a suggested Near Mint value of $25-75.)			
—Capitol albums above have black "rainbow" labels.—					
Capitol SABB-11045	(S)	Rock Of Ages (2 LPs)	1972	10.00	25.00
—Capitol albums above have red labels with a purple "C" logo.—					
Mobile Fidelity MFSL-039	(S)	Music From Big Pink	198?	15.00	45.00

BAND OF GYPSYS: *Refer to* JIMI HENDRIX

BANDITS, THE

The Bandits feature Glen Campbell.

Label & Catalog #		Title	Year	VG+	NM
World Pacific T-1833	(M)	The Electric 12 String	1964	8.00	20.00
World Pacific ST-1833	(S)	The Electric 12 String	1964	10.00	25.00

BANKS, DARRELL

Label & Catalog #		Title	Year	VG+	NM
Atco 33-216	(M)	Darrell Banks Is Here	1967	10.00	25.00
Atco SD-33-216	(S)	Darrell Banks Is Here	1967	12.00	30.00
		("Open The Door To Your Heart" is rechanneled for this album.)			
Volt VOS-6002	(S)	Here To Stay	1969	10.00	25.00

BANTAMS, THE

Label & Catalog #		Title	Year	VG+	NM
Warner Bros. W-1625	(M)	Beware The Bantams	1966	8.00	20.00
Warner Bros. WS-1625	(S)	Beware The Bantams	1966	10.00	25.00

BAR-KAYS, THE

Label & Catalog #		Title	Year	VG+	NM
Volt 417	(M)	Soul Finger	1967	10.00	25.00
Volt S-417	(S)	Soul Finger	1967	12.00	30.00
Volt S-6004	(S)	Gotta Groove	1969	10.00	25.00

Label & Catalog #		Title	Year	VG+	NM
Volt S-6011	(S)	**Black Rock**	1971	10.00	25.00
Volt S-8001	(S)	**Do You See What I See?**	1972	10.00	25.00
Volt S-6023	(S)	**Cold Blooded**	1974	10.00	25.00
BARBARIANS, THE					
Laurie LLP-2033	(M)	**Are You A Boy Or Are You A Girl?**	1966	40.00	100.00
Laurie SLP-2033	(S)	**Are You A Boy Or Are You A Girl?**	1966	60.00	150.00
BARDOT, BRIGITTE					
Refer to Ray Ventura.					
Poplar 33-1002	(M)	**The Girl In The Bikini** (*Soundtrack*)	1952	200.00	400.00
Decca DL-8685	(M)	**And God Created Woman** (*Soundtrack*)	1957	80.00	200.00
Warner Bros. W-1371	(M)	**Behind Brigitte Bardot**	1960	16.00	40.00
Warner Bros. WS-1371	(S)	**Behind Brigitte Bardot**	1960	20.00	50.00
Everest LPBR-5056	(M)	**Love Is My Profession** (*Soundtrack*)	1960	20.00	50.00
Everest SDBR-1056	(S)	**Love Is My Profession** (*Soundtrack*)	1960	30.00	75.00
Philips PC-204	(M)	**Brigitte Bardot Sings**	1963	12.00	30.00
Philips PCC-604	(S)	**Brigitte Bardot Sings**	1963	16.00	40.00
Burlington-Cameo 1000	(DJ)	**Special Bardot** (*TV Soundtrack*)	1968	80.00	200.00
BARE, BOBBY					
RCA Victor LPM-2776	(M)	**Detroit City And Other Hits**	1963	10.00	25.00
RCA Victor LSP-2776	(S)	**Detroit City And Other Hits**	1963	12.00	30.00
RCA Victor LPM-2835	(M)	**500 Miles Away From Home**	1963	10.00	25.00
RCA Victor LSP-2835	(S)	**500 Miles Away From Home**	1963	12.00	30.00
RCA Victor LPM-2955	(M)	**The Travelin' Bare**	1964	10.00	25.00
RCA Victor LSP-2955	(S)	**The Travelin' Bare**	1964	12.00	30.00
RCA Victor LPM-3336	(M)	**Tunes For Two**	1965	8.00	20.00
RCA Victor LSP-3336	(S)	**Tunes For Two**	1965	10.00	25.00
RCA Victor LPM-3395	(M)	**Constant Sorrow**	1965	8.00	20.00
RCA Victor LSP-3395	(S)	**Constant Sorrow**	1965	10.00	25.00
RCA Victor LPM-3479	(M)	**The Best Of Bobby Bare**	1965	8.00	20.00
RCA Victor LSP-3479	(S)	**The Best Of Bobby Bare**	1965	10.00	25.00
RCA Victor LPM-3515	(M)	**Talk Me Some Sense**	1966	8.00	20.00
RCA Victor LSP-3515	(S)	**Talk Me Some Sense**	1966	10.00	25.00
RCA Victor LPM-3618	(M)	**The Streets Of Baltimore**	1966	8.00	20.00
RCA Victor LSP-3618	(S)	**The Streets Of Baltimore**	1966	10.00	25.00
RCA Victor LPM-3688	(M)	**This I Believe**	1966	8.00	20.00
RCA Victor LSP-3688	(S)	**This I Believe**	1966	10.00	25.00
RCA Victor LPM-3764	(M)	**The Game Of Triangles**	1967	10.00	25.00
RCA Victor LSP-3764	(S)	**The Game Of Triangles**	1967	8.00	20.00
RCA Victor LPM-3831	(M)	**A Bird Named Yesterday**	1967	10.00	25.00
RCA Victor LSP-3831	(S)	**A Bird Named Yesterday**	1967	8.00	20.00
RCA Victor LPM-3896	(M)	**The English Country Side**	1967	10.00	25.00
RCA Victor LSP-3896	(S)	**The English Country Side**	1967	8.00	20.00
RCA Victor LPM-3994	(M)	**The Best Of Bobby Bare, Volume II**	1968	12.00	30.00
RCA Victor LSP-3994	(S)	**The Best Of Bobby Bare, Volume II**	1968	6.00	15.00
		—RCA albums above have black labels.—			
RCA Victor DJL1-0079	(DJ)	**Singing In The Kitchen—**			
		The Bobby Bare & Family Radio Show	1974	10.00	25.00
BARE, BOBBY, & SKEETER DAVIS					
RCA Victor LPM-3336	(M)	**Tunes For Two**	1965	8.00	20.00
RCA Victor LSP-3336	(S)	**Tunes For Two**	1965	10.00	25.00
		—RCA albums above have black labels.—			
BARGE, GENE					
Checker LP-2994	(M)	**Dance With Daddy G**	1965	20.00	50.00
BARKER, WARREN					
Warner Bros. W-1205	(M)	**"The King And I" For Orchestra**	1958	10.00	25.00
Warner Bros. WS-1205	(S)	**"The King And I" For Orchestra**	1958	12.00	30.00
Warner Bros. W-1289	(M)	**77 Sunset Strip**	1959	16.00	40.00
Warner Bros. WS-1289	(S)	**77 Sunset Strip**	1959	20.00	50.00
Warner Bros. W-1290	(M)	**TV Guide—Top Television Themes**	1959	12.00	30.00
Warner Bros. WS-1290	(S)	**TV Guide—Top Television Themes**	1959	16.00	40.00
Warner Bros. W-1308	(M)	**William Holden Presents**			
		A Musical Touch Of Far Away Places	1959	12.00	30.00

Label & Catalog #		Title	Year	VG+	NM
Warner Bros. WS-1308	(S)	**William Holden Presents**			
		A Musical Touch Of Far Away Places	1959	16.00	40.00
Warner Bros. W-1331	(M)	**Warren Barker Is In**	1959	8.00	20.00
Warner Bros. WS-1331	(S)	**Warren Barker Is In**	1959	10.00	25.00
BARNES, GEORGE					
Decca DL-8658	(M)	**Guitars By George**	1957	16.00	40.00
BARNES, J. J., & STEVE MANCHA					
Volt VOS-6001	(S)	**Rare Stamps**	1969	10.00	25.00
BARNETT, BOBBY					
Sims LP-198	(M)	**Bobby Barnett At The World Famous**			
		Crystal Palace, Tombstone, Arizona	1964	10.00	25.00
Sims LPS-198	(S)	**Bobby Barnett At The World Famous**			
		Crystal Palace, Tombstone, Arizona	1964	12.00	30.00
BAROQUES, THE					
Chess LP-1516	(M)	**The Baroques**	1967	20.00	50.00
Chess LPS-1516	(S)	**The Baroques**	1967	30.00	75.00
BARRACUDAS, THE					
Justice JLP-143	(M)	**A Plane View**	1968	200.00	400.00
BARRIER BROTHERS, THE					
Philips PHM-200-003	(M)	**Golden Bluegrass Hits**	1962	10.00	25.00
Philips PHS-600-003	(S)	**Golden Bluegrass Hits**	1962	12.00	30.00
Philips PHM-200-049	(M)	**More Golden Bluegrass Hits**	1962	10.00	25.00
Philips PHS-600-049	(S)	**More Golden Bluegrass Hits**	1962	12.00	30.00
Philips PHM-200-083	(M)	**Gospel Songs, Bluegrass Style**	1962	10.00	25.00
Philips PHS-600-083	(S)	**Gospel Songs, Bluegrass Style**	1962	12.00	30.00
BARRY, GENE					
RCA Victor LPM-2975	(M)	**The Star Of "Burke's Law"**			
		Sings Of Love And Things	1964	10.00	25.00
RCA Victor LSP-2975	(S)	**The Star Of "Burke's Law"**			
		Sings Of Love And Things	1964	14.00	35.00
BARRY, LEN					
Len Barry was formerly a member of The Dovells.					
Decca DL-4720	(M)	**1-2-3**	1965	12.00	30.00
Decca DL-74720	(S)	**1-2-3** *("Lip Sync" is rechanneled)*	1965	16.00	40.00
RCA Victor LPM-3823	(M)	**My Kind Of Soul**	1967	10.00	25.00
RCA Victor LSP-3823	(S)	**My Kind Of Soul**	1967	8.00	20.00
BARRY, MARGARET					
Margaret Barry is a traditonal Irish street singer and banjo player.					
Riverside RLP-12-602	(M)	**Songs Of An Irish Tinker Lady**	195?	12.00	30.00
BARRY & BARRY					
Barry McGuire and Barry Kane, both of The New Christy Minstrels.					
Horizon WP-1608	(M)	**Here And Now!**	1962	10.00	25.00
Horizon ST-1608	(M)	**Here And Now!**	1962	12.00	30.00
BARRY & THE TAMERLANES					
Valiant LP-406	(M)	**I Wonder What She's Doing Tonight**	1963	80.00	200.00
Valiant LPS-406	(S)	**I Wonder What She's Doing Tonight**	1963	300.00	500.00
BARTHOLOMEW, DAVE					
Imperial LP-9162	(M)	**Fats Domino Presents David Bartholomew**	1961	40.00	100.00
Imperial LP-12076	(S)	**Fats Domino Presents David Bartholomew**	1961	60.00	150.00
Imperial LP-9217	(M)	**New Orleans House Party**	1963	40.00	100.00
Imperial LP-12217	(S)	**New Orleans House Party**	1963	60.00	150.00

BARTLEY, CHARLENE: *Refer to* GOLDMINE'S PRICE GUIDE TO COLLECTIBLE JAZZ ALBUMS

BARTON, BILLY: *Refer to* JOHNNY HORTON / BILLY BARTON / DON HUGHES

Label & Catalog #		Title	Year	VG+	NM
BARTON BROTHERS, THE					
Jalyn JLP-139	(M)	**Virginia Bluegrass**	196?	10.00	25.00
BASKERVILLE HOUNDS, THE					
Dot DLP-3823	(M)	**The Baskerville Hounds**	1967	16.00	40.00
Dot DLP-25823	(S)	**The Baskerville Hounds**	1967	20.00	50.00
BASS, FONTELLA					
Checker LP-2997	(M)	**The New Look**	1966	30.00	75.00
Checker LPS-2997	(S)	**The New Look**	1966	40.00	100.00
— Checker albums above have blue labels with red & black checkers on top.—					
Checker LP-2997	(M)	**The New Look**	1967	14.00	35.00
Checker LPS-2997	(S)	**The New Look**	1967	20.00	50.00
— Checker albums above have blue & white labels.—					
Paula LPS-2203	(S)	**Free**	1972	12.00	30.00
BASSEY, SHIRLEY					
MGM E-3834	(M)	**The Bewitching Miss Bassey**	1960	8.00	20.00
MGM SE-3834	(S)	**The Bewitching Miss Bassey**	1960	10.00	25.00
MGM E-3862	(M)	**The Fabulous Shirley Bassey**	1961	8.00	20.00
MGM SE-3862	(S)	**The Fabulous Shirley Bassey**	1961	10.00	25.00
United Arts. UAL-3169	(M)	**Shirley Bassey**	1962	8.00	20.00
United Arts. UAS-6169	(S)	**Shirley Bassey**	1962	10.00	25.00
United Arts. UAL-3237	(M)	**Shirley Bassey Sings The Hit From "Oliver"** **(& 11 Other Musical Tunes)**	1962	8.00	20.00
United Arts. UAS-6237	(S)	**Shirley Bassey Sings The Hit From "Oliver"** **(& 11 Other Musical Tunes)**	1962	10.00	25.00
United Arts. SP-104	(DJ)	**The Sassy Miss Bassey**	196?	10.00	25.00
BATTERED ORNAMENTS					
Harvest SKAO-422	(S)	**Mantle-Piece**	1970	16.00	40.00
BAUGH, PHIL					
Longhorn LP-002	(M)	**Country Guitar**	1965	24.00	60.00
Toro T-502	(M)	**Country Guitar II**	1965	16.00	40.00
Era ES-801	(S)	**California Guitar**	196?	12.00	30.00

BAXTER, LES

Les Baxter's earl;y work stands as the precursor to what is now referred to as "exotic music." His other efforts in this rather esoteric field including acting as Yma Sumac's original producer and writing many of the songs that made Martin Denny a success. . .

Capitol H-288	(10")	**Le Sacre Du Sauvage**	1952	40.00	100.00
Capitol H-???	(10")	**Music Out Of The Moon**	195?	40.00	100.00
Capitol H-???	(10")	**Music For Peace Of Mind**	195?	40.00	100.00
Capitol T-288	(M)	**Le Sacre Du Sauvage**	1954	20.00	50.00
Capitol T-390	(M)	**Music Out Of The Moon /** **Music For Peace Of Mind**	1954	20.00	50.00
Capitol T-474	(M)	**Thinking Of You**	1954	20.00	50.00
Capitol LAL-486	(M)	**The Passions**	1954	20.00	50.00
Capitol T-594	(M)	**Kaleidoscope**	1955	20.00	50.00
Capitol T-655	(M)	**Tamboo!**	1956	20.00	50.00
Capitol T-733	(M)	**Caribbean Moonlight**	1956	20.00	50.00
Capitol T-774	(M)	**Skins!**	1957	20.00	50.00
Capitol T-780	(M)	**'Round The World**	1957	20.00	50.00
Capitol T-843	(M)	**Midnight On The Cliffs**	1957	20.00	50.00
Capitol T-868	(M)	**Ports Of Pleasure**	1957	20.00	50.00
Capitol T-968	(M)	**Space Escapade**	1958	20.00	50.00
Capitol T-1012	(M)	**Selections From "South Pacific"**	1958	20.00	50.00
— Capitol albums above have turquoise or gray labels.—					
Capitol T-1293	(M)	**The Sacred Idol** *(Soundtrack)*	1960	20.00	50.00
Capitol ST-1293	(S)	**The Sacred Idol** *(Soundtrack)*	1960	30.00	75.00
Capitol T-1388	(M)	**Baxter's Best**	1960	12.00	30.00
Capitol DT-1388	(E)	**Baxter's Best**	1960	8.00	20.00
Capitol T-1537	(M)	**Jewels Of The Sea**	1961	10.00	25.00
Capitol ST-1537	(S)	**Jewels Of The Sea**	1961	12.00	30.00
Capitol T-1661	(M)	**The Sensational Les Baxter**	1962	10.00	25.00
Capitol ST-1661	(S)	**The Sensational Les Baxter**	1962	12.00	30.00
— Capitol albums above have black "rainbow" labels with the logo on the left.—					

Label & Catalog #		Title	Year	VG+	NM
American Inter. 100M	(M)	**Barbarian** (Soundtrack)	1960	20.00	50.00
American Inter. 100S	(M)	**Barbarian** (Soundtrack)	1960	40.00	100.00
		(A.I. 100 is the soundtrack for "Goliath And The Barbarian.")			
Vee Jay LP-6000	(M)	**Alakazam The Great** (Soundtrack)	1961	20.00	50.00
Reprise R-6079	(M)	**Academy Award Winners 1963 (& Other**			
		Outstanding Motion Picture Themes)	1963	10.00	25.00
Reprise R9-6079	(S)	**Academy Award Winners 1963 (& Other**			
		Outstanding Motion Picture Themes)	1963	12.00	30.00
Sidewalk ST-5919	(S)	**Hell's Belles** (Soundtrack)	1969	12.00	30.00
American Inter. STA-1028	(S)	**The Dunwich Horror** (Soundtrack)	1970	10.00	25.00
American Inter. STA-1029	(S)	**Bora, Bora** (Soundtrack)	1970	10.00	25.00
BAYSIDERS, THE					
Everest LPBR-5124	(M)	**Over The Rainbow**	1961	80.00	200.00
Everest BRST-5124	(S)	**Over The Rainbow**	1961	150.0	300.00
BE-BOP DELUXE					
Harvest SPRO-???	(DJ)	**Live! In The Air Age** (EP)	1977	12.00	30.00
Harvest SPRO-???	(DJ)	**Live Kicks** (EP)	1977	12.00	30.00
Harvest SPRO-8531	(DJ)	**Be-Bop's Biggest** (EP)	1978	12.00	30.00

BEACH BOYS, THE
Original members were Brian Wilson with brothers Carl and Dennis, cousin Mike Love, and neighbor Al Jardine. Jardine left in 1963 and returned in 1964, replaced during that time by David Marks. With Brian's increasing involvement in producing the group's albums, his role in the touring band was filled by Bruce Johnston. Johnston left in 1971 over difficulties with management; he returned in 1978. From 1971 through 1973, Rickie Fataar and Blondie Chaplin, formerly of The Flame, were Beach Boys.

The group initially laid down a set of tracks in the tiny studios of Hite Morgan; their first single, "Surfin'" / "Luau," was issued on Morgan's "X" and Candix labels in November 1961. They also released a second Morgan single on Randy as Kenny & The Cadets. After signing with Capitol in '62, their early recordings languished until the end of the decades, when they were issued on the budget label, Era. They have since appeared on sundry labels, several of which are hard to find. The first section below lists several of those albums; note that along with the Candix and Randy sides, there are several outtakes and filler from other Morgan groups.

The Beach Boys were produced by Brian Wilson through 1967, although Capitol staff producer is credited on the first two albums and the group is credited on "Smiley Smile" and "Wild Honey." Brian is virtually deaf in one ear so he works exclusively in mono; stereo mixes that exist during this time were done by engineer Chuck Britz. Capitol 1890, 1981, 2164 and 2198 were issued completely in stereo; 1998, 2027 and 2110 are partially stereo. The other albums—1808, 2269, 2354, 2398, 2458, 2545, 2813, 2859 and Brother 9001—are "duophonically" (sic) rechanneled. On SKAO-133 "Do It Again" and "Time To Get Alone" are rechanneled while the original 1966 tracks for "Our Prayer" and "Cabinessence" are mono with additional stereo overdubs.

The listings of the group's Capitol catalog below include every known variation of the original black rainbow label, record club versions and other important reissues. Several albums remained in print through the '70s and '80s; the prefix was changed to "SM" and at least five albums were reissued with a yellow label. In the early '80s several albums—including the long out of print post '66 tiles—were reinstated as part of the label's budget series (the 16000 series with green labels). At this time, most of these reissues are easily found. . .

For more listtings refer to Annette; Jan & Dean; Mike Love & Dean Torrence; Brian Wilson; Carl Wilson; Dennis Wilson; and Murray Wilson. The interested reader can peruse the Capitol listings in the Various Artists section and safely assume that any surf or hot rod compilation features The Beach Boys. Of particlular note are 1918 (the first Shut Down, an automotive sampler compiled without the group's knowledge and from whence Shut Down, Volume 2 derived its name) and both 1995 and 2024 along with PRO 2396 and 2480. These albums could easily function as Beach Boys titles.

1. The Capitol Years, 1962-69

Capitol T-1808	(M)	**Surfin' Safari**	1962	20.00	50.00
Capitol DT-1808	(E)	**Surfin' Safari**	1962	40.00	100.00
		(Original pressings of DT-1808 have covers that read			
		"Full Dimensional Stereo" across the top.)			
Capitol DT-1808	(E)	**Surfin' Safari**	1962	16.00	40.00
		(Later covers have the correct "Duophonic" banner across the top.)			

Label & Catalog #		Title	Year	VG+	NM
Capitol DT-1808	(E)	**Surfin' Safari**	1962	80.00	200.00
		(Some pressings of DT-1808 have covers with both the "Duophonic"			
		and the "Full Dimensional Stereo" banners across the top.)			
Capitol T-1890	(M)	**Surfin' U.S.A.**	1963	14.00	35.00
Capitol ST-1890	(S)	**Surfin' U.S.A.**	1963	20.00	50.00
Capitol T-1981	(M)	**Surfer Girl**	1963	14.00	35.00
Capitol ST-1981	(S)	**Surfer Girl**	1963	18.00	45.00
		(Original covers mention the influence of The Four Freshmen			
		style on "Your Summer Dreams" in the liner notes on the back.)			
Capitol T-1981	(M)	**Surfer Girl**	1963	16.00	40.00
Capitol ST-1981	(S)	**Surfer Girl**	1963	20.00	50.00
		(Later pressings make mention of "Their other new single-			
		record hit Little Deuce Coupe" in the liner notes on the back.)			
Capitol T-1998	(M)	**Little Deuce Coupe**	1963	14.00	35.00
Capitol ST-1998	(S)	**Little Deuce Coupe**	1963	18.00	45.00
Capitol T-2027	(M)	**Shut Down, Volume 2**	1964	14.00	35.00
Capitol ST-2027	(P)	**Shut Down, Volume 2**	1964	18.00	45.00
		("Fun, Fun, Fun" is a shorter, different mix on the stereo album.)			
Capitol T-2110	(M)	**All Summer Long**	1964	20.00	50.00
Capitol ST-2110	(S)	**All Summer Long**	1964	24.00	60.00
		(Original pressings of Capitol 2110 have front covers that erron-			
		eously list the last song on the album as "Don't Break Down.")			
Capitol T-2110	(M)	**All Summer Long**	1964	14.00	35.00
Capitol ST-2110	(P)	**All Summer Long**	1964	16.00	40.00
		(Later covers correctly lists the song as "Don't Back Down.")			
Capitol T-2164	(M)	**The Beach Boys' Christmas Album**	1964	14.00	35.00
Capitol ST-2164	(S)	**The Beach Boys' Christmas Album**	1964	16.00	40.00
		("Merry Christmas Baby" is 28 seconds longer on the stereo album			
		than on the mono.)			
Capitol PRO-3133	(DJ)	**The Beach Boys Christmas Special**	1964	300.00	600.00
		(Promotional radio show built around the group's new LP.)			
Capitol TAO-2198	(M)	**Beach Boys Concert**	1964	14.00	35.00
Capitol STAO-2198	(S)	**Beach Boys Concert**	1964	16.00	40.00
Capitol STAO-8-2198	(S)	**Beach Boys Concert** *(Record Club)*	1964	30.00	75.00
Capitol T-2269	(M)	**The Beach Boys Today!**	1965	16.00	40.00
Capitol DT-2269	(E)	**The Beach Boys Today!**	1965	14.00	35.00
Capitol DT-8-2269	(E)	**The Beach Boys Today!** *(Record Club)*	1965	30.00	75.00
Capitol T-2354	(M)	**Summer Days (And Summer Nights!!)**	1965	16.00	40.00
Capitol DT-2354	(E)	**Summer Days (And Summer Nights!!)**	1965	30.00	75.00
		(Original pressings of DT-2354 have covers that read			
		"Full Dimensional Stereo" across the top.)			
Capitol DT-2354	(E)	**Summer Days (And Summer Nights!!)**	1965	14.00	35.00
		(Later covers have the correct "Duophonic" banner across the top.)			
Capitol MAS-2398	(M)	**Beach Boys Party!**	1965	16.00	40.00
Capitol DMAS-2398	(E)	**Beach Boys Party!**	1965	12.00	30.00
		(Issued with a sheet of perforated, full-color wallet photos.)			
Capitol MAS-2398	(M)	**Beach Boys Party!** *(Without the photos)*	1965	14.00	35.00
Capitol DMAS-2398	(E)	**Beach Boys Party!** *(Without the photos)*	1965	10.00	25.00
Capitol T-2458	(M)	**Pet Sounds**	1966	14.00	35.00
Capitol DT-2458	(E)	**Pet Sounds**	1966	10.00	25.00
Capitol T-2545	(M)	**Best Of The Beach Boys, Volume 1**	1966	10.00	25.00
Capitol DT-2545	(E)	**Best Of The Beach Boys, Volume 1**	1966	8.00	20.00
		(Original pressings of Capitol 2545 have black "rainbow" label.)			
Capitol T-2545	(M)	**Best Of The Beach Boys, Volume 1**	1966	12.00	30.00
Capitol DT-2545	(E)	**Best Of The Beach Boys, Volume 1**	1966	10.00	25.00
		(Second pressings have black Starline labels.)			
Capitol T-2545	(M)	**Best Of The Beach Boys, Volume 1**	1967	16.00	40.00
Capitol DT-2545	(E)	**Best Of The Beach Boys, Volume 1**	1967	6.00	15.00
		(Thirs pressings have red & white "bullseye" Starline labels.)			
Capitol DT-2545	(E)	**Best Of The Beach Boys, Volume 1**	1969	10.00	25.00
		(Fourth pressings of DY-2545 fave red & white "star" Starline label.)			
Capitol T-2580	(M)	**Smile**	1966		See below
Capitol DT-2580	(E)	**Smile**	1966		See below
		("Smile" remains Brian Wilson's legendary unreleased masterpiece.			
		For Christmas 1966 Capitol printed 400,000 front and back cover			
		slicks and a similar number of booklets with graphics and lyrics.			
		Both the cover slicks and the booklets are priced separately below.			
		Note: Reproductions of both are in circulation.)			

Examples of two different types of printing errors that can turn an album into a collectible: In the case of Surfin' Safari, *the machine that applies the front and back cover slicks goofed and the "Full Dimensional Stereo" banner that should be covered by the "Duophonic" banner ended up beneath it! More interesting is the erroneous crediting of a song on* All Summer Long: *The cover reads "Don't Break Down" instead of "Don't Back Down." Prophetically, the song's writer, head Beach Boy Brian Wilson was to suffer a mild nervous breakdown shortly afterwards. . .*

Label & Catalog #		Title	Year	VG+	NM
Capitol T/DT-2580		**Smile Cover Slick**	1966		*See below*
		(Front/back cover slicks for "Smile" are rare with a			
		a suggested Near Mint value of $500-1,500.)			
Capitol T/DT-2580		**Smile Bonus Book**	1966	100.00	300.00
Capitol T-2706	(M)	**Best Of The Beach Boys, Volume 2**	1967	10.00	25.00
Capitol DT-2706	(E)	**Best Of The Beach Boys, Volume 2**	1967	6.00	15.00
		(Red & white "bullseye" Starline label.)			
Brother T-9001	(M)	**Smiley Smile**	1967	12.00	30.00
Brother ST-9001	(E)	**Smiley Smile**	1967	8.00	20.00
		(Original pressings of Brother 9001 do not credit			
		Barry Turnbull on the back cover.)			
Brother T-9001	(M)	**Smiley Smile**	1967	10.00	25.00
Brother ST-9001	(E)	**Smiley Smile**	1967	6.00	15.00
		(Later pressings read "Title for this album by Barry Turnbull"			
		on the back cover)			
Capitol TCL-2813	(M)	**The Beach Boys Deluxe Set** *(3 LP box)*	1967	80.00	200.00
		(The mono box has a black border and contains standard copies			
		of the albums with a "T" prefix.)			
Capitol DTCL-2813	(E)	**The Beach Boys Deluxe Set** *(3 LP box)*	1967	30.00	75.00
		(The stereo box has a maroon border and contains custom copies			
		of the albums with a "DTCL" prefix.)			
Capitol DTCL-8-2813	(E)	**The Beach Boys Deluxe Set** *(Record Club)*	1967	100.00	250.00
		(The stereo box has a blue border and contains custom copies			
		of the albums with a "DTCL" prefix.)			
Capitol T-2859	(M)	**Wild Honey**	1967	12.00	30.00
Capitol ST-2859	(E)	**Wild Honey**	1967	8.00	20.00
Capitol ST-8-2891	(E)	**Smiley Smile** *(Record Club)*	1968	150.00	300.00
Capitol DKAO-2893	(E)	**Stack O' Tracks** *(With booklet)*	1968	20.00	50.00
Capitol DKAO-2893	(E)	**Stack O' Tracks** *(Without booklet)*	1968	16.00	40.00
Capitol DKAO-8-2893	(E)	**Stack O' Tracks** *(Record Club with booklet)*	1968	60.00	150.00
Capitol ST-2895	(S)	**Friends**	1968	10.00	25.00
Capitol SKAO-133	(P)	**20/20** *(Gatefold cover)*	1969	10.00	25.00
		(Original pressings of SKAO-138 have black "rainbow" labels.)			
Capitol SKAO-133	(P)	**20/20** *(Gatefold cover)*	1969	12.00	30.00
		(Later pressings have red & white "star" Starline label.)			
Capitol SKAO-8-0133	(P)	**20/20** *(Record Club. Black label)*	1969	16.00	40.00
Capitol SKAO-8-0133	(P)	**20/20** *(Record Club. Green label)*	197?	20.00	50.00
Capitol SWBB-253	(E)	**Close-Up** *(2 LPs. Black rainbow label)*	1969	10.00	25.00
Capitol SWBB-253	(E)	**Close-Up** *(2 LPs. Green label)*	197?	16.00	40.00
Sears SPS-609	(E)	**Summertime Blues**	1970	20.00	50.00
Capitol ST-442	(P)	**Good Vibrations** *(Green label)*	1970	10.00	25.00
Capitol DT-8-442	(P)	**Good Vibrations** *(Record Club)*	1970	10.00	25.00
Capitol STBB-500	(E)	**All Summer Long / California Girls** *(2 LPs)*	1970	10.00	25.00
		(Lime label. Two single albums, edited versions of 2110 and			
		2354, bound together with a Special Double Play sticker.			
Capitol STBB-500	(E)	**All Summer Long / California Girls** *(2 LPs)*	1970	12.00	30.00
		(Orange label with a purple "C" on top. This is two single			
		albums bound together with a Special Double Play sticker.)			
Capitol SF-702/DF-703	(P)	**Fun, Fun, Fun / Dance, Dance, Dance** *(2 LPs.)*	1971	12.00	30.00
		(Orange label with a purple "C" on top. This is two single			
		albums bound together with a Special Double Play sticker.)			

3. The Brother/Reprise Years, 1970-1978

Label & Catalog #		Title	Year	VG+	NM
Reprise RS-6382	(S)	**Sunflower** *(White label promo)*	1970	16.00	40.00
Reprise RS-6382	(S)	**Sunflower** *(Orange label)*	1970	30.00	75.00
Reprise SKAO-93352	(S)	**Sunflower** *(Capitol Record Club)*	1970	60.00	150.00
Reprise RS-6453	(S)	**Surf's Up** *(White label promo with insert)*	1971	16.00	40.00
Asylum R-113793	(S)	**Surf's Up** *(RCA Record Club)*	1971	60.00	150.00
Reprise 2MS-2083	(S)	**Carl And The Passion-So Tough /**			
		Pet Sounds *(2 LPs. White label promo)*	1972	20.00	50.00
Reprise 2MS-2083	(S)	**Carl And The Passion-So Tough /**			
		Pet Sounds *(2 LPs)*	1972	10.00	25.00
		(While "So Tough" is in stereo, "Pet Sounds" is in mono.)			
Reprise MS-2118	(S)	**Holland** *(Test pressing with "We Got Love")*	1973	300.00	500.00
Reprise MS-2118	(S)	**Holland** *(White label promo)*	1973	16.00	40.00
		(The value includes a white label promo 7" mini-LP,			
		"Mt. Vernon & Fairway," with picture sleeve.)			

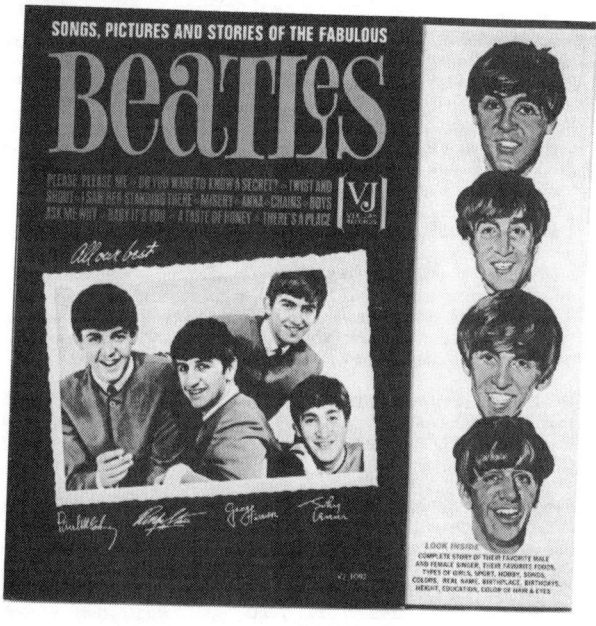

After Capitol turned down the option to pick up the first album (Please Please Me, EMI/Parlophone, 1963) by the soon-to-be world's greatest faverave most popular ever group, Vee Jay picked up the rights and issued Introducing The Beatles for the Christmas season of '63. When the Fab Four broke loose in '64, the little label from Chicago flooded the market with a veritable potpourri of Beatles albums, all using the same fourteen tracks in one configuration after another. These two were the most popular with sales of Introducing impossible to estimate due to the plethora of unauthorized pressings—probably from Vee Jay after they lost their rights to the material—and out-and-out counterfeits, all of which found their way onto the retail racks of America. So, if you are not experienced, beware, as there are more phonies than originals on the collectors market. . .

Label & Catalog #		Title	Year	VG+	NM
Reprise 2MS-6484	(S)	**Beach Boys In Concert** *(2 LPs. White label)*	1973	**16.00**	**40.00**
Reprise 2MS-2166	(E)	**Wild Honey / 20/20** *(2 LPs. Promo label.)*	1974	**12.00**	**30.00**
Reprise 2MS-2167	(S)	**Friends / Smiley Smile** *(2 LPs. Promo label)*	1974	**12.00**	**30.00**
Reprise *(No number)*	(DJ)	**The Beach Boys Radio Special Promo Spot**	1976	**20.00**	**50.00**

— Reprise albums above have yellow labels without the Warner Communication logo.—

BEACON STREET UNION
The Beacon Street Union later recorded as Eagle.

MGM E-4517	(M)	**The Eyes Of The Beacon Street Union**	1968	**10.00**	**25.00**
MGM SE-4517	(S)	**The Eyes Of The Beacon Street Union**	1968	**12.00**	**30.00**
MGM SE-4568	(S)	**The Clown Died In Marvin Gardens**	1968	**12.00**	**30.00**

BEALE STREET SHEIKS, THE: *Refer to* **THE MISSISSIPPI SHEIKS / THE BEALE STREET SHEIKS**

BEAN, ORSON
Fantasy F-7009	(M)	**Orson Bean At The Hungry i** *(Red vinyl)*	1960	**20.00**	**50.00**
Fantasy F-7009	(M)	**Orson Bean At The Hungry i**	1960	**10.00**	**25.00**

BEASLEY, JIMMY
Modern LMP-1214	(M)	**The Fabulous Jimmy Beasley**	1956	**200.00**	**400.00**
Crown CLP-5014	(M)	**The Fabulous Jimmy Beasley**	1957	**60.00**	**150.00**
Crown CLP-5247	(M)	**Twist With Jimmy Beasley**	1961	**20.00**	**50.00**
Crown CST-247	(E)	**Twist With Jimmy Beasley**	1961	**8.00**	**20.00**

(Crown 5014 and 5247 are reissues of Modern 1214.)

BEAT OF THE EARTH
Ardish AS-001	(S)	**Beat Of The Earth**	196?	**150.00**	**300.00**

BEATLES, THE
Prior to international stardom, John Lennon, Paul McCartney and George Harrison with drummer Pete Best backed up Tony Sheridan on a number of studio sessions recorded in Hamburg, Germany, in 1961 (they were billed as "The Beat Brothers"). After the group's initial U.S. success in 1964, a number of companies recycled these sessions on various 45s and LPs. By 1962 Mr. Best was history and Richard Starkey, a.k.a. Ringo Starr, was about to make history as The Beatles' irrepressible drummer. Their now legendary audition for Decca Records (who, ahem, saw no commercial potential in a British beat group) made the rounds of various labels after a copyright lapse in 1982. For chronological purposes, the Decca and Hamburg material (including live recordings) are listed below in Section 1, "Early Recordings 1962."

The group finally signed with Parlophone, an EMI subsidiary, which was both a last ditch effort (Parlophone was a budget label with no major stars to claim) and arguably their greatest stroke of luck, as it placed them under the talented and sympathetic wing of staff producer George Martin. After taking most of the civilized world by storm in 1963, EMI offered them to their American licensee, Capitol, who, like Decca U.K., saw no reason to bite. Consequently, their first recordings ended up on a variety of smaller, independent U.S. labels, the most significant being Vee Jay (aside from being the only label to have enough material to issue an LP).

Section 2, "Vee Jay 1963-1964," lists the many attempts of that company to successfully package the fourteen tracks to which they possessed the rights. As Vee Jay issued mono albums with stereo labels, check for an "S" suffix on the master number in the trail-off vinyl. Also, many counterfeits of the Vee Jay albums exist.

Section 3, "Capitol Originals 1964-1967," covers the main period of the group's history in this country. During this time all of the group's new recordings were issued on Capitol, who had finally picked up their option on the group's American releases in late 1963, except the new songs prepared for the film "A Hard Day's Night," to which United Artists had the rights in this country. So the third section collects the Capitol releases, including later pressings, and Capitol Record Club issues (designated with an "8" added to their catalogue number), along with the United Artists material. This section also includes what must surely be the most collectible album in the world, the now-legendary Beatles butcher cover. . .

These albums were all issued on Capitol's classic black label with the rainbow perimeter. This particular label is not to be confused with two later permutations: The original '60s version has the perimeter data along the bottom in white print on the black label and reads "Mfd. by Capitol Records, Inc., U.S.A." A second version of this label, used briefly in 1969, is identical to the above except the perimeter data reads "Mfd. by Capitol Records, Inc. A Subsidiary of Capitol Industries, Inc. U.S.A." After undergoing several major color changes through the next fourteen years, Capitol returned to the black label in 1983 except this time the perimeter data was in black print in the rainbow.

Label & Catalog #		Title	Year	VG+	NM

With the formation of their own Apple Records in 1968, things become complicated: Aside from new titles being issued exclusively on Apple (listed in Section 5, "Apple Originals, 1968-1973"), the earlier catalog titles were kept in print on Capitol and reissued on Apple with the same covers and catalog numbers. Further complicating matters is the fact that early pressings of the Apple reissues can be found inside Capitol covers. (And, for the O/C, later copies of Meet The Beatles, The Beatles' Second Album, Beatles '65, Beatles VI and "Yesterday" ...And Today can be found with and without the RIAA Gold Record seal on the cover.) The reissues can be found in Section 4, "Capitol & Apple Reissues 1968-1974."

After the collapse of Apple, the material reverted to Capitol and has remained in print since. From 1976-78 the entire catalog of albums were reissued with an orange label followed by a purple label during 1978-83. From 1983-88 the company brought back the black rainbow label (noted above). It was during this time that Capitol issued the Parlophone versions for the first time. Finally, in 1988, a second purple label was used and all of the albums were reissued, this time with new catalog numbers (the Parlophone versions were also in print on this label). While these variations are nor listed below, most are readily found in shops and shows fetching $6-12 each. Note: The orange label pressings and the latter purple label issues are quickly escalating in value and may bring $15 or more from completists.

Section 6, "Capitol Repackagings 1976-1984," lists the new titles composed of previously released material including Capitol's finally releasing the original Parlophone versions of the first seven albums. Section 7, "Miscellaneous Releases," collects a few odds 'n' ends while while Section 8 collect the Original Master Recording and Ultra High Quality Recording audiophile releases from Mobile Fidelity Sound Labs.

Approximately half of three albums— "A Hard Day's Night," "Help!" and "Yellow Submarine"— contain incidental soundtrack music by George Martin's Orchestra. A number of Beatles recordings are rather difficult to track down in stereo, especially if the reader has a basic collection made up of the American albums. For more information on how to assemble a more or less complete stereo catalog, refer to the appendix "The Beatles Uncommon Stereo."

In the wake of 1964's Beatlemania in the U.S., the inevitable exploitation of the group, their sound and their image, commenced with a vengeance. While countless artists recorded Lennon-McCartney songs and several entire albums of the Fabs' music, it is the "exploitation records" that attract some collectors interest. For those with a taste for the obscure, the hilarious, the offensive and, occasionally, the creative, refer to The Beagle & The Four Liverpool Whigs; The Bearcuts; Beat-A-Mania; The Beatle Buddies; The Beats; Pete Best (yes, he was a Beatle briefly but this is exploitational nonetheless); The Blue Beats; B. Brock & The Sultans; The Buggs; Louise Harrison Caldwell (George's sister tells all); The Liverpool Lads; The Liverpools; The Merseybeats; The Merseyboys; Sing Along With The Beatles; The Sparrows; and The Weasels. Also refer to Elvis Presley / The Silver Beatles.

Note: The Beatles are the single most collectible group in the hobby; every variation in sound, label or cover is pursued, documented and valued among aficionados. While the listings here are more than adequate for most dealers and collectors to assess their acquisitions, they may be less so for the completist. I recommend The Beatles Price Guide For American Records by Perry Cox and Joe Lindsay. For more information on this book, contact Perry Cox Ent., P.O. Box 82278, Phoenix, AZ 85071.

1. Early Recordings 1962

—*Tony Sheridan Sessions*—

Label & Catalog #		Title	Year	VG+	NM
Savage BM-69	(M)	**The Savage Young Beatles**	1964	80.00	200.00
		(This album of dubious legality collects Tony Sheridan material with and without The Beat Brothers. Orange label and a yellow cover. Counterfeits have "Stereo" in the upper right corner of the cover.)			
Savage BM-69	(M)	**The Savage Young Beatles**	1964		See below
		(Some copies have a yellow label and a glossy orange cover. Rare with a suggested Near Mint value of $1,500-2,000.)			
Atco 33-169	(DJ)	**Ain't She Sweet** *(White label promo)*	1964	600.00	1,200.00
Atco 33-169	(M)	**Ain't She Sweet**	1964	150.00	300.00
Atco SD-33-169	(S)	**Ain't She Sweet**	1964	175.00	350.00
		(Original stereo pressings have purple & brown labels.)			
Atco SD-33-169	(S)	**Ain't She Sweet**	1969	300.00	500.00
		(Later pressings have yellow labels with a white border on the cover.)			
MGM E-4215	(M)	**The Beatles With Tony Sheridan & Their Guests & Others**	1964	80.00	200.00
MGM SE-4215	(S)	**The Beatles With Tony Sheridan & Their Guests & Others**	1964	300.00	500.00
MGM E-4215	(M)	**The Beatles With Tony Sheridan & Their Guests**	1964	60.00	150.00
MGM SE-4215	(S)	**The Beatles With Tony Sheridan & Their Guests**	1964	300.00	600.00
		(Later pressings drop "& Others" from the cover title.)			

Label & Catalog #		Title	Year	VG+	NM
Metro M-563	(M)	**This Is Where It Started**	1966	**40.00**	**100.00**
Metro MS-563	(S)	**This Is Where It Started**	1966	**50.00**	**125.00**
		(Metro 563 is a reissue of MGM 4215.)			
Clarion 601	(M)	**The Amazing Beatles**			
		& Other Great English Group Sounds	1966	**40.00**	**100.00**
Clarion SD-601	(S)	**The Amazing Beatles**			
		& Other Great English Group Sounds	1966	**30.00**	**175.00**
		(Clarion 601 is a reissue of Atco 169.)			
Polydor SKAO-93199	(S)	**The Beatles Circa 1960—In The Beginning**			
		Featuring Tony Sheridan *(Record Club)*	1970	**16.00**	**40.00**
Polydor PD-4504	(S)	**In The Beginning: The Beatles**	197?	**16.00**	**40.00**
		(This rare reissue alters the LP's title on the record label.)			

— Live In Germany —

Lingasong LS-2-7001	(DJ)	**Live! At The Star-Club In Hamburg,**			
		Germany; 1962 *(2 LPs. Blue vinyl)*	1977	**175.00**	**350.00**
Lingasong LS-2-7001	(DJ)	**Live! At The Star-Club In Hamburg,**			
		Germany; 1962 *(2 LPs. Red vinyl)*	1977	**100.00**	**250.00**
Lingasong LS-2-7001	(DJ)	**Live! At The Star-Club In Hamburg,**			
		Germany; 1962 *(2 LPs. Black vinyl)*	1977	**100.00**	**250.00**
		(White label promo with different running order for the tracks.)			
Lingasong LS-2-7001	(DJ)	**Live! At The Star-Club In Hamburg,**			
		Germany; 1962 *(2 LPs. Black vinyl)*	1977	**16.00**	**40.00**
Pickwick BAN-90051	(M)	**Recorded Live In Hamburg, Vol. 1**	1978	**14.00**	**35.00**
Pickwick BAN-90061	(M)	**Recorded Live In Hamburg, Vol. 2**	1978	**14.00**	**35.00**
Pickwick BAN-90071	(M)	**Recorded Live In Hamburg, Vol. 3**	1978	**20.00**	**50.00**
Hall Of Music HM1-2200	(M)	**Live 1962 Hamburg, Germany**	1981	**14.00**	**35.00**

— Decca Audition Sessions —

Backstage BSR-1111	(M)	**Like Dreamers Do** *(Gray vinyl promo)*	1982	**20.00**	**50.00**
Backstage BSR-1111	(M)	**Like Dreamers Do** *(White vinyl promo)*	1982	**20.00**	**50.00**
Backstage BSR-1111	(M)	**Like Dreamers Do** *(3 LPs)*	1982	**20.00**	**50.00**
		(Two picture discs, one an interview and one from the Decca sessions with a white vinyl LP that duplicates the Decca disc. Contains ten of the fifteen Decca audition tracks.)			
Backstage 2-201	(M)	**Like Dreamers Do** *(2 LPs)*	1982	**14.00**	**35.00**
		(Double album of the above with one picture disc and the white LP. Contains ten of the fifteen Decca audition tracks.)			
Pac UDL-2333	(M)	**Dawn Of The Silver Beatles**	1981	**30.00**	**75.00**
		(First pressings were hand numbered on the label and back cover. Contains ten of the fifteen Decca audition tracks.)			
Pac UDL-2333	(M)	**Dawn Of The Silver Beatles** *(With the card)*	1981	**30.00**	**75.00**
Pac UDL-2333	(M)	**Dawn Of The Silver Beatles** *(Without card)*	1981	**20.00**	**50.00**
		(Second pressings included numbered registration cards. Contains ten of the fifteen Decca audition tracks.)			
Audio Fidelity PD-339	(M)	**First Movement** *(Picture disc)*	1982	**16.00**	**40.00**
Orange ORC-12280	(M)	**The Silver Beatles** *(Half-speed master)*	1985	**150.00**	**300.00**
		(Test pressing in a plain jacket with a full-color cover-slick insert. Contains all fifteen of the Decca audition tracks.)			
Orange ORC-12280	(M)	**The Silver Beatles** *(Half-speed master)*	1985	**80.00**	**200.00**
		(Test pressing in a plain cardboard jacket with a title sticker. Contains all fifteen of the Decca audition tracks.)			

2. Vee Jay, 1963-1964 "Introducing The Beatles"

*Vee Jay 1062 may be the most counterfeited album ever released. There are so mnmay unauthorized reproductions at this point that they difficult to keep track of and more keep turning up. I will attempt here to delineate certain points to look for in real copies and tell-tale signs in the repros, but first, a little background. After the initial success of The Beatles in the UK, thier label, Parlophone, a budget subsidiary of EMI, optioned the group to its American lecensee, Capitol. who saw no reason to market a British beat group in the States. Vee Jay's contract to release Beatles material in the US was cancelled in August 1963 due to the company's inability to pay royalties on the minisculke sales of already released Beates product. Apparently either an agreement of sorts was reached or there was litigation involved, as Vee Jay continued to release Beatles recordings through much of 1964. The first version of **Introducing The Beatles** featured "Love Me Do" and "P.S. I Love You," two songs that was part of its legal problems. While the LP (with the two songs) had already been pressed as early as July, when the covers were manufactured later in the year, Vee Jay altered the planned back cover, which would have been similar to that of the EMI/Parlophone*

Label & Catalog #		Title	Year	VG+	NM
Vee Jay LP-1062	(M)	**Introducing The Beatles** ("Ad back")	1963		See below
Vee Jay SR-1062	(P)	**Introducing The Beatles** ("Ad back")	1963		See below
		(Includes "Love Me Do" and "P.S. I Love You." The back cover has ads for 25 other Vee Jay albums. Mono copies have a suggested Near Mint value of $3,000-4,000; stereo copies have a suggested Near Mint value of $8,000-12,000.)			
Vee Jay LP-1062	(M)	**Introducing The Beatles** ("Blank back")	1963	1,000.00	1,500.00
Vee Jay SR-1062	(P)	**Introducing The Beatles** ("Blank back")	1963	2,800.00	4,000.00
		(Includes "Love Me Do" and "P.S. I Love You." The back cover is completely blank.)			
Vee Jay LP-1062	(M)	**Introducing The Beatles**	1963	360.00	600.00
		(Includes "Love Me Do" and "P.S. I Love You." Black rainbow label with an oval logo. The back cover lists the song titles.)			
Vee Jay LP-1062	(M)	**Introducing The Beatles**	1963	500.00	800.00
		(Includes "Love Me Do" and "P.S. I Love You." Black rainbow label with a brackets logo. The back cover lists the song titles.)			
Vee Jay LP-1062	(M)	**Introducing The Beatles**	1964		See below
		(Second pressings of LP-1062 replace "Love Me Do" and "P.S. I Love You" with "Please Please Me" and "Ask Me Why." There are five label variations for the mono pressings: 1) a black "rainbow" label with the "Vee Jay" logo in an oval; 2) a black "rainbow" label with the "Vee Jay" logo in brackets; 3) a solid black label with a plain "VJ" logo; 4) a solid black label with the "VJ" logo in an oval; and 5) a solid black label with "VJ" logo in brackets. These mono variations have a suggested Near Mint value of $300-400 each.)			
Vee Jay SR-1062	(S)	**Introducing The Beatles**	1964		See below
		(Second pressings of SR-1062 replace "Love Me Do" and "P.S. I Love You" with "Please Please Me" and "Ask Me Why." There are three label variations for the stereo pressing: 1) a black "rainbow" label with a "Vee Jay" logo in an oval; 2) a black "rainbow" label with a "Vee Jay' logo in brackets; and 3) a solid black label with a plain "VJ" logo. These stereo variations s are very rare with a suggested Near Mint value of $1,500-2,500 each.)			
Vee Jay LP-1085	(M)	**The Beatles And Frank Ifield On Stage**	1964	100.00	250.00
Vee Jay LPS-1085	(P)	**The Beatles And Frank Ifield On Stage**	1964	300.00	500.00
		(The cover has a drawing of a Victorian gentleman with a Beatles haircut. Original covers have printing along the spine.)			
Vee Jay LP-1085	(M)	**The Beatles And Frank Ifield On Stage**	1964		See below
Vee Jay LPS-1085	(P)	**The Beatles And Frank Ifield On Stage**	1964		See below
		(The cover has a full-color, painted portrait of John, Paul, George, and Ringo There are three label variations for both the mono and stereo pressings; 1) a black "rainbow" label with a "Vee Jay" logo in an oval; 2) a black "rainbow" label with a "Vee Jay" logo in brackets; and 3) a solid black label with silver print. While the monos have a suggested Near Mint value of $3,000-5,000 while stereo copies have a suggested NM value of $8,000-12,000.)			
Vee Jay DX-30	(M)	**The Beatles Vs. The Four Seasons** (2 LPs)	1964		See below
Vee Jay DXS-30	(M)	**The Beatles Vs. The Four Seasons** (2 LPs)	1964		See below
		(Vee Jay 30 repackages 1065, "Golden Hits Of The Four Seasons," with the second version of 1062 that includes "Please Please Me" and "Ask Me Why." Original front covers must read "Free Bonus 8" x 15" Full Color Beatle Picture Suitable For Framing," worth an additional $300 in NM.. The mono version has a suggested NM value of $500-1,000 while the stereo pressing is very rare with a suggested NM value of $$2,500-3,500.)			
Vee Jay VJ-1092	(M)	**Songs, Pictures And Stories Of The Fabulous Beatles** (Gatefold cover)	1964		See below
Vee Jay VJS-1092	(S)	**Songs, Pictures And Stories Of The Fabulous Beatles** (Gatefold cover)	1964		See below
		(Vee Jay 1092 is a repackage of the second version of Vee Jay 1062. The front flap of the gatefold cover is 8" wide thus exposing drawings of the four mop- tops printed on the inner cover. There are three label variations for both the mono and stereo pressings; 1) a black "rainbow" label with a "Vee Jay" logo in an oval; 2) a black "rainbow" label with a "Vee Jay" logo in brackets; and 3) a solid black label with silver print. While the monos have a suggested Near Mint value of $300-400 each, the stereo versions are very rare with a suggested NM value of $1,500-2,500 each.)			

Label & Catalog #		Title	Year	VG+	NM
Vee Jay PRO-202	(DJ)	**Hear The Beatles Tell All** (White label)	1964		See note below
		(PRO-202 is rare with a suggested NM value of $6,000-10,000.)			
Vee Jay PRO-202	(M)	**Hear The Beatles Tell All**	1964	60.00	150.00
		(Original pressings have black rainbow labels. Counterfeits have plain black labels and no print on the spine of the cover.)			
Vee Jay 202	(M)	**Hear The Beatles Tell All**	1964	100.00	250.00
		(Later pressings have black rainbow labels but drop the "PRO" prefix from the catalog number.)			

3. Capitol Originals 1964-1967

Label & Catalog #		Title	Year	VG+	NM
Capitol T-2047	(M)	**Meet The Beatles**	1964	60.00	150.00
Capitol ST-2047	(P)	**Meet The Beatles**	1964	30.00	75.00
		(Original covers for Capitol 2047 have "Beatles!" in brown print.)			
Capitol T-2047	(M)	**Meet The Beatles**	1964	50.00	125.00
Capitol ST-2047	(P)	**Meet The Beatles**	1964	24.00	60.00
		(Later front covers have "Beatles!" in olive green print.)			
Capitol ST-8-2047	(P)	**Meet The Beatles** (Record Club)	1964	200.00	400.00
Capitol T-2080	(M)	**The Beatles' Second Album**	1964	60.00	150.00
Capitol ST-2080	(P)	**The Beatles' Second Album**	1964	24.00	60.00
Capitol ST-8-2080	(P)	**The Beatles' Second Album** (Record Club)	1964	300.00	500.00
United Artists SP-2359	(DJ)	**A Hard Day's Night Open-End Interview**	1964	1,000.00	1,500.00
		(Issued with a script in a plain cardboard jacket.)			
United Artists SP-2362	(DJ)	**A Hard Day's Night Radio Spots**	1964	800.00	1,200.00
		(Issued in a plain cardboard jacket.)			
United Artists UAL-3366	(DJ)	**A Hard Day's Night** (White label)	1964		See below
		(Rare with suggested values in collectible condition of 2,000-3,000.)			
United Artists UAL-3366	(M)	**A Hard Day's Night** (Soundtrack)	1964	80.00	200.00
		(Black label. The back cover correctly lists "I'll Cry Instead.")			
United Artists UAL-3366	(M)	**A Hard Day's Night** (Soundtrack)	1964	60.00	150.00
		(Black label. The back cover incorrectly lists "I Cry Instead.")			
United Artists UAS-6366	(P)	**A Hard Day's Night** (Soundtrack)	1964	80.00	200.00
		(Black label. The back cover correctly lists "I'll Cry Instead.")			
United Artists UAS-6366	(P)	**A Hard Day's Night** (Soundtrack)	1964	60.00	150.00
		(Black label. The back cover incorrectly lists "I Cry Instead.")			
United Artists T-90828	(M)	**A Hard Day's Night** (Soundtrack)	1964	660.00	1,000.00
United Artists ST-90828	(P)	**A Hard Day's Night** (Soundtrack)	1964	360.00	600.00
		(U.A. 90828 is a Capitol Record Club issue.)			
United Artists UAS-6366	(P)	**A Hard Day's Night** (Soundtrack)	1968	16.00	40.00
		(Pink & orange label)			
United Artists UAS-6366	(P)	**A Hard Day's Night** (Soundtrack)	1970	12.00	30.00
		(Pink & black label)			
United Artists UAS-6366	(P)	**A Hard Day's Night** (Soundtrack)	1971	60.00	150.00
		(Tan label. The back cover is completely blank.)			
Capitol T-2108	(M)	**Something New**	1964	60.00	150.00
Capitol ST-2108	(S)	**Something New**	1964	24.00	60.00
Capitol ST-8-2108	(S)	**Something New** (Record Club)	1964	175.00	350.00
Capitol TBO-2222	(M)	**The Beatles' Story** (2 LPs)	1964	80.00	200.00
Capitol STBO-2222	(P)	**The Beatles' Story** (2 LPs)	1969	50.00	125.00
		(Capitol 2222 was produced by Gary Usher and Roger Christian.)			
Capitol T-2228	(M)	**Beatles '65**	1964	50.00	125.00
Capitol ST-2228	(P)	**Beatles '65**	1964	24.00	60.00
Capitol T-2309	(M)	**The Early Beatles**	1965	60.00	150.00
Capitol ST-2309	(P)	**The Early Beatles**	1965	24.00	60.00
Capitol T-2358	(M)	**Beatles VI**	1965	50.00	125.00
Capitol ST-2358	(P)	**Beatles VI**	1965	24.00	60.00
		(The back cover reads "See label for correct playing order.")			
Capitol T-2358	(M)	**Beatles VI**	1965	40.00	100.00
Capitol ST-2358	(P)	**Beatles VI**	1965	20.00	50.00
		(The back cover lists the tracks in correct order.)			
Capitol ST-8-2358	(P)	**Beatles VI** (Record Club)	1965	300.00	500.00
United Artists Help-A/B	(DJ)	**Help! Radio Spots**	1965	660.00	1,000.00
		(Issued in a plain cardboard jacket.)			
United Artists Help-INT	(DJ)	**Help! Open-End Interview**	1965	1,200.00	1,600.00
		(Issued with a script in a plain cardboard jacket.)			
United Artists Help-Show	(DJ)	**Help!** (One-sided open-end interview)	1965	1,600.00	2,400.00
		(Issued with a script in a plain cardboard jacket.)			

Label & Catalog #		Title	Year	VG+	NM
Capitol MAS-2386	(M)	**Help!** (Soundtrack)	1965	**60.00**	**150.00**
Capitol SMAS-2386	(P)	**Help!** (Soundtrack)	1965	**24.00**	**60.00**
Capitol SMAS-8-2386	(P)	**Help!** (Soundtrack. Record Club)	1965	**200.00**	**400.00**
		(The cover catalogue number is SMAS-2386.)			
Capitol SMAS-8-2386	(P)	**Help!** (Soundtrack. Record Club)	1965	**360.00**	**600.00**
		(The cover catalogue number is SMAS-8-2386.)			
Capitol T-2442	(M)	**Rubber Soul**	1965	**50.00**	**125.00**
Capitol ST-2442	(S)	**Rubber Soul**	1965	**24.00**	**60.00**
Capitol ST-8-2442	(S)	**Rubber Soul** (Record Club)	1965	**200.00**	**400.00**

The "Yesterday" ...And Today "Butcher" Cover

Capitol 2553, "Yesterday" ...And Today was a U.S. only compilation of tracks cribbed from the group's previous EMI album releases. The original cover photo for this album depicted the smiling Fabs dressed in butcher's smocks, covered with pieces of raw meat and baby doll parts. Capitol, after pressing up hundreds of thousands of covers and sending out advance copies, did a turnabout and pulled the album from distribution almost immediately. A new cover with an innocuous photo of an unsmiling, some might say dour, group posing around a steamer trunk, was designed. Rather than destroy the original covers, Capitol simply pasted this new "trunk" cover over the "butcher cover" and sent them back out to their distributors. This has created a situation for collectors where this album has a variety of terms applied to it according to the state the cover is in:

"First state" refers to the original cover as it was manufactured. That is, the butcher cover has never had the trunk cover pasted over it. First-state butcher covers are the most talked-about and widely sought-after LPs in and outside of the hobby. The Beatles Price Guide For American Records recommends "to lightly moisten a small piece of tissue paper. Gently press the moistened tissue on any area of the front cover and allow to dry. If the cover is a true first-state the tissue will brush or blow off easily. If the [tissue] paper sticks to the cover, it is most likely not a first-state." (That is, it is a third state, discussed below.)

"Second state" refers to the album as it was sent out for sale with the trunk cover pasted over the original butcher cover. Whether or not a copy of the album is a second-state is readily apparent: The black "V" of Ringo's sweater on the original cover can be seen through the paste-over midway up the right side of the cover, beneath the album title. Second states are also referred to as "paste-overs."

"Third state" refers to the various attempts to make a second state a first state. That is, to remove the trunk cover from the butcher cover. These are also referred to as "peel jobs." The success of the peel would dictate the value; the closer to Near Mint the more it would be worth to a collector seeking a first-state but unable or unwilling to pay for a first-state. Poorly peeled copies are a staple of the hobby and yet, even covers that have been decimated by hasty fingers are in demand and fetch hundreds of dollars from some would-be owner. If a lightly moistened piece of tissue paper drys and adheres to what appears to be a first-state cover, it indicates that is more than likely a first-rate peel. Note: The easiest way to detect a first-state from a peel: Stand the cover om its spine alongside any other Beatles Capitol album. Paste-over jackets were cropped 3/16" along the mouth!

Due to the fact that so many collectors are interested in owning an original butcher cover, the stock of second states are being depleted (especially in light of the contemporary means of removing the extraneous cover using chemicals that dissolve the adhesive without marring the paper). Collectors—and historians—should consider the fact that it is the existence of the second state covers that are the centerpiece for this bit of cultural history and that without them, the story is incomplete. Should every collector remove their trunk cover to reveal the butcher cover below, eventually the second state covers would become rarer than the first states.

Of particular note are still-sealed "butcher cover." Sealed first and second-state butchers command a hefty premium, but it is the first state that deserves some attention here. A still-sealed first-state stereo butcher cover currently ranks as the most sought-after album in the hobby. In the past few years, at least four copies have sold in excess of $10,000 with two of them topping $15,000. The next few years will probably see this particular item reach undreamt of heights. . .

Capitol T-2553	(M)	**"Yesterday" ...And Today** ("Butcher cover")	1966		See below
Capitol ST-2553	(P)	**"Yesterday" ...And Today** ("Butcher cover")	1966		See below

(First state butcher cover; refer to the notes above. Mono covers have a suggested Near Mint value of $3,000-4,000. Stereo copies have a suggested Near Mint value of $6,000-10,000. Please note that the value is for the cover; the record is of negligible value in this case. First state mono butcher cover still-sealed in factory shrinkwrap have a suggested value of $4,000-6,000. Still-sealed first state stereo butcher covers have a suggested value of $15,000-20,000.)

Label & Catalog #		Title	Year	VG+	NM
Capitol T-2553	(M)	**"Yesterday" ...And Today** ("Butcher cover")	1966		See below
Capitol ST-2553	(P)	**"Yesterday" ...And Today** ("Butcher cover")	1966		See below
		(Second state butcher cover; refer to the notes above. Mono covers have a suugested Near Mint value of $800-1,200. Stereo copies have a suggested Near Mint value of $2,000-3,000. Please note that the value is for the cover; the record is of negligible value in this case. Second state mono butcher cover still-sealed in factory shrinkwrap have a suggested value of $2,000-3,000. Still-sealed second state stereo butcher covers have a suggested value of $5,000-7,000.)			
Capitol T-2553	(M)	**"Yesterday" ...And Today** ("Butcher cover")	1966		See below
Capitol ST-2553	(P)	**"Yesterday" ...And Today** ("Butcher cover")	1966		See below
		(Third state, or "peeled," butcher cover; refer to the notes above. Mono covers in collectible condition (i.e., VG-NM) have suggested values of $200-1,000. Stereo covers in collectible condition have suggested values of $400-1,600.)			
Capitol T-2553	(M)	**"Yesterday" ...And Today** ("Trunk cover")	1966	60.00	150.00
Capitol ST-2553	(P)	**"Yesterday" ...And Today** ("Trunk cover")	1966	24.00	60.00
		(Trunk cover. Black rainbow label without "A Subsidiary of Capitol." All subsequent pressings of this album feature this "trunk cover." Refer to the notes above.)			
Capitol ST-8-2553	(P)	**"Yesterday" ...And Today** (Record Club)	1966	175.00	350.00
Capitol T-2576	(M)	**Revolver**	1966	60.00	150.00
Capitol ST-2576	(S)	**Revolver**	1966	24.00	60.00
Capitol ST-8-2576	(S)	**Revolver** (Record Club)	1966	200.00	400.00
Capitol MAS-2653	(M)	**Sgt. Pepper's Lonely Heart's Club Band**	1967	100.00	250.00
Capitol SMAS-2653	(S)	**Sgt. Pepper's Lonely Heart's Club Band**	1967	24.00	60.00
		(Issued in a gatefold cover with a sheet of cutouts and a psychedelic inner sleeve. Counterfeits were issued in a standard, single-pocket jacket, a plain white inner sleeve and without the cut-outs.)			
Capitol MAL-2835	(M)	**Magical Mystery Tour**	1967	150.00	300.00
		(Gatefold covers; counterfeits have single-pocket covers.)			
Capitol SMAL-2835	(P)	**Magical Mystery Tour**	1967	24.00	60.00

— Capitol albums above have black labels without "A Subsidiary of Capitol" on the bottom.—

4. Capitol & Apple Reissues 1968-1974

Label & Catalog #		Title	Year	VG+	NM
Capitol ST-2047	(P)	**Meet The Beatles**	1969	16.00	40.00
Capitol ST-2080	(P)	**The Beatles' Second Album**	1969	16.00	40.00
Capitol ST-2108	(S)	**Something New**	1969	16.00	40.00
Capitol STBO-2222	(P)	**The Beatles' Story**	1969	20.00	50.00
Capitol ST-2228	(P)	**Beatles '65**	1969	16.00	40.00
Capitol ST-2309	(P)	**The Early Beatles**	1969	16.00	40.00
Capitol ST-2358	(P)	**Beatles VI**	1969	16.00	40.00
Capitol SMAS-8-2386	(P)	**Help!** (Soundtrack)	1969	16.00	40.00
Capitol ST-2442	(S)	**Rubber Soul**	1969	16.00	40.00
Capitol ST-2553	(P)	**"Yesterday" ...And Today**	1969	16.00	40.00
Capitol ST-2576	(S)	**Revolver**	1969	16.00	40.00
Capitol SMAS-2653	(S)	**Sgt. Pepper's Lonely Heart's Club Band**	1969	16.00	40.00
Capitol SMAL-2835	(P)	**Magical Mystery Tour**	1969	16.00	40.00

— Capitol albums above have black rainbow labels with "A Subsidiary of Capitol" on the bottom.—

Label & Catalog #		Title	Year	VG+	NM
Capitol ST-2047	(P)	**Meet The Beatles**	1969	16.00	40.00
Capitol ST-8-2047	(P)	**Meet The Beatles** (Record Club)	1969	60.00	150.00
Capitol ST-2080	(P)	**The Beatles' Second Album**	1969	16.00	40.00
Capitol ST-8-2080	(P)	**The Beatles' Second Album** (Record Club)	1969	80.00	200.00
Capitol ST-2108	(S)	**Something New**	1969	16.00	40.00
Capitol ST-8-2108	(S)	**Something New** (Record Club)	1969	60.00	150.00
Capitol ST-8-2108	(S)	**Something New** (Longines Sym. issue)	1969	100.00	250.00
Capitol STBO-2222	(P)	**The Beatles' Story** (2 LPs)	1969	20.00	50.00
Capitol ST-2228	(P)	**Beatles '65**	1969	16.00	40.00
Capitol ST-2309	(P)	**The Early Beatles**	1969	16.00	40.00
Capitol ST-2358	(P)	**Beatles VI**	1969	16.00	40.00
Capitol ST-8-2358	(P)	**Beatles VI** (Record Club)	1969	80.00	200.00
Capitol SMAS-2386	(P)	**Help!** (Soundtrack)	1969	16.00	40.00
Capitol SMAS-8-2386	(P)	**Help!** (Soundtrack. Record Club)	1969	200.00	400.00
		(On a rare pressing of this Capitol Record Club issue, the cover catalogue number is SMAS-8-2386.)			

Label & Catalog #		Title	Year	VG+	NM
Capitol SMAS-8-2386	(P)	**Help!** *(Soundtrack. Record Club)*	1969	80.00	200.00
		(The cover catalogue number is SMAS-2386.)			
Capitol ST-2442	(S)	**Rubber Soul**	1969	16.00	40.00
Capitol ST-8-2442	(S)	**Rubber Soul** *(Record Club)*	1969	60.00	150.00
Capitol ST-2553	(P)	**"Yesterday" ...And Today**	1969	16.00	40.00
Capitol ST-8-2553	(P)	**"Yesterday" ...And Today** *(Record Club)*	1969	60.00	150.00
Capitol ST-2576	(S)	**Revolver**	1969	12.00	30.00
Capitol ST-8-2576	(S)	**Revolver** *(Record Club)*	1969	60.00	150.00
Capitol ST-2576	(S)	**Revolver** *(Red label. Canadian)*	197?	300.00	500.00
Capitol ST-8-2576	(S)	**Revolver** *(Record Club. Orange label)*	197?	200.00	400.00
Capitol SMAS-2653	(S)	**Sgt. Pepper's Lonely Heart's Club Band**	1969	16.00	40.00
Capitol SMAL-2835	(P)	**Magical Mystery Tour**	1969	16.00	40.00

— Capitol albums above have lime-green labels except where noted.—

Apple ST-2047	(P)	**Meet The Beatles**	1969	16.00	40.00
Apple ST-2080	(P)	**The Beatles' Second Album**	1969	16.00	40.00
Apple ST-2108	(S)	**Something New**	1969	16.00	40.00
Apple ST-2222	(P)	**The Beatles' Story** *(2 LPs)*	1969	20.00	50.00
Apple ST-2228	(P)	**Beatles '65**	1969	16.00	40.00
Apple ST-2309	(P)	**The Early Beatles**	1969	16.00	40.00
Apple ST-2358	(P)	**Beatles VI**	1969	16.00	40.00
Apple ST-2386	(P)	**Help!** *(Soundtrack)*	1969	16.00	40.00
Apple ST-2442	(S)	**Rubber Soul**	1969	16.00	40.00
Apple ST-2553	(P)	**"Yesterday" ...And Today**	1969	16.00	40.00
Apple ST-2576	(S)	**Revolver**	1969	16.00	40.00
Apple SMAS-2653	(S)	**Sgt. Pepper's Lonely Heart's Club Band**	1969	16.00	40.00
Apple SMAL-2835	(P)	**Magical Mystery Tour**	1969	16.00	40.00

— Apple albums above have green Apple labels with "A Subsidiary of Capitol" on the bottom.—

5. Apple Originals 1968-1974

Apple SWBO-101	(S)	**The Beatles** *(2 LPs)*	1968	40.00	100.00
		(First pressing labels read "A subsidiary of Capitol" on the bottom. *First pressing covers have "The Beatles" in raised white letters* *and are sequentially numbered 1-3,000,000 in black. Copies with* *numbers under #10,000 affect the value— under #1,000, the value* *is raised substantially. Issued with a fold-open poster/lyric sheet* *and four glossy, full-color portraits of the group, included in the* *price. Note: Because of the lack of graphics on the front and back* *cover, this album is also known as "The White Album.")*			
Apple SWBO-101	(S)	**The Beatles** *(2 LPs)*	1968	300.00	500.00
		(First pressing same as above with a large, fluorescent *red sticker on the front cover with song titles, etc.)*			
Apple SWBO-101	(S)	**The Beatles** *(2 LPs)*	1968	150.00	300.00
		(First pressing same as above with a small sticker *on the back cover with song titles, etc.)*			
Apple SWBO-101	(S)	**The Beatles** *(2 LPs)*	1968	28.00	70.00
		(First pressing without the poster and photos.)			
Apple SWBO-101	(S)	**The Beatles** *(2 LPs)*	1969	24.00	60.00
		(Second pressing label read "Manufactured by Apple" on the bottom. *Covers are similar to the first except there is no number stamped* *on the cover. Issued with the poster and the four glossy photos.)*			
Apple SWBO-101	(S)	**The Beatles** *(2 LPs)*	1969	12.00	30.00
		(Second pressing without the poster and photos.)			
Apple SWBO-101	(S)	**The Beatles** *(2 LPs)*	1975	24.00	60.00
		(Third pressing labels have an "All rights reserved" disclaimer. *This and all subsequent pressings have the title printed in black* *on the cover and the photos are on thin stock with less gloss.)*			
Apple KAL-1004	(DJ)	**Yellow Submarine** *(Radio spots)*	1968	1,000.00	Rare
		(Near Mint copies have a suggested value of $2,000-4,000.)			
Apple SW-153	(P)	**Yellow Submarine**	1969	10.00	25.00
		(First pressing labels read "A subsidiary of Capitol" on the bottom.)			
Apple SO-383	(S)	**Abbey Road**	1969	16.00	40.00
		(The labels read "A subsidiary of Capitol" on the bottom. *"Her Majesty" is listed on the cover and the label.)*			
Apple SO-383	(S)	**Abbey Road**	1969	20.00	50.00
		(The labels read "A subsidiary of Capitol" on the bottom. *"Her Majesty" is not listed on either the cover or the label.)*			

Label & Catalog #		Title	Year	VG+	NM
Apple SO-385	(S)	**Beatles Again** (Alternate covers)	1970		See below
		(At least two variations were made for this album when its title was "Beatles Again." One has the same photos but the back cover is purple while the other has the front and back photos reversed. Suggested values in collectible condition are $5,000-10,000 each.)			
Apple SW-385	(S)	**Hey Jude/The Beatles Again**	1970	10.00	25.00
		(Second pressings read "Manufactured by Apple" on the label. and have an "SW" prefix. While the title on the cover is "Hey Jude," on the label it is "The Beatles Again.")			
Apple SW-385	(S)	**Hey Jude**	1970	20.00	50.00
		(Third pressings read "Manufactured by Capitol" on the label. Both the cover and the label on this and all subsequent Apple and Capitol pressings list the title as "Hey Jude.")			
Apple AR-34001	(S)	**Let It Be**	1970	10.00	25.00
		(Red Apple label. Originals have "Bell Sound" stamped in the trail-off vinyl; counterfeits do not.)			
Apple SBC-100	(M)	**The Beatles Christmas Album** (Fan club)	1970	100.00	250.00
		(Convincing counterfeits exist: Both the photos on the cover— especially the background details— and the print in the trail-off vinyl are slightly blurred.)			
Apple SKBO-3403	(P)	**The Beatles 1962-1966** (2 LPs)	1973	12.00	30.00
		(First pressings have custom Apple labels.)			
Apple SKBO-3403	(P)	**The Beatles 1962-1966** (2 LPs)	1975	20.00	50.00
		(Second pressing labels have an "All rights reserved" disclaimer.)			
Apple SKBO-3404	(P)	**The Beatles 1967-1970** (2 LPs)	1973	12.00	30.00
		(First pressings have custom Apple labels.)			
Apple SKBO-3404	(P)	**The Beatles 1967-1970** (2 LPs)	1975	20.00	50.00
		(Second pressing labels have an "All rights reserved" disclaimer.)			
Capitol SKBO-3403	(P)	**The Beatles 1962-1966** (2 LPs. Red labels)	1976	10.00	25.00
Capitol SKBO-3403	(P)	**The Beatles 1962-1966** (2 LPs. Blue labels)	1976	20.00	50.00
Capitol SKBO-3404	(P)	**The Beatles 1967-1970** (2 LPs. Blue labels)	1976	14.00	35.00
Apple (No number)	(P)	**The Beatles Special Limited Edition**	1974	660.00	1,000.00
		(Promotional boxed set of nine Apple label albums.)			

6. Capitol Repackagings 1976-1983

Label & Catalog #		Title	Year	VG+	NM
Capitol (No number)	(DJ)	**The Beatles 10th Anniversary Box Set**	1974	1,400.00	2,000.00
		(Boxed set of seventeen Apple label albums.)			
Capitol SMAS-11638	(DJ)	**The Beatles At The Hollywood Bowl**	1977	225.00	450.00
		(White label issued in a plain white jacket.)			
Capitol SEAX-11711	(S)	**Love Songs** (2 LPs. White label promo)	1978	150.00	300.00
		(Advance copy/test pressing with printed labels.)			
Capitol SEAX-11840	(S)	**Sgt. Pepper** (Picture disc)	1978	10.00	25.00
Capitol SEBX-11841	(S)	**The Beatles** (2 LPs. White vinyl)	1978	16.00	40.00
Capitol SEBX-11842	(P)	**The Beatles 1962-1966** (2 LPs. Red vinyl)	1978	12.00	30.00
Capitol SEBX-11843	(P)	**The Beatles 1967-1970** (2 LPs. Blue vinyl)	1978	12.00	30.00
Capitol SEAX-11900	(S)	**Abbey Road** (Picture disc)	1978	16.00	40.00
Capitol SN-12009	(P)	**The Beatles Rarities** (Green label)	1978	150.00	300.00
		(Withdrawn prior to release, Capitol 12009 is a reissue of the EMI/ Parlophone release with 17 tracks and was issued without a cover.)			
Capitol/EMI BC-13	(P)	**The Beatles Collection** (14 LP numbered box)	1978	100.00	250.00
Capitol SPRO-8969	(DJ)	**The Beatles Rarities** (Purple label)	1978	16.00	40.00
Capitol SV-12199	(DJ)	**Reel Music** (Gold vinyl with booklet)	1982	20.00	50.00
		(Back cover stamped with a "Limited Edition" number.)			
Capitol SV-12199	(S)	**Reel Music** (Gold vinyl)	1982	12.00	30.00
		(Without the "Limited Edition" number with program.)			
Capitol (No number)	(DJ)	**The Platinum Collection** (18 LP box)	1984	465.00	700.00
Capitol BBX1-91302	(DJ)	**The Deluxe Box Set** (14 LP box)	1984	80.00	200.00
Capitol C1-90445	(S)	**Beatles VI**	1988	30.00	75.00

7. Miscellaneous Releases

Label & Catalog #		Title	Year	VG+	NM
INS Radio News DOC-1	(DJ)	**Beatlemania Tour Coverage**	1964	660.00	1,000.00
		(Open-end interview issued with a script in a plain cardboard jacket.)			
Radio Pulsebeat #2	(M)	**American Tour With Ed Rudy**	1964	60.00	150.00
		(Yellow label with booklet. Counterfeits are on flexible vinyl with no writing in the trail-off area.)			

Beginning as a five man group, The Beau Brummels emulated the sound of the British Invasion, achieving big chart success in 1964-65 with "Laugh Laugh," "Just A Little" and "Tell Me Why." By 1967 the group was a studio trio. Both of these albums are astonishing; Ron Elliot's guitar(s) and Sal Valentino's vocals are breath-taking. 1967's Triangle is a minor masterpiece of late '60s mood music while 1968's Bradley's Barn was one of the earliest forays into country rock, recorded in Owen Bradley's famed Nashville studios with local pickers.

Label & Catalog #		Title	Year	VG+	NM
Radio Pulsebeat	(M)	**1965 Talk Album, Ed Rudy With New U.S. Tour**	1965	80.00	200.00
		(Original covers have "The Beatles" in black print under the photo; counterfeit covers have "The Beatles" in red print above the photo.)			
Sterling Prod. 8895-6481	(M)	**I Apologize** (With bonus photo)	1966	300.00	500.00
Sterling Prod. 8895-6481	(M)	**I Apologize** (Without photo)	1966	175.00	350.00
PBR Int. 7005/6	(M)	**The Beatles Tapes** (2 LPs. Blue vinyl)	1978	20.00	50.00
PBR Int. 7005/6	(M)	**The Beatles Tapes** (2 LPs. Black vinyl)	1980	20.00	50.00
		(PBR 7005/6 contains the David Wogg interviews.)			
Adirondack Group AG-8146	(S)	**Happy Michelmas**	1981	12.00	30.00
Desert Vibrat. HSRD-SP1	(S)	**Christmas Reflections**	1982	12.00	30.00

8. Original Master Recordings & UHQRs

—Mobile Fidelity made test pressings for each of the Beatles' albums as potential Ultra High Quality Recordings titles. These are all very rare with a suggested Near Mint value of $1,500-2,500 per album.—

Label & Catalog #		Title	Year	VG+	NM
Mobile Fidelity MFSL-023	(S)	**Abbey Road**	1979	15.00	45.00
Mobile Fidelity MFSL-047	(P)	**Magical Mystery Tour**	1980	20.00	60.00
Mobile Fidelity MFSL-072	(S)	**The Beatles** (2 LPs)	1982	20.00	60.00
Mobile Fidelity MFSL-100	(S)	**Sgt. Pepper's Lonely Heart's Club Band**	1982	16.00	40.00
Mobile Fidelity MFQR-100	(S)	**Sgt. Pepper's Lonely Heart's Club Band**	1982	100.00	300.00
		(Issued in a box with a Geodisc cartridge alignment tool.)			
Mobile Fidelity MFSL-101	(P)	**Please Please Me**	1986	10.00	30.00
Mobile Fidelity MFSL-102	(S)	**With The Beatles**	1986	70.00	210.00
Mobile Fidelity MFSL-103	(S)	**A Hard Day's Night**	1986	10.00	30.00
Mobile Fidelity MFSL-104	(S)	**Beatles For Sale**	1986	10.00	30.00
Mobile Fidelity MFSL-105	(S)	**Help!**	1986	10.00	30.00
Mobile Fidelity MFSL-106	(S)	**Rubber Soul**	1986	15.00	45.00
Mobile Fidelity MFSL-107	(S)	**Revolver**	1987	10.00	30.00
Mobile Fidelity MFSL-108	(P)	**Yellow Submarine**	1987	15.00	45.00
Mobile Fidelity MFSL-109	(S)	**Let It Be**	1987	10.00	30.00
Mobile Fidelity MFSL-110	(DJ)	**Rarities** (One-sided test pressing)	1987	200.00	400.00
Mobile Fidelity BC-1	(P)	**The Beatles: The Collection** (14 LP box)	1982	300.00	500.00

BEATS, THE

Label & Catalog #		Title	Year	VG+	NM
Design 170	(M)	**The New Merseyside Sound**	1964	20.00	50.00
		(This was also released on Rondo credited to The Liverpool Beats.)			

BEAU BRUMMELS, THE
Originally Ron Elliot, Declan Mulligan, Ron Meagher, John Petersen and Sal Valentino, by 1967 The Beau Brummels were a duo, Valentino and Elliot.

Label & Catalog #		Title	Year	VG+	NM
Autumn LP-103	(M)	**Introducing The Beau Brummels**	1965	16.00	40.00
Autumn SLP-103	(S)	**Introducing The Beau Brummels**	1965	20.00	50.00
		("I Would Be Happy" is in mono on this album.)			
Autumn LP-104	(M)	**The Beau Brummels, Volume 2**	1965	16.00	40.00
Autumn SLP-104	(S)	**The Beau Brummels, Volume 2**	1965	20.00	50.00
Warner Bros. WS-1644	(M)	**Beau Brummels '66**	1966	10.00	25.00
Warner Bros. WS-1644	(S)	**Beau Brummels '66**	1966	12.00	30.00
Warner Bros. W-1692	(M)	**Triangle**	1967	8.00	20.00
Warner Bros. WS-1692	(S)	**Triangle**	1967	10.00	25.00
Warner Bros. WS-1760	(S)	**Bradley's Barn**	1968	10.00	25.00

BEAUREGARDE

Label & Catalog #		Title	Year	VG+	NM
F-Empire	(S)	**Beauregarde**	196?	30.00	75.00

BEAVER, PAUL

Label & Catalog #		Title	Year	VG+	NM
Rapture 11111	(S)	**Perchance To Dream**	196?	20.00	50.00

BEAVER & KRAUSE/PAUL BEAVER & BERNIE KRAUSE

Label & Catalog #		Title	Year	VG+	NM
Limelight 86069	(S)	**Ragnarok**	1969	12.00	30.00

BECK, JEFF

Label & Catalog #		Title	Year	VG+	NM
Epic HE-43409	(S)	**Blow By Blow** (Half-speed master)	1982	15.00	45.00
Epic HE-43849	(S)	**Wired** (Half-speed master)	1982	15.00	45.00

BEDIENT, JACK, & THE CHESSMEN

Label & Catalog #		Title	Year	VG+	NM
Executive Prods.	(M)	**Jack Bedient**	196?	20.00	50.00
Trophy 101	(M)	**Two Sides Of Jack Bedient**	1964	20.00	50.00
Fantasy 3365	(M)	**Live At Harvey's**	1965	20.00	50.00
Satori LP-1001	(M)	**Where Did She Go?**	1966	30.00	75.00

Molly Bee was a child star with Rex Allen in the '40s, signed with Capitol as a teen star in the '50s where she released her first album (top) and then found her way to MGM, where she cut another pair in the mid-'60s. She also found success on stage and screen and scored some minor country hits in the '70s.

Label & Catalog #		Title	Year	VG+	NM

BEE, MOLLY
Molly Bee is a pseudonym for Molly Beachboard.

Capitol T-1097	(M)	**Young Romance**	1958	20.00	50.00
MGM E-4303	(M)	**It's Great, It's Molly Bee**	1965	8.00	20.00
MGM SE-4303	(S)	**It's Great, It's Molly Bee**	1965	10.00	25.00
MGM E-4423	(M)	**Swingin' Country**	1967	8.00	20.00
MGM SE-4423	(S)	**Swingin' Country**	1967	10.00	25.00

BEE GEES, THE
The Bee Gees are the brothers Gibb: Barry, Maurice and Robin.

Atco 33-223	(M)	**The Bee Gees First**	1967	10.00	25.00
Atco SD-33-223	(S)	**The Bee Gees First**	1967	8.00	20.00
Atco 33-233	(M)	**Horizontal**	1968	12.00	30.00
Atco SD-33-233	(S)	**Horizontal**	1968	8.00	20.00
Atco 33-253	(M)	**Idea** *(White label promo)*	1968	20.00	50.00
Atco SD-33-253	(S)	**Idea**	1968	8.00	20.00
Atco 33-264	(M)	**Rare, Precious And Beautiful** *(White label)*	1968	20.00	50.00
Atco SD-33-264	(E)	**Rare, Precious And Beautiful**	1968	8.00	20.00

— Atco stereo albums above have brown & purple labels.—

Atco ST-142	(DJ)	**Odessa** *(In-store sampler)*	1969	30.00	75.00
Atco SD-2-702	(S)	**Odessa** *(Red felt cover)*	1969	12.00	30.00
Atco SD-2-702	(S)	**Odessa** *(Record Club. Plain red cover)*	1969	20.00	50.00
Atco 33-321	(M)	**Rare, Precious And Beautiful, Volume 2** *(White label promo)*	1970	20.00	50.00
Atco SD-33-321	(E)	**Rare, Precious And Beautiful, Volume 2**	1970	5.00	12.00

— Atco albums above have yellow labels with an 1841 Broadway address on the bottom.—

RSO PRO-033	(DJ)	**Saturday Night Fever Special Disco Version**	1977	20.00	50.00

(RSO 033 contains extended remixes of five Bee Gees tracks from the film.)

RSO SMP-1	(DJ)	**The Words And Music Of Maurice, Barry And Robin Gibb**	1979	20.00	50.00
RSO PUB-1000	(DJ)	**Unichapel Publisher's Sampler**	1980	20.00	50.00

(Both RSP 1 and 1000 are publishers samplers.)

Nautilus NR-42	(DJ)	**Living Eyes** *(Test pressing)*	1981	30.00	90.00

BEE GEES, THE / RAY CHARLES

Atlantic	(DJ)	**Rare, Precious And Beautiful / The Other Ray Charles**	1969	20.00	50.00

(Sampler with each side devoted to one artist's latest album.)

BEEFHEART, CAPTAIN: *Refer to* **CAPTAIN BEEFHEART & THE MAGIC BAND**

BEERS, EVELYNE [FOLK]

Prestige Int. PRLP-13053	(M)	**The Gentle Art**	1962	12.00	30.00

BEETHOVEN SOUL, THE

Dot DLP-3821	(M)	**The Beethoven Soul**	1967	8.00	20.00
Dot DLP-25821	(S)	**The Beethoven Soul**	1967	10.00	25.00

BEGINNING OF THE END, THE

Alston SD-33-379	(S)	**Funky Nassau**	1971	10.00	25.00

BELAFONTE, HARRY
Harry Belafonte popularized West Indian folk-based music— especially calyps— in the States in the '50s.

RCA Victor LPM-1022	(M)	**Mark Twain & Other Folk Favorites**	1954	20.00	50.00
RCA Victor LPM-1150	(M)	**Belafonte**	1955	20.00	50.00
RCA Victor LPM-1248	(M)	**Calypso**	1956	12.00	30.00
RCA Victor LPM-1402	(M)	**An Evening With Belafonte**	1957	12.00	30.00
RCA Victor LPM-1505	(M)	**Belafonte Sings Of The Caribbean**	1957	12.00	30.00
RCA Victor LPM-1887	(M)	**To Wish You A Merry Christmas**	1958	10.00	25.00
RCA Victor LPM-1927	(M)	**Love Is A Gentle Thing**	1959	8.00	20.00
RCA Victor LSP-1927	(S)	**Love Is A Gentle Thing**	1959	10.00	25.00
RCA Victor LPM-1972	(M)	**Belafonte Sings The Blues**	1959	8.00	20.00
RCA Victor LSP-1972	(S)	**Belafonte Sings The Blues**	1959	10.00	25.00
RCA Victor LOC-1507	(M)	**Porgy And Bess**	1959	8.00	20.00
RCA Victor LSO-1507	(S)	**Porgy And Bess**	1959	10.00	25.00
RCA Victor LOC-6006	(M)	**Belafonte At Carnegie Hall** *(2 LPs)*	1959	8.00	20.00
RCA Victor LSO-6006	(S)	**Belafonte At Carnegie Hall** *(2 LPs)*	1959	10.00	25.00
RCA Victor LPM-2022	(M)	**My Lord What A Mornin'**	1960	8.00	20.00

Label & Catalog #		Title	Year	VG+	NM
RCA Victor LPM-2022	(M)	My Lord What A Mornin'	1960	8.00	20.00
RCA Victor LSP-2022	(S)	My Lord What A Mornin'	1960	10.00	25.00
RCA Victor LOC-6007	(M)	Belafonte Returns To Carnegie Hall (2 LPs)	1960	8.00	20.00
RCA Victor LSO-6007	(S)	Belafonte Returns To Carnegie Hall (2 LPs)	1960	10.00	25.00
		("Returns To Carnegie Hall" also introduces The Chad Mitchell Trio.)			
RCA Victor LPM-2194	(M)	Swing Dat Hammer	1960	8.00	20.00
RCA Victor LSP-2194	(S)	Swing Dat Hammer	1960	10.00	25.00
RCA Victor LPM-2309	(M)	At Home And Abroad	1961	8.00	20.00
RCA Victor LSP-2309	(S)	At Home And Abroad	1961	10.00	25.00
RCA Victor LPM-2388	(M)	Jump Up Calypso	1961	8.00	20.00
RCA Victor LSP-2388	(S)	Jump Up Calypso	1961	10.00	25.00
RCA Victor LPM-2449	(M)	The Midnight Special	1962	12.00	30.00
RCA Victor LSP-2449	(S)	The Midnight Special	1962	16.00	40.00
		(RCA 2499 features Bob Dylan's first appearance on record, playing harmonica on one track.)			
RCA Victor LPM-2574	(M)	The Many Moods Of Belafonte	1962	8.00	20.00
RCA Victor LSP-2574	(S)	The Many Moods Of Belafonte	1962	10.00	25.00
RCA Victor LPM-2626	(M)	To Wish You A Merry Christmas	1962	8.00	20.00
RCA Victor LSP-2626	(S)	To Wish You A Merry Christmas	1962	10.00	25.00
RCA Victor LPM-2695	(M)	Streets I Have Walked	1963	8.00	20.00
RCA Victor LSP-2695	(S)	Streets I Have Walked	1963	10.00	25.00
		— RCA mono albums above have "Long Play" on the bottom of the label; stereo albums have "Living Stereo" on the bottom. —			

BELEW, CARL

Decca DL-4074	(M)	Carl Belew	1960	12.00	30.00
Decca DL-74074	(S)	Carl Belew	1960	16.00	40.00
Wrangler WR-1007	(M)	Carl Belew	1962	16.00	40.00
Wrangler WRS-31007	(S)	Carl Belew	1962	20.00	50.00
RCA Victor LPM-2848	(M)	Hello Out There	1964	8.00	20.00
RCA Victor LSP-2848	(S)	Hello Out There	1964	10.00	25.00
RCA Victor LPM-3381	(M)	Am I That Easy To Forget?	1965	8.00	20.00
RCA Victor LSP-3381	(S)	Am I That Easy To Forget?	1965	10.00	25.00
Pickwick/Hilltop JM-6013	(M)	Another Lonely Night	1965	8.00	20.00
Pickwick/Hilltop JS-6013	(S)	Another Lonely Night	1965	10.00	25.00
RCA Victor LPM-3919	(M)	Twelve Shades Of Belew	1968	20.00	50.00
RCA Victor LSP-3919	(S)	Twelve Shades Of Belew	1968	8.00	20.00

BELL, ARCHIE, & THE DRELLS

Atlantic 8181	(M)	Tighten Up	1968	12.00	30.00
Atlantic SD-8181	(S)	Tighten Up	1968	16.00	40.00
Atlantic SD-8204	(S)	I Can't Stop Dancing	1968	16.00	40.00
Atlantic SD-8226	(S)	There's Gonna Be A Showdown	1969	16.00	40.00

BELL, FREDDIE, & THE BELL BOYS

Mercury MG-20289	(M)	Rock And Roll—All Flavors	1958	60.00	150.00
20th Century TF-4146	(M)	Bells Are Swinging	1964	10.00	25.00
20th Century TFS-4146	(S)	Bells Are Swinging	1964	12.00	30.00

BELL, WILLIAM

Stax 719	(M)	Soul Of A Bell	1967	16.00	40.00
Stax S-719	(S)	Soul Of A Bell	1967	20.00	50.00
Stax ST-2014	(M)	Bound To Happen (Promo)	1969	16.00	40.00
Stax STS-2014	(S)	Bound To Happen	1969	14.00	35.00
Stax STS-2037	(S)	Wow...	1971	14.00	35.00
Stax STS-3005	(S)	Phases To Reality	1973	12.00	30.00
Stax STS-5502	(S)	Relating	1974	10.00	25.00

BELLAMY, RALPH

Camden CAL-1032	(M)	Stories And Songs Of The Civil War	1960	10.00	25.00

BELLUS, TONY

N.R.C. LPA-8	(M)	Robbin' The Cradle	1960	60.00	150.00

BELMONTS, THE
Refer to Dion & The Belmonts.

Sabina SALP-5001	(M)	The Belmonts' Carnival Of Hits	1962	60.00	150.00
Dot DLP-25949	(S)	Summer Love	1969	12.00	30.00
Buddah BDS-5123	(S)	Cigars, Acappella, Candy	1972	20.00	50.00

Label & Catalog #		Title	Year	VG+	NM

BELVIN, JESSE
Refer to Brook Benton / Jesse Belvin.

Crown CLP-5145	(M)	**The Casual Jessie Belvin**	1959	16.00	40.00
Crown CLP-5187	(M)	**The Unforgettable Jessie Belvin**	1959	16.00	40.00
RCA Victor LPM-2089	(M)	**Just Jesse Belvin**	1959	14.00	35.00
RCA Victor LSP-2089	(S)	**Just Jesse Belvin**	1959	20.00	50.00
RCA Victor LPM-2105	(M)	**Mr. Easy**	1960	12.00	30.00
RCA Victor LSP-2105	(S)	**Mr. Easy**	1960	16.00	40.00

— *RCA mono albums above have black labels with "Long Play" on the bottom; stereo albums have "Living Stereo" on the bottom.* —

BENDER, BILL
Bill Bender is a guitar player and singer of traditional folk songs.

| Stinson SLP-18 | (10") | **Frontier Ballads And Cowboy Songs** | 195? | 30.00 | 75.00 |

BENDIX, WILLIAM

| Cricket CR-30 | (M) | **Famous Pirate Stories** | 1959 | 20.00 | 50.00 |

BENET, VICKI

Decca DL-8233	(M)	**Woman Of Paris**	1956	20.00	50.00
Decca DL-8381	(M)	**The French Touch**	1957	20.00	50.00
Decca DL-8987	(M)	**a' Paris**	1959	14.00	35.00
Decca DL-78987	(S)	**a' Paris**	1959	20.00	50.00
Liberty LRP-3103	(M)	**Sing To Me Of Love**	1960	10.00	25.00
Liberty LST-7103	(S)	**Sing To Me Of Love**	1960	14.00	35.00

BENNETT, BETTY: *Refer to* **GOLDMINE'S PRICE GUIDE TO COLLECTIBLE JAZZ ALBUMS**

BENNETT, BOYD

| King 395-594 | (M) | **Boyd Bennett** | 1955 | | See below |

(King 594 has a suggested Near Mint value of $3,000-6,000.)

BENNETT, CONNIE, & BILL SMYTH & THE HARLEM-AIRES

| Hollywood LPH-30 | (M) | **Rhythm 'N Blues In The Night** | 1957 | 300.00 | 600.00 |

(The cover, a generic pretty white girl common on R&B albums of the time, features a very young— and scantily clad— Julie Newmar.)

BENNETT, MARJORY
Marjory Bennett is backed by Marty King.

| Judson J-3028 | (M) | **Sing A Song Of Childhood** | 195? | 16.00 | 40.00 |

BENNETT, TONY

Columbia CL-6221	(10")	**Because Of You**	1952	30.00	75.00
Columbia CL-2507	(10")	**Alone At Last With Tony Bennett**	1955	20.00	50.00
Columbia CL-2550	(10")	**Because Of You** (Reissue of 6221)	1956	20.00	50.00
Columbia CL-621	(M)	**Cloud Seven**	1955	16.00	40.00

— *Columbia albums above have "Long Playing" on the bottom.* —

Columbia CL-938	(M)	**Tony**	1957	14.00	35.00
Columbia CL-1079	(M)	**The Beat Of My Heart**	1957	14.00	35.00
Columbia CL-1186	(M)	**Long Ago And Far Away**	1958	14.00	35.00
Columbia CL-1229	(M)	**Tony's Greatest Hits**	1958	14.00	35.00
Columbia CL-1292	(M)	**Blue Velvet**	1959	14.00	35.00
Columbia CL-2343	(M)	**If I Ruled The World**	1959	14.00	35.00
Columbia CL-1294	(M)	**Tony Bennett In Person!** (With Count Basie)	1959	10.00	25.00
Columbia CS-8104	(S)	**Tony Bennett In Person!** (With Count Basie)	1959	14.00	35.00
Columbia CL-1301	(M)	**Hometown, My Hometown**	1959	10.00	25.00
Columbia CS-8107	(S)	**Hometown, My Hometown**	1959	14.00	35.00
Columbia CL-1429	(M)	**To My Wonderful One**	1960	10.00	25.00
Columbia CS-8226	(S)	**To My Wonderful One**	1960	14.00	35.00
Columbia CL-1446	(M)	**Tony Sings For Two**	1960	10.00	25.00
Columbia CS-8242	(S)	**Tony Sings For Two**	1960	14.00	35.00
Columbia CL-1471	(M)	**Alone Together**	1960	10.00	25.00
Columbia CS-8262	(S)	**Alone Together**	1960	14.00	35.00
Columbia CL-1535	(M)	**More Tony's Greatest Hits**	1960	10.00	25.00
Columbia CS-8335	(S)	**More Tony's Greatest Hits**	1960	10.00	25.00
Columbia CL-1559	(M)	**Tony Bennett Sings A String Of Harold Arlen**	1960	10.00	25.00
Columbia CS-8359	(S)	**Tony Bennett Sings A String Of Harold Arlen**	1960	12.00	30.00
Roulette R-25072	(M)	**Count Basie Swings/Tony Sings**	1961	10.00	25.00
Roulette SR-25072	(S)	**Count Basie Swings/Tony Sings**	1961	12.00	30.00

Jesse Lorenzo Belvin is another virtually unsung mover of the '50s rhythm 'n blues scene. Aside from recording with several groups (including The Three Dots & A Dash for Jig Jay McNeely, The Capris, The Chargers and The Cliques), he had a hand in the writing of "Earth Angel" and "Goodnight My Love." He was beginning to enjoy success outside of rhythm 'n blues as a pop singer (ala Sam Cooke) for RCA Victor when he was tragically killed in an automobile accident in 1960.

Label & Catalog #		Title	Year	VG+	NM
Roulette R-25231	(M)	**Bennett And Basie Strike Up The Band**	1963	8.00	20.00
Roulette SR-25231	(S)	**Bennett And Basie Strike Up The Band**	1963	10.00	25.00
Columbia CL-1658	(M)	**My Heart Sings**	1961	10.00	25.00
Columbia CS-8458	(S)	**My Heart Sings**	1961	12.00	30.00
Columbia CL-1763	(M)	**Mr. Broadway**	1962	10.00	25.00
Columbia CS-8563	(S)	**Mr. Broadway**	1962	12.00	30.00
Columbia CL-1813	(M)	**On The Glory Road**	1962	10.00	25.00
Columbia CS-8613	(S)	**On The Glory Road**	1962	12.00	30.00
Columbia CL-1852	(M)	**Tony's Greatest Hits**	1962	8.00	20.00
Columbia CS-8652	(E)	**Tony's Greatest Hits**	1962	6.00	15.00
		(Columbia 18/6852 is a reissue of 1229.)			
Columbia CL-1869	(M)	**I Left My Heart In San Francisco**	1962	10.00	25.00
Columbia CS-8669	(S)	**I Left My Heart In San Francisco**	1962	12.00	30.00
Columbia C2L-23	(M)	**Tony Bennett At Carnegie Hall** *(2 LPs)*	1962	12.00	30.00
Columbia C2S-823	(S)	**Tony Bennett At Carnegie Hall** *(2 LPs)*	1962	16.00	40.00
Columbia CL-1905	(S)	**Tony Bennett At Carnegie Hall, Vol. 1**	1962	8.00	20.00
Columbia CS-8705	(S)	**Tony Bennett At Carnegie Hall, Vol. 1**	1962	10.00	25.00
Columbia CL-1906	(S)	**Tony Bennett At Carnegie Hall, Vol. 2**	1962	8.00	20.00
Columbia CS-8706	(S)	**Tony Bennett At Carnegie Hall, Vol. 2**	1962	10.00	25.00
— Columbia albums above have three white "eye" logos on each side of the spindle hole.—					
Columbia OL-6550	(M)	**The Oscar** *(Soundtrack)*	1966	20.00	50.00
Columbia OS-2950	(S)	**The Oscar** *(Soundtrack)*	1966	24.00	60.00
Mobile Fidelity MFSL-117	(S)	**The Bennett/Evans Album**	1981	12.00	36.00

BENNY, JACK
Refer to Benny Fields.

Capitol T-3241	(M)	**Jack Benny Plays The Bee** *(With Mel Blanc)*	195?	24.00	60.00

BENSON, GEORGE

Mobile Fidelity MFSL-011	(S)	**Breezin'**	1979	10.00	30.00

BENT WIND

Trend T-1015	(S)	**Sussex** *(Canadian)*	196?	2,000.00	See below
		(Rare with a suggested Near Mint alue of $3,000-6,000.)			

BENTON, BROOK

Epic LG-3573	(M)	**Brook Benton At His Best**	1959	16.00	40.00
Mercury MG-20421	(M)	**It's Just A Matter Of Time**	1959	16.00	40.00
Mercury SR-60077	(S)	**It's Just A Matter Of Time**	1959	20.00	50.00
Mercury MG-20464	(M)	**Brook Benton**	1959	12.00	30.00
Mercury SR-60146	(S)	**Brook Benton**	1959	16.00	40.00
Mercury MG-20565	(M)	**So Many Ways I Love You**	1959	12.00	30.00
Mercury SR-60225	(S)	**So Many Ways I Love You**	1959	16.00	40.00
Mercury MG-20602	(M)	**Songs I Love To Sing**	1960	8.00	20.00
Mercury SR-60602	(S)	**Songs I Love To Sing**	1960	12.00	30.00
Mercury MG-20607	(M)	**Brook Benton's Golden Hits**	1961	8.00	20.00
Mercury SR-60607	(S)	**Brook Benton's Golden Hits**	1961	12.00	30.00
Mercury MG-20619	(M)	**If You Believe**	1961	8.00	20.00
Mercury SR-60619	(S)	**If You Believe**	1961	10.00	25.00
Mercury MG-20641	(M)	**The Boll Weevil Song**	1961	8.00	20.00
Mercury SR-60641	(S)	**The Boll Weevil Song**	1961	10.00	25.00
Mercury MG-20673	(M)	**There Goes That Song Again**	1962	8.00	20.00
Mercury SR-60673	(S)	**There Goes That Song Again**	1962	10.00	25.00
Mercury MG-20740	(M)	**Singing The Blues**	1962	8.00	20.00
Mercury SR-60740	(S)	**Singing The Blues**	1962	10.00	25.00
Mercury MG-20774	(M)	**Brook Benton's Golden Hits, Volume 2**	1963	8.00	20.00
Mercury SR-60774	(S)	**Brook Benton's Golden Hits, Volume 2**	1963	10.00	25.00
Mercury MG-20830	(M)	**Best Ballads Of Broadway**	1963	8.00	20.00
Mercury SR-60830	(S)	**Best Ballads Of Broadway**	1963	10.00	25.00
Mercury MG-20886	(M)	**Born To Sing The Blues**	1964	8.00	20.00
Mercury SR-60886	(S)	**Born To Sing The Blues**	1964	10.00	25.00
—Mercury albums above have black labels with silver print.—					

BENTON, BROOK, & DINAH WASHINGTON

Mercury MG-20588	(M)	**The Two Of Us**	1960	8.00	20.00
Mercury SR-60244	(S)	**The Two Of Us**	1960	10.00	25.00

BERGEN, FRANCES

Columbia CL-873	(M)	**Beguiling Miss**	1956	12.00	30.00

Label & Catalog #		Title	Year	VG+	NM
BERGEN, POLLY					
Jubilee JGL-14	(10")	Polly Bergen	1955	20.00	50.00
Columbia CL-994	(M)	Bergen Sings Morgan	1957	12.00	30.00
Columbia CL-1031	(M)	The Party's Over	1957	12.00	30.00
Columbia CL-1138	(M)	Polly And Her Pop	1958	10.00	25.00
Columbia OL-2014	(M)	First Impressions	1959	10.00	25.00
Columbia CL-1218	(M)	My Heart Sings	1959	8.00	20.00
Columbia CS-8018	(S)	My Heart Sings	1959	10.00	25.00
Columbia CL-1300	(M)	All Alone By The Telephone	1959	8.00	20.00
Columbia CS-8100	(S)	All Alone By The Telephone	1959	10.00	25.00
Columbia CL-1481	(M)	Four Seasons Of Love	1960	8.00	20.00
Columbia CS-8246	(S)	Four Seasons Of Love	1960	10.00	25.00
Columbia CL-1632	(M)	"Do Re Mi" And "Annie Get Your Gun"	1961	8.00	20.00
Columbia CS-8432	(S)	"Do Re Mi" And "Annie Get Your Gun"	1961	10.00	25.00

— Columbia albums above have three white "eye" logos on each side of the spindle hole.—

BERGMAN, INGRID					
Caedmon TC-1118	(M)	The Human Voice	1960	12.00	30.00

BERLE, MILTON					
Refer to Benny Fields.					
Forum F-9005	(M)	Songs My Mother Loved	196?	12.00	30.00
Forum SF-9005	(S)	Songs My Mother Loved	196?	16.00	40.00

BERNARD, ROD					
Jin LP-4007	(M)	Rod Bernard	196?	20.00	50.00

BERRY, BROOKS, & SCRAPPER BLACKWELL					
Bluesville BVLP-1074	(M)	My Heart Struck Sorrow	1963	40.00	100.00

— Bluesville albums above have bright blue labels with silver print.—

Bluesville BVLP-1074	(M)	My Heart Struck Sorrow	1964	12.00	30.00

— Bluesville albums above have blue labels with a trident logo on the right side.—

BERRY, CHUCK					
Mr. Berry also recorded with Bo Diddley.					
Chess LP-1426	(M)	After School Session *(White label promo)*	1958	250.00	500.00
Chess LP-1426	(M)	After School Session	1958	80.00	200.00
Chess LP-1432	(M)	One Dozen Berrys *(White label promo)*	1958	250.00	500.00
Chess LP-1432	(M)	One Dozen Berrys	1958	80.00	200.00
Chess LP-1435	(M)	Berry Is On Top *(White label promo)*	1959	20.00	400.00
Chess LP-1435	(M)	Berry Is On Top	1959	80.00	200.00
Chess LP-1448	(M)	Rockin' At The Hops *(White label promo)*	1960	200.00	400.00
Chess LP-1448	(M)	Rockin' At The Hops	1960	80.00	200.00
Chess LP-1456	(M)	New Juke Box Hits *(White label promo)*	1961	200.00	400.00
Chess LP-1456	(M)	New Juke Box Hits	1961	80.00	200.00
Chess LP-1465	(M)	Chuck Berry Twist *(White label promo)*	1962	150.00	300.00
Chess LP-1465	(M)	Chuck Berry Twist	1962	40.00	100.00
Chess LP-1465	(M)	More Chuck Berry *(White label promo)*	1963	150.00	300.00
Chess LP-1465	(M)	More Chuck Berry	1963	40.00	100.00
Chess LP-1480	(M)	Chuck Berry On Stage *(White label promo)*	1963	150.00	300.00
Chess LP-1480	(M)	Chuck Berry On Stage	1963	40.00	100.00
Chess LP-1485	(M)	Chuck Berry's Greatest Hits *(White label)*	1964	80.00	200.00
Chess LP-1485	(M)	Chuck Berry's Greatest Hits	1964	20.00	50.00
Chess LP-1488	(M)	St. Louis To Liverpool *(White label promo)*	1964	80.00	200.00
Chess LP-1488	(M)	St. Louis To Liverpool	1964	20.00	50.00
Chess LPS-1488	(S)	St. Louis To Liverpool	1964	30.00	75.00

— Chess albums above have black or blue & silver labels.—

Chess LP-1495	(DJ)	Chuck Berry In London *(White label promo)*	1965	80.00	200.00
Chess LP-1495	(M)	Chuck Berry In London	1965	16.00	40.00
Chess LPS-1495	(S)	Chuck Berry In London	1965	20.00	50.00
Chess LP-1498	(DJ)	Fresh Berry's *(White label promo)*	1965	80.00	200.00
Chess LP-1498	(M)	Fresh Berry's	1965	16.00	40.00
Chess LPS-1498	(S)	Fresh Berry's	1965	20.00	50.00

— Chess albums above have blue labels with a gold logo on top.—

Chess LPS-1480	(E)	Chuck Berry On Stage	1966	16.00	40.00
Chess LPS-1485	(E)	Chuck Berry's Greatest Hits	1966	16.00	40.00

— Chess albums above have black labels with a gold logo on top.—

Mercury MG-21103	(M)	Chuck Berry's Golden Hits	1967	8.00	20.00
Mercury SR-61103	(S)	Chuck Berry's Golden Hits	1967	10.00	25.00

Label & Catalog #		Title	Year	VG+	NM
Mercury SR-61123	(S)	Chuck Berry In Memphis	1967	16.00	40.00
Mercury MG-21138	(M)	Live At The Fillmore Auditorium	1967	12.00	30.00
Mercury SR-61138	(S)	Live At The Fillmore Auditorium	1967	16.00	40.00
		(On Mercury 2/61138, Berry is backed by The Steve Miller Band.)			
Mercury SR-61176	(S)	From St. Louis To Frisco	1968	10.00	25.00
Mercury SR-61223	(S)	Concerto In B. Goode	1969	10.00	25.00

BERRY, KEN

Barnaby Z-30014	(S)	R. F. D.	197?	10.00	25.00

BERRY, RICHARD, & THE DREAMERS

Crown CLP-5371	(M)	Richard Berry And The Dreamers	1963	30.00	75.00
Crown CST-371	(E)	Richard Berry And The Dreamers	1963	14.00	35.00

BERRY, RICHARD, & THE SOUL SEARCHERS

Pam 1001	(M)	Live At The Century Club	196?	20.00	50.00
Pam 1002	(M)	Wild Berry	196?	20.00	50.00

BEST, PETE
Best was a member of the Beatles before they recorded for EMI/Parlophone.

Savage BM-71	(M)	Best Of The Beatles	1965	80.00	200.00
		(Original pressings of Savage 71 have orange labels; the cover has a white circle around Best. Counterfeits have red labels and a blue circle around Best.)			

BEVERLY HILL BILLIES, THE
The Hill Billies are a studio concoction featuring Elton Britt.

Rar-Arts 1000	(M)	Those Fabulous Beverly Hill Billies (Gold vinyl)	1961	40.00	100.00

BIBB, LEON
Leon Bibb is a folksinger and guitar player.

Vanguard VRS-9067	(M)	Love Songs	1960	8.00	20.00
Vanguard VSD-2067	(S)	Love Songs	1960	10.00	25.00
Vanguard VRS-9041	(M)	Folksongs	1961	8.00	20.00
Vanguard VSD-2041	(S)	Folksongs	1961	10.00	25.00
Vanguard VRS-9058	(M)	Tol' My Captain	1961	8.00	20.00
Vanguard VSD-2058	(S)	Tol' My Captain	1961	10.00	25.00
Liberty LRP-3327	(M)	Encore! Leon Bibb In Concert	1963	8.00	20.00
Liberty LST-7327	(S)	Encore! Leon Bibb In Concert	1963	10.00	25.00

BICKERSONS, THE: Refer to DON AMECHE & FRANCES LANGFORD

BIG BEATS, THE

Liberty LRP-3407	(M)	The Big Beats Live	1965	8.00	20.00
Liberty LST-7407	(S)	The Big Beats Live	1965	10.00	25.00

BIG BOPPER, THE
The Big Bopper is a pseudonym for J. P. "Jape" Richardson.

Mercury MG-20402	(M)	Chantilly Lace (Black label)	1959	200.00	400.00
Mercury MG-20402	(M)	Chantilly Lace	1964	80.00	200.00
		(Red label with black & white logo on top.)			
Mercury MG-20402	(M)	Chantilly Lace	1971	10.00	25.00
		(Red label with twelve oval logos around the perimeter.)			

BIG BROTHER

All American 5770	(M)	Big Brother Featuring Ernie Joseph	1970	60.00	150.00

BIG BROTHER & THE HOLDING COMPANY
BB&THC were Peter Albin, Sam Andrews, David Getz and James Gurley. The first two albums feature Janis Joplin; the final two feature Nick Gravenites.

Mainstream 56099	(M)	Big Brother & The Holding Company	1967	12.00	30.00
Mainstream S-6099	(S)	Big Brother & The Holding Company	1967	10.00	25.00
Columbia KCL-2900	(M)	Cheap Thrills	1968	20.00	50.00
Columbia KCS-9700	(S)	Cheap Thrills ("360 Sound" label)	1968	8.00	20.00
Columbia C-30222	(S)	Be A Brother	1970	10.00	25.00
Columbia C-30738	(S)	How Hard It Is	1971	10.00	25.00

Label & Catalog #		Title	Year	VG+	NM

BIG DADDY
Gee G-704	(M)	Big Daddy's Blues (Red label)	1960	40.00	100.00
Gee SG-704	(S)	Big Daddy's Blues (Red label)	1960	80.00	200.00
Regent MG-6106	(M)	Twist Party	1962	30.00	75.00

BIG MAYBELLE
Savoy MG-14005	(M)	Big Maybelle Sings	1957	50.00	150.00
Savoy MG-14011	(M)	Blues, Candy And Big Maybelle	1958	50.00	150.00
Brunswick BL-54107	(M)	What More Can A Woman Do	1962	10.00	25.00
Brunswick BL-754107	(S)	What More Can A Woman Do	1962	12.00	30.00
Brunswick BL-54142	(M)	The Gospel Soul Of Big Maybelle	1962	8.00	20.00
Brunswick BL-754142	(S)	The Gospel Soul Of Big Maybelle	1962	10.00	25.00
Scepter S-522	(M)	The Soul Of Big Maybelle	1964	8.00	20.00
Scepter SS-522	(S)	The Soul Of Big Maybelle	1964	12.00	30.00
Epic EE-22011	(M)	Gabbin' Blues	196?	10.00	25.00
Epic EE-22012	(E)	Gabbin' Blues	196?	6.00	15.00
Rojac R-522	(M)	Got A Brand New Bag	1967	12.00	30.00
Rojac RS-522	(S)	Got A Brand New Bag	1967	20.00	50.00
Rojac RS-123	(S)	Saga Of The Good Life And Hard Times	196?	12.00	30.00

BIG STAR
Big Star features Alex Chilton, formerly of The Box Tops.
Ardent ADS-2803	(S)	#1 Record	1972	10.00	25.00
Ardent ADS-1501	(S)	Radio City ("O My Soul" is in mono)	1974	10.00	25.00
PVC 7903	(S)	Big Star's Third	1978	14.00	35.00

BIG THREE, THE
The Big Three are Cass Elliot, James Hendricks and Tim Rose.
FM 307	(M)	The Big Three	1963	12.00	30.00
FM FS-307	(S)	The Big Three	1963	16.00	40.00
FM 311	(M)	The Big Three Live At The Recording Studio	1964	12.00	30.00
FM FS-311	(S)	The Big Three Live At The Recording Studio	1964	16.00	40.00
Roulette R-42000	(M)	The Big Three Featuring Cass Elliot	1967	10.00	25.00
Roulette SR-42000	(S)	The Big Three Featuring Cass Elliot	1967	12.00	30.00

BIKEL, THEODORE
Multi-instrumentalist Theodore Bikel is a singer of traditonal folk songs in many languages..
Elektra EKL-32	(10")	Folksongs Of Israel	195?	20.00	50.00
Elektra EKL-105	(M)	An Actor's Holiday—			
		Folksongs Of Many Lands	195?	14.00	35.00
Elektra EKL-132	(M)	Folksongs Of Israel	195?	14.00	35.00
		(Elektra 132 is a reissue of 32 with five additional tracks)			
Elektra EKL-141	(M)	Theodore Bikel Sings Jewish Folk Songs	1959	14.00	35.00
Elektra EKL-175	(M)	Bravo Bikel	1959	12.00	30.00
Elektra EKS-7175	(S)	Bravo Bikel	1959	14.00	35.00
Elektra EKL-200	(M)	From Bondage To Freedom	1961	8.00	20.00
Elektra EKS-7200	(S)	From Bondage To Freedom	1961	10.00	25.00
Elektra EKL-210	(M)	A Harvest Of Israeli Songs	1962	8.00	20.00
Elektra EKS-7210	(S)	A Harvest Of Israeli Songs	1962	10.00	25.00
Elektra EKL-220	(M)	Poetry And Prophecy Of The Old Testament	1962	8.00	20.00
Elektra EKS-7220	(S)	Poetry And Prophecy Of The Old Testament	1962	10.00	25.00
Elektra EKL-225	(M)	Best Of Theodore Bikel	1962	8.00	20.00
Elektra EKS-7225	(S)	Best Of Theodore Bikel	1962	10.00	25.00
Elektra EKL-230	(M)	Theodore Bikel On Tour	1963	8.00	20.00
Elektra EKS-7230	(S)	Theodore Bikel On Tour	1963	10.00	25.00
Elektra EKL-250	(M)	A Folksinger's Choice	1964	8.00	20.00
Elektra EKS-7250	(S)	A Folksinger's Choice	1964	10.00	25.00
Elektra EKL-281	(M)	Theodore Bikel	1964	8.00	20.00
Elektra EKS-7281	(S)	Theodore Bikel	1964	10.00	25.00
Elektra EKL-326	(M)	Songs Of The Earth	1967	8.00	20.00
Elektra EKS-7326	(S)	Songs Of The Earth	1967	10.00	25.00

BIKEL, THEODORE, & GEULA GILL
Elektra EKL-150	(M)	Russian Gypsy	1959	8.00	20.00
Elektra EKS-7150	(S)	Russian Gypsy	1959	10.00	25.00
Elektra EKL-161	(M)	Folk Songs From Just About Everywhere	1959	8.00	20.00
Elektra EKS-7161	(S)	Folk Songs From Just About Everywhere	1959	10.00	25.00
Elektra EKL-185	(M)	Songs Of Russia, Old And New	1960	8.00	20.00
Elektra EKS-7185	(S)	Songs Of Russia, Old And New	1960	10.00	25.00

Label & Catalog #		Title	Year	VG+	NM

BIKEL, THEODORE, & CYNTHIA GOODING
Refer to Cynthia Gooding.

| Elektra EKL-109 | (M) | A Young Man And A Maid | 195? | 14.00 | 35.00 |

BIRMINGHAM SUNDAY

| All-American | (S) | Birmingham Sunday | 197? | 300.00 | 500.00 |

BIRTH CONTROL

| Prophesy PRS-1002 | (S) | Birth Control—A New German Rock Group | 1970 | 10.00 | 25.00 |

BISHOP, JOEY

| ABC-Paramount 408 | (M) | Joey Bishop Sings Country & Western | 1962 | 10.00 | 25.00 |
| ABC-Paramount S-408 | (S) | Joey Bishop Sings Country & Western | 1962 | 12.00 | 30.00 |

BLACK, BILL
Bill Black was Elvis Presley's bass player from 1954 through his first golden era with RCA, 1956-1959.

Hi HL-12001	(M)	Smokie	1960	24.00	60.00
		—Hi albums above have a black label with a red & silver logo on top.—			
Hi HL-12001	(M)	Smokie	1960	12.00	40.00
Hi SHL-32001	(E)	Smokie	1964	8.00	20.00
Hi HL-12002	(M)	Saxy Jazz	1960	12.00	40.00
Hi SHL-32002	(E)	Saxy Jazz	196?	8.00	20.00
Hi HL-12003	(M)	Solid And Raunchy	1960	12.00	40.00
Hi SHL-32003	(E)	Solid And Raunchy	1960	8.00	20.00
Hi HL-12004	(M)	That Wonderful Feeling	1961	8.00	20.00
Hi SHL-32004	(S)	That Wonderful Feeling	1961	10.00	30.00
Hi HL-12005	(M)	Movin'	1961	8.00	20.00
Hi SHL-32005	(S)	Movin'	1961	10.00	30.00
Hi HL-12006	(M)	Bill Black's Record Hop	1961	8.00	20.00
Hi SHL-32006	(S)	Bill Black's Record Hop	1961	10.00	30.00
Hi HL-12006	(M)	Let's Twist Her	1962	8.00	20.00
Hi SHL-32006	(S)	Let's Twist Her	1962	10.00	25.00
		("Let's Twist Her" is a repackage of "Bill Black's Record Hop.")			
Hi HL-12009	(M)	The Untouchable Sound Of Bill Black	1963	8.00	20.00
Hi SHL-32009	(S)	The Untouchable Sound Of Bill Black	1963	10.00	25.00
Hi SR-8689	(DJ)	Sears-Silvertone Presents Hi Records: The Untouchable Sound Of Bill Black	1963	12.00	30.00
Hi HL-12015	(M)	Bill Black Plays The Blues	1964	8.00	20.00
Hi SHL-32015	(S)	Bill Black Plays The Blues	1964	10.00	25.00
Hi HL-12017	(M)	Bill Black Plays Tunes By Chuck Berry	1964	8.00	20.00
Hi SHL-32017	(S)	Bill Black Plays Tunes By Chuck Berry	1964	10.00	25.00

BLACK, CILLA

| Capitol T-2308 | (M) | Is It Love? | 1965 | 12.00 | 30.00 |
| Capitol ST-2308 | (S) | Is It Love? | 1965 | 16.00 | 40.00 |

BLACK, JEANNE

| Capitol T-1513 | (M) | A Little Bit Lonely | 1961 | 8.00 | 20.00 |
| Capitol ST-1513 | (S) | A Little Bit Lonely | 1961 | 10.00 | 25.00 |

BLACK MERDA

| Chess LP-1551 | (S) | Black Merda | 1970 | 30.00 | 75.00 |

BLACK ORCHIDS, THE

| "NR" 4680 | (S) | The Black Orchids *(No cover)* | 1972 | 30.00 | 75.00 |

BLACK PEARL

| Atlantic SD-8220 | (S) | Black Pearl | 1969 | 10.00 | 25.00 |
| Prophesy PRS-1001 | (S) | Black Pearl Live | 1970 | 10.00 | 25.00 |

BLACK SABBATH
The original Sabbath featured Ozzie Osbourne, later replaced by Ronnie James Dio and Ian Gillan.

Warner Bros. WS-1871	(S)	Black Sabbath *(White label promo)*	1969	20.00	50.00
Warner Bros. WS-1887	(S)	Paranoid *(White label promo)*	1971	14.00	35.00
Warner Bros. BS-2562	(S)	Master Of Reality *(White label promo)*	1971	14.00	35.00
Warner Bros. BS-2562	(S)	Master Of Reality *(Green label with poster)*	1971	16.00	40.00
Warner Bros. BS-2602	(S)	Black Sabbath, Volume 4 *(White label)*	1972	14.00	35.00
Warner Bros. WS4-1887	(Q)	Paranoid	1974	10.00	25.00

Label & Catalog #		Title	Year	VG+	NM
Mercury SRM-1-61288	(S)	**The Ultimate Prophecy**	1970	20.00	50.00
BLACKHORSE					
DSDA 001	(S)	**Blackhorse**	197?	30.00	75.00
BLACKMAN, HONOR [P&P]					
London LL-3408	(M)	**Everything I've Got** *("Goldfinger" cover)*	1964	12.00	30.00
London PS-408	(S)	**Everything I've Got** *("Goldfinger" cover)*	1964	16.00	40.00
BLACKWELL, OTIS					
Davis 109	(M)	**Singin' The Blues**	1956	200.00	400.00
BLACKWELL, SCRAPPER					
Scrapper also recorded with Brooks Berry.					
Bluesville BVLP-1047	(M)	**Mr. Scrapper's Blues**	1962	60.00	150.00
— Bluesville albums above have bright blue labels with silver print.—					
Bluesville BVLP-1047	(M)	**Mr. Scrapper's Blues**	1964	16.00	40.00
—Bluesville albums above have blue labels with a trident logo on the right side.—					
BLAINE, HAL					
Refer to The Folkswingers.					
RCA Victor LPM-2834	(M)	**Deuces, "T's," Roadsters & Drums**	1963	40.00	100.00
RCA Victor LSP-2834	(S)	**Deuces, "T's," Roadsters & Drums**	1963	60.00	150.00
(RCA 2834 credits Hal Blaine & The Young Cougars.)					
Dunhill D-50002	(M)	**Drums! Drums! A Go Go**	1966	10.00	25.00
Dunhill DS-50002	(S)	**Drums! Drums! A Go Go**	1966	12.00	30.00
Dunhill D-50019	(M)	**Psychedelic Percussion**	1967	12.00	30.00
Dunhill DS-50019	(S)	**Psychedelic Percussion**	1967	20.00	50.00
Dunhill D-50035	(M)	**Have Fun!!! Play Drums!!!** *(With book)*	1969	16.00	40.00
Dunhill DS-50035	(S)	**Have Fun!!! Play Drums!!!** *(With book)*	1969	20.00	50.00
(Dunhill 50035 was issued with an instruction booklet.)					
Dunhill D-50035	(M)	**Have Fun!!! Play Drums!!!** *(Without book)*	1969	12.00	30.00
Dunhill DS-50035	(S)	**Have Fun!!! Play Drums!!!** *(Without book)*	1969	16.00	40.00
BLAINE, VIVIAN					
Mercury MG-20233	(M)	**Vivian Blaine Sings** **Songs From The Ziegfield Follies**	1957	20.00	50.00
Mercury MG-20234	(M)	**Vivian Blaine Sings** **Songs From "The Great White Way"**	1957	20.00	50.00
Mercury MG-20321	(M)	**Vivian Blaine Sings Songs From "Pal Joey"**	1958	20.00	50.00
Wing MGW-12166	(M)	**Broadway's All Time Hits**	1963	10.00	25.00
Wing SRW-16166	(S)	**Broadway's All Time Hits**	1963	12.00	30.00

BLAIR, SALLIE: *Refer to* GOLDMINE'S PRICE GUIDE TO COLLECTIBLE JAZZ ALBUMS

BLAKE, BETTY: *Refer to* GOLDMINE'S PRICE GUIDE TO COLLECTIBLE JAZZ ALBUMS

BLANC, MEL
Mel Blanc was the extraordinary voice behind most of the Looney Tunes & Merrie Melodies characters, including Bugs Bunny and Daffy Duck. Many of the records that include his work can be found in the "Cartoon Character" listings in this book. Refer to Jack Benny.

Capitol H-436 (10")	(M)	**Party Panic**	1953	40.00	100.00
MBA (No number)	(DJ)	**Mel Blanc Takes A Humorous Look At Commercials...** **Past, Present & Future**	1966	40.00	100.00
(Promotional record issued without a cover and with an insert.)					
BLAND, BOBBY "BLUE"					
Duke DLP-74	(M)	**Two Steps From The Blues**	1961	50.00	150.00
Duke DLP-75	(M)	**Here's The Man**	1961	50.00	150.00
— Duke albums above have purple & yellow/orange labels.—					
Duke DLP-74	(M)	**Two Steps From The Blues** *(Red vinyl)*	1962	50.00	150.00
Duke DLP-74	(M)	**Two Steps From The Blues**	1962	30.00	75.00
Duke DLPS-74	(E)	**Two Steps From The Blues**	196?	20.00	50.00
Duke DLP-75	(M)	**Here's The Man**	1962	20.00	50.00
Duke DLPS-75	(S)	**Here's The Man**	1962	50.00	150.00
(Original pressings of DLPS-75 have a spoken on "36-22-36.")					
Duke DLPS-75	(S)	**Here's The Man**	196?	30.00	75.00
(Later pressings delete the spoken intro.)					
Duke DLP-77	(M)	**Call On Me**	1963	20.00	50.00

Label & Catalog #		Title	Year	VG+	NM
Duke DLP-77	(M)	Call On Me	1963	20.00	50.00
Duke DLP-78	(M)	Ain't Nothing You Can Do	1964	20.00	50.00
Duke DLP-79	(M)	The Soul Of The Man	1966	12.00	30.00
Duke DLPS-79	(S)	The Soul Of The Man	1966	16.00	40.00
Duke DLP-84	(M)	The Best Of Bobby Bland	1967	6.00	20.00
Duke DLPS-84	(P)	The Best Of Bobby Bland	1967	6.00	25.00
Duke DLP-88	(M)	Touch Of The Blues	1967	10.00	25.00
Duke DLPS-88	(S)	Touch Of The Blues	1967	6.00	25.00
Duke DLP-86	(M)	The Best Of Bobby Bland, Volume 2	1968	12.00	30.00
Duke DLPS-86	(P)	The Best Of Bobby Bland, Volume 2	1968	10.00	25.00
Duke DLPS-89	(S)	Spotlighting The Man	1969	10.00	25.00
Duke X-90	(S)	If Loving You Is Wrong	1970	10.00	25.00
Duke X-92	(S)	Introspective Of The Early Years	1970	10.00	25.00
		— Duke albums above have orange labels. —			

BLAND, BOBBY "BLUE" / JIMMY SOUL / JOHNNY "GUITAR" WATSON

Crown CLP-5358	(M)	Bobby Bland-Jimmy Soul-Johnny Watson	196?	10.00	25.00
Crown CST-358	(E)	Bobby Bland-Jimmy Soul-Johnny Watson	196?	4.00	10.00

BLASTERS, THE

Crown CLP-5392	(M)	Sounds Of The Drags	1963	8.00	20.00
Crown CST-392	(S)	Sounds Of The Drags	1963	10.00	25.00

BLASTERS, THE

Rollin' Rock 021	(S)	American Music	1980	30.00	75.00

BLAZERS, THE: *Refer to* THE HARMONY BLAZERS

BLENDELLS, THE: *Refer to* SONNY & CHER

BLENTONES, THE

Success SLP-1010	(M)	Only For Teenagers	1963	80.00	200.00

BLESSED END

T. N. S.	(M)	Movin' On	1971	80.00	200.00

BLOCKER, DAN
Also refer to Lorne Greene & Dan Blocker & Mike Landon & Pernell Roberts.

Trey TLP-903	(M)	Tales For Young 'Uns	196?	20.00	50.00
RCA Victor LPM-2896	(M)	Our Land, Our Heritage	1964	16.00	40.00
RCA Victor LSP-2896	(S)	Our Land, Our Heritage	1964	20.00	50.00

BLONDE ON BLONDE

Janus JLS-3003	(S)	Contrasts	1969	10.00	25.00

BLONDIE
Blondie features Debbie Harry, formerly of Wind In The Willows.

Private Stock PS-2035	(S)	Blondie	1975	8.00	20.00
Chrysalis CHS-24	(DJ)	At Home With Debbie Harry & Chris Stein	1981	10.00	25.00
		(Open-end interview with script.)			
Mobile Fidelity MFSL-50	(S)	Parallel Lines	1981	10.00	30.00

BLOOD, SWEAT & TEARS
Originally the brainchild of Blues Project members Al Kooper and Steve Katz, by the second album BS&T was later fronted by David Clayton-Thomas.

Columbia HC-49619	(S)	Child Is Father To The Man (Half-speed)	1981	25.00	75.00
Direct Disk SD-16605	(S)	Blood, Sweat And Tears	198?	20.00	60.00
Direct Disk SD-16605	(S)	Blood, Sweat And Tears (DBX encoded)	198?	6.00	30.00

BLOOMFIELD, MIKE, & AL KOOPER & STEVE STILLS

Columbia CS-9701	(S)	Super Session ("360 Sound" label)	1968	8.00	20.00
Columbia PCQ-9701	(Q)	Super Session (Gold label)	1974	10.00	25.00

BLUE BARONS, THE

Philips PHM-200-017	(M)	Twist To The Great Blues Hits	1962	8.00	20.00
Philips PHS-600-017	(S)	Twist To The Great Blues Hits	1962	10.00	25.00

BLUE BEATS, THE

A.A. 133	(M)	The Beatle Beat	1964	20.00	50.00

Label & Catalog #		Title	Year	VG+	NM

BLUE CHEER
The original Blue Cheer was Dickie Peterson, Leigh Stevens and Paul Whaley.

Label & Catalog #		Title	Year	VG+	NM
Philips PHM-200-264	(M)	Vincebus Eruptum	1968	16.00	40.00
Philips PHS-600-264	(S)	Vincebus Eruptum	1968	12.00	30.00
Philips PHS-600-278	(S)	Outsideinside	1968	12.00	30.00
Philips PHS-600-305	(S)	New! Improved! Blue Cheer	1969	12.00	30.00
Philips PHS-600-333	(S)	Blue Cheer	1970	12.00	30.00

— *Philips albums above have black labels with no print on the bottom perimeter.* —

BLUE DIAMONDS, THE

London LL-3235	(M)	Ramona	1963	10.00	25.00

BLUE JAYS, THE

Milestone MLP-1001	(M)	The Blue Jays Meet Little Caesar	196?	20.00	50.00

BLUE MOUNTAIN EAGLE
BLUE OYSTER CULT

Columbia AS-40	(DJ)	The Live Bootleg *(No cover)*	1972	30.00	75.00
		(Counterfeits of Columbia AS-40 exist.)			

BLUE RIDGE MOUNTAIN BOYS, THE

Time T-2083	(M)	Hootenanny And Bluegrass	1963	8.00	20.00
Time ST-2083	(S)	Hootenanny And Bluegrass	1963	10.00	25.00
Time S-2103	(M)	Bluegrass Down Home	1963	8.00	20.00
Time ST-2103	(S)	Bluegrass Down Home	1963	10.00	25.00

BLUE SKY BOYS, THE
The Blue Sky Boys were brothers Bill and Earl Bollick.

Camden CAL-797	(M)	The Blue Sky Boys	1963	10.00	25.00
Camden CAS-797	(E)	The Blue Sky Boys	1963	6.00	15.00
Starday SLP-205	(M)	Rare Treasury Of Old Song Gems	1963	20.00	50.00
Starday SLP-257	(M)	Together Again	1964	20.00	50.00
Starday SLP-269	(M)	The Blue Sky Boys	1964	20.00	50.00
Capitol T-2483	(M)	Presenting The Blue Sky Boys	1966	8.00	20.00
Capitol ST-2483	(S)	Presenting The Blue Sky Boys	1966	10.00	25.00

BLUE THINGS, THE

RCA Victor LPM-3603	(M)	The Blue Things	1966	40.00	100.00
RCA Victor LSP-3603	(S)	The Blue Things	1966	60.00	150.00

BLUE VELVET BAND, THE

Warner Bros. WS-1802	(S)	Sweet Moments	1969	12.00	30.00

BLUEBIRD

Piccadilly PIC-	(S)	Bluebird	1980	16.00	40.00

BLUES CLIMAX

Horne JC-333	(S)	Blues Climax	196?	20.00	50.00

BLUES MAGOOS, THE

Mercury MG-21096	(M)	Psychedelic Lollipop	1966	12.00	30.00
Mercury SR-61096	(S)	Psychedelic Lollipop	1966	16.00	40.00
Mercury MG-21104	(M)	Electric Comic Book	1967	16.00	40.00
Mercury SR-61104	(S)	Electric Comic Book	1967	20.00	50.00
		(The price includes a small black & white comic book.)			
Mercury MG-21104	(M)	Electric Comic Book	1967	12.00	30.00
Mercury SR-61104	(S)	Electric Comic Book	1967	16.00	40.00
		(The price here is for the album without the comic book.)			
Mercury SR-61167	(M)	Basic Blues Magoos	1968	8.00	20.00
Mercury SR-61167	(S)	Basic Blues Magoos	1968	10.00	25.00

— *Mercury albums above have red labels with a black & white logo on top.* —

ABC S-697	(S)	Never Goin' Back To Georgia	1969	10.00	25.00
ABC S-710	(S)	Gulf Coast Bound	1970	10.00	25.00

BLUES PROJECT, THE
The Blues Project consisted of Roy Blumenfeld, Tommy Flanders, Danny Kalb, Steve Katz, Al Kooper and Andy Kulberg. Refer to Blood, Sweat & Tears; Seatrain.

Verve/Folkways FV-9024	(M)	Live At The Cafe Au-Go-Go	1966	10.00	25.00
Verve/Folkways FVS-9024	(S)	Live At The Cafe Au-Go-Go	1966	12.00	30.00

Label & Catalog #		Title	Year	VG+	NM
Verve/Folkways FT-3000	(M)	**Live At The Cafe Au-Go-Go**	1966	8.00	20.00
Verve/Folkways FTS-3000	(S)	**Live At The Cafe Au-Go-Go**	1966	10.00	25.00
		(Folkways 3000 is a reissue of 9024.)			
Verve/Forecast FT-3008	(M)	**Projections**	1966	8.00	20.00
Verve/Forecast FTS-3008	(S)	**Projections**	1966	10.00	25.00
Verve/Forecast FT-3025	(M)	**Live At Town Hall**	1967	8.00	20.00
Verve/Forecast FTS-3025	(S)	**Live At Town Hall**	1967	10.00	25.00
Verve/Forecast FTS-3046	(S)	**Planned Obsolescence**	1968	10.00	25.00
Verve/Forecast FTS-3069	(S)	**Flanders/Kalb/Katz, Etc.**	1969	10.00	25.00

BLUES SPECTRUM, THE

DB 8970	(S)	**We Were The Blues Spectrum**	1970	60.00	150.00

BLYTHE, STERLING

Sage C-14	(M)	**Night At The Showboat** (Red vinyl)	1962	20.00	50.00
		(Original pressings of C-14 have red & black lettering on the label.)			
Sage C-14	(M)	**Night At The Showboat** (Red vinyl)	1963	10.00	25.00
		(Later pressings have multi-colored lettering on the label.)			
Crown CLP-5179	(M)	**Sterling Blythe Sings**	1963	10.00	25.00

BO STREET RUNNERS, THE

B.T. Puppy BTPS-1026	(S)	**The Bo Street Runners**	1969	660.00	1,000.00

BOA

Snakefield SN-001	(S)	**Wrong Road**	1969	80.00	200.00

BOAZ

Blue Moon	(S)	**Three Of A Kind**	1978	40.00	100.00

BOB & EARL
Bob Garrett and Earl Cosby.

Tip TLP-1011	(M)	**Harlem Shuffle**	1964	14.00	35.00
Tip TLS-9011	(P)	**Harlem Shuffle**	1964	20.00	50.00
Crestview CRS-3055	(S)	**Bob & Earl**	196?	12.00	30.00

BOB & RAY

Unicorn 1001	(10")	**Bob & Ray**	1954	30.00	75.00
RCA Victor LPM-2131	(M)	**On A Platter**	1960	10.00	25.00
RCA Victor LSP-2131	(S)	**On A Platter**	1960	12.00	30.00

BOBB B. SOXX & THE BLUE JEANS
The Blue Jeans feature Darlene Love. Produced by Phil Spector.

Philles PHLP-4002	(DJ)	**Zip-A-Dee-Doo-Dah** (White label)	1963	500.00	1,000.00
Philles PHLP-4002	(M)	**Zip-A-Dee-Doo-Dah**	1963	200.00	400.00

BOETCHER, CURT
Produced by Gary Usher. Boetcher was formerly a member of Milennium.

Elektra EKS-75037	(DJ)	**There's An Innocent Face**	1972	6.00	15.00
Elektra EKS-75037	(S)	**There's An Innocent Face**	1972	10.00	25.00

BOGARDE, DIRK

London LL-3147	(M)	**Lyrics For Lovers**	1960	10.00	25.00

BOGGS, DOCK
Dock Boggs is a banjo player and singer of traditional American folk music.

Folkways FA-2351	(M)	**Dock Boggs**	196?	10.00	25.00
Folkways FA-2392	(M)	**Songs Of The Cumberland**	196?	10.00	25.00
Folkways FA-3903	(M)	**Dock Boggs (Volume 3)**	196?	10.00	25.00
Folkways 5458	(M)	**Dock Boggs Interview**	196?	10.00	25.00
Verve/Folkways FV-9025	(M)	**The Legendary Dock Boggs**	1965	10.00	25.00
Verve/Folkways FVS-9025	(E)	**The Legendary Dock Boggs**	1965	6.00	15.00

BOGGS, NOEL

Shasta SHLP-503	(M)	**Magic Steel Guitar** (Red cover)	1960	20.00	50.00
Shasta SHLP-530	(M)	**Hollywood And Vine**	196?	20.00	50.00
Shasta SHLP-531	(M)	**Noel Boggs With Friends**	196?	20.00	50.00
Repeat 100-10	(M)	**Anytime**	196?	20.00	50.00
Repeat 310-8	(M)	**Western Swing**	1965	20.00	50.00

Label & Catalog #		Title	Year	VG+	NM
BOGUSLAV, RAPHAEL					
Riverside RLP-12-638	(M)	Songs From a Village Garret	195?	12.00	30.00
BOHEMIAN VENDETTA					
Mainstream 56106	(M)	Bohemian Vendetta	1968	14.00	35.00
Mainstream S-6106	(S)	Bohemian Vendetta	1968	20.00	50.00
BOK, GORGON					
Gordon Bok is a folk-based guitar player, singer and songwriter. Refer to Clearwater; The Golden Ring.					
Verve/Forecast FT-3016	(M)	Gordon Bok	1966	8.00	20.00
Verve/Forecast FTS-3016	(S)	Gordon Bok	1966	10.00	25.00
BOLDER DAMN					
Hit HRI-5061	(S)	Mourning	1971	800.00	1,200.00
BOLGER, RAY					
Disneyland WD-3930	(M)	The Story Of The Scarecrow Of Oz	1965	12.00	30.00
Disneyland ST-3930	(S)	The Story Of The Scarecrow Of Oz	1965	16.00	40.00
BONADUCE, DANNY					
Lion LN-1015	(S)	Danny Bonaduce	1973	20.00	50.00
BOND, EDDIE					
Philips Int. PLP-1980	(M)	The Greatest Country Gospel Hits	1961	200.00	400.00
BOND, JOHNNY					
Johnny also recorded with Merle Travis.					
Starday SLP-147	(M)	That Wild, Wicked, But Wonderful West	1961	20.00	50.00
Starday SLP-187	(M)	Live It Up And Laugh It Up	1962	16.00	40.00
Starday SLP-227	(M)	Songs That Made Him Famous	1963	16.00	40.00
Starday SLP-298	(M)	Hot Rod Lincoln	1964	24.00	60.00
Starday SLP-333	(M)	Ten Little Bottles	1965	16.00	40.00
Starday SLP-354	(M)	Famous Hot Rodders I Have Known	1965	30.00	75.00
Starday SLP-368	(M)	The Man Who Comes Around	1966	12.00	30.00
Starday SLP-378	(M)	Bottles Up	1966	12.00	30.00
Starday SLP-388	(M)	The Branded Stock Of Johnny Bond	1966	12.00	30.00
Starday SLP-402	(M)	Ten Nights In A Barroom	1967	12.00	30.00
		— Starday albums above have yellow labels.—			
BONDS, GARY U.S.					
Refer to Chubby Checker / Gary U.S. Bonds.					
Legrand LLP-3001	(M)	Dance 'Til Quarter To Three	1961	40.00	100.00
Legrand LLP-3002	(M)	Twist Up Calypso	1962	30.00	75.00
Legrand LLP-3003	(M)	Greatest Hits Of Gary U.S. Bonds	1962	30.00	75.00
BONFA, LUIZ: *Refer to* **GOLDMINE'S PRICE GUIDE TO COLLECTIBLE JAZZ ALBUMS**					
BONNEVILLES, THE					
Drum Boy DLM-1001	(M)	Meet The Bonnevilles	1963	40.00	100.00
Drum Boy DLS-1001	(S)	Meet The Bonnevilles	1963	60.00	150.00
BONNEVILLES, THE					
Justice JLP-146	(S)	Bringing It Home	196?	360.00	600.00
BONNIE LOU					
King 595	(M)	Bonnie Lou Sings	1958	60.00	150.00
BONNIWELL'S MUSIC MACHINE *Refer to* **THE MUSIC MACHINE**					
BONYUN, BILL					
Bill Bonyun is a guitar player and singer of traditional folk songs.					
Folkways LP-2	(10")	Who Built America?	195?	30.00	75.00
Folkways FC-7402	(10")	Who Built America?	195?	30.00	75.00
Heirloom HL-500	(M)	Yankee Legend *(With Gene Bonyun)*	1958	12.00	30.00
Heirloom HL-502	(M)	The Story Of The American Revolution	1958	12.00	30.00
BONZO DOG BAND, THE/THE BONZO DOG DOO DAH BAND					
Imperial LP-9370	(M)	Gorilla *(Includes booklet)*	1968	12.00	30.00
Imperial LP-12370	(S)	Gorilla *(Includes booklet)*	1968	12.00	30.00

Label & Catalog #		Title	Year	VG+	NM
Imperial LP-9370	(M)	**Gorilla** *(Without booklet)*	1968	10.00	25.00
Imperial LP-12370	(S)	**Gorilla** *(Without booklet)*	1968	10.00	25.00
Imperial LP-12432	(S)	**Urban Spaceman** *(Includes booklet)*	1969	12.00	30.00
Imperial LP-12432	(S)	**Urban Spaceman** *(Without booklet)*	1969	10.00	25.00
Imperial LP-12445	(S)	**Tadpoles**	1969	10.00	25.00
Imperial LP-12457	(S)	**Keynsham**	1970	10.00	25.00
BOOGIE KINGS, THE					
Montel LP-104	(M)	**The Boogie Kings**	1966	10.00	25.00
Montel LP-109	(M)	**Blue Eyed Soul**	1967	10.00	25.00
BOOKER T. & THE M.G.'S					
Refer to The Mar-Keys & Booket T. & The M.G.'s					
Stax ST-701	(M)	**Green Onions**	1962	20.00	50.00
Stax STS-701	(E)	**Green Onions**	1966	10.00	25.00
Stax ST-705	(M)	**Soul Dressing**	1965	20.00	40.00
Stax STS-705	(E)	**Soul Dressing**	1966	10.00	25.00
Stax ST-711	(M)	**And Now... Booker T. & The M.G.'s**	1966	12.00	30.00
Stax STS-711	(S)	**And Now... Booker T. & The M.G.'s**	1966	20.00	40.00
Stax ST-713	(M)	**In The Christmas Spirit**	1966	200.00	400.00
Stax STS-713	(S)	**In The Christmas Spirit**	1966	200.00	400.00
		(Original pressings of Stax 713 have a drawing of fingers and piano keys on a green cover.)			
Stax ST-713	(M)	**In The Christmas Spirit**	1967	80.00	200.00
Stax STS-713	(S)	**In The Christmas Spirit**	1967	80.00	200.00
		(Reissues have multiple images of Santa Claus.)			
Stax ST-717	(M)	**Hip Hug-Her**	1967	10.00	25.00
Stax STS-717	(S)	**Hip Hug-Her**	1967	12.00	30.00
Stax ST-724	(M)	**Doin' Our Thing**	1968	12.00	30.00
Stax STS-724	(S)	**Doin' Our Thing**	1968	10.00	25.00
Stax STS-2001	(S)	**Soul Limbo**	1968	10.00	25.00
Stax STS-2006	(S)	**Up Tight**	1968	10.00	25.00
Stax STS-2009	(S)	**Booker T. Set**	1969	10.00	25.00
Stax STS-2027	(S)	**McLemore Avenue**	1971	10.00	25.00
BOONE, PAT					
Dot DLP-3012	(M)	**Pat Boone**	1956	20.00	50.00
Dot DLP-3030	(M)	**Howdy!**	1956	20.00	50.00
		— Dot albums above have maroon labels.—			
Dot DLP-3012	(M)	**Pat Boone**	1957	12.00	30.00
Dot DLP-25012	(E)	**Pat Boone**	196?	6.00	15.00
Dot DLP-3030	(M)	**Howdy!**	1957	12.00	30.00
Dot DLP-25030	(E)	**Howdy!**	196?	6.00	15.00
Dot DLP-3050	(M)	**Pat**	1957	12.00	30.00
Dot DLP-25050	(E)	**Pat**	196?	6.00	15.00
Dot DLP-3068	(M)	**Hymns We Love**	1957	12.00	30.00
Dot DLP-25068	(S)	**Hymns We Love**	1957	12.00	30.00
Dot DLP-3071	(M)	**Pat's Great Hits**	1957	10.00	25.00
Dot DLP-25071	(P)	**Pat's Great Hits**	1957	12.00	30.00
Dot DLP-9000	(M)	**April Love**	1957	12.00	30.00
Dot DLP-3077	(M)	**Pat Boone Sings Irving Berlin**	1958	10.00	25.00
Dot DLP-25077	(S)	**Pat Boone Sings Irving Berlin**	1958	12.00	30.00
Dot DLP-3118	(M)	**Star Dust**	1958	10.00	25.00
Dot DLP-25118	(S)	**Star Dust**	1958	12.00	30.00
Dot DLP-3121	(M)	**Yes Indeed!**	1958	10.00	25.00
Dot DLP-3158	(M)	**Pat Boone Sings**	1959	10.00	25.00
Dot DLP-25158	(S)	**Pat Boone Sings**	1959	12.00	30.00
Dot DLP-3180	(M)	**Tenderly**	1959	10.00	25.00
Dot DLP-25180	(S)	**Tenderly**	1959	12.00	30.00
Dot DLP-3181	(M)	**Great Millions**	1959	10.00	25.00
Dot DLP-25181	(S)	**Great Millions**	1959	12.00	30.00
Dot DLP-3199	(M)	**Side By Side**	1959	10.00	25.00
Dot DLP-25199	(S)	**Side By Side**	1959	12.00	30.00
Dot DLP-3222	(M)	**White Christmas**	1959	10.00	25.00
Dot DLP-25222	(S)	**White Christmas**	1959	12.00	30.00
Dot DLP-3234	(M)	**He Leadeth Me**	1960	8.00	20.00
Dot DLP-25234	(S)	**He Leadeth Me**	1960	10.00	25.00
Dot DLP-3261	(M)	**Pat's Great Hits, Volume 2**	1960	8.00	20.00
Dot DLP-25261	(S)	**Pat's Great Hits, Volume 2**	1960	10.00	25.00

Label & Catalog #		Title	Year	VG+	NM
Dot DLP-3270	(M)	Moonglow	1960	8.00	20.00
Dot DLP-25270	(S)	Moonglow	1960	10.00	25.00
Dot DLP-25270	(S)	Moonglow (Blue vinyl)	1960	20.00	50.00
Dot DLP-3501	(M)	Pat Boone Sings Guess Who?	1963	20.00	50.00
Dot DLP-25501	(S)	Pat Boone Sings Guess Who?	1963	30.00	75.00
		("White Bucks" Boone sings "Blue Suede" Presley.)			

BOONE, RANDY

Decca DL-4619	(M)	The Singing Star Of The Virginian	1965	12.00	30.00
Decca DL-74619	(S)	The Singing Star Of The Virginian	1965	16.00	40.00
Decca DL-4663	(M)	Ramblin' Randy	1965	10.00	25.00
Decca DL-74663	(S)	Ramblin' Randy	1965	12.00	30.00

BOOT

Agape 2601	(S)	Boot	197?	10.00	25.00

BOOTSY / BOOTSY'S RUBBER BAND: *Refer to* **WILLIAM COLLINS**

BORGE, VICTOR

Columbia CL-1313	(M)	Victor Borge	1959	8.00	20.00
Columbia CLS-8113	(S)	Victor Borge	1959	10.00	25.00

BORDERSONG
Ann and Nancy Wilson of Heart provide backing vocals on "It's Time Again."

Real Good 1001	(S)	Morning	1975	24.00	60.00

BOSTIC, EARL

King 295-64	(10")	Earl Bostic & His Alto Sax, Vol. 1 (Red vinyl)	195?	40.00	100.00
King 295-64	(10")	Earl Bostic & His Alto Sax, Vol. 1	195?	24.00	60.00
King 295-65	(10")	Earl Bostic & His Alto Sax, Vol. 2 (Red vinyl)	195?	40.00	100.00
King 295-65	(10")	Earl Bostic & His Alto Sax, Vol. 2	195?	24.00	60.00
King 295-66	(10")	Earl Bostic & His Alto Sax, Vol. 3 (Red vinyl)	195?	40.00	100.00
King 295-66	(10")	Earl Bostic & His Alto Sax, Vol. 3	195?	24.00	60.00
King 295-72	(10")	Earl Bostic & His Alto Sax, Vol. 4	195?	24.00	60.00
King 295-76	(10")	Earl Bostic & His Alto Sax, Vol. 5	195?	24.00	60.00
King 295-77	(10")	Earl Bostic & His Alto Sax, Vol. 6	195?	24.00	60.00
King 295-78	(10")	Earl Bostic & His Alto Sax, Vol. 7	195?	24.00	60.00
King 295-79	(10")	Earl Bostic & His Alto Sax, Vol. 8	195?	24.00	60.00
King 295-95	(10")	Earl Bostic Plays Old St&ards	195?	24.00	60.00
King 295-103	(10")	Earl Bostic & His Alto Sax	195?	24.00	60.00
King 395-500	(M)	The Best Of Earl Bostic	1956	14.00	35.00
King 395-503	(M)	Bostic For You	1956	14.00	35.00
King 395-515	(M)	Alto-Tude	1956	14.00	35.00
King 395-525	(M)	Dance Time	1956	14.00	35.00
King 395-529	(M)	Let's Dance With Earl Bostic	1958	12.00	30.00
King 395-547	(M)	Invitation To Dance	1958	12.00	30.00
King 395-558	(M)	C'mon And Dance With Earl Bostic	1958	12.00	30.00
King KSD-558	(S)	C'mon And Dance With Earl Bostic	1958	20.00	50.00
King 395-571	(M)	Bostic Rocks	1958	12.00	30.00
King 395-583	(M)	Showcase Of Swinging Dance Hits	1958	12.00	30.00
King 395-597	(M)	Alto Magic In Hi-Fi	1958	12.00	30.00
King 395-602	(M)	Sweet Tunes Of The Fantastic Fifties	1959	12.00	30.00
King KSD-602	(S)	Sweet Tunes Of The Fantastic Fifties	1959	20.00	50.00
King 395-613	(M)	Workshop	1959	12.00	30.00
King 395-620	(M)	Sweet Tunes From The Roaring twenties	1959	12.00	30.00
King 632	(M)	Sweet Tunes Of The Swinging Forties	1959	10.00	25.00
King 640	(M)	Sweet Tunes Of The Sentimental Forties	1959	10.00	25.00
King 395- 620	(M)	Sweet Tunes From The Roaring twenties	1959	12.00	30.00
King 662	(M)	Musical Pearls	1959	10.00	25.00
King 705	(M)	Hit Tunes Of Big Broadway Shows	1960	10.00	25.00
King 725	(M)	25 Years Of Rhythm And Blues Hits	1960	10.00	25.00
King 786	(M)	By Popular Demand	1962	10.00	25.00
King 827	(M)	Earl Bostic Plays Bossa Nova	1963	10.00	25.00
King 838	(M)	Fantastic Fifties	1963	10.00	25.00
King 846	(M)	Jazz As I Feel It	1963	10.00	25.00
King 881	(M)	The Best Of Earl Bostic	1964	10.00	25.00
King 900	(M)	New Sound	1964	10.00	25.00
King 921	(M)	The Great Hits Of 1964	1964	10.00	25.00

— King albums above have "crownless" black labels.—

Label & Catalog #		Title	Year	VG+	NM
Philips PHS-600-262	(S)	**The Song Is Not Ended**	1967	10.00	25.00
King KS-1048	(S)	**Harlem Nocturne**	1969	10.00	25.00
BOSTON					
Epic HE-34188	(S)	**Boston** (Half-speed master)	1981	15.00	45.00
Epic HE-44188	(S)	**Boston** (Half-speed master)	1982	12.00	35.00
Epic E99-45050	(S)	**Don't Look Back** (Promo picture disc)	1982	10.00	25.00
Epic HE-45050	(S)	**Don't Look Back** (Half-speed master)	1982	25.00	75.00
BOSTON TEA PARTY, THE					
Flick Disc 45000	(S)	**The Boston Tea Party**	1968	10.00	25.00
American Inter. ST-A-1033	(S)	**The Cycle Savages** (Soundtrack)	1970	12.00	30.00

BOSWELL, CONNEE: *Refer to* GOLDMINE'S PRICE GUIDE TO COLLECTIBLE JAZZ ALBUMS

BOWEN, JIMMY
Jimmy also recorded with Buddy Knox.

Roulette R-25004	(M)	**Jimmy Bowen** (Black label)	1957	80.00	200.00
Reprise R-6210	(M)	**Sunday Morning With The Comics**	1966	12.00	30.00
Reprise RS-6210	(S)	**Sunday Morning With The Comics**	1966	16.00	40.00

BOWIE, DAVID
Refer to Mott The Hoople; Iggy Pop.

Deram DE-16003	(M)	**David Bowie** (White label promo)	1967	100.00	250.00
Deram DE-16003	(M)	**David Bowie**	1967	50.00	125.00
Deram DES-18003	(S)	**David Bowie**	1967	80.00	200.00
Mercury SR-61246	(M)	**Man Of Words, Man Of Music** (White label)	1969	100.00	250.00
Mercury SR-61246	(S)	**Man Of Words, Man Of Music**	1969	70.00	175.00
Mercury SR-61325	(M)	**The Man Who Sold The World** (White label)	1971	60.00	150.00
Mercury SR-61325	(S)	**The Man Who Sold The World**	1971	30.00	75.00
		(The matrix number is stamped in the trail-off vinyl of originals; counterfeits have those numbers hand-etched.)			
London 628/9	(P)	**Images 1966-1967** (2 LPs)	1973	12.00	30.00
RCA Victor LSP-4813	(S)	**Space Oddity**	1972	12.00	30.00
		(Orange label with fold-open poster.)			
RCA Victor LSP-4816	(S)	**Man Who Sold The World**	1972	12.00	30.00
		(Orange label with fold-open poster.)			
RCA Victor CPL1-0576	(S)	**Diamond Dogs**	1974		See below
		(Original covers show the Bowie-dog's genitals clearly. This was withdrawn and the offending member airbrushed out for release. Rare with a suggested Near Mint value of $3,000-6,000.)			
RCA Victor JD-11306	(DJ)	**Peter And The Wolf** (Black vinyl)	1978	16.00	40.00
RCA Victor DJL1-2697	(DJ)	**Bowie Now**	1978	14.00	35.00
RCA Victor DJL1-3016	(DJ)	**An Evening With David Bowie**	1978	30.00	75.00
		(Originals have a black border along the bottom of the cover.)			
RCA Victor DJL1-3545	(DJ)	**1980 All Clear**	1979	10.00	25.00
RCA Victor DJL1-3829	(DJ)	**Special Radio Series, Volume 1: Scary Monsters Interview Album**	1980	10.00	25.00
RCA Victor DJL1-3829	(DJ)	**College Radio Series, Volume 1: Scary Monsters Interview Album**	1980	12.00	30.00
RCA Victor DJL1-3840	(DJ)	**Scary Monsters Interview Album**	1980	12.00	30.00
RCA Victor CPL2-4862	(DJ)	**Ziggy Stardust, The Motion Picture** (2 LPs)	1983	40.00	100.00
		(Promo issued on clear vinyl.)			
EMI SPRO-9960/1	(DJ)	**Let's Talk**	1983	12.00	30.00
EMI SPRO-79112/3	(DJ)	**Never Let Me Down: The Interview**	1987	30.00	75.00
Mobile Fidelity MFSL-064	(S)	**The Rise & Fall Of Ziggy Stardust & The Spiders From Mars**	1981	15.00	45.00
Rykodisc LSD-4702	(DJ)	**The Rise & Fall Of Ziggy Stardust & The Spiders From Mars**	1990	40.00	100.00
		(Rykodisc 4702 contains an album and a CD.)			

BOWIE, PAT: *Refer to* GOLDMINE'S PRICE GUIDE TO COLLECTIBLE JAZZ ALBUMS

BOWMAN, DON, & SKEETER DAVIS

RCA Victor LPM-3920	(M)	**Funny Folk Flops**	1968	20.00	50.00
RCA Victor LSP-3920	(S)	**Funny Folk Flops**	1968	10.00	25.00

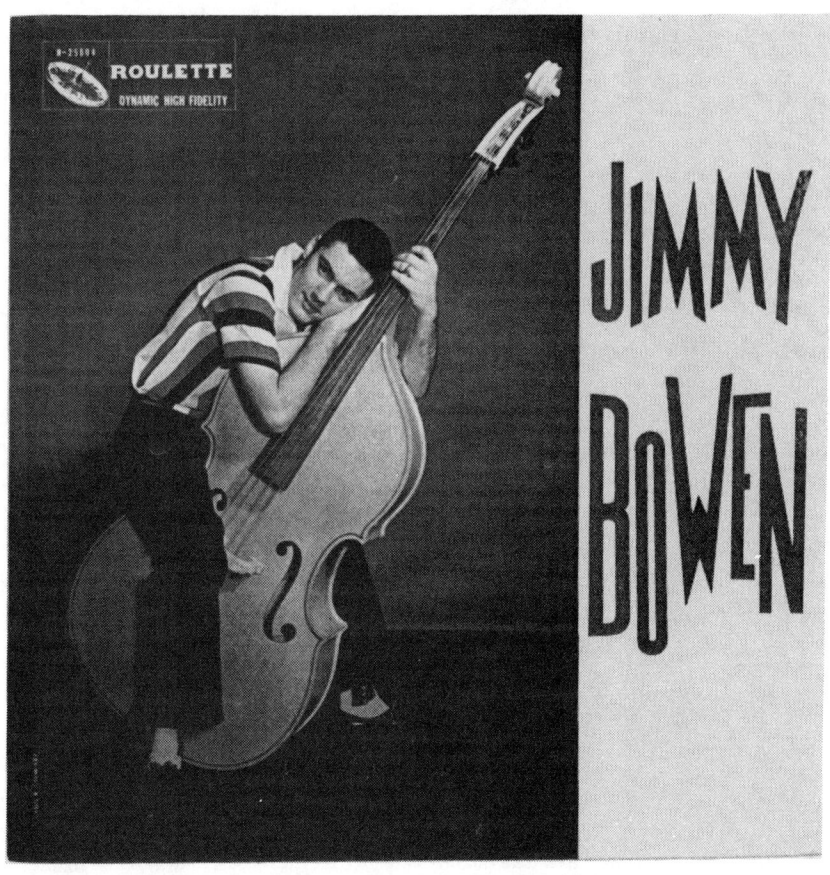

Jimmy Bowen's first album for Roulette was his last until the mid-'60s. During that time he worked as a songwriter and producer.

Label & Catalog #		Title	Year	VG+	NM

BOWN, ALAN: *Refer to* THE ALAN BOWN

BOX TOPS, THE
The Box Tops feature Alex Chilton. Refer to Big Star.

Bell 6011	(M)	The Letter/Neon Rainbow	1967	10.00	25.00
Bell S-6011	(S)	The Letter/Neon Rainbow	1967	12.00	30.00
Bell S-6017	(S)	Cry Like A Baby	1968	10.00	25.00
Bell S-6023	(S)	Non-Stop	1968	10.00	25.00

BOYCE, TOMMY, & BOBBY HART
Refer to Dolenz, Jones, Boyce & Hart.

A&M LP-126	(M)	Test Patterns	1967	8.00	20.00
A&M SP-4126	(S)	Test Patterns	1967	10.00	25.00
A&M LP-143	(M)	I Wonder What She's Doing Tonight	1968	10.00	25.00
A&M SP-4143	(S)	I Wonder What She's Doing Tonight	1968	12.00	30.00
A&M SP-4162	(S)	It's All Happening On The Inside	1968	10.00	25.00

BOYD, BILLY

Crown CLP-5196	(M)	Twangy Guitars	1960	10.00	25.00
Crown CST-196	(E)	Twangy Guitars	1960	4.00	10.00
Crown CST-196	(E)	Twangy Guitars (Red vinyl)	1960	20.00	50.00

BOYD, EDDIE

| Epic BN-26409 | (S) | 7936 South Rhodes | 1968 | 16.00 | 40.00 |
| London PS-554 | (S) | I'll Dust My Broom | 1969 | 16.00 | 40.00 |

BOYER, CHARLES

| Valiant VLM-5001 | (M) | Where Does Love Go? | 1966 | 10.00 | 25.00 |
| Valiant VLS-5001 | (S) | Where Does Love Go? | 1966 | 14.00 | 35.00 |

BRACKEN, EDDIE

| Sea Horse CSH-7002 | (M) | Bat Masterson | 1960 | 20.00 | 50.00 |

BRADBURY, RAY

| Tower ST-5172 | (S) | Dark Carnival | 1968 | 12.00 | 30.00 |

BRADFORD, ALEX

| Specialty SP-2108 | (M) | Too Close To Heaven | 1959 | 40.00 | 100.00 |

BRADLEY, OWEN

Coral CRL-56012	(10")	Christmas Time	195?	30.00	75.00
Coral CRL-56022	(10")	Strauss Waltzes	195?	30.00	75.00
Coral CRL-56035	(10")	Lazy River	195?	30.00	75.00
Coral CRL-56047	(10")	Singin' In The Rain	195?	30.00	75.00
Coral CRL-56065	(10")	Cherished Hymns	195?	30.00	75.00
Decca DL-8724	(M)	Bandstand Hop	1958	12.00	30.00
Decca DL-8868	(M)	Big Guitar	1958	12.00	30.00
Decca DL-78868	(S)	Big Guitar	1958	16.00	40.00
Decca DL-4078	(M)	Paradise Island	1960	10.00	25.00
Decca DL-74078	(S)	Paradise Island	1960	12.00	30.00

BRADLEY, WILL: *Refer to* GOLDMINE'S PRICE GUIDE TO COLLECTIBLE JAZZ ALBUMS

BRADSHAW, TINY

King 295-74	(10")	Off And On	1955	175.00	400.00
King 395-501	(M)	Selections	1958	200.00	500.00
King 653	(M)	Great Composer	1959	80.00	200.00
King 953	(M)	24 Great Songs	1966	10.00	25.00

BRADY BUNCH, THE
Refer to Chris Knight & Maureen McCormick.

Paramount PAS-6032	(S)	Meet The Brady Bunch	1972	20.00	50.00
Paramount PAS-6037	(S)	The Kids From The Brady Bunch	1972	14.00	35.00
Paramount PAS-5026	(S)	Merry Christmas From The Brady Bunch	1972	30.00	75.00
Paramount PAS-6058	(S)	The Brady Bunch Phonograph Record	1973	30.00	75.00

Label & Catalog #		Title	Year	VG+	NM

BRAND, OSCAR
Oscar Brand is a guitar player, singer and songwriter covering folk, country and pop material. Refer to Ed McCurdy / Oscar Brand / Jack Elliott; Jean Ritchie.

Label & Catalog #		Title	Year	VG+	NM
Chesterfield CMS-101	(10")	Backtoom Ballads	195?	20.00	50.00
Riverside RLP-12-630	(M)	American Drinking Songs	195?	12.00	30.00
Riverside RLP-12-639	(M)	G. I. American Army Songs	195?	12.00	30.00
Riverside RLP-12-825	(M)	Absolute Nonsense	195?	12.00	30.00
Riverside RLP-12-835	(M)	Songs Inane Only	1959	12.00	30.00
Riverside RLP-12-844	(M)	Songs Of The U.S. Army	1960	12.00	30.00
Tradition TLP-1014	(M)	Laughing America	195?	12.00	30.00
Tradition TLP-1022	(M)	Pie In The Sky	195?	12.00	30.00
Tradition TLP-2053	(M)	The Best Of Oscar Brand	1957	12.00	30.00
Audio Fidelity ADFL-906	(10")	Bawdy Songs & Back Room Ballads, Vol. 1	1957	14.00	35.00
Audio Fidelity LP-1906	(M)	Bawdy Songs & Back Room Ballads, Vol. 1	1957	10.00	25.00
Audio Fidelity LP-1806	(M)	Bawdy Songs & Back Room Ballads, Vol. 2	1957	10.00	25.00
Audio Fidelity LP-1824	(M)	Bawdy Songs & Back Room Ballads, Vol. 3	1957	10.00	25.00
Audio Fidelity LP-1847	(M)	Bawdy Songs & Back Room Ballads, Vol. 4	1958	10.00	25.00
Audio Fidelity SD-5847	(S)	Bawdy Songs & Back Room Ballads, Vol. 4	1958	12.00	30.00
Audio Fidelity LP-1884	(M)	Bawdy Sea Shanties (Volume 5)	1959	10.00	25.00
Audio Fidelity SD-5884	(S)	Bawdy Sea Shanties (Volume 5)	1959	12.00	30.00
Audio Fidelity LP-1920	(M)	Bawdy Western Songs	1960	10.00	25.00
Audio Fidelity SD-5920	(S)	Bawdy Western Songs	1960	12.00	30.00
Audio Fidelity LP-1952	(M)	Bawdy Songs Goes To College	1961	10.00	25.00
Audio Fidelity SD-5952	(S)	Bawdy Songs Goes To College	1961	12.00	30.00
Audio Fidelity LP-1971	(M)	Sing-A-Long Bawdy Songs	1962	10.00	25.00
Audio Fidelity SD-5971	(S)	Sing-A-Long Bawdy Songs	1962	12.00	30.00
Audio Fidelity LP-2121	(M)	Bawdy Hootenanny	1964	8.00	20.00
Audio Fidelity SD-6121	(S)	Bawdy Hootenanny	1964	10.00	25.00
Elektra EKL-169	(M)	Every Inch A Sailor	1960	8.00	20.00
Elektra EKS-7169	(S)	Every Inch A Sailor	1960	10.00	25.00
Elektra EKL-174	(M)	Tell It To The Marines	1960	8.00	20.00
Elektra EKS-7174	(S)	Tell It To The Marines	1960	10.00	25.00
Elektra EKL-178	(M)	Out Of The Blue	1960	8.00	20.00
Elektra EKS-7178	(S)	Out Of The Blue	1960	10.00	25.00
Elektra EKL-183	(M)	Boating Songs & All That Bilge	1960	8.00	20.00
Elektra EKS-7183	(S)	Boating Songs & All That Bilge	1960	10.00	25.00
Elektra EKL-188	(M)	Sports Car Songs For Big Wheels	1960	10.00	25.00
Elektra EKS-7188	(S)	Sports Car Songs For Big Wheels	1960	12.00	30.00
Elektra EKL-198	(M)	Up In The Air With Oscar Brand	1961	8.00	20.00
Elektra EKS-7198	(S)	Up In The Air With Oscar Brand	1961	10.00	25.00
Elektra EKL-204	(M)	For Doctors Only	1961	8.00	20.00
Elektra EKS-7204	(S)	For Doctors Only	1961	10.00	25.00
Elektra EKL-228	(M)	Snow Job For Skiers	1962	8.00	20.00
Elektra EKS-7228	(S)	Snow Job For Skiers	1962	10.00	25.00
Offbeat O-4021		The Drinking Man's Songbook	1961	10.00	25.00
ABC-Paramount ABC-388	(M)	Oscar Brand Sings For Adults	1961	10.00	25.00
ABC-Paramount ABCS-388	(S)	Oscar Brand Sings For Adults	1961	12.00	30.00
Decca DL-4275	(M)	Folk Songs For Fun	1962	8.00	20.00
Decca DL-74275	(S)	Folk Songs For Fun	1962	10.00	25.00
Impulse A-25	(M)	Morality	1962	10.00	25.00
Impulse AS-25	(S)	Morality	1962	12.00	30.00

BRASSELLE, KEEFE

Coral CRL-57295	(M)	Minstrel Man	1959	8.00	20.00
Coral CRL-757295	(S)	Minstrel Man	1959	10.00	25.00

BRAUTIGAN, RICHARD

Harvest ST-424	(S)	Listening To Richard Brautigan	1969	12.00	30.00

BRAZOS VALLEY BOYS, THE
The Brazos Valley Boys are Hank Thompson's backing group.

Warner Bros. W-1664	(M)	Where Is The Circus	1966	8.00	20.00
Warner Bros. WS-1664	(S)	Where Is The Circus	1966	10.00	25.00
Warner Bros. W-1679	(M)	The Countrypolitan Sound	1967	8.00	20.00
Warner Bros. WS-1679	(S)	The Countrypolitan Sound	1967	10.00	25.00
Warner Bros. W-1686	(M)	The Gold Standard Collection	1967	8.00	20.00
Warner Bros. WS-1686	(S)	The Gold Standard Collection	1967	10.00	25.00

Label & Catalog #		Title	Year	VG+	NM
BREEDLOVE, JIM					
Camden CAL-430	(M)	**Rock 'N' Roll Hits**	1958	12.00	30.00
BRENDA & THE TABULATIONS					
Dionn LPM-2000	(M)	**Dry Your Eyes**	1967	14.00	35.00
Dionn LPS-2000	(S)	**Dry Your Eyes** ("Dry" is rechanneled)	1967	20.00	50.00
BRENNAN, WALTER					
Dot DLP-3309	(M)	**Dutchman's Gold**	1960	10.00	25.00
Dot DLP-25309	(M)	**Dutchman's Gold**	1960	12.00	30.00
Everest LPBR-5103	(M)	**World Of Miracles**	1960	10.00	25.00
Everest SDBR-1103	(S)	**World Of Miracles**	1960	12.00	30.00
Everest LPBR-5123	(M)	**The President—A Musical Biography Of Our Chief Executive**	1960	10.00	25.00
Everest SDBR-1123	(S)	**The President—A Musical Biography Of Our Chief Executive**	1960	12.00	30.00
R.P.C. 108	(M)	**By The Fireside**	1962	10.00	25.00
R.P.C. 108S	(S)	**By The Fireside**	1962	12.00	30.00
Liberty LRP-3233	(M)	**Old Rivers**	1962	8.00	20.00
Liberty LST-7233	(S)	**Old Rivers**	1962	10.00	25.00
Liberty LRP-3241	(M)	**The President—A Musical Biography Of Our Chief Executive**	1962	8.00	20.00
Liberty LST-7241	(S)	**The President—A Musical Biography Of Our Chief Executive**	1962	10.00	25.00
		(Liberty3/7241 is a reissue of Everest 5/1123.)			
Liberty LRP-3244	(M)	**World Of Miracles**	1962	8.00	20.00
Liberty LST-7244	(S)	**World Of Miracles**	1962	10.00	25.00
		(Liberty3/7244 is a reissue of Everest 5/1103.)			
Liberty LRP-3257	(M)	**'Twas The Night Before Christmas Back Home**	1962	8.00	20.00
Liberty LST-7257	(S)	**'Twas The Night Before Christmas Back Home**	1962	10.00	25.00
Liberty LRP-3266	(M)	**Mama Sang A Song**	1963	8.00	20.00
Liberty LST-7266	(S)	**Mama Sang A Song**	1963	10.00	25.00
Liberty LRP-3317	(M)	**Talkin' From The Heart**	1964	8.00	20.00
Liberty LST-7317	(S)	**Talkin' From The Heart**	1964	10.00	25.00
Liberty LRP-3372	(M)	**Gunfight At The O.K. Corral**	1964	8.00	20.00
Liberty LST-7372	(S)	**Gunfight At The O.K. Corral**	1964	10.00	25.00
BREWER, TERESA					
London APB-1006	(10")	**Teresa Brewer**	1952	16.00	40.00
Coral CRL-56072	(10")	**A Bouquet Of Hits**	1952	16.00	40.00
Coral CRL-56093	(10")	**Till I Waltz Again With You**	1954	16.00	40.00
Coral CRL-57027	(M)	**Music, Music, Music**	1956	12.00	30.00
Coral CRL-57053	(M)	**Teresa**	1956	12.00	30.00
Coral CRL-57135	(M)	**For Teenagers In Love**	1957	12.00	30.00
Coral CRL-57144	(M)	**Teresa Brewer At Christmas Time**	1957	12.00	30.00
Coral CRL-57179	(M)	**Miss Music**	1958	12.00	30.00
Coral CRL-57232	(M)	**Time For Teresa**	1958	12.00	30.00
Coral CRL-57245	(M)	**Teresa Brewer And The Dixieland Band**	1959	8.00	20.00
Coral CRL-757245	(S)	**Teresa Brewer And The Dixieland Band**	1959	10.00	25.00
Coral CRL-57257	(M)	**When Your Lover Has Gone**	1959	8.00	20.00
Coral CRL-757257	(S)	**When Your Lover Has Gone**	1959	10.00	25.00
Coral CRL-57297	(M)	**Heavenly Lover**	1959	8.00	20.00
Coral CRL-757297	(S)	**Heavenly Lover**	1959	10.00	25.00
Coral CRL-57315	(M)	**Ridin' High**	1960	8.00	20.00
Coral CRL-757315	(S)	**Ridin' High**	1960	10.00	25.00
Coral CRL-57329	(M)	**Naughty, Naughty, Naughty**	1960	8.00	20.00
Coral CRL-757329	(S)	**Naughty, Naughty, Naughty**	1960	10.00	25.00
Coral CRL-57351	(M)	**My Golden Favorites**	1960	8.00	20.00
Coral CRL-757351	(E)	**My Golden Favorites**	1960	8.00	20.00
Coral CRL-57361	(M)	**Songs Everybody Knows**	1961	8.00	20.00
Coral CRL-757361	(S)	**Songs Everybody Knows**	1961	10.00	25.00
Coral CRL-57374	(M)	**Aloha From Teresa**	1961	8.00	20.00
Coral CRL-757374	(S)	**Aloha From Teresa**	1961	10.00	25.00
Coral CRL-57414	(M)	**Don't Mess With Tess**	1962	8.00	20.00
Coral CRL-757414	(S)	**Don't Mess With Tess**	1962	10.00	25.00

— Coral albums above have maroon labels.—

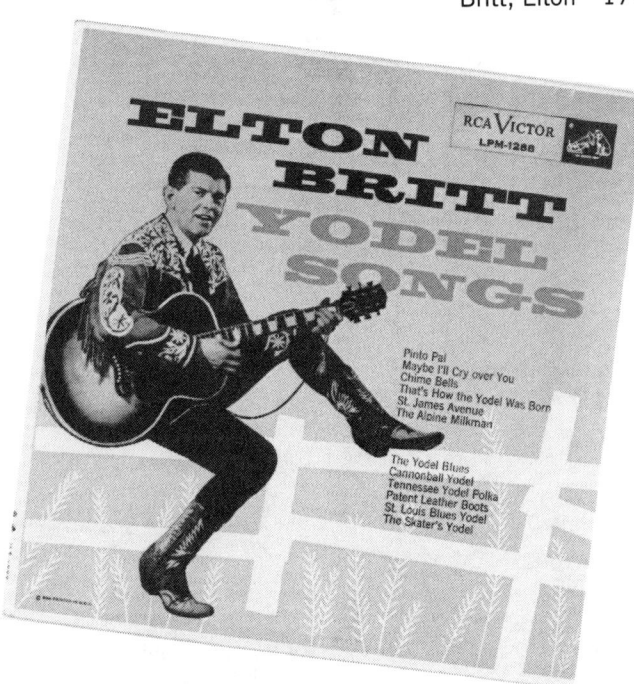

Elton Britt's first two LPs are pictured above, although Yodel Songs originally appeared as a 10" a few years prior. Born James Britt Baker, he was one of country's biggest stars during the '40s. By the time of the release of these LPs, he was past his hit-making days, although he remained influential on many young country singers.

Label & Catalog #		Title	Year	VG+	NM
BRICE, FANNY, & HELEN MORGAN					
Vik LVA-1007	(M)	**Torch Songs**	1955	30.00	75.00
BRIDGES, LLOYD					
Carlton CHH-17	(M)	**Hear How To Skin Dive**	195?	16.00	40.00
BRIGADE					
Band'n Vocal BVRS-1066	(S)	**Last Laugh**	1970	1,000.00	See below
		(Near Mint copies have a suggested value of $1,500-2,500)			
BRIGG					
Susquehanna LP-301	(S)	**Brigg**	1973	60.00	150.00
BRIGMAN, GEORGE					
Solid SR-001	(S)	**Jungle Rot**	1975	40.00	100.00
BRILL, MARTY					
Mercury MG-20178	(M)	**The Roving Balladeer**	1956	12.00	30.00
BRILLIANT, ASHLEIGH					
Dorash 1001	(M)	**In The Haight-Ashbury** (Documentary)	1967	40.00	100.00
BRIMSTONE					
"S" 30534	(M)	**Paper Winged Dreams**	1968	70.00	175.00
BRITT, ELTON					
Elton Britt also recorded as a member of The Beverly Hill Billies. Refer to Rosalie Allen / Elton Britt.					
RCA Victor LPM-3222	(10")	**Yodel Songs**	1954	60.00	150.00
RCA Victor LPM-1288	(M)	**Yodel Songs**	1956	30.00	75.00
ABC-Paramount ABC-293	(M)	**The Wandering Cowboy**	1959	14.00	35.00
ABC-Paramount ABCS-293	(S)	**The Wandering Cowboy**	1959	20.00	50.00
ABC-Paramount ABC-322	(M)	**Beyond The Sunset**	1960	10.00	25.00
ABC-Paramount ABCS-322	(S)	**Beyond The Sunset**	1960	14.00	35.00
ABC-Paramount ABC-331	(M)	**I Heard A Forest Praying**	1960	10.00	25.00
ABC-Paramount ABCS-331	(S)	**I Heard A Forest Praying**	1960	14.00	35.00
ABC-Paramount ABC-521	(M)	**The Singing Hills**	1965	8.00	20.00
ABC-Paramount ABCS-521	(S)	**The Singing Hills**	1965	10.00	25.00
ABC-Paramount ABC-566	(M)	**Somethin' For Everybody**	1966	8.00	20.00
ABC-Paramount ABCS-566	(S)	**Somethin' For Everybody**	1966	10.00	25.00
RCA Victor LPM-2669	(M)	**The Best Of Elton Britt**	1963	12.00	30.00
		— RCA albums above have "Lng Play" on the bottom of the label.—			
BRITTON, GEORGE					
Folkways FP-615	(10")	**Pennsylvania Dutch Folk Songs**	1955	30.00	75.00
Folkways FA-2215	(10")	**Pennsylvania Dutch Folk Songs**	1955	30.00	75.00
BROCK, B., & THE SULTANS					
Crown CLP-5399	(M)	**Do The Beetle**	1964	16.00	40.00
Crown CST-399	(S)	**Do The Beetle**	1964	20.00	50.00
BROLIN, JAMES					
Artco LPC-1099	(M)	**James Brolin Sings**	1974	12.00	30.00
BROOKS, DONNA: *Refer to* **GOLDMINE'S PRICE GUIDE TO COLLECTIBLE JAZZ ALBUMS**					
BROOKS, DONNIE					
Era EL-105	(M)	**The Happiest**	1961	60.00	150.00
BROOKS, HADDA					
Modern LMP-1210	(M)	**Femme Fatale**	1956	100.00	250.00
Crown CLP-5010	(M)	**Femme Fatale** (Black label)	1957	30.00	75.00
		(Crown 5010 is a reissue of Modern 1210.)			
Crown CLP-5374	(M)	**Hadda Brooks Sings And Swings**	1963	10.00	25.00
Crown CST-374	(E)	**Hadda Brooks Sings And Swings**	1963	4.00	10.00
BROOKS, HADDA / PETE JOHNSON					
Crown CLP-5058	(M)	**Boogie**	1958	20.00	50.00

Label & Catalog #		Title	Year	VG+	NM

BROOKS, JOHN BENSON
| Vik LX-1083 | (M) | Folk Jazz, U.S.A. | 195? | 14.00 | 35.00 |

BROOKS, MEL, & CARL REINER
| World Pacific WP-1401 | (M) | 2,000 Years | 1960 | 20.00 | 50.00 |

BROONZY, BIG BILL
Big Bill is a country-blues guitar player, fiddler, singer and songwriter. Refer to Pete Seeger.
Dial 306	(10')	Blues Concert	1952	80.00	200.00
EmArcy MG-26034	(10')	Folk Blues	1954	70.00	175.00
EmArcy MG-36137	(M)	Blues By Broonzy	1958	40.00	100.00
		(EmArcy 36137 is a reissue of 26034.)			
Period SLP-1114	(M)	Big Bill Broonzy Sings	1956	40.00	100.00
Period SLP-1209	(M)	Big Bill Broonzy Sings			
		And Josh White Comes A-Visiting	1958	30.00	75.00
Folkways FA-2315	(M)	Big Bill Broonzy	1957	20.00	50.00
Folkways FA-2326	(M)	Country Blues	1957	20.00	50.00
Folkways FG-3586	(M)	His Songs & Story *(Studs Terkel interview)*	1957	20.00	50.00
Columbia WL-111	(M)	Big Bill's Blues *(Gold label)*	1958	30.00	75.00
Verve MGV-3000-5	(M)	The Big Bill Broonzy Story *(5 LP box)*	1959	80.00	200.00
Verve MGV-3001	(M)	Last Session, Part 1	1959	24.00	60.00
Verve MGV-3002	(M)	Last Session, Part 2	1959	24.00	60.00
Verve MGV-3003	(M)	Last Session, Part 3	1959	24.00	60.00
		(The "Last Sessions" are taken from the boxed set above.)			
Riverside RLP-12-125	(M)	Big Bill Broonzy	195?	30.00	75.00
Mercury MG-20822	(M)	Big Bill Broonzy—Memorial	1963	12.00	30.00
Mercury SR-60822	(E)	Big Bill Broonzy—Memorial	1963	8.00	20.00
Mercury MG-20905	(M)	Remembering Big Bill Broonzy	1964	12.00	30.00
Mercury SR-60905	(E)	Remembering Big Bill Broonzy	1964	8.00	20.00
Epic EE-22017	(M)	Big Bill's Blues	1969	12.00	30.00

BROONZY, BIG BILL, & SONNY TERRY & BROWNIE McGHEE
| Folkways FA-3817 | (M) | Big Bill Broonzy, | | | |
| | | **Sonny Terry And Brownie McGhee** | 1959 | 20.00 | 50.00 |

BROONZY, BIG BILL, & WASHBOARD SAM
Chess LP-1468	(M)	Big Bill Broonzy			
		And Washboard Sam *(White label promo)*	1962	250.00	500.00
Chess LP-1468	(M)	Big Bill Broonzy And Washboard Sam	1962	80.00	200.00

BROTHER FOX & TAR BABY
| Oracle 1001 | (S) | Brother Fox & Tar Baby | 1969 | 16.00 | 40.00 |
| Capitol ST-544 | (S) | Brother Fox & Tar Baby | 1969 | 10.00 | 25.00 |

BROTHERHOOD
| BH 501 | (S) | Stavia | 1972 | 50.00 | 125.00 |

BROWN, AL
Al Brown's band backed countless New York vocal groups in the '50s and '60s.
Moon LPBA-1	(M)	Al Brown Presents DynaSounds	196?	250.00	500.00
		(Various artists compilation with all groups backed by Brown.)			
Amy A-1	(M)	The Madison Dance Party	1960	16.00	40.00
Amy AS-1	(S)	The Madison Dance Party	1960	20.00	50.00
		("The Madison" is rechanneled for this album.)			

BROWN, ARTHUR
| Atlantic/Track SD-8198 | (S) | The Crazy World Of Arthur Brown | 1968 | 10.00 | 25.00 |

BROWN, BOBBY
| Destiny 4002 | (S) | The Enlightening Beam Of Axonda | 1972 | 10.00 | 25.00 |

BROWN, BOOTS, & HIS BLOCKBUSTERS / DAN DREW & HIS DAREDEVILS
Both the "artists" on this album are pseudonyms for two different groups of jazz luminaries including Shelly Manne, Gerry Mulligan and Shorty Rogers (as the West Coast's Blockbusters) and Al Cohn, Elliott Lawrence and Nick Travis (the East Coast's Daredevils).
| Groove LG-1000 | (M) | Rock That Beat | 1958 | 150.00 | 300.00 |

Label & Catalog #		Title	Year	VG+	NM

BROWN, BUSTER

Fire FLP-101	(M)	The New King Of The Blues	1960	400.00	800.00
Fire FLP-104	(M)	The New King Of The Blues	1960	300.00	600.00

(Original covers for Fire 104—a reissue of 101—are blue with a small photo of Brown in the lower right corner and a drawing of a crown above his head.)

Fire FLP-104	(M)	The New King Of The Blues	1960	250.00	500.00

(Later covers are white with the photo of Brown enlarged to fill the entire cover. While this is a "second pressing cover," it is more desirable than the first because of the attractively redone cover.)

BROWN, CHARLES

Aladdin LP-702	(10")	Mood Music (Red vinyl)	1955		See below

(Red vinyl copies of Aladdin 702 have suggested values in VG of $1,000-2,000; in VG+ of $3,000-4,000; & in NM of $6,000-10,000.)

Aladdin LP-702	(10")	Mood Music	1955		See below

(Black vinyl copies of Aladdin 702 have suggested values in VG of $300-600; in VG+ of $1,000-2,000; and in NM of $3,000-5,000.)

Aladdin LP-809	(M)	Mood Music	1955		Unreleased
Score SLP-4011	(M)	Driftin' Blues	1958	200.00	400.00
Score SLP-4036	(M)	More Blues With Charles Brown	1958		Unreleased
Imperial LP-9178	(M)	Charles Brown Sings Million Sellers	1961	200.00	500.00
King 775	(M)	Charles Brown Sings Christmas Songs	1961	80.00	200.00
King 878	(M)	The Great Charles Brown	1963	60.00	150.00
Mainstream 56035	(M)	Ballads My Way	1965	8.00	20.00
Mainstream S-6035	(S)	Ballads My Way	1965	12.00	30.00
BluesWay BLS-6039	(S)	Charles Brown—Legend	1970	10.00	25.00

BROWN, CHARLES / AMOS MILBURN

Grand Prix K-421	(M)	Original Blues Sounds	196?	10.00	25.00
Grand Prix KS-421	(E)	Original Blues Sounds	196?	4.00	10.00

BROWN, HELEN GURLEY

Crescendo GNP-604	(M)	Lessons In Love	196?	8.00	20.00
Crescendo GNP-604ST	(S)	Lessons In Love	196?	10.00	25.00

BROWN, HYLO

Capitol T-1168	(M)	Hylo Brown	1959	30.00	75.00
Starday SLP-185	(M)	Bluegrass Balladeer	196?	24.00	60.00
Starday SLP-204	(M)	Bluegrass Goes To College	196?	20.00	50.00
Starday SLP-220	(M)	Hylo Brown Meets The Lonesome Pine Fiddlers	196?	20.00	50.00
Starday SLP-249	(M)	Sing Me A Bluegrass Song	196?	16.00	40.00

— Starday albums above have yellow labels.—

BROWN, JAMES/JAMES BROWN & HIS FAMOUS FLAMES

Refer to Hank Ballard; Bobby Byrd; Lynn Collins; Bill Doggett; Dee Felice; Fred & The New JB's; Martha High; The JB's; Anna King; Maceo; Sweet Charles; Fred Wesley; Marva Whitney.

King 610	(M)	Please Please Please	1958		See below

(Original pressings of King 610 have black labels with the small, 2" wide "King" on top. The cover features a photo of a woman's legs ascending steps. Rare with suggested values in VG of $200-400; in VG+ of $600-1,000; and in NM of $1,200-2,000.)

King 610	(M)	Please Please Please	196?		See below

(Second pressings have black labels with the large, 3" wide "King" on top and has the same cover of a woman's legs ascending steps. Rare with suggested values in VG of $150-300; in VG+ of $500-800; and in NM of $1,000-1,600.)

King 635	(M)	Try Me!	1959		See below

(Original pressings of King 635 have black labels with the small, 2" wide "King" on top. The cover features a drawing of a woman holding a cigarette and a smoking gun. Rare with suggested values in VG of $150-300; in VG+ of $500-800; and in NM of $1,000-1,600.)

King 635	(M)	Try Me!	196?		See below

(Second pressings have black labels with the large, 3" wide "King" on top and the same cover of a woman holding a cigarette and a smoking gun. Rare with suggested values in VG of $100-200; in VG+ of $400-600; and in NM of $800-1,200.)

James Brown and His Famous Flames' first long-player, the impossible to find King 610, Please Please
Please. *This original pressing—there are two pressings on the crownless King label; refer to the listings—
has been referred to as the "stairs cover" and the "legs cover." Since this was the '50s, it was deemed more
saleable to feature the flesh of a white woman than that of a black woman. Perhaps more interesting, just
exactly what is the carefully cropped photo supposed to be depicting?*

Label & Catalog #		Title	Year	VG+	NM
King 683	(M)	**Think!**	1960		*See below*
		(Original pressings of King 683 have black labels with the small, 2" wide "King" on top. The cover features a photo of a baby. Rare with suggested values in VG of $150-300; in VG+ of $500-800; and in NM of $1,000-1,600.)			
King 683	(M)	**Think!**	196?		*See below*
		(Second pressings have black labels with the large, 3" wide "King" on top and the same cover with a baby. Rare with suggested values in VG of $100-200; in VG+ of $400-600; and in NM of $800-1,200.)			
King 683	(M)	**Think!**	1963	150.00	300.00
		(Later covers have a photo of James Brown.)			
King 743	(M)	**The Amazing James Brown**	1961	300.00	600.00
		(Original covers for King 743 have JB in a fine suit.)			
King 743	(M)	**The Amazing James Brown**	1963	60.00	150.00
		(Later pressings have a white title covers.)			
King 771	(M)	**Night Train** *(White label promo)*	1961		*See below*
		(White label promos of King 771 are rare with a suggested Near Mint value of $900-1,800.)			
King 771	(M)	**Night Train**	1961	150.00	300.00
King 771	(M)	**Twist Around**	1962	100.00	250.00
King 771	(M)	**Jump Around**	1963	80.00	200.00
King KS-771	(S)	**Jump Around**	1963	150.00	300.00
		(King 771 with its three different titles s a various artists album featuring JB on the cover and is considered part of his oeuvre.)			
King 780	(M)	**Shout And Shimmy** *(White label promo)*	1962		*See below*
		(White label promos of King 780 are rare with a suggested Near Mint value of $750-1,500.)			
King 780	(M)	**Shout And Shimmy**	1962	100.00	250.00
		(The covers and labels for King 780 read "Shout And Shimmy.")			
King 780	(M)	**Shout And Shimmy/Good Good Twistin'**	1962	80.00	200.00
		(A "Shout And Shimmy" cover with a "Good Good Twistin'" record.)			
King 780	(M)	**Excitement**	1963	60.00	150.00
		("Excitement" is a reissue of "Shout And Shimmy.")			
King 804	(M)	**James Brown & His Famous Flames Tour The U.S.A.** *(White label promo)*	1962		*See below*
		(White label promos of King 804 are rare with a suggested Near Mint value of $750-1,500.)			
King 804	(M)	**James Brown & His Famous Flames Tour The U.S.A.**	1962	100.00	250.00
King 826	(M)	**Live At The Apollo!** *(White label promo)*	1963		*See below*
		(White label promos of King 826, which are specially banded for airplay, are rare with a suggested Near Mint value of $600-1,000.)			
King 826	(M)	**Live At The Apollo!**	1963	80.00	200.00
King KS-826	(S)	**Live At The Apollo!**	1963	150.00	300.00
		(Original pressings for King 826 have custom back covers.]			
King 826	(M)	**Live At The Apollo!**	1963	60.00	150.00
King KS-826	(S)	**Live At The Apollo!**	1963	80.00	200.00
		(Later covers have house ads for other King albums on the back.)			
King 851	(M)	**Prisoner Of Love**	1963	80.00	200.00
		(Original pressings for King 851 have custom back covers.)			
King 851	(M)	**Prisoner Of Love**	1963	40.00	100.00
		(Later covers have house ads for other King albums on the back.)			
King 883	(M)	**Pure Dynamite! Live At The Royal** *(Promo)*	1964		*See below*
		(White label promos of King 883, which are specially banded for airplay, are rare with a suggested Near Mint value of $600-1,000.)			
King 883	(M)	**Pure Dynamite! Live At The Royal**	1964	80.00	200.00
King 909	(M)	**Please Please Please**	1964	40.00	100.00
King 919	(M)	**The Unbeatable James Brown—16 Hits**	1964	40.00	100.00
		(King 919 is a reissue of 635.)			
King 938	(M)	**Papa's Got A Brand New Bag** *(Red cover)*	1965	30.00	75.00
King LPS-938	(P)	**Papa's Got A Brand New Bag** *(Red cover)*	1965	40.00	100.00
King 938	(M)	**Papa's Got A Brand New Bag** *(Green cover)*	1966	20.00	50.00
King LPS-938	(P)	**Papa's Got A Brand New Bag** *(Green cover)*	1966	30.00	75.00
King 946	(M)	**I Got You (I Feel Good)**	1966	40.00	100.00
King KSD-946	(S)	**I Got You (I Feel Good)**	1966	60.00	150.00
King 961	(M)	**Mighty Instrumentals**	1966	40.00	100.00

—*King mono albums above have crownless black labels; stereo albums have crownless blue labels. The logo on the covers have a crown with "King" in open capital block letters below.*—

Label & Catalog #		Title	Year	VG+	NM
King 683	(M)	Think! (JB cover)	1966	20.00	50.00
King KSD-683	(E)	Think! (JB cover)	1966	16.00	40.00
King 743	(M)	The Amazing James Brown	1966	20.00	50.00
King KS-743	(E)	The Amazing James Brown	1966	16.00	40.00
King 780	(M)	Excitement	1966	20.00	50.00
King KS-780	(E)	Excitement	1966	20.00	50.00
King 804	(M)	James Brown & His Famous Flames Tour The U.S.A.	1966	20.00	50.00
King KS-804	(E)	James Brown & His Famous Flames Tour The U.S.A.	1966	16.00	40.00
King 826	(M)	Live At The Apollo!	1966	20.00	50.00
King KS-826	(S)	Live At The Apollo!	1966	30.00	75.00
King 851	(M)	Prisoner Of Love	1966	20.00	50.00
King KS-851	(E)	Prisoner Of Love	1966	16.00	40.00
King 883	(M)	Pure Dynamite! Live At The Royal	1966	20.00	50.00
King KS-883	(E)	Pure Dynamite! Live At The Royal	1966	16.00	40.00
King 909	(M)	Please Please Please	1966	20.00	50.00
King KS-909	(E)	Please Please Please	1966	16.00	40.00
King 919	(M)	The Unbeatable James Brown—16 Hits	1966	20.00	50.00
King KS-919	(E)	The Unbeatable James Brown—16 Hits	1966	16.00	40.00
King 938	(M)	Papa's Got A Brand New Bag	1966	16.00	40.00
King LPS-938	(P)	Papa's Got A Brand New Bag	1966	20.00	50.00
King 946	(M)	I Got You (I Feel Good)	1966	16.00	40.00
King KSD-946	(S)	I Got You (I Feel Good)	1966	20.00	50.00
King 985	(M)	It's A Man's Man's Man's World	1966	20.00	50.00
King KS-985	(S)	It's A Man's Man's Man's World	1966	30.00	75.00
King 1010	(M)	Christmas Songs	1966	40.00	100.00
King KS-1010	(S)	Christmas Songs	1966	60.00	150.00
		(Original pressings of King 1010 have a wreath on a gray wall on the front cover and no titles on the back cover.)			
King 1010	(M)	Christmas Songs	1967	30.00	75.00
King KS-1010	(S)	Christmas Songs	1967	40.00	100.00
		(Later pressings have a wreath on a white wall on the front cover with titles on the back cover.)			
King 1016	(M)	Raw Soul	1967	20.00	50.00
King KS-1016	(P)	Raw Soul	1967	30.00	75.00
King 1018	(M)	Live At The Garden	1967	200.00	400.00
		(Black label promo banded for air-play.)			
King 1018	(M)	Live At The Garden	1967	30.00	75.00
King KS-1018	(S)	Live At The Garden	1967	40.00	100.00
King K-1020	(M)	Cold Sweat	1967	20.00	50.00
King KS-1020	(P)	Cold Sweat	1967	30.00	75.00
King KS-1022	(S)	Live At The Apollo, Vol. 2 (2 LPs)	1968	30.00	75.00
King KS-1024	(S)	JB Presents His Show Of Tomorrow	1968	20.00	50.00
		(King 1024 is actually a various artists album.)			
King KS-1030	(S)	I Can't Stand Myself (When You Touch Me)	1968	20.00	50.00
King KS-1031	(S)	I Got The Feelin'	1968	20.00	50.00
King KS-1034	(S)	JB Plays Nothing But Soul	1968	20.00	50.00
King KS-1038	(S)	Thinking About Little Willie John And A Few Nice Things	1968	20.00	50.00
King KS-1040	(S)	A Soulful Christmas	1968	30.00	75.00
King KS-1047	(S)	Say It Loud—I'm Black And I'm Proud	1969	20.00	50.00
King KS-1051	(S)	Gettin' Down To It	1969	20.00	50.00
—King mono albums above have black labels with a crown on top; stereo albums have blue or red labels with a crown on top. The covers have a crown with "King" in open capital block letters.—					
King KSD-1055	(S)	The Popcorn	1969	16.00	40.00
King KS-1063	(S)	It's A Mother	1969	20.00	50.00
King KSD-1092	(S)	Ain't It Funky	1970	16.00	40.00
King KS-1095	(S)	It's A New Day—Let A Man Come In	1970	24.00	60.00
King KS-1100	(S)	Soul On Top	1970	16.00	40.00
King KSD-1110	(S)	Sho Is Funky Down Here	1971	16.00	40.00
King KSD-1115	(S)	Sex Machine (2 LPs)	1970	20.00	50.00
King KSD-1124	(S)	Hey, America!	1970	20.00	50.00
King KS-1127	(S)	Super Bad	1971	16.00	40.00
Smash MGS-27054	(M)	Showtime	1964	12.00	30.00
Smash SRS-67054	(S)	Showtime	1964	16.00	40.00
Smash MGS-27057	(M)	Grits And Soul	1965	12.00	30.00
Smash SRS-67057	(S)	Grits And Soul	1965	16.00	40.00

Label & Catalog #		Title	Year	VG+	NM
Smash MGS-27058	(S)	**Out Of Sight**	1965	40.00	100.00
Smash SRS-67058	(S)	**Out Of Sight**	1965	60.00	150.00
		(Smash 2/67058 was deleted shortly after release.)			
Smash MGS-27072	(M)	**JB Plays JB Today And Yesterday**	1965	12.00	30.00
Smash SRS-67072	(S)	**JB Plays JB Today And Yesterday**	1965	16.00	40.00
Smash MGS-27080	(M)	**JB Plays New Breed—The Boo-Ga-Loo**	1966	12.00	30.00
Smash SRS-67080	(S)	**JB Plays New Breed—The Boo-Ga-Loo**	1966	16.00	40.00
Smash MGS-27084	(M)	**Handful Of Soul**	1966	12.00	30.00
Smash SRS-67084	(S)	**Handful Of Soul**	1966	16.00	40.00
Smash MGS-27087	(M)	**The James Brown Show**	1967	12.00	30.00
Smash SRS-67087	(S)	**The James Brown Show**	1967	16.00	40.00
		("The JB Show" is a various artists album.)			
Smash MGS-27093	(M)	**JB Plays The Real Thing**	1967	12.00	30.00
Smash SRS-67093	(S)	**JB Plays The Real Thing**	1967	16.00	40.00
Smash SRS-67109	(S)	**James Brown Sings Out Of Sight**	1968	12.00	30.00
		(Smash 67109 is a reissue of 67058 minus one track.)			
Mercury SMX-7083	(S)	**Soulful James Brown**	197?	30.00	75.00
Polydor PD-4054	(S)	**Hot Pants**	1971	16.00	40.00
Polydor PD2-3003	(S)	**Revolution Of The Mind /**			
		Live At The Apollo, Vol. III *(2 LPs)*	1971	30.00	75.00
Polydor PD-5028	(S)	**There It Is**	1972	16.00	40.00
Polydor PD-5401	(S)	**Soul Classics**	1972	10.00	25.00
Polydor PD2-3004	(S)	**Get On The Good Foot** *(2 LPs)*	1972	30.00	75.00
Polydor PD1-6014	(S)	**Black Caesar** *(Soundtrack)*	1973	24.00	60.00
Polydor PD1-6015	(S)	**Slaughter's Big Rip Off** *(Soundtrack)*	1973	20.00	50.00
Polydor PD-5402	(S)	**Soul Classics, Volume 2**	1973	10.00	25.00
Polydor PD2-3007	(S)	**The Payback** *(2 LPs)*	1974	20.00	50.00
Polydor PD2-9001	(S)	**Hell** *(2 LPs)*	1974	30.00	75.00
Polydor PD1-6039	(S)	**Reality**	1975	16.00	40.00
Polydor PD1-6042	(S)	**Sex Machine Today**	1975	16.00	40.00
Polydor PD1-6054	(S)	**Everybody's Doin' The Hustle**			
		& Dead On The Double Bump	1975	16.00	40.00
Polydor PD2-6059	(S)	**Hot**	1976	16.00	40.00
Polydor PD2-9004	(S)	**Sex Machine Live** *(2 LPs)*	1976	20.00	50.00
Polydor PD1-6071	(S)	**Get Up Offa That Thing**	1976	16.00	40.00
Polydor PD1-6093	(S)	**Bodyheat**	1976	16.00	40.00
Polydor PD1-6111	(S)	**Mutha's Nature**	1977	16.00	40.00
Polydor PD1-6140	(S)	**Jam 1980s**	1973	16.00	40.00
HRB 1004	(S)	**The Fabulous James Brown** *(2 LPs)*	1978	10.00	25.00
Polydor PD1-6181	(S)	**Take A Look At Those Cakes**	1979	12.00	30.00
Polydor PD1-6212	(S)	**The Original Disco Man**	1979	10.00	25.00
Polydor PD1-6258	(S)	**People**	1980	12.00	30.00
Polydor PD2-6290	(S)	**Live—Hot On The One** *(2 LPs)*	1980	20.00	50.00
Polydor PD1-6318	(S)	**Nonstop!**	1981	12.00	30.00

BROWN, MAXINE
Maxine Brown also recorded with Chuck Jackson.

Label & Catalog #		Title	Year	VG+	NM
Wand WD-656	(M)	**The Fabulous Sound Of Maxine Brown**	1963	14.00	35.00
Wand WDS-656	(S)	**The Fabulous Sound Of Maxine Brown**	1963	20.00	50.00
Wand WD-663	(M)	**Spotlight On Maxine Brown**	1965	10.00	25.00
Wand WDS-663	(S)	**Spotlight On Maxine Brown**	1965	14.00	35.00
Wand WD-684	(M)	**Maxine Brown's Greatest Hits**	1967	8.00	20.00
Wand WDS-684	(P)	**Maxine Brown's Greatest Hits**	1967	10.00	25.00

BROWN, MILTON, & HIS MUSICAL BROWNIES

Label & Catalog #		Title	Year	VG+	NM
Decca DL-5561	(10")	**Dance-O-Rama #1**	1955	200.00	400.00
Western WS-101	(10")	**Dance-O-Rama #1**	1955	60.00	150.00

BROWN, NAPPY

Label & Catalog #		Title	Year	VG+	NM
Savoy MG-14002	(M)	**Nappy Brown Sings**	1958	150.00	300.00
Savoy MG-14025	(M)	**The Right Time**	1960	80.00	200.00

BROWN, ROY

Label & Catalog #		Title	Year	VG+	NM
King 956	(M)	**Roy Brown Sings 24 Hits**	1966	20.00	50.00
King KS-956	(E)	**Roy Brown Sings 24 Hits**	1966	20.00	50.00
BluesWay BLS-6019	(S)	**The Blues Are Brown**	1968	10.00	25.00
BluesWay BLS-6056	(S)	**Hard Times**	197?	10.00	25.00
King KS-1130	(M)	**Hard Luck Blues**	1971	10.00	25.00
Epic BG-30473	(S)	**Live At Monterey**	1971	10.00	25.00

One has only to see these two items to realize that one doesn't see them too often. Like many artists who have not taken the hold of the collectors' group-mind, these albums are mush rarer, especially in nearly mint condition, than their modest values indicate. Jim Ed, Maxine and Bonnie Brown enjoyed success on the country'n western charts through the '50s and most of the '60s before their star faded and tastes changed. And yes, they are siblings.

Label & Catalog #		Title	Year	VG+	NM

BROWN, ROY / WYNONIE HARRIS

| King 607 | (M) | Battle Of The Blues, Volume 1 | 1958 | 250.00 | 500.00 |
| King 627 | (M) | Battle Of The Blues, Volume 2 | 1959 | 300.00 | 600.00 |

BROWN, ROY / WYNONIE HARRIS / EDDIE VINSON

| King 668 | (M) | Battle Of The Blues, Volume 4 | 1960 | | See below |

(King 668 is rare with suggested values in VG of $250-500; in VG+, $800-1,200; and in Near Mint of $1,500-2,500.)

BROWN, RUTH

Atlantic 115	(10")	Ruth Brown Sings Favorites	1952		Unreleased
Atlantic 8004	(M)	Ruth Brown	1957	70.00	175.00
Atlantic 8026	(M)	Miss Rhythm	1959	70.00	175.00
Atlantic 8026	(M)	Miss Rhythm (White "bullseye" label)	1959	100.00	250.00
Atlantic 1308	(M)	Late Date With Ruth Brown	1959	80.00	200.00
Atlantic SD-1308	(S)	Late Date With Ruth Brown	1959	150.00	300.00

— Atlantic mono albums above have black labels; stereo albums have green labels.—

Atlantic 8004	(M)	Ruth Brown	196?	10.00	25.00
Atlantic 8026	(M)	Miss Rhythm	196?	10.00	25.00
Atlantic 1308	(M)	Late Date With Ruth Brown	196?	10.00	25.00
Atlantic SD-1308	(S)	Late Date With Ruth Brown	196?	12.00	30.00

— Atlantic albums above have multi-colored labels with the "fan" logo on the right side.—

Atlantic 8080	(M)	The Best Of Ruth Brown	1963	16.00	40.00
Philips PHM-200-028	(M)	Along Comes Ruth	1962	16.00	40.00
Philips PHS-600-028	(S)	Along Comes Ruth	1962	20.00	50.00
Philips PH-200-055	(M)	Gospel Time	1962	12.00	30.00
Philips PHS-600-055	(S)	Gospel Time	1962	16.00	40.00
Mainstream 16034	(S)	Ruth Brown '65	1965	10.00	25.00
Mainstream S-6034	(S)	Ruth Brown '65	1965	12.00	30.00

BROWN, WALT

| Warner Bros. W-1568 | (M) | The Walt Brown Show With Bill Collins | 1965 | 8.00 | 20.00 |
| Warner Bros. WS-1568 | (S) | The Walt Brown Show With Bill Collins | 1965 | 10.00 | 25.00 |

BROWN'S FERRY FOUR, THE

Country "supergroup" features Granpa Jones, The Delmore Brothers and Merle Travis.

King 551	(M)	Sacred Songs	1957	40.00	100.00
King 590	(M)	Sacred Songs	1958	40.00	100.00
King 943	(M)	Sacred Songs	1964	16.00	40.00

BROWNE, JACKSON

| (No label) | (DJ) | "Jackson Browne's First Album" (2 LPs) | 1967 | 1,000.00 | See below |

(This is a publishers demo issued in plain cardboard jackets. Near Mint copis have a suggested value of $1,500-2,500.)

| Asylum SD-5051 | (S) | Jackson Browne (With burlap cover) | 1972 | 12.00 | 30.00 |
| Asylum SD-5067 | (S) | For Everyman | 1973 | 10.00 | 25.00 |

(Asylum 5051-5067 have white labels with a door-in-a-circle logo.)

Asylum EQ-1017	(Q)	Late For The Sky	1974	12.00	30.00
Reprise RS-	(S)	Late For The Sky	1973	12.00	30.00
Mobile Fidelity MFSL-055	(S)	The Pretender	1983	10.00	30.00

BROWNS, THE

The Browns are Bonnie, Jim Ed and Maxine.

RCA Victor LPM-1438	(M)	Jim Edward, Maxine And Bonnie Brown	1957	20.00	50.00
RCA Victor LPM-2144	(M)	Sweet Sounds By The Browns	1959	12.00	30.00
RCA Victor LSP-2144	(S)	Sweet Sounds By The Browns	1959	16.00	40.00
RCA Victor LPM-2174	(M)	Town And Country	1960	8.00	20.00
RCA Victor LSP-2174	(S)	Town And Country	1960	10.00	25.00
RCA Victor LPM-2260	(M)	The Browns Sing Their Hits	1960	8.00	20.00
RCA Victor LSP-2260	(S)	The Browns Sing Their Hits	1960	10.00	25.00
RCA Victor LPM-2333	(M)	Our Favorite Folk Songs	1961	8.00	20.00
RCA Victor LSP-2333	(S)	Our Favorite Folk Songs	1961	10.00	25.00
RCA Victor LPM-2345	(M)	The Little Brown Church Hymnal	1961	8.00	20.00
RCA Victor LSP-2345	(S)	The Little Brown Church Hymnal	1961	10.00	25.00

— RCA mono albums above have "Long Play" on the bottom of the label; stereo albums have "Living Stereo" on the bottom.—

BROWNSVILLE STATION

| Palladium P-1004 | (S) | Brownsville Station | 1970 | 12.00 | 30.00 |

Label & Catalog #		Title	Year	VG+	NM
BRUCE, CAROL					
Tops L-1574	(M)	Carol Bruce Sings	195?	10.00	25.00
BRUCE, ED					
RCA Victor LPM-3948	(M)	If I Could Just Go Home	1968	20.00	50.00
RCA Victor LSP-3948	(S)	If I Could Just Go Home	1968	10.00	25.00
BRUCE, LENNY					
Refer to Lawrence Schiller.					
Fantasy 7001	(M)	Interviews Of Our Times *(Dark red vinyl)*	1959	40.00	100.00
Fantasy 7001	(M)	Interviews Of Our Times	1959	16.00	40.00
Fantasy 7003	(M)	The Sick Humor			
		Of Lenny Bruce *(Dark red vinyl)*	1959	40.00	100.00
Fantasy 7003	(M)	The Sick Humor Of Lenny Bruce	1959	16.00	40.00
Fantasy 7007	(M)	I Am Not A Nut, Elect Me *(Dark red vinyl)*	1960	40.00	100.00
Fantasy 7007	(M)	I Am Not A Nut, Elect Me	1960	16.00	40.00
Fantasy 7011	(M)	Lenny Bruce, American *(Dark red vinyl)*	1962	40.00	100.00
Fantasy 7011	(M)	Lenny Bruce, American	1962	16.00	40.00
		— Fantasy albums above have red labels on non-flexible vinyl.—			
Fantasy 7001	(M)	Interviews Of Our Times *(Clear red vinyl)*	196?	16.00	40.00
Fantasy 7001	(M)	Interviews Of Our Times	196?	8.00	20.00
Fantasy 7003	(M)	The Sick Humor			
		Of Lenny Bruce*(Clear red vinyl)*	196?	16.00	40.00
Fantasy 7003	(M)	The Sick Humor Of Lenny Bruce	196?	8.00	20.00
Fantasy 7007	(M)	I Am Not A Nut, Elect Me *(Clear red vinyl)*	196?	16.00	40.00
Fantasy 7007	(M)	I Am Not A Nut, Elect Me *(Clear red vinyl)*	196?	8.00	20.00
Fantasy 7011	(M)	Lenny Bruce, American *(Clear red vinyl)*	196?	16.00	40.00
Fantasy 7011	(M)	Lenny Bruce, American	196?	8.00	20.00
Fantasy 7012	(M)	The Best Of Lenny Bruce *(Clear red vinyl)*	1962	20.00	50.00
Fantasy 7012	(M)	The Best Of Lenny Bruce	1962	8.00	25.00
		— Fantasy albums above have red labels on flexible vinyl.—			
Philles PHLP-4010	(M)	Lenny Bruce Is Out Again	1966	30.00	75.00
Philles LB-3001/2	(M)	Lenny Bruce Is Out Again	196?	100.00	250.00
		(LB-3001/2 has the same cover as Philles 4101 except Bruce's address is on the back cover and the LP has plain white labels.)			
Philles LB-9001/2	(M)	Recordings Submitted As Evidence In The San			
		Francisco Obscenity Trial In March, 1962	196?	250.00	500.00
United Arts. UAL-3580	(M)	Lenny Bruce/Midnight Concert	1967	10.00	25.00
United Arts. UAS-6580	(E)	Lenny Bruce/Midnight Concert	1967	6.00	15.00
		(The complete concert from which this album was taken was later issued as United Arts. 9800, "Lenny Bruce At Carnegie Hall.")			
Bizarre 2XS-6329	(M)	The Berkeley Concert *(2 LPs)*	1969	10.00	25.00
BRUNSON, FRANKIE					
Gee G-704	(M)	Big Daddy's Blues	1959	20.00	50.00
Gee SG-704	(S)	Big Daddy's Blues	1959	30.00	75.00
BRUTE FORCE					
Columbia CL-2615	(M)	I, Brute Force—Confections Of Love	1967	8.00	20.00
Columbia CS-9415	(M)	I, Brute Force—Confections Of Love	1967	10.00	25.00
Embryo 522	(S)	Brute Force	1970	10.00	25.00
B.T. Puppy BTPS-1015	(S)	Extemporaneous	1971		*See below*
		(Preposterously rare, scatalogically live-in-the-studio album with a suggested Near Mint value of $1,000-2,000.)			
BRYAN, JOY: *Refer to* **GOLDMINE'S PRICE GUIDE TO COLLECTIBLE JAZZ ALBUMS**					
BRYANT, ANITA					
Carlton LP-118	(M)	Anita Bryant	1959	8.00	20.00
Carlton STLP-118	(S)	Anita Bryant	1959	12.00	30.00
Carlton LP-127	(M)	Hear Anita Bryant In Your Home Tonight	1960	8.00	20.00
Carlton STLP-127	(S)	Hear Anita Bryant In Your Home Tonight	1960	10.00	25.00
Carlton LP-132	(M)	In My Little Corner Of The World	1961	8.00	20.00
Carlton STLP-132	(S)	In My Little Corner Of The World	1961	10.00	25.00
BRYANT, BOUDLEAUX					
Monument MLP-8007	(M)	Boudleaux Bryant's Best Sellers	1963	8.00	20.00
Monument SLP-18007	(S)	Boudleaux Bryant's Best Sellers	1963	10.00	25.00

Label & Catalog #		Title	Year	VG+	NM

BRYANT, JIMMY
Bryant also recorded with Speedy West.

Label & Catalog #		Title	Year	VG+	NM
Capitol T-1314	(M)	Country Cabin Jazz	1960	40.00	100.00
Capitol ST-1314	(S)	Country Cabin Jazz	1960	60.00	150.00
Dolton BLP-16505	(M)	Play Country Guitar With Jimmy Bryant	1965	8.00	20.00
Dolton BST-17505	(S)	Play Country Guitar With Jimmy Bryant	1965	10.00	25.00
Imperial LP-9310	(M)	Bryant's Back In Town	1966	8.00	20.00
Imperial LP-12310	(S)	Bryant's Back In Town	1966	10.00	25.00
Imperial LP-9315	(M)	Laughing Guitar, Crying Guitar	1966	8.00	20.00
Imperial LP-12315	(S)	Laughing Guitar, Crying Guitar	1966	10.00	25.00
Imperial LP-9338	(M)	We Are Young	1966	8.00	20.00
Imperial LP-12338	(S)	We Are Young	1966	10.00	25.00
Imperial LP-9349	(M)	Wingin' It With Norval & Ivy	1967	8.00	20.00
Imperial LP-12349	(S)	Wingin' It With Norval & Ivy	1967	10.00	25.00
Imperial LP-9360	(M)	The Fastest Guitar In The Country	1967	8.00	20.00
Imperial LP-12360	(S)	The Fastest Guitar In The Country	1967	10.00	25.00

BRYNNER, YUL

Vanguard VRS-9256	(M)	The Gypsy And I	1967	10.00	25.00
Vanguard VSD-79256	(S)	The Gypsy And I	1967	12.00	30.00

BUBBLE GUM MACHINE, THE

Senate 1002	(M)	The Bubble Gum Machine	1967	10.00	25.00
Senate 21002	(S)	The Bubble Gum Machine	1967	12.00	30.00

BUBBLE PUPPY
Bubble Puppy later recorded as Demian.

International Arts. 10	(S)	A Gathering Of Promises	1969	30.00	75.00
International Arts. 10	(S)	A Gathering Of Promises	1979	10.00	25.00

(Reissues have "Masterfonics" stamped in the trail-off vinyl.)

BUCCANEER
A recent warehouse find has halved the value of these records.

Blunderbuss	(S)	Buccaneer	1980	20.00	50.00

(The title on the cover is gold; issued with two singles.)

Blunderbuss	(S)	Buccaneer	198?	12.00	30.00

(Second pressings: the title on the cover is red.)

BUCHANAN, ROY

Bioya MM-519	(S)	Buch & The Snake Stretchers	1971	80.00	200.00

(MM-519 was issued in a burlap bag)

BUCHANAN & GOODMAN

Rori 3301	(M)	The Many Heads Of Buchanan & Goodman	195?	40.00	100.00

BUCHANAN BROTHERS, THE
The Buchanan Brothers are Terry Cashman, Gene Pistilli and Tommy West.

Event ES-101	(S)	Medicine Man	1969	10.00	25.00

BUCKAROOS, THE
Buck Owens' Buckaroos are Tom Brumley, Doyle Holly, Don Rich and Jerry Wiggens.

Capitol T-2436	(M)	The Buck Owens' Songbook	1965	10.00	25.00
Capitol ST-2436	(S)	The Buck Owens' Songbook	1965	12.00	30.00
Capitol T-2722	(M)	America's Most Wanted Band	1967	10.00	25.00
Capitol ST-2722	(S)	America's Most Wanted Band	1967	12.00	30.00
Capitol T-2828	(M)	Again	1967	10.00	25.00
Capitol ST-2828	(S)	Again	1967	10.00	25.00
Capitol ST-2902	(S)	A Night On The Town	1968	10.00	25.00
Capitol ST-2973	(S)	Meanwhile, Back At The Ranch	1968	10.00	25.00
Capitol ST-194	(S)	Anywhere, U.S.A.	1969	10.00	25.00

— Capitol albums above have black "rainbow" labels.—

BUCKINGHAM/NICKS
Lindsay Buckingham and Stevie Nicks. Refer to Fleetwood Mac.

Polydor PD-5058	(S)	Buckingham/Nicks (Gatefold cover)	1973	20.00	50.00
Polydor PD-5058	(S)	Buckingham/Nicks (Standard cover)	1973	10.00	25.00

Label & Catalog #		Title	Year	VG+	NM

BUCKINGHAMS, THE

U.S.A. 107	(M)	Kind Of A Drag	1967	300.00	500.00

(Original mono pressings of USA 107 contain "I'm A Man."
Should a stereo copy be found with this track it would
have a suggested Near Mint value of $500-1,000.)

U.S.A. 107	(M)	Kind Of A Drag	1967	10.00	25.00
U.S.A. 107	(S)	Kind Of A Drag	1967	12.00	30.00
Columbia CL-2669	(M)	Time And Charges	1967	8.00	20.00
Columbia CS-9469	(S)	Time And Charges	1967	10.00	25.00
Columbia CL-2798	(M)	Portraits	1968	12.00	30.00
Columbia CS-9598	(S)	Portraits	1968	8.00	20.00
Columbia CS-9703	(S)	In One Ear And Gone Tomorrow	1968	10.00	25.00

— Columbia albums above have "360 Sound " on the bottom of the label.—

BUCKLEY, BRUCE
Bruce Buckley is a guitar and dulcimer player and singer of traditional folk songs.

Folkways FP-23	(10")	Ohio Valley Ballads	195?	30.00	75.00
Folkways FA-2025	(10")	Ohio Valley Ballads	195?	30.00	75.00

BUCKLEY, TIM

Straight STS-1060	(S)	Blue Afternoon	1969	10.00	25.00

BUD & TRAVIS
Bud Dashiell and Travis Edmonson.

Liberty LRP-3125	(M)	Bud & Travis	1959	14.00	35.00
Liberty LST-7125	(S)	Bud & Travis	1959	16.00	50.00
Liberty LDR-8001	(M)	Bud & Travis In Concert	1960	10.00	25.00
Liberty LDS-12001	(S)	Bud & Travis In Concert	1960	12.00	30.00
Liberty LRP-3138	(M)	Spotlight On Bud & Travis	1961	10.00	25.00
Liberty LST-7138	(S)	Spotlight On Bud & Travis	1961	12.00	30.00
Liberty LRP-3222	(M)	Bud & Travis In Concert, Volume 2	1962	10.00	25.00
Liberty LST-7222	(S)	Bud & Travis In Concert, Volume 2	1962	12.00	30.00
Liberty LRP-3295	(M)	Naturally	1963	8.00	20.00
Liberty LST-7295	(S)	Naturally	1963	10.00	25.00
Liberty LRP-3341	(M)	Perspective On Bud & Travis	1964	8.00	20.00
Liberty LST-7341	(S)	Perspective On Bud & Travis	1964	10.00	25.00
Liberty LRP-3386	(M)	Bud & Travis In Person	1964	8.00	20.00
Liberty LST-7386	(S)	Bud & Travis In Person	1964	10.00	25.00
Liberty LRP-3398	(M)	Bud & Travis' Latin Album	1965	8.00	20.00
Liberty LST-7398	(S)	Bud & Travis' Latin Album	1965	10.00	25.00

BUDDIES, THE

Wing MGW-12293	(M)	The Buddies And The Compacts	1965	16.00	40.00
Wing SRW-16293	(S)	The Buddies And The Compacts	1965	20.00	50.00
Wing MGW-12306	(M)	Go Go With The Buddies	1965	16.00	40.00
Wing SRW-16306	(S)	Go Go With The Buddies	1965	20.00	50.00

BUDGIE

Kapp KS-3656	(S)	Budgie	1971	16.00	40.00
Kapp KS-3669	(S)	Squawk	1972	12.00	30.00

BUFFALO NICKEL JUGBAND, THE

Happy Tiger 1018	(S)	The Buffalo Nickel Jugband	1971	10.00	25.00

BUFFALO SPRINGFIELD, THE
The Springfield consisted of Neil Young, Steve Stills, Richie Furay, Dewey Martin and Bruce Palmer,
replaced by Jim Messina in 1968. Refer to The Au Go-Go Singers.

Atco 33-200	(M)	Buffalo Springfield	1966	40.00	100.00
Atco SD-33-200	(S)	Buffalo Springfield	1966	60.00	150.00

(First pressings of Atco 200 contain "Baby Don't Scold Me."
"Burned" is rechanneled on all stereo pressings of this album.)

Atco 33-200-A	(M)	Buffalo Springfield	1967	16.00	40.00
Atco SD-33-200-A	(S)	Buffalo Springfield	1967	10.00	25.00

(Later pressings replace "Scold" with "For What It's Worth.")

Atco 33-226	(M)	Buffalo Springfield Again	1967	20.00	50.00
Atco SD-33-226	(S)	Buffalo Springfield Again	1967	10.00	25.00
Atco 33-256	(M)	Last Time Around (White label promo)	1968	40.00	100.00
Atco SD-33-256	(S)	Last Time Around	1968	16.00	40.00

— Atco stereo albums above purple & brown labels.—

Label & Catalog #		Title	Year	VG+	NM
Atco 33-283	(M)	**Retrospective** (White label promo)	1969	**20.00**	**50.00**
—Atco albums above yellow labels with "Atlantic Recording Co." on the bottom.—					
Atco SD-33-283	(S)	**Retrospective**	1969	**20.00**	**50.00**
		(Gold & gray label with laminated cover manufactured for export.)			

BUFFALO SPRINGFIELD, THE / IRON BUTTERFLY

Atlantic SP-	(DJ)	**Retrospective / Ball**	1969	**20.00**	**50.00**
		(Sampler with one side devoted to each artist's latest album.)			

BUFFALO SPRINGFIELD, THE / KING CURTIS

Atlantic SP-	(DJ)	**Last Time Around / Sweet Soul**	1968	**20.00**	**50.00**
		(Sampler with one side devoted to each artist's latest album.)			

BUFFETT, JIMMY

Barnaby Z-30093	(S)	**Down To Earth**	197?	**16.00**	**40.00**
Barnaby BR-6014	(S)	**High Cumberland Jubilee**	1976	**16.00**	**40.00**

BUGALOOS, THE

Capitol ST-621	(S)	**The Bugaloos**	1970	**12.00**	**30.00**

BUMP

Pioneer	(S)	**Bump** (Canadian)	1970	**100.00**	**250.00**

BUNKERS, THE: *Refer to* **O' CONNOR, CARROLL, & JEAN STAPLETON**

BURDON, ERIC, & THE ANIMALS: *Refer to* **THE ANIMALS**

BURGHOFF, GARY

Shalom 651	(S)	**Just For Fun**	197?	**20.00**	**50.00**

BURKE, SOLOMON
Refer to Ray Charles / Solomon Burke.

Apollo ALP-498	(M)	**Solomon Burke**	1962	**300.00**	**600.00**
Kenwood LP-498	(M)	**Solomon Burke**	1964	**100.00**	**250.00**
		(Kenwood 498 is a reissue of Apollo 498.)			
Atlantic 8067	(M)	**Solomon Burke's Greatest Hits**	1962	**20.00**	**50.00**
Atlantic SD-8067	(S)	**Solomon Burke's Greatest Hits**	1962	**30.00**	**75.00**
Atlantic 8085	(M)	**If You Need Me**	1963	**20.00**	**50.00**
Atlantic SD-8085	(S)	**If You Need Me**	1963	**30.00**	**75.00**
Atlantic 8096	(M)	**Rock 'N' Soul**	1964	**20.00**	**50.00**
Atlantic SD-8096	(S)	**Rock 'N' Soul**	1964	**30.00**	**75.00**
Atlantic 8109	(M)	**The Best Of Solomon Burke**	1965	**12.00**	**30.00**
Atlantic SD-8109	(S)	**The Best Of Solomon Burke**	1965	**16.00**	**40.00**
Atlantic SD-8158	(S)	**King Solomon**	1968	**10.00**	**25.00**
Atlantic SD-8185	(S)	**I Wish I Knew**	1968	**10.00**	**25.00**

BURNETTE, J. HENRY : *Refer to* **T-BONE BURNETTE**

BURNETTE, DORSEY

Era EL-102	(M)	**Tall Oak Tree**	1960	**80.00**	**200.00**
Era ES-102	(S)	**Tall Oak Tree**	1960	**200.00**	**400.00**
Dot DLP-3456	(M)	**Dorsey Burnette Sings**	1963	**16.00**	**40.00**
Dot DLP-25456	(S)	**Dorsey Burnette Sings**	1963	**20.00**	**50.00**
Era ES-800	(S)	**Dorsey Burnette's Greatest Hits**	1969	**10.00**	**25.00**

BURNETTE, JOHNNY, & THE ROCK 'N' ROLL TRIO

Coral CRL-57080	(M)	**Johnny Burnette & The Rock 'N' Roll Trio**	1956	**2,000.00**	*See below*
		(Original copies of CRL-57080 have printing on the spine and "Made in USA" on the lower right back cover; counterfeits do not. Near Mint copies of CRL-57080 are rare with a suggested value of $4,000-8,000. There are no blue label promos for this album.)			
Solid Smoke SS-8001	(M)	**Tear It Up!** (Blue vinyl)	1978	**10.00**	**25.00**
		("Tear It Up" repackages the Coral album with bonus tracks.)			

BURNETTE, JOHNNY

Liberty LRP-3179	(M)	**Dreamin'**	1960	**16.00**	**40.00**
Liberty LST-7179	(S)	**Dreamin'**	1960	**20.00**	**50.00**
Liberty LRP-3183	(M)	**Johnny Burnette**	1961	**16.00**	**40.00**
Liberty LST-7183	(S)	**Johnny Burnette**	1961	**20.00**	**50.00**

Label & Catalog #		Title	Year	VG+	NM
Liberty LRP-3190	(M)	Johnny Burnette Sings	1961	16.00	40.00
Liberty LST-7190	(S)	Johnny Burnette Sings	1961	20.00	50.00
Liberty LRP-3206	(M)	Hits And Other Favorites	1962	16.00	40.00
Liberty LST-7206	(S)	Hits And Other Favorites	1962	20.00	50.00
Liberty LRP-3255	(M)	Roses Are Red	1962	16.00	40.00
Liberty LST-7255	(S)	Roses Are Red	1962	20.00	50.00
Liberty LRP-3389	(M)	The Johnny Burnette Story	1964	16.00	40.00
Liberty LST-7389	(S)	The Johnny Burnette Story	1964	20.00	50.00

BURNETTE, SMILEY

Starday SLP-191	(M)	Ole Frog (Yellow label)	1962	16.00	40.00

BURNETTE, T-BONE
T-Bone is a pseudonym for J. Henry Burnette.

Uni 73125	(S)	The B-52 Band & The Fabulous Skyhawks	1972	12.00	30.00

BURNS, RANDY, & THE SKY DOG BAND

ESP-Disk' 1039S	(S)	Sons Of Love And War	1966	10.00	25.00
ESP-Disk' 1089S	(S)	Evening Of The Magician	1968	10.00	25.00

BURNT SUITE

B. J. W. 9	(M)	Burnt Suite	1967	80.00	200.00

BURRITO BROTHERS: *Refer to* FLYING BURRITO BROTHERS

BURROUGHS, WILLIAM

ESP-Disk' 1050	(M)	Call Me Burroughs	196?	40.00	100.00

BURROWS, ABE

Columbia CL-6128	(10")	Abe Burrows Sings	195?	16.00	40.00
Decca DL-5288	(10")	The Girl With The Three Blue Eyes	1950	16.00	40.00

BURTON, JAMES
Refer to Longbranch Pennywhistle; Ralph Mooney; Elvis Presley.

A&M SP-4293	(S)	James Burton	1971	10.00	25.00

BUSH, JOHNNY

Million 1001	(M)	The Best Of Johnny Bush	1972	16.00	40.00

BUSH, KATE

Harvest SW-11761	(S)	The Kick Inside	1978	16.00	40.00
EMI SSA-3020	(DJ)	Self Portrait/The Kate Bush Radio Special	1979	60.00	150.00
Steve Strout SSA-3020	(DJ)	Kate Bush Interview Album	1982	100.00	250.00
		(EMI issued this promo with a note to DJs inside regular covers of "The Kick Inside" with a special wrapper around the jacket identifying the contents as a special interview album.)			
EMI ST-17171	(DJ)	Hounds Of Love (With folder and press kit)	1986	60.00	150.00
EMI ST-17171	(DJ)	Hounds Of Love (Marble vinyl)	1986	16.00	40.00

BUSHES, THE

Growth LPS-200-08	(S)	Assorted Shrubbery	197?	40.00	100.00

BUTCH

Sunndial	(S)	The Bitch Of Rock & Roll	1977	30.00	75.00

BUTERA, SAM, & THE WITNESSES
Refer to Louis Prima.

Capitol T-1098	(M)	The Big Horn	1959	10.00	25.00
Capitol ST-1098	(S)	The Big Horn	1959	14.00	35.00
Capitol S-1521	(M)	The Big Sax And The Big Voice	1960	10.00	25.00
Capitol ST-1521	(S)	The Big Sax And The Big Voice	1960	14.00	35.00
Capitol S-1677	(M)	The Continental Twist (Soundtrack)	1961	8.00	20.00
Capitol ST-1677	(S)	The Continental Twist (Soundtrack)	1961	10.00	25.00
Dot DLP-3272	(M)	The Wildest Clan	1960	8.00	20.00
Dot DLP-25272	(S)	The Wildest Clan	1960	10.00	25.00
Dot DLP-3306	(M)	Sam Butera Plays Music From The Rat Race	1961	8.00	20.00
Dot DLP-25306	(S)	Sam Butera Plays Music From The Rat Race	1961	10.00	25.00
Dot DLP-3381	(M)	Apache	1961	8.00	20.00
Dot DLP-25381	(S)	Apache	1961	10.00	25.00

Label & Catalog #		Title	Year	VG+	NM
BUTLER, BILLY					
OKeh OKM-12115	(M)	**Right Track**	1966	8.00	20.00
OKeh OKS-12115	(S)	**Right Track**	1966	10.00	25.00
BUTLER, CARL					
Columbia CL-2002	(M)	**Don't Let Me Cross Over**	1963	8.00	20.00
Columbia CS-8802	(S)	**Don't Let Me Cross Over**	1963	10.00	25.00
BUTLER, FREDDY					
Kapp KL-1519	(M)	**With A Dab Of Soul**	1968	10.00	25.00
Kapp KS-3519	(S)	**With A Dab Of Soul**	1968	14.00	35.00
BUTLER, JERRY					
Jerry Butler was originally lead singer with The Impressions. Refer to The Ice Man's Band.					
Abner R-2001	(M)	**Jerry Butler Esquire**	1959	200.00	400.00
Vee Jay LP-1027	(M)	**Jerry Butler Esquire**	1960	40.00	100.00
		(Vee Jay 1027 is a reissue of the Abner album.)			
Vee Jay LP-1029	(M)	**He Will Break Your Heart**	1960	30.00	75.00
Vee Jay LP-1034	(M)	**Love Me**	1961	14.00	35.00
		(Vee Jay 1034 is a reissue of 1027.)			
Vee Jay LP-1038	(M)	**Aware Of Love**	1961	10.00	25.00
Vee Jay SR-1038	(S)	**Aware Of Love**	1961	12.00	30.00
Vee Jay LP-1046	(M)	**Moon River**	1962	10.00	25.00
Vee Jay SR-1046	(S)	**Moon River**	1962	12.00	30.00
Vee Jay LP-1048	(M)	**The Best Of Jerry Butler**	1962	10.00	25.00
Vee Jay SR-1048	(P)	**The Best Of Jerry Butler**	1962	12.00	30.00
Vee Jay LP-1057	(M)	**Folk Songs**	1963	10.00	25.00
Vee Jay SR-1057	(S)	**Folk Songs**	1963	12.00	30.00
Vee Jay LP-1075	(M)	**For Your Precious Love**	1963	10.00	25.00
Vee Jay VJS-1075	(S)	**For Your Precious Love**	1963	12.00	30.00
Vee Jay LP-1076	(M)	**Giving Up On Love/Need To Belong**	1963	10.00	25.00
Vee Jay VJS-1076	(S)	**Giving Up On Love/Need To Belong**	1963	12.00	30.00
Vee Jay LP-1119	(M)	**More Of The Best Of Jerry Butler**	1965	10.00	25.00
Vee Jay VJS-1119	(S)	**More Of The Best Of Jerry Butler**	1965	12.00	30.00
BUTLER, JERRY, & BETTY EVERETT					
Vee Jay LP-1099	(M)	**Delicious Together**	1964	8.00	20.00
Vee Jay VJS-1099	(S)	**Delicious Together**	1964	10.00	25.00
BUTLER BROTHERS, THE					
Jalyn JLP-142	(M)	**West Virginia Bluegrass**	196?	10.00	25.00
BUTTERFIELD, PAUL/THE BUTTERFIELD BLUES BAND					
Butterfield's original band included Jerome Arnold, Elvin Bishop, Mike Bloomfield and Mark Naftalin.					
Elektra EKL-294	(M)	**Paul Butterfield Blues Band**	1965	8.00	20.00
Elektra EKS-7294	(S)	**Paul Butterfield Blues Band**	1965	10.00	25.00
Elektra EKL-315	(M)	**East-West**	1966	8.00	20.00
Elektra EKS-7315	(S)	**East-West**	1966	10.00	25.00
		— Elektra albums above have gold labels.—			
BUTTERFINGERS					
Pot SLP-457	(S)	**Butterfingers**	1972	500.00	1,000.00
BUTTERSWORTH, MARY: *Refer to* MARY BUTTERSWORTH					
BYRD, BILLY					
Warner Bros. W-1327	(M)	**I Love A Guitar**	1960	8.00	20.00
Warner Bros. WS-1327	(S)	**I Love A Guitar**	1960	10.00	25.00
Reprise R-6040	(M)	**Lonesome Country Songs**	1962	8.00	20.00
Reprise R9-6040	(S)	**Lonesome Country Songs**	1962	10.00	25.00
Warner Bros. W-1576	(M)	**The Golden Guitar Of Billy Byrd**	1964	8.00	20.00
Warner Bros. WS-1576	(S)	**The Golden Guitar Of Billy Byrd**	1964	10.00	25.00
BYRD, BOBBY					
Bobby Byrd originally recorded as Bobby Day.					
King KS-1118	(S)	**I Need Help** *(Produced by James Brown)*	1970	100.00	250.00

Label & Catalog #		Title	Year	VG+	NM

BYRD, JERRY

Jerry also recorded as a member of The Country All-Stars.

Label & Catalog #		Title	Year	VG+	NM
Mercury MG-25077	(10")	Nani Hawaii	1954	40.00	100.00
Mercury MG-25134	(10")	Pagan Love Song	1954	40.00	100.00
Mercury MG-25169	(10")	Byrd's Expedition	1954	40.00	100.00
Decca DL-8643	(M)	Hi Fi Guitar	1958	20.00	50.00
Decca DL-4078	(M)	Paradise Island	1961	10.00	25.00
Decca DL-74078	(S)	Paradise Island	1961	14.00	35.00
Mercury MG-20230	(M)	On The Shores Of Waikiki	1960	14.00	35.00
Mercury SR-60230	(S)	On The Shores Of Waikiki	1960	20.00	50.00
Mercury MG-20345	(M)	Steel Guitar Favorites	1961	14.00	35.00
Mercury SR-60345	(S)	Steel Guitar Favorites	1961	20.00	50.00
Mercury MG-20693	(M)	Hawaiian Golden Hits	1962	14.00	35.00
Mercury SR-60693	(S)	Hawaiian Golden Hits	1962	20.00	50.00
Mercury MG-20856	(M)	Blue Hawaiian Steel Guitar	1963	14.00	35.00
Mercury SR-60856	(S)	Blue Hawaiian Steel Guitar	1963	20.00	50.00
Mercury MG-20932	(M)	The Man Of Steel	1964	14.00	35.00
Mercury SR-60932	(S)	The Man Of Steel	1964	20.00	50.00
Monument MLP-4003	(M)	Byrd Of Paradise	1961	8.00	20.00
Monument SLP-14003	(S)	Byrd Of Paradise	1961	10.00	25.00
Monument MLP-4008	(M)	Memories Of Maria	1962	8.00	20.00
Monument SLP-14008	(S)	Memories Of Maria	1962	10.00	25.00
Monument MLP-8009	(M)	Byrd Of Paradise	1961	8.00	20.00
Monument SLP-18009	(S)	Byrd Of Paradise	1961	10.00	25.00
Monument MLP-8018	(M)	Admirable Byrd	1963	8.00	20.00
Monument SLP-18018	(S)	Admirable Byrd	1963	10.00	25.00
		—Monument albums above have "swirl" labels.—			
Monument MLP-8033	(M)	Satin Strings Of Steel	1965	10.00	25.00
Monument SLP-18033	(S)	Satin Strings Of Steel	1965	12.00	30.00

BYRD, JERRY / SHOT JACKSON

Label & Catalog #		Title	Year	VG+	NM
Sesac PA-228	(M)	Just A Minute	195?	40.00	100.00

BYRDS, THE

It was The Byrds' melding of electric rock music with the lyrics of Bob Dylan and more traditional folk music that led to the coining of the phrase "folk-rock." Gene Clark, David Crosby and Jim McGuinn originally recorded as The Jet Set (refer to Early L.A. on Together in the various artists section) and then a lone single for Elektra as The Beefeaters with no success. With Chris Hillman and Michael Clarke they formed The Byrds, recording a series of demos in 1964 eventually released in 1969 on as Prefylte.

After signing with Columbia the original five man band last through two album as Clark leaves at the beginning of the Fifth Dimension sessions. While Notorious Byrd Brothers features all of the members in some capacity— Clark plays tambourine and possibly contributes backing vocals on a track or two— it is basically McGuinn and Hillman backed by studio musicians.

By Sweetheart of The Rodeo the members are McGuinn (now Roger) and Hillman with Gram Parsons and Kevin Kelly. For Dr. Byrds it is McGuinn with Gene Parsons, Clarence White and John York, who is replaced by Skip Battin in late 1969. Finally, the five original members reunited for the eponymous album on Asylum. Refer to The International Submarine Band; The Kentucky Colonels; The Flying Buritto Brothers; The Scottsville Squirrel Barkers.

Unless noted otherwise, "Mr. Tambourine Man," "I Knew I'd Want You," and "Turn! Turn! Turn!" are in rechenneld stereo on all Columbia albums. "Younger Than Yesterday," "Notorious Byrd Brothers" and "Sweetheart Of The Rodeo" were produced by Gary Usher.

Label & Catalog #		Title	Year	VG+	NM
Columbia CL-2372	(M)	Mr. Tambourine Man (White label promo)	1965	60.00	150.00
Columbia CL-2372	(M)	Mr. Tambourine Man	1965	20.00	50.00
		(Original mono pressing labels read "Guaranteed High Fidelity.")			
Columbia CL-2372	(M)	Mr. Tambourine Man	1965	12.00	30.00
Columbia CS-9172	(S)	Mr. Tambourine Man	1965	10.00	25.00
Columbia CL-2454	(M)	Turn! Turn! Turn! (White label promo)	1965	40.00	100.00
Columbia CL-2454	(M)	Turn! Turn! Turn!	1965	12.00	30.00
Columbia CS-9254	(S)	Turn! Turn! Turn!	1965	10.00	25.00
Columbia CL-2549	(M)	5D (Fifth Dimension) (White label promo)	1966	40.00	100.00
Columbia CL-2549	(M)	5D (Fifth Dimension)	1966	12.00	30.00
Columbia CS-9349	(S)	5D (Fifth Dimension)	1966	10.00	25.00
Columbia CL-2642	(M)	Younger Than Yesterday (White label)	1967	40.00	100.00
Columbia CL-2642	(M)	Younger Than Yesterday	1967	16.00	40.00
Columbia CS-9442	(S)	Younger Than Yesterday	1967	10.00	25.00

Label & Catalog #		Title	Year	VG+	NM
MGM E-4484	(M)	**Don't Make Waves** (Soundtrack)	1967	8.00	20.00
MGM SE-4484	(S)	**Don't Make Waves** (Soundtrack)	1967	10.00	25.00
Columbia CL-2716	(M)	**The Byrds' Greatest Hits** (White label)	1967	30.00	75.00
Columbia CL-2716	(M)	**The Byrds' Greatest Hits**	1967	12.00	30.00
Columbia CS-9516	(S)	**The Byrds' Greatest Hits**	1967	8.00	20.00
Columbia CL-2775	(M)	**The Notorious Byrd Brothers** (White label)	1968	30.00	75.00
Columbia CL-2775	(M)	**The Notorious Byrd Brothers**	1968	20.00	50.00
Columbia CS-9575	(S)	**The Notorious Byrd Brothers**	1968	8.00	20.00
Columbia CS-9670	(S)	**Sweetheart Of The Rodeo** (White label)	1968	20.00	50.00
Columbia CS-9755	(S)	**Dr. Byrds And Mr. Hyde** (White label)	1969	20.00	50.00
Columbia CS-9942	(S)	**Ballad Of Easy Rider** (White label promo)	1969	20.00	50.00

—Columbia albums above have "360 Sound" on the bottom of the label.—

Together ST-1-1001	(S)	**Preflyte**	1969	10.00	25.00

(ST-1001 collectis demos recorded in 1964 at World Pacific Studios.)

BYRNES, ED "KOOKIE"

Label & Catalog #		Title	Year	VG+	NM
Warner Bros. W-1309	(M)	**Kookie** (With bonus photo)	1959	50.00	125.00
Warner Bros. WS-1309	(S)	**Kookie** (With bonus photo)	1959	60.00	150.00
Warner Bros. W-1309	(M)	**Kookie** (Without the photo)	1959	30.00	75.00
Warner Bros. WS-1309	(S)	**Kookie** (Without the photo)	1959	40.00	100.00

These two lovely covers, very much a part of the psychedelic era in which they were conceived, house some truly marvelous music. The mono version of Younger Than Yesterday contains slightly different mixes, punching up the bass in particular. This is no small endorsement, as Chris Hillman's bass playing on this album ranks with the finest in Rock's history, on a par with McCartney on Sgt. Pepper. And, while the hits package is just as lovely, the cover is rather unfair: Seven of the eleven tracks, including both of their #1 songs, were recorded by the five original members. Gene Clark is notably missing from the cover.

C

C. A. QUINTET, THE

Candy Floss 7764	(M)	**A Trip Through Hell**	1969	1,000.00	1,500.00

("A Trip Through Hell" is in stereo on this album.)

C. C. S.

Rak KZ-30559	(S)	**Whole Lotta Love**	1971	12.00	30.00
Rak KZ-31569	(S)	**C. C. S.**	1972	12.00	30.00

CABOT, SEBASTIAN

MGM E-4431	(M)	**Sebastian Cabot, Actor/Bob Dylan, Poet**	1967	10.00	25.00
MGM SE-4431	(S)	**Sebastian Cabot, Actor/Bob Dylan, Poet**	1967	14.00	35.00

CADETS, THE
The Cadets also recorded as The Jacks. Refer to Aaron Collins.

Modern LPM-1215	(M)	**Rockin' 'N' Reelin**	1956	*Unreleased*	
Crown CLP-5015	(M)	**Rockin' 'N' Reelin**	1957	100.00	300.00

(Crown 5015 is a reissue of the unreleased Modern 1215.)

Crown CLP-5370	(M)	**The Cadets**	1963	60.00	150.00
Crown CST-370	(E)	**The Cadets**	1963	50.00	100.00

(Crown 5370 is a reissue of 5015.)

CADILLACS, THE

Jubilee JGM-1045	(M)	**The Fabulous Cadillacs**	1957	250.00	500.00

—Jubilee albums above have blue labels.—

Jubilee JGM-1045	(M)	**The Fabulous Cadillacs**	1959	100.00	250.00
Jubilee JGM-1089	(M)	**The Crazy Cadillacs**	1959	150.00	300.00

—Jubilee albums above have flat black labels.—

Jubilee JGM-1045	(M)	**The Fabulous Cadillacs**	1960	40.00	100.00
Jubilee JGM-1089	(M)	**The Crazy Cadillacs**	1960	40.00	100.00
Jubilee JGM-5009	(M)	**Twisting With The Cadillacs**	1962	150.00	300.00

—Jubilee albums above have glossy black labels.—

CADILLACS, THE / THE ORIOLES

Jubilee JGM-1117	(M)	**The Cadillacs Meet The Orioles**	1961	100.00	250.00

CAIN

A.S.I. 204	(S)	**A Pound Of Flesh**	1974	24.00	60.00
A.S.I. 214	(S)	**Stinger**	1975	12.00	30.00

CAIN, JACKIE, & ROY KRAL: *Refer to* GOLDMINE'S PRICE GUIDE TO COLLECTIBLE JAZZ ALBUMS

CAIOLA, AL
Al also recorded with Johnny Mathis

Savoy MG-12033	(M)	**Deep In A Dream**	1955	16.00	40.00
Savoy MG-12057	(M)	**Serenade In Blue**	1956	16.00	40.00
RCA Victor LPM-2031	(M)	**High Strung**	1959	10.00	25.00
RCA Victor LSP-2031	(S)	**High Strung**	1959	14.00	35.00
Atco 33-117	(M)	**Music For Space Squirrels**	1960	10.00	25.00
Atco SD-33-117	(S)	**Music For Space Squirrels**	1960	14.00	35.00
Chancellor CHL-5008	(M)	**Great Pickin'** *(With Don Arone)*	1960	12.00	30.00
Chancellor CHS-5008	(S)	**Great Pickin'** *(With Don Arone)*	1960	10.00	25.00
Roulette R-25108	(M)	**Salute Italia**	1960	8.00	20.00
Roulette SR-25108	(S)	**Salute Italia**	1960	10.00	25.00
Time 52006	(M)	**Percussion Espanol**	1960	8.00	20.00
Time S-2006	(S)	**Percussion Espanol**	1960	10.00	25.00
Time 52039	(M)	**Spanish Guitars**	1960	8.00	20.00
Time S-2039	(S)	**Spanish Guitars**	1960	10.00	25.00
Time 52101	(M)	**Gershwin And Guitars**	1961	8.00	20.00
Time S-2101	(S)	**Gershwin And Guitars**	1961	10.00	25.00
United Arts. UAL-3299	(M)	**Cleopatra And All That Jazz**	1963	12.00	30.00
United Arts. UAS-6299	(S)	**Cleopatra And All That Jazz**	1963	10.00	25.00

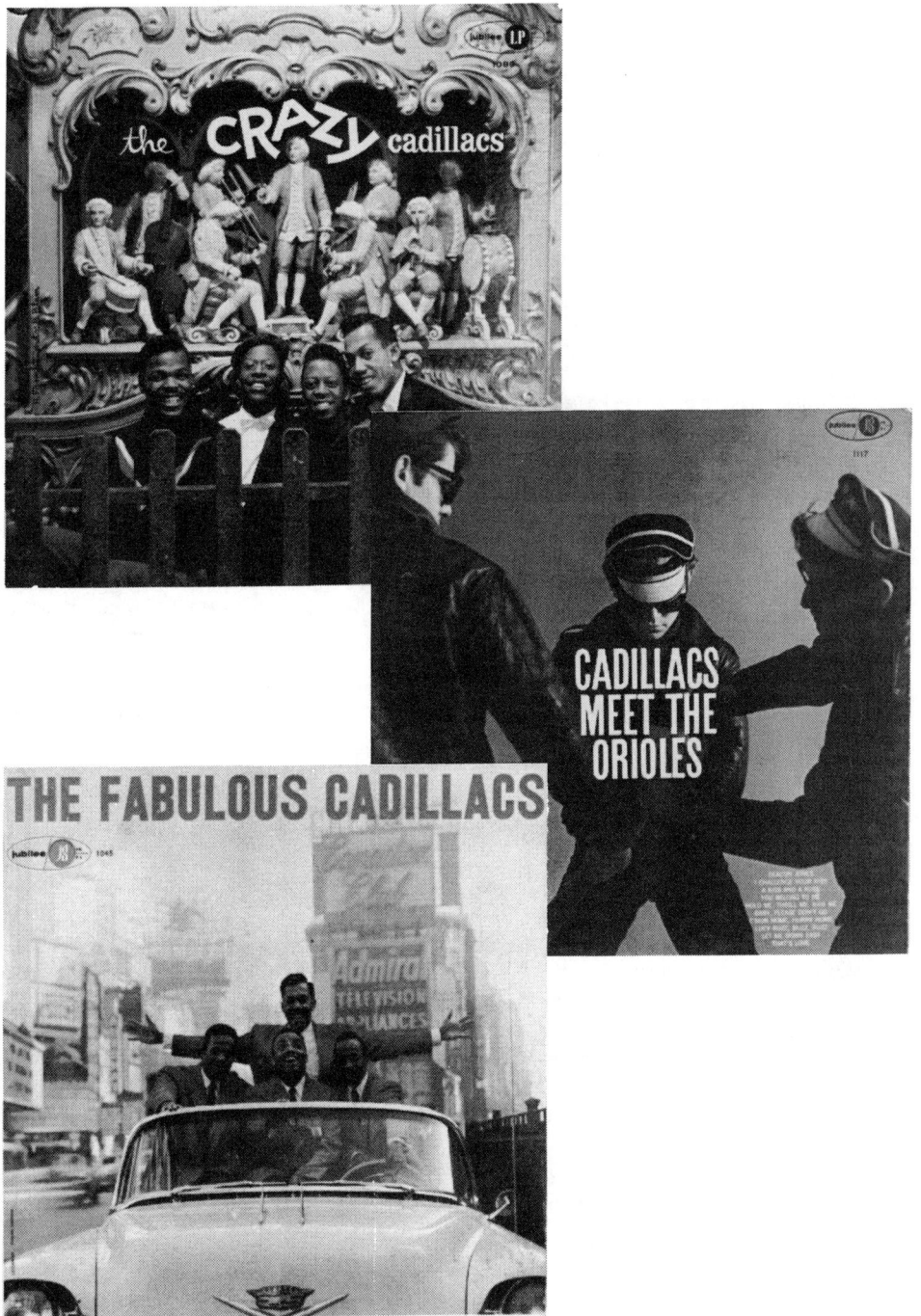

The Cadillacs were one of the few rhythm 'n blues vocal groups to be graced by the powers-that-be with an album. While they eventually recorded for Mercury/Smash and Capitol, it was well past the heyday of doo wop and these companies never released any albums, leaving the group's entire LP catalog to Jubilee.

Label & Catalog #		Title	Year	VG+	NM
CAJUN PETE					
Mercury MG-20633	(M)	**Tales Of The Bayou**	1961	8.00	20.00
Mercury SR-60633	(S)	**Tales Of The Bayou**	1961	10.00	25.00
CAKE, THE					
Decca DL-4927	(M)	**The Cake**	1967	8.00	20.00
Decca DL-74927	(S)	**The Cake**	1967	10.00	25.00
Decca DL-75039	(S)	**A Slice Of The Cake**	1968	10.00	25.00
CALDWELL, LOUISE HARRISON					
Recar 2012	(M)	**Questions All About The Beatles Answered By Louise Harrison Caldwell**	1965	60.00	150.00

(Louise Harrison Caldwell is the sister of George Harrison and this is a wonderful exploitation of her sibling's fame as a Beatle.. Issued with an explanatory insert, worth an additional $50.)

CALE, JOHN					

Cale was formerly a member of the Velvet Underground.

Columbia CS-1037	(P)	**Vintage Violence** ("360 Sound" label)	1970	8.00	20.00
Island IXP-2	(DJ)	**Hear Fear** (Interview)	1976	10.00	25.00
Spy/IRS SP-004	(DJ)	**Sabotage** (Live)	1980	10.00	25.00
CALIFORNIA POPPY PICKERS, THE					

The C.P.P.'s was a house name for various artists who recorded without credit. While rumors that Gene Clark was involved remain unconfirmed, Wilson McKinley can he found on "Honkey Tonk Women."

Alshire S-51??	(S)	**Sounds Of '69**	1969	14.00	35.00
Alshire S-5153	(S)	**Hair-Aquarius**	1969	14.00	35.00
Alshire S-51??	(S)	**Today's Chart Busters**	1969	14.00	35.00
Alshire S-51??	(S)	**Honkey Tonk Women**	1969	20.00	50.00
CALLIER, TERRY					
Prestige PRLP-7383	(M)	**The New Folk Sound Of Terry Callier**	1966	8.00	20.00
Prestige PRST-7383	(S)	**The New Folk Sound Of Terry Callier**	1966	10.00	25.00
CALLIOPE					

Calliope features Danny O'Keefe.

Buddah BDS-5023	(S)	**Steamed**	1968	10.00	25.00

CALLOWAY, CAB: *Refer to* **GOLDMINE'S PRICE GUIDE TO COLLECTIBLE JAZZ ALBUMS**

CAMERON, ISLA					

Isla Camron is a Scottish singer of traditional folk songs of the British Isles.

Tradition TLP-1001	(M)	**Through Bushes And Briars**	195?	12.00	30.00
Prestige Inter. PR-13042	(M)	**The Best Of Isla Cameron**	1961	12.00	30.00
CAMERON, ISLA, & LOU KILLEN					
Prestige Inter. PR-13059	(M)	**The Waters Of Tyne**	1962	12.00	30.00
CAMILLERI, CHARLES					
MGM E-3856	(M)	**Spectacular Accordions**	1960	8.00	20.00
MGM SE-3856	(S)	**Spectacular Accordions**	1960	10.00	25.00

CAMP CREEK BOYS, THE: *Refer to* **KYLE CREED**

CAMP MEETIN' CHOIR, THE					
Mercury MG-25083	(10")	**Spirituals, Vol. 1**	195?	40.00	100.00
Mercury MG-25084	(10")	**Spirituals, Vol. 2**	195?	40.00	100.00
CAMPBELL, ALEX, & OLA BELLE REED					
Starday SLP-214	(M)	**16 Radio Favorites**	1963	12.00	30.00
Starday SLP-342	(M)	**Travel On**	1965	12.00	30.00
CAMPBELL, ARCHIE					
Starday SLP-162	(M)	**Make Friends With Archie Campbell**	1962	14.00	35.00
Starday SLP-167	(M)	**Bedtime Stories For Adults**	1962	14.00	35.00
Starday SLP-223	(M)	**The Joker Is Wild**	1963	14.00	35.00
Starday SLP-377	(M)	**The Grand Ole Opry's Good Humor Man**	1966	10.00	25.00

— *Starday albums above have yellow labels.*—

While Glen Campbell's first two albums seem to present the young singer as a folksy country neophyte, he had already established himself as one of the premier guitar players in American with his astounding session work with sundry Los Angeles recording studios. Big Bluegrass Special, *often credited to The Green River Boys, is among the hottest and most collectible of all bluegrass albums.*

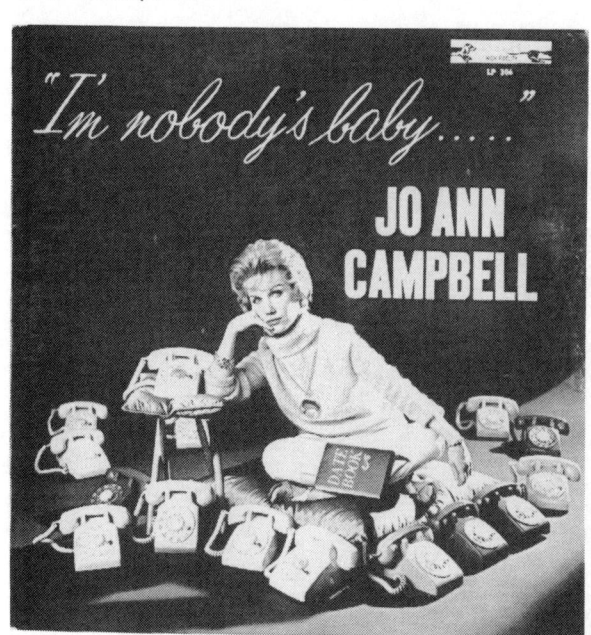

After the success of her only real hit, "(I'm The Girl On) Wolverton Mountain," Ms. Campbell married Troy Seals and the two teamed up as Jo Ann & Troy, to little success. Later, Seals formed another duo, this time with Dash Crofts. . .

Label & Catalog #		Title	Year	VG+	NM
CAMPBELL, CECIL					
Starday SLP-254	(M)	**Steel Guitar Jamboree** *(Yellow label)*	1963	16.00	40.00
CAMPBELL, CHOKER					
Motown 620	(M)	**Hits Of The Sixties**	1965	12.00	30.00
Motown MS-620	(S)	**Hits Of The Sixties**	1965	16.00	40.00
CAMPBELL, DICK					
Mercury MG-21060	(M)	**Dick Campbell Sings Where It's At**	1966	12.00	30.00
Mercury SR-61060	(S)	**Dick Campbell Sings Where It's At**	1966	16.00	40.00
CAMPBELL, GERALD					
London LL-1714	(M)	**The Wandering Minstrel**	195?	12.00	30.00
CAMPBELL, GLEN					
Refer to The Bandits; The Folkswingers; Tennessee Ernie Ford & Glen Campbell; The In Group.					
Capitol T-1810	(M)	**Big Bluegrass Special**	1962	40.00	100.00
Capitol T-1810	(S)	**Big Bluegrass Special**	1962	60.00	150.00
		(Capitol 1810 credits The Green River Boys & Glen Campbell.)			
Capitol T-1881	(M)	**Too Late To Worry, Too Blue To Cry**	1963	8.00	20.00
Capitol ST-1881	(S)	**Too Late To Worry, Too Blue To Cry**	1963	10.00	25.00
Capitol SW-11722	(DJ)	**Basic** *(Picture disc)*	1978	20.00	50.00
Sears SPS-465	(S)	**One Hundred Miles From Home**	1969	14.00	35.00
CAMPBELL, JO ANN					
End LP-306	(M)	**I'm Nobody's Baby.....**	1959	60.00	150.00
ABC-Paramount 393	(M)	**Twistin' And Listenin'**	1962	40.00	100.00
ABC-Paramount S-393	(S)	**Twistin' And Listenin'**	1962	60.00	150.00
Cameo C-1026	(M)	**I'm The Girl From Wolverton Mountain—** **All The Hits By Jo Ann Campbell**	1962	20.00	50.00
Cameo SC-1026	(S)	**I'm The Girl From Wolverton Mountain—** **All The Hits By Jo Ann Campbell**	1962	40.00	100.00
Roulette R-25168	(M)	**Hey, Let's Twist** *(Soundtrack)*	1962	16.00	40.00
Roulette SR-25168	(S)	**Hey, Let's Twist** *(Soundtrack)*	1962	20.00	50.00
CAMPUS SINGERS, THE					
Argo LP-4023	(M)	**The Campus Singers At The Fickle Pickle**	1963	8.00	20.00
Argo LPS-4023	(S)	**The Campus Singers At The Fickle Pickle**	1963	10.00	25.00
CANADIAN BEADLES, THE					
Tide 2005	(M)	**Three Faces North**	1964	20.00	50.00
CANADIAN SWEETHEARTS, THE					
The Sweethearts feature Lucille Starr.					
A&M LP-106	(M)	**Introducing The Canadian Sweethearts**	1964	8.00	20.00
A&M SP-106	(S)	**Introducing The Canadian Sweethearts**	1964	12.00	30.00
CANARIES, THE					
B.T. Puppy BTS-1007	(S)	**Flying High With The Canaries**	1970	40.00	100.00
CANDY STORE, THE					
Decca DL-75147	(S)	**Turned On Christmas**	1969	10.00	25.00
CANNED HEAT					
Liberty LRP-3526	(M)	**Canned Heat**	1967	10.00	25.00
Liberty LST-7526	(S)	**Canned Heat**	1967	12.00	30.00
Liberty LST-7541	(S)	**Boogie With Canned Heat**	1968	10.00	25.00
Liberty LST-7618	(S)	**Hallelujah**	1968	10.00	25.00
Liberty LST-27200	(S)	**Living The Blues**	1968	10.00	25.00
Wand WDS-693	(S)	**Live At Topanga Canyon**	1970	10.00	25.00
CANNED HEAT & JOHN LEE HOOKER					
Liberty LST-35002	(S)	**Hooker 'N' Heat** *(2 LPs)*	1971	10.00	25.00
CANNIBAL & THE HEADHUNTERS					
Rampart RM-3302	(M)	**Land Of 1,000 Dances**	1966	20.00	50.00
Rampart RS-3302	(S)	**Land Of 1,000 Dances**	1966	30.00	75.00
Date TEM-3001	(M)	**Land Of 1,000 Dances**	1966	16.00	40.00
Date TES-3001	(S)	**Land Of 1,000 Dances**	1966	20.00	50.00

Label & Catalog #		Title	Year	VG+	NM
CANNON, ACE					
Hi HL-12007	(M)	**Tuff Sax**	1962	10.00	25.00
Hi SHL-32007	(S)	**Tuff Sax**	1962	12.00	30.00
Hi HL-12008	(M)	**Looking Back**	1962	10.00	25.00
Hi SHL-32008	(S)	**Looking Back**	1962	12.00	30.00
Hi HL-12014	(M)	**The Moanin' Sax Of Ace Cannon**	1963	10.00	25.00
Hi SHL-32014	(S)	**The Moanin' Sax Of Ace Cannon**	1963	12.00	30.00
Hi HL-12016	(M)	**Aces Hi**	1964	8.00	20.00
Hi SHL-32016	(S)	**Aces Hi**	1964	10.00	25.00
Hi HL-12019	(M)	**The Great Show Tunes**	1964	8.00	20.00
Hi SHL-32019	(S)	**The Great Show Tunes**	1964	10.00	25.00
Hi HL-12022	(M)	**Christmas Cheers**	1964	8.00	20.00
Hi SHL-32022	(S)	**Christmas Cheers**	1964	10.00	25.00
		— Hi albums above have silver labels.—			
CANNON, FREDDY					
Swan LP-502	(M)	**The Explosive! Freddie Cannon**	1960	60.00	150.00
Swan LPS-502	(S)	**The Explosive! Freddie Cannon**	1960	160.00	300.00
		("Way Down Yonder In New Orleans" and "Okefenokee" are rechanneled while "Tallahassee Lassie" was rerecorded.)			
Swan LP-504	(M)	**Happy Shades Of Blue**	1960	60.00	150.00
Swan LP-505	(M)	**Solid Gold Hits**	1961	60.00	150.00
Swan LP-506	(M)	**Twistin' All Night Long**	1961	60.00	150.00
		(Freddy is backed by Danny & The Juniors.)			
Swan LP-507	(M)	**Freddie Cannon At Palisades Park**	1962	60.00	150.00
Swan LP-511	(M)	**Freddie Cannon Steps Out**	1963	60.00	150.00
Warner Bros. W-1544	(M)	**Freddie Cannon**	1964	10.00	25.00
Warner Bros. WS-1544	(S)	**Freddie Cannon**	1964	12.00	30.00
Warner Bros. W-1612	(M)	**Action!**	1965	10.00	25.00
Warner Bros. WS-1612	(S)	**Action!**	1965	12.00	30.00
Warner Bros. W-1628	(M)	**Freddie Cannon's Greatest Hits**	1966	8.00	20.00
Warner Bros. WS-1628	(S)	**Freddie Cannon's Greatest Hits**	1966	10.00	25.00
CANNON, GUS					
Stax ST-702	(M)	**Walk Right In**	1962	350.00	750.00
CANSLER, LOMAN					
Loman Cansler is a guitar player and singer of traditional folk songs.					
Folkways FH-5324	(M)	**Missouri Folk Songs**	1959	12.00	30.00
CANTELON, WILLARD					
Supreme M-113	(M)	**L.S.D. Battle For The Mind**	1966	12.00	30.00
Supreme S-113	(S)	**L.S.D. Battle For The Mind**	1966	16.00	40.00
CANTOR, EDDIE					
Vik LXA-1119	(M)	**The Best Of Eddie Cantor**	195?	20.00	50.00
CAPITOLS, THE					
Atco 33-190	(M)	**Dance The Cool Jerk**	1966	16.00	40.00
Atco SD-33-190	(S)	**Dance The Cool Jerk**	1966	20.00	50.00
Atco 33-201	(M)	**We Got A Thing That's In The Groove**	1966	16.00	40.00
Atco SD-33-201	(S)	**We Got A Thing That's In The Groove**	1966	20.00	50.00
CAPTAIN BEEFHEART & THE MAGIC BAND					
The Captain also recorded with Frank Zappa.					
Buddah BDM-1001	(M)	**Safe As Milk** *(White label promo)*	1967	80.00	200.00
Buddah BDM-1001	(M)	**Safe As Milk** *(With bonus sticker)*	1967	24.00	60.00
Buddah BDS-5001	(S)	**Safe As Milk** *(White label promo)*	1967	80.00	200.00
Buddah BDS-5001	(S)	**Safe As Milk** *(With bonus sticker)*	1967	30.00	75.00
		("Safe As Mil" was issued with a "Baby Jesus" bumper sticker.)			
Buddah BDM-1001	(M)	**Safe As Milk** *(Without the sticker)*	1967	14.00	35.00
Buddah BDS-5001	(S)	**Safe As Milk** *(Without the sticker)*	1967	20.00	50.00
Buddah BDS-5063	(S)	**Safe As Milk**	1969	8.00	20.00
Buddah BDS-5077	(S)	**Mirror Man** *(Fold open, die-cut cover)*	1971	16.00	40.00
Verve/Forecast FTS-3054	(S)	**Captain Beefheart & The Magic Band**	1968	Unreleased	
Blue Thumb BTS-1	(S)	**Strictly Personal**	1968	30.00	75.00
		(First pressings of BTS-1 have black labels with unbanded, continuous play tracks.)			

Label & Catalog #		Title	Year	VG+	NM
Blue Thumb BTS-1	(S)	**Strictly Personal**	1969	12.00	30.00
		(Second pressings have white labels with unbanded, continuous play tracks.)			
Blue Thumb BTS-1	(S)	**Strictly Personal**	1969	8.00	20.00
		(Later pressings have white labels with banded tracks.)			
Bizarre 2MS-2027	(S)	**Trout Mask Replica** (2 LPs with book)	1969	30.00	75.00
		("2MS-2027" was issued with a bonus booklet.)			
Bizarre 2MS-2027	(S)	**Trout Mask Replica** (2 LPs without book)	1969	20.00	50.00
Reprise 2MS-2027	(S)	**Trout Mask Replica** (2 LPs)	1972	10.00	25.00
		(2MS-2027 was produced by Frank Zappa.)			
Straight RS-6420	(S)	**Lick My Decals Off, Baby** (With lyric sheet)	1970	16.00	40.00
Reprise MS-2050	(S)	**Spotlight Kid** (White label promo)	1971	20.00	50.00
Reprise MS-2050	(S)	**Spotlight Kid**	1971	10.00	25.00
Reprise MS-2115	(S)	**Clear Spot** (Issued in a clear plastic jacket)	1972	16.00	40.00
Warner Bros.	(DJ)	**Bat Chain Puller** (Test pressing)	1978	200.00	400.00
		(Original test pressings for "Bat Chain Puller" have a different track			

selection.)

CAPTAIN BEEFHEART / RY COODER

Reprise PRO-447	(DJ)	**Capt. Beefheart / Ry Cooder Interview**	1972	200.00	400.00

CARAVELLES, THE

Smash MGS-27044	(M)	**You Don't Have To Be A Baby To Cry**	1963	30.00	75.00
Smash SRS-67044	(E)	**You Don't Have To Be A Baby To Cry**	1963	30.00	75.00

CARAWAN, GUY
Guy Carawan is a singer and multi-instrumentalist in the traditional folk field.

Folkways FA-3544	(M)	**Guy Carawan**	195?	8.00	20.00

CARE PACKAGE

Liberty LST-7647	(S)	**Keep On Keepin' On**	1969	10.00	25.00

CAREFREES, THE

London LL-3379	(M)	**From England! The Carefrees**	1964	30.00	75.00
London PS-379	(S)	**From England! The Carefrees**	1964	40.00	100.00

CATANOOGA CATS, THE

Forward ST-F-1018	(S)	**The Catanooga Cats**	1969	12.00	30.00

CARLISLES, THE
The Carlisle are brothers Bill and Clifford.

Mercury MG-20359	(M)	**On Stage With The Carlisles**	1958	20.00	50.00
King 643	(M)	**Fresh From The Country**	1959	40.00	100.00

CARLTON, JOHN

Craftsmen C-8002	(M)	**Movie Themes** (With Kim Novak cover)	195?	20.00	50.00

CARLTON, LARRY

Uni 73036	(S)	**With A Little Help From My Friends**	1968	6.00	15.00

CARMAN, JENKS "TEX"

Modern MLP-7037	(M)	**Country Caravan**	195?	40.00	100.00
Sage C-9	(M)	**Jenks "Tex" Carman**	1960	20.00	50.00
Sage C-26	(M)	**The Ole Indian** (Red vinyl)	1962	20.00	50.00
Sage C-40	(M)	**Jenks "Tex" Carman Sings And Plays**	1963	20.00	50.00

CARMICHAEL, HOAGY: Refer to GOLDMINE'S PRICE GUIDE TO COLLECTIBLE JAZZ ALBUMS

CARNEY, ART

Columbia CL-2595	(10")	**Doodle-Li-Boops And Rhinocelopes**	1954	30.00	75.00
Golden GLP-153	(M)	**The Wizard Of Oz**	1962	20.00	50.00

CAROLINA SLIM

Sharp 2002	(M)	**Blues From The Cotton Fields**	195?	100.00	300.00

CAROLINA TAR HEELS, THE
The Tar Heels are an old-time hillbilly band that has featured Clarence Ashley, Garley Foster, Gwen Foster and Dock Walsh.

Folk/Legacy FSA-24	(M)	**The Carloina Tar Heels**	1962	10.00	25.00

Label & Catalog #		Title	Year	VG+	NM
CARPENTER, IKE					
Discovery DL-3003	(10")	**Dancers In Love**	1949	150.00	300.00
Intro 950	(10")	**Lights Out**	1952	150.00	300.00
Aladdin LP-811	(M)	**Lights Out**	1956		See below
		(Contrary to previous listings, Aladdin 811 does not, in fact, exist.)			
Score SLP-4010	(M)	**Lights Out**	1957	70.00	175.00
		(Score 4010 is a reissue of Intro 950.)			
CARPENTERS, THE					
The Carpenters are siblings Karen and Richard.					
A&M SP-4205	(S)	**Offering**	1969	16.00	40.00
A&M QU-54271	(Q)	**Close To You**	1973	10.00	25.00
A&M QU-53502	(Q)	**Carpenters**	1973	10.00	25.00
A&M QU-53511	(Q)	**A Song For You**	1973	10.00	25.00
A&M QU-53519	(Q)	**Now & Then**	1973	10.00	25.00
A&M QU-53601	(Q)	**The Singles 1969-1973**	1973	10.00	25.00
A&M QU-54530	(Q)	**Horizon**	1975	10.00	25.00
CARR, CATHY					
Fraternity 1005	(M)	**Ivory Tower**	1957	60.00	150.00
Dot DLP-3674	(M)	**Ivory Tower**	1964	10.00	25.00
Dot DLP-25674	(S)	**Ivory Tower**	1964	10.00	25.00

CARR, GEORGIA: Refer to GOLDMINE'S PRICE GUIDE TO COLLECTIBLE JAZZ ALBUMS

CARR, HELEN: Refer to GOLDMINE'S PRICE GUIDE TO COLLECTIBLE JAZZ ALBUMS

Label & Catalog #		Title	Year	VG+	NM
CARR, JAMES					
Goldwax 3001S	(S)	**You've Got My Mind Messed Up**	1968	50.00	125.00
Goldwax 3002S	(S)	**A Man Needs A Woman**	1968	50.00	125.00
CARR, JOE "FINGERS"					
Refer to Pee Wee Hunt & Joe "Fingers" Carr.					
Capitol T-280	(M)	**Bar Room Piano**	1952	10.00	25.00
Capitol T-345	(M)	**Roughhouse Piano**	1953	10.00	25.00
Capitol T-443	(M)	**Joe "Fingers" Carr & His Ragtime Band**	1954	10.00	25.00
Capitol T-527	(M)	**Fireman's Ball**	1954	10.00	25.00
Capitol T-1151	(M)	**"Fingers" And The Flapper**	1959	8.00	20.00
Capitol ST-1151	(S)	**"Fingers" And The Flapper**	1959	10.00	25.00
Capitol T-1217	(M)	**Joe "Fingers" Carr & His Swingin' String Band**	1959	8.00	20.00
Capitol ST-1217	(S)	**Joe "Fingers" Carr & His Swingin' String Band**	1959	10.00	25.00
CARR, LEROY					
Columbia CL-1911	(M)	**Blues Before Sunrise**	1962	12.00	30.00
Columbia CS-8511	(E)	**Blues Before Sunrise**	1962	8.00	20.00
CARROLL, ANDREA / BEVERLY WARREN					
B.T. Puppy BP-1017	(S)	**Andrea Carroll And Beverly Warren**	1971	60.00	150.00
CARROLL, DIAHANN					
RCA Victor LPM-1467	(M)	**Diahann Carroll Sings Harold Arlen**	1957	14.00	35.00
United Arts. UAL-4021	(M)	**Porgy And Bess** (With Andre Previn)	1960	8.00	20.00
United Arts. UAS-5021	(S)	**Porgy And Bess** (With Andre Previn)	1960	10.00	25.00
United Arts. UAL-3069	(M)	**Diahann Carroll And Andre Previn**	1960	8.00	20.00
United Arts. UAS-6069	(S)	**Diahann Carroll And Andre Previn**	1960	10.00	25.00
United Arts. UAL-3080	(M)	**Diahann Carroll At The Persian Room**	1960	8.00	20.00
United Arts. UAS-6080	(S)	**Diahann Carroll At The Persian Room**	1960	10.00	25.00
Atlantic 8048	(M)	**Fun Life**	1961	8.00	20.00
Atlantic SD-8048	(S)	**Fun Life**	1961	12.00	30.00
		—Atlantic albums above have multi-color labels with a white "fan" logo on the right.—			
United Arts. UAL-4091	(M)	**Goodbye Again** (Soundtrack)	1961	14.00	35.00
United Arts. UAS-5091	(S)	**Goodbye Again** (Soundtrack)	1961	20.00	50.00
CARROLL BROTHERS, THE					
Cameo C-1015	(M)	**College Twist Party**	1962	8.00	20.00
Cameo CS-1015	(S)	**College Twist Party**	1962	12.00	30.00

Ike Carpenter, brother to Nat, originally recorded Lights Out *on the Intro label in 1952. It was scheduled to be reissued as Aladdin 811 but was withdrawn prior to release. It was then picked up and issued by Score in 1957.*

Label & Catalog #		Title	Year	VG+	NM
CARS, THE					
Elektra 5E-567	(DJ)	**Shake It Up** (KMET FM picture disc)	1981	20.00	50.00
Elektra 5E-567	(DJ)	**Shake It Up** (Picture disc with a blank back)	1981	16.00	40.00
CARSON, JOHNNY					
Columbia CL-2199	(M)	**Johnny Carson's Introduction**			
		To New York And The World's Fair	1964	10.00	25.00
Columbia CS-8999	(S)	**Johnny Carson's Introduction**			
		To New York And The World's Fair	1964	14.00	35.00
CARSON, MARTHA LOU					
RCA Victor LPM-1145	(M)	**Journey To The Sky**	1955	20.00	50.00
RCA Victor LPM-1490	(M)	**Rock-A My Soul**	1957	20.00	50.00
Sims LP-100	(M)	**Martha Carson**	195?	12.00	30.00
Sims LP-109	(M)	**Martha Carson**	195?	12.00	30.00
Capitol T-1507	(M)	**Satisfied**	1960	8.00	20.00
Capitol ST-1507	(S)	**Satisfied**	1960	12.00	30.00
CARTER, ANITA					
Refer to The Carter Family.					
Mercury MG-20770	(M)	**Folk Songs Old And New**	1963	10.00	25.00
Mercury SR-60770	(S)	**Folk Songs Old And New**	1963	12.00	30.00
Mercury MG-260847	(M)	**Anita Carter Of The Carter Family**	1964	10.00	25.00
Mercury SR-60847	(S)	**Anita Carter Of The Carter Family**	1964	12.00	30.00

CARTER, BETTY: *Refer to* GOLDMINE'S PRICE GUIDE TO COLLECTIBLE JAZZ ALBUMS

Label & Catalog #		Title	Year	VG+	NM
CARTER, CALVIN					
Vee Jay LP-1041	(M)	**Twist Along With Calvin Carter**	1962	30.00	75.00
Vee Jay LPS-1041	(S)	**Twist Along With Calvin Carter**	1962	40.00	100.00
CARTER, CLARENCE					
Atlantic SD-8192	(S)	**This Is Clarence Carter**	1968	12.00	30.00
Atlantic SD-8199	(S)	**The Dynamic Clarence Carter**	1969	12.00	30.00
Atlantic SD-8238	(S)	**Testifyin'**	1969	12.00	30.00
Atlantic SD-8267	(S)	**Patches**	1970	12.00	30.00
Atlantic SD-8282	(S)	**The Best Of Clarence Carter**	1971	8.00	20.00
ABC X-633	(S)	**Real**	1974	8.00	20.00
ABC X-943	(S)	**A Heart Full Of Song**	1976	8.00	20.00
CARTER, LYNDA					
Epic JE-35308	(S)	**Portrait** (Picture disc)	1978	12.00	30.00
CARTER, "MOTHER" MAYBELLE					
Maybelle Carter of The Carter Family is a guitar and autoharp player and singer of traditional folk music.					
Ambassador 98069	(M)	**Mother Maybelle Carter**	195?	80.00	200.00
Briar LP-101	(M)	**Mother Maybelle Carter**	195?	20.00	50.00
Autoharp 688S-1674	(M)	**Autoharp For Students And Educators**	195?	20.00	50.00
		(*"Autoharp"* is an instructional album issued with a how-to booklet.)			
Smash MGS-27025	(M)	**Mother Maybelle Carter And Her Autoharp**	1963	10.00	25.00
Smash SRS-67025	(S)	**Mother Maybelle Carter And Her Autoharp**	1963	14.00	35.00
Smash MGS-27041	(M)	**Mother Maybelle Carter Pickin' And Singin'**	1963	10.00	25.00
Smash SRS-67041	(S)	**Mother Maybelle Carter Pickin' And Singin'**	1963	14.00	35.00
Kapp KL-1413	(M)	**Queen Of The Autoharp**	1964	10.00	25.00
Kapp KS-3413	(S)	**Queen Of The Autoharp**	1964	14.00	35.00
Columbia CL-2475	(M)	**Mother Maybelle Carter—A Living Legend**	1965	10.00	25.00
Columbia CS-9275	(S)	**Mother Maybelle Carter—A Living Legend**	1965	14.00	30.00
Cumberland MGC-69524	(M)	**Mother Maybelle Carter**			
		Sings Carter Family Favorites	1967	8.00	20.00
Cumberland SRC-69524	(S)	**Mother Maybelle Carter**			
		Sings Carter Family Favorites	1967	8.00	25.00
CARTER, MEL					
Derby LPM-702	(M)	**When A Boy Falls In Love**	1963	200.00	400.00
CARTER FAMILY, THE					
The original Carters were A.P., Maybelle and Sara; later Carters included Anita, Helen and June. The Carters have been referred to as "the first family of traditional American music."					
Acme LP-1	(M)	**All Time Favorites**	195?	100.00	250.00

Label & Catalog #		Title	Year	VG+	NM
Acme LP-2	(M)	In Memory Of A. P. Carter	195?	100.00	250.00
Liberty LRP-3230	(M)	The Carter Family Album	1962	14.00	35.00
Liberty LST-7230	(S)	The Carter Family Album	1962	20.00	50.00
Starday SLP-248	(M)	Echoes Of The Carter Family (Yellow label)	1963	16.00	40.00
RCA Victor LPM-2772	(M)	'Mid The Green Fields Of Virginia	1963	16.00	40.00
RCA Victor LSP-2772	(E)	'Mid The Green Fields Of Virginia	1963	8.00	20.00
		—RCA albums above have black labels.—			
Decca DL-4404	(M)	A Collection Of Favorites			
		By The Carter Family	1963	12.00	30.00
Decca DL-74404	(E)	A Collection Of Favorites			
		By The Carter Family	1963	8.00	20.00
Decca DL-4557	(M)	More Favorites By The Carter Family	1964	12.00	30.00
Decca DL-74557	(E)	More Favorites By The Carter Family	1964	8.00	20.00

CARTOONE
Atlantic SD-8219	(S)	Cartoone (With Jimmy Page)	1969	10.00	25.00

CARTWRIGHT, ANGELA
Star-Bright HLP-102	(M)	Angela Cartwright Sings	195?	16.00	40.00

CASCADES
Valiant W-405	(M)	Rhythm Of The Rain	1963	60.00	150.00
Valiant WS-405	(S)	Rhythm Of The Rain	1963	150.00	300.00
		("Rhythm Of The Rain" is rechanneled.)			
Cascade 681001	(S)	What Goes On	1968	20.00	50.00
Uni 73069	(S)	Maybe The Rain Will Fall	1969	10.00	25.00

CASE, ALAN
Columbia CL-1402	(M)	The "Deputy" Sings	1960	8.00	20.00
Columbia CS-8202	(S)	The "Deputy" Sings	1960	12.00	30.00

CASEY, AL
Refer to The Exotic Guitars.
Prestige W-2007	(M)	Buck Jumpin'	1960	20.00	50.00
Prestige MV-12	(M)	The Al Casey Quartet	1961	16.00	40.00
Stacy STM-100	(M)	Surfin' Hootenanny (Surf-colored vinyl)	1963	40.00	100.00
Stacy STMS-100	(S)	Surfin' Hootenanny (Surf-colored vinyl)	1963	60.00	150.00

CASH, ALVIN, & THE REGISTERS
Mar-V-Lus 1827	(M)	Twine Time	196?	14.00	35.00

CASH, JOHNNY
Johnny Cash is a singer, guitar player and songwriter of country music loosely associated with rockabilly through his Sun recordings. He was backed by The Tennessee Two, Luther Perkins and Marshall Grant. Refer to The Carter Family; The Tennessee Three.

Sun SLP-1220	(M)	Johnny Cash With His Hot & Blue Guitar	1956	40.00	100.00
Sun SLP-1235	(M)	The Songs That Made Him Famous	1958	40.00	100.00
Sun SLP-1240	(M)	Johnny Cash's Greatest!	1959	20.00	50.00
Sun SLP-1245	(M)	Johnny Cash Sings Hank Williams	1960	20.00	50.00
Sun SLP-1255	(M)	Now Here's Johnny Cash	1961	20.00	50.00
Sun SLP-1270	(M)	All Aboard The Blue Train	1963	20.00	50.00
Sun SLP-1275	(M)	The Original Sun Sound Of Johnny Cash	1965	20.00	50.00
Columbia CL-1253	(M)	The Fabulous Johnny Cash	1958	10.00	25.00
Columbia CS-8122	(S)	The Fabulous Johnny Cash	1958	20.00	50.00
Columbia CL-1284	(M)	Hymns By Johnny Cash	1959	12.00	30.00
Columbia CS-8125	(S)	Hymns By Johnny Cash	1959	16.00	40.00
Columbia CL-1339	(M)	Songs Of Our Soil	1959	12.00	30.00
Columbia CS-8148	(S)	Songs Of Our Soil	1959	16.00	40.00
Columbia CL-1463	(M)	Now, There Was A Song!	1960	12.00	30.00
Columbia CS-8254	(S)	Now, There Was A Song!	1960	16.00	40.00
Columbia CL-1464	(M)	Ride This Train	1960	12.00	30.00
Columbia CS-8255	(S)	Ride This Train	1960	16.00	40.00
Columbia CL-1622	(M)	The Lure Of The Grand Canyon	1961	16.00	40.00
Columbia CS-8422	(S)	The Lure Of The Grand Canyon	1961	20.00	50.00
Columbia CL-1722	(M)	Hymns From The Heart	1962	8.00	20.00
Columbia CS-8522	(S)	Hymns From The Heart	1962	12.00	30.00
Columbia CL-1802	(M)	The Sound Of Johnny Cash	1962	8.00	20.00
Columbia CS-8602	(S)	The Sound Of Johnny Cash	1962	12.00	30.00

—Columbia albums above have three white "eye" logos on each side of the spindle hole.—

Label & Catalog #		Title	Year	VG+	NM
Columbia CL-1930	(M)	**Blood, Sweat And Tears**	1963	8.00	20.00
Columbia CS-8730	(S)	**Blood, Sweat And Tears**	1963	10.00	25.00
Columbia CL-2053	(M)	**Ring Of Fire/The Best Of Johnny Cash**	1963	8.00	20.00
Columbia CS-8853	(S)	**Ring Of Fire/The Best Of Johnny Cash**	1963	10.00	25.00
Columbia CL-2117	(M)	**Christmas Spirit**	1963	10.00	25.00
Columbia CS-8917	(S)	**Christmas Spirit**	1963	12.00	30.00
Columbia CL-2190	(M)	**I Walk The Line**	1964	8.00	20.00
Columbia CS-8990	(S)	**I Walk The Line**	1964	10.00	25.00
Columbia CL-2248	(M)	**Bitter Tears**	1964	8.00	20.00
Columbia CS-9048	(S)	**Bitter Tears**	1964	10.00	25.00
Columbia C2L-838	(M)	**Ballads Of The True West** (2 LPs)	1965	10.00	25.00
Columbia C2S-838	(S)	**Ballads Of The True West** (2 LPs)	1965	10.00	25.00
Columbia CL-2309	(M)	**Orange Blossom Special**	1965	8.00	20.00
Columbia CS-9109	(S)	**Orange Blossom Special**	1965	10.00	25.00
Columbia CL-2446	(M)	**Mean As Hell**	1965	8.00	20.00
Columbia CS-9246	(S)	**Mean As Hell**	1965	10.00	25.00
Columbia OL-6420	(M)	**The Sons Of Katie Elder** (Soundtrack)	1965	75.00	150.00
Columbia OS-2820	(S)	**The Sons Of Katie Elder** (Soundtrack)	1965	100.00	200.00
		— Columbia albums above have "360 Sound" labels.—			

CASINOS, THE

Fraternity LP-1019	(M)	**Then You Can Tell Me Goodbye**	1967	18.00	45.00
Fraternity LPS-1019	(S)	**Then You Can Tell Me Goodbye**	1967	24.00	60.00

CASSIDY, DAVID
David was formerly a member of The Partridge Family.

Bell 1312	(S)	**Cassidy Live**	1974	10.00	25.00
RCA Victor APL1-1066	(S)	**The Higher They Climb...** (Blue vinyl promo)	1975	40.00	100.00
RCA Victor APL1-1852	(S)	**Gettin' It In The Street**	1976	16.00	40.00

CASTELLS, THE

Era EL-109	(M)	**So This Is Love**	1962	60.00	150.00
Era ES-109	(S)	**So This Is Love**	1962	200.00	400.00

CASTLE, PAULA: *Refer to* **GOLDMINE'S PRICE GUIDE TO COLLECTIBLE JAZZ ALBUMS**

CASTOR BUNCH, JIMMY

Smash MGS-27091	(M)	**Hey Leroy!**	1967	10.00	25.00
Smash SRW-67091	(S)	**Hey Leroy!**	1967	14.00	35.00

CATALINAS, THE
The Catalinas feature Bruce Johnston and Terry Melcher.

Ric M-1006	(M)	**Fun, Fun, Fun**	1964	40.00	100.00
Ric S-1006	(S)	**Fun, Fun, Fun**	1964	60.00	150.00

CATHEDRAL

Delta DRC-1002	(S)	**Stained Glass Stories**	197?	150.00	300.00

CATHY JEAN & THE ROOMATES

Valmor 789	(M)	**At The Hop!**	1961	150.00	300.00
Valmor 78	(M)	**Great Oldies**	1962	200.00	400.00
		(Valmor 78 is a reissue of 789 with a various artists-like cover, making it difficult to identify as Cathy Jean & The Roomates.)			

CENTURIONS, THE

Del-Fi DFLP-1228	(M)	**Surfer's Pajama Party**	1963	20.00	50.00
Del-Fi DFST-1228	(S)	**Surfer's Pajama Party**	1963	30.00	75.00
		(Del-Fi 1228 has the same title, catalog number and cover as The Bruce Johnston Surfing Band, but plays The Centurions.)			

CEYLIB PEOPLE, THE
The Cetlib People feature Ry Cooder.

Vault LP-117	(S)	**Tanyet**	1968	16.00	40.00

CHAD & JEREMY/CHAD STUART & JEREMY CLYDE

Columbia CL-2374	(M)	**Before And After**	1965	8.00	20.00
Columbia CS-9174	(S)	**Before And After**	1965	10.00	25.00
Columbia CL-2398	(M)	**I Don't Want To Lose You Baby**	1965	8.00	20.00
Columbia CS-9198	(S)	**I Don't Want To Lose You Baby**	1965	10.00	25.00

After modest success as a sort of easy rocking, folk-type duo, Chad Stuart and Jeremy Clyde were infected with a bit of the old consciousness expansion. Their final brace of long-players became curiouser and curiouser: Of Cabbages And Kings (from Lewis Carroll, of course) features a colorful if somewhat ludicrous flower-power cover and "The Progress Suite, Movements 1 Thru 5" taking up all of Side 2. The Ark features a marvelous painting by Charles Bragg and "Painted Dayglow Smile." Both albums are wonderful listening, far better than the self-conscious hipness of the song titles would have the discerning customer believe, and I have always been baffled that they are not thought more highly of by psych fans. PS: Supposedly Gary Usher's willingness to indulge Chad Stuart's arrangements with expensive productions led to his dismissal as a Columbia staff producer, in light of much success elsewhere, notably The Byrds.

Label & Catalog #		Title	Year	VG+	NM
Columbia CL-2564	(M)	**Distant Shores**	1966	8.00	20.00
Columbia CS-9364	(S)	**Distant Shores**	1966	10.00	25.00
		("Distant Shores" is rechanneled.)			
Columbia CL-2671	(M)	**Of Cabbages And Kings**	1967	8.00	20.00
Columbia CS-9471	(S)	**Of Cabbages And Kings**	1967	10.00	25.00
Columbia CL-2899	(M)	**The Ark**	1968	10.00	25.00
Columbia CS-9699	(S)	**The Ark**	1968	8.00	20.00

CHAIRMEN OF THE BOARD

Invictus SKAO-7300	(S)	**Chairmen Of The Board**	1970	16.00	40.00
Invictus SKAO-7304	(S)	**In Session**	1971	16.00	40.00
Invictus ST-9801	(S)	**Bittersweet**	1972	16.00	40.00
Invictus KZ-32526	(S)	**The Skin I'm In**	1974	16.00	40.00

CHALKER, CURLY

Columbia CL-2496	(M)	**Big Hits On Big Steel**	1965	12.00	30.00
Columbia CS-9296	(S)	**Big Hits On Big Steel**	1965	16.00	40.00

CHALLENGERS, THE
The Challengers also recorded as The Good Guys. Refer to The Surfaris.

Vault LP-100	(M)	**Surfbeat**	1963	20.00	50.00
Vault VS-100	(S)	**Surfbeat**	1963	30.00	75.00
Vault VS-100	(S)	**Surfbeat** *(Orange vinyl)*	1963	80.00	200.00
Vault VS-100	(S)	**Surfbeat** *(Red vinyl)*	1963	80.00	200.00
Vault VS-100	(S)	**Surfbeat** *(Yellow vinyl)*	1963	80.00	200.00
Vault LP-101	(M)	**Surfing**	1963	20.00	50.00
Vault VS-101	(S)	**Surfing**	1963	30.00	75.00
Vault VS-101	(S)	**Surfing** *(Orange vinyl)*	1963	80.00	200.00
Vault VS-101	(S)	**Surfing** *(Red vinyl)*	1963	80.00	200.00
Vault VS-101	(S)	**Surfing** *(Yellow vinyl)*	1963	80.00	200.00
Vault VS-101	(S)	**Surfing** *(Blue vinyl)*	1963	80.00	200.00
Vault LP-102	(M)	**The Challengers On The Move**	1963	14.00	35.00
Vault VS-102	(S)	**The Challengers On The Move**	1963	20.00	50.00
Vault LP-107	(M)	**K-39**	1964	30.00	75.00
Vault LP-109	(M)	**The Surf's Up**	1965	20.00	50.00
Vault VS-109	(S)	**The Surf's Up**	1965	14.00	35.00
Vault LP-110	(M)	**The Challengers A Go Go**	1966	14.00	35.00
Vault VS-110	(S)	**The Challengers A Go Go**	1966	20.00	50.00
Vault LP-111	(M)	**The Challengers' Greatest Hits**	1967	10.00	25.00
Vault VS-111	(S)	**The Challengers' Greatest Hits**	1967	8.00	20.00
Triumph TR-100	(M)	**Sidewalk Surfing**	1965	8.00	20.00
Triumph TRS-100	(S)	**Sidewalk Surfing**	1965	10.00	25.00
Crescendo GNP-2010	(M)	**The Challengers At The Teenage Fair**	1965	8.00	20.00
Crescendo GNPS-2010	(S)	**The Challengers At The Teenage Fair**	1965	10.00	25.00
Crescendo GNP-2018	(M)	**The Man From U.N.C.L.E.**	1965	8.00	20.00
Crescendo GNPS-2018	(S)	**The Man From U.N.C.L.E.**	1965	10.00	25.00
Crescendo GNP-2025	(M)	**California Kicks**	1966	8.00	20.00
Crescendo GNPS-2025	(S)	**California Kicks**	1966	10.00	25.00
Crescendo GNP-2030	(M)	**Billy Strange And The Challengers**	1966	8.00	20.00
Crescendo GNPS-2030	(S)	**Billy Strange And The Challengers**	1966	10.00	25.00
Crescendo GNP-2031	(M)	**Wipe Out**	1966	8.00	20.00
Crescendo GNPS-2031	(S)	**Wipe Out**	1966	10.00	25.00
Crescendo GNP-609	(M)	**25 Great Instrumental Hits** *(2 LPs)*	1967	8.00	20.00
Crescendo GNPS-609	(S)	**25 Great Instrumental Hits** *(2 LPs)*	1967	10.00	25.00
Crescendo GNPS-2045	(S)	**Light My Fire With Classical Gas**	1968	10.00	25.00
Crescendo GNPS-2056	(S)	**Vanilla Funk**	1970	10.00	25.00
		— GNP Crescendo albums above have red labels.—			

CHALLENGERS, THE

Nariel LPMS-104	(S)	**The Challengers**	196?	60.00	150.00

CHAMBERLAIN, RICHARD

MGM E-4088	(M)	**Richard Chamberlain Sings**	1963	8.00	20.00
MGM SE-4088	(S)	**Richard Chamberlain Sings**	1963	10.00	25.00
MGM E-4287	(M)	**Joy In The Morning**	1964	8.00	20.00
MGM SE-4287	(S)	**Joy In The Morning**	1964	10.00	25.00
Metro M-564	(M)	**Theme From "Dr. Kildare"**	1966	8.00	20.00
Metro MS-564	(S)	**Theme From "Dr. Kildare"**	1966	10.00	25.00

Like many Vee Jay albums, the stereo release of Gene Chandler's Duke Of Earl *is damn near impossible to find. Complicating the matter was the dumping of counterfeits on the market years ago. While collectors have tended to use the existence of the "Stereophonic" across the top of the front cover or the stereo notice on top of the back cover that begins "Important Notice" in identifying originals from fakes, both of these can be found on the counterfeit covers! But. . . thus far there are no known counterfeits of the stereo disc. So, when purchasing this or any other stereo Vee Jay album, check the record.*

Label & Catalog #		Title	Year	VG+	NM

CHAMBERS BROTHERS, THE
The Chambers Brothers also recorded with Barbara Dane.

Label & Catalog #		Title	Year	VG+	NM
Vault LP-9003	(M)	People Get Ready	1966	8.00	20.00
Vault VS-9003	(S)	People Get Ready	1966	10.00	25.00
Vault LP-115	(M)	The Chambers Brothers Now	1967	8.00	20.00
Vault VS-115	(S)	The Chambers Brothers Now	1967	10.00	25.00
Columbia CL-2722	(M)	The Time Has Come	1967	10.00	25.00
Columbia CS-9522	(S)	The Time Has Come ("360 Sound" label)	1967	10.00	25.00
Roxbury RLX-106	(S)	Live In Concert On Mars	1976	12.00	30.00

CHAMPS, THE

Challenge CHL-601	(M)	Go Champs Go (Blue vinyl)	1958		See below
		(CHL-501 has a suggested Near Mint value of $1,500-3,000.)			
Challenge CHL-601	(M)	Go Champs Go	1958	150.00	300.00
Challenge CHL-605	(M)	Everybody's Rockin' With The Champs	1959	60.00	150.00
Challenge CHS-250?	(S)	Everybody's Rockin' With The Champs	1959	80.00	200.00
Challenge CHL-613	(M)	Great Dance Hits	1962	30.00	75.00
Challenge CHS-2513	(S)	Great Dance Hits	1962	40.00	100.00
Challenge CHL-614	(M)	All American Music From The Champs	1962	30.00	75.00
Challenge CHS-2514	(S)	All American Music From The Champs	1962	40.00	100.00

CHANDLER, GENE
Gene Chandler also recorded with Jerry Butler.

Vee Jay MR-1040	(M)	The Duke Of Earl	1962	60.00	150.00
Vee Jay SR-1040	(S)	The Duke Of Earl	1962		See below

(Original copies of SR-1040 have "Stereophonic" across the top of the front cover and a notice across the top of the back cover that begins "Important Notice. . . This is a Stereophonic Record. These are rare with a suggested Near Mint value of $500-1,000. Later pressings, referred to as counterfeits, have "Stereophonic" on the front cover but lack the "Important Notice" on the back. These covers generally contain mono albums and are worth $25-50..)

Constellation LP-1421	(M)	Greatest Hits By Gene Chandler	1964	12.00	30.00
Constellation LP-1423	(M)	Just Be True	1964	12.00	30.00
Constellation LP-1425	(M)	Gene Chandler/Live On Stage In '65	1965	12.00	30.00
Checker LP-3003	(M)	The Duke Of Soul	1967	12.00	30.00
Checker LPS-3003	(E)	The Duke Of Soul	1967	8.00	20.00

CHANDLER, JEFF

Liberty LRP-3067	(M)	Jeff Chandler Sings To You	1957	20.00	50.00
Liberty LRP-3074	(M)	Warm And Easy	1957	20.00	50.00

CHANNEL, BRUCE

Smash MGS-27008	(M)	Hey! Baby	1962	40.00	100.00
Smash SRS-67008	(E)	Hey! Baby	1962	30.00	75.00

CHANNING, CAROL

Vanguard VRS-9041	(M)	Carol Channing	1959	8.00	20.00
Vanguard VSD-2041	(S)	Carol Channing	1959	10.00	25.00
Vanguard VRS-9056	(M)	Previous Hits	1959	8.00	20.00
Vanguard VSD-2056	(S)	Previous Hits	1959	10.00	25.00

CHANTAYS, THE

Downey DLP-1002	(M)	Pipeline	1963	60.00	150.00
Downey DLPS-1002	(S)	Pipeline	1963	80.00	200.00
Dot DLP-3516	(M)	Pipeline	1963	16.00	40.00
Dot DLP-25516	(S)	Pipeline	1963	20.00	50.00
		(Dot 3/25515 is a reissue of Downey 1002.)			
Dot DLP-3771	(M)	Two Sides Of The Chantays	1966	16.00	40.00
Dot DLP-25771	(S)	Two Sides Of The Chantays	1966	20.00	50.00

CHANTELS, THE

End LP-301	(M)	We're The Chantels	1958	500.00	See below

(Original pressings of End 301 have gray labels and a cover photo of the group dressed in Southern plantation finery that brought accusations of racial stereotyping and was quickly withrawn. Rare in Near Mint with a suggested value of $1,000-2,000.)

Label & Catalog #		Title	Year	VG+	NM
End LP-301	(M)	We're The Chantels	1959	150.00	300.00
		(Second pressings have gray labels but the covers replace the group with a photo of a jukebox.)			
End LP-301	(M)	We're The Chantels	1962	60.00	150.00
		(Third pressings have gray labels with 1962 in the trail-off vinyl and were issued in the jukebox cover.)			
End LP-301	(M)	We're The Chantels	1965	20.00	50.00
		(Later pressings have a color label with 1965 in the trail-off vinyl and were issued in the jukebox cover.)			
Carlton LP-144	(M)	The Chantels On Tour	1961	80.00	200.00
Carlton STLP-144	(P)	The Chantels On Tour	1961	150.00	300.00
		(Carlton 144 contains tracks by Chris Montez, The Imeprials, and Gus Backus in mono and the Chantels' tracks in stereo.)			
End LP-312	(M)	There's Our Song Again	1962	40.00	100.00
Forum 9104	(M)	The Chantels Sing Their Favorites	196?	10.00	25.00

CHAPIN BROTHERS, THE
The Chapin Brothers are Harry and Tom.

Rockland 66	(M)	Chapin Music	1966	12.00	30.00

CHARIOTEERS, THE

Columbia CL-6014	(10")	Sweet And Low	1950	150.00	300.00

CHARITY

Uni 73061	(S)	Charity Now	1969	10.00	25.00

CHARLATANS, THE

Philips PHS-600-309	(S)	The Charlatans	1969	24.00	60.00

CHARLES, LEE

Riverside RLP-12-651	(M)	Swing Low, Sweet Chariot	195?	12.00	30.00

CHARLES, RAY
Refer to The Bee Gees / Ray Charles. Hollywood 504 and 505 contain Ray's pre-Atlantic recordings.

Hollywood 504	(M)	Ray Charles	1959	30.00	75.00
Hollywood 505	(M)	The Fabulous Ray Charles	1959	30.00	75.00
Atlantic 8006	(M)	Ray Charles	1957	30.00	75.00
Atlantic 8006	(M)	Hallelujah!	195?	20.00	50.00
Atlantic 1259	(M)	The Great Ray Charles	1957	20.00	50.00
Atlantic SD-1259	(S)	The Great Ray Charles	1959	30.00	75.00
Atlantic 1279	(M)	Soul Brothers (With Milt Jackson)	1958	20.00	50.00
Atlantic SD-1279	(S)	Soul Brothers (With Milt Jackson)	1959	30.00	75.00
Atlantic 1289	(M)	Ray Charles At Newport	1958	20.00	50.00
Atlantic SD-1289	(S)	Ray Charles At Newport	1958	30.00	75.00
Atlantic 8025	(M)	Yes, Indeed! (Screaming girls on cover)	1959	20.00	50.00
Atlantic 8029	(M)	What'd I Say (White "bullseye" label)	1959	60.00	150.00
Atlantic 8029	(M)	What'd I Say	1959	20.00	50.00
Atlantic 8039	(M)	Ray Charles In Person	1960	16.00	40.00
		("Ray Charles In Person" is a repackage of "What'd I Say.")			
Atlantic 1312	(M)	The Genius Of Ray Charles	1960	16.00	40.00
Atlantic SD-1312	(S)	The Genius Of Ray Charles	1960	20.00	50.00
		—Atlantic albums above have black labels; stereo albums have green labels.—			
Atlantic 8054	(M)	Do The Twist With Ray Charles!	1961	10.00	25.00
Atlantic 1360	(M)	Soul Meeting (With Milt Jackson)	1961	10.00	25.00
Atlantic SD-1360	(S)	Soul Meeting (With Milt Jackson)	1961	14.00	35.00
		—Atlantic albums above have muti-colored labels with a white "fan" logo on the right side.—			
Atlantic 2-900	(M)	The Ray Charles Story (2 LPs)	1962	12.00	30.00
		—Atlantic albums above have muti-colored labels with a black "fan" logo on the right side.—			
Atlantic SD-7101	(S)	Great Hits Recorded On 8-Track Stereo	1964	10.00	25.00
ABC-Paramount ABC-335	(M)	The Genius Hits The Road	1960	8.00	20.00
ABC-Paramount ABCS-335	(S)	The Genius Hits The Road	1960	12.00	30.00
ABC-Paramount ABC-355	(M)	Dedicated To You	1961	8.00	20.00
ABC-Paramount ABCS-355	(S)	Dedicated To You	1961	12.00	30.00
		—ABC albums above have black labels with "ABC-PARAMOUNT" on the top and "Am-Par Record Corp." on the bottom.—			
ABC-Paramount ABC-410	(M)	Modern Sounds In Country And Western	1962	10.00	25.00
ABC-Paramount ABCS-410	(S)	Modern Sounds In Country And Western	1962	12.00	30.00
		(Original covers do not bear the RIAA Gold Record Award seal.)			
		—ABC albums above have black labels with "ABC-Paramount" on top.—			

Label & Catalog #		Title	Year	VG+	NM
ABC 2-590	(M)	**A Man And His Soul** (2 LPs)	1967	8.00	20.00
ABC Y-2-590	(S)	**A Man And His Soul** (2 LPs)	1967	10.00	25.00
Impulse A-2	(M)	**Genius + Soul = Jazz**	1961	12.00	30.00
Impulse AS-2	(S)	**Genius + Soul = Jazz**	1961	16.00	40.00

CHARLES, RAY, & BETTY CARTER

ABC-Paramount ABC-385	(M)	**Ray Charles And Betty Carter**	1961	20.00	50.00
ABC-Paramount ABCS-385	(S)	**Ray Charles And Betty Carter**	1961	30.00	75.00

CHARLES VALLEY RIVER BOYS, THE

Folklore FRLP-14017	(M)	**Bluegrass And Old Timey Music**	1964	10.00	25.00
Folklore FRST-14017	(S)	**Bluegrass And Old Timey Music**	1964	12.00	30.00
Folklore FRLP-14024	(M)	**Bluegrass Get Together** (With Tex Logan)	1964	10.00	25.00
Folklore FRST-14024	(S)	**Bluegrass Get Together** (With Tex Logan)	1964	12.00	30.00
Elektra EKL-4006	(M)	**Beatles Country**	1967	8.00	20.00
Elektra ES-74006	(S)	**Beatles Country**	1967	10.00	25.00

CHARLIE

Janus/GRT JXS-7036	(DJ)	**Lines** (Picture disc)	1978	20.00	50.00

CHARMER

Illusion CM-1070	(S)	**Your Presence Requested**	1976	40.00	100.00
Illusion CM-1071	(S)	**Do It To It**	1976	40.00	100.00

CHARTBUSTERS, THE: *Refer to* THE MANCHESTERS

CHASE, LINCOLN

Liberty LRP-3076	(M)	**The Explosive Lincoln Chase**	1958	16.00	40.00

CHEAP TRICK

Epic AS-518	(DJ)	**From Tokyo To You** (Live EP)	1978	12.00	30.00
Epic 35773	(DJ)	**Dream Police** (Picture disc)	1979	12.00	30.00

CHEATWOOD, BILLY

Tradition TLPS-2077	(S)	**Anthology Of The Banjo**	195?	10.00	25.00

CHECKER, CHUBBY
Chubby Checker is a pseudonym for Ernest Evans. Refer to Bobby Rydell; Dee Dee Sharp.

Parkway 5001	(M)	**Chubby Checker**	1960	30.00	75.00
Parkway P-7001	(M)	**Twist With Chubby Checker**	1960	20.00	50.00
Parkway P-7002	(M)	**For Twisters Only**	1960	20.00	50.00
Parkway P-7003	(M)	**It's Pony Time**	1961	20.00	50.00
Parkway P-7004	(M)	**Let's Twist Again**	1961	20.00	50.00
Parkway P-7007	(M)	**Your Twist Party**	1961	20.00	50.00
Parkway P-7008	(M)	**Twistin' Round The World**	1962	20.00	50.00
Parkway SP-7008	(P)	**Twistin' Round The World**	1962	40.00	100.00
Parkway P-7009	(M)	**For Teen Twisters Only**	1962	20.00	50.00
Parkway SP-7009	(S)	**For Teen Twisters Only**	1962	40.00	100.00
Parkway P-7011	(M)	**Don't Knock The Twist** (Soundtrack)	1962	40.00	100.00
Parkway P-7014	(M)	**All The Hits For Your Dancin' Party**	1962	20.00	50.00
Parkway P-7020	(M)	**Limbo Party**	1962	20.00	50.00
Parkway SP-7020	(S)	**Limbo Party**	1962	40.00	100.00
Parkway P-7022	(M)	**Chubby Checker's Biggest Hits**	1962	20.00	50.00
Parkway SP-7022	(E)	**Chubby Checker's Biggest Hits**	1962	20.00	50.00
Parkway P-7026	(M)	**Chubby Checker In Person**	1963	20.00	50.00
Parkway SP-7026	(S)	**Chubby Checker In Person**	1963	40.00	100.00
Parkway P-7027	(M)	**Let's Limbo Some More**	1963	20.00	50.00
Parkway SP-7027	(S)	**Let's Limbo Some More**	1963	40.00	100.00
Parkway P-7030	(M)	**Beach Party**	1963	20.00	50.00
Parkway SP-7030	(S)	**Beach Party**	1963	40.00	100.00
Parkway P-7036	(M)	**Chubby Checker With Sy Oliver**	1964	20.00	50.00
Parkway SP-7036	(S)	**Chubby Checker With Sy Oliver**	1964	40.00	100.00
Parkway P-7040	(M)	**Folk Album**	1964	20.00	50.00
Parkway SP-7040	(S)	**Folk Album**	1964	40.00	100.00
Parkway P-7045	(M)	**Discotheque**	1965	20.00	50.00
Parkway SP-7045	(S)	**Discotheque**	1965	40.00	100.00
Parkway P-7048	(M)	**Chubby Checker's Eighteen Golden Hits**	1966	20.00	50.00
Parkway SP-7048	(P)	**Chubby Checker's Eighteen Golden Hits**	1966	40.00	100.00

Label & Catalog #		Title	Year	VG+	NM
CHECKMATES, THE					
Justice JLP-149	(S)	The Checkmates	1966	150.00	300.00
CHECKMATES LTD., THE					
Ikon 122	(M)	Live At Harvey's	1965	10.00	25.00
Capitol T-2840	(M)	Live At Caesar's Palace	1966	8.00	20.00
Capitol ST-2840	(S)	Live At Caesar's Palace	1966	10.00	25.00
A&M SP-4183	(S)	Love Is All We Have To Give	1969	10.00	25.00
		(SP-4183 was produced by Phil Spector.)			
CHELSEA					
Chelsea features Peter Criss, later of Kiss.					
Decca DL-75262	(S)	The Chelsea Album	1972	40.00	100.00
CHER					
Refer to Sonny & Cher.					
Imperial LP-9292	(M)	All I Really Want To Do	1965	8.00	20.00
Imperial LP-12292	(S)	All I Really Want To Do	1965	10.00	25.00
Imperial LP-9301	(M)	The Sonny Side Of Cher	1966	8.00	20.00
Imperial LP-12301	(S)	The Sonny Side Of Cher	1966	10.00	25.00
		— Imperial albums above have green, white & black labels.—			
CHEVALIER, MAURICE					
MGM E-3738	(M)	Maurice Chevalier Sings Broadway	1959	8.00	20.00
MGM SE-3738	(S)	Maurice Chevalier Sings Broadway	1959	12.00	30.00
MGM E-3773	(M)	A Tribute To Al Jolson	1959	8.00	20.00
MGM SE-3773	(S)	A Tribute To Al Jolson	1959	12.00	30.00
MGM E-3801	(M)	Life Is Just A Bowl Of Cherries	1960	8.00	20.00
MGM SE-3801	(S)	Life Is Just A Bowl Of Cherries	1960	12.00	30.00
MGM E-3835	(M)	Thank Heaven For Little Girls	1960	8.00	20.00
MGM SE-3835	(S)	Thank Heaven For Little Girls	1960	12.00	30.00
MGM E-4015	(M)	Maurice Chevalier Sings			
		Lerner, Loewe & Chevalier	1962	8.00	20.00
MGM SE-4015	(S)	Maurice Chevalier Sings			
		Lerner, Loewe & Chevalier	1962	10.00	25.00
MGM E-4120	(M)	Paris To Broadway	1963	8.00	20.00
MGM SE-4120	(S)	Paris To Broadway	1963	10.00	25.00
RCA Victor LPM-2076	(M)	Thank Heaven For Maurice Chevalier	1960	8.00	20.00
RCA Victor LSP-2076	(S)	Thank Heaven For Maurice Chevalier	1960	12.00	30.00
Time 52072	(M)	Maurice Chevalier	1963	8.00	20.00
Time S-2072	(S)	Maurice Chevalier	1963	10.00	25.00
CHEVRONS, THE					
The Chevrons feature Terry Cashman.					
Time 10008	(M)	Sing A Long Rock & Roll	1961	30.00	75.00
CHI-LITES, THE					
Brunswick BL-754152	(S)	Give It Away	1969	10.00	25.00
Brunswick BL-754165	(S)	I Like Your Lovin', Do You Like Mine?	1971	10.00	25.00
Brunswick BL-754170	(S)	Give More Power To The People	1971	10.00	25.00
Brunswick BL-754179	(S)	Lonely Man	1972	10.00	25.00
Brunswick BL-754184	(S)	The Chi-Lites Greatest Hits	1972	10.00	25.00
Brunswick BL-754188	(S)	A Letter To Myself	1973	10.00	25.00
Brunswick BL-754197	(S)	The Chi-Lites	1973	10.00	25.00
Brunswick BL-754200	(S)	Toby	1974	10.00	25.00
Brunswick BL-754204	(S)	Half A Love	1974	10.00	25.00
CHICAGO/CHICAGO TRANSIT AUTHORITY					
Columbia GP-8	(S)	Chicago Transit Authority *(2 LPs)*	1969	16.00	40.00
Columbia KGP-24	(S)	Chicago *(2 LPs)*	1970	20.00	50.00
		— Columbia albums above have "360 Sound" on the bottom of the label.—			
Columbia GQ-33255	(Q)	Chicago Transit Authority *(2 LPs)*	1975	10.00	25.00
Columbia GQ-33258	(Q)	Chicago *(2 LPs)*	1975	10.00	25.00
Columbia C2Q-30110	(Q)	Chicago III *(2 LPs)*	1974	12.00	30.00
Columbia C4X-30865	(S)	Chicago At Carnegie Hall *(4 LP box)*	1971	12.00	30.00
Columbia C4Q-30865	(Q)	Chicago At Carnegie Hall *(4 LP box)*	1974	30.00	75.00
		(Columbia 30865 collects 30863 and 30864.)			
Columbia CQ-31102	(Q)	Chicago V	1974	10.00	25.00
Columbia CQ-32400	(Q)	Chicago VI	1974	10.00	25.00

Label & Catalog #		Title	Year	VG+	NM
Columbia C2Q-32810	(Q)	**Chicago VII** *(2 LPs)*	1974	**12.00**	**30.00**
Columbia PCQ-33100	(Q)	**Chicago VIII**	1975	**10.00**	**25.00**
Columbia PCQ-33900	(Q)	**Chicago IX/Greatest Hits**	1975	**10.00**	**25.00**
Columbia HC-43900	(S)	**Chicago IX/Greatest Hits** *(Half-speed)*	1982	**12.00**	**30.00**
Columbia PCQ-34200	(Q)	**Chicago X**	1976	**10.00**	**25.00**
Columbia HC-44200	(S)	**Chicago X** *(Half-speed master)*	1982	**10.00**	**25.00**
Columbia *(No number)*	(DJ)	**Chicago** *(17 LP box)*	1976	**10.00**	**250.00**

(Promotional boxed set of Chicago's first ten albums—a total of seventeen stock copies stamped "Demonstration-Not For Sale." The silver box has a photo cover on one side,. Complete sets include a side panel with the album titles embossed that was taped to the box to keep the albums from sliding out, and a paper wrap-around that lists the ten album titles. Approximately 60% of the listed value is for the box with the panel and the wrap-around.)

Mobile Fidelity MFSL-128	(S)	**Chicago Transit Authority** *(2 LPs)*	1983	**15.00**	**45.00**

CHICKEN SHACK
Chicken Shack features Christine Perfect a.k.a. Christine McVie, later of Fleetwood Mac.

Epic LN-24414	(M)	**Forty Blue Fingers, Freshly Packed And Ready To Serve**	1968	**40.00**	**100.00**
Epic BN-26414	(S)	**Forty Blue Fingers, Freshly Packed And Ready To Serve**	1968	**12.00**	**30.00**
Blue Horizon BH-7705	(S)	**O.K. Ken?**	1969	**10.00**	**25.00**
Blue Horizon BH-7706	(S)	**100 Ton Chicken**	1969	**10.00**	**25.00**
Blue Horizon BH-4809	(S)	**Accept Chicken Shack**	1970	**10.00**	**25.00**

CHIEF THUNDERCLOUD

Prestige Inter. PRLP-13076	(M)	**A Child's Introduction To The American Indian**	1963	**12.00**	**30.00**

CHIFFONS, THE
Refer to The Islaey Brothers / The Chiffons.

Laurie LLP-2018	(M)	**He's So Fine**	1963	**60.00**	**150.00**
Laurie DT-90075	(E)	**He's So Fine** *(Capitol Record Club)*	1963	**80.00**	**200.00**
Laurie LLP-2020	(M)	**One Fine Day**	1963	**60.00**	**150.00**
Laurie LLP-2036	(M)	**Sweet Talkin' Guy**	1966	**30.00**	**75.00**
Laurie SLP-2036	(S)	**Sweet Talkin' Guy**	1966	**40.00**	**100.00**

("Nobody Knows What's Goin' On" is rechanneled on this album.)

B.T. Puppy S-1011	(S)	**My Secret Love**	1970	**30.00**	**75.00**

CHILD'S ART

Gold 3000	(S)	**Uncut**	1982	**24.00**	**60.00**

CHILDRE, LEW

Starday SLP-153	(M)	**Old Time Get-Together** *(Yellow label)*	1961	**12.00**	**30.00**

CHILDREN, THE

Cinema CLP-1	(S)	**Rebirth**	1968	**30.00**	**75.00**

CHIPMUNKS, THE
The Chipmunks are the creation of Ross Bagdasarian, a.k.a. David Seville.

Liberty LRP-3132	(M)	**Let's All Sing With The Chipmunks** *(Red vinyl)*	1959	**30.00**	**75.00**
Liberty LRP-3132	(M)	**Let's All Sing With The Chipmunks**	1959	**14.00**	**35.00**
Liberty LST-7132	(S)	**Let's All Sing With The Chipmunks** *(Red vinyl)*	1959	**40.00**	**100.00**
Liberty LST-7132	(S)	**Let's All Sing With The Chipmunks**	1959	**20.00**	**50.00**

(Original covers feature "realistic" drawings of the Chipmunks.—
—Liberty mono albums above have turquoise labels; stereo albums have black & silver labels.

Liberty LRP-3132	(M)	**Let's All Sing With The Chipmunks**	1961	**10.00**	**25.00**
Liberty LST-7132	(S)	**Let's All Sing With The Chipmunks**	1961	**12.00**	**30.00**

(Later covers feature the more familiar cartoon Chipmunks.)

Liberty LRP-3159	(M)	**Sing Again With The Chipmunks**	1960	**14.00**	**35.00**
Liberty LST-7159	(S)	**Sing Again With The Chipmunks**	1960	**20.00**	**50.00**

(Original covers feature "realistic" drawings of the Chipmunks.—

Liberty LRP-3159	(M)	**Sing Again With The Chipmunks**	1961	**10.00**	**25.00**
Liberty LST-7159	(S)	**Sing Again With The Chipmunks**	1961	**12.00**	**30.00**

(Later covers feature the more familiar cartoon Chipmunks.)

Patricia Bennett, Judy Craig, Barbara Lee and Sylvia Patterson, four young women from the Bronx, virtually define "girl group" for many collectors. And, unlike so many others of the genre, they made several albums to go along with their classic singles. Both of their first two LPs on Laurie are far more difficult to find in collectible condition than their current market value indicates.

Label & Catalog #		Title	Year	VG+	NM
Liberty LRP-3170	(M)	**Around The World With The Chipmunks**	1960	14.00	35.00
Liberty LST-7170	(S)	**Around The World With The Chipmunks**	1960	20.00	50.00
		(Original covers feature "realistic" drawings of the Chipmunks.—			
Liberty LRP-3170	(M)	**Around The World With The Chipmunks**	1961	10.00	25.00
Liberty LST-7170	(S)	**Around The World With The Chipmunks**	1961	12.00	30.00
		(Later covers feature the more familiar cartoon Chipmunks.)			
Liberty LRP-3209	(M)	**The Alvin Show** *(TV Soundtrack)*	1961	14.00	35.00
Liberty LST-7209	(S)	**The Alvin Show** *(TV Soundtrack)*	1961	20.00	50.00
Liberty LRP-3229	(M)	**The Chipmunks Songbook**	1962	10.00	25.00
Liberty LST-7229	(S)	**The Chipmunks Songbook**	1962	12.00	30.00
Liberty LRP-3256	(M)	**Christmas With The Chipmunks**	1962	10.00	25.00
Liberty LST-7256	(S)	**Christmas With The Chipmunks**	1962	12.00	30.00
Liberty LRP-3334	(M)	**Christmas With The Chipmunks, Volume 2**	1963	10.00	25.00
Liberty LST-7334	(S)	**Christmas With The Chipmunks, Volume 2**	1963	12.00	30.00
Liberty LRP-3388	(M)	**The Chipmunks Sing The Beatles Hits**	1964	12.00	30.00
Liberty LST-7388	(S)	**The Chipmunks Sing The Beatles Hits**	1964	16.00	40.00
Liberty LRP-3424	(M)	**The Chipmunks A Go-Go**	1965	8.00	20.00
Liberty LST-7424	(S)	**The Chipmunks A Go-Go**	1965	10.00	25.00
Liberty LRP-3405	(M)	**The Chipmunks Sing With Children**	1965	8.00	20.00
Liberty LST-7405	(S)	**The Chipmunks Sing With Children**	1965	10.00	25.00

CHOATE, BILL

Sims LP-123	(M)	**True Country & Western Songs**	1964	40.00	100.00

CHOATES, HARRY

"D" 7000	(M)	**Jole Blon**	195?	20.00	50.00

CHOCO & HIS MALIMBA DRUM RHYTHMS

Audio Fidelity AFLP-2102	(M)	**African Latin Voodoo Drums**	1962	8.00	20.00
Audio Fidelity AFSD-6102	(S)	**African Latin Voodoo Drums**	1962	12.00	30.00

CHOCOLATE WATCH BAND, THE

Tower T-5096	(M)	**No Way Out**	1967	80.00	200.00
Tower ST-5096	(S)	**No Way Out**	1967	100.00	250.00
Tower T-5016	(M)	**The Inner Mystique**	1968	80.00	200.00
Tower ST-5016	(S)	**The Inner Mystique**	1968	100.00	250.00
Tower ST-5153	(S)	**One Step Beyond**	1969	80.00	200.00
		(Original copies of ST-5153 s have printing on the spine			
		and "Printed in USA" on the cover; counterfeits do not.)			

CHORDETTES, THE

Columbia CL-6111	(10")	**Harmony Time**	1950	20.00	50.00
Columbia CL-6170	(10")	**Harmony Time, Volume 2**	1951	20.00	50.00
Columbia CL-6218	(10")	**Harmony Encores**	1952	20.00	50.00
Columbia CL-6285	(10")	**Your Requests**	1953	20.00	50.00
Columbia CL-2519	(10")	**The Chordettes**	1955	20.00	50.00
Columbia CL-956	(M)	**Listen**	1957	16.00	40.00
Cadence CLP-1002	(10")	**Close Harmony**	1955	20.00	50.00
Cadence CLP-3001	(M)	**The Chordettes**	1957	16.00	40.00
Cadence CLP-3002	(M)	**Close Harmony**	1957	16.00	40.00
Cadence CLP-3056	(M)	**Never On Sunday**	1962	8.00	20.00
Cadence CLP-25056	(S)	**Never On Sunday**	1962	12.00	30.00

CHRISTIE, LOU

Lou Christie is a pseudonym for Lugee Sacco. Refer to The Critters & The Young Rascals & Lou Christie.

Roulette R-25208	(M)	**Lou Christie**	1963	14.00	35.00
Roulette SR-25208	(P)	**Lou Christie**	1963	20.00	50.00
MGM E-4360	(M)	**Lightnin' Strikes**	1966	8.00	20.00
MGM SE-4360	(S)	**Lightnin' Strikes**	1966	10.00	25.00
Co&Ce LP-1231	(M)	**Lou Christie Strikes Back**	1966	16.00	40.00
Colpix CP-4001	(M)	**Lou Christie Strikes Again**	1966	10.00	25.00
Colpix SCP-4001	(S)	**Lou Christie Strikes Again**	1966	16.00	40.00
Roulette R-25332	(M)	**Lou Christie Strikes Again**	1966	8.00	20.00
Roulette SR-25332	(S)	**Lou Christie Strikes Again**	1966	10.00	25.00
		(Roulette 25332 is a reissue of Colpix 4001.)			
MGM E-4394	(M)	**Painter Of Hits**	1966	8.00	20.00
MGM SE-4394	(S)	**Painter Of Hits**	1966	10.00	25.00
		("Rhapsody In The Rain" is in mono.)			

Label & Catalog #		Title	Year	VG+	NM
CHRISTOPHER					
Chris Tee	(S)	**What'cha Gonna Do?** (Orange cover)	1969	660.00	1,000.00
Rockadelic	(S)	**What'cha Gonna Do?** (Reissue)	1990	16.00	40.00
CHRISTOPHER					
Metromedia 1024	(DJ)	**Christopher**	197?	150.00	300.00
CHRISTY, JUNE					
Capitol H-516	(10")	**Something Cool**	1954	30.00	75.00
Capitol T-516	(M)	**Something Cool** (Blue cover)	1955	20.00	50.00
Capitol T-656	(M)	**Duets**	1955	16.00	40.00
Capitol T-725	(M)	**The Misty Miss Christy**	1955	16.00	40.00
Capitol T-833	(M)	**June Fair And Warmer**	1957	16.00	40.00
Capitol T-902	(M)	**Gone For The Day**	1957	16.00	40.00
Capitol T-1006	(M)	**This Is June Christy!**	1958	16.00	40.00
		— Capitol albums above have turquoise labels.—			
Capitol T-1076	(M)	**June's Got Rhythm**	1958	12.00	30.00
Capitol ST-1076	(M)	**June's Got Rhythm**	1958	16.00	40.00
Capitol T-1114	(M)	**The Song Is June!**	1959	12.00	30.00
Capitol ST-1114	(M)	**The Song Is June!**	1959	16.00	40.00
Capitol T-1202	(M)	**June Christy Recalls Those Kenton Days**	1959	12.00	30.00
Capitol ST-1202	(M)	**June Christy Recalls Those Kenton Days**	1959	16.00	40.00
Capitol T-1308	(M)	**Ballads For Night People**	1959	12.00	30.00
Capitol ST-1308	(M)	**Ballads For Night People**	1959	16.00	40.00
Capitol TBO-1327	(M)	**Road Show** (2 LPs)	1960	12.00	30.00
Capitol STBO-1327	(S)	**Road Show** (2 LPs)	1960	16.00	40.00
		(Capitol 1327 features side 1 by Stan Kenton, side 2 by Ms. Christy, side 3 by the Freshmen and side 4 is ensemble.)			
Capitol T-1398	(M)	**The Cool School**	1960	12.00	30.00
Capitol ST-1398	(S)	**The Cool School**	1960	16.00	40.00
Capitol T-1498	(M)	**Off Beat**	1961	16.00	40.00
Capitol ST-1498	(S)	**Off Beat**	1961	20.00	50.00
Capitol T-1586	(M)	**Do Re Mi**	1961	16.00	40.00
Capitol ST-1586	(S)	**Do Re Mi**	1961	20.00	50.00
Capitol T-1605	(M)	**That Time Of Year**	1961	16.00	40.00
Capitol ST-1605	(S)	**That Time Of Year**	1961	20.00	50.00
		— Capitol albums above have black labels with the Capitol logo on the left side.—			
Capitol T-1693	(M)	**The Best Of June Christy**	1962	10.00	25.00
Capitol ST-1693	(S)	**The Best Of June Christy**	1962	12.00	30.00
Capitol T-1845	(M)	**Big Band Specials**	1962	12.00	30.00
Capitol ST-1845	(S)	**Big Band Specials**	1962	16.00	40.00
Capitol T-1953	(M)	**The Intimate June Christy**	1962	12.00	30.00
Capitol ST-1953	(S)	**The Intimate June Christy**	1962	16.00	40.00
Capitol T-2410	(M)	**Something Broadway, Something Latin**	1965	12.00	30.00
Capitol ST-2410	(S)	**Something Broadway, Something Latin**	1965	16.00	40.00
		— Capitol albums above have black label with the Capitol logo on the top.—			
CIRCUIT RIDER					
C.R. 666	(S)	**Circuit Rider**	1980	30.00	75.00
CIRCUS MAXIMUS					
Circus Maximus features Jerry Jeff Walker.					
Vanguard VRS-9260	(M)	**Circus Maximus**	1967	8.00	20.00
Vanguard VSD-79260	(S)	**Circus Maximus**	1967	10.00	25.00
Vanguard VSD-79274	(S)	**Never Land Revisited**	1968	12.00	30.00
CITY					
City features Carole King.					
Ode Z12-44012	(S)	**Now That Everything's Been Said**	1969	20.00	50.00
		(Original copies of Ode 44012 have color covers; counterfeits have black & white covers.)			
CITY BLUES, THE					
Nouveau NR-5001	(M)	**Blues For Laurence Street**	1967	80.00	200.00
CLANCY BROTHERS, THE, & TOMMY MAKEM					
Liam, Paddy and Tom Clancy with Tommy Makem are a traditional Irish-American folk group					
Tradition TLP-1006	(M)	**The Rising Of The Moon**	1956	12.00	30.00
Tradition TLP-1032	(M)	**Come Fill Your Glass With Us**	1957	12.00	30.00

Label & Catalog #		Title	Year	VG+	NM
Tradition TLP-1042	(M)	The Clancy Brothers And Tommy Makem	1961	8.00	20.00
Tradition TLPS-1042	(S)	The Clancy Brothers And Tommy Makem	1961	10.00	25.00

CLANTON, JIMMY

Ace 1001	(M)	Just A Dream	1959	40.00	100.00
Ace 1007	(M)	Jimmy's Happy	1960	40.00	100.00
Ace 1007	(M)	Jimmy's Happy (Red vinyl)	1960	60.00	150.00
Ace 1008	(M)	Jimmy's Blue	1960	40.00	100.00
Ace 1008	(M)	Jimmy's Blue (Blue vinyl)	1960	60.00	150.00
		(The records for "Jimmy's Happy" and "Jimmy's Blue" on red and blue vinyl have both the single album catalog numbers, 1007-8 and the double album catalog number, 100, on their labels.)			
Ace DLP-100	(M)	Jimmy's Happy/Blue (2 LPs. Colored vinyl)	1960	150.00	300.00
		(Issued with a poster, priced separately below.)			
Ace DLP-100		Jimmy's Happy/Jimmy's Blue Poster	1960	20.00	50.00
Ace 1011	(M)	My Best To You	1961	40.00	100.00
Ace 1014	(M)	Teenage Millionaire	1961	40.00	100.00
Ace 1026	(M)	Venus In Bluejeans	1962	40.00	100.00
Philips PHM-200-154	(M)	The Best Of Jimmy Clanton	1964	8.00	20.00
Philips PHS-600-154	(S)	The Best Of Jimmy Clanton	1964	10.00	25.00
		(Philips 154 contains rerecorded versions of the Ace material.)			

CLAP

Nova Sol 1001	(S)	Have You Reached Yet?	1970	660.00	1,000.00

CLAPTON, ERIC
Refer to Blind Faith; Cream; Delaney & Bonnie; Derek & The Dominos; John Mayall; The Yardbirds.

Atco SD-33-329	(S)	Eric Clapton	1970	80.00	200.00
		(Some early pressings of Atco 329 were erroneously mastered with alternate takes and can be identified by the matrix number, "STC 701879-1A CTH," in the trail-off vinyl.)			
RSO QD-4801	(Q)	461 Ocean Boulevard	1974	10.00	25.00
RSO QD-4806	(Q)	There's One In Every Crowd	1975	10.00	25.00
RSO 035	(DJ)	Slowhand (White vinyl)	1978	12.00	30.00
RSO 1009	(DJ)	Backless (White vinyl)	1978	10.00	25.00
RSO PRO-22-015	(DJ)	Classic Cuts (2 LPs)	1980	12.00	30.00
Mobile Fidelity MFSL-030	(S)	Slowhand	1980	16.00	50.00
Nautilus NR-32	(S)	Just One Night	198?	16.00	50.00

CLARK, CHRIS

Motown 664	(M)	Soul Sounds	1967	16.00	40.00
Motown MS-664	(S)	Soul Sounds	1967	20.00	50.00
Weed 801	(S)	C. C. Rides Again	1969	16.00	40.00

CLARK, CLAUDINE

Chancellor CHL-5029	(M)	Party Lights	1962	50.00	200.00

CLARK, DAVE/THE DAVE CLARK FIVE

Crown CLP-5400	(M)	The Dave Clark Five With The Playbacks	1964	12.00	30.00
Crown CST-400	(E)	The Dave Clark Five With The Playbacks	1964	8.00	20.00
Crown CLP-5473	(M)	Chaquita/In Your Heart	1964	12.00	30.00
Crown CST-473	(E)	Chaquita/In Your Heart	1964	8.00	20.00
Cortleigh C-1073	(M)	The Dave Clark Five With Ricky Astor	1964	12.00	30.00
Cortleigh CS-1073	(E)	The Dave Clark Five With Ricky Astor	1964	8.00	20.00
Epic LN-24093	(M)	Glad All Over	1964	40.00	100.00
Epic BN-26093	(E)	Glad All Over	1964	30.00	75.00
		(On original covers for Epic 24/26093, the photo of the band has them without their instruments.)			
Epic LN-24093	(M)	Glad All Over	1964	16.00	40.00
Epic BN-26093	(E)	Glad All Over	1964	12.00	30.00
		(On later covers, the band has their instruments.)			
Epic LN-24104	(M)	The Dave Clark Five Return	1964	16.00	40.00
Epic BN-26104	(E)	The Dave Clark Five Return	1964	12.00	30.00
Epic LN-24117	(M)	American Tour, Volume 1	1964	16.00	40.00
Epic BN-26117	(E)	American Tour, Volume 1	1964	12.00	30.00
Epic XEM-77238	(DJ)	The Dave Clark 5 Interview	1964	300.00	500.00
Radio Pulsebeat	(M)	Interview With Ed Rudy	1964	100.00	250.00
Epic LN-24128	(M)	Coast To Coast	1965	16.00	40.00
Epic BN-26128	(E)	Coast To Coast	1965	12.00	30.00

Gene Clark With The Gosdin Brothers *features the original Byrds' first outing as a solo. While the material is basically solid if unexciting, the playing is first rate, including then Byrds Chris Hillman and Mike Clarke, future Byrd Clarence White, and Gene's soon to be partner, Doug Dillard. Had Clark remained a Byrd and the best material here used by the group on their third and fourth albums, both would have gained...*

Label & Catalog #		Title	Year	VG+	NM
Epic LN-24139	(M)	**Weekend In London**	1965	16.00	40.00
Epic BN-26139	(E)	**Weekend In London**	1965	12.00	30.00
Warner Bros. SP-3248	(DJ)	**Having A Wild Weekend Radio Spots**	1965	150.00	300.00
Warner Bros. 3296	(DJ)	**Having A Wild Weekend Interview**	1965	300.00	500.00
Epic LN-24162	(M)	**Having A Wild Weekend** *(Soundtrack)*	1965	16.00	40.00
Epic BN-26162	(E)	**Having A Wild Weekend** *(Soundtrack)*	1965	12.00	30.00
Epic LN-24178	(M)	**I Like It Like That**	1965	16.00	40.00
Epic BN-26178	(E)	**I Like It Like That**	1965	12.00	30.00
Epic LN-24185	(M)	**Greatest Hits**	1966	12.00	30.00
Epic BN-26185	(E)	**Greatest Hits**	1966	10.00	25.00
Epic BN-26185	(E)	**Greatest Hits** *(Orange label)*	1973	16.00	40.00
Epic LN-24198	(M)	**Try Too Hard**	1966	12.00	30.00
Epic BN-26198	(E)	**Try Too Hard**	1966	10.00	25.00
Epic LN-24212	(M)	**Satisfied With You**	1966	12.00	30.00
Epic BN-26212	(E)	**Satisfied With You**	1966	10.00	25.00
Epic LN-24221	(M)	**More Greatest Hits**	1966	12.00	30.00
Epic BN-26221	(E)	**More Greatest Hits**	1966	10.00	25.00
Epic LN-24236	(M)	**Five By Five**	1967	10.00	25.00
Epic BN-26236	(S)	**Five By Five**	1967	12.00	30.00
Epic LN-24312	(M)	**You Got What It Takes**	1967	10.00	25.00
Epic BN-26312	(S)	**You Got What It Takes**	1967	12.00	30.00
Epic LN-24354	(M)	**Everybody Knows**	1968	10.00	25.00
Epic BN-26354	(S)	**Everybody Knows**	1968	12.00	30.00
Epic EG-30434	(S)	**The Dave Clark Five** *(2 LPs. Yellow label)*	1971	40.00	100.00
Epic EG-30434	(S)	**The Dave Clark Five** *(2 LPs Orange label)*	1971	30.00	75.00

(Epic 30434 is a collection of sides in honestogod stereo.)
— *Epic albums above have yellow labels with a oval logo on top.*—

Epic KEG-33459	(M)	**Glad All Over Again** *(2 LPs)*	1975	14.00	35.00

CLARK, DEE

Abner LP-2000	(M)	**Dee Clark**	1959	40.00	100.00
Abner SR-2000	(S)	**Dee Clark** *(Counterfeits exist)*	1959	80.00	200.00
Abner LP-2002	(M)	**How About That**	1960	30.00	75.00
Abner SR-2002	(S)	**How About That**	1960	40.00	100.00
Vee Jay LP-2000	(M)	**Dee Clark**	196?		See below

(This is a Vee Jay reissue of the original Abner release with the Abner catalog number.. The copy found was in the Abner jacket. Rare with a suggested Near Mint value of $100-200.)

Vee Jay LP-1019	(M)	**You're Looking Good**	1960	20.00	50.00
Vee Jay LP-1037	(M)	**Hold On, It's Dee Clark**	1961	20.00	50.00
Vee Jay SR-1037	(S)	**Hold On, It's Dee Clark**	1961	30.00	75.00
Vee Jay LP-1047	(M)	**The Best Of Dee Clark**	1964	20.00	50.00
Vee Jay SR-1047	(S)	**The Best Of Dee Clark**	1964	30.00	75.00

CLARK, DICK: *Refer to* **THE KEYMEN**

CLARK, GENE
Clark was formerly a member of The Byrds. Refer to Dillard & Clark; McGuinn, Clark & Hillman

Columbia CL-2618	(M)	**Gene Clark With The Gosdin Brothers**	1967	12.00	30.00
Columbia CS-9418	(S)	**Gene Clark With The Gosdin Brothers**	1967	20.00	50.00

CLARK, GUY

RCA Victor APL1-1303	(S)	**Old No. 1**	1975	10.00	25.00
RCA Victor APL1-1944	(S)	**Texas Cookin'**	1976	10.00	25.00
Warner Bros. WBMS-???	(DJ)	**Warner Brothers Music Show Live Album**	1979	20.00	50.00

CLARK, KEITH
Keith Clark is a guitar and banjo player, singer and writer of traditionally-based folk music.

Folkways FA-2080	(10")	**Ballads Of LaSalle County, Illinois**	1956?	20.00	50.00

CLARK, KEN, & DON ANTHONY

Starday SLP-114	(M)	**Fiddlin' Country Style** *(Yellow label)*	1959	20.00	50.00

CLARK, PETULA

Imperial LP-9079	(M)	**Pet Clark**	1959	20.00	50.00
Imperial LP-12027	(S)	**Pet Clark**	1959	30.00	75.00
Imperial LP-9281	(M)	**Uptown With Petula Clark**	1965	8.00	20.00
Imperial LP-12281	(S)	**Uptown With Petula Clark**	1965	10.00	25.00

(Imperial 9/12281 is a reissue of 9/12079.)

Label & Catalog #		Title	Year	VG+	NM
Coca-Cola 103	(DJ)	Petula Clark Swings The Jingle	1965	60.00	150.00
MGM PRO-1667	(DJ)	Goodbye, Mr. Chips (Soundtrack interview)	1969	30.00	75.00
Warner Bros. ST-93215	(S)	Hits... My Way (2 LPs, Capitol Record Club)	1969	10.00	25.00
		("The Other Man's Grass Is Always Greener" is rechanneled.)			

CLARK, ROGIE
Classically trained Edgar Rogie Clark is a singer of Afro-American folk songs.

Allegro AL-8	(10")	Legend Of John Henry	1950	24.00	60.00

CLARK, SANFORD

L.H.I. 12003	(S)	The Return Of The Fool	1968	20.00	50.00

CLARK, TODD
Todd originally recorded with Eyes.

World Theatre	(S)	We're Not Safe	197?	150.00	300.00

CLARK, "YODELING SLIM"

Remington 1017	(10")	Cowboy Songs	195?	20.00	50.00
Playhouse 2017	(10")	Western Songs And Dances	1954	20.00	50.00
Continental C-1505	(M)	Cowboy And Yodel Songs	1962	20.00	50.00
Masterseal MS-57	(M)	Cowboy Songs	1963	12.00	30.00
Masterseal MS-112	(M)	Songs By Yodeling Slim Clark	1964	12.00	30.00
Masterseal MS-135	(M)	Cowboy Songs (Volume 2)	1964	12.00	30.00
Palomino 300	(M)	Yodeling Slim Clark Sings The Legendary Jimmie Rodgers Songs	1966	20.00	50.00
Palomino 301	(M)	Yodeling Slim Clark Sings And Yodels Favorite Montana Slim Songs Of The Mountains And Plains, Vol. 1	1966	16.00	40.00
Palomino 303	(M)	Yodeling Slim Clark Sings And Yodels Favorite Montana Slim Songs Of The Mountains And Plains, Vol. 2	1966	16.00	40.00
Palomino 306	(M)	I Feel A Trip Coming On	1966	16.00	40.00
Palomino 307	(M)	Old Chestnuts	1967	16.00	40.00
Palomino 310	(M)	Yodeling Slim Clark Happens Again	1968	16.00	40.00
Palomino 311	(M)	The Ballad Of Billy Venero	1966	16.00	40.00
Palomino 314	(M)	50th Anniversary Album (Gold vinyl)	1968	16.00	40.00

CLARK SISTERS, THE
The Clark Sisters are Ann, Jean, Mary and Peggy Clark.

Dot DLP-3104	(M)	Sing Sing Sing!	1957	12.00	30.00
Dot DLP-3137	(M)	The Clark Sisters Swing Again	1958	10.00	25.00
Dot DLP-25137	(S)	The Clark Sisters Swing Again	1958	12.00	30.00
Coral CRL-57290	(M)	Beauty Shop Beat	1960	8.00	20.00
Coral CRL-757290	(S)	Beauty Shop Beat	1960	10.00	25.00

CLASH, THE

Epic AS-913	(DJ)	Sandanista Now! (Sampler)	1981	10.00	25.00
Epic AS-952	(DJ)	Interchords/If Music Could Talk	1981	12.00	30.00
Epic FE-37689	(DJ)	Combat Rock (Camouflage colored vinyl)	1982	6.00	30.00
Epic AS-99-1592	(DJ)	Combat Rock (Picture disc)	1982	6.00	30.00
Epic AS-1594	(DJ)	The World According To The Clash	1982	12.00	30.00

CLASS-AIRES, THE

Honey Bee	(M)	Tears Start To Fall	195?	150.00	300.00

CLAUSON, WILLIAM
William Clauson is a guitar player and singer of traditional folk songs in many languages.

RCA Victor LPM-1286	(M)	Folk Songs	1956	16.00	40.00
Capitol Int. T-10158	(M)	Concert	1957	12.00	30.00

CLAY, CASSIUS
World champion boxer Cassius Clay later appeared on vinyl under his adopted Muslim name, Muhammad Ali.

Columbia CL-2093	(M)	I Am The Greatest!	1963	16.00	40.00
Columbia CS-8893	(S)	I Am The Greatest!	1963	20.00	50.00

CLAY, JUDY, & BILLY VERA

Atlantic 8174	(M)	Storybook Children	1967	8.00	20.00
Atlantic 8174	(S)	Storybook Children	1967	10.00	25.00

Label & Catalog #		Title	Year	VG+	NM

CLAYTON, PAUL
Paul Clayton is a guitar and dulcimer player and singer of traditional folk music. Refer to Jean Ritchie..

Folkways FP-47	(10")	Bay State Ballads	195?	40.00	100.00
Folkways FA-2007	(10")	Cumberland Mountain Folksongs	195?	40.00	100.00
Folkways FA-2106	(10")	Bay State Ballads	195?	40.00	100.00
Folkways FA-2110	(10")	Folksongs And Ballads Of Virginia	195?	40.00	100.00
Riverside RLP-12-615	(M)	Bloody Ballads	1957	12.00	30.00
Riverside RLP-12-640	(M)	Wanted For Murder—American Folksongs Of Outlaws And Desperados	1958	12.00	30.00
Riverside RLP-12-648	(M)	Timber-r-r!— Folk Songs & Ballads Of The Lumberjack	1958	12.00	30.00
Riverside RLP-12-836	(M)	Concert Of British And American Folksongs	1958	12.00	30.00
Elektra EKL-147	(M)	Unholy Matrimony	1958	12.00	30.00
Elektra EKL-155	(M)	Bobby Burns' Merry Muses Of Caledonia	1958	12.00	30.00
Stinson SLP-69	(10")	Whaling Songs And Ballads	1958	16.00	40.00
Stinson SLP-70	(10")	Waters Of Tyne— English North Country Songs	1958	16.00	40.00
Folkways FA-2310	(M)	Folkways-Viking Record Of Folk Ballads	1958	12.00	30.00
Folkways FA-2378	(M)	American Broadside Ballads In Popular Tradition	1958	12.00	30.00
Folkways FA-2382	(M)	Dulcimer Songs And Solos	1958	12.00	30.00
Folkways FA-2429	(M)	Foc'sle Songs And Shanties	195?	12.00	30.00
Folkways FW-8708	(M)	British Broadside Ballads In Popular Tradition	195?	12.00	30.00
Tradition TLP-1005	(M)	Whaling And Sailing Songs From The Days Of Moby Dick	1956	12.00	30.00
Monument MLP-8017	(M)	Folk Singer	1965	8.00	20.00
Monument SLP-18017	(S)	Folk Singer	1965	10.00	25.00

CLEANLINESS & GODLINESS SKIFFLE BAND, THE

Vanguard VSD-79285	(S)	Greatest Hits	1968	12.00	30.00

CLEAR LIGHT

Elektra EKL-4011	(M)	Clear Light	1967	8.00	20.00
Elektra EKS-74011	(S)	Clear Light	1967	10.00	25.00

CLEARY, DON

Palomino 302	(M)	Traditional Cowboy Songs	1966	16.00	40.00

CLEAVER, ELDRIDGE

More 4000	(M)	Soul On Wax—Recorded At Syracuse	1968	10.00	25.00

CLEFTONES, THE

Gee GLP-705	(M)	Heart And Soul	1961	80.00	200.00
Gee SGLP-705	(P)	Heart And Soul	1961	200.00	450.00
Gee GLP-707	(M)	For Sentimental Reasons	1962	80.00	200.00
Gee SGLP-707	(P)	For Sentimental Reasons	1962	350.00	800.00
		— Gee albums above have gray labels.—			

CLIFF, JIMMY

Veep VPS-16536	(S)	Can't Get Enough Of It	1968	14.00	35.00

CLIFFORD, BUZZ

Columbia CL-1616	(M)	Baby Sittin' With Buzz	1961	30.00	75.00
Columbia CS-8416	(S)	Baby Sittin' With Buzz	1961	40.00	100.00
Dot DLP-25965	(S)	See Your Way Clear	1969	10.00	25.00

CLIFFORD, MIKE

United Arts. UAL-3409	(M)	For The Love Of Mike	1965	8.00	20.00
United Arts. UAS-6409	(P)	For The Love Of Mike	1965	10.00	25.00

CLIFTON, BILL, & THE DIXIE MOUNTAIN BOYS
Bill Clifton is a bluegrass guitar player and singer.

Starday SLP-111	(M)	Mountain Folk Songs	1959	20.00	50.00
Starday SLP-146	(M)	Carter Family Memorial Album	1961	16.00	40.00
Starday SLP-159	(M)	The Bluegrass Sound Of Bill Clifton	1961	16.00	40.00
Starday SLP-213	(M)	Soldier, Sing Me A Song	1963	12.00	30.00
Starday SLP-271	(M)	Code Of The Mountains	1965	12.00	30.00

Label & Catalog #		Title	Year	VG+	NM

CLINE, PATSY
Refer to Cowboy Copas / Hawkshaw Hawkins / Patsy Cline.

Decca DL-8611	(M)	**Patsy Cline**	1957	40.00	100.00
		— Decca albums above have black labels with "silver print.—			
Decca DL-8611	(M)	**Patsy Cline**	1958	20.00	50.00
Decca DL-4202	(M)	**Patsy Cline Showcase**	1961	16.00	40.00
Decca DL-74202	(S)	**Patsy Cline Showcase**	1961	20.00	50.00
Decca DL-4282	(M)	**Sentimentally Yours**	1962	12.00	30.00
Decca DL-74282	(S)	**Sentimentally Yours**	1962	16.00	40.00
Decca DXB-176	(M)	**The Patsy Cline Story** *(2 LPs with booklet)*	1963	14.00	35.00
Decca DXSB-7176	(S)	**The Patsy Cline Story** *(2 LPs with booklet)*	1963	16.00	40.00
Decca DL-4508	(M)	**A Portrait Of Patsy Cline**	1964	12.00	30.00
Decca DL-74508	(S)	**A Portrait Of Patsy Cline**	1964	14.00	35.00
Decca DL-4586	(M)	**That's How A Heartache Begins**	1964	12.00	30.00
Decca DL-74586	(S)	**That's How A Heartache Begins**	1964	14.00	35.00
		— Decca albums above have black labels with "Mfrd. by Decca" beneath the rainbow.—			
Decca DL-4854	(M)	**Patsy Cline's Greatest Hits**	1967	8.00	20.00
Decca DL-74854	(S)	**Patsy Cline's Greatest Hits**	1967	10.00	25.00
Sears SPS-127	(E)	**In Care Of The Blues**	1968	10.00	25.00

CLOONEY, ROSEMARY
Refer to The Clooney Sisters; Bing Crosby & Rosemary Clooney; The Ferrers; Prez Prado; The Reprise Repertory Theatre.

Columbia CL-6224	(10")	**Hollywood's Best**	1952	24.00	60.00
Columbia CL-6297	(10")	**Rosemary Clooney**	1954	24.00	60.00
Columbia CL-6338	(10")	**White Christmas**	1954	24.00	60.00
Columbia CL-6282	(10")	**Red Garters** *(Soundtrack)*	1954	50.00	100.00
Columbia CL-2525	(10")	**Tenderly**	1955	24.00	60.00
Columbia CL-2569	(10")	**Children's Favorites**	1956	24.00	60.00
Columbia CL-2572	(10")	**A Date With The King**	1956	24.00	60.00
Columbia CL-2581	(10")	**On Stage**	1956	24.00	60.00
Columbia CL-2597	(10")	**My Fair Lady**	1956	24.00	60.00
MGM E-3153	(M)	**Deep In My Heart** *(Soundtrack in a box)*	1954	40.00	100.00
MGM E-3153	(M)	**Deep In My Heart** *(Soundtrack in a jacket)*	1955	20.00	50.00
Columbia CL-585	(M)	**Hollywood's Best**	1955	20.00	50.00
Columbia CL-872	(M)	**Blue Rose**	1956	16.00	30.00
Columbia CL-969	(M)	**Clooney Tunes**	1957	30.00	75.00
Columbia CL-1230	(M)	**Rosie's Greatest Hits**	1958	16.00	40.00
		— Columbia albums above have three white "eye" logos on each side of the spindle hole.—			
Harmony HL-7123	(M)	**Rosemary Clooney In High Fidelity**	195?	10.00	25.00
Harmony HL-7213	(M)	**Hollywood Hits**	195?	10.00	25.00
Coral CRL-57266	(M)	**Swing Around Rosie**	1958	12.00	30.00
Coral CRL-757266	(S)	**Swing Around Rosie**	1958	16.00	40.00
MGM E-3687	(M)	**Oh, Captain!**	1958	16.00	40.00
MGM E-3782	(M)	**Hymns From The Heart**	1959	12.00	30.00
MGM SE-3782	(S)	**Hymns From The Heart**	1959	16.00	40.00
MGM E-3834	(M)	**Rosie Swings Softly**	1960	12.00	30.00
MGM SE-3834	(S)	**Rosis Clooney Swings Softly**	1960	16.00	40.00
RCA Victor LPM-1854	(M)	**Fancy Meeting You Here**	1958	8.00	20.00
RCA Victor LSP-1854	(S)	**Fancy Meeting You Here**	1958	12.00	30.00
RCA Victor LPM-2133	(M)	**A Touch Of Tabasco**	1960	8.00	20.00
RCA Victor LSP-2133	(S)	**A Touch Of Tabasco**	1960	12.00	30.00
RCA Victor LPM-2212	(M)	**Clap Hands, Here Comes Rosie**	1960	8.00	20.00
RCA Victor LSP-2212	(S)	**Clap Hands, Here Comes Rosie**	1960	12.00	30.00
RCA Victor LPM-2265	(M)	**Rosie Solves The Swingin' Riddle**	1961	8.00	20.00
RCA Victor LSP-2265	(S)	**Rosie Solves The Swingin' Riddle**	1961	12.00	30.00
RCA Victor LPM-2565	(M)	**Country Hits From The Heart**	1963	8.00	20.00
RCA Victor LSP-2565	(S)	**Country Hits From The Heart**	1963	12.00	30.00
		— Mono RCA albums above have "Long Play" on the bottom of the label;			
		stereo albums have "Living Stereo" on the bottom.—			
Reprise R-6088	(M)	**Love**	1963	12.00	30.00
Reprise R-96088	(S)	**Love**	1963	16.00	40.00
Reprise R-6108	(M)	**Thanks For Nothing**	1964	12.00	30.00
Reprise R-96108	(S)	**Thanks For Nothing**	1964	16.00	40.00

CLOONEY, ROSEMARY, & THE HI-LO'S

| Columbia CL-1006 | (M) | **Ring Around Rosie** *(With The Hi-Los)* | 1958 | 16.00 | 40.00 |

Label & Catalog #		Title	Year	VG+	NM

CLOONEY SISTERS, THE
The Sisters feature Rosemary Clooney.

Epic LN-3160	(M)	**The Clooney Sisters With Tony Pastor**	1955	24.00	60.00

CLOVERS, THE

Atlantic LP-1248	(M)	**The Clovers**	1956	300.00	700.00
Atlantic LP-8009	(M)	**The Clovers**	1957	200.00	400.00
Atlantic LP-8009	(M)	**The Clovers** *(White "bullseye" label)*	1959	250.00	500.00
		(Atlantic 8009 is a reissue of 1248.)			
Atlantic LP-8034	(M)	**Dance Party** *(White "bullseye" label)*	1959	250.00	500.00
Atlantic LP-8034	(M)	**Dance Party**	1959	200.00	400.00
		—Atlantic albums above have black labels.—			
Atlantic LP-8009	(M)	**The Clovers**	196?	80.00	200.00
Atlantic LP-8034	(M)	**Dance Party**	196?	80.00	200.00
		—Atlantic albums above have purple & orange labels.—			
Poplar 1001	(M)	**In Clover**	1958	150.00	400.00
United Arts. UAL-3033	(M)	**In Clover**	1959	150.00	300.00
United Arts. UAS-6033	(E)	**In Clover**	1959	100.00	250.00
United Arts. UAL-3099	(M)	**Love Potion Number Nine**	1959	150.00	300.00
United Arts. UAS-6099	(S)	**Love Potion Number Nine**	1959	200.00	400.00
		("Love Potion Number Nine" and "Lovey Dovey"			
		were rerecorded for this album.)			
Design DLP-	(M)	**Love Potion Number Nine**	196?	16.00	40.00
Design DSLP-	(E)	**Love Potion Number Nine**	196?	6.00	15.00
Grand Prix K-428	(M)	**The Original Love Potion Number Nine**	1964	12.00	30.00
Grand Prix KS-428	(E)	**The Original Love Potion Number Nine**	1964	6.00	15.00

COASTERS, THE
Refer to The Drifters / The Coasters.

Atco 33-101	(M)	**The Coasters**	1958	200.00	400.00
Atco 33-111	(M)	**The Coasters' Greatest Hits**	1959	80.00	200.00
Atco 33-123	(M)	**One By One**	1960	80.00	200.00
		—Atco albums above have yellow labels with a harp on top.—			
Atco 33-101	(M)	**The Coasters**	1960	40.00	100.00
Atco SD-33-101	(E)	**The Coasters**	196?	30.00	75.00
Atco 33-111	(M)	**The Coasters' Greatest Hits**	1960	20.00	50.00
Atco SD-33-111	(E)	**The Coasters' Greatest Hits**	196?	10.00	25.00
Atco 33-123	(M)	**One By One**	1960	40.00	100.00
Atco SD-33-123	(S)	**One By One**	1960	60.00	150.00
Atco 33-135	(M)	**Coast Along With The Coasters**	1962	40.00	100.00
Atco SD-33-135	(P)	**Coast Along With The Coasters**	1962	60.00	150.00
		—Atco mono albums above have gold & gray labels; stereo albums have purple & brown labels.—			
Clarion 605	(M)	**That's Rock And Roll**	1964	16.00	40.00
Clarion 605	(P)	**That's Rock And Roll**	1964	20.00	50.00
King KS-1146	(M)	**The Coasters On Broadway**	1973	10.00	25.00

COCHRAN, EDDIE

Liberty LRP-3061	(M)	**Singin' To My Baby** *(Green label)*	1957	300.00	600.00
Liberty LRP-3061	(M)	**Singin' To My Baby** *(Black label)*	1960	100.00	250.00
Liberty LRP-3172	(DJ)	**Eddie Cochran** *(White label promo)*	1960	200.00	400.00
Liberty LRP-3172	(M)	**Eddie Cochran**	1960	60.00	150.00
Liberty LRP-3220	(M)	**Never To Be Forgotten**	1962	30.00	75.00
Sunset SUM-1123	(M)	**Summertime Blues**	1966	14.00	35.00
Sunset SUS-5123	(E)	**Summertime Blues**	1966	10.00	25.00
United Arts. UAS-9959	(M)	**Legendary Master** *(2 LPs)*	1971	10.00	25.00

COCHRAN, HANK

RCA Victor LPM-3303	(M)	**Hits From The Heart**	1965	8.00	20.00
RCA Victor LSP-3303	(S)	**Hits From The Heart**	1965	10.00	25.00
RCA Victor LPM-3431	(M)	**Going In Training**	1965	8.00	20.00
RCA Victor LSP-3431	(S)	**Going In Training**	1965	10.00	25.00
Monument SLP-18089	(S)	**The Heart Of Eddie Cochran**	1968	8.00	20.00

COCHRAN, STEVIE

(No label)	(DJ)	**No Need To Worry** *(Test pressing)*	1984	60.00	150.00

COCHRAN, WAYNE/WAYNE COCHRAN & THE C.C. RIDERS

Chess LP-1519	(M)	**Wayne Cochran**	1967	12.00	30.00
Chess LPS-1519	(S)	**Wayne Cochran**	1967	16.00	40.00

Label & Catalog #		Title	Year	VG+	NM
COE, DAVID ALLAN					
SSS Inter. 9	(S)	**Penitentiary Blues**	1977	20.00	50.00
COGAN, MIKE					
Columbia HL-9007	(10")	**Sagebrush Swing**	195?	30.00	75.00
COHEN, JOHN					
John Cohen also recorded with The New Lost City Ramblers.					
Folkways FA-2317	(M)	**Mountain Music Of Kentucky**	1960	12.00	30.00
COLD SUN: Refer to DARK SHADOWS					
COLDER, BEN					
Ben Colder is a pseudonym for Shelby "Sheb" Wooley.					
MGM E-4117	(M)	**Spoofing The Big Ones**	1961	14.00	35.00
MGM SE-4117	(S)	**Spoofing The Big Ones**	1961	20.00	50.00
MGM E-4173	(M)	**Ben Colder**	1963	12.00	30.00
MGM SE-4173	(S)	**Ben Colder**	1963	16.00	40.00
COLE, COZY					
Cozy Cole's main catalogue can be found in "Goldmine's Price Guide To Collectible Jazz Albums."					
Love 500M	(M)	**Topsy**	195?	40.00	100.00
Love 500S	(S)	**Topsy**	195?	80.00	200.00
		("Topsy" was rerecorded in stereo for this album.)			
COLE, IKE					
Dee Cee LPM-4001	(M)	**Ike Cole's Tribute To His Brother Nat**	195?	20.00	50.00
Bally BLP-12020	(M)	**Get A Load O' Cole**	195?	12.00	30.00
COLE, JERRY, & HIS SPACEMEN					
Mr. Cole also recorded as Jerry Kole.					
Capitol T-2044	(M)	**Outer Limits**	1963	16.00	40.00
Capitol ST-2044	(S)	**Outer Limits**	1963	20.00	50.00
Capitol T-2061	(M)	**Hot Rod Dance Party**	1964	20.00	50.00
Capitol ST-2601	(S)	**Hot Rod Dance Party**	1964	30.00	75.00
Capitol T-2112	(M)	**Surf Age**	1964	30.00	75.00
Capitol ST-2112	(S)	**Surf Age**	1964	40.00	100.00
		(Capitol 2112 ncludes the bonus single "Thunder Wave" / "Spanish Kiss" by Dick Dale in aspecial " pocket" on the front cover.)			
Capitol T-2112	(M)	**Surf Age** (Without the single)	1964	20.00	50.00
Capitol ST-2112	(S)	**Surf Age** (Without the single)	1964	30.00	75.00
Liberty LRP-3362	(M)	**Sounds Of The Big Irons**	1964	16.00	40.00
Liberty LST-7362	(S)	**Sounds Of The Big Irons**	1964	20.00	50.00
COLE, MARIA					
Kapp 102	(10")	**Maria Cole**	1954	20.00	50.00
COLE, NAT "KING"					
Aladdin LP-705	(10")	**The King Cole Trio** (Red vinyl)	1954	300.00	600.00
Aladdin LP-705	(10")	**The King Cole Trio**	1954	200.00	400.00
Score SLP-4019	(M)	**The Lester Young-King Cole Trio**	1958	60.00	150.00
		(Score 4019 is a reissue of Aladdin 705.)			
Capitol H-8	(10")	**The King Cole Trio**	1950	20.00	50.00
Capitol H-29	(10")	**The King Cole Trio, Volume 2**	1950	20.00	50.00
Capitol H-59	(10")	**The King Cole Trio, Volume 3**	1950	20.00	50.00
Capitol L-156	(10")	**Nat King Cole At The Piano**	1950	20.00	50.00
Capitol H-177	(10")	**The King Cole Trio, Volume 4**	1950	20.00	50.00
Capitol L-213	(10")	**Harvest Of Hits**	1950	20.00	50.00
Capitol H-220	(10")	**The Nat King Cole Trio, Volume 1**	1950	20.00	50.00
Capitol H-332	(10")	**Penthouse Serenade**	1952	20.00	50.00
Capitol H-357	(10")	**Unforgettable**	1952	16.00	40.00
Capitol H-420	(10")	**Two In Love**	1954	20.00	50.00
Capitol H-514	(10")	**Tenth Anniversary Album**	1954	20.00	50.00
Capitol H-9110	(10")	**8 Top Pops**	1954	16.00	40.00
Capitol T-332	(M)	**Penthouse Serenade**	1954	16.00	40.00
Capitol T-357	(M)	**Unforgettable**	1954	12.00	30.00
Capitol T-420	(M)	**Two In Love**	1954	16.00	40.00
Capitol W-514	(M)	**Tenth Anniversary Album**	1954	16.00	40.00
Capitol T-591	(M)	**Vocal Classics**	1955	12.00	30.00

Label & Catalog #		Title	Year	VG+	NM
Capitol T-592	(M)	Instrumental Classics	1955	16.00	40.00
Capitol T-680	(M)	Ballads Of The Day	1956	12.00	30.00
Capitol W-689	(M)	The Piano Style Of Nat King Cole	1956	16.00	40.00
Capitol W-782	(M)	After Midnight	1956	16.00	40.00
— Capitol albums above have "Long Playing" on the bottom of the label.—					
Decca DL-8260	(M)	In The Beginning	1956	16.00	40.00
Score SLP-4019	(M)	The King Cole Trio And Lester Young	1957	30.00	75.00
Capitol W-824	(M)	Love Is The Thing	1957	10.00	25.00
Capitol T-870	(M)	This Is Nat King Cole	1957	10.00	25.00
Capitol W-903	(M)	Just One Of Those Things	1958	10.00	25.00
Capitol W-993	(M)	Saint Louis Blues (Soundtrack)	1958	16.00	40.00
— Capitol albums above have "Long Playing High Fidelity" on the bottom of the label.—					
Capitol SW-824	(S)	Love Is The Thing	1958	12.00	30.00
Capitol SW-903	(S)	Just One Of Those Things	1958	12.00	30.00
Capitol SW-993	(S)	Saint Louis Blues (Soundtrack)	1958	16.00	40.00
Capitol W-1031	(M)	Cole Espanol	1958	10.00	25.00
Capitol DW-1031	(E)	Cole Espanol	196?	5.00	12.00
Capitol W-1084	(M)	The Very Thought Of You	1958	8.00	20.00
Capitol SW-1084	(S)	The Very Thought Of You	1958	10.00	25.00
Capitol W-1120	(M)	Welcome To The Club	1959	8.00	20.00
Capitol SW-1120	(S)	Welcome To The Club	1959	10.00	25.00
Capitol W-1190	(M)	To Whom It May Concern	1959	8.00	20.00
Capitol SW-1190	(S)	To Whom It May Concern	1959	10.00	25.00
Capitol W-1220	(M)	A Mis Amigos	1959	8.00	20.00
Capitol SW-1220	(S)	A Mis Amigos	1959	10.00	25.00
Capitol T-1249	(M)	Every Time I Feel The Spirit	1960	8.00	20.00
Capitol ST-1249	(S)	Every Time I Feel The Spirit	1960	10.00	25.00
Capitol W-1331	(M)	Tell Me All About Yourself	1960	8.00	20.00
Capitol SW-1331	(S)	Tell Me All About Yourself	1960	10.00	25.00
Capitol WAK-1392	(M)	Wild Is Love	1960	8.00	20.00
Capitol SWAK-1392	(S)	Wild Is Love	1960	10.00	25.00
Capitol W-1444	(M)	The Magic Of Christmas	1960	8.00	20.00
Capitol␣W-1444	(S)	The Magic Of Christmas	1960	10.00	25.00
Capitol WCL-1613	(M)	The Nat King Cole Story (3 LPs)	1961	10.00	25.00
Capitol SWCL-1613	(P)	The Nat King Cole Story (3 LPs)	1961	12.00	30.00
Capitol TCL-2873	(M)	Nat King Cole Deluxe Set (3 LP box)	1967	10.00	25.00
Capitol STCL-2873	(P)	Nat King Cole Deluxe Set (3 LP box)	1967	10.00	25.00
— Capitol albums above have black labels with the Capitol logo on top.—					
Mobile Fidelity MFSL-081	(S)	Nat King Cole Sings/George Shearing Plays	198?	16.00	50.00

COLLECTORS, THE

Warner Bros. WS-1746	(S)	The Collectors	1968	10.00	25.00
Warner Bros. WS-1774	(S)	Grass And Wild Strawberries	1969	10.00	25.00

COLLEGIANS, THE

Winley LP-6004	(M)	Sing Along With The Collegians	195?	150.00	300.00

COLLIER, MITTY

Chess LP-1492	(M)	Shades Of Genius	1965	14.00	35.00
Chess LPS-1492	(S)	Shades Of Genius	1965	20.00	50.00

COLLINS, AARON

Aaron Collins was the lead singer for The Cadets and The Jacks.

Crown CLP-5028	(M)	Calypso U.S.A.	1958	300.00	600.00

COLLINS, ALBERT

TCF-Hall 8002	(M)	The Cool Sound Of Albert Collins	1965	80.00	200.00
Imperial LP-12428	(S)	Love Can Be Found Anywhere	1968	12.00	30.00
Imperial LP-12438	(S)	Trash Talkin'	1969	12.00	30.00
Imperial LP-12449	(S)	The Complete Albert Collins	1969	12.00	30.00
Blue Thumb BTS-8	(S)	Truckin' With Albert Collins	1969	10.00	25.00
(Blue Thumb 8 is a reissue of TCF Hall 8002.)					

COLLINS, DOROTHY

Coral CRL-57105	(M)	Dorothy Collins At Home	1957	10.00	25.00
Coral CRL-57106	(M)	Songs By Dorothy Collins	1957	10.00	25.00
Coral CRL-57150	(M)	Picnic	1958	10.00	25.00
Top Rank RM-340	(M)	A New Way To Travel	1961	10.00	25.00
Top Rank RM-340	(S)	A New Way To Travel	1961	14.00	35.00

Label & Catalog #		Title	Year	VG+	NM

COLLINS, JOAN: *Refer to* PETER SELLERS & JOAN COLLINS & ANTHONY NEWLEY

COLLINS, TOMMY

Label & Catalog #		Title	Year	VG+	NM
Capitol T-776	(M)	Words And Music Country Style	1957	40.00	100.00
Capitol T-1125	(M)	Light Of The Lord	1959	60.00	150.00
Capitol T-1196	(M)	This Is Tommy Collins	1959	30.00	75.00
Capitol T-1436	(M)	Songs I Love To Sing	1961	24.00	60.00
Capitol ST-1436	(S)	Songs I Love To Sing	1961	30.00	75.00
Tower T-5021	(M)	Let's Live A Little	1966	16.00	40.00
Tower DT-5021	(E)	Let's Live A Little	1966	10.00	25.00
Tower T-5107	(M)	Shindig	1968	20.00	50.00
Tower DT-5107	(E)	Shindig	1968	16.00	40.00
Columbia CL-2510	(M)	The Dynamic Tommy Collins	1966	14.00	35.00
Columbia CS-9310	(S)	The Dynamic Tommy Collins	1966	20.00	50.00
Columbia CL-2778	(M)	Tommy Collins On Tour	1968	30.00	75.00
Columbia CS-9578	(S)	Tommy Collins On Tour	1968	20.00	50.00
Starday SLP-474	(M)	Callin'	1972	10.00	25.00

COLWELL-WINFIELD BLUES BAND, THE

Label & Catalog #		Title	Year	VG+	NM
Verve/Forecast FVS-3056	(S)	Cold Wind Blues	1968	10.00	25.00
Verve/Forecast FVS-3072	(S)	Colwell-Winfield Blues Band	1969	*Unreleased*	
ZaZoo 1	(S)	Live Bust	1971	12.00	30.00

COMMON PEOPLE, THE

Label & Catalog #		Title	Year	VG+	NM
Capitol ST-266	(S)	Of The People, By The People	1969	50.00	125.00

COMO, PERRY

Label & Catalog #		Title	Year	VG+	NM
RCA Victor LPM-51	(10")	Merry Christmas	1951	16.00	40.00
RCA Victor LPM-3013	(10")	TV Favorites	1952	16.00	40.00
RCA Victor LPM-3035	(10")	A Sentimental Date With Perry Como	1952	16.00	40.00
RCA Victor LPM-3044	(10")	Supper Club Favorites	1952	16.00	40.00
RCA Victor LPM-3124	(10")	Hits From Broadway Shows	1953	16.00	40.00
RCA Victor LPM-3133	(10")	Around The Christmas Tree	1953	16.00	40.00
RCA Victor LPM-3188	(10")	I Believe	1954	16.00	40.00
RCA Victor LPM-3224	(10")	Como's Golden Records	1954	16.00	40.00
RCA Victor LPM-1085	(M)	So Smooth	1955	12.00	30.00
RCA Victor LPM-1172	(M)	I Believe	1956	12.00	30.00
RCA Victor LPM-1176	(M)	Relaxing With Perry Como	1956	12.00	30.00
RCA Victor LPC-1177	(M)	A Sentimental Date With Perry Como	1956	12.00	30.00
RCA Victor LPM-1191	(M)	Hits From Broadway Shows	1956	12.00	30.00
RCA Victor LPM-1243	(M)	Merry Christmas Music	1956	12.00	30.00
RCA Victor LPM-1463	(M)	We Get Letters	1957	12.00	30.00
RCA Victor LOP-1004	(M)	Saturday Night With Mr. C	1958	12.00	30.00
RCA Victor LOP-1007	(M)	Como's Golden Records	1958	12.00	30.00
RCA Victor LPM-1885	(M)	When You Come To The End Of The Day	1958	8.00	20.00
RCA Victor LSP-1885	(S)	When You Come To The End Of The Day	1958	12.00	30.00
RCA Victor LPM-1971	(M)	Saturday Night With Mr. C	1959	8.00	20.00
RCA Victor LSP-1971	(E)	Saturday Night With Mr. C	1959	6.00	15.00
		(RCA 1971 is a reissue of 1004.)			
RCA Victor LPM-1981	(M)	Como's Golden Records	1959	8.00	20.00
RCA Victor LSP-1981	(E)	Como's Golden Records	1959	6.00	15.00
		(RCA 1981 is a reissue of 1007.)			
RCA Victor LPM-2010	(M)	Como Swings	1959	8.00	20.00
RCA Victor LSP-2010	(S)	Como Swings	1959	10.00	25.00
RCA Victor LPM-2066	(M)	Season's Greetings	1959	8.00	20.00
RCA Victor LSP-2066	(S)	Season's Greetings	1959	10.00	25.00

— RCA mono albums above have "Long Play" on the bottom of the label stereo albums have "Living Stereo" on the bottom. —

COMPETITORS, THE
The Competitors are a creation of Gary Usher & Co.

Label & Catalog #		Title	Year	VG+	NM
Dot DLP-3542	(M)	Hits Of The Street And Strip	1963	60.00	150.00
Dot DLP-25542	(S)	Hits Of The Street And Strip	1963	80.00	200.00

COMSTOCK, BOBBY, & THE COUNTS

Label & Catalog #		Title	Year	VG+	NM
Ascot ALM-13026	(M)	Out Of Sight	1966	10.00	25.00
Ascot ALS-16026	(S)	Out Of Sight	1966	14.00	35.00

Label & Catalog #		Title	Year	VG+	NM
CONDELLO					
Scepter SP-542	(M)	**Phase 1**	1968	8.00	20.00
Scepter SPS-542	(S)	**Phase 1**	1968	10.00	25.00
CONLEY, ARTHUR					
Atco 33-215	(M)	**Sweet Soul Music**	1967	16.00	40.00
Atco SD-33-215	(E)	**Sweet Soul Music**	1967	12.00	30.00
Atco 33-220	(M)	**Shake, Rattle And Roll**	1967	16.00	40.00
Atco SD-33-220	(E)	**Shake, Rattle And Roll**	1967	12.00	30.00
Atco SD-33-243	(S)	**Soul Directions**	1968	12.00	30.00
Atco SD-33-276	(S)	**More Sweet Soul**	1969	12.00	30.00
CONNELLY, PEGGY: *Refer to* GOLDMINE'S PRICE GUIDE TO COLLECTIBLE JAZZ ALBUMS					
CONNERY, SEAN					
Sean Connnery, of course, is one of the leadingest of male actors in the past thirty years of film. . .					
London PM-55005	(M)	**Peter & The Wolf—The**			
		Young Person's Guide To The Orchestra	196?	16.00	40.00
London SPC-21007	(S)	**Peter & The Wolf—The**			
		Young Person's Guide To The Orchestra	196?	20.00	50.00
CONNOR, CHRIS: *Refer to* GOLDMINE'S PRICE GUIDE TO COLLECTIBLE JAZZ ALBUMS					
CONRAD, RAY					
Prestige Int. PRLP-13039	(M)	**A Cotton Pickin' Lift Tower**	1962	10.00	25.00
CONRIED, HANS					
RCA Victor LPM-1923	(M)	**Monster Rally**	1959	20.00	50.00
RCA Victor LSP-1923	(S)	**Monster Rally**	1959	30.00	75.00
CONTOURS, THE					
Gordy G-901	(M)	**Do You Love Me**	1962	200.00	400.00
COODER, RY					
Refer to Capt. Beefheart / Ry Cooder; The Ceylib People; Longbranch Pennywhistle					
Reprise PRO-558	(DJ)	**The Ry Cooder Radio Show**	1976	12.00	30.00
Warner Bros. PRO-	(DJ)	**Borderlive/Live In Europe**	1981	12.00	30.00
Mobile Fidelity MFSL-085	(S)	**Jazz**	1984	100.00	300.00
COOK, BARBARA					
Urania ULM-9126	(M)	**From The Heart—Songs Of Rodgers & Hart**	196?	10.00	25.00
Urania ULS-9126	(S)	**From The Heart—Songs Of Rodgers & Hart**	196?	12.00	30.00
COOKE, SAM					
Refer to The Soul Stirrers.					
Keen A-2001	(M)	**Sam Cooke**	1958	80.00	200.00
Keen A-2003	(M)	**Encore**	1958	80.00	200.00
Keen A-2004	(M)	**Tribute To The Lady—Billie Holiday**	1959	60.00	150.00
Keen AS-2004	(S)	**Tribute To The Lady—Billie Holiday**	1959	80.00	200.00
Keen 86101	(M)	**Hit Kit**	1959	100.00	250.00
Keen 86103	(M)	**I Thank God**	1960	200.00	450.00
Keen 86106	(M)	**The Wonderful World Of Sam Cooke**	1960	150.00	350.00
RCA Victor LPM-2221	(M)	**Cooke's Tour**	1960	16.00	40.00
RCA Victor LSP-2221	(S)	**Cooke's Tour**	1960	20.00	50.00
RCA Victor LPM-2236	(M)	**Hits Of The 50's**	1960	16.00	40.00
RCA Victor LSP-2236	(S)	**Hits Of The 50's**	1960	20.00	50.00
RCA Victor LPM-2293	(M)	**Swing Low**	1960	16.00	40.00
RCA Victor LSP-2293	(S)	**Swing Low**	1960	20.00	50.00
RCA Victor LPM-2392	(M)	**My Kind Of Blues**	1961	16.00	40.00
RCA Victor LSP-2392	(S)	**My Kind Of Blues**	1961	20.00	50.00
RCA Victor LPM-2555	(M)	**Twistin' The Night Away**	1962	16.00	40.00
RCA Victor LSP-2555	(S)	**Twistin' The Night Away**	1962	20.00	50.00
RCA Victor LPM-2625	(M)	**The Best Of Sam Cooke**	1962	12.00	30.00
RCA Victor LPM-2673	(M)	**Mr. Soul**	1963	12.00	30.00
RCA Victor LSP-2673	(S)	**Mr. Soul**	1963	16.00	40.00
RCA Victor LPM-2709	(M)	**Night Beat**	1963	12.00	30.00
RCA Victor LSP-2709	(S)	**Night Beat**	1963	16.00	40.00

— RCA mono albums above have "Long Play" on the bottom of the label;
stereo albums have "Living Stereo" on the bottom.—

Label & Catalog #		Title	Year	VG+	NM
RCA Victor LPM-2899	(M)	Ain't That Good News	1964	10.00	25.00
RCA Victor LSP-2899	(S)	Ain't That Good News	1964	12.00	30.00
RCA Victor LPM-2970	(M)	Sam Cooke At The Copa	1964	10.00	25.00
RCA Victor LSP-2970	(S)	Sam Cooke At The Copa	1964	12.00	30.00
RCA Victor LPM-3367	(M)	Shake	1965	10.00	25.00
RCA Victor LSP-3367	(S)	Shake	1965	12.00	30.00
RCA Victor LPM-3373	(M)	The Best Of Sam Cooke, Volume 2	1965	8.00	20.00
RCA Victor LSP-3373	(P)	The Best Of Sam Cooke, Volume 2	1965	10.00	25.00
RCA Victor LPM-3435	(M)	Try A Little Love	1965	10.00	25.00
RCA Victor LSP-3435	(S)	Try A Little Love	1965	12.00	30.00
RCA Victor LPM-3517	(M)	The Unforgettable Sam Cooke	1966	8.00	20.00
RCA Victor LSP-3517	(S)	The Unforgettable Sam Cooke	1966	10.00	25.00
RCA Victor LSP-3991	(S)	The Man Who Invented Soul	1968	10.00	25.00
		— RCA albums above have black labels.—			
Famous F-502	(M)	Sam's Songs	1969	20.00	50.00
Famous F-505	(M)	Only Sixteen	1969	20.00	50.00
Famous F-508	(M)	So Wonderful	1969	20.00	50.00
Famous F-509	(M)	You Send Me	1969	20.00	50.00
Famous F-512	(M)	Cha-Cha-Cha	1969	20.00	50.00
		(The Famous albums above repackage the Keen material.)			

COOKIES, THE / LITTLE EVA / CAROLE KING

Dimension DLP-6001	(M)	The Dimension Dolls	1964	100.00	250.00

COOL, CALVIN, & THE SURF KNOBS

Charter CLP-103	(M)	The Surfer's Beat	1963	14.00	35.00
Charter CLS-103	(S)	The Surfer's Beat	1963	20.00	50.00

COOLEY, SPADE
Spade Cooley is a pseudonym for Don Cooley.

Columbia HL-9007	(10")	Sagebrush Swing	1949	100.00	250.00
Decca DL-5563	(10")	Dance-O-Rama #3	1955	200.00	400.00
Raynote R-5007	(M)	Fidoolin'	1959	20.00	50.00
Raynote RS-5007	(S)	Fidoolin'	1959	30.00	75.00
Roulette R-25145	(M)	Fidoolin'	1961	16.00	40.00
Roulette SR-25145	(M)	Fidoolin'	1961	20.00	50.00
		(Roulette 25145 is a reissue of Raynote 5007.)			

COOPER, ALICE
Alice Cooper has become pseudonymous with leader Vince Furnier. Refer to The Billion Dollar Babies.

Straight STS-1051	(S)	Pretties For You (White label promo)	1969	60.00	150.00
Straight STS-1051	(S)	Pretties For You (Yellow label)	1969	30.00	75.00
Straight STS-1051	(S)	Pretties For You (Pink label)	1969	20.00	50.00
Straight WS-1845	(S)	Easy Action (White label promo)	1970	40.00	100.00
Straight WS-1845	(S)	Easy Action (Pink label)	1970	20.00	50.00
		(Original covers for Straight 1845 have "Alice Cooper" in black.)			
Straight WS-1845	(S)	Easy Action (Pink label)	1970	12.00	30.00
		(Later covers have "Alice Cooper" iin white.)			
Straight WS-1883	(S)	Love It to Death (White label promo)	1971	40.00	100.00
Straight WS-1883	(S)	Love It to Death (Pink label)	1971	20.00	50.00
Warner Bros. WS-1883	(S)	Love It to Death	1971	12.00	30.00
		(On original covers for WS-1883 Cooper is gripping his cape in			
		such a manner that his right thumb has a phallic appearance.)			
Warner Bros. WS-1883	(S)	Love It to Death	197?	20.00	50.00
		(Some later covers have a white border around the front.)			
Warner Bros. BS-2567	(S)	Killer (With calendar and poster)	1971	12.00	30.00
Warner Bros. BS-2623	(DJ)	School's Out (With panties & report card)	1972	30.00	75.00
Warner Bros. BS-2623	(S)	School's Out (With panties)	1972	16.00	40.00
Warner Bros. BS4-2685	(Q)	Billion Dollar Babies	1974	10.00	25.00
Warner Bros. BS4-2748	(Q)	Muscle Of Love	1974	10.00	25.00
Warner Bros. K-56018	(S)	Muscle Of Love	1974	16.00	40.00
		(W.B. 56108 was made in the U.S. for export to the U.K.)			
Warner Bros. BS4-22803	(Q)	Alice Copper's Greatest Hits	1974	10.00	25.00
Warner Bros. PRO-789	(DJ)	The Alice Cooper Radio Show	1978	10.00	25.00
Mobile Fidelity MFSL-063	(S)	Welcome To My Nightmare	1980	12.00	35.00

COOPER, CLARENCE

Elektra EKL-27	(10")	Goin' Down The Road	195?	20.00	50.00

Label & Catalog #		Title	Year	VG+	NM

COOPER, JACKIE
| Dot DLP-3146 | (M) | The Movies Swing! | 1958 | 16.00 | 40.00 |
| Signature SM-1049 | (M) | Hennesey (Soundtrack) | 195? | 30.00 | 75.00 |

COOPER, LES, & THE SOUL ROCKERS
| Everlast ELP-202 | (M) | Wiggle Wobble | 1963 | 16.00 | 40.00 |

COOPER, STONEY & WILMA LEE
Harmony HL-7233	(M)	Sacred Songs	1960	12.00	30.00
Harmony HS-7233	(E)	Sacred Songs	1960	8.00	20.00
Harmony HL-11178	(M)	Sunny Side Of The Mountain	1966	8.00	20.00
Harmony HS-11178	(E)	Sunny Side Of The Mountain	1966	6.00	15.00
Hickory LPM-100	(M)	(There's A) Big Wheel	1960	10.00	25.00
Hickory LPM-106	(M)	Family Favorites	1962	10.00	25.00
Hickory LPM-112	(M)	Songs Of Inspiration	1962	10.00	25.00
Decca DL-4784	(M)	Wilma Lee And Stoney Cooper Sing	1966	8.00	20.00
Decca DL-74784	(S)	Wilma Lee And Stoney Cooper Sing	1966	10.00	25.00

COPAS, COWBOY
King 553	(M)	His All-Time Hits	1957	60.00	150.00
King 556	(M)	Favorite Scared Songs	1957	40.00	100.00
King 619	(M)	Sacred Songs	1960	40.00	100.00
King 714	(M)	Tragic Tales Of Love And Life	1960	40.00	100.00
King 720	(M)	Broken Hearted Melodies	1960	40.00	100.00
King 817	(M)	Country Gentleman Of Song	1963	20.00	50.00
King 824	(M)	As You Remember Cowboy Copas	1963	20.00	50.00
Starday SLP-118	(M)	All Time Country Music Great	1960	16.00	40.00
Starday SLP-133	(M)	Inspirational Songs	1961	16.00	40.00
Starday SLP-144	(M)	Cowboy Copas	1961	16.00	40.00
Starday SLP-157	(M)	Opry Star Spotlight On Cowboy Copas	1962	16.00	40.00
Starday SLP-175	(M)	Mr. Country Music	1962	16.00	40.00
Starday SLP-184	(M)	Songs That Made Him Famous	1962	16.00	40.00
Starday SLP-208	(M)	Country Music Entertainer #1	1963	16.00	40.00
Starday SLP-212	(M)	Beyond The Sunset	1963	16.00	40.00
Starday SLP-234	(M)	The Unforgettable Cowboy Copas	1963	16.00	40.00
Starday SLP-247	(M)	Star Of The Grand Ole Opry	1963	16.00	40.00
Starday SLP-268	(M)	Cowboy Copas And His Friends	1964	16.00	40.00
Starday SLP-317	(M)	The Legend Lives On	1965	12.00	30.00
Starday SLP-347	(M)	The Cowboy Copas Story (2 LPs)	1965	12.00	30.00
Starday SLP-371	(M)	Shake A Hand	1967	12.00	30.00
		— Starday albums above have yellow labels.—			

COPAS, COWBOY / HAWKSHAW HAWKINS
King 835	(M)	In Memory	1963	20.00	50.00
King 850	(M)	Legend Of Cowboy Copas And Hawkshaw Hawkins	1964	20.00	50.00
King 984	(M)	24 Great Hits	1966	12.00	30.00

COPAS, COWBOY / HAWKSHAW HAWKINS / PATSY CLINE
| Starday SLP-346 | (M) | Gone, But Not Forgotten (Yellow label) | 1965 | 16.00 | 40.00 |

COPPER PLATED INTEGRATED CIRCUIT, THE
| Command CS-945 | (S) | Plugged In Pop | 1969 | 10.00 | 25.00 |

CORBIN, HAROLD
| Roulette R-25079 | (M) | Soul Brother | 1961 | 8.00 | 20.00 |
| Roulette SR-25079 | (S) | Soul Brother | 1961 | 10.00 | 25.00 |

COREY, JILL
| Columbia CL-1095 | (M) | Sometime's I'm Happy, Sometime's I'm Blue | 1957 | 12.00 | 30.00 |

CORNELL, DON
Coral CRL-57133	(M)	For Teenagers Only!	1957	12.00	30.00
Dot DLP-3160	(M)	Don Cornell's Great Hits	1959	10.00	25.00
Dot DLP-26160	(S)	Don Cornell's Great Hits	1959	12.00	30.00
Signature SM-1001	(M)	Don Cornell Sings Love Songs	196?	8.00	20.00
Signature SS-1001	(S)	Don Cornell Sings Love Songs	196?	10.00	25.00

Dave "Baby" Cortez Clowney began his career as singer and organist for The Pearls. After "The Happy Organ" hit the national charts for Clock in 1959, RCA Victor leased the material and issued his first album. By 1963 he was on Chess, who recycled the photo of Dave for their album art. . .

Label & Catalog #		Title	Year	VG+	NM
CORNELLS, THE					
Garex LPGA-100	(M)	**Beach Bound**	1963	**300.00**	**600.00**
CORPORATION, THE					
Age of Aquarius 4150	(S)	**Get On Our Swing**	1969	10.00	25.00
Age of Aquarius 4250	(S)	**Hassles In My Mind**	1969	10.00	25.00
Capitol ST-175	(S)	**The Corporation**	1969	16.00	40.00
CORPUS					
Acorn 1001	(S)	**Creation: A Child**	1972	150.00	300.00
CORTEZ, DAVE "BABY"					
RCA Victor LPM-2099	(M)	**The Happy Organ**	1959	30.00	75.00
RCA Victor LSP-2099	(P)	**The Happy Organ**	1959	40.00	100.00
Clock C-331	(M)	**Dave "Baby" Cortez**	1960	14.00	35.00
Clock CS-331	(P)	**Dave "Baby" Cortez**	1960	20.00	50.00
Clock MG-20647C	(M)	**Dave "Baby" Cortez**	1960	14.00	35.00
Clock SR-60647C	(P)	**Dave "Baby" Cortez**	1960	20.00	50.00
Chess LP-1473	(M)	**Rinky Dink**	1962	20.00	50.00
Roulette R-25298	(M)	**Organ Shindig**	1965	8.00	20.00
Roulette SR-25298	(S)	**Organ Shindig**	1965	10.00	25.00
Roulette R-25315	(M)	**Tweety Pie**	1966	8.00	20.00
Roulette SR-25315	(S)	**Tweety Pie**	1966	10.00	25.00
Roulette R-25328	(M)	**In Orbit With Dave "Baby" Cortez**	1966	8.00	20.00
Roulette SR-25328	(S)	**In Orbit With Dave "Baby" Cortez**	1966	10.00	25.00
COSTA, DON					
ABC Paramount ABC-362	(M)	**Don Costa Conducts His 15 Hits**	1961	8.00	20.00
ABC Paramount ABCS-362	(S)	**Don Costa Conducts His 15 Hits**	1961	10.00	25.00
COSTELLO, ELVIS/ELVIS COSTELLO & THE ATTRACTIONS					
CBS CDN-10	(DJ)	**Live At The El Mocambo** (Canadian)	1978	60.00	150.00
		(Counterfeits have excessive tape hiss.)			
Columbia (No number)	(DJ)	**My Aim Is True /**			
		This Year's Model (Picture disc)	1979	20.00	50.00
Costello AS-847	(DJ)	**Taking Liberties** (Radio sampler)	1980	10.00	25.00
Columbia AS-958	(DJ)	**The Tom Snyder Interview**	1981	10.00	25.00
Columbia AS-1318	(DJ)	**Almost Blue**	1981	10.00	25.00
		(Radio sampler with introductions to each track by EC)			
Columbia HC-48157	(S)	**Imperial Bedroom** (Half-speed master)	1982	15.00	45.00
COSTELLO, ELVIS / NICK LOWE / MINK DeVILLE					
Columbia/Capitol AS-443	(DJ)	**Radio Radio** (Orange vinyl)	1979	10.00	25.00
COTTEN, ELIZABETH "LIBBA"					
Libba a singer, guitar player and writer of traditional Black American folk music.					
Folkways FG-3526	(M)	**Negro Folk Songs And Tunes**	195?	16.00	40.00
Folkways FTS-31003	(M)	**Elizabeth Cotten Vol. 2—Shake Sugaree**	1967	10.00	25.00
COTTON, JAMES/THE JAMES COTTON BLUES BAND					
Verve/Forecast FT-3023	(M)	**James Cotton Blues Band**	1967	8.00	20.00
Verve/Forecast FTS-3023	(S)	**James Cotton Blues Band**	1967	10.00	25.00
Verve/Forecast FTS-3038	(S)	**Pure Cotton**	1968	10.00	25.00
COTTON PICKERS, THE					
Philips PHM-200-025	(M)	**Country Guitar**	1962	8.00	20.00
Philips PHS-600-025	(S)	**Country Guitar**	1962	10.00	25.00
COUCH, ORVILLE					
Vee Jay LP-1087	(M)	**Hello Trouble**	1964	8.00	20.00
Vee Jay LPS-1087	(S)	**Hello Trouble**	1964	16.00	40.00
COUGAR, JOHN: *Refer to* **JOHN COUGAR MELLENCAMP**					
COUNT FIVE, THE					
Double Shot DSM-1001	(M)	**Psychotic Reaction**	1966	16.00	40.00
Double Shot DSS-5001	(E)	**Psychotic Reaction**	1966	12.00	30.00
		(Reproductions of Double Shot DSS-5001 exist.)			

Label & Catalog #		Title	Year	VG+	NM

COUNTRY ALL-STARS, THE
The All-Stars feature Chet Atkins, Jerry Byrd and Henry "Homer" Haynes.

RCA Victor LPM-3167	(10")	**String Dustin'**	1953	80.00	200.00

COUNTRY CUT-UPS, THE

Town House 1000	(M)	**The Country Cut-Ups Go To College**	195?	30.00	75.00

COUNTRY GENTLEMEN, THE
The original Country Gentlemen— Eddie Adcock, Jim Cox, John Duffey and Charlie Waller— were the first of the progressive bluegrass bands of the '50s and '60s. When Adcock and Duffey left in 1969 they were replaced by Bill Emerson and Jimmy Gaudreau, respectively. Personnel changes have continued since.

Starday SLP-109	(M)	**Traveling Dobro Blues**	1959	20.00	50.00
Starday SLP-174	(M)	**Bluegrass At Carnegie Hall**	1962	16.00	40.00
Starday SLP-311	(M)	**Songs Of The Pioneers**	1965	12.00	30.00
		— Starday albums above have yellow labels.—			
Cimarron 2001	(M)	**Songs Of The Pioneers**	1962	12.00	30.00
Mercury MG-20858	(M)	**Folk Session Inside**	1963	8.00	20.00
Mercury SR-60858	(S)	**Folk Session Inside**	1963	10.00	25.00

COUNTRY GENTLEMEN, THE
This Country Gentlemen is a Washington, D,C., based folk/bluegrass group.

Folkways FA-2409	(M)	**Country Songs, Old & New**	1960	10.00	25.00
Folkways FA-2410	(M)	**Folksongs & Bluegrass**	1960	10.00	25.00
Folkways FA-2411	(M)	**On The Road**	1960	10.00	25.00

COUNTRY GOSPEL-AIRES, THE

Starday SLP-105	(M)	**The Church Back Home** *(Yellow label)*	1959	16.00	40.00

COUNTRY JOE & THE FISH
Country Joe MacDonald with Fish Barry Melton, Chicken Hirsch, Bruce Barthol and David Cohen.

Vanguard VRS-9244	(M)	**Electric Music For The Mind And Body**	1967	20.00	50.00
Vanguard VSD-79244	(S)	**Electric Music For The Mind And Body**	1967	16.00	40.00
		— Vanguard albums above have black labels.—			
Vanguard VRS-9244	(M)	**Electric Music For The Mind And Body**	1967	10.00	25.00
Vanguard VSD-79244	(S)	**Electric Music For The Mind And Body**	1967	8.00	20.00
Vanguard VRS-9266	(M)	**I-Feel-Like-I'm-Fixin'-To-Die**	1967	10.00	25.00
Vanguard VSD-79266	(S)	**I-Feel-Like-I'm-Fixin'-To-Die**	1967	8.00	20.00
		(Originally issued with a fold-open, "Fish game" poster, priced separately below.)			
Vanguard		**I-Feel-Like-I'm-Fixin'-To-Die Fish Game**	1967	8.00	20.00
		— Vanguard albums above have gold labels.—			

COUNTRY JOE/JOE McDONALD

Custom Fidelity CFS-2348	(S)	**Joe McDonald**	1968	200.00	400.00
		(CFS-2348 was recorded in 1964 and 200 copies were pressed in 1968 in plain jackets solely for Joe's use.)			

COUNTRY WEATHER

(No label)	(S)	**Country Weather** *(One-sided demo)*	1968	60.00	150.00

COUSIN WILBUR

C.W. LP-100	(M)	**The Cousin Wilbur Show**	195?	24.00	60.00

COVAY, DON

Atlantic 8104	(M)	**Mercy**	1965	16.00	40.00
Atlantic SD-8104	(S)	**Mercy**	1965	20.00	50.00
Atlantic 8120	(M)	**See Saw**	1966	16.00	40.00
Atlantic SD-8120	(S)	**See Saw**	1966	20.00	50.00
Atlantic SD-8237	(S)	**The House Of Blue Lights**	1969	10.00	25.00

COWARD, NOEL, & GERTRUDE LAWRENCE
For more on Mr. Coward refer to Mary Martin & Noel Coward.

RCA Victor LPM-1156	(M)	**Noel And Gertie**	1955	12.00	30.00

COWSILLS, THE

London 587	(S)	**On My Side**	1971	12.00	30.00

Label & Catalog #		Title	Year	VG+	NM
COX, DANNY					
Pioneer 2125	(S)	**Sunny**	1966	12.00	30.00
Together ZR-1011	(S)	**Birth Announcement** (2 LPs)	1970	12.00	30.00
		(ZR-1001 was produced by Gary Usher.)			
COXAN'S ARMY					
Coxan's Army features Pat Benatar.					
(Label unknown)	(S)	**Coxan's Army**	1972	150.00	300.00
CRADDOCK, BILLY "CRASH"					
King 912	(M)	**I'm Tore Up**	1964	40.00	100.00
CRAIN, JIMMY					
Ray-O LP-2005	(M)	**Miles To Go**	196?	50.00	125.00
CRAMER, FLOYD					
Refer to Chet Atkins, Floyd Cramer & Boots Randolph; Chet Atkins, Floyd Cramer & Danny Davis.					
MGM E-3502	(M)	**That Honky-Tonk Piano**	1957	16.00	40.00
CRANE, BOB					
Epic LN-246224	(M)	**The Funny Side Of TV**	1967	16.00	40.00
Epic BN-26224	(S)	**The Funny Side Of TV**	1967	20.00	50.00
CRANE, BOB, & PAT BUTTRAM					
KNX 1070	(M)	**Laffter, Sweet And ZProfane**	196?	12.00	30.00
CRAWFORD, JOAN					
Universal Int. DCLA-1086	(DJ)	**Personal Interview With**			
		The Star Of "Female On The Beach"	195?	40.00	100.00
		(One-sided interview on red vinyl)			
CRAWFORD, JOHNNY					
Del-Fi DFLP-1220	(M)	**The Captivating Johnny Crawford**	1962	16.00	40.00
Del-Fi DFLP-1223	(M)	**A Young Man's Fancy**	1963	12.00	30.00
Del-Fi DFST-1223	(S)	**A Young Man's Fancy**	1963	16.00	40.00
Del-Fi DFLP-1224	(M)	**Rumors**	1963	12.00	30.00
Del-Fi DFST-1224	(S)	**Rumors**	1963	16.00	40.00
Del-Fi DFLP-1229	(M)	**Johnny Crawford: His Greatest Hits**	1963	12.00	30.00
Del-Fi DFST-1229	(S)	**Johnny Crawford: His Greatest Hits**	1963	16.00	40.00
Del-Fi DFLP-1248	(M)	**Greatest Hits, Volume 2**	1964	8.00	20.00
Del-Fi DFST-1248	(S)	**Greatest Hits, Volume 2**	1964	12.00	30.00
Guest Star GS-1470	(M)	**Johnny Crawford**	196?	8.00	20.00
Guest Star GSS-1470	(S)	**Johnny Crawford**	196?	10.00	25.00
Supreme S-210	(S)	**Songs From "The Restless Ones"**	196?	12.00	30.00
CRAYTON, PEE WEE					
Crown CLP-5175	(M)	**Pee Wee Crayton**	1959	40.00	100.00
CREAM					
Cream was Ginger Baker, Jack Bruce, and Eric Clapton with Felix Pappalardi.					
Atco 33-206	(M)	**Fresh Cream** (Without "I Feel Free.)	1967	16.00	40.00
Atco SD-33-206	(S)	**Fresh Cream** (Without "I Feel Free.)	1967	12.00	30.00
Atco 33-206	(M)	**Fresh Cream** (Includes "I Feel Free")	1967	10.00	25.00
Atco SD-33-206	(S)	**Fresh Cream** (Includes "I Feel Free")	1967	8.00	20.00
Atco 33-232	(M)	**Disraeli Gears**	1967	20.00	50.00
Atco SD-33-232	(S)	**Disraeli Gears**	1967	12.00	30.00
Atco 2-700	(M)	**Wheels Of Fire** (2 LPs. White label promo)	1968	40.00	100.00
Atco SD-2-700	(S)	**Wheels Of Fire** (2 LPs)	1968	16.00	40.00
		(Original covers have a silver foil-like backing.)			
Atco SD-7001	(S)	**Goodbye** (With bonus poster)	1969	16.00	40.00
Atco SD-7001	(S)	**Goodbye** (Without the poster)	1969	12.00	30.00
		—Atco stereo albums above have purple & brown labels.—			
Atco SD-33-291	(S)	**Best Of Cream** (White label promo)	1969	20.00	50.00
RSO-015	(DJ)	**Classic Cuts** (2 LPs)	1975	16.00	40.00
Mobile Fidelity MFSL-066	(S)	**Wheels Of Fire**	1980	15.00	45.00
CREAM / THE NEW YORK ROCK 'N' ROLL ENSEMBLE					
Atco TLST-119/20	(DJ)	**Wheels Of Fire /**			
		The New York Rock 'N' Roll Ensemble	1968	30.00	75.00

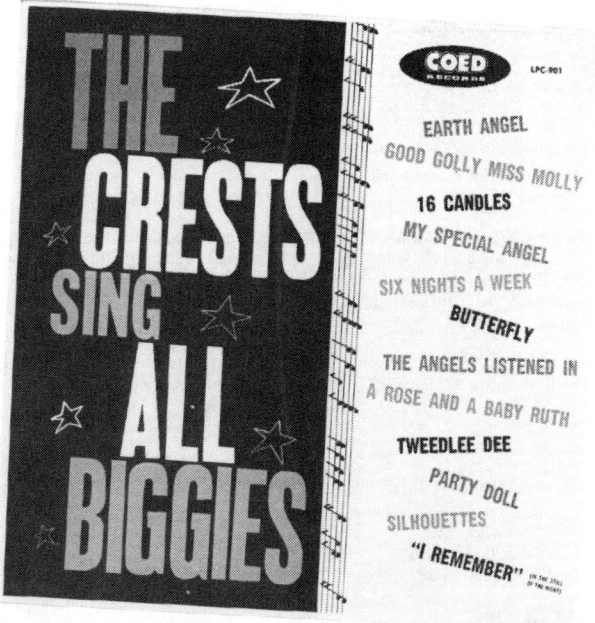

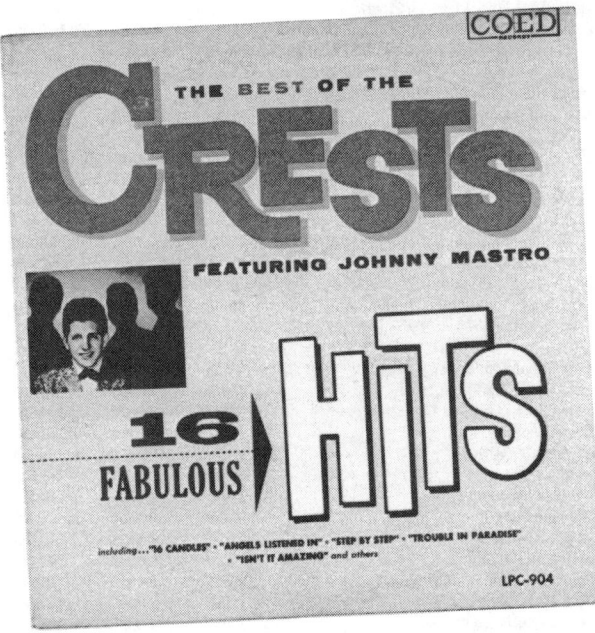

The Crests featuring Johnny Maestro are one of the few white groups that collectors of '50s rhythm'n blues group vocal records take to with great affinity, a testament to the sincerity conveyed by the young Maestro's pipes. Their two albums on Coed are both difficult to find in collectible condition. Neither are known to have been recorded in stereo, but a stereo cover for 904 was found but it contained a mono album. I would assume that the disc intended for such a jacket (and how come there's only one stereo jacket?) would be rechanneled stereo. Nonetheless, should a stereo record be found, it would easily fetch four figures as one of the rarest albums in the hobby.

Label & Catalog #		Title	Year	VG+	NM

CREAM / THE VANILLA FUDGE

| Atco TLST-141/2 | (DJ) | Goodbye / Rock'n Roll | 1969 | 30.00 | 75.00 |
| | | (Atco 119/20 and 141/2 above are samplers with one side devoted to each artist's latest album.) | | | |

CREATION OF SUNLIGHT

| Windi 1001 | (S) | Creation Of Sunlight | 196? | 300.00 | 500.00 |

CREEDENCE CLEARWATER/CREEDENCE CLEARWATER REVIVAL

CCR was John and Tom Fogerty, Stu Cook and Doug Clifford, who originally recorded as The Golliwogs. Note: CCR albums on Liberty— other titles may exist— were manufactured for either record club or foreign distribution and have suggested Near Mint values of $50-100 each.)

Fantasy F-8382	(S)	Creedence Clearwater Revival	1968	10.00	25.00
		(Original pressings of F-8382 do not have a blurb for "Suzie Q" on the front cover.)			
Mobile Fidelity MFSL-037	(S)	Cosmo's Factory	1979	25.00	75.00
Sweet Thunder 13	(S)	Green River	198?	30.00	90.00

CREME SODA

| Trinity CST-11 | (S) | Tricky Zingers (Group photo cover) | 1975 | 40.00 | 100.00 |
| Trinity CST-11 | (S) | Tricky Zingers (Plain white cover) | 1976 | 20.00 | 50.00 |

CRESCENDOS, THE

| Guest Star G-1453 | (M) | Oh Julie | 196? | 20.00 | 50.00 |
| Guest Star GS-1453 | (E) | Oh Julie | 196? | 10.00 | 25.00 |

CRESTS, THE

The Crests feature Johnny Maestro. Refer to The Brooklyn Bridge.

Coed LPC-901	(M)	The Crests Sing All The Biggies (Red label)	1960		See below
		(Red label pressings of Coed 901 used as audition copies are rare with a suggested Near Mint value of $1,500-2,500.)			
Coed LPC-901	(M)	The Crests Sing All The Biggies	1960	125.00	300.00
Coed LPC-904	(M)	The Best Of The Crests	1961	150.00	400.00
		(A single stereo cover of Coed 904 was found with a mono record inside. Should a stereo copy be found, it would have a suggested value of $1,000-5,000 in virtually any playable condition.)			
Post 3000	(E)	The Crests Sing	196?	20.00	50.00
		(Post 3000 is a reissue of Coed 904.)			

CRESWELL, GRACE

Grace Creswell is a guitar, autoharp and dulcimer player and singer of traditional folk songs.

| Rebel 411 | (M) | Tragic Ballads | 1959 | 12.00 | 30.00 |

CREW CUTS, THE

Mercury MG-25200	(10")	The Crew Cuts On The Campus	1956	30.00	75.00
Mercury MG-20067	(M)	The Crew Cuts Go Longhair	1956	20.00	50.00
Mercury MG-20140	(M)	The Crew Cuts On The Campus	1957	20.00	50.00
Mercury MG-20143	(M)	Crew Cut Capers	1957	20.00	50.00
Mercury MG-20144	(M)	Rock And Roll Bash	1957	30.00	75.00
Mercury MG-20199	(M)	Music Ala Carte	1957	20.00	50.00
RCA Victor LPM-1933	(M)	Surprise Package	1958	14.00	35.00
RCA Victor LSP-1933	(S)	Surprise Package	1958	20.00	50.00
RCA Victor LPM-2037	(M)	The Crew Cuts Sing	1959	14.00	35.00
RCA Victor LSP-2037	(S)	The Crew Cuts Sing	1959	20.00	50.00
RCA Victor LPM-2067	(M)	You Must Have Been A Beautiful Baby	1960	14.00	35.00
RCA Victor LSP-2067	(S)	You Must Have Been A Beautiful Baby	1960	20.00	50.00
RCA Victor PR-102	(DJ)	The Crew Cuts Sing Out!	1960	10.00	25.00
RCA Victor CR-129	(DJ)	The Crew Cuts Have A Ball + Bowling Tips	1960	10.00	25.00
Wing MGW-12145	(M)	The Crew Cuts On The Campus	1962	8.00	20.00
Wing MGW-12177	(M)	The Crew Cuts	1962	8.00	20.00
Wing MGW-12180	(M)	High School Favorites	1962	8.00	20.00
Wing MGW-12195	(M)	The Crew Cuts Sing The Masters	1962	8.00	20.00
Camay CA-1002	(M)	The Crew Cuts Sing Folk	196?	8.00	20.00
Camay CA-3002	(S)	The Crew Cuts Sing Folk	196?	10.00	25.00

CREWE, BOB/THE BOB CREWE GENERATION

Bob Crewe, as producer, writer and performer, was the "fifth" Four Season.

| Warwick W-2009 | (M) | Kicks | 1960 | 10.00 | 25.00 |
| Warwick W-2009ST | (S) | Kicks | 1960 | 20.00 | 50.00 |

When Jerry Allison, Charles Hardin Holley, Joel Mauldin and Nikki Sullivan signed with Brunswick, their contract allowed them to record as a group, The Crickets, for the parent label, and their singer, guitarist and songwriter, known professionally as Buddy Holly, to record as a solo for their Coral subsidiary. The Chirping Crickets was their sole album released during Buddy's life, cut short by the now legendary airplane crash in the winter of 1959 that also took the lives of Ritchie Valens and The Big Bopper ("the day the music died"). In Style With The Crickets was the first album the trio made following their leader's death; the rare stereo version is listed here for the first time.

Label & Catalog #		Title	Year	VG+	NM
Warwick W-2034	(M)	**Crazy In The Heart**	1961	10.00	25.00
Warwick W-2034ST	(S)	**Crazy In The Heart**	1961	20.00	50.00
Philips PHM-200-150	(M)	**All The Song Hits Of The Four Seasons' Hits**	1964	10.00	25.00
Philips PHS-600-150	(S)	**All The Song Hits Of The Four Seasons' Hits**	1964	12.00	30.00
Philips PHM-200-238	(M)	**Bob Crewe Plays The Four Seasons' Hits**	1967	8.00	20.00
Philips PHS-600-238	(S)	**Bob Crewe Plays The Four Seasons' Hits**	1967	10.00	25.00

CRICKETS, THE
The Crickets featured Buddy Holly; refer to Holly for more listings. Original members were Jerry Allison, Don Guess and Sonny Curtis; later members included Tommy Allsup, Glen Hardin, and Niki Sullivan. Refer to Bobby Vee; The Ventures.

Coral CRL-57320	(M)	**In Style With The Crickets** *(Blue label promo)*	1960	300.00	600.00
Coral CRL-57320	(M)	**In Style With The Crickets**	1960	80.00	200.00
Coral CRL-757320	(S)	**In Style With The Crickets**	1960	150.00	300.00
		("Deborah," "When You Ask About Love," "Time Will Tell," "I Fought The Law," and "Love's Made A Fool Of You" are rechanneled.)			
Liberty LRP-3272	(M)	**Something Old, Something New**	1962	40.00	100.00
Liberty LST-7272	(S)	**Something Old, Something New**	1962	60.00	150.00
Liberty LRP-7351	(M)	**California Sun**	1964	30.00	75.00
Liberty LST-7351	(S)	**California Sun**	1964	40.00	100.00

CRISS, PETER
Refer to Chelsea; Kiss.

Casablanca NBLP-7240	(S)	**Out Of Control**	1980	10.00	25.00

CRITTERS, THE

Kapp KL-1485	(M)	**Younger Girl**	1966	14.00	35.00
Kapp KS-3485	(S)	**Younger Girl**	1966	16.00	40.00

CRITTERS, THE / THE YOUNG RASCALS / LOU CHRISTIE

Boutique CA-1079	(M)	**A Taste Of The Critters & The Young Rascals & Lou Christie**	1966	16.00	40.00

CROCE, JIM

Croce *(No number)*	(S)	**Faucets**	1966	150.00	300.00
Capitol SMAS-315	(S)	**Jim And Ingrid Croce**	1969	20.00	50.00
Mobile Fidelity MFSL-079	(S)	**You Don't Mess Around With Jim**	1980	12.00	35.00

CROSBY, BING
Due to Der Bingle's prolific career, his albums are listed chronologically by label with no interruptions. Refer to Al Jolson; The Reprise Repertory Theatre; Frank Sinatra.

Decca DL-5000	(10")	**Hits From Musical Comedies**	1949	20.00	50.00
Decca DL-5001	(10")	**Jerome Kern Songs**	1949	20.00	50.00
Decca DL-5010	(10")	**Stephen Foster Songs**	1949	20.00	50.00
Decca DL-5011	(10")	**El Bingo**	1949	20.00	50.00
Decca DL-5019	(10")	**Merry Christmas**	1949	20.00	50.00
Decca DL-5020	(10")	**Christmas Greetings**	1949	20.00	50.00
Decca DL-5028	(10")	**Auld Lang Syne**	1950	20.00	50.00
Decca DL-5037	(10")	**St. Patrick's Day**	1950	20.00	50.00
Decca DL-5039	(10")	**St. Valentine's Day**	1950	20.00	50.00
Decca DL-5042	(10")	**Blue Skies**	1950	20.00	50.00
Decca DL-5052	(10")	**Going My Way / The Bells Of St. Mary's** *(Soundtrack)*	1950	40.00	100.00
Decca DL-5060	(10")	**Showboat Selections** *(Soundtrack)*	1950	30.00	75.00
Decca DL-5063	(10")	**Don't Fence Me In**	1950	20.00	50.00
Decca DL-5064	(10")	**Cole Porter Songs**	1950	20.00	50.00
Decca DL-5081	(10")	**Songs By Gershwin**	1950	20.00	50.00
Decca DL-5092	(10")	**Holiday Inn** *(Soundtrack)*	1950	30.00	75.00
Decca DL-5102	(10")	**Blue Of The Night**	1950	20.00	50.00
Decca DL-5105	(10")	**Blue Of The Night**	1950	20.00	50.00
Decca DL-5107	(10")	**Cowboy Songs**	1950	20.00	50.00
Decca DL-5119	(10")	**Drifting And Dreaming**	1950	20.00	50.00
Decca DL-5122	(10")	**Hawaiian Songs**	1950	20.00	50.00
Decca DL-5126	(10")	**Stardust**	1950	20.00	50.00
Decca DL-5129	(10")	**Cowboy Songs, Volume 2**	1950	20.00	50.00
Decca DL-5207	(10")	**South Pacific**	1950	20.00	50.00
Decca DL-5220	(10")	**Bing Sings Hits**	1950	20.00	50.00
Decca DL-5272	(10")	**Top O' The Morning**	1950	20.00	50.00
Decca DL-5284	(10")	**Mr. Music**	1950	20.00	50.00

After der Bingle had settled down and become a ubiquitous part of the American landscape, his gift and his achievements were all but forgotten. Will Friedwald claims that Crosby created, along with that other perennially underestimated singer, Louis Armstrong, "virtually the entire vocabulary of twentieth-century vocal music" (Jazz Singing, Quartet Books, 1990, page 48). These two Decca 12" albums show a mature Bing quite at home on the range (both covers were shot at the same time) and are hard to find. Again, another artist who does not receive his due from collectors.

Label & Catalog #		Title	Year	VG+	NM
Decca DL-5298	(10")	Hits From Broadway Shows	1951	20.00	50.00
Decca DL-5299	(10")	Favorite Hawaiian Songs	1951	20.00	50.00
Decca DL-5302	(10")	Go West, Young Man	1951	20.00	50.00
Decca DL-5310	(10")	Way Back Home	1951	20.00	50.00
Decca DL-5323	(10")	Bing And The Dixieland Bands	1951	20.00	50.00
Decca DL-5326	(10")	Yours Is My Heart Alone	1951	20.00	50.00
Decca DL-5331	(10")	Country Style	1951	20.00	50.00
Decca DL-5340	(10")	Down Memory Lane	1951	20.00	50.00
Decca DL-5343	(10")	Down Memory Lane, Volume 2	1951	20.00	50.00
Decca DL-5351	(10")	Beloved Hymns	1951	20.00	50.00
Decca DL-5355	(10")	Bing Sings Victor Herbert	1951	20.00	50.00
Decca DL-5403	(10")	When Irish Eyes Are Smiling	1952	20.00	50.00
Decca DL-5417	(10")	Just For You	1952	20.00	50.00
Decca DL-5444	(10")	The Road To Bali (Soundtrack)	1952	30.00	75.00
Decca DL-5499	(10")	Song Hits Of Paris/Le Bing	1953	20.00	50.00
Decca DL-5508	(10")	Some Fine Old Chestnuts	1954	20.00	50.00
Decca DL-5520	(10")	Bing Sings The Hits	1954	20.00	50.00
Decca DL-5556	(10")	Country Girl	1953	20.00	50.00
Decca DL-6000	(10")	The Small One /			
		The Happy Prince (Soundtrack)	1950	30.00	75.00
Decca DL-6001	(10")	Ichabod Crane	1951	20.00	50.00
Decca DL-6008	(10")	Collector's Classics	1951	20.00	50.00
Decca DL-6009	(10")	Two For Tonight	1951	20.00	50.00
Decca DL-6010	(10")	Rhythm On The Range (Soundtrack)	1951	40.00	100.00
Decca DL-6011	(10")	Waikiki Wedding (Soundtrack)	1951	30.00	75.00
Decca DL-6012	(10")	Collector's Classics	1951	20.00	50.00
Decca DL-6013	(10")	The Star Maker (Soundtrack)	1951	30.00	75.00
Decca DL-6014	(10")	Collector's Classics	1951	20.00	50.00
Decca DL-6015	(10")	The Road To Singapore (Soundtrack)	1951	30.00	75.00
		—Decca 6008-6015 are a series of "Collector's Classics" from Bing's '30s recordings; soundtrack titles are listed where known.—			
Decca DX-151	(M)	A Musical Autobiography (5 LP box)	1954	60.00	150.00
		(The five albums were released separately as Decca 8702-8706.)			
Decca DX-152	(M)	Old Masters (3 LPs)	1954	60.00	150.00
Decca DL-8020	(M)	A Man Without A Country	1954	16.00	40.00
Decca DL-8083	(M)	White Christmas (Soundtrack)	1954	20.00	50.00
Decca DL-8110	(M)	Lullabye Time	1955	16.00	40.00
Decca DL-8128	(M)	Merry Christmas	1955	16.00	40.00
Decca DL-8207	(M)	Shillelaghs And Shamrocks	1956	16.00	40.00
Decca DL-8210	(M)	Home On The Range	1956	16.00	40.00
Decca DL-8262	(M)	When Irish Eyes Are Smiling	1956	16.00	40.00
Decca DL-8268	(M)	Drifting And Dreaming	1956	16.00	40.00
Decca DL-8269	(M)	Blue Hawaii	1956	16.00	40.00
Decca DL-8272	(M)	High Tor (Soundtrack)	1956	200.00	400.00
Decca DL-8318	(M)	Anything Goes (Soundtrack)	1956	16.00	40.00
Decca DL-8352	(M)	Songs I Wish I Had Sung	1956	16.00	40.00
Decca DL-8365	(M)	Twilight On The Trail	1956	16.00	40.00
Decca DL-8374	(M)	Some Fine Old Chestnuts	1957	16.00	40.00
Decca DL-8419	(M)	A Christmas Sing Around The World	1957	16.00	40.00
Decca DL-8493	(M)	Bing And The Dixieland Bands	1957	16.00	40.00
Decca DL-8575	(M)	New Tricks	1957	16.00	40.00
Decca DL-8687	(M)	Around The World	1958	16.00	40.00
Decca DL-8702	(M)	A Musical Autobiography 1927-1934	1958	16.00	40.00
Decca DL-8703	(M)	A Musical Autobiography 1934-1941	1958	16.00	40.00
Decca DL-8704	(M)	A Musical Autobiography 1941-1944	1958	16.00	40.00
Decca DL-8705	(M)	A Musical Autobiography 1944-1947	1958	16.00	40.00
Decca DL-8706	(M)	A Musical Autobiography 1947-1953	1958	16.00	40.00
Decca DL-8780	(M)	Bing In Paris	1958	16.00	40.00
Decca DL-8781	(M)	That Christmas Feeling	1958	16.00	40.00
		—Decca albums above have black labels with silver print.—			
Decca DL-8846	(M)	In A Little Spanish Town	1959	12.00	30.00
Decca DL-4086	(M)	My Golden Favorites	1961	10.00	25.00
Decca DL-4250	(M)	Easy To Remember	1962	10.00	25.00
Decca DL-4251	(M)	Pennies From Heaven	1962	10.00	25.00
Decca DL-4252	(M)	Pocketful Of Dreams	1962	10.00	25.00
Decca DL-4253	(M)	East Side Of Heaven	1962	10.00	25.00
Decca DL-4254	(M)	The Road Begins	1962	10.00	25.00
Decca DL-4255	(M)	Only Forever	1962	10.00	25.00
Decca DL-4256	(M)	Holiday Inn	1962	10.00	25.00

Label & Catalog #		Title	Year	VG+	NM
Decca DL-4257	(M)	**Swinging On A Star**	1962	10.00	25.00
Decca DL-4258	(M)	**Accentuate The Positive**	1962	10.00	25.00
Decca DL-4259	(M)	**Blue Skies**	1962	10.00	25.00
Decca DL-4260	(M)	**But Beautiful**	1962	10.00	25.00
Decca DL-4261	(M)	**Sunshine Cake**	1962	10.00	25.00
Decca DL-4262	(M)	**Cool Of The Evening**	1962	10.00	25.00
Decca DL-4263	(M)	**Zing A Little Zong**	1962	10.00	25.00
Decca DL-4264	(M)	**Anything Goes**	1962	10.00	25.00
		— Decca 4250-4264 above are known as "Bing's Hollywood Series" and			
		collect a variety of his earlier soundtrack recordings onto LP.—			
Decca DL-4281	(M)	**Holiday In Europe**	1962	8.00	20.00
Decca DL-74281	(S)	**Holiday In Europe**	1962	10.00	25.00
Decca DL-4283	(M)	**The Small One**	1962	8.00	20.00
Decca DL-74283	(S)	**The Small One**	1962	10.00	25.00
Decca DL-4415	(M)	**Songs Everybody Knows**	1964	8.00	20.00
Decca DL-74415	(S)	**Songs Everybody Knows**	1964	10.00	25.00
Decca DX-184	(M)	**The Best Of Bing Crosby** *(2 LPs)*	1965	8.00	20.00
Decca DXSB-184	(P)	**The Best Of Bing Crosby** *(2 LPs)*	1965	8.00	20.00
		— Decca albums above have black labels with "Mfrd By Decca" beneath the rainbow.—			
Columbia CL-6027	(10")	**Crosby Classics, Volume 1**	1949	20.00	50.00
Columbia CL-6105	(10")	**Crosby Classics, Volume 2**	1950	20.00	50.00
Columbia CL-2502	(10")	**Der Bingle**	1955	16.00	40.00
Brunswick BL-58000	(10")	**Bing Crosby, Volume 1**	1950	20.00	50.00
Brunswick BL-58001	(10")	**Bing Crosby, Volume 2**	1950	20.00	50.00
Brunswick BL-54005	(M)	**The Voice Of Bing In The 30s**	1955	10.00	25.00
"X" XLVA-4250	(M)	**Young Bing Crosby**	1955	20.00	50.00
Verve V-2020	(M)	**Bing Sings Whilst Bregman Swings**	1956	20.00	50.00
		— Verve albums above have "Verve Records Inc" on the bottom of the label.—			
Verve V-2020	(M)	**Bing Sings Whilst Bregman Swings**	1961	10.00	25.00
		— Verve albums above have "MGM Records" on the bottom of the label.—			
Capitol W-750	(M)	**High Society** *(Soundtrack)*	1956	16.00	40.00
United Arts. UAL-4001	(M)	**Paris Holiday** *(Soundtrack)*	1958	14.00	35.00
Grand Award 298:20	(M)	**Ali Baba And The Forty Thieves**	1957	8.00	20.00
Grand Award 298:21	(M)	**Christmas Story**	1957	8.00	20.00
RCA Victor LPM-1473	(M)	**Bing With A Beat**	1957	16.00	40.00
RCA Victor LPM-2071	(M)	**Young Bing Crosby**	1959	16.00	40.00
RCA Victor LPM-2314	(M)	**High Time** *(Soundtrack)*	1960	20.00	50.00
RCA Victor LSP-2314	(S)	**High Time** *(Soundtrack)*	1960	30.00	75.00
Liberty LOM-16002	(M)	**The Road To Hong Kong** *(Soundtrack)*	1962	14.00	35.00
Liberty LOS-17002	(S)	**The Road To Hong Kong** *(Soundtrack)*	1962	20.00	50.00

CROSBY, BING, & THE ANDREWS SISTERS

Decca DL-5019	(10")	**Merry Christmas**	1949	20.00	50.00

CROSBY, BING, & LOUIS ARMSTRONG

MGM E-3882	(M)	**Bing And Satch**	1960	16.00	40.00
MGM SE-3882	(E)	**Bing And Satch**	1960	8.00	20.00

CROSBY, BING, & ROSEMARY CLOONEY

RCA Victor LPM-1854	(M)	**Fancy Meeting You Here**	1958	12.00	30.00
RCA Victor LSP-1854	(S)	**Fancy Meeting You Here**	1958	20.00	50.00
Capitol T-2300	(M)	**That Travelin' Two-Beat**	1965	10.00	25.00
Capitol ST-2300	(S)	**That Travelin' Two-Beat**	1965	12.00	30.00

CROSBY, BING, & CONNEE BOSWELL

Decca DL-5390	(10")	**Bing And Connee**	1951	20.00	50.00

CROSBY, BING / WALTER HUSTON

Decca DL-9109	(M)	**Bing Crosby Read "Ichabod Crane" /**			
		Walter Huston Reads "Rip Van Winkle"	1959	10.00	25.00

CROSBY, STILLS & NASH
David Crosby of The Byrds, Stephen Stills of The Buffalo Springfield, and Graham Nash of The Hollies.

Nautilus NR-48	(S)	**Crosby, Stills & Nash**	1982	20.00	60.00

CROSBY, STILLS, NASH & YOUNG
The aforementioned trio plus ex-Buffalo Springfield Neil Young.

Atlantic 7200	(M)	**Deja Vu** *(White label promo)*	1970	60.00	150.00
Atlantic SD-7200	(S)	**Deja Vu** *(White label promo)*	1970	20.00	50.00

Label & Catalog #		Title	Year	VG+	NM
Atlantic 2-902	(M)	**4 Way Street** *(2 LPs. White label promo)*	1973	40.00	100.00
Atlantic SD-2-902	(S)	**4 Way Street** *(2 LPs. White label promo)*	1973	24.00	60.00
Atlantic PR-18102	(DJ)	**A Rap With C, S, N & Y** *(Interview)*	1973	20.00	50.00
Atlantic PR-165	(DJ)	**Celebration/CSNY Month** *(Sampler)*	1973	20.00	50.00
Mobile Fidelity MFSL-088	(S)	**Deja Vu**	1983	50.00	150.00
CROSSFIRES, THE					
Strand SL-1083	(M)	**Limbo Rock**	1963	8.00	20.00
Strand SLS-1083	(S)	**Limbo Rock**	1963	10.00	25.00
CROSSRODE					
Strawberry Jamm 801	(S)	**Crossrode**	1980	30.00	75.00
CROTHERS, SCATMAN					
Tops 1511	(M)	**Rock 'N Roll With Scatman**	1956	40.00	100.00
Craftsman 8036	(M)	**Gone With Scatman**	1960	16.00	40.00
CRUDUP, ARTHUR "BIG BOY"					
Fire 103	(M)	**Mean Ol' Frisco**	1960	500.00	1,000.00
Delmark DS-614	(S)	**Look On Yonders Wall**	1969	10.00	25.00
Delmark DS-621	(S)	**Crudup's Mood**	1969	10.00	25.00
RCA Victor LVP-573	(M)	**Father Of Rock And Roll**	1971	8.00	20.00

CRUM, SIMON
Simon Crum is a pseudonym for Ferlin Husky.

Capitol T-1880	(M)	**The Unpredictable Simon Crum**	1963	30.00	75.00
Capitol ST-1880	(S)	**The Unpredictable Simon Crum**	1963	50.00	100.00

CRUZ, ALONZO

Cook Laboratories 5019	(M)	**Mexican Love Songs** **By The Blind Troubador Of Oaxaca**	195?	16.00	40.00

CRYAN' SHAMES, THE
The Cryan' Shames feature Isaac Guillory.

Columbia CL-2589	(M)	**Sugar And Spice**	1966	10.00	25.00
Columbia CS-9389	(S)	**Sugar And Spice**	1966	12.00	30.00
		("Sugar & Spice," "Ben Franklin's Almanac," "We Could Be Happy" and "I Wanna Meet You" are rechanneled on this album.)			
Columbia CL-9586	(M)	**A Scratch In The Sky**	1967	8.00	20.00
Columbia CS-9586	(S)	**A Scratch In The Sky**	1967	10.00	25.00
		— Columbia albums above have red labels with "360 Sound" on the bottom.—			

CRYSTAL HAZE

(No label)	(S)	**Crystal Haze**	1977	30.00	75.00

CRYSTAL CIRCUS
Crystal Circus features the former lead singer of The Strawberry Alarm Clock.

All-American	(S)	**Crystal Circus** *(Issued without a cocer)*	197?	300.00	500.00
		(The printed labels read "Strawberry SAC" with new labels that read "Crystal Circus" pasted over the old..)			

CRYSTALS, THE
The Crystals were produced by Phil Spector.

Philles PHLP-4000	(M)	**Twist Uptown** *(White label promo)*	1962	600.00	1,200.00
Philles PHLP-4000	(M)	**Twist Uptown** *(Blue label)*	1962	250.00	500.00
Philles T-90722	(M)	**Twist Uptown** *(Capitol Record Club)*	1963	300.00	600.00
Philles DT-90722	(E)	**Twist Uptown** *(Capitol Record Club)*	1963	900.00	1,500.00
Philles PHLP-4001	(M)	**He's A Rebel** *(White label promo)*	1963	600.00	1,200.00
Philles PHLP-4001	(M)	**He's A Rebel** *(Blue label)*	1963	200.00	400.00
Philles PHLP-4003	(M)	**The Greatest Hits** *(Blue label)*	1963	350.00	700.00

CUEVAS, LOLITA

Folkways FP-811	(10")	**Haitian Folk Songs**	1953	20.00	50.00
Folkways FW-6811	(10")	**Haitian Folk Songs**	1953	20.00	50.00

CUGAT, XAVIER

Columbia CL-110	(10")	**Cugat's Rhumba**	1949	20.00	50.00
Columbia ML-6005	(10")	**Cugat's Rhumba**	1949	20.00	50.00
Columbia ML-6036	(10")	**Rhumba With Cugat**	1949	20.00	50.00

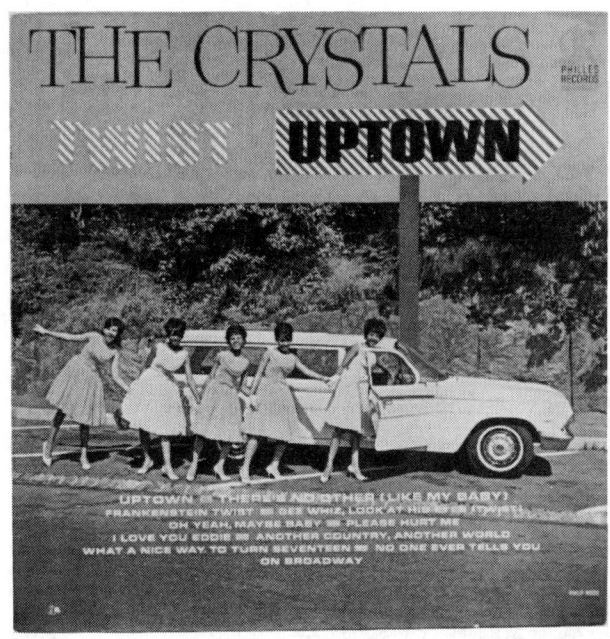

Barbara Alston, Lala Brooks, Dee Dee Kennibrew, Mary Thomas and Patricia Wright, better known as The Crystals, fared far better than the average protege of Phil Spector, realizing two full albums under Uncle Phil's magic production wand. As with all Philles albums, Spector cut post-production costs as much as possible, using low quality (read "cheap") vinyl and plating on all his product. Decades later, it is almost a miracle to find any of the Philles albums in a condition that plays without surface noise. (Note that two of the group's biggest hits, "He's A Rebel" and "He's Sure The Boy I Love," were sung not by them at all; they both feature Darlene Love's Blossoms, a typical Spectorian move. . .)

Label & Catalog #		Title	Year	VG+	NM
Columbia ML-6077	(10")	Conga With Cugat	1950	20.00	50.00
Columbia ML-6086	(10")	Tropical Bouquet	1950	20.00	50.00
Columbia ML-6121	(10")	Dance Date	1950	20.00	50.00
Columbia ML-6213	(10")	Mambo At The Waldorf	1953	20.00	50.00
Columbia ML-6234	(10")	Tango With Cugat	1953	20.00	50.00
Columbia ML-6236	(10")	Samba With Cugat	1953	20.00	50.00
Columbia CL-515	(M)	Quiet Music	1954	14.00	35.00
Columbia CL-537	(M)	Dance With Cugat	1954	14.00	35.00
Columbia CL-579	(M)	Favorite Rhumbas	1955	14.00	35.00
Columbia CL-618	(M)	Ole	1955	14.00	35.00
— Columbia albums above have "Long Playing" on the bottom of the label.—					
Columbia CL-718	(M)	Cha Cha Cha	1956	14.00	35.00
Columbia CL-1094	(M)	Cugat Calvacade	1958	10.00	25.00
Columbia CS-8055	(S)	Cugat Calvacade	1959	14.00	35.00
Columbia CL-1143	(M)	Waltzes	1959	10.00	25.00
Columbia CS-8059	(S)	Waltzes	1959	14.00	35.00
— Columbia albums above have six white-on-black "eye" logos on each side of the spindle hole.—					
Mercury MG-20065	(M)	Cugat's Favorites	1956	14.00	35.00
Mercury MG-20???	(M)	Music For Latin Lovers	1956	14.00	35.00
Mercury MG-20108	(M)	Mambo	1957	14.00	35.00
— Mercury albums above have black labels with silver print.—					
RCA Victor LPM-1882	(M)	King Plays Some Aces	1958	10.00	25.00
RCA Victor LSP-1882	(S)	King Plays Some Aces	1958	14.00	35.00
RCA Victor LPM-1894	(M)	Cugat's Spain	1958	10.00	25.00
RCA Victor LSP-1894	(S)	Cugat's Spain	1958	14.00	35.00
RCA Victor LPM-2087	(M)	Dancing Beat Of The Latin Bands	1959	10.00	25.00
RCA Victor LSP-2087	(S)	Dancing Beat Of The Latin Bands	1959	14.00	35.00
RCA Victor LPM-2173	(M)	Xavier Cugat In Spain, France and Italy	1960	10.00	25.00
RCA Victor LSP-2173	(S)	Xavier Cugat In Spain, France and Italy	1960	14.00	35.00
— RCA mono albums above "Long Play" on the bottom of the label; stereo albums have "Living Stereo" on the bottom.—					
Mercury MG-20745	(M)	Cugat	1963	8.00	20.00
Mercury SR-60745	(S)	Cugat	1963	10.00	25.00
Mercury MG-20832	(M)	Cugi's Cocktail	1963	8.00	20.00
Mercury SR-60832	(S)	Cugi's Cocktail	1963	10.00	25.00
— Mercury albums above have black labels with silver print.—					

CUMBERLAND THREE, THE
The Cumberland Three features John Stewart, later of The Kingston Trio.

Roulette R-25121	(M)	Folk Scene, U.S.A.	1960	10.00	25.00
Roulette SR-25121	(S)	Folk Scene, U.S.A.	1960	12.00	30.00
Roulette R-25132	(M)	Civil War Almanac—The Yankees	1960	10.00	25.00
Roulette SR-25132	(S)	Civil War Almanac—The Yankees	1960	12.00	30.00
Roulette R-25133	(M)	Civil War Almanac—The Rebels	1960	10.00	25.00
Roulette SR-25133	(S)	Civil War Almanac—The Rebels	1960	12.00	30.00

CUMMINGS, BOB

Renner RC-100	(M)	Sounds Of Aviation	195?	10.00	25.00

CURB, MIKE

Forward STF-1023	(S)	The Original Hot Wheels	197?	10.00	25.00

CURLESS, DICK

Tiffany 1016	(M)	Songs Of The Open Country	1958	40.00	100.00
Tiffany 1028	(M)	Singing Just For Fun	1959	40.00	100.00
Tiffany 1033	(M)	I Love To Tell A Story	1960	40.00	100.00

CURTIS, KEN

Capitol T-2418	(M)	Gunsmoke's Festus	1965	12.00	30.00
Capitol ST-2418	(S)	Gunsmoke's Festus	1965	16.00	40.00
Dot DLP-3859	(M)	Gunsmoke's Festus Calls Out Ken Curtis	1967	10.00	25.00
Dot DLP-25859	(S)	Gunsmoke's Festus Calls Out Ken Curtis	1967	12.00	30.00

CURTIS, SONNY
Curtis was formerly a member of The Crickets.

Imperial LP-9276	(M)	Beatle Hits Flamenco Style	1964	16.00	40.00
Imperial LP-12276	(S)	Beatle Hits Flamenco Style	1964	20.00	50.00
Viva V-36012	(S)	The First Of Sonny Curtis	1968	10.00	25.00
Viva V-36021	(S)	The Sonny Curtis Style	1969	10.00	25.00

Label & Catalog #		Title	Year	VG+	NM

CYCLONES, THE: *Refer to* THE CHAMPS / THE CYCLONES

CYKLE, THE

| Label 9-261 | (S) | The Cykle | 1969 | 150.00 | 300.00 |

CYMBAL, JOHNNY

| Kapp KL-1324 | (M) | Mr. Bass Man | 1963 | 16.00 | 40.00 |
| Kapp KS-3324 | (S) | Mr. Bass Man | 1963 | 20.00 | 50.00 |

CYRKLE, THE

| Columbia CL-2544 | (M) | Red Rubber Ball | 1966 | 10.00 | 25.00 |
| Columbia CS-9344 | (S) | Red Rubber Ball | 1966 | 16.00 | 40.00 |

D

DAILEY, DON

Crown CLP-5314	(M)	Surf Stompin'	1963	16.00	40.00
Crown CST-314	(E)	Surf Stompin'	1963	8.00	20.00

DALE, DICK/DICK DALE & HIS DEL-TONES
Refer to Jerry Cole.

Deltone LPM-1001	(M)	Surfer's Choice	1962	40.00	100.00
Deltone T-1886	(M)	Surfer's Choice	1962	16.00	40.00
Deltone DT-1886	(E)	Surfer's Choice	1962	12.00	30.00
Capitol T-1930	(M)	King Of The Surf Guitar	1963	16.00	40.00
Capitol ST-1930	(S)	King Of The Surf Guitar	1963	20.00	50.00
Capitol T-2002	(M)	Checkered Flag	1963	20.00	50.00
Capitol ST-2002	(S)	Checkered Flag	1963	30.00	75.00
Capitol T-2053	(M)	Mr. Eliminator	1964	20.00	50.00
Capitol ST-2053	(S)	Mr. Eliminator	1964	30.00	75.00
Capitol T-2111	(M)	Summer Surf	1964	20.00	50.00
Capitol ST-2111	(S)	Summer Surf	1964	30.00	75.00
		(Includes the bonus single "Racing Waves" / "Movin' Surf"			
		by Jerry Cole in a special "pocket" on the front cover.)			
Capitol T-2111	(M)	Summer Surf *(Without the single)*	1964	16.00	40.00
Capitol ST-2111	(S)	Summer Surf *(Without the single)*	1964	27.00	65.00
Capitol T-2293	(M)	Rock Out—Live At Ciro's	1965	40.00	100.00
Capitol ST-2293	(S)	Rock Out—Live At Ciro's	1965	60.00	150.00

DALE, DICK / THE HOLLYWOOD SURFERS

Dub Tone LP-1246	(M)	The Surf Family	1964	14.00	35.00

DALE, DICK / THE STOMPERS

Cloister CLP-6301	(M)	Silver Sounds Of The Surf *(Felt cover)*	1963	80.00	200.00

DALE & GRACE

Montel LP-100	(M)	I'm Leaving It Up To You	1964	40.00	100.00

DALEY, JIMMY

Decca DL-8429	(M)	Rock Pretty Baby *(Soundtrack)*	1958	40.00	100.00
Decca DL-8714	(M)	Summer Love *(Soundtrack)*	1958	40.00	100.00

DALHART, VERNON: *Refer to* **GENE AUSTIN & VERNON DALHART & JIMMIE RODGERS**

DALLAS, DEAN, & THE DOUGHBOYS
Dean Dallas is a pseudonym for Pete Drake.

Cumberland MGC-29516	(M)	Golden Country Hits	1965	8.00	20.00
Cumberland SRC-69516	(S)	Golden Country Hits	1965	10.00	25.00

DALLAS, MARIA

RCA Victor LPM-3950	(M)	Tumblin' Down	1968	12.00	30.00
RCA Victor LSP-3950	(S)	Tumblin' Down	1968	6.00	15.00

DALTREY, ROGER
Mr. Daltrey is a member of The Who.

Polydor SA-038	(DJ)	McVicar On Record *(Interview)*	1980	16.00	40.00

DAMIN EIH & BROTHER CLARK

Demelot 7310	(S)	Never Mind	1974	80.00	200.00

DAMITA JO

ABC-Paramount ABC-378	(M)	The Big Fifteen	1961	30.00	75.00
ABC-Paramount ABCS-378	(S)	The Big Fifteen	1961	40.00	100.00
		(ABC 378 features backing by Steve Gibson's Red Caps.)			
Mercury MG-20642	(M)	I'll Save The Last Dance For You	1961	10.00	25.00
Mercury SR-60642	(S)	I'll Save The Last Dance For You	1961	12.00	30.00

The first album from the "King of the Surf Guitar" (above) was originally issued on his own Deltone label as LPM-1001. After signing with Capitol it was reissued on the Deltone label but with a Capitol catalog number, T-1886 (DT-1886 for the Duophonic stereo release), where it made the charts in the first quarter of 1963. Summer Surf (below) was one of a series of surf related albums that Capitol issued with a special bonus single tucked inside a "pocket" on the front cover.

Label & Catalog #		Title	Year	VG+	NM
Mercury MG-20734	(M)	**Sing A Country Song**	1962	10.00	25.00
Mercury SR-60734	(S)	**Sing A Country Song**	1962	12.00	30.00
Mercury MG-20703	(M)	**Damita Jo At The Diplomat**	1962	10.00	25.00
Mercury SR-60703	(S)	**Damita Jo At The Diplomat**	1962	12.00	30.00
Vee Jay LP-1137	(M)	**Damita Jo Sings**	1965	10.00	25.00
Vee Jay SR-1137	(S)	**Damita Jo Sings**	1965	20.00	50.00

DAMON
Damon features Atlee Yeager.

Ankh 968	(M)	**Song Of A Gypsy** *(Gatefold cover)*	1970	2,000.00	3,000.00
Ankh 968	(M)	**Song Of A Gypsy** *(Regular cover)*	1970	1,000.00	1,500.00

DAMONE, VIC

Mercury MG-25028	(10")	**Vic Damone**	1950	16.00	40.00
Mercury MG-25029	(10")	**Vic Damone**	1950	16.00	40.00
Mercury MG-25045	(10")	**Vic Damone**	1950	16.00	40.00
Mercury MG-25054	(10")	**Song Hits**	1950	16.00	40.00
Mercury MG-25092	(10")	**Christmas Favorites**	1951	16.00	40.00
Mercury MG-25100	(10")	**Vic Damone And Others**	1952	16.00	40.00
Mercury MG-25131	(10")	**The Night Has A Thousand Eyes**	1952	16.00	40.00
Mercury MG-25132	(10")	**Vocals By Vic**	1952	16.00	40.00
Mercury MG-25133	(10")	**April In Paris**	1952	16.00	40.00
Mercury MG-25156	(10")	**Vic Damone**	1952	16.00	40.00
Mercury MG-25202	(10")	**Athena** *(Soundtrack)*	1954	80.00	200.00
MGM E-86 (10")	(M)	**Rich, Young And Pretty** *(Soundtrack)*	1951	40.00	100.00
MGM E-3153	(M)	**Deep In My Heart** *(Soundtrack. Boxed set)*	1954	40.00	100.00
MGM E-3153	(M)	**Deep In My Heart** *(Soundtrack)*	1955	20.00	50.00
MGM E-3236	(M)	**Rich, Young And Pretty** *(Soundtrack)*	1955	20.00	50.00
Mercury MG-20163	(M)	**Yours For A Song**	1957	10.00	25.00
Mercury MG-20193	(M)	**My Favorites**	1957	10.00	25.00
Columbia CL-900	(M)	**That Towering Feeling!**	1956	10.00	25.00
Columbia CL-950	(M)	**The Stingiest Man In Town** *(Soundtrack)*	1956	20.00	50.00
Columbia CL-1113	(M)	**The Gift Of Love** *(Soundtrack)*	1958	40.00	100.00
— Columbia albums above have three white "eye" logos on each side of the spindle hole.—					
RCA Victor LOC-1132	(M)	**Arrivederci Baby** *(Soundtrack)*	1966	8.00	20.00
RCA Victor LSO-1132	(S)	**Arrivederci Baby** *(Soundtrack)*	1966	10.00	25.00

DAN & DALE

Tifton M-8002	(M)	**Batman And Robin**	1966	12.00	30.00
Tifton S-78002	(S)	**Batman And Robin**	1966	16.00	40.00

DANE, BARBARA
Barbara Dane is a guitar player and singer of "peoples songs" with folk, jazz and blues influences.

San Francisco 33014	(M)	**Trouble In Mind**	1957	20.00	50.00
Barbary Coast 33014	(M)	**Trouble In Mind**	1959	16.00	40.00
		(Barbary Coast 33014 is a reissue of San Francisco 33014.)			
Dot DLP-3177	(M)	**Livin' With The Blues**	1959	16.00	40.00
Dot DLP-25177	(S)	**Livin' With The Blues**	1959	20.00	50.00
Capitol T-1758	(M)	**On My Way**	1962	12.00	30.00
Capitol ST-1758	(S)	**On My Way**	1962	14.00	35.00
Folkways FA-2468	(S)	**Barbara Dane & The Chambers Brothers**	1966	20.00	50.00

DANIELS, CHARLIE

Epic HE-44365	(S)	**Fire On The Mountain** *(Half-speed master)*	1982	8.00	25.00
Epic HE-45751	(S)	**Million Mile Reflections** *(Half-speed master)*	1982	8.00	25.00

DANIELS, CHARLOTTE, & PAT WEBB

Prestige Inter. PR-13037	(M)	**Charlotte Daniels And Pat Webb**	1961	12.00	30.00

DANIELS, SLOPPY

Dooto DTL-266	(M)	**Sloppy's House Party**	1959	10.00	25.00

DANTE, RON
Dante was the mastermind behind The Detergents; The Archies; Mercy.

Kirshner KES-106	(S)	**Ron Dante**			
		Brings You Up *(With bonus photo)*	1970	10.00	25.00
Kirshner KES-106	(S)	**Ron Dante Brings You Up** *(Without photo)*	1970	6.00	15.00

Born Walden Robert Cassotto, Bobby Darin's biography is painful, exasperating and touching, as the young singer and songwriter overcame a host of physical and emotional problems to top the charts as a rock'n roller emulating Elvis, pack them into Vegas as a crooner following the style of Sinatra, and earning '60s respectability as a folk/rock/pop artist ala Tim Hardin. Several of his Atco and Atlantic albums are inexplicably scarce in stereo, the most cited being If I Were A Carpenter. But others, including Things & Other Things, pictured here, are also more difficult for stereo collectors to find in nearly mint condition than their modest values would indicate.

Label & Catalog #		Title	Year	VG+	NM
DANTE & THE EVERGREENS					
Madison MA-1002	(M)	**Dante & The Evergreens**	1961	100.00	250.00
DARIN, BOBBY					
Bobby Darin is a pseudonym for Walden Robert Cassotto.					
Atco 33-102	(M)	**Bobby Darin**	1958	40.00	100.00
Atco 33-104	(M)	**That's All**	1959	20.00	50.00
Atco SD-33-104	(S)	**That's All**	1959	40.00	100.00
Atco 33-115	(M)	**This Is Darin**	1960	20.00	50.00
Atco SD-33-115	(S)	**This Is Darin**	1960	30.00	75.00
Atco 33-122	(M)	**Darin At The Copa**	1960	20.00	50.00
Atco SD-33-122	(S)	**Darin At The Copa**	1961	30.00	75.00
Atco SP-1001	(M)	**For Teenagers Only**	1960	80.00	200.00
		(Gatefold cover with insert and fold-open poster)			
Atco SP-1001	(M)	**For Teenagers Only**	1960	60.00	150.00
		(Gatefold cover without the insert or poster.)			
Atco 33-124	(M)	**It's You Or No One**	1960	20.00	50.00
Atco SD-33-124	(S)	**It's You Or No One**	1960	30.00	75.00
Atco 33-125	(M)	**The 25th Of December**	1960	20.00	50.00
Atco SD-33-125	(S)	**The 25th Of December**	1960	30.00	75.00
Colpix CP-507	(M)	**Pepe** *(Soundtrack)*	1960	16.00	40.00
Colpix SCP-507	(S)	**Pepe** *(Soundtrack)*	1960	20.00	50.00
Atco 33-126	(M)	**Two Of A Kind**	1961	16.00	40.00
Atco SD-33-126	(S)	**Two Of A Kind**	1961	20.00	50.00
Atco 33-131	(M)	**The Bobby Darin Story** *(White cover)*	1961	16.00	40.00
Atco SD-33-131	(P)	**The Bobby Darin Story** *(White cover)*	1961	20.00	50.00
Atco 33-134	(M)	**Love Swings**	1961	16.00	40.00
Atco SD-33-134	(S)	**Love Swings**	1961	20.00	50.00
Atco 33-138	(M)	**Twist With Bobby Darin**	1961	16.00	40.00
Atco SD-33-138	(S)	**Twist With Bobby Darin**	1961	20.00	50.00
— Atco albums above have yellow labels with a harp on top.—					
Atco 33-102	(M)	**Bobby Darin**	196?	12.00	30.00
Atco 33-104	(M)	**That's All**	196?	8.00	20.00
Atco SD-33-104	(S)	**That's All**	196?	10.00	25.00
Atco 33-115	(M)	**This Is Darin**	196?	8.00	20.00
Atco SD-33-115	(S)	**This Is Darin**	196?	10.00	25.00
Atco 33-122	(M)	**Darin At The Copa**	196?	8.00	20.00
Atco SD-33-122	(S)	**Darin At The Copa**	196?	10.00	25.00
Atco 33-124	(M)	**It's You Or No One**	196?	8.00	20.00
Atco SD-33-124	(S)	**It's You Or No One**	196?	10.00	25.00
Atco 33-125	(M)	**The 25th Of December**	196?	8.00	20.00
Atco SD-33-125	(S)	**The 25th Of December**	196?	10.00	25.00
Atco 33-126	(M)	**Two Of A Kind**	196?	8.00	20.00
Atco SD-33-126	(S)	**Two Of A Kind**	196?	10.00	25.00
Atco 33-131	(M)	**The Bobby Darin Story** *(Black cover)*	196?	8.00	20.00
Atco SD-33-131	(S)	**The Bobby Darin Story** *(Black cover)*	196?	10.00	25.00
Atco 33-134	(M)	**Love Swings**	196?	8.00	20.00
Atco SD-33-134	(S)	**Love Swings**	196?	10.00	25.00
Atco 33-138	(M)	**Twist With Bobby Darin**	196?	8.00	20.00
Atco SD-33-138	(S)	**Twist With Bobby Darin**	196?	10.00	25.00
Atco 33-140	(M)	**Bobby Darin Sings Ray Charles**	1962	10.00	25.00
Atco SD-33-140	(S)	**Bobby Darin Sings Ray Charles**	1962	12.00	30.00
Dot DLP-9011	(M)	**State Fair** *(Soundtrack)*	1962	12.00	30.00
Dot DLP-25011	(S)	**State Fair** *(Soundtrack)*	1962	16.00	40.00
Atco 33-146	(M)	**Things And Other Things**	1962	10.00	25.00
Atco SD-33-146	(S)	**Things And Other Things**	1962	12.00	30.00
Atco 33-124	(M)	**It's You Or No One**	1963	10.00	25.00
Atco SD-33-124	(S)	**It's You Or No One**	1963	12.00	30.00
Atco 33-167	(M)	**Winners**	1964	10.00	25.00
Atco SD-33-167	(S)	**Winners**	1964	12.00	30.00
— Atco mono albums above have gold & gray labels; stereo albums have purple & brown labels.—					
Capitol T-1791	(M)	**Oh! Look At Me Now**	1962	10.00	25.00
Capitol ST-1791	(S)	**Oh! Look At Me Now**	1962	12.00	30.00
Capitol T-1826	(M)	**Earthy**	1963	10.00	25.00
Capitol ST-1826	(S)	**Earthy**	1963	12.00	30.00
Capitol T-1866	(M)	**You're The Reason I'm Living**	1963	10.00	25.00
Capitol ST-1866	(S)	**You're The Reason I'm Living**	1963	12.00	30.00
Capitol T-1942	(M)	**18 Yellow Roses**	1963	10.00	25.00
Capitol ST-1942	(S)	**18 Yellow Roses**	1963	12.00	30.00

Label & Catalog #		Title	Year	VG+	NM
Capitol T-2007	(M)	**Golden Folk Hits**	*1963*	10.00	**25.00**
Capitol ST-2007	(S)	**Golden Folk Hits**	*1963*	12.00	**30.00**
Capitol T-2194	(M)	**From "Hello Dolly" To "Goodbye Charlie"**	*1964*	10.00	**25.00**
Capitol ST-2194	(S)	**From "Hello Dolly" To "Goodbye Charlie"**	*1964*	12.00	**30.00**
Decca DL-9119	(M)	**The Lively Set** *(Soundtrack)*	*1964*	14.00	**35.00**
Decca DL7-9119	(S)	**The Lively Set** *(Soundtrack)*	*1964*	20.00	**50.00**
Capitol T-2322	(M)	**Venice Blue**	*1965*	10.00	**25.00**
Capitol ST-2322	(S)	**Venice Blue**	*1965*	12.00	**30.00**
Capitol T-2571	(M)	**The Best Of Bobby Darin**	*1966*	8.00	**20.00**
Capitol ST-2571	(S)	**The Best Of Bobby Darin**	*1966*	10.00	**25.00**
Atlantic 8121	(M)	**The Shadow Of Your Smile**	*1966*	8.00	**20.00**
Atlantic SD-8121	(S)	**The Shadow Of Your Smile**	*1966*	10.00	**25.00**
Atlantic 8126	(M)	**In A Broadway Bag**	*1966*	8.00	**20.00**
Atlantic SD-8126	(S)	**In A Broadway Bag**	*1966*	10.00	**25.00**
Atlantic 8135	(M)	**If I Were A Carpenter**	*1966*	10.00	**25.00**
Atlantic SD-8135	(S)	**If I Were A Carpenter**	*1966*	20.00	**50.00**
Atlantic 8142	(M)	**Inside Out**	*1967*	10.00	**25.00**
Atlantic SD-8142	(S)	**Inside Out**	*1967*	12.00	**30.00**
Atlantic 8154	(M)	**Bobby Darin Sings Doctor Doolittle**	*1967*	8.00	**20.00**
Atlantic SD-8154	(S)	**Bobby Darin Sings Doctor Doolittle**	*1967*	10.00	**25.00**
Direction 1936	(S)	**Born Walden Robert Cassotto**	*1968*	10.00	**25.00**
Direction 1937	(S)	**Commitment**	*1969*	10.00	**25.00**

DARIUS

Chartmaker 1102	(S)	**Darius**	*1969*	100.00	**250.00**

DARK SHADOWS

Rockadelic LP-2.5	(S)	**Dark Shadows**	*198?*	40.00	**100.00**

("Dark Shadows" was recorded by the group Cold Sun. An acetate of that album exists. Due to technical reasons, Rockadelic had to release this credited to Dark Shadows.)

DARLING, ERIC

Eric Darling is a singer and a guitar and banjo player in the contemporary folk scene. Refer to The Kossoy Sisters; Ed McCurdy; The Rooftop Singers; The Tarriers.

Elektra EKL-154	(M)	**Erik Darling—Folksongs**	*196?*	10.00	**25.00**
Vanguard VRS-9099	(M)	**True Religion**	*1961*	10.00	**25.00**
Vanguard VRS-9131	(M)	**Train Time**	*1962*	8.00	**20.00**
Vanguard VSD-2131	(S)	**Train Time**	*1962*	10.00	**25.00**

DARREN, JAMES

Colpix CLP-406	(M)	**James Darren**	*1960*	20.00	**50.00**
Colpix CLP-406	(M)	**James Darren** *(Green vinyl)*	*1960*	60.00	**150.00**
Colpix CLP-406	(M)	**James Darren** *(Red vinyl)*	*1960*	60.00	**150.00**
Colpix CLP-418	(M)	**Gidget Goes Hawaiian**	*1961*	14.00	**35.00**
Colpix SCP-418	(S)	**Gidget Goes Hawaiian**	*1961*	20.00	**50.00**
Colpix CLP-424	(M)	**James Darren Sings For All Sizes**	*1962*	14.00	**35.00**
Colpix SCP-424	(S)	**James Darren Sings For All Sizes**	*1962*	20.00	**50.00**
Colpix CLP-428	(M)	**Love Among The Young**	*1962*	14.00	**35.00**
Colpix SCP-428	(S)	**Love Among The Young**	*1962*	20.00	**50.00**
Colpix CLP-454	(M)	**Bye Bye Birdie**	*1963*	14.00	**35.00**
Colpix SCP-454	(S)	**Bye Bye Birdie**	*1963*	20.00	**50.00**
Decca DL-9119	(M)	**The Lively Set** *(Soundtrack)*	*1964*	14.00	**35.00**
Decca DL7-9119	(S)	**The Lively Set** *(Soundtrack)*	*1964*	20.00	**50.00**

DARREN, JAMES / SHELLY FABARES / PAUL PETERSEN

Colpix CP-444	(M)	**Teenage Triangle**	*1962*	16.00	**40.00**
Colpix SCP-444	(E)	**Teenage Triangle**	*1962*	20.00	**50.00**
Colpix CP-468	(M)	**More Teenage Triangle**	*1964*	16.00	**40.00**
Colpix SCP-468	(P)	**More Teenage Triangle**	*1964*	30.00	**75.00**

DARTELLS, THE

Dot DLP-3522	(M)	**Hot Pastrami**	*1963*	12.00	**30.00**
Dot DLP-25522	(S)	**Hot Pastrami**	*1963*	16.00	**40.00**

DARTS, THE

Del-Fi DF-1244	(M)	**Hollywood Drag**	*1963*	12.00	**30.00**
Del-Fi DFST-1244	(S)	**Hollywood Drag**	*1963*	16.00	**40.00**

Label & Catalog #		Title	Year	VG+	NM
DASHIEL, BUD, & THE KINSMEN					
Refer to Bud & Travis.					
Warner Bros. W-1429	(M)	**Folk Music In A Contemporary Manner**	1961	10.00	25.00
Warner Bros. WS-1429	(S)	**Folk Music In A Contemporary Manner**	1961	14.00	35.00
Warner Bros. W-1432	(M)	**Live Concert Extraordinary-Bud Dashiell & The Kinsmen Sing Everybody's Hits**	1962	10.00	25.00
Warner Bros. WS-1432	(S)	**Live Concert Extraordinary-Bud Dashiell & The Kinsmen Sing Everybody's Hits**	1962	14.00	35.00
DAVE DEE, DOZY, BEAKY, MICK & TICH					
Fontana MGF-27567	(M)	**Greatest Hits**	1967	12.00	30.00
Fontana SRF-67567	(S)	**Greatest Hits**	1967	16.00	40.00
		("Bend It" and "Hold Tight" are rechanneled on this album.)			
Imperial LP-12402	(S)	**Time To Take Off**	1968	16.00	40.00
		("Zabadak" is rechanneled on this album.)			
DAVEY & THE BADMEN					
Gothic WA-63054	(M)	**Wanted**	1963	80.00	200.00
DAVID, THE					
V.M.C. 124	(S)	**Another Day, Another Lifetime**	1968	30.00	75.00
DAVIE, HUTCH					
Atco 33-105	(M)	**Much Hutch**	1959	20.00	50.00
DAVIS, BETTE					
Citadel CT-7030	(M)	**Miss Bette Davis Sings!**	1976	12.00	30.00
DAVIS, ELLABELLE					
London LS-182	(10")	**Recital Of Negro Spirituals**	1950	30.00	75.00
DAVIS, "REVEREND" GARY					
Gary Davis is a guitar and banjo player, singer and writer of blues, spirituals and ragtime music. Refer to Pink Anderson / Rev. Gary Davis.					
Stinson SLP-56	(10")	**The Singing Reverend**	195?	40.00	100.00
Bluesville BVLP-1015	(M)	**Harlem Street Singer**	1961	50.00	125.00
Bluesville BVLP-1032	(M)	**A More Little Faith**	1961	50.00	125.00
Bluesville BVLP-1049	(M)	**Say No To The Devil**	1962	40.00	100.00
		— Bluesville albums above have bright blue labels with silver print.—			
Bluesville BVLP-1015	(M)	**Harlem Street Singer**	1964	16.00	40.00
Bluesville BVLP-1032	(M)	**A More Little Faith**	1964	16.00	40.00
Bluesville BVLP-1049	(M)	**Say No To The Devil**	1964	16.00	40.00
		— Bluesville albums above have blue labels with a trident logo on the right side.—			
Folklore FRLP-14028	(M)	**Pure Religion**	1964	14.00	35.00
Folklore FRST-14028	(S)	**Pure Religion**	1964	16.00	40.00
		(Folklore 14028 is a reissue of Bluesville 1015.)			
Folklore FRLP-14033	(M)	**Guitar And Banjo**	1964	14.00	35.00
Folklore FRST-14033	(S)	**Guitar And Banjo**	1964	16.00	40.00
DAVIS, JIMMIE					
Refer to Red Foley / Jimmie Davis.					
Decca DL-5500	(10")	**Jimmie Davis**	1954	20.00	50.00
Decca DL-8174	(M)	**Near The Cross**	1955	12.00	30.00
Decca DL-8572	(M)	**Hymn Time**	1957	12.00	30.00
Decca DL-8729	(M)	**The Door Is Always Open**	1958	12.00	30.00
Decca DL-8786	(M)	**Hail Him With A Song**	1958	12.00	30.00
Decca DL-8896	(M)	**You Are My Sunshine**	1959	8.00	20.00
Decca DL-78896	(S)	**You Are My Sunshine**	1959	12.00	30.00
Decca DL-8953	(M)	**Suppertime**	1960	8.00	20.00
Decca DL-78953	(S)	**Suppertime**	1960	12.00	30.00
		— Decca albums above have black labels with silver print.—			

DAVIS, JOHNNY: *Refer to* GOLDMINE'S PRICE GUIDE TO COLLECTIBLE JAZZ ALBUMS

DAVIS, LINK					
Mercury SR-61243	(S)	**Cajun Crawdaddy**	1969	10.00	25.00

Born Mary Frances Penick, Skeeter Davis was signed by RCA Victor, sent out on tour with their biggest stars, Eddy Arnold and Elvis Presley, and then scored a succession of hits on the country cgharts from 1958 through the early '70s. Her first two albums were both clever concepts: On I'll Sing You And Song And Harmonize, Too she was multi-tracked providing all of her own harmonies, quite a novelty in 1960. On Here's The Answer she sang "answer songs" (all the rage for a year years in the early '60s) to a half-dozen of the biggest hits of the day.

Label & Catalog #		Title	Year	VG+	NM
DAVIS, MAXWELL					
Aladdin LP-709	*(10")*	**Maxwell Davis**	*1954*	150.00	300.00
Aladdin LP-804	*(M)*	**Maxwell Davis**	*1956*	80.00	200.00
Score SLP-4106	*(M)*	**Blue Tango**	*1957*	80.00	200.00
DAVIS, PAUL					
Bang BLPS-223	*(S)*	**A Little Bit Of Soap**	*1970*	14.00	35.00
DAVIS, SAMMY, JR.					
Refer to The Reprise Repertory Theatre.					
Decca DL-8118	*(M)*	**Starring Sammy Davis, Jr.**	*1955*	12.00	30.00
Decca DL-8170	*(M)*	**Just For Lovers**	*1955*	12.00	30.00
Decca DL-9032	*(M)*	**Mr. Wonderful** *(Soundtrack)*	*1956*	16.00	40.00
Decca DL-8351	*(M)*	**Here's Looking At You**	*1956*	10.00	25.00
Decca DL-8486	*(M)*	**Sammy Swings**	*1957*	10.00	25.00
Decca DL-8641	*(M)*	**It's All Over But The Swingin'**	*1957*	10.00	25.00
Decca DL-8676	*(M)*	**Mood To Be Wooed**	*1958*	10.00	25.00
Decca DL-8779	*(M)*	**All The Way And Then Some**	*1958*	10.00	25.00
Decca DL-8841	*(M)*	**Sammy Davis, Jr. At Town Hall**	*1959*	8.00	20.00
Decca DL-78841	*(S)*	**Sammy Davis, Jr. At Town Hall**	*1959*	12.00	30.00
Decca DL-8854	*(M)*	**Porgy And Bess**	*1959*	8.00	20.00
Decca DL-78854	*(S)*	**Porgy And Bess**	*1959*	12.00	30.00
Decca DL-8921	*(M)*	**Sammy Awards**	*1960*	8.00	20.00
Decca DL-78921	*(S)*	**Sammy Awards**	*1960*	12.00	30.00
Decca DL-8981	*(M)*	**I Got A Right To Swing**	*1960*	8.00	20.00
Decca DL-78981	*(S)*	**I Got A Right To Swing**	*1960*	12.00	30.00
		— Decca albums above have black & silver labels.—			
United Arts. UAL-4111	*(M)*	**Johnny Cool** *(Soundtrack)*	*1963*	10.00	25.00
United Arts. UAS-5111	*(S)*	**Johnny Cool** *(Soundtrack)*	*1963*	12.00	30.00
Capitol VAS-2124	*(M)*	**Golden Boy** *(Soundtrack)*	*1964*	10.00	25.00
Capitol SVAS-2124	*(S)*	**Golden Boy** *(Soundtrack)*	*1964*	12.00	30.00
Reprise R-6180	*(M)*	**A Man Called Adam** *(Soundtrack)*	*1966*	10.00	25.00
Reprise RS-6180	*(S)*	**A Man Called Adam** *(Soundtrack)*	*1966*	12.00	30.00
		— Reprise albums above have pink, gold & green labels.—			
Motown MS-710	*(S)*	**Something For Everyone**	*1970*	12.00	30.00
DAVIS, JR., SAMMY, & CARMEN McRAE					
Decca DL-8490	*(M)*	**Boy Meets Girl**	*1957*	12.00	30.00
DAVIS, SKEETER					
Refer to Babby Bare & Skeeter Davis; Don Bowman & Skeeter Davis; George Hamilton IV & Skeeter Davis;					
Sandy Posey / Skeeter Davis; Porter Wagoner & Skeeter Davis.					
RCA Victor LPM-2197	*(M)*	**I'll Sing You A Song And Harmonize, Too**	*1960*	12.00	30.00
RCA Victor LSP-2197	*(S)*	**I'll Sing You A Song And Harmonize, Too**	*1960*	16.00	40.00
RCA Victor LPM-2327	*(M)*	**Here's The Answer**	*1961*	12.00	30.00
RCA Victor LSP-2327	*(S)*	**Here's The Answer**	*1961*	16.00	40.00
RCA Victor LPM-2699	*(M)*	**The End Of The World**	*1962*	12.00	30.00
RCA Victor LSP-2699	*(S)*	**The End Of The World**	*1962*	16.00	40.00
RCA Victor LPM-2736	*(M)*	**Cloudy, With Occasional Tears**	*1963*	12.00	30.00
RCA Victor LSP-2736	*(S)*	**Cloudy, With Occasional Tears**	*1963*	16.00	40.00
		— RCA mono albums above have "Long Play" on the bottom of the label;			
		stereo albums have "Living Stereo" on the bottom.—			
RCA Victor LPM-2980	*(M)*	**Let Me Get Close To You**	*1964*	10.00	25.00
RCA Victor LSP-2980	*(S)*	**Let Me Get Close To You**	*1964*	12.00	30.00
RCA Victor LPM-3374	*(M)*	**The Best Of Skeeter Davis**	*1965*	10.00	25.00
RCA Victor LSP-3374	*(S)*	**The Best Of Skeeter Davis**	*1965*	12.00	30.00
RCA Victor LPM-3382	*(M)*	**Written By The Stars**	*1965*	10.00	25.00
RCA Victor LSP-3382	*(S)*	**Written By The Stars**	*1965*	12.00	30.00
RCA Victor LPM-3463	*(M)*	**Skeeter Sings Standards**	*1965*	10.00	25.00
RCA Victor LSP-3463	*(S)*	**Skeeter Sings Standards**	*1965*	12.00	30.00
RCA Victor LPM-3567	*(M)*	**Singin' In The Summer Sun**	*1966*	10.00	25.00
RCA Victor LSP-3567	*(S)*	**Singin' In The Summer Sun**	*1966*	12.00	30.00
RCA Victor LPM-3667	*(M)*	**My Heart's In The Country**	*1966*	10.00	25.00
RCA Victor LSP-3667	*(S)*	**My Heart's In The Country**	*1966*	12.00	30.00
RCA Victor LPM-3763	*(M)*	**Hand In Hand With Jesus**	*1967*	14.00	35.00
RCA Victor LSP-3763	*(S)*	**Hand In Hand With Jesus**	*1967*	10.00	25.00
RCA Victor LPM-3790	*(M)*	**Skeeter Davis Sings Buddy Holly**	*1967*	20.00	50.00
RCA Victor LSP-3790	*(S)*	**Skeeter Davis Sings Buddy Holly**	*1967*	20.00	50.00

For many, Ms. Day will always be the effervescently cute actress with the almost chipmunk like smile that made many mundane movies for the family in the '50s and '60s. But, as Day In Hollywood illustrates, she was originally discovered as a big band singer because she was a beautiful woman with a pleasing set of pipes.

Label & Catalog #		Title	Year	VG+	NM
RCA Victor LPM-3876	(M)	**What Does It Take**	1967	14.00	35.00
RCA Victor LSP-3876	(S)	**What Does It Take**	1967	10.00	25.00
RCA Victor LPM-3960	(M)	**Why So Lonely?**	1968	20.00	50.00
RCA Victor LSP-3960	(S)	**Why So Lonely?**	1968	10.00	25.00

— RCA albums above have black labels.—

DAVIS, SPENCER/THE SPENCER DAVIS GROUP
Steve Winwood is featured on each album except 6652.

United Arts. UAL-3578	(M)	**Gimme Some Lovin'**	1967	20.00	50.00
United Arts. UAS-6578	(E)	**Gimme Some Lovin'**	1967	16.00	40.00
United Arts. UAL-3589	(M)	**I'm A Man**	1967	16.00	40.00
United Arts. UAS-6589	(P)	**I'm A Man**	1967	20.00	50.00
United Arts. UAS-6641	(P)	**Spencer Davis' Greatest Hits**	1968	10.00	25.00
United Arts. UAS-6652	(S)	**With Their New Face On**	1968	10.00	25.00
United Arts. UAS-6691	(S)	**Heavies**	1969	10.00	25.00

DAWE, TIM
Dawe was formerly a member of Iron Butterfly.

Straight STS-1058	(S)	**Penrod**	1969	20.00	50.00
Warner Bros. WS-1841	(S)	**Penrod**	1970	8.00	20.00

DAY, BOBBY
Bobby Day is a pseudonym for Bobby Byrd.

Class LP-5002	(M)	**Rockin' With Robin**	1959	200.00	400.00
Rendezvous M-1312	(M)	**Rockin' With Robin**	196?	40.00	100.00

(Rendezvous 1312 is a reissue of Class 5002.)

DAY, CARA LEE: *Refer to* **GOLDMINE'S PRICE GUIDE TO COLLECTIBLE JAZZ ALBUMS**

DAY, DORIS
Ms. Day also recorded with Frank Sinatra.

Columbia CL-6071	(10")	**You're My Thrill**	1949	20.00	50.00
Columbia CL-6106	(10")	**Young Man With A Horn** (Soundtrack)	1950	40.00	100.00
Columbia CL-6149	(10")	**Tea For Two** (Soundtrack)	1950	40.00	100.00
Columbia CL-6168	(10")	**Lullaby Of Broadway** (Soundtrack)	1951	40.00	100.00
Columbia CL-6186	(10")	**On Moonlight Bay** (Soundtrack)	1951	40.00	100.00
Columbia CL-6198	(10")	**I'll See You In My Dreams** (Soundtrack)	1951	40.00	100.00
Columbia CL-6248	(10")	**By The Light Of The Silvery Moon** (Soundtrack)	1953	40.00	100.00
Columbia CL-6273	(10")	**Calamity Jane** (Soundtrack)	1953	40.00	100.00
Columbia CL-2518	(10")	**Lights, Cameras, Action**	1955	20.00	50.00
Columbia CL-2530	(10")	**Boys And Girls Together**	1955	20.00	50.00
Columbia CL-2534	(10")	**Hot Canaries** (With Peggy Lee)	1955	20.00	50.00
Columbia CL-582	(M)	**Young Man With A Horn**	1954	16.00	40.00
Columbia CL-624	(M)	**Day Dreams**	1955	16.00	40.00
Columbia CL-710	(M)	**Love Me Or Leave Me** (Soundtrack)	1955	20.00	50.00

— Columbia albums above have "Long Playing" on the bottom of the label.—

Columbia CL-582	(M)	**Young Man With A Horn**	1955	10.00	25.00
Columbia CL-624	(M)	**Day Dreams**	1955	10.00	25.00
Columbia CL-710	(M)	**Love Me Or Leave Me** (Soundtrack)	1955	10.00	25.00
Columbia CL-749	(M)	**Day In Hollywood**	1955	10.00	25.00
Columbia CL-942	(M)	**Day By Day**	1957	10.00	25.00
Columbia OL-5210	(M)	**The Pajama Game** (Soundtrack)	1957	10.00	25.00
Columbia CL-1210	(M)	**Doris Day's Greatest Hits**	1958	10.00	25.00
Columbia CS-8635	(P)	**Doris Day's Greatest Hits**	1958	10.00	25.00
Columbia C2L-5	(M)	**Hooray For Hollywood** (2 LPs)	1959	12.00	30.00

— Columbia albums above have three white "eye" logos on each side of the spindle hole.—

DAY, DORIS, & ROCK HUDSON

U.I. DCLA-1316	(DJ)	**Selections From "Pillow Talk"** (One sided)	195?	20.00	50.00

DAY, JIMMY

Philips PHM-200-016	(M)	**Golden Steel Guitar Hits**	1962	12.00	30.00
Philips PHS-600-016	(S)	**Golden Steel Guitar Hits**	1962	16.00	40.00
Philips PHM-200-075	(M)	**Steel And Strings**	1962	12.00	30.00
Philips PHS-600-075	(S)	**Steel And Strings**	1962	16.00	40.00

DAY BLINDNESS

Studio 10 DBX-101	(S)	**Day Blindness**	1969	16.00	40.00

Yvonne De Carlo's album is primarily sought after by collectors of "personality" records. That is, albums by people who would not otherwise be given a recording contract if it wasn't for the fact that they were already established personalities in another field, primarily for the big screen (movies) and the little (television). A sub-field of personality records is the ever-growing "golden throat" field: Vocal albums so [unintentionally] bad as to defy rational belief. Ms. De Carlo apparently has avoided that, er, distinction.

Label & Catalog #		Title	Year	VG+	NM
DAYBREAK					
R. P. C.	(S)	**Daybreak**	1971	300.00	600.00
DE-FENDERS, THE					
The De-Fenders feature Bruce Johnston.					
World Pacific WP-1810	(M)	**The Big Ones**	1963	20.00	50.00
World Pacific ST-1810	(S)	**The Big Ones**	1963	30.00	75.00
World Pacific ST-1810	(S)	**The Big Ones** (Green vinyl)	1963	60.00	150.00
World Pacific ST-1810	(S)	**The Big Ones** (Red vinyl)	1963	60.00	150.00
Del-Fi DFLP-1242	(M)	**Drag Beat**	1963	20.00	50.00
Del-Fi DFSP-1242	(S)	**Drag Beat**	1963	30.00	75.00
DEAD BOYS, THE					
Sire SR-6038	(S)	**Young, Loud And Snotty**	1977	10.00	25.00
Sire SRK-6054	(S)	**We Have Come For Your Children**	1978	10.00	25.00
DEADLY ONES, THE					
Vee Jay LP-1090	(M)	**It's Monster Surfing Time**	1964	20.00	50.00
Vee Jay VS-1090	(S)	**It's Monster Surfing Time**	1964	40.00	100.00
DEAN, AL					
Warrior 506	(M)	**Fragile Heart**	195?	50.00	125.00
DEAN, EDDIE					
Sage & Sand C-1	(M)	**Greatest Westerns**	1956	20.00	50.00
Sage & Sand C-5	(M)	**Hi-Country**	1957	20.00	50.00
Sound LP-603	(M)	**Greatest Westerns**	1957	12.00	30.00
Sage & Sand C-16	(M)	**Hillbilly Heaven**	1961	12.00	30.00
King 686	(M)	**Favorites Of Eddie Dean**	1960	20.00	50.00
DEAN, JAMES					
Coral CRL-57009	(M)	**The James Dean Story**	1956	40.00	100.00
Capitol W-881	(M)	**The James Dean Story**	1957	40.00	100.00
Imperial LP-9031	(M)	**A Tribute To James Dean**	1958	40.00	100.00
		(Imperial 9031 contains excerpts from Deans' films "Rebel Without A Cause" and "East Of Eden.")			
DEAN, JIMMY					
Mercury MG-20319	(M)	**Television Favorites**	1956	20.00	50.00
Columbia CL-1025	(M)	**Hour Of Prayer**	1957	16.00	40.00
King 686	(M)	**Favorites Of Jimmy Dean**	1961	30.00	75.00
DEAN, JIMMY / JOHNNY HORTON					
LaBrea L-8014	(M)	**Bummin' Around**	1961	30.00	75.00
Starday SLP-325	(M)	**Bummin' Around** (Yellow label)	1965	12.00	30.00
DEARIE, BLOSSOM: *Refer to* GOLDMINE'S PRICE GUIDE TO COLLECTIBLE JAZZ ALBUMS					
DEBRIS					
Static Disposal	(S)	**Debris**	1976	20.00	50.00
DeCARLO, YVONNE					
Masterseal *(No number)*	(M)	**Yvonne DeCarlo Sings**	1957	30.00	75.00
DeCASTRO SISTERS, THE					
Abbott 5002	(M)	**The DeCastro Sisters**	1960	20.00	50.00
Capitol T-1402	(M)	**The DeCastros Sing**	1960	8.00	20.00
Capitol ST-1402	(S)	**The DeCastros Sing**	1960	10.00	25.00
Capitol T-1501	(M)	**The Rockin' Beat**	1960	8.00	20.00
Capitol ST-1501	(S)	**The Rockin' Beat**	1960	10.00	25.00
DECKER, EVA / HARLEY LUSE					
Imperial FD-102	(10")	**American Folk Dance**	195?	20.00	50.00
DECORMIER, BOB & LOUISE					
Stinson SLP-68	(10")	**Ballads And Folksongs**	195?	20.00	50.00
Stinson SLP-72	(10")	**Catskill Mountain Folk Songs**	195?	20.00	50.00
Judson J-3025	(M)	**Songs Children Sing In Italy**	195?	10.00	25.00

Label & Catalog #		Title	Year	VG+	NM

DEE, JOEY/JOEY DEE & THE STARLIGHTERS

Label & Catalog #		Title	Year	VG+	NM
Roulette R-25166	(M)	Doin' The Twist	1961	16.00	40.00
Roulette SR-25166	(S)	Doin' The Twist	1961	20.00	50.00
Roulette R-25168	(M)	Hey, Let's Twist (Soundtrack)	1961	20.00	50.00
Roulette SR-25168	(S)	Hey, Let's Twist (Soundtrack)	1961	30.00	75.00
Roulette R-25171	(M)	All The World Is Twistin'	1961	12.00	30.00
Roulette SR-25171	(S)	All The World Is Twistin'	1961	16.00	40.00
Roulette R-25173	(M)	Back To The Peppermint Lounge Twistin'	1961	12.00	30.00
Roulette SR-25173	(S)	Back To The Peppermint Lounge Twistin'	1961	16.00	40.00
Columbia SP-1986	(DJ)	Two Tickets To Paris Radio Spots	1963	30.00	75.00
Roulette R-25182	(M)	Two Tickets To Paris (Soundtrack)	1961	10.00	25.00
Roulette SR-25182	(S)	Two Tickets To Paris (Soundtrack)	1961	12.00	30.00
Roulette R-25197	(M)	Joey Dee	1961	10.00	25.00
Roulette SR-25197	(S)	Joey Dee	1961	12.00	30.00
Roulette R-25221	(M)	Dance, Dance, Dance	1961	10.00	25.00
Roulette SR-25221	(S)	Dance, Dance, Dance	1961	12.00	30.00
Scepter S-503	(M)	The Peppermint Twisters	1962	8.00	20.00
Scepter SS-503	(S)	The Peppermint Twisters	1962	10.00	25.00
Jubilee JLP-8000	(M)	Hitsville	1966	8.00	20.00
Jubilee JLS-8000	(S)	Hitsville	1966	10.00	25.00

DEE, MERCY

Label & Catalog #		Title	Year	VG+	NM
Arhoolie 1007	(M)	Mercy Dee	1961	10.00	25.00

DEEP, THE

Label & Catalog #		Title	Year	VG+	NM
Parkway P-7051	(M)	Psychedelic Moods	1966	60.00	150.00
Parkway SP-7051	(S)	Psychedelic Moods	1966	80.00	200.00

DEEP PURPLE

Deep Purple features Ritchie Blackmore, Ian Paice and Jon Lord. Refer to Green Bullfrog.

Label & Catalog #		Title	Year	VG+	NM
Tetragrammaton T-102	(S)	Shades Of Deep Purple	1968	10.00	25.00
Tetragrammaton T-107	(S)	Book Of Taliesyn	1968	10.00	25.00
Tetragrammaton T-119	(S)	Deep Purple	1968	10.00	25.00
Tetragrammaton T-131	(S)	Deep Purple & The Royal Philharmonic	1968	150.00	300.00
Warner Bros. BS4-2607	(Q)	Machine Head	1974	10.00	25.00
Warner Bros. BS4-2832	(Q)	Stormbringer	1974	10.00	25.00
Harvest SHVL-751	(S)	Book Of Taliesyn	197?	60.00	150.00
Harvest SHVL-777	(S)	Deep Purple In Rock	197?	60.00	150.00

(Harvest 751 and 777 are US discs inside UK jackets manufactured for export during the early '70s. While the label and catalog number are British, the label reads "Made in USA.")

DEEP RIVER BOYS, THE

Label & Catalog #		Title	Year	VG+	NM
Waldorf Music Hall 108	(10")	The Deep River Boys Sing Songs Of Jubilee (Group photo cover)	195?	200.00	400.00
Waldorf Music Hall 108	(10")	The Deep River Boys Sing Songs Of Jubilee (Cartoon cover)	195?	80.00	200.00
Waldorf Music Hall 120	(10")	The Deep River Boys Sing Spirituals	195?	80.00	200.00
"X" LXA-1019	(M)	Presenting The Deep River Boys	1956	60.00	150.00
Vik LX-11??	(M)	Presenting The Deep River Boys	1956	40.00	100.00
Camden CAL-303	(M)	Presenting The Deep River Boys	1957	20.00	50.00

(The Vik and Camden albums are reissues of "X" 1019.)

Label & Catalog #		Title	Year	VG+	NM
Que FLS-104	(M)	Midnight Magic	1957	80.00	200.00

DEERFIELD

Label & Catalog #		Title	Year	VG+	NM
Flat Rock FRS-1	(S)	Nil Desperandum	196?	40.00	100.00

DeJOHN SISTERS, THE

Label & Catalog #		Title	Year	VG+	NM
Epic LN-1116	(M)	The DeJohn Sisters	195?	10.00	25.00

DEKKER, DESMOND

Label & Catalog #		Title	Year	VG+	NM
Uni 73059	(S)	Israelites	1969	12.00	30.00

("Tip Of My Finger," "Too Much Too Soon" and "Nincompoop" are rechanneled.)

DEL SATINS, THE

Label & Catalog #		Title	Year	VG+	NM
B.T. Puppy BTS-1019	(S)	Out To Lunch	1972	150.00	300.00

Label & Catalog #		Title	Year	VG+	NM

DEL VIKINGS, THE

The original all-black Del Vikings were Corinthian "Kripp" Johnson and Samuel Patterson, both lead, with Don Jackson, Clarence Quick and Bernard Robertson. Jackson, Patterson and Robertson were replaced by Norman Wright and white members Dave Lerchey and Donald "Gus" Backus. The all-black group recorded the acapella material that showed up on the Luniverse album (with strings over-dubbed), even though the cover depicts the later, racially integrated group. When their manager signed the group to Mercury, Johnson formed a second group, sometimes called The Dell Vikings, for Fee Bee. The group on the Mercury albums consisted of Backus, Lerchey, Quick, Wright and William Blakely; the group on the Dot album was original members Kripp Johnson and Don Jackson with Arthur Budd, Eddie Everette and Chuck Jackson*. Refer to The Chantels.

Luniverse LP-1000	(M)	Come Go With The Del Vikings	1957	250.00	600.00
		(Original copies of Luniverse 1000 have eight tracks with the cover slick pasted on the jacket. Counterfeits have ten or twelve tracks with a wraparound cover on the jacket.)			
Mercury MG-20314	(M)	They Sing-They Swing	1957	200.00	400.00
Mercury MG-20353	(M)	A Swinging, Singing Record Session	1958	150.00	300.00
Dot DLP-3695	(M)	Come Go With Me	1966	150.00	300.00
Dot DLP-25695	(E)	Come Go With Me	1966	200.00	400.00

DEL VIKINGS, THE / THE SONNETS

| Crown CLP-5368 | (M) | The Del Vikings And The Sonnets | 1963 | 16.00 | 40.00 |
| Crown CST-368 | (E) | The Del Vikings And The Sonnets | 1963 | 8.00 | 20.00 |

DELEGATES, THE: *Refer to* GOLDMINE'S PRICE GUIDE TO COLLECTIBLE JAZZ ALBUMS

DELFONICS, THE

The Delfonics featrue Major Harris.

Philly Groove 1150	(S)	La La Means I Love You	1968	24.00	60.00
Philly Groove 1151	(S)	The Sexy Sound Of Soul	1969	24.00	60.00
Philly Groove 1152	(S)	The Delfonics' Super Hits	1969	20.00	50.00
Philly Groove 1153	(S)	The Delfonics	1970	20.00	50.00
Philly Groove 1154	(S)	Tell Me This Is A Dream	1972	20.00	50.00
Philly Groove 1501	(S)	Alive & Kicking	1974	20.00	50.00

DELLER, ALFRED

Alfred Deller is a guitar and lute player and singer of traditonal English folk music.

| Vanguard VRS-479 | (M) | The Three Ravens | 195? | 16.00 | 40.00 |
| Vanguard VRS-499 | (M) | The Holly And The Ivy— Christmas Carols Of Old England | 1956 | 16.00 | 40.00 |

DELLS, THE

Vee Jay LP-1010	(M)	Oh What A Nite (Maroon label)	1959	300.00	600.00
Vee Jay LP-1010	(M)	Oh What A Nite (Black label)	1959	150.00	300.00
Vee Jay LP-1141	(M)	It's Not Unusual	1965	20.00	50.00
Vee Jay LPS-1141	(S)	It's Not Unusual	1965	40.00	100.00
Cadet LPS-804	(S)	There Is	1968	20.00	50.00
Cadet LPS-822	(S)	Musical Menu / Always Together	1969	20.00	50.00
Cadet LPS-824	(S)	The Dells' Greatest Hits	1969	20.00	50.00
Cadet LPS-829	(S)	Love Is Blue	1969	20.00	50.00
Cadet LPS-837	(S)	Like It Is, Like It Was	1970	20.00	50.00
Cadet 50037	(S)	Give Your Baby A Standing Ovation	1973	14.00	35.00
Cadet 50046	(S)	The Dells	1973	14.00	35.00

DELLWOODS, THE: *Refer to* MAD MAGAZINE

DELMORE BROTHERS, THE

Altona and Rabon Delmore were guitar players, singers and songwriters. They also recorded as members of The Brown's Ferry Four.

King 589	(M)	Songs By The Delmore Brothers	1958	150.00	300.00
King 589	(M)	16 All-Time Favorites	1958	60.00	150.00
		("Favorites" is a reissue of "Songs By.")			
King 785	(M)	30th Anniversary Album	1962	40.00	100.00
King 910	(M)	In Memory	1964	20.00	50.00
King 920	(M)	In Memory, Volume 2	1964	20.00	50.00
King 983	(M)	24 Great Country Songs	1966	16.00	40.00
King KS-983	(E)	24 Great Country Songs	1966	12.00	30.00

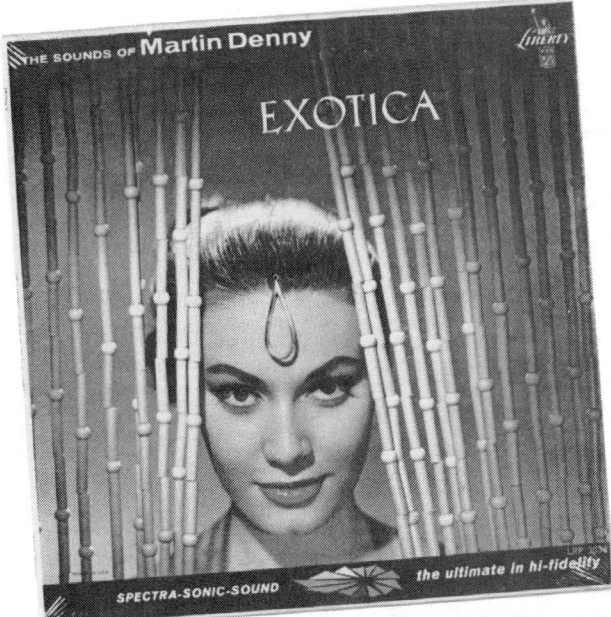

Martin Denny is currently collected as the leading progenitor of "exotic" music, and his first two albums for Liberty virtually define the genre. Denny's albums also attract interest to their wonderfully lush covers, many of them highlighted by the eroticism of the model, the exquisite Sandy warner, gracing both of the cover above.

Label & Catalog #		Title	Year	VG+	NM

DELTA RHYTHM, BOYS, THE

Label & Catalog #		Title	Year	VG+	NM
Mercury MG-25153	(10")	The Delta Rhythm Boys	1952	150.00	300.00
RCA Victor LPM-3085	(10")	Dry Bones	1953	80.00	200.00
Camden CAL-313	(M)	The Delta Rhythm Boys	1957	40.00	100.00
Elektra EKL-138	(M)	The Delta Rhythm Boys	1957	40.00	100.00
Jubilee LP-1022	(M)	Delta Rhythm Boys In Sweden (Red vinyl)	1957	150.00	300.00
Jubilee LP-1022	(M)	Delta Rhythm Boys In Sweden	1957	80.00	200.00
Coral CRL-57358	(M)	Singin' Spirituals	1961	20.00	50.00
Coral CRL-757358	(S)	Singin' Spirituals	1961	30.00	75.00

DeLUGG, MILTON

Milton DeLugg conducts his own composition, the TV show's theme, plus other ghoulish goodies.

Label & Catalog #		Title	Year	VG+	NM
Epic LN-24125	(M)	Music For Monsters, Munsters, Mummies (& Other TV Friends)	1964	40.00	100.00
Epic BN-26125	(S)	Music For Monsters, Munsters, Mummies (& Other TV Friends)	1964	60.00	150.00

DEMEMSIONS, THE

Label & Catalog #		Title	Year	VG+	NM
Coral CRL-57430	(M)	My Foolish Heart	1963	50.00	150.00
Coral CRL-757430	(S)	My Foolish Heart	1963	100.00	300.00

DEMIAN

Demian originally recorded as Bubble Puppy.

Label & Catalog #		Title	Year	VG+	NM
ABC ABCS-718	(S)	Demian	1970	20.00	50.00

DENNY, MARTIN

Martin Denny is a pioneer in the creation of "exotic" music; i.e., music with a Pacific-like ambience created in the studio. Melding various aspects of Hawaiian music with, among other things, mostly unknown (to your average American household) Afro-Cubano percussion instruments, South and Central American rhythms and melodies, and a Hollywood flair for effects (many of the bird and frog calls, etc., were provided by the vocal chords of various band members), he created a bit of a stir in the late '50s when his first album reached #1 two years after its initial release. His group included both Julius Wechter, later to found the Baja Marimba Band, and Arthur Lyman, another collectible band leader. With the current vogue among vinyl collectors for "incredibly strange music," Denny is a cult figure whose time has come!

Label & Catalog #		Title	Year	VG+	NM
Liberty LRP-3034	(M)	Exotica	1957	16.00	40.00
Liberty LST-7034	(E)	Exotica	1959	10.00	25.00
Liberty LRP-3077	(M)	Exotica, Volume II	1957	12.00	30.00
Liberty LST-7006	(S)	Exotica, Volume II	1958	16.00	40.00
Liberty LRP-3081	(M)	Forbidden Island (Girl in jungle cover)	1958	12.00	30.00
Liberty LST-7001	(S)	Forbidden Island (Girl in jungle cover)	1958	16.00	40.00
Liberty LRP-3087	(M)	Primitiva	1958	12.00	30.00
Liberty LST-7023	(S)	Primitiva	1958	16.00	40.00
Liberty LRP-3102	(M)	Hypnotique	1959	14.00	35.00
Liberty LST-7102	(S)	Hypnotique	1959	20.00	50.00
Liberty LRP-3111	(M)	Afro-Desia	1959	12.00	30.00
Liberty LST-7111	(S)	Afro-Desia	1959	16.00	40.00
Liberty LRP-3116	(M)	Exotica, Vol. III	1959	12.00	30.00
Liberty LST-7116	(S)	Exotica, Vol. III	1959	16.00	40.00
Liberty LRP-3122	(M)	Quiet Village	1959	12.00	30.00
Liberty LST-7122	(S)	Quiet Village	1959	16.00	40.00
Liberty LRP-3141	(M)	The Enchanted Sea	1959	12.00	30.00
Liberty LST-7141	(S)	The Enchanted Sea	1959	16.00	40.00

— Liberty mono albums above have turquoise & silver labels; stereo albums have black & silver labels.—

Label & Catalog #		Title	Year	VG+	NM
Liberty LRP-3081	(M)	Forbidden Island (White foil cover)	1960	10.00	25.00
Liberty LST-7001	(S)	Forbidden Island (White foil cover)	1960	12.00	30.00
Liberty LRP-3158	(M)	Exotic Sounds From The Silver Screen (Colored vinyl)	1960	24.00	60.00
Liberty LRP-3158	(M)	Exotic Sounds From The Silver Screen	1960	10.00	25.00
Liberty LST-7158	(S)	Exotic Sounds From The Silver Screen (Colored vinyl)	1960	40.00	100.00
Liberty LST-7158	(S)	Exotic Sounds From The Silver Screen	1960	12.00	30.00
Liberty LRP-3163	(M)	Exotic Sounds Visits Broadway	1960	10.00	25.00
Liberty LST-7163	(S)	Exotic Sounds Visits Broadway	1960	12.00	30.00
Liberty LRP-3168	(M)	Exotic Percussion	1961	10.00	25.00
Liberty LST-7168	(S)	Exotic Percussion	1961	12.00	30.00
Liberty LMM-13020	(M)	Exotica Suite (With Si Zentner)	1962	12.00	30.00
Liberty LSS-14020	(S)	Exotica Suite (With Si Zentner)	1962	16.00	40.00
Liberty LST-7621	(S)	Exotic Moog	1969	16.00	40.00

Label & Catalog #		Title	Year	VG+	NM
DENVER DARLING					
Audio Lab AL-1507	(M)	**Denver Darling**	1958	80.00	200.00
DePAUR INFANTRY CHORUS, THE					
Columbia AL-45	(10")	**Swing Low**	1953	30.00	75.00
Columbia ML-2119	(10")	**Work Songs And Spirituals**	195?	30.00	75.00
DEREK & THE DOMINOS					
Derek is Eric Clapton while the Dominos feature Duane Allman.					
Atco 2-704	(M)	**Layla** *(2 LPs. White label promo)*	1970	40.00	100.00
Atco SD-2-704	(S)	**Layla** *(2 LPs. White label promo)*	1970	80.00	200.00
Atco SD-2-704	(S)	**Layla** *(2 LPs)*	1970	12.00	30.00
Direct Disk SD-16629	(S)	**Layla** *(2 LPs)*	198?	25.00	75.00
DeSANTO, SUGAR PIE					
Checker LP-2979	(M)	**Sugar Pie DeSanto**	1961	60.00	150.00
DeSHANNON, JACKIE					
Liberty LRP-3320	(M)	**Jackie DeShannon**	1963	16.00	40.00
Liberty LST-7320	(S)	**Jackie DeShannon**	1963	20.00	50.00
Liberty LRP-3390	(M)	**Breakin' It Up On The Beatles Tour**	1964	20.00	50.00
Liberty LST-7390	(S)	**Breakin' It Up On The Beatles Tour**	1964	30.00	75.00
Imperial LP-9286	(M)	**This Is Jackie DeShannon**	1965	8.00	20.00
Imperial LP-12286	(S)	**This Is Jackie DeShannon**	1965	10.00	25.00
Imperial LP-9294	(M)	**You Won't Forget Me**	1965	8.00	20.00
Imperial LP-12294	(S)	**You Won't Forget Me**	1965	10.00	25.00
Imperial LP-9296	(M)	**In The Wind**	1965	8.00	20.00
Imperial LP-12296	(S)	**In The Wind**	1965	10.00	25.00
		—Imperial albums above have black, white & pink labels.—			
DESMOND, JOHNNY					
Columbia CL-1394	(M)	**Once Upon A Time**	1959	8.00	20.00
Columbia CS-8194	(S)	**Once Upon A Time**	1959	10.00	25.00
DETERGENTS, THE					
The Detergents feature Ron Dante.					
Roulette R-25308	(M)	**The Many Faces Of The Detergents**	1965	40.00	100.00
Roulette SR-25308	(E)	**The Many Faces Of The Detergents**	1965	30.00	75.00
DETROIT EMERALDS, THE					
Westbound WB-2013	(S)	**You Want It, You Got It**	197?	20.00	50.00
DEUCE COUPES, THE					
Del Fi DFLP-1243	(M)	**Hotrodder's Choice**	1963	16.00	40.00
Del Fi DFS-1243	(S)	**Hotrodder's Choice**	1963	20.00	50.00
DEUCE COUPES, THE					
Crown CLP-5393	(M)	**The Shut Downs**	1963	8.00	20.00
Crown CST-393	(S)	**The Shut Downs**	1963	10.00	25.00
DEVIANTS, THE					
Sire SES-97001	(S)	**Ptooff!**	1968	24.00	60.00
Sire SES-97005	(S)	**Disposable**	1969	24.00	60.00
Sire SES-97016	(S)	**No. 3**	1969	24.00	60.00
DEVIL'S ANVIL, THE					
Columbia CL-2664	(M)	**Hard Rock From The Middle East**	1967	10.00	25.00
Columbia CS-9464	(S)	**Hard Rock From The Middle East**	1967	14.00	35.00
DEVO					
Warner Bros. WBMS-115	(DJ)	**Devo Live**	1980	16.00	40.00
DEVROE, BILLY, & THE DEVILAIRES					
Tampa TP-31	(M)	**Billy Devroe & The Devilaires, Vol. 1** *(Colored vinyl)*	1957	30.00	75.00
Tampa TP-31	(M)	**Billy Devroe & The Devilaires, Vol. 1**	1958	16.00	40.00
Tampa TP-39	(M)	**Billy Devroe & The Devilaires, Vol. 2** *(Colored vinyl)*	1958	30.00	75.00
Tampa TP-39	(M)	**Billy Devroe & The Devilaires, Vol. 2**	1958	16.00	40.00

Label & Catalog #		Title	Year	VG+	NM
DEXTER, AL					
Al Dexter is a pseudonym for Albert Poindexter.					
Columbia CL-9005	(10")	**Songs Of The Southwest**	1954	**24.00**	**60.00**
Harmony HL-7293	(M)	**Pistol Packin' Mama**	1961	**10.00**	**25.00**
Capitol T-1701	(M)	**His Greatest Hits**	1962	**16.00**	**40.00**
Capitol ST-1701	(S)	**His Greatest Hits**	1962	**20.00**	**50.00**
DIALOGUE					
Cold Studio	(M)	**Dialogue** (White cover includes insert)	196?	**60.00**	**150.00**
Cold Studio	(M)	**Dialogue** (Orange cover includes insert)	196?	**20.00**	**50.00**
DIAMOND, LEO					
RCA Victor LPM-1165	(M)	**Skin Diver Suite (And Other Selections)**	1955	**30.00**	**75.00**
Reprise R-6002	(M)	**Exciting Sounds Of The South Seas**	1961	**12.00**	**30.00**
Reprise R9-6002	(S)	**Exciting Sounds Of The South Seas**	1961	**16.00**	**40.00**
Reprise R-6009	(M)	**Themes From Great Foreign Films**	1961	**10.00**	**25.00**
Reprise R9-6009	(S)	**Themes From Great Foreign Films**	1961	**12.00**	**30.00**
Reprise R-6024	(M)	**Off Shore**	1962	**10.00**	**25.00**
Reprise R9-6024	(S)	**Off Shore**	1962	**12.00**	**30.00**
DIAMOND, NEIL					
Refer to Diana Ross / Neil Diamond.					
Bang BLP-214	(M)	**The Feel Of Neil**	1966	**16.00**	**40.00**
		(Note: Some copies of BLP-214 play stereo.)			
Bang BLPS-214	(S)	**The Feel Of Neil**	1966	**30.00**	**75.00**
Bang BLP-217	(M)	**Just For You**	1967	**12.00**	**30.00**
Bang BLPS-217	(S)	**Just For You**	1967	**16.00**	**40.00**
		(First pressings of Bang 217 have a printed blurb for "Thank The Lord For The Nighttime" on the front cover. "The Long Way Home," "You'll Forget" and the single version of "Solitary Man" are rechanneled on this and all subsequent pressings..)			
Bang BLP-217	(M)	**Just For You**	1967	**12.00**	**30.00**
Bang BLPS-217	(S)	**Just For You**	1967	**16.00**	**40.00**
		(Later pressings of Bang 217 have a sticker promoting "Shiloh" pasted over the blurb for "Thank The Lord" on the cover.)			
Bang BLP-217	(M)	**Just For You**	1967	**10.00**	**25.00**
Bang BLPS-217	(S)	**Just For You**	1967	**12.00**	**30.00**
		(Second pressings of Bang 217 promote "Shiloh" on the cover.)			
Bang BLPS-219	(S)	**Neil Diamond's Greatest Hits**	1968	**12.00**	**30.00**
		("Do It," "Kentucky Woman" and the single version of "Solitary Man" are rechanneled on this LP.)			
Bang BLPS-219	(S)	**Neil Diamond's Greatest Hits**	1968	**10.00**	**25.00**
		("Solitary Man" is rerecorded in stereo on later pressings.)			
Bang BLPS-221	(S)	**Shilo**	1970	**12.00**	**30.00**
Bang BLPS-224	(S)	**Do It!**	1970	**10.00**	**25.00**
		("Some Day Baby" is in mono while "Shot Down," "You'll Forget" and "The Long Way Home" are rechanneled.)			
Bang BLPS-227	(S)	**Double Gold** (2 LPs)	1970	**10.00**	**25.00**
		—Bang albums above have red & white labels.—			
Uni ND-11	(DJ)	**Neil Diamond** (Radio sampler)	1970	**80.00**	**200.00**
Uni ST-1913	(DJ)	**Open-End Interview**	1971	**150.00**	**300.00**
Frog King AAR-1	(S)	**Early Classics** (Includes songbook)	1972	**20.00**	**50.00**
Frog King AAR-1	(S)	**Early Classics** (Without songbook)	1972	**12.00**	**30.00**
		("Kentucky Woman" is in stereo on this while "Do It" is mono.)			
Columbia PCQ032919	(Q)	**Serenade**	1974	**10.00**	**25.00**
Columbia HC-42550	(S)	**Jonathan Livingston Seagull** (Half-speed)	1982	**16.00**	**50.00**
Columbia HC-42625	(S)	**You Don't Bring Me Flowers** (Half-speed)	1982	**13.00**	**40.00**
Columbia HC-42628	(S)	**On The Way To The Sky** (Half-speed)	1982	**16.00**	**50.00**
Columbia HC-48068	(S)	**His 12 Greatest Hits, Volume 2** (Half-speed)	1982	**13.00**	**40.00**
Columbia HC-48359	(S)	**Heartlight** (Half-speed master)	1982	**13.00**	**40.00**
Mobile Fidelity MFSL-024	(S)	**Hot August Night**	1979	**10.00**	**30.00**
Mobile Fidelity MFSL-071	(S)	**Jazz Singer**	1981	**8.00**	**25.00**
Direct Disk SD-16612	(S)	**His 12 Greatest Hits**	1982	**16.00**	**50.00**
DIAMONDS, THE					
Mercury MG-20213	(M)	**Collection Of Golden Hits**	1956	**60.00**	**150.00**
Mercury MG-20309	(M)	**The Diamonds**	1957	**60.00**	**150.00**
Mercury MG-20368	(M)	**The Diamonds Meet Pete Rugolo**	1958	**30.00**	**75.00**
Mercury SR-60076	(S)	**The Diamonds Meet Pete Rugolo**	1958	**40.00**	**100.00**

The Feel Of Neil Diamond *remains a hard to find and undervalued piece of '60s pop, especially the improbably rare—and vastly undervalued—stereo pressing. The mono pressing shown here has a sticker affixed to the cover calling the potential customer's attention to the inclusion of the hit single, "I Got The Feelin' (Oh No No)."*

Label & Catalog #		Title	Year	VG+	NM
Mercury MG-20480	(M)	**Songs From The Old West**	1959	30.00	75.00
Mercury SR-60159	(S)	**Songs From The Old West**	1959	40.00	100.00
Wing MGW-12112	(M)	**America's Famous Song Stylists**	1962	12.00	30.00
Wing MGW-12178	(M)	**Pop Hits By The Diamonds**	1962	12.00	30.00

DICK & DEE DEE
Dick St. John and Dee Dee Sperling.

Label & Catalog #		Title	Year	VG+	NM
Liberty LRP-3236	(M)	**Tell Me/The Mountain's High**	1962	16.00	40.00
Liberty LST-7236	(E)	**Tell Me/The Mountain's High**	1962	12.00	30.00
Warner Bros. W-1500	(M)	**Young And In Love**	1963	10.00	25.00
Warner Bros. WS-1500	(S)	**Young And In Love**	1963	12.00	30.00
Warner Bros. W-1538	(M)	**Turn Around**	1964	10.00	25.00
Warner Bros. WS-1538	(S)	**Turn Around**	1964	12.00	30.00
Warner Bros. W-1586	(M)	**Thou Shalt Not Steal**	1965	10.00	25.00
Warner Bros. WS-1586	(S)	**Thou Shalt Not Steal**	1965	12.00	30.00
Warner Bros. W-1623	(M)	**Songs We've Sung On "Shindig"**	1966	10.00	25.00
Warner Bros. WS-1623	(S)	**Songs We've Sung On "Shindig"**	1966	12.00	30.00

DICKENS, LITTLE JIMMY

Label & Catalog #		Title	Year	VG+	NM
Columbia CL-9053	(10")	**The Old Country Church**	1954	60.00	150.00
Columbia CL-1047	(M)	**Raisin' The Dickens**	1957	30.00	75.00
Columbia CL-1545	(M)	**Big Songs**	1960	12.00	30.00
Columbia CS-8345	(S)	**Big Songs By**	1960	16.00	40.00
Columbia CL-1887	(M)	**Out Behind The Barn**	1962	12.00	30.00
Columbia CS-8687	(S)	**Out Behind The Barn**	1962	16.00	40.00

— Columbia albums above have three white "eye" logos on each side of the spindle hole.—

DICKY DOO & THE DON'TS

Label & Catalog #		Title	Year	VG+	NM
United Arts. UAL-3094	(M)	**The Madison & Other Dances**	1959	16.00	40.00
United Arts. UAS-6094	(S)	**The Madison & Other Dances**	1959	20.00	50.00
United Arts. UAL-3097	(M)	**Teen Scene**	1959	16.00	40.00
United Arts. UAS-6097	(S)	**Teen Scene**	1959	20.00	50.00
(No label)	(DJ)	**Dicky Doo & The Don'ts Live**	1962	500.00	1,000.00

DIDDLEY, BO
Bo Diddley is a pseudonym for Ellas McDaniel.

Label & Catalog #		Title	Year	VG+	NM
Checker LP-1431	(M)	**Bo Diddley** *(White label promo)*	1958	250.00	600.00
Checker LP-1431	(M)	**Bo Diddley**	1958	80.00	200.00
Checker LP-1436	(M)	**Go Bo Diddley** *(White label promo)*	1959	250.00	600.00
Checker LP-1436	(M)	**Go Bo Diddley**	1959	60.00	150.00
Checker LP-2974	(M)	**Have Guitar, Will Travel** *(White label promo)*	1960	200.00	500.00
Checker LP-2974	(M)	**Have Guitar, Will Travel**	1960	60.00	150.00
Checker LP-2976	(M)	**Bo Diddley In The Spotlight** *(White label)*	1960	200.00	500.00
Checker LP-2976	(M)	**Bo Diddley In The Spotlight**	1960	60.00	150.00
Checker LP-2977	(M)	**Bo Diddley Is A Gunslinger** *(White label)*	1960	200.00	500.00
Checker LP-2977	(M)	**Bo Diddley Is A Gunslinger**	1960	60.00	150.00
Checker LP-2980	(M)	**Bo Diddley Is A Lover** *(White label promo)*	1961	200.00	500.00
Checker LP-2980	(M)	**Bo Diddley Is A Lover**	1961	60.00	150.00
Checker LP-2982	(M)	**Bo Diddley's A Twister** *(White label promo)*	1962	200.00	500.00
Checker LP-2982	(M)	**Bo Diddley's A Twister**	1962	40.00	100.00
Checker LP-2984	(M)	**Bo Diddley** *(White label promo)*	1962	200.00	500.00
Checker LP-2984	(M)	**Bo Diddley**	1962	40.00	100.00
Checker LP-2985	(M)	**Bo Diddley And Company** *(White label)*	1963	200.00	500.00
Checker LP-2985	(M)	**Bo Diddley And Company**	1963	60.00	150.00
Checker LP-2987	(M)	**Surfin' With Bo Diddley** *(White label promo)*	1964	150.00	300.00
Checker LP-2987	(M)	**Surfin' With Bo Diddley**	1964	40.00	100.00
Checker LPS-2987	(E)	**Surfin' With Bo Diddley**	1964	24.00	60.00
Checker LP-2988	(M)	**Bo Diddley's Beach Party** *(White label)*	1963	150.00	300.00
Checker LP-2988	(M)	**Bo Diddley's Beach Party**	1963	40.00	100.00
Checker LPS-2988	(E)	**Bo Diddley's Beach Party**	1963	24.00	60.00
Checker LP-2989	(M)	**16 All Time Greatest Hits**	1964	20.00	50.00
Checker LPS-2989	(E)	**16 All Time Greatest Hits**	1964	16.00	40.00
Checker LP-2992	(M)	**Hey! Good Lookin'** *(White label promo)*	1965	150.00	300.00
Checker LP-2992	(M)	**Hey! Good Lookin'**	1965	24.00	60.00
Checker LPS-2992	(E)	**Hey! Good Lookin'**	1965	16.00	40.00
Checker LP-2996	(M)	**500% More Man** *(White label promo)*	1965	150.00	300.00
Checker LP-2996	(M)	**500% More Man**	1965	24.00	60.00
Checker LPS-2996	(E)	**500% More Man**	1965	16.00	40.00

— Checker albums above have black or maroon labels with silver print—

While the covers of Dick and Dee Dee's albums depict them as the modicum of the then popular "boy/girl next door" fixation of American parents everywhere, Richard St. John was a rather progressive record maker and many of the duo's finest sides stand as testaments to his ability to mold a classic pop single.

Label & Catalog #		Title	Year	VG+	NM
Checker LP-2987	(M)	**Surfin' With Bo Diddley**	196?		*See below*
		(A copy of this album was found with a gold version of the original Checker label. . . Rare with no established value.)			
Checker LPS-2992	(E)	**Hey! Good Lookin'**	1966	12.00	30.00
Checker LPS-2996	(E)	**500% More Man**	1966	12.00	30.00
		— Checker albums above have blue labels with checkers on top.—			
Checker LP-2982	(M)	**Road Runner**	1967	30.00	75.00
Checker LPS-2982	(E)	**Road Runner**	1967	20.00	50.00
		("Road Runner" is a repackage of "Bo Diddley's A Twister.")			
Checker LP-3001	(M)	**The Originator**	1966	12.00	30.00
Checker LPS-3001	(S)	**The Originator**	1966	16.00	40.00
Checker LP-3006	(M)	**Go Bo Diddley**	1967	20.00	50.00
Checker LPS-3006	(E)	**Go Bo Diddley**	1967	16.00	40.00
		(Checker 3006 is a reissue of 1436.)			
Checker LP-3007	(M)	**Boss Man**	1967	30.00	75.00
Checker LPS-3007	(E)	**Boss Man**	1967	20.00	50.00
		(Checker 3007 is a reissue of 1431.)			
		— Checker albums above have blue labels with checkers on top.—			
Checker LPS-3013	(S)	**The Black Gladiator**	1968	12.00	30.00
Chess CH-50001	(S)	**Another Dimension**	1971	16.00	40.00
Chess 2CH-60005	(E)	**Got My Own Bag Of Tricks** *(2 LPs)*	1972	10.00	25.00
Chess CH-50016	(S)	**Where It All Began**	1972	16.00	40.00
Chess CH-50029	(S)	**The London Bo Diddley Sessions**	1973	10.00	25.00
Chess CH-50047	(S)	**Big Bad Bo**	1974	10.00	25.00
M.F. 2002	(S)	**I'm A Man** *(2 LPs)*	1977	40.00	100.00

DIDDLEY, BO, & CHUCK BERRY

Checker LP-2991	(M)	**Two Great Guitars**	1964	30.00	75.00
Checker LPS-2991	(E)	**Two Great Guitars**	1964	16.00	40.00
		— Checker albums above have black labels with silver print—			
Checker LPS-2991	(E)	**Two Great Guitars**	1966	12.00	30.00
		— Checker albums above have blue labels with checkers on top.—			

DIDDLEY, BO, & MUDDY WATERS & LITTLE WALTER

Checker LP-3008	(M)	**Super Blues Band**	1968	20.00	50.00
Checker LPS-3008	(S)	**Super Blues Band**	1968	16.00	40.00

DIDDLEY, BO, & MUDDY WATERS & HOWLIN' WOLF

Checker LP-3010	(M)	**Super, Super Blues Band**	1968	20.00	50.00
Checker LPS-3010	(S)	**Super, Super Blues Band**	1968	16.00	40.00

DIETRICH, MARLENE

Decca DL-5100	(10")	**Souvenir Album**	1950	30.00	75.00
Vox PL-3040	(10")	**Marlene Dietrich Sings**	1951	30.00	75.00
Columbia GL-105	(M)	**American Songs In German For The OSS**	1952	30.00	75.00
Columbia WL-164	(M)	**Dietrich In Rio**	1953	30.00	75.00
Columbia ML-4975	(M)	**Cafe De Paris**	1955	20.00	50.00
Decca DL-8465	(M)	**Marlene Dietrich**	1957	16.00	40.00
Columbia CL-1275	(M)	**Lili Marlene**	1959	12.00	30.00
Capitol Int. T-10397	(M)	**Marlene**	1965	10.00	25.00
Capitol Int. DT-10397	(E)	**Marlene**	1965	8.00	20.00
Capitol OTCR-300	(M)	**The Magic Of Marlene**	1969	10.00	25.00

DIGA RHYTHM BAND, THE
The Digas are Mickey Hart and Bill Kreutzmann of the Grateful Dead.

Round RX-110	(S)	**The Diga Rhythm Band**	1976	12.00	30.00

DILL, DANNY

MGM E-3819	(M)	**Folk Songs Of The Wild West**	1960	8.00	20.00
MGM SE-3819	(S)	**Folk Songs Of The Wild West**	1960	10.00	25.00

DILLARD, DOUG

Together STT-1003	(S)	**Banjo Album**	1970	30.00	75.00

DILLARD & CLARK
Doug Dillard and Gene Clark.

A&M SP-4158	(S)	**The Fantastic Expedition Of Dillard & Clark** *(Brown label)*	1969	10.00	25.00

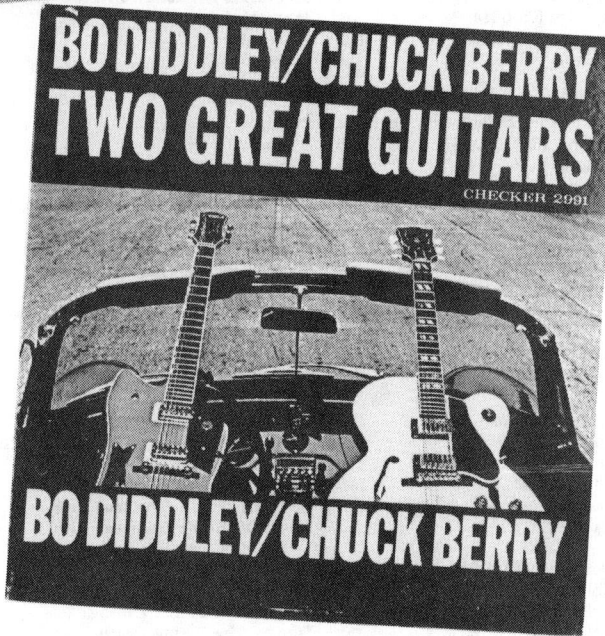

Ellas McDaniel took his moniker from a single-stringed African instrument known as a "bo diddley." After hitting big with the single of the same name, he just up and called the rhythmic progression, based squarely on that of the vaudevillian "shave-and-a-haircut" pattern, "bo diddley." While the album on top depicts a typically jauntily humorous Bo, the bottom is a guitar classic long out of print.

Label & Catalog #		Title	Year	VG+	NM

DILLARDS, THE

Label & Catalog #		Title	Year	VG+	NM
Elektra EKL-232	(M)	Back Porch Bluegrass	1963	10.00	25.00
Elektra EKS-7232	(S)	Back Porch Bluegrass	1963	14.00	35.00
Elektra EKL-265	(M)	The Dillards, Live!!! Almost!!!	1964	8.00	20.00
Elektra EKS-726	(S)	The Dillards, Live!!! Almost!!!	1964	10.00	25.00
Elektra EKL-285	(M)	Pickin' And Fiddlin' (With Byron Berline)	1965	8.00	20.00
Elektra EKS-7285	(S)	Pickin' And Fiddlin' (With Byron Berline)	1965	10.00	25.00

DIMENSIONS, THE

Label & Catalog #		Title	Year	VG+	NM
(No label)	(M)	From All Dimensions	1966	800.00	1,200.00

DINNING, MARK

Label & Catalog #		Title	Year	VG+	NM
MGM E-3828	(M)	Teen Angel	1960	40.00	100.00
MGM SE-3828	(S)	Teen Angel	1960	60.00	150.00
MGM E-3855	(M)	Wanderin'	1960	30.00	75.00
MGM SE-3855	(S)	Wanderin'	1960	40.00	100.00

DINNING SISTERS, THE

Label & Catalog #		Title	Year	VG+	NM
Capitol H-318	(10")	The Dinning Sisters	195?	16.00	40.00

DINO, DESI & BILLY
Dino Martin, Desi Arnaz Jr, and Billy Hinsche.

Label & Catalog #		Title	Year	VG+	NM
Reprise R-6176	(M)	I'm A Fool	1965	8.00	20.00
Reprise RS-6176	(S)	I'm A Fool	1965	10.00	25.00
Reprise R-6194	(M)	Our Times Are Coming	1966	8.00	20.00
Reprise RS-6194	(S)	Our Times Are Coming	1966	10.00	25.00
Reprise R-6198	(M)	Memories Are Made Of This	1966	8.00	20.00
Reprise RS-6198	(S)	Memories Are Made Of This	1966	10.00	25.00
Reprise R-6224	(M)	Souvenir	1966	10.00	25.00
Reprise RS-6224	(S)	Souvenir	1966	12.00	30.00

DION
Dion Dimucci formerly recorded backed by The Belmonts.

Label & Catalog #		Title	Year	VG+	NM
Laurie LLP-2004	(M)	Alone With Dion	1960	40.00	100.00
Laurie LLP-2009	(M)	Runaround Sue (Green vinyl)	1961	250.00	500.00
Laurie LLP-2009	(M)	Runaround Sue	1961	40.00	100.00
Laurie T-91027	(M)	Runaround Sue (Capitol Record Club)	196?	60.00	150.00
Laurie DT-91027	(E)	Runaround Sue (Capitol Record Club)	196?	60.00	150.00
Laurie LLP-2012	(M)	Lovers Who Wander	1962	30.00	75.00
Laurie LLP-2013	(M)	Dion Sings His Greatest Hits	1962	20.00	50.00
Laurie SLP-2013	(E)	Dion Sings His Greatest Hits	1962	12.00	30.00
		(Laurie 2018 features two of Dion's solo hits and ten with The Belmonts.)			
Laurie T-90386	(M)	Dion Sings His Greatest Hits	1962	60.00	150.00
Laurie DT-90386	(E)	Dion Sings His Greatest Hits	1962	60.00	150.00
		(Capitol Record Club)			
Laurie LLP-2015	(M)	Love Came To Me	1963	30.00	75.00
Laurie LLP-2017	(M)	Dion Sings To Sandy (& All His Other Girls!)	1963	30.00	75.00
Laurie LLP-2019	(M)	Dion Sings The 15 Million Sellers	1963	20.00	50.00
Laurie LLP-2022	(M)	More Of Dion's Greatest Hits	1963	20.00	50.00
Laurie T-91128	(M)	More Of Dion's Greatest Hits	1963	60.00	150.00
Laurie DT-91128	(E)	More Of Dion's Greatest Hits	1963	60.00	150.00
		(Capitol Record Club)			
Columbia CL-2010	(M)	Ruby Baby	1963	10.00	25.00
Columbia CS-8810	(S)	Ruby Baby	1963	12.00	30.00
Columbia CL-2107	(M)	Donna The Prima Donna	1963	10.00	25.00
Columbia CS-8907	(S)	Donna The Prima Donna	1963	12.00	30.00

DION & THE BELMONTS
Refer to The Belmonts.

Label & Catalog #		Title	Year	VG+	NM
Laurie LLP-1002	(M)	Presenting Dion & The Belmonts	1959	200.00	400.00
		(First pressing have gold labels and the covers have "Master-works" under the Laurie label in the upper right corner.)			
Laurie LLP-2002	(M)	Presenting Dion & The Belmonts	1959	60.00	150.00
		(Second pressings have the gold & white label.)			
Laurie LLPS-2002	(E)	Presenting Dion & The Belmonts	1959		See below
		(LLPS-2002 has a suggested Near Mint value of $1,000-2,000.)			
Laurie LLP-2006	(M)	Wish Upon A Star	1959	150.00	300.00
Laurie LLP-2016	(M)	Together (On Records)	1963	20.00	50.00

After achieving massive success as a doo-wop group with The Belmonts, Dion DiMucci branched out into a lucrative solo career, first with Laurie and then with Columbia. As the quintessential Italian kid making good, Dion was the idol of virtually every white kid on the streets on New York, much the same role that Frankie Lymon played for every black kid in New York. (Elvis wasn't the king everywhere, at least not then.)

Label & Catalog #		Title	Year	VG+	NM
ABC 599	(M)	**Dion & The Belmonts—Together Again**	1967	12.00	30.00
ABC S-599	(S)	**Dion & The Belmonts—Together Again**	1967	12.00	30.00
Reprise BS-2664	(S)	**Dion & The Belmonts Live 1972**	1973	12.00	30.00
DIRE STRAITS					
Warner Bros. WBMS-109	(DJ)	**Dire Straits Live**	1980	16.00	40.00
DIRTY BLUES BAND, THE					
BluesWay BLS-6010	(S)	**The Dirty Blues Band**	1968	10.00	25.00
BluesWay BLS-6020	(S)	**Stone Dirt**	1968	10.00	25.00
DIXIE CUPS, THE					
Red Bird RB-20-100	(M)	**Chapel Of Love**	1964	20.00	50.00
Red Bird RBS-20-100	(S)	**Chapel Of Love**	1964	30.00	75.00
Red Bird RB-20-103	(M)	**Iko Iko**	1965	20.00	50.00
ABC-Paramount ABC-525	(M)	**Riding High**	1965	20.00	50.00
ABC-Paramount ABCS-525	(S)	**Riding High**	1965	30.00	75.00
DIXIE DREGS, THE					
No label	(S)	**The Great Spectacular**	1975	60.00	150.00
Direct Disk SD-16620	(S)	**Dregs Of The Earth**	198?	13.00	40.00
DIXIEBELLES, THE					
Sound Stage-7 SSM-5000	(M)	**Down At Papa Joe's**	1963	20.00	50.00
Sound Stage-7 SSS-15000	(E)	**Down At Papa Joe's**	1963	16.00	40.00
DIXON, WILLIE					
Bluesville BVLP-1003	(M)	**Willie's Blues**	1960	60.00	150.00
		—Bluesville albums above have bright blue labels with silver print.—			
Bluesville BVLP-1003	(M)	**Willie's Blues**	1964	16.00	40.00
		—Bluesville albums above have blue labels with a trident logo on the right side.—			
DIXON, WILLIE, & MEMPHIS SLIM					
Verve MGV-3007	(M)	**Blues Every Which Way**	1960	50.00	125.00
		—Verve albums above have "Verve Records, Inc." on the bottom of the label.—			
Battle BV-6122	(M)	**In Paris**	1963	8.00	20.00
Battle BVS-6122	(S)	**In Paris**	1963	10.00	25.00
DOBKINS, CARL, JR.					
Decca DL-8938	(M)	**Carl Dobkins, Jr.**	1959	40.00	100.00
Decca DL-78938	(S)	**Carl Dobkins, Jr.**	1959	60.00	150.00
DOBSON, BONNIE					
Prestige Int. PRLP-13021	(M)	**Like A Swallow**	1962	12.00	30.00
Prestige Int. PRLP-13034	(M)	**Dear Companion**	1962	12.00	30.00
Prestige Int. PRLP-13064	(M)	**Merry-Go-Round Of Children's Songs**	1962	12.00	30.00
Folklore FRLP-14007	(M)	**Dear Companion**	1964	8.00	20.00
Folklore FRST-14007	(S)	**Dear Companion**	1964	10.00	25.00
		(Folklore 14007 is a reissue of Prestige 13034.)			
Folklore FRLP-14015	(M)	**She's Like A Swallow**	1964	8.00	20.00
Folklore FRST-14015	(S)	**She's Like A Swallow**	1964	10.00	25.00
		(Folklore 14015 is a reissue of Prestige 13021.)			
Folklore FRLP-14018	(M)	**Hootenanny With Bonnie Gibson**	1964	8.00	20.00
Folklore FRST-14018	(S)	**Hootenanny With Bonnie Gibson**	1964	10.00	25.00
DR. FEELGOOD & THE INTERNS					
Dr. Feelgood also recorded as Piano Red.					
OKeh OKM-12101	(M)	**Doctor Feelgood & The Interns**	1962	30.00	75.00
OKeh OKS-14101	(S)	**Doctor Feelgood & The Interns**	1962	60.00	150.00
DR. ROSS					
Fortune F-3011	(M)	**Doctor Ross, The Harmonica Boss**	1962	20.00	50.00
Fortune FS-3011	(S)	**Doctor Ross, The Harmonica Boss**	1962	30.00	75.00
DODD, DICK					
Dodd was formerly a member of The Standells.					
Tower ST-5142	(S)	**First Evolution Of Dick Dodd**	1968	20.00	50.00

Label & Catalog #		Title	Year	VG+	NM
DODD, JIMMIE					
Mercury MG-20315	(M)	500 Miles To Glory	1957	24.00	60.00
Imperial LP-9089	(M)	Lonely Guitar	1959	12.00	40.00
Imperial LP-9121	(M)	Swing-A-Spell	1960	12.00	40.00
Imperial LP-12121	(S)	Swing-A-Spell	1960	20.00	50.00
Disneyland DQ-1235	(M)	Sing Along With Jimmie Dodd	1962	12.00	30.00

DODSON, MARGE:*Refer to* **GOLDMINE'S PRICE GUIDE TO COLLECTIBLE JAZZ ALBUMS**

Label & Catalog #		Title	Year	VG+	NM
DOGGETT, BILL					
King 295-82	(10")	Bill Doggett—His Organ And Combo	1955	40.00	100.00
King 295-83	(10")	Bill Doggett—His Organ And Combo, Vol. 2	1955	40.00	100.00
King 295-89	(10")	All-Time Christmas Favorites	1955	80.00	200.00
		(King 89 may have been the first rhythm'n blues Christmas album.)			
King 295-102	(10")	Sentimentally Yours	1956	40.00	100.00
King 395-502	(M)	Moondust	1957	16.00	40.00
King 395-514	(M)	Hot Doggett	1957	16.00	40.00
King 395-523	(M)	As You Desire	1958	16.00	40.00
King 395-531	(M)	Everybody Dance To The Honky Tonk	1958	16.00	40.00
King 395-532	(M)	Dame Dreaming	1958	16.00	40.00
King 395-533	(M)	A Salute To Ellington	1958	16.00	40.00
King 395-557	(M)	The Doggett Beat For Dancing Feet	1958	16.00	40.00
King 395-563	(M)	Candle Glow	1958	16.00	40.00
King 395-582	(M)	Swingin' Easy	1959	16.00	40.00
King 395-585	(M)	Dance Awhile	1959	16.00	40.00
King 395-600	(M)	Bill Doggett Christmas	1959	16.00	40.00
King 395-609	(M)	Hold It	1959	16.00	40.00
King 633	(M)	High And Wide	1959	12.00	30.00
King 641	(M)	Big City Dance Party	1959	12.00	30.00
King 667	(M)	Bill Doggett On Tour	1959	12.00	30.00
King 706	(M)	For Reminiscent Lovers, Romantic Songs	1960	12.00	30.00
King 723	(M)	Back Again With More	1960	12.00	30.00
King 759	(M)	Bonanza Of 24 Songs	1960	12.00	30.00
King 778	(M)	The Many Moods Of Bill Doggett	1963	12.00	30.00
King 830	(M)	American Songs In The Bossa Nova Style	1963	12.00	30.00
King 868	(S)	Impressions	1964	12.00	30.00
King 908	(S)	The Best Of Bill Doggett	1964	12.00	30.00
King 959	(S)	Bonanza Of 24 Hit Songs	1966	12.00	30.00
		— King albums above have crownless black or blue labels. The logo on the covers			
		have a crown with "King" in open capital block letters below.—			
King KSD-1078	(S)	Honky Tonk Popcorn	1969	20.00	50.00
		(King 1078 was produced by James Brown.)			

DOHERTY, DENNY
Mr. Doherty was formerly a member of The Mugwumps; The Mamas & The Papas.

Label & Catalog #		Title	Year	VG+	NM
Dunhill DS-50096	(S)	Watcha' Gonna Do?	1970	10.00	25.00

DOJO

Label & Catalog #		Title	Year	VG+	NM
Eclipse ES-7309	(S)	Down For The Last Time	1971	10.00	25.00

DOLENZ, JONES, BOYCE & HART
Mickey Dolenz, Davey Jones, Tommy Boyce and Bobby Hart. Refer to The Monkees.

Label & Catalog #		Title	Year	VG+	NM
Capitol ST-11513	(S)	Dolenz, Jones, Boyce And Hart	1976	10.00	25.00

DOMINO, FATS

Label & Catalog #		Title	Year	VG+	NM
Imperial LP-9004	(M)	Rock And Rollin' With Fats Domino	1956	80.00	200.00
Imperial LP-9009	(M)	Rock And Rollin'	1956	80.00	200.00
Imperial LP-9028	(M)	This Is Fats Domino!	1957	80.00	200.00
Imperial LP-9038	(M)	Here Stands Fats Domino	1957	80.00	200.00
Imperial LP-9040	(M)	This Is Fats	1957	80.00	200.00
		— Original Imperial albums above have maroon labels.—			
Imperial LP-9004	(M)	Rock And Rollin' With Fats Domino	1958	40.00	100.00
Imperial LP-9009	(M)	Rock And Rollin'	1958	40.00	100.00
Imperial LP-9028	(M)	This Is Fats Domino!	1958	40.00	100.00
Imperial LP-9038	(M)	Here Stands Fats Domino	1958	40.00	100.00
Imperial LP-9040	(M)	This Is Fats	1958	40.00	100.00
Imperial LP-9055	(M)	The Fabulous Mr. D	1958	40.00	100.00
Imperial LP-9062	(M)	Fats Domino Swings	1959	40.00	100.00
Imperial LP-9065	(M)	Let's Play Fats Domino	1959	40.00	100.00

Label & Catalog #		Title	Year	VG+	NM
Imperial LP-9103	(M)	Million Record Hits	1960	40.00	100.00
Imperial LP-9127	(M)	A Lot Of Dominos	1961	40.00	100.00
Imperial LP-12066	(S)	A Lot Of Dominos	1961	60.00	150.00
Imperial LP-9138	(M)	I Miss You So	1961	40.00	100.00
Imperial LP-12398	(E)	I Miss You So	1961	30.00	75.00
Imperial LP-9153	(M)	Let The Four Winds Blow	1961	40.00	100.00
Imperial LP-12073	(S)	Let The Four Winds Blow	1961	60.00	150.00
Imperial LP-9164	(M)	What A Party	1962	30.00	75.00
Imperial LP-9170	(M)	Twistin' The Stomp	1962	30.00	75.00
Imperial LP-9195	(M)	Million Sellers By Fats	1962	24.00	60.00
Imperial LP-9208	(M)	Just Domino	1962	24.00	60.00
Imperial LP-9227	(M)	Walking To New Orleans	1963	20.00	50.00
Imperial LP-9239	(M)	Let's Dance With Domino	1963	20.00	50.00
Imperial LP-9248	(M)	Here He Comes Again	1963	20.00	50.00

— Imperial mono albums above have black labels with colored stars on top; stereo album have black labels with silver print.—

Imperial LP-9004	(M)	Rock And Rollin' With Fats Domino	1964	12.00	30.00
Imperial LP-12387	(E)	Rock And Rollin' With Fats Domino	1964	8.00	20.00
Imperial LP-9009	(M)	Rock And Rollin'	1964	12.00	30.00
Imperial LP-12388	(E)	Rock And Rollin'	1964	8.00	20.00
Imperial LP-9028	(M)	This Is Fats Domino!	1964	12.00	30.00
Imperial LP-12389	(E)	This Is Fats Domino!	1964	8.00	20.00
Imperial LP-9038	(M)	Here Stands Fats Domino	1964	12.00	30.00
Imperial LP-12390	(E)	Here Stands Fats Domino	1964	8.00	20.00
Imperial LP-9040	(M)	This Is Fats	1964	12.00	30.00
Imperial LP-12391	(E)	This Is Fats	1964	8.00	20.00
Imperial LP-9055	(M)	The Fabulous Mr. D	1964	12.00	30.00
Imperial LP-12394	(E)	The Fabulous Mr. D	1964	8.00	20.00
Imperial LP-9062	(M)	Fats Domino Swings	1964	12.00	30.00
Imperial LP-12091	(E)	Fats Domino Swings	1964	8.00	20.00
Imperial LP-9065	(M)	Let's Play Fats Domino	1964	12.00	30.00
Imperial LP-12395	(E)	Let's Play Fats Domino	1964	8.00	20.00
Imperial LP-9103	(M)	Million Record Hits	1964	12.00	30.00
Imperial LP-12103	(E)	Million Record Hits	1964	8.00	20.00
Imperial LP-9127	(M)	A Lot Of Dominos	1964	12.00	30.00
Imperial LP-12066	(S)	A Lot Of Dominos	1964	14.00	35.00
Imperial LP-9138	(M)	I Miss You So	1964	12.00	30.00
Imperial LP-12398	(E)	I Miss You So	1964	8.00	20.00
Imperial LP-9153	(M)	Let The Four Winds Blow	1964	12.00	30.00
Imperial LP-12073	(S)	Let The Four Winds Blow	1964	16.00	40.00
Imperial LP-9195	(M)	Million Sellers By Fats	1964	12.00	30.00
Imperial LP-12195	(E)	Million Sellers By Fats	1964	8.00	20.00
Imperial LP-9227	(M)	Walking To New Orleans	1964	12.00	30.00
Imperial LP-12227	(E)	Walking To New Orleans	1964	8.00	20.00
Imperial LP-9239	(M)	Let's Dance With Domino	1964	12.00	30.00
Imperial LP-12239	(E)	Let's Dance With Domino	1964	8.00	20.00
Imperial LP-9248	(M)	Here He Comes Again	1964	12.00	30.00
Imperial LP-12248	(E)	Here He Comes Again	1964	8.00	20.00

— Imperial albums above have black, white & pink labels.—

ABC Paramount ABC-455	(M)	Here Comes Fats Domino	1963	8.00	20.00
ABC Paramount ABCS-455	(S)	Here Comes Fats Domino	1963	10.00	25.00
ABC Paramount ABC-479	(M)	Fats On Fire	1964	8.00	20.00
ABC Paramount ABCS-479	(S)	Fats On Fire	1964	10.00	25.00
ABC Paramount ABC-510	(M)	Getaway With Fats Domino	1965	8.00	20.00
ABC Paramount ABCS-510	(S)	Getaway With Fats Domino	1965	10.00	25.00
Mercury MG-21039	(M)	Fats Domino '65	1965	10.00	25.00
Mercury SR-61039	(S)	Fats Domino '65	1965	16.00	40.00
Reprise RS-6439	(S)	Fats (Test pressing)	1971	200.00	400.00
United Arts. UAMG-104	(DJ)	The Fats Domino Sound	1973	14.00	35.00

(Promo only with edited versions of 30 tracks.)

United ArtS. LA-122	(DJ)	Cookin' With Fats (2 LPs)	1974	300.00	500.00

(Promo with one LP on black and one on multi-color vinyL)

United Arts. LA-122	(M)	Cookin' With Fats (2 LPs)	1974	12.00	30.00

DON & DEWEY

Don "Sugarcane" Harris and Dewey Terry.

Specialty SPS-2131	(E)	They're Rockin' Til Midnight, Rollin' Til Dawn	1970	16.00	40.00

("Pink Champagne" and "Mammer Jammer" are stereo on this LP.)

Label & Catalog #		Title	Year	VG+	NM
DON & EDDIE					
Modern MST-814	(S)	**Rock And Roll Party**	196?	16.00	40.00
DON & THE GOOD TIMES					
Refer to Jim Valley.					
Burdette 300	(M)	**Don & The Goodtimes' Greatest Hits**	1966	40.00	100.00
Burdette 300-S	(S)	**Don & The Goodtimes' Greatest Hits**	1966	100.00	250.00
Burdette 300-S	(E)	**Don & The Goodtimes' Greatest Hits**	1966	20.00	50.00
Wand WDS-679	(S)	**Where The Action Is**	1969	12.00	30.00
DON, DICK & JIMMY					
Modern LMP-1205	(M)	**Spring Fever**	195?	20.00	50.00
Verve MGV-2084	(M)	**Medium Rare**	1958	16.00	40.00
Verve MGV-2107	(M)	**Songs For The Hearth**	1959	16.00	40.00
		— Verve albums above have "Verve Records, Inc" on the bottom of the label.—			
DONEGAN, LONNIE					
Mercury MG-20229	(M)	**An Englishman Sings American Folk Songs**	1957	30.00	75.00
Dot DLP-3159	(M)	**Lonnie Donegan**	1959	14.00	35.00
Dot DLP-25159	(S)	**Lonnie Donegan**	1959	20.00	50.00
Dot DLP-3394	(M)	**Lonnie Donegan**	1961	14.00	35.00
Dot DLP-25394	(S)	**Lonnie Donegan**	1961	16.00	40.00
		(Dot 3/25394 was originally issued with a wrap-around paper sleeve advertiting the hit, "Does Your Chewing Gum Lose Its Flaor.")			
Dot DLP-3394	(M)	**Lonnie Donegan**	1961	10.00	25.00
Dot DLP-25394	(S)	**Lonnie Donegan**	1961	12.00	30.00
Atlantic 8038	(M)	**Skiffle Folk Music**	1960	20.00	50.00
Atlantic SD-8038	(S)	**Skiffle Folk Music**	1960	30.00	75.00
		— Atlantic mono albums above have black labels; stereo albums have green labels.—			
Atlantic 8038	(M)	**Skiffle Folk Music**	196?	8.00	20.00
Atlantic SD-8038	(S)	**Skiffle Folk Music**	196?	10.00	25.00
		— Atlantic albums above have muti-colored labels with a white "fan" logo on the right side.—			
ABC-Paramount-433	(M)	**Sing Hallelujah**	1963	8.00	20.00
ABC-Paramount S-433	(S)	**Sing Hallelujah**	1963	10.00	25.00
DONNER, RAL					
Gone LP-5012	(M)	**Takin' Care Of Business**	1961	150.00	300.00
DONNER, RAL / RAY SMITH / BOBBY DALE					
Crown CLP-5335	(M)	**Ral Donner, Ray Smith And Bobby Dale**	1963	12.00	30.00
Crown CST-335	(E)	**Ral Donner, Ray Smith And Bobby Dale**	1963	6.00	15.00
DONNIE & THE DELCHORDS					
Taurus 1000	(S)	**Donnie & The Delchords With The Neons**	1967	50.00	125.00
DONOVAN					
Billed as "Great Britain's answer to Dylan," Singer, songwriter and guitar player Donovan Leitch's early work was in the contemporary folk vein. By 1966 he was working in an eclectic pop style					
Hickory LPM-123	(M)	**Catch The Wind**	1965	10.00	25.00
Hickory LPS-123	(E)	**Catch The Wind**	1965	8.00	20.00
Hickory LPM-127	(M)	**Fairy Tale**	1965	8.00	20.00
Hickory LPS-127	(S)	**Fairy Tale** *("Colours" is rechanneled)*	1965	10.00	25.00
Hickory LPM-135	(M)	**The Real Donovan**	1966	8.00	20.00
Hickory LPS-135	(P)	**The Real Donovan**	1966	10.00	25.00
		(While this compilation features rechanneled stereo tracks from Hickory 127, the other tracks, including "Colours," are stereo.)			
Epic LN-24217	(M)	**Sunshine Superman**	1966	10.00	25.00
Epic BN-26217	(E)	**Sunshine Superman**	1966	5.00	12.00
Epic LN-24239	(M)	**Mellow Yellow**	1967	10.00	25.00
Epic BN-26239	(E)	**Mellow Yellow**	1967	5.00	12.00
Epic L2N-171	(M)	**A Gift From A Flower To A Garden**	1968	16.00	40.00
Epic B2N-171	(S)	**A Gift From A Flower To A Garden**	1968	10.00	25.00
		(Epic 171 is a boxed set of the two previous albums, "Wear Your Love Like Heaven" and "For Little Ones." Issued with a portfolio of lyrics, drawings, and poetry, which are included in the price.)			
		— Epic albums above have yellow labels.—			
DOOBIE BROTHERS, THE					
Nautilus NR-5	(S)	**The Captain And Me**	1980	13.00	40.00

Label & Catalog #		Title	Year	VG+	NM

DOORS, THE
The Doors are John Densmore, Robbie Krieger, Ray Manzarek and Jim Morrison.

Elektra EKL-4007	(M)	**The Doors**	1967	60.00	150.00
Elektra EKS-74007	(S)	**The Doors**	1967	10.00	25.00
Elektra EKL-4014	(M)	**Strange Days**	1967	80.00	200.00
Elektra EKS-74014	(S)	**Strange Days**	1967	10.00	25.00
Elektra EKL-4024	(M)	**Waiting For The Sun**	1968	100.00	250.00
Elektra EKS-74024	(S)	**Waiting For The Sun** *(White label promo)*	1968	30.00	75.00
Elektra EKS-74024	(S)	**Waiting For The Sun**	1968	10.00	25.00
		— Elektra albums above have brown labels.—			
Elektra EKS-75007	(S)	**Morrison Hotel/Hard Rock Cafe** *(White label)*	1970	30.00	75.00
Elektra EKS-75007	(S)	**Morrison Hotel/Hard Rock Cafe**	1970	6.00	15.00
		— Elektra albums above have red labels.—			
Elektra EKS-2-9002	(S)	**Absolutely Live** *(2 LPs. White label promo)*	1970	24.00	60.00
Elektra EKS-2-9002	(S)	**Absolutely Live** *(2 LPs)*	1970	10.00	25.00
Elektra EKS-74079	(S)	**The Doors 13** *(White label promo)*	1970	16.00	40.00
Elektra EKS-74079	(S)	**The Doors 13**	1970	6.00	15.00
Elektra EKS-75011	(S)	**L.A. Woman** *(White label promo)*	1971	24.00	60.00
Elektra EKS-75011	(S)	**L.A. Woman**	1971	10.00	25.00
		(Originally issued in a cover with a die-cut window and a yellow inner sleeve with a photo of the group.)			
Elektra EQ-5035	(Q)	**Best Of The Doors**	1973	10.00	25.00
		— Elektra albums above have "butterfly" labels.—			
Mobile Fidelity MSFL-051	(S)	**The Doors**	1980	20.00	60.00
Elektra 60345	(S)	**The Best Of The Doors** *(2 LPs)*	1985	16.00	40.00
		(White label promo pressed on "high quality audiophile vinyl.")			

DORS, DIANA

Columbia CL-1436	(M)	**Swinging Dors**	1960	30.00	75.00
Columbia CS-8236	(S)	**Swinging Dors**	1960	40.00	100.00

DORSEY, LEE

Fury 1002	(M)	**Ya Ya**	1962	150.00	300.00
Sphere Sound SR-7003	(M)	**Ya Ya**	1963	20.00	50.00
Sphere Sound SSR-7003	(E)	**Ya Ya**	1963	16.00	40.00
		(Sphere Sound 7003 is a reissue of Fury 1002.)			
Amy 8010	(M)	**Ride Your Pony**	1966	12.00	30.00
Amy S-8010	(S)	**Ride Your Pony**	1966	16.00	40.00
Amy 8011	(M)	**The New Lee Dorsey**	1966	10.00	25.00
Amy S-8011	(S)	**The New Lee Dorsey**	1966	12.00	30.00

DORSEY, WILLA, & THE MIGHTY FAITH INCREASERS

King 806	(M)	**Willa Dorsey And The Mighty Faith Increasers**	1962	40.00	100.00

DOUBLE SIX OF PARIS, THE: *Refer to* **GOLDMINE'S PRICE GUIDE TO COLLECTIBLE JAZZ ALBUMS**

DOUGLAS, GLENN

Decca DL-8748	(M)	**Heartbreak Alley**	1958	20.00	50.00

DOUGLAS, K. C.

Cook LP-5002	(M)	**Road Recordings**	1954	200.00	500.00
Bluesville BVLP-1023	(M)	**K. C.'s Blues**	1961	30.00	75.00
Bluesville BVLP-1050	(M)	**Big Road Blues**	1962	30.00	75.00
		— Bluesville albums above have bright blue labels with silver print.—			
Bluesville BVLP-1023	(M)	**K. C.'s Blues**	1964	12.00	30.00
Bluesville BVLP-1050	(M)	**Big Road Blues**	1964	12.00	30.00
		— Bluesville albums above have blue labels with a trident logo on the right side.—			

DOVELLS, THE
The Dovells feature Len Barry. Refer to the Orlons.

Parkway P-7006	(M)	**The Bristol Stomp**	1961	40.00	100.00
Parkway P-7010	(M)	**All The Hits Of The Teen Groups**	1962	40.00	100.00
Parkway P-7011	(M)	**Don't Knock The Twist** *(Soundtrack)*	1962	40.00	100.00
Parkway P-7021	(M)	**For Your Hully Gully Party**	1963	30.00	75.00
Parkway P-7025	(M)	**You Can't Sit Down**	1963	30.00	75.00
Cameo C-1082	(M)	**Len Barry Sings With The Dovells**	1964	20.00	50.00

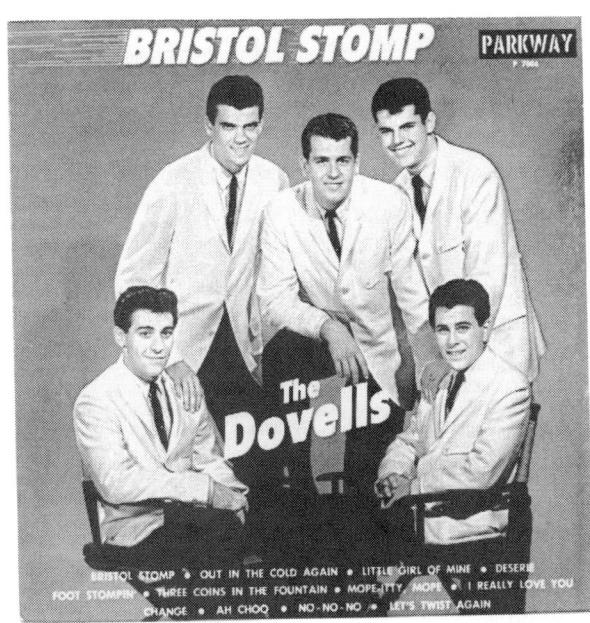

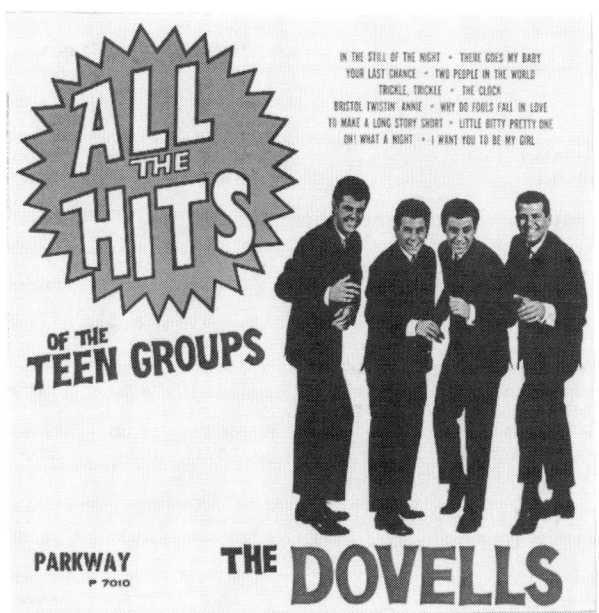

Philadelphia's Dovells featured lead singer Len Barry (born Leonard Borisoff) with Danny Brooks (Born Jim Meeley), Mike Dennis (born Mike Freda, Jerry Summers (born Jerry Gross) and Arnie Silver. The uptempo jive group scored several hits, including two biggies with 1961's "Bristol Stomp" and '63's "You Can't Sit Down." By the time their singles stopped making the charts, both Brooks and Barry had left, the latter for a brief spell in the spotlight as a solo. The other members later recorded as The magistrates on MGM. Their LPs are hard to find in nearly mint condition but not a lot of collectors seem to care. . .

Label & Catalog #		Title	Year	VG+	NM
DOWELL, JOE					
Smash MGS-27000	(M)	**Wooden Heart**	1961	14.00	35.00
Smash SRS-67000	(S)	**Wooden Heart**	1961	20.00	50.00
Smash MGS-27011	(M)	**German American Hits**	1962	10.00	25.00
Smash SRS-67011	(S)	**German American Hits**	1962	12.00	30.00
DOWN FROM NOTHING					
No label	(S)	**Down From Nothing**	197?	100.00	250.00
DOWNS, HUGH					
Epic LN-3597	(M)	**An Evening With Hugh Downs**	1961	10.00	25.00
Epic BN-341	(S)	**An Evening With Hugh Downs**	1961	14.00	35.00
DOYLE, BOBBY/THE BOBBY DOYLE THREE					
The BD3 features Kenny Rogers.					
Columbia CL-1858	(M)	**In A Most Unusual Way**	1962	8.00	20.00
Columbia CS-8658	(S)	**In A Most Unusual Way**	1962	10.00	25.00
DOYLE, MIKE					
Fleetwood FLP-3018	(M)	**The Secrets Of Surfing**	1963	20.00	50.00
DOZIER, GENE, & THE BROTHERHOOD					
Minit 40010	(M)	**Blues Power**	1967	12.00	30.00
Minit 240010	(S)	**Blues Power**	1967	12.00	30.00
DRAGONFLY					
Megaphone MS-1202	(S)	**Dragonfly**	1968	60.00	150.00
DRAGONWYCK					
(No label)	(S)	**Dragonwyck** *(Test pressing without a cover)*	197?	500.00	1,000.00
(No label)	(S)	**Dragonwyck 2** *(Acetate without a cover)*	197?		*See below*
		(Near Mint acetates have a suggested value of $1,000-2,000.)			
DRAGSTERS, THE					
Wing MGW-12269	(M)	**Hot Rod Hits**	1964	20.00	50.00
Wing SRW-16269	(S)	**Hot Rod Hits**	1964	30.00	75.00
DRAKE, DONNA: *Refer to* GOLDMINE'S PRICE GUIDE TO COLLECTIBLE JAZZ ALBUMS					
DRAKE, NICK					
Island SMAS-9307	(S)	**Nick Drake**	1971	10.00	25.00
DRAKE, PETE					
Drake also recorded as Dean Dallas.					
Starday SLP-180	(M)	**The Fabulous Steel Guitar Of Pete Drake**	1962	20.00	50.00
Starday SLP-319	(M)	**The Amazing And Incredible Pete Drake**	1964	16.00	40.00
		— Starday albums above have yellow labels.—			
Cumberland MGC-29053	(M)	**Country Steel Guitar**	1963	8.00	20.00
Cumberland SRC-69053	(S)	**Country Steel Guitar**	1963	10.00	25.00
DRAMATICS, THE					
Volt VOS-6018	(S)	**Whatcha See Is Whatcha Get**	1972	10.00	25.00
Volt VOS-6019	(S)	**A Dramatic Experience**	1973	10.00	25.00
DRAPER, RUSTY					
Mercury MG-20068	(M)	**Music For A Rainy Night**	1956	16.00	40.00
Mercury MG-20117	(M)	**Encores**	1957	16.00	40.00
Mercury MG-20118	(M)	**Songs By Rusty Draper**	1957	16.00	40.00
Mercury MG-20173	(M)	**Rusty Meets Hoagy**	1957	16.00	40.00
Mercury MG-20499	(M)	**Hits That Sold A Million**	1960	12.00	30.00
Mercury SR-60176	(S)	**Hits That Sold A Million**	1960	16.00	40.00
Mercury MG-20657	(M)	**Country And Western Golden Greats**	1961	12.00	30.00
Mercury SR-60657	(S)	**Country And Western Golden Greats**	1961	16.00	40.00
DREAM 6					
Dream 6 features Johnette Napolitano, later of Concrete Blond.					
Happy Hermit Co. HH-1983	(S)	**Dream 6**	1983	20.00	50.00

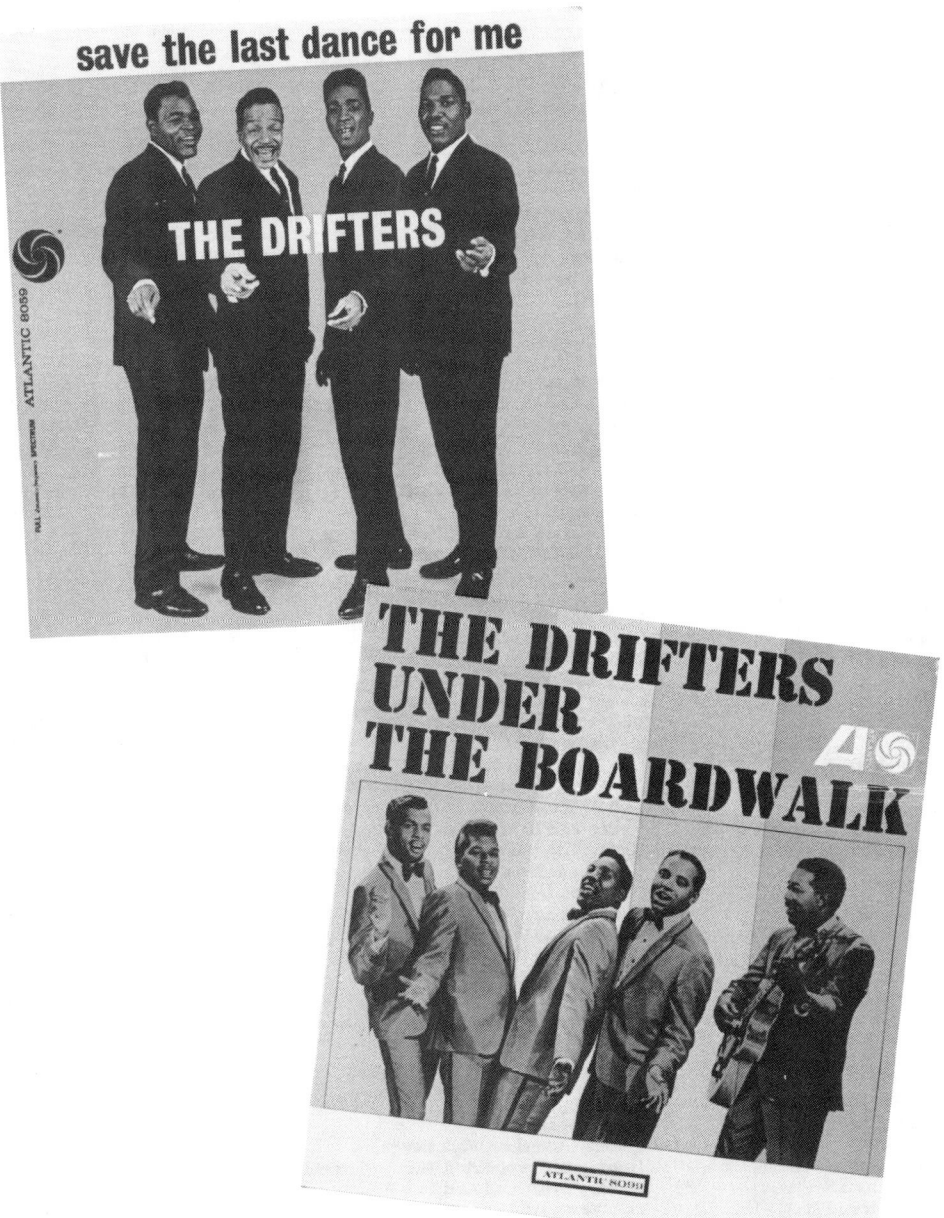

The Drifters were a groundbreakingly influential rhythm'n blues vocal group. But just who was the group? Originally formed under the wing of lead vocalist Clyde McPhatter, they set the standard for '50s groups, influencing just about every black singer to follow and more than a few white ones, including Elvis, who idolized Clyde. By the time of the Save The Last Dance For Me album above, there were all new members, the lead singer was Benjamin Nelson, better known as Ben. E. King, and the group was geared towards pop/R&B. An entirely different set of pipes paced Under The Boardwalk, especially lead singer Johnny Moore. There were more personnel changes than most readers would want to read about.

Label & Catalog #		Title	Year	VG+	NM
DREAMLOVERS, THE					
Columbia CL-2020	(M)	The Bird/Other Golden Dancing Grooves	1963	16.00	40.00
Columbia CS-8820	(S)	The Bird/Other Golden Dancing Grooves	1963	20.00	50.00
DREW, DORIS					
Mode MOD-126	(M)	Delightful Doris Drew	1957	40.00	100.00
DREW, PATTI					
Capitol T-2804	(M)	Tell Him	1967	8.00	20.00
Capitol ST-2804	(S)	Tell Him	1967	10.00	25.00
Capitol ST-408	(DJ)	Wild Is Love (Picture disc)	1979	16.00	40.00
DRIFTERS, THE					
Originally formed by Clyde McPhatter, other lead singers over the years included Johnny Moore, Bobby Hendricks and Ben E. King.					
Atlantic 8003	(M)	Clyde McPhatter & The Drifters	1956	200.00	500.00
Atlantic 8022	(M)	Rockin' And Driftin' (White "bullseye" label)	1958	250.00	600.00
Atlantic 8022	(M)	Rockin' And Driftin'	1958	200.00	500.00
Atlantic 8041	(M)	The Drifters' Greatest Hits	1959	200.00	500.00
		—Atlantic albums above have black labels.—			
Atlantic 8003	(M)	Clyde McPhatter & The Drifters	196?	80.00	200.00
Atlantic 8022	(M)	Rockin' And Driftin'	196?	80.00	200.00
Atlantic 8041	(M)	The Drifters' Greatest Hits	196?	60.00	150.00
Atlantic 8059	(M)	Save The Last Dance For Me	1962	60.00	150.00
Atlantic SD-8059	(S)	Save The Last Dance For Me	1962	100.00	250.00
		—Atlantic albums above multi-color labels with a white "fan" logo on the right side.—			
Atlantic 8003	(M)	Clyde McPhatter & The Drifters	1963	40.00	100.00
Atlantic 8022	(M)	Rockin' And Driftin'	1963	40.00	100.00
Atlantic 8041	(M)	The Drifters' Greatest Hits	1963	30.00	75.00
Atlantic 8059	(M)	Save The Last Dance For Me	1963	30.00	75.00
Atlantic SD-8059	(S)	Save The Last Dance For Me	1963	40.00	100.00
Atlantic 8073	(M)	Up On The Roof	1963	40.00	100.00
Atlantic SD-8073	(S)	Up On The Roof	1963	60.00	150.00
Atlantic 8093	(M)	Our Biggest Hits	1964	30.00	75.00
Atlantic SD-8093	(S)	Our Biggest Hits	1964	40.00	100.00
Atlantic 8099	(M)	Under The Boardwalk (White cover)	1964	30.00	75.00
Atlantic SD-8099	(S)	Under The Boardwalk (White cover)	1964	40.00	100.00
Atlantic 8099	(M)	Under The Boardwalk (Multi-colored cover)	1964	20.00	50.00
Atlantic SD-8099	(S)	Under The Boardwalk (Multi-colored cover)	1964	30.00	75.00
Atlantic 8103	(M)	The Good Life With The Drifters	1965	20.00	50.00
Atlantic SD-8103	(S)	The Good Life With The Drifters	1965	30.00	75.00
Atlantic 8113	(M)	I'll Take You Where The Music's Playing	1965	20.00	50.00
Atlantic SD-8113	(S)	I'll Take You Where The Music's Playing	1965	30.00	75.00
Atlantic 8153	(M)	The Drifters' Golden Hits	1968	10.00	25.00
Atlantic SD-8153	(P)	The Drifters' Golden Hits	1968	12.00	30.00
		—Atlantic albums above multi-color labels with a black "fan" logo on the right side.—			
Clarion 608	(M)	The Drifters	1964	8.00	20.00
Clarion SD-608	(P)	The Drifters	1964	12.00	30.00
DRIFTWOOD, JIMMIE					
RCA Victor LPM-1635	(M)	Newly Discovered Early American Folk Songs	1958	24.00	60.00
RCA Victor LPM-1994	(M)	Jimmie Driftwood And The Wilderness Road	1959	16.00	40.00
RCA Victor LSP-1994	(S)	Jimmie Driftwood And The Wilderness Road	1959	24.00	60.00
RCA Victor LPM-2171	(M)	The Westward Movement	1959	16.00	40.00
RCA Victor LSP-2171	(S)	The Westward Movement	1959	24.00	60.00
RCA Victor LPM-2228	(M)	Tall Tales In Song	1960	12.00	30.00
RCA Victor LSP-2228	(S)	Tall Tales In Song	1960	16.00	40.00
RCA Victor LPM-2316	(M)	Songs Of Billy Yank And Johnny Reb	1961	12.00	30.00
RCA Victor LSP-2316	(S)	Songs Of Billy Yank And Johnny Reb	1961	16.00	40.00
RCA Victor LPM-2443	(M)	Driftwood At Sea—Sea Shanties	1962	12.00	30.00
RCA Victor LSP-2443	(S)	Driftwood At Sea—Sea Shanties	1962	16.00	40.00
		—RCA mono albums above have black labels with "Long Play" on the bottom; stereo albums have "Living Stereo" on the bottom.—			
Monument MLP-8006	(M)	Voice Of The People	1963	8.00	20.00
Monument SLP-18006	(S)	Voice Of The People	1963	10.00	25.00
Monument MLP-8019	(M)	Down In The Arkansas	1965	8.00	20.00
Monument SLP-18019	(S)	Down In The Arkansas	1965	10.00	25.00

Label & Catalog #		Title	Year	VG+	NM
DRUIDS OF STONEHENGE, THE					
Uni 3004	(M)	**Creation**	1967	16.00	40.00
Uni 73004	(S)	**Creation**	1967	20.00	50.00
DRUSKY, ROY					
Decca DL-4160	(M)	**Anymore With Roy Drusky**	1961	8.00	20.00
Decca DL-74160	(S)	**Anymore With Roy Drusky**	1961	12.00	30.00
		—Decca albums above have black labels with silver print.—			
DRY CITY SCAT BAND, THE					
Elektra EKL-292	(M)	**Dry City Scat Band**	1965	10.00	25.00
Elektra EKS-7292	(S)	**Dry City Scat Band**	1965	12.00	30.00
DRYEWATER					
J. T. B. NRS-122	(S)	**Dryewater**	1974	30.00	75.00
DUALS, THE					
Sue LP-2002	(M)	**Stick Shift** *(Cartoon cover)*	1961	200.00	400.00
Sue LP-2002	(M)	**Stick Shift** *(Photo cover)*	1964	150.00	300.00
DUBS, THE					
Josie JM-4001	(M)	**The Dubs Meet The Shells**	1962	150.00	300.00
Josie JSS-4001	(P)	**The Dubs Meet The Shells**	1962	300.00	600.00
DUDLEY, DAVE					
Golden Ring G-110	(M)	**Six Days On The Road**	1963	60.00	150.00
DUKE, PATTY, & NORMAN VINCENT PEALE					
Guideposts GP-101	(M)	**Guideposts For Christmas**	1963	30.00	75.00
DUKE, PATTY					
United Arts. UAL-4131	(M)	**Billie** *(Soundtrack)*	1965	8.00	20.00
United Arts. UAS-5131	(S)	**Billie** *(Soundtrack)*	1965	10.00	25.00
United Arts. UAS-6632	(S)	**Songs From The Valley Of The Dolls**	1968	10.00	25.00
DUKE OF IRON, THE [MOR]					
Prestige Int. PRLP-13068	(M)	**Limbo, Limbo, Limbo**	1963	12.00	30.00
DUKE OF PADUCAH, THE					
Starday SLP-148	(M)	**Button Shoes, Belly Laughs And Monkey Business** *(Yellow label)*	1961	16.00	40.00
DULLEA, KEIR					
Platypus SLP-5001	(S)	**Keir Dullea**	197?	10.00	25.00
DUNBAR, AYNSLEY					
Aynsley Dunbar also recorded as a Mother with Frank Zappa.					
Blue Thumb BTS-4	(S)	**Retaliation**	1968	10.00	25.00
Blue Thumb BTS-6	(S)	**Doctor Dunbar's Prescription**	1969	10.00	25.00
Blue Thumb BTS-16	(S)	**To Mum, From Aynsley And The Boys**	1970	10.00	25.00
DUNBAR, MAX					
Folkways FW-3006	(M)	**Songs And Ballads Of The Scottish Wars**	195?	10.00	25.00
DUNCAN, BILL					
King 825	(M)	**A Scene Near My Country Home**	1962	12.00	30.00
DUNCAN, TODD					
Allegro ALG-3022	(M)	**Spirituals**	195?	12.00	30.00
DUNNE, IRENE: *Refer to* DICK VAN DYKE / IRENE DUNNE					
DUPREE, "CHAMPION" JACK					
Refer to King Curtis & Jack Dupree.					
Atlantic 8019	(M)	**Blues From The Gutter**	1959	80.00	200.00
Atlantic SD-8019	(S)	**Blues From The Gutter**	1959	150.00	300.00
		—Atlantic mono albums above have black labels; stereos have green labels.—			
Atlantic 8019	(M)	**Blues From The Gutter**	196?	14.00	35.00
Atlantic SD-8019	(S)	**Blues From The Gutter**	196?	20.00	50.00

Label & Catalog #		Title	Year	VG+	NM
Atlantic 8045	(S)	Natural And Soulful Blues	196?	14.00	35.00
Atlantic SD-8045	(S)	Natural And Soulful Blues	196?	20.00	50.00
Atlantic 8056	(M)	Champion Of The Blues	1961	20.00	50.00
—Atlantic albums above have muti-colored labels with a white "fan" logo on the right side.—					
Atlantic 8019	(M)	Blues From The Gutter	196?	8.00	20.00
Atlantic SD-8019	(S)	Blues From The Gutter	196?	10.00	25.00
Atlantic 8045	(S)	Natural And Soulful Blues	196?	8.00	20.00
Atlantic SD-8045	(S)	Natural And Soulful Blues	196?	10.00	25.00
Atlantic 8056	(M)	Champion Of The Blues	196?	10.00	25.00
—Atlantic albums above have muti-colored labels with a black "fan" logo on the right side.—					
King LP-735	(M)	Champion Jack Dupree Sings The Blues	1961	175.00	350.00
Folkways FS-3825	(M)	Women Blues Of Champion Jack Dupree	1961	10.00	25.00
OKeh OKM-12103	(M)	Cabbage Greens	1963	12.00	30.00
Blue Horizon 7702	(S)	When You Feel The Feeling	1969	10.00	25.00

DUPREE, "CHAMPION" JACK, & MICKEY BAKER

Sire SES-97010	(S)	In Heavy Blues	1969	14.00	35.00

DUPREE, "CHAMPION" JACK / JIMMY RUSHING

Audio Lab AL-1512	(M)	Two Shades Of Blue	1959	80.00	200.00

DUPREE, SIMON, & THE BIG SOUND

Tower ST-5097	(S)	Without Reservations	1968	10.00	25.00

DUPREES, THE

Coed LPC-905	(M)	You Belong To Me	1962	150.00	300.00
Coed LPC-906	(M)	Have You Heard	1963	100.00	250.00
Heritage HTS-35002	(S)	Total Recall	1968	12.00	30.00

DURAN DURAN

Capitol SPRO-79097/8	(DJ)	Duran Duran Goes Dutch	1987	20.00	50.00

DURANTE, JIMMY

Lion L-70053	(M)	Jimmy Durante In Person	1959	10.00	25.00
Decca DL-9040	(M)	Club Durante	1959	10.00	25.00
Decca DL-79040	(S)	Club Durante	1959	12.00	30.00
Roulette R-25123	(M)	Jimmy Durante At The Copacabana	1961	8.00	20.00
Roulette SR-25123	(S)	Jimmy Durante At The Copacabana	1961	10.00	25.00
Warner Bros. W-1506	(M)	September Song	1963	8.00	20.00
Warner Bros. WS-1506	(S)	September Song	1963	10.00	25.00
Warner Bros. W-1531	(M)	Hello Young Lovers	1964	8.00	20.00
Warner Bros. WS-1531	(S)	Hello Young Lovers	1964	10.00	25.00

DURBIN, DEANNA

Decca DL-8785	(M)	Deanna Durbin	1958	20.00	50.00

DWARR

Brand-X	(S)	Starting Over	1985	14.00	35.00
Brand-X	(S)	Animals	1986	14.00	35.00

DYER-BENNET, RICHARD

Richard Dyer-Bennett is a singer, guitar and lute player, and songwriter who is referred to as a "20th Century minstrel" for his way with traditional folk material. Refer to Tom Glazer / Richard Dyer-Bennett.

Decca DLP-5046	(10")	Richard Dyer-Bennett (Folk Songs)	1949	20.00	50.00
Stinson SLP-2	(10")	The 20th Century Minstrel	195?	20.00	50.00
Stinson SLP-35	(10")	Ballads	195?	20.00	50.00
Stinson SLP-60	(10")	More Songs By The 20th Century Minstrel	195?	20.00	50.00
Stinson SLP-61	(10")	Concert	195?	20.00	50.00
Remington 199-34	(M)	Ballads	195?	12.00	30.00
Dyer-Bennet RD-B 1	(M)	Richard Dyer-Bennet Songs, Volume 1	1955	12.00	30.00
Dyer-Bennet DYB-2000	(M)	Richard Dyer-Bennet Songs, Volume 2	1956	12.00	30.00
Dyer-Bennet DYB-3000	(M)	Richard Dyer-Bennet Songs, Volume 3	1956	12.00	30.00
Dyer-Bennet RD-B 4	(M)	Richard Dyer-Bennet Songs, Volume 4	1957	12.00	30.00
Dyer-Bennet DYB-5000	(M)	Richard Dyer-Bennet Songs, Volume 5	1958	12.00	30.00
Dyer-Bennet DYB-6000	(M)	Songs With Young People In Mind	1958	12.00	30.00
Dyer-Bennet DYB-1601	(M)	Mark Twain's 1601	1962	12.00	30.00
Decca DL-9102	(M)	Twentieth Century Minstrel	1960	12.00	30.00
Decca DL-79102	(E)	Twentieth Century Minstrel	1960	8.00	20.00
		(Decca 9102 is a reissue of 5046.)			

Jersey City's Duprees hit big in 1962 with a remake of Jo Stafford's "You Belong To Me" and then scored three more hits and a few chart entries before disbanding. Both of their Coed albums are sought after by collectors of early '60s white vocal groups, and are hard to find. Members of the group, including lead singer Joey Vann (born Joseph Canzano), later formed the Italian Asphalt & Pavement Company.

Label & Catalog #		Title	Year	VG+	NM

DYKE & THE BLAZERS

Original Sound LP-8876	(M)	The Funky Broadway	1967	16.00	40.00
Original Sound LPS-8876	(S)	The Funky Broadway	1967	20.00	50.00
Original Sound LPS-8877	(S)	Dyke's Greatest Hits	1968	20.00	50.00

DYLAN, BOB

Bob Dylan, born Robert Zimmerman, is a singer, guitar and harmonica player, and writer of songs. At the beginning of his career he was the single most important figure in contemporary folk music since Woody Guthrie. By 1966 he was the single most important white artist in rock & roll since Elvis. To avoid confusing label changes, the albums below are listed first in mono, then stereo. Refer to Harry Belafonte; Barry Goldberg; George Harrison & Friends; Carolyn Hester; The New World Singers; Doug Sahm; Victoria Spivey; The Traveling Wilburys.

| Columbia CL-1779 | (M) | Bob Dylan | 1962 | 200.00 | 400.00 |

(First pressing labels of CL-1779 have three white "eye" logo on each side of the spindle hole. The label is stamped promo and the cover has a "A New Star On Columbia" sticker.)

| Columbia CL-1779 | (M) | Bob Dylan | 1962 | 150.00 | 300.00 |

(First pressing labels of CL-1779 have three white "eye" logo on each side of the spindle hole.)

| Columbia CL-1779 | (M) | Bob Dylan | 1963 | 16.00 | 40.00 |

(Second pressings have "Guaranteed High Fidelity" labels.)

| Columbia CL-1779 | (M) | Bob Dylan | 1967 | 12.00 | 30.00 |

(Third pressings have "360 Sound Mono" labels.)

| Columbia CS-8579 | (S) | Bob Dylan | 1962 | 300.00 | 500.00 |

(First pressing labels of CS-8579 have three white "eye" logo on each side of the spindle hole. The label is stamped promo and the cover has a "A New Star On Columbia" sticker.)

| Columbia CS-8579 | (S) | Bob Dylan | 1962 | 200.00 | 400.00 |

(First pressing labels of CS-8579 have three white "eye" logo on each side of the spindle hole.)

| Columbia CS-8579 | (S) | Bob Dylan | 1965 | 16.00 | 40.00 |

(Second pressings have "360 Sound Stereo" in black on the bottom of the label.)

| Columbia CS-8579 | (S) | Bob Dylan | 1967 | 10.00 | 25.00 |

(Third pressings have "360 Sound Stereo" in white on the bottom of the label.)

| Columbia CL-1986 | (M) | The Freewheelin' Bob Dylan | 1963 | | See below |

(First pressings of CL-1986 have "Guaranteed High Fidelity" labels and include "Let Me Die In My Footsteps," "Talkin' John Birch Blues," ""Ramblin' Gamblin' Willie" and "Rocks & Gravel." These four were replaced on all subsequent pressings with "Masters Of War," "Girl From North Country," "Talkin' World War III Blues," and "Bob Dylan's Dream." All known mono copies with the deleted tracks list the later songs on the label, but the matrix number in the trail-off vinyl ends with a "— 1" and a [irrelevant to the case] letter. Rare with a suggested Near Mint value of $10,000-20,000.)

| Columbia CS-8786 | (S) | The Freewheelin' Bob Dylan | 1963 | | See below |

(First pressings of CS-8786 have "360 Sound Stereo" in black without arrows on the bottom of the label and include "Let Me Die In My Footsteps," "Talkin' John Birch Blues," ""Ramblin' Gamblin' Willie" and Rocks & Gravel." These four tracks were deleted and replaced on all subsequent pressings with "Masters Of War," "Girl From North Country," "Talkin' World War III Blues," and "Bob Dylan's Dream." Both of the stereo copies found list these songs on the label; refer to the article "The World's Most Valuable Album" in this book for more information. Rare with a suggested minimum Near Mint value of $20,000. I wouldn't even hazard an estimate on the ceiling for a Near Mint copy of this record. . .)

| Columbia CL-1986 | (M) | The Freewheelin' Bob Dylan (White label) | 1963 | | See below |

(Both the label and the timing strip on the cover list the original deleted tracks but the album plays the replacement tracks. Rare with a suggested Near Mint value of $3,000-5,000.)

| Columbia 1986 | | The Freewheelin' Bob Dylan Insert | 1963 | 150.00 | 300.00 |

(Some copies of the original promos above were issued with an approximately 4" x 11" note that reads "NOTICE: Please note that on Side 1, Band 3 and Band 6 are reversed." This is in reference to the original track line-up where those songs, "Let Me Die In My Footsteps" and "A Hard Rain's A-Gonna Fall," respectively, were transposed on the master after the labels had been printed.)

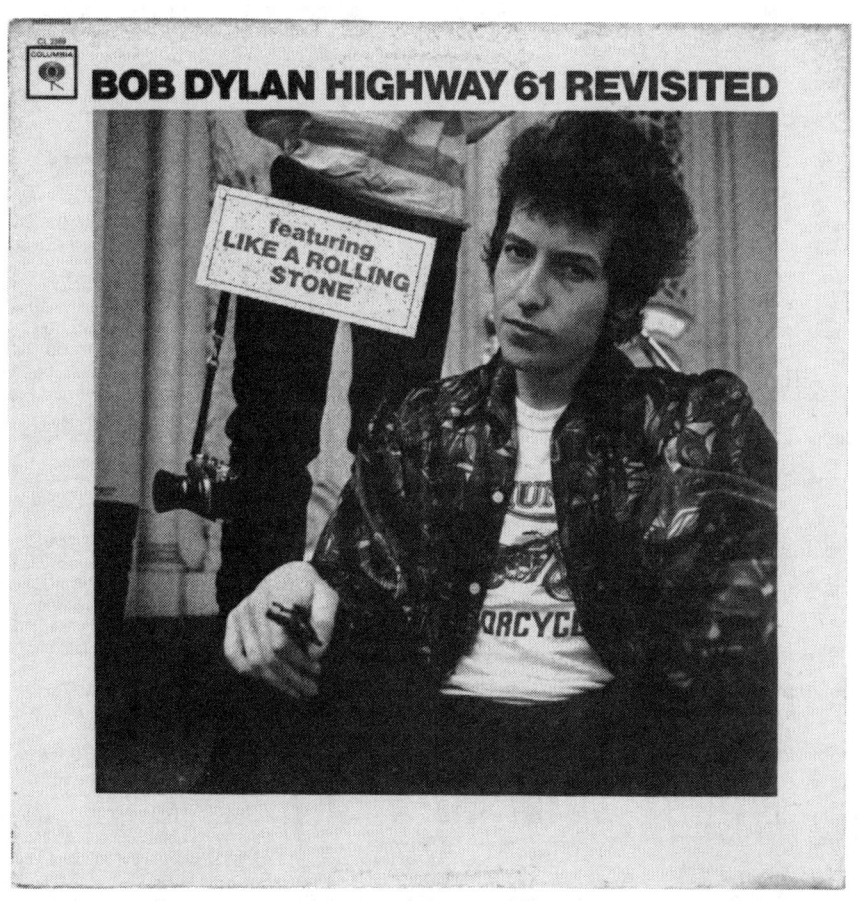

Bob Dylan (born Robert Zimmerman) set the stage for the development of the "folk/rock" movement with his fourth and fifth albums, although it was The Byrds' debut album, Mr. Tambourine Man, in 1965 that defined the genre. Dylan followed the group's album with his first all electric outing, the essential Highway 61 Revisited later in '65. First mono pressings were mastered with an alternate take of "Like A Buick 6" and can be identified by the matrix number in the trail-off vinyl (see listing).

Label & Catalog #		Title	Year	VG+	NM
Columbia CL-1986	(M)	**The Freewheelin' Bob Dylan** (White label)	1963	**660.00**	**1,000.00**
		(The label lists the original deleted tracks while the timing strip on the cover lists the replacement tracks. The album, of course, plays the replacement tracks.)			
Columbia CL-1986	(M)	**The Freewheelin' Bob Dylan** (White label)	1963	**500.00**	**750.00**
		(The timing strip on the cover lists the original deleted tracks. The cover and labels list, and the album plays, the replacement tracks.)			
Columbia CL-1986	(M)	**The Freewheelin' Bob Dylan** (White label)	1963	**300.00**	**500.00**
		(The timing strip on the cover lists the replacement tracks. The cover and labels list, and the album plays, the replacement tracks.)			
Columbia CL-1986	(M)	**The Freewheelin' Bob Dylan**	1963	**16.00**	**40.00**
		(First pressings of CL-1986 have "Guaranteed High Fidelity" labels.)			
Columbia CL-1986	(M)	**The Freewheelin' Bob Dylan**	1967	**12.00**	**30.00**
		(Second pressings have "360 Sound Mono" labels.)			
Columbia CS-8786	(S)	**The Freewheelin' Bob Dylan**	1963	**20.00**	**50.00**
		(First pressings of CS-8786 have "360 Sound Stereo" in black without arrows on the bottom of the label.)			
Columbia CS-8786	(S)	**The Freewheelin' Bob Dylan**	1965	**16.00**	**40.00**
		(Second pressings have "360 Sound Stereo" in black on the bottom of the label with arrows pointing upwards on both sides.)			
Columbia CS-8786	(S)	**The Freewheelin' Bob Dylan**	1967	**10.00**	**25.00**
		(Third pressings have "360 Sound Stereo" in white on the label.)			
Columbia CL-2105	(M)	**The Times They Are A-Changin'** (White label)	1964	**200.00**	**400.00**
Columbia CL-2105	(M)	**The Times They Are A-Changin'**	1964	**16.00**	**40.00**
		(First pressings of CL-2105 have "Guaranteed High Fidelity" labels. This and most subsequent pressings were issued with a sheet continuing "11 Outlined Epitaphs" from the back cover.)			
Columbia CL-2105	(M)	**The Times They Are A-Changin'**	1967	**12.00**	**30.00**
		(Second pressings have "360 Sound Mono" labels.)			
Columbia CS-8905	(S)	**The Times They Are A-Changin'**	1964	**16.00**	**40.00**
		(First pressings of CS-8905 have "360 Sound Stereo" in black on the bottom of the label.)			
Columbia CS-8905	(S)	**The Times They Are A-Changin'**	1967	**10.00**	**25.00**
		(Second pressings have "360 Sound Stereo" in white on the label.)			
Columbia CL-2193	(M)	**Another Side Of Bob Dylan** (White label)	1964	**300.00**	**500.00**
Columbia CL-2193	(M)	**Another Side Of Bob Dylan**	1964	**16.00**	**40.00**
		(First pressings of CL-2193 have "Guaranteed High Fidelity" labels.)			
Columbia CL-2193	(M)	**Another Side Of Bob Dylan**	1967	**12.00**	**30.00**
		(Second pressings have "360 Sound Mono" labels.)			
Columbia CS-8993	(S)	**Another Side Of Bob Dylan**	1964	**16.00**	**40.00**
		(First pressings of CS-8993 have "360 Sound Stereo" in black on the bottom of the label.)			
Columbia CS-8993	(S)	**Another Side Of Bob Dylan**	1967	**10.00**	**25.00**
		(Second pressings have "360 Sound Stereo" in white on the bottom of the label.)			
Columbia CL-2302	(M)	**Bob Dylan In Concert**	1965		Unreleased
Columbia CS-9102	(S)	**Bob Dylan In Concert**	1965		Unreleased
		(Front cover slicks have a suggested NM value of $3,000-5,000.)			
Columbia CL-2328	(M)	**Bringing It All Back Home** (White label)	1965	**200.00**	**400.00**
Columbia CL-2328	(M)	**Bringing It All Back Home**	1965	**20.00**	**50.00**
		(First pressings of CL-2328 have "Guaranteed High Fidelity" labels.)			
Columbia CL-2328	(M)	**Bringing It All Back Home**	1967	**16.00**	**40.00**
		(Second pressings have "360 Sound Mono" labels.)			
Columbia CS-9128	(S)	**Bringing It All Back Home**	1965	**16.00**	**40.00**
		(First pressings of CS-9128 have "360 Sound Stereo" in black on the bottom of the label.)			
Columbia CS-9128	(S)	**Bringing It All Back Home**	1967	**10.00**	**25.00**
		(Second pressings have "360 Sound Stereo" in white on the label.)			
Columbia CL-2389	(M)	**Highway 61 Revisited** (White label promo)	1965	**200.00**	**400.00**
Columbia CL-2389	(M)	**Highway 61 Revisited**	1965	**30.00**	**75.00**
Columbia CS-9189	(S)	**Highway 61 Revisited**	1965	**150.00**	**300.00**
		(Original pressings of CS-9189 contain an alternate take of "From A Buick 6." The matrix number in the trail-off vinyl on the first side ends with a "– 1" and a [irrelevant to the case] letter.)			
Columbia CS-9189	(S)	**Highway 61 Revisited**	1965	**12.00**	**30.00**
		(Remastered first pressings of have "360 Sound Stereo" labels.)			
Columbia		**Highway 61 Revisited Poster**	1965	**60.00**	**150.00**
		(Album-size ink line drawing of Dylan by Lambert. This may have been included with other Dylan albums during 1965.)			

Label & Catalog #		Title	Year	VG+	NM
Columbia C2L-41	(M)	**Blonde On Blonde** (2 LPs. White label)	1966	660.00	1,000.00
Columbia C2L-41	(M)	**Blonde On Blonde** (2 LPs)	1966	40.00	100.00
Columbia C2S-841	(S)	**Blonde On Blonde** (2 LPs)	1966	20.00	50.00
		(First pressings of 41/841 have "360 Sound" labels. Origina gatefold covers have nine photos on the inside, including one of actress Claudia Cardinale.)			
Columbia C2L-41	(M)	**Blonde On Blonde** (2 LPs)	1966		See below
Columbia C2S-841	(S)	**Blonde On Blonde** (2 LPs)	1966	16.00	40.00
		(Second pressings with the "360 Sound" labels have an altered cover: Two of the inner photos, including the one of Ms. Cardinale, were deleted, leaving seven photos. While the stereo cover is common, the mono is rare with a suggested NM value of $200-400.)			
Columbia KCL-2663	(M)	**Bob Dylan's Greatest Hits**	1967	20.00	50.00
Columbia KCS-9463	(S)	**Bob Dylan's Greatest Hits**	1967	12.00	30.00
		(First pressings of KCS-9463 have "360 Sound Stereo" labels. Virtually all pressings of this album through the '70s were issued with a fold-open poster of Dylan by artist Peter Max worth $5-10.)			
Warner/7-Arts. 221567	(DJ)	**"The Bob Dylan Whitmark Demos"**	1967		See below
		(One-sided album in a plain cardboard jacket compiled by Whitmark Publishers to showcase twelve of Dylan's [then] unreleased. Rare with a suggested Near Mint value of $500-1,500.)			
Columbia CL-2804	(M)	**John Wesley Harding** (White label promo)	1968	150.00	300.00
Columbia CL-2804	(M)	**John Wesley Harding**	1968	60.00	150.00
Columbia CS-9604	(S)	**John Wesley Harding**	1968	12.00	30.00
		(First pressings of CS-9604 have "360 Sound Stereo" labels.)			
Columbia KCS-9825	(S)	**Nashville Skyline**	1969	12.00	30.00
		(First pressings of KCS-9825 have "360 Sound Stereo" labels.)			
Columbia CQ-32825	(Q)	**Nashville Skyline**	1973	12.00	30.00
Columbia HE-49825	(S)	**Nashville Skyline** (Half-speed master)	1975	25.00	75.00
Columbia C2X-30050	(S)	**Self Portrait** (2 LPs)	1970	60.00	150.00
		(First pressings of C2X-30050 have "360 Sound Stereo" labels.)			
Asylum 7E-1003	(S)	**Planet Waves** (White label promo)	1974	20.00	50.00
Asylum EQ-1003	(Q)	**Planet Waves**	1974	20.00	50.00
Island AB-201	(S)	**Before The Flood** (2 LPs)	1974	16.00	40.00
Asylum AB-201	(S)	**Before The Flood** (2 LPs. White label promo)	1974	20.00	50.00
Columbia PC-33235	(DJ)	**Blood On The Tracks** (Test pressing)	1975		See below
		(Original test pressings of PC-33235 include completely different recordings of "Idiot Wind," "Lily, Rosemary & The Jack Of Hearts," "Tangled Up In Blue," "If You See Her Say Hello" and "You're A Big Girl Now." Rare with a suggested Near Mint value of $4,000-6,000.)			
Columbia PC-33235	(S)	**Blood On The Tracks** (White label promo)	1975	16.00	40.00
Columbia PC-33235	(S)	**Blood On The Tracks** ("Mural cover")	1976	10.00	25.00
		(Second pressing covers feature a full-cover drawing on the back.)			
Columbia HC-43235	(S)	**Blood On The Tracks** (Half-speed master)	1975	25.00	75.00
Columbia CS2-33682	(S)	**The Basement Tapes** (2 LPs. White label)	1975	16.00	40.00
Columbia PC-33893	(S)	**Desire** (White label promo)	1976	12.00	30.00
Columbia PCQ-33893	(Q)	**Desire**	1976	14.00	35.00
Columbia PC-34349	(S)	**Hard Rain** (White label promo)	1976	12.00	30.00
Columbia AS-422	(DJ)	**Renaldo And Clara**	1976	14.00	35.00
		(Original copies of AS-422 have a title sticker on the cover. Counterfeits have the title printed on the cover.)			
Columbia JC-35453	(S)	**Street Legal** (White label promo)	1978	10.00	25.00
Columbia PC2-36067	(S)	**Bob Dylan At Budokan** (2 LPs. White label)	1979	12.00	30.00
Columbia FC-36120	(S)	**Slow Train Coming** (White label promo)	1979	10.00	25.00
Columbia AS-798	(S)	**Saved** (White label promo)	1980	10.00	25.00
Columbia C5S-38830	(P)	**Biograph** (5 LPs)	1985	10.00	25.00
Columbia CAS-2222	(DJ)	**Time Passes Slowly: Biograph Sampler**	1985	10.00	25.00

DYLAN, BOB, & ALAN J. WEBERMAN

Folkways FB-5322	(M)	**Bob Dylan Versus A. J. Weberman**	1977	150.00	300.00
		(Folkways 5322 consists of a porrly taped telephone conversation between Mr. Webereman and Mr. Zimmerman.)			

DYNAMICS, THE

Bolo BLP-8001	(M)	**The Dynamics With Jimmy Hanna**	1963	20.00	50.00

EAGLES, THE
Eagles have been Don Felder, Glenn Frey, Don Henley, Bernie Leadon, Randy meisner, Timothy Schmidt and Joe Walsh.

Mobile Fidelity MFSL-126	(S)	**Hotel California**	*1981*	**30.00**	**90.00**

EAGLIN, "BLIND" SNOOKS

Folkways FA-2476	(M)	**New Orleans Street Singer**	*1959*	**20.00**	**50.00**
Bluesville BVLP-1046	(M)	**That's All Right**	*1962*	**30.00**	**75.00**

— Bluesville albums above have bright blue labels with silver print.—

Bluesville BVLP-1046	(M)	**That's All Right**	*1964*	**10.00**	**25.00**

— Bluesville albums above have blue labels with a trident logo on the right side.—

EARLS, THE

Old Town LP-104	(M)	**Remember Me Baby**	*1963*	**200.00**	**500.00**

(Original records have blue labels on thick vinyl. Covers have the catalog number stamped on the front with printing on the spine.)

EARTH ISLAND

Philips 600-340	(S)	**We Must Survive**	*1970*	**10.00**	**25.00**

EARTH, WIND & FIRE

Columbia HC-45647	(S)	**Best Of Earth, Wind & Fire** *(Half-speed)*	*1981*	**13.00**	**40.00**
Columbia HC-45730	(S)	**I Am** *(Half-speed master)*	*1981*	**10.00**	**30.00**
Columbia HC-47548	(S)	**Raise** *(Half-speed master)*	*1982*	**10.00**	**30.00**
Columbia HC-48367	(S)	**Powerlight** *(Half-speed master)*	*1982*	**16.00**	**50.00**

EARTHEN VESSEL

NRS 2587	(S)	**Everlasting Life**	*1971*	**60.00**	**150.00**

EASTWOOD, CLINT

Cameo C-1056	(M)	**Clint Eastwood Sings Cowboy Favorites**	*1963*	**40.00**	**100.00**
Cameo CS-1056	(S)	**Clint Eastwood Sings Cowboy Favorites**	*1963*	**60.00**	**150.00**

EASTWOOD, CLINT, & LEE MARVIN & JEAN SEBERG

Garrison Sys. 1609/10	(DJ)	**"Paint Your Wagon" Radio Special**	*106?*	**40.00**	**100.00**

EASY CHAIR, THE
The Easy Chair features Jeff Simmons.

Vanco 1004	(M)	**The Easy Chair** *(One sided. No cover)*	*1968*	**150.00**	**300.00**

EASY RIDERS, THE

Columbia CL-990	(M)	**Marianne And Other Songs**	*1957*	**20.00**	**50.00**
Columbia CL-1302	(M)	**Wanderin' Folk Songs**	*1959*	**14.00**	**35.00**
Epic LN-24033	(M)	**Easy Riders**	*1962*	**8.00**	**20.00**
Epic BN-26033	(S)	**Easy Riders**	*1962*	**12.00**	**30.00**

EASYBEATS, THE

United Arts. UAL-3588	(M)	**Friday On My Mind**	*1967*	**16.00**	**40.00**
United Arts. UAS-6588	(S)	**Friday On My Mind**	*1967*	**20.00**	**50.00**

("Make You Feel Alright" is rechanneled.)

United Arts. UAS-6667	(S)	**Falling Off The Edge Of The World**	*1968*	**16.00**	**40.00**

("Women" is rechanneled.)

EBON-KNIGHTS, THE

Stepheny MF-4001	(M)	**First Date With The Ebon-Knights**	*1963*	**600.00**	**1,500.00**

EBSEN, BUDDY

Reprise R-6174	(M)	**Buddy Ebsen Says Howdy**	*1965*	**10.00**	**25.00**
Reprise R9-6174	(S)	**Buddy Ebsen Says Howdy**	*1965*	**12.00**	**30.00**

ECKSTINE, BILLY: *Refer to* **GOLDMINE'S PRICE GUIDE TO COLLECTIBLE JAZZ ALBUMS**

Label & Catalog #		Title	Year	VG+	NM
EDDY, DUANE					
Jamie JLP-3000	(M)	Have "Twangy" Guitar-Will Travel	1958	50.00	125.00
Jamie JLPS-3000	(P)	Have "Twangy" Guitar-Will Travel	1958	150.00	300.00
		(Original pressings of Jamie 3000 have yellow labels with the title on			
		the front cover in white print. On JLPS-3000, "Lonesome Road,"			
		I Almost Lost My Mind," "Three-30-Blues," "Detour," "Anytime"			
		and "Loving You" are in stereo.)			
Jamie JLPM-3000	(M)	Have "Twangy" Guitar-Will Travel	1959	20.00	50.00
Jamie JLPS-3000	(P)	Have "Twangy" Guitar-Will Travel	1959	40.00	100.00
		(Second pressings have gold & white label with the title on the cover			
		is in red print. The early stereo pressings with the gold & white label			
		have the same stereo content as above. Subsequent stereo pressings			
		are completely rechanneled.)			
Jamie JLPS-3000	(E)	Have "Twangy" Guitar-Will Travel	196?	20.00	50.00
		(Gold & white label with electronic stereo.)			
Jamie JLPM-3006	(M)	Especially For You....	1959	24.00	60.00
Jamie JLPS-3006	(S)	Especially For You....	1959	40.00	100.00
Jamie JLPM-3009	(M)	The "Twangs" The "Thang"	1959	24.00	60.00
Jamie JLPS-3009	(S)	The "Twangs" The "Thang"	1959	40.00	100.00
Jamie ST-91301	(S)	The "Twangs"			
		The "Thang" *(Capitol Record Club)*	1965	24.00	60.00
Jamie JLPM-3011	(M)	Songs Of Our Heritage *(Gatefold cover)*	1960	40.00	100.00
Jamie JLPS-3011	(S)	Songs Of Our Heritage *(Gatefold cover)*	1960	60.00	150.00
Jamie JLPS-3011	(S)	Songs Of Our Heritage *(Blue vinyl)*	1960	200.00	400.00
Jamie JLPS-3011	(S)	Songs Of Our Heritage *(Red vinyl)*	1960	200.00	400.00
		(Original pressings of Jamie 301 on black and colored vinyl above			
		have gatefold covers with a fold-open poster bound to the inside.			
		Subtract 20-40% if the poster has been removed.)			
Jamie JLPM-3011	(M)	Songs Of Our Heritage *(Standard cover)*	1960	12.00	30.00
Jamie JLPS-3011	(S)	Songs Of Our Heritage *(Standard cover)*	1960	16.00	40.00
Jamie JLPM-3014	(M)	$1,000,000 Worth Of Twang	1960	20.00	50.00
Jamie JLPS-3014	(E)	$1,000,000 Worth Of Twang	1960	16.00	40.00
Jamie JLPM-3019	(M)	Girls! Girls! Girls!	1961	20.00	50.00
Jamie JLPS-3019	(E)	Girls! Girls! Girls!	1961	16.00	40.00
Jamie JLPM-3021	(M)	$1,000,000 Worth Of Twang, Volume 2	1962	20.00	50.00
Jamie JLPS-3021	(E)	$1,000,000 Worth Of Twang, Volume 2	1962	16.00	40.00
Jamie JLPM-3022	(M)	Twistin' With Duane Eddy	1962	16.00	40.00
Jamie JLPS-3022	(S)	Twistin' With Duane Eddy	1962	20.00	50.00
		("Rebel Rouser Twist," "Cannon Ball Twist," "Movin' 'N Groovin'			
		Twist," "Ramrod Twist" and "Twisting Up & Down" are rechanneled.)			
Jamie JLPM-3024	(M)	Surfin'	1963	20.00	50.00
Jamie JLPS-3024	(S)	Surfin'	1963	30.00	75.00
Jamie JLPM-3025	(M)	Duane Eddy & The Rebels-In Person	1963	16.00	40.00
Jamie JLPS-3025	(S)	Duane Eddy & The Rebels-In Person	1963	20.00	50.00
Jamie ST-90663	(S)	Duane Eddy & The Rebels-			
		In Person *(Capitol Record Club)*	1964	24.00	60.00
Jamie JLPM-3026	(M)	16 Greatest Hits	1964	20.00	50.00
Jamie JLPS-3026	(E)	16 Greatest Hits	1964	16.00	40.00
		—*Jamie albums above have gold & white labels.*—			
RCA Victor LPM-2525	(M)	Twistin' And Twangin'	1962	8.00	20.00
RCA Victor LSP-2525	(S)	Twistin' And Twangin'	1962	12.00	30.00
RCA Victor LPM-2576	(M)	Twangy Guitar, Silky Strings	1962	8.00	20.00
RCA Victor LSP-2576	(S)	Twangy Guitar, Silky Strings	1962	12.00	30.00
RCA Victor LPM-2648	(M)	Dance With The Guitar Man	1962	8.00	20.00
RCA Victor LSP-2648	(S)	Dance With The Guitar Man	1962	12.00	30.00
RCA Victor LPM-2681	(M)	Twang A Country Song	1963	8.00	20.00
RCA Victor LSP-2681	(S)	Twang A Country Song	1963	12.00	30.00
RCA Victor LPM-2700	(M)	Twangin' Up A Storm	1963	8.00	20.00
RCA Victor LSP-2700	(S)	Twangin' Up A Storm	1963	12.00	30.00
		—*RCA mono albums above have "Long Play" on the bottom of the label;*			
		stereo albums have "Living Stereo" on the bottom.—			
RCA Victor LPM-2798	(M)	Lonely Guitar	1964	8.00	20.00
RCA Victor LSP-2798	(S)	Lonely Guitar	1964	12.00	30.00
RCA Victor LPM-2918	(M)	Water Skiing	1964	8.00	20.00
RCA Victor LSP-2918	(S)	Water Skiing	1964	12.00	30.00
RCA Victor LPM-2993	(M)	Twangin' The Golden Hits	1965	8.00	20.00
RCA Victor LSP-2993	(S)	Twangin' The Golden Hits	1965	12.00	30.00
RCA Victor LPM-3432	(M)	Twangsville	1965	8.00	20.00
RCA Victor LSP-3432	(S)	Twangsville	1965	12.00	30.00

Label & Catalog #		Title	Year	VG+	NM
RCA Victor LPM-3477	(M)	The Best Of Duane Eddy	1966	8.00	20.00
RCA Victor LSP-3477	(P)	The Best Of Duane Eddy	1966	10.00	25.00
		— RCA albums above have black labels.—			
Colpix CP-490	(M)	Duane A-Go-Go	1965	14.00	35.00
Colpix CPS-490	(S)	Duane A-Go-Go	1965	20.00	50.00
Colpix CP-494	(M)	Duane Eddy Does Bob Dylan	1965	20.00	50.00
Colpix CPS-494	(S)	Duane Eddy Does Bob Dylan	1965	30.00	75.00
Reprise R-6218	(M)	The Biggest Twang Of Them All	1966	8.00	20.00
Reprise RS-6218	(S)	The Biggest Twang Of Them All	1966	10.00	25.00
Reprise R-6240	(M)	The Roaring Twangies	1967	8.00	20.00
Reprise RS-6240	(S)	The Roaring Twangies	1967	10.00	25.00
Sire SASH-3707	(P)	Vintage Years (2 LPs)	1975	10.00	25.00

EDEN, BARBARA

Label & Catalog #		Title	Year	VG+	NM
Dot DLP-3795	(M)	Miss Barbara Eden	1967	16.00	40.00
Dot DLP-25795	(S)	Miss Barbara Eden	1967	24.00	60.00

EDGE, THE

Label & Catalog #		Title	Year	VG+	NM
Nose NRS-48003	(S)	The Edge	1970	16.00	40.00

EDMONSON, TRAVIS
Refer to Bud & Travis; The Gateway Singers.

Label & Catalog #		Title	Year	VG+	NM
Reprise R-6035	(M)	Travis On His Own	1962	10.00	25.00
Reprise R9-6035	(S)	Travis On His Own	1962	12.00	30.00
Horizon T-1606	(M)	Travis On Cue	1962	8.00	20.00
Horizon ST-1606	(S)	Travis On Cue	1962	10.00	25.00

EDMUNDS, DAVE
Edmunds was formerly a member of Love Sculpture.

Label & Catalog #		Title	Year	VG+	NM
MAM 3	(S)	Rockpile (Counterfeits exist)	1972	10.00	25.00
Atlantic PR-320	(DJ)	College Network Interview (Colored label)	1978	12.00	30.00

EDWARDS, ALF

Label & Catalog #		Title	Year	VG+	NM
Prestige Int. PRLP-13060	(M)	Art Of The Concertina	1962	12.00	30.00

EDWARDS, JONATHAN & DARLENE

Label & Catalog #		Title	Year	VG+	NM
Westminster WGAP-68104	(M)	American Popular Songs	195?	10.00	25.00
Columbia CL-1513	(M)	In Paris	1960	8.00	20.00
Columbia CS-8313	(S)	In Paris	1960	10.00	25.00

EDWARDS, TOMMY

Label & Catalog #		Title	Year	VG+	NM
Regent MG-6096	(M)	Tommy Edwards Sings	195?	30.00	75.00
Lion L-70120	(M)	Tommy Edwards	1959	12.00	30.00
		(Lion 70120 is a reissue of Regent 6096.)			
MGM E-3732	(M)	It's All In The Game	1959	12.00	30.00
MGM SE-3732	(S)	It's All In The Game	1959	20.00	50.00
MGM E-3760	(M)	For Young Lovers	1959	12.00	30.00
MGM SE-3760	(S)	For Young Lovers	1959	20.00	50.00
		— MGM albums above have yellow labels.—			
MGM E-3805	(M)	You Started Me Dreaming	1960	8.00	20.00
MGM SE-3805	(S)	You Started Me Dreaming	1960	12.00	30.00
MGM E-3822	(M)	Step Out Singing	1960	8.00	20.00
MGM SE-3822	(S)	Step Out Singing	1960	12.00	30.00
MGM E-3838	(M)	Tommy Edwards In Hawaii	1960	8.00	20.00
MGM SE-3838	(S)	Tommy Edwards In Hawaii	1960	12.00	30.00
MGM E-3884	(M)	Tommy Edwards' Greatest Hits	1961	8.00	20.00
MGM SE-3884	(S)	Tommy Edwards' Greatest Hits	1961	12.00	30.00
MGM E-3959	(M)	Golden Country Hits	1961	8.00	20.00
MGM SE-3959	(S)	Golden Country Hits	1961	12.00	30.00
MGM E-4020	(M)	Stardust	1962	8.00	20.00
MGM SE-4020	(S)	Stardust	1962	12.00	30.00
MGM E-4060	(M)	Soft Strings And Two Guitars	1962	8.00	20.00
MGM SE-4060	(S)	Soft Strings And Two Guitars	1962	12.00	30.00
MGM E-4141	(M)	The Very Best Of Tommy Edwards	1963	8.00	20.00
MGM SE-4141	(S)	The Very Best Of Tommy Edwards	1963	10.00	25.00
		— MGM albums above have black labels.—			

Label & Catalog #		Title	Year	VG+	NM

EDWARDS, VINCENT
Vince Edwards is better known as Dr. Ben Casey from the television series of the same name.

Decca DL-4311	(M)	**Vincent Edwards Sings**	1962	10.00	25.00
Decca DL-74311	(S)	**Vincent Edwards Sings**	1962	12.00	30.00
Decca DL-4399	(M)	**In Person At The Riviera, Las Vegas**	1963	10.00	25.00
Decca DL-74399	(S)	**In Person At The Riviera, Las Vegas**	1963	12.00	30.00

EIRE APPARENT

| Buddah BDS-5031 | (S) | **Sunrise** *(Produced by Jimi Hendrix)* | 1969 | 14.00 | 35.00 |

EL CAMPO JADES, THE

| Golden Eagle LP-101 | (M) | **The El Campo Jades** | 1966 | 40.00 | 100.00 |

EL DORADOS, THE / THE MAGNIFICENTS

| Vee Jay LP-1001 | (M) | **Crazy Little Mama** | 1959 | 300.00 | 700.00 |

(First pressings of V.J. 1001 have maroon labels with a thick silver band around the perimeter. Ten of the twelve tracks on this album are by The El Dorados; the other two are by The Magnificents.)

| Vee Jay LP-1001 | (M) | **Crazy Little Mama** | 1960 | 200.00 | 500.00 |

(Second pressings have maroon labels with a thin silver band.)

| Vee Jay LP-1001 | (M) | **Crazy Little Mama** | 196? | 150.00 | 300.00 |

(Later pressings have black labels.)

ELBERT, DONNIE

| King 629 | (M) | **The Sensational Donnie Elbert Sings** | 1959 | 150.00 | 400.00 |

ELECTRIC FLAG, THE
The original Flag includes Mike Bloomfield, Barry Goldberg and Nick Gravenites.

| Sidewalk T-5908 | (M) | **The Trip** *(Soundtrack)* | 1967 | 12.00 | 30.00 |
| Sidewalk ST-5908 | (S) | **The Trip** *(Soundtrack)* | 1967 | 16.00 | 40.00 |

ELECTRIC LIGHT ORCHESTRA, THE/ELO
ELO features was founded by Roy Wood and Jeff Lynne, although Wood left soon after formation and the group fell into Lynne's hands exclusively. Refer to The Idle Race; The Move; The Traveling Wilburys.

United Arts. LA823	(DJ)	**Out Of The Blue** *(2 LPs. Blue vinyl)*	1977	10.00	25.00
United Arts. SP-123	(DJ)	**Ole ELO** *(Gold vinyl in black & white cover)*	1978	40.00	100.00
United Arts. SP-123	(DJ)	**Ole ELO** *(Gold vinyl & no cover)*	1978	20.00	50.00
United Arts. SP-123	(DJ)	**Ole ELO** *(Red vinyl & no cover)*	1978	30.00	75.00
United Arts. SP-123	(DJ)	**Ole ELO** *(Blue vinyl & no cover)*	1978	30.00	75.00
United Arts. SP-123	(DJ)	**Ole ELO** *(White vinyl & no cover)*	1978	30.00	75.00

("Ole" was first issued promotionally on gold vinyl in a black & white photo cover. It was pressed surreptitiously on gold, red, white and blue vinyl by an employee. U.A. issued the album commercially with the same cover as the original gold vinyl LP except in color.)

United Arts./Jet HZ-45769	(S)	**Discovery** *(Half-speed master)*	1981	10.00	30.00
United Arts./Jet HZ-46310	(S)	**ELO's Greatest Hits** *(Half-speed master)*	1981	13.00	40.00
United Arts./Jet HZ-47371	(S)	**Time** *(Half-speed master)*	1981	10.00	30.00
United Arts./Jet HZ-48490	(S)	**Secret Messages** *(Half-speed master)*	1983	16.00	50.00

ELECTRIC PRUNES, THE

Reprise R-6248	(M)	**I Had Too Much To Dream**	1967	16.00	40.00
Reprise RS-6248	(S)	**I Had Too Much To Dream**	1967	20.00	50.00
Reprise R-6262	(M)	**Underground**	1967	14.00	35.00
Reprise RS-6262	(S)	**Underground**	1967	16.00	40.00
Reprise R-6275	(M)	**Mass In F Minor**	1967	14.00	35.00
Reprise RS-6275	(S)	**Mass In F Minor**	1967	10.00	25.00
Reprise R-6316	(M)	**Release Of An Oath**	1968	14.00	35.00
Reprise RS-6316	(S)	**Release Of An Oath**	1968	10.00	25.00

— Reprise albums above have pink, gold & green labels.—

| Reprise RS-6342 | (S) | **Just Good Rock N' Roll** | 1969 | 10.00 | 25.00 |

ELECTRIC TOILET

| Nasco 9004 | (S) | **In The Hands Of Karma** | 1970 | 40.00 | 100.00 |

ELECTROMAGNETS, THE
The Electromagnets feature Eric Johnson, formerly of Mariani.

| E.C.M. 1001 | (S) | **The Electromagnets** *(Green cover)* | 197? | 60.00 | 150.00 |
| E.C.M. 1001 | (S) | **The Electromagnets** *(Red/orange cover)* | 197? | 50.00 | 125.00 |

Label & Catalog #		Title	Year	VG+	NM
ELEPHANT'S MEMORY					
For additional listings refer to John Lennon & Yoko Ono.					
Apple SMAS-3389	(S)	**Elephants Memory** *(Prod. by John & Yoko)*	1972	10.00	25.00
ELF					
Epic KE-31789	(S)	**Elf**	1972	10.00	25.00
ELGINS, THE					
V.I.P. 400	(M)	**Darling Baby**	1966	16.00	40.00
V.I.P. S-400	(S)	**Darling Baby**	1966	20.00	50.00
ELIMINATORS, THE					
Liberty LRP-3365	(M)	**Liverpool! Dragsters! Cycles! Surfing!**	1964	16.00	40.00
Liberty LST-7365	(S)	**Liverpool! Dragsters! Cycles! Surfing!**	1964	20.00	50.00
ELIRAN, RON					
Prestige Int. PRLP-13046	(M)	**Twilight Songs Of Israel**	1962	12.00	30.00
Prestige Int. PRLP-13054	(M)	**New Sounds Of Israel**	1962	12.00	30.00
Prestige Int. PRLP-13063	(M)	**Ladino**	1962	12.00	30.00
Prestige Int. PRLP-13069	(M)	**Golden Songs Of Israel**	1962	12.00	30.00
ELLINGTON, HARVEY					
Stepheny MF-4010	(M)	**I Can't Hide The Blues**	1959	40.00	100.00
ELLIOTT, DEAN					
Capitol T-????	(M)	**Zounds! What Sounds!**	196?	14.00	35.00
Capitol ST-????	(S)	**Zounds! What Sounds!**	196?	20.00	50.00
ELLIOTT, "RAMBLIN'" JACK					
Jack Elliott, the "Singing Cowboy from Brooklyn," is a pseudonym for Elliott Adnopoz, a singer, guitar					
player and writer of tradiitional and topical folk songs. Refer to Ed McCurdy / Oscar Brand / Jack Elliott;					
Topic T-14	(10")	**The Rambling Boys** *(With Derroll Adams)*	1958	16.00	40.00
Topic T-15	(10")	**Jack Takes The Floor**	1958	16.00	40.00
Prestige Int. PRLP-13016	(M)	**The Songs Of Woody Guthrie**	1961	12.00	30.00
Prestige Int. PRLP-13033	(M)	**Ramblin'**	1961	12.00	30.00
Prestige Int. PRLP-13045	(M)	**Country Style**	1962	12.00	30.00
Prestige Int. PRLP-13065	(M)	**At The Second Fret**	1962	12.00	30.00
Monitor MF-379	(M)	**Ramblin' Cowboy**	1962	10.00	25.00
Monitor MF-380	(M)	**Sings Woody Guthrie And Jimmie Rodgers**	1962	10.00	25.00
Monitor MS-380	(S)	**Sings Woody Guthrie And Jimmie Rodgers**	1962	10.00	25.00
Vanguard VRS-9151	(M)	**Jack Elliott**	1964	8.00	20.00
Vanguard VSD-79151	(S)	**Jack Elliott**	1964	10.00	25.00
Folklore FRLP-14011	(M)	**The Songs Of Woody Guthrie**	1964	10.00	25.00
Folklore FRST-14011	(S)	**The Songs Of Woody Guthrie**	1964	12.00	30.00
		(Folklore 14011 is a reissue of Prestige Int. 13016.)			
Folklore FRLP-14014	(M)	**Ramblin'**	1964	10.00	25.00
Folklore FRST-14014	(S)	**Ramblin'**	1964	12.00	30.00
		(Folklore 14014 is a reissue of Prestige Int. 13033.)			
Folklore FRLP-14019	(M)	**Hootenanny With Jack Elliott**	1964	10.00	25.00
Folklore FRST-14019	(S)	**Hootenanny With Jack Elliott**	1964	12.00	30.00
Folklore FRLP-14029	(M)	**Country Style**	1964	10.00	25.00
Folklore FRST-14029	(S)	**Country Style**	1964	12.00	30.00
Delmark DL-801	(M)	**Talking Woody Guthrie**	1966	10.00	25.00
Delmark DS-801	(S)	**Talking Woody Guthrie**	1966	10.00	25.00
ELLIOT, RON					
Ron Elliott was formerly a member of the Beau Brummels.					
Warner Bros. WS-1833	(S)	**Candlestickmaker** *(With booklet)*	1969	10.00	25.00
ELLIS, ANITA: *Refer to* **GOLDMINE'S PRICE GUIDE TO COLLECTIBLE JAZZ ALBUMS**					
ELLIS, JIMMY					
Boblo 78-829	(S)	**Ellis Sings Elvis By Request**	1978	30.00	75.00
ELLIS, RED, & THE HURON VALLEY BOYS					
Starday SLP-168	(M)	**Holy Cry From The Cross**	1962	12.00	30.00
Starday SLP-203	(M)	**The Sacred Sound Of Bluegrass Music**	1962	12.00	30.00
Starday SLP-273	(M)	**Old Time Religion Bluegrass Style**	1963	12.00	30.00
		— Starday albums above have yellow labels.—			

These two albums on Prestige's Folklore label show a mature Elliott in a relaxed cowboy setting, more than befitting this excellent troubadour long noted for his songs and tales of the cowboy's travails.

Label & Catalog #		Title	Year	VG+	NM
ELLIS, SHIRLEY					
Congress CGL-3002	(M)	**Shirley Ellis In Action**	1964	10.00	25.00
Congress CGS-3002	(S)	**Shirley Ellis In Action**	1964	12.00	30.00
Congress CGL-3003	(M)	**The Name Game**	1965	10.00	25.00
Congress CGS-3003	(S)	**The Name Game**	1965	12.00	30.00
Columbia CL-2679	(M)	**Sugar, Let's Shing-A-Ling**	1967	8.00	20.00
Columbia CS-9479	(S)	**Sugar, Let's Shing-A-Ling**	1967	10.00	25.00
ELLIS, STEVE, & THE STARFIRES					
I.G.L. 105	(M)	**The Steve Ellis Songbook**	1967	150.00	300.00
ELMER CITY RAMBLING DOGS, THE					
Dog Dirt DD-1	(S)	**Jam It**	1975	10.00	25.00
ELMER GANTRY'S VELVET OPERA					
Epic BN-26415	(S)	**Elmer Gantry's Velvet Opera**	1968	20.00	50.00
EMBERS, THE					
J.C.P. Recording 2006	(M)	**The Embers Roll Eleven**	196?	70.00	175.00
J.C.P. Recording 2009	(M)	**Just For The Birds**	196?	40.00	100.00
E.E.E. 1069	(S)	**The Embers Burn You A New One**	197?	12.00	30.00
EMERSON, LAKE & PALMER					
Atlantic PR-281	(DJ)	**On Tour With Emerson, Lake & Palmer**	1977	16.00	40.00
Mobile Fidelity MFSL-031	(S)	**Pictures At An Exhibition**	1980	8.00	25.00
EMERSON'S OLD TIMEY CUSTARD-SUCKIN' BAND					
ESP-Disk' 2006	(S)	**Emerson's Old Timey**			
		Custard-Suckin' Band	1969	12.00	30.00
EMERY, TIM					
Ros-Sound 130	(S)	**Alias Red Garrett**	1978	20.00	50.00
EMMAUS ROAD BAND, THE					
Members of The E.R.B. originally recorded as Maranatha.					
(No label)	(S)	**This Could Be The Beginning**	197?	80.00	200.00
EMMONS, BUDDY					
Refer to Longbranch Pennywhistle.					
Mercury MG-20843	(M)	**Steel Guitar Jazz**	1963	40.00	100.00
Mercury SR-60843	(S)	**Steel Guitar Jazz**	1963	60.00	150.00
Emmons ELP-1001	(M)	**Buddy Emmons—The Black Album**	196?	10.00	25.00
EMMONS, BUDDY, & SHOT JACKSON					
Starday SLP-230	(M)	**Singing Strings Of Steel And Dobro**	196?	20.00	50.00
		— Starday albums above have yellow labels.—			
Nashville NLP-2026	(M)	**Steel Guitar And Dobro Sounds**	1965	20.00	50.00
EMPEROR HUDSON					
Hook 100	(M)	**The Adventures Of Emperor Hudson**	196?	10.00	25.00
END, THE					
London PS-560	(S)	**Introspection** (Produced by Bill Wyman)	1969	20.00	50.00
ENDLE ST. CLOUD					
International Arts. 12	(S)	**Thank You All Very Much**	1968	16.00	40.00
ENGEL, SCOTT, & JOHN STEWART					
Refer to Scott Walker; The Walker Brothers.					
Tower T-5026	(M)	**I Only Came To Dance With You**	1966	8.00	20.00
Tower ST-5026	(S)	**I Only Came To Dance With You**	1966	10.00	25.00
ENGLISH, LOGAN					
Logan English is a guitar player and singer of traditional American folk material.					
Folkways FA-2136	(10")	**Kentucky Ballads**	195?	16.00	40.00
Folkways FH-5255	(M)	**The Days Of '49**	195?	12.00	30.00
Riverside RLP-12-643	(M)	**Gambling Songs**	195?	12.00	30.00

Label & Catalog #		Title	Year	VG+	NM
ENNIS, ETHEL					
Jubilee JLP-1021	(M)	**Lullabies For Losers**	1956	20.00	50.00
Capitol T-941	(M)	**Changes Of Scenery**	1957	16.00	40.00
Capitol T-1078	(M)	**Have You Forgotten?**	1958	16.00	40.00
Jubilee JLP-5024	(M)	**Ethel Ennis Sings**	1963	8.00	20.00
Jubilee SDJLP-5024	(S)	**Ethel Ennis Sings**	1963	10.00	25.00
RCA Victor LPM-2786	(M)	**This Is Ethel Ennis**	1964	8.00	20.00
RCA Victor LSP-2786	(S)	**This Is Ethel Ennis**	1964	10.00	25.00
RCA Victor LPM-2862	(M)	**Once Again**	1964	8.00	20.00
RCA Victor LSP-2862	(S)	**Once Again**	1964	10.00	25.00
RCA Victor LPM-2984	(M)	**Eyes For You**	1964	8.00	20.00
RCA Victor LSP-2984	(S)	**Eyes For You**	1964	10.00	25.00
ENNIS, SEAMUS					
Seamus Ennis is a piper, singer and storyteller of traditional Irish folk material.					
Tradition TLP-1013	(M)	**The Bonny Bunch Of Roses**	195?	12.00	30.00
ENTWISTLE, JOHN					
Mr. Entwistle is a member of The Who.					
Decca DL-79183	(S)	**Smash Your Head Against The Wall**	1971	10.00	25.00
Decca DL-79190	(S)	**Whistle Rhymes**	1972	10.00	25.00
MCA/Track 1926	(S)	**Who's Ox** *(Promo sampler)*	1975	20.00	50.00
EPPS, PRESTON					
Original Sound LPM-5002	(M)	**Bongo, Bongo, Bongo**	1960	20.00	50.00
Original Sound LPS-8851	(S)	**Bongo, Bongo, Bongo**	1960	30.00	75.00
		("Bongo Rock" is rechanneled.)			
Top Rank RM-349	(M)	**Bongola**	1961	14.00	35.00
Top Rank RS-649	(S)	**Bongola**	1961	20.00	50.00
Original Sound OS-8872	(M)	**Surfin' Bongos** *(With The Bongo Teens)*	1963	12.00	30.00
Original Sound OSS-8872	(S)	**Surfin' Bongos** *(With The Bongo Teens)*	1963	16.00	40.00
EQUALS, THE					
Laurie LP-2045	(M)	**Unequalled**	1967	10.00	25.00
Laurie SLP-2045	(S)	**Unequalled**	1967	12.00	30.00
ERHARDT, CAPT. FRANK					
RCA Victor LBY-1013	(M)	**Adventures In Sound And Space**	1958	20.00	50.00
RCA Victor LBYS-1013	(S)	**Adventures In Sound And Space**	1958	40.00	100.00
ERICA					
ESP-Disk' 1099	(S)	**You Used To Think**	1968	40.00	100.00
ESCORTS, THE					
Teo LPM-5000	(M)	**The Escorts Bring Down The House**	1966	60.00	150.00
ESKIN, SAM					
Sam Eskin is a guitar player and singer of traditional American folk songs.					
Folkways FA-2019	(10")	**Shanty Men**	195?	16.00	40.00
Cook Laborator.1020	(10")	**Songs Of All Times**	195?	16.00	40.00
SQUERITA					
Capitol T-1186	(M)	**Esquerita**	1959	500.00	1,000.00
ESQUIRES, THE					
Bunky 300	(S)	**Get On Up And Get Away**	1968	10.00	25.00
ESQUIVEL					
RCA Victor LPM-1345	(M)	**To Love Again**	1957	20.00	50.00
RCA Victor LPM-1749	(M)	**Four Corners Of The World**	1958	10.00	25.00
RCA Victor LSP-1749	(S)	**Four Corners Of The World**	1958	20.00	50.00
RCA Victor LPM-1753	(M)	**Other Worlds, Other Sounds**	1958	10.00	25.00
RCA Victor LSP-1753	(S)	**Other Worlds, Other Sounds**	1958	20.00	50.00
RCA Victor LPM-1978	(M)	**Exploring New Sounds In Hi Fi**	1959	12.00	30.00
RCA Victor LSP-1978	(S)	**Exploring New Sounds In Stereo**	1959	24.00	60.00
RCA Victor LPM-1988	(M)	**Strings Aflame**	1959	10.00	25.00
RCA Victor LSP-1988	(S)	**Strings Aflame**	1959	20.00	50.00
RCA Victor LPM-2225	(M)	**Infinity In Sound**	1960	12.00	30.00
RCA Victor LSP-2225	(S)	**Infinity In Sound**	1960	24.00	60.00

Label & Catalog #		Title	Year	VG+	NM
RCA Victor LPM-2296	(M)	**Infinity In Sound, Vol. 2**	1961	12.00	30.00
RCA Victor LSP-2296	(S)	**Infinity In Sound, Vol. 2**	1961	24.00	60.00
RCA Victor LPM-2418	(M)	**Latin-esque** (Standard cover)	1962	8.00	20.00
RCA Victor LSP-2418	(S)	**Latin-esque** (Die-cut cover with inner sleeve)	1962	24.00	60.00
RCA Victor LSP-2418	(S)	**Latin-esque** (Standard cover)	1962	16.00	40.00
		— RCA mono albums above have "Long Play" on the bottom of the label; stereo albums have "Living Stereo" on the bottom.—			
Reprise R-6046	(M)	**More Of Other Worlds Other Sounds**	1962	10.00	25.00
Reprise R9-6046	(S)	**More Of Other Worlds Other Sounds**	1962	20.00	50.00

ESSEX, THE

Roulette R-25234	(M)	**Easier Said Than Done**	1963	16.00	40.00
Roulette SR-25234	(S)	**Easier Said Than Done**	1963	20.00	50.00
Roulette R-25235	(M)	**A Walkin' Miracle**	1963	12.00	30.00
Roulette SR-25235	(S)	**A Walkin' Miracle**	1963	15.00	40.00
Roulette R-25246	(M)	**Young And Lively**	1964	12.00	30.00
Roulette SR-25246	(S)	**Young And Lively**	1964	16.00	40.00

ESTES, "SLEEPY" JOHN
Singer, guitar player and songwriter John Estes is one of the few bluesmen to have been recorded prior to the Great Depression.

Delmark DL-603	(M)	**The Legend Of Sleepy John Estes**	1966	20.00	50.00
Delmark DS-603	(E)	**The Legend Of Sleepy John Estes**	1966	12.00	30.00
Delmark DL-608	(M)	**Broke And Hungry**	1966	20.00	50.00
Delmark DS-608	(E)	**Broke And Hungry**	1966	12.00	30.00
Delmark DS-613	(E)	**Sleepy John Estes**	1969	12.00	30.00
Delmark DS-619	(E)	**Electric Sheep**	1969	12.00	30.00

ETC.

Windi WLPS-1011	(S)	**Etc. Is The Name Of The Band!**	1976	20.00	50.00

ETERNITY'S CHILDREN

Tower ST-5123	(S)	**Eternity's Children**	1968	10.00	25.00
Tower ST-5144	(S)	**Timeless** (Canadian)	1968	12.00	30.00

EUPHORIA

Capitol SKAO-363	(S)	**A Gift From Euphoria**	1969	60.00	150.00

EUPHORIA

Rainbow 1003	(S)	**Lost In Trance**	197?	100.00	250.00

EVANS, DALE
Ms. Evans also recorded with her hubby, Roy Rogers.

Capitol T-2772	(M)	**It's Real**	1967	8.00	20.00
Capitol ST-2772	(S)	**It's Real**	1967	10.00	25.00

EVANS, PAUL

Guaranteed GUL-1000	(M)	**Fabulous Teens**	1960	20.00	50.00
Guaranteed GUS-1000	(S)	**Fabulous Teens**	1960	30.00	75.00
Carlton TLP-129	(M)	**Hear Paul Evans In Your Home Tonight**	1961	14.00	35.00
Carlton STLP-129	(S)	**Hear Paul Evans In Your Home Tonight**	1961	20.00	50.00
		("Seven Little Girls" is rechanneled on this album.)			
Carlton TLP-130	(M)	**Folk Songs Of Many Lands**	1961	14.00	35.00
Carlton STLP-130	(S)	**Folk Songs Of Many Lands**	1961	20.00	50.00
Kapp KL-1346	(M)	**21 Years In A Tennessee Jail**	1964	8.00	20.00
Kapp KS-3346	(S)	**21 Years In A Tennessee Jail**	1964	10.00	25.00
Kapp KL-1475	(M)	**Another Town, Another Jail**	1966	8.00	20.00
Kapp KS-3475	(S)	**Another Town, Another Jail**	1966	10.00	25.00

EVEN DOZEN JUG BAND, THE
Stefan Grossman and Peter Siegel's loosely assembled Jug Band included— at one time or another— Maria D'Amato (later Maria Muldauer), David Grisman, Steve Katz, Joshua Rifkin and John Sebastian.

Elektra EKL-246	(M)	**The Even Dozen Jug Band**	1965	12.00	30.00
Elektra ES-7246	(S)	**The Even Dozen Jug Band**	1965	20.00	50.00

EVERETT, BETTY
Ms. Everett also recorded with Jerry Butler.

Vee Jay LP-1077	(M)	**You're No Good**	1964	20.00	50.00
Vee Jay LPS-1077	(S)	**You're No Good**	1964	30.00	75.00

Label & Catalog #		Title	Year	VG+	NM
Vee Jay LP-1077	(M)	It's In His Kiss	1964	14.00	35.00
Vee Jay VJS-1077	(S)	It's In His Kiss	1964	20.00	50.00
		("It's In His Kiss" is a reissue of "You're No Good.")			
Vee Jay LP-1122	(M)	The Very Best Of Betty Everett	1965	8.00	20.00
Vee Jay VJS-1122	(S)	The Very Best Of Betty Everett	1965	12.00	30.00

EVERLY BROTHERS, THE

Of Don and Phil's Cadence repertoire, only "Let It Be Me," "Like Strangers," "Love Of My Life," "Poor Jenny," "Take A Message To Mary," "Til I Kissed You," and "When Will I Be Loved" were released in stereo.

Label & Catalog #		Title	Year	VG+	NM
Cadence CLP-3003	(M)	The Everly Brothers	1958	40.00	100.00
Cadence CLP-3106	(M)	Songs Our Daddy Taught Us	1958	40.00	100.00
Cadence CLP-3025	(M)	The Everly Brothers' Best	1969	30.00	75.00
Cadence CLP-3040	(M)	The Fabulous Style Of The Everly Brothers	1960	20.00	50.00
Cadence CLP-25040	(P)	The Fabulous Style Of The Everly Brothers	1960	40.00	100.00
		— Cadence albums above have burgundy labels with silver print.—			
Cadence CLP-3003	(M)	The Everly Brothers	1963	20.00	50.00
Cadence CLP-3025	(M)	The Everly Brothers' Best	1963	12.00	30.00
Cadence CLP-3040	(M)	The Fabulous Style Of The Everly Brothers	1963	12.00	30.00
Cadence CLP-25040	(P)	The Fabulous Style Of The Everly Brothers	1963	20.00	50.00
Cadence CLP-3059	(M)	Folk Songs Of The Everly Brothers	1963	20.00	50.00
Cadence CLP-25059	(E)	Folk Songs Of The Everly Brothers	1963	16.00	40.00
		(Cadence 3/25059 is a reissue of 3106.)			
Cadence CLP-3062	(M)	15 Everly Hits 15	1963	16.00	40.00
Cadence CLP-25062	(P)	15 Everly Hits 15	1963	20.00	50.00
		— Cadence albums above have red labels with black print.—			
Warner Bros. PRO-134	(10")	It's Everly Time Souvenir Sampler *(Promo)*	1960	300.00	600.00
Warner Bros. W-1381	(M)	It's Everly Time	1960	12.00	30.00
Warner Bros. WS-1381	(S)	It's Everly Time	1960	16.00	40.00
Warner Bros. W-1395	(M)	A Date With The Everly Brothers *(With bonus photos)*	1960	16.00	40.00
Warner Bros. WS-1395	(S)	A Date With The Everly Brothers *(With bonus photos)*	1960	20.00	50.00
Warner Bros. W-1395	(M)	A Date With The Everly Brothers *(Without the photos)*	1960	12.00	30.00
Warner Bros. WS-1395	(S)	A Date With The Everly Brothers *(Without the photos)*	1960	16.00	40.00
Warner Bros. W-1418	(M)	Both Sides Of An Evening	1961	12.00	30.00
Warner Bros. WS-1418	(S)	Both Sides Of An Evening	1961	16.00	40.00
Warner Bros. W-1430	(M)	Instant Party	1962	12.00	30.00
Warner Bros. WS-1430	(S)	Instant Party	1962	16.00	40.00
Warner Bros. W-1471	(M)	The Everly Brothers' Golden Hits	1962	10.00	25.00
Warner Bros. WS-1471	(S)	The Everly Brothers' Golden Hits	1962	14.00	35.00
		— Warner mono albums above have grey labels; stereo albums have gold labels.—			
Warner Bros. W-1483	(M)	Christmas With The Everly Brothers	1962	16.00	40.00
Warner Bros. WS-1483	(S)	Christmas With The Everly Brothers	1962	20.00	50.00
Warner Bros. W-1513	(M)	Great Country Hits	1963	12.00	30.00
Warner Bros. WS-1513	(S)	Great Country Hits	1963	16.00	40.00
Warner Bros. W-1554	(M)	Very Best Of The Everly Brothers	1964	12.00	30.00
Warner Bros. WS-1554	(S)	Very Best Of The Everly Brothers	1964	16.00	40.00
		(Original covers for Warner Bros. 1554 have a yellow cover.)			
Warner Bros. W-1554	(M)	The Very Best Of The Everly Brothers	1965	8.00	20.00
Warner Bros. WS-1554	(S)	The Very Best Of The Everly Brothers	1965	10.00	25.00
		(Later pressings have a white cover.)			
Warner Bros. ST-91343	(S)	The Very Best Of The Everly Brothers *(Capitol Record Club)*	1965	16.00	40.00
Warner Bros. W-1578	(M)	Rock N' Soul	1965	16.00	40.00
Warner Bros. WS-1578	(S)	Rock N' Soul	1965	20.00	50.00
Warner Bros. W-1585	(M)	Gone, Gone, Gone	1965	16.00	40.00
Warner Bros. WS-1585	(S)	Gone, Gone, Gone	1965	20.00	50.00
Warner Bros. W-1605	(M)	Beat N' Soul	1965	16.00	40.00
Warner Bros. WS-1605	(S)	Beat N' Soul	1965	20.00	50.00
Warner Bros. W-1620	(M)	In Our Image	1966	16.00	40.00
Warner Bros. WS-1620	(S)	In Our Image	1966	20.00	50.00
		— Warner albums above have grey labels with a black & white logo.—			
Warner Bros. W-1646	(M)	Two Yanks In London	1966	16.00	40.00
Warner Bros. WS-1646	(S)	Two Yanks In London	1966	20.00	50.00
		(Although uncredited, The Hollies wrote many of the songs and back up the Everlys throughout this album, produced by Ron Richards.)			

Label & Catalog #		Title	Year	VG+	NM
Warner Bros. W-1676	(M)	**The Hit Sound Of The Everly Brothers**	1967	16.00	40.00
Warner Bros. WS-1676	(S)	**The Hit Sound Of The Everly Brothers**	1967	20.00	50.00
Warner Bros. W-1708	(M)	**The Everly Brothers Sing**	1967	16.00	40.00
Warner Bros. WS-1708	(S)	**The Everly Brothers Sing**	1967	20.00	50.00
		— *Warner albums above have gold labels.—*			
Warner Bros. WS-1752	(S)	**Roots**	1968	12.00	30.00
Warner Bros. ST-91601	(S)	**Roots** *(Capitol Record Club)*	1968	16.00	40.00
Warner Bros. WS-1858	(S)	**The Everly Brothers' Show**	1970	8.00	20.00
Warner Bros. STBO-93286	(S)	**The Everly Brothers' Show** *(Capitol Record Club)*	1970	10.00	25.00
Passport 4006DJ	(S)	**Reunion Concert** *(Promo label)*	1983	20.00	50.00
EVERPRESENT FULLNESS					
White Whale 7132	(S)	**Everpresent Fullness**	1970	12.00	30.00
EVERYTHING IS EVERYTHING					
Vanguard VSD-6512	(S)	**Everything Is Everything**	1969	10.00	25.00
EVESLAGE, ROBERT					
Mark 5208	(M)	**Reflecting/Portraits Of Loneliness**	196?	20.00	50.00
EXCITERS, THE					
United Arts. UAL-3264	(M)	**Tell Him**	1963	14.00	35.00
United Arts. UAS-6264	(S)	**Tell Him**	1963	20.00	50.00
Roulette R-25326	(M)	**The Exciters**	1966	10.00	25.00
Roulette RS-25326	(S)	**The Exciters**	1966	14.00	35.00
EXCURSIONS					
No label	(S)	**Excursions**	197?	60.00	150.00
EYES, THE					
World Theatre	(S)	**New Gods: Aardvark Thru Zymurgy**	1977	300.00	500.00

While Faine Jade is almost always referred to and listed as a group (as in this volume), the name, in fact, refers to the individual responsible for this sought-after psychedelic album. So, if he wants to be a group, who am I to argue?

FABARES, SHELLY
Refer to James Darren / Shelly Fabares / Paul Petersen.

Colpix CLP-426	(M)	**Shelly**	1962	60.00	150.00
Colpix SCP-426	(S)	**Shelly**	1962	300.00	500.00
Colpix CLP-431	(M)	**The Things We Did Last Summer**	1962	60.00	150.00
Colpix SCP-431	(S)	**The Things We Did Last Summer**	1962	200.00	400.00
MGM SE-4540	(S)	**A Time To Sing** *(Soundtrack)*	1968	10.00	25.00

FABIAN

Chancellor CHL-5003	(M)	**Hold That Tiger**	1959	30.00	75.00
Chancellor CHLS-5003	(S)	**Hold That Tiger**	1959	40.00	100.00
Chancellor CHL-5005	(M)	**The Fabulous Fabian**	1959	30.00	75.00
Chancellor CHLX-5005	(S)	**The Fabulous Fabian**	1959	40.00	100.00
Chancellor CHL-5012	(M)	**The Good Old Summertime**	1960	30.00	75.00
Chancellor CHLS-5012	(S)	**The Good Old Summertime**	1960	40.00	100.00
Chancellor CHL-69802	(M)	**Fabian Facade** *(Felt, die-cut cover)*	1960	40.00	100.00
Chancellor CHL-5019	(M)	**Rockin' Hot**	1961	30.00	75.00
Chancellor CHL-5024	(M)	**Fabian's 16 Fabulous Hits**	1962	30.00	75.00

FABIAN / FRANKIE AVALON

Chancellor CHL-5009	(M)	**The Hit Makers**	1960	20.00	50.00

FACES, THE: *Refer to* THE SMALL FACES

FAHEY, JOHN

Takoma 1002	(M)	**Blind Joe Death**	1959	10.00	25.00
Takoma 1003	(S)	**Death Chants, Break Downs And Military Waltzes**	1963	10.00	25.00
Takoma 1004	(S)	**Dance Of Death (& Other Plantation Favorites)**	1965	10.00	25.00

FAIER, BILLY
Billy Faier is a banjo player, singer and writer of contemporary folk-based music. Refer to Ed McCurdy;
Dick Weissman, Billy Faier & Eric Weissberg..

Riverside RLP-12-427	(M)	**Travelin' Man**	195?	12.00	30.00
Riverside RLP-12-813	(M)	**The Art Of The Five String Banjo**	195?	12.00	30.00

FAINE JADE

R.S.V.P. 8002	(S)	**Introspection—A Faine Jade Recital**	1968	100.00	200.00

FAIRPORT CONVENTION
Fairport Convention plays traditional British folk music on electric instruments. The group has had many personnel changes and members have included Sandy Denny, Ashley Hutchings, Ian Matthews and Richard Thompson. Refer to Steeleye Span.

Cotillion SO-9024	(S)	**Fairport Convention**	1969	10.00	25.00

FAITH, ADAM

MGM E-3951	(M)	**England's Top Singer**	1961	16.00	40.00
MGM SE-3951	(S)	**England's Top Singer**	1961	20.00	50.00
Amy 8005	(M)	**Adam Faith**	1965	10.00	25.00
Amy S-8005	(S)	**Adam Faith**	1965	12.00	30.00

FAITHFULL, MARIANNE

London LL-3423	(M)	**Marianne Faithfull**	1965	10.00	25.00
London PS-423	(E)	**Marianne Faithfull**	1965	8.00	20.00
London LL-3452	(M)	**Go Away From My World**	1965	8.00	20.00
London PS-452	(S)	**Go Away From My World** ("*Summer Nights*" *is rechanneled.*)	1965	10.00	25.00
London LL-3482	(M)	**Faithfull Forever**	1966	8.00	20.00
London PS-482	(S)	**Faithfull Forever**	1966	10.00	25.00

Label & Catalog #		Title	Year	VG+	NM

FALCONAIRES, THE
The Falconaires feature Steve Alaimo, Keith Allison and Mark Lindsay of Paul Revere's Raiders.

USAF 70-3/4	(S)	Something From The Falconaires	1970	20.00	50.00

FALLEN ANGELS, THE

Roulette SR-25358	(S)	The Fallen Angels	1968	20.00	50.00
Roulette SR-42011	(S)	It's A Long Way Down	1968	100.00	250.00

FAME, GEORGIE
Refer to Shorty.

Imperial LP-9282	(M)	Yeh, Yeh	1965	10.00	25.00
Imperial LP-12282	(S)	Yeh, Yeh ("Yeh Yeh" is rechanneled)	1965	12.00	30.00
Imperial LP-9331	(M)	Get Away	1966	10.00	25.00
Imperial LP-12331	(E)	Get Away	1966	8.00	20.00
Epic BN-26368	(S)	The Ballad Of Bonnie And Clyde	1968	10.00	25.00

FANKHAUSER, MERRELL
Refer to Fapardokly; The Impacts; Mu.

Shamley SS-701	(S)	Things	197?	10.00	25.00
Maui 101	(S)	Merrell Fankhauser	1976	24.00	60.00

FANTASTIC BAGGYS, THE
The Baggys are the creation of Steve Barri and Phil Sloan.

Imperial LP-9270	(M)	Tell 'Em I'm Surfin'	1964	40.00	100.00
Imperial LP-12270	(S)	Tell 'Em I'm Surfin'	1964	60.00	150.00

FANTASTIC DEE JAY'S, THE

Stone SLP-4003	(S)	The Fantastic Dee Jay's	196?	600.0	1,500.00

FANTASTIC FOUR, THE

Soul 717	(P)	Best Of The Fantastic Four	1969	12.00	30.00

FANTASTIC JOHNNY C, THE

Phil-L.A. 4000	(S)	Boogaloo Down Broadway	1968	20.00	50.00

FAPARDOKLY
Fapardokly is Merrell Fankhauser.

U.I.P. 2500	(S)	Fapardokly	1966	100.00	250.00

FARLOWE, CHRIS/CHRIS FARLOWE & THE THUNDERBIRDS

Columbia CL-2593	(M)	The Fabulous Chris Farlowe	1966	14.00	35.00
Columbia CS-9393	(E)	The Fabulous Chris Farlowe	1966	10.00	25.00

FARM

Series-2 F2001	(S)	The Inner Most Limits Of Pure Fun *(Issued with an insert cover.)*	197?	40.00	100.00

FARM BAND, THE

Mantra 777	(S)	The Farm Band *(2 LPs with poster)*	197?	14.00	35.00

FARRELL, EILEEN

Columbia CL-1465	(M)	I've Got A Right To Sing The Blues	1960	8.00	20.00
Columbia CS-8256	(S)	I've Got A Right To Sing The Blues	1960	12.00	30.00
Columbia CL-1653	(M)	Here I Go Again	1961	8.00	20.00
Columbia CS-8453	(S)	Here I Go Again	1961	10.00	25.00
Columbia CL-1739	(M)	This Fling Called Love	1962	8.00	20.00
Columbia CS-8539	(S)	This Fling Called Love	1962	10.00	25.00

FAT

Dream Merchant OU812	(S)	Footloose	1976	10.00	25.00

FATHER YOD

Higher Key 3301	(S)	Kohoutek	1973	60.00	150.00
Higher Key 3302	(S)	To Our Children	1973	80.00	200.00
Higher Key 3304	(S)	All Or Nothing At All	1974	60.00	150.00
Higher Key 3306	(S)	The Savage Sons Of Yo Ho Wa	1974	60.00	150.00
Higher Key 3307	(S)	An Aquarian Symphony—Penetration	1974	60.00	150.00
Higher Key 3309	(S)	I'm Gonna Take You Home	1975	60.00	150.00

Label & Catalog #		Title	Year	VG+	NM

FAUN
Members of Faun later founded Journey.

Gregar 7000	(S)	**Faun**	1969	12.00	30.00

FAYE, FRANCES: *Refer to* GOLDMINE'S PRICE GUIDE TO COLLECTIBLE JAZZ ALBUMS

FEATHER

Magic	(S)	**Feather**	1978	16.00	40.00

FELICE, DEE DEE

Bethlehem B-1000	(S)	**In The Heat** *(Produced by James Brown)*	1969	10.00	25.00

FELT

Nasco 9006	(S)	**Felt**	1971	30.00	75.00

FENDERMEN, THE

Soma MG-1240	(M)	**Mule Skinner Blues** *(Blue vinyl)*	1960	2,000.00	4,000.00
Soma MG-1240	(M)	**Mule Skinner Blues**	1960		See below

(There are two black vinyl pressings of Soma 1240: The more common one is on normal, opaque black vinyl with a suggested Near Mint value of $600-1,200. The second is pressed on non-opaque black vinyl. That is, when held up to a light source, the light will shine through the black vinyl with a reddish-brown glow. These have a suggested Near Mint value of $1,000-2,000.)

Point P-213	(M)	**Mule Skinner Blues** *(Black label)*	1960	150.00	300.00
Point P-213	(M)	**Mule Skinner Blues** *(Green label)*	196?	60.00	150.00

(The Canadian Point pressings are listed here because they have become a more affordable alternative to their US counterparts.)

FENDERS, THE

(No label)	(M)	**Second Time 'Round**	1966	20.00	50.00

FERLINGHETTI, LAWRENCE
Refer to Kenneth Rexroth & Lawrence Ferlinghetti.

Fantasy 7004	(M)	**Impeachment Of Eisenhower** *(Red vinyl)*	1958	80.00	200.00
Fantasy 7004	(M)	**Impeachment Of Eisenhower**	1958	40.00	100.00

FERRERS, THE
Mr. and Mrs. Jose Ferrer. Mrs. Ferrer also recorded under her maiden name, Rosemary Clooney.

MGM E-3709	(M)	**The Ferrers At Home**	1958	16.00	40.00

FERRIER, KATHLEEN

London LS-48	(10")	**Folk Songs**	195?	16.00	40.00
London LS-538	(10")	**Folk Songs**	195?	16.00	40.00
London LL-5411	(M)	**Folk Songs**	195?	16.00	40.00

(London 5411 collects both 48 and 538.)

FEVER TREE

Uni 73024	(S)	**The Fever Tree**	1968	10.00	25.00
Uni 73040	(S)	**Another Time, Another Place**	1968	10.00	25.00
Uni 73067	(S)	**Creation**	1970	10.00	25.00
Uni 73091	(S)	**Angels Die Hard** *(Soundtrack)*	1970	10.00	25.00
Ampex A-10113	(S)	**For Sale**	1970	10.00	25.00

FIELD, SALLY

Colgems COL-106	(M)	**Star Of "The Flying Nun"**	1967	10.00	25.00
Colgems COS-106	(S)	**Star Of "The Flying Nun"**	1967	12.00	30.00

FIELDING, JANE: *Refer to* GOLDMINE'S PRICE GUIDE TO COLLECTIBLE JAZZ ALBUMS

FIELDS, BENNY

Mercury MG-20224	(M)	**Two Days At The Palace**	1957	14.00	35.00
Coplix CP-501	(M)	**Benny Fields & His Minstrel Men**	196?	14.00	35.00

(The Minstrel Men are fellow comedians Jack Benny, Milton Berle, George Burns and Phil Silvers.)

FIELDS, GRACIE

Liberty LRP-3059	(M)	**Our Gracie**	1957	20.00	50.00

Label & Catalog #		Title	Year	VG+	NM
FIFTH ESTATE, THE					
Jubilee JGM-8005	(M)	Ding Dong The Witch Is Dead	1967	10.00	25.00
Jubilee JGS-8005	(S)	Ding Dong The Witch Is Dead	1967	12.00	30.00
FIFTY FOOT HOSE					
Limelight 86062	(S)	Cauldron	1969	20.00	50.00
FILET OF SOUL					
Mongoloid	(M)	Freedom	196?	60.00	150.00
FINCHLEY BOYS, THE					
Golden Throat 200-19	(S)	Everlasting Tribute	1971	40.00	100.00
FIRE ESCAPE, THE					
Crescendo GNP-2034	(M)	Psychotic Reaction (Red label)	1967	12.00	30.00
Crescendo GNPS-2034	(S)	Psychotic Reaction (Red label)	1967	12.00	30.00
FIREBALLS, THE/JIMMY GILMER & THE FIREBALLS					
Top Rank RM-324	(M)	The Fireballs	1960	80.00	200.00
Top Rank RM-343	(M)	Vaquero	1960	80.00	200.00
Top Rank RS-643	(S)	Vaquero	1960	150.00	300.00
Warwick W-2042	(M)	Here Are The Fireballs	1961	80.00	200.00
Warwick WST-2042	(S)	Here Are The Fireballs	1961	150.00	300.00
Dot DLP-3512	(M)	Torquay	1963	14.00	35.00
Dot DLP-25512	(S)	Torquay	1963	20.00	50.00
Dot DLP-3545	(M)	Sugar Shack	1963	14.00	35.00
Dot DLP-25545	(S)	Sugar Shack	1963	20.00	50.00
Dot DLP-3577	(M)	Buddy's Buddy	1964	20.00	50.00
Dot DLP-25577	(S)	Buddy's Buddy	1964	30.00	75.00
Dot DLP-3643	(M)	Lucky 'Leven	1965	10.00	25.00
Dot DLP-25643	(S)	Lucky 'Leven	1965	12.00	30.00
Dot DLP-3668	(M)	Folkbeat	1965	10.00	25.00
Dot DLP-25668	(S)	Folkbeat	1965	12.00	30.00
Dot DLP-3709	(M)	Campusology	1966	10.00	25.00
Dot DLP-25709	(S)	Campusology	1966	12.00	30.00
Dot DLP-25856	(S)	Firewater	1968	10.00	25.00
		("Daisy Petal Pickin'" is rechanneled).			
Atco SD-33-239	(S)	Bottle Of Wine	1968	10.00	25.00
Atco SD-33-275	(S)	Come On, React!	1969	10.00	25.00
FIREBIRDS, THE					
Crown CST-589	(S)	Light My Fire	1968	30.00	75.00
FIREFLIES, THE					
Taurus S-1002	(S)	You Were Mine	1967	150.00	300.00
		(The 1959 hit, "You Were Mine," was rerecorded in stereo.)			
FIRESIGN THEATRE					
Philip Austin, Peter Bergman, David Ossman And Philip Proctor.					
Columbia CL-2719	(M)	Waiting For The Electrician	1968	10.00	25.00
Columbia CS-9519	(S)	Waiting For The Electrician	1968	6.00	15.00
— Columbia albums above have "360 Sound" on the bottom of the label. —					
Columbia CQ-30737	(Q)	I Think We're All Bozos On This Bus	1971	10.00	25.00
Columbia AS-41	(DJ)	A Firesign Chat With Papoon	1972	16.00	40.00
Columbia CQ-33141	(Q)	Everything You Know Is Wrong	1974	10.00	25.00
FIRST CHIPS, THE					
Clay Pigeon CPP-SFCV1	(S)	First Chips, Volume 1	1972	60.00	150.00
FIRST EDITION, THE/KENNY ROGERS & THE FIRST EDITION					
Kenny Rogers originally recorded with The Bobby Doyle Three.					
Reprise R-6276	(M)	The First Edition	1967	10.00	25.00
Reprise RS-6276	(S)	The First Edition	1967	12.00	30.00
FIRST FRIDAY					
Webster's Last Word 2895	(S)	First Friday	197?	40.00	100.00

Label & Catalog #		Title	Year	VG+	NM
FISCHER, WILD MAN					
Bizarre 2XS-6332	(S)	**An Evening WithWild Man Fischer**	1969	12.00	30.00
		(2 LPs "produced" by Frank Zappa.)			
FISHER, AL, & LOU MARKS					
Cameo C-1081	(M)	**Home On The Range**	1964	6.00	15.00
Cameo SC-1081	(S)	**Home On The Range**	1964	10.00	25.00
Swan LP-514	(M)	**It's A Beatle (Coo Coo) World**	1964	20.00	50.00
FISHER, CHIP					
RCA Victor LPM-1797	(M)	**Chipper At The Sugar Bowl**	1958	20.00	50.00
RCA Victor LSP-1797	(S)	**Chipper At The Sugar Bowl**	1958	30.00	75.00
FISHER, EDDIE					
RCA Victor LPM-3025	(10")	**Fisher Sings**	1952	20.00	50.00
RCA Victor LPM-3058	(10")	**I'm In The Mood For Love**	1952	20.00	50.00
RCA Victor LPM-3065	(10")	**Christmas With Fisher**	1952	20.00	50.00
RCA Victor LPM-3122	(10")	**Irving Berlin Favorites**	1954	20.00	50.00
RCA Victor LPM-3185	(10")	**May I Sing To You?**	1954	20.00	50.00
RCA Victor LPM-3375	(10")	**The Best Of Eddie Fisher**	1954	20.00	50.00
RCA Victor LOC-1024	(M)	**Academy Award Winners**	1955	16.00	40.00
RCA Victor LPM-1097	(M)	**I Love You**	1955	16.00	40.00
RCA Victor LPM-1180	(M)	**I'm In The Mood For Love**	1955	16.00	40.00
RCA Victor LPM-1181	(M)	**May I Sing To You?**	1955	16.00	40.00
RCA Victor LPM-1399	(M)	**Bundle Of Joy** (Soundtrack)	1956	16.00	40.00
RCA Victor LPM-1548	(M)	**Thinking Of You**	1957	16.00	40.00
RCA Victor LPM-1647	(M)	**As Long As There's Music**	1958	16.00	40.00
RCA Victor LSP-1647	(S)	**As Long As There's Music**	1958	20.00	50.00
Ramrod T-6001	(M)	**Scent Of Mystery** (Soundtrack)	1960	16.00	40.00
		(The previous edition of this book erroneously listed this record, T-6001, at $300.)			
Ramrod ST-6001	(S)	**Scent Of Mystery** (Soundtrack)	1960	200.00	400.00
RCA Victor LPM-2504	(M)	**Eddie Fisher's Greatest Hits**	1962	8.00	20.00
RCA Victor LSP-2504	(S)	**Eddie Fisher's Greatest Hits**	1962	10.00	25.00
		— RCA mono albums above have "Long Play" on the bottom of the label; stereo albums have "Living Stereo" on the bottom. —			
Ramrod RR-1	(M)	**Eddie Fisher At The Winter Garden**	1963	8.00	20.00
Ramrod RRS-1	(S)	**Eddie Fisher At The Winter Garden**	1963	10.00	25.00
FISHER, KEVIN					
P. Pan P-101	(S)	**The First Of Fisher**	1977	60.00	150.00
FISHER, MISS TONI					
Signet WP-509	(S)	**The Big Hurt** ("The Big Hurt" is rechanneled)	1960	20.00	50.00
FISK JUBILEE SINGERS, THE					
Folkways FA-2372	(M)	**The Fisk Jubilee Singers**	195?	12.00	30.00
FITZGERALD, ELLA: Refer to GOLDMINE'S PRICE GUIDE TO COLLECTIBLE JAZZ ALBUMS					
FIVE AMERICANS, THE					
HBR HLP-8503	(M)	**I See The Light**	1966	8.00	20.00
HBR HST-9503	(S)	**I See The Light**	1966	10.00	25.00
FIVE EMPREES, THE					
Freeport FR-3001	(M)	**The Five Emprees**	1965	40.00	100.00
Freeport FRS-4001	(S)	**The Five Emprees**	1965	60.00	150.00
Freeport FR-3001	(M)	**Little Miss Sad**	1966	20.00	50.00
Freeport FRS-4001	(S)	**Little Miss Sad**	1966	30.00	75.00
		("Little Miss Sad" is a reissue of "The Five Emprees.")			
FIVE KEYS, THE					
Aladdin LP-806	(M)	**The Best Of The Five Keys** (Blue label)	1956		See below
		(Note: Should a copy of Aladdin 806 with a blue label— long rumored to exist— be found, it would have a suggested Near Mint value of at least twice that of the maroon label below.)			
Aladdin LP-806	(M)	**The Best Of The Five Keys** (Maroon label)	1956	1,000.00	2,000.00
Score LP-4003	(M)	**The Five Keys On The Town**	1957	300.00	750.00

The Five Satins, under the leadership of Fred Parris, recorded, under less than ideal conditions, as was all too typical of black vocal groups of the time, one of the quintessential vocal classics with their enormous hit of 1956, "In The Still Of The Nite." If the group had disbanded and gone their separate ways immediately thereafter, they would live eternally on every "oldies but goodies" show or chart in the country.

Label & Catalog #		Title	Year	VG+	NM
Capitol T-828	(M)	**The Five Keys On Stage**	1957	200.00	400.00
		(Original covers have a photo of the five members positioned back to front. The first man's pose is such that the thumb of his right hand is exposed just enough to appear as a dangling penis. . .)			
Capitol T-828	(M)	**The Five Keys On Stage**	1957	250.00	500.00
		(Later covers, much rarer than the originals, have the offending thumb airbrushed out.)			
King 688	(M)	**The Five Keys**	1960	200.00	400.00
King 692	(M)	**Rhythm & Blues Hits Past And Present**	1960	200.00	400.00
		— King albums above have crownless black labels.—			
Capitol T-1769	(M)	**The Fantastic Five Keys**	1962	80.00	200.00

FIVE ROYALES, THE

Label & Catalog #		Title	Year	VG+	NM
Apollo LP-488	(M)	**The Rockin' 5 Royales** (Purple label)	1956		See below
		(Apollo 488 with the purple label with silver print is rare with suggested values in VG of 500-1,000; in VG+, $1,500-2,500; and in NM, $4,000-6,000.)			
Apollo LP-488	(M)	**The Rockin' 5 Royales** (Green label)	1956		See below
		(Apollo 488 with the green label is rare with suggested values in VG of 250-500; in VG+, $750-1,500; and in NM, $2,000-3,000.)			
Apollo LP-488	(M)	**The Rockin' 5 Royales** (Yellow label)	1956	300.00	750.00
		(Counterfeits of all three versions of Apollo 488 exist.)			
King 580	(M)	**Dedicated To You**	1957	200.00	400.00
King 616	(M)	**The 5 Royales Sing For You**	1959	100.00	250.00
King 678	(M)	**The Five Royales**	1960	100.00	250.00
King 955	(M)	**24 All Time Hits**	1966	40.00	100.00
		— King albums above have crownless black labels.—			

FIVE SATINS, THE
Refer to Fred Parris & The Satins.

Label & Catalog #		Title	Year	VG+	NM
Ember ELP-100	(M)	**The Five Satins Sing** (Blue vinyl)	1957		See below
		(Original pressings of ELP-100 on blue vinyl has a suggested Near Mint value of $1,000-2,000.)			
Ember ELP-100	(M)	**The Five Satins Sing**	1957	200.00	500.00
		(Original pressings of ELP-100 have a red label and a red cover with a group photo.)			
Ember ELP-100	(M)	**The Five Satins Sing**	1959	100.00	300.00
		(Second pressings have a "logs logo" label and a red cover with a group photo.)			
Ember ELP-100	(M)	**The Five Satins Sing**	1959	80.00	200.00
		(Later pressings with the "logs" label have a black & gold title cover.)			
Ember ELP-100	(M)	**The Five Satins Sing**	1961	40.00	100.00
		(Third pressings have a black label and a black & gold title cover.)			
Ember ELP-401	(M)	**Encore, Volume 2**	1960	80.00	200.00
		(First pressings of ELP-401 have a "logs logo" label.)			
Ember ELP-401	(M)	**Encore, Volume 2**	1961	40.00	100.00
		(Second pressings have a black label.)			
Mt. Vernon 108	(M)	**The Five Satins Sing**	196?	12.00	30.00
Celebrity Show. JB-7671	(M)	**The Best Of The Five Satins**	1970	10.00	25.00

FIVE STAIRSTEPS, THE

Label & Catalog #		Title	Year	VG+	NM
Windy C 6000	(M)	**The Five Stairsteps**	1967	8.00	20.00
Windy C S-6000	(S)	**The Five Stairsteps**	1967	10.00	25.00

FLAIRS, THE

Label & Catalog #		Title	Year	VG+	NM
Crown CLP-5356	(M)	**The Flairs**	1963	24.00	60.00
Crown CST-356	(E)	**The Flairs**	1963	10.00	25.00

FLAME, THE
Features Blondie Chaplin And Rickie Fataar, later of The Beach Boys.

Label & Catalog #		Title	Year	VG+	NM
Brother BR-2500	(S)	**Flame** (With poster)	1970	10.00	25.00
		(Brother 2500 was recorded in compatible stereo/quadraphonic.)			

FLAMIN' GROOVIES, THE

Label & Catalog #		Title	Year	VG+	NM
Snazz R-2371 (10")	(S)	**Sneekers**	1969	30.00	75.00
Epic BN-26487	(S)	**Supersnazz**	1969	16.00	40.00
Kama Sutra KSBS-2021	(S)	**Flamingo** (Pink label in a gatefold cover)	1970	10.00	25.00
Kama Sutra KSBS-2031	(S)	**Teenage Head** (Pink label)	1971	10.00	25.00

Lester Flatt, mandolin, and Earl Scruggs, banjo, are one of the pre-eminent bluegrass duos in country'n western's lengthy history. The two met while members of Bill Monroe's band, developed a mutual musical kinship and left to go their own way. While they were never all that big on the charts, they placed ten sides in the top 20 over a period of years, reaching the #1 spot in 1962 with the national exposure they received by providing the unforgettable theme for the popular television series, "The Beverly Hillbillies." (Actually, the title of the song that topped the charts was "The Ballad Of Jed Clampett.")

Label & Catalog #		Title	Year	VG+	NM

FLAMING YOUTH
Flaming Youth features Phil Collins, later of of Genesis.

Uni 73075	(S)	**Ark 2**	1969	12.00	30.00

FLAMINGOS, THE

Checker LP-1433	(M)	**The Flamingos** (Black label)	1959	150.00	400.00
Checker LP-1433	(M)	**The Flamingos** (Blue label)	1965	40.00	100.00
Checker LPS-1433	(E)	**The Flamingos** (Blue label)	1965	30.00	75.00
End LP-304	(M)	**Flamingo Serenade**	1959	80.00	200.00
End LPS-304	(S)	**Flamingo Serenade**	1959	200.00	400.00
		(Original covers for LPS-304 correctly list the record as Stereo.			
		"But Not For Me" is rechanneled on all stereo pressings.)			
End STLP-304	(S)	**Flamingo Serenade**	196?	80.00	200.00
		(Later covers incorrectly read Rechanneled Stereo.)			
End LP-307	(M)	**Flamingo Favorites**	1960	40.00	100.00
End LPS-307	(E)	**Flamingo Favorites**	1960	30.00	75.00
End LP-308	(M)	**Requestfully Yours**	1960	40.00	100.00
End LPS-308	(E)	**Requestfully Yours**	1960	30.00	75.00
End LP-316	(M)	**The Sound Of The Flamingos**	1962	40.00	100.00
End LPS-316	(S)	**The Sound Of The Flamingos**	1962	100.00	250.00
		(Stereo copies read "Stereo" in the upper right corner of the cover.)			
End LPS-316	(E)	**The Sound Of The Flamingos**	1962	30.00	75.00
Constellation CS-3	(M)	**Collectors Showcase: The Flamingos**	1964	40.00	100.00
		(First pressing with "hot flamingo" pink lettering on the cover.)			
Constellation CS-3	(M)	**Collectors Showcase: The Flamingos**	1964	20.00	50.00
		(Later pressing with cooler, dark pink lettering on the cover.)			
Philips PHM-200-206	(M)	**Their Hits-Then And Now**	1966	10.00	25.00
Philips PHS-600-206	(S)	**Their Hits-Then And Now**	1966	14.00	35.00

FLAMINGOS, THE / THE MOONGLOWS

Vee Jay LP-1052	(M)	**The Flamingos Meet The Moonglows**	1962	60.00	150.00

FLARES, THE

Press PR-73001	(M)	**Encore Of Foot Stompin' Hits**	1961	30.00	75.00
Press PRS-83001	(S)	**Encore Of Foot Stompin' Hits**	1961	50.00	125.00

FLAT EARTH SOCIETY

Fleetwood 3027	(S)	**Waleeco**	1968	150.00	300.00

FLATT & SCRUGGS/LESTER FLATT & EARL SCRUGGS

Columbia CL-1019	(M)	**Foggy Mountain Jamboree**	1957	20.00	50.00
Mercury MG-20358	(M)	**Country Music**	1958	16.00	40.00
Mercury MG-20542	(M)	**Lester Flatt & Earl Scruggs**	1959	20.00	50.00
Mercury MG-20773	(M)	**The Original Sound Of Flatt & Scruggs**	1963	10.00	25.00
Mercury SR-60773	(E)	**The Original Sound Of Flatt & Scruggs**	1963	6.00	15.00
Columbia CL-1424	(M)	**Songs Of Glory**	1960	10.00	25.00
Columbia CS-8224	(S)	**Songs Of Glory**	1960	12.00	30.00
Columbia CL-1564	(M)	**Foggy Mountain Banjo**	1961	10.00	25.00
Columbia CS-8364	(S)	**Foggy Mountain Banjo**	1961	12.00	30.00
Columbia CL-1664	(M)	**Songs Of The Famous Carter Family**	1961	10.00	25.00
Columbia CS-8464	(S)	**Songs Of The Famous Carter Family**	1961	12.00	30.00
Columbia CL-1830	(M)	**Folk Songs Of Our Land**	1962	10.00	25.00
Columbia CS-8630	(S)	**Folk Songs Of Our Land**	1962	12.00	30.00
		— Columbia albums above have three white "eye" logos on each side of the spindle hole.—			
Columbia CL-1951	(M)	**Hard Travelin'/The Ballad Of Jed Clampett**	1963	8.00	20.00
Columbia CS-8751	(S)	**Hard Travelin'/The Ballad Of Jed Clampett**	1963	10.00	25.00
Columbia CL-2045	(M)	**Flatt & Scruggs At Carnegie Hall**	1963	8.00	20.00
Columbia CS-8845	(S)	**Flatt & Scruggs At Carnegie Hall**	1963	10.00	25.00
Columbia CL-2134	(M)	**Flatt & Scruggs Live At Vanderbilt University**	1964	8.00	20.00
Columbia CS-8934	(S)	**Flatt & Scruggs Live At Vanderbilt University**	1964	10.00	25.00
Columbia CL-2255	(M)	**The Fabulous Sound Of Flatt & Scruggs**	1964	8.00	20.00
Columbia CS-9055	(S)	**The Fabulous Sound Of Flatt & Scruggs**	1964	10.00	25.00
Columbia CL-2354	(M)	**Pickin', Strummin' And Singin'**	1965	8.00	20.00
Columbia CS-9154	(S)	**Pickin', Strummin' And Singin'**	1965	10.00	25.00
Columbia CL-2443	(M)	**Town And Country**	1965	8.00	20.00
Columbia CS-9243	(S)	**Town And Country**	1965	10.00	25.00
Columbia CL-2513	(M)	**When The Saints Go Marching In**	1966	8.00	20.00
Columbia CS-9313	(S)	**When The Saints Go Marching In**	1966	10.00	25.00
		— Columbia albums above have "360 Sound" on the bottom of the label.—			

Label & Catalog #		Title	Year	VG+	NM

FLATT & SCRUGGS / JIM & JESSE
| Starday SLP-365 | (M) | **Stars Of The Grand Ole Opry** (Yellow label) | 1966 | 12.00 | 30.00 |

FLEETWOOD MAC
Over the years Mick Fleetwood and John McVie have hosted a revolving door of members including Peter Green, Jeremy Spencer, Christine McVie, Bob Welch, Lindsay Buckingham and Stevie Nicks.
Epic BN-26402	(S)	**Fleetwood Mac** (Yellow label)	1968	12.00	30.00
Epic BN-26446	(S)	**English Rose** (Yellow label)	1969	12.00	30.00
Warner Bros. PRO-652	(DJ)	**Rumours** (Embossed promo cover)	1976	20.00	50.00
Warner Bros. PRO	(DJ)	**The Fleetwood Mac Story** (2 LPs)	1979	20.00	50.00
Mobile Fidelity MFSL-012	(S)	**Fleetwood Mac**	1980	13.00	40.00
Mobile Fidelity MFSL-119	(S)	**Mirage**	198?	12.00	35.00
Nautilus NR-8	(S)	**Rumours**	1980	8.00	25.00

FLEETWOOD MAC & OTIS SPANN
Blue Horizon BH-66227	(S)	**Blues Jam At Chess**	1969	12.00	30.00
Blue Horizon BH-4802	(S)	**The Biggest Thing Since Colossus**	1970	14.00	35.00
Blue Horizon BH-4803	(S)	**Blues Jam In Chicago, Volume 1**	1970	10.00	25.00
Blue Horizon BH-4803	(S)	**Blues Jam In Chicago, Volume 2**	1970	10.00	25.00
Blue Horizon BH-3801	(S)	**Blues Jam In Chicago** (2 LPs)	1970	12.00	30.00

FLEETWOODS, THE
Dolton BLP-2001	(M)	**Mr. Blue**	1959	30.00	75.00
Dolton BST-8001	(S)	**Mr. Blue** ("Mr. Blue" is rechanneled)	1959	40.00	100.00
Dolton BLP-2002	(M)	**The Fleetwoods**	1960	20.00	50.00
Dolton BST-8002	(S)	**The Fleetwoods**	1960	30.00	75.00
Dolton BLP-2005	(M)	**Softly**	1961	20.00	50.00
Dolton BST-8005	(S)	**Softly** ("Come Softly To Me" is rechanneled)	1961	30.00	75.00
Dolton BLP-2007	(M)	**Deep In A Dream**	1961	16.00	40.00
Dolton BST-8007	(S)	**Deep In A Dream**	1961	20.00	50.00
Dolton BLP-2011	(M)	**The Best Of The Oldies**	1962	16.00	40.00
Dolton BST-8011	(S)	**The Best Of The Oldies**	1962	20.00	50.00
—*Dolton albums above have light blue labels with the fish logo above the spindle hole.*—					
Dolton BLP-2018	(M)	**The Fleetwoods' Greatest Hits**	1962	8.00	20.00
Dolton BST-8018	(P)	**The Fleetwoods' Greatest Hits**	1962	12.00	30.00
Dolton BLP-2025	(M)	**Goodnight My Love**	1963	8.00	20.00
Dolton BST-8025	(S)	**Goodnight My Love**	1963	12.00	30.00
Dolton BLP-2020	(M)	**The Fleetwoods Sing For Lovers By Night**	1963	8.00	20.00
Dolton BST-8020	(S)	**The Fleetwoods Sing For Lovers By Night**	1963	12.00	30.00
Dolton BLP-2030	(M)	**Before And After**	1965	8.00	20.00
Dolton BST-8030	(S)	**Before And After**	1965	12.00	30.00
Dolton BLP-2039	(M)	**Folk Rock**	1965	8.00	20.00
Dolton BST-8039	(S)	**Folk Rock**	1965	12.00	30.00
—*Dolton albums above have dark blue labels with a color logo on the left side.*—					

FLEMING, RHONDA
| Columbia CL-1080 | (M) | **Rhonda** | 1958 | 30.00 | 75.00 |

FLEMONS, WADE
| Vee Jay LP-1011 | (M) | **Wade Flemons** (Maroon label) | 1959 | 40.00 | 100.00 |
| Vee Jay LP-1011 | (M) | **Wade Flemons** (Black label) | 196? | 20.00 | 50.00 |

FLINT, SHELBY
Valiant LP-401	(M)	**Shelby Flint—The Quiet Girl**	1961	14.00	35.00
Valiant LPS-401	(S)	**Shelby Flint—The Quiet Girl**	1961	20.00	50.00
Valiant LP-403	(M)	**Shelby Flint Sings Folk**	1962	14.00	35.00
Valiant LPS-403	(S)	**Shelby Flint Sings Folk**	1962	20.00	50.00
Valiant VL-25003	(M)	**Cast Your Fate To The Wind**	1966	10.00	25.00
Valiant VLS-25003	(S)	**Cast Your Fate To The Wind**	1966	14.00	35.00

FLOYD, EDDIE
Eddie Floyd was formerly with The Falcons.
Stax ST-714	(M)	**Knock On Wood**	1967	12.00	30.00
Stax STS-714	(S)	**Knock On Wood**	1967	16.00	40.00
Stax STS-2002	(S)	**I've Never Found A Girl**	1968	12.00	30.00
Stax STS-2011	(S)	**Rare Stamps**	1969	10.00	25.00
		("Big Bird" and "Things Get Better" are rechanneled on this album.)			
Stax STS-2017	(S)	**You've Got To Have Eddie**	1969	10.00	25.00
Stax STS-2029	(S)	**California Girl**	1970	10.00	25.00

Label & Catalog #		Title	Year	VG+	NM
Stax ST-2041	(M)	**Down To Earth** (White label promo)	1971	16.00	40.00
Stax STS-2041	(S)	**Down To Earth**	1971	10.00	25.00
Stax STS-3016	(S)	**Baby Lay Your Head Down**	1973	10.00	25.00

FLYING BURRITO BROTHERS, THE/THE BURRITO BROTHERS
The FBB feature Chris Hillman and Gram Parsons amongst a cast of thousands.

A&M SP-8070	(DJ)	**Hot Burrito** (Sampler)	1975	20.00	50.00

FLYNN, ERROL / BASIL RATHBONE

Columbia CL-4162	(10")	**Errol Flynn Reads "The Three Musketeers" /**			
		Basil Rathbone Reads "Oliver Twist"	195?	20.00	50.00
Columbia CL-674	(M)	**Errol Flynn Reads "The Three Musketeers" /**			
		Basil Rathbone Reads "Oliver Twist"	1955	16.00	40.00

FOGELBERG, DAN

Full Moon A2S-1335	(DJ)	**Interchords** (2 LPs)	1982	10.00	25.00

FOGGY RIVER BOYS, THE

Intern. Arts. LPS-5004	(S)	**I Believe In Music**	197?	14.00	35.00

FOLEY, RED
Red Foley is a pseudonym for Clyde Julian Foley.

Decca DL-5303	(10")	**Souvenir Album**	1951	40.00	100.00
Decca DL-5338	(10")	**Lift Up Your Voice**	1951	40.00	100.00
Decca DL-8294	(M)	**Souvenir Album**	1956	24.00	60.00
Decca DL-8296	(M)	**Red Foley Beyond The Sunset**	1956	24.00	60.00
Decca DL-8767	(M)	**He Walks With Thee**	1958	20.00	50.00
Decca DL-8806	(M)	**My Keepsake Album**	1958	20.00	50.00
Decca DL-8847	(M)	**Let's All Sing With Red Foley**	1959	20.00	50.00
Decca DL-78847	(S)	**Let's All Sing With Red Foley**	1959	24.00	60.00
Decca DL-8903	(M)	**Let's All Sing To Him**	1959	20.00	50.00
Decca DL-88903	(S)	**Let's All Sing To Him**	1959	24.00	60.00
		— Decca albums above have black labels with silver print. —			
Decca DL-36068	(DJ)	**Gratefully**	1958	40.00	100.00
		(DL-36068 was issued promotionally for the Dickies Company.)			
Decca DL-4107	(M)	**Red Foley's Golden Favorites**	1961	10.00	25.00
Decca DL-74107	(S)	**Red Foley's Golden Favorites**	1961	12.00	30.00
Decca DL-4140	(M)	**Company's Comin'**	1961	10.00	25.00
Decca DL-74140	(S)	**Company's Comin'**	1961	12.00	30.00
Decca DL-4198	(M)	**Songs Of Devotion**	1961	10.00	25.00
Decca DL-74198	(S)	**Songs Of Devotion**	1961	12.00	30.00
Decca DL-4290	(M)	**Dear Hearts And Gentle People**	1962	8.00	20.00
Decca DL-74290	(S)	**Dear Hearts And Gentle People**	1962	10.00	25.00
Decca DL-4341	(M)	**The Red Foley Show**	1963	8.00	20.00
Decca DL-74341	(S)	**The Red Foley Show**	1963	10.00	25.00
Decca DXB-177	(M)	**The Red Foley Story** (2 LPs)	1964	8.00	20.00
Decca DXSB-7177	(S)	**The Red Foley Story** (2 LPs)	1964	10.00	25.00
Decca DL-4603	(M)	**Songs Everybody Knows**	1965	8.00	20.00
Decca DL-74603	(S)	**Songs Everybody Knows**	1965	10.00	25.00
		— Decca albums above have black labels with "Mfrd by Decca" beneath the rainbow. —			

FOLEY, RED, & ERNEST TUBB

Decca DL-8298	(M)	**Red And Ernie**	1956	24.00	60.00
		— Decca albums above have black labels with silver print. —			

FOLK SINGERS, THE

Elektra EKL-157	(M)	**Run Come Hear**	1958	12.00	30.00

FOLK STRINGERS, THE

Prestige PRLP-7371	(M)	**The Folk Stringers**	1965	10.00	25.00
Prestige PRST-7371	(S)	**The Folk Stringers**	1965	12.00	30.00
		— Prestige albums above have blue labels with a trident logo on the left side. —			

FOLKMASTERS, THE

Folkways FP-28	(10")	**Get On Board**	195?	30.00	75.00
Folkways FA-2028	(10")	**Get On Board**	195?	30.00	75.00

FOLKNIKS, THE

Hifi LP-1017	(M)	**The Folkniks**	196?	8.00	20.00

Clyde "Red" Foley was a consistent country chart-topper through the '40s and the '50s as a solo or duet-ting with such stars as Ernest Tubb and Kitty Wells. It was Red's recording of "Old Shep" (highlighted on Souvenir Album above) that inspired a young Elvis Presley to sing in public and Presley later covered Foley's "Peace In The Valley" for his first gospel recordings. Gratefully, also illustrated, was issued as a promotional vehicle for Dickies manufacturers.

Label & Catalog #		Title	Year	VG+	NM

FOLKSINGERS, THE
| Elektra EKL-157 | (M) | **Run Come Here** | 1958 | 14.00 | 35.00 |

FOLKSMITHS, THE
The Folksmiths, a group dedicated to traditional folk music, features Joe Hickerson.
| Folkways FA-2407 | (M) | **We've Got Some Singing To Do—** | | | |
| | | **Folksongs With The Folksmiths** | 195? | 12.00 | 30.00 |

FOLKSWINGERS, THE
The Folkswingers, featuring Hal Blaine and Glen Campbell, also recorded with Tut Taylor.
World Pacific WP-1812	(M)	**12 String Guitar**	1963	10.00	25.00
World Pacific ST-1812	(S)	**12 String Guitar** (Red vinyl)	1963	24.00	60.00
World Pacific ST-1812	(S)	**12 String Guitar**	1963	12.00	30.00
World Pacific WP-1814	(M)	**12 String Guitar, Volume 2**	1963	10.00	25.00
World Pacific ST-1814	(S)	**12 String Guitar, Volume 2**	1963	12.00	30.00
World Pacific WP-1846	(M)	**Raga Rock**	1966	10.00	25.00
World Pacific ST-1846	(S)	**Raga Rock**	1966	12.00	30.00

FONDA, HENRY
| Coral CRL-57308 | (M) | **Voices Of The 20th Century** | 1959 | 20.00 | 50.00 |
| Caedmon TC-1570 | (M) | **The Grapes Of Wrath** | 1978 | 10.00 | 25.00 |

FONTANA, WAYNE, & THE MINDBENDERS
| Fontana MGF-27542 | (M) | **The Game Of Love** | 1965 | 12.00 | 30.00 |
| Fontana SRF-67542 | (E) | **The Game Of Love** | 1965 | 10.00 | 25.00 |

FONTANA, WAYNE
| MGM E-4459 | (M) | **Wayne Fontana** | 1967 | 8.00 | 20.00 |
| MGM SE-4459 | (S) | **Wayne Fontana** | 1967 | 10.00 | 25.00 |

FONTANE SISTERS, THE
| Dot DLP-3004 | (M) | **The Fontanes Sing** (Maroon label) | 1956 | 16.00 | 40.00 |
| Dot DLP-3042 | (M) | **A Visit With The Fontane Sisters** | 1957 | 12.00 | 30.00 |

FORBES, GRAHAM
| Phillips Inter. PLP-1955 | (M) | **The Martini Set** | 1959 | 40.00 | 100.00 |

FORD, FRANKIE
| Ace LP-1005 | (M) | **Let's Take A Sea Cruise** | 1959 | 150.00 | 300.00 |

FORD, MARY
Refer to Les Paul & Mary Ford.
| Challenge CHS-623 | (S) | **A Brand New Ford** | 1966 | 12.00 | 30.00 |
| | | *(This appears to have been manufactured for Ford distributors.)* | | | |

FORD, NEAL, & THE FANATICS
| Hickory LPS-141 | (S) | **Neal Ford & The Fanatics** | 1968 | 12.00 | 30.00 |

FORD, ROCKY BILL
| Audio Lab AL-1561 | (M) | **A New Singing Star** | 1960 | 60.00 | 150.00 |

FORD, TENNESSE ERNIE
Refer to Brenda Lee / Ernie Ford.
Capitol T-700	(M)	**This Lusty Land!**	1956	12.00	30.00
Capitol T-756	(M)	**Hymns**	1957	12.00	30.00
Capitol T-818	(M)	**Spirituals**	1957	12.00	30.00
Capitol T-841	(M)	**Tennessee Ernie Ford Favorites**	1957	12.00	30.00
Capitol T-888	(M)	**Ol' Rockin' Ern'**	1957	20.00	50.00
Capitol T-1005	(M)	**Nearer The Cross**	1958	12.00	30.00
		— Capitol albums above have torquoise or grey labels.—			
Capitol T-1380	(M)	**Sixteen Tons**	1960	10.00	25.00
		— Capitol albums above have black labels with the logo on the side.—			

FOREST
| Harvest SKAO-419 | (S) | **Forest** | 1970 | 20.00 | 50.00 |

FORREST, HELEN: *Refer to* GOLDMINE'S PRICE GUIDE TO COLLECTIBLE JAZZ ALBUMS

Label & Catalog #		Title	Year	VG+	NM
FORRESTER, HOWDY					
Cub 8008	(M)	**Fancy Fiddlin' Country Style**	1960	16.00	40.00
MGM E-4035	(M)	**Fancy Fiddlin' Country Style**	1962	12.00	30.00
United Arts. UAL-3295	(M)	**Fiddlin' Country Style**	1963	10.00	25.00
United Arts. UAS-6295	(S)	**Fiddlin' Country Style**	1963	12.00	30.00
FORTUNE, JOHNNY					
Park Avenue P-1301	(M)	**Soul Surfer**	1963	40.00	100.00
Park Avenue PS-401	(S)	**Soul Surfer**	1963	60.00	150.00
FORTUNE-TELLER					
R.M.T. 4956	(S)	**Inner-City Scream**	1978	60.00	150.00
FORTUNES, THE					
Press PR7-3002	(M)	**The Fortunes**	1965	14.00	35.00
Press PRS-83002	(S)	**The Fortunes**	1965	20.00	50.00
Coca-Cola (No number)	(DJ)	**It's The Real Thing**	1969	24.00	60.00
FORTY-NINTH PARALLEL, THE					
Maverick MAS-7001	(S)	**The Forty-Ninth Parallel**	1969	80.00	200.00

FOSTER, GWEN: *Refer to* **TOM ASHLEY & GWEN FOSTER**

Label & Catalog #		Title	Year	VG+	NM
FOSTER, CHUCK					
Phillips Inter. PLP-1965	(M)	**Chuck Foster At Hotel Peabdoy**	1961	40.00	100.00

FOSTER, PAT
Pat Foster is a 12-string guitar player and singer of traditional American folk songs. Both the Counterpoint and Riverside album feature accompaniment by Dick Weissman.

Counterpoint CPT-550	(M)	**Documentary Talking Blues**	195?	16.00	40.00
Riverside RLP-12-654	(M)	**Gold In California**	195?	16.00	40.00

FOTHERINGAY
Fotheringay features Sandy Denny.

A&M SP-4289	(S)	**Fotheringay**	1970	10.00	25.00

FOUL DOGS, THE

Rhythm Sound GA-481	(M)	**No. 1**	1966	150.00	300.00

FOUNDATIONS, THE

Uni 73016	(S)	**Baby, Now That I've Found You**	1968	12.00	30.00
		("Baby, Now That I've Found You" is rechanneled on this album.)			
Uni 73043	(S)	**Build Me Up Buttercup**	1969	12.00	30.00
		(Side 1 is in stereo; side 2 is rechanneled.)			
Uni 73058	(S)	**Digging The Foundations**	1969	12.00	30.00

FOUR ACES, THE
The lead Ace was Al Alberts.

Decca DL-5429	(10")	**The Four Aces**	1952	30.00	75.00
Decca DL-8122	(M)	**The Mood For Love**	1955	20.00	50.00
Decca DL-8191	(M)	**Merry Christmas**	1956	20.00	50.00
Decca DL-8227	(M)	**Sentimental Souvenirs**	1956	20.00	50.00
Decca DL-8228	(M)	**Heart And Soul**	1956	20.00	50.00
Decca DL-8312	(M)	**She Sees All The Hollywood Hits**	1957	20.00	50.00
Decca DL-8424	(M)	**Written On The Wind** (Soundtrack)	1957	40.00	100.00
Decca DL-8567	(M)	**Shuffling Along**	1957	20.00	50.00
Decca DL-8693	(M)	**Hits From Hollywood**	1958	20.00	50.00
Decca DL-8766	(M)	**The Swingin' Aces**	1958	14.00	35.00
Decca DL-78766	(S)	**The Swingin' Aces**	1958	20.00	50.00
Decca DL-8855	(M)	**Hits From Broadway**	1959	14.00	35.00
Decca DL-78855	(S)	**Hits From Broadway**	1959	20.00	50.00
Decca DL-8944	(M)	**Beyond The Blue Horizon**	1959	14.00	35.00
Decca DL-78944	(S)	**Beyond The Blue Horizon**	1959	20.00	50.00
		—Decca albums above have black labels with silver print.—			
Decca DL-4013	(M)	**The Golden Hits Of The Four Aces**	1960	8.00	20.00
Decca DL-74013	(P)	**The Golden Hits Of The Four Aces**	1960	10.00	25.00
United Arts. UAL-3337	(M)	**Record Oldies**	1963	8.00	20.00
United Arts. UAS-6337	(S)	**Record Oldies**	1963	10.00	25.00

Label & Catalog #		Title	Year	VG+	NM
FOUR COINS, THE					
Epic LN-1104	(M)	The Four Coins	1955	20.00	50.00
Epic LN-3445	(M)	The Four Coins In Shangri La	1958	14.00	35.00
FOUR FRESHMEN, THE					
Capitol H-522	(10")	Voices In Modern	1955	20.00	50.00
Capitol T-522	(M)	Voices In Modern	1955	16.00	40.00
Capitol T-683	(M)	Four Freshmen And Five Trombones	1956	16.00	40.00
Capitol T-743	(M)	Freshmen Favorites	1956	16.00	40.00
Capitol T-763	(M)	Four Freshmen And Five Trumpets	1957	16.00	40.00
Capitol T-844	(M)	Four Freshmen And Five Saxes	1957	16.00	40.00
Capitol T-922	(M)	Voices In Latin	1958	16.00	40.00
Capitol T-1008	(M)	The Four Freshmen In Person	1958	16.00	40.00
Capitol ST-1008	(S)	The Four Freshmen In Person	1958	20.00	50.00
		— Capitol albums above have turquoise or gray labels.—			
Capitol T-522	(M)	Voices In Modern	195?	10.00	25.00
Capitol T-683	(M)	Four Freshmen And Five Trombones	195?	10.00	25.00
Capitol T-743	(M)	Freshmen Favorites	195?	10.00	25.00
Capitol T-763	(M)	Four Freshmen And Five Trumpets	195?	10.00	25.00
Capitol T-844	(M)	Four Freshmen And Five Saxes	195?	10.00	25.00
Capitol T-922	(M)	Voices In Latin	195?	10.00	25.00
Capitol T-1008	(M)	The Four Freshmen In Person	195?	10.00	25.00
Capitol ST-1008	(S)	The Four Freshmen In Person	195?	12.00	30.00
Capitol T-1074	(M)	Voices In Love	1958	10.00	25.00
Capitol ST-1074	(S)	Voices In Love	1958	12.00	30.00
Capitol T-1103	(M)	Freshmen Favorites, Volume 2	1959	10.00	25.00
Capitol ST-1103	(S)	Freshmen Favorites, Volume 2	1959	12.00	30.00
Capitol T-1189	(M)	Love Lost	1959	10.00	25.00
Capitol ST-1189	(S)	Love Lost	1959	12.00	30.00
Capitol T-1255	(M)	The Four Freshmen And Five Guitars	1960	10.00	25.00
Capitol ST-1255	(S)	The Four Freshmen And Five Guitars	1960	10.00	25.00
Capitol T-1295	(M)	Voices And Brass	1960	10.00	25.00
Capitol ST-1295	(S)	Voices And Brass	1960	10.00	25.00
Capitol TBO-1327	(M)	Road Show (2 LPs)	1960	12.00	30.00
Capitol STBO-1327	(S)	Road Show (2 LPs)	1960	16.00	40.00
		(Capitol 1327 features side 1 by Stan Kenton, side 2 by June Christy, side 3 by the Freshmen and side 4 is ensemble.)			
Capitol T-1378	(M)	First Affair	1960	8.00	20.00
Capitol ST-1378	(S)	First Affair	1960	10.00	25.00
Capitol T-1485	(M)	Freshmen Year	1961	8.00	20.00
Capitol ST-1485	(S)	Freshmen Year	1961	10.00	25.00
Capitol T-1543	(M)	Voices In Fun	1961	8.00	20.00
Capitol ST-1543	(S)	Voices In Fun	1961	10.00	25.00
Capitol T-1640	(M)	The Best Of The Four Freshmen	1962	8.00	20.00
Capitol ST-1640	(S)	The Best Of The Four Freshmen	1962	10.00	25.00
Capitol T-1682	(M)	Stars In Our Eyes	1962	8.00	20.00
Capitol ST-1682	(S)	Stars In Our Eyes	1962	10.00	25.00
		— Capitol albums above have black "rainbow" labels with the logo on the left side.—			
FOUR KNIGHTS, THE					
Capitol H-346	(10")	Spotlight Songs	1953	80.00	200.00
Capitol T-346	(M)	Spotlight Songs	1956	40.00	100.00
Coral CRL-57221	(M)	The Four Knights	1959	40.00	100.00
Coral CRL-57309	(M)	Million Dollar Baby	1960	20.00	50.00
Coral CRL-757309	(S)	Million Dollar Baby	1960	30.00	75.00
FOUR LADS, THE					
Columbia CL-6329	(10")	Stage Show	1954	24.00	60.00
Columbia CL-2545	(10")	The Four Lads Sing Frank Loesser	1956	20.00	50.00
Columbia CL- 2577	(10")	Stage Show	1956	20.00	50.00
Columbia CL-861	(M)	The Four Lads With Frankie Laine	1956	16.00	40.00
Columbia CL-912	(M)	On The Sunny Side	1956	16.00	40.00
Columbia CL-950	(M)	The Stingiest Man In Town (Soundtrack)	1956	20.00	50.00
Columbia CL-1045	(M)	The Four Lads Sing Frank Loesser	1957	20.00	50.00
Columbia CL-1235	(M)	The Four Lads' Greatest Hits	1958	12.00	30.00
Columbia CL-1???	(M)	Breezin' Along	1959	10.00	25.00
Columbia CS-8035	(S)	Breezin' Along	1959	12.00	30.00
Columbia CL-1111	(M)	Four On The Aisle	1959	10.00	25.00
Columbia CS-8047	(S)	Four On The Aisle	1959	12.00	30.00

Label & Catalog #		Title	Year	VG+	NM
Columbia CL-1299	(M)	**The Four Lads Swing Along**	1959	10.00	25.00
Columbia CS-8106	(S)	**The Four Lads Swing Along**	1959	12.00	30.00
Columbia CL-1407	(M)	**High Spirits!**	1959	10.00	25.00
Columbia CS-8203	(S)	**High Spirits!**	1959	12.00	30.00
Columbia CL-1502	(M)	**Love Affair**	1960	8.00	20.00
Columbia CS-8293	(S)	**Love Affair**	1960	10.00	25.00
Columbia CL-1550	(M)	**Everything Goes**	1960	8.00	20.00
Columbia CS-8350	(S)	**Everything Goes**	1960	10.00	25.00

— Columbia albums above have three white "eye" logos on each side of the spindle hole.—

FOUR LOVERS, THE
Members Frankie Valli, Nick DeVito and Hank Majewski formed the Four Seasons.

RCA Victor LPM-1317	(M)	**Joyride**	1956	250.00	500.00

FOUR PREPS, THE

Capitol T-994	(M)	**The Four Preps** (Turquoise label)	1958	14.00	35.00
Capitol T-994	(M)	**The Four Preps**	1958	10.00	25.00
Capitol T-1090	(M)	**The Things We Did Last Summer**	1958	10.00	25.00
Capitol T-1216	(M)	**Dancing And Dreaming**	1959	8.00	20.00
Capitol ST-1216	(S)	**Dancing And Dreaming**	1959	12.00	30.00
Capitol T-1291	(M)	**Early In The Morning**	1960	10.00	25.00
Capitol DT-1291	(E)	**Early In The Morning**	1960	6.00	15.00
Capitol T-1566	(M)	**Four Preps On Campus**	1961	8.00	20.00
Capitol ST-1566	(S)	**Four Preps On Campus**	1961	10.00	25.00
Capitol T-1647	(M)	**Campus Encore**	1962	8.00	20.00
Capitol ST-1647	(S)	**Campus Encore**	1962	10.00	25.00

— Capitol albums above have black "rainbow" labels with the logo on the left side.—

FOUR SEASONS, THE/FRANKIE VALLI & THE FOUR SEASONS
Refer to The Beatles; Bob Crewe; The Four Lovers; Frankie Valli.

Vee Jay LP-1053	(M)	**Sherry And 11 Others**	1962	12.00	30.00
Vee Jay SR-1053	(P)	**Sherry And 11 Others**	1962	16.00	40.00
Vee Jay LP-1055	(M)	**Four Seasons' Greetings**	1963	12.00	30.00
Vee Jay SR-1055	(S)	**Four Seasons' Greetings**	1963	16.00	40.00
Vee Jay LP-1056	(M)	**Big Girls Don't Cry**	1963	12.00	30.00
Vee Jay SR-1056	(P)	**Big Girls Don't Cry**	1963	16.00	40.00
Vee Jay LP-1059	(M)	**Ain't That A Shame**	1963	10.00	25.00
Vee Jay SR-1059	(P)	**Ain't That A Shame**	1963	16.00	40.00
Vee Jay LP-1065	(M)	**Golden Hits Of The Four Seasons**	1963	14.00	35.00
Vee Jay SR-1065	(P)	**Golden Hits Of The Four Seasons**	1963	20.00	50.00

— Vee Jay albums above have black "rainbow" labels with an oval logo on top.—

Vee Jay LP-1082	(M)	**Folk-Nanny**	1963	10.00	25.00
Vee Jay SR-1082	(S)	**Folk-Nanny**	1963	16.00	40.00

*("Connie-O," "Soon," "Silver Wings" and "Star Maker"
are rechanneled on this album.)*

Vee Jay LP-1082	(M)	**Stay & Other Great Hits**	1964	8.00	20.00
Vee Jay SR-1082	(S)	**Stay & Other Great Hits**	1964	12.00	30.00

("Stay" is a repackage of "Folk-Nanny.")

Vee Jay LP-1088	(M)	**More Golden Hits By The Four Seasons**	1964	12.00	30.00
Vee Jay SR-1088	(P)	**More Golden Hits By The Four Seasons**	1964	16.00	40.00

(First pressings includes "Long Lonely Nights.")

Vee Jay LP-1088	(M)	**More Golden Hits By The Four Seasons**	1965	8.00	20.00
Vee Jay SR-1088	(P)	**More Golden Hits By The Four Seasons**	1965	10.00	25.00

(Later pressings replace "Nights" with "Apple Of My Eye.")

Vee Jay LP-1121	(M)	**We Love Girls**	1965	12.00	30.00
Vee Jay SR-1121	(S)	**We Love Girls**	1965	16.00	40.00
Vee Jay LP-1154	(M)	**Recorded Live On Stage**	1965	12.00	30.00
Vee Jay SR-1154	(S)	**Recorded Live On Stage**	1965	16.00	40.00
Coca-Cola TX-94	(DJ)	**The Four Seasons Swing The Jingle**	1964	100.00	250.00
Philips PHM-200-124	(M)	**Dawn (Go Away) & 11 Other Great Songs**	1964	8.00	20.00
Philips PHS-600-124	(S)	**Dawn (Go Away) & 11 Other Great Songs**	1964	10.00	25.00
Philips PHM-200-129	(M)	**Born To Wander**	1964	8.00	20.00
Philips PHS-600-129	(S)	**Born To Wander**	1964	10.00	25.00
Philips PHM-200-146	(M)	**Rag Doll**	1964	8.00	20.00
Philips PHS-600-146	(P)	**Rag Doll**	1964	10.00	25.00
Philips PHM-200-146	(M)	**Rag Doll**	1964	8.00	20.00
Philips PHS-600-146	(P)	**Rag Doll**	1964	10.00	25.00

*(Second pressings of Philips 145 have a yellow seal noting "Save
It For Me" on the cover. "Rag Doll" is in mono on this album.)*

Label & Catalog #		Title	Year	VG+	NM
Philips PHM-200-164	(M)	**The Four Seasons Entertain You**	1965	10.00	25.00
Philips PHS-600-164	(S)	**The Four Seasons Entertain You**	1965	12.00	30.00
		(The cover has an orange seal noting "Bye Bye Baby.")			
Philips PHM-200-164	(M)	**The Four Seasons Entertain You**	1965	10.00	25.00
Philips PHS-600-164	(S)	**The Four Seasons Entertain You**	1965	12.00	30.00
		(Cover has an orange seal noting "Bye Bye Baby" and "Toy Soldier.")			
Philips PHM-200-164	(M)	**The Four Seasons Entertain You**	1965	8.00	20.00
Philips PHS-600-164	(S)	**The Four Seasons Entertain You**	1965	10.00	25.00
		(The cover has a blue seal noting "Bye Bye Baby" and "Toy Soldier.")			
Philips PHM-200-193	(M)	**Big Hits By Bacharach, David & Dylan**	1965	8.00	20.00
Philips PHS-600-193	(S)	**Big Hits By Bacharach, David & Dylan**	1965	10.00	25.00
		(The cover has a medieval motif.)			
Philips PHM-200-193	(M)	**Big Hits By Bacharach, David & Dylan**	1965	12.00	30.00
Philips PHS-600-193	(S)	**Big Hits By Bacharach, David & Dylan**	1965	16.00	40.00
		(The cover features photos of the group.)			
Philips PHM-200-196	(M)	**Gold Vault Of Hits**	1965	8.00	20.00
Philips PHS-600-196	(S)	**Gold Vault Of Hits**	1965	10.00	25.00
		(The title on the cover is in unadorned red print; the group photo on the back cover features Charlie Calello.)			
Philips PHM-200-201	(M)	**Working My Way Back To You**	1966	8.00	20.00
Philips PHS-600-201	(S)	**Working My Way Back To You**	1966	10.00	25.00
Philips PHM-200-222	(M)	**Lookin' Back**	1966	8.00	20.00
Philips PHS-600-222	(S)	**Lookin' Back**	1966	10.00	25.00
Philips PHM-200-223	(M)	**The Four Seasons' Christmas Album**	1966	10.00	25.00
Philips PHS-600-223	(S)	**The Four Seasons' Christmas Album**	1966	12.00	30.00
Philips PHS-2-6501	(P)	**Edizone D'Oro** (2 LPs)	1969	12.00	30.00
		(The "4" on the cover is in unadorned red on a gold foil. "Rag Doll" is in stereo on all pressings of this album.)			
Philips PHS-2-6501	(P)	**Edizone D'Oro** (2 LPs)	1969	16.00	40.00
		(The "4" on the cover is white or red with black trim on gold foil.)			
Philips PHS-2-6501	(P)	**Edizone D'Oro** (2 LPs)	1969	16.00	40.00
		(The "4" on the cover is in white print on a gold board.)			
Philips PHS-600290	(S)	**Genuine Imitation Life Gazette**	1969	10.00	25.00
		(Original covers are yellow newspaper.)			
Sears SPS-609	(S)	**Brotherhood Of Man**	1970	16.00	40.00
Longines Sym. 95833	(P)	**The Greatest Hits Of**			
		Frankie Valli & The Four Seasons (4 LPs)	197?	10.00	25.00
		(The cover reads "As seen on TV.")			
Sweet Thunder 3	(S)	**Reunited Live**	198?	10.00	30.00

FOUR TOPS, THE
Refer to The Supremes & The Four Tops.

Label & Catalog #		Title	Year	VG+	NM
Workshop 217	(M)	**Jazz Impressions**	1962	Unreleased	
Motown 622	(M)	**The Four Tops**	1964	12.00	30.00
Motown MS-622	(S)	**The Four Tops**	1964	16.00	40.00
Motown 634	(M)	**The Four Tops, No. 2**	1964	12.00	30.00
Motown MS-634	(S)	**The Four Tops, No. 2**	1965	16.00	40.00
Motown 647	(M)	**The Four Tops On Top**	1966	12.00	30.00
Motown MS-647	(S)	**The Four Tops On Top**	1966	16.00	40.00
Motown 654	(M)	**The Four Tops Live**	1966	10.00	25.00
Motown MS-654	(S)	**The Four Tops Live**	1966	12.00	30.00
Motown 657	(M)	**The Four Tops On Broadway**	1967	8.00	20.00
Motown MS-657	(S)	**The Four Tops On Broadway**	1967	10.00	25.00
Motown 660	(M)	**Reach Out**	1967	8.00	20.00
Motown MS-660	(S)	**Reach Out**	1967	10.00	25.00
Motown M-669	(M)	**Yesterday Dreams**	1968	12.00	30.00
Command QD-40011	(Q)	**Keeper Of The Castle**	1974	10.00	25.00
Command QD-40012	(Q)	**Main Street People**	1974	10.00	25.00

FOUR TUNES, THE

Label & Catalog #		Title	Year	VG+	NM
Jubilee LP-1039	(M)	**12 X 4**	1957	200.00	600.00

FOWLEY, KIM

Label & Catalog #		Title	Year	VG+	NM
Tower T-5080	(M)	**Love Is Alive And Well**	1967	10.00	25.00
Tower ST-5080	(S)	**Love Is Alive And Well**	1967	12.00	30.00
Imperial LP-12413	(S)	**Born To Be Wild**	1968	12.00	30.00
Imperial LP-12423	(S)	**Outrageous**	1969	12.00	30.00
Imperial LP-12443	(S)	**Good Clean Fun**	1969	12.00	30.00

Label & Catalog #		Title	Year	VG+	NM

FOWLER, WALLY
Wally Fowler was the founder of the original Oak Ridge Quartet in 1945. . .

Decca DL-8560	(M)	**Call Of The Cross**	1958	24.00	60.00
King 702	(M)	**Gospel Song Festival**	1960	60.00	150.00
Starday SLP-112	(M)	**All Nite Singing Gospel Concert**	1960	20.00	50.00
		(Both King 702 and Starday 112 feature The Oak Ridge Quartet.)			
Starday SLP-301	(M)	**More All Nite Singing Concert**	1964	16.00	40.00
		— Starday albums above have yellow labels.—			

FOX, CURLY, & TEXAS RUBY

Starday SLP-235	(M)	**Curly Fox And Texas Ruby** *(Yellow label)*	1963	16.00	40.00
Harmony HL-7302	(M)	**Travelling Blues**	196?	10.00	25.00

FOXX, INEZ & CHARLIE

Symbol SYM-4400	(M)	**Mockingbird**	1963	60.00	150.00
Sue LP-1037	(M)	**Inez And Charlie Foxx**	1966	24.00	60.00
Sue LP-1037	(S)	**Inez And Charlie Foxx**	1966	40.00	100.00
Dynamo D-7000	(M)	**Come By Here**	1967	8.00	20.00
Dynamo DS-8000	(S)	**Come By Here**	1967	10.00	25.00
Dynamo D-7003	(M)	**Inez And Charlie Foxx's Greatest Hits**	1967	8.00	20.00
Dynamo DS-8003	(S)	**Inez And Charlie Foxx's Greatest Hits**	1967	10.00	25.00
		(Contains rerecorded stereo versions of earlier Symbol material.)			

FOXX, RED
Red Foxx is a pseudonym for John Elroy Sanford.

Dooto DTL-270	(M)	**Side Splitter**	1959	10.00	25.00
Dooto DTL-274	(M)	**Best Party Fun**	1960	10.00	25.00
Dooto DTL-290	(M)	**Funn**	1960	10.00	25.00
Dooto DTL-???	(M)	**Laff-A-Rama**	1961	10.00	25.00
Dooto DTL-804	(M)	**Wild Party**	1961	10.00	25.00
Dooto DTL-809	(M)	**This Is Foxx**	1961	10.00	25.00
Dooto DTL-815	(M)	**He's Funny That Way**	1962	10.00	25.00
Dooto DTL-828	(M)	**Hearty Party Laffs**	1962	10.00	25.00
Dooto DTL-834	(M)	**Crack Up**	1963	10.00	25.00
Dooto DTL-836	(M)	**Round One & Two**	1964	10.00	25.00
Dooto DTL-838	(M)	**Naughties But Goodies**	1965	10.00	25.00

FRACTION

Angelus WR-5005	(S)	**Moon Blood**	197?	2,000.00	3,000.00
		(Issued in a die-cut cover with a red cellophane window that allows the moon pictured on the inner sleeve to show through.)			

FRAMPTON, PETER
Peter Frampton formerly recorded with The Herd.

A&M SP-27200	(DJ)	**The Peter Frampton Radio Special**	197?	10.00	25.00
Sweet Thunder	(S)	**Frampton Comes Alive** *(2 LPs. Half-speed)*	198?	35.00	100.00

FRANCIS, CONNIE

MGM E-3686	(M)	**Who's Sorry Now?**	1958	40.00	100.00
MGM E-3761	(M)	**The Exciting Connie Francis**	1959	30.00	75.00
MGM SE-3761	(S)	**The Exciting Connie Francis**	1959	40.00	100.00
		— MGM albums above have yellow labels.—			
MGM E-3686	(M)	**Who's Sorry Now?**	1959	16.00	40.00
MGM SE-3686	(E)	**Who's Sorry Now?**	1959	10.00	25.00
MGM E-3761	(M)	**The Exciting Connie Francis**	1959	12.00	30.00
MGM SE-3761	(S)	**The Exciting Connie Francis**	1959	16.00	40.00
MGM E-3776	(M)	**My Thanks To You**	1959	12.00	30.00
MGM SE-3776	(S)	**My Thanks To You**	1959	16.00	40.00
MGM E-3791	(M)	**Italian Favorites**	1959	12.00	30.00
MGM SE-3791	(S)	**Italian Favorites**	1959	16.00	40.00
MGM E-3792	(M)	**Christmas In My Heart**	1959	12.00	30.00
MGM SE-3792	(S)	**Christmas In My Heart**	1959	16.00	40.00
MGM E-3793	(M)	**Connie's Greatest Hits**	1960	14.00	35.00
MGM SE-3793	(E)	**Connie's Greatest Hits**	1960	10.00	25.00
MGM E-3794	(M)	**Rock 'N' Roll Million Sellers**	1960	12.00	30.00
MGM SE-3794	(S)	**Rock 'N' Roll Million Sellers**	1960	16.00	40.00
MGM E-3795	(M)	**Country And Western Golden Hits**	1960	12.00	30.00
MGM SE-3795	(S)	**Country And Western Golden Hits**	1960	16.00	40.00

Label & Catalog #		Title	Year	VG+	NM
MGM E-3853	(M)	Spanish And Latin American Favorites	1960	12.00	30.00
MGM SE-3853	(S)	Spanish And Latin American Favorites	1960	16.00	40.00
MGM E-3869	(M)	Jewish Favorites	1961	12.00	30.00
MGM SE-3869	(S)	Jewish Favorites	1961	16.00	40.00
MGM E-3871	(M)	More Italian Favorites	1961	12.00	30.00
MGM SE-3871	(S)	More Italian Favorites	1961	16.00	40.00
MGM E-3893	(M)	Songs To A Swinging Band	1961	12.00	30.00
MGM SE-3893	(S)	Songs To A Swinging Band	1961	16.00	40.00
MGM E-3913	(M)	Connie At The Copa	1961	12.00	30.00
MGM SE-3913	(S)	Connie At The Copa	1961	16.00	40.00
		(MGM 3913 was released with two different covers.)			
MGM E-3942	(M)	More Greatest Hits	1961	12.00	30.00
MGM SE-3942	(S)	More Greatest Hits	1961	16.00	40.00
MGM E-3965	(M)	Never On Sunday	1961	12.00	30.00
MGM SE-3965	(S)	Never On Sunday	1961	16.00	40.00
MGM E-3969	(M)	Folk Song Favorites	1961	12.00	30.00
MGM SE-3969	(S)	Folk Song Favorites	1961	16.00	40.00
MGM E-4013	(M)	Irish Favorites	1962	12.00	30.00
MGM SE-4013	(S)	Irish Favorites	1962	16.00	40.00
MGM E-4022	(M)	Do The Twist With Connie Francis	1962	12.00	30.00
MGM SE-4022	(S)	Do The Twist With Connie Francis	1962	16.00	40.00
MGM E-4022	(M)	Dance Party	196?	10.00	25.00
MGM SE-4022	(S)	Dance Party	196?	12.00	30.00
		("Dance Party" is a repackage of "Do The Twist.")			
MGM L-70126	(M)	Fun Songs For Children	196?	40.00	100.00
MGM E-4023	(M)	Fun Songs For Children	1962	20.00	50.00
MGM E-4048	(M)	Award Winning Motion Picture Hits	1962	10.00	25.00
MGMS E-4048	(S)	Award Winning Motion Picture Hits	1962	12.00	30.00
MGM E-4049	(M)	Second Hand Love And Other Hits	1962	10.00	25.00
MGM SE-4049	(S)	Second Hand Love And Other Hits	1962	12.00	30.00
MGM E-4079	(M)	Country Music, Connie Style	1962	10.00	25.00
MGM SE-4079	(S)	Country Music, Connie Style	1962	12.00	30.00
MGM E-4102	(M)	Modern Italian Hits	1963	10.00	25.00
MGM SE-4102	(S)	Modern Italian Hits	1963	12.00	30.00
MGM E-4123	(M)	Follow The Boys (Soundtrack)	1963	10.00	25.00
MGM SE-4123	(S)	Follow The Boys (Soundtrack)	1963	12.00	30.00
MGM E-4124	(M)	German Favorites	1963	10.00	25.00
MGM SE-4124	(S)	German Favorites	1963	12.00	30.00
MGM E-4145	(M)	Greatest American Waltzes	1963	10.00	25.00
MGM SE-4145	(S)	Greatest American Waltzes	1963	12.00	30.00
MGM E-4161	(M)	Mala Femmina And Big Hits From Italy	1963	10.00	25.00
MGM SE-4161	(S)	Mala Femmina And Big Hits From Italy	1963	12.00	30.00
MGM E-4167	(M)	The Very Best Of Connie Francis	1963	10.00	25.00
MGM SE-4167	(S)	The Very Best Of Connie Francis	1963	12.00	30.00
MGM E-4210	(M)	In The Summer Of His Years	1964	10.00	25.00
MGM SE-4210	(S)	In The Summer Of His Years	1964	12.00	30.00
MGM E-4229	(M)	Looking For Love (Soundtrack)	1964	10.00	25.00
MGM SE-4229	(S)	Looking For Love (Soundtrack)	1964	12.00	30.00
MGM E-4253	(M)	A New Kind Of Connie	1964	10.00	25.00
MGM SE-4253	(S)	A New Kind Of Connie	1964	12.00	30.00
MGM E-4294	(M)	For Mama	1965	10.00	25.00
MGM SE-4294	(S)	For Mama	1965	12.00	30.00
MGM E-4298	(M)	All Time International Hits	1965	10.00	25.00
MGM SE-4298	(S)	All Time International Hits	1965	12.00	30.00
MGM E-4355	(M)	Jealous Heart	1965	10.00	25.00
MGM SE-4355	(S)	Jealous Heart	1965	12.00	30.00
MGM E-4382	(M)	Movie Greats Of The 60's	1966	10.00	25.00
MGM SE-4382	(S)	Movie Greats Of The 60's	1966	12.00	30.00
MGM E-4399	(M)	Connie's Christmas	1966	10.00	25.00
MGM SE-4399	(S)	Connie's Christmas	1966	12.00	30.00
		(MGM SE-4399 is a repackage of 3792.)			
MGM E-4411	(M)	Live At The Sahara In Las Vegas	1966	10.00	25.00
MGM SE-4411	(S)	Live At The Sahara In Las Vegas	1966	12.00	30.00
Lion LE-903	(M)	Connie Francis And The Kids Next Door	1966	20.00	50.00
Lion LES-903	(S)	Connie Francis And The Kids Next Door	1966	30.00	75.00
MGM E-4448	(M)	Love, Italian Style	1967	10.00	25.00
MGM SE-4448	(S)	Love, Italian Style	1967	12.00	30.00
MGM E-4472	(M)	Connie Francis On Broadway Today	1967	10.00	25.00
MGM SE-4472	(S)	Connie Francis On Broadway Today	1967	12.00	30.00

Label & Catalog #		Title	Year	VG+	NM
MGM E-4474	(M)	Grandes Exitos del Cine de los Anos 60	1967	10.00	25.00
MGM SE-4474	(S)	Grandes Exitos del Cine de los Anos 60	1967	12.00	30.00
MGM E-4487	(M)	My Heart Cries For You	1967	10.00	25.00
MGM SE-4487	(S)	My Heart Cries For You	1967	12.00	30.00
		—MGM albums above have black labels.—			
MGM E-4522	(M)	Hawaii: Connie	1968	40.00	100.00
MGM SE-4522	(S)	Hawaii: Connie	1968	60.00	150.00
MGM SE-4573	(S)	Connie & Clyde	1968	10.00	25.00
MGM SE-4585	(S)	Connie Francis Sings Bacharach & David	1968	10.00	25.00
MGM ST-91145	(S)	My Best To You (Capitol Record Club)	1968	10.00	25.00
MGM SE-4637	(S)	The Wedding Cake	1969	10.00	25.00
MGM SE-4655	(S)	The Songs Of Les Reed	1969	10.00	25.00
MGM GAS-109	(S)	Greatest Golden Groovy Goodies	1970	12.00	30.00
MGM E6PS-2	(S)	A Connie Francis Spectacular (5 LP box)	197?	20.00	50.00
Metro M-519	(M)	Connie Francis	1964	8.00	20.00
Metro MS-519	(S)	Connie Francis	1964	10.00	25.00
Metro M-538	(M)	Folk Favorites	1965	8.00	20.00
Metro MS-538	(S)	Folk Favorites	1965	10.00	25.00
Metro M-571	(M)	Songs Of Love	1966	8.00	20.00
Metro MS-571	(S)	Songs Of Love	1966	10.00	25.00
Metro M-603	(M)	The Incomparable Connie Francis	1967	8.00	20.00
Metro MS-603	(S)	The Incomparable Connie Francis	1967	10.00	25.00

FRANCIS, CONNIE, & HANK WILLIAMS, JR.

MGM E-4251	(M)	Great Country Favorites	1964	12.00	30.00
MGM SE-4251	(S)	Great Country Favorites	1964	16.00	40.00

FRANKLIN, ALAN/THE ALAN FRANKLIN EXPLOSION

Horne JC-888	(S)	The Blues Climax	1969	50.00	125.00
Aladdin 104049	(S)	Come Home, Baby	1979	20.00	50.00

FRANKLIN, ARETHA

Columbia CL-1612	(M)	Aretha	1961	20.00	50.00
Columbia CS-8412	(S)	Aretha	1961	30.00	75.00
Columbia CL-1761	(M)	The Electrifying Aretha Franklin	1962	16.00	40.00
Columbia CS-8561	(S)	The Electrifying Aretha Franklin	1962	20.00	50.00
Columbia CL-1876	(M)	The Tender... Swinging Aretha Franklin	1962	16.00	40.00
Columbia CS-8676	(S)	The Tender... Swinging Aretha Franklin	1962	20.00	50.00
		— Columbia albums above have three white "eye" logos on each side of the spindle hole.—			
Columbia CL-2079	(M)	Laughing On The Outside	1963	8.00	20.00
Columbia CS-8879	(S)	Laughing On The Outside	1963	10.00	25.00
Columbia CL-2163	(M)	Unforgettable	1964	8.00	20.00
Columbia CS-8963	(S)	Unforgettable	1964	10.00	25.00
Columbia CL-2281	(M)	Runnin' Out Of Fools	1964	8.00	20.00
Columbia CS-9081	(S)	Runnin' Out Of Fools	1964	10.00	25.00
Columbia CL-2351	(M)	Yeah!!!	1965	8.00	20.00
Columbia CS-9151	(S)	Yeah!!!	1965	10.00	25.00
Columbia CL-2521	(M)	Soul Sister	1966	8.00	20.00
Columbia CS-9321	(S)	Soul Sister	1966	10.00	25.00
Columbia CL-2629	(M)	Take It Like You Give It	1967	8.00	20.00
Columbia CS-9429	(S)	Take It Like You Give It	1967	10.00	25.00
Columbia CL-2673	(M)	Aretha Franklin's Greatest Hits	1967	8.00	20.00
Columbia CS-9473	(S)	Aretha Franklin's Greatest Hits	1967	10.00	25.00
Columbia CL-2754	(M)	Take A Look	1967	8.00	20.00
Columbia CS-9554	(S)	Take A Look	1967	10.00	25.00
Columbia CS-9601	(S)	Aretha Franklin's Greatest Hits, Volume 2	1968	8.00	20.00
Columbia CS-9776	(S)	Soft And Beautiful	1969	8.00	20.00
		—Columbia albums above have "360 Sound" on the bottom of the label.—			
Atlantic 8139	(M)	I Never Loved A Man (The Way I Love You)	1967	10.00	25.00
Atlantic SD-8139	(S)	I Never Loved A Man (The Way I Love You)	1967	8.00	20.00
Atlantic 8150	(M)	Aretha Arrives	1967	10.00	25.00
Atlantic SD-8150	(S)	Aretha Arrives	1967	8.00	20.00
Atlantic 8176	(M)	Lady Soul	1968	12.00	30.00
Atlantic SD-8176	(S)	Lady Soul	1968	8.00	20.00
Atlantic SD-8186	(S)	Aretha Now	1968	8.00	20.00
		—Atlantic stereo albums above have green & blue labels.—			
Atlantic QD-7205	(Q)	Live At The Fillmore West	1974	10.00	25.00
Atlantic QD-8305	(Q)	The Best Of Aretha Franklin	1974	12.00	30.00

Label & Catalog #		Title	Year	VG+	NM
FRANKLIN, ERMA					
Epic LN-3824	(S)	**Her Name Is Erma**	1962	10.00	25.00
Epic BN-619	(S)	**Her Name Is Erma**	1962	12.00	30.00
FRANKLIN, PETE					
Bluesville BVLP-1068	(M)	**Guitar Pete's Blues**	1963	30.00	75.00
		— Bluesville albums above have bright blue labels with silver print.—			
Bluesville BVLP-1068	(M)	**Guitar Pete's Blues**	1964	10.00	25.00
		— Bluesville albums above have blue labels with a trident logo on the right side.—			
FRANTIC FREDDIE & THE REFLECTIONS					
Tom Rice	(M)	**Music Power**	1967	80.00	200.00
FRATERNITY OF MAN, THE					
ABC S-647	(S)	**The Fraternity Of Man**	1968	12.00	30.00
Dot DLP-25955	(S)	**Get It On**	1969	12.00	30.00
FRAWLEY, WILLIAM					
Dot DLP-3061	(M)	**The Old Ones**	1957	16.00	40.00
FRAZIER, DALLAS					
Capitol T-2552	(M)	**Elvira**	1966	10.00	25.00
Capitol ST-2552	(S)	**Elvira**	1966	12.00	30.00
Capitol T-2764	(M)	**Tell It Like It Is**	1967	10.00	25.00
Capitol ST-2764	(S)	**Tell It Like It Is**	1967	12.00	30.00
FREAK SCENE, THE					
Columbia CL-2656	(M)	**Psychedelic Psoul**	1967	30.00	75.00
Columbia CS-9456	(S)	**Psychedelic Psoul**	1967	40.00	100.00
FREBERG, STAN					
Capitol T-777	(M)	**A Child's Garden Of Freberg**	1957	20.00	50.00
		— Capitol albums above have turquoise labels.—			
Capitol WBO-1035	(M)	**The Best Of The Stan Freberg Show**	1958	20.00	50.00
Capitol T-1242	(M)	**Stan Freberg With The Original Cast**	1959	12.00	30.00
No label	(M)	**Oregon! Oregon!** *(Original cast)*	1959	100.00	300.00
		(Privately pressed album of Freberg's musical comedy *for the Oregon State Centennial of 1959.)*			
Capitol W-1573	(M)	**The United States Of America**	1961	10.00	25.00
Capitol SW-1573	(S)	**The United States Of America**	1961	12.00	30.00
Capitol T-1694	(M)	**Face The Funnies**	1962	10.00	25.00
Capitol ST-1694	(S)	**Face The Funnies**	1962	12.00	30.00
		— Capitol albums above have black labels with the Capitol logo on the left side.—			
Capitol T-1816	(M)	**Madison Avenue Werewolf**	1962	10.00	25.00
Capitol T-2020	(M)	**The Best Of Stan Freberg**	1964	10.00	25.00
Freberg Ltd. (No number)	(M)	**More Here Than Meets The Ear**	1965	40.00	100.00
		("More Here" is a promo for SF's ad agency.)			
Capitol T-2551	(M)	**Underground Show #1**	1966	8.00	20.00
Capitol ST-2551	(S)	**Underground Show #1**	1966	10.00	25.00
		— Capitol albums above have black labels with the Capitol logo on top.—			
FRED, JOHN, & HIS PLAYBOY BAND					
Paula LP-2191	(M)	**John Fred And His Playboys**	1966	8.00	20.00
Paula LPS-2191	(S)	**John Fred And His Playboys**	1966	10.00	25.00
Paula LP-2193	(M)	**34:40 Of John Fred And His Playboys**	1967	8.00	20.00
Paula LPS-2193	(S)	**34:40 Of John Fred And His Playboys**	1967	10.00	25.00
Paula LP-2197	(M)	**Agnes English**	1967	8.00	20.00
Paula LPS-2197	(S)	**Agnes English**	1967	10.00	25.00
Paula LPS-2197	(S)	**Judy In Disguise With Glasses**	1968	10.00	25.00
		("Judy" is a repackage of "Agnes.")			
FRED & THE NEW JB'S: *Refer to* **FRED WESLEY & THE JB'S**					
FREDDIE & THE DREAMERS					
Tower T-5003	(M)	**I'm Telling You Now**	1965	10.00	25.00
Tower DT-5003	(E)	**I'm Telling You Now**	1965	8.00	20.00
		(While Tower 5003 pictures Freddie & The Dreamers on the cover, *it is actually a various artists comp with only two tracks by F&TDs.)*			

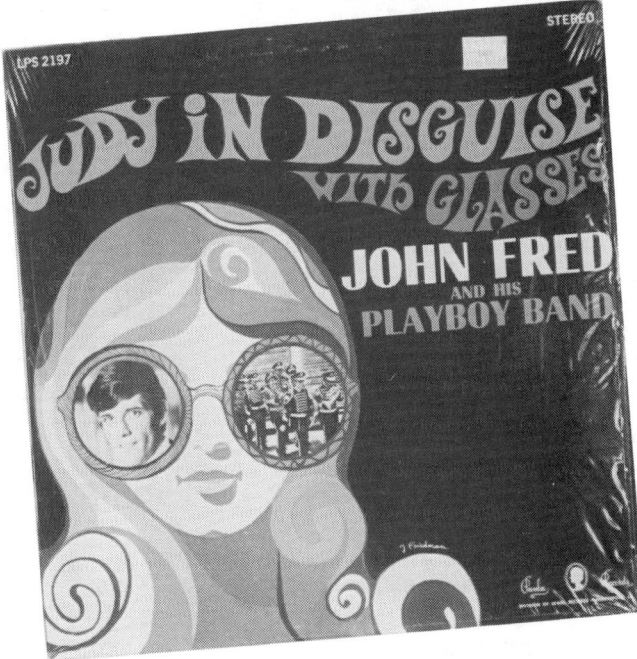

John Fred Gourrier had been a regional success for more than a decade when the ridiculously wonderful "Judy In Disguise (With Glasses)" spoofed Sgt. Pepper on its way to the top of the charts. After the single's unexpected success, Paula 2197, Agnes English, was rechristened, given gear new cover art (a big improvement over the drab original) and sent back out into the field for retail exposure.

Label & Catalog #		Title	Year	VG+	NM
Mercury MG-21017	(M)	**Freddie & The Dreamers**	1965	10.00	25.00
Mercury SR-61017	(E)	**Freddie & The Dreamers**	1965	8.00	20.00
Mercury MG-21026	(M)	**Do The Freddie**	1965	8.00	20.00
Mercury SR-61026	(S)	**Do The Freddie**	1965	10.00	25.00
Mercury MG-21031	(M)	**Seaside Swingers** (Soundtrack)	1965	8.00	20.00
Mercury SR-61031	(S)	**Seaside Swingers** (Soundtrack)	1965	10.00	25.00
Mercury MG-21053	(M)	**Frantic Freddie**	1965	8.00	20.00
Mercury SR-61053	(S)	**Frantic Freddie**	1965	10.00	25.00
Mercury MG-21061	(M)	**Fun Lovin' Freddie**	1966	8.00	20.00
Mercury SR-61061	(S)	**Fun Lovin' Freddie**	1966	10.00	25.00
FREDRIC					
Forte 301	(S)	**Phases And Faces**	1968	360.00	600.00
FREEBORNE					
Monitor MPS-607	(S)	**Peak Impressions**	1967	30.00	75.00
FREED, ALAN					
MGM E-293	(10")	**The Big Beat**	1956	80.00	200.00
Coral CRL-57063	(M)	**Alan Freed's Rock 'N Roll Dance Party, Vol. 1**	1956	60.00	150.00
Coral CRL-57115	(M)	**Alan Freed's Rock 'N Roll Dance Party, Vol. 2**	1957	60.00	150.00
Coral CRL-57177	(M)	**Go Go Go—Alan Freed's TV Record Hop**	1957	60.00	150.00
Coral CRL-57213	(M)	**Rock Around The Block**	1958	60.00	150.00
Coral CRL-57216	(M)	**Alan Freed Presents The King's Henchmen**	1958	60.00	150.00
Brunswick BL-54043	(M)	**The Alan Freed Rock & Roll Show**	1959	60.00	150.00
FREEMAN, BOBBY					
Jubilee JLP-1086	(M)	**Do You Wanna Dance?**	1959	50.00	125.00
Jubilee JLPS-1086	(S)	**Do You Wanna Dance?**	1959	80.00	200.00
Jubilee JGM-5010	(M)	**Twist With Bobby Freeman**	1962	30.00	75.00
Autumn LP-102	(M)	**C'mon And S-W-I-M**	1964	20.00	50.00
King 930	(M)	**The Lovable Style Of Bobby Freeman**	1965	150.00	300.00
Josie JM-4007	(M)	**Get In The Swim With Bobby Freeman**	1965	12.00	30.00
Josie JGS-4007	(E)	**Get In The Swim With Bobby Freeman**	1965	10.00	25.00
FREEMAN, ERNIE					
Imperial LP-9022	(M)	**Ernie Freeman Plays Irving Berlin**	1957	20.00	50.00
Imperial LP-9030	(M)	**Jivin' Around**	1957	20.00	50.00
Imperial LP-9057	(M)	**Ernie Freeman**	1958	20.00	50.00
Imperial LP-9067	(M)	**Dark At The Top Of The Stairs**	1959	12.00	30.00
Imperial LP-12067	(S)	**Dark At The Top Of The Stairs**	1959	16.00	40.00
Imperial LP-9081	(M)	**Twistin' Time**	1960	12.00	30.00
Imperial LP-12081	(S)	**Twistin' Time**	1960	16.00	40.00
Imperial LP-9148	(M)	**The Stripper**	1962	10.00	25.00
Imperial LP-12193	(S)	**The Stripper**	1962	12.00	30.00
Liberty LRP-3283	(M)	**Limbo Dance Party**	1963	10.00	25.00
Liberty LST-7283	(S)	**Limbo Dance Party**	1963	12.00	30.00
Liberty LRP-3331	(M)	**Comin' Home, Baby**	1963	10.00	25.00
Liberty LST-7331	(S)	**Comin' Home, Baby**	1963	12.00	30.00
FREHELY, ACE: *Refer to* **KISS**					
FREIGHT TRAIN					
Fly-by-Nite LPFBN-1001	(S)	**Just The Beginning**	1971	20.00	50.00
FRIAR TUCK					
Mercury MG-21111	(M)	**Friar Tuck & His Psychedelic Guitar**	1967	10.00	25.00
Mercury SR-61111	(S)	**Friar Tuck & His Psychedelic Guitar**	1967	12.00	30.00
FRIJID PINK					
Parrot PAS-71033	(S)	**Frijid Pink**	1970	10.00	25.00
Parrot PAS-71041	(S)	**Frijid Pink Defrosted**	1970	10.00	25.00
		(The inner sleeve is a full-color photo of the group.)			
FRIZZELL, LEFTY					
Refer to Carl Smith / Lefty Frizzell / Marty Robbins.					
Columbia HL-9019	(10")	**Lefty Frizzell Sings** **The Songs Of Jimmie Rodgers**	1951	100.00	300.00
Columbia HL-9021	(10")	**Listen To Lefty**	1952	100.00	300.00

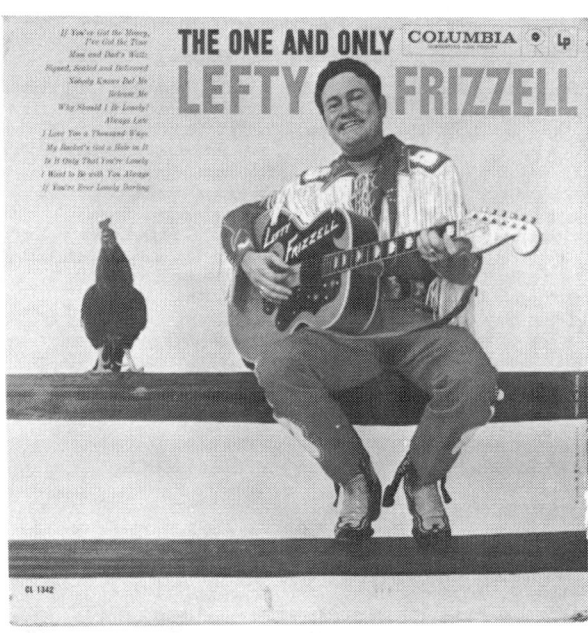

William "Lefty" Frizzell is a country'n western legend who was a mainstay on country stations through the '50s and '60s. His few LPs from the '50s are very rare and always in demand, even by rock collectors who recognize Lefty as a seminal influence on rock'n roll.

Label & Catalog #		Title	Year	VG+	NM
Columbia CL-1342	(M)	**The One And Only Lefty Frizzell**	1959	60.00	150.00
		— Columbia albums above have three white "eye" logos on each side of the spindle hole.—			
Harmony HL-7241	(M)	**Lefty Frizzell Sings**			
		The Songs Of Jimmie Rodgers	1960	10.00	25.00
Columbia CL-2169	(M)	**Saginaw, Michigan**	1964	14.00	35.00
Columbia CS-8969	(S)	**Saginaw, Michigan**	1964	16.00	40.00
Columbia CL-2386	(M)	**The Sad Side Of Love**	1965	14.00	35.00
Columbia CS-9186	(S)	**The Sad Side Of Love**	1965	16.00	40.00
Columbia CL-2488	(M)	**Lefty Frizzell's Greatest Hits**	1966	14.00	35.00
Columbia CS-9288	(S)	**Lefty Frizzell's Greatest Hits**	1966	16.00	40.00
Columbia CL-2772	(M)	**Puttin' On**	1967	20.00	50.00
Columbia CS-9572	(S)	**Puttin' On**	1967	16.00	40.00
		—Columbia albums above have "360 Sound Mono/Stereo" on the bottom of the label.—			

FROGGIE BEAVER

Label & Catalog #		Title	Year	VG+	NM
Froggie Beaver 7301	(S)	**From The Pond**	1973	12.00	30.00

FROLK HAVEN

Label & Catalog #		Title	Year	VG+	NM
LRS RF-6023	(S)	**At The Apex Of High**	197?	60.00	150.00

FROM BRITAIN WITH BEAT

Label & Catalog #		Title	Year	VG+	NM
Modern Sound 544	(M)	**From Britain With Beat**	196?	30.00	75.00

FROMAN, JANE

Label & Catalog #		Title	Year	VG+	NM
Decca DL-6021	(10")	**Souvenirs**	1952	20.00	50.00
RCA Victor LPT-3055	(10")	**Gems From Gershwin**	1952	20.00	50.00
Capitol L-309	(10")	**With A Song In My Heart** (Soundtrack)	1952	40.00	100.00
Capitol S-310	(10")	**Pal Joey** (Soundtrack)	1952	40.00	100.00
Capitol H-354	(10")	**Yours Alone**	1952	20.00	50.00
Capitol T-309	(M)	**With A Song In My Heart** (Soundtrack)	1955	16.00	40.00
Capitol T-310	(M)	**Pal Joey** (Soundtrack)	1952	40.00	100.00
Capitol T-726	(M)	**Faith**	1956	12.00	30.00
Capitol T-889	(M)	**Songs At Sunset**	1957	12.00	30.00

FROST, THE

Label & Catalog #		Title	Year	VG+	NM
Vanguard VSD-6520	(S)	**Frost Music**	1969	10.00	25.00
Vanguard VSD-6541	(S)	**Rock And Roll Music**	1969	10.00	25.00
Vanguard VSD-6556	(S)	**Through The Eyes Of Music**	1970	10.00	25.00

FROST, FRANK, & THE NIGHTHAWKS

Label & Catalog #		Title	Year	VG+	NM
Phillips Int. PLP-1975	(M)	**Hey Boss Man!**	1961	2,000.00	4,000.00

FROST, MAX, & THE TROOPERS

Label & Catalog #		Title	Year	VG+	NM
Tower ST-5147	(S)	**Shape Of Things To Come**	1968	20.00	50.00

FRUT

Label & Catalog #		Title	Year	VG+	NM
Westbound WB-2005	(S)	**Keep On Truckin'**	1971	10.00	25.00
Westbound WB-2008	(S)	**Spoiled Rotten**	1972	10.00	25.00

FUGITIVES, THE

Label & Catalog #		Title	Year	VG+	NM
Hideout 1001	(M)	**The Fugitives At Dave's Hideout**	1968	500.00	1,500.00
Justice JLP-141	(S)	**The Fugitives On The Run**	1967	100.00	250.00

FUGS, THE/THE VILLAGE FUGS

The Fugs are ex-Beats poets Tuli Kupferburg and Ed Sanders with Ken Weaver. The Broadside and ESP albums feature backing by Peter Stampfel and Steve Weber, later The Holy Modal Rounders.

Label & Catalog #		Title	Year	VG+	NM
Broadside 304	(M)	**The Village Fugs Sing Ballads Of**			
		Contemporary Protest (With insert)	1966	100.00	250.00
Broadside 304	(M)	**The Village Fugs Sing Ballads Of**			
		Contemporary Protest (Without insert)	1966	80.00	200.00
ESP-Disk' 1018	(M)	**The Fugs First Album**	1966	16.00	40.00
		(Cover reads "Reissue of Broadside 304.)			
ESP-Disk' 1018	(M)	**The Fugs First Album**	1966	60.00	150.00
		(Turquoise & black cover with different back cover)			
ESP-Disk' 1017	(M)	**The Fugs First Album**	196?	12.00	30.00
		(The cover makes no mention of the Broadside original.)			
ESP-Disk' 1017	(M)	**The Fugs First Album**	196?	20.00	50.00
		(Psychedelic wizard cover)			

Label & Catalog #		Title	Year	VG+	NM
ESP-Disk' 1028	(S)	The Fugs	196?	20.00	50.00
		(Black & white cover with the photos on the back staggered.)			
ESP-Disk' 1028	(S)	The Fugs	196?	14.00	35.00
		(Black & white cover with the photos on the back straight.)			
ESP-Disk' 1028	(S)	The Fugs	196?	30.00	75.00
		(The cover is a psychedelic color shield.)			
ESP-Disk' 1038	(S)	Virgin Fugs	1967	40.00	100.00
		(The cover has a sticker that reads " For Adults Minds Only" and was issued with a poster, a flip book, and stickers. This and all subsequent pressings are in partial mono and partial stereo.)			
ESP-Disk' 1038	(S)	Virgin Fugs	1967	20.00	50.00
		(The cover has a sticker that reads " For Adults Minds Only" without the inserts.)			
ESP-Disk' 1038	(S)	Virgin Fugs	1967	20.00	50.00
		("For Adult Minds" is stamped on the back cover.)			
ESP-Disk' 1038	(S)	Virgin Fugs	1967	14.00	35.00
		("For Adult Minds" printed on the front cover.)			
ESP-Disk' 2018	(S)	Fugs 4, Rounders Score	1967	30.00	75.00
Reprise R-6280	(M)	Tenderness Junction	1967	14.00	35.00
Reprise RS-6280	(S)	Tenderness Junction	1967	10.00	25.00
Reprise RS-6305	(S)	It Crawled Into My Hand, Honest	1968	10.00	25.00
Reprise RS-6359	(S)	Belle Of Avenue A	1969	10.00	25.00
Reprise RS-6396	(S)	Golden Filth	1970	10.00	25.00
Olufsen 5009	(S)	Buckets Of Love	1985	20.00	50.00

FULLER, BOBBY/THE BOBBY FULLER FOUR
Mustang M-900	(M)	KRLA King Of The Wheels	1965	60.00	150.00
Mustang MS-900	(S)	KRLA King Of The Wheels	1965	100.00	250.00
Mustang M-901	(M)	I Fought The Law	1966	30.00	75.00
Mustang MS-901	(S)	I Fought The Law	1966	100.00	200.00
		(The mono and stereo versions of "I Fought The Law" contain different takes of several songs. Both Mustang 900 and 901 have been convincingly counterfeited in mono.)			

FULLER, JERRY
| Lin LP-100 | (M) | Teenage Love | 1960 | 100.00 | 250.00 |

FULLER, JESSE
Jesse Fuller is a blues guitar, bass, harmonica and kazzoo and singer and writer of old-time folk music.
World Song EG-027	(10")	Working On The Railroad	195?	60.00	150.00
Cavalier CAV-5006	(10")	Frisco Bound	1955	150.00	300.00
Cavalier CAV-6009	(M)	Frisco Bound	195?	200.00	400.00
Good Time Jazz L-12031	(M)	Work Songs, Blues, Spirituals	1958	16.00	40.00
Good Time Jazz L-10039	(M)	The Lone Cat	1961	16.00	40.00
Good Time Jazz S-10039	(S)	The Lone Cat	1961	20.00	50.00
Folklore FRLP-14006	(M)	San Francisco Bay Blues	1964	10.00	25.00
Folklore FRST-14006	(S)	San Francisco Bay Blues	1964	12.00	30.00

FULSOM, LOWELL/LOWELL FOLSOM
Jewel LP-5003	(M)	In A Heavy Bag	1965	16.00	40.00
Jewel LPS-5003	(S)	In A Heavy Bag	1965	20.00	50.00
Jewel LP-5009	(M)	I've Got The Blues	1965	16.00	40.00
Jewel LPS-5009	(S)	I've Got The Blues	1965	20.00	50.00
Kent KLP-5016	(M)	Lowell Fulson	1965	12.00	30.00
Kent KST-516	(S)	Lowell Fulson	1965	16.00	40.00
Kent KLP-5020	(M)	Tramp	1967	12.00	30.00
Kent KST-520	(S)	Tramp	1967	16.00	40.00
Kent KST-531	(S)	Lowell Fulson Now	1969	12.00	30.00

FUN & GAMES, THE
| Uni 73042 | (S) | Elephant Candy | 1968 | 10.00 | 25.00 |

FUNICELLO, ANNETTE: Refer to ANNETTE

FUNKADELIC
Funkadelic, who also recorded as Parliament, is the brainchild of George Clinton.
Westbound 2000	(S)	Funkadelic	1970	20.00	50.00
Westbound 2001	(S)	Free Your Mind And Your Ass Will Follow	1970	20.00	50.00
Westbound 2007	(S)	Maggot Brain	1971	20.00	50.00

Label & Catalog #		Title	Year	VG+	NM
Westbound 2020	(S)	**America Eats Its Young**	1972	20.00	50.00
Westbound 2022	(S)	**Cosmic Slop**	1973	20.00	50.00
Westbound 1001	(S)	**Standing On The Verge Of Getting It On**	1974	20.00	50.00
Westbound 1004	(S)	**Funkadelic's Greatest Hits**	1975	20.00	50.00
Westbound 215	(S)	**Let's Take It To The Stage**	1975	20.00	50.00
Westbound 216	(S)	**Funkadelic**	1975	14.00	35.00
		(Westbound 216 is a reissue of 2000.)			
Westbound 227	(S)	**Tales Of Kidd Funkadelic**	1976	20.00	50.00
Westbound 303	(S)	**The Best Of The Early Years**	1977	16.00	40.00
— *Westbound albums above have thick vinyl and thick cardboard covers.*—					
Westbound 2001	(S)	**Free Your Mind And Your Ass Will Follow**	198?	8.00	20.00
Westbound 2007	(S)	**Maggot Brain**	198?	8.00	20.00
Westbound 2020	(S)	**America Eats Its Young**	198?	8.00	20.00
Westbound 2022	(S)	**Cosmic Slop**	198?	8.00	20.00
Westbound 1001	(S)	**Standing On The Verge Of Getting It On**	198?	8.00	20.00
Westbound 1004	(S)	**Funkadelic's Greatest Hits**	198?	8.00	20.00
Westbound 215	(S)	**Let's Take It To The Stage**	198?	8.00	20.00
Westbound 216	(S)	**Funkadelic**	1975	8.00	20.00
Westbound 227	(S)	**Tales Of Kidd Funkadelic**	198?	8.00	20.00
Westbound 303	(S)	**The Best Of The Early Years**	198?	8.00	20.00
— *Westbound reissues above have thinner vinyl and thinner cardboard jackets*					
with a space for the UPC bar code on the back cover.—					
Warner Bros. BS-2973	(S)	**Hardcore Jollies**	1976	12.00	30.00
Warner Bros. BS-3209	(S)	**One Nation Under A Groove**	1978	12.00	30.00
Warner Bros. BSK-3371	(S)	**Uncle Jam Wants You**	1979	12.00	30.00
Warner Bros. 3BSK-482	(S)	**The Electric Spanking Of War Babies**	1981	12.00	30.00

FUSE

Fuse features Rick Nielson And Tom Peterson, later of Cheap Trick.

Epic BN-26502	(S)	**Fuse** *(Counterfeits exist)*	1970	16.00	40.00

G. T. O. 'S
Girls Together Outrageously were produced by Frank Zappa.

Straight STS-1059	(S)	**Permanent Damage** *(With booklet)*	1969	50.00	125.00
Straight STS-1059	(S)	**Permanent Damage** *(Without booklet)*	1969	40.00	100.00
Reprise RS-6390	(S)	**Permanent Damage** *(With booklet)*	1970	40.00	100.00
Reprise RS-6390	(S)	**Permanent Damage** *(Without booklet)*	1970	30.00	75.00

GABLES, THE

Fleetwood GAB-1	(M)	**Snake Dance**	196?	150.00	300.00

GABRIEL, PETER
Gabriel was formerly the leader of Genesis.

Direct Disk SD-16615	(S)	**Peter Gabriel**	198?	25.00	75.00
Geffen PRO-	(DJ)	**Peter Gabriel Plays Live**	1983	10.00	25.00

GABRIEL BONDAGE

Dharma D-804	(S)	**Angel Dust** *(Blue vinyl)*	1973	20.00	50.00
Dharma D-808	(S)	**Another Trip To Earth** *(Blue vinyl)*	1979	20.00	50.00
Dharma D-808	(S)	**Another Trip To Earth** *(Red vinyl)*	1979	20.00	50.00
Dharma D-808	(S)	**Another Trip To Earth** *(White vinyl)*	1979	20.00	50.00

GAINER, PATRICK
Patrick Gainer is a rebec player and singer of traditional West Virginia mountain music.

Folk Heritage DB-2122-3	(M)	**Folk Songs Of The Allegheny Mountains**	195?	12.00	30.00

GALAHADS, THE

Liberty LRP-3371	(M)	**The Galahads**	1964	8.00	20.00
Liberty LST-7371	(S)	**The Galahads**	1964	10.00	25.00

GALE, SUNNY

RCA Victor LPM-1277	(M)	**Sunny And Blue**	1956	16.00	40.00
Warwick W-2018	(M)	**Sunny**	1960	12.00	30.00

GALVIN, PATRICK

Stinson SLP-83	(10")	**Irish Rebel Songs, Vol. 1**	195?	16.00	40.00
Stinson SLP-84	(10")	**Irish Rebel Songs, Vol. 2**	195?	16.00	40.00
Stinson SLP-835	(10")	**Irish Rebel Songs, Vol. 3**	195?	16.00	40.00
Riverside RLP-12-604	(M)	**Irish Drinking Songs**	195?	12.00	30.00
Riverside RLP-12-608	(M)	**Irish Love Songs**	195?	12.00	30.00
Riverside RLP-12-613	(M)	**Irish Street Songs**	195?	12.00	30.00
Riverside RLP-12-616	(M)	**Irish Humor Songs**	195?	12.00	30.00

GANDALF

Capitol ST-121	(S)	**Gandalf**	1969	80.00	200.00

GANDALF THE GREY

G.W.R. 7	(S)	**The Grey Wizard Am I**	196?	150.00	300.00

GANT, CECIL

Red Mill *(No number)*	(M)	**Cecil Gant** *(Red vinyl)*	1956	150.00	300.00
King 671	(M)	**Cecil Gant**	1958	60.00	150.00
Sound 601	(M)	**The Incomparable Cecil Gant**	1958	40.00	100.00

GANTS, THE

Liberty LRP-3432	(M)	**Road Runner**	1965	12.00	30.00
Liberty LST-7432	(S)	**Road Runner**	1965	16.00	40.00
		("Road Runner" is rechanneled.)			
Liberty LRP-3455	(M)	**The Gants Galore**	1966	12.00	30.00
Liberty LST-7455	(S)	**The Gants Galore**	1966	16.00	40.00
Liberty LRP-3473	(M)	**The Gants Again**	1966	12.00	30.00
Liberty LST-7473	(S)	**The Gants Again**	1966	16.00	40.00

Label & Catalog #		Title	Year	VG+	NM
GARAGIOLA, JOE					
Joe was formerly a member of The Pittsburgh Pirates.					
United Arts. UAL-3032	(M)	**That Holler Guy**	1959	16.00	40.00
United Arts. UAS-6032	(S)	**That Holler Guy**	1959	20.00	50.00
GARBO, GRETA					
MGM E-4201	(M)	Garbo	1964	16.00	40.00
MGM SE-4201	(E)	Garbo	1964	12.00	30.00
GARCIA, JERRY					
Refer to The Grateful Dead; Old & In The Way; Merl Saunders; Howard Wales.					
Warner Bros. BS-2582	(S)	**Garcia**	1972	10.00	25.00
Round RX-102	(S)	**Garcia**	1974	10.00	25.00
Round RX-107	(S)	**Reflections**	1975	10.00	25.00
GARDELL, TONY					
Cavalier LP-6005	(M)	**A-Roving With Tony Gardell**	1958	12.00	30.00
GARDNER, "BROTHER" DAVE					
RCA Victor LPM-2083	(M)	**Rejoice, Dear Hearts**	1959	8.00	20.00
RCA Victor LSP-2083	(S)	**Rejoice, Dear Hearts**	1959	10.00	25.00
RCA Victor LPM-2239	(M)	**Kick Thy Own Self**	1960	8.00	20.00
RCA Victor LSP-2239	(S)	**Kick Thy Own Self**	1960	10.00	25.00
RCA Victor LPM-2335	(M)	**Ain't That Weird**	1961	8.00	20.00
RCA Victor LSP-2335	(S)	**Ain't That Weird**	1961	10.00	25.00
RCA Victor LPM-2498	(M)	**Did You Ever...**	1962	8.00	20.00
RCA Victor LSP-2498	(S)	**Did You Ever...**	1962	10.00	25.00
RCA Victor LPM-2628	(M)	**All Seriousness Aside**	1963	8.00	20.00
RCA Victor LSP-2628	(S)	**All Seriousness Aside**	1963	10.00	25.00
		—RCA mono albums above have "Long Play" on the bottom of the label; stereo albums have "Living Stereo" on the bottom.—			
GARDNER, DON, & DEE DEE FORD					
Fire LP-105	(M)	**Need Your Lovin'**	1962	200.00	400.00
Sue LP-1044	(M)	**Don Gardner & Dee Dee Ford In Sweden**	1965	40.00	100.00
GARDNERS, THE					
Prestige Int. PRLP-13062	(M)	**Folk Songs Far And Near**	1962	12.00	30.00
GARFUNKEL, ART					
Refer to Simon & Garfunkel.					
Columbia JC-34975	(S)	**Watermark** *(With unreleased tracks)*	1978	40.00	100.00
		(Original test and stock pressings of JC-34975 contain several tracks deleted from subsequent pressings. Test pressings with these tracks are also worth $100 in Near Mint condition.)			
GARLAND, HANK					
Hank also recorded as a member of The Nashville All-Stars.					
Sesac N-2301/2	(M)	**Subtle Swing**	196?	40.00	100.00
Columbia CL-1572	(M)	**Jazz Winds From A New Direction**	1961	16.00	40.00
Columbia CS-8372	(S)	**Jazz Winds From A New Direction**	1961	20.00	50.00
Columbia CL-1913	(M)	**The Unforgettable Guitar Of Hank Garland**	1962	16.00	40.00
Columbia CS-8713	(S)	**The Unforgettable Guitar Of Hank Garland**	1962	20.00	50.00
		— Columbia albums above have six white-on-black "eye" logos around the perimeter of the label.—			
H.G. 1001 LPS	(S)	**Jazz In New York**	197?	20.00	50.00
GARLAND, JUDY					
MGM E-501	(10")	**Tills The Clouds Roll By** *(Soundtrack)*	1950	40.00	100.00
MGM E-502	(10")	**Easter Parade** *(Soundtrack)*	1950	40.00	100.00
MGM E-505	(10")	**Words And Music** *(Soundtrack)*	1950	40.00	100.00
MGM E-519	(10")	**Summer Stock** *(Soundtrack)*	1950	40.00	100.00
MGM E-21	(10")	**The Pirate / Summer Stock** *(Soundtracks)*	1951	40.00	100.00
MGM E-82	(10")	**Judy Garland Sings**	1951	30.00	75.00
MGM E-3149	(M)	**If You Feel Like Singing, Sing**	1955	30.00	75.00
MGM E-3227	(M)	**Easter Parade** *(Soundtrack)*	1955	30.00	75.00
MGM E-3231	(M)	**Tills The Clouds Roll By** *(Soundtrack)*	1955	30.00	75.00
MGM E-3232	(M)	**In The Good Old Summertime** *(Soundtrack)*	1955	30.00	75.00
MGM E-3233	(M)	**Words And Music** *(Soundtrack)*	1955	30.00	75.00
MGM E-3234	(M)	**Summer Stock / The Pirate** *(Soundtracks)*	1955	30.00	75.00

Former player Joe Garagiola met with great success as a sportscaster, where his flamboyant, exclama-
tory style earned him the nickname "that holler guy," from whence the title of this album. While it is
doubtful that collectors of any known musical form would have this on their want-list, the fact that ol'
Joe is posing with, from left to right, Mickey Mantle, Stan Musial, Yogi Berra and Ken Boyer, should
make this of interest to baseball fans in general and Yankees and Cardinals fans in particular. Which
means this is one of those albums that has more value as a sports collectible than as a record!

Label & Catalog #		Title	Year	VG+	NM
MGM E-3249	(M)	**Judy Garland With The MGM Orchestra**	1956	30.00	75.00
MGM E-3464	(M)	**The Wizard Of Oz** (Soundtrack)	1956	50.00	125.00
		(Original covers are yellow with a photo.)			
MGM E-3770	(M)	**Tills The Clouds Roll By** (Soundtrack)	1959	20.00	50.00
MGM E-3771	(M)	**Words & Music / Good News** (Soundtracks)	1959	20.00	50.00
		— MGM albums above have yellow labels.—			
MGM E-3464	(M)	**The Wizard Of Oz** (Yellow photo cover)	1959	40.00	100.00
MGM E-3464	(M)	**The Wizard Of Oz** (White drawing cover)	1962	12.00	30.00
MGM E-3989	(M)	**The Star Years**	1962	12.00	30.00
MGM E-3996	(M)	**The Wizard Of Oz**	1962	12.00	30.00
MGM SE-3996	(E)	**The Wizard Of Oz**	1962	10.00	25.00
MGM E-4005	(M)	**The Hollywood Years**	1962	12.00	30.00
MGM E-4204	(M)	**The Very Best Of Judy Garland**	1962	12.00	30.00
		— MGM albums above have black labels.—			
Capitol T-676	(M)	**Miss Show Business**	1955	16.00	40.00
Capitol T-734	(M)	**Judy**	1956	16.00	40.00
Capitol T-835	(M)	**Alone**	1957	14.00	35.00
		— Capitol albums above have turquoise labels.—			
Capitol T-1036	(M)	**In Love**	1958	14.00	35.00
Capitol ST-1036	(S)	**In Love**	1958	20.00	50.00
Capitol T-1118	(M)	**Garland At The Grove**	1959	14.00	35.00
Capitol ST-1118	(S)	**Garland At The Grove**	1959	20.00	50.00
Capitol T-1188	(M)	**The Letter** (With letter attached to cover)	1959	20.00	50.00
Capitol ST-1188	(S)	**The Letter** (With letter attached to cover)	1959	30.00	75.00
Capitol T-1188	(M)	**The Letter** (Without the letter)	1959	12.00	30.00
Capitol ST-1188	(S)	**The Letter** (Without the letter)	1959	16.00	40.00
Capitol T-1467	(M)	**That's Entertainment**	1960	10.00	25.00
Capitol ST-1467	(S)	**That's Entertainment**	1960	14.00	35.00
Capitol WBO-1569	(M)	**Judy At Carnegie Hall**	1961	10.00	25.00
Capitol SWBO-1569	(S)	**Judy At Carnegie Hall**	1961	14.00	35.00
		— Capitol albums above have black labels with the Capitol logo on the left side.—			
Capitol W-1710	(M)	**The Garland Touch**	1962	10.00	25.00
Capitol SW-1710	(S)	**The Garland Touch**	1962	12.00	30.00
Capitol W-1861	(M)	**I Could Go On Singing** (Soundtrack)	1963	20.00	50.00
Capitol SW-1861	(S)	**I Could Go On Singing** (Soundtrack)	1963	30.00	75.00
Capitol T-1941	(M)	**Our Love Letter**	1963	10.00	25.00
Capitol ST-1941	(S)	**Our Love Letter**	1963	12.00	30.00
Capitol T-1999	(M)	**The Hits Of Judy Garland**	1963	8.00	20.00
Capitol ST-1999	(S)	**The Hits Of Judy Garland**	1963	10.00	25.00
Capitol W-2062	(M)	**Just For Openers**	1964	8.00	20.00
Capitol DW-2062	(S)	**Just For Openers**	1964	10.00	25.00
Capitol STCL-2988	(S)	**The Judy Garland Deluxe Set** (3 LP box)	1967	16.00	40.00
		— Capitol albums above have black labels with the Capitol logo on top.—			
Decca DL-6020 (10")	(M)	**Judy At The Palace**	1952	30.00	75.00
Decca DL-5152 (10")	(M)	**The Wizard Of Oz**	1951	50.00	125.00
Decca DL-5412 (10")	(M)	**Girl Crazy** (Soundtrack)	1953	40.00	100.00
Decca DL-8190	(M)	**Judy Garland's Greatest Performances**	1955	16.00	40.00
Decca DL-8387	(M)	**The Wizard Of Oz**	1957	16.00	40.00
Decca DL-8498	(M)	**Meet Me In St. Louis /**			
		The Harvey Girls (Soundtracks)	1957	60.00	150.00
Decca DL-4199	(M)	**The Magic Of Judy Garland**	1961	12.00	30.00
Decca DXB-172	(M)	**The Best Of Judy Garland** (2 LPs)	1964	8.00	20.00
Decca DXSB-7172	(S)	**The Best Of Judy Garland** (2 LPs)	1964	10.00	25.00
Columbia CL-1101	(M)	**A Star Is Born** (Soundtrack; boxed set)	1958	54.00	100.00
Columbia CL-1101	(M)	**A Star Is Born** (Soundtrack)	1958	20.00	50.00
Columbia CL-1940	(M)	**A Star Is Born** (Soundtrack)	1963	10.00	25.00
Columbia CS-8740	(E)	**A Star Is Born** (Soundtrack)	1963	6.00	15.00
Colpix CP-507	(M)	**Pepe** (Soundtrack)	1961	30.00	75.00
Colpix SCP-507	(S)	**Pepe** (Soundtrack)	1961	50.00	125.00
Warner Bros. B-1479	(M)	**Gay Purr-ee** (Soundtrack)	1962	20.00	50.00
Warner Bros. BS-1479	(S)	**Gay Purr-ee** (Soundtrack)	1962	30.00	75.00
ABC 620	(M)	**Judy Garland At Home At The Palace**	1967	8.00	20.00
ABC S-620	(S)	**Judy Garland At Home At The Palace**	1967	10.00	25.00
Mark-56	(S)	**Live In San Francisco** (Picture disc)	1978	20.00	50.00

GARNETT, GALE

RCA Victor LPM-2833	(M)	**My Kind Of Folk Songs**	1964	8.00	20.00
RCA Victor LSP-2833	(S)	**My Kind Of Folk Songs**	1964	10.00	25.00

Label & Catalog #		Title	Year	VG+	NM
RCA Victor LSP-3305	(M)	Lovin' Place	1965	8.00	20.00
RCA Victor LSP-3305	(S)	Lovin' Place	1965	10.00	25.00
RCA Victor LPM-3325	(M)	The Many Faces Of Gale Garnett	1965	8.00	20.00
RCA Victor LSP-3325	(S)	The Many Faces Of Gale Garnett	1965	10.00	25.00
RCA Victor LPM-3498	(M)	Variety Is The Spice Of Gale Garnett	1966	8.00	20.00
RCA Victor LSP-3498	(S)	Variety Is The Spice Of Gale Garnett	1966	10.00	25.00
RCA Victor LPM-3586	(M)	New Adventures	1966	8.00	20.00
RCA Victor LSP-3586	(S)	New Adventures	1966	10.00	25.00
RCA Victor LPM-3747	(M)	Flying And Rainbows And Love	1967	8.00	20.00
RCA Victor LSP-3747	(S)	Flying And Rainbows And Love	1967	10.00	25.00

GARY, JOHN
Refer to Ann-Margret & John Gary.

LaBrea 8010	(M)	John Gary	1961	10.00	25.00
LaBrea S-8010	(S)	John Gary	1961	12.00	30.00

GARY, SAM

Transition TRLP-F-1	(M)	Spirituals And Worksongs	1958	12.00	30.00

GATES, HEN, & HIS GATERS

Masterseal M-700	(M)	Let's Go Dancing To Rock And Roll	195?	20.00	50.00
Plymouth R12-144	(M)	Rock And Roll	1956	20.00	50.00

GATEWAY SINGERS, THE
The Gateway Singers—Travis Edmonson, Lou Gottlieb, Elmerlee Thomas and Jerry Walter—are a contemporary folk/pop group. Refer to The Limeliters.

Decca DL-8413	(M)	Puttin' On The Style	1958	16.00	40.00
Decca DL-8671	(M)	The Gateway Singers At The Hungry i	1958	16.00	40.00
Decca DL-8742	(M)	The Gateway Singers In Hi Fi	1958	16.00	40.00
Warner Bros. W-1295	(M)	The Gateway Singers On The Lot	1959	12.00	30.00
Warner Bros. WS-1295	(S)	The Gateway Singers On The Lot	1959	16.00	40.00
Warner Bros. W-1334	(M)	Wagons West	1960	12.00	30.00
Warner Bros. WS-1334	(S)	Wagons West	1960	16.00	40.00
MGM E-3905	(M)	Down In The Valley	1961	10.00	25.00
MGM SE-3905	(S)	Down In The Valley	1961	12.00	30.00
MGM E-4154	(M)	Hootenanny	1963	10.00	25.00
MGM SE-4154	(S)	Hootenanny	1963	12.00	30.00

GATLIN BROTHERS, THE

Columbia HC-48135	(S)	Sure Feels Like Love *(Half-soeed master)*	198?	25.00	75.00

GAUCHOS, THE

ABC-Paramount ABC-506	(M)	The Gauchos Featuring Jim Doval	1965	10.00	25.00
ABC-Paramount ABCS-506	(S)	The Gauchos Featuring Jim Doval	1965	12.00	30.00

GAVIN, KEVIN: *Refer to* **GOLDMINE'S PRICE GUIDE TO COLLECTIBLE JAZZ ALBUMS**

GAYE, MARVIN
Marvin also recorded with Diana Ross; Mary Wells & Marvin Gaye.

Tamla T-221	(M)	Soulful Moods Of Marvin Gaye	1961	500.00	1,000.00
Tamla T-239	(M)	That Stubborn Kind Of Fella	1963	300.00	600.00
Tamla T-242	(M)	Recorded Live On Stage	1963	150.00	300.00
Tamla T-251	(M)	When I'm Alone I Cry	1964	60.00	150.00
Tamla T-252	(M)	Marvin Gaye's Greatest Hits	1964	10.00	25.00
Tamla TS-252	(S)	Marvin Gaye's Greatest Hits	1964	12.00	30.00
Tamla T-258	(M)	How Sweet It Is To Be Loved By You	1965	16.00	40.00
Tamla TS-258	(S)	How Sweet It Is To Be Loved By You	1965	20.00	50.00
Tamla T-259	(M)	Hello Broadway, This Is Marvin	1965	16.00	40.00
Tamla TS-259	(S)	Hello Broadway, This Is Marvin	1965	20.00	50.00
Tamla T-261	(M)	Tribute To The Great Nat King Cole	1965	16.00	40.00
Tamla TS-261	(S)	Tribute To The Great Nat King Cole	1965	20.00	50.00
Tamla T-266	(M)	Moods Of Marvin Gaye	1966	12.00	30.00
Tamla TS-266	(S)	Moods Of Marvin Gaye	1966	16.00	40.00
Tamla T-278	(M)	Marvin Gaye's Greatest Hits, Volume 2	1967	10.00	25.00
Tamla TS-278	(S)	Marvin Gaye's Greatest Hits, Volume 2	1967	12.00	30.00

—Tamla albums above have two side-by-side circles at the top of the label.—

Tamla T-285	(M)	In The Groove	1968	20.00	50.00
Tamla TS-285	(S)	In The Groove	1968	12.00	30.00

Label & Catalog #		Title	Year	VG+	NM
Tamla TS-285	(S)	I Heard It Through The Grapevine	1968	10.00	25.00
		("Grapevine" is a repackage of "In The Groove.")			
Tamla TS-292	(S)	M. P. G.	1969	10.00	25.00
Tamla TS-293	(S)	Marvin Gaye And His Girls	1969	10.00	25.00
		(Duets with Tammi Terrell and Kim Weston.)			

GAYE, MARVIN, & TAMI TERRELL

Label & Catalog #		Title	Year	VG+	NM
Tamla T-277	(M)	United	1967	10.00	25.00
Tamla TS-277	(S)	United	1967	12.00	30.00
		—Tamla albums above have two side-by-side circles at the top of the label.—			
Tamla T-284	(M)	You're All I Need (White label promo)	1968	20.00	50.00
Tamla TS-284	(S)	You're All I Need	1968	10.00	25.00
Tamla TS-294	(S)	Easy	1969	10.00	25.00

GAYE, MARVIN, & KIM WESTON

Label & Catalog #		Title	Year	VG+	NM
Tamla T-270	(M)	Marvin Gaye And Kim Weston	1966	12.00	30.00
Tamla TS-270	(S)	Marvin Gaye And Kim Weston	1966	16.00	40.00
		—Tamla albums above have two side-by-side circles at the top of the label.—			

GAYLE, CRYSTAL

Label & Catalog #		Title	Year	VG+	NM
United Artists LA-856	(DJ)	Somebody Loves You (Picture disc)	1978	20.00	50.00

GAYLORDS, THE

Label & Catalog #		Title	Year	VG+	NM
Mercury MG-25198	(10")	By Request	1955	20.00	50.00
Mercury MG-20186	(M)	Italia	1957	14.00	35.00
Mercury MG-20356	(M)	Let's Have A Pizza Party	1958	10.00	25.00
Mercury SR-60075	(S)	Let's Have A Pizza Party	1959	14.00	35.00
Mercury MG-20???	(M)	That's Amore	1959	10.00	25.00
Mercury SR-60102	(S)	That's Amore	1959	14.00	35.00
Mercury MG-20620	(M)	American Hits In Italian	1961	8.00	20.00
Mercury SR-60620	(S)	American Hits In Italian	1961	10.00	25.00
Mercury MG-20695	(M)	The Gaylords At The Shamrock	1962	8.00	20.00
Mercury SR-60695	(S)	The Gaylords At The Shamrock	1962	10.00	25.00
Mercury MG-20742	(M)	Party Style	1963	8.00	20.00
Mercury SR-60742	(S)	Party Style	1963	10.00	25.00
		—Mercury albums above have black labels with silver print.—			

GAYNOR, MITZI

Label & Catalog #		Title	Year	VG+	NM
Verve MGV-2110	(M)	Mitzi	1959	16.00	40.00
Verve MGVS-6014	(S)	Mitzi	1959	20.00	50.00
Verve MGV-2115	(M)	Mitzi Gaynor Sings The Lyrics Of Ira Gershwin	1959	16.00	40.00
Verve MGVS-6049	(S)	Mitzi Gaynor Sings The Lyrics Of Ira Gershwin	1959	20.00	50.00

GEEZINSLAW BROTHERS, THE
The Geezinslaws are Sam Allred and Dwayne Smith.

Label & Catalog #		Title	Year	VG+	NM
Columbia CS-8900	(M)	The Rocky World Of The Geezinslaw Brothers	1963	8.00	20.00
Columbia CS-8900	(S)	The Rocky World Of The Geezinslaw Brothers	1963	10.00	25.00

GENE & DEBBIE

Label & Catalog #		Title	Year	VG+	NM
T.R.X. LPS-1001	(S)	Hear And Now	1968	10.00	25.00

GENESIS
Genesis features Peter Gabriel And Phil Collins.

Label & Catalog #		Title	Year	VG+	NM
Impulse ASD-9205	(S)	Trespass	1971	10.00	25.00
Mobile Fidelity MFSL-062	(S)	A Trick Of The Tail	1981	13.00	40.00

GENTLE SOUL

Label & Catalog #		Title	Year	VG+	NM
Epic BN-26374	(S)	Gentle Soul	1968	10.00	25.00

GENTRYS, THE

Label & Catalog #		Title	Year	VG+	NM
MGM E-4336	(M)	Keep On Dancing	1965	10.00	25.00
MGM SE-4336	(P)	Keep On Dancing	1965	12.00	30.00
MGM E-4346	(M)	Time	1966	10.00	25.00
MGM SE-4346	(S)	Time	1966	12.00	30.00
Sun 117	(S)	The Gentrys	1970	20.00	50.00

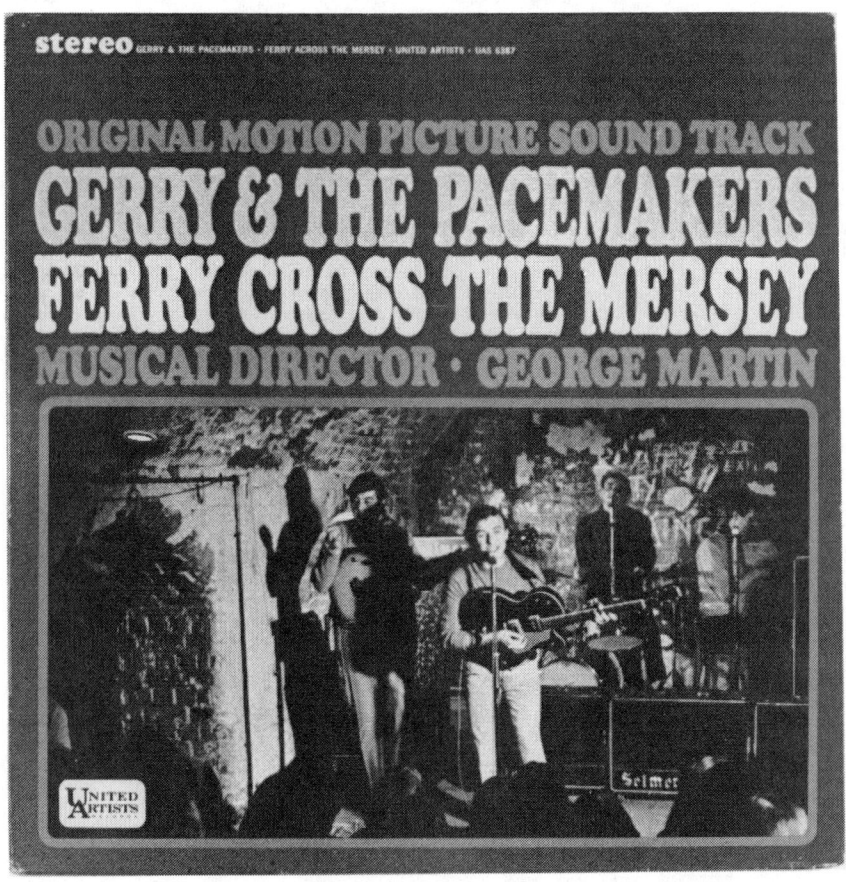

Gerry Marsden and his Pacemakers were one of the Merseyside's top talents, considered by some as on a par with The Beatles in 1962. When the Fan Four intentionally did a poor performance of the song that their label had chosen for them as their first single, the song was handed to Marsden, who took "How Do You Do It" to the top of the British charts, the first local act to achieve the #1 spot. While the group's star has diminished over the years, their one film effort, Ferry Cross The Mersey, remains a highlight of the British Invasion, perhaps not in the league with A Hard Day's Night, but certainly one of the best rock'n roll movies of the '60s. The soundtrack cover features a great photo of the Pacemakers performing in Liverpool's legendary Cavern.

Label & Catalog #		Title	Year	VG+	NM
GEORDIE					
MGM SE-4903	(S)	**Hope You Like It**	1973	12.00	30.00
GEORGE, BARBARA					
A.F.O. 5001	(M)	**I Know (You Don't Love Me Anymore)**	1962	100.00	250.00
GERONIMO BLACK					
Uni 73132	(S)	**Geronimo Black**	1972	10.00	25.00
GERRY & THE PACEMAKERS					
Laurie LLP-2024	(M)	**Don't Let The Sun Catch You Crying**	1964	16.00	40.00
Laurie SLP-2024	(E)	**Don't Let The Sun Catch You Crying**	1964	14.00	35.00
Laurie DT-90555	(E)	**Don't Let The Sun Catch You Crying** (Capitol Record Club)	1965	20.00	50.00
Laurie LLP-2027	(M)	**Gerry & The Pacemakers' Second Album**	1964	16.00	40.00
Laurie SLLP-2027	(E)	**Gerry & The Pacemakers' Second Album**	1964	14.00	35.00
Laurie LLP-2030	(M)	**I'll Be There**	1964	16.00	40.00
Laurie SLLP-2030	(E)	**I'll Be There**	1964	14.00	35.00
United Arts. UAL-3387	(M)	**Ferry Cross The Mersey** (Soundtrack)	1965	14.00	35.00
United Arts. UAS-6387	(S)	**Ferry Cross The Mersey** (Soundtrack)	1965	20.00	50.00
Capitol T-90812	(M)	**Ferry Cross The Mersey** (Soundtrack)	1965	20.00	50.00
Capitol ST-90812	(S)	**Ferry Cross The Mersey** (Soundtrack)	1965	30.00	75.00
		(Capitol Record Club release with completely different front cover.)			
Laurie LLP-2031	(M)	**Gerry & The Pacemakers' Greatest Hits**	1965	12.00	30.00
Laurie SLLP-2031	(E)	**Gerry & The Pacemakers' Greatest Hits**	1965	12.00	30.00
Laurie T-90384	(M)	**Gerry & The Pacemakers' Greatest Hits** (Capitol Record Club)	1965	16.00	40.00
Laurie LLP-2037	(M)	**Girl On A Swing**	1966	14.00	35.00
Laurie SLP-2037	(E)	**Girl On A Swing**	1966	14.00	35.00
GHOULS, THE					
The Ghouls are a creation of Gary Usher & Co.					
Capitol T-2215	(M)	**Dracula's Deuce**	1965	60.00	150.00
Capitol ST-2215	(S)	**Dracula's Deuce**	1965	80.00	200.00
GIBB, ROBIN					
Robin Gibb is a member of The Bee Gees.					
Atco SD-33-323	(S)	**Robin's Reign**	1970	8.00	20.00
GIBBS, GEORGIA					
Coral CRL-56037	(10")	**Ballin' The Jack**	1951	20.00	50.00
Mercury MG-25175	(10")	**Georgia Gibbs Sings Oldies**	1953	20.00	50.00
Mercury MG-25199	(10")	**The Man That Got Away**	1954	20.00	50.00
Mercury MG-20071	(M)	**Music And Memories**	1956	16.00	40.00
Mercury MG-20114	(M)	**Song Favorites**	1956	16.00	40.00
Mercury MG-20170	(M)	**Swingin' With Her Nibs**	1956	16.00	40.00
Coral CRL-57183	(M)	**Her Nibs**	1957	12.00	35.00
GIBSON, BOB					
Bob Gibson was a guitar and banjo player, singer and songwriter whose early '50s work in the popular folk vein paved the way for the boom of the latter half of that decade.					
Stinson SLP-76	(10")	**Folksongs Of Ohio**	195?	20.00	50.00
Riverside RLP-12-802	(M)	**Offbeat Folk Songs**	1957	16.00	40.00
Riverside RLP-12-806	(M)	**I Come For To Sing**	1957	16.00	40.00
Riverside RLP-12-816	(M)	**Carnegie Concert**	1958	16.00	40.00
Riverside RLP-12-830	(M)	**There's A Meetin' Here Tonight**	1958	16.00	40.00
Riverside RLP-1111	(S)	**There's A Meetin' Here Tonight**	1959	20.00	50.00
Elektra EKL-177	(M)	**Ski Songs**	1959	10.00	25.00
Elektra EKS-7177	(S)	**Ski Songs**	1959	12.00	30.00
Elektra EKL-197	(M)	**Yes I See**	1961	8.00	20.00
Elektra EKS-7197	(S)	**Yes I See**	1961	10.00	25.00
Elektra EKL-239	(M)	**Where I'm Bound**	1963	8.00	20.00
Elektra EKS-7239	(S)	**Where I'm Bound**	1963	10.00	25.00
Riverside RLP-542	(M)	**Hootenanny At Carnegie**	1963	8.00	20.00
Riverside RS-9542	(S)	**Hootenanny At Carnegie**	1963	8.00	20.00
GIBSON, BOB, & BOB CAMP					
Elektra EKL-207	(M)	**At The Gate Of Horn**	1961	8.00	20.00
Elektra EKS-7207	(S)	**At The Gate Of Horn**	1961	10.00	25.00

Label & Catalog #		Title	Year	VG+	NM
GIBSON, DON					
Refer to Dottie West & Don Gibson.					
Lion L-70069	(M)	**Songs By Don Gibson**	1958	40.00	100.00
RCA Victor LPM-1743	(M)	**Oh Lonesome Me**	1958	16.00	50.00
RCA Victor LPM-1918	(M)	**No One Stands Alone**	1959	14.00	35.00
RCA Victor LSP-1918	(S)	**No One Stands Alone**	1959	20.00	50.00
RCA Victor LPM-2038	(M)	**That Gibson Boy**	1959	14.00	35.00
RCA Victor LSP-2038	(S)	**That Gibson Boy**	1959	20.00	50.00
RCA Victor LPM-2184	(M)	**Look Who's Blue**	1960	14.00	35.00
RCA Victor LSP-2184	(S)	**Look Who's Blue**	1960	20.00	50.00
RCA Victor LPM-2269	(M)	**Sweet Dreams**	1960	14.00	35.00
RCA Victor LSP-2269	(S)	**Sweet Dreams**	1960	20.00	50.00
RCA Victor LPM-2361	(M)	**Girls, Guitars And Gibson**	1961	14.00	35.00
RCA Victor LSP-2361	(S)	**Girls, Guitars And Gibson**	1961	20.00	50.00
RCA Victor LPM-2448	(M)	**Some Favorites Of Mine**	1962	14.00	35.00
RCA Victor LSP-2448	(S)	**Some Favorites Of Mine**	1962	20.00	50.00
RCA Victor LPM-2702	(M)	**I Wrote A Song**	1963	14.00	35.00
RCA Victor LSP-2702	(S)	**I Wrote A Song**	1963	20.00	50.00
		— RCA mono albums above have "Long Play" on the bottom of the label;			
		stereo albums have "Living Stereo" on the bottom. —			
RCA Victor LPM-2878	(M)	**God Walks These Hills**	1964	8.00	20.00
RCA Victor LSP-2878	(S)	**God Walks These Hills**	1964	10.00	25.00
RCA Victor LPM-3376	(M)	**The Best Of Don Gibson**	1965	8.00	20.00
RCA Victor LSP-3376	(S)	**The Best Of Don Gibson**	1965	10.00	25.00
RCA Victor LPM-3470	(M)	**Too Much Hurt**	1965	8.00	20.00
RCA Victor LSP-3470	(S)	**Too Much Hurt**	1965	10.00	25.00
RCA Victor LPM-3594	(M)	**Don Gibson With Spanish Guitar**	1966	8.00	20.00
RCA Victor LSP-3594	(S)	**Don Gibson With Spanish Guitar**	1966	10.00	25.00
RCA Victor LPM-3680	(M)	**Great Country Songs**	1966	8.00	20.00
RCA Victor LSP-3680	(S)	**Great Country Songs**	1966	10.00	25.00
RCA Victor LPM-3843	(M)	**All My Love**	1967	8.00	20.00
RCA Victor LSP-3843	(S)	**All My Love**	1967	10.00	25.00
RCA Victor LPM-3974	(M)	**The King Of Country Soul**	1968	20.00	50.00
RCA Victor LSP-3974	(S)	**The King Of Country Soul**	1968	8.00	20.00
RCA Victor LSP-4053	(S)	**More Country Soul**	1968	8.00	20.00
		— RCA albums above have black labels. —			
GIBSON, STEVE, & THE RED CAPS					
Many of The Red Caps' sides feature vocalist Damita Jo.					
Mercury MG-25115	(10")	**You're Driving Me Crazy**	1954	200.00	400.00
Mercury MG-25116	(10")	**Blueberry Hill**	1954	200.00	400.00
GILBERT, ANN: *Refer to* **GOLDMINE'S PRICE GUIDE TO COLLECTIBLE JAZZ ALBUMS**					
GILBERT, JOHN					
(No label)	(S)	**Mead River**	1971	30.00	75.00
GILBERTO, ASTRUD: *Refer to* **GOLDMINE'S PRICE GUIDE TO COLLECTIBLE JAZZ ALBUMS**					
GILES, GILES & FRIPP					
GG&F features Robert Fripp, later of King Crimson.					
Deram DES-18019	(S)	**Cheerful Insanity Of Giles, Giles & Fripp**	1968	16.00	40.00
GILKYSON, TERRY					
Decca DL-5263	(10")	**Folk Songs**	1950	20.00	50.00
Decca DL-5457	(10")	**Golden Minutes Of Folk Music**	1952	20.00	50.00
GILL, GEULA: *Refer to* **THEODORE BIKEL & GEULA GILL**					
GILLESPIE, DARLENE					
Disneyland WDL-3010	(M)	**Top Tunes Of The '50s**	1958	40.00	100.00
Disneyland WDL-1006	(M)	**Top Tunes Of The '50s**	196?	20.00	50.00
		(WDL-1006 is a reissue of 3010.)			
GILLEY, MICKEY					
Astro 101	(M)	**Lonely Wine**	1964	150.00	300.00
Paula LP-2195	(M)	**Down The Line**	1967	16.00	40.00
Paula LPS-2195	(S)	**Down The Line**	1967	20.00	50.00

Label & Catalog #		Title	Year	VG+	NM

GILMER, JIMMY, & THE FIREBALLS: *Refer to* THE FIREBALLS

GILMER, JULIA ANN

ABC-Paramount ABC-168	(M)	**Cads, Blackguards And False True-Loves**	195?	12.00	30.00

GINANDES, SHEP
Shep Ginandes is a guitar and vielle player and singer of traditional folk songs in many languages.

Elektra EKL-4	(10")	**British Traditional Ballads In America**	195?	20.00	50.00
Elektra EKL-7	(10")	**American Folksongs For Children**	195?	20.00	50.00
Elektra EKL-133	(M)	**Shep Ginandes Sings Folksongs**	195?	12.00	30.00

GINNY & GALLIONS

Downey DS-1003	(S)	**Two Sides Of Ginny And Gallions**	1964	14.00	35.00

GINSBERG, ALLEN

Fantasy F-7006	(M)	**Howl And Other Poems** *(Red vinyl)*	1959	150.000	300.00
Fantasy F-7006	(M)	**Howl And Other Poems** *(Black vinyl)*	1959	75.00	150.00
		—Fantasy albums above have red labels on non-flexible vinyl.—			
Atlantic 4001	(M)	**Allen Ginsberg Reads Kaddish**	1966	10.00	25.00

GITTER, DEAN

Riverside RLP-12-636	(M)	**Ghost Ballads**	195?	12.00	30.00

GLACIERS, THE

Mercury MG-20895	(M)	**From Sea To Ski**	1964	8.00	20.00
Mercury SR-60895	(S)	**From Sea To Ski**	1964	10.00	25.00

GLASER, JIM
Refer to Tompall Glaser & The Glaser Brothers.

Starday SLP-158	(M)	**Just Looking For A Home** *(Yellow label)*	1961	20.00	50.00

GLASER, JOE

Folkways FA-2039	(10")	**The Songs Of Joe Hill**	195?	30.00	75.00

GLASER, TOMPALL
Tompall and his brothers Charlie and Jim Glaser.

United Arts. UAL-3540	(M)	**The Ballad Of Namu The Killer Whale**	1966	8.00	20.00
United Arts. UAS-6540	(S)	**The Ballad Of Namu The Killer Whale**	1966	10.00	25.00

GLASER, TOMPALL, & THE GLASER BROTHERS)
Tompall and his brothers Charlie and Jim Glaser.

Decca DL-4041	(M)	**This Land**	1960	12.00	30.00
Decca DL-74041	(S)	**This Land**	1960	16.00	40.00

GLASS HARP, THE
The Glass Harp features lead guitarist Phil Keaggy.

Decca DL-75261	(S)	**Glass Harp**	1971	10.00	25.00
Decca DL-75306	(S)	**Synergy**	1971	12.00	30.00
Decca DL-75358	(S)	**It Makes Me Glad**	1972	12.00	30.00

GLAZER, JOE
Joe Glazer, a.k.a. "The Political Minstrel" and "Labor's Troubador," is a guitar player, singer and writer of traditional and topical folk songs.

Folkways FP-39	(10")	**Songs Of Joe Hill**	195?	30.00	75.00
Folkways FA-2039	(10")	**Songs Of Joe Hill**	195?	30.00	75.00

GLAZER, TOM / RICHARD DYER-BENNETT
Refer to Richard Dyer-Bennett.

Mercury MG-20007	(M)	**Olden Ballads**	1955	20.00	50.00

GLAZER, TOM
Tom Glazer is a singer, storyteller and writer of folk-based songs for children and adults.

Washington WC-301	(M)	**The Tom Glazer Concert For And With Children**	1959	10.00	25.00

GLEASON, JACKIE

Capitol H-352	(10")	**Music For Lovers Only**	1952	12.00	30.00
Capitol H-366	(10")	**Lover's Rhapsody**	1953	12.00	30.00
Capitol H-455	(10")	**Music To Make You Misty**	1954	12.00	30.00

Label & Catalog #		Title	Year	VG+	NM
Capitol L-471	(10")	Tawny	1954	12.00	30.00
Capitol H-511	(10")	And Awaaay We Go! (TV Soundtrack)	1954	20.00	50.00
Capitol H-627	(10")	Lonesome Echo	1955	12.00	30.00
Capitol T-352	(M)	Music For Lovers Only	1953	10.00	25.00
Capitol T-455	(M)	Music To Make You Misty	1954	10.00	25.00
Capitol T-471	(M)	Tawny	1954	10.00	25.00
Capitol T-475	(M)	Music For Lovers Only /			
		Music To Make You Misty (2 LPs)	1954	16.00	40.00
Capitol T-509	(M)	Music, Martinis And Memories	1954	10.00	25.00
Capitol T-511	(M)	And Awaaay We Go! (TV Soundtrack)	1955	16.00	40.00
Capitol T-568	(M)	Romantic Jazz	1955	10.00	25.00
Capitol T-570	(M)	Music To Remember Her	1955	10.00	25.00
Capitol T-627	(M)	Lonesome Echo	1955	10.00	25.00
Capitol T-632	(M)	Music To Change Her Mind	1956	10.00	25.00
Capitol T-717	(M)	Night Winds	1956	10.00	25.00
Capitol T-758	(M)	Merry Christmas	1956	10.00	25.00
Capitol T-816	(M)	Music For The Love Hours	1957	10.00	25.00
Capitol T-859	(M)	Velvet Brass	1957	10.00	25.00
Capitol T-905	(M)	Jackie Gleason Presents "Oooo!"	1957	10.00	25.00
Capitol W-961	(M)	The Torch With The Blue Flame	1958	10.00	25.00
Capitol W-1020	(M)	Riff Jazz	1958	10.00	25.00
		— Capitol albums above have turquoise or gray labels.—			
RCA Victor LOC-1050	(M)	Take Me Along (Soundtrack)	1959	12.00	30.00
RCA Victor LSO-1050	(S)	Take Me Along (Soundtrack)	1959	16.00	40.00
Capitol W-1250	(M)	Aphrodisia	1960	8.00	20.00
Capitol SW-1250	(S)	Aphrodisia	1960	10.00	25.00
Capitol W-1519	(M)	The Gentle Touch	1961	8.00	20.00
Capitol SW-1519	(S)	The Gentle Touch	1961	10.00	25.00
		— Capitol albums above have black "rainbow" labels with the logo on the left.—			
Capitol W-1754	(M)	Gigot (Soundtrack)	1962	12.00	30.00
Capitol SW-1754	(S)	Gigot (Soundtrack)	1962	16.00	40.00
		— Capitol albums above have black "rainbow" labels with the logo on top.—			

GLENFOLK FOUR, THE

London LL-3413	(M)	The Glenfolk Four	1965	8.00	20.00
London PS-413	(S)	The Glenfolk Four	1965	10.00	25.00

GLENN, DARRELL

NRC LPA-5	(M)	Crying In The Chapel	1959	10.00	25.00
NRC SLPA-5	(S)	Crying In The Chapel	1959	12.00	30.00

GLENN, LLOYD

Swing Time 1901	(10")	Lloyd Glenn	1954	1,500.00	3,000.00
Aladdin LP-808	(M)	Chica Boo	1956	200.00	500.00
Aladdin LP-808	(M)	Chica Boo (Red vinyl)	1956	350.00	800.00
Score SLP-4006	(M)	Piano Stylings Of Lloyd Glenn	1957	200.00	400.00
Score SLP-4020	(M)	After Hours	1958	200.00	400.00
Imperial LP-9174	(M)	Chica Boo	1962	60.00	150.00
Imperial LP-12174	(S)	Chica Boo	1962	80.00	200.00
Imperial LP-9175	(M)	After Hours	1962	60.00	150.00
Imperial LP-12175	(S)	After Hours	1962	80.00	200.00

GLORY

Texas Revolution CFS-2531	(S)	A Meat Music Sampler	197?	20.00	50.00

GLORY

Avalanche LA148	(S)	Glory	1973	10.00	25.00

GOBEL, GEORGE

Decca DL-4163	(M)	Lonesome George	1962	8.00	20.00
Decca DL-74163	(S)	Lonesome George	1962	10.00	25.00

GODCHAUX, KEITH & DONNA
Refer to The Grateful Dead; The Heart Of Gold Band.

Round RX-104	(S)	Keith And Donna	1975	12.00	30.00

GODZ, THE

ESP-Disk' 1037	(M)	Contact High With The Godz	1967	12.00	30.00
ESP-Disk' 1037	(S)	Contact High With The Godz	1967	12.00	30.00

Label & Catalog #		Title	Year	VG+	NM
ESP-Disk' 1047	(S)	**Godz 2**	*1968*	**12.00**	**30.00**
ESP-Disk' 1077	(S)	**Third Testament**	*1969*	**12.00**	**30.00**
ESP-Disk' 2017	(S)	**Godzundheit**	*1970*	**12.00**	**30.00**
GIONS BROTHERS, THE					
Jalyn JLP-131	(M)	**Bluegrass Country**	*196?*	**10.00**	**25.00**
GOLDBERG, BARRY					
Refer to The Electric Flag.					
Epic LN-24199	(M)	**Blowing My Mind**	*1966*	**12.00**	**30.00**
Epic BN-26199	(S)	**Blowing My Mind**	*1966*	**16.00**	**40.00**
Buddah BDS-5012	(S)	**The Barry Goldberg Reunion**	*1968*	**10.00**	**25.00**
Buddah BDS-5029	(S)	**Barry Goldberg Recorded Live**	*1970*	**10.00**	**25.00**
GOLDEN DAWN					
International Art. 4	(S)	**Power Plant**	*1968*	**20.00**	**50.00**
International Art. 4	(S)	**Power Plant**	*1979*	**6.00**	**15.00**
		(Reissues have "Masterfonics" stamped in the trail-off vinyl.)			
GOLDEN EARRING					
Capitol T-2823	(M)	**Winter Harvest**	*1967*	**20.00**	**50.00**
Capitol ST-2823	(E)	**Winter Harvest**	*1967*	**16.00**	**40.00**
Capitol ST-164	(S)	**Miracle Mirror**	*1969*	**16.00**	**40.00**
Atlantic SD-8244	(S)	**Eight Miles High**	*1969*	**10.00**	**25.00**
Track 396	(S)	**Moontan** *(Nude dancer cover)*	*1973*	**10.00**	**25.00**
GOLDEN GATE QUARTET, THE					
Mercury MG-25063	(10")	**Spirituals**	*1950*	**80.00**	**200.00**
Columbia CL-6102	(10")	**The Golden Gate Spirituals**	*1953*	**80.00**	**200.00**
Camden CAL-308	(M)	**The Golden Gate Quartet** *(Purple label)*	*1956*	**40.00**	**100.00**
Harmony HL-7018	(M)	**That Golden Chariot** *(Maroon label)*	*1957*	**40.00**	**100.00**
GOLDENROD					
Chartmaker CSG-1101	(S)	**Goldenrod**	*1968*	**60.00**	**150.00**
GOLDSBORO, BOBBY					
United Arts. UAL-3358	(M)	**The Bobby Goldsboro Album**	*1964*	**10.00**	**25.00**
United Arts. UAS-6358	(S)	**The Bobby Goldsboro Album**	*1964*	**12.00**	**30.00**
United Arts. UAL-3381	(M)	**I Can't Stop Loving You**	*1964*	**10.00**	**25.00**
United Arts. UAS-6381	(S)	**I Can't Stop Loving You**	*1964*	**12.00**	**30.00**
United Arts. UAL-3425	(M)	**Little Things**	*1965*	**10.00**	**25.00**
United Arts. UAS-6425	(S)	**Little Things**	*1965*	**12.00**	**30.00**
United Arts. UAL-3471	(M)	**Broomstick Cowboy**	*1966*	**8.00**	**20.00**
United Arts. UAS-6471	(S)	**Broomstick Cowboy**	*1966*	**10.00**	**25.00**
United Arts. UAL-3486	(M)	**It's Too Late**	*1966*	**8.00**	**20.00**
United Arts. UAS-6486	(S)	**It's Too Late**	*1966*	**10.00**	**25.00**
United Arts. UAL-3552	(M)	**Blue Autumn**	*1966*	**8.00**	**20.00**
United Arts. UAS-6552	(S)	**Blue Autumn**	*1966*	**10.00**	**25.00**
GOLDTONES, THE					
LaBrea L-8011	(M)	**The Goldtones Featuring Randy Seol**	*1961*	**20.00**	**50.00**
LaBrea LS-8011	(S)	**The Goldtones Featuring Randy Seol**	*1961*	**30.00**	**75.00**
GOLLIWOGS, THE					
The Golliwogs was an early incarnation of Creedence Clearwater Revival.					
Fantasy F-9474	(M)	**Pre-Creedence**	*1975*	**10.00**	**25.00**
GOMEZ, VINCENTE					
Decca DL-5380	(10")	**Blood And Sand** *(Soundtrack)*	*1952*	**40.00**	**100.00**
Decca DL-5415	(10")	**The Fighter** *(Soundtrack)*	*1952*	**40.00**	**100.00**
Decca DL-8279	(M)	**Blood And Sand** *(Soundtrack)*	*1956*	**20.00**	**50.00**
Decca DL-8439	(M)	**Romantic Guitar**	*1957*	**12.00**	**30.00**
Decca DL-8965	(M)	**The Artistry Of Vincente Gomez**	*1959*	**8.00**	**20.00**
Decca DL-78965	(S)	**The Artistry Of Vincente Gomez**	*1959*	**12.00**	**30.00**
GOOD & PLENTY					
Senate 21001	(S)	**The World Of Good & Plenty**	*196?*	**12.00**	**30.00**

Lesley Gore was teenage singing sensation, topping the charts with her first single and following with three more top tenners in a row! As an album artist, she was rather less successful, although her LPs are uniformly well-crafted and impeccably performed. Oddly, as the '60s progressed, Ms. Gore's albums became increasingly harder to find in stereo, generally the opposite of what one should expect. Possibly, as they sold poorly, initial press runs were primarily mono, the demand not justifying later runs, where the bulk of the stereo pressings would have been. California Nights is one such album sought after by stereo collectors. Rarer still is the second volume of Golden Hits, an album which many collectors have never seen!

Label & Catalog #		Title	Year	VG+	NM

GOOD GUYS, THE
The Good Guys is a pseudonym for The Challengers.
| Crescendo GNP-2001 | (M) | **Sidewalk Surfing** *(Red label)* | 1964 | 8.00 | 20.00 |
| Crescendo GNPS-2001 | (S) | **Sidewalk Surfing** *(Red label)* | 1964 | 10.00 | 25.00 |

GOOD OLD BOYS, THE
| Round 576 | (S) | **Pistol Packin' Mama** | 1976 | 10.00 | 25.00 |

GOOD RATS, THE
| Kapp KS-3580 | (S) | **The Good Rats** | 1969 | 10.00 | 25.00 |
| Passport SP-20 | (DJ) | **Rats The Way You Like It-Live** | 1978 | 6.00 | 30.00 |

GOODIES, THE
| Hip HIS-7002 | (S) | **Candy Coated Goodies** | 1969 | 10.00 | 25.00 |

GOODING, CYNTHIA
Ms. Gooding is a guitar player and singer of folk songs in many languages. Refer to Theodore Bikel.
Elektra EKL-8	(10")	**Mexican Folksongs**	1953	16.00	40.00
Elektra EKL-11	(10")	**Queen Of Hearts**	195?	16.00	40.00
Elektra EKL-16	(10")	**Turkish And Spanish Folk Songs**	195?	16.00	40.00
Elektra EKL-17	(10")	**Italian Folk Songs**	195?	16.00	40.00
Elektra EKL-107	(M)	**Faithful Lovers And Other Phenomena**	195?	12.00	30.00
Elektra EKL-128	(M)	**Turkish, Spanish And Mexican Folk Songs**	195?	16.00	40.00
Elektra EKL-131	(M)	**Queen Of Hearts**	195?	12.00	30.00
Riverside RLP-12-830	(M)	**Languages Of Love**	195?	12.00	30.00

GOODMAN, DICKIE
Refer to Buchanan & Goodman.
| Rori 3301 | (M) | **The Many Heads Of Dickie Goodman** | 1962 | 30.00 | 75.00 |
| Comet 69 | (M) | **My Son, The Joke** | 196? | 16.00 | 40.00 |

GOODMAN, DODY
| Coral CRL-57196 | (M) | **Dody Goodman Sings** | 1957 | 12.00 | 30.00 |

GORDON, HONI: *Refer to* **GOLDMINE'S PRICE GUIDE TO COLLECTIBLE JAZZ ALBUMS**

GORDON, LUCK: *Refer to* **JIMMY DEAN / LUCK GORDON**

GORE, CHARLIE
| Audio Lab AL-1526 | (M) | **The Country Gentleman** | 1959 | 80.00 | 200.00 |

GORE, LESLEY
Mercury MG-20805	(M)	**I'll Cry If I Want To**	1963	12.00	30.00
Mercury SR-60805	(S)	**I'll Cry If I Want To**	1963	16.00	40.00
Mercury MG-20849	(M)	**Lesley Gore Sings Of Mixed Up Hearts**	1963	12.00	30.00
Mercury SR-60849	(S)	**Lesley Gore Sings Of Mixed Up Hearts**	1963	16.00	40.00
Mercury MG-20901	(M)	**Boys, Boys, Boys**	1964	12.00	30.00
Mercury SR-60901	(S)	**Boys, Boys, Boys**	1964	16.00	40.00
Mercury MG-20943	(M)	**Girl Talk**	1964	12.00	30.00
Mercury SR-60943	(S)	**Girl Talk**	1964	16.00	40.00
Mercury MG-21024	(M)	**The Golden Hits Of Lesley Gore**	1965	8.00	20.00
Mercury SR-61024	(S)	**The Golden Hits Of Lesley Gore** *(12 tracks)*	1965	12.00	30.00
		(The stereo "Look Of Love," "You Don't Own Me" and "I Don't Wanna Be A Loser" are different takes than the mono versions.)			
Mercury MG-21042	(M)	**My Town, My Guy And Me**	1965	10.00	25.00
Mercury SR-61042	(S)	**My Town, My Guy And Me**	1965	16.00	40.00
Mercury MG-21066	(M)	**All About Love**	1966	10.00	25.00
Mercury SR-61066	(S)	**All About Love**	1966	16.00	40.00
Mercury MG-21120	(M)	**California Nights**	1967	10.00	25.00
Mercury SR-61120	(S)	**California Nights**	1967	16.00	40.00
Mercury SR-61185	(S)	**Lesley Gore's Golden Hits, Vol. 2**	1968	16.00	40.00
Wing SRW-16350	(S)	**Girl Talk**	1968	10.00	25.00
		(Wing SRW-16350 is a reissue of Mercury 60943.)			
Wing SRW-16382	(S)	**Love, Love, Love**	1968	10.00	25.00
		(Wing 16382 is a reissue of Mercury 61066.)			
Wing PKW-2-119	(S)	**The Sound Of Young Love** *(2 LPs)*	1969	12.00	30.00
		(Wing 119 repackages 16350 and 16382.)			
Mowest MW-117L	(S)	**Someplace Else Now**	1972	10.00	25.00

Born Audrey Brown, Miss Gogi Grant was responsible for one of the biggest pop hits of the '50s with "The Wayward Wind," recorded for Era in 1956 and one of the few singles in that year to keep something by Elvis out of the top spot. When she signed with RCA Victor, their A&R staff aimed her at an older, easy-listening audience, not unusual for the outrageously conservative major labels, and her hits

Label & Catalog #		Title	Year	VG+	NM
GORME, EYDIE					
Refer to Steve Lawrence & Eydie Gorme.					
Coral CRL-57109	(M)	**Delight**	1957	14.00	35.00
ABC-Paramount ABC-150	(M)	**Eydie Gorme**	1957	14.00	35.00
ABC-Paramount ABC-192	(M)	**Eydie Swings The Blues**	1957	14.00	35.00
ABC-Paramount ABC-218	(M)	**Eydie Gorme Vamps The Roaring '20s**	1958	10.00	25.00
ABC-Paramount ABCS-218	(S)	**Eydie Gorme Vamps The Roaring '20s**	1958	14.00	35.00
ABC-Paramount ABC-246	(M)	**Eydie In Love**	1958	10.00	25.00
ABC-Paramount ABCS-246	(S)	**Eydie In Love**	1958	14.00	35.00
ABC-Paramount ABC-254	(M)	**Showstoppers**	1958	10.00	25.00
ABC-Paramount ABCS-254	(S)	**Showstoppers**	1958	14.00	35.00
ABC-Paramount ABC-273	(M)	**Love Is A Season**	1958	10.00	25.00
ABC-Paramount ABCS-273	(S)	**Love Is A Season**	1958	14.00	35.00
ABC-Paramount ABC-307	(M)	**Eydie Gorme On Stage**	1959	10.00	25.00
ABC-Paramount ABCS-307	(S)	**Eydie Gorme On Stage**	1959	14.00	35.00
ABC-Paramount ABC-343	(M)	**Eydie Gorme In Dixieland**	1960	8.00	20.00
ABC-Paramount ABCS-343	(S)	**Eydie Gorme In Dixieland**	1960	10.00	25.00
GOSDIN BROTHERS, THE					
Vern and Rex Gosdin. Refer to Gene Clark; The Hillmen.					
Capitol ST-2852	(S)	**Sounds Of Goodbye**	1968	12.00	30.00
GOSPEL STARS, THE					
Tamla TM-222	(M)	**The Great Gospel Stars**	1961		See below
		(Tamla 222 is one of the rarest of Motown albums, apparently distributed only in Detroit. Very rare with a suggested Near Mint value of $2,000-4.000.)			
GOULDMAN, GRAHAM					
RCA Victor LPM-3954	(M)	**Graham Gouldman Thing**	1968	20.00	50.00
RCA Victor LSP-3954	(S)	**Graham Gouldman Thing**	1968	30.00	75.00
GOWDY, CURT					
Mod. Ed. Sys. PS1-72521	(S)	**Curt Gowdy Tells You How To Watch Pro Football** *(With booklet)*	1972	12.00	30.00
GRACEFUL HEAD					
Excelsior	(S)	**Graceful Head**	198?	40.00	100.00
GRACEN, THELMA: *Refer to GOLDMINE'S PRICE GUIDE TO COLLECTIBLE JAZZ ALBUMS*					
GRACIOUS					
Gracious features Paul Davis.					
Capitol ST-602	(S)	**Gracious**	1970	16.00	40.00
GRAMMER, BILLY					
Monument MLP-4000	(M)	**Travelin' On**	1959	16.00	40.00
GRAND FUNK RAILROAD/GRAND FUNK					
Mark Farner, Don Brewer, Mel Schacher and Craig Frost. Refer to Terry Knight.					
Capitol SMAS-11207	(DJ)	**We're An American Band** *(Gold vinyl)*	1973	10.00	25.00
GRAND THEFT					
No label	(S)	**Grand Theft** *(Issued without a cover)*	197?	200.00	400.00
GRANDMA'S ROCKERS					
Fredlo 6727	(M)	**Homemade Apple Pie**	1967	1,000.00	1,500.00
GRANT, GOGI					
Era 20001	(M)	**Suddenly There's Gogi Grant** *(Red vinyl)*	1956	40.00	100.00
Era 20001	(M)	**Suddenly There's Gogi Grant**	1957	20.00	50.00
RCA Victor LOC-1030	(M)	**The Helen Morgan Story** *(Soundtrack)*	1957	20.00	50.00
RCA Victor LPM-1717	(M)	**Welcome To My Heart**	1958	16.00	40.00
RCA Victor LPM-1940	(M)	**Torch Time**	1959	12.00	30.00
RCA Victor LSP-1940	(S)	**Torch Time**	1959	16.00	40.00
RCA Victor LPM-1984	(M)	**Kiss Me, Kate**	1959	12.00	30.00
RCA Victor LSP-1984	(S)	**Kiss Me, Kate**	1959	16.00	40.00

Label & Catalog #		Title	Year	VG+	NM
RCA Victor LPM-2000	(M)	**Granted... It's Gogi**	1960	12.00	30.00
RCA Victor LSP-2000	(S)	**Granted... It's Gogi**	1960	16.00	40.00
		— RCA mono albums above have black labels with "Long Play" on the bottom;			
		stereo albums have "Living Stereo" on the bottom.—			
Liberty LRP-3144	(M)	**If You Want To Get To Heaven, Shout**	1959	12.00	30.00
Liberty LST-7144	(S)	**If You Want To Get To Heaven, Shout**	1959	16.00	40.00
Era EL-106	(M)	**The Wayward Wind**	1960	16.00	40.00

GRASS ROOTS, THE
Originally a studio concoction of Steve Barri and Phil Sloan (Dunhill 50011), their initial success lead to the formation of a "real" group based around vocalist Rob Grill.

Dunhill D-50011	(M)	**Where Were You When I Needed You?**	1966	20.00	50.00
Dunhill DS-50011	(S)	**Where Were You When I Needed You?**	1966	30.00	75.00
Dunhill D-50020	(M)	**Let's Live For Today**	1967	10.00	25.00
Dunhill DS-50020	(S)	**Let's Live For Today**	1967	12.00	30.00
Dunhill D-50027	(M)	**Feelings**	1968	10.00	25.00
Dunhill DS-50027	(S)	**Feelings**	1968	10.00	25.00
Command QD-40013	(Q)	**Their 16 Greatest Hits**	1974	10.00	25.00

GRATEFUL DEAD, THE
Original members were Jerry Garcia, Bill Kreutzmann, Phil Lesh, Ron "Pig Pen" McKernan (died 1973), Bob Weir and lyricist Robert Hunter. Mickey Hart joined in 1967, left 1970 and rejoined 1974. Tom Constanten was a member from 1968-70; Keith and Donna Godchaux during 1971-1978; and Brent Mydland, 1979 through his death in 1990. Refer to Ken Kesey; Kingfish; The Rhythm Devils; Touchstone.

Warner Bros. W-1689	(M)	**The Grateful Dead**	1967	30.00	75.00
Warner Bros. WS-1689	(S)	**The Grateful Dead**	1967	16.00	40.00
		— Warner albums above have gold labels.—			
Warner Bros. WS-1689	(S)	**The Grateful Dead**	1968	10.00	25.00
Warner Bros. WS-1749	(S)	**Anthem Of The Sun** *(Purple cover)*	1968	10.00	25.00
Warner Bros. WS-1790	(S)	**Aoxomoxoa**	1969	10.00	25.00
Warner Bros. 2WS-1830	(S)	**Live/Dead** *(2 LPs with booklet)*	1970	14.00	35.00
		— Warner albums above have green labels with a "W7" logo on top.—			
Warner Bros. WS-1749	(S)	**Anthem Of The Sun** *(White cover)*	197?	20.00	50.00
		(Rare version of "Anthem" remixed by Phil Lesh.)			
Warner Bros. 2WS-1935	(S)	**Grateful Dead** *(2 LPs with sticker)*	1971	10.00	25.00
		(2WS-1935 was issued with a bonus Skull & Roses" sticker.)			
		— Warner albums above have green labels with a "WB" logo on top.—			
Sunflower SUN-5001	(S)	**Vintage Dead**	1970	10.00	25.00
		(Counterfeits are 1/4" shorter than normal album covers.)			
Sunflower SNF-5004	(S)	**Historic Dead**	1971	10.00	25.00
Pride PRD-0016	(S)	**History Of The Grateful Dead**	1972	12.00	30.00
Grateful Dead GD-01	(S)	**Wake Of The Flood** *(Green vinyl)*	1973	200.00	400.00
		(The green vinyl was issued to members of the fan club.			
		Most of the copies were damaged by local flooding!)			
Grateful Dead GD-01	(S)	**Wake Of The Flood**	1975	6.00	15.00
		(Original covers of GD-01 do not list contributors on the back.)			
Grateful Dead GD-01	(S)	**Wake Of The Flood**	1975	10.00	25.00
		(Later covers have contributing artists listed on the back.)			
Grateful Dead GD-102	(S)	**From The Mars Hotel**	1974	10.00	25.00
United Arts. SP-114	(DJ)	**For Dead Heads**	1975	12.00	30.00
Arista SP-35	(DJ)	**Grateful Dead Sampler**	1977	12.00	30.00
Arista AL-7001	(DJ)	**Terrapin Station** *(Banded for air-play)*	1977	12.00	30.00
Mobile Fidelity MFSL-014	(S)	**American Beauty**	1980	20.00	60.00
Mobile Fidelity MFSL-172	(S)	**From The Mars Hotel**	1984	12.00	30.00
Direct Disk SD-16619	(S)	**Terrapin Station**	1980	50.00	150.00

GRAVITY ADJUSTERS EXPANSION BAND

Nocturne NRS-302	(S)	**One**	1973	80.00	200.00

GRAY, BILLY

Decca DL-5567	(10")	**Dance-O-Rama #7**	1955	200.00	400.00

GRAY, DOBIE
Dobie Gray later recorded with Pollution.

Stripe LPM-2001	(M)	**Look-Dobie Gray**	1963	40.00	100.00
Charger CHR-M-2002	(M)	**Dobie Gray Sings For In Crowders**	1965	20.00	50.00
Charger CHR-S-2002	(S)	**Dobie Gray Sings For In Crowders**	1965	30.00	75.00

Label & Catalog #		Title	Year	VG+	NM
GRAY, DOLORES					
Capitol T-897	(M)	**Warm Brandy**	1957	12.00	30.00
GRAYCO, HELEN					
Vik LX-1066	(M)	**After Midnight**	1957	10.00	25.00
GRAYSON, KATHRYN					
MGM E-551	(10")	**Kathryn Grayson**	1952	20.00	50.00
MGM E-3077	(10")	**Kiss Me Kate** (Soundtrack)	1953	40.00	100.00
RCA Victor LOC-3000	(10")	**So This Is Love** (Soundtrack)	1953	40.00	100.00
RCA Victor LPM-3105	(10")	**The Desert Song** (Soundtrack)	1953	40.00	100.00
MGM E-3257	(M)	**Kathryn Grayson Sings**	1956	16.00	40.00
Lion L-7055	M)	**Kathryn Grayson**	1959	10.00	25.00
GREAT SOCIETY, THE					

The Great Society features Grace Slick, later of Jefferson Airplane.

Columbia CS-9624	(S)	**Conspicuous Only In Its Absence**	1968	10.00	25.00
Columbia CS-9702	(S)	**How It Was**	1968	10.00	25.00

— Columbia albums above have "360 Sound" on the bottom of the label. —

GRECO, BUDDY					
Coral CRL-57022	(M)	**Buddy Greco At Mister Kelly's**	1956	10.00	25.00
Kapp KL-1033	(M)	**Broadway Melodies**	1956	10.00	25.00
GRECO, JULIETTE					
Columbia CL-569	(M)	**Juliette Greco**	1954	12.00	30.00
Columbia CL-992	(M)	**Greco**	1957	12.00	30.00
GREEK FOUNTAIN RIVER FRONT BAND, THE					
Montel LLP-110	(M)	**The Greek Fountain** **River Front Band Takes Requests**	1965	30.00	75.00
GREEN, AL					
Hot Line 1500	(M)	**Back Up Train**	1967	20.00	50.00
Hot Line 1500	(S)	**Back Up Train**	1967	30.00	75.00

(Al Green's name is spelled "Al Greene" on this album.)

GREEN, GRIZ					
Sand & Sage C-50	(M)	**West Of Yesterday**	195?	12.00	30.00
GREEN, LLOYD					
Time T-2152	(M)	**Big Steel Guitar**	1964	16.00	40.00
Time ST-2152	(S)	**Big Steel Guitar**	1964	20.00	50.00
GREEN, VERNON, & THE MEDALLIONS					
Dooto DLT-857	(M)	**Vernon Green & The Medallions**	197?	12.00	30.00
GREEN BULLFROG					

Green Bullfrog features Richie Blackmore and Jon Lord of Deep Purple.

Decca DL-75269	(S)	**Green Bullfrog**	1971	10.00	25.00
GREEN ON RED					
Green On Red 714	(S)	**Green On Red** (Red vinyl)	1981	40.00	100.00

GREEN RIVER BOYS, THE: *Refer to* GLEN CAMPBELL

GREENE, AL: *Refer to* AL GREEN

GREENE, BERNIE, & HIS STEREO MAD-MEN					
RCA Victor LPM-1929	(M)	**Musically Mad**	1958	24.00	60.00
RCA Victor LSP-1929	(S)	**Musically Mad**	1958	40.00	100.00

(RCA 1929 features a delightfully idiotic painting of Mad Magazine's poster boy Alfred E. Neuman by Norman Mingo.)

GREENE, DODO: *Refer to* GOLDMINE'S PRICE GUIDE TO COLLECTIBLE JAZZ ALBUMS

This wondrous work attracts a broad spectrum of collectors, primarily Mad collectors obviously, as the painting by Norman Mingo, Alfred E. Newman's official portrait painter, justifies adding it to an otherwise comic book oriented collection, and stereophiles, as it is a great example of Victor's "Living Stereo." For another look at this creation of Bill Gaines, Harvey Kurtzman, Al Feldstein and company, refer to Mad in the 'M's.

Label & Catalog #		Title	Year	°VG+	NM

GREENE, LORNE

Label & Catalog #		Title	Year	°VG+	NM
RCA Victor LPM-2661	(M)	Young At Heart	1963	12.00	30.00
RCA Victor LSP-2661	(S)	Young At Heart	1963	16.00	40.00

—RCA mono albums above have black labels with "Long Play" on the bottom;
stereo albums have "Living Stereo" on the bottom.—

Label & Catalog #		Title	Year	VG+	NM
RCA Victor LPM-2843	(M)	Welcome To The Ponderosa	1964	12.00	30.00
RCA Victor LSP-2843	(S)	Welcome To The Ponderosa	1964	16.00	40.00
RCA Victor SP-33-327	(DJ)	Palaver With The Man (Interveiw with script)	1965	20.00	50.00
RCA Victor LM-2783	(M)	Peter And The Wolf	1964	10.00	25.00
RCA Victor LCS-2783	(M)	Peter And The Wolf	1964	12.00	30.00
RCA Victor LPM-3302	(M)	Lorne Greene-The Man	1965	10.00	25.00
RCA Victor LSP-3302	(S)	Lorne Greene-The Man	1965	12.00	30.00
RCA Victor LPM-3409	(M)	Lorne Greene's American West	1965	10.00	25.00
RCA Victor LSP-3409	(S)	Lorne Greene's American West	1965	12.00	30.00
RCA Victor LPM-3410	(M)	Have A Happy Holiday	1965	10.00	25.00
RCA Victor LSP-3410	(S)	Have A Happy Holiday	1965	12.00	30.00
RCA Victor LPM-3678	(M)	Portrait Of The West	1966	10.00	25.00
RCA Victor LSP-3678	(S)	Portrait Of The West	1966	12.00	30.00
MGM YDS-303	(S)	The Robin Hood Of El Dorado	196?	12.00	30.00
Guideposts GP-116	(S)	Who Are The Peacemakers?	1968	12.00	30.00
Camden CAS-2391	(S)	Five Card Stud	1970	10.00	25.00

GREENE, LORNE, & DAN BLOCKER & MIKE LANDON & PERNELL ROBERTS
The actors from TV's "Bonanza" play and sing country music, more or less.

Label & Catalog #		Title	Year	VG+	NM
RCA Victor LPM-2583	(M)	Bonanza—Ponderosa Party Time!	1962	12.00	30.00
RCA Victor LSP-2583	(S)	Bonanza—Ponderosa Party Time!	1962	16.00	40.00

—RCA mono albums above have black labels with "Long Play" on the bottom;
stereo albums have "Living Stereo" on the bottom.—

GREENHILL, MITCH

Label & Catalog #		Title	Year	VG+	NM
Folklore FRLP-14026	(M)	Pickin' The City Blues	1964	10.00	25.00
Folklore FRST-14026	(S)	Pickin' The City Blues	1964	12.00	30.00
Prestige PRLP-7438	(M)	Shepherd Of The Highway	1966	8.00	20.00
Prestige PRST-7438	(S)	Shepherd Of The Highway	1966	10.00	25.00

GREENSLEEVES, EDDIE

Label & Catalog #		Title	Year	VG+	NM
Cameo C-1031	(M)	Humorous Folk Songs	1963	8.00	20.00
Cameo SC-1031	(S)	Humorous Folk Songs	1963	10.00	25.00

GREENWAY, JOHN

Label & Catalog #		Title	Year	VG+	NM
Riverside RLP-12-619	(M)	The Great American Bum—Hobo And Migratory Worker's Songs	195?	12.00	30.00

GREENWICH, ELLIE
Ms. Greenwich was formerly a member of The Raindrops.

Label & Catalog #		Title	Year	VG+	NM
United Arts. UAS-6648	(S)	Composes, Produces And Sings	1968	10.00	25.00

GREER

Label & Catalog #		Title	Year	VG+	NM
Sugarbush SBS-109	(S)	Between Two Worlds	197?	60.00	150.00

GREGG, BOBBY

Label & Catalog #		Title	Year	VG+	NM
Epic LN-24051	(M)	"Let's Stomp" And "Wild Weekend"	1963	8.00	20.00
Epic BN-26051	(S)	"Let's Stomp" And "Wild Weekend"	1963	12.00	30.00

GRIFFIN, JIMMY
Jimmy Griffin later recorded as James Griffin with Bread.

Label & Catalog #		Title	Year	VG+	NM
Reprise R-6091	(M)	Summer Holiday	1963	20.00	50.00
Reprise R9-6091	(S)	Summer Holiday	1963	30.00	75.00

GRIFFIN, MERV

Label & Catalog #		Title	Year	VG+	NM
Carlton LP-12-134	(M)	Merv Griffin's Dance Party	196?	12.00	30.00
Carlton STLP-12-134	(S)	Merv Griffin's Dance Party	196?	16.00	40.00

GRIFFITH, ANDY

Label & Catalog #		Title	Year	VG+	NM
Capitol T-962	(M)	Just For Laughs	1958	16.00	40.00
Capitol T-1105	(M)	Andy Griffith Shouts The Blues And Old Timey Songs	1959	16.00	40.00
Capitol ST-1105	(S)	Andy Griffith Shouts The Blues And Old Timey Songs	1959	20.00	50.00

Label & Catalog #		Title	Year	VG+	NM
Capitol T-1215	(M)	**This Here Andy Griffith**	1959	12.00	30.00
Capitol ST-1215	(S)	**This Here Andy Griffith**	1959	16.00	40.00
Capitol T-1611	(M)	**Songs, Themes And Laughs From**			
		The Andy Griffith Show *(TV Soundtrack)*	1961	16.00	40.00
Capitol ST-1611	(S)	**Songs, Themes And Laughs From**			
		The Andy Griffith Show *(TV Soundtrack)*	1961	20.00	50.00
Capitol T-2066	(M)	**Andy And Cleopatra**	1964	8.00	20.00
Capitol ST-2066	(S)	**Andy And Cleopatra**	1964	10.00	25.00

GRIFFITH, SHIRLEY

Bluesville BVLP-1087	(M)	**The Blues Of Shirley Griffith**	1964	20.00	50.00

— Bluesville albums above have bright blue labels with silver print.—

Bluesville BVLP-1087	(M)	**The Blues Of Shirley Griffith**	1964	10.00	25.00

— Bluesville albums above have blue labels with a trident logo on the right side.—

GRIMES, ANNE
Ms. Grimes is a autoharp, banjo, dulcimer, psaltery and zither player and singer of American folk songs.

Folkways FH-5217	(M)	**Ballads Of Ohio**	195?	12.00	30.00

GRIND, JODY

United Arts. UAS-6774	(S)	**One Step On**	1970	12.00	30.00

GROOM, DEWEY, & THE TEXAS LONGHORNS

Longhorn LP-004	(M)	**Last Of The Big Bands**	196?	30.00	75.00

GROOV-U

Gateway GLP-3010	(M)	**Groov-U On Campus**	196?	16.00	40.00

GROUNDHOGS, THE

Cleve CH-82871	(S)	**The Groundhogs**			
		With John Lee Hooker And John Mayall	1968	30.00	75.00
World Pacific WPS-21892	(S)	**Scratching The Surface**	1968	16.00	40.00
Imperial LP-12452	(S)	**Blues Obituary**	1969	16.00	40.00
Liberty LST-7644	(S)	**Thank Christ For The Bomb**	1970	14.00	35.00
United Arts. UAS-5513	(S)	**The Groundhogs Split**	1971	10.00	25.00
United Arts. UAS-5570	(S)	**Who Will Save The World**	1972	10.00	25.00
United Arts. LA008	(S)	**Hogwash**	1973	10.00	25.00
United Arts. LA603	(S)	**Crosscut Saw**	1976	10.00	25.00
United Arts. LA680	(S)	**Black Diamond**	1976	10.00	25.00

GROUNDSTAR

Stellar SR-2549	(S)	**Forced Landing**	1980	12.00	30.00

GROUP, THE

RCA Victor LPM-2663	(M)	**The Group**	1963	8.00	20.00
RCA Victor LSP-2663	(S)	**The Group**	1963	10.00	25.00

GROUPIES, THE

Earth ELPS-1000	(S)	**The Groupies** *(Documentary)*	196?	10.00	25.00

GROVE, BOBBY

King 831	(M)	**It Was For You**	1963	16.00	40.00

GROWING CONCERN, THE

Mainstream 56108	(M)	**Growing Concern**	1968	16.00	40.00
Mainstream S-6108	(S)	**Growing Concern**	1968	16.00	40.00

GRYPHON

(No label)	(S)	**Gryphon**	197?	24.00	60.00

GUARD, DAVE, & THE WHISKEYHILL SINGERS
Dave Guard's Whiskeyhill Singers feature Judy Henske. Refer to The Kingston Trio.

Capitol T-1728	(M)	**Dave Guard & The Whiskeyhill Singers**	1962	12.00	30.00
Capitol ST-1728	(S)	**Dave Guard & The Whiskeyhill Singers**	1962	16.00	40.00
MGM 1E-5	(M)	**How The West Was Won** *(Soundtrack)*	1963	10.00	25.00
MGM S1E-5	(S)	**How The West Was Won** *(Soundtrack)*	1963	12.00	30.00

Label & Catalog #		Title	Year	VG+	NM

GUESS WHO, THE
The original group was formed by Chad Allan, who left in 1965, and Randy Bachman, who left in 1970.
Burton Cummings joined in 1965. Refer to Chad Allan & The Expressions; Brave Belt.

Wand WDS-691	(P)	**Born In Canada**	1969	10.00	25.00
		("Shakin' All Over," "Clock On The Wall," and			
		"Tossin' And Turnin'" are reprocessed.)			
MGM SE-4645	(S)	**The Guess Who**	1969	10.00	25.00
RCA Victor LSP-4141	(S)	**Wheatfield Soul**	1969	10.00	25.00
RCA Victor LSP-4779	(S)	**Live At The Paramount**	1972	12.00	30.00
RCA Victor LSP-4830	(S)	**Artificial Paradise** *(With paper bag)*	1972	10.00	25.00
RCA Victor APD1-0130	(Q)	**Guess Who No. 10**	1973	10.00	25.00
RCA Victor APD1-0269	(Q)	**The Best Of The Guess Who, Volume 2**	1974	10.00	25.00
RCA Victor APD1-0405	(Q)	**Road Food**	1974	10.00	25.00
		— RCA albums above have orange labels.—			
Hilltak PR-331	(DJ)	**Track And Dialogue**	1979	10.00	25.00

GUILD, THE
The Guild is a creation of Gary Usher & Co.

Elektra EKS-	(S)	**The Guild**	1972	10.00	25.00

GUITAR, BONNIE

Dot DLP-3069	(M)	**Moonlight And Shadows**	1957	20.00	50.00
Dot DLP-3151	(M)	**Whispering Hope**	1958	14.00	35.00
Dot DLP-25151	(S)	**Whispering Hope**	1958	20.00	50.00
Dot DLP-3335	(M)	**Dark Moon**	1961	10.00	25.00
Dot DLP-25335	(E)	**Dark Moon**	1961	8.00	20.00
Dot DLP-3696	(M)	**Two Worlds**	1966	8.00	20.00
Dot DLP-25696	(S)	**Two Worlds**	1966	10.00	25.00
Dot DLP-3737	(M)	**Miss Bonnie Guitar**	1966	8.00	20.00
Dot DLP-25737	(S)	**Miss Bonnie Guitar**	1966	10.00	25.00
Dot DLP-3746	(M)	**Merry Christmas From Bonnie Guitar**	1966	8.00	20.00
Dot DLP-25746	(S)	**Merry Christmas From Bonnie Guitar**	1966	10.00	25.00
Dot DLP-3793	(M)	**Award Winner**	1967	8.00	20.00
Dot DLP-25793	(S)	**Award Winner**	1967	10.00	25.00

GUITAR JR.
Refer to Mississippi Fred McDowll / Guitar Jr.

Goldband 1085	(M)	**Pick Me Up On Your Way Down**	1960	10.00	25.00

GUNS N' ROSES

Uzi Suicide USR-001	(S)	**Live! Like A Suicide**	1986	60.00	150.00

GUNTER, ARTHUR

Excello 8017	(E)	**Black And Blues**	1971	10.00	25.00

GUTHRIE, WOODY
Guitar player, singer and songwriter Woody Guthrie, father to Arlo Guthrie, is the quintessential, 20th
Century American romantic folk hero/artist. Refer to Will Greer / Dick Wingfield; The Almanac Singers.

Folkways FP-11	(10")	**Dust Bowl Ballads**	1950	300.00	600.00
Folkways FA-2011	(10")	**Dust Bowl Ballads**	195?	300.00	600.00
Folkways FP-715	(10")	**Songs To Grow On (For Mother And Child)**	195?	250.00	500.00
Folkways FC-7015	(10")	**Songs To Grow On (For Mother And Child)**	195?	250.00	500.00
Folkways FP-78	(M)	**Bound For Glory**	195?	60.00	150.00
Folkways FA-2481	(M)	**The Songs And Strory Of Woody Guthrie**	195?	60.00	150.00
		(FA-2481 is narrated by Will Greer.)			
Folkways FA-2483	(M)	**Woody Guthrie Sings Folk Songs**	195?	24.00	60.00
		(FA-2483 features Cico Houston, Bess Hawes,			
		Leadbelly and Sonny Terry.)			
Folkways FA-2484	(M)	**Woody Guthrie Sings Folk Songs, Vol. 2**	195?	24.00	60.00
		(Folkways 2483 features Cico Houston and Sonny Terry.)			
Folkways FA-2485	(M)	**Struggle**	195?	24.00	60.00
Folkways FH-5212	(M)	**Dust Bowl Ballads**	195?	12.00	30.00
Folkways FH-5485	(M)	**Ballads Of Sacco & Venzetti**	195?	12.00	30.00
Elektra EKL-271	(M)	**Library Of Congress Recordings** *(3 LPs)*	1964	12.00	30.00
Elektra EKS-7271	(E)	**Library Of Congress Recordings** *(3 LPs)*	1964	10.00	25.00
RCA Victor LPV-502	(M)	**Dust Bowl Ballads**	1964	10.00	25.00
Verve/Folkways FV-9007	(M)	**Bed On The Floor**	1965	12.00	30.00
Verve/Folkways FVS-9007	(E)	**Bed On The Floor**	1965	8.00	20.00

Label & Catalog #		Title	Year	VG+	NM
Verve/Folkways FV-9036	(M)	**Bonneville Dam**			
		& Other Columbia River Songs	1965	12.00	30.00
Verve/Folkways FVS-9036	(E)	**Bonneville Dam**			
		& Other Columbia River Songs	1965	8.00	20.00

GUTHRIE, WOODY, & CISCO HOUSTON

Stinson SLP-32	(10")	**Cowboy Songs**	195?	80.00	200.00
Stinson SLP-44	(10")	**Folk Songs, Vol. 1**	195?	80.00	200.00
Stinson SLP-53	(10")	**More Songs**	195?	80.00	200.00

GUTHRIE, WOODY / SONNY TERRY / ALEK STEWART

Stinson SLP-7	(10")	**Chain Gang, Volume I**	195?	80.00	200.00
Stinson SLP-8	(10")	**Chain Gang, Volume 2**	195?	80.00	200.00

GUY, BUDDY

Chess LP-1527	(M)	**Left My Blues In San Francisco**	1967	12.00	30.00
Chess LPS-1527	(S)	**Left My Blues In San Francisco**	1967	16.00	40.00
Vanguard VSD-79272	(S)	**A Man And The Blues**	1968	12.00	30.00
Vanguard VSD-79290	(S)	**This Is Buddy Guy**	1969	12.00	30.00

GUY, BUDDY, & JUNIOR WELLS

Blue Thumb BYS-20	(S)	**Buddy And The Juniors** (Colored vinyl)	1970	20.00	50.00
Blue Thumb BYS-20	(S)	**Buddy And The Juniors**	1970	10.00	25.00

H

H. P. LOVECRAFT

Philips PHM-200-252	(M)	H. P. Lovecraft	1967	10.00	25.00
Philips PHS-600-252	(S)	H. P. Lovecraft	1967	12.00	30.00
Philips PHS-600-279	(S)	Lovecraft II	1968	12.00	30.00

HA' PENNYS, THE

Fersch FL-1110	(M)	Love Is Not The Same	1968	200.00	400.00

HAGAR, ERNIE

Sage C-42	(M)	Swinging Steel Guitar	195?	20.00	50.00

HAGGARD, MERLE/MERLE HAGGARD & THE STRANGERS
Refer to George Jones & Merle Haggard; The Strangers.

Capitol T-2373	(M)	Strangers	1965	10.00	25.00
Capitol ST-2373	(S)	Strangers	1965	12.00	30.00
Capitol T-2585	(M)	Swinging Doors	1966	10.00	25.00
Capitol ST-2585	(S)	Swinging Doors	1966	12.00	30.00
Capitol T-2702	(M)	I'm A Lonesome Fugitive	1967	10.00	25.00
Capitol ST-2702	(S)	I'm A Lonesome Fugitive	1967	12.00	30.00
Capitol T-2789	(M)	Branded Man/I Threw Away The Rose	1967	10.00	25.00
Capitol ST-2789	(S)	Branded Man/I Threw Away The Rose	1967	12.00	30.00
Capitol T-2848	(M)	Sing Me Back Home	1968	12.00	30.00
Capitol ST-2848	(S)	Sing Me Back Home	1968	10.00	25.00
Capitol ST-2912	(S)	Legend Of Bonnie & Clyde	1968	10.00	25.00
Capitol SKAO-2951	(S)	Best Of Merle Haggard	1968	10.00	25.00
Capitol ST-2972	(S)	Mama Tried	1969	10.00	25.00
Capitol SKAO-168	(S)	Pride In What I Am	1969	10.00	25.00
Capitol SWBB-223	(S)	Same Train, A Different Time (2 LPs)	1969	12.00	30.00
		— Capitol albums above have black "rainbow" labels.—			
Capitol ST-638	(S)	Tribute To The Best Damn Fiddle Player - Or, My Salute To Bob Wills	1970	10.00	25.00
Capitol ST-803	(S)	Land Of Many Churches (2 LPs)	1971	20.00	50.00
Capitol ST-823	(S)	Truly The Best Of Merle Haggard	1971	16.00	40.00
Capitol ST-835	(S)	Someday We'll Look Back	1972	10.00	25.00
Capitol ST-882	(S)	Let Me Tell You About A Song	1972	10.00	25.00
		— Capitol albums above have green labels.—			

HAGGARD, MERLE, & BONNIE OWENS

Capitol T-2453	(M)	Just Between The Two Of Us	1966	10.00	25.00
Capitol ST-2453	(S)	Just Between The Two Of Us	1966	12.00	30.00

HAINES, CONNIE

Coral CRL-56055	(10")	Connie Haines Sings	1955	60.00	150.00
Tops L-1606	(M)	Connie Haines Sings Helen Morgan	1959	10.00	25.00
RCA Victor LPM-2264	(M)	Faith, Hope And Charity	1961	8.00	20.00
RCA Victor LSP-2264	(S)	Faith, Hope And Charity	1961	12.00	30.00

HALE, CORKY: Refer to GOLDMINE'S PRICE GUIDE TO COLLECTIBLE JAZZ ALBUMS

HALEY, BILL, & HIS COMETS
Refer to Trini Lopez / Scott Gregory.

Essex LP-202	(M)	Rock With Bill Haley And The Comets	1955	100.00	400.00
Trans World 202	(M)	Rock With Bill Haley And The Comets	1956	150.00	300.00
		(Transworld 202 is a reissue of Essex 202.)			
Somerset P-4600	(M)	Rock With Bill Haley And The Comets	1957	50.00	150.00
Decca DL-5560	(10")	Shake, Rattle And Roll	1955		See below
		(Decca 5560 is rare with suggested values in VG of $100-200; in VG+ of $300-400; and in Near Mint of $600-1,000.)			
Decca DL-8225	(M)	Rock Around The Clock	1956	60.00	150.00
		(Black label with "Decca" on top and "Long Play" on the bottom.)			

Illustrated here are two attempts by smaller labels to overcome the financial hurdle of issuing albums in two different formats: Both Juanita Hall's album on Counterpoint and Toni Fisher's on Signet were issued in "compatible mono/stereo," meaning that the grooves were cut to allow either a mono or stereo stylus to pick up the appropriate waves and replay either monophonically or stereophonically. This system did not go over well and separate mono and stereo pressings continued through the late '60s, when mono was simply dumped by the industry.

Label & Catalog #		Title	Year	VG+	NM
Decca DL-78225	(E)	Rock Around The Clock	1958	30.00	75.00
		(Black label with "Decca Stereo" on top.)			
Decca DL-8225	(M)	Rock Around The Clock	1960	16.00	40.00
Decca DL-78225	(E)	Rock Around The Clock	1960	10.00	25.00
		(Black label with "Decca" in a rainbow band across the middle and			
		"Mfrd. by Decca Records Inc New York" beneath the band.)			
Decca DL-8315	(M)	Music For The Boyfriend	1956	60.00	150.00
Decca DL-8345	(M)	Rock And Roll Stage Show	1956	80.00	200.00
Decca DL-8569	(M)	Rockin' The Oldies	1957	60.00	150.00
Decca DL-8692	(M)	Rockin' Around The World	1958	60.00	150.00
Decca DL-8775	(M)	Rockin' The Joint	1958	60.00	150.00
Decca DL-8821	(M)	Bill Haley's Chicks	1959	40.00	100.00
Decca DL-78821	(S)	Bill Haley's Chicks	1959	60.00	150.00
Decca DL-8964	(M)	Strictly Instrumental	1960	40.00	100.00
Decca DL-78964	(S)	Strictly Instrumental	1960	60.00	150.00
— Decca mono albums above have black labels with "Long Play 33 1/3 RPM" on the bottom;					
stereo albums have black labels with "Decca Stereo" on top.—					
Warner Bros. W-1378	(M)	Bill Haley And His Comets	1960	20.00	50.00
Warner Bros. WS-1378	(S)	Bill Haley And His Comets	1960	30.00	75.00
Warner Bros. W-1391	(M)	Bill Haley's Jukebox	1960	20.00	50.00
Warner Bros. WS-1391	(S)	Bill Haley's Jukebox	1960	30.00	75.00
Roulette R-25174	(M)	Twistin' Knights At The Roundtable	1962	40.00	100.00
Roulette SR-25174	(S)	Twistin' Knights At The Roundtable	1962	40.00	100.00
Vocalion VL-3696	(M)	Bill Haley And The Comets	1963	10.00	25.00
Guest Star GS-1454	(M)	Rock Around The Clock King	1964	10.00	25.00
Guest Star GSS-1454	(E)	Rock Around The Clock King	1964	6.00	15.00
Decca DL-5027	(M)	Bill Haley's Greatest Hits	1967	12.00	30.00
Decca DL-75027	(S)	Bill Haley's Greatest Hits	1967	8.00	20.00
Kama Sutra KLPS-2104	(S)	Scrapbook/Live At The Bitter End	1970	12.00	30.00
Janus 3035	(S)	Travelin' Band	1970	10.00	25.00

HALL, BECKY: Refer to GOLDMINE'S PRICE GUIDE TO COLLECTIBLE JAZZ ALBUMS

HALL, DICKSON/DIXON HALL

MGM E-329	(10")	Outlaws Of The Old West	1954	30.00	75.00
MGM E-3263	(M)	Outlaws Of The Old West	1956	20.00	50.00
Kapp KL-1067	(M)	Fabulous Country Hits Way Out West	1957	16.00	40.00
Epic LN-3427	(M)	25 All-Time Country And Western Hits	1958	12.00	30.00
Perfect P-14016	(M)	Country & Western Million Sellers	1960	10.00	25.00
Perfect PS-14016	(S)	Country & Western Million Sellers	1960	12.00	30.00

HALL, JOANIE, & THE FRONTIERSMEN

Sage & Sand C-34	(M)	Western Meets Country	1962	12.00	30.00

HALL, JUANITA

Counterpoint 556	(S)	Jaunita Hall Sings The Blues	1958	80.00	200.00
		(Counterpoint 556 was issued in compatible mono/stereo.)			

HALL, LARRY

Strand 1005	(M)	Sandy	1960	30.00	75.00
Strand S-1005	(S)	Sandy	1960	60.00	150.00

HALL, ROY, & THE BLUE RIDGE ENTERTAINERS

County LPS-406	(S)	Roy Hall & The Blue Ridge Entertainers	197?	4.00	10.00

HALL, VERA: Refer to DOCK REED & VERA HALL

HALLYDAY, JOHNNY

Philips PHM-200-019	(M)	America's Rockin' Hits	1961	30.00	75.00
Philips PHS-600-019	(S)	America's Rockin' Hits	1961	40.00	100.00

HALOS, THE

Warwick W-2046	(M)	The Halos	1962	175.00	400.00

HAMBLEN, STUART
Refer to Webb Pierce / Marvin Rainwater / Stuart Hamblen.

RCA Victor LPM-3265	(10")	It Is No Secret	1954	30.00	75.00
RCA Victor LPM-1253	(M)	It Is No Secret	1956	20.00	50.00
RCA Victor LPM-1436	(M)	Grand Old Hymns	1957	20.00	50.00

Label & Catalog #		Title	Year	VG+	NM
Harmony HL-7009	(M)	**Hymns**	1957	10.00	25.00
Camden CAL-537	(M)	**Beyond The Sun**	1959	10.00	25.00
Coral CRL-57254	(M)	**Remember Me**	1960	10.00	25.00
Columbia CL-1588	(M)	**The Spell Of The Yukon**	1961	8.00	20.00
Columbia CS-8388	(S)	**The Spell Of The Yukon**	1961	10.00	25.00
Columbia CL-1769	(M)	**Of God I Sing**	1962	8.00	20.00
Columbia CS-8569	(S)	**Of God I Sing**	1962	10.00	25.00

— Columbia albums above have three white "eye" logos on each side of the spindle hole.—

HAMILTON, GEORGE, IV

Label & Catalog #		Title	Year	VG+	NM
ABC-Paramount ABC-220	(M)	**George Hamilton IV On Campus**	1958	14.00	35.00
ABC-Paramount ABCS-220	(S)	**George Hamilton IV On Campus**	1958	20.00	50.00
ABC-Paramount ABC-251	(M)	**Sing Me A Sad Song—**			
		A Tribute To Hank Williams	1958	14.00	35.00
ABC-Paramount ABCS-251	(S)	**Sing Me A Sad Song—**			
		A Tribute To Hank Williams	1958	20.00	50.00
ABC-Paramount ABC-461	(M)	**Big Fifteen**	1963	12.00	30.00
ABC-Paramount ABCS-461	(S)	**Big Fifteen**	1963	12.00	40.00
		("Little Tom," "Even Tho," "Why Don't They Understand,"			
		and "One Heart" are rechanneled on this album.)			
ABC-Paramount ABC-535	(M)	**By George**	1966	8.00	20.00
ABC-Paramount ABCS-535	(S)	**By George**	1966	10.00	25.00
RCA Victor LPM-2373	(M)	**To You And Yours From Me And Mine**	1961	8.00	20.00
RCA Victor LSP-2373	(S)	**To You And Yours From Me And Mine**	1961	10.00	25.00

— RCA mono albums above have black labels with "Long Play" on the bottom;
stereo albums have "Living Stereo" on the bottom.—

HAMILTON, ROY

Label & Catalog #		Title	Year	VG+	NM
Epic LN-1103	(10")	**The Voice Of Roy Hamilton**	195?	60.00	150.00
Epic LN-3176	(M)	**Roy Hamilton**	1955	20.00	50.00
Epic LN-3294	(M)	**You'll Never Walk Alone**	1956	20.00	50.00
Epic BN-632	(E)	**You'll Never Walk Alone**	1962	8.00	20.00
Epic LN-3364	(M)	**Golden Boy**	1957	20.00	50.00
Epic LN-3519	(M)	**With All My Love**	1958	12.00	30.00
Epic BN-518	(S)	**With All My Love**	1959	16.00	40.00
Epic LN-3545	(M)	**Why Fight The Feeling?**	1959	10.00	25.00
Epic BN-525	(S)	**Why Fight The Feeling?**	1959	12.00	30.00
Epic LN-3561	(M)	**Come Out Swingin'**	1959	10.00	25.00
Epic BN-530	(S)	**Come Out Swingin'**	1959	12.00	30.00
Epic LN-3580	(M)	**Have Blues, Must Travel**	1959	12.00	30.00
Epic BN-535	(S)	**Have Blues, Must Travel**	1959	12.00	30.00
Epic LN-3628	(M)	**Roy Hamilton At His Best**	1960	20.00	50.00
Epic LN-3654	(M)	**Spirituals**	1960	10.00	25.00
Epic BN-551	(S)	**Spirituals**	1960	12.00	30.00
Epic LN-3717	(M)	**Soft 'N Warm**	1960	10.00	25.00
Epic BN-578	(S)	**Soft 'N Warm**	1960	12.00	30.00
Epic LN-3775	(M)	**You Can Have Her**	1961	12.00	30.00
Epic BN-595	(S)	**You Can Have Her**	1961	16.00	40.00
Epic LN-3807	(M)	**Only You**	1962	10.00	25.00
Epic BN-610	(S)	**Only You**	1962	12.00	30.00
Epic LN-24000	(M)	**Mr. Rock And Soul**	1962	10.00	25.00
Epic BN-26000	(S)	**Mr. Rock And Soul**	1962	12.00	30.00
Epic LN-24009	(M)	**Roy Hamilton's Greatest Hits**	1962	8.00	20.00
Epic BN-26009	(S)	**Roy Hamilton's Greatest Hits**	1962	10.00	25.00
Epic LN-24316	(M)	**Roy Hamilton's Greatest Hits, Vol. 2**	1963	8.00	20.00
Epic BN-26316	(S)	**Roy Hamilton's Greatest Hits, Vol. 2**	1963	10.00	25.00

—Epic albums above have yellow labels with black spokes along the perimeter.—

HAMILTON, RUSS

Label & Catalog #		Title	Year	VG+	NM
Kapp KL-1076	(M)	**Rainbow**	1957	30.00	75.00

HAMMER, JACK

Label & Catalog #		Title	Year	VG+	NM
Warwick W-2014	(M)	**Revolution: Jack Hammer Reads**			
		Songs And Poems Of The Beat Generation	1960	30.00	75.00

HAMMOND, JOHN. JR.
Refer to Larry Johnson.

Label & Catalog #		Title	Year	VG+	NM
Vanguard VRS-9132	(M)	**John Hammond**	1963	12.00	30.00
Vanguard VSD-2148	(S)	**John Hammond**	1963	16.00	40.00

Label & Catalog #		Title	Year	VG+	NM
Vanguard VRS-9153	(M)	**Big City Blues**	1964	10.00	25.00
Vanguard VSD-79153	(S)	**Big City Blues**	1964	12.00	30.00
Vanguard VRS-9178	(M)	**So Many Roads**	1966	12.00	30.00
Vanguard VSD-79178	(S)	**So Many Roads**	1966	16.00	40.00
Vanguard VRS-9198	(M)	**Country Blues**	1966	10.00	25.00
Vanguard VSD-79198	(S)	**Country Blues**	1966	12.00	30.00
Vanguard VRS-9245	(M)	**Mirrors**	1967	12.00	30.00
Vanguard VSD-79245	(S)	**Mirrors**	1967	16.00	40.00
		(Vanguard 9178 and 9245 feature Levon Helm, Garth Hudson and Robbie Robertson.)			
Atlantic 8152	(M)	**I Can Tell**	1967	16.00	40.00
Atlantic SD-8152	(S)	**I Can Tell**	1967	20.00	50.00
		(Atlantic 8152 features Robertson, Rick Danko and Bill Wyman.)			
Atlantic SD-8206	(S)	**Sooner Or Later**	1968	8.00	20.00

HANGMEN, THE

Monument MLP-8077	(M)	**Bitter Sweet**	1967	8.00	20.00
Monument SLP-18077	(S)	**Bitter Sweet**	1967	10.00	25.00

HANKINS, ESCO

Audio Lap AL-1547	(M)	**Country Style**	1959	80.00	200.00

HAPPENINGS, THE

B.T. Puppy BT-1001	(M)	**The Happenings**	1966	10.00	25.00
B.T. Puppy BTS-1001	(S)	**The Happenings**	1966	12.00	30.00
B.T. Puppy BT-1003	(M)	**Psycle**	1967	10.00	25.00
B.T. Puppy BTS-1003	(S)	**Psycle**	1967	12.00	30.00
B.T. Puppy BTS-1004	(S)	**The Happenings' Golden Hits!**	1968	16.00	40.00
Jubilee JGS-8028	(S)	**Piece Of Mind**	1969	10.00	25.00
Jubilee JGS-8030	(S)	**The Happenings' Greatest Hits!**	1969	10.00	25.00

HAPPY DRAGON BAND, THE

Fiddler's Music 1157	(S)	**The Happy Dragon Band**	1977	40.00	100.00

HAPSHASH & THE COLOURED COAT

Imperial LP-12377	(S)	**Hapshash & The Coloured Coat**	1968	12.00	30.00
Imperial LP-12430	(S)	**Western Flyer**	1969	12.00	30.00

HARD TIMES, THE

World Pacific WP-1867	(M)	**Blew Mind**	1968	10.00	25.00
World Pacific ST-1867	(S)	**Blew Mind**	1968	12.00	30.00

HARDIN, TIM
Tim Hardin is a guitar player, singer and songwriter in the contemporary folk vein.

Verve/Folkways FT-3004	(M)	**Tim Hardin 1**	1966	8.00	20.00
Verve/Folkways FTS-3004	(S)	**Tim Hardin 1**	1966	10.00	25.00
Atco 33-210	(M)	**Tim Hardin**	1967	12.00	30.00
Atco SD-33-210	(E)	**Tim Hardin**	1967	6.00	15.00

HARDWATER
Hardwater originally recorded as The Astronauts.

Capitol ST-2954	(S)	**Hardwater**	1968	16.00	40.00

HARDY, FRANCOISE

Four Corners FC-4231	(M)	**Francoise**	196?	10.00	25.00
Four Corners FCS-4231	(S)	**Francoise**	196?	12.00	30.00
Four Corners FC-4238	(M)	**Je Vous Aime**	196?	10.00	25.00
Four Corners FCS-4238	(S)	**Je Vous Aime**	196?	12.00	30.00
Reprise RS-6290	(S)	**Francoise Hardy**	1968	12.00	30.00

HARLEM-AIRES, THE: *Refer to* CONNIE BENNETT, BILL SMYTH & THE HARLEM-AIRES

HARMONETTES, THE

Sherwood G-1172	(M)	**People Say**	196?	80.00	200.00

HARMONY BLAZERS, THE

Harmony HL-7103	(M)	**Ten Big Hits**	195?	10.00	25.00
Harmony HL-7126	(M)	**Ten Big Hits, Vol. II**	195?	10.00	25.00

While Francoise Hardy was a talented singer and songwriter being sold to the American folk scene, her style owed more to French cabaret singers than to, say, Bob Dylan. She was also an extraordinarily photogenic woman, as evidenced by these two hard to find Reprise albums.

Label & Catalog #		Title	Year	VG+	NM

HARNELL, JOE: *Refer to* GOLDMINE'S PRICE GUIDE TO COLLECTIBLE JAZZ ALBUMS

HARPER, ARTHUR LEE
Mr. Harper also recorded as Arthur.

Nocturne NRS-905	(S)	Love Is The Revolution	1975	150.00	300.00

HARPER, ROY

World Pacific WPS-21888	(S)	Folkjokeopus	1969	10.00	25.00
Chrysalis PRO-620	(DJ)	Introduction To Roy Harper *(Sampler)*	1975	12.00	30.00

HARPER, TONI: *Refer to* GOLDMINE'S PRICE GUIDE TO COLLECTIBLE JAZZ ALBUMS

HARRIS, DAVE

Decca DL-4113	(M)	Dinner Music For A Pack Of Hungry Cannibals	1961	8.00	20.00
Decca DL7-4113	(S)	Dinner Music For A Pack Of Hungry Cannibals	1961	12.00	30.00

HARRIS, EMMYLOU

Jubilee JGS-8031	(S)	Gliding Bird *(Full color cover)*	1969	40.00	100.00
		(White label counterfeits of Jubilee 8031 have black & white covers.)			
Mobile Fidelity MFSL-015	(S)	Quarter Moon In A Ten Cent Town	1979	10.00	30.00

HARRIS, PEPPERMINT

Time 5	(M)	Peppermint Harris	1962	80.00	200.00

HARRIS, ROLF

Epic LN-24053	(M)	The Original Sun Arise & Tie Me Kangaroo Down, Sport	1963	12.00	30.00
Epic BN-26053	(S)	The Original Sun Arise & Tie Me Kangaroo Down, Sport	1963	16.00	40.00
Epic LN-24110	(M)	The Court Of King Caractacus (& Other Fun Songs)	1964	12.00	30.00
Epic BN-26110	(S)	The Court Of King Caractacus (& Other Fun Songs)	1964	16.00	40.00

— Epic albums above have yellow labels with "A Product of CBS" on the bottom.—

HARRIS, SHAUN
Harris was formerly a member of The West Coast Pop Art Experimental Band.

Capitol ST-11168	(S)	Shaun Harris	1973	12.00	30.00

HARRIS, WYNONIE
Refer to Roy Brown; Amos Milburn.

King KS-1086	(E)	Good Rockin' Blues	1970	10.00	25.00

HARRISON, GEORGE
Harrison was formerly a member of The Fab Four. Refer to The Beatles; Jackie Lomax; Bill;y Preston; The Radha Krsna Temple Leon Russell; Ravi Shankar; The Traveling Wilburys; Doris Troy.

Apple ST-3350	(S)	Wonderwall Music	1969	60.00	150.00
		(Apple labels read "A Subsidiary of Capitol" on the bottom. Issued with a 10" x 10" bonus photo, worth $10.)			
Apple ST-3350	(S)	Wonderwall Music	1969	10.00	25.00
		(Apple labels read "Manufactured by Apple" on the bottom. Issued with a 10" x 10" bonus photo, worth $10.)			
Zapple ST-3358	(S)	Electronic Sound	1969	14.00	35.00
Apple STCH-639	(S)	All Things Must Pass *(3 LP box)*	1970	16.00	40.00
		(First pressings have orange Apple labels on the first two LPs and a custom label on the third with "Mfd. by Apple" on the inside front cover. Includes a poster and a lyric sheet. Produced by Phil Spector)			
Dark Horse *(No number)*	(DJ)	Dark Horse Radio Special	1975	200.00	400.00
Dark Horse PRO-649	(DJ)	Personal Music Dialogue At 33 & 1/3	1976	20.00	50.00
Dark Horse 23734	(DJ)	Gone Troppo *(Promo with Quiex II vinyl)*	1982	12.00	30.00
Dark Horse DHK-3255	(S)	George Harrison *(Columbia Record Club)*	1979	20.00	50.00
Capitol STCH-639	(S)	All Things Must Pass *(Orange label)*	1976	12.00	30.00
Capitol STCH-639	(S)	All Things Must Pass *(Purple label)*	1976	10.00	25.00
Capitol STCH-639	(S)	All Things Must Pass *(Black label)*	1983	40.00	100.00
Capitol STCH-639	(S)	All Things Must Pass *(Apple label)*	1983	20.00	50.00
		(Capitol box contains LPs with original Apple label but have a large "S" in the trail-off vinyl.)			

Label & Catalog #		Title	Year	VG+	NM
Capitol STCH-639	(S)	**All Things Must Pass** (Apple label)	1983	30.00	75.00
		(Capitol box contains LPs with original Apple label but have a large "S" in the trail-off vinyl. Some copies printed with a special slick with titles and credits affixed to the back cover.)			
Capitol ST-11578	(S)	**Best Of George Harrison** (Orange label)	1976	50.00	125.00
Capitol ST-11578	(S)	**Best Of George Harrison**	1989	12.00	30.00
		(Purple "Manufactured" label)			
Capitol SN-16216	(S)	**Living In The Material World** (Green label)	1980	10.00	25.00
Capitol SN-16217	(S)	**Extra Texture** (Green label)	1980	10.00	25.00

HARRISON, GEORGE, & FRIENDS
Features performances by Ravi Shankar, Harrison, Billy Preston, Ringo, Leon Russell, amd Bob Dylan, featuring Badfinger as everybody's band. Produced by Harrison and Phil Spector.

Apple STCX-3385	(S)	**The Concert For Bangla Desh** (3 LP box)	1972	12.00	30.00
		(Custom Apple labels with photo booklet.)			
Apple STCX-3385	(S)	**The Concert For Bangla Desh** (3 LP box)	1972	20.00	50.00
		(Custom "All rights reserved" Apple labels with photo booklet.)			
Capitol SABB-12248	(S)	**The Concert For Bangla Desh** (2 LPs)	1982	150.00	300.00
		(Abridged two-album reissue of the original Apple box.)			

HARRISON, NOEL

London LL-3459	(M)	**Noel Harrison**	1965	8.00	20.00
London PS-459	(S)	**Noel Harrison**	1965	10.00	25.00

HARRISON, WILBERT

Sphere Sound SR-7000	(M)	**Kansas City**	1965	40.00	100.00
Sphere Sound SSR-7000	(E)	**Kansas City**	1965	30.00	75.00
Sue SSLP-8801	(S)	**Let's Work Together**	1970	20.00	50.00
Juggernaut ST-8803	(S)	**Shoot You Full Of Love**	1971	20.00	50.00
Buddah BDS-5092	(S)	**Wilbert Harrison**	1971	14.00	35.00
Wet Soul 1001	(S)	**Anything You Want**	197?	20.00	50.00

HARROW, NANCY: *Refer to* **GOLDMINE'S PRICE GUIDE TO COLLECTIBLE JAZZ ALBUMS**

HART, FREDDIE/FREDDIE HART & THE HEARTBEATS

Columbia CL-1792	(M)	**The Spirited Freddie Hart**	1962	12.00	30.00
Columbia CS-8592	(E)	**The Spirited Freddie Hart**	1962	8.00	20.00

HART, MICKEY
Refer to The Diga Rhythm Band; The Grateful Dead; The Heart Of Gold Band.

Warner Bros. BS-2635	(S)	**Rolling Thunder** (With insert)	1972	16.00	40.00

HARTMAN, JOHNNY: *Refer to* **GOLDMINE'S PRICE GUIDE TO COLLECTIBLE JAZZ ALBUMS**

HARUMI

Verve/Forecast FTS-3030	(S)	**Harumi**	1968	10.00	25.00

HARVEST FLIGHT

Destiny D-3303	(S)	**One Way**	197?	40.00	100.00

HASKELL, JIMMIE

Imperial LP-9068	(M)	**Countdown**	1959	14.00	35.00
Imperial LP-12015	(S)	**Countdown**	1959	20.00	50.00

HASTINGS, BOB

Home HR-101	(M)	**Bob Hastings Sings For The Family**	1968	12.00	30.00

HAWKINS, DALE

Chess LP-1429	(M)	**Oh! Suzie-Q**	1958	500.00	See below
		(Near Mint copies have a suggested value of $800-1,200.)			
Roulette R-25175	(M)	**Let's All Twist At The Miami Beach Peppermint Lounge**	1962	60.00	150.00
Roulette SR-25175	(S)	**Let's All Twist At The Miami Beach Peppermint Lounge**	1962	80.00	200.00
Bell 6036	(S)	**L.A., Memphis And Tyler, Texas**	1969	16.00	40.00

HAWKINS, DOLORES

Epic LN-3250	(M)	**Dolores**	195?	16.00	40.00

Label & Catalog #		Title	Year	VG+	NM

HAWKINS, HAWKSHAW
Refer to Cowboy Copas / Hawkshaw Hawkins.

Gladwynne G-2006	(M)	Country Western Cavalcade	195?	60.00	150.00
King 587	(M)	Hawkshaw Hawkins	1958	60.00	150.00
King 592	(M)	Grand Ole Opry Favorites	1958	60.00	150.00
King 599	(M)	Hawkshaw Hawkins	1959	60.00	150.00
LaBrea 8020	(M)	Hawkshaw Hawkins	1961	40.00	100.00
LaBrea S-8020	(S)	Hawkshaw Hawkins	1961	40.00	100.00
King 808	(M)	The All New Hawkshaw Hawkins	1963	40.00	100.00
King KS-808	(S)	The All New Hawkshaw Hawkins	1963	60.00	150.00
King 858	(M)	Taken From Our Vaults, Volume 1	1963	20.00	50.00
King 870	(M)	Taken From Our Vaults, Volume 2	1963	20.00	50.00
King 873	(M)	Taken From Our Vaults, Volume 3	1963	20.00	50.00

Original King albums above have crownless black or blue labels with silver print.—

HAWKINS, RONNIE
The Hawks, a.k.a. The Band, is Ronnie's group on many of the Roulette sides.

Roulette R-25078	(M)	Ronnie Hawkins	1959	40.00	100.00
Roulette SR-25078	(S)	Ronnie Hawkins	1959	80.00	200.00
Roulette SR-25078	(S)	Ronnie Hawkins (Red vinyl)	1959	250.00	500.00
Roulette R-25102	(M)	Mr. Dynamo	1960	40.00	100.00
Roulette SR-25102	(S)	Mr. Dynamo	1960	80.00	200.00
Roulette SR-25102	(S)	Mr. Dynamo (Red vinyl)	1960	250.00	500.00
Roulette R-25120	(M)	The Folk Ballads Of Ronnie Hawkins	1960	30.00	75.00
Roulette SR-25120	(S)	The Folk Ballads Of Ronnie Hawkins	1960	60.00	150.00
Roulette R-25137	(M)	The Songs Of Hank Williams	1960	30.00	75.00
Roulette SR-25137	(S)	The Songs Of Hank Williams	1960	60.00	150.00
Roulette SR-42045	(S)	The Best Of Ronnie Hawkins & His Band	1970	10.00	25.00

(Roulette 42045 contains early '60s recordings with The Band.)

HAWKINS, "SCREAMIN' JAY"

Epic LN-3448	(M)	At Home With Screamin' Jay Hawkins	1958	500.00	See below

(Near Mint copies have a suggested value of $800-1,200.)

Epic LN-3457	(M)	I Put A Spell On You	1959	200.00	400.00
Epic BN-26457	(E)	I Put A Spell On You	1969	20.00	50.00

(Epic 26457 is a reissue of 3457.)

Philips PHS-600-319	(S)	What That Is	1969	16.00	40.00
Philips PHS-600-336	(S)	Screamin' Jay Hawkins	1970	16.00	40.00
Sounds Of Hawaii 5015	(S)	A Night At Forbidden City	196?	20.00	50.00

HAWKS, BILLY: *Refer to* **GOLDMINE'S PRICE GUIDE TO COLLECTIBLE JAZZ ALBUMS**

HAYDEN, WILLIE

Dooto DTL-293	(M)	Blame It On The Blues (Maroon label)	1960	200.00	400.00
Dooto DTL-293	(M)	Blame It On The Blues (Multi-color label)	196?	60.00	150.00

HAYES, BILL/BILL HAYES & THE BUCKLE BUSTERS

ABC-Paramount ABC-194	(M)	Bill Hayes Sings The Best Of Disney	1957	14.00	35.00
Kapp KL-1106	(M)	Jimmy Crack Corn	1958	12.00	30.00
Daybreak DR-2020	(S)	The Look Of Love	1972	10.00	25.00

HAYES, CATHY

Hifi R-416	(M)	It's All Right With Me	1959	16.00	40.00

HAYES, ISAAC

Enterprise E-100	(M)	Presenting Isaac Hayes	1968	12.00	30.00
Enterprise ES-100	(S)	Presenting Isaac Hayes	1968	10.00	25.00

HAYES, MARTHA: *Refer to* **GOLDMINE'S PRICE GUIDE TO COLLECTIBLE JAZZ ALBUMS**

HAYES, ROLAND
Classical trained tenor Roland Hayes is also a singer of Afro-American spirituals, or, as he terms them, "religious folkslieder."

Vanguard VRS-7016	(10")	Christmas Carols Of The Nations	195?	20.00	50.00
Vanguard VRS-462	(M)	Life Of Christ In Folk Song	1954	12.00	30.00
Vanguard VRS-494	(M)	My Songs, Aframerican Religious Folk-Songs	1955	12.00	30.00
A440 Records AC-1203	(M)	Recital	1953	16.00	40.00

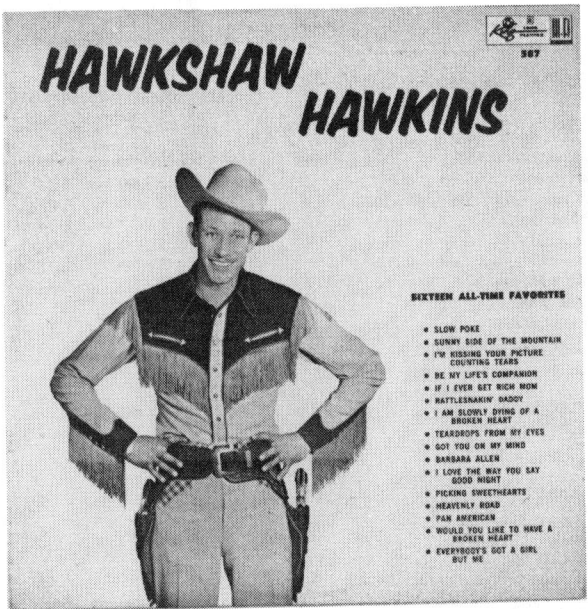

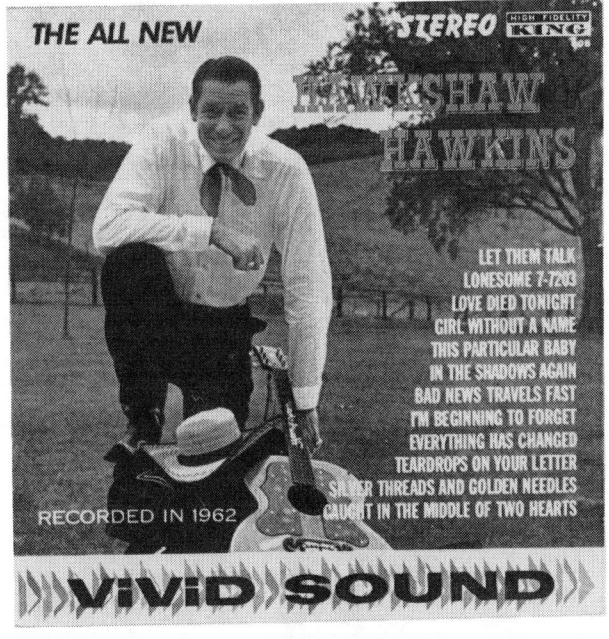

Harold "Hawkshaw" Hawkins was a country star during the '40s and '50s. Pictured here are his first LP for King, 1958's Hawkshaw Hawkins, *subtitled* Sixteen All-Time Favorites, *and his final release, 1963's* The All New Hawkshaw Hawkins, *in its rare stereo version (all King albums in stereo prior to 1966 are rare). On March 5, 1963, Hawkins was traveling with Patsy Cline and Cowboy Copas in a small airplane that crashed into the side of a Tennessee mountain. There were no survivors.*

Label & Catalog #		Title	Year	VG+	NM
HAYMARKET SQUARE					
Chaparral 201	(S)	**Magic Lantern**	1968	1,000.00	1,500.00
HAYMES, DICK					
Decca DL-5012	(10")	**Souvenir Album**	1949	20.00	50.00
Decca DL-5022	(10")	**Chrsimas Songs**	1949	20.00	50.00
Decca DL-5023	(10")	**Dick Haymes Sings Irving Berlin**	1950	20.00	50.00
Decca DL-5038	(10")	**Little Shamrocks**	1950	20.00	50.00
Capitol T-713	(M)	**Rain Or Shine**	1956	12.00	30.00
Capitol T-787	(M)	**Moondreams**	1956	12.00	30.00
Hallmark 301	(M)	**The Name's Haymes**	195?	12.00	30.00
Hollywood 138	(M)	**Look At Me Now**	195?	12.00	30.00
Decca DL-8773	(M)	**Little White Lies**	1959	20.00	50.00
Warwick W-2023	(M)	**Richard The Lion-Hearted**	1961	12.00	30.00
HAYNES, WALTER					
Mercury MG-20715	(M)	**Steel Guitar Sounds**	1962	12.00	30.00
Mercury SR-60715	(S)	**Steel Guitar Sounds**	1962	16.00	40.00
HAYSTACKERS, THE					
London APB-1008	(10")	**Square Dances**	195?	12.00	30.00
HAYWARD, JUSTIN, & JOHN LODGE					
Hayward and Lodge are members of The Moody Blues.					
Threshold THSX-1	(DJ)	**Blue Jays** *(Open-end interview with script)*	1975	20.00	50.00
HAYWOOD, LEON					
Galaxy 206	(S)	**The Mellow, Mellow Leon Haywood**	1967	20.00	50.00
HAZEL, EDDIE					
Eddie Hazel is a member of the Parliament/Funkadelic community.					
Warner Bros. 3058	(S)	**Games, Dames And Guitar Thangs**	1977	10.00	25.00
HAZLEWOOD, LEE					
Refer to Nancy Sinatra & Lee Hazlewood.					
Mercury MG-20860	(M)	**Trouble Is A Lonesome Town**	1964	8.00	20.00
Mercury SR-60860	(S)	**Trouble Is A Lonesome Town**	1964	10.00	25.00
HEAD, JIM, & HIS DEL RAYS					
"HP" 22893	(M)	**Jim Head & His Del Rays**	1964	80.00	200.00
HEAD, ROY					
TNT 101	(M)	**Roy Head And The Traits**	1965	40.00	100.00
Scepter S-532	(M)	**Treat Me Right**	1965	12.00	30.00
Scepter SS-532	(S)	**Treat Me Right**	1965	16.00	40.00
HEAD SHOP, THE					
Epic BN-26476	(S)	**The Head Shop**	1969	20.00	50.00
HEADSTONE					
Starr 740539	(S)	**Still Looking**	1974	60.00	150.00
HEART					
Heart features Ann and Nancy Wilson. Refer to Bordersong.					
Mushroom MRS-5008	(DJ)	**Magazine** *(Picture disc)*	1978	12.00	30.00
Portrait HR-44799	(S)	**Little Queen** *(Half-speed master)*	1981	10.00	30.00
Nautilus NR-3	(S)	**Dreamboat Annie**	1980	12.00	35.00
HEARTBEATS, THE					
The Heartbeats are James "Shep" Sheppard with Albert Crump, Wally Roker, Vernon Sievers and Robbie Tatum. Refer to Shep & The Limelites.					
Roulette R-25107	(M)	**A Thousand Miles Away**	1960	150.00	300.00
Roulette SR-25107	(E)	**A Thousand Miles Away**	1960	80.00	200.00
— Roulette albums above have white labels with four crossed color bars.—					
Emus ES-12033	(E)	**A Thousand Miles Away** *(Emus 12033 is a reissue of Roulette 25107.)*	1980	10.00	25.00

HEARTBEATS, THE: *Refer to* **FREDDIE HEART & THE HEARTBEATS**

Label & Catalog #		Title	Year	VG+	NM

HEARTS, THE
The Hearts feature Baby Washington.

Zells 337	(M)	**I Feel So Good**	195?	200.00	400.00

HEARTS & FLOWERS
Heart & Flowers features Rick Cunha. Linda Ronstadt supplies backing vocals.

Capitol T-2762	(M)	**Now Is The Time For Hearts And Flowers**	1967	12.00	30.00
Capitol ST-2762	(S)	**Now Is The Time For Hearts And Flowers**	1967	16.00	40.00
Capitol ST-2868	(S)	**Of Horses, Kids And Forgotten Women**	1968	20.00	50.00

HEATHER BLACK

American Playboy 1001	(S)	**Heather Black** *(2 LPs)*	197?	60.00	150.00
American Playboy 1001	(S)	**Heather Black** *(Single LP)*	197?	24.00	60.00
Double Bayou 2000	(S)	**Heather Black**	197?	12.00	30.00

HEAVEN

W.W. 8701	(S)	**Heaven**	197?	12.00	30.00

HEAVY BALLOON, THE

Elephant EVS-104	(S)	**32,000 Lbs.**	196?	14.00	35.00

HEBB, BOBBY

Philips PHM-200-212	(M)	**Sunny**	1966	10.00	25.00
Philips PHS-600-212	(S)	**Sunny**	1966	12.00	30.00

HEFTI, NEAL
Neal Hefti has had a long career as musician, composer and conductor in jazz, pop and soundtracks. The title listed below are those from his catalog of general interest...

Epic LN-3113	(M)	**Singing Instrumentals**	195?	20.00	50.00
Reprise R-6018	(M)	**Themes From TV's Top 12**	1962	10.00	25.00
Reprise R9-6018	(S)	**Themes From TV's Top 12**	1962	12.00	30.00
RCA Victor LPM-3573	(M)	**Batman Theme**	1966	16.00	40.00
RCA Victor LSP-3573	(S)	**Batman Theme**	1966	20.00	50.00
RCA Victor LPM-3621	(M)	**Hefti In Gotham City**	1966	20.00	50.00
RCA Victor LSP-3621	(S)	**Hefti In Gotham City**	1966	24.00	60.00

HELL, RICHARD, & THE VOIDOIDS

Sire SR-6037	(S)	**Blank Generation**	1977	10.00	25.00

HELMS, BOBBY

Decca DL-8638	(M)	**Bobby Helms Sings To My Special Angel**	1957	60.00	150.00
Columbia CL-2060	(M)	**The Best Of Bobby Helms**	1963	10.00	25.00
Columbia CS-8860	(S)	**The Best Of Bobby Helms**	1963	12.00	30.00

HELMS, DON

Smash MGS-27001	(M)	**Steel Guitar Sounds Of Hank Williams**	1963	10.00	25.00
Smash SRS-67001	(S)	**Steel Guitar Sounds Of Hank Williams**	1963	12.00	30.00
Smash MGS-27019	(M)	**Don Helms' Steel Guitar**	1963	10.00	25.00
Smash SRS-67019	(S)	**Don Helms' Steel Guitar**	1963	12.00	30.00

HELP

Decca DL-75257	(S)	**Help**	1971	10.00	25.00
Decca DL-75304	(S)	**Second Coming**	1971	10.00	25.00

HEMSWORTH, WADE

Folkways FP-821	(10")	**Canadian Northwest Ballads**	195?	20.00	50.00
Folkways FW-6821	(10")	**Canadian Northwest Ballads**	195?	20.00	50.00

HENDERSON, BILL: *Refer to* **GOLDMINE'S PRICE GUIDE TO COLLECTIBLE JAZZ ALBUMS**

HENDERSON, BUGS

Armadillo LP-78-1	(S)	**The Bugs Henderson Group At Last**	195?	12.00	30.00

HENDERSON, JOE

Todd MT-2701	(M)	**Snap Your Fingers**	1962	16.00	40.00
Todd ST-2701	(S)	**Snap Your Fingers**	1962	20.00	50.00
Capitol T-1765	(M)	**You'd Be So Nice To Come Home To**	1962	10.00	25.00
Capitol ST-1765	(S)	**You'd Be So Nice To Come Home To**	1962	12.00	30.00

Label & Catalog #		Title	Year	VG+	NM

HENDRICKS, JON: *Refer to* GOLDMINE'S PRICE GUIDE TO COLLECTIBLE JAZZ ALBUMS

HENDRIX, JIMI/THE JIMI HENDRIX EXPERIENCE
The Experience featured Hendrix with Noel Reding, replaced by Billy Cox in 1969. and Mitch Mitchell.
Refer to Eire Apparent; The Isley Brothers; Love; Martha Velez.

Label & Catalog #		Title	Year	VG+	NM
Reprise R-6261	(M)	**Are You Experienced?** (White label promo)	1967	150.00	300.00
Reprise R-6261	(M)	**Are You Experienced?**	1967	40.00	100.00
Reprise RS-6261	(S)	**Are You Experienced?**	1967	16.00	40.00
Reprise R-6281	(M)	**Axis: Bold As Love** (White label promo)	1968	360.00	600.00
Reprise R-6281	(M)	**Axis: Bold As Love**	1968	660.00	1,000.00
Reprise RS-6281	(S)	**Axis: Bold As Love**	1968	16.00	40.00
		— Reprise albums have pink, gold & green labels.—			
Reprise 2R-6307	(M)	**Electric Ladyland** (2 LPs. White label)	1968		See below
		(The mono white label promo for Reprise 6231 is rare with a suggested Near Mint value of $1,500-3,000.)			
Reprise 2RS-6307	(S)	**Electric Ladyland** (2 LPs. White label promo)	1968	80.00	200.00
Reprise 2RS-6307	(S)	**Electric Ladyland** (2 LPs)	1968	16.00	40.00
Reprise MS-2025	(S)	**Smash Hits** (White label promo)	1969	50.00	125.00
Reprise MS-2025	(P)	**Smash Hits** (With poster)	1969	24.00	60.00
Reprise MS-2025	(P)	**Smash Hits** (Without poster)	1969	10.00	25.00
		(Original covers advertised a poster in the lower right corner.)			
		— Reprise albums above have brown & orange labels.—			
Capitol STAO-472	(S)	**Band Of Gypsys** (Red label)	1970	10.00	25.00
Capitol R-104148	(S)	**Band Of Gypsys** (RCA Record Club)	1970	14.00	35.00
Capitol SJ-12416	(S)	**Band Of Gypsys 2** (Mispressing)	1986	60.00	150.00
		(Band Of Gypsys also includes Billy Cox and Buddy Miles. Original pressings were erroneously mastered with a completely different second side consisting of four unreleased tracks. The cover and label list the normal three tracks for side two so the disc must be viewed.)			
Reprise MS-2034	(S)	**The Cry Of Love** (White label promo)	1971	20.00	50.00
Reprise MS-2040	(S)	**Rainbow Bridge**	1971	10.00	25.00
Reprise MS-2049	(S)	**Hendrix In The West**	1972	10.00	25.00
Reprise MS-2103	(S)	**War Heroes** (White label promo)	1972	20.00	50.00
Reprise 2RS-6481	(S)	**Soundtrack Recordings From The Film "Jimi Hendrix"** (2 LPs)	1973	10.00	25.00
Reprise MS-2204	(S)	**Crash Landing** (Promo label)	1975	10.00	25.00
Reprise MS-2229	(S)	**Midnight Lightning** (Promo label)	1975	10.00	25.00
Reprise PRO-A-840	(DJ)	**The Jimi Hendrix Medley**	1979	30.00	75.00
		— Reprise albums above have brown labels.—			
MFP 5278	(S)	**What'd I Say** (U.S. pressing LP in U.K. jacket)	1970	16.00	40.00
Crawdaddy 5-1975	(DJ)	**The Jimi Hendrix Interview LP**	1975	80.00	200.00
Nutmeg NUT-1001	(S)	**High, Live 'N' Dirty** (Red vinyl)	1978	10.00	25.00
Nutmeg NUT-1001	(S)	**High, Live 'N' Dirty** (Black vinyl)	1978	10.00	25.00
Rhino RNDF-254	(M)	**The Jimi Hendrix Interview** (Black vinyl test pressing)	1982	10.00	25.00
Rhino RNDF-254	(M)	**The Jimi Hendrix Interview** (Picture disc)	1982	10.00	25.00

HENDRIX, JIMI, & CURTIS KNIGHT
Knight's group features a young Jimi Hendrix on guitar.

Label & Catalog #		Title	Year	VG+	NM
Capitol T-2856	(M)	**Get That Feeling**	1967	30.00	75.00
Capitol ST-2856	(S)	**Get That Feeling**	1967	20.00	50.00
Capitol T-2894	(M)	**Flashing**	1968	40.00	100.00
Capitol ST-2894	(S)	**Flashing**	1968	20.00	50.00

HENDRIX, JIMI / OTIS REDDING

Label & Catalog #		Title	Year	VG+	NM
Reprise MS-2029	(S)	**Historic Performances Recorded At The Monterey International Pop Festival**	1970	10.00	25.00

HENDRIX, JIMI, & LONNIE YOUNGBLOOD
Note: While the Maple album does in fact contain tapes of Jimi backing Youngblood, all of the other releases of this material contain doctored tapes using a Hendrix imitator!

Label & Catalog #		Title	Year	VG+	NM
Maple LPM-6004	(S)	**Two Great Experiences Together**	1971	14.00	35.00

HENRI, ADRIAN, & ROGER McGOUGH: *Refer to* THE LIVERPOOL SCENE

HENRY, CLARENCE "FROGMAN"

Label & Catalog #		Title	Year	VG+	NM
Argo LP-4009	(M)	**You Always Hurt The One You Love**	1961	50.00	150.00
Roulette SR-42039	(S)	**Alive And Well And Living In New Orleans**	1969	10.00	25.00

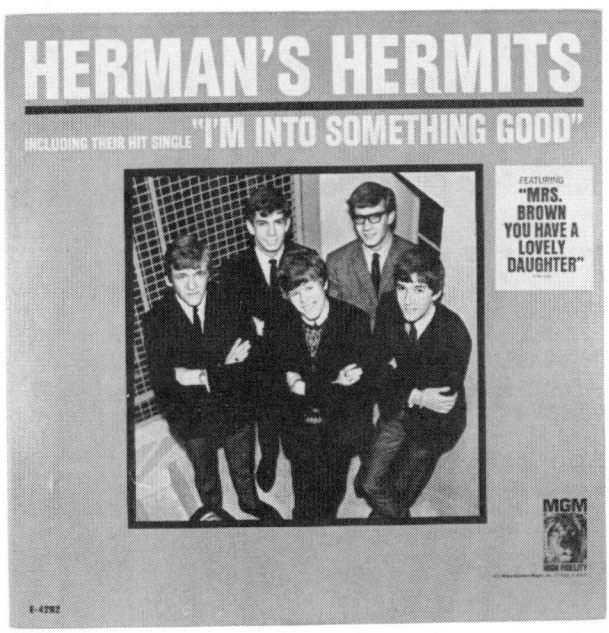

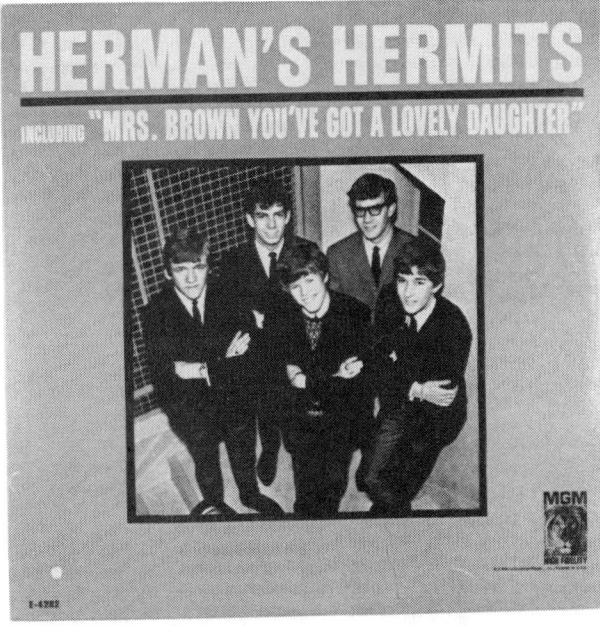

You can argue over The Beatles and The Stones in the beat battle of the world that took place in 1964-65, but on this side of the Atlantic it was Herman's Hermits that fought for chart supremacy with the Fab Four, scoring eighteen straight top 40 hits before their popularity waned in 1967. Each of their ten MGM albums made the charts, five of them achieving RIAA Gold Records. Original pressings of their first MGM album (above) read "Including Their Hit Single I'm Into Something Good" (the copy here has a sticker applied to the cover noting—and mistitling—their next single). After the unexpected success of "Mrs. Brown You've Got A Lovely Daughter," the cover of all subsequent pressings was amended (below).

Label & Catalog #		Title	Year	VG+	NM
HENSKE & YESTER					
Judy Henske and hubby Jerry Yester. Refer to The Lovin' Spoonful; The Modern Folk Quartet.					
Straight STS-1052	(S)	**Farewell Aldebaran**	1968	20.00	**50.00**
Reprise RS-6388	(S)	**Farewell Aldebaran**	1971	10.00	**25.00**
HENSON, COUSIN HERB, & THE TRADING POST GANG					
Tally	(M)	**Herb Henson & The Trading Post Gang**	195?	40.00	**100.00**
HEPTONES, THE					
Studio One SO-1108	(S)	**The Best Of The Heptones**	1976	14.00	**35.00**
HERD, THE					
The Herd features Peter Frampton.					
Fontana SRF-67579	(S)	**Lookin' Thru You**	1968	10.00	**25.00**
		("Understand Me" and "William" are rechanneled on this album.)			
HERE COMES EVERYBODY					
Cab 101	(S)	**Here Comes Everybody**	1971	16.00	**40.00**
HERMAN, MICHAEL/MICHAEL HERMAN'S FOLK DANCE ORCHESTRA					
RCA Victor LPM-1620	(M)	**Happy Folk Dances**	1958	12.00	**30.00**
RCA Victor LPM-1621	(M)	**Festival Folk Dances**	1958	12.00	**30.00**
RCA Victor LPM-1622	(M)	**Folk Dances For All Ages**	1958	12.00	**30.00**
RCA Victor LPM-1623	(M)	**All Purpose Dances**	1958	12.00	**30.00**
RCA Victor LPM-1624	(M)	**Folk Dances For Fun**	1958	12.00	**30.00**
RCA Victor LPM-1625	(M)	**First Folk Dances**	1958	12.00	**30.00**
HERMAN, PEE WEE					
Fatima	(S)	**The Pee Wee Herman Show** *(Picture disc)*	1981	20.00	**50.00**
HERMAN'S HERMITS					
Note: MGM dramatically over-estimated the long term impact of The Hermits, manufacturing copious quantities of all of their albums, Consequently, a diligent searcher can obtain still-sealed copies of most of the group's mono and stereo catalog for [comfortably] under $10 each. . .					
MGM E-4282	(M)	**Introducing Herman's Hermits**	1965	10.00	**25.00**
MGM SE-4282	(E)	**Introducing Herman's Hermits**	1965	8.00	**20.00**
		(Original covers on MGM 4282 read "Including Their Hit Singl " I'm Into Something Good.")			
MGM DT-90613	(E)	**Best Of Herman's Hermits** *(Cap. Rec. Club)*	1965	10.00	**25.00**
HERMON KNIGHTS, THE					
C.O. 2323	(S)	**The Hermon Knights**	1968	20.00	**50.00**
HESITATIONS, THE					
Kapp KL-1525	(M)	**Soul Superman**	1967	10.00	**25.00**
Kapp KS-3525	(S)	**Soul Superman**	1967	10.00	**25.00**
Kapp KS-3548	(S)	**The New Born Free**	1968	10.00	**25.00**
Kapp KS-3561	(S)	**Where We're At**	1968	10.00	**25.00**
Kapp KS-3574	(S)	**Solid Gold**	1968	10.00	**25.00**
HESS, CHUCK, & HIS CHUCK-RIDERS					
Strand SL-1084	(M)	**Country & Western Favorites**	1960	10.00	**25.00**
Strand SLS-1084	(S)	**Country & Western Favorites**	1960	12.00	**30.00**
HESTER, BENNY					
V.M.I. 72001	(S)	**Benny Hester**	1972	20.00	**50.00**
HESTER, CAROLYN					
Carolyn Hester is a guitar player and singer of contemporary folk material.					
Coral CRL-57143	(M)	**Carolyn Hester**	1957	20.00	**50.00**
Tradition TLP-1043	(M)	**Carolyn Hester**	1961	14.00	**35.00**
Columbia CL-1796	(M)	**Carolyn Hester**	1962	20.00	**50.00**
Columbia CS-8596	(S)	**Carolyn Hester**	1962	30.00	**75.00**
		(On her first Columbia album, Ms Hester is harmonica-ally [sic] backed by Bob Dylan on "Swing And Turn Jubilee," "I'll Fly Away" and "Come Back, Baby." A rare and important Dylan artifact.)			
Columbia CL-2032	(M)	**This Life I'm Living**	1963	8.00	**20.00**
Columbia CS-8832	(S)	**This Life I'm Living**	1963	10.00	**25.00**
Metromedia MD-1022	(S)	**Magazine**	197?	30.00	**75.00**

Label & Catalog #		Title	Year	VG+	NM

HEYWOOD, EDDIE: *Refer to* GOLDMINE'S PRICE GUIDE TO COLLECTIBLE JAZZ ALBUMS

HI-LITES, THE
| Dandee DLP-206 | (M) | **For Your Precious Love** | 1958 | 400.00 | *See below* |

(Near Mint copies have a suggested value of $800-1,200.)

HI-LO'S, THE
Refer to Rosemary Clooney & The Hi-Lo's; The Reprise Repertory Theatre.
Starlite 6004	(10")	**Listen!**	1955	20.00	75.00
Starlite 6005	(10")	**The Hi-Lo's, I Presume**	1955	20.00	75.00
Starlite 7005	(M)	**Under Glass**	1956	16.00	50.00
Starlite 7006	(M)	**Listen!**	1956	16.00	50.00
Starlite 7007	(M)	**The Hi-Lo's, I Presume**	1956	16.00	50.00
Starlite 7008	(M)	**On Hand**	1956	16.00	50.00
Kapp KL-1027	(M)	**The Hi-Lo's And The Jerry Fielding Band**	1956	12.00	40.00
Kapp KL-1184	(M)	**Under Glass**	1959	12.00	30.00
Kapp KL-1194	(M)	**On Hand**	1960	12.00	30.00
Omega SL-11	(S)	**The Hi-Lo's In Stereo**	195?	12.00	30.00
Columbia CL-952	(M)	**Suddenly It's The Hi-Lo's**	1957	16.00	40.00
Columbia CL-1023	(M)	**Now Hear This**	1957	16.00	40.00
Columbia CL-1259	(M)	**The Hi-Lo's And All That Jazz**	1959	12.00	30.00
Columbia CS-8077	(S)	**The Hi-Lo's And All That Jazz**	1959	16.00	40.00
Columbia CL-1416	(M)	**Broadway Playbill**	1959	12.00	30.00
Columbia CS-8213	(S)	**Broadway Playbill**	1959	16.00	40.00
Columbia CL-1509	(M)	**All Over The Place**	1960	10.00	25.00
Columbia CS-8300	(S)	**All Over The Place**	1960	12.00	30.00
Columbia CL-1723	(M)	**This Time It's Love**	1962	10.00	25.00
Columbia CS-8523	(S)	**This Time It's Love**	1962	12.00	30.00

— Columbia albums above have three white on black "eye" logos around the perimeter of each labels.—
| Reprise R-6066 | (M) | **The Hi-Lo's Happen To Bossa Nova** | 1963 | 8.00 | 20.00 |
| Reprise RS-6066 | (S) | **The Hi-Lo's Happen To Bossa Nova** | 1963 | 10.00 | 25.00 |

HI-TONES, THE
| Hi HL-31011 | (M) | **Raunchy Sounds** | 1963 | 8.00 | 20.00 |
| Hi SHL-32011 | (S) | **Raunchy Sounds** | 1963 | 10.00 | 25.00 |

HIBBLER, AL: *Refer to* GOLDMINE'S PRICE GUIDE TO COLLECTIBLE JAZZ ALBUMS

HICKMAN, DWAYNE
| Capitol T-1441 | (M) | **Dobie!** | 1960 | 14.00 | 35.00 |
| Capitol ST-1441 | (S) | **Dobie!** | 1960 | 20.00 | 50.00 |

HIGGINS, CHUCK
| Combo LP-300 | (M) | **Pachuko Hop** | 1960 | 300.00 | 750.00 |

(Original covers for Combo 800 picture a delightfully naked woman.)
| Combo LP-300 | (M) | **Pachuko Hop** | 1961 | 150.00 | 400.00 |

(Later covers picture a photo of a fully attired Higgins.)

HIGGINS, CHUCK / ROY MILTON
| Dooto DTL-223 | (M) | **Rock 'N' Roll Versus Rhythm And Blues** | 1959 | 150.00 | 400.00 |
| Authentic AUL-223 | (M) | **Rock 'N' Roll Versus Rhythm And Blues** | 196? | 60.00 | 150.00 |

(Authentic 223 is a reissue of Dooto 223.)

HIGH TIDE
| Liberty LST-7638 | (S) | **Sea Shanties** | 1969 | 10.00 | 25.00 |

HIGH TREASON
| Abbott ABS-1209 | (S) | **High Treason** | 197? | 20.00 | 50.00 |

HIGHTOWER, DEAN
| ABC-Paramount 312 | (M) | **Guitar-Twangy With A Beat** | 1959 | 10.00 | 25.00 |
| ABC-Paramount S-312 | (S) | **Guitar-Twangy With A Beat** | 1959 | 14.00 | 35.00 |

HIGHTOWER, DONNA: *Refer to* GOLDMINE'S PRICE GUIDE TO COLLECTIBLE JAZZ ALBUMS

HIGHWAY, THE
| *(No label)* | (S) | **The Highway** | 197? | 60.00 | 150.00 |

Label & Catalog #		Title	Year	VG+	NM
HILDEGARDE					
Decca DL-8656	(M)	**Souvenir Album**	1958	10.00	25.00
HILL, GOLDIE/GOLDIE HILL SMITH					
Decca DL-4034	(M)	**Goldie Hill**	1960	12.00	30.00
Decca DL-74034	(S)	**Goldie Hill**	1960	16.00	40.00
Decca DL-4148	(M)	**Lonely Heartaches**	1961	8.00	20.00
Decca DL-74148	(S)	**Lonely Heartaches**	1961	12.00	30.00
Decca DL-4219	(M)	**According To My Heart**	1962	8.00	20.00
Decca DL-74219	(S)	**According To My Heart**	1962	10.00	25.00
Decca DL-4492	(M)	**Country Hit Parade**	1964	8.00	20.00
Decca DL-74492	(S)	**Country Hit Parade**	1964	10.00	25.00
HILL, Z. Z.					
Kent KLP-5018	(M)	**The Soul Stirrings Of Z. Z. Hill**	1965	16.00	40.00
Kent KST-518	(S)	**The Soul Stirrings Of Z. Z. Hill**	1965	20.00	50.00
HILLEL & AVIVA					
Riverside RLP-12-803	(M)	**Land Of Milk And Honey**	195?	12.00	30.00
Elektra EKL-171	(M)	**A Concert With Hillel And Aviva**	1959	10.00	25.00
Elektra EKS-7171	(S)	**A Concert With Hillel And Aviva**	1959	12.00	30.00

HILLMEN, THE
These 1963-64 recordings are actually by The Golden State Boys: Vern and Rex Gosdin, Chris Hillmen and Don Parmley. The album was named The Hillmen due to Hillman's success with The Byrds and The Flying Buritto Brothers. Refer to The Gosdin Brothers; The Scottsville Squirrel Barkers.

Together STT-1012	(S)	**The Hillmen**	1970	30.00	75.00
Sugar Hill SH-3719	(S)	**The Hillmen**	1981	4.00	10.00
HILLOW HAMMET					
House Of Fox 2	(S)	**Hammer**	197?	24.00	60.00
L & BJ 14028	(S)	**Hammer**	197?	40.00	100.00

HILLTOPPERS, THE
The Hilltoppers feature future MOR master Billy Vaughn.

Dot DLP-3003	(M)	**The Hilltoppers Present Tops In Pops**	1955	20.00	50.00
		(Original covers of Dot 3003 feature a cartoon of a young female fan.)			
Dot DLP-3003	(M)	**The Hilltoppers Present Tops In Pops**	1956	14.00	35.00
		(Later covers feature four collegiate caps with a "W" on each.)			
Dot DLP-3029	(M)	**The Towering Hilltoppers**	1957	14.00	35.00
Dot DLP-3073	(M)	**Love In Bloom**	1958	14.00	35.00

HILTON, L. M.
Lavoli Hilton is a singer of Mormon folk songs.

Folkways FP-36	(10")	**Mormon Folk Songs**	1952	20.00	50.00
Folkways FA-2036	(10")	**Mormon Folk Songs**	1952	20.00	50.00
HINES, ERNIE					
WeProduce 1902	(S)	**Electrified**	1972	20.00	50.00
HINES, MIMI					
Decca DL-8434	(M)	**Mimi Hines Is A Happening**	1958	10.00	25.00
Decca DL-78434	(S)	**Mimi Hines Is A Happening**	1958	12.00	30.00
HINSON, DON, & THE RIGORMORTICIANS					
Capitol T-2219	(M)	**Monster Dance Party**	1964	14.00	35.00
Capitol ST-2219	(S)	**Monster Dance Party**	1964	20.00	50.00
HINTON, JOE					
Backbeat B-60	(M)	**Funny (How Time Slips Away)**	1965	14.00	35.00
Backbeat B-60	(S)	**Funny (How Time Slips Away)**	1965	20.00	50.00
Dule 91	(M)	**Duke-Peacock Remembers**	1969	8.00	20.00

HINTON, SAM
Sam Hinton was a singer and multi-instrumental player of traditional folk music.

Decca DL-8108	(M)	**Singing Across The Land**	1956	14.00	35.00
Decca DL-8418	(M)	**A Family Tree Of Folk Songs**	1957	14.00	35.00

Label & Catalog #		Title	Year	VG+	NM

HIRT, AL
Al Hirt combined Dixieland swing with pop music over a lengthy and successful career. The sole entry here is of general interest. His early jazz work can be found in Goldmine's Price Guide To Collectible Jazz Albums. Refer to Ann-Margret & Al Hirt.

Label & Catalog #		Title	Year	VG+	NM
RCA Victor LPM-3716	(M)	The Horn Meets The Hornet	1966	10.00	25.00
RCA Victor LSP-3716	(S)	The Horn Meets The Hornet	1966	12.00	30.00
		(Original covers for RCA 3715 feature TV's Green Hornet.)			

HITCHCOCK, ALFRED

Imperial LP-9052	(M)	Music To Be Murdered By	1958	40.00	100.00
Imperial LP-12052	(S)	Music To Be Murdered By	1958	60.00	150.00
Golden GLP-89	(M)	Alfred Hitchcock's Ghost Stories For Young People	1962	30.00	75.00

HOBBITS, THE

Decca DL-4290	(M)	Down To Middle Earth	1967	12.00	30.00
Decca DL-74290	(S)	Down To Middle Earth	1967	16.00	40.00
Decca DL-5009	(M)	Men And Doors	1968	8.00	20.00
Decca DL-75009	(S)	Men And Doors	1968	10.00	25.00
Perception	(S)	Return To Middle Earth	1971	12.00	30.00

HOFFMAN, ABBIE

Big Toe 1	(M)	Wake Up, America!	196?	12.00	30.00

HOFNER, ADOLPH

Decca DL-5564	(10")	Dance-O-Rama #4	1955	200.00	400.00

HOGAN, CLAIRE

MGM E-3349	(M)	Just Imagine	1956	16.00	40.00
MGM E-4501	(M)	Boozers And Losers	1967	8.00	20.00
MGM SE-4501	(S)	Boozers And Losers	1967	10.00	25.00

HOGAN'S HEROES

Sunset SUM-1137	(M)	The Best Of World War II	1966	8.00	20.00
Sunset SUS-5137	(S)	The Best Of World War II	1966	10.00	25.00

HOGG, ANDREW "SMOKEY"

Time 6	(M)	Smokey Hogg	1962	40.00	100.00
Crown CLP-5226	(M)	Smokey Hogg Sings The Blues	1962	20.00	50.00

HOLCOMB, ROSCOE
Roscoe Holcomb is a guitar, banjo and harp player and singer of traditional American folk music.

Folkways FA-2317	(M)	Mountain Music Of Kentucky	1959	12.00	30.00
Folkways FA-2368	(M)	The High Lonesome Sound *(Soundtrack)*	1962	12.00	30.00
Folkways FA-2374	(M)	Close To Home	1963	12.00	30.00

HOLCOMB, ROSCOE, & WADE WARD

Folkways FA-2363	(M)	The Music Of Roscoe Holcomb & Wade Ward	1962	12.00	30.00

HOLDEN, RANDY
Holden was formerly a member of The Other Half; Blue Cheer.

Hobbit 5002	(S)	Population II	1968	40.00	200.00

HOLDEN, RON

Donna DLP-2111	(M)	I Love You So	1960	100.00	250.00
Donna DLPS-2111	(S)	I Love You So	1960	300.00	500.00

HOLIDAY, BILLIE: *Refer to* **GOLDMINE'S PRICE GUIDE TO COLLECTIBLE JAZZ ALBUMS**

HOLIDAY, JIMMY

Minit LP-40005	(M)	Turning Point	1966	8.00	20.00
Minit LP-24005	(S)	Turning Point	1966	10.00	25.00

HOLLAND, EDDIE

Motown 604	(M)	Eddie Holland	1963	100.00	250.00

HOLLIDAY, JUDY

Columbia OL-5170	(M)	Bells Are Ringing *(Original Cast)*	1956	16.00	40.00

Label & Catalog #		Title	Year	VG+	NM
Columbia CL-1153	(M)	**Trouble Is A Man**	1958	12.00	30.00
Columbia CS-8041	(S)	**Trouble Is A Man**	1959	16.00	40.00
Capitol W-1435	(M)	**Bells Are Ringing** (Soundtrack)	1960	8.00	20.00
Capitol SW-1435	(S)	**Bells Are Ringing** (Soundtrack)	1960	12.00	30.00

HOLLIES, THE
Original members include Allan Clarke, Graham Nash, Tony Hicks, Eric Haydock and Donald Rathbone. Rathbone was replaced by Bobby Elliott in 1963; Haydock by Bernie Calvert, 1966; and Nash by Terry Sylvester, 1968. Mikael Rikfors replaced Clarke on "Romany." Refer to The Everly Brothers.

Imperial LP-9265	(M)	**Here I Go Again**	1964	40.00	100.00
Imperial LP-12265	(E)	**Here I Go Again**	1964	30.00	75.00
		— Imperial albums above have black labels with colored stars and rays on top.—			
Imperial LP-9265	(M)	**Here I Go Again**	1964	20.00	50.00
Imperial LP-12265	(E)	**Here I Go Again**	1964	14.00	35.00
Imperial LP-9299	(M)	**Hear! Here!**	1965	20.00	50.00
Imperial LP-12299	(E)	**Hear! Here!**	1965	16.00	40.00
Imperial LP-9312	(M)	**The Hollies—Beat Group**	1966	12.00	30.00
Imperial LP-12312	(S)	**The Hollies—Beat Group**	1966	16.00	40.00
Imperial LP-9330	(M)	**Bus Stop**	1966	16.00	40.00
Imperial LP-12330	(E)	**Bus Stop**	1966	12.00	30.00
		— Imperial albums above have black, pink & white labels.—			
United Arts. UAL-4148	(M)	**After The Fox** (Soundtrack)	1966	10.00	25.00
United Arts. UAS-5148	(S)	**After The Fox** (Soundtrack)	1966	12.00	30.00
		(The Hollies back Peter Sellers on "After The Fox," which is rechanneled on 5148.)			
Imperial LP-9330	(M)	**Bus Stop**	1966	10.00	25.00
Imperial LP-12330	(E)	**Bus Stop**	1966	8.00	20.00
Imperial LP-9339	(M)	**Stop! Stop! Stop!**	1966	10.00	25.00
Imperial LP-12339	(S)	**Stop! Stop! Stop!**	1966	12.00	30.00
Imperial LP-9350	(M)	**The Hollies' Greatest Hits**	1967	8.00	20.00
Imperial LP-12350	(P)	**The Hollies' Greatest Hits**	1967	10.00	25.00
		— Imperial albums above have black, green & white labels.—			
Epic LN-24315	(M)	**Evolution**	1967	8.00	20.00
Epic BN-26315	(S)	**Evolution**	1967	10.00	25.00
Epic LN-24344	(M)	**Dear Eloise/King Midas In Reverse**	1967	8.00	20.00
Epic BN-26344	(S)	**Dear Eloise/King Midas In Reverse**	1967	10.00	25.00
Epic BN-26447	(S)	**Words And Music By Bob Dylan**	1968	10.00	25.00
Epic BN-26538	(S)	**He Ain't Heavy, He's My Brother**	1969	10.00	25.00
Epic KE-30255	(S)	**Moving Finger**	1970	10.00	25.00
		— Epic albums above have yellow labels.—			

HOLLIN'S FERRY

Port City	(S)	**Hollin's Ferry**	197?	30.00	75.00

HOLLOWAY, BRENDA

Tamla T-257	(M)	**Every Little Bit Hurts**	1964	100.00	250.00
Tamla TS-257	(E)	**Every Little Bit Hurts**	1964	80.00	200.00

HOLLY, BUDDY/BUDDY HOLLY & THE CRICKETS
Buddy Holly originally signed to Decca as a solo with Decca, who tried to record him as country singer. He then signed with his group, The Crickets, to Brunswick and as a solo with that label's subsidiary, Coral. Aside from "The Chirping Crickets" album, his recordings with and without the group were collected on Coral albums. In the wake of his death, The Crickets continued as a group while producer Norman Petty took Holly's demos and overdubbed rock'n roll backing tracks by The Fireballs onto the tapes for a "fuller, more commercial" sound. Refer to Buddy Knox & Jimmy Bowen; The Crickets; Terry Noland; and Norman Petty.

Decca DL-8707	(M)	**That'll Be The Day** (Pink label promo)	1958	1,000.00	1,500.00
Decca DL-8707	(M)	**That'll Be The Day**	1958	1,400.00	2,000.00
		(Original pressings of DL-8707 have black labels with silver print.)			
Decca DL-8707	(M)	**That'll Be The Day**	196?	100.00	200.00
		(Later pressings have a black label with a rainbow band through the center and were pressed on thick vinyl. Counterfeits from the '70s have poor cover reproduction and were pressed on thin vinyl.)			
Brunswick BL-54038	(M)	**The Chirping Crickets** (Yellow label promo)	1957		See below
		(Promos of BL-54038 have suggested values in VG of $300-600; in VG+ of $1,000-2,000; and in NM of $3,000-5,000.)			
Brunswick BL-54038	(M)	**The Chirping Crickets**	1957	400.00	800.00
Coral CRL-57210	(M)	**Buddy Holly** (Blue label promo)	1958	500.00	1,000.00
Coral CRL-57210	(M)	**Buddy Holly**	1958	150.00	300.00

The Hollies ran up an impressive string of hits on the UK charts, ranking them with The Beatles and The Rolling Stones among Great Britain's hit-makers of the '60s. Unfortunately, precious little of their always excellent, often incredible singles made it big on the American charts. Like may British groups, their catalog of material included updates of oldies, as witness their first two U.S. albums above. While the first is mediocre, their second, Hear! Here!, can sit comfortably alongside any of The Beatles albums of the period as a wondrous example of British beat at its best!

Label & Catalog #		Title	Year	VG+	NM
Coral CRL-57279	(M)	The Buddy Holly Story (Blue label promo)	1959	500.00	750.00
Coral CRL-57279	(M)	The Buddy Holly Story	1959	150.00	300.00
		(The print on the back cover is in red and black.)			
Coral CRL-57279	(M)	The Buddy Holly Story	1959	80.00	200.00
Coral CRL-757279	(E)	The Buddy Holly Story	1959	70.00	175.00
		(The print on the back cover is in black only.)			
Coral CRL-57326	(M)	Buddy Holly Story, Vol. 2 (Blue label promo)	1959	500.00	750.00
Coral CRL-57326	(M)	Buddy Holly Story, Vol. 2	1959	60.00	150.00
Coral CRL-57405	(M)	Buddy Holly & The Crickets (Blue label)	1962	500.00	750.00
Coral CRL-57405	(M)	Buddy Holly & The Crickets	1962	80.00	200.00
Coral CRL-757405	(E)	Buddy Holly & The Crickets	1962	60.00	150.00
		(Coral 57405 is a reissue of Brunswick 54038.)			
Coral CRL-57426	(M)	Reminiscing (Yellow label promo)	1963	300.00	500.00
Coral CRL-57426	(M)	Reminiscing	1963	80.00	200.00
Coral CRL-757426	(E)	Reminiscing	1963	60.00	150.00
		— Coral albums above have maroon labels.—			
Coral CRL-57210	(M)	Buddy Holly	1963	40.00	100.00
Coral CRL-57279	(M)	The Buddy Holly Story	1963	30.00	75.00
Coral CRL-757279	(E)	The Buddy Holly Story	1963	20.00	50.00
Coral CRL-57326	(M)	The Buddy Holly Story, Vol. 2	1963	30.00	75.00
Coral CRL-757326	(E)	The Buddy Holly Story, Vol. 2	1963	20.00	50.00
Coral CRL-57426	(M)	Reminiscing	1964	30.00	75.00
Coral CRL-757426	(E)	Reminiscing	1964	20.00	50.00
Coral CRL-57450	(M)	Showcase (Yellow label promo)	1964	100.00	250.00
Coral CRL-57450	(M)	Showcase	1964	40.00	100.00
Coral CRL-757450	(E)	Showcase	1964	30.00	75.00
Coral CRL-57463	(M)	Holly In The Hills (Yellow label promo)	1965	100.00	250.00
Coral CRL-57463	(M)	Holly In The Hills	1965	50.00	125.00
Coral CRL-757463	(E)	Holly In The Hills	1965	40.00	100.00
Coral CXB-8	(M)	The Best Of Buddy Holly (Yellow label)	1966	100.00	200.00
Coral CXB-8	(M)	The Best Of Buddy Holly	1966	30.00	75.00
Coral CXSB-8	(E)	The Best Of Buddy Holly	1966	20.00	50.00
Coral CRL-57492	(M)	Buddy Holly's Greatest Hits	1967	30.00	75.00
Coral CRL-757492	(E)	Buddy Holly's Greatest Hits	1967	20.00	50.00
Coral CRL-757504	(E)	Giant (Yellow label promo)	1969	60.00	150.00
Coral CRL-757504	(E)	Giant	1969	20.00	50.00
		— Coral albums above have black labels that read "A subsidiary of Decca."—			
Vocalion VL-3811	(M)	The Great Buddy Holly	1967	30.00	75.00
Vocalion VL-73811	(E)	The Great Buddy Holly	1967	20.00	50.00
		(Vocalion 3811 is a repackage of "That'll Be The Day.")			
Vocalion VL-73923	(E)	Good Rockin'	1971	40.00	100.00
Decca DXSE-207	(M)	A Rock & Roll Collection (2 LPs)	1972	14.00	35.00
MCA 2-4009	(M)	A Rock & Roll Collection (2 LPs)	1973	10.00	25.00
		(Reissue of Decca 207. Original pressings have liner notes.)			

HOLLYWOOD SOUNDSTAGE ORCHESTRA, THE

Label & Catalog #		Title	Year	VG+	NM
Somerset P-1500	(M)	Songs Of The Golden West / Songs Of The Deep South	195?	10.00	25.00

HOLLYRIDGE STRINGS, THE

Label & Catalog #		Title	Year	VG+	NM
Capitol T-2156	(M)	The Beach Boys Songbook	1964	8.00	20.00
Capitol ST-2156	(S)	The Beach Boys Songbook	1964	10.00	25.00
Capitol T-2221	(M)	Hits Made Famous By Elvis Presley	1964	8.00	20.00
Capitol ST-2221	(S)	Hits Made Famous By Elvis Presley	1964	10.00	25.00
Capitol T-2749	(M)	The Beach Boys Songbook, Volume 2	1967	8.00	20.00
Capitol ST-2749	(S)	The Beach Boys Songbook, Volume 2	1967	10.00	25.00

HOLLYWOOD ARGYLES, THE

The Hollywood Argyles feature Gary Paxton.

Label & Catalog #		Title	Year	VG+	NM
Lute L-101	(M)	The Hollywood Argyles	1960	200.00	500.00
Lute L-9001	(M)	The Hollywood Argyles	1960	200.00	500.00
		(It is possible that two pressings with above catalog numbers exist or that covers designate the album L-101 while the record labels carries the L-9001 number.)			

HOLLYWOOD PERSUADERS, THE

Label & Catalog #		Title	Year	VG+	NM
Original Sound LPM-5013	(M)	Drums A Go-Go	1965	20.00	50.00
Original Sound LPS-8874	(S)	Drums A Go-Go	1965	30.00	75.00

Country's favorite comedy duo consisted of Henry "Homer" Haynes and Kenneth "Jethro" Burns, who played their way through three decades of country music, lampooning each and every change in artistic style or public taste. The cover for Barefoot Ballads, *electric guitar anomaly included, readily displays their vaudevillian cornpone ("Hee haw!") approach to humor.* Life Can Miserable, *an early example of RCA's "Living Stereo," boasts a marvelous drawing by former EC horror master Jack Davis.*

Label & Catalog #		Title	Year	VG+	NM
HOLMAN, EDDIE					
ABC S-701	(S)	**I Love You**	1969	12.00	30.00
HOLMAN, LIBBY					
Evergreen MR-6501	(M)	**The Legendary Libby Holman** (With book)	1965	10.00	25.00
Evergreen MRS-6501	(S)	**The Legendary Libby Holman** (With book)	1965	12.00	30.00
HOLMES, MARVIN, & JUSTICE					
Brown Door MH-6573	(S)	**Summer Of '73**	1973	10.00	25.00
Brown Door MH-6581	(S)	**Honor Thy Father**	1975	10.00	25.00
HOLT, WILL					
Will Holt is a a musician, composer and singer of many types of music, including folk based songs.					
Stinson SLP-64	(10")	**Songs And Ballads**	195?	16.00	40.00
Coral CRL-57114	(M)	**The World Of Will Holt**	1957	16.00	40.00
HOLT, WILL, & DOLLY JONAH					
Atlantic 8051	(M)	**On The Brink**	1961	8.00	20.00
Atlantic SD-8051	(S)	**On The Brink**	1961	10.00	25.00
HOLY MACKEREL					
Holy Mackerel features Paul Williams.					
Reprise RS-6311	(S)	**Holy Mackerel**	1968	10.00	25.00
HOLY MODAL ROUNDERS, THE					
The Rounders are Peter Stampfel and Steve Weber. Refer to The Fugs.					
Folklore FRLP-14031	(M)	**The Holy Modal Rounders**	1964	30.00	75.00
Prestige PRLP-7410	(M)	**The Holy Modal Rounders 2** (Blue label)	1966	14.00	35.00
Prestige PRLP-7451	(M)	**The Holy Modal Rounders** (Blue label)	1966	14.00	35.00
		(Prestige 7451 is a reissue of Folklore 14031.)			
ESP-Disk' 1068	(M)	**Indian War Whoop**	1967	16.00	40.00
ESP-Disk' 1068	(S)	**Indian War Whoop**	1967	16.00	40.00
Elektra EKS-74026	(S)	**The Moray Eels**			
		Eat The Holy Modal Rounders	1968	12.00	30.00
Metromedia MD-1039	(S)	**Good Taste Is Timeless**	1971	12.00	30.00
HOMBRES, THE					
Verve/Forecast FT-3036	(M)	**Let It Out**	1967	10.00	25.00
Verve/Forecast FTS-3036	(S)	**Let It Out**	1967	12.00	30.00
HOMER					
Universal Rec. Art. HS-101	(S)	**Grown In U.S.A**	197?	150.00	300.00
HOMER & JETHRO					
Country comedians/musicians Henry "Homer" Haynes and Kenny "Jethro" Burns. Refer to The Country All-Stars; The Nashville String Band.					
RCA Victor LPM-3112	(10")	**Homer & Jethro Fracture Frank Loesser**	1953	80.00	200.00
Audio Lab AL-1513	(M)	**Musical Madness**	1958	80.00	200.00
King 639	(M)	**They Sure Are Corny**	1959	60.00	150.00
King 848	(M)	**Cornier Than Corn**	1963	40.00	100.00
RCA Victor LPM-1412	(M)	**Barefoot Ballads**	1957	20.00	50.00
RCA Victor LPM-1560	(M)	**The Worst Of Homer & Jethro**	1957	20.00	50.00
RCA Victor LPM-1880	(M)	**Life Can Be Miserable**	1958	14.00	35.00
RCA Victor LSP-1880	(S)	**Life Can Be Miserable**	1958	20.00	50.00
RCA Victor LPM-2181	(M)	**At The Country Club**	1960	12.00	30.00
RCA Victor LSP-2181	(S)	**At The Country Club**	1960	16.00	40.00
RCA Victor LPM-2286	(M)	**Songs My Mother Never Sang**	1961	12.00	30.00
RCA Victor LSP-2286	(S)	**Songs My Mother Never Sang**	1961	16.00	40.00
RCA Victor LPM-2455	(M)	**Zany Songs Of The '30s**	1962	12.00	30.00
RCA Victor LSP-2455	(S)	**Zany Songs Of The '30s**	1962	16.00	40.00
RCA Victor LPM-2459	(M)	**Playing It Straight**	1962	12.00	30.00
RCA Victor LSP-2459	(S)	**Playing It Straight**	1962	16.00	40.00
RCA Victor LPM-2492	(M)	**Homer & Jethro At The Convention**	1962	12.00	30.00
RCA Victor LSP-2492	(S)	**Homer & Jethro At The Convention**	1962	16.00	40.00
RCA Victor LPM-2674	(M)	**Homer & Jethro Go West**	1963	12.00	30.00
RCA Victor LSP-2674	(S)	**Homer & Jethro Go West**	1963	16.00	40.00

— RCA mono albums above have "Long Play" on the bottom of the label;
stereo albums have "Living Stereo" on the bottom. —

John Lee Hooker is a prime mover in the transition from the classic acoustic blues of the pre-World War II era and the electronically amplified blues of the post-war period, which led directly to the formation of th sub-genre, "rhythm'n blues." John Lee Hooker Plays & Sings The Blues is a classic from the early '60s; had it not contained the excellent music within, its beautiful cover alone could have made it a collectible!

Label & Catalog #		Title	Year	VG+	NM
RCA Victor LPM-2743	(M)	Ooh, That's Corny	1963	10.00	25.00
RCA Victor LSP-2743	(S)	Ooh, That's Corny	1963	12.00	30.00
RCA Victor LPM-2928	(M)	Cornfucius Say	1964	10.00	25.00
RCA Victor LSP-2928	(S)	Cornfucius Say	1964	12.00	30.00
RCA Victor LPM-2954	(M)	Fractured Folk Songs	1964	10.00	25.00
RCA Victor LSP-2954	(S)	Fractured Folk Songs	1964	12.00	30.00
RCA Victor LPM-3357	(M)	Homer & Jethro Sing Tenderly	1965	10.00	25.00
RCA Victor LSP-3357	(S)	Homer & Jethro Sing Tenderly	1965	12.00	30.00
RCA Victor LPM-3462	(M)	The Old Crusty Minstrels	1965	10.00	25.00
RCA Victor LSP-3462	(S)	The Old Crusty Minstrels	1965	12.00	30.00
RCA Victor LPM-3474	(M)	The Best Of Homer & Jethro	1966	10.00	25.00
RCA Victor LSP-3474	(S)	The Best Of Homer & Jethro	1966	12.00	30.00
RCA Victor LPM-3538	(M)	Any News From Nashville	1966	10.00	25.00
RCA Victor LSP-3538	(S)	Any News From Nashville	1966	12.00	30.00
RCA Victor LPM-3673	(M)	Wanted For Murder	1966	10.00	25.00
RCA Victor LSP-3673	(S)	Wanted For Murder	1966	10.00	25.00
RCA Victor LPM-3701	(M)	It Ain't Necessarily Square	1967	20.00	50.00
RCA Victor LSP-3701	(S)	It Ain't Necessarily Square	1967	10.00	25.00
RCA Victor LPM-3822	(M)	Nashville Cats	1967	20.00	50.00
RCA Victor LSP-3822	(S)	Nashville Cats	1967	10.00	25.00
RCA Victor LPM-3877	(M)	Somethin' Stupid	1967	20.00	50.00
RCA Victor LSP-3877	(S)	Somethin' Stupid	1967	10.00	25.00
RCA Victor LPM-3973	(M)	There's Nothing Like An Old Hippie	1968	40.00	100.00
RCA Victor LSP-3973	(S)	There's Nothing Like An Old Hippie	1968	10.00	25.00
RCA Victor LSP-4001	(S)	Cool Crazy Christmas	1968	10.00	25.00
RCA Victor LSP-4024	(S)	Live At Vanderbilt U	1968	10.00	25.00
		— RCA albums above have black labels.—			

HONDELLS, THE
The Hondells are a creation of Gary Usher & Co. featuring Chuck Girard.

Mercury MG-20940	(M)	Go Little Honda	1964	14.00	35.00
Mercury SR-60940	(S)	Go Little Honda	1964	20.00	50.00
Mercury MG-20982	(M)	The Hondells	1965	20.00	50.00
Mercury SR-60982	(S)	The Hondells	1965	30.00	75.00

HONEYCOMBS, THE

Vee Jay IN-88001	(M)	Here Are The Honeycombs	1964	20.00	50.00
Vee Jay IN-88001	(E)	Here Are The Honeycombs	1964	16.00	40.00
Interphon IN-88001	(M)	Here Are The Honeycombs	1964	16.00	40.00
Interphon IN-88001	(E)	Here Are The Honeycombs	1964	12.00	30.00

HONEYDREAMERS, THE: *Refer to* GOLDMINE'S PRICE GUIDE TO COLLECTIBLE JAZZ ALBUMS

HOOKER, D. R.

On XTL-1029	(S)	The Truth	1972	100.00	200.00
On 40725	(S)	Armaggedon	1979	12.00	30.00

HOOKER, JOHN LEE
Singer, guitar player and writer John Lee Hooker is a pivotal figure in the development of amplified post-WWII blues, rhythm'n blues, and, consequently, rock'n roll. Refer to Canned Heat; The Groundhogs; Albert King & John Lee Hooker; Sticks McGhee; and Big Maceo Merriweather.

Vee Jay LP-1007	(M)	I'm John Lee Hooker	1959	80.00	200.00
		— Vee Jay albums above have maroon labels.—			
Vee Jay LP-1007	(M)	I'm John Lee Hooker	1960	30.00	75.00
Vee Jay LP-1023	(M)	Travelin'	1960	30.00	75.00
Vee Jay LP-1033	(M)	The Folk Lore Of John Lee Hooker	1961	20.00	50.00
Vee Jay SR-1033	(S)	The Folk Lore Of John Lee Hooker	1961	30.00	75.00
Vee Jay LP-1043	(M)	Burnin'	1962	20.00	50.00
Vee Jay SR-1043	(S)	Burnin'	1962	40.00	100.00
Vee Jay LP-1049	(M)	The Best Of John Lee Hooker	1962	20.00	50.00
Vee Jay LP-1049	(P)	The Best Of John Lee Hooker	1962	30.00	75.00
Vee Jay LP-1066	(M)	The Big Soul Of John Lee Hooker	1963	20.00	50.00
Vee Jay SR-1066	(S)	The Big Soul Of John Lee Hooker	1963		See below
Vee Jay LP-1078	(M)	John Lee Hooker At Newport	1964	20.00	50.00
Vee Jay SR-1078	(S)	John Lee Hooker At Newport	1964		See below
		(Should stereo copies of Vee Jay 1066 or 1078 exist, they would carry a suggested Near Mint value of $100-200 each.)			
		— Vee Jay albums above have black "rainbow" labels.—			

Label & Catalog #		Title	Year	VG+	NM
Riverside RLP-12-838	(M)	**Folk Blues**	1959	40.00	100.00
Riverside RLP-12-321	(M)	**That's My Story**	1960	40.00	100.00
King 727	(M)	**John Lee Hooker Sings The Blues**	1960	200.00	500.00
Chess LP-1438	(M)	**House Of The Blues**	1960	150.00	300.00
Chess LP-1454	(M)	**John Lee Hooker Plays And Sings The Blues**	1961	150.00	300.00
		— Chess albums above have black labels.—			
Chess LPS-1438	(E)	**House Of The Blues**	196?	20.00	50.00
Chess LP-1454	(M)	**John Lee Hooker Plays And Sings The Blues**	196?	20.00	50.00
		— Chess albums above have blue & white labels.—			
Crown CLP-5157	(M)	**The Blues**	1960	16.00	40.00
Crown CLP-5232	(M)	**John Lee Hooker Sings The Blues**	1962	16.00	40.00
Crown CST-???	(E)	**John Lee Hooker Sings The Blues**	1962	6.00	15.00
Crown CLP-5295	(M)	**Folk Blues**	1962	16.00	40.00
Crown CST-???	(E)	**Folk Blues**	1962	6.00	15.00
Crown CLP-5333	(M)	**The Great John Lee Hooker**	1963	16.00	40.00
Crown CST-???	(E)	**The Great John Lee Hooker**	1963	6.00	15.00
Galaxy 201	(M)	**I'm John Lee Hooker**	1962	100.00	250.00
Galaxy 8201	(S)	**I'm John Lee Hooker**	1962	100.00	250.00
Atco 33-151	(M)	**Don't Turn Me**			
		From Your Door (White label promo)	1963	100.00	250.00
Atco 33-151	(M)	**Don't Turn Me From Your Door**	1963	40.00	100.00
Atco SD-33-151	(E)	**Don't Turn Me From Your Door**	1967	20.00	50.00
Verve/Folkways FT-3003	(M)	**John Lee Hooker And Seven Nights**	1965	10.00	25.00
Verve/Folkways FTS-3003	(S)	**John Lee Hooker And Seven Nights**	1965	14.00	35.00
Chess LP-1508	(M)	**Real Folk Blues**	1966	20.00	50.00
Chess LPS-1508	(E)	**Real Folk Blues**	1966	14.00	35.00
Exodus 325	(M)	**Is He The World's Greatest Blues Singer?**	1966	10.00	25.00
Impulse A-9103	(M)	**It Serve You Right To Suffer**	1966	12.00	30.00
Impulse AS-9103	(S)	**It Serve You Right To Suffer**	1966	16.00	40.00
BluesWay BL-6002	(M)	**Live At Cafe Au-Go-Go**	1966	8.00	20.00
BluesWay BLS-6002	(S)	**Live At Cafe Au-Go-Go**	1966	10.00	25.00
BluesWay BL-6012	(M)	**Urban Blues**	1967	8.00	20.00
BluesWay BLS-6012	(S)	**Urban Blues**	1967	10.00	25.00
BluesWay BLS-6023	(S)	**Simply The Truth**	1968	10.00	25.00
BluesWay BLS-6038	(S)	**If You Miss 'Im**	1969	10.00	25.00
BluesWay BLS-6052	(S)	**Live At Kabuki Wuki**	1973	6.00	15.00
Kent KLP-5025	(M)	**The Original Folk Blues**	1967	10.00	25.00
Kent KST-525	(E)	**The Original Folk Blues**	1967	6.00	15.00
HOOTCH					
Pro-gress PRS-4844	(S)	**Hootch**	1974	500.00	800.00
HOPE, BOB					
RCA Victor LPM-3275	(10")	**Seven Little Foys** (Soundtrack)	1955	30.00	75.00
Imperial LP-9041	(M)	**Beau James** (Soundtrack)	1957	20.00	50.00
Decca DL-4396	(M)	**Hope In Russia And Other Places**	1963	8.00	20.00
Decca DL-74396	(S)	**Hope In Russia And Other Places**	1963	10.00	25.00
Kin Koc 1226	(S)	**Thanks For The Memories** (3 LP box)	1968	40.00	100.00
HOPE, LYNN					
Aladdin LP-707	(10")	**Lynn Hope And His Tenor Sax**	1953	250.00	600.00
Aladdin LP-805	(M)	**Lynn Hope And His Tenor Sax**	1955		See below
		(Contrary to previous;y published listings, Aladdin 805 was not released.)			
Score SLP-4015	(M)	**Tenderly**	1957	80.00	200.00
King 717	(M)	**Maharaja Of The Saxophone**	1961	60.00	150.00
Imperial LP-9177	(M)	**Tenderly**	1962	20.00	50.00
Imperial LP-12177	(S)	**Tenderly**	1962	30.00	75.00
HOPKIN, MARY					
Apple SW-3351	(S)	**Postcard** (Produced by Paul McCartney)	1969	10.00	25.00
Apple SW-53351	(S)	**Postcard** (Record club)	1969	14.00	35.00
		("Those Were The Days" is in stereo on both versions of "Postcard." .)			
Apple SMAS-3381	(S)	**Earth Song/Ocean Song**	1969	10.00	25.00
Apple SW-3395	(S)	**Those Were The Days**	1972	16.00	40.00
		("Those Were The Days," "Temma Harbour," "Think About Your Children" and "Knock Knock Who's There?" are in mono.)			
Paramount PAS-5005	(S)	**Where's Jack** (Soundtrack)	1969	16.00	40.00

Label & Catalog #		Title	Year	VG+	NM

HOPKINS, LIGHTNIN'

Sam "Lightnin'" Hopkins is a guitar player, singer and songwriter in the country/blues mode.

Label & Catalog #		Title	Year	VG+	NM
Score SLP-4022	(M)	**Lightnin' Hopkins Strums The Blues**	1958	500.00	1,000.00
Herald LP-1012	(M)	**Lightnin' And The Blues**	1959	750.00	1,500.00
Fire LP-104	(M)	**Mojo Hand**	1960	600.00	1,200.00
Tradition TLP-1035	(M)	**Country Blues**	1960	10.00	25.00
Tradition TLP-1040	(M)	**Autobiography In Blues**	1961	10.00	25.00
Tradition TLP-2056	(M)	**The Best Of Lightnin' Hopkins**	1964	8.00	20.00
Tradition TLP-2103	(M)	**Lightnin' Strikes**	1972	6.00	15.00
Time 1	(M)	**Blues/Folk**	196?	60.00	150.00
Time 3	(M)	**Blues/Folk, Volume 2**	196?	60.00	150.00
Time T-70004	(M)	**Last Of The Great Blues Singers**	1961	60.00	150.00
Time ST-70004	(S)	**Last Of The Great Blues Singers**	1961	60.00	150.00
Candid CM-8010	(M)	**Lightnin' In New York**	1961	60.00	150.00
Candid CS-9010	(S)	**Lightnin' In New York**	1961	80.00	200.00
Bluesville BVLP-1019	(M)	**Lightnin'**	1961	40.00	100.00
Bluesville BVLP-1029	(M)	**Last Night Blues**	1961	40.00	100.00
Bluesville BVLP-1045	(M)	**Blues In My Bottle**	1962	40.00	100.00
Bluesville BVLP-1057	(M)	**Walkin' This Street**	1962	40.00	100.00
Bluesville BVLP-1061	(M)	**Lightnin' & Co.**	1963	40.00	100.00
Bluesville BVLP-1070	(M)	**Smokes Like Lightnin'**	1963	40.00	100.00
Bluesville BVLP-1073	(M)	**Goin' Away**	1963	40.00	100.00
		— Bluesville albums above have bright blue labels with silver print.—			
Bluesville BVLP-1019	(M)	**Lightnin'**	1964	12.00	30.00
Bluesville BVLP-1045	(M)	**Blues In My Bottle**	1964	12.00	30.00
Bluesville BVLP-1057	(M)	**Walkin' This Street**	1964	12.00	30.00
Bluesville BVLP-1061	(M)	**Lightnin' & Co.**	1964	12.00	30.00
Bluesville BVLP-1070	(M)	**Smokes Like Lightnin'**	1964	12.00	30.00
Bluesville BVLP-1073	(M)	**Goin' Away**	1964	12.00	30.00
Bluesville BVLP-1081	(M)	**Gotta Move Your Baby**	1964	16.00	40.00
		(Bluesville 1081 is a reissue of 1029.)			
Bluesville BVLP-1084	(M)	**Lightnin' Hopkins' Greatest Hits**	1964	16.00	40.00
Bluesville BVLP-1086	(M)	**Down Home Blues**	1964	10.00	25.00
		— Bluesville albums above have blue labels with a trident logo on the right side.—			
Dart D-8000	(M)	**Lightning Strikes Again**	1962	100.00	250.00
Crown CLP-5224	(M)	**Lightnin' Hopkins Sings The Blues**	1962	40.00	100.00
		(Plain black label)			
Crown CLP-5224	(M)	**Lightnin' Hopkins Sings The Blues**	1962	20.00	50.00
		(Gray label)			
Crown CLP-5224	(M)	**Lightnin' Hopkins Sings The Blues**	1962	10.00	25.00
		(Black label with color logo)			
Folkways FS-3822	(M)	**Lightnin' Hopkins**	1962	20.00	50.00
Vee Jay LP-1044	(M)	**Lightnin' Strikes**	1962	24.00	60.00
		— Vee Jay albums above have black "rainbow" labels with an oval logo on top.—			
Vee Jay LP-1138	(M)	**Coffee House Blues**	1965	20.00	50.00
		(Vee Jay 1138 also features Sonny Terry & Brownie McGhee.)			
		— Vee Jay albums above have black "rainbow" labels with a brackets logo on top.—			
Verve V-8453	(M)	**Fast Life Woman**	1962	16.00	40.00
Imperial LP-9180	(M)	**Lightnin' Hopkins On Stage**	1962	60.00	150.00
Imperial LP-9186	(M)	**Lightnin' Hopkins Sings The Blues**	1962	60.00	150.00
Imperial LP-9211	(M)	**Lightnin' Hopkins And The Blues**	1963	40.00	100.00
Imperial LP-12211	(E)	**Lightnin' Hopkins And The Blues**	1963	40.00	75.00
		(Imperial 92111 is a reissue of 9135.)			
World Pacific WP-1817	(M)	**First Meetin'**	1963	12.00	30.00
World Pacific ST-1817	(S)	**First Meetin'**	1963	16.00	40.00
World Pacific ST-1817	(S)	**First Meetin'** *(Red vinyl)*	1963	30.00	75.00
Guest Star G-1458	(M)	**"Live" At The Bird Lounge, Houston, Texas**	1964	10.00	25.00
Mt. Vernon 104	(M)	**Nothin' But The Blues**	196?	10.00	25.00
		(Mt. Vernon 104 is a reissue of Herald 1012.)			
Verve/Folkways FV-9000	(M)	**The Roots Of Lightnin' Hopkins**	1965	10.00	25.00
Verve/Folkways FVS-9000	(S)	**The Roots Of Lightnin' Hopkins**	1965	12.00	30.00
Verve/Folkways FV-9022	(M)	**Lightnin' Strikes**	1965	10.00	25.00
Verve/Folkways FVS-9022	(S)	**Lightnin' Strikes**	1965	12.00	30.00
Verve/Folkways FT-3013	(M)	**Something Blue**	1967	8.00	20.00
Verve/Folkways FTS-3013	(S)	**Something Blue**	1967	10.00	25.00
Verve/Folkways FTS-3031	(S)	**Lightnin' Strikes**	1968	8.00	20.00
		(Folkways 3031 is a reissue of 9022.)			
Folklore FRLP-14021	(M)	**Hootin' The Blues**	1964	24.00	60.00
Folklore FRST-14021	(S)	**Hootin' The Blues**	1964	30.00	75.00

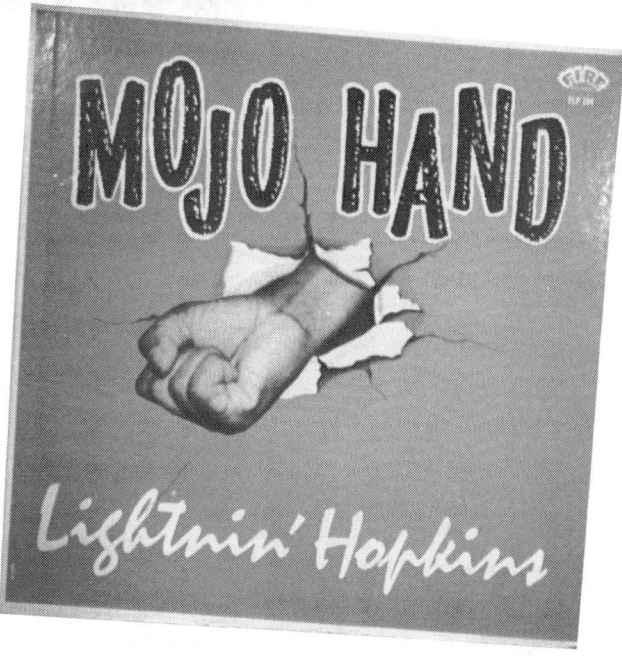

The observant reader will note quite a bit of change in the basic discography of Samuel "Lightnin' Hopkins' from the third edition of this book to the one listed here. Aside from adding missing titles, the basic chronology has been adjusted. While Lightnin' Hopkins Strums The Blues*(not shown here) has been determined to have been his first LP release, it is his second and third albums that have attracting the most attention in recent years.* Lightnin' And The Blues *has become what many believe to be the most sought-after blues album in the business; the listed value of $1,500 may be conservative for a truly near mint copy.* Mojo Hand *is close behind in both rarity and demand. (Oh, and there's some pretty good music between the grooves of all three of them. . .)*

Label & Catalog #		Title	Year	VG+	NM
Prestige PRLP-7370	(M)	My Life With The Blues *(2 LPs)*	1965	24.00	60.00
Prestige PRST-7370	(S)	My Life With The Blues *(2 LPs)*	1965	30.00	75.00
Prestige PRLP-7377	(M)	Soul Blues	1966	20.00	50.00
Prestige PRST-7377	(S)	Soul Blues	1966	24.00	60.00
International Art. LP-6	(S)	Free Form Patterns	1968	80.00	200.00
		(Original pressings of I.A. 6 have a picture of Hopkins on the cover.)			
International Art. LP-6	(S)	Free Form Patterns	1968	20.00	50.00
		(Later pressings have a pseudo-psychedelic art cover.)			
Vault 129	(S)	California Mudslide	1969	10.00	25.00
Poppy 60002	(S)	Lightnin'	1969	10.00	25.00

HOPNEY

Illusion CM-1032	(S)	End And Means	197?	80.00	200.00
Illusion CM-1033	(S)	Perils Of Love	197?	100.00	250.00
Illusion CM-1034	(S)	Cosmic Rockout	197?	300.00	500.00

HORN, SHIRLEY: *Refer to* **GOLDMINE'S PRICE GUIDE TO COLLECTIBLE JAZZ ALBUMS**

HORNE, LENA

MGM E-545	(10")	Lena Horne Sings	1952	20.00	50.00
Tops L-910	(10")	Moanin' Low	195?	14.00	35.00
Tops L-931	(10")	Lena Horne Sings	195?	14.00	35.00
RCA Victor LPT-3061	(10")	This Is Lena Horne	1952	20.00	50.00
RCA Victor LPM-1148	(M)	It's Love	1955	20.00	50.00
RCA Victor LPM-1375	(M)	Stormy Weather	1956	20.00	50.00
RCA Victor LOC-1028	(M)	Lena Horne At The Waldorf Astoria	1957	14.00	35.00
RCA Victor LSO-1028	(S)	Lena Horne At The Waldorf Astoria	1957	20.00	50.00
RCA Victor LOC-1036	(M)	Jamaica *(Soundtrack)*	1957	14.00	35.00
RCA Victor LSO-1036	(S)	Jamaica *(Soundtrack)*	1957	20.00	50.00
Jazztone J-1262	(M)	Lena And Ivie	1957	20.00	50.00
RCA Victor LPM-1879	(M)	Give The Lady What She Wants	1958	14.00	35.00
RCA Victor LSP-1879	(S)	Give The Lady What She Wants	1958	20.00	50.00
RCA Victor LPM-1895	(M)	Songs Of Burke And Van Heusen	1959	14.00	35.00
RCA Victor LSP-1895	(S)	Songs Of Burke And Van Heusen	1959	20.00	50.00
RCA Victor LOC-1507	(M)	Porgy And Bess *(Soundtrack)*	1959	10.00	25.00
RCA Victor LSO-1507	(S)	Porgy And Bess *(Soundtrack)*	1959	14.00	35.00
RCA Victor LPM-2364	(M)	Lena Horne At The Sands	1961	8.00	20.00
RCA Victor LSP-2364	(S)	Lena Horne At The Sands	1961	12.00	30.00
RCA Victor LPM-2465	(M)	On The Blue Side	1962	8.00	20.00
RCA Victor LSP-2465	(S)	On The Blue Side	1962	12.00	30.00

—RCA mono albums above have "Long Play" on the bottom of the label;
stereo albums have "Living Stereo" on the bottom.—

HORNETS, THE

Liberty LRP-3348	(M)	Motorcycles U.S.A.	1963	16.00	40.00
Liberty LST-7348	(S)	Motorcycles U.S.A.	1963	20.00	50.00
Liberty LRP-3364	(M)	Big Drag Boats U.S.A.	1964	20.00	50.00
Liberty LST-7364	(S)	Big Drag Boats U.S.A.	1964	30.00	75.00

HORSES
Horses features future TV star Don Johnson.

White Whale WWS-7121	(S)	Horses	1970	16.00	40.00

HORTON, JOHNNY
Refer to Jimmy Dean / Johnny Horton.

Briar Int. 104	(M)	Done Rovin'	195?	50.00	125.00
Sesac 1201/2	(M)	Free And Easy Songs	1959	60.00	150.00
Mercury MG-20478	(M)	The Fantastic Johnny Horton	1959	20.00	50.00
Columbia CL-1362	(M)	The Spectacular Johnny Horton	1960	12.00	30.00
Columbia CS-8167	(S)	The Spectacular Johnny Horton	1960	16.00	40.00
Columbia CL-1478	(M)	Johnny Horton Makes History	1960	12.00	30.00
Columbia CS-8269	(S)	Johnny Horton Makes History	1960	16.00	40.00
Columbia CL-1596	(M)	Greatest Hits *(With bonus photo)*	1961	20.00	50.00
Columbia CS-8396	(S)	Greatest Hits *(With bonus photo)*	1961	24.00	60.00
Columbia CL-1596	(M)	Greatest Hits *(Without the photo)*	1961	12.00	30.00
Columbia CS-8396	(S)	Greatest Hits *(Without the photo)*	1961	16.00	40.00
Columbia CL-1721	(M)	Honky-Tonk Man	1962	12.00	30.00
Columbia CS-8779	(E)	Honky-Tonk Man	1962	10.00	25.00

— Columbia albums above have three white "eye" logos on each side of the spindle hole.—

Label & Catalog #		Title	Year	VG+	NM
Dot DLP-3221	(M)	**Johnny Horton**	1962	12.00	30.00
Dot DLP-25221	(E)	**Johnny Horton**	196?	6.00	15.00
Columbia CL-2299	(M)	**I Can't Forget You**	1965	10.00	25.00
Columbia CS-9099	(E)	**I Can't Forget You**	1965	6.00	15.00
Columbia CL-2566	(M)	**Johnny Horton On The Louisiana Hayride**	1966	8.00	20.00
Columbia CS-9366	(S)	**Johnny Horton On The Louisiana Hayride**	1966	10.00	25.00
		— Columbia albums above have "360 Sound" on the bottom of the label.—			
Sears SPS-110	(E)	**The Legend Of Johnny Horton**	196?	12.00	30.00

HORTON, ROBERT
Columbia CL-2202	(M)	**The Very Thought Of You**	1964	8.00	20.00
Columbia CS-9002	(S)	**The Very Thought Of You**	1964	10.00	25.00
Columbia CL-2408	(M)	**The Man Called Shenendoah**	1965	10.00	25.00
Columbia CS-9208	(S)	**The Man Called Shenendoah**	1965	12.00	30.00

HORTON, WALTER "SHAKEY"
Refer to Elmore James & Walter Horton.
| Argo LP-4037 | (M) | **The Soul Of Blues Harmonica** | 1964 | 40.00 | 100.00 |

HORTON'S PINETOPPERS
| Decca DL-8348 | (M) | **Saturday Night Barn Dance** | 1956 | 12.00 | 30.00 |

HOT DOGGERS, THE
The Hot Doggers feature Bruce Johnston.
| Epic LN-24054 | (M) | **Surfin' USA** | 1963 | 60.00 | 150.00 |
| Epic BN-26054 | (S) | **Surfin' USA** | 1963 | 80.00 | 200.00 |

HOT POOP
| Hot Poop 3072 | (S) | **Hot Poop Does Their Own Stuff** | 1975 | 30.00 | 75.00 |

HOTLEGS
Hotlegs features Lol Creme, Kevin Godley, later of 10CC, and Eric Stewart.
| Capitol ST-587 | (S) | **Hotlegs Thinks: School Stinks** | 1971 | 10.00 | 25.00 |

HOTZ, JIMMY
| Vision VR-777 | (S) | **Beyond The Crystal Sea** | 1980 | 60.00 | 150.00 |

HOUK, RALPH
| Carlton CHH-16 | (M) | **Hear How To Play Better Baseball** | 196? | 24.00 | 60.00 |

HOUR GLASS, THE
Hour Glass features Duane and Gregg Allman.
Liberty LRP-3536	(M)	**The Hour Glass**	1967	10.00	25.00
Liberty LST-7536	(S)	**The Hour Glass**	1967	12.00	30.00
Liberty LRP-3555	(M)	**The Power Of Love**	1968	12.00	30.00
Liberty LST-7555	(S)	**The Power Of Love**	1968	12.00	30.00

HOUSE, SON
Son House is a preeminent Delta blues singer, guitar player and songwrtiter and a forerunner of Robert Johnson and Muddy Waters.
Columbia CL-2417	(M)	**Father Of The Folk Blues**	1965	8.00	20.00
Columbia CS-9217	(S)	**Father Of The Folk Blues**	1965	10.00	25.00
		— Columbia albums above have "360 Sound" labels.—			

HOUSE, SON, & J. D. SHORT
| Verve/Folkways FV-9035 | (M) | **Blues From The Mississippi Delt** | 1966 | 12.00 | 30.00 |
| Verve/Folkways FVS-9035 | (E) | **Blues From The Mississippi Delta** | 1966 | 8.00 | 20.00 |

HOUSE, WALLACE
Professor Wallace House is a lute player and singer of folk music from many lands.
Folkways FP-48	(10")	**Ballads Of War** (4 LP box)	195?	80.00	200.00
Folkways FH-2151	(10")	**Ballads Of The Revolution 1767-1775**	195?	20.00	50.00
Folkways FH-2152	(10")	**Ballads Of The Revolution 1776-1781**	195?	20.00	50.00
Folkways FA-2163	(10")	**Ballads Of The War Of 1812, Vol. 1**	195?	20.00	50.00
Folkways FA-2164	(10")	**Ballads Of The War Of 1812, Vol. 2**	195?	20.00	50.00
Folkways FP-823	(10")	**English Folk Songs**	195?	20.00	50.00
Folkways FW-6823	(10")	**English Folk Songs**	195?	20.00	50.00
Folkways FP-839	(10")	**Robin Hood Ballads**	195?	20.00	50.00
Folkways FW-6839	(10")	**Robin Hood Ballads**	195?	20.00	50.00

Label & Catalog #		Title	Year	VG+	NM

HOUSTON, CISCO

Cisco Houston is a guitar player, singer and writer of traditional and topical folk music. He also recorded with Woody Guthrie.

Label & Catalog #		Title	Year	VG+	NM
Folkways FP-13	(10")	900 Miles And Other Railroad Ballads	1952	40.00	100.00
Folkways FA-2013	(10")	900 Miles And Other Railroad Ballads	1952	40.00	100.00
Folkways FP-22	(10")	Cisco Houston Sings Cowboy Ballads	1952	40.00	100.00
Folkways FA-2022	(10")	Cisco Houston Sings Cowboy Ballads	1952	40.00	100.00
Folkways FP-42	(10")	Hard Travelin'	1954	40.00	100.00
Folkways FA-2042	(10")	Hard Travelin'	1954	40.00	100.00
Folkways FA-2346	(M)	Cisco Houston Sings Folk Songs	195?	20.00	50.00
Folkways FA-2480	(M)	Songs Of The Open Road	1964	10.00	25.00
Folkways FTS-31012	(M)	Cisco Houston Sings American Folk Songs	196?	6.00	15.00
Stinson SLP-37	(10")	Traditional Songs Of The Old West	195?	40.00	100.00
Vanguard VRS-9057	(M)	Cisco Special	1961	12.00	30.00
Vanguard VSD-2042	(S)	Cisco Special	1961	16.00	40.00
Vanguard VRS-9107	(M)	I Ain't Got No Home	1962	10.00	25.00
Vanguard VSD-2107	(S)	I Ain't Got No Home	1962	12.00	30.00
Vanguard VRS-9131	(M)	Cisco Houston Sings The Songs Of Woody Guthrie	1963	10.00	25.00
Vanguard VSD-2131	(S)	Cisco Houston Sings The Songs Of Woody Guthrie	1963	12.00	30.00
Verve/Folkways FV-9002	(M)	Passing Through	1965	8.00	20.00
Verve/Folkways FVS-9002	(S)	Passing Through	1965	10.00	25.00

HOUSTON, JOE

Label & Catalog #		Title	Year	VG+	NM
Modern LMP-1206	(M)	Joe Houston Blows All Night Long	1956	200.00	500.00
Tops L-1518	(M)	Rock And Roll	1958	20.00	50.00
Crown CLP-5006	(M)	Joe Houston Rocks & Rolls All Nite Long *(Red cover)*	1958	200.00	500.00
Crown CLP-5006	(M)	Joe Houston Rocks & Rolls All Nite Long *(Black cover)* *(Crown 5006 is a reissue of Modern 1206.)*	1959	40.00	100.00

— Crown albums above have black labels.—

Label & Catalog #		Title	Year	VG+	NM
Combo LP-100	(M)	Joe Houston *(Silver cover with saxophone)*	1960	200.00	500.00
Combo LP-100	(M)	Joe Houston *(Photo cover)*	1960	150.00	300.00
Combo LP-400	(M)	Rockin' At The Drive In	1960	150.00	350.00
Crown CLP-5203	(M)	Wild Man Of The Tenor Sax	1962	20.00	50.00
Crown CLP-5246	(M)	Doin' The Twist	1962	20.00	50.00
Crown CLP-5313	(M)	Surf Rockin'	1963	20.00	50.00
Crown CST-313	(E)	Surf Rockin'	1963	10.00	25.00
Crown CLP-5319	(M)	Limbo	1963	20.00	50.00
Crown CST-319	(E)	Limbo	1963	10.00	25.00

— Crown albums above have gray labels.—

HOWARD, DAVE: Refer to GOLDMINE'S PRICE GUIDE TO COLLECTIBLE JAZZ ALBUMS

HOWARD, HARLAN

Label & Catalog #		Title	Year	VG+	NM
Capitol T-1631	(M)	Harlan Howard Sings Harlan Howard	1961	16.00	40.00
Capitol ST-1631	(S)	Harlan Howard Sings Harlan Howard	1961	20.00	50.00
Monument MLP-8038	(M)	All-Time Favorite Country Songwriter	1965	10.00	25.00
Monument SLP-18038	(S)	All-Time Favorite Country Songwriter	1965	12.00	30.00
RCA Victor LPM-3729	(M)	Mr. Songwriter	1967	8.00	20.00
RCA Victor LSP-3729	(S)	Mr. Songwriter	1967	10.00	25.00
RCA Victor LPM-3886	(M)	Down To Earth	1968	20.00	50.00
RCA Victor LSP-3886	(S)	Down To Earth	1968	10.00	25.00

— RCA albums above have black labels.—

HOWARD, JAN

Refer to Bill Anderson & Jan Howard.

Label & Catalog #		Title	Year	VG+	NM
Wrangler 1005	(M)	Jan Howard	1962	12.00	30.00
Wrangler S-1005	(S)	Jan Howard	1962	16.00	40.00
Capitol T-1779	(M)	Sweet And Sentimental	1962	8.00	20.00
Capitol ST-1779	(S)	Sweet And Sentimental	1962	12.00	30.00

HOWARD UNIVERSITY CHOIR, THE

Label & Catalog #		Title	Year	VG+	NM
RCA Victor LM-2126	(M)	Spirituals	1957	12.00	30.00

While the veneration of the guitar as the prime instrument in the history of rock 'n roll continues to this day, few seem to recall that it was the saxophone of such artists as Joe Houston that was the driving force behind much of the earliest rhythm 'n blues derived rock 'n roll.

Label & Catalog #		Title	Year	VG+	NM

HOWLIN' WOLF
Howlin' Wolf is a pseudonym for Chester Burnett. Refer to Bo Diddley.

Label & Catalog #		Title	Year	VG+	NM
Chess LP-1434	(M)	**Moanin' In The Moonlight** *(White label)*	1958		*See below*
		(White label promos of Chess 1434 are rare with			
		a suggested Near Mint value of $1,000-2,000.)			
Chess LP-1434	(M)	**Moanin' In The Moonlight**	1958	200.00	500.00
Chess LP-1469	(M)	**Howlin' Wolf** *(White label promo)*	1962		*See below*
		(White label promos of Chess 1469 are rare with			
		a suggested Near Mint value of $1,000-2,000.)			
Chess LP-1469	(M)	**Howlin' Wolf**	1962	200.00	500.00
		— Chess albums above have black & silver labels.—			
Chess LP-1502	(M)	**The Real Folk Blues**	1966	20.00	50.00
Chess LP-1512	(M)	**More Real Folk Blues**	1967	20.00	50.00
		— Chess albums above have dark blue labels with a color logo on top.—			
Crown CLP-5240	(M)	**Howlin' Wolf Sings The Blues**	1962	10.00	25.00
Custom CM-2055	(M)	**Big City Blues**	196?	14.00	35.00
Custom CS-2055	(E)	**Big City Blues**	196?	8.00	20.00
Kent KLP-526	(M)	**Original Folk Blues**	1967	10.00	25.00
Cadet 319	(S)	**This Is Howlin' Wolf's New Album**	1969	10.00	25.00
Chess LP-1540	(M)	**Evil**	1969	10.00	25.00
Chess CH-60016	(E)	**Howlin' Wolf A.K.A. Chester Burnett** *(2 LPs)*	1972	10.00	25.00
		— Chess albums above have blue & white labels.—			
Chess CH509332	(S)	**Howlin' Wolf** *(5 LP box)*	1991	16.00	40.00

HRANT, OUDI

Label & Catalog #		Title	Year	VG+	NM
Bluesville BVLP-1089	(M)	**Turkish Delights**	1964	10.00	25.00

HUDSON, ROCK
Refer to Doris Day & Rock Hudson

Label & Catalog #		Title	Year	VG+	NM
Stanyan 10014	(S)	**Rock Gently** *(With poster)*	1971	14.00	35.00
Stanyan 10014	(S)	**Rock Gently** *(Without poster)*	1971	10.00	25.00
Brunswick BL-754157	(S)	**Baby Boy**	1970	5.00	12.00

HUGHES, JIMMY

Label & Catalog #		Title	Year	VG+	NM
Vee Jay VJ-1102	(M)	**Steal Away**	1965	10.00	25.00
Vee Jay SR-1102	(E)	**Steal Away**	1965	8.00	20.00
Atco 33-209	(M)	**Why Not Tonight**	1967	10.00	25.00
Atco SD-33-209	(E)	**Why Not Tonight**	1967	8.00	20.00
Volt VOS-6003	(S)	**Something Special**	1969	10.00	25.00

HUGHES, LANGSTON: Refer to GOLDMINE'S PRICE GUIDE TO COLLECTIBLE JAZZ ALBUMS

HUGHES, RHETA: Refer to GOLDMINE'S PRICE GUIDE TO COLLECTIBLE JAZZ ALBUMS

HULLABALOO SINGERS, THE

Label & Catalog #		Title	Year	VG+	NM
Columbia CL-2410	(M)	**The Hullabaloo Show**	1965	8.00	20.00
Columbia CS-9210	(S)	**The Hullabaloo Show**	1965	10.00	25.00

HULLABALOOS, THE

Label & Catalog #		Title	Year	VG+	NM
Roulette R-25297	(M)	**England's Newest Singing Sensations**	1965	20.00	50.00
Roulette SR-25297	(S)	**England's Newest Singing Sensations**	1965	24.00	60.00
		("Can't You Tell," "I'm Gonna Love You Too," "Party Doll" and			
		"Why Do Fools Fall In Love" are rechanneled on this album.)			
Roulette R-25310	(M)	**The Hullabaloos On Hullabaloo**	1965	20.00	50.00
Roulette SR-25310	(S)	**The Hullabaloos On Hullabaloo**	1965	24.00	60.00
		("Don't Cha Know," "Learning The Game," "Rave On" and			
		"That'll Be The Day" are rechanneled on this album.)			

HUMAN BEINZ, THE / THE MAMMALS

Label & Catalog #		Title	Year	VG+	NM
Gateway GLP-3012	(S)	**Nobody But Me**	1968	16.00	40.00

HUMAN BEINZ, THE

Label & Catalog #		Title	Year	VG+	NM
Capitol ST-2906	(S)	**Nobody But Me**	1968	12.00	30.00
Capitol ST-2926	(S)	**Evolutions**	1968	12.00	30.00

HUMAN ZOO, THE

Label & Catalog #		Title	Year	VG+	NM
Accent ACS-5055	(S)	**The Human Zoo**	1971	40.00	100.00

Label & Catalog #		Title	Year	VG+	NM

HUMBLE PIE

Immediate 101	(S)	**As Safe As Yesterday Is**	1968	10.00	25.00

HUMES, HELEN: *Refer to* **GOLDMINE'S PRICE GUIDE TO COLLECTIBLE JAZZ ALBUMS**

HUMPERDINCK, ENGELBERT
Engelbert Humperdinck is a pseudonym for Gerry Dorsey.

Epic/Mam PAL-35020	(DJ)	**Last Of The Romantics** *(Picture disc)*	1978	20.00	50.00

HUNGER

Public 1006	(S)	**Strictly From Hunger**	1969	150.00	300.00

HUNT, TOMMY
Hunt was formerly a member of the Flamingos.

Scepter 506	(M)	**I Just Don't Know What To Do With Myself**	1962	14.00	35.00
Scepter SS-506	(S)	**I Just Don't Know What To Do With Myself**	1962	20.00	50.00
Dynamo D-7001	(M)	**Tommy Hunt's Greatest Hits**	1967	8.00	20.00
Dynamo DS-8001	(S)	**Tommy Hunt's Greatest Hits**	1967	10.00	25.00
		(Dynamo 7/8001 contains rerecordings of Hunt's former glories.)			

HUNTER, IVORY JOE

MGM E-3488	(M)	**I Get That Lonesome Feeling**	1957	150.00	400.00
King 605	(M)	**16 Of His Greatest Hits**	1958	150.00	400.00
Atlantic 8008	(M)	**Ivory Joe Hunter**	1957	100.00	250.00
Atlantic 8015	(M)	**The Old & The New**	1958	100.00	250.00
		—Atlantic albums above have black labels.—			
Atlantic 8008	(M)	**Ivory Joe Hunter**	1960	40.00	100.00
Atlantic 8015	(M)	**The Old & The New**	1960	40.00	100.00
		—Atlantic albums above have purple & orange labels.—			
Sage & Sand C-603	(M)	**Ivory Joe Hunter**	1959	60.00	150.00
Lion L-70068	(M)	**I Need You So**	1959	60.00	150.00
Goldisc 403	(M)	**The Fabulous Ivory Joe Hunter**	1961	30.00	75.00
Smash MGS-27037	(M)	**Ivory Joe Hunter's Golden Hits**	1963	14.00	35.00
Smash SRS-67037	(S)	**Ivory Joe Hunter's Golden Hits**	1963	20.00	50.00
Dot DLP-3569	(M)	**This Is Ivory Joe Hunter**	1964	14.00	35.00
Dot DLP-25569	(S)	**This Is Ivory Joe Hunter**	1964	20.00	50.00

HUNTER, LURLEAN: *Refer to* **GOLDMINE'S PRICE GUIDE TO COLLECTIBLE JAZZ ALBUMS**

HUNTER, ROBERT
Refer to The Grateful Dead.

Round RX-101	(S)	**Tales Of The Great Rum Runners**	1974	12.00	30.00
Round RX-105	(S)	**Tiger Rose**	1975	12.00	30.00

HUNTER, TAB

Warner Bros. W-1221	(M)	**Tab Hunter**	1958	12.00	30.00
Warner Bros. WS-1221	(S)	**Tab Hunter**	1958	16.00	40.00
Warner Bros. W-1292	(M)	**When I Fall In Love**	1959	12.00	30.00
Warner Bros. WS-1292	(S)	**When I Fall In Love**	1959	16.00	40.00
Warner Bros. W-1367	(M)	**R. F. D. Tab Hunter**	1960	12.00	30.00
Warner Bros. WS-1367	(S)	**R. F. D. Tab Hunter**	1960	16.00	40.00
Dot DLP-3370	(M)	**Young Love**	1961	8.00	20.00
Dot DLP-25370	(S)	**Young Love**	1961	12.00	30.00

HUNTER MUSKETT

Bradley 1003	(S)	**Hunter Muskett**	1969	30.00	75.00

HUNTINGTON, E. G.
E. G. "Gale" Huntington is a guitar and fiddle player and singer of traditional folk songs.

Folkways FA-2032	(10")	**Folk Songs Of Martha's Vineyard**	195?	20.00	50.00

HURD, PETER
Peter Hurd is a guitar player and singer of Spanish and Mexican folk-based songs.

Folkways FP-604	(10")	**Peter Hurd Sings Ranchera Songs**	195?	20.00	50.00
Folkways FA-2204	(10")	**Peter Hurd Sings Ranchera Songs**	1957	20.00	50.00

HURT, MISSISSIPPI JOHN
John Hurt is a blues guitar player, singer and songwriter.

Piedmont PLP-13157	(M)	**Folk Songs And Blues**	1963	30.00	75.00

Label & Catalog #		Title	Year	VG+	NM
Piedmont PLP-13161	(M)	Worried Blues	1964	24.00	60.00
Piedmont PLP-131??	(M)	Mississippi John Hurt Live	1964	24.00	60.00
Vanguard VRS-9145	(M)	Blues At Newport	1965	10.00	25.00
Vanguard VSD-79145	(S)	Blues At Newport	1965	12.00	30.00
Vanguard VRS-9220	(M)	Mississippi John Hurt/Today	1966	10.00	25.00
Vanguard VSD-79220	(S)	Mississippi John Hurt/Today	1966	12.00	30.00
Vanguard VRS-9248	(M)	The Immortal Mississippi John Hurt (2 LP)	1967	10.00	25.00
Vanguard VSD-79248	(S)	The Immortal Mississippi John Hurt (2 LP)	1967	12.00	30.00

HURVITZ, SANDY

Verve V6-5064	(S)	Sandy's Album Is Here At Last	1969	12.00	30.00
		(Produced by Frank Zappa.)			

HUSKY, FERLIN
Husky also recorded as Simon Crum.

Capitol T-718	(M)	Songs Of The Home And Heart	1956	30.00	75.00
Capitol T-880	(M)	Boulevard Of Broken Dreams	1957	20.00	50.00
Capitol T-976	(M)	Sittin' On A Rainbow	1958	20.00	50.00
		— Capitol albums above have turquoise labels.—			
King 647	(M)	Country Tunes Sung From The Heart	1959	40.00	100.00
King 728	(M)	Easy Livin'	1960	40.00	100.00
Capitol T-976	(M)	Sittin' On A Rainbow	1958	12.00	30.00
Capitol ST-976	(S)	Sittin' On A Rainbow	1958	20.00	50.00
Capitol T-1204	(M)	Born To Lose	1959	12.00	40.00
Capitol T-1280	(M)	Ferlin's Favorites	1959	12.00	40.00
Capitol T-1383	(M)	Gone	1960	12.00	40.00
Capitol T-1546	(M)	Walkin' And Hummin'	1961	10.00	25.00
Capitol ST-1546	(S)	Walkin' And Hummin'	1961	12.00	30.00
Capitol T-1633	(M)	Memories Of Home	1961	10.00	25.00
Capitol ST-1633	(S)	Memories Of Home	1961	12.00	30.00
		— Capitol albums above have black labels with the Capitol logo on the side.—			

HUSKY, FERLIN / SONNY JAMES / TOMMY SANDS / GENE VINCENT

Capitol T-1009	(M)	Teen Age Rock!	1959	20.00	50.00

HUTTON, BETTY

Capitol H-256	(10")	Square In The Social Circle	1950	24.00	60.00
MGM E-509	(10")	Annie Get Your Gun (Soundtrack)	1950	40.00	100.00
RCA LPM-3097	(10")	Somebody Loves Me (Soundtrack)	1952	40.00	100.00
Capitol L-547	(10")	Satins And Spurs (TV Soundtrack)	1954	50.00	125.00
MGM E-3227	(M)	Annie Get Your Gun (Soundtrack)	1955	16.00	40.00
Warner Bros. W-1267	(M)	At The Saints And Sinners Ball	1959	8.00	20.00
Warner Bros. WS-1267	(S)	At The Saints And Sinners Ball	1959	10.00	25.00

HUTTON, DANNY
Danny Hutton was a member of Three Dog Night.

MGM SE-4664	(S)	Pre-Dog Night	1970	12.00	30.00

HUTTON, JUNE

Capitol T-643	(M)	Afterglow	1955	12.00	30.00
Venise 10017	(M)	Dream	195?	12.00	30.00

HYLAND, BRIAN

Kapp KL-1202	(M)	The Bashful Blonde	1960	20.00	50.00
Kapp KS-3202	(S)	The Bashful Blonde	1960	30.00	75.00
ABC-Paramount ABC-400	(M)	Let Me Belong To You	1961	14.00	35.00
ABC-Paramount ABCS-400	(S)	Let Me Belong To You	1961	20.00	50.00
ABC-Paramount ABC-431	(M)	Sealed With A Kiss	1962	14.00	35.00
ABC-Paramount ABCS-431	(S)	Sealed With A Kiss	1962	20.00	50.00
		("Sealed With A Kiss" is rechanneled on this album.)			
ABC-Paramount 463	(M)	Country Meets Folk	1964	12.00	30.00
ABC-Paramount S-463	(S)	Country Meets Folk	1964	16.00	40.00
Philips PHM-200-136	(M)	Here's To Our Love	1964	8.00	20.00
Philips PHS-600-136	(S)	Here's To Our Love	1964	10.00	25.00
Philips PHM-200-158	(M)	Rockin' Folk	1965	8.00	20.00
Philips PHS-600-158	(S)	Rockin, Folk	1965	10.00	25.00
Philips PHM-200-217	(M)	The Joker Went Wild	1966	8.00	20.00
Philips PHS-600-217	(S)	The Joker Went Wild	1966	10.00	25.00

easy livin'
FERLIN HUSKY

IF YOU DON'T BELIEVE I'M LEAVING	I WISHED A THOUSAND TIMES	MY PRECIOUS BABY GIRL	NEVER AGAIN
LET'S GROW OLD TOGETHER	HARD HEARTED	DEADLY WEAPON	CRYING HEART BLUES
HEART OF STONE	SAY WHEN	ECHOES IN MY HEART	THE ROAD TO HEAVEN

Ferlin Husky is best known to collectors of rock'n roll music for his 1957 smash, "Gone," one of his four pop hits. Country'n western fans know him as the singer who placed over four dozen sides on the country charts during the '50s, '60s and '70s. Husky also recorded as Terry Preston and as the humorous Simon Crum, under whose name he recorded a highly sought after album for Capitol in 1963, found under Crum in this book.

I

IAN, JANIS
Janis Ian is a guitar and piano player, singer and songwriter of contemporary folk and pop music.

Verve V-5027	(M)	**Society's Child**	1967	8.00	20.00
Verve V6-5027	(S)	**Society's Child**	1967	10.00	25.00

IAN & SYLVIA
Ian Tyson and Sylvia Fricker are a Canadian vocal and instrumental duo playing urban folk music.

Vanguard VRS-9109	(M)	**Ian And Sylvia**	1963	10.00	25.00
Vanguard VSD-2113	(S)	**Ian And Sylvia**	1963	12.00	30.00
Vanguard VRS-9133	(M)	**Four Strong Winds**	1963	8.00	20.00
Vanguard VSD-2149	(S)	**Four Strong Winds**	1963	10.00	25.00
Vanguard VRS-9154	(M)	**Northern Journey**	1964	8.00	20.00
Vanguard VSD-79154	(S)	**Northern Journey**	1964	10.00	25.00
Vanguard VRS-9175	(M)	**Early Morning Rain**	1965	8.00	20.00
Vanguard VSD-79175	(S)	**Early Morning Rain**	1965	10.00	25.00
Vanguard VRS-9215	(M)	**Play One More**	1966	8.00	20.00
Vanguard VSD-79215	(S)	**Play One More**	1966	10.00	25.00
Vanguard VRS-9241	(M)	**So Much For Dreaming**	1967	8.00	20.00
Vanguard VSD-79241	(S)	**So Much For Dreaming**	1967	10.00	25.00

IAN & THE ZODIACS

Philips PHM-200-176	(M)	**Ian And The Zodiacs**	1965	16.00	40.00
Philips PHS-600-176	(S)	**Ian And The Zodiacs**	1965	20.00	50.00

ID, THE

RCA Victor LPM-3805	(M)	**The Inner Sounds Of The Id**	1967	12.00	30.00
RCA Victor LSP-3805	(S)	**The Inner Sounds Of The Id**	1967	10.00	25.00
		("The Rake" is rechanneled on this album.)			
Aura 1000	(S)	**Where Are We Going?**	1976	12.00	30.00

IDLE, ERIC, & NEIL INNES
Refer to The Rutles; Monty Python.

Passport PPSD-98018	(S)	**The Rutland Weekend Television Songbook**	1976	10.00	25.00

IDLE RACE, THE
The Idle Race features Jeff Lynne. Refer to The Electric Light Orchestra; The Move.

Liberty LST-7603	(S)	**Birthday Party**	1969	20.00	50.00
		("Sitting In My Tree" is in mono on this album.)			

IFIELD, FRANK
Refer to The Beatles.

Vee Jay LP-1054	(M)	**I Re-mem-ber You**	1963	12.00	30.00
Vee Jay SR-1054	(S)	**I Re-mem-ber You**	1963	20.00	50.00
Capitol Int. T-10356	(M)	**I'm Confessin'**	1964	8.00	20.00
Capitol Int. ST-10356	(S)	**I'm Confessin'**	1964	10.00	25.00
Hickory LPM-132	(M)	**The Best Of Frank Ifield**	1966	8.00	20.00
Hickory LPS-132	(S)	**The Best Of Frank Ifield**	1966	10.00	25.00
Hickory LPM-136	(M)	**Tale Of Two Cities**	1967	8.00	20.00
Hickory LPS-136	(S)	**Tale Of Two Cities**	1967	10.00	25.00

IKETTES, THE
The Ikettes backed Ike & Tina Turner during the '60s.

Modern M-102	(M)	**Soul Hits**	1965	12.00	30.00
Modern MST-102	(S)	**Soul Hits**	1965	16.00	40.00

ILL WIND

ABC S-641	(S)	**Flashes**	1968	12.00	30.00

ILLUSION

Sinergia SR-7654	(S)	**Illusion**	1974	30.00	75.00

Label & Catalog #		Title	Year	VG+	NM
ILLUSTRATION					
Janus 3010	(S)	**Illustration**	1969	10.00	25.00
ILMO SMOKEHOUSE					
Beautiful Sound 3002	(S)	**Ilmo Smokehouse**	1971	14.00	35.00
IMMIGRANTS, THE					
Justice JLP-???	(M)	**The Immigrants '66**	1966	150.00	300.00
IMPACS, THE					
King 886	(M)	**Impact!**	1964	30.00	75.00
King KS-886	(S)	**Impact!**	1964	60.00	150.00
King 916	(M)	**Weekend With The Impacs**	1964	30.00	75.00
King KS-916	(S)	**Weekend With The Impacs**	1964	60.00	150.00
IMPACTS, THE					
The Impacts feature Merrel Fankhauser.					
Del-Fi DFLP-1234	(M)	**Wipe Out**	1963	14.00	35.00
Del-Fi DFS-1234	(S)	**Wipe Out**	1963	20.00	50.00
IMPALA SYNDROME, THE					
Parallax 4002	(S)	**The Impala Syndrome**	1970	12.00	30.00
IMPALAS, THE					
Cub 8003	(M)	**Sorry (I Ran All The Way Home)**	1959	200.00	400.00
Cub S-8003	(S)	**Sorry (I Ran All The Way Home)**	1959	300.00	600.00
IMPRESSIONS, THE					
The Impressions feature Curtis Mayfield. Refer to Jerry Butler.					
ABC-Paramount ABC-450	(M)	**The Impressions**	1963	10.00	25.00
ABC-Paramount ABCS-450	(S)	**The Impressions**	1963	12.00	30.00
ABC-Paramount ABC-468	(M)	**Never Ending Impressions**	1964	10.00	25.00
ABC-Paramount ABCS-468	(S)	**Never Ending Impressions**	1964	12.00	30.00
ABC-Paramount ABC-493	(M)	**Keep On Pushing**	1964	10.00	25.00
ABC-Paramount ABCS-493	(S)	**Keep On Pushing**	1964	12.00	30.00
ABC-Paramount ABC-505	(M)	**People Get Ready**	1965	10.00	25.00
ABC-Paramount ABCS-505	(S)	**People Get Ready**	1965	12.00	30.00
ABC-Paramount ABC-515	(M)	**The Impressions' Greatest Hits**	1965	8.00	20.00
ABC-Paramount ABCS-515	(S)	**The Impressions' Greatest Hits**	1965	10.00	25.00
ABC-Paramount ABC-523	(M)	**One By One**	1965	8.00	20.00
ABC-Paramount ABCS-523	(S)	**One By One**	1965	10.00	25.00
ABC-Paramount ABC-545	(M)	**Ridin' High**	1966	10.00	25.00
ABC-Paramount ABCS-545	(S)	**Ridin' High**	1966	12.00	30.00
ABC 606	(M)	**The Fabulous Impressions**	1967	8.00	20.00
ABC S-606	(S)	**The Fabulous Impressions**	1967	10.00	25.00
IN-SECT, THE					
Camden CAL-909	(M)	**Introducing The In-Sect**	1965	16.00	40.00
Camden CAS-909	(S)	**Introducing The In-Sect**	1965	20.00	50.00
INCREDIBLE STRING BAND, THE					
Elektra EKL-322	(M)	**The Incredible String Band**	1967	8.00	20.00
Elektra EKS-7322	(S)	**The Incredible String Band**	1967	10.00	25.00
Elektra EKL-4010	(M)	**The 5,000 Spirits**	1967	8.00	20.00
Elektra EKS-74010	(S)	**The 5,000 Spirits**	1967	10.00	25.00
Elektra EKS-4021	(M)	**The Hangman's Beautiful Daughter**	1968	8.00	20.00
Elektra EKS-74021	(S)	**The Hangman's Beautiful Daughter**	1968	10.00	25.00
Elektra EKS-74036	(S)	**Wee Tam**	1969	10.00	25.00
Elektra EKS-74037	(S)	**The Big Huge**	1969	10.00	25.00
		— Elektra albums above have brown labels.—			
Decca DL-79181	(S)	**Taking Off** *(Soundtrack)*	1971	16.00	40.00
INDEX, THE					
Members of The Index later recorded as Just Us.					
D. C. *(No number)*	(M)	**The Index**	1968	2,100.00	3,000.00

(Original records and covers list "New York Mining Disaster."
Many copies of the original album were issued in second pressing
covers; these are worth 50-60% of the values above.)

Label & Catalog #		Title	Year	VG+	NM
D. C. *(No number)*	*(M)*	**The Index**	1968	1,000.00	1,500.00
		(Second pressing records and covers feature "Fire Eyes.")			
INGMANN, JORGEN					
Mercury MG-20200	*(M)*	**Swinging Guitar**	1956	30.00	75.00
Mercury MG-20292	*(M)*	**Swing Softly**	1956	30.00	75.00
Atco 33-130	*(M)*	**Apache**	1961	16.00	40.00
Atco 33-139	*(M)*	**The Many Guitars Of Jorgen Ingmann**	1962	16.00	40.00
INK SPOTS, THE					
Waldorf Music 33-144	*(10")*	**The Ink Spots**	195?	30.00	75.00
Waldorf Music 33-152	*(10")*	**The Ink Spots**	195?	30.00	75.00
Waldorf Music 33-W2A	*(10")*	**America's Favorite Music** *(2 LPs)*	195?	30.00	75.00
		(Waldorf 2A collects the two 10" albums plus eight others.)			
Decca DL-5056	*(10")*	**The Ink Spots, Volume 1**	1950	20.00	50.00
Decca DL-5071	*(10")*	**The Ink Spots, Volume 2**	1950	20.00	50.00
Decca DL-5333	*(10")*	**Precious Memories**	1951	20.00	50.00
Decca DL-5541	*(10")*	**Street Of Dreams**	1954	20.00	50.00
Decca DL-8154	*(M)*	**The Ink Spots**	1955	16.00	40.00
Decca DL-8232	*(M)*	**Time Out For Tears**	1956	16.00	40.00
Decca DL-8768	*(M)*	**Torch Time**	1958	16.00	40.00
Decca DL-4297	*(M)*	**Our Golden Favorites**	1962	10.00	25.00
Decca DL-74297	*(E)*	**Our Golden Favorites**	1962	6.00	15.00
Decca DXB-182	*(M)*	**The Best Of The Ink Spots** *(2 LPs)*	1965	12.00	30.00
Decca DXSB-182	*(P)*	**The Best Of The Ink Spots** *(2 LPs)*	1965	8.00	20.00
Grand Award GA-33-328	*(M)*	**The Ink Spots' Greatest, Volume 1**	1956	10.00	25.00
Grand Award GA-33-354	*(M)*	**The Ink Spots' Greatest, Volume 2**	1956	10.00	25.00
King LP-535	*(M)*	**Something Old, Something New**	1958	200.00	400.00
King LP-642	*(M)*	**Songs That Will Live Forever**	1959	100.00	300.00
Colortone 4901	*(M)*	**The Ink Spots**	1958	30.00	75.00
Colortone 4947	*(M)*	**The Ink Spots (Volume 2)**	1959	30.00	75.00
Grand LP-328	*(M)*	**The Ink Spots' Greatest**	1959	10.00	25.00
Grand LP-354	*(M)*	**The Ink Spots' Greatest, Volume 2**	1959	10.00	25.00
Verve MGV-2124	*(M)*	**The Ink Spots' Favorites**	1960	10.00	25.00
Verve MGVS-6096	*(S)*	**The Ink Spots' Favorites**	1960	16.00	40.00
Crown CST-175	*(E)*	**The Ink Spots** *(Red vinyl)*	196?	20.00	50.00
Crown CST-1??	*(E)*	**The Ink Spots' Greatest Hits** *(Red vinyl)*	196?	20.00	50.00
Crown CST-2??	*(E)*	**The Sensational Ink Spots** *(Red vinyl)*	196?	20.00	50.00
Mayfair 9685S	*(M)*	**In The Spotlight** *(Yellow vinyl)*	196?	20.00	50.00
INMAN, AUTRY					
Mountain Dew 7022	*(M)*	**Autry Inman**	1963	8.00	20.00
Mountain Dew S-7022	*(S)*	**Autry Inman**	1963	10.00	25.00
Sims 107	*(M)*	**Autry Inman At The Frontier Club**	1964	8.00	20.00
Sims S-107	*(S)*	**Autry Inman At The Frontier Club**	1964	10.00	25.00
Jubilee JGM-2055	*(M)*	**Discotheque Saterday Night**	1964	8.00	20.00
Jubilee JGS-2055	*(S)*	**Discotheque Saterday Night**	1964	10.00	25.00
Jubilee JGM-2056	*(M)*	**New Year's Eve With Autry Inman**	1964	8.00	20.00
Jubilee JGS-2056	*(S)*	**New Year's Eve With Autry Inman**	1964	10.00	25.00
INNOCENCE, THE					
The Innocence is Pete Anders and Vinnie Poncia.					
Kama Sutra KLP-8059	*(M)*	**The Innocence**	1967	6.00	15.00
Kama Sutra KLPS-8059	*(S)*	**The Innocence**	1967	12.00	30.00
INNOCENTS, THE					
The Innocents also recorded with Kathy Young.					
Indigo 503	*(M)*	**Innocently Yours**	1961	300.00	800.00
		(Advance copies designated as promos were issued in plain white covers with "The Innocents" printed in blue letters on the front.)			
Indigo 503	*(M)*	**Innocently Yours**	1961	80.00	200.00
INSECT TRUST, THE					
Capitol SKAO-109	*(S)*	**The Insect Trust**	1968	16.00	40.00
Atco SD-33-313	*(S)*	**Hoboken Saturday Night**	1970	14.00	35.00
INTERNATIONAL SUBMARINE BAND, THE					
The I.S.B. features Gram Parsons.					
L.H.I. 12001	*(S)*	**Safe At Home** *(Multi-color label)*	1968	40.00	100.00
		(Originals have multi-color labels; counterfeits have white labels.)			

Label & Catalog #		Title	Year	VG+	NM
INTRIGUES, THE					
Yew YS-777	(S)	**In A Moment**	1970	16.00	40.00
INTRUDERS, THE					
Gamble 5001	(M)	**The Intruders Are Together**	1967	16.00	40.00
Gamble KZ-5001	(P)	**The Intruders Are Together**	1967	20.00	50.00
Gamble KZ-5004	(P)	**Cowboys To Girls**	1968	20.00	50.00
Gamble KZ-5005	(P)	**The Intruders' Greatest Hits**	1969	16.00	40.00
Gamble KZ-5008	(S)	**When We Get Married**	1970	20.00	50.00
INVADERS, THE					
Justice JLP-125	(M)	**On The Right Track**	196?	150.00	300.00
INVADERS, THE					
Duane 1006	(M)	**Spacing Out**	1968	40.00	100.00
INVICTAS, THE					
M80-P-5817	(M)	**The Invictas**	1963	100.00	250.00
Sahara 101	(M)	**The Invictas A-Go-Go**	1965	40.00	100.00

IRON BUTTERFLY
Refer to The Buffalo Springfield / Iron Butterfly.

Atco 33-227	(M)	**Heavy**	1967	10.00	25.00
Atco SD-33-227	(S)	**Heavy**	1967	8.00	20.00
Atco 33-250	(M)	**In-A-Gadda-Da-Vida**	1968	14.00	35.00
Atco SD-33-250	(S)	**In-A-Gadda-Da-Vida**	1968	10.00	25.00

— Atco stereo albums above have purple & brown labels.—

IRON MAIDEN

Capitol SEAX-12219	(S)	**Number Of The Beast** *(Picture disc)*	19??	20.00	50.00
Capitol SEAX-12306	(S)	**Piece Of Mind** *(Picture disc)*	19??	20.00	50.00
		(Contains one bonus track, "Cross Eyed Mary.")			

ISAACSON, DAN
Dan Isaacson is a guitar player and singer of traditional folk songs.

Cornell CRS-10021	(10")	**Ballads**	1954	16.00	40.00

ISLEY, TEX: *Refer to* **TOM ASHLEY & TEX ISLEY**

ISLEY BROTHERS, THE
Refer to Jimi Hendrix / The Isley Brothers.

RCA Victor LPM-2156	(M)	**Shout!**	1959	40.00	100.00
RCA Victor LSP-2156	(S)	**Shout!**	1959	60.00	150.00
Wand WD-653	(M)	**Twist And Shout**	1962	30.00	75.00
Wand WDS-653	(S)	**Twist And Shout**	1962	40.00	100.00
United Arts. UAL-3313	(M)	**The Famous Isley Brothers**	1963	20.00	50.00
United Arts. UAS-6313	(S)	**The Famous Isley Brothers**	1963	30.00	75.00
Scepter SC-552	(M)	**Take Some Time Out For The Isley Brothers**	1966	12.00	30.00
Scepter SCS-552	(S)	**Take Some Time Out For The Isley Brothers**	1966	16.00	40.00
Tamla T-269	(M)	**This Old Heart Of Mine**	1966	8.00	20.00
Tamla TS-269	(S)	**This Old Heart Of Mine**	1966	10.00	25.00
Tamla 275	(M)	**Soul On The Rocks**	1967	8.00	20.00
Tamla TS-275	(S)	**Soul On The Rocks**	1967	10.00	25.00
Tamla TS-287	(S)	**Doin' Their Thing**	1969	8.00	20.00

ISLEY BROTHERS, THE / THE CHIFFONS
Refer to The Chiffons.

Spin-O-Rama SP-127	(M)	**The Islaey Brothers And The Chiffons**	1964	10.00	25.00
Spin-O-Rama SPS-127	(E)	**The Islaey Brothers And The Chiffons**	1964	4.00	10.00

ISLEY BROTHERS, THE / MARVIN & JOHNNY
Refer to Marvin & Johnny.

Crown CLP-5352	(M)	**The Isley Brothers And Marvin & Johnny**	196?	10.00	25.00
Crown CST-352	(E)	**The Isley Brothers And Marvin & Johnny**	196?	4.00	10.00

ISAACS, BUD

Jabs 101	(M)	**The Best Of Bud Isaacs**	195?	80.00	200.00

Label & Catalog #		Title	Year	VG+	NM

IT'S A BEAUTIFUL DAY

Label & Catalog #		Title	Year	VG+	NM
Columbia CS-9768	(S)	It's A Beautiful Day	1969	16.00	40.00
Columbia CS-1058	(S)	Marrying Maiden	1970	10.00	25.00
— Columbia albums above have "360 Sound" labels.—					
San Fran. Sound 11790	(S)	It's A Beautiful Day (Half-speed master)	1985	10.00	30.00
San Fran. Sound 04800	(S)	Marrying Maiden (Half-speed master)	1985	10.00	30.00

IVES, BURL
Burl Ives is a guitar and banjo player and singer of folk and pop music as well as a successful screen actor.

Stinson SLP-1	(10")	The Wayfaring Stranger	1949	20.00	50.00
Columbia CL-6058	(10")	The Return Of The Wayfaring Stranger	1949	20.00	50.00
Columbia CL-6109	(10")	The Wayfaring Stranger	1950	20.00	50.00
Columbia CL-6144	(10")	More Folksongs	1950	20.00	50.00
Columbia CL-2570	(10")	Children's Favorites	1954	20.00	50.00
Columbia CL-628	(M)	The Wayfaring Stranger	1955	12.00	30.00
Columbia CL-980	(M)	Burl Ives Sings Songs For All Ages	1957	12.00	30.00
Columbia CL-1459	(M)	Return Of The Wayfaring Stranger	1960	12.00	30.00
Decca DL-5013	(10")	Ballads And Folk Songs, Volume 1	1949	20.00	50.00
Decca DL-5080	(10")	Ballads And Folk Songs, Volume 2	1949	20.00	50.00
Decca DL-5093	(10")	Ballads, Folk And Country Songs	1949	20.00	50.00
Decca DL-5428	(10")	Christmas Day In The Morning	1952	20.00	50.00
Decca DL-5467	(10")	Folk Songs Dramatic And Dangerous	1953	20.00	50.00
Decca DL-5490	(10")	Women: Folk Songs About The Fair	1954	20.00	50.00
Decca DL-8080	(M)	Coronation Concert	1956	10.00	25.00
Decca DL-8107	(M)	The Wild Side Of Life	1956	10.00	25.00
Decca DL-8125	(M)	Men	1956	10.00	25.00
Decca DL-8245	(M)	Down To The Sea In Ships	1956	10.00	25.00
Decca DL-8246	(M)	Women	1956	10.00	25.00
Decca DL-8247	(M)	In The Quiet Of Night	1956	10.00	25.00
Decca DL-8248	(M)	Burl Ives Sings For Fun	1956	10.00	25.00
Decca DL-8391	(M)	Christmas Eve With Ives	1957	10.00	25.00
Decca DL-78391	(E)	Christmas Eve With Ives	196?	4.00	10.00
Decca DL-8444	(M)	Songs Of Ireland	1958	10.00	25.00
Decca DL-8637	(M)	Old Time Varieties	1958	10.00	25.00
Decca DL-8587	(M)	Captain Burl Ives' Ark	1958	10.00	25.00
Decca DL-8749	(M)	Australian Folk Songs	1958	10.00	25.00
Decca DL-8886	(M)	Cheers	1959	10.00	25.00
Decca DL-78886	(S)	Cheers	1959	12.00	30.00
Encyclopedia Brit. Films I	(M)	Songs Of The Colonies	195?	12.00	30.00
Encyclopedia Brit. Films II	(M)	Songs Of The Revolution	195?	12.00	30.00
Encyclopedia Brit. Films III	(M)	Songs Of North And South	195?	12.00	30.00
Encyclopedia Brit. Films IV	(M)	Songs Of The Sea	195?	12.00	30.00
Encyclopedia Brit. Films V	(M)	Songs Of The Frontier	195?	12.00	30.00
Encyclopedia Brit. Films VI	(M)	Songs Of The Expanding America	195?	12.00	30.00
Decca DL-4815	(M)	Rudolph The Red-Nosed Reindeer	1966	12.00	30.00
Decca DL-74815	(S)	Rudolph The Red-Nosed Reindeer	1966	16.00	40.00

IVEYS, THE
The Iveys later recorded as Badfinger.

Apple SAPCOR-8S	(S)	Maybe Tomorrow (Italian. Green label)	1968	500.00	1,000.00
		(Copies of this album with a black label are counterfeits. This album was also issued in several other countries, including Japan and West Germany.)			

IVORY, JACKIE

Atco 33-178	(M)	Soul Discovery	1965	8.00	20.00
Atco SD-33-178	(S)	Soul Discovery	1965	10.00	25.00

IVY LEAGUE, THE

Cameo C-2000	(M)	Tossing And Turning	1965	10.00	25.00
Cameo CS-2000	(E)	Tossing And Turning	1965	8.00	20.00

IVY LEAGUE TRIO, THE

Reprise R-6087	(M)	Folk Ballads From The World Of Edgar Allan Poe	1963	8.00	20.00
Reprise R9-6087	(S)	Folk Ballads From The World Of Edgar Allan Poe	1963	10.00	25.00

The eclectic Burl Ives is often dismissed as a sort of novelty actor type who had a few pop hits in the '60s. Unfortunately, that does a great disservice to Mr. Ives, one of this country's best-loved folk singers during the '40s and '50s. The Wayfaring Stranger may be his best known folk song and the best album with which to get to know that aspect of his multi-talented persona.

J. A. BLUEZY
Apollo Music ERK-0782	(S)	**At The Delta Lady**	*1980*	**30.00**	**75.00**

J. TEAL BAND, THE
Mother Cleo MCPLP-7721	(S)	**The J. Teal Band Cooks**	*1977*	**24.00**	**60.00**

JACKIE & ROY: *Refer to* **GOLDMINE'S PRICE GUIDE TO COLLECTIBLE JAZZ ALBUMS**

JACKS, THE
The Jacks also recorded as The Cadets. Refer to Aaron Collins.
RPM LRP-3006	(M)	**Jumpin' With The Jacks**	*1956*	**500.00** *See below*
		(RPM 3006 has a suggested Near Mint value of $1,000-2,000.)			
Crown CLP-5021	(M)	**Jumpin' With The Jacks**	*195?*	**80.00**	**200.00**
Crown CLP-5372	(M)	**Jumpin' With The Jacks**	*1962*	**40.00**	**100.00**
Crown CST-372	(E)	**Jumpin' With The Jacks**	*1962*	**20.00**	**50.00**
		(Crown 5021 and 5372 are reissues of RPM 3006.)			

JACKSON, BULL MOOSE
Audio Lab LP-1524	(M)	**Bull Moose Jackson**	*1959*	**250.00**	**750.00**

JACKSON, CHUCK
Wand WD-650	(M)	**I Don't Want To Cry**	*1961*	**16.00**	**40.00**
Wand WDS-650	(S)	**I Don't Want To Cry**	*1961*	**20.00**	**50.00**
Wand WD-654	(M)	**Any Day Now**	*1962*	**16.00**	**40.00**
Wand WDS-654	(S)	**Any Day Now**	*1962*	**20.00**	**50.00**
Wand WD-655	(M)	**Encore**	*1963*	**12.00**	**30.00**
Wand WDS-655	(S)	**Encore**	*1963*	**16.00**	**40.00**
Wand WD-658	(M)	**Chuck Jackson On Tour**	*1964*	**12.00**	**30.00**
Wand WDS-658	(S)	**Chuck Jackson On Tour**	*1964*	**16.00**	**40.00**
Wand WD-667	(M)	**Mr. Everything**	*1965*	**12.00**	**30.00**
Wand WDS-667	(S)	**Mr. Everything**	*1965*	**16.00**	**40.00**
Wand WD-673	(M)	**A Tribute To Rhythm & Blues**	*1966*	**12.00**	**30.00**
Wand WDS-673	(S)	**A Tribute To Rhythm & Blues**	*1966*	**16.00**	**40.00**
Wand WD-676	(M)	**A Tribute To Rhythm & Blues, Volume 2**	*1966*	**12.00**	**30.00**
Wand WDS-676	(S)	**A Tribute To Rhythm & Blues, Volume 2**	*1966*	**16.00**	**40.00**
Wand WD-680	(M)	**Dedicated To The King!!**	*1966*	**12.00**	**30.00**
Wand WDS-680	(S)	**Dedicated To The King!!**	*1966*	**16.00**	**40.00**
Wand WD-683	(M)	**Chuck Jackson's Greatest Hits**	*1967*	**8.00**	**20.00**
Wand WDS-683	(S)	**Chuck Jackson's Greatest Hits**	*1967*	**10.00**	**25.00**
Motown M-667	(M)	**Chuck Jackson Arrives!**	*1968*	**16.00**	**40.00**
Motown MS-667	(S)	**Chuck Jackson Arrives!**	*1968*	**10.00**	**25.00**
Motown MS-687	(S)	**Goin' Back To Chuck Jackson**	*1969*	**10.00**	**25.00**

JACKSON, CHUCK, & MAXINE BROWN
Wand WD-669	(M)	**Saying Something**	*1965*	**12.00**	**30.00**
Wand WDS-669	(S)	**Saying Something**	*1965*	**16.00**	**40.00**
Wand WD-678	(M)	**Hold On, We're Coming**	*1966*	**12.00**	**30.00**
Wand WDS-678	(S)	**Hold On, We're Coming**	*1966*	**16.00**	**40.00**

JACKSON, CHUCK, & TAMMI TERRELL
Wand LP-682	(M)	**The Early Show**	*1967*	**12.00**	**30.00**
Wand WDS-682	(S)	**The Early Show**	*1967*	**16.00**	**40.00**

JACKSON, DEON
Atco 33-188	(M)	**Love Makes The World Go Round**	*1966*	**12.00**	**30.00**
Atco SD-33-188	(S)	**Love Makes The World Go Round**	*1966*	**16.00**	**40.00**

JACKSON, GRAHAM
Westminster WP-6048	(M)	**Spirituals**	*195?*	**12.00**	**30.00**

Label & Catalog #		Title	Year	VG+	NM
JACKSON, J. J.					
Calla C-1101	(M)	**But It's Alright/I Dig Girls**	1967	8.00	20.00
CaMla CS-1101	(S)	**But It's Alright/I Dig Girls**	1967	10.00	25.00
JACKSON, LIL' SON					
Imperial LP-9142	(M)	**Rockin' And Rollin'**	1961	150.00	300.00
JACKSON, MICHAEL					
Michael was a member of The Jacksons.					
Motown M-755	(S)	**Ben** *(Soundtrack. Cover features a rat)*	1972	16.00	40.00
Epic HE-47545	(S)	**Off The Wall** *(Half-speed master)*	1982	15.00	45.00
Epic HE-48112	(S)	**Thriller** *(Half-speed master)*	1982	15.00	45.00
JACKSON, "AUNT" MOLLY					
Molly Jackson was a singer and songwriter of traditional and topical folk music.					
Folkways 5457	(M)	**The Songs And Stories Of Aunt Molly Jackson**	1961	12.00	30.00
JACKSON, SAMMY					
Arvee M-434	(M)	**Ladies' Man**	1962	24.00	60.00
JACKSON, SHOT					
Starday SLP-230	(M)	**The Singing Strings Of Steel Guitar And Dobro** *(Yellow label)*	1962	16.00	40.00
Cumberland SRC-69513	(M)	**Bluegrass Dobro**	1965	8.00	20.00
Cumberland MGC-29513	(S)	**Bluegrass Dobro**	1965	10.00	25.00
JACKSON, STONEWALL					
Columbia CL-1391	(M)	**The Dynamic Stonewall Jackson**	1959	12.00	30.00
Columbia CS-8186	(S)	**The Dynamic Stonewall Jackson**	1959	16.00	40.00
Columbia CL-1770	(M)	**Sadness In A Song**	1962	10.00	25.00
Columbia CS-8570	(S)	**Sadness In A Song**	1962	12.00	30.00
		— Columbia albums above have three white "eye" logos on each side of the spindle hole.—			
Columbia CL-2059	(M)	**I Love A Song**	1963	8.00	20.00
Columbia CS-8859	(S)	**I Love A Song**	1963	10.00	25.00
Columbia CL-2278	(M)	**Trouble And Me**	1965	8.00	20.00
Columbia CS-9078	(S)	**Trouble And Me**	1965	10.00	25.00
		— Columbia albums above have "360 Sound" on the bottom of the label.—			
JACKSON, TOMMY					
Dot DLP-3015	(M)	**Popular Square Dance Music**	1957	12.00	30.00
Dot DLP-3085	(M)	**Square Dance Tonight!**	1958	12.00	30.00
Mercury MG-20346	(M)	**Square Dance Fiddle Favorites**	1958	12.00	30.00
Decca DL-78950	(M)	**Square Dancs Without Calls**	1959	8.00	20.00
Decca DL-78950	(S)	**Square Dancs Without Calls**	1959	10.00	25.00
Dot DLP-3471	(M)	**Greatest Bluegrass Hits**	1962	8.00	20.00
Dot DLP-25471	(S)	**Greatest Bluegrass Hits**	1962	10.00	25.00
JACKSON, WALTER					
OKeh OKM-12107	(M)	**It's All Over**	1965	8.00	20.00
OKeh OKS-14107	(S)	**It's All Over**	1965	10.00	25.00
OKeh OKM-12108	(M)	**Welcome Home**	1965	8.00	20.00
OKeh OKS-14108	(S)	**Welcome Home**	1965	10.00	25.00
OKeh OKM-12120	(M)	**Speak Her Name**	1967	8.00	20.00
OKeh OKS-14120	(S)	**Speak Her Name**	1967	10.00	25.00
JACKSON, WANDA/WANDA JACKSON & THE PARTY TIMERS					
Capitol T-1041	(M)	**Wanda Jackson**	1958	150.00	300.00
Capitol T-1384	(M)	**Rockin' With Wanda!**	1960	300.00	500.00
		(T-1384 collects Ms. Jackson's earlier rockabilly singles.)			
Capitol T-1384	(M)	**Rockin' With Wanda!** *(Gold Starline label)*	1962	150.00	300.00
Capitol T-1384	(M)	**Rockin' With Wanda!** *(Black Starline label)*	1963	60.00	150.00
Capitol T-1511	(M)	**There's A Party Goin' On**	1961	150.00	300.00
Capitol ST-1511	(S)	**There's A Party Goin' On**	1961	200.00	400.00
Capitol T-1596	(M)	**Right Or Wrong**	1961	16.00	40.00
Capitol ST-1596	(S)	**Right Or Wrong**	1961	20.00	50.00
		— Capitol albums above have black labels with the Capitol logo on the side.—			
Decca DL-4224	(M)	**Lovin' Country Style**	1962	20.00	50.00
Decca DL-74224	(E)	**Lovin' Country Style**	1962	12.00	30.00
		(DL-4224 contains Ms Jackson's pre-Capitol country recordings.)			

Label & Catalog #		Title	Year	VG+	NM
Capitol T-1776	(M)	**Wonderful Wanda**	1962	10.00	25.00
Capitol ST-1776	(S)	**Wonderful Wanda**	1962	12.00	30.00
Capitol T-1911	(M)	**Love Me Forever**	1963	10.00	25.00
Capitol ST-1911	(S)	**Love Me Forever**	1963	12.00	30.00
Capitol T-2030	(M)	**Two Sides Of Wanda Jackson**	1964	12.00	30.00
Capitol ST-2030	(S)	**Two Sides Of Wanda Jackson**	1964	16.00	40.00
Capitol T-2306	(M)	**Blues In My Heart**	1964	12.00	30.00
Capitol ST-2306	(S)	**Blues In My Heart**	1964	16.00	40.00
Capitol T-2438	(M)	**Wanda Jackson Sings Country Songs**	1966	10.00	25.00
Capitol ST-2438	(S)	**Wanda Jackson Sings Country Songs**	1966	12.00	30.00

— Capitol albums above have black labels with the Capitol logo on top.—

JACKSON FIVE, THE/THE JACKSONS
The Jacksons feature Jackie, Jermaine and Michael Jackson.

Motown MS-700	(S)	**Diana Ross Presents The Jackson Five**	1970	10.00	25.00
Motown MS-709	(S)	**ABC**	1970	10.00	25.00
Motown MS-713	(S)	**Christmas Won't Be The Same This Year**	1970	10.00	25.00
National Res. NR-4013TI	(S)	**Boogie**	1979		*See below*

(National Resource 4013 is a compilation of Motown tracks with-drawn from release after The Jacksons threatened litigation. Rare with no established value at this time.)

Epic PAL-34835	(DJ)	**Goin' Places** *(Picture disc)*	1978	20.00	50.00
Epic HE-46424	(S)	**Triumph** *(Half-speed master)*	1981	13.00	40.00

JACKSON HEIGHTS
Mercury SR-61331	(S)	**King Progress**	1970	10.00	25.00
Verve V6-5089	(S)	**Jackson Heights**	1973	8.00	20.00

JACOBS, FREDDY
Westminster WP-6087	(M)	**Swingin' Folk Tunes**	195?	10.00	25.00

JACOBS, HANK
Sue LP-1023	(M)	**So Far Away**	1964	40.00	100.00

JADE
Gar 11311	(M)	**The Faces Of Jade**	196?	20.00	50.00

JADE STONE & LUV
Jade JS-4351	(S)	**Mosaics-Pieces Of Stone**	1977	50.00	125.00

JADES, THE
Jarrett 21517	(M)	**Live At The Disc A-Go-Go**	196?	60.00	150.00

JAGGER, MICK
Both of the soundtracks below feature only one track by Jagger but as he was each films' star and is featured on the cover the LPs are listed here. Refer to The Rolling Stones.

United Arts. UAS-5213	(S)	**Ned Kelly** *(Soundtrack)*	1970	10.00	25.00
		("Wild Colonial Boy" is rechanneled on this album..)			
Warner Bros. BS-1846	(S)	**Performance** *(Soundtrack)*	1970	10.00	25.00

JAIM
Ethereal 1001	(S)	**Prophesy Fulfilled**	1970	20.00	50.00

JALOPY FIVE, THE
Modern Sound M-525	(M)	**Draggin' & Surfin'**	196?	20.00	50.00
Modern Sound MS-525	(S)	**Draggin' & Surfin'**	196?	24.00	60.00
Modern Sound M-536	(M)	**Draggin' & Surfin'**	196?	20.00	50.00
Modern Sound MS-536	(S)	**Draggin' & Surfin'**	196?	24.00	60.00
Modern Sound M-561	(M)	**I Love That West Coast Sound**	1965	10.00	25.00
Modern Sound MS-561	(S)	**I Love That West Coast Sound**	1965	12.00	30.00

JAMES, ELMORE
Crown CLP-5168	(M)	**Blues After Hours** *(Black label)*	1961	100.00	250.00
Sphere Sound SR-7002	(M)	**The Sky Is Crying**	1965	80.00	200.00
Sphere Sound SSR-7002	(E)	**The Sky Is Crying**	1965	40.00	100.00
Sphere Sound SR-7008	(M)	**I Need You**	1966	80.00	200.00
Sphere Sound SSR-7008	(E)	**I Need You** *(Red label)*	1966	40.00	100.00
Sphere Sound SSR-7008	(E)	**I Need You** *(Yellow label)*	196?	20.00	50.00

Joan Carmello Babbo, better known to collectors around the world as Miss Joni James, is one the hottest of the white female pop singers in the field of collecting records. Her albums, mono or stereo, first pressing or second, have been consistently good sellers and consistently rising prices for many years. While there may be arguments over which is her best album, and most fans prefer her earlier recordings, it may be Merry Christmas From Joni, issued for the 1956 Yuletide that is her rarest and most valuable

Label & Catalog #		Title	Year	VG+	NM
Kent KLP-5022	(M)	**Original Folk Blues**	1964	16.00	40.00
Kent KST-522	(E)	**Original Folk Blues**	1964	10.00	25.00
Chess LP-1537	(S)	**Whose Muddy Shoes**	1969	10.00	25.00
Bell 6037	(S)	**Elmore James**	1969	10.00	25.00
JAMES, ETTA					
Crown CLP-5209	(M)	**Miss Etta James**	1961	40.00	100.00
		(Original covers of Crown 5209 have a framed picture of Etta.)			
Crown CLP-5209	(M)	**Miss Etta James**	1962	20.00	50.00
		(Later covers are white and read "Miss Etta James.")			
Crown CLP-5250	(M)	**Twist With Etta James**	1962	20.00	50.00
Kent KLP-5000	(M)	**Miss Etta James**	1964	12.00	30.00
Kent KST-500	(E)	**Miss Etta James** *(Red vinyl)*	1964	30.00	75.00
Kent KST-500	(E)	**Miss Etta James**	1964	10.00	25.00
		(Kent 5000 is a reissue of Crown 5209.)			
Argo LP-4003	(M)	**At Last**	1961	14.00	35.00
Argo LPS-4003	(S)	**At Last**	1961	20.00	50.00
Argo LP-4011	(M)	**The Second Time Around**	1961	14.00	35.00
Argo LPS-4011	(S)	**The Second Time Around**	1961	20.00	50.00
Argo LP-4013	(M)	**Etta James**	1962	14.00	35.00
Argo LPS-4013	(S)	**Etta James**	1962	20.00	50.00
		("Spoonful" and "If I Can't Have You" are rechanneled on this album.)			
Argo LP-4018	(M)	**Etta James Sings For Lovers**	1962	14.00	35.00
Argo LPS-4018	(S)	**Etta James Sings For Lovers**	1962	20.00	50.00
Argo LP-4025	(M)	**Top Ten**	1963	14.00	35.00
Argo LPS-4025	(S)	**Top Ten**	1963	20.00	50.00
Argo LP-4032	(M)	**Etta James Rocks The House**	1964	40.00	100.00
Argo LPS-4032	(S)	**Etta James Rocks The House**	1964	60.00	150.00
Argo LP-4040	(M)	**The Queen Of Soul**	1965	14.00	35.00
Argo LPS-4040	(S)	**The Queen Of Soul**	1965	20.00	50.00
Caedt LP-802	(M)	**Tell Mama**	1967	8.00	20.00
Caedt LPS-802	(S)	**Tell Mama**	1967	10.00	25.00
JAMES, JONI					
MGM E-222	(10")	**Let There Be Love**	1953	60.00	150.00
MGM E-234	(10")	**Award Winning Album**	1954	60.00	150.00
MGM E-272	(10")	**Little Girl Blue**	1956	60.00	150.00
MGM E-3328	(M)	**In The Still Of The Night**	1956	30.00	75.00
MGM E-3240	(M)	**When I Fall In Love**	1956	30.00	75.00
MGM E-3346	(M)	**Award Winning Album**	1956	30.00	75.00
MGM E-3347	(M)	**Little Girl Blue**	1956	30.00	75.00
MGM E-3348	(M)	**Let There Be Love**	1956	30.00	75.00
MGM E-3449	(M)	**Songs By Victor Young And Frank Loesser**	1956	30.00	75.00
MGM E-3468	(M)	**Merry Christmas From Joni**	1956	40.00	100.00
MGM E-3528	(M)	**Give Us This Day**	1957	30.00	75.00
MGM E-3533	(M)	**Songs By Kern & Warren**	1957	30.00	75.00
MGM E-3602	(M)	**Among My Souvenirs**	1958	30.00	75.00
MGM SE-3602	(S)	**Among My Souvenirs**	1958	40.00	100.00
MGM E-3623	(M)	**Ti Voglio Bene**	1958	30.00	75.00
MGM SE-3623	(S)	**Ti Voglio Bene**	1958	40.00	100.00
MGM E-3702	(M)	**Award Winning Album, Volume 2**	1958	30.00	75.00
MGM SE-3702	(S)	**Award Winning Album, Volume 2**	1958	40.00	100.00
MGM E-3718	(M)	**Je T'aime (I Love You)**	1958	30.00	75.00
MGM SE-3718	(S)	**Je T'aime (I Love You)**	1958	40.00	100.00
MGM E-3739	(M)	**Songs Of Hank Williams**	1959	30.00	75.00
MGM SE-3739	(S)	**Songs Of Hank Williams**	1959	40.00	100.00
MGM E-3749	(M)	**Irish Favorites**	1959	30.00	75.00
MGM SE-3749	(S)	**Irish Favorites**	1959	40.00	100.00
MGM E-3755	(M)	**100 Strings And Joni**	1959	30.00	75.00
MGM SE-3755	(S)	**100 Strings And Joni**	1959	40.00	100.00
		— MGM albums above have yellow labels. —			
MGM E-3328	(M)	**In The Still Of The Night**	196?	12.00	30.00
MGM E-3240	(M)	**When I Fall In Love**	196?	12.00	30.00
MGM E-3346	(M)	**Award Winning Album**	196?	12.00	30.00
MGM E-3347	(M)	**Little Girl Blue**	196?	12.00	30.00
MGM E-3348	(M)	**Let There Be Love**	196?	12.00	30.00
MGM E-3449	(M)	**Songs By Victor Young And Frank Loesser**	196?	12.00	30.00
MGM E-3468	(M)	**Merry Christmas From Joni**	196?	20.00	50.00
MGM E-3528	(M)	**Give Us This Day**	196?	12.00	30.00

Label & Catalog #		Title	Year	VG+	NM
MGM E-3533	(M)	Songs By Kern & Warren	196?	12.00	30.00
MGM E-3602	(M)	Among My Souvenirs	196?	12.00	30.00
MGM SE-3602	(S)	Among My Souvenirs	196?	16.00	40.00
MGM E-3623	(M)	Ti Voglio Bene	196?	12.00	30.00
MGM SE-3623	(S)	Ti Voglio Bene	196?	16.00	40.00
MGM E-3702	(M)	Award Winning Album, Volume 2	196?	12.00	30.00
MGM SE-3702	(S)	Award Winning Album, Volume 2	196?	16.00	40.00
MGM E-3718	(M)	Je T'aime (I Love You)	196?	12.00	30.00
MGM SE-3718	(S)	Je T'aime (I Love You)	196?	16.00	40.00
MGM E-3739	(M)	Songs Of Hank Williams	196?	12.00	30.00
MGM SE-3739	(S)	Songs Of Hank Williams	196?	16.00	40.00
MGM E-3749	(M)	Irish Favorites	196?	12.00	30.00
MGM SE-3749	(S)	Irish Favorites	196?	16.00	40.00
MGM E-3755	(M)	100 Strings And Joni	196?	12.00	30.00
MGM SE-3755	(S)	100 Strings And Joni	196?	16.00	40.00
MGM E-3772	(M)	Joni James Swings Sweet	1959	20.00	50.00
MGM SE-3772	(S)	Joni James Swings Sweet	1959	30.00	75.00
MGM E-3800	(M)	Joni James At Carnegie Hall	1959	20.00	50.00
MGM SE-3800	(S)	Joni James At Carnegie Hall	1959	30.00	75.00
MGM E-3837	(M)	I'm In The Mood For Love	1960	20.00	50.00
MGM SE-3837	(S)	I'm In The Mood For Love	1960	24.00	60.00
MGM E-3839	(M)	100 Strings And Joni On Broadway	1960	20.00	50.00
MGM SE-3839	(S)	100 Strings And Joni On Broadway	1960	24.00	60.00
MGM E-3840	(M)	100 Strings And Joni In Hollywood	1960	20.00	50.00
MGM SE-3840	(S)	100 Strings And Joni In Hollywood	1960	24.00	60.00
MGM E-3885	(M)	More Joni Hits	1960	16.00	40.00
MGM SE-3885	(P)	More Joni Hits	1960	20.00	50.00
MGM E-3892	(M)	100 Voices, 100 Strings	1960	16.00	40.00
MGM SE-3892	(S)	100 Voices, 100 Strings	1960	20.00	50.00
MGM E-3958	(M)	Folk Songs By Joni James	1961	16.00	40.00
MGM SE-3958	(S)	Folk Songs By Joni James	1961	20.00	50.00
MGM E-3987	(M)	The Mood Is Swinging	1961	16.00	40.00
MGM SE-3987	(S)	The Mood Is Swinging	1961	20.00	50.00
MGM E-3990	(M)	The Mood Is Romance	1961	16.00	40.00
MGM SE-3990	(S)	The Mood Is Romance	1961	20.00	50.00
MGM E-3991	(M)	The Mood Is Blue	1961	16.00	40.00
MGM SE-3991	(S)	The Mood Is Blue	1961	20.00	50.00
MGM E-4053	(M)	I Feel A Song Comin' On	1962	16.00	40.00
MGM SE-4053	(S)	I Feel A Song Comin' On	1962	20.00	50.00
MGM E-4054	(M)	I'm Your Girl	1962	16.00	40.00
MGM SE-4054	(S)	I'm Your Girl	1962	20.00	50.00
MGM E-4088	(M)	After Hours	1962	16.00	40.00
MGM SE-4088	(S)	After Hours	1962	20.00	50.00
MGM E-4101	(M)	Country Girl Style	1962	16.00	40.00
MGM SE-4101	(S)	Country Girl Style	1962	20.00	50.00
MGM E-4151	(M)	The Very Best Of Joni James	1963	12.00	30.00
MGM SE-4151	(S)	The Very Best Of Joni James	1963	16.00	40.00
MGM E-4158	(M)	Something For The Boys	1963	12.00	30.00
MGM SE-4158	(S)	Something For The Boys	1963	16.00	40.00
MGM E-4182	(M)	Three O' Clock In The Morning	1963	12.00	30.00
MGM SE-4182	(S)	Three O' Clock In The Morning	1963	16.00	40.00
MGM E-4200	(M)	My Favorite Things	1963	12.00	30.00
MGM SE-4200	(S)	My Favorite Things	1963	16.00	40.00
MGM E-4208	(M)	Italianissime!	1963	12.00	30.00
MGM E-4208	(S)	Italianissime!	1963	16.00	40.00
MGM E-4248	(M)	Put On A Happy Face	1964	12.00	30.00
MGM SE-4248	(S)	Put On A Happy Face	1964	16.00	40.00
MGM E-4255	(M)	Joni James Sings The Gershwins	1964	12.00	30.00
MGM SE-4255	(S)	Joni James Sings The Gershwins	1964	16.00	40.00
MGM E-4263	(M)	Beyond The Reef	1964	12.00	30.00
MGM SE-4263	(S)	Beyond The Reef	1964	16.00	40.00
MGM E-4286	(M)	Bossa Nova Style	1965	12.00	30.00
MGM SE-4286	(S)	Bossa Nova Style	1965	16.00	40.00
		— MGM albums above have black labels. —			

JAMES, LEONARD

| Decca DL-8772 | (M) | Boppin' And A Strollin' | 1958 | 20.00 | 50.00 |

Label & Catalog #		Title	Year	VG+	NM

JAMES, SKIP

Skip James was a blues guitar player, pianist, singer and songwriter.

Melodeon MLP-7321	(M)	**Greatest Of The Dleta Blues Singers**	*196?*	**30.00**	**75.00**
Vanguard VSR-9219	(M)	**Skip James Today!**	*1966*	**10.00**	**25.00**
Vanguard VSD-79219	(S)	**Skip James Today!**	*1966*	**12.00**	**30.00**
Vanguard VSD-79273	(S)	**Devil Got My Woman**	*1968*	**10.00**	**25.00**

JAMES, SONNY/SONNY JAMES & THE SOUTHERN GENTLEMEN

Sonny James is a pseudonym for James Loden. Collectors Note: The hit single version of "Young Love" can only be found on Capitol albums. Those on Dot, Hamilton and RCA Camden are rerecordings. Refer to Ferlin Husky / Sonny James / Tommy Sands / Gene Vincent..

Capitol T-779	(M)	**The Southern Gentleman**	*1957*	**24.00**	**60.00**
Capitol T-867	(M)	**Sonny**	*1957*	**24.00**	**60.00**
Capitol T-988	(M)	**Honey**	*1958*	**24.00**	**60.00**
Capitol T-1178	(M)	**This Is Sonny James**	*1959*	**20.00**	**50.00**
		— Capitol albums above have turquoise labels.—			
Dot DLP-3462	(M)	**Young Love**	*1962*	**16.00**	**40.00**
Dot DLP-25462	(S)	**Young Love**	*1962*	**20.00**	**50.00**
Capitol T-779	(M)	**The Southern Gentleman**	*1964*	**10.00**	**25.00**
Capitol T-867	(M)	**Sonny**	*1964*	**10.00**	**25.00**
Capitol T-988	(M)	**Honey**	*1964*	**10.00**	**25.00**
Capitol T-1178	(M)	**This Is Sonny James**	*1964*	**10.00**	**25.00**
Capitol T-2017	(M)	**The Minute You're Gone**	*1964*	**8.00**	**20.00**
Capitol ST-2017	(S)	**The Minute You're Gone**	*1964*	**10.00**	**25.00**
Capitol T-2209	(M)	**You're The Only World I Know**	*1965*	**8.00**	**20.00**
Capitol ST-2209	(S)	**You're The Only World I Know**	*1965*	**10.00**	**25.00**
Capitol T-2317	(M)	**I'll Keep Holding On**	*1965*	**8.00**	**20.00**
Capitol ST-2317	(S)	**I'll Keep Holding On**	*1965*	**10.00**	**25.00**
Capitol T-2415	(M)	**Behind The Tear**	*1965*	**8.00**	**20.00**
Capitol ST-2415	(S)	**Behind The Tear**	*1965*	**10.00**	**25.00**
Capitol T-2500	(M)	**True Love's A Blessing**	*1966*	**8.00**	**20.00**
Capitol ST-2500	(S)	**True Love's A Blessing**	*1966*	**10.00**	**25.00**
Capitol T-2561	(M)	**Till The Last Leaf Shall Fall**	*1966*	**8.00**	**20.00**
Capitol ST-2561	(S)	**Till The Last Leaf Shall Fall**	*1966*	**10.00**	**25.00**
Capitol T-2589	(M)	**My Christmas Dream**	*1966*	**8.00**	**20.00**
Capitol ST-2589	(S)	**My Christmas Dream**	*1966*	**10.00**	**25.00**
Capitol T-2615	(M)	**The Best Of Sonny James**	*1966*	**8.00**	**20.00**
Capitol ST-2615	(P)	**The Best Of Sonny James**	*1966*	**10.00**	**25.00**
		(First pressings of Capitol 2615 have black Starline labels.)			
Capitol T-2703	(M)	**Need You**	*1967*	**10.00**	**25.00**
Capitol ST-2703	(S)	**Need You**	*1967*	**8.00**	**20.00**
Capitol T-2788	(M)	**I'll Never Find Another You**	*1967*	**10.00**	**25.00**
Capitol ST-2788	(S)	**I'll Never Find Another You**	*1967*	**8.00**	**20.00**
Capitol T-2884	(M)	**A World Of Our Own**	*1968*	**12.00**	**30.00**
Capitol ST-2884	(S)	**A World Of Our Own**	*1968*	**10.00**	**25.00**
Capitol ST-2937	(S)	**Heaven Says Hello**	*1968*	**10.00**	**25.00**
Capitol ST-111	(S)	**Born To Be With You**	*1968*	**10.00**	**25.00**
Capitol ST-193	(S)	**Only The Lonely**	*1969*	**10.00**	**25.00**
		— Capitol albums above have black labels with the Capitol logo on top.—			
Capitol SPRO-4941/42	(DJ)	**The #1 Hits Of Sonny James**	*1969*	**10.00**	**25.00**

JAMES, TOMMY, & THE SHONDELLS

Members of The Shondells also recordeed as Hog Heaven.

Roulette R-25336	(M)	**Hanky Panky**	*1966*	**10.00**	**25.00**
Roulette SR-25336	(S)	**Hanky Panky** (*"Hanky" is rechanneled*)	*1966*	**12.00**	**30.00**
Roulette R-25344	(M)	**It's Only Love**	*1967*	**10.00**	**25.00**
Roulette SR-25344	(S)	**It's Only Love**	*1967*	**12.00**	**30.00**
Roulette R-25353	(M)	**I Think We're Alone Now**	*1967*	**10.00**	**25.00**
Roulette SR-25353	(S)	**I Think We're Alone Now**	*1967*	**16.00**	**40.00**
		(Original covers of Roulette 25353 feature a photo of the group.)			
Roulette SR-25353	(S)	**I Think We're Alone Now**	*1968*	**10.00**	**25.00**
		(Later covers are black with footprints drawn across the center.			
		"I Think We're Alone Now" is rechanneled on both oressings..)			
Roulette SR-25355	(P)	**Something Special!**	*1968*	**10.00**	**25.00**
Roulette SR-25357	(S)	**Gettin' Together**	*1968*	**10.00**	**25.00**
Roulette SR-42012	(P)	**Mony Mony**	*1968*	**10.00**	**25.00**
Roulette SR-42023	(S)	**Crimson And Clover**	*1968*	**10.00**	**25.00**

Label & Catalog #		Title	Year	VG+	NM

JAN & DEAN
Jan Berry and Dean Torrence. Refer to Mike Love & Dean Torrence.

Label & Catalog #		Title	Year	VG+	NM
Dore LP-101	(M)	**Jan & Dean** *(Light blue label)*	1960	150.00	300.00
		(Issued with a bonus photo, priced separately below.)			
Dore LP-101		**Jan & Dean Bonus Photo**	1960	80.00	200.00
Liberty LRP-3248	(M)	**Jan & Dean's Golden Hits**	1962	16.00	40.00
Liberty LST-7248	(S)	**Jan & Dean's Golden Hits**	1962	20.00	50.00
		("Baby Talk," "We Go Together," "Heart And Soul" and "Jenny Lee" are rechanneled.)			
Liberty LRP-3294	(M)	**Jan & Dean Take Linda Surfing**	1963	20.00	50.00
Liberty LST-7294	(S)	**Jan & Dean Take Linda Surfing**	1963	30.00	75.00
		(The Beach Boys provide backing on "Surfin'" and "Surfin' Safari.")			
Liberty LRP-3314	(M)	**Surf City**	1963	12.00	30.00
Liberty LST-7314	(S)	**Surf City**	1963	16.00	40.00
Liberty LRP-3339	(M)	**Drag City**	1963	16.00	40.00
Liberty LST-7339	(S)	**Drag City**	1963	20.00	50.00
		(The Beach Boys provide backing on "Little Deuce Coupe..")			
Liberty LRP-3361	(M)	**Dead Man's Curve/New Girl In School**	1964	16.00	40.00
Liberty LST-7361	(S)	**Dead Man's Curve/New Girl In School**	1964	20.00	50.00
		(Original covers for Liberty 3/7361 are black & white with pink overtones.)			
Liberty LRP-3361	(M)	**Dead Man's Curve/New Girl In School**	1964	12.00	30.00
Liberty LST-7361	(S)	**Dead Man's Curve/New Girl In School**	1964	16.00	40.00
		(Second pressing cover photos are in full color.)			
Liberty LRP-3361	(M)	**New Girl In School/Dead Man's Curve**	1964	12.00	30.00
Liberty LST-7361	(S)	**New Girl In School/Dead Man's Curve**	1964	16.00	40.00
		(Third pressings flip-flop the title.)			
Columbia FLP-177	(DJ)	**Ride The Wild Surf Radio Spots**	1964	60.00	150.00
		(FLP-177 is a one-sided promo with a short segment with J&D.)			
Columbia FLP-177 A/B	(DJ)	**Ride The Wild Surf Radio Spots**	1964	60.00	150.00
		(FLP-177 A/B is two-sided with Frank Gifford voice-overs on the second side. This does not feature J&D's voices!)			
Liberty LRP-3368	(M)	**Ride The Wild Surf** *(Soundtrack)*	1964	12.00	30.00
Liberty LST-7368	(S)	**Ride The Wild Surf** *(Soundtrack)*	1964	16.00	40.00
Liberty LRP-3377	(M)	**Little Old Lady From Pasadena**	1964	12.00	30.00
Liberty LST-7377	(S)	**Little Old Lady From Pasadena**	1964	16.00	40.00
Liberty LRP-3403	(M)	**Command Performance**	1965	12.00	30.00
Liberty LST-7403	(S)	**Command Performance**	1965	14.00	35.00
Liberty LRP-3414	(M)	**Jan & Dean's Pop Symphony No.1**	1965	30.00	75.00
Liberty LST-7414	(S)	**Jan & Dean's Pop Symphony No.1**	1965	50.00	125.00
Liberty LRP-3417	(M)	**Jan & Dean's Golden Hits, Volume 2**	1965	10.00	25.00
Liberty LST-7417	(S)	**Jan & Dean's Golden Hits, Volume 2**	1965	12.00	30.00
Liberty CRC-LST-7417	(S)	**Jan & Dean's Golden Hits, Volume 2** *(Columbia Record Club)*	1965	12.00	30.00
Liberty LRP-3431	(M)	**Folk 'N' Roll**	1965	10.00	25.00
Liberty LST-7431	(S)	**Folk 'N' Roll**	1965	12.00	30.00
Liberty LRP-3441	(M)	**Filet Of Soul (A "Live" One)**	1966	8.00	20.00
Liberty LST-7441	(S)	**Filet Of Soul (A "Live" One)**	1966	10.00	25.00
Liberty LRP-3444	(M)	**Jan & Dean Meet Batman**	1966	16.00	40.00
Liberty LST-7444	(S)	**Jan & Dean Meet Batman**	1966	20.00	50.00
Liberty LRP-3458	(M)	**Popsicle**	1966	12.00	30.00
Liberty LST-7458	(S)	**Popsicle**	1966	12.00	30.00
Liberty LRP-3460	(M)	**Jan & Dean's Golden Hits, Volume 3**	1966	8.00	20.00
Liberty LST-7460	(S)	**Jan & Dean's Golden Hits, Volume 3**	1966	10.00	25.00
L-J 101	(M)	**Jan & Dean With The Soul Surfers**	1963	10.00	25.00
Coca-Cola TX-98	(DJ)	**Jan & Dean Swing The Jingle**	1965	300.00	500.00
		(Both sides contain the same five cuts, ranging from ten to 90 seconds in length. Issued with a color cover.)			
Columbia CL-2661	(M)	**Save For A Rainy Day**	1967		See below
Columbia CS-9461	(S)	**Save For A Rainy Day**	1967		See below
		(Columbia had this album prepared then pulled it. It saw the light of day in the U.S. as J&D 101 [below]. Columbia did release this album in Japan; this should not be confused with the apparently non-existent American pressing. Should an actual U.S. pressing be discovered, it could easily fetch several thousands of dollars. . .)			
J&D 101	(M)	**Save For A Rainy Day**	1967	150.00	300.00
United Arts. UAS-9961	(P)	**The Jan & Dean Anthology Album** *(2 LPs)*	1971	10.00	25.00

Label & Catalog #		Title	Year	VG+	NM
Deadman's Curve	(M)	**Jan & Dean Live At The Keystone Berkeley**	1981	20.00	50.00
		(The Keystone album is a private pressing taken from an audience tape, and authorized for release by Jan and Dean. It was originally issued in plain jackets with front and back cover inserts.)			
Deadman's Curve	(M)	**Jan & Dean Live At The Keystone Berkeley**	1981	10.00	25.00
		(Later pressings have the front and back slicks pasted on.)			

JANIS, JOHNNY
ABC-Paramount ABC-140	(M)	**For The First Time**	1956	20.00	50.00

JANSSEN, DAVID
Epic LN-24150	(M)	**Hidden Island**	1965	8.00	20.00
Epic BN-26150	(S)	**Hidden Island**	1965	10.00	25.00

JARRETT, MERRICK
Canadian Merrick Jarrett is a singer of traditional folk songs.
Riverside RLP-12-631	(M)	**The Old Chisholm Trail**	1956	16.00	40.00

JASPER WRATH
Sunflower SNF-5003	(S)	**Jasper Wrath** *(With insert)*	1971	10.00	25.00

JAY, MERRILL/THE MERRILL JAY SINGERS
Cabot CAB-5003	(M)	**Songs Of The Railroad**	1957	20.00	50.00

JAY & THE AMERICANS
United Arts. UAL-3222	(M)	**She Cried**	1962	14.00	35.00
United Arts. UAS-6222	(S)	**She Cried**	1962	20.00	50.00
United Arts. UAL-3300	(M)	**At The Cafe Wha?**	1963	14.00	35.00
United Arts. UAS-6300	(S)	**At The Cafe Wha?**	1963	20.00	50.00
United Arts. UAL-3407	(M)	**Come A Little Bit Closer**	1964	10.00	25.00
United Arts. UAS-6407	(S)	**Come A Little Bit Closer**	1964	12.00	30.00
United Arts. UAL-3417	(M)	**Blockbusters**	1965	10.00	25.00
United Arts. UAS-6417	(S)	**Blockbusters**	1965	12.00	30.00
United Arts. UAL-3453	(M)	**Jay & The Americans' Greatest Hits**	1965	8.00	20.00
United Arts. UAS-6453	(P)	**Jay & The Americans' Greatest Hits**	1965	10.00	25.00
United Arts. UAS-ST-90814	(P)	**Jay & The Americans' Greatest Hits** *(Capitol Record Club)*	1966	10.00	25.00
United Arts. UAL-3474	(M)	**Sunday And Me**	1966	8.00	20.00
United Arts. UAS-6474	(S)	**Sunday And Me**	1966	10.00	25.00
United Arts. UAL-3534	(M)	**Livin' Above Your Head**	1966	8.00	20.00
United Arts. UAS-6534	(S)	**Livin' Above Your Head**	1966	10.00	25.00
United Arts. UAL-3555	(M)	**Jay & The Americans' Greatest Hits, Vol. 2**	1966	8.00	20.00
United Arts. UAS-6555	(S)	**Jay & The Americans' Greatest Hits, Vol. 2**	1966	10.00	25.00
United Arts. ST-90815	(S)	**Jay & The Americans' Greatest Hits, Vol. 2** *(Capitol Record Club)*	1966	10.00	25.00
United Arts. UAL-3562	(M)	**Try Some Of This**	1967	8.00	20.00
United Arts. UAS-6562	(S)	**Try Some Of This**	1967	10.00	25.00
		— U.A. albums above have black labels.—			

JAY & THE TECHNIQUES
Smash MGS-27095	(M)	**Apples, Peaches, Pumpkin Pie**	1967	10.00	25.00
Smash SRS-67095	(S)	**Apples, Peaches, Pumpkin Pie**	1967	12.00	30.00
Smash SRS-67102	(S)	**Love Lost And Found**	1968	12.00	30.00

JAYNETTES, THE
Tuff LP-13	(M)	**Sally Go Round The Roses**	1963	150.00	300.00

JB'S, THE/THE JB'S INTERNATIONAL
The JB's are James Brown's backing group and were produced by JB. Refer to Fred Wesley.
People PE-5601	(S)	**Food For Thought**	1972	20.00	50.00
People PE-5603	(S)	**Doing It To Death**	1973	20.00	50.00

JEFFERSON
Janus JLS-3006	(S)	**Baby, Take Me In Your Arms**	1969	10.00	25.00

JEFFERSON, BLIND LEMON
Jefferson was a blues guitar player, singer and songwriter.
Riverside 1014	(10")	**The Folk Blues Of Blind Lemon Jefferson**	1953	100.00	300.00
Riverside 1053	(10")	**Penitentiary Blues**	1955	100.00	300.00

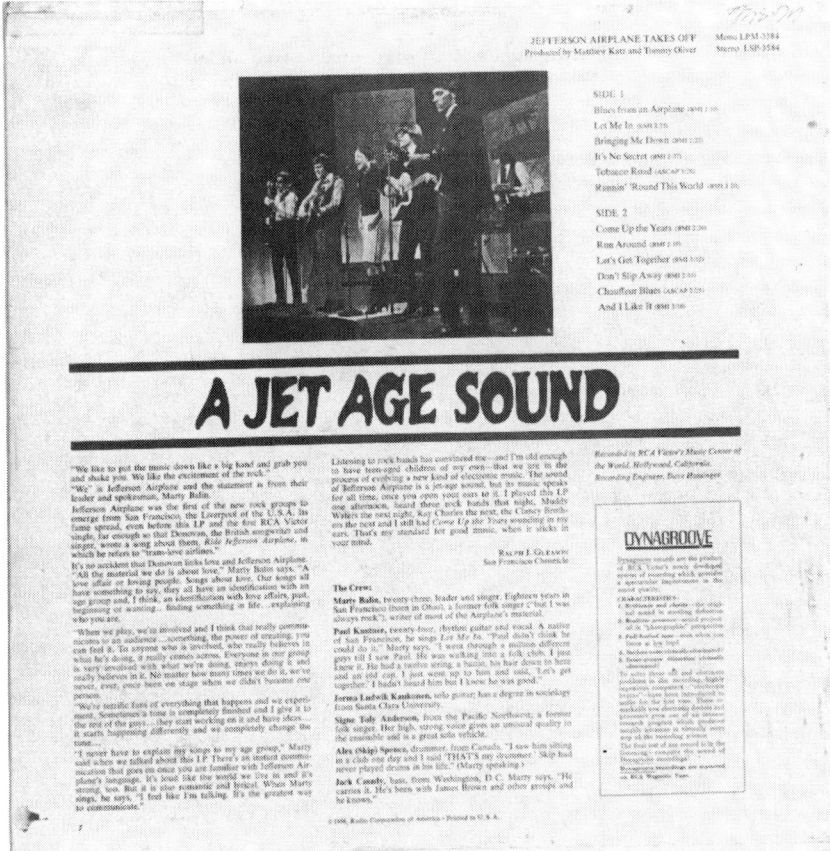

Original mono pressings of Jefferson Airplane Takes Off *contained a version of "Let Me In" that featured lyrics that hinted at acid-assisted sex and a sixth song on the first side, "Runnin' 'Round This World," both deleted from all subsequent pressings. Pictured here is the back cover with the track listing of twelve songs. Collectors should note that many covers with this listing do not contain the original twelve-track album but the regular eleven-track reissue, so always check the first side label. There are only mono copies of the record and album known to exist with the twelve tracks. (Note: "Runnin' 'Round This World" was eventually reissued in 1974 on* Early Flight *while the risque version of "Let Me In" had to wait until 1992's boxed CD set,* Jefferson Airplane Loves You.*)*

Label & Catalog #		Title	Year	VG+	NM
Riverside RLP-12-125	(M)	**Classic Folk Blues**	*1957*	50.00	150.00
Riverside RLP-12-126	(M)	**Blind Lemon Jefferson**	*1957*	50.00	150.00
Riverside RLP-12-136	(M)	**Blind Lemon Jefferson, Vol. 2**	*1958*	50.00	150.00
Milestone MLP-2004	(M)	**The Immortal Blind Lemon Jefferson**	*1968*	10.00	25.00
Milestone MLP-2007	(M)	**The Immortal Blind Lemon Jefferson, Vol. 2**	*1969*	10.00	25.00
Milestone MLP-2013	(M)	**Black Snake Moan**	*1970*	10.00	25.00

JEFFERSON, EDDIE: *Refer to* GOLDMINE'S PRICE GUIDE TO COLLECTIBLE JAZZ ALBUMS

JEFFERSON AIRPLANE

The original group on "Takes Off" was founder Marty Balin with Signe Andersson, Jack Casady, Paul Kantner, Jorma Kaukonen and Alexander Spence. Andersson and Spence left in 1966, replaced by Grace Slick, formerly of The Great Society, and Spencer Dryden, replaced in 1970 by Joey Covington and then John Barbata (1972). "Papa" John Creach joined in 1970. In 1971 Balin left his group in disgust and, by 1974, what's left of the Airplane became (shudder) Jefferson Starship. Refer to Hot Tuna; Moby Grape.

RCA Victor LPM-3584	(M)	**Jefferson Airplane Takes Off!**	*1965*		*See below*

(LPM-3584 was originally issued with "Runnin' Round This World," deleted from all subsequent pressings, and a version of "Let Me In" deemed risque, which was rerecorded for subsequent pressings. Rare with a suggested Near Mint value of $2,000-4,000. Stereo copies [LSP-3584] with these tracks are not known to exist; should one turn up, it would be worth considerably more than the mono. Note: Copies of this cover usually contain late pressings of the album and should be listened to first. . .)

RCA Victor LPM-3584	(M)	**Jefferson Airplane Takes Off!**	*1966*	12.00	30.00
RCA Victor LSP-3584	(S)	**Jefferson Airplane Takes Off!**	*1966*	10.00	25.00
RCA Victor LPM-3766	(M)	**Surrealistic Pillow**	*1967*	20.00	50.00
RCA Victor LSP-3766	(S)	**Surrealistic Pillow**	*1967*	10.00	25.00
RCA Victor LOP-1511	(M)	**After Bathing At Baxter's**	*1967*	20.00	50.00
RCA Victor LSO-1511	(S)	**After Bathing At Baxter's**	*1967*	10.00	25.00
RCA Victor LSP-4058	(S)	**Crown Of Creation**	*1968*	12.00	30.00

— RCA albums above have black labels with Nipper on top.—

RCA Victor APD1-0320	(Q)	**Volunteers** *(Yellow label)*	*1973*	20.00	50.00
RCA Victor APD1-0320	(Q)	**Volunteers** *(Brown label)*	*1975*	16.00	40.00

("Volunteers," "We Can Be Together," "Wooden Ships" and "Hey Frederick" are alternate takes from the stereo album.)

JEFFREY, JOE

Wand WDS-686	(S)	**My Pledge Of Love**	*1969*	14.00	35.00

JEFFRIES, FRAN

Warwick W-2020	(M)	**Fran Can Really Hang You Up The Most**	*1960*	8.00	20.00
Warwick WST-2020	(S)	**Fran Can Really Hang You Up The Most**	*1960*	12.00	30.00

JELLY BEAN BANDITS, THE

Mainstream 56103	(M)	**Jelly Bean Bandits**	*1967*	14.00	35.00
Mainstream S-6103	(S)	**Jelly Bean Bandits**	*1967*	20.00	50.00

JEMISON, EUGENE

Eugene Emison is a guitar player and singer of traditional folk music.

Folkways FP-23	(10")	**Solomon Valley Ballads**	*1954*	20.00	50.00
Folkways FA-2023	(10")	**Solomon Valley Ballads**	*1954*	20.00	50.00

JENKINS, GORDON

Capitol T-766	(M)	**The Complete Manhattan Tower**	*1956*	12.00	30.00

JENNINGS, WAYLON

Bat 1001	(M)	**Waylon Jennings At JD's**	*1964*	300.00	600.00
Sounds 1001	(M)	**Waylon Jennings At JD's**	*1964*	150.00	300.00
RCA Victor LPM-3523	(M)	**Folk Country**	*1966*	12.00	30.00
RCA Victor LSP-3523	(S)	**Folk Country**	*1966*	16.00	40.00
RCA Victor LPM-3620	(M)	**Leavin' Town**	*1966*	12.00	30.00
RCA Victor LSP-3620	(S)	**Leavin' Town**	*1966*	16.00	40.00
RCA Victor LPM-3660	(M)	**Waylon Sings Ol' Harlan**	*1967*	16.00	40.00
RCA Victor LSP-3660	(S)	**Waylon Sings Ol' Harlan**	*1967*	20.00	50.00
RCA Victor LPM-3736	(M)	**Nashville Rebel** *(Soundtrack)*	*1967*	12.00	30.00
RCA Victor LSP-3736	(S)	**Nashville Rebel** *(Soundtrack)*	*1967*	10.00	25.00
RCA Victor LPM-3825	(M)	**Love Of The Common People**	*1967*	12.00	30.00
RCA Victor LSP-3825	(S)	**Love Of The Common People**	*1967*	10.00	25.00

Label & Catalog #		Title	Year	VG+	NM
RCA Victor LPM-3918	(M)	Hangin' On	1968	40.00	100.00
RCA Victor LSP-3918	(S)	Hangin' On	1968	10.00	25.00
RCA Victor LSP-4023	(S)	Only The Greatest	1968	10.00	25.00
		—RCA albums above have black labels.—			
A&M SP-4238	(S)	Don't Think Twice	1969	16.00	40.00
RCA Victor SPS-570	(DJ)	Get Into Waylon Jennings	1972	20.00	50.00

JENNINGS, WAYLON, & WILLIE NELSON

RCA Victor AFL1-2686	(S)	Waylon And Willie (Gold vinyl promo)	1978	10.00	25.00

JENSEN, KRIS

Hickory LPM-110	(M)	Torture	1963	14.00	35.00
Hickory LPS-110	(S)	Torture	1963	20.00	50.00

JENSEN, KURT

Holltwood LPH-137	(M)	An Evening With Jayne	195?	20.00	50.00
		(LPH-137 is an easy-listening album with a photo of Jatne Mansfield on the cover.)			

JEREMY'S FRIENDS

Warwick W-2019	(M)	Jeremy's Friends	1960	20.00	50.00

JESSE & THE BANDITS

Re-Car 2001	(M)	Top Teen Hits	1965	50.00	125.00

JETHRO TULL

Reprise MS-2072	(S)	Thick As A Brick (Promo sampler)	1972	12.00	30.00
Chrysalis CHR-1040	(S)	A Passion Play (Promo edited for airplay)	1973	10.00	25.00
Chrysalis CH4-1044	(Q)	Aqualung	1973	16.00	40.00
Chrysalis CH4-1067	(Q)	War Child	1974	16.00	40.00
Chrysalis PRO-623	(S)	The Jethro Tull Radio Show	1975	20.00	50.00
Mobile Fidelity MFSL-061	(S)	Aqualung (Test pressing)	1980		See below
		(Original test pressings of MFSL-061 have alternate takes and can be identified by the "A5" and "B5" in the trail-off vinyl. Rare with a suggested Near Mint value of $300-600.)			
Mobile Fidelity MFSL-061	(S)	Aqualung	1980	25.00	75.00
Mobile Fidelity MFSL-092	(S)	The Broadsword And The Beast	1982	10.00	30.00
Mobile Fidelity MFSL-187	(S)	Thick As A Brick	1985	10.00	30.00

JETT, JOAN

Blackheart JJ-707	(S)	Bad Reputation	1980	20.00	50.00

JEWISH YOUNG FOLKSINGERS, THE

Stinson SLP-67	(10")	The Jewish Young Folksingers	195?	16.00	40.00

JIVE FIVE, THE

United Arts. UAL-3455	(M)	The Jive Five	1965	14.00	35.00
United Arts. UAS-6455	(S)	The Jive Five	1965	20.00	50.00

JO, DAMITA: *Refer to* DAMITA JO

JOE & EDDIE

Crescendo GNP-86	(M)	There's A Meetin' Here Tonight	1964	8.00	20.00
Crescendo GNPS-86	(S)	There's A Meetin' Here Tonight	1964	10.00	25.00
Crescendo GNP-96	(M)	Coast To Coast	1964	8.00	20.00
Crescendo GNPS-96	(S)	Coast To Coast	1964	10.00	25.00
Crescendo GNP-99	(M)	Joe And Eddie	1964	8.00	20.00
Crescendo GNPS-99	(S)	Joe And Eddie	1964	10.00	25.00
Crescendo GNP-2005	(M)	Tear Down The Walls	1965	8.00	20.00
Crescendo GNPS-2005	(S)	Tear Down The Walls	1965	10.00	25.00
Crescendo GNP-2007	(M)	Joe And Eddie Live In Hollywood	1965	8.00	20.00
Crescendo GNPS-2007	(S)	Joe And Eddie Live In Hollywood	1965	10.00	25.00
Crescendo GNP-2014	(M)	Walkin' Down The Line	1965	8.00	20.00
Crescendo GNPS-2014	(S)	Walkin' Down The Line	1965	10.00	25.00
Crescendo GNP-2021	(M)	The Magic Of Their Singing	1966	8.00	20.00
Crescendo GNPS-2021	(S)	The Magic Of Their Singing	1966	10.00	25.00

Label & Catalog #		Title	Year	VG+	NM

JOEL, BILLY
Billy Joel originally recorded with The Hassles; Attila.

Label & Catalog #		Title	Year	VG+	NM
Family Prod. 2700	(S)	**Cold Spring Harbor**	1971	20.00	50.00
		(Originals have color labels; counterfeits have white labels.)			
Columbia AS-326	(DJ)	**Souvenir** *(One-sided live album)*	1976	10.00	30.00
April-Blackwood ABS-1	(S)	**Billy Joel Professional Sampler**	1979	20.00	50.00
		(Promotional boxed set of five albums with book.)			
Columbia HC-34987	(S)	**The Stranger** *(Half-speed master)*	1981	13.00	40.00
Columbia HC-44987	(S)	**The Stranger** *(Half-speed master)*	1982	8.00	25.00
Columbia HC-45609	(S)	**52nd Street** *(Half-speed master)*	1982	8.00	25.00
Columbia HC-47461	(S)	**Songs In The Attic** *(Half-speed master)*	1982	8.00	25.00
Columbia HC-48837	(S)	**An Innocent Man** *(Half-speed master)*	1983	12.00	35.00

JOHN, ELTON

Label & Catalog #		Title	Year	VG+	NM
Viking 105	(S)	**The Games** *(Soundtrack)*	1970	80.00	200.00
Paramount DJ-1	(DJ)	**Friends** *(Open-end interview)*	1971	80.00	200.00
Paramount PAS-6004	(S)	**Friends** *(Soundtrack)*	1971	10.00	25.00
MCA 2142	(DJ)	**Capt. Fantastic & The Brown Dirt Cowboy**	1975	150.00	300.00
		(Brown vinyl. All copies are autographed by Elton and Bernie.)			
MCA L33-1995	(DJ)	**A Single Man** *(Picture disc)*	1979	16.00	40.00
Nautilus NR-43	(S)	**Greatest Hits**	198?	35.00	100.00
Direct Disk 10003	(S)	**Goodbye Yellow Brick Road** *(2 LPs)*	1980	12.00	35.00
Mobile Fidelity MFSL-160	(S)	**Goodbye Yellow Brick Road** *(2 LPs)*	1990	8.00	25.00

JOHN, LITTLE WILLIE

Label & Catalog #		Title	Year	VG+	NM
King 395-564	(M)	**Fever** *(Brwon cover with nurse)*	1956	500.00	1,000.00
King 595-564	(M)	**Fever** *(White "Fever" cover)*	1957	250.00	500.00
King 395-596	(M)	**Talk To Me**	1958	150.00	300.00
King 603	(M)	**Mister Little Willie John**	1958	150.00	300.00
King 691	(M)	**Action**	1960	150.00	350.00
King 739	(M)	**Sure Things**	1961	60.00	150.00
King 767	(M)	**The Sweet, The Hot, The Teenage Beat**	1961	60.00	150.00
King 802	(M)	**Come On And Join Little Willie John**	1962	60.00	150.00
King 895	(M)	**These Are My Favorite Songs**	1964	30.00	75.00
King K-949	(M)	**Little Willie Sings All Originals**	1966	20.00	50.00
King KS-949	(S)	**Little Willie Sings All Originals**	1966	40.00	100.00
		—*King albums above have crownless black labels.*—			
King KS-1081	(M)	**Free At Last**	1970	16.00	40.00
		("Leave My Kitten Alone" and "Free At Last" are in stereo.)			
BluesWay BLS-6069	(P)	**Free At Last**	1970	10.00	25.00

JOHN STREET ROCKETS, THE

Label & Catalog #		Title	Year	VG+	NM
Confidential SCR-5001	(S)	**Rot And Roll The Hard Way**	1979	20.00	50.00

JOHN'S CHILDREN

Label & Catalog #		Title	Year	VG+	NM
White Whale WWS-7128	(S)	**Orgasm**	1970	80.00	200.00

JOHNNIE & JACK
Johnnie Wright and Jack Anglin.

Label & Catalog #		Title	Year	VG+	NM
RCA Victor LPM-1587	(M)	**The Tennessee Mountain Boys**	1957	16.00	40.00
RCA Victor LPM-2017	(M)	**Hits By Johnnie & Jack**	1959	16.00	40.00
RCA Victor LSP-2017	(E)	**Hits By Johnnie & Jack**	1959	10.00	25.00
Decca DL-4308	(M)	**Smiles And Tears**	1962	8.00	20.00
Decca DL-74308	(S)	**Smiles And Tears**	1962	10.00	25.00

JOHNNY & THE BLUE BEATS

Label & Catalog #		Title	Year	VG+	NM
Winsor R-1001	(M)	**Smile**	196?	10.00	25.00
Winsor RL-1001	(S)	**Smile**	196?	12.00	30.00

JOHNNY & THE HURRICANES

Label & Catalog #		Title	Year	VG+	NM
Warwick W-2007	(M)	**Johnny & The Hurricanes**	1959	60.00	150.00
Warwick WST-2007	(S)	**Johnny & The Hurricanes**	1959	100.00	250.00
		("Red River Rock" is rechanneled on this album.)			
Warwick W-2010	(M)	**Stormsville**	1960	60.00	150.00
Warwick WST-2010	(S)	**Stormsville**	1960	100.00	250.00
Big Top 12-1302	(M)	**Big Sound Of Johnny & The Hurricanes**	1960	60.00	150.00
Big Top ST-1302	(S)	**Big Sound Of Johnny & The Hurricanes**	1960	100.00	250.00
Attila 1030	(M)	**Live At The Star Club**	1965	150.00	300.00

Label & Catalog #		Title	Year	VG+	NM

JOHNSON, BETTY

Atlantic 8017	(M)	Betty Johnson	1958	20.00	50.00
Atlantic 8027	(M)	The Song You Heard When You Fell In Love	1959	20.00	50.00
Atlantic SD-8027	(S)	The Song You Heard When You Fell In Love	1959	30.00	75.00

— Atlantic mono albums above have black labels; stereo albums have green labels.—

Atlantic 8027	(M)	The Song You Heard When You Fell In Love	196?	8.00	20.00
Atlantic SD-8027	(S)	The Song You Heard When You Fell In Love	196?	10.00	25.00

— Atlantic albums above have multi-colored labels with a white "fan" logo on the right side.—

JOHNSON, BOB, & THE LONESOME TRAVELERS

Parkway P-7017	(M)	12 Shades Of Bluegrass	1963	20.00	50.00

JOHNSON, BUBBER

King 395-569	(M)	Come Home	1957	100.00	250.00
King 624	(M)	Sings Sweet Love Songs	1959	60.00	150.00

JOHNSON, BUDDY

Wing MGW-12111	(M)	Rock 'N' Roll Stage Show	1956	60.00	150.00
Mercury MG-20072	(M)	Buddy Johnson Wails	1958	40.00	100.00
Mercury MG-20209	(M)	Rock 'N' Roll	1958	40.00	100.00
Mercury MG-20322	(M)	Walkin'	1958	40.00	100.00

JOHNSON, BUDDY & ELLA

Mercury MG-20347	(M)	Swing Me	1958	40.00	100.00
Roulette R-25085	(M)	Go Ahead And Rock And Roll	1959	40.00	100.00
Roulette SR-25085	(S)	Go Ahead And Rock And Roll	1959	60.00	150.00

JOHNSON, CANDY

Canjo LP-1001	(M)	The Candy Johnson Show	1964	16.00	40.00
Canjo LP-1002	(M)	Bikini Beach	1964	12.00	30.00

JOHNSON, LONNIE

King 395-520	(M)	Lonesome Road	1958	1,000.00	2,000.00
Bluesville BVLP-1007	(M)	Blues By Lonnie	1960	40.00	100.00
Bluesville BVLP-1011	(M)	Blues And Ballads	1960	40.00	100.00
Bluesville BVLP-1024	(M)	Losing Game	1961	40.00	100.00
Bluesville BVLP-1062	(M)	Another Night To Cry	1963	40.00	100.00

— Bluesville albums above have bright blue labels with silver print.—

Bluesville BVLP-1007	(M)	Blues By Lonnie	1964	12.00	30.00
Bluesville BVLP-1011	(M)	Blues And Ballads	1964	12.00	30.00
Bluesville BVLP-1024	(M)	Losing Game	1964	12.00	30.00
Bluesville BVLP-1062	(M)	Another Night To Cry	1964	12.00	30.00

— Bluesville albums above have blue labels with a trident logo on the right side.—

King K-958	(M)	Lonnie Johnson 24 Twelve Bar Blues	1966	30.00	75.00
King KS-958	(S)	Lonnie Johnson 24 Twelve Bar Blues	1966	40.00	100.00
King KS-1083	(S)	Tomorrow Night	1970	10.00	25.00

JOHNSON, LONNIE, & VICTORIA SPIVEY

Lonnie Johnson also recorded with Victoria Spivey.

Bluesville BVLP-1044	(M)	Idle Hours	1962	40.00	100.00
Bluesville BVLP-1054	(M)	Woman Blues	1962	40.00	100.00

— Bluesville albums above have bright blue labels with silver print.—

Bluesville BVLP-1044	(M)	Idle Hours	1964	12.00	30.00
Bluesville BVLP-1054	(M)	Woman Blues	1964	12.00	30.00

— Bluesville albums above have blue labels with a trident logo on the right side.—

JOHNSON, MARV

United Arts. UAL-3081	(M)	Marvelous Marv Johnson	1960	40.00	100.00
United Arts. UAS-6081	(P)	Marvelous Marv Johnson	1960	60.00	150.00
United Arts. UAL-3118	(M)	More Marv Johnson	1960	40.00	100.00
United Arts. UAS-6118	(P)	More Marv Johnson	1960	60.00	150.00
United Arts. UAL-3187	(M)	I Believe	1962	30.00	75.00
United Arts. UAS-6187	(S)	I Believe	1962	40.00	100.00

JOHNSON, OLLIE

RCA Victor LPM-1369	(M)	A Bit Of The Blues	1957	16.00	40.00

Label & Catalog #		Title	Year	VG+	NM

JOHNSON, ROBERT

Columbia CL-1654	(M)	**King Of The Delta Blues Singers**	1961	40.00	100.00
	— Columbia albums above have six white-on-black "eye" logos around the perimeter.—				
Columbia CL-1654	(M)	**King Of The Delta Blues Singers**	1963	12.00	30.00
	— Columbia albums above have "Guaranteed High Fidelity" labels.—				
Columbia CL-1654	(M)	**King Of The Delta Blues Singers**	1965	10.00	25.00
	— Columbia albums above have "360 Sound Mono" labels.—				
Columbia C3-46222	(M)	**The Complete Recordings Of Robert Johnson** (3 LP box)	1990	16.00	40.00

JOHNSON, SYL

Twinight LPS-1002	(S)	**Is It Because I'm Black?**	1972	16.00	40.00

JOHNSON, "BLIND" WILLIE

Folkways FG-3585	(M)	**Blind Willie Johnson: His Story** (Documentary)	195?	40.00	100.00
RBF 10	(M)	**Blind Willie Johnson 1927-1930**	1965	30.00	75.00

JOHNSTON, BRUCE

Bruce Johnston also recorded as a member of The Beach Boys; The Catalinas; The Centurions; The Defenders; The Hot Doggers; The Rip Chords; The Vettes.

Del-Fi DFLP-1228	(M)	**Surfers' Pajama Party**	1963	30.00	75.00
Del-Fi DFST-1228	(S)	**Surfers' Pajama Party**	1963	40.00	100.00
Columbia CL-2057	(M)	**Surfin' 'Round The World**	1963	60.00	150.00
Columbia CS-8857	(S)	**Surfin' 'Round The World**	1963	80.00	200.00

JOLSON, AL

Decca 5006	(10")	**Jolson Sings Again** (Soundtrack)	1949	16.00	40.00
Decca DLP-5026	(10")	**In Songs He Made Famous**	1949	16.00	40.00
Decca DLP-5029	(10")	**Souvenir Album, Vol. 2**	1949	16.00	40.00
Decca DLP-5030	(10")	**Al Jolson**	1949	16.00	40.00
Decca DLP-5031	(10")	**Souvenir Album, Vol. 4**	1949	16.00	40.00
Decca DL-5308	(10")	**Stephen Foster Songs**	1950	40.00	100.00
Decca DL-5314	(10")	**Souvenir Album, Vol. 5**	1951	20.00	50.00
Decca DL-5315	(10")	**Souvenir Album, Vol. 6**	1951	20.00	50.00
Decca DL-5316	(10")	**Al Jolson And Bing Crosby**	1951	20.00	50.00
	(Decca 5316 is a collection of Jolson duets including two each woth Crosby, the Mills Brothers, and the Andrews Sisters.)				
Decca DL-9034	(M)	**You Made Me Love You**	1957	10.00	25.00
Decca DL-9035	(M)	**Rock A Bye Your Baby**	1957	10.00	25.00
Decca DL-9036	(M)	**Rainbow 'Round My Shoulder**	1957	10.00	25.00
Decca DL-9037	(M)	**You Ain't Heard Nothing Yet**	1957	10.00	25.00
Decca DL-9038	(M)	**Memories**	1957	10.00	25.00
Decca DL-9050	(M)	**Among My Souvenirs**	1957	10.00	25.00
Decca DL-9063	(M)	**The Immortal Al Jolson**	1958	10.00	25.00
Decca DL-9070	(M)	**Overseas**	1959	16.00	40.00
Decca DL-9074	(M)	**The World's Greatest Entertainer**	1959	10.00	25.00
Decca DL-9095	(M)	**Al Jolson With Oscar Levant At The Piano**	1961	12.00	30.00
	— Decca albums above have black or burgundy labels with silver print.—				

JOLSON, AL / EDDIE CANTOR

Epic LN-1128	(10")	**The Immortals - Jolson And Cantor**	1957	24.00	60.00

JONES, ANN, & HER AMERICAN SWEETHEARTS

Audio Lab AL-1521	(M)	**Ann Jones & Her American Sweethearts**	195?	80.00	200.00
Audio Lab AL-1556	(M)	**Hit And Run**	195?	80.00	200.00

JONES, BRIAN

Brian Jones was formerly a member of The Rolling Stones.

Roll. Stones RSR-49100	(S)	**Pipes Of Pan At Joujouka** (With inserts)	1971	20.00	50.00

JONES, CURTIS

Bluesville BVLP-1022	(M)	**Trouble Blues**	1961	30.00	75.00
	— Bluesville albums above have bright blue labels with silver print.—				
Bluesville BVLP-1022	(M)	**Trouble Blues**	1964	10.00	25.00
	— Bluesville albums above have blue labels with a trident logo on the right side.—				
Delmar DL-605	(M)	**Lonesome Bedroom Blues**	1963	16.00	40.00

Label & Catalog #		Title	Year	VG+	NM

JONES, DAVY
Davy Jones was a member of The Monkees.

Colpix CP-493	(M)	David Jones	1965	10.00	25.00
Colpix SCP-493	(S)	David Jones	1965	16.00	40.00

JONES, DEAN

Valiant LP-407	(M)	Introducing Dean Jones	1962	12.00	30.00
Valiant LPS-407	(S)	Introducing Dean Jones	1962	20.00	50.00

JONES, ETTA: *Refer to* GOLDMINE'S PRICE GUIDE TO COLLECTIBLE JAZZ ALBUMS

JONES, GEORGE
Refer to The Jones Boys; Dolly Parton.

Starday SLP-101	(M)	The Grand Ole Opry's New Star	1958	600.00	1,200.00
Starday SLP-125	(M)	The Crown Prince Of Country Music	1960	60.00	150.00
Starday SLP-150	(M)	George Jones Sings His Greatest Hits	1962	20.00	50.00
Starday DT-90080	(E)	George Jones Sings His Greatest Hits *(Capitol Record Club)*	196?	30.00	75.00
Starday SLP-151	(M)	The Fabulous Country Music Sound Of George Jones	1962	20.00	50.00
Starday SLP-335	(M)	George Jones	1965	16.00	40.00
Starday SLP-344	(M)	Long Live King George	1965	16.00	40.00
Starday SLP-366	(M)	The George Jones Story *(With bonus photo)*	1966	20.00	50.00
Starday SLP-366	(M)	The George Jones Story *(Without photo)*	1966	12.00	30.00
Starday SLP-401	(M)	The George Jones Song Book & Picture Album *(With 32 page book)*	1967	20.00	50.00
Starday SLP-401	(M)	The George Jones Song Book & Picture Album *(Without the book)*	1967	12.00	30.00
Starday SLP-440	(M)	The Golden Country Hits Of George Jones	1969	12.00	30.00
		— Starday albums above have yellow labels.—			
Mercury MG-20282	(M)	Hillbilly Hit Parade, Volume 1	1957	60.00	150.00
		(This is actually a various artists album but features five tracks by George, one by George with Benny barnes, and the rest by Barnes, Earl Aycock, James O' Gwynn, Leon Payne and so is listed here.)			
Mercury MG-20306	(M)	14 Country Favorites	1957	60.00	150.00
Mercury MG-20462	(M)	Country Church Time	1959	80.00	200.00
Mercury MG-20477	(M)	White Lightning & Other Favorites	1959	60.00	150.00
Mercury MG-20596	(M)	George Jones Salutes Hank Williams	1960	30.00	75.00
Mercury SR-60596	(S)	George Jones Salutes Hank Williams	1960	40.00	100.00
Mercury MG-20621	(M)	George Jones' Greatest Hits	1961	14.00	35.00
Mercury SR-60621	(S)	George Jones' Greatest Hits	1961	20.00	50.00
Mercury MG-20624	(M)	Country And Western Hits	1961	14.00	35.00
Mercury SR-60624	(S)	Country And Western Hits	1961	20.00	50.00
Mercury MG-20694	(M)	From The Heart	1962	14.00	35.00
Mercury SR-60694	(S)	From The Heart	1962	20.00	50.00
Mercury MG-20793	(M)	The Novelty Side Of George Jones	1963	30.00	75.00
Mercury SR-60793	(S)	The Novelty Side Of George Jones	1963	40.00	100.00
Mercury MG-20836	(M)	The Ballad Side Of George Jones	1963	14.00	35.00
Mercury SR-60836	(S)	The Ballad Side Of George Jones	1963	20.00	50.00
		— Mercury albums above have black labels with silver print.—			
Mercury MG-20906	(M)	Blue And Lonesome	1964	10.00	25.00
Mercury SR-60906	(S)	Blue And Lonesome	1964	14.00	35.00
Mercury MG-20937	(M)	Country & Western #1 Male Singer	1964	10.00	25.00
Mercury SR-60937	(S)	Country & Western #1 Male Singer	1964	14.00	35.00
Mercury MG-20990	(M)	Heartaches And Tears	1965	10.00	25.00
Mercury SR-60990	(S)	Heartaches And Tears	1965	14.00	35.00
Mercury MG-21029	(M)	Singing The Blues	1965	10.00	25.00
Mercury SR-61029	(S)	Singing The Blues	1965	14.00	35.00
Mercury MG-21048	(M)	George Jones' Greatest Hits, Volume 2	1965	10.00	25.00
Mercury SR-61048	(S)	George Jones' Greatest Hits, Volume 2	1965	14.00	35.00
		— Mercury albums above have red labels.—			
United Arts. UAL-3193	(M)	The New Favorites Of George Jones	1962	12.00	30.00
United Arts. UAS-6193	(S)	The New Favorites Of George Jones	1962	16.00	40.00
United Arts. UAL-3218	(M)	The Hits Of His Country Cousins	1962	12.00	30.00
United Arts. UAS-6218	(S)	The Hits Of His Country Cousins	1962	16.00	40.00
United Arts. UAL-3219	(M)	Homecoming In Heaven	1962	12.00	30.00
United Arts. UAS-6219	(S)	Homecoming In Heaven	1962	16.00	40.00
United Arts. UAL-3220	(M)	My Favorites Of Hank Williams	1962	16.00	40.00
United Arts. UAS-6220	(S)	My Favorites Of Hank Williams	1962	20.00	50.00

Label & Catalog #		Title	Year	VG+	NM
United Arts. UAL-3221	(M)	George Jones Sings Bob Wills	1962	16.00	40.00
United Arts. UAS-6221	(S)	George Jones Sings Bob Wills	1962	20.00	50.00
United Arts. UAL-3270	(M)	I Wish Tonight Would Never End	1963	10.00	25.00
United Arts. UAS-6270	(S)	I Wish Tonight Would Never End	1963	16.00	40.00
United Arts. UAL-3291	(M)	The Best Of George Jones	1963	10.00	25.00
United Arts. UAS-6291	(S)	The Best Of George Jones	1963	12.00	30.00
United Arts. UAL-3338	(M)	More New Favorites	1964	12.00	30.00
United Arts. UAS-6338	(S)	More New Favorites	1964	16.00	40.00
United Arts. UAL-3364	(M)	George Jones Sings Like The Dickens	1964	20.00	50.00
United Arts. UAS-6364	(S)	George Jones Sings Like The Dickens	1964	20.00	50.00
United Arts. UAL-3388	(M)	I Get Lonely In A Hurry	1964	12.00	30.00
United Arts. UAS-6388	(S)	I Get Lonely In A Hurry	1964	16.00	40.00
United Arts. UAL-3408	(M)	Trouble In Mind	1965	12.00	30.00
United Arts. UAS-6408	(S)	Trouble In Mind	1965	16.00	40.00
United Arts. UAL-3422	(M)	The Race Is On (Photo cover)	1965	12.00	30.00
United Arts. UAS-6422	(S)	The Race Is On (Photo cover)	1965	16.00	40.00
United Arts. UAL-3442	(M)	King Of Broken Hearts	1965	12.00	30.00
United Arts. UAS-6442	(S)	King Of Broken Hearts	1965	16.00	40.00
United Arts. UAL-3457	(M)	The Great George Jones	1966	12.00	30.00
United Arts. UAS-6457	(S)	The Great George Jones	1966	16.00	40.00
United Arts. UAL-3532	(M)	George Jones' Golden Hits, Volume 1	1966	8.00	20.00
United Arts. UAS-6532	(S)	George Jones' Golden Hits, Volume 1	1966	10.00	25.00
United Arts. UAL-3558	(M)	The Young George Jones	1967	12.00	30.00
United Arts. UAS-6558	(S)	The Young George Jones	1967	8.00	20.00
United Arts. UAL-3566	(M)	George Jones' Golden Hits, Volume 2	1967	10.00	25.00
United Arts. UAS-6566	(S)	George Jones' Golden Hits, Volume 2	1967	8.00	20.00
		—U.A. albums above have black labels.—			
Musicor MM-2060	(M)	New Country Hits	1965	12.00	30.00
Musicor MS-3060	(S)	New Country Hits	1965	16.00	40.00
Musicor MM-2061	(M)	Old Brush Arbors	1966	12.00	30.00
Musicor MS-3061	(S)	Old Brush Arbors	1966	16.00	40.00
Musicor MM-2088	(M)	Love Bug	1966	12.00	30.00
Musicor MS-3088	(S)	Love Bug	1966	16.00	40.00
Musicor P2-5094	(M)	Country Heart	1966	12.00	30.00
Musicor P2S-5094	(S)	Country Heart	1966	16.00	40.00
Musicor MM-2099	(M)	I'm A People	1966	10.00	25.00
Musicor MS-3099	(S)	I'm A People	1966	12.00	30.00
Musicor MM-2106	(M)	We Found Heaven Right Here On Earth	1966	10.00	25.00
Musicor MS-3106	(S)	We Found Heaven Right Here On Earth	1966	12.00	30.00
Musicor MM-2116	(M)	George Jones' Greatest Hits	1967	10.00	25.00
Musicor MS-3116	(S)	George Jones' Greatest Hits	1967	10.00	25.00
Musicor MM-2119	(M)	Walk Through This World With Me	1967	12.00	30.00
Musicor MS-3119	(S)	Walk Through This World With Me	1967	10.00	25.00
Musicor MM-2124	(M)	Cup Of Loneliness	1967	12.00	30.00
Musicor MS-3124	(S)	Cup Of Loneliness	1967	10.00	25.00
Musicor MM-2128	(M)	Hits By George	1967	12.00	30.00
Musicor MS-3128	(S)	Hits By George	1967	10.00	25.00
Musicor MS-3149	(S)	The Songs Of Dallas Frazier	1968	10.00	25.00
Musicor MS-3158	(S)	If My Heart Had Windows	1968	10.00	25.00
Musicor MS-3159	(S)	The Musical Loves, Life And Sorrows Of America's Great Country Star	1968	12.00	30.00
Musicor MS-3169	(S)	My Country	1969	10.00	25.00
Musicor MS-3177	(S)	I'll Share My World With You	1969	10.00	25.00
Musicor MS-3181	(S)	Where Grass Won't Grow	1969	10.00	25.00
Musicor MS-3188	(S)	Will You Visit Me On Sunday?	1970	10.00	25.00
Musicor MS-3191	(S)	The Best Of George Jones	1970	10.00	25.00
Musicor MS-3194	(S)	With Love	1971	10.00	25.00
Musicor MS-3203	(S)	The Best Of Sacred Music	1971	10.00	25.00
Musicor MS-3204	(S)	The Great Songs Of Leon Payne	1971	10.00	25.00
		—Musicor albums above have black labels.—			
Sears SPS-125	(E)	Maybe, Little Baby	196?	20.00	50.00

JONES, GEORGE, & MELBA MONTGOMERY

Label & Catalog #		Title	Year	VG+	NM
United Arts. UAL-3301	(M)	What's In Our Hearts	1963	12.00	30.00
United Arts. UAS-6301	(S)	What's In Our Hearts	1963	16.00	40.00
United Arts. UAL-3352	(M)	Bluegrass Hootenanny	1964	12.00	30.00
United Arts. UAS-6352	(S)	Bluegrass Hootenanny	1964	16.00	40.00
United Arts. UAL-3472	(M)	Blue Moon Of Kentucky	1966	10.00	25.00
United Arts. UAS-6472	(S)	Blue Moon Of Kentucky	1966	12.00	30.00

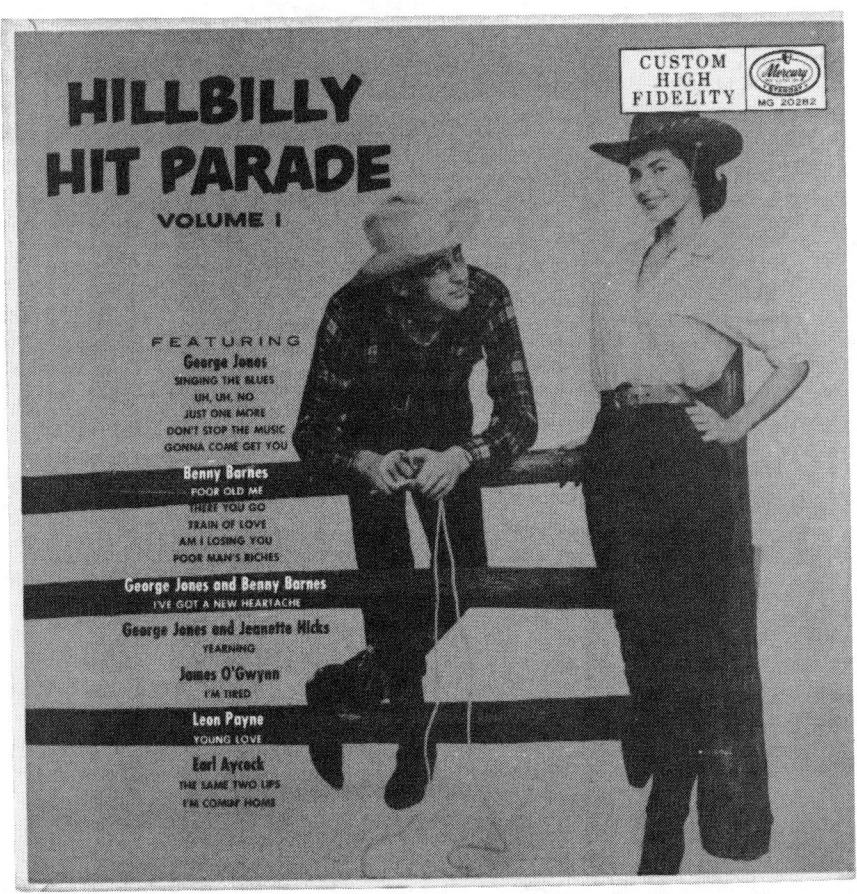

Hillbilly Hit Parade, Volume 1 *is technically a various artists album containing sixteen tracks by a half-dozen artists. Because the bulk of the material features George Jones—five solo and two duets, it is generally considered to be Jones debut with Mercury, containing his first three sides to make the country charts for his new label: "Yearning" and the double-sided hit, "Don't Stop The Music" / "Uh, Uh, No." (Note: This album was erroneously listed in the previous volume of this book as a Starday release.)*

Label & Catalog #		Title	Year	VG+	NM
Musicor M-3079	(M)	**Famous Country Duets**	*1965*	8.00	20.00
Musicor MS-3079	(S)	**Famous Country Duets**	*1965*	10.00	25.00
Musicor M-3109	(M)	**Close Together As You And Me**	*1966*	8.00	20.00
Musicor MS-3109	(S)	**Close Together As You And Me**	*1966*	10.00	25.00
Musicor M-3127	(M)	**Let's Get Together/Boy Meets Girl**	*1967*	8.00	20.00
Musicor MS-3127	(S)	**Let's Get Together/Boy Meets Girl**	*1967*	10.00	25.00
		— Musicor albums above have black labels.—			

JONES, GEORGE / MELBA MONTGOMERY / JUDY LYNN

Label & Catalog #		Title	Year	VG+	NM
United Arts. UAL-3367	(M)	**A King And Two Queens**	*1964*	8.00	20.00
United Arts. UAS-6367	(S)	**A King And Two Queens**	*1964*	10.00	25.00

JONES, GEORGE, & MELBA MONTGOMERY & GENE PITNEY

Label & Catalog #		Title	Year	VG+	NM
Musicor M-3079	(M)	**Famous Country Duets**	*1965*	8.00	20.00
Musicor MS-3079	(S)	**Famous Country Duets**	*1965*	10.00	25.00
		— Musicor albums above have black labels.—			

JONES, GEORGE, & GENE PITNEY

Label & Catalog #		Title	Year	VG+	NM
Musicor M-2044	(M)	**For The First Time! Two Great Singers**	*1965*	10.00	25.00
Musicor MS-3044	(S)	**For The First Time! Two Great Singers**	*1965*	12.00	30.00
Musicor M-2044	(M)	**Recorded In Nashville**	*1965*	10.00	25.00
Musicor MS-3044	(S)	**Recorded In Nashville**	*1965*	12.00	30.00
Musicor M-3065	(M)	**It's Country Time Again!**	*1965*	10.00	25.00
Musicor MS-3065	(S)	**It's Country Time Again!**	*1965*	12.00	30.00
		— Musicor albums above have black labels.—			

JONES, GEORGE, & MARGE SINGLETON

Label & Catalog #		Title	Year	VG+	NM
Mercury MG-20747	(M)	**Duets Country Style**	*1962*	12.00	30.00
Mercury SR-60747	(S)	**Duets Country Style**	*1962*	16.00	40.00

JONES, GRANPA
Granpa also recorded as a member of The Brown's Ferry Four.

Label & Catalog #		Title	Year	VG+	NM
King 554	(M)	**Granpa Jones Sings His Greatest Hits**	*1958*	60.00	150.00
King 625	(M)	**Strictly Country Tunes**	*1959*	60.00	150.00
King 809	(M)	**Rollin' Along With Granpa Jones**	*1963*	40.00	100.00
King 822	(M)	**16 Sacred Gospel Songs**	*1963*	40.00	100.00
King 845	(M)	**Do You Remember?**	*1963*	40.00	100.00
King 888	(M)	**The Other Side Of Granpa Jones**	*1964*	30.00	75.00
Decca DL-4364	(M)	**An Evening With Granpa Jones**	*1963*	10.00	25.00
Decca DL-74364	(S)	**An Evening With Granpa Jones**	*1963*	12.00	30.00
Monument MLP-4006	(M)	**Granpa Jones Makes The Rafters Ring**	*1962*	10.00	25.00
Monument SLP-14006	(S)	**Granpa Jones Makes The Rafters Ring**	*1962*	12.00	30.00
Monument MLP-8001	(M)	**Yodeling Hits**	*1963*	10.00	25.00
Monument SLP-18001	(S)	**Yodeling Hits**	*1963*	12.00	30.00
Monument MLP-8021	(M)	**Real Folk Songs**	*1964*	10.00	25.00
Monument SLP-18021	(S)	**Real Folk Songs**	*1964*	12.00	30.00
Monument MLP-8041	(M)	**Remembers The Brown's Ferry Four**	*1966*	10.00	25.00
Monument SLP-18041	(S)	**Remembers The Brown's Ferry Four**	*1966*	12.00	30.00
Monument SLP-18083	(S)	**Everybody's Grandpa**	*1968*	10.00	25.00
King KS-1042	(E)	**The Living Legend Of Country Music**	*1969*	10.00	25.00

JONES, JIM, & THE CHAUNTEYS

Label & Catalog #		Title	Year	VG+	NM
Sunglow SLP-113	(S)	**Soul Clap**	*196?*	20.00	50.00

JONES, JIMMY

Label & Catalog #		Title	Year	VG+	NM
MGM E-3847	(M)	**Good Timin'**	*1960*	60.00	150.00
MGM SE-3847	(E)	**Good Timin'**	*1960*	80.00	200.00
		("I Just Go For You" is in stereo on this album.)			

JONES, JOE

Label & Catalog #		Title	Year	VG+	NM
Roulette R-25143	(M)	**You Talk Too Much**	*1961*	50.00	125.00
Roulette SR-25143	(E)	**You Talk Too Much**	*1961*	20.00	50.00

JONES, LINDA

Label & Catalog #		Title	Year	VG+	NM
Loma 5907	(S)	**Hypnotized**	*1967*	10.00	25.00
Turbo 7007	(S)	**Your Precious Love**	*196?*	10.00	25.00

Known as the "King of Corn," band leader Spike Jones was leaving laughter in his wake for decades prior to his death in 1964. Using a wide variety of tools, toys, and other appropriate implements, his stage act and recordings were laced with nonsensical special effects, some of which still sound funny ages after their novelty should have worn off. These two albums from 1960 are of note not only as Jones vehicles, but the cover art makes them of some import to collectors of horror images, comics in particular. Thank You, Music Lovers, a collection of older sides, boasts a cover by Jack Davis, the hot in the advertising field after years as the artist for the Crypt-Keeper in EC Comics' "Tales From The Crypt." The painting on the cover of Spike Jones In Stereo, subtitled "A Spooktacular in Screaming Sound," features a wolfman, a mummy, a vampire, a Frankenstein monster, Vampira and, horror of horrors, a two-headed beatnik.

Label & Catalog #		Title	Year	VG+	NM
JONES, PAUL					
Paul Jones was formerly a member of Manfred Mann.					
Uni 3005	(M)	**Privilege** *(Soundtrack)*	1967	8.00	20.00
Uni 73005	(S)	**Privilege** *(Soundtrack)*	1967	10.00	25.00
Capitol T-2795	(M)	**Songs From The Film "Privilege"**	1967	8.00	20.00
Capitol ST-2795	(S)	**Songs From The Film "Privilege"**	1967	10.00	25.00
JONES, RICKIE LEE					
Mobile Fidelity MFSL-089	(S)	**Rickie Lee Jones**	1980	50.00	150.00
Mobile Fidelity MFQR-089	(S)	**Rickie Lee Jones** *(UHQR test pressing)*	1980	250.00	750.00
JONES, RUFUS					
Cameo C-1076	(M)	**Five On Eight**	1964	10.00	25.00
Cameo SC-1076	(S)	**Five On Eight**	1964	16.00	40.00
JONES, SHIRLEY, & JACK CASSIDY					
Columbia CL-991	(M)	**Speaking Of Love**	1957	14.00	35.00
Columbia CL-1255	(M)	**With Love From Hollywood**	1959	12.00	30.00
JONES, SPIKE					
RCA Victor LPT-18	(10")	**Spike Jones Plays The Charleston**	1952	80.00	200.00
RCA Victor LPM-3054	(10")	**Bottoms Up**	1952	80.00	200.00
RCA Victor LPM-3128	(10")	**Spike Jones Murders Carmen**	1953	80.00	200.00
Verve MGV-2021	(M)	**Let's Sing A Song For Christmas**	1956	20.00	50.00
Verve MGV-4005	(M)	**Dinner Music For People Who Aren't Very Hungry**	1957	20.00	50.00
Verve MGV-8564	(M)	**35 Reasons Why Christmas Can Be Fun**	1958	20.00	50.00
— Verve albums above have "Verve Records, Inc." on the bottom of the label.—					
Verve V-2021	(M)	**Let's Sing A Song For Christmas**	1961	10.00	25.00
Verve V-4005	(M)	**Dinner Music For People Who Aren't Very Hungry**	1961	10.00	25.00
Verve V-8564	(M)	**35 Reasons Why Christmas Can Be Fun**	1961	10.00	25.00
— Verve albums above have "MGM Records" on the bottom of the label.—					
Liberty LRP-3140	(M)	**Omnibust**	1959	20.00	50.00
Liberty LST-7140	(S)	**Omnibust**	1959	30.00	75.00
Liberty LST-7140	(S)	**Omnibust** *(Red vinyl)*	1959	60.00	150.00
Liberty LRP-3154	(M)	**60 Years Of Music America Hates Best**	1959	20.00	50.00
Liberty LST-7154	(S)	**60 Years Of Music America Hates Best**	1959	30.00	75.00
Warner Bros. B-1332	(M)	**Spike Jones In Hi Fi**	1960	14.00	35.00
Warner Bros. WS-1332	(S)	**Spike Jones In Stereo**	1960	20.00	50.00
Liberty LRP-3338	(M)	**Washington Square**	1963	8.00	20.00
Liberty LST-7338	(S)	**Washington Square**	1963	10.00	25.00
Liberty LRP-3349	(M)	**Spike Jones' New Band**	1963	12.00	30.00
Liberty LST-7349	(S)	**Spike Jones' New Band**	1963	16.00	40.00
Liberty LRP-3401	(M)	**Spike Jones Plays Hank Williams Hits**	1965	8.00	20.00
Liberty LST-7401	(S)	**Spike Jones Plays Hank Williams Hits**	1965	10.00	25.00
RCA Victor LPM-2224	(M)	**Thank You, Music Lovers**	1960	20.00	50.00
RCA Victor LOC-3235	(M)	**Spike Jones Is Murdering The Classics**	1965	12.00	30.00
RCA Victor LSC-3235	(E)	**Spike Jones Is Murdering The Classics**	1965	10.00	25.00
RCA Victor LPM-3849	(M)	**The Best Of Spike Jones**	1967	10.00	25.00
RCA Victor LSP-3849	(E)	**The Best Of Spike Jones**	1967	8.00	20.00
JONES, STAN					
Disneyland WDL-1005	(M)	**Songs Of The National Parks**	1957	20.00	50.00
		(Original pressings of WDL-1005 have custom back covers.)			
Disneyland WDL-1005	(M)	**Songs Of The National Parks**	1963	10.00	25.00
		(Later pressings have ads for other LPs on the back cover.)			
Disneyland WDL-3015	(M)	**Creakin' Leather**	1958	20.00	50.00
Disneyland WDL-3033	(M)	**This Was The West**	1961	10.00	25.00
Buena Vista BV-3306	(M)	**Ghost Riders In The Sky**	1961	14.00	35.00
Buena Vista BV-3315	(M)	**Creakin' Leather**	1962	14.00	35.00
		(BV-3315 is a reissue of Disneyland 3015.)			
JONES, TAMIKO					
December DEC-8500	(S)	**Tamiko**	196?	12.00	30.00
JONES, TOM					
Parrot XPAS-1	(DJ)	**Special Tom Jones Interview**	1970	30.00	75.00
		(Open-end interview issued in a gatefold cover with script.)			

Label & Catalog #		Title	Year	VG+	NM

JONES BOYS, THE
George Jones' boys.

Musicor M-2017	(M)	Country & Western Songbook	1964	12.00	30.00
Musicor MS-3017	(S)	Country & Western Songbook	1964	16.00	40.00
Musicor MS-3182	(S)	My Boys, The Jones Boys	1970	10.00	25.00
		—Musicor albums above have black labels.—			

JOPLIN, JANIS
Janis was formerly a member of Big Brother & The Holding Company. Refer to Hot Tuna.

Columbia PC-37569	(DJ)	A Farewell Song *(Banded for air-play)*	1982	14.00	35.00
Mobile Fidelity MFSL-154	(S)	Pearl *(Test pressing)*	1984	200.00	400.00
Mobile Fidelity MFSL-154	(S)	Pearl	1984		*Unreleased*

JORDAN, KING

Coral CRL-57372	(M)	Phantom Guitar	1962	8.00	20.00
Coral CRL-757372	(S)	Phantom Guitar	1962	10.00	25.00

JORDAN, LOUIS

Score SLP-4007	(M)	Go Blow Your Horn	1957	80.00	200.00
Mercury MG-20242	(M)	Somebody Up There Digs Me	1957	50.00	125.00
Mercury MG-20331	(M)	Man, We're Wailin'	1958	50.00	125.00
Decca DL-8551	(M)	Let The Good Times Roll	1958	40.00	100.00
Wing MGW-12126	(M)	Somebody Up There Digs Me	1962	10.00	25.00
Wing SRW-16126	(E)	Somebody Up There Digs Me	1962	4.00	10.00
Decca DL-5035	(M)	Let The Good Times Roll	1968	12.00	30.00

JORDAN, SHEILA: *Refer to* GOLDMINE'S PRICE GUIDE TO COLLECTIBLE JAZZ ALBUMS

JORDANAIRES, THE
While The Jordanaires have built a solid career as a white gospel group, they have also backed scores of country singers, achieving lasting fame backing Elvis on virtually all of his RCA sides through 1966.

RCA Victor LPM-3081	(10")	Beautiful City	1953	40.00	100.00
Decca DL-8681	(M)	Peace In The Valley	1957	20.00	50.00
Sesac 1401	(M)	Of Rivers And Plains	195?	30.00	75.00
Capitol T-1011	(M)	Heavenly Spirit	1958	16.00	40.00
Capitol T-1167	(M)	Gloryland	1959	16.00	40.00
Capitol T-1311	(M)	Land Of Jordan	1960	14.00	35.00
Capitol ST-1311	(S)	Land Of Jordan	1960	16.00	40.00
Capitol T-1742	(M)	Spotlight On The Jordanaires	1962	10.00	25.00
Capitol ST-1742	(S)	Spotlight On The Jordanaires	1962	12.00	30.00
Capitol T-1559	(M)	To God Be The Glory	1961	8.00	20.00
Capitol ST-1559	(S)	To God Be The Glory	1961	10.00	25.00

JOSEFUS

Hookah 330	(S)	Dead Man	1969	80.00	200.00
Mainstream 6127	(S)	Josefus	1970	20.00	50.00

JOSEPH

Scepter 674	(S)	Stoned Age Man	1970	16.00	40.00

JOSEPH, MARGIE

Volt VOS-6012	(S)	Margie Joseph Makes A New Impression	1971	12.00	30.00
Volt VOS-6016	(S)	Phase II	1971	12.00	30.00

JOSIE & THE PUSSYCATS
Cheryl Ladd is the voice of Josie.

Capitol ST-665	(S)	Josie And The Pussycats	1970	80.00	200.00

JOURNEY

Mobile Fidelity MFSL-144	(S)	Escape	1986	50.00	150.00

JOURNEYMEN, THE
The vocal and instrumental Journeymen were John Phillips, Scott McKenzie and Dick Weissman.

Capitol T-1629	(M)	The Journeymen	1961	12.00	30.00
Capitol ST-1629	(S)	The Journeymen	1961	16.00	40.00
Capitol T-1770	(M)	Coming Attraction—Live!	1962	12.00	30.00
Capitol ST-1770	(S)	Coming Attraction—Live!	1962	16.00	40.00
Capitol T-1951	(M)	New Directions In Folk Music	1963	10.00	25.00
Capitol ST-1951	(S)	New Directions In Folk Music	1963	12.00	30.00

Label & Catalog #		Title	Year	VG+	NM
JOY DIVISION					
Members of Joy Division later recorded as New Order.					
Rough Trade FACT-6	(S)	**Closer** *(Purple tinted vinyl)*	1980	20.00	50.00
Rough Trade FACT-6	(S)	**Closer** *(Red tinted vinyl)*	1980	10.00	25.00
JUDAS PRIEST					
Visa IMP-7001	(S)	**Rocka-Rolla**	1974	10.00	25.00
Ovation 1751	(S)	**Sad Wines Of Destiny**	1976	10.00	25.00
JULIAN, DON					
Amazon 1009	(M)	**Greatest Oldies**	1963	24.00	60.00
JULY					
Epic BN-26416	(E)	**July**	1969	80.00	200.00
JUPITER					
Jupiter 1005	(S)	**Multiple Choice**	1980	16.00	40.00
JUST IV					
Liberty LRP-3340	(M)	**First Twelve Sides**	1964	8.00	20.00
Liberty LST-7340	(S)	**First Twelve Sides**	1964	10.00	25.00
JUST US					
Just Us features former members of The Index.					
Valord AR-2634	(S)	**The U.S.A. From The Air**	197?	40.00	100.00
JUSTICE, JIMMY					
Kapp KL-1308	(M)	**Justice For All**	1964	10.00	25.00
Kapp KS-3308	(S)	**Justice For All**	1964	14.00	35.00
JUSTIS, BILL					
Phillips Inter. PLP-1950	(M)	**Cloud Nine**	1959	250.00	500.00

K. O. BOSSY
Toga TSTLP-2003	(S)	**K. O. Bossy**	197?	12.00	30.00

K-DOE, ERNIE
Ernie K-Doe is a pseudonym for Ernest Kador.
Minit LP-4002	(M)	**Mother-In-Law**	1961	80.00	200.00
Minit LP-24002	(E)	**Mother-In-Law**	1961	100.00	250.00

KAILUA, PRINCE, & THE TROPICAL ISLANDERS
Prince Kailua is a pseudonym for Roy Smeck.
Epic LN-24055	(M)	**Hawaii's Greatest Hits**	1963	10.00	25.00
Epic BN-26055	(S)	**Hawaii's Greatest Hits**	1963	12.00	30.00

KAK
Epic BN-26429	(S)	**Kak**	1969	70.00	175.00

KALABASH CORP., THE
Uncle Bill KB-3114	(S)	**The Kalabash Corp.**	197?	30.00	75.00

KALEIDOSCOPE
Epic LN-24304	(M)	**Side Trips**	1967	12.00	30.00
Epic BN-26304	(S)	**Side Trips**	1967	16.00	40.00
Epic LN-24333	(M)	**Beacon From Mars**	1967	16.00	40.00
Epic BN-26333	(S)	**Beacon From Mars**	1967	20.00	50.00
Epic BN-26467	(S)	**Incredible Kaleidoscope**	1969	10.00	25.00
Epic BN-26508	(S)	**Bernice**	1970	8.00	20.00

KALIN TWINS, THE
Decca DL-8812	(M)	**The Kalin Twins**	1959	40.00	100.00

KALLEN, KITTY
Mercury MG-25206	(10")	**Pretty Kitty Kallen Sings**	1955	20.00	50.00
Decca DL-8397	(M)	**It's A Lonesome Old Town**	1958	16.00	40.00
Vocalion VL-3679	(M)	**Little Things Mean A Lot**	1959	10.00	25.00
Columbia CL-1404	(M)	**If I Give My Heart To You**	1960	8.00	20.00
Columbia CS-8204	(S)	**If I Give My Heart To You**	1960	10.00	25.00
Columbia CL-1662	(M)	**Honky Tonk Angel**	1961	8.00	20.00
Columbia CS-8462	(S)	**Honky Tonk Angel**	1961	10.00	25.00
RCA Victor LPM-2640	(M)	**My Coloring Book**	1963	8.00	20.00
RCA Victor LSP-2640	(S)	**My Coloring Book**	1963	10.00	25.00

KAMMERZELL
Artco-Alpha 50-1209	(S)	**Hot For Your Love**	1979	30.00	75.00

KANNON, JACKIE
Roulette R-502	(M)	**Prose From The Cons**	1959	10.00	25.00
Rat Fink 1313	(M)	**Music For Ratfink Lovers**	196?	20.00	50.00
Roulette R-25312	(M)	**Live From The Ratfink Room**	1965	8.00	20.00
Roulette SR-25312	(S)	**Live From The Ratfink Room**	1965	10.00	25.00

KANSAS
Kirshner HZ-44224	(S)	**Leftoverture** *(Half-speed master)*	1982	12.00	35.00
Kirshner HZ-44929	(S)	**Point Of Know Return** *(Half-speed master)*	1982	13.00	40.00
Kirshner JZ-44929	(DJ)	**Point Of Know Return** *(Picture disc)*	1982	20.00	50.00
Kirshner HZ-46008	(S)	**Monolith** *(Half-speed master)*	1982	16.00	50.00
Kirshner HZ-48002	(S)	**Vinyl Confessions** *(Half-speed master)*	1982	10.00	30.00

KANSAS CITY JAMMERS, THE
(No label)	(S)	**Got Good (If You Get It)**	197?	20.00	50.00

Label & Catalog #		Title	Year	VG+	NM
KANTNER, PAUL, & THE JEFFERSON STARSHIP					
RCA Victor LSP-4448	(S)	**Blows Against The Empire** (Clear vinyl)	1970	100.00	250.00
KARLOFF, BORIS					
Cricket CR-32	(M)	**Tales Of Mystery And Imagination**	1959	20.00	50.00
Mercury MG-20815	(M)	**Tales Of The Frightened, Volume 1**	1963	14.00	35.00
Mercury SR-60815	(S)	**Tales Of The Frightened, Volume 1**	1963	16.00	40.00
Mercury MG-20816	(M)	**Tales Of The Frightened, Volume 2**	1963	14.00	35.00
Mercury SR-60816	(S)	**Tales Of The Frightened, Volume 2**	1963	16.00	40.00
Decca DL-4833	(M)	**An Evening With Karloff And His Friends**	1967	8.00	20.00
Decca DL-74833	(S)	**An Evening With Karloff And His Friends**	1967	10.00	25.00
Caedmon TC-1038	(M)	**Just So Stories, Vol. 1**	196?	10.00	25.00
Caedmon TC-1074	(M)	**The Reluctant Dragon**	196?	10.00	25.00
Caedmon TC-1075	(M)	**The Pied Piepr / The Hunting Of The Snark**	196?	10.00	25.00
Caedmon TC-1088	(M)	**Just So Stories, Vol. 2**	196?	10.00	25.00
Caedmon TC-1100	(M)	**Kipling's Jungle Books: How Fear Came**	196?	10.00	25.00
Caedmon TC-1117	(M)	**The Little Match Girl**	196?	10.00	25.00
Caedmon TC-1109	(M)	**The Ugly Duckling**	196?	10.00	25.00
Caedmon TC-1129	(M)	**The Three Little Pigs**	1962	10.00	25.00
Caedmon TC-1139	(M)	**The Cat Who Walked By Herself**	196?	10.00	25.00
Caedmon TC-1176	(M)	**Kipling's Jungle Books:**			
		Toomai Of The Elephants	196?	10.00	25.00
Caedmon TC-1182	(M)	**Let's Listen** (10" album with Julie Harris)	196?	10.00	25.00
Caedmon TC-1221	(M)	**Aesop's Fables**	1967	10.00	25.00
KATZ, FRED: Refer to **GOLDMINE'S PRICE GUIDE TO COLLECTIBLE JAZZ ALBUMS**					
KAUFMANN, BOB					
L.H.I. 12002	(S)	**Trip Through A Blown Mind**	1967	20.00	50.00
KAY, JOHN/JOHN KAY & SPARROW					
John Kay is the former lead singer for Steppenwolf.					
Columbia CS-9758	(S)	**John Kay & Sparrow** ("360 Sound" label)	1970	10.00	25.00
		(Sparrow as an early incarnation of Steppenwolf;.)			
KAYE, DANNY					
Columbia CL-6023	(10")	**Danny Kaye** (Custom yellow cover)	1949	24.00	60.00
Columbia CL-6023	(10")	**Danny Kaye** (Title cover)	1949	16.00	40.00
Columbia CL-6249	(10")	**Danny Kaye Entertains** (Custom blue cover)	1949	24.00	60.00
Columbia CL-6249	(10")	**Danny Kaye Entertains** (Title cover)	1949	16.00	40.00
Decca DLP-5033	(10")	**Danny Kaye**	1949	16.00	40.00
Decca DL-5094	(10")	**Gilbert And Sullivan And Danny Kaye**	1949	40.00	100.00
Decca DL-5433	(10")	**Hans Christian Andersen** (Soundtrack)	1952	20.00	50.00
Decca DL-6024	(10")	**Danny At The Palace**	1953	16.00	40.00
Decca DL-5527	(10")	**Knock On Wood** (Soundtrack)	1954	40.00	100.00
Decca DL-8212	(M)	**The Court Jester**	1955	40.00	100.00
Decca DL-8461	(M)	**Danny At The Palace**	1957	16.00	40.00
		(Decca 8561 is a reissue of 6024.)			
Decca DL-8479	(M)	**Hans Christian Andersen** (Soundtrack)	1957	40.00	100.00
		— Decca albums above have black & silver labels.—			
Capitol T-937	(M)	**Mommy Gimme A Drinka Water**	1958	16.00	40.00
Capitol T-1016	(M)	**Merry Andrew** (Soundtrack)	1958	20.00	50.00
Dena XTV-92557	(M)	**Rambler Dealers Presnet Danny Kaye**	195?	16.00	40.00
Decca DL-8212	(M)	**The Court Jester**	1959	30.00	75.00
Decca DL-8461	(M)	**Danny At The Palace**	1959	10.00	25.00
Decca DL-8479	(M)	**Hans Christian Andersen** (Soundtrack)	1959	12.00	30.00
Decca DL-78479	(E)	**Hans Christian Andersen** (Soundtrack)	1962	6.00	15.00
Decca DL-8726	(M)	**For Children**	1959	10.00	25.00
Decca DL-78726	(E)	**For Children**	1959	8.00	20.00
Decca DXB-175	(M)	**The Best Of Danny Kaye** (2 LPs)	1962	12.00	30.00
Decca DXSB-7175	(E)	**The Best Of Danny Kaye** (2 LPs)	1962	8.00	20.00
KAYE, MARY/THE MARY KAYE TRIO					
Decca DL-8238	(M)	**The Mary Kaye Trio**	1956	12.00	30.00
Decca DL-8454	(M)	**Music On A Silver Platter**	1957	12.00	30.00
Decca DL-8650	(M)	**You Don't Know What Love Is**	1958	12.00	30.00
Warner Bros. W-1263	(M)	**Jackpot**	1959	8.00	20.00
Warner Bros. WS-1263	(S)	**Jackpot**	1959	10.00	25.00

Label & Catalog #		Title	Year	VG+	NM
Warner Bros. W-1342	(M)	On Sunset Strip	1959	8.00	20.00
Warner Bros. WS-1342	(S)	On Sunset Strip	1959	10.00	25.00
Verve MGV-2142	(M)	Up Front!	1960	16.00	40.00
— Verve albums above have "Verve Records, Inc." on the bottom of the label.—					
Verve V-8446	(M)	For The Record	1962	8.00	20.00
Verve V6-8446	(S)	For The Record	1962	10.00	25.00

KAZEE, BUELL H.
Buell Kazee is a banjo player and singer of traditional Kentucky folk music.

Folkways FS-3810	(M)	Buell Kazee Sings And Plays His Songs And Music	195?	12.00	30.00

KEENE, BOB

Del-Fi DFLP-1202	(M)	Unforgettable	1959	12.00	30.00
Del-Fi DFLP-1203	(M)	Masque D' Afrique	1959	12.00	30.00
Del-Fi DFLP-1222	(M)	Twist To Radio KRLA	1962	12.00	30.00
Del-Fi DFST-1222	(S)	Twist To Radio KRLA	1962	20.00	50.00

KEITH, BARBARA
Ms. Keith also recorded with Kangaroo.

Warner Bros. MS-2087	(S)	Barbara Keith	1972	20.00	50.00

KEITH, BILL, & JIM ROONEY

Folklore FRLP-14002	(M)	Living On The Mountain	1964	8.00	20.00
Folklore FRST-14002	(S)	Living On The Mountain	1964	10.00	25.00

KELLER, JERRY

Kapp KL-1178	(M)	Here Comes Jerry Keller	1960	14.00	35.00
Kapp KS-3178	(S)	Here Comes Jerry Keller	1960	20.00	50.00

KELLERMAN, SALLY

Decca DL-75359	(S)	Roll With The Feelin'	1972	10.00	25.00

KELLY, BEVERLY: *Refer to* **GOLDMINE'S PRICE GUIDE TO COLLECTIBLE JAZZ ALBUMS**

KELLY, EMMETT

Roulette R-25130	(M)	Sing Along With Emmett Kelly	1960	10.00	25.00
Roulette SR-25130	(S)	Sing Along With Emmett Kelly	1960	12.00	30.00

KELLY, GENE

Columbia JL-8001	(10")	Nursery Songs	1949	30.00	75.00

KELLY BROTHERS, THE

King 810	(M)	The Kelly Brothers Sing A Page Of Songs From The Good Book	1962	40.00	100.00
Excello 8007	(M)	Sweet Soul	196?	20.00	50.00

KELTNER, JIM, & RON TUTT

Sheffield Lab	(S)	The Sheffield Drum Record *(Direct-to-disc)*	198?	10.00	30.00

KENNEDY, JERRY
Refer to Tom & Jerry.

Smash MGS-27004	(M)	Dancing Guitars Rock Elvis' Hits	1962	12.00	30.00
Smash SRS-67004	(S)	Dancing Guitars Rock Elvis' Hits	1962	16.00	40.00
Smash MGS-27024	(M)	Jerry Kennedy's Guitars And Strings Play The Golden Standards	1963	10.00	25.00
Smash SRS-67024	(S)	Jerry Kennedy's Guitars And Strings Play The Golden Standards	1963	12.00	30.00
Smash MGS-27066	(M)	From Nashville To Soulville	1965	10.00	25.00
Smash SRS-67066	(S)	From Nashville To Soulville	1965	12.00	30.00

KENNEDY, ROBERT F.
Former U.S. Attorney General and Presidential aspirant Senator Robert F. Kennedy was shot and killed in 1968 . The autopsy showed that he was killed by several bullets that entered him from the rear and that had been fired at a range so close that powder burns stained his jacket. Nonetheless, the assassination was pinned on a demented student, Sirhan Sirhan, who fired his shots at Senator Kennedy from the front at a range no closer than approximately two feet away. . .

Columbia D2S-792	(S)	Robert F. Kennedy—A Memorial	1968	10.00	25.00

Label & Catalog #		Title	Year	VG+	NM
KENNER, CHRIS					
Atlantic 8117	(M)	**Land Of 1,000 Dances**	1965	20.00	50.00
KENNEY, BEVERLY: *Refer to* GOLDMINE'S PRICE GUIDE TO COLLECTIBLE JAZZ ALBUMS					
KENNY, BILL					
Mr. Kenny is a member of The Ink Spots.					
Warwick W-2021	(M)	**Mr. Ink Spot**	1962	10.00	25.00
Warwick W-2021ST	(M)	**Mr. Ink Spot**	1962	20.00	50.00
KENNY & THE KASUALS					
Mark LP-5000	(M)	**The Impact Sound Of Kenny & The Kasuals**			
		Live At The Studio Club	1966		*See below*
		(Mark 5000 has a suggested Near Mint value of $600-1,000.)			
Mark LP-5000	(M)	**The Impact Sound Of Kenny & The Kasuals**			
		Live At The Studio Club	1977	20.00	50.00
Mark LP-6000	(M)	**Teen Dreams** *(Red vinyl)*	1978	100.00	250.00
		(Mark 6000 is a signed, numbered edition of 200 copies.)			
Mark LP-7000	(S)	**Garage Kings**	1979	20.00	50.00
KENTUCKY COLONELS, THE					
The KCs are Roger Bush, Billy Latham, and Clarence and Roland White. Refer to The Byrds; Tut Taylor.					
World Pacific T-1821	(M)	**Appalachian Swing**	1964	16.00	40.00
World Pacific ST-1821	(S)	**Appalachian Swing**	1964	20.00	50.00
Briar BT-7202	(S)	**Livin' In The Past**	1975	10.00	25.00
Briar Inter. 109	(S)	**The New Sounds Of Bluegrass America**	1976	16.00	40.00
KEROUAC, JACK					
Refer to Charles Laughton.					
Dot DLP-3154	(M)	**Poetry For The Beat Generation**	1959		*See below*
		(After little more than 100 copies of Dot 3154 had been pressed, the album was pulled by the company president, who deemed it unfit for children's listening! Rare both as a recorded and a literary artifact with a suggested Near Mint value of $5,000-10,000.)			
Hanover HML-5000	(M)	**Poetry For The Beat Generation**	1959	200.00	400.00
Hanover HML-5006	(M)	**Blues And Haikus**	1959	200.00	400.00
Verve MGV-15005	(M)	**Readings On The Beat Generation**	1959	100.00	250.00
Rhino/Word Beat	(M)	**The Jack Kerouac Collection**	1990	20.00	50.00
		(Boxed set of four LPs collects the works above plus outtakes.)			
KERSHAW, DOUG & RUSTY					
Hickory LPM-103	(M)	**Louisiana Man (& Other Favorites)**	1969	10.00	25.00
Hickory LPS-103	(S)	**Louisiana Man (& Other Favorites)**	1969	12.00	30.00
KESEY, KEN					
Sound City 27690	(M)	**The Acid Test** *(With the Grateful Dead)*	1967	200.00	400.00
KESSEL, BARNEY					
Emerald 1201	(M)	**On Fire**	1965	20.00	50.00
Emerald 2201	(S)	**On Fire**	1965	30.00	75.00
		(Jazz guitarist Kessel's sole album is included here due to Emerald being a subsidiary of Philles and a must for Spector completists.)			
KESSINGER, CLARK					
Folkways FA-2336	(M)	**The Legend Of Clark Kessinger**	1959	12.00	30.00
KEYMEN, THE					
Coral CRL-57112	(M)	**Vocal Sounds Of The Keymen**	1957	14.00	35.00
ABC-Paramount ABC-288	(M)	**Dance With Dick Clark**	1958	14.00	35.00
ABC-Paramount ABCS-288	(S)	**Dance With Dick Clark**	1958	20.00	50.00
ABC-Paramount ABC-288	(M)	**Dance With Dick Clark, Volume 2**	1959	14.00	35.00
ABC-Paramount ABCS-288	(S)	**Dance With Dick Clark, Volume 2**	1959	20.00	50.00
KEYMEN, THE					
Goldust LPS-153	(S)	**The Keymen Live**	196?	20.00	50.00
KHAN, ALI AKBAR					
Bluesville BVLP-1079	(M)	**Classical Music Of India**	1964	10.00	25.00

Label & Catalog #		Title	Year	VG+	NM

KICKSTANDS, THE
The Kickstands are a creation of Gary Usher & Co.

Capitol T-2078	(M)	**Black Boots And Bikes** *(With bonus photo)*	1964	40.00	100.00
Capitol ST-2078	(S)	**Black Boots And Bikes** *(With bonus photo)*	1964	50.00	125.00
Capitol T-2078	(M)	**Black Boots And Bikes** *(Without the photo)*	1964	30.00	75.00
Capitol ST-2078	(S)	**Black Boots And Bikes** *(Without the photo)*	1964	40.00	100.00

(Capitol 2078 was issued with a 12" x 10" folded photo of a bike with a hot rod calatog on the back.)

KILGORE, MERLE

| Starday SLP-251 | (M) | **There's Gold In Them Thar Hills** *(Yellow label)* | 1963 | 16.00 | 40.00 |

KILLING FLOOR
Killing Floor features Rory Gallagher.

| Sire SES-97019 | (S) | **Killing Floor** | 1970 | 20.00 | 50.00 |

KINCAID, BRADLEY

| Varsity LP-6988 | (10") | **American Ballads** | 195? | 30.00 | 75.00 |
| Varsity LP-34 | (M) | **American Ballads And Folk Siongs** | 195? | 20.00 | 50.00 |

KINES, TOM

| Elektra EKL-137 | (M) | **Of Maids And Mistresses** | 1958` | 12.00 | 30.00 |

KING, ALBERT

King 852	(M)	**Big Blues**	1963	200.00	400.00
Stax ST-723	(M)	**Born Under A Bad Sign**	1967	30.00	75.00
Stax STS-723	(S)	**Born Under A Bad Sign**	1967	60.00	150.00
Stax STS-2003	(S)	**Live Wire/Blues Power**	1968	10.00	25.00
King KS-1060	(S)	**Travelin' To California**	1969	10.00	25.00
Atlantic SD-8213	(S)	**King Of The Blues Guitar**	1969	10.00	25.00
Stax STS-2010	(S)	**Years Gone By**	1969	10.00	25.00
Stax STS-2015	(S)	**King Does The King's Thing**	1969	10.00	25.00

KING, ALBERT, & STEVE CROPPER, & POP STAPLES

| Stax STS-2020 | (S) | **Jammed Together** | 1971 | 10.00 | 25.00 |

KING, ALBERT, & OTIS RUSH

| Chess LPS-1538 | (S) | **Door To Door** | 1969 | 10.00 | 25.00 |

KING, ANNA

| Smash MGS-27059 | (M) | **Back To Soul** *(Produced by James Brown)* | 1964 | 12.00 | 30.00 |
| Smash SRS-67059 | (S) | **Back To Soul** *(Produced by James Brown)* | 1964 | 16.00 | 40.00 |

KING, B. B.

Crown CLP-5020	(M)	**Singin' The Blues**	1957	30.00	75.00
Crown CST-???	(E)	**Singin' The Blues**	196?	8.00	20.00
Crown CLP-5063	(M)	**The Blues**	1958	30.00	75.00
Crown CST-???	(E)	**The Blues**	196?	8.00	20.00
Crown CLP-5115	(M)	**B. B. King Wails**	1959	30.00	75.00
Crown CST-147	(E)	**B. B. King Wails**	196?	8.00	20.00
Crown CST-147	(E)	**B. B. King Wails** *(Red vinyl)*	196?	40.00	100.00
Crown CLP-5119	(M)	**B. B. King Sings Spirituals**	1960	20.00	50.00
Crown CST-152	(E)	**B. B. King Sings Spirituals**	1960	8.00	20.00
Crown CST-152	(E)	**B. B. King Sings Spirituals** *(Red vinyl)*	1960	40.00	100.00
Crown CLP-5143	(M)	**The Great B. B. King**	1961	20.00	50.00
Crown CST-???	(E)	**The Great B. B. King**	1961	8.00	20.00
Crown CLP-5167	(M)	**King Of The Blues**	1961	20.00	50.00
Crown CST-195	(E)	**King Of The Blues**	1961	8.00	20.00
Crown CST-195	(E)	**King Of The Blues** *(Red vinyl)*	1961	40.00	100.00
Crown CLP-5188	(M)	**My Kind Of Blues**	1961	16.00	40.00
Crown CST-???	(E)	**My Kind Of Blues**	1961	8.00	20.00
Crown CLP-5230	(M)	**More B. B. King**	1962	16.00	40.00
Crown CST-???	(E)	**More B. B. King**	1962	8.00	20.00
Crown CLP-5248	(M)	**Twist With B. B. King**	1962	16.00	40.00
Crown CST-???	(E)	**Twist With B. B. King**	1962	8.00	20.00
Crown CLP-5286	(M)	**Easy Listening Blues**	1962	16.00	40.00
Crown CST-???	(E)	**Easy Listening Blues**	1962	8.00	20.00
Crown CLP-5309	(M)	**Blues In My Heart**	1962	16.00	40.00
Crown CST-309	(E)	**Blues In My Heart**	1962	8.00	20.00

Label & Catalog #		Title	Year	VG+	NM
Crown CLP-5359	(M)	B. B. King	1963	16.00	40.00
Crown CST-359	(E)	B. B. King	1963	8.00	20.00
Galaxy 202	(M)	The Best Of B. B. King	1962	30.00	75.00
Galaxy 8202	(S)	The Best Of B. B. King	1962	40.00	100.00
ABC-Paramount ABC-456	(M)	Mr. Blues	1963	12.00	30.00
ABC-Paramount ABCS-456	(S)	Mr. Blues	1963	16.00	40.00
ABC-Paramount ABC-509	(M)	Live At The Regal	1965	16.00	40.00
ABC-Paramount ABCS-509	(S)	Live At The Regal	1965	20.00	50.00
ABC-Paramount ABC-528	(M)	Confessin' The Blues	1965	12.00	30.00
ABC-Paramount ABCS-528	(S)	Confessin' The Blues	1965	16.00	40.00
BluesWay BL-6001	(S)	Blues Is King	1967	8.00	20.00
BluesWay BLS-6001	(S)	Blues Is King	1967	10.00	25.00
BluesWay BLS-6011	(S)	Blues On Top Of Blues	1968	10.00	25.00
BluesWay BLS-6016	(S)	Lucille	1968	10.00	25.00
Direct Disk SD-16616	(S)	Midnight Believer	1980	10.00	30.00

KING, BEN E.
Ben E. King was formerly a member of The Drifters.

Atco SD-33-133	(M)	Spanish Harlem	1961	30.00	75.00
Atco SD-33-133	(S)	Spanish Harlem	1961	60.00	150.00
		—Atco albums above have yellow "harp" labels.—			
Atco SD-33-133	(M)	Spanish Harlem	1962	16.00	40.00
Atco SD-33-133	(S)	Spanish Harlem	1962	20.00	50.00
Atco SD-33-137	(M)	Ben E. King Sings For Soulful Lovers	1962	16.00	40.00
Atco SD-33-137	(S)	Ben E. King Sings For Soulful Lovers	1962	20.00	50.00
Atco SD-33-142	(M)	Don't Play That Song	1962	16.00	40.00
Atco SD-33-142	(S)	Don't Play That Song	1962	20.00	50.00
Atco SD-33-165	(M)	Ben E. King's Greatest Hits	1964	12.00	30.00
Atco SD-33-165	(S)	Ben E. King's Greatest Hits	1964	16.00	40.00
Atco SD-33-174	(M)	Seven Letters	1965	12.00	30.00
Atco SD-33-174	(S)	Seven Letters	1965	16.00	40.00
		—Atco mono albums above have gold & gray labels; stereo albums have purple & brown labels.—			
Clarion 606	(M)	Young Boy Blues	1964	8.00	20.00
Clarion 606	(S)	Young Boy Blues	1964	10.00	25.00
Mandala MLP-3008	(DJ)	Audio Biography (Radio interview)	1972	10.00	25.00

KING, CAROLE
Refer to City; The Cookies / Little Eva / Carole King.

Epic/Ode HE-44946	(S)	Tapestry (Half-speed master)	1980	25.00	75.00

KING, CLAUDE

Columbia CL-1810	(M)	Meet Claude King	1962	10.00	25.00
Columbia CS-8610	(S)	Meet Claude King	1962	16.00	40.00
		—Columbia albums above have six eye logos around the perimeter of the label.—			
Columbia CL-2415	(M)	Tiger Woman	1965	8.00	20.00
Columbia CS-9215	(S)	Tiger Woman	1965	10.00	25.00
		—Columbia albums above have "350 Sound" labels.—			

KING, FREDDIE

King 762	(M)	Freddie King Sings The Blues	1961	60.00	150.00
King 773	(M)	Let's Hide Away And Dance Away	1961	60.00	150.00
King 821	(M)	Bossa Nova And Blues	1962	40.00	100.00
King 856	(M)	Freddie King Goes Surfin'	1963	20.00	50.00
King 856	(S)	Freddie King Goes Surfin'	1963	30.00	75.00
King 928	(M)	A Bonanza Of Instrumentals	1965	14.00	35.00
King 928	(S)	A Bonanza Of Instrumentals	1965	20.00	50.00
King 964	(M)	24 Vocals And Instrumentals	1966	10.00	25.00
King KS-1059	(S)	Hide Away	1969	10.00	25.00

KING, FREDDIE, & LULA REED & SONNY THOMPSON

King 777	(M)	Boy-Girl-Boy	1962	60.00	150.00

KING, JONATHAN

Parrot PA-61013	(M)	Or Then Again	1967	16.00	40.00
Parrot PAS-71013	(S)	Or Then Again	1967	20.00	50.00
		("Where The Sun Has Never Shown" is rechanneled on this album.)			
UK S-53101	(S)	Bubble Rock Is Here To Stay	1972	10.00	25.00
UK S-53104	(S)	Pandora's Box	1973	10.00	25.00

Morgana King started in Basin Street and related New York clubs in the '50s. Her background allowed her to record jazz and pop for a variety of labels through the '50s and '60s. While her recordings veered from jazzy to poppish to folkie, searching for a market, she nonetheless maintained a degree of credibility with fans of jazz vocals, who are very accepting of female singers' need to stray afield.

Label & Catalog #		Title	Year	VG+	NM
KING, DR. MARTIN LUTHER					
Dooto DTL-831	(M)	**Martin Luther King At Zion Hill**	1962	12.00	30.00
Mr. Maestro 1000	(M)	**The March On Washington**	1963	12.00	30.00
20th Century TFM-3100	(M)	**Freedom March On Washington**	1963	12.00	30.00
Gordy G-906	(M)	**The Great March To Freedom**	1963	12.00	30.00
Gordy G-908	(M)	**The Great March On Washington**	1963	12.00	30.00
Gordy G-929	(M)	**...Free At Last** (Gatefold cover)	1968	12.00	30.00
Gordy G-929	(M)	**...Free At Last** (Standard cover)	1968	8.00	20.00
KING, MORGANA					
EmArcy MG-36079	(M)	**For You, For Me, Forever More**	1956	30.00	75.00
		— EmArcy albums above have blue labels with silver print.—			
Mercury MG-20231	(M)	**Morgana King Sings The Blues**	1958	30.00	75.00
		— Mercury albums above have black labels with silver print.—			
United Arts. UAL-3020	(M)	**Let Me Love You**	1960	20.00	50.00
United Arts. UAS-6020	(S)	**Let Me Love You**	1960	30.00	75.00
		— U.A. albums above have red & black mono or gold & black stereo labels.—			
United Arts. UAL-3028	(M)	**Folk Songs Ala King**	1960	16.00	40.00
United Arts. UAS-6028	(S)	**Folk Songs Ala King**	1960	20.00	50.00
Camden CAL-543	(M)	**The Greatest Songs Ever Swung**	1959	8.00	20.00
Camden CAS-543	(S)	**The Greatest Songs Ever Swung**	1959	12.00	30.00
Ascot ALM-13014	(M)	**The Winter Of My Discontent**	1965	10.00	25.00
Ascot ALS-16014	(S)	**The Winter Of My Discontent**	1965	12.00	30.00
Ascot ALM-13019	(M)	**The End Of A Love Affair**	1965	10.00	25.00
Ascot ALS-16019	(S)	**The End Of A Love Affair**	1965	12.00	30.00
		(Ascot 13019 is a reissue of U.A. 40020.)			
Ascot ALM-13020	(M)	**Everybody Loves Saturday Night**	1965	10.00	25.00
Ascot ALS-16020	(S)	**Everybody Loves Saturday Night**	1965	12.00	30.00
Ascot ALM-13025	(M)	**More Morganna**	1965	10.00	25.00
Ascot ALS-16025	(S)	**More Morganna**	1965	12.00	30.00
Mainstream 56015	(M)	**With A Taste Of Honey**	1965	8.00	20.00
Mainstream S-6015	(S)	**With A Taste Of Honey**	1965	10.00	25.00
Mainstream 56052	(M)	**Miss Morgana King**	1965	8.00	20.00
Mainstream S-6052	(S)	**Miss Morgana King**	1965	10.00	25.00
Reprise R-6192	(M)	**It's A Quiet Thing**	1965	8.00	20.00
Reprise RS-6192	(S)	**It's A Quiet Thing**	1965	10.00	25.00
Reprise R-6205	(M)	**Wild Is Love**	1966	8.00	20.00
Reprise RS-6205	(S)	**Wild Is Love**	1966	10.00	25.00
Reprise R-6257	(M)	**Gemini Changes**	1967	8.00	20.00
Reprise RS-6257	(S)	**Gemini Changes**	1967	10.00	25.00
Verve V-5061	(M)	**I Know How It Feels**	1968	8.00	20.00
Verve V6-5061	(S)	**I Know How It Feels**	1968	10.00	25.00
KING, PEE WEE, & THE (NEW) GOLDEN WEST COWBOYS					
Pee Wee King is a pseudonym for Frank Kuczynski. The Golden West Cowboys feature Redd Stewart.					
RCA Victor LPM-3028	(10")	**Pee Wee King**	1954	40.00	100.00
RCA Victor LPM-3071	(10")	**Western Hits**	1954	40.00	100.00
RCA Victor LPM-3109	(10")	**Waltzes**	1955	40.00	100.00
RCA Victor LPM-3280	(10")	**Swing West**	1955	40.00	100.00
RCA Victor LPM-1237	(M)	**Swing West**	1955	20.00	50.00
Longhorn 1236	(M)	**The Legendary Pee Wee King**	1967	10.00	25.00
Briar M-102	(M)	**Golden Olde-Tyme Dances**	196?	20.00	50.00
Starday SLP-284	(M)	**Back Again With Songs**			
		That Made Them Famous (Yellow label)	1964	16.00	40.00
KING, PEGGY					
Columbia CL-2549	(10")	**Wish Upon A Star**	1955	20.00	50.00
Columbia CL-713	(M)	**Girl Meets Boy**	1955	14.00	35.00
Imperial LP-9026	(M)	**Peggy King**	1959	8.00	20.00
Imperial LP-12026	(S)	**Peggy King**	1959	12.00	30.00
KING CRIMSON					
Mobile Fidelity MFSL-075	(S)	**In The Court Of The Crimson King**	1980	20.00	60.00
Warner Bros. WBMS-119	(DJ)	**The Return Of King Crimson** (Interview)	1981	16.00	40.00
KING CURTIS					
Refer to The Buffalo Springfield / King Curtis.					
Atco 33-113	(M)	**Have Tenor Sax, Will Blow**	1959	30.00	75.00
Atco SD-33-113	(S)	**Have Tenor Sax, Will Blow**	1959	40.00	100.00

Label & Catalog #		Title	Year	VG+	NM
New Jazz NJLP-8237	(M)	The New Scene Of King Curtis	1960	30.00	75.00
		—New Jazz albums above have purple labels.—			
New Jazz NJLP-8237	(M)	The New Scene Of King Curtis	1965	12.00	30.00
		—New Jazz albums above have blue labels with a trident logo on the right side.—			
Everest LPBR-5121	(M)	Azure	1961	20.00	50.00
Everest SDBR-1121	(S)	Azure	1961	30.00	75.00
Tru-Sound TS-15001	(M)	Trouble In Mind	1961	20.00	50.00
Tru-Sound TS-15008	(M)	It's Party Time	1962	20.00	50.00
Tru-Sound TS-15009	(M)	Doin' The Dixie Twist	1962	20.00	50.00
Prestige PRLP-7222	(M)	Soul Meeting	1962	20.00	50.00
Prestige PRST-7222	(S)	Soul Meeting	1962	30.00	75.00
RCA Victor LPM-2492	(M)	Arthur Murray's Music			
		For Dancing: The Twist!	1962	10.00	25.00
RCA Victor LSM-2492	(S)	Arthur Murray's Music			
		For Dancing: The Twist!	1962	12.00	30.00
Enjoy ENLP-2001	(M)	Soul Twist	1962	40.00	100.00
Capitol T-1756	(M)	Country Soul	1963	12.00	30.00
Capitol ST-1756	(S)	Country Soul	1963	16.00	40.00
Capitol T-2095	(M)	Soul Serenade	1964	12.00	30.00
Capitol ST-2095	(S)	Soul Serenade	1964	16.00	40.00
Capitol T-2341	(M)	King Curtis Plays The Hits			
		Made Famous By Sam Cooke	1965	12.00	30.00
Capitol ST-2341	(S)	King Curtis Plays The Hits			
		Made Famous By Sam Cooke	1965	16.00	40.00
Capitol ST-2858	(S)	The Best Of King Curtis	1968	10.00	25.00
Clarion 615	(M)	The Great "K" Curtis	1964	10.00	25.00
Clarion SD-615	(S)	The Great "K" Curtis	1964	12.00	30.00
		(Clarion 615 is a reissue of Atco 113.)			
Atco 33-189	(M)	That Lovin' Feeling	1966	10.00	25.00
Atco SD-33-189	(S)	That Lovin' Feeling	1966	12.00	30.00
Atco 33-198	(M)	Live At Small's Paradise	1966	10.00	25.00
Atco SD-33-198	(S)	Live At Small's Paradise	1966	12.00	30.00
Atco 33-211	(M)	King Curtis Plays The Great Memphis Hits	1967	10.00	25.00
Atco SD-33-211	(S)	King Curtis Plays The Great Memphis Hits	1967	12.00	30.00
Atco 33-231	(M)	King Size Soul	1967	10.00	25.00
Atco SD-33-231	(S)	King Size Soul	1967	12.00	30.00
Atco 33-247	(M)	Sweet Soul	1968	10.00	25.00
Atco SD-33-247	(S)	Sweet Soul	1968	10.00	25.00
		—Atco albums above have multi-colored labels.—			
KING ERRISSON					
Westbound W-224	(S)	The Magic Man	1976	20.00	50.00
KING PINS, THE					
King 865	(M)	It Won't Be This Way Always	1963	60.00	150.00
KING'S HENCHMEN, THE: *Refer to* ALAN FREED					
KINGDOM					
Specialty 2135	(S)	Kingdom	1970	40.00	100.00

KINGSLEY, GERSHON
Gershon Kingsley is a composer, arranger and performer of "20th Century music," notably for the Moog synthesizer. Refer to Perrey-Kingsley.

Audio Fidelity AFSD-6222	(S)	Music To Moog By	1971	16.00	40.00
Audio Fidelity AFSD-6254	(S)	Popcorn—First Moog Quartet	1972	16.00	40.00
KINGSMEN, THE					
Wand WD-657	(M)	The Kingsmen In Person	1964	10.00	25.00
Wand WDS-657	(P)	The Kingsmen In Person	1964	12.00	30.00
Wand WD-659	(M)	More Great Sounds	1964	10.00	25.00
Wand WDS-659	(S)	More Great Sounds	1964	12.00	30.00
		(Wand 659 was originally issued with "Death Of An Angel")			
Wand WD-659	(M)	More Great Sounds	1964	8.00	20.00
Wand WDS-659	(S)	More Great Sounds	196?	10.00	25.00
		("Death Of An Angel" replaced by an uncredited instrumental)			
Wand WD-662	(M)	The Kingsmen, Volume 3	1965	8.00	20.00
Wand WDS-662	(S)	The Kingsmen, Volume 3	1965	10.00	25.00

Label & Catalog #		Title	Year	VG+	NM
Wand WD-670	(M)	The Kingsmen On Campus	1965	8.00	20.00
Wand WDS-670	(S)	The Kingsmen On Campus	1965	10.00	25.00
Wand WD-674	(M)	15 Great Hits	1966	8.00	20.00
Wand WDS-674	(P)	15 Great Hits	1966	10.00	25.00
Wand WD-675	(M)	Up And Away	1966	8.00	20.00
Wand WDS-675	(S)	Up And Away	1966	10.00	25.00

KINGSTON TRIO, THE

The most popular and influential vocal and instrumental group of the '50s' urban folk revival, members were Dave Guard, Nick Reynolds and Bob Shane. When Guard left in 1961 to assemble The Whiskeyhill Sinmgers he was replaced by John Stewart.

Label & Catalog #		Title	Year	VG+	NM
Capitol T-996	(M)	The Kingston Trio	1958	20.00	50.00
		— Capitol albums above have turquoise labels.—			
Capitol T-996	(M)	The Kingston Trio	1958	16.00	40.00
Capitol T-1107	(M)	From The Hungry i	1959	16.00	40.00
Capitol ST-1183	(S)	Stereo Concert	1959	20.00	50.00
Capitol T-1199	(M)	The Kingston Trio At Large	1959	12.00	30.00
Capitol ST-1199	(S)	The Kingston Trio At Large	1959	16.00	40.00
Capitol T-1258	(M)	Here We Go Again	1959	12.00	30.00
Capitol ST-1258	(S)	Here We Go Again	1959	16.00	40.00
Capitol T-1352	(M)	Sold Out	1960	12.00	30.00
Capitol ST-1352	(S)	Sold Out	1960	16.00	40.00
Capitol T-1407	(M)	String Along	1960	12.00	30.00
Capitol ST-1407	(S)	String Along	1960	16.00	40.00
Capitol T-1446	(M)	The Last Month Of The Year	1960	12.00	30.00
Capitol ST-1446	(S)	The Last Month Of The Year	1960	16.00	40.00
Capitol T-1474	(M)	Make Way!	1961	12.00	30.00
Capitol ST-1474	(S)	Make Way!	1961	16.00	40.00
Capitol T-1564	(M)	Goin' Places	1961	12.00	30.00
Capitol ST-1564	(S)	Goin' Places	1961	16.00	40.00
Capitol T-1612	(M)	Encores	1961	12.00	30.00
Capitol DT-1612	(E)	Encores	1961	8.00	20.00
Capitol T-1642	(M)	Close Up	1961	12.00	30.00
Capitol ST-1642	(S)	Close Up	1961	16.00	40.00
		— Capitol albums above have black labels with the logo on the left side.—			
Capitol T-1658	(M)	College Concert	1962	8.00	20.00
Capitol ST-1658	(S)	College Concert	1962	10.00	25.00
Capitol T-1747	(M)	Something Special	1962	8.00	20.00
Capitol ST-1747	(S)	Something Special	1962	10.00	25.00
Capitol T-1809	(M)	New Frontier	1962	8.00	20.00
Capitol ST-1809	(S)	New Frontier	1962	10.00	25.00
Capitol T-1871	(M)	Kingston Trio #16	1963	8.00	20.00
Capitol ST-1871	(S)	Kingston Trio #16	1963	10.00	25.00
Capitol T-1935	(M)	Sunny Side!	1963	8.00	20.00
Capitol ST-1935	(S)	Sunny Side!	1963	10.00	25.00
Capitol KAO-2005	(M)	Sing A Song With The Kingston Trio	1964	10.00	25.00
Capitol SKAO-2005	(S)	Sing A Song With The Kingston Trio	1964	12.00	30.00
		(Capitol 2005 features "instrumental background re-creations of their biggest hits!")			
Capitol T-2011	(M)	Time To Think	1963	10.00	25.00
Capitol ST-2011	(S)	Time To Think	1963	12.00	30.00
Capitol T-2081	(M)	Back In Town	1964	8.00	20.00
Capitol ST-2081	(S)	Back In Town	1964	10.00	25.00
Capitol TCL-2180	(M)	The Folk Era *(3 LPs with booklet)*	1964	16.00	40.00
Capitol STCL-2180	(S)	The Folk Era *(3 LPs with booklet)*	1964	20.00	50.00
		— Capitol albums above have black labels with the logo on top.—			
Decca DL-4613	(M)	The Kingston Trio: Nick-Bob-John	1965	12.00	30.00
Decca DL-74613	(S)	The Kingston Trio: Nick-Bob-John	1965	14.00	35.00
Decca DL-4656	(M)	Stay Awhile	1965	12.00	30.00
Decca DL-74656	(S)	Stay Awhile	1965	14.00	35.00
Decca DL-4694	(M)	Somethin' Else	1965	12.00	30.00
Decca DL-74694	(S)	Somethin' Else	1965	14.00	35.00
Decca DL-4758	(M)	Children In The Morning	1966	14.00	35.00
Decca DL-74758	(S)	Children In The Morning	1966	16.00	40.00
Tetragrammaton 5101	(S)	Once Upon A Time	1969	10.00	25.00
Longines SYS-5569-5574	(P)	American Gold *(6 LPs)*	1973	20.00	50.00

Label & Catalog #		Title	Year	VG+	NM

KINKS, THE

The original Kinks were Ray and Dave Davies, Mick Avory and Pete Quaife, replaced by John Dalton in '66.

Label & Catalog #		Title	Year	VG+	NM
Reprise R-6143	(M)	**You Really Got Me** *(White label promo)*	1965	200.00	400.00
Reprise R-6143	(M)	**You Really Got Me**	1965	16.00	40.00
Reprise RS-6143	(S)	**You Really Got Me**	1965	20.00	50.00
Reprise R-6158	(M)	**Kinks Size** *(White label promo)*	1965	80.00	200.00
Reprise R-6158	(M)	**Kinks Size**	1965	20.00	50.00
Reprise RS-6158	(E)	**Kinks Size**	1965	16.00	40.00
Reprise R-6173	(M)	**Kinda Kinks** *(White label promo)*	1965	80.00	200.00
Reprise R-6173	(M)	**Kinda Kinks**	1965	20.00	50.00
Reprise RS-6173	(E)	**Kinda Kinks**	1965	16.00	40.00
Reprise R-6184	(M)	**Kinks' Kinkdom** *(White label promo)*	1965	80.00	200.00
Reprise R-6184	(M)	**Kinks' Kinkdom**	1965	20.00	50.00
Reprise RS-6184	(E)	**Kinks' Kinkdom**	1965	16.00	40.00
Reprise R-6197	(M)	**Kink Kontroversy** *(White label promo)*	1966	80.00	200.00
Reprise R-6197	(M)	**Kink Kontroversy**	1966	20.00	50.00
Reprise RS-6197	(E)	**Kink Kontroversy**	1966	16.00	40.00
Reprise R-6217	(M)	**The Kinks' Greatest Hits**	1966	14.00	35.00
Reprise RS-6217	(E)	**The Kinks' Greatest Hits**	1966	10.00	25.00
Reprise RS-6217	(E)	**The Kinks' Greatest Hits** *(RCA Record Club)*	1966	20.00	50.00
Reprise R-6228	(M)	**Face To Face**	1967	16.00	40.00
Reprise RS-6228	(P)	**Face To Face**	1967	16.00	40.00
		(1/3 of RS-6228 is in bad stereo while the rest is rechanneled.)			
Reprise R-6260	(M)	**Live Kinks**	1967	14.00	35.00
Reprise RS-6260	(S)	**Live Kinks**	1967	10.00	25.00
Reprise R-6272	(M)	**Something Else By The Kinks** *(White label)*	1968	150.00	300.00
Reprise RS-6272	(S)	**Something Else By The Kinks**	1968	14.00	35.00
		— Reprise albums above have pink, gold & green labels. —			
Reprise RS-6327	(S)	**The Kinks Are The Village Green Preservation Society**	1969	14.00	35.00
Reprise PRO-328	(P)	**God Save The Kinks Box**	1969	200.00	400.00
		(PRO-328 is a promotional boxed set includes a postcard, a decal, a bag of grass, a Union Jack pin, a letter, Kinks consumer guide, a "God Save The Kinks" button and an album, "Then, Now And In Between," all included in the price.)			
Reprise PRO-328	(P)	**Then, Now And In Between**	1969	40.00	100.00
		("Then, Now" was included in the "God Save The Kinks" box above.)			
Reprise RS-6366	(S)	**Arthur (Or The Decline & Fall Of The British Empire)**	1969	10.00	25.00
Reprise SMAS-93034	(S)	**Arthur (Or The Decline & Fall Of The British Empire)** *(Capitol Record Club)*	1971	14.00	35.00
Reprise RS-6423	(S)	**Lola Vs. The Powerman & The Moneygoround, Part 1**	1970	10.00	25.00
		— Reprise albums above have brown & orange labels with a "W7" and ":r" logos on top. —			
Reprise MS-2127	(P)	**The Great Lost Kinks Album**	1973	20.00	50.00
RCA Victor LSP-4644	(S)	**Muswell Hillbillie** *(Orange label)*	1971	12.00	30.00
Arista AL-4106	(S)	**Sleepwalker** *(White label promo)*	1977	10.00	25.00
Arista AL-4167	(S)	**Misfits** *(White label promo)*	1978	10.00	25.00
Arista SP-69	(S)	**Low Budget Radio Interview**	1979	16.00	40.00
MCA 17281	(S)	**A Look At "Think Visual"** *(Plain jacket)*	1986	20.00	50.00

KIRBY, BEECHER "PETE": *Refer to* BROTHER OSWALD

KIRBY STONE FOUR, THE

Label & Catalog #		Title	Year	VG+	NM
Cadence CLP-1023	(M)	**Man I Flipped**	1958	12.00	30.00
Columbia CL-1211	(M)	**Baubles, Bangles And Beads**	1958	8.00	20.00
Columbia CS-8014	(S)	**Baubles, Bangles And Beads**	1959	10.00	25.00
Columbia CL-1290	(M)	**The "Go" Sound Of The Kirby Stone Four**	1959	8.00	20.00
Columbia CS-8130	(S)	**The "Go" Sound Of The Kirby Stone Four**	1959	10.00	25.00
Columbia CL-1356	(M)	**The Kirny Stone Touch**	1959	8.00	20.00
Columbia CS-8164	(S)	**The Kirny Stone Touch**	1959	10.00	25.00
Columbia CL-1646	(M)	**The Kirby Stone Four At The Playboy Club**	1960	8.00	20.00
Columbia CS-8446	(S)	**The Kirby Stone Four At The Playboy Club**	1960	10.00	25.00
Columbia CL-1714	(M)	**Guys And Dolls**	1961	8.00	20.00
Columbia CS-8514	(S)	**Guys And Dolls**	1961	10.00	25.00

— Columbia albums above have three white "eye" logos on each side of the spindle hole. —

Label & Catalog #		Title	Year	VG+	NM

KISS

The original Kiss consisted of Peter Criss, Ace Frehley, Gene Simmons and Paul Stanley. Criss left in '81 and was replaced by Eric Carr; while Frehely left in '82 was replaced by Vinnie Vincent.

Casablanca NBLP-9001	(S)	**Kiss** (White label promo)	1974	60.00	150.00
Casablanca NBLP-9001	(S)	**Kiss**	1974	20.00	50.00
Casablanca NBLP-7001	(S)	**Kiss**	1974	10.00	25.00
Casablanca NBLP-7006	(S)	**Hotter Than Hell**	1974	10.00	25.00
Casablanca NBLP-7016	(S)	**Dressed To Kill** (Embossed cover)	1975	10.00	25.00
Casablanca NBLP-7020	(S)	**Alive!**	1975	10.00	25.00
Casablanca NBLP-7025	(S)	**Destroyer**	1976	10.00	25.00
		— Casablanca albums above have blue/grey with a smoking man on the left. —			
Casablanca NBLP-7032	(S)	**Kiss: The Originals**	1976	60.00	150.00
		(Issued with a bonus booklet, four Kiss cards and a Kiss Army sticker. Repackages 7001, 7006 and 7016.)			
Casablanca NBLP-7032	(S)	**Kiss: The Originals** (Without inserts)	1976	40.00	100.00
Casablanca NBLP-7037	(DJ)	**Rock And Roll Over Special Edition**	1976	16.00	40.00
		— Casablanca albums above have labels with a desert scene with three camels and "Casablanca" on top. —			
Casablanca NBLP-7032	(S)	**Kiss: The Originals** (Includes inserts)	1977	40.00	100.00
Casablanca NBLP-7032	(S)	**Kiss: The Originals** (Without inserts)	1977	30.00	75.00
Casablanca NBLP-7057	(S)	**Love Gun** (Includes a punchout sheet)	1977	10.00	25.00
Casablanca NBLP-7076	(S)	**Alive II** (Includes booklet and "tattoos.")	1977	40.00	100.00
		(Original pressing covers of Casablanca 7076 erroneously list "Take Me," "Hooligan" and "Do You Love Me" on the back.)			
Casablanca NBLP-7076	(S)	**Alive II** (Includes booklet and "tattoos.")	1977	10.00	25.00
Casablanca NBLP-7100	(S)	**Double Platinum** (2 LPs)	1978	12.00	30.00
		(Issued with a bonus cardboard platinum album award.)			
Casablanca NBLP-7120	(S)	**Gene Simmons** (With poster)	1978	14.00	35.00
Casablanca NBLP-7120	(S)	**Gene Simmons** (Without poster)	1978	10.00	25.00
Casablanca NBLP-7122	(S)	**Gene Simmons** (Picture disc)	1978	20.00	50.00
Casablanca NBLP-7121	(S)	**Ace Frehley** (With poster)	1978	14.00	35.00
Casablanca NBLP-7121	(S)	**Ace Frehley** (Without poster)	1978	10.00	25.00
Casablanca NBLP-7121	(S)	**Ace Frehley** (Picture disc)	1978	20.00	50.00
Casablanca NBLP-7122	(S)	**Peter Criss** (With poster)	1978	14.00	35.00
Casablanca NBLP-7122	(S)	**Peter Criss** (Without poster)	1978	10.00	25.00
Casablanca NBLP-7122	(S)	**Peter Criss** (Picture disc)	1978	20.00	50.00
Casablanca NBLP-7123	(S)	**Paul Stanley** (With poster)	1978	14.00	35.00
Casablanca NBLP-7123	(S)	**Paul Stanley** (Without poster)	1978	10.00	25.00
Casablanca NBLP-7123	(S)	**Paul Stanley** (Picture disc)	1978	20.00	50.00
		— Casablanca albums above have labels with a desert scene with a film crew and "Manufactured by Casablanca" on the bottom. —			
Casablanca NBLP-7261	(S)	**Music From The Elder** (Soundtrack)	1981	14.00	35.00
		(Includes a paper inner sleeve with lyrics on it.)			
		— Casablanca albums above have labels with a desert scene with a film crew and "Manufactured by Polygram" on the bottom. —			
Mercury 836 8871-	(S)	**Smashes, Thrashes And Hits** (Picture disc)	1988	12.00	30.00
		— Special Promotional Albums —			
Integrity Entertainment	(S)	**Wherehouse Albums Of The Wereek 5/5/78**	1978	30.00	75.00
		(In-store sampler features tracks from "Double Platinum" on one side and tracks from the "FM" soundtrack on the other.)			
Casablanca Kiss-76	(DJ)	**Special Album For Their Summer Tour**	1978	30.00	75.00
Casablanca NB 20128	(DJ)	**A Taste Of Platinum**	1978	16.00	40.00
Casablanca NB 20137	(DJ)	**Solo Album Sampler**	1978	16.00	40.00
Mercury 792	(DJ)	**First Kiss, Last Licks**	1990	40.00	100.00

KIT KATS, THE

Jamie LPM-3029	(M)	**It's Just A Matter Of Time**	1966	20.00	50.00
Jamie LPS-3029	(E)	**It's Just A Matter Of Time**	1966	16.00	40.00
Jamie LPM-3032	(M)	**Do Their Thing Live**	1967	16.00	40.00
Jamie LPS-3032	(S)	**Do Their Thing Live**	1967	20.00	50.00

KITCHEN CINQ, THE

L.H.I. 12000	(M)	**Everything But The Kitchen Cinq**	1967	10.00	25.00
L.H.I. 12000	(S)	**Everything But The Kitchen Cinq**	1967	12.00	30.00

KITT, EARTHA

RCA Victor LOC-1008	(M)	**New Faces Of 1952** (Original Cast)	1952	30.00	75.00
RCA Victor LPM-3062	(10")	**Songs**	1953	30.00	75.00
RCA Victor LPM-3187	(10")	**That Bad Eartha**	1953	30.00	75.00
RCA Victor LPM-1109	(M)	**Down To Eartha**	1955	20.00	50.00

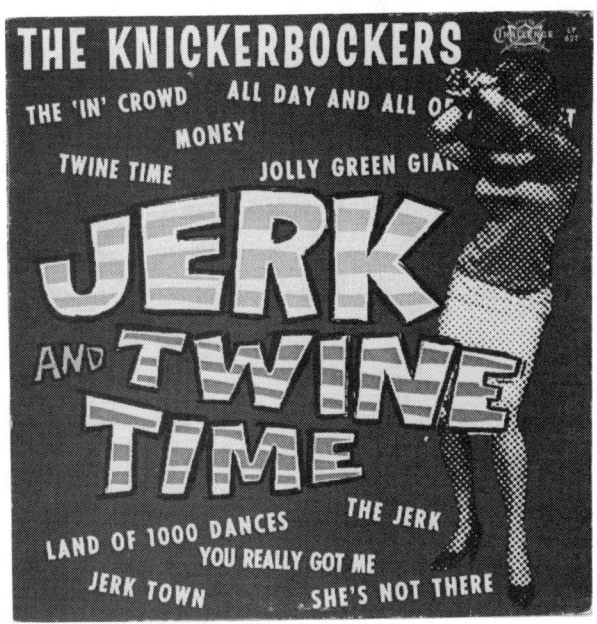

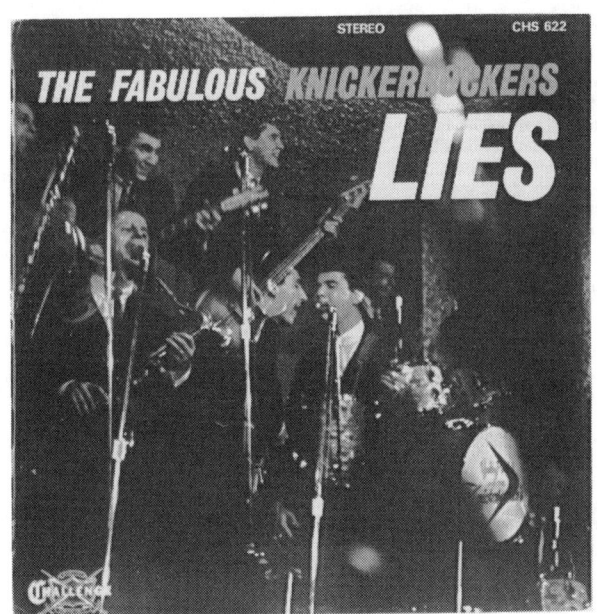

The Knickerbockers, featuring former Royal Teen Buddy Randell as lead singer, were able to imitate many of the '60s rock and soul greats: Their live shows often featured impeccably righteous versions of "You've Lost That Lovin' Feeling." Their first album, Sing And Sync Along With Lloyd (Not shown here), is a "trick track" album, with five sets of parallel grooves on the both sides. When the needle is dropped onto the outer edge of the disc, where exactly it lands decides which song is played. Their second— and rarest— album is Jerk And Twine Time and, while no stereo copies are known to exist, most of the other Challenge albums of this period were issued in both mono and stereo. Their third album contains their big hit, "Lies," a remarkable Beatles sound-alike that convinced more than a few people that it was the Fab Four's follow-up to "Yesterday."

Label & Catalog #		Title	Year	VG+	NM
RCA Victor LPM-1183	(M)	**That Bad Eartha**	1955	20.00	50.00
RCA Victor LPM-1300	(M)	**Thursday's Child**	1956	20.00	50.00
RCA Victor LPM-1661	(M)	**St. Louis Blues**	1958	14.00	35.00
RCA Victor LSP-1661	(S)	**St. Louis Blues**	1958	20.00	50.00
		— RCA mono albums above have "Long Play" on the bottom of the label;			
		stereo albums have "Living Stereo" on the bottom.—			
Kapp KL-1162	(M)	**The Fabulous Eartha Kitt**	1959	10.00	25.00
Kapp KS-3046	(S)	**The Fabulous Eartha Kitt**	1959	14.00	35.00
Kapp KL-1192	(M)	**Eartha Kitt Revisited**	1960	10.00	25.00
Kapp KS-3192	(S)	**Eartha Kitt Revisited**	1960	14.00	35.00
MGM E-4009	(M)	**Bad But Beautiful**	1962	10.00	25.00
MGM SE-4009	(S)	**Bad But Beautiful**	1962	14.00	35.00
Decca DL-4635	(M)	**Eartha Kitt Sings In Spanish**	1965	12.00	30.00
Decca DL-74635	(S)	**Eartha Kitt Sings In Spanish**	1965	16.00	40.00

KNICKERBOCKERS, THE

Label & Catalog #		Title	Year	VG+	NM
Challenge LP-12-6-64	(DJ)	**Sing And Sync Along With Lloyd**	1964	60.00	150.00
Challenge CH-621	(M)	**Jerk And Twine Time**	1965	150.00	300.00
Challenge CHS-621	(S)	**Jerk And Twine Time**	1965	*Unreleased?*	
Challenge CH-622	(M)	**Lies** *(White label promo)*	1966	60.00	150.00
Challenge CH-622	(M)	**Lies**	1966	30.00	75.00
Challenge CHS-622	(S)	**Lies**	1966	60.00	150.00

KNIGHT, CHRIS, & MAUREEN McCORMICK

Label & Catalog #		Title	Year	VG+	NM
Paramount PAS-6062	(S)	**Chris Knight And Maureen McCormick**	1973	40.00	100.00
		(Chris and Maureen were members of TV's Brady Bunch			
		and this LP could be considered the group's last album.)			

KNIGHT, CURTIS, & JIMI HENDRIX: *Refer to* **JIMI HENDRIX & CURTIS KNIGHT**

KNIGHT, GLADYS, & THE PIPS

Label & Catalog #		Title	Year	VG+	NM
Fury 1003	(M)	**Letter Full Of Tears**	1962	200.00	400.00
Maxx 3000	(M)	**Gladys Knight & The Pips**	1964	40.00	100.00
Sphere Sound SR-7006	(M)	**Gladys Knight & The Pips**	1965	20.00	50.00
Sphere Sound SSR-7006	(E)	**Gladys Knight & The Pips**	1965	16.00	40.00
Soul S-706	(M)	**Everybody Needs Love**	1967	8.00	20.00
Soul SS-706	(S)	**Everybody Needs Love**	1967	10.00	25.00
Soul S-707	(M)	**Feelin' Bluesy** *(Promo label)*	1968	16.00	40.00
Soul SS-707	(S)	**Feelin' Bluesy**	1968	10.00	25.00

KNIGHT, JEAN

Label & Catalog #		Title	Year	VG+	NM
Stax STS-2045	(S)	**Mr. Big Stuff**	1971	10.00	25.00

KNIGHT, ROBERT

Label & Catalog #		Title	Year	VG+	NM
Sound Stage-7 SSM-7000	(M)	**Everlasting Love**	1967	12.00	30.00
Sound Stage-7 SM-17000	(S)	**Everlasting Love**	1967	16.00	40.00

KNIGHT, SONNY

Label & Catalog #		Title	Year	VG+	NM
Aura AR-3001	(M)	**If You Want This Love**	1964	8.00	20.00
Aura AS-3001	(S)	**If You Want This Love**	1964	10.00	25.00

KNIGHT, TERRY, & THE PACK
The Pack features Mark Farner and Don Brewer, later of Grand Funk Railroad.

Label & Catalog #		Title	Year	VG+	NM
Lucky Eleven LE-8000	(M)	**Terry Knight & The Pack**	1966	10.00	25.00
Lucky Eleven LES-8000	(S)	**Terry Knight & The Pack**	1966	12.00	30.00
Lucky Eleven LE-8001	(S)	**Track On!**	1966	10.00	25.00
Lucky Eleven LES-8001	(S)	**Track On!**	1966	12.00	30.00

KNIGHTS, THE
The Knights are a creation of Gary Usher & Co.

Label & Catalog #		Title	Year	VG+	NM
Capitol T-2189	(M)	**Hot Rod High**	1964	100.00	250.00
Capitol DT-2189	(E)	**Hot Rod High**	1964	150.00	300.00

KNIGHTS, THE

Label & Catalog #		Title	Year	VG+	NM
Ace MG-200854	(M)	**Across The Road**	1966	60.00	150.00
Ace MG-201303	(M)	**The Knights 1967**	1967	50.00	125.00

KNIGHTS, THE

Label & Catalog #		Title	Year	VG+	NM
Justice JLP-156	(S)	**On The Move**	196?	150.00	300.00

Label & Catalog #		Title	Year	VG+	NM
KNOCKOUTS, THE					
Tribute 1202	(M)	Go Ape With The Knockouts	1964	80.00	200.00
KNOWBODY ELSE					
Members of Knowbody Else later recorded as Black Oak Arkansas.					
Hip HIS-7003	(S)	Knowbody Else	1969	40.00	100.00
KNOTTS, DON					
United Arts. UAL-4090	(M)	An Evening With Me	1961	8.00	20.00
United Arts. UAS-5090	(S)	An Evening With Me	1961	10.00	25.00
KNOX, BUDDY					
Roulette R-25003	(M)	Buddy Knox (White label promo)	1957	100.00	400.00
Roulette R-25003	(M)	Buddy Knox (Black label)	1957	60.00	150.00
Liberty LRP-3251	(M)	Buddy Knox's Golden Hits	1962	12.00	30.00
Liberty LSP-7251	(P)	Buddy Knox's Golden Hits	1962	16.00	40.00
		(Contains rerecorded versions of the Roulette material.)			
United Arts. UAS-6689	(S)	Gypsy Man	1969	10.00	25.00
KNOX, BUDDY, & JIMMY BOWEN					
Roulette R-25048	(M)	Buddy Knox & Jimmy Bowen (Black label)	1958	60.00	150.00
		(Buddy Holly plays guitar on "All For You.")			
KODAKS, THE / THE STARLITES					
Sphere Sound SR-7005	(M)	The Kodaks Vs. The Starlites	1965	60.00	150.00
Sphere Sound SRR-7005	(E)	The Kodaks Vs. The Starlites	1965	40.00	100.00
KOERNER, "SPIDER" JOHN					
Elektra EKL-290	(M)	Spider Blues	1965	10.00	25.00
Elektra EKS-7290	(S)	Spider Blues	1965	12.00	30.00
Elektra EKS-74041	(S)	Running, Jumping, Standing Still	1969	10.00	25.00
KOERNER, JOHN; DAVE RAY & TONY GLOVER					
Elektra EKL-240	(M)	Blue Rags And Hollers	1963	10.00	25.00
Elektra EKS-7240	(S)	Blue Rags And Hollers	1963	12.00	30.00
Elektra EKL-267	(M)	Lots More Blues Rags And Hollers	1964	10.00	25.00
Elektra EKS-7267	(S)	Lots More Blues Rags And Hollers	1964	12.00	30.00
Elektra EKL-305	(M)	The Return Of Koerner, Ray & Glover	1966	8.00	20.00
Elektra EKS-7305	(S)	The Return Of Koerner, Ray & Glover	1966	10.00	25.00
KOFFMAN, MOE: *Refer to* **GOLDMINE'S PRICE GUIDE TO COLLECTIBLE JAZZ ALBUMS**					
KOLE, JERRY, & THE STROKERS					
Jerry Kole is a pseudonym for Jerry Cole. Refer to Ritchie Valens / Jerry Kole.					
Crown CLP-5385	(M)	Hot Rod Alley	1963	12.00	30.00
Crown CST-385	(S)	Hot Rod Alley	1963	16.00	40.00
KOOL & THE GANG					
De-Lite DSR-2003	(S)	Kool & The Gang	1969	10.00	25.00
KOPPERFIELD					
Kopperdisc 5014N5	(S)	Tales Untold	1974	200.00	400.00
KORNER, ALEXIS					
Warner Bros. 2XS-1966	(S)	Bootleg Him (2 LPs with Charlie Watts)	1972	10.00	25.00
KOSSOY SISTERS, THE					
Irene Kossoy are autoharp, banjo, guitar and mandolin players and singers of traditional folk songs.					
Tradition TLP-1018	(M)	Bowling Green & Other Folksongs From The			
		Southern Mountains (With Erik Darling)	1956	12.00	30.00
KOTTKE, LEO					
Oblivion 1	(S)	Live At The Scholar Coffee House	197?	10.00	25.00
KRABER, TONY					
Tony Kraber is a singer of traditional folk songs. Refer to Jean Ritchie & Tony Kraber.					
Mercury MG-20003	(10")	Songs Of The Old Chisolm Trail	1950	20.00	50.00
Mercury MG-20008	(M)	Songs Of The Old Chisolm Trail	1956	12.00	30.00

Label & Catalog #		Title	Year	VG+	NM

KRACKER
| Primo PS-001 | (S) | **Kracker** | 1978 | 12.00 | 30.00 |

KRAL, IRENE: *Refer to* GOLDMINE'S PRICE GUIDE TO COLLECTIBLE ALBUMS

KRAMER, BILLY J., & THE DAKOTAS
Imperial LP-9267	(M)	**Little Children**	1964	20.00	50.00
Imperial LP-12267	(P)	**Little Children**	1964	30.00	75.00
		— Imperial mono albums above have black labels with stars on top;			
		stereo albums are black with silver print.—			
Imperial LP-9267	(M)	**Little Children**	1964	12.00	30.00
Imperial LP-12267	(P)	**Little Children**	1964	16.00	40.00
Imperial LP-9273	(M)	**I'll Keep You Satisfied/From A Window**	1964	12.00	30.00
Imperial LP-12273	(S)	**I'll Keep You Satisfied/From A Window**	1964	16.00	40.00
		("I'll Keep You Satisfied," "Sugar Babe," "I'll Be On My Way," "From A			
		Window," "Second To None," and "The Cruel Surf" are rechanneled.)			
Imperial LP-9291	(M)	**Trains And Boats And Planes**	1965	14.00	35.00
Imperial LP-12291	(E)	**Trains And Boats And Planes**	1965	10.00	25.00
		— Imperial albums above have black & pink labels.—			

KRAZY KATS, THE
| Damon 12478 | (S) | **Movin' Out** | 196? | 30.00 | 75.00 |

KREED
| Visions Of Sound 71-56 | (S) | **This Is Kreed** | 1971 | 360.00 | 600.00 |

KRISTYL
| (No label) | (M) | **Kristyl** | 196? | 150.00 | 300.00 |

KUBAN, BOB, & THE IN-MEN
| Musicland LP-3500 | (M) | **Look Out For The Cheater** | 1966 | 12.00 | 30.00 |
| Musicland SLP-3500 | (S) | **Look Out For The Cheater** | 1966 | 16.00 | 40.00 |

KUBIKS, THE
| Prestige Int. PRLP-13051 | (M) | **Czechoslovakian Folk Songs** | 1962 | 12.00 | 30.00 |

KUPFERBERG, TULI
Tuli was formerly a member of The Fugs.
| ESP-Disk' 1035 | (M) | **No Deposit No Return** *(Gold vinyl)* | 1967 | 24.00 | 60.00 |
| ESP-Disk' 1035 | (M) | **No Deposit No Return** | 1967 | 16.00 | 40.00 |

KUSTOM KINGS, THE
| Smash MGS-27051 | (M) | **Kustom City, U.S.A.** | 1964 | 50.00 | 125.00 |
| Smash SRS-67051 | (S) | **Kustom City, U.S.A.** | 1964 | 80.00 | 200.00 |

KWESKIN, JIM/JIM KWESKIN & THE JUG BAND
The Jug Band consisted of Maria D'Amato (later Maria Muldauer), Richard Greene, Bill Keith, Mel Lyman, Geoff Muldauer and Fritz Richmond.
Vanguard VRS-9139	(M)	**Jim Kweskin & The Jug Band**	1965	8.00	20.00
Vanguard VSD-2158	(S)	**Jim Kweskin & The Jug Band**	1965	10.00	25.00
Vanguard VRS-9163	(M)	**Jug Band Music**	1966	8.00	20.00
Vanguard VSD-79163	(S)	**Jug Band Music**	1966	10.00	25.00
Vanguard VRS-9188	(M)	**Relax Your Mind**	1966	8.00	20.00
Vanguard VSD-79188	(S)	**Relax Your Mind**	1966	10.00	25.00
Vanguard VRS-9234	(M)	**See Reverse Side For Title**	1966	8.00	20.00
Vanguard VSD-79234	(S)	**See Reverse Side For Title**	1966	10.00	25.00
Vanguard VRS-9243	(M)	**Jump For Joy**	1967	8.00	20.00
Vanguard VSD-79243	(S)	**Jump For Joy**	1967	8.00	20.00
Vanguard VSD-79270	(S)	**The Best Of Jim Kweskin & The Jug Band**	1968	10.00	25.00
Vanguard VSD-79278	(S)	**Whatever Happened To Those Good Old Days**	1968	8.00	20.00
Reprise R-6266	(M)	**Garden Of Joy**	1967	8.00	20.00
Reprise RS-6266	(S)	**Garden Of Joy**	1967	10.00	25.00

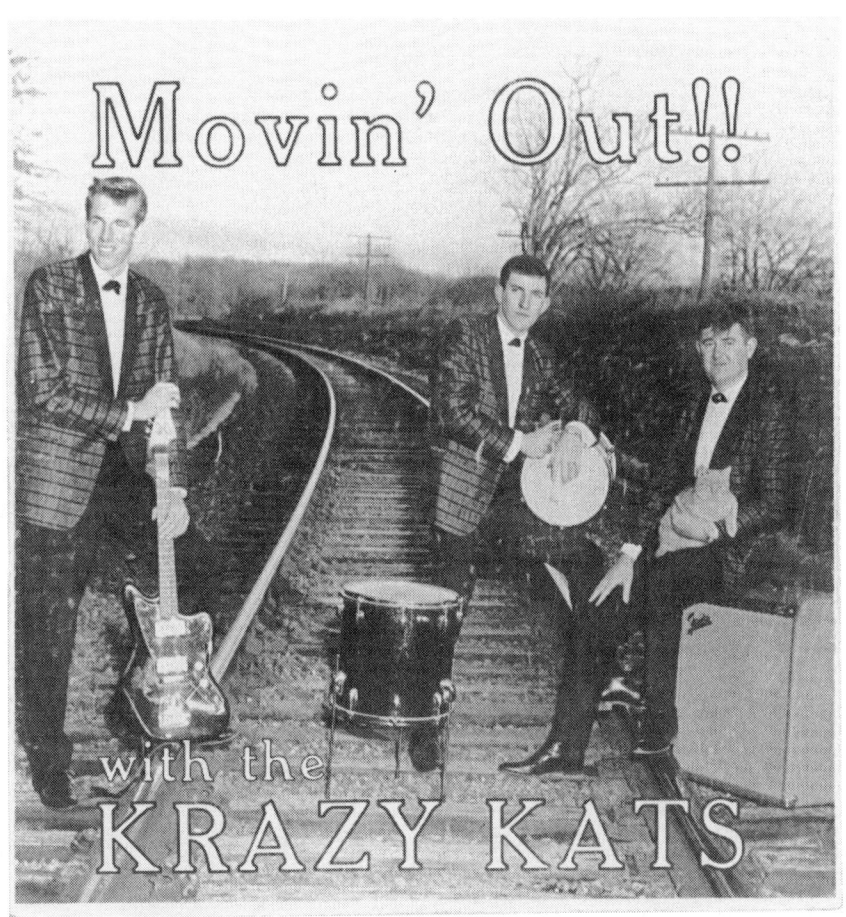

What can I say about the Krazy Kats? That they named themselves after the whimsically surreal creation of George Herriman. That they were a trio. That the guitar player's guitar casts a shadow but that he doesn't. And neither do the others. Can I therefore say that they were undead?

L

LaBELLE, PATTI &THE BLUEBELLES/THE BLUEBELLES

Newtown 631	(M)	Sweethearts Of The Apollo	1963	200.00	400.00
Newtown 632	(M)	Sleigh Bells, Jingle Bells And Blue Bells	1963	150.00	300.00
Parkway P-7043	(M)	The Bluebelles On Stage (With bonus single)	1965	60.00	150.00
Parkway P-7043	(M)	The Bluebelles On Stage (Without single)	1965	50.00	125.00
Atlantic 8119	(M)	Over The Rainbow	1966	12.00	30.00
Atlantic SD-8119	(S)	Over The Rainbow	1966	16.00	40.00
Atlantic 8147	(M)	Dreamer	1967	12.00	30.00
Atlantic SD-8147	(S)	Dreamer	1967	16.00	40.00

LABRECQUE, JACQUES

London LB-957	(10")	Canadian Folksongs (Chansons Populaires du Canada)	1954	20.00	50.00
Folkways FG-3560	(M)	Folk Songs Of French Canada	195?	12.00	30.00

LaFARGE, PETER
Peter LaFarge, of Pima Indian heritage, was a guitar player, singer and writer of topical folk music.

Verve/Folkways FV-9004	(M)	Peter LaFarge Sings Women Blues	1965	8.00	20.00
Verve/Folkways FVS-9004	(S)	Peter LaFarge Sings Women Blues	1965	10.00	25.00

LAINE, DENNY
Denny Laine was an original member of The Moody Blues.

Capitol ST-11588	(S)	Holly Days (Produced by Paul McCartney)	1976	20.00	50.00
		(Original copies were issued as advanced promos in plain cardboard jackets with a 1976 copyright date on the label.)			

LAINE, FRANKIE
Refer to The Four Lads; Jo Stafford & Frankie Laine.

Mercury MG-25007	(10")	Favorites	1949	20.00	50.00
Mercury MG-25024	(10")	Songs From The Heart	1950	20.00	50.00
Mercury MG-25025	(10")	Frankie Laine	1950	20.00	50.00
Mercury MG-25026	(10")	Frankie Laine	1950	20.00	50.00
Mercury MG-25027	(10")	Frankie Laine	1950	20.00	50.00
Mercury MG-25097	(10")	Mr. Rhythm Sings	1951	20.00	50.00
Mercury MG-25082	(10")	Christmas Favorites	1951	20.00	50.00
Mercury MG-25124	(10")	Listen To Laine	1952	20.00	50.00
Mercury MG-20069	(M)	Songs By Frankie Laine	1956	14.00	35.00
Mercury MG-20080	(M)	That's My Desire	1957	14.00	35.00
Mercury MG-20083	(M)	Frankie Laine Sings For Us	1957	14.00	35.00
Mercury MG-20085	(M)	Concert Date	1957	14.00	35.00
Mercury MG-20105	(M)	With All My Heart	1957	14.00	35.00
Mercury MG-20587	(M)	Frankie Laine's Golden Hits	1960	10.00	25.00
Columbia CL-6200	(10")	One For My Baby	1952	20.00	50.00
Columbia CL-6278	(10")	Mr. Rhythm	1954	20.00	50.00
Columbia CL-2504	(10")	Lover's Laine	1955	20.00	50.00
Columbia CL-2548	(10")	One For My Baby	1955	20.00	50.00
Columbia CL-625	(M)	Command Performance	1956	14.00	35.00
Columbia CL-808	(M)	Jazz Spectacular	1956	12.00	30.00
Columbia CL-975	(M)	Rockin'	1957	12.00	30.00
Columbia CL-1116	(M)	Foreign Affair	1958	12.00	30.00
Columbia CL-1231	(M)	Frankie Laine's Greatest Hits	1959	10.00	25.00
Columbia CL-1224	(M)	Torchin'	1959	8.00	20.00
Columbia CS-8024	(S)	Torchin'	1959	10.00	25.00
Columbia CL-1287	(M)	Reunion In Rhythm	1959	8.00	20.00
Columbia CS-8087	(S)	Reunion In Rhythm	1959	10.00	25.00
Columbia CL-1319	(M)	You Are My Love	1959	8.00	20.00
Columbia CS-8119	(S)	You Are My Love	1959	10.00	25.00
Columbia CL-1388	(M)	Frankie Laine, Balladeer	1959	8.00	20.00
Columbia CS-8188	(S)	Frankie Laine, Balladeer	1959	10.00	25.00
Columbia CL-1615	(M)	Hell Bent For Leather!	1959	10.00	25.00
Columbia CS-8415	(S)	Hell Bent For Leather!	1959	12.00	30.00

Label & Catalog #		Title	Year	VG+	NM
Columbia CL-1696	(M)	**Deuces Wild**	1959	8.00	20.00
Columbia CS-8496	(S)	**Deuces Wild**	1959	10.00	25.00
		— Columbia albums above have three white "eye" logos on each side of the spindle hole.—			

LAMBERT, DAVE: *Refer to* GOLDMINE'S PRICE GUIDE TO COLLECTIBLE JAZZ ALBUMS

LAMBERT, HENDRICKS & BAVAN: *Refer to* GOLDMINE'S PRICE GUIDE TO COLLECTIBLE JAZZ ALBUMS

LAMBERT, HENDRICKS & ROSS: *Refer to* GOLDMINE'S PRICE GUIDE TO COLLECTIBLE JAZZ ALBUMS

LAMEGO, DANNY, & HIS JUMPIN' JACKS

Forget-Me-Not 105A	(M)	**The Big Weekend**	1964	40.00	100.00

LAMOUR, DOROTHY

Decca DL-5115	(10")	**Favorite Hawaiian Songs**	1950	30.00	75.00
Design DLP-45	(M)	**The Road To Romance**	196?	14.00	35.00
Design SDLP-45	(E)	**The Road To Romance**	196?	8.00	20.00

LANCE, MAJOR

OKeh OKM-12105	(M)	**The Monkey Time**	1963	12.00	30.00
OKeh OKS-14105	(S)	**The Monkey Time**	1963	16.00	40.00
		("Monkey Time" and "Mama Didn't Know" are rechanneled.)			
OKeh OKM-12106	(M)	**Um, Um, Um, Um, Um, Um**	1964	12.00	30.00
OKeh OKS-14106	(P)	**Um, Um, Um, Um, Um, Um**	1964	16.00	40.00
OKeh OKM-12110	(M)	**Major Lance's Greatest Hits**	1965	10.00	25.00
OKeh OKS-14110	(S)	**Major Lance's Greatest Hits**	1965	12.00	30.00
		("Monkey Time" is rechanneled on this album.)			

LANCELOT LINK

ABC S-715	(S)	**Lancelot Link & The Evolution Revolution**	1970	10.00	25.00

LANCERS, THE

Trend TL-1009	(10")	**The Lancers**	1954	16.00	40.00
Coral CRL-57100	(M)	**Dixieland Ball**	1957	10.00	25.00

LANCERS, THE

Imperial LP-9075	(M)	**Concert In Contrasts**	1959	14.00	35.00
Imperial LP-12023	(S)	**Concert In Contrasts**	1959	20.00	50.00

LANCHESTER, ELSA

Verve MGV-15015	(M)	**Cockney London**	1960	16.00	40.00
Verve MGV-15024	(M)	**Elsa Lanchester Herself**	1961	16.00	40.00
		— Verve albums above have "Verve Records, Inc." on the bottom of the label.—			

LANDON, MICHAEL: *Refer to* LORNE GREENE & DAN BLOCKER & MIKE LANDON & PERNELL ROBERTS

LANE, ABBE

Mercury MG-20643	(M)	**Abbe Lane** **With Xavier Cugat & His Orchestra**	1961	10.00	25.00
Mercury SR-60643	(S)	**Abbe Lane** **With Xavier Cugat & His Orchestra**	1961	12.00	30.00

LANE, VICKI

RCA Victor LPM-2056	(M)	**I Swing For You**	1959	12.00	30.00

LANGFORD, FRANCIS

Chanford KB-2175/6	(DJ)	**The Francis Langford Show**	1960	60.00	150.00
		(This TV soundtrack includes the Three Stooges singing "Que Sea Sera" to Doris Day's mother!)			

LANGDON, DORY

Verve V-2101	(M)	**Leprechauns Are Upon Me**	1957	16.00	40.00
		— Verve albums above have "Verve Records, Inc." on the bottom of the label.—			

Label & Catalog #		Title	Year	VG+	NM

LANGSTAFF, JOHN
Classically trained John Langstaff is a singer of traditional folk songs.

Tradition TLP-1009	(M)	**John Langstaff Sings Folksongs And Ballads**	1956	12.00	30.00

LARKS, THE
The Larks feature Don Julian.

Money MY-1102	(M)	**The Jerk**	1965	12.00	30.00
Money MS-1102	(S)	**The Jerk**	1965	16.00	40.00
Money MY-1107	(M)	**Soul Kaleidoscope**	1966	12.00	30.00
Money MS-1107	(S)	**Soul Kaleidoscope**	1966	16.00	40.00
Money MY-1110	(M)	**Superslick**	1967	12.00	30.00
Money MS-1110	(S)	**Superslick**	1967	16.00	40.00

LaROSA, JULIUS

RCA Victor LPM-1299	(M)	**Julius LaRosa**	1956	16.00	40.00
Cadence CLP-1007	(M)	**Julius LaRosa**	1957	12.00	30.00
Roulette R-25054	(M)	**Love Songs A LaRosa**	1959	8.00	20.00
Roulette SR-25054	(S)	**Love Songs A LaRosa**	1959	12.00	30.00
Roulette R-25083	(M)	**On The Sunny Side**	1960	8.00	20.00
Roulette SR-25083	(S)	**On The Sunny Side**	1960	10.00	25.00

LaRUE, MICHAEL, & THE DRINKING GOURD SINGERS

Esoteric ES-560	(M)	**Follow The Drinking Gourd**	195?	12.00	30.00

LAST DAYS, THE

(No label)	(S)	**The Last Days**	197?	20.00	50.00

LAST POETS, THE

Juggernaut 8802	(S)	**Right On**	1971	10.00	25.00
Douglas Z-30583	(S)	**This Is Madness**	1971	10.00	25.00
Douglas Z-30811	(S)	**Last Poets**	1971	10.00	25.00

LAUGHTON, CHARLES

Decca DL-8031	(M)	**Readings From The Bible**	1955	12.00	30.00
RCA Victor LPM-1136	(M)	**Night Of The Hunter** (Soundtrack)	1955	100.00	250.00
Capitol TBO-1650	(M)	**The Story Teller** (2 LPs)	1962	10.00	25.00
Capitol STBO-1650	(S)	**The Story Teller** (2 LPs)	1962	12.00	30.00

(Capitol 1650 includes Mr. Laughton reading a Kerouac piece.)

LAUREL RIVER VALLEY BOYS, THE

Judson J-3031	(M)	**Music For Moonshiners**	195?	12.00	30.00

LAUREN, ROD

RCA Victor LPM-2176	(M)	**I'm Rod Lauren**	1961	8.00	20.00
RCA Victor LSP-2176	(S)	**I'm Rod Lauren**	1961	12.00	30.00

LAURIE, ANNIE

Audio Lab AL-1510	(M)	**...It Hurts To Be In Love!**	1959	200.00	400.00
Palace 793	(M)	**Annie Laurie**	1964	20.00	50.00

LAURIE SISTERS, THE

Camden CAL-545	(M)	**Hits Of The Great Girl Groups**	1960	8.00	20.00
Camden CAS-545	(S)	**Hits Of The Great Girl Groups**	1960	12.00	30.00

LAWRENCE, EDDIE

Coral CRL-57103	(M)	**The Old Philosopher**	1957	10.00	25.00
Coral CRL-57155	(M)	**Eddie "The Old Philosopher" Lawrence**	1957	10.00	25.00
Coral CRL-57203	(M)	**The Kingdom Of Eddie Lawrence**	1958	10.00	25.00
Signature SM-1003	(M)	**A Garden Of Eddie Lawrence**	1959	10.00	25.00

LAWRENCE, GERTRUDE
Refer to Noel Coward & Gertude Lawrence.

Decca DL-5418	(10")	**Souvenir Album**	1952	20.00	50.00
Decca DL-8673	(M)	**A Remembrance**	1958	12.00	30.00

LAWRENCE, STEVE

Coral CRL-57050	(M)	**About That Girl**	1956	16.00	40.00
Coral CRL-57182	(M)	**Songs By Steve Lawrence**	1957	16.00	40.00
Coral CRL-57204	(M)	**Here's Steve Lawrence**	1958	16.00	40.00

Label & Catalog #		Title	Year	VG+	NM
Coral CRL-57268	(M)	All About Love	1959	2.00	30.00
Coral CRL-757268	(S)	All About Love	1959	16.00	40.00
Coral CRL-57434	(M)	Songs Everybody Knows	1963	10.00	25.00
Coral CRL-757434	(S)	Songs Everybody Knows	1963	12.00	30.00
King 395-593	(M)	Steve Lawrence	1959	40.00	100.00
ABC-Paramount ABC-290	(M)	Swing Softly With Me	1959	10.00	25.00
ABC-Paramount ABCS-290	(S)	Swing Softly With Me	1959	12.00	30.00
ABC-Paramount ABC-392	(M)	The Best Of Steve Lawrence	1960	8.00	20.00
ABC-Paramount ABCS-392	(S)	The Best Of Steve Lawrence	1960	10.00	25.00
United Arts. UAL-3098	(M)	The Steve Lawrence Sound	1960	8.00	20.00
United Arts. UAS-6098	(S)	The Steve Lawrence Sound	1960	10.00	25.00
United Arts. UAL-3114	(M)	Steve Lawrence Goes Latin	1960	8.00	20.00
United Arts. UAS-6114	(S)	Steve Lawrence Goes Latin	1960	10.00	25.00
United Arts. UAL-3150	(M)	Portrait Of My Love	1961	8.00	20.00
United Arts. UAS-6150	(S)	Portrait Of My Love	1961	10.00	25.00
United Arts. UAL-3190	(M)	The Very Best Of Steve Lawrence	1962	8.00	20.00
United Arts. UAS-6190	(S)	The Very Best Of Steve Lawrence	1962	10.00	25.00
United Arts. UAL-3265	(M)	People Will Say We're In Love	1963	8.00	20.00
United Arts. UAS-6265	(S)	People Will Say We're In Love	1963	10.00	25.00
United Arts. UAL-3368	(M)	Steve Lawrence Conquers Broadway	1963	8.00	20.00
United Arts. UAS-6368	(S)	Steve Lawrence Conquers Broadway	1963	10.00	25.00
Columbia KOL-6040	(M)	What Makes Sammy Run? (Soundtrack)	1964	14.00	35.00
Columbia KOS-2040	(S)	What Makes Sammy Run? (Soundtrack)	1964	20.00	50.00

LAWRENCE, STEVE, & EYDIE GORME

Label & Catalog #		Title	Year	VG+	NM
ABC-Paramount ABC-300	(M)	We Got Us	1960	8.00	20.00
ABC-Paramount ABCS-300	(S)	We Got Us	1960	10.00	25.00
ABC-Paramount ABC-311	(M)	Steve & Eydie Sing The Golden Hits	1960	8.00	20.00
ABC-Paramount ABCS-311	(S)	Steve & Eydie Sing The Golden Hits	1960	10.00	25.00
ABC-Paramount ABC-469	(M)	Our Best To You	1964	8.00	20.00
ABC-Paramount ABCS-469	(S)	Our Best To You	1964	10.00	25.00
ABC-Paramount (No #)	(M)	Songs From "The Golden Circle"	196?	20.00	50.00
		(TV Soundtrack manufactured for sale through the John Oster Company.)			
United Arts. WWL-4509	(M)	Cozy	1961	8.00	20.00
United Arts. WWS-8509	(S)	Cozy	1961	10.00	25.00
United Arts. UAL-3191	(M)	The Very Best Of Eydie & Steve	1962	8.00	20.00
United Arts. UAS-6191	(S)	The Very Best Of Eydie & Steve	1962	10.00	25.00
United Arts. UAL-3267	(M)	The Golden Hits Of Eydie & Steve	1962	8.00	20.00
United Arts. UAS-6267	(S)	The Golden Hits Of Eydie & Steve	1962	10.00	25.00
United Arts. WWL-4518	(M)	Two On The Aisle	1963	8.00	20.00
United Arts. WWS-8518	(S)	Two On The Aisle	1963	10.00	25.00

LAWSON, DEE: Refer to GOLDMINE'S PRICE GUIDE TO COLLECTIBLE JAZZ ALBUMS

LAWSON, LINDA

Label & Catalog #		Title	Year	VG+	NM
Chancellor CHL-5010	(M)	Introducing Linda Lawson	1960	6.00	15.00
Chancellor CHLS-5010	(S)	Introducing Linda Lawson	1960	10.00	25.00

LAY, SAM

Label & Catalog #		Title	Year	VG+	NM
Blue Thumb BTS-14	(S)	Sam Lay In Bluesland	1968	10.00	25.00

LAZAR, BILLY

Label & Catalog #		Title	Year	VG+	NM
Scarlett 100	(M)	Surfin' Around	1963	40.00	100.00

LAZY LESTER

Label & Catalog #		Title	Year	VG+	NM
Excello LP-8006	(M)	True Blues	1966	100.00	250.00

LAZY SMOKE

Label & Catalog #		Title	Year	VG+	NM
Onyx 6903	(M)	Corridor Of Faces	196?	800.00	1,200.00

LEA, BARBARA: Refer to GOLDMINE'S PRICE GUIDE TO COLLECTIBLE JAZZ ALBUMS

LEA, TERREA

Label & Catalog #		Title	Year	VG+	NM
ABC-Paramount ABC-161	(M)	Terrea Lea And Her Singing Guitar	195?	12.00	30.00
Hifi R-404	(M)	Folk Songs And Ballads	195?	12.00	30.00

LEACH, CURTIS

Label & Catalog #		Title	Year	VG+	NM
Longhorn 003	(M)	Indescribable	1965	20.00	50.00

Label & Catalog #		Title	Year	VG+	NM

LEADBELLY

Leadbelly was a nickname for Huddie "Leadbelly" Ledbetter was a guitar player, singer and writer of folk songs in the traditional Black American vein. His life and work is, along with that of Woody Guthrie, the basis for the entire folk process that followed.. Refer to The Lonesome Blues Singer.

Label & Catalog #		Title	Year	VG+	NM
Folkways FP-4	*(10")*	**Take This Hammer**	1950	80.00	200.00
Folkways FA-2004	*(10")*	**Take This Hammer**	1950	80.00	200.00
Folkways FP-14	*(10")*	**Rock Island Line—Leadbelly's Legacy, Vol. 2**	1951	80.00	200.00
Folkways FA-2014	*(10")*	**Rock Island Line—Leadbelly's Legacy, Vol. 2**	1951	80.00	200.00
Folkways FP-24	*(10")*	**Leadbelly's Legacy, Vol. 3**	1951	80.00	200.00
Folkways FA-2024	*(10")*	**Leadbelly's Legacy, Vol. 3**	1951	80.00	200.00
Folkways FP-34	*(10")*	**Easy Rider—Leadbelly's Legacy, Vol. 4**	1951	80.00	200.00
Folkways FA-2034	*(10")*	**Easy Rider—Leadbelly's Legacy, Vol. 4**	1951	80.00	200.00
Stinson SLP-17	*(10")*	**Leadbelly Memorial, Volume I** *(Red vinyl)*	1951	60.00	150.00
Stinson SLP-19	*(10")*	**Leadbelly Memorial, Volume II** *(Red vinyl)*	1951	60.00	150.00
Stinson SLP-39	*(10")*	**Play-Party Songs** *(Red vinyl)*	1951	60.00	150.00
Stinson SLP-41	*(10")*	**More Play-Party Songs** *(Red vinyl)*	1951	60.00	150.00
Stinson SLP-48	*(10")*	**Leadbelly Memorial, Volume III** *(Red vinyl)*	1951	60.00	150.00
Stinson SLP-51	*(10")*	**Leadbelly Memorial, Volume IV**	1951	30.00	75.00
Stinson SLP-72	*(10")*	**Leadbelly Memorial**	1951	30.00	75.00
Allegro 4027	*(10")*	**Sinful Songs**	195?	150.00	300.00
Capitol H-369	*(10")*	**Classics In Jazz**	1952	150.00	300.00
Folkways FP-241	*(M)*	**Leadbelly's Last Sessions, Vol. 1** *(2 LPs)*	1958	16.00	40.00
Folkways FA-2941	*(M)*	**Leadbelly's Last Sessions, Vol. 1** *(2 LPs)*	1958	16.00	40.00
Folkways FP-242	*(M)*	**Leadbelly's Last Sessions, Vol. 2** *(2 LPs)*	1958	16.00	40.00
Folkways FA-2942	*(M)*	**Leadbelly's Last Sessions, Vol. 2** *(2 LPs)*	1958	16.00	40.00
Folkways FA-3106	*(M)*	**Leadbelly Sings Folk Songs**	1959	12.00	30.00
Capitol T-1821	*(M)*	**Leadbelly—Huddie Ledbetter's Best**	1962	20.00	50.00
Capitol DT-1891	*(E)*	**Leadbelly—Huddie Ledbetter's Best**	1962	16.00	40.00
Verve/Folkways FV-9001	*(M)*	**Take This Hammer**	1965	10.00	25.00
Verve/Folkways FVS-9001	*(E)*	**Take This Hammer**	1965	6.00	15.00
Verve/Folkways FT-9021	*(M)*	**Keep Your Hands Off Her**	1965	10.00	25.00
Verve/Folkways FTS-9021	*(E)*	**Keep Your Hands Off Her**	1965	6.00	15.00
Verve/Folkways FT-3019	*(M)*	**From The Last Sessions**	1967	10.00	25.00
Verve/Folkways FTS-3019	*(E)*	**From The Last Sessions**	1967	6.00	15.00
RCA Victor LPV-505	*(M)*	**Midnight Special**	1964	20.00	50.00
Elektra EKL-301/2	*(M)*	**Library Of Congress Recordings** *(2 LPs)*	1966	10.00	25.00

LEARY, TIMOTHY

Broadside 601	*(M)*	**The Psychedelic Experience** *(With booklet)*	1966	40.00	100.00
Pixie CA-1069	*(M)*	**L.S.D.**	1966	30.00	75.00
ESP-Disk' 1027	*(M)*	**Turn On, Tune In, Drop Out**	1966	60.00	150.00
Mercury MG-21131	*(M)*	**Turn On, Tune In, Drop Out** *(Soundtrack)*	1967	16.00	40.00
Mercury SR-61131	*(S)*	**Turn On, Tune In, Drop Out** *(Soundtrack)*	1967	20.00	50.00
Douglas 1	*(M)*	**You Can Be Anyone This Time Around**	196?	40.00	100.00
		(Douglas 1 features Jimi Hendrix on guitar.)			

LEATHERCOATED MINDS, THE

The Minds feature J.J. Cale.

Viva V-36003	*(M)*	**Trip Down Sunset Strip**	1967	16.00	40.00
Viva VS-36003	*(S)*	**Trip Down Sunset Strip**	1967	20.00	50.00

LEAVES, THE

Mira LP-3005	*(M)*	**Hey Joe**	1966	16.00	40.00
Mira LPS-3005	*(S)*	**Hey Joe**	1966	20.00	50.00
Surrey LPS-3005	*(S)*	**Hey Joe**	1966		See below
		(While copies of Surrey 3005 were pressed, they were apparently issued in Mira covers. Thus the price here is for a Surrey disc in a Mira jacket Rare with a suggested Near Mint value of $100-200.)			
Capitol T-2638	*(M)*	**All The Good That's Happening**	1967	10.00	25.00
Capitol ST-2638	*(S)*	**All The Good That's Happening**	1967	12.00	30.00

LED ZEPPELIN

LZ was Jimmy Page, Robert Plant, John Bonham and John Paul Jones. Refer to Eric Clapton/ Jeff Beck / Jimmy Page; Lord Sutch; The Yardbirds.

Atlantic 8216	*(M)*	**Led Zeppelin** *(White label promo)*	1969	150.00	300.00
Atlantic SD-8216	*(S)*	**Led Zeppelin** *(White label promo)*	1969	80.00	200.00
Atlantic SD-8216	*(S)*	**Led Zeppelin** *(Purple & brown label)*	1969	80.00	200.00
		(Copies of Atlantic 8216 were pressed with the purple & brown, Atco-style label. These may have been errors or first pressings.)			

Label & Catalog #		Title	Year	VG+	NM
Atlantic 8236	(M)	**Led Zeppelin II** (White label promo)	1969	150.00	300.00
Atlantic SD-8236	(S)	**Led Zeppelin II** (White label promo)	1969	80.00	200.00
Atlantic SD-8236	(S)	**Led Zeppelin II**	1969	10.00	25.00
		(Original pressings of SD-8236 issued in a textured gatefold cover.)			
Atlantic 7201	(M)	**Led Zeppelin III** (White label promo)	1970	150.00	300.00
Atlantic SD-7201	(S)	**Led Zeppelin III** (White label promo)	1970	80.00	200.00
Atlantic SD-7208	(S)	**Led Zeppelin IV** (White label promo)	1971	80.00	200.00
Atlantic 7255	(M)	**Houses Of The Holy** (White label promo)	1973	150.00	300.00
Atlantic SD-7255	(S)	**Houses Of The Holy** (White label promo)	1973	80.00	200.00
		—Atlantic albums above have green & orange labels with "1841 Broadway" on the bottom.—			
Mobile Fidelity MFSL-065	(S)	**Led Zeppelin II**	1980	40.00	100.00

LED ZEPPELIN / DUSTY SPRINGFIELD

Atlantic SP-135	(DJ)	**Led Zeppelin / Dusty In Memphis**	1969	100.00	250.00
		(Album sampler with one side devoted to each artist's new album. Known among Zep collectors as "Climb Aboard Led Zeppelin.")			

LEE, BRENDA

Decca DL-8873	(M)	**Grandma, What Great Songs You Sang**	1959	20.00	50.00
Decca DL-78873	(S)	**Grandma, What Great Songs You Sang**	1959	30.00	75.00
		—Decca albums above have black labels with silver print.—			
Decca DL-8873	(M)	**Grandma, What Great Songs You Sang**	1960	12.00	30.00
Decca DL-78873	(S)	**Grandma, What Great Songs You Sang**	1960	16.00	40.00
Decca DL-4039	(M)	**Brenda Lee**	1960	12.00	30.00
Decca DL-74039	(S)	**Brenda Lee**	1960	16.00	40.00
Decca DL-4082	(M)	**This Is Brenda**	1960	12.00	30.00
Decca DL-74082	(S)	**This Is Brenda**	1960	16.00	40.00
Decca DL-4104	(M)	**Emotions**	1961	10.00	25.00
Decca DL-74104	(S)	**Emotions**	1961	12.00	30.00
Decca DL-4176	(M)	**All The Way**	1961	10.00	25.00
Decca DL-74176	(S)	**All The Way**	1961	12.00	30.00
Decca DL-4216	(M)	**Sincerely, Brenda Lee**	1962	10.00	25.00
Decca DL-74216	(S)	**Sincerely, Brenda Lee**	1962	12.00	30.00
Decca DL-4326	(M)	**That's All**	1962	8.00	20.00
Decca DL-74326	(S)	**That's All**	1962	10.00	25.00
Decca DL-4370	(M)	**All Alone Am I**	1963	8.00	20.00
Decca DL-74370	(S)	**All Alone Am I**	1963	10.00	25.00
Decca DL-4439	(M)	**Let Me Sing**	1963	8.00	20.00
Decca DL-74439	(S)	**Let Me Sing**	1963	10.00	25.00
Decca DL-4509	(M)	**By Request**	1964	8.00	20.00
Decca DL-74509	(S)	**By Request**	1964	10.00	25.00
Decca DL-4583	(M)	**Merry Christmas From Brenda Lee**	1964	8.00	20.00
Decca DL-74583	(S)	**Merry Christmas From Brenda Lee**	1964	10.00	25.00
Decca DL-4626	(M)	**Top Teen Hits**	1965	8.00	20.00
Decca DL-74626	(S)	**Top Teen Hits**	1965	10.00	25.00
		—Decca albums above have black "rainbow" labels with "Mfrd by Decca" beneath the rainbow.—			

LEE, BRENDA / TENNESSEE ERNIE FORD

Decca MG-9226	(M)	**The Show For Christmas Seals**	1962	12.00	30.00
Decca MG-79226	(S)	**The Show For Christmas Seals**	1962	16.00	40.00

LEE, DICKIE

Smash MGS-27020	(M)	**Tales Of Patches**	1962	12.00	30.00
Smash SRS-67020	(S)	**Tales Of Patches**	1962	16.00	40.00

LEE, JEANNE: *Refer to* GOLDMINE'S PRICE GUIDE TO COLLECTIBLE JAZZ ALBUMS

LEE, JULIA: *Refer to* GOLDMINE'S PRICE GUIDE TO COLLECTIBLE JAZZ ALBUMS

LEE, KATIE

Specialty 5000	(M)	**Spicy Songs For Cool Knights**	195?	12.00	30.00
Commentary	(M)	**Songs Of Couch And Consultation**	1960	12.00	30.00
Reprise R-6025	(M)	**Songs Of Couch And Consultation**	1961	10.00	25.00

LEE, PEGGY

Ms. Lee also recorded with Doris Day.

Columbia CL-6033	(10")	**Benny Goodman And Peggy Lee**	1949	20.00	50.00
Capitol H-151	(10")	**Rendezvous With Peggy Lee**	1952	30.00	75.00
Capitol H-204	(10")	**My Best To You**	1952	30.00	75.00

Label & Catalog #		Title	Year	VG+	NM
Decca DL-5482	(10")	**Black Coffee**	1953	40.00	100.00
Decca DL-5539	(10")	**Song In Intimate Style**	1953	30.00	75.00
Decca DL-5557	(10")	**The Lady And The Tramp** (Soundtrack)	1955	50.00	125.00
Decca DL-8083	(M)	**White Christmas** (Soundtrack)	1954	30.00	75.00
Decca DL-8166	(M)	**Songs From Pete Kelly's Blues** (Soundtrack)	1955	24.00	60.00
Decca DL-8358	(M)	**Black Coffee**	1956	30.00	75.00
Decca DL-8411	(M)	**Dream Street**	1956	20.00	50.00
Decca DL-8462	(M)	**The Lady And The Tramp** (Soundtrack)	1957	40.00	100.00
Decca DL-8591	(M)	**Sea Shells**	1958	20.00	50.00
Decca DL-8816	(M)	**Miss Wonderful**	1959	20.00	50.00
		— Decca albums above have black labels with silver print. —			
Decca DL-4478	(M)	**Lover**	1964	10.00	25.00
Decca DL-74478	(E)	**Lover**	1964	5.00	12.00
Decca DL-4461	(M)	**The Fabulous Peggy Lee**	1964	10.00	25.00
Decca DL-74461	(E)	**The Fabulous Peggy Lee**	1964	5.00	12.00
Decca DXB-164	(M)	**The Best Of Peggy Lee** (2 LPs)	1964	12.00	30.00
Decca DXSB-164	(E)	**The Best Of Peggy Lee** (2 LPs)	1964	6.00	15.00
Capitol T-151	(M)	**Rendezvous With Peggy Lee**	1954	20.00	50.00
Capitol T-204	(M)	**My Best To You**	1954	20.00	50.00
Capitol W-864	(M)	**The Man I Love**	1957	20.00	50.00
		(The orchestra on Capitol 864 was conducted by Frank Sinatra.)			
Capitol T-975	(M)	**Jump For Joy**	1957	16.00	40.00
		— Capitol albums above have turquoise or gray labels. —			
Capitol T-151	(M)	**Rendezvous With Peggy Lee**	1954	10.00	25.00
Capitol T-204	(M)	**My Best To You**	1954	10.00	25.00
Capitol W-864	(M)	**The Man I Love**	1959	10.00	25.00
Capitol SW-864	(S)	**The Man I Love**	1959	12.00	30.00
Capitol T-975	(M)	**Jump For Joy**	1959	10.00	25.00
Capitol ST-975	(S)	**Jump For Joy**	1959	12.00	30.00
Capitol T-1049	(M)	**Things Are Swingin'**	1959	10.00	25.00
Capitol ST-1049	(S)	**Things Are Swingin'**	1959	12.00	30.00
Capitol T-1131	(M)	**I Like Men**	1959	10.00	25.00
Capitol ST-1131	(S)	**I Like Men**	1959	12.00	30.00
Capitol T-1213	(M)	**Alright, Okay, You Win**	1960	10.00	25.00
Capitol ST-1213	(S)	**Alright, Okay, You Win**	1960	12.00	30.00
Capitol T-1219	(M)	**Beauty And The Beat**	1960	10.00	25.00
Capitol ST-1219	(S)	**Beauty And The Beat**	1960	12.00	30.00
		— Capitol albums above have black "rainbow" labels with the logo on the left side. —			
Capitol T-1290	(M)	**Latin Ala Lee!**	1960	8.00	20.00
Capitol ST-1290	(S)	**Latin Ala Lee!**	1960	10.00	25.00
Capitol T-1366	(M)	**All Aglow Again**	1960	8.00	20.00
Capitol ST-1366	(S)	**All Aglow Again**	1960	10.00	25.00
Capitol T-1401	(M)	**Pretty Eyes**	1960	8.00	20.00
Capitol ST-1401	(S)	**Pretty Eyes**	1960	10.00	25.00
Capitol T-1423	(M)	**Christmas Carousel**	1960	8.00	20.00
Capitol ST-1423	(S)	**Christmas Carousel**	1960	10.00	25.00
Capitol T-1475	(M)	**Ole A La Lee**	1960	8.00	20.00
Capitol ST-1475	(S)	**Ole A La Lee**	1960	10.00	25.00
Capitol T-1520	(M)	**Basin Street East**	1960	8.00	20.00
Capitol ST-1520	(S)	**Basin Street East**	1960	10.00	25.00
Capitol T-1630	(M)	**If You Go**	1961	8.00	20.00
Capitol ST-1630	(S)	**If You Go**	1961	10.00	25.00
Capitol T-1671	(M)	**Blue Cross Country**	1961	8.00	20.00
Capitol ST-1671	(S)	**Blue Cross Country**	1961	10.00	25.00
Capitol T-1743	(M)	**Bewitching Lee**	1962	10.00	25.00
Capitol DT-1743	(E)	**Bewitching Lee**	1962	6.00	15.00
		(Capitol 1743 is a reissue of 151 and 204.)			
Capitol T-1772	(M)	**Sugar 'N' Spice**	1962	8.00	20.00
Capitol ST-1772	(S)	**Sugar 'N' Spice**	1962	10.00	25.00
Capitol T-1850	(M)	**Mink Jazz**	1963	10.00	25.00
Capitol ST-1850	(S)	**Mink Jazz**	1963	12.00	30.00
Capitol ST-105	(S)	**Two Shows Nightly**	1969		See below
		(Unsatisfied with her performances, Ms. Lee had "Two Shows Nightly" withdrawn immediatley after, or prior, to release. Rare with a suggested Near Mint value of $150-300.)			
		— Capitol albums above have black labels with the logo on top. —			

LEE, PINKY

Decca DL-8421	(M)	**The Surprise Party**	1957	20.00	50.00

Label & Catalog #		Title	Year	VG+	NM

LEE, WILMA, & STONEY COOPER

Hickory LPM-100	(M)	There's A Big Wheel	1960	12.00	30.00
Hickory LPM-100	(S)	There's A Big Wheel	1960	16.00	40.00
Hickory LPS-106	(M)	Family Favorites	1960	12.00	30.00
Hickory LPS-106	(S)	Family Favorites	1960	16.00	40.00

LEFEVRE, RAYMOND

| Atlantic 8044 | (M) | Romantica | 1960 | 8.00 | 20.00 |
| Atlantic SD-8044 | (S) | Romantica | 1960 | 10.00 | 25.00 |

—Atlantic albums above have multi-color labels with a white "fan" logo on the right side.—

LEFT BANKE, THE

The Left Banke features Michael Brown. Refer to The Beckies; Montage; Stories.

Smash MGS-27088	(M)	Walk Away Renee / Pretty Ballerina	1967	20.00	50.00
Smash SRS-67088	(P)	Walk Away Renee / Pretty Ballerina	1967	20.00	50.00
Smash SRS-67113	(P)	Left Banke, Too	1968	20.00	50.00

(Both stereo albums have been poorly counterfeited.)

LEGEND

| Bell 6027 | (S) | Legend | 1969 | 16.00 | 40.00 |

LEGEND

| Megaphone 101 | (S) | Legend | 1970 | 30.00 | 75.00 |

LEGEND

| Empire 11186 | (S) | From The Fjords (With insert) | 1979 | 150.00 | 300.00 |

LEGENDS, THE

| Columbia CL-1707 | (M) | Hit Sounds Of Today's Smash Hit Combos | 1961 | 12.00 | 30.00 |
| Columbia CS-8507 | (S) | Hit Sounds Of Today's Smash Hit Combos | 1961 | 16.00 | 40.00 |

LEGENDS, THE

Ermine 101	(M)	The Legends Let Loose	1963	60.00	150.00
Capitol T-1925	(M)	The Legends Let Loose	1963	20.00	50.00
Capitol ST-1925	(S)	The Legends Let Loose	1963	20.00	50.00

LeGRAND, MICHEL

Columbia CL-647	(M)	Holiday In Rome	1955	10.00	25.00
Columbia CL-706	(M)	Vienna Holiday	1956	10.00	25.00
Columbia CL-888	(M)	Castles In Spain	1957	10.00	25.00

LEHRER, TOM

Tom Lehrer is a pianist, singer and writer of topical songs with a satirical bent.

Rivoli 4	(10")	Song Satires	1954	20.00	50.00
Lehrer 101	(10")	Songs By Tom Lehrer	1954	20.00	50.00
Lehrer TL-101	(M)	Songs By Tom Lehrer	1958	12.00	30.00
Lehrer TL-202	(M)	An Evening Wasted With Tom Lehrer	1958	8.00	20.00
Lehrer TL-202S	(S)	An Evening Wasted With Tom Lehrer	1958	12.00	30.00
Lehrer TL-102	(M)	More Of Tom Lehrer	1958	8.00	20.00
Lehrer TL-102S	(M)	More Of Tom Lehrer	1958	12.00	30.00

(Lehrer 102 contains the same live tracks as Lehrer 202 with
Tom's spoken commentary and the audience sounds edited out.)

LEIBER, JERRY

| Kapp KL-1127 | (M) | Scooby-Doo | 1959 | 20.00 | 50.00 |

LEIBER, JERRY, & MIKE STOLLER: *Refer to* ELVIS PRESLEY'S "SOUNDTRACK RADIO SPOTS, ETC."

LEIBER & STOLLER BIG BAND, THE

The Big Band is Atlantic's house band under the direction of Jerry Leiber and Mike Stoller. Refer to Elvis
Presley's "Soundtrack Radio Spots & Interviews."

| Atlantic 8047 | (M) | Yakety Yak | 1960 | 16.00 | 40.00 |
| Atlantic SD-8047 | (S) | Yakety Yak | 1960 | 20.00 | 50.00 |

—Atlantic albums above have multi-colored labels with a white "fan" logo on the right side.—

| Atlantic 8047 | (M) | Yakety Yak | 196? | 8.00 | 20.00 |
| Atlantic SD-8047 | (S) | Yakety Yak | 196? | 10.00 | 25.00 |

—Atlantic albums above have muti-colored labels with a black "fan" logo on the right side.—

Label & Catalog #		Title	Year	VG+	NM
LEMMON, JACK					
Epic LN-3491	(M)	**A Twist Of Lemmon**	1959	14.00	35.00
Epic BN-3491	(S)	**A Twist Of Lemmon**	1959	20.00	50.00
Epic LN-3551	(M)	**Music From "Some Like It Hot"**	1959	14.00	35.00
Epic BN-3551	(S)	**Music From "Some Like It Hot"**	1959	20.00	50.00
Riverside RLP-12-849	(M)	**Jack Lemmon Reads**			
		E.B. White's "Here Is New York"	196?	12.00	30.00
Capitol T-1943	(M)	**Piano Selections From "Irma La Douce"**	1963	12.00	30.00
Capitol ST-1943	(S)	**Piano Selections From "Irma La Douce"**	1963	16.00	40.00
LEMON PIPERS, THE					
Refer to 1910 Fruitgum Co. / The Lemon Pipers.					
Buddah BD-5009	(M)	**Green Tambourine**	1968	8.00	20.00
Buddah BDS-5009	(S)	**Green Tambourine**	1968	10.00	25.00
LENNON, JOHN/JOHN LENNON & THE PLASTIC ONO BAND					
Refer to The Beatles; Elephant's Memory; Nilsson; Yoko Ono; David Peel.					
United Arts. FLP-671010	(DJ)	**How I Won The War** (Radio spots)	1965	300.00	500.00
		(The listed values are based on the assumption that John is not present on the spots. Should he indeed prove to be on the record, the values would likely double. . .)			
Apple SW-3362	(S)	**Live Peace In Toronto** (With calendar)	1969	16.00	40.00
Apple SW-3362	(S)	**Live Peace In Toronto** (Without calendar)	1969	12.00	30.00
		(Apple label reads "A Subsidiary of Capitol" on the bottom and credits The Plastic Ono Band. Issued with a 16 page 1970 calendar.)			
Adam VIII 8018	(S)	**Roots: John Lennon Sings**			
		The Great Rock & Roll Hits	1975		*See below*
		(Adam 8018 was widely counterfeited in the wake of the lawsuit by Lennon that forced its withdrawal from the market! Original covers have the art printed on the jacket cardboard. On the back cover there are ads for other albums: The song titles for "20 Solid Gold Hits" are clearly legible. The print on the jacket's spine reads "John Lennon Sings The Great Rock & Roll Hits." Copies with the cover slicks affixed to the jacket, illegible print on the back cover ad, or spines that read "John Lennon Sings The Greatest Rock & Roll Hits" are easy ways to spot a reproduction. Finally, the single most defining aspect of an original: Originals must have "A-8018" hand-etched into the paper label. Rare with a suggested Near Mint value of $500-1,000.)			
Capitol SW-3362	(S)	**Live Peace In Toronto 1969** (Black label)	1983	10.00	25.00
Capitol SW-3414	(S)	**Mind Games** (Purple label)	1978	12.00	30.00
Capitol SK-3419	(S)	**Rock 'N' Roll** (Purple label)	1978	16.00	40.00
Capitol R-144136	(S)	**Menlove Ave.** (RCA Record Club)	1986	14.00	35.00
Geffen GHSP-2023	(S)	**The John Lennon**			
		Collection (Promo on Quiex II vinyl)	1982	20.00	50.00
Mobile Fidelity MFSL-153	(S)	**Imagine**	1982	10.00	25.00
LENNON, JOHN, & YOKO ONO					
Apple T-5001	(S)	**Two Virgins: Unfinished Music No. 1**	1968	60.00	150.00
		(Issued in a brown paper outer sleeve that is the same size as the album jacket and opens on the right. Originals have glossy labels with "MR" machine-stamped in the trail-off vinyl. Reissued in 1985 with non-glossy labels; these are worth $10-15.)			
Zapple ST-3357	(S)	**Unfinished Music #2: Life With The Lions**	1969	10.00	25.00
Apple 3361	(S)	**Wedding Album**	1969	60.00	150.00
		(Boxed set contains photos, postcard, poster of wedding photos, poster of lithographs, a booklet of press clippings, duplicate of marriage certificate, a "bagism" bag.)			
Apple SVBB-3392	(DJ)	**Some Time In New York City** (2 LPs)	1972	500.00	800.00
		(White label promo)			
Apple SVBB-3392	(S)	**Some Time In New York City** (2 LPs)	1972	12.00	30.00
		(Label credits John & Yoko/Plastic Ono Band With Elephant's Memory And Invisible Strings. Issued with a bonus photo and a petiton to the government to allow John to stay in the U.S.)			
Capitol SVBB-3392	(S)	**Some Time In New York City**	1978	10.00	25.00
		(Purple label in a double pocket, gatefold jacket.)			
Capitol SVBB-3392	(S)	**Some Time In New York City**	1978	100.00	250.00
		(Purple label in a single pocket, gatefold jacket.)			
Geffen GHS-2001	(S)	**Double Fantasy** (Off-white label)	1986	12.00	30.00
Geffen GHS-2001	(S)	**Double Fantasy** (Black label)	1986	20.00	50.00

The John Lennon Collection *was a posthumous collection of his post-Beatles hits covering that inexplicably omits such chart hits as "Cold Turkey," "Mother," "Woman Is The Nigger Of The World" and "Stand By Me" with album tracks "Jealous Guy" "Love," "Dear Yoko" and "I'm Losing You." The promo was issued as a Limited Edition Pressing on Quiex II vinyl, making it desirable both as a Lennon item and as an audiophile collectible.*

Label & Catalog #		Title	Year	VG+	NM
Geffen GHS-2001	(S)	**Double Fantasy**	1980	20.00	50.00
		(Columbia Record Club with "CH" on the label)			
Geffen R-104689	(S)	**Double Fantasy** *(RCA Record Club)*	1980	10.00	25.00
Nautilus NR-47	(S)	**Double Fantasy**	1980	200.00	400.00
		(Promo issued in a white jacket with a nautilus shell			
		and record bar logo on the front.)			
Nautilus NR-47	(S)	**Double Fantasy** *(Includes a poster)*	1980	16.00	50.00
Nautilus NR-47	(S)	**Double Fantasy** *(Alternate cover)*	1980		See below
		(This alternate cover has yellowish markings added to the back-			
		ground and a red heart drawn on Yoko's chest. There is one known			
		copies and no transactions; the suggested Near Mint value of			
		$3,000-6,000 is made with reservations. . .)			
Capitol C1-591425	(S)	**Double Fantasy** *(Columbia Record Club)*	1989	20.00	50.00
Polydor 817-160-1	(S)	**Milk And Honey** *(Green vinyl)*	1984	60.00	150.00
Polydor 817-160-1	(S)	**Milk And Honey** *(Gold vinyl)*	1984	50.00	125.00
		(These are unauthorized pressings done by a Polydor			
		company employee "after hours." Issued without a cover.)			
Polydor 817-160-1	(S)	**Milk And Honey** *(Columbia Record Club)*	1984	20.00	50.00
Silhouette SM-10012	(DJ)	**Reflections And Poetry** *(2 LPs with poster)*	1984	30.00	75.00

LENNON SISTERS, THE

Brunswick BL-54031	(M)	**Let's Get Acquainted**	1957	10.00	25.00
Brunswick BL-54039	(M)	**Lawrence Welk Presents The Lennon Sisters**	1958	10.00	25.00

LESLIE, NORMAN

Tops L-1652	(M)	**Gigi** *(With Mary Tyler Moore cover)*	195?	14.00	35.00

LESTER, BOBBY, & THE MOONGLOWS: *Refer to* **THE MOONGLOWS**

LESTER, KETTY

Era EL-108	(M)	**Love Letters**	1963	16.00	40.00
Era ES-108	(S)	**Love Letters**	1963	20.00	50.00
RCA Victor LPM-2945	(M)	**Soul Of Me**	1964	8.00	20.00
RCA Victor LSP-2945	(S)	**Soul Of Me**	1964	10.00	25.00
RCA Victor LPM-3326	(M)	**Where Is Love**	1965	8.00	20.00
RCA Victor LSP-3326	(S)	**Where Is Love**	1965	10.00	25.00

LETTERMEN, THE

Capitol SPRO-6218/9	(DJ)	**The Lettermen At The Waldorf**	196?	12.00	30.00

LEVENSON, SAM

Signature SM-1026	(M)	**But Seriously Folks**	1959	10.00	25.00

LEVIATHAN

Mach XMA-12501	(S)	**Leviathan**	1974	14.00	35.00

LEWIS, BARBARA

Atlantic 8086	(M)	**Hello Stranger**	1963	14.00	35.00
Atlantic SD-8086	(S)	**Hello Stranger**	1963	20.00	50.00
Atlantic 8090	(M)	**Snap Your Fingers**	1964	14.00	35.00
Atlantic SD-8090	(S)	**Snap Your Fingers**	1964	20.00	50.00
Atlantic 8110	(M)	**Baby, I'm Yours**	1965	10.00	25.00
Atlantic SD-8110	(S)	**Baby, I'm Yours**	1965	14.00	35.00
Atlantic 8118	(M)	**It's Magic**	1966	8.00	20.00
Atlantic SD-8118	(S)	**It's Magic**	1966	10.00	25.00
Atlantic SD-8173	(S)	**Workin' On A Groovy Thing**	1968	10.00	25.00
Enterprise ENS-1006	(S)	**The Many Grooves Of Barbara Lewis**	1970	10.00	25.00

LEWIS, BOBBY

Beltone 4000	(M)	**Tossin' And Turnin'**	1961	70.00	175.00

LEWIS, FURRY

Refer to Mississippi Fred McDoweel / Furry Lewis.

Bluesville BVLP-1036	(M)	**Back On My Feet Again**	1961	40.00	100.00
Bluesville BVLP-1037	(M)	**Done Changed My Mind**	1961	40.00	100.00
		—Bluesville albums above have bright blue labels with silver print.—			
Bluesville BVLP-1036	(M)	**Back On My Feet Again**	1964	12.00	30.00
Bluesville BVLP-1037	(M)	**Done Changed My Mind**	1964	12.00	30.00
		—Bluesville albums above have blue labels with a trident logo on the right side.—			

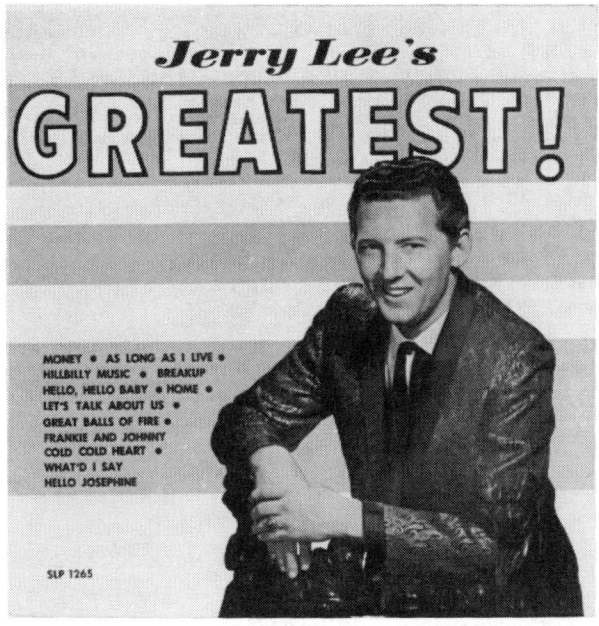

Not only one of the great rock 'n rollers, nor merely one of the great country 'n westerners (sic), Mr. Lewis is one of the great American singers. . . period. While Jerry Lee has yet to receive an RIAA Gold Record, he has placed twenty albums on the charts, although the Sun material had to wait until Shelby Singleton's repackages in 1969 to see the best-seller lists. Collectors should note that a rare white label promo exists for Sun 1265, Jerry Lee's Greatest (below) that commands big buckaroos. . .

Label & Catalog #		Title	Year	VG+	NM
LEWIS, GARY/GARY LEWIS & THE PLAYBOYS					
Liberty LRP-3408	(M)	**This Diamond Ring**	1965	8.00	20.00
Liberty LST-7408	(S)	**This Diamond Ring**	1965	10.00	25.00
Liberty LRP-3487	(M)	**You Don't Have To Paint Me A Picture**	1967	16.00	40.00
Liberty LST-7487	(S)	**You Don't Have To Paint Me A Picture**	1967	20.00	50.00
		(Some copies of Liberty 3/7487 were erroneously mastered with "Ice Melts The Sun" playing on the first side, although the cover and label list "Tina." This must be heard to be identified.)			
LEWIS, JERRY					
Decca DL-8410	(M)	**Jerry Lewis Just Sings**	1956	30.00	75.00
Decca DL-8595	(M)	**More Jerry Lewis**	1956	30.00	75.00
Decca DL-8936	(M)	**Big Songs For Little People**	1959	20.00	50.00
Decca DL-78936	(S)	**Big Songs For Little People**	1969	30.00	75.00
Dot DLP-8001	(M)	**Cinderfella** *(Soundtrack. Colored vinyl)*	1960	40.00	100.00
Dot DLP-8001	(M)	**Cinderfella** *(Soundtrack)*	1960	16.00	40.00
Dot DLP-38001	(S)	**Cinderfella** *(Soundtrack. Colored vinyl)*	1960	60.00	150.00
Dot DLP-38001	(S)	**Cinderfella** *(Soundtrack)*	1960	20.00	50.00
Capitol J-3267	(M)	**Nagger**	1963	12.00	30.00
LEWIS, JERRY LEE					
Refer to Johnny Cash / Jerry Lee Lewis; Johnny Cash, Jerry Lee Lewis & Carl Perkins.					
Sun SLP-1230	(M)	**Jerry Lee Lewis**	1958	80.00	200.00
Sun SLP-1265	(M)	**Jerry Lee's Greatest** *(White label promo)*	1961	250.00	750.00
Sun SLP-1265	(M)	**Jerry Lee's Greatest**	1961	100.00	250.00
Design DLP-165	(M)	**Rockin' With Jerry Lee Lewis**	1963	10.00	25.00
Design DSP-165	(E)	**Rockin' With Jerry Lee Lewis**	1963	8.00	20.00
Smash MGS-27040	(M)	**The Golden Hits Of Jerry Lee Lewis**	1964	10.00	25.00
Smash SRS-67040	(S)	**The Golden Hits Of Jerry Lee Lewis**	1964	14.00	35.00
Smash SRS-67040	(S)	**The Golden Rock Hits Of Jerry Lee Lewis**	1969	6.00	15.00
		("Golden Rock Hits" is a reissue of "Golden Hits.")			
Smash MGS-27056	(M)	**The Greatest Live Show On Earth**	1964	30.00	75.00
Smash SRS-67056	(S)	**The Greatest Live Show On Earth**	1964	40.00	100.00
Smash MGS-27063	(M)	**The Return Of Rock**	1965	14.00	35.00
Smash SRS-67063	(S)	**The Return Of Rock**	1965	20.00	50.00
Smash MGS-27071	(M)	**Country Songs For City Folks**	1965	6.00	15.00
Smash SRS-67071	(S)	**Country Songs For City Folks**	1965	10.00	25.00
Smash SRS-67071	(S)	**All Country**	1969	6.00	15.00
		("All Country" is a reissue of "Country Songs For City Folks.")			
Smash MGS-27079	(M)	**Memphis Beat**	1966	8.00	20.00
Smash SRS-67079	(S)	**Memphis Beat**	1966	12.00	30.00
Smash MGS-27086	(M)	**By Request**	1966	8.00	20.00
Smash SRS-67086	(S)	**By Request**	1966	12.00	30.00
Smash MGS-27097	(M)	**Soul My Way**	1967	12.00	30.00
Smash SRS-67097	(S)	**Soul My Way**	1967	16.00	40.00
Mercury SR-61318	(S)	**In Loving Memories**	1971	10.00	25.00
Mercury SR-61343	(S)	**Touching Home** *(Drawing cover)*	1971	10.00	25.00
Mercury MK-3	(DJ)	**Southern Roots Radio Special**	1972	20.00	50.00
Mercury SRM-2-803	(S)	**The Session** *(2 LPs)*	1973	10.00	25.00
LEWIS, LINDA GAIL					
Smash SRS-67119	(S)	**Two Sides Of Linda Gail Lewis**	1969	10.00	25.00
LEWIS, KATHERINE HANDY					
Folkways FG-3540	(M)	**W.C. Handy Blues**	196?	10.00	25.00
LEWIS, MEADE LUX: *Refer to* GOLDMINE'S PRICE GUIDE TO COLLECTIBLE JAZZ ALBUMS					
LEWIS, SHARI					
RCA Victor LBY-1006	(M)	**Fun In Shariland**	1954	30.00	75.00
Camden CAL-1052	(M)	**Jack And The Beanstalk & Other Stories**	1964	10.00	25.00
Camden CAS-1052	(S)	**Jack And The Beanstalk & Other Stories**	1964	10.00	25.00
Golden GLP-39	(M)	**Shari Lewis Songfest** *(With Lampchop)*	1962	20.00	50.00
LEWIS, SMILEY					
Imperial LP-9141	(M)	**I Hear You Knocking** *(Green vinyl)*	1961	*See below*	
		(Green vinyl copies of LP-9141 are rare with a suggested Near Mint value of $3,000-5,000.)			
Imperial LP-9141	(M)	**I Hear You Knocking**	1961	250.00	500.00

Label & Catalog #		Title	Year	VG+	NM

LEWIS FAMILY, THE

Starday SLP-121	(M)	Singin' Time Down South	1960	16.00	40.00
Starday SLP-161	(M)	Anniversary Celebration	1962	16.00	40.00
Starday SLP-193	(M)	Gospel Special	1962	16.00	40.00
Starday SLP-238	(M)	Sing Me A Gospel Song	1962	16.00	40.00
Starday SLP-252	(M)	All Night Singing Convention	1963	16.00	40.00
Starday SLP-289	(M)	Singin' In My Soul	1964	16.00	40.00
Starday SLP-331	(M)	The First Family Of Gospel Music	1965	16.00	40.00
Starday SLP-381	(M)	The Lewis Family Sings The Gospel With Carl Story	1965	16.00	40.00
Starday SLP-381	(M)	The Lewis Family Album	1965	16.00	40.00
Starday SLP-395	(M)	Shall We Gather At The River	1966	16.00	40.00
Starday SLP-408	(M)	Time Is Moving On	1966	16.00	40.00

— Starday albums above have yellow labels. —

LEWIS & CLARKE EXPEDITION, THE

| Colgems COM-105 | (M) | The Lewis & Clarke Expedition | 1967 | 10.00 | 25.00 |
| Colgems COS-105 | (S) | The Lewis & Clarke Expedition | 1967 | 12.00 | 30.00 |

LIBERACE

Advance 7	(10")	Piano	1951	12.00	30.00
Columbia CL-6217	(10")	Liberace At The Piano	1952	10.00	25.00
Columbia CL-6239	(10")	An Evening With Liberace	1953	10.00	25.00
Columbia CL-6251	(10")	Liberace By Candlelight	1953	10.00	25.00
Columbia CL-6269	(10")	Concertos For You	1953	10.00	25.00
Columbia CL-6283	(10")	Concertos For You, Volume 2	1954	10.00	25.00
Columbia CL-6327	(10")	Liberace Plays Chopin	1954	10.00	25.00
Columbia ML-6328	(10")	Liberace Plays Chopin, Volume 2	1954	10.00	25.00
Columbia ML-4764	(10")	Concertos For You	1954	10.00	25.00
Columbia CL-800	(M)	Sincerely Yours *(Soundtrack)*	1955	14.00	35.00
Columbia CL-2516	(10")	Piano Reverie	1955	10.00	25.00
Columbia CL-2592	(10")	Kiddin' On The Keys	1956	10.00	25.00

LIBERMAN, JEFFREY

Librah 1545	(S)	Jeffrey Liberman	1975	30.00	75.00
Librah 6969	(S)	Solitude Within	1975	40.00	100.00
Librah 12157	(S)	Synergy	1978	40.00	100.00

LIC

| Big Dog BD-1001 | (S) | Just A Taste | 1979 | 20.00 | 50.00 |

LIGGINS, JOE

| Mercury MG-20731 | (M) | Honeydripper | 1962 | 20.00 | 50.00 |
| Mercury SR-60731 | (S) | Honeydripper | 1962 | 30.00 | 75.00 |

LIGHTCRUST DOUGHBOYS, THE

The Doughboys were Johnny Gimble, Leon McAuliffe, W. Lee O' Daniel and Bob Wills.

| Audio Lab LP-1525 | (M) | The Lightcrust Doughboys | 1959 | 100.00 | 250.00 |

LIGHTFOOT, GORDON

Canadian Gordon Lightfoot is a guitar player, singer and writer of popular songs with a folkie flavor.

United Arts. UAL-3487	(M)	Lightfoot	1965	8.00	20.00
United Arts. UAS-6487	(S)	Lightfoot	1965	10.00	25.00
United Arts. UAL-3587	(M)	The Way I Feel	1967	8.00	20.00
United Arts. UAS-6587	(S)	The Way I Feel	1967	10.00	25.00
Mobile Fidelity MFSL-018	(S)	Sundown	1979	12.00	35.00

LIGHTNIN' SLIM

| Excello 8000 | (M) | Rooster Blues | 1960 | 200.00 | 400.00 |
| Excello 8004 | (M) | Lightnin' Slim's Bell Ringer | 1965 | 100.00 | 250.00 |

LIGHTNING

| P.I.P. 6807 | (S) | Lightning | 1971 | 12.00 | 30.00 |

LILLIE, BEATRICE

Liberty Music 1002	(10")	Thirty Minutes With Beatrice	1952	20.00	50.00
Decca DL-5453	(10")	Souvenir Album	1953	20.00	50.00
London LL-1373	(M)	An Evening With Beatrice Lillie	1957	10.00	25.00

Label & Catalog #		Title	Year	VG+	NM

LILLY BROTHERS, THE/THE LILLY BROTHERS & DON STOVER
Everett and Mitchell "Bea" Lilly with banjoist Don Stover have been one of the country's premier bluerass ensembles since the '40s.

Folkways FA-2433	(M)	Folk Songs From The Southern Mountains	196?	10.00	25.00
Folklore FRLP-14010	(M)	Bluegrass Breakdown	1964	8.00	20.00
Folklore FRST-14010	(S)	Bluegrass Breakdown	1964	10.00	25.00
Folklore FRLP-14035	(M)	Country Songs	1964	8.00	20.00
Folklore FRST-14035	(S)	Country Songs	1964	10.00	25.00

LIMELITERS, THE
The Limeliters— Lou Gottlieb, Alex Hassilev and Glenn Yarbrough— are a vocal/instrumental group from the urban folk movement of the '50s. Refer to The Gateway Singers; Jimmie Rodgers / The Limeliters.

Elektra EKL-180	(M)	The Limeliters	1960	8.00	20.00
Elektra EKS-7180	(S)	The Limeliters	1960	10.00	25.00
RCA Victor LPM-2272	(M)	Tonight: In Person	1961	8.00	20.00
RCA Victor LSP-2272	(S)	Tonight: In Person	1961	10.00	25.00
RCA Victor LPM-2393	(M)	The Slightly Fabulous Limeliters	1961	8.00	20.00
RCA Victor LSP-2393	(S)	The Slightly Fabulous Limeliters	1961	10.00	25.00
RCA Victor LPM-2445	(M)	The Limeliters Sing Out!	1962	8.00	20.00
RCA Victor LSP-2445	(S)	The Limeliters Sing Out!	1962	10.00	25.00
RCA Victor LPM-2512	(M)	Through Children's Eyes	1962	8.00	20.00
RCA Victor LSP-2512	(S)	Through Children's Eyes	1962	10.00	25.00
RCA Victor LPM-2547	(M)	Folk Matinee	1962	8.00	20.00
RCA Victor LSP-2547	(S)	Folk Matinee	1962	10.00	25.00
RCA Victor LPM-2588	(M)	Makin' A Joyful Noise	1963	8.00	20.00
RCA Victor LSP-2588	(S)	Makin' A Joyful Noise	1963	10.00	25.00
RCA Victor LPM-2609	(M)	Our Men In San Francisco	1963	8.00	20.00
RCA Victor LSP-2609	(S)	Our Men In San Francisco	1963	10.00	25.00
RCA Victor LPM-2671	(M)	Fourteen 14K Folk Songs	1963	8.00	20.00
RCA Victor LSP-2671	(S)	Fourteen 14K Folk Songs	1963	10.00	25.00

— RCA mono albums above have "Long Play" on the bottom of the label; stereo albums have "Living Stereo" on the bottom.—

LINCOLN, ABBEY: *Refer to* GOLDMINE'S PRICE GUIDE TO COLLECTIBLE JAZZ ALBUMS

LINCOLN, PHILAMORE
The uncredited backing group for Lincoln is Jimmy Page's Yardbirds.

Epic BN-26497	(S)	North Wind Blew South	1970	10.00	25.00

LINCOLN STREET EXIT

Mainstream S-6126	(S)	Drive It	1970	12.00	30.00

LIND, BOB

Verve/Forecast FT-3005	(M)	Elusive Bob Lind	1966	10.00	25.00
Verve/Forecast FTS-3005	(S)	Elusive Bob Lind	1966	12.00	30.00
World Pacific WP-1841	(M)	Don't Be Concerned	1966	10.00	25.00
World Pacific ST-21841	(S)	Don't Be Concerned	1966	12.00	30.00
World Pacific WP-1851	(M)	Photographs Of Feeling	1966	8.00	20.00
World Pacific ST-21851	(S)	Photographs Of Feeling	1966	10.00	25.00

LINDE, DENNIS

Intrepid 4004	(M)	Linde Manor	1966	8.00	20.00
Intrepid 74004	(S)	Linde Manor	1966	10.00	25.00

LINDEN, KATHY

Felsted 7501	(M)	That Certain Boy	1958	30.00	75.00

LINDSEY, GEORGE

Capitol T-2965	(M)	Goober Sings!	1968	10.00	25.00
Capitol ST-2965	(S)	Goober Sings!	1968	12.00	30.00
Capitol ST-230	(S)	96 Miles To Bakersfield	1969	10.00	25.00

LINKLETTER, ART

Columbia CL-703	(M)	Howlers, Boners And Shockers	1955	14.00	35.00
Capitol T1-284	(M)	House Party Music Time	1958	14.00	35.00

LINTON, SHERWOOD, & THE COTTON KINGS

Re-Car 2108	(S)	Sherwood Linton & The Cotton Kings	1968	30.00	75.00

Originally The Imperials (as illustrated here by their first LP for End), they changed their name to Little Anthony & The Imperials for obvious reasons. This, their first album, has a wonderful photo that poses the question "Why was Anthony called Little when he's obviously taller than the others?" I know, I know. He's standing on something and they're not. . .

Label & Catalog #		Title	Year	VG+	NM
LIPSCOMB, MANCE					
Mance Lipscomb was a blues guitar player and singer.					
Reprise R-2012	(M)	**Trouble In Mind**	1961	10.00	25.00
Reprise R9-2012	(S)	**Trouble In Mind**	1961	14.00	35.00
LIPTON, PEGGY					
Ode Z12-44006	(S)	**Peggy Lipton**	1968	10.00	25.00
LIQUID SMOKE					
Avco Embassy AVE-33005	(S)	**Liquid Smoke**	196?	10.00	25.00
LISTENING					
Vanguard VSD-6504	(S)	**Listening**	1968	10.00	25.00
LITE STORM					
Beverly Hills 1135	(S)	**Lite Storm Warning**	1973	16.00	40.00
LITTER, THE					
Warick UR-5M-1940	(M)	**Distortions**	1967	300.00	500.00
Hexagon HX-681	(S)	**$100 Fine**	1968	200.00	400.00
Probe CPLP-4504	(S)	**Emerge**	1969	16.00	40.00
LITTLE ANTHONY/LITTLE ANTHONY & THE IMPERIALS					
Little Anthony is Anthony Guardine. Refer to The Chantels.					
End 303	(M)	**We Are The Imperials Featuring Little Anthony**	1959	150.00	300.00
End 311	(M)	**Shades Of The 40's**	1960	60.00	150.00
DCP DCL-3801	(M)	**I'm On The Outside Looking In**	1964	10.00	25.00
DCP DCS-6801	(S)	**I'm On The Outside Looking In**	1964	12.00	30.00
DCP DCL-3808	(M)	**Goin' Out Of My Head**	1965	10.00	25.00
DCP DCS-6808	(S)	**Goin' Out Of My Head**	1965	12.00	30.00
DCP DCL-3809	(M)	**Best Of Little Anthony & The Imperials**	1966	8.00	20.00
DCP DCS-6809	(S)	**Best Of Little Anthony & The Imperials**	1966	10.00	25.00
Roulette R-25294	(M)	**Little Anthony & The Imperials' Greatest Hits**	1965	8.00	20.00
Roulette SR-25294	(S)	**Little Anthony & The Imperials' Greatest Hits**	1965	10.00	25.00
LITTLE BOY BLUES					
Fontana MGF-27578	(M)	**In The Woodland Of Weir**	1967	10.00	25.00
Fontana SRF-67578	(S)	**In The Woodland Of Weir**	1967	12.00	30.00
LITTLE CAESAR & THE ROMANS					
Del-Fi DFLP-1218	(M)	**Memories Of Those Oldies But Goodies**	1961	150.00	300.00
LITTLE ESTHER: *Refer to* **ESTHER PHILLIPS**					
LITTLE EVA					
Little Eva is Eva Boyd. Refer to The Cookies / Little Eva / Carole King.					
Dimension DLP-6000	(M)	**L-L-L-L-Loco-Motion**	1962	50.00	125.00
Dimension DLPS-6000	(E)	**L-L-L-L-Loco-Motion**	1962	60.00	150.00
(First pressings do not contain "Keep Your Hands Off Of My Baby.")					
Dimension DLP-6000	(M)	**L-L-L-L-Loco-Motion**	1962	70.00	175.00
Dimension DLPS-6000	(E)	**L-L-L-L-Loco-Motion**	1962	80.00	200.00
(Later pressings contain "Keep Your Hands Off Of My Baby.")					
LITTLE FEAT					
The Feat were formed and led by Lowell George.					
Mobile Fidelity MFSL-013	(S)	**Waiting For Columbus** (2 LPs)	1978	25.00	75.00
Nautilus NR-24	(S)	**Time Loves A Hero**	198?	20.00	60.00
LITTLE MILTON					
Little Milton is a pseudonym for Milton Campbell. Refer to Albert King & Little Milton.					
Checker LP-2995	(M)	**We're Gonna Make It** (Black label)	1965	40.00	100.00
Checker LP-3002	(M)	**Little Milton Sings Big Blues**	1966	20.00	50.00
LITTLE MISS CORNSHUCKS					
Chess LP-1453	(M)	**Little Miss Cornshucks**	1961	20.00	50.00

Label & Catalog #		Title	Year	VG+	NM

LITTLE RICHARD

The ever-raucous, flamboyantly joyous Little Richard Penniman is one of the archetypes of rock'n roll and a pivotal figure in the genre's development.. Refer to Canned Heat & Little Richard; Jimi Hendrix & Little Richard.

Label & Catalog #		Title	Year	VG+	NM
Camden CAL-420	(M)	Little Richard	1956	80.00	200.00
Specialty 100	(M)	Here's Little Richard	1957	250.00	500.00
Specialty 2100	(M)	Here's Little Richard	1957	80.00	200.00
Specialty SP-2103	(M)	Little Richard	1957	80.00	200.00
Specialty SP-2104	(M)	The Fabulous Little Richard	1958	80.00	200.00
Specialty SP-2111	(E)	Little Richard—His Biggest Hits	1963	20.00	50.00
Specialty SP-2113	(E)	Little Richard's Grooviest 17 Original Hits	1968	10.00	25.00
Specialty SP-2136	(M)	Well Alright!	1970	10.00	25.00

("Poor Boy Paul," "Bama-Lama Bama-Loo," "Annie Is Back" and "Shakle A Hand" are in stereo on this album.)

— Specialty albums above have black & gold labels.—

Label & Catalog #		Title	Year	VG+	NM
20th Century FXG-5010	(M)	Little Richard Sings Gospel	1959	30.00	75.00
20th Century SGM-5010	(S)	Little Richard Sings Gospel	1959	40.00	100.00
Mercury MG-20656	(M)	It's Real	1961	14.00	35.00
Mercury SR-60656	(S)	It's Real	1961	20.00	50.00
Crown CLP-5362	(M)	Little Richard Sings Freedom Songs	1963	10.00	25.00
Crown CST-362	(E)	Little Richard Sings Freedom Songs	1963	4.00	10.00
Coral CRL-57446	(M)	Coming Home	1963	12.00	30.00
Coral CRL-757446	(S)	Coming Home	1963	16.00	40.00
Specialty SP-2111	(M)	Little Richard's Biggest Hits	1963	16.00	40.00
Wing MGW-122288	(M)	King Of The Gospel Singers	1964	8.00	20.00
Wing SRW-162288	(S)	King Of The Gospel Singers	1964	10.00	25.00
Vee Jay LP-1107	(M)	Little Richard Is Back	1964	14.00	35.00
Vee Jay SR-1107	(S)	Little Richard Is Back	1964	20.00	50.00

(Vee Jay 1107 reputedly features Jimi Hendrix on guitar on "Whole Lotta Shakin'," "Hound Dog," "Going Home Tomorrow," "Goodnight Irene," "Money honey" and "Lawdy Miss Clawdy.")

Label & Catalog #		Title	Year	VG+	NM
Vee Jay LP-1124	(M)	Little Richard's Greatest Hits	1965	10.00	25.00
Vee Jay SR-1124	(S)	Little Richard's Greatest Hits	1965	16.00	40.00
Vee Jay VJS-2-100	(S)	Little Richard's Gold (2 LPs)	196?	10.00	25.00
Audio Encores 1002	(S)	Little Richard	1980	10.00	25.00

LITTLE SONNY

Label & Catalog #		Title	Year	VG+	NM
Enterprise ENS-1005	(S)	New King Of The Blues Harmonica	1970	14.00	35.00
Enterprise ENS-1018	(S)	Black And Blue	1971	14.00	35.00
Enterprise ENS-1036	(S)	Hard Goin' Up	1973	14.00	35.00

LITTLE WALTER

Refer to Bo Diddley.

Label & Catalog #		Title	Year	VG+	NM
Checker LP-1428	(M)	The Best Of Little Walter	1958	150.00	500.00
Checker LP-3005	(M)	The Best Of Little Walter	1967	14.00	35.00
Checker LPS-3005	(E)	The Best Of Little Walter	1967	10.00	25.00

(Checker 3004 is a reissue of 1428.)

— Checker albums above have blue labels with checkers on top.—

Label & Catalog #		Title	Year	VG+	NM
Chess LPS-1535	(S)	Hate To See You Go	1969	10.00	25.00

LIVELY ONES, THE

Label & Catalog #		Title	Year	VG+	NM
Del-Fi DFLP-1226	(M)	Surf-Rider	1963	12.00	30.00
Del-Fi DFST-1226	(S)	Surf-Rider	1963	16.00	40.00
Del-Fi DFLP-1231	(M)	Surf Drums	1963	12.00	30.00
Del-Fi DFST-1231	(S)	Surf Drums	1963	16.00	40.00
Del-Fi DFLP-1237	(M)	This Is Surf City	1963	12.00	30.00
Del-Fi DFST-1237	(S)	This Is Surf City	1963	16.00	40.00
Del-Fi DFLP-1238	(M)	Great Surf Hits	1963	12.00	30.00
Del-Fi DFST-1238	(S)	Great Surf Hits	1963	16.00	40.00
Del-Fi DFLP-1240	(M)	Surfin' South Of The Border	1964	12.00	30.00
Del-Fi DFST-1240	(S)	Surfin' South Of The Border	1964	16.00	40.00

LIVERPOOL BEATS, THE

Label & Catalog #		Title	Year	VG+	NM
Rondo 2026	(M)	The New Merseyside Sound	1964	20.00	50.00

(This was also released on Design credited to The Beats.)

Label & Catalog #		Title	Year	VG+	NM
LIVERPOOL FIVE, THE					
Refer to The Astronauts / The Liverpool Five.					
RCA Victor LPM-3583	(M)	The Liverpool Five Arrive	1966	10.00	25.00
RCA Victor LSP-3583	(S)	The Liverpool Five Arrive	1966	12.00	30.00
RCA Victor LPM-3682	(M)	Out Of Sight	1967	10.00	25.00
RCA Victor LSP-3682	(S)	Out Of Sight	1967	12.00	30.00
LIVERPOOL LADS, THE					
This album features The Liverpool Lads in the studio overdubbed by crowd noise from a Beatles concert!					
Lloyds ER-MC-Ltd.	(M)	The Great American Tour:			
		1965 Live Beatlemania Concert	1965	300.00	500.00
LIVERPOOL SCENE, THE/ADRIAN HENRI & ROGER McGOUGH					
Epic LN-24336	(M)	The Incredible New Liverpool Scene	1967	8.00	20.00
Epic BN-26336	(S)	The Incredible New Liverpool Scene	1967	10.00	25.00
		(Epic 24/26336 credits Henri & McGough.)			
LIVIN' BLUES					
Dwarf 2003	(S)	Dutch Treat	1971	12.00	30.00
LLOYD, A. L.					
A. L. Lloyd is an Englisgh singer of traditional folk music with a British origin.					
Riverside RLP-12-606	(M)	Australian Bush Songs	195?	12.00	30.00
Riverside RLP-12-614	(M)	English Street Songs	195?	12.00	30.00
Riverside RLP-12-618	(M)	English Drinking Songs	195?	12.00	30.00
Tradition TLP-1016	(M)	The Foggy Dew			
		(& Other Traditional English Love Songs)	1956	12.00	30.00
Prestige Int. PRLP-13066	(M)	The Best Of A. L. Lloyd	1963	12.00	30.00
LLOYD, A. L., & EWAN MacCOLL					
Refer to Ewan MacColl.					
Stinson SLP-80	(10")	Haul On The Bowlin'	195?	16.00	40.00
Stinson SLP-81	(10")	Off To Sea Once More	195?	16.00	40.00
Riverside RLP-12-621	(M)	The English And Scottish Popular Ballads	1956	12.00	30.00
Riverside RLP-12-622	(M)	The English And Scottish Popular Ballads	1956	12.00	30.00
Riverside RLP-12-623	(M)	The English And Scottish Popular Ballads	1956	12.00	30.00
Riverside RLP-12-624	(M)	The English And Scottish Popular Ballads	1956	12.00	30.00
Riverside RLP-12-625	(M)	The English And Scottish Popular Ballads	1956	12.00	30.00
Riverside RLP-12-627	(M)	The English And Scottish Popular Ballads	1956	12.00	30.00
Riverside RLP-12-628	(M)	The English And Scottish Popular Ballads	1956	12.00	30.00
Riverside RLP-12-629	(M)	Great British Ballads	1956	12.00	30.00
Riverside RLP-12-635	(M)	That She Blows! (Whaling Ballads & Songs)	195?	12.00	30.00
Riverside RLP-12-652	(M)	Champions And Sporting Blades	195?	12.00	30.00
Tradition TLP-1026	(M)	Blow Boys, Blow (Songs Of The Sea)	195?	12.00	30.00
Prestige Inter. PRLP-13043	(M)	A Sailor's Garland	1961	12.00	30.00
LOADING ZONE, THE					
Umbrella US-101	(S)	One For All	1967	30.00	75.00
RCA Victor LSP-3959	(S)	The Loading Zone	1968	10.00	25.00
LOCKLIN, HANK					
Refer to Hank Snow / Hank Locklin / Porter Wagoner.					
RCA Victor LPM-1673	(M)	Foreign Love	1958	30.00	75.00
RCA Victor LPM-2291	(M)	Please Help Me, I'm Falling			
		(& 11 Other Hank Locklin Favorites)	1960	14.00	35.00
RCA Victor LSP-2291	(S)	Please Help Me, I'm Falling			
		(& 11 Other Hank Locklin Favorites)	1960	20.00	50.00
King 672	(M)	The Best Of Hank Locklin	1961	40.00	100.00
King 738	(M)	Encores	1961	40.00	100.00
RCA Victor LPM-2464	(M)	Happy Journey	1962	10.00	25.00
RCA Victor LSP-2464	(S)	Happy Journey	1962	14.00	35.00
RCA Victor LPM-2597	(M)	A Tribute To Roy Acuff	1962	10.00	25.00
RCA Victor LSP-2597	(S)	A Tribute To Roy Acuff	1962	14.00	35.00
RCA Victor LPM-2680	(M)	The Ways Of Love	1963	10.00	25.00
RCA Victor LSP-2680	(S)	The Ways Of Love	1963	14.00	35.00
		—*RCA mono albums above have "Long Play" on the bottom of the label;*			
		stereo albums have "Living Stereo" on the bottom.—			
RCA Victor LPM-2801	(M)	Irish Songs, Country Style	1964	8.00	20.00
RCA Victor LSP-2801	(S)	Irish Songs, Country Style	1964	10.00	25.00

Label & Catalog #		Title	Year	VG+	NM
RCA Victor LPM-2997	(M)	Hank Locklin Sings Hank Williams	1964	8.00	20.00
RCA Victor LSP-2997	(S)	Hank Locklin Sings Hank Williams	1964	10.00	25.00
RCA Victor LPM-3391	(M)	Hank Locklin Sings Eddy Arnold	1965	8.00	20.00
RCA Victor LSP-3391	(S)	Hank Locklin Sings Eddy Arnold	1965	10.00	25.00
RCA Victor LPM-3465	(M)	Once Over Lightly	1965	8.00	20.00
RCA Victor LSP-3465	(S)	Once Over Lightly	1965	10.00	25.00
RCA Victor LPM-3559	(M)	The Best Of Hank Locklin	1966	10.00	25.00
RCA Victor LSP-3559	(S)	The Best Of Hank Locklin	1966	10.00	25.00
		("Fraulein," "Send Me The Pillow You Dream On," "Geisha Girl" and "It's A Little More Like Heaven" are rechanneled.)			
RCA Victor LPM-3588	(M)	The Girls Get Prettier	1966	8.00	20.00
RCA Victor LSP-3588	(S)	The Girls Get Prettier	1966	10.00	25.00
RCA Victor LPM-3656	(M)	The Gloryland Way	1966	8.00	20.00
RCA Victor LSP-3656	(S)	The Gloryland Way	1966	10.00	25.00
RCA Victor LPM-3770	(M)	Send Me The Pillow You Dream On	1967	10.00	25.00
RCA Victor LSP-3770	(S)	Send Me The Pillow You Dream On	1967	8.00	20.00
RCA Victor LPM-3841	(M)	Nashville Women	1967	10.00	25.00
RCA Victor LSP-3841	(S)	Nashville Women	1967	8.00	20.00
RCA Victor LPM-3946	(M)	Country Hall Of Fame	1968	40.00	100.00
RCA Victor LSP-3946	(S)	Country Hall Of Fame	1968	8.00	20.00
		— RCA Victor albums above have black labels.—			
Wrangler W-1004	(M)	Hank Locklin	1962	12.00	30.00
Wrangler WS-1004	(S)	Hank Locklin	1962	12.00	30.00
Sears SPS-104	(E)	Send Me The Pillow You Dream On	196?	10.00	25.00

LODI

Mowest 101	(S)	Lodi	1972	10.00	25.00

LOFGREN, NILS
Refer to Crazy Horse; Grin.

A&M SP-8362	(DJ)	Authorized Bootleg (Counterfeits exist)	1976	10.00	25.00

LOGAN, TEX: *Refer to* THE CHARLES VALLEY RIVER BOYS

LOGGINS & MESSINA
Kenny Loggins and Jim Messina.

Columbia HC-44388	(S)	Best Of Friends (Half-speed master)	1982	8.00	25.00

LOGSDON, JIMMIE

King 843	(M)	Howdy, Neighbors	1963	30.00	75.00

LOLLIPOP SHOPPE, THE
The Lollipop Shoppe features Nik Pascal Raicevic.

Tower ST-5128	(S)	Angels From Hell (Soundtrack)	1968	12.00	30.00
Uni 73019	(S)	The Lollipop Shoppe	1968	16.00	40.00

LOMAX, JACKIE

Apple ST-3354	(S)	Is This What You Want	1969	10.00	25.00
		(Apple 3354 was produced by George Harrison.)			
Warner Bros. PRO-520	(DJ)	An Interview With Jackie Lomax	1972	16.00	40.00

LOMAX, JOHN A., JR.

Folkways FG-3508	(M)	American Folksongs	195?	12.00	30.00

LONDON, JULIE

Liberty LRP-3006	(M)	Julie Is Her Name	1956	20.00	50.00
Liberty LST-7027	(S)	Julie Is Her Name (Blue vinyl)	1958	40.00	100.00
Liberty LST-7027	(S)	Julie Is Her Name (Red vinyl)	1958	40.00	100.00
Liberty LST-7027	(S)	Julie Is Her Name	1958	16.00	40.00
Liberty LRP-3012	(M)	Lonely Girl	1956	20.00	50.00
Liberty LST-7029	(S)	Lonely Girl	1958	16.00	40.00
Liberty SL-9002	(M)	Calendar Girl (Gatefold cover)	1956	40.00	100.00
Liberty LRP-3043	(M)	About The Blues	1957	16.00	40.00
Liberty LST-7012	(S)	About The Blues	1958	16.00	40.00
Liberty LRP-3060	(M)	Make Love To Me	1957	16.00	40.00
Liberty LRP-3096	(M)	Julie	1957	16.00	40.00
Liberty LST-7004	(S)	Julie	1958	16.00	40.00
Liberty LRP-3100	(M)	Julie Is Her Name, Volume 2	1958	12.00	30.00
Liberty LST-7100	(S)	Julie Is Her Name, Volume 2	1958	16.00	40.00

Label & Catalog #		Title	Year	VG+	NM
Liberty LRP-3105	(M)	London By Night	1958	12.00	30.00
Liberty LST-7105	(S)	London By Night	1958	16.00	40.00
Liberty LRP-3119	(M)	Swing Me An Old Song	1959	12.00	30.00
Liberty LST-7119	(S)	Swing Me An Old Song	1959	16.00	40.00
Liberty LRP-3130	(M)	Your Number Please	1959	12.00	30.00
Liberty LST-7130	(S)	Your Number Please	1959	16.00	40.00
		—Liberty mono albums above have green labels; stereo albums have silver on black labels.—			
Liberty LRP-3152	(M)	Julie... At Home	1960	10.00	25.00
Liberty LST-7152	(S)	Julie... At Home *(Blue vinyl)*	1960	30.00	75.00
Liberty LST-7152	(S)	Julie... At Home	1960	12.00	30.00
Liberty LRP-3164	(M)	Around Midnight	1960	10.00	25.00
Liberty LST-7164	(S)	Around Midnight	1960	12.00	30.00
Liberty LRP-3171	(M)	Send For Me	1961	10.00	25.00
Liberty LST-7171	(S)	Send For Me	1961	12.00	30.00
Liberty LRP-3192	(M)	Whatever Julie Wants	1961	10.00	25.00
Liberty LST-7192	(S)	Whatever Julie Wants	1961	12.00	30.00
Liberty LRP-3203	(M)	Sophisticated Lady	1962	10.00	25.00
Liberty LST-7203	(S)	Sophisticated Lady	1962	12.00	30.00
Liberty LRP-3231	(M)	Love Letters	1962	10.00	25.00
Liberty LST-7231	(S)	Love Letters	1962	12.00	30.00
Liberty LRP-5501	(M)	The Best Of Julie London	1962	8.00	20.00
Liberty LST-6601	(S)	The Best Of Julie London	1962	10.00	25.00
Liberty LRP-3249	(M)	Love On The Rocks	1963	10.00	25.00
Liberty LST-7249	(S)	Love On The Rocks	1963	12.00	30.00
Liberty LRP-3278	(M)	Latin In A Satin Mood	1963	10.00	25.00
Liberty LST-7278	(S)	Latin In A Satin Mood	1963	12.00	30.00
Liberty LRP-3291	(M)	Julie's Golden Greats *(White cover)*	1963	8.00	20.00
Liberty LST-7291	(S)	Julie's Golden Greats *(White cover)*	1963	10.00	25.00
Liberty LRP-3291	(M)	Julie's Golden Greats *(Black cover)*	1963	8.00	20.00
Liberty LST-7291	(S)	Julie's Golden Greats *(Black cover)*	1963	10.00	25.00
		(Liberty 32/7291 is a compilation with one new track.)			
Liberty LRP-3300	(M)	The End Of The World	1963	8.00	20.00
Liberty LST-7300	(S)	The End Of The World	1963	10.00	25.00
Liberty LRP-3324	(M)	The Wonderful World Of Julie London	1964	8.00	20.00
Liberty LST-7324	(S)	The Wonderful World Of Julie London	1964	10.00	25.00
Liberty LRP-3342	(M)	Julie London	1964	8.00	20.00
Liberty LST-7342	(S)	Julie London	1964	10.00	25.00
Liberty LRP-3375	(M)	Julie London In Person At The Americana	1964	8.00	20.00
Liberty LST-7375	(S)	Julie London In Person At The Americana	1964	10.00	25.00
Liberty LRP-3392	(M)	Our Fair Lady	1965	8.00	20.00
Liberty LST-7392	(S)	Our Fair Lady	1965	10.00	25.00
Liberty LRP-3416	(M)	Feeling Good	1965	8.00	20.00
Liberty LST-7416	(S)	Feeling Good	1965	10.00	25.00
Liberty LRP-3434	(M)	All Through The Night	1965	8.00	20.00
Liberty LST-7434	(S)	All Through The Night	1965	10.00	25.00
Liberty LRP-3478	(M)	For The Night People	1966	8.00	20.00
Liberty LST-7478	(S)	For The Night People	1966	10.00	25.00
Liberty LRP-3493	(M)	Nice Girls Don't Stay For Breakfast	1967	8.00	20.00
Liberty LST-7493	(S)	Nice Girls Don't Stay For Breakfast	1967	10.00	25.00
Liberty LRP-3514	(M)	With Body And Soul	1967	8.00	20.00
Liberty LST-7514	(S)	With Body And Soul	1967	10.00	25.00
Liberty LST-7546	(S)	Easy Does It	1968	10.00	25.00
Liberty LST-7609	(S)	Yummy, Yummy, Yummy	1969	10.00	25.00
Liberty RC-1	(M)	By Myself	196?	10.00	25.00
Liberty SRC-1	(S)	By Myself	196?	12.00	30.00
		—Liberty albums above have black labels with a gold & white logo on the side.—			

LONDON, LAURIE
Capitol T-10169	(M)	Laurie London	1958	12.00	30.00

LONE STAR RAMBLERS, THE
Longhorn LP-600	(M)	Texas Square Dancing At The 60 Club	196?	10.00	25.00

LONESOME BLUES SINGERS, THE
The Lonesome Blues Singer is a pseudonym for Leadbelly.
Royale 18131	(10")	Blues Songs	1954	80.00	200.00

Label & Catalog #		Title	Year	VG+	NM
LONESOME PINE FIDDLERS, THE					
The LPF feature Charlie, Ezra and "Curly" Ray Cline. Refer to Hylo Brown					
Starday SLP-155	(M)	**14 Mountain Songs**			
		Featuring 5-String Banjo	1961	16.00	40.00
Starday SLP-194	(M)	**Bluegrass**	1962	16.00	40.00
Starday SLP-222	(M)	**More Bluegrass**	1963	16.00	40.00
		— Starday albums above have yellow labels.—			
LONESOME VALLEY SINGERS, THE					
Diplomat D-2622	(M)	**Song Of The Dragsters**	196?	12.00	30.00
Diplomat DS-2622	(S)	**Song Of The Dragsters**	196?	16.00	40.00
LONG, BARBARA: *Refer to* **GOLDMINE'S PRICE GUIDE TO COLLECTIBLE JAZZ ALBUMS**					
LONG, SHORTY, & THE SEARCHERS					
Ford FXM-712	(M)	**Country Jamboree**	1963	10.00	25.00
LONGBRANCH PENNYWHISTLE					
Members include J.D. Souther, Glen Frey, James Burton, Ry Cooder, Doug Kershaw; Buddy Emmons.					
Amos AAS-7007	(S)	**Longbranch Pennywhistle**	1969	20.00	50.00
LONZO & OSCAR					
Starday SLP-119	(M)	**America's Greatest Country Comedians**	1960	16.00	40.00
Starday SLP-244	(M)	**Country Music Time**	1963	16.00	40.00
		— Starday albums above have yellow labels.—			
LOOSE					
Necturne 906	(S)	**Freaky Billie, The Wheelie King**	1970	12.00	30.00
LOPEZ, TRINI					
King 863	(M)	**Teenage Love Songs**	1963	30.00	75.00
King 877	(M)	**More Of Trini Lopez**	1964	30.00	75.00
King 962	(M)	**24 Songs By The Great Trini Lopez**	1966	12.00	30.00
LOPEZ, TRINI / SCOTT GREGORY					
This album includes early, rare tracks by Bill Haley a.k.a. Scott Gregory.					
Guest Star GS-1499	(M)	**Trini Lopez And Scott Gregory**	1964	20.00	50.00
Guest Star GSS-1499	(E)	**Trini Lopez And Scott Gregory**	1964	8.00	20.00
LOPEZ, VINCENT / ENOCH LIGHT					
Waldorf Music Hall 33-1214	(M)	**Moments To Remember**	195?	20.00	50.00
		(Waldorf 1214 is an easy listening album			
		with Jayne Mansfield on the cover.)			
LORD, BOBBY					
Harmony HL-7322	(M)	**Bobby Lord's Best**	1964	12.00	30.00
Harmony HS-7322	(E)	**Bobby Lord's Best**	1964	8.00	20.00
LORD BUCKLEY					
RCA Victor LPM-3246	(10")	**Hipsters, Flipsters, And Finger**			
		Poppin' Daddies, Knock Me Your Lobes	1955	150.00	300.00
Vaya VLP-101/2	(10")	**Euphoria**	1955	80.00	200.00
Vaya CPM-10-1715LP	(10")	**Euphoria** *(Red vinyl)*	1955	150.00	300.00
Vaya VLP-101/2	(M)	**Euphoria, Volume 1**	1957	60.00	150.00
Vaya VLP-107/8	(M)	**Euphoria, Volume 2**	1957	60.00	150.00
World Pacific WP-1279	(M)	**The Way Out Humor Of Lord Buckley**	1959	60.00	150.00
Crestview CRV-801	(M)	**The Best Of Lord Buckley**	1963	20.00	50.00
Crestview CRV7-801	(S)	**The Best Of Lord Buckley**	1963	20.00	50.00
World Pacific WP-1815	(M)	**Lord Buckley In Concert**	1964	20.00	50.00
		(World Pacific 1815 is a reissue of WP 1279.)			
World Pacific WP-1849	(M)	**Blowing His Mind (And Yours, Too)**	1966	20.00	50.00
World Pacific WPS-21879	(S)	**Buckley's Best**	1968	14.00	35.00
World Pacific WPS-21889	(S)	**Bad Rapping Of The Marquis De Sade**	1969	14.00	35.00
Elektra EKS-74047	(S)	**The Best Of Lord Buckley**	1969	10.00	25.00
		(Elektra 74047 is a reissue of Crestview 801.)			
Straight STS-1054	(S)	**A Most Immaculately Hip Aristocrat**	1970	14.00	35.00
Reprise RS-6389	(S)	**A Most Immaculately Hip Aristocrat**	1970	10.00	25.00

Label & Catalog #		Title	Year	VG+	NM
LORD SITAR					
Capitol ST-3916	(S)	**Lord Sitar**	1968	12.00	30.00
LORD SUTCH					
Cotillion SD-9015	(S)	**Lord Sutch And His Heavy Friends**	1972	12.00	30.00
		(The good Lord's heavy friends include Led Zep's Jimmy Page			
		and John Bonham with Jeff Beck and Noel Redding.)			
Cotillion SD-9049	(S)	**Hands Of Jack The Ripper**	1972	12.00	30.00
LOREN, DONNA					
Capitol T-2323	(M)	**Beach Blanket Bingo**	1965	16.00	40.00
Capitol ST-2323	(S)	**Beach Blanket Bingo**	1965	20.00	50.00
LOREN, SOPHIA					
Ms. Loren also recorded with Peter Sellers.					
Columbia CL-1222	(M)	**Houseboat** (Soundtrack)	1958	80.00	200.00
RCA Victor Int. FOC-5	(M)	**Boccaccio '70** (Soundtrack)	1962	20.00	50.00
RCA Victor Int. FSO-5	(S)	**Boccaccio '70** (Soundtrack)	1962	30.00	75.00
		(Although the cover pictures Romy Schneider and Anita Ekberg			
		with Ms. Loren, neither of them appear on the record.)			
Columbia OL-6310	(M)	**Sophia Loren In Rome** (TV Soundtrack)	1964	10.00	25.00
Columbia OS-2710	(S)	**Sophia Loren In Rome** (TV Soundtrack)	1964	12.00	30.00
LOS BRAVOS					
Los Bravos features Mike Kennedy.					
Press PR-73003	(M)	**Black Is Black**	1966	16.00	40.00
		(Features the original single version of "Black Is Black.")			
Press PAS-83003	(E)	**Black Is Black**	1966	12.00	30.00
Parrot PAS-71021	(S)	**Bring A Little Lovin**	1968	16.00	40.00
LOS INDIOS TABAJARAS					
RCA Victor LPM-1788	(M)	**Sweet And Savage**	1958	14.00	35.00
RCA Victor LSP-1788	(S)	**Sweet And Savage**	1958	20.00	50.00
RCA Victor LPM-2822	(M)	**Maria Elena**	1963	8.00	20.00
RCA Victor LSP-2822	(S)	**Maria Elena**	1963	10.00	25.00
		(RCA 2822 is a reissue of 1788.)			
LOS LOBOS/LOS LOBOS DEL ESTE DE LOS ANGELES					
Pan American 101	(S)	**Si Se Puede!**	1976	100.00	200.00
New Vista 1001	(S)	**Just Another Band From East L.A.**	1978	200.00	400.00
LOS MORENOS					
Prestige Int. PRLP-13052	(M)	**The Sound Of Flamenco**	1962	12.00	30.00
LOS SEVEN DAYS					
Eco 314	(M)	**Sha-La-La**	196?	20.00	50.00
LOST & FOUND					
International Art. 3	(S)	**Everybody's Here**	1968	20.00	50.00
International Art. 3	(S)	**Everybody's Here**	1979	6.00	15.00
		(Reissues have "Masterfonics" stamped in the trail-off vinyl.)			
LOTHAR & THE HAND PEOPLE					
Capitol ST-2997	(S)	**Presenting Lothar & The Hand People**	1968	16.00	40.00
Capitol ST-247	(S)	**Space Hymn**	1969	16.00	40.00
LOUDERMILK, JOHN D.					
RCA Victor LPM-2434	(M)	**Language Of Love**	1961	8.00	20.00
RCA Victor LSP-2434	(S)	**Language Of Love**	1961	10.00	25.00
RCA Victor LPM-2539	(M)	**Twelve Sides Of Loudermilk**	1962	8.00	20.00
RCA Victor LSP-2539	(S)	**Twelve Sides Of Loudermilk**	1962	10.00	25.00
		— RCA mono albums above have "Long Play" on the bottom of the label;			
		stereo albums have "Living Stereo" on the bottom. —			
RCA Victor LPM-3497	(M)	**A Bizarre Collection Of... Unusual Songs**	1965	10.00	25.00
RCA Victor LSP-3497	(S)	**A Bizarre Collection Of... Unusual Songs**	1965	12.00	30.00
LOUDON, DOROTHY					
Coral CRL-57265	(M)	**Live At The Blue Angel**	1959	6.00	15.00
Coral CRL-757265	(S)	**Live At The Blue Angel**	1959	10.00	25.00

Wow! Was she ever beeyooteefool! While Miss Louise appeared on other album covers, she was merely—and I bite my tongue using that word in reference to her—a model. On this one, she sings. This is the original mono only release on Concert Hall; later pressings on Urania were issued in stereo, which are even rarer than the Concert Hall.

Label & Catalog #		Title	Year	VG+	NM
LOUISE, TINA					
Concert Hall H-1503	*(M)*	**Tina Louise—Her Portrait In Hi Fi**	*1957*	**20.00**	**50.00**
		(CH-1503 is an instrumental album with Ms. Louise on the cover.)			
Concert Hall H-1521	*(M)*	It's Time For Tina	*1958*	**150.00**	**300.00**
Urania ULM-2005	*(M)*	It's Time For Tina	*1958*	**80.00**	**200.00**
Urania USD-2005	*(S)*	It's Time For Tina	*1958*	**150.00**	**300.00**
		(Urania 2005 is a reissue of CH-1521.)			
LOUISIANA HONEY DRIPPERS, THE					
Prestige Int. PRLP-13035	*(M)*	**Bluegrass**	*1961*	**12.00**	**30.00**
LOUISIANA RED					
Roulette R-25200	*(M)*	**The Lowdown Back Porch Blues**	*1963*	**14.00**	**35.00**
LOUVIN, CHARLIE					
Capitol T-2208	*(M)*	**Less And Less**	*1965*	**8.00**	**20.00**
Capitol ST-2208	*(S)*	**Less And Less**	*1965*	**10.00**	**25.00**
Capitol T-2437	*(M)*	**The Many Moods Of Charlie Louvin**	*1966*	**8.00**	**20.00**
Capitol ST-2437	*(S)*	**The Many Moods Of Charlie Louvin**	*1966*	**10.00**	**25.00**
Capitol T-2482	*(M)*	**Lonesome Is Me**	*1966*	**8.00**	**20.00**
Capitol ST-2482	*(S)*	**Lonesome Is Me**	*1966*	**10.00**	**25.00**
		— Capitol albums above have black "rainbow" labels.—			
LOUVIN, IRA					
Capitol T-2413	*(M)*	**The Unforgettable Ira Louvin**	*1965*	**10.00**	**25.00**
Capitol ST-2413	*(S)*	**The Unforgettable Ira Louvin**	*1965*	**12.00**	**30.00**
		— Capitol albums above have black "rainbow" labels.—			
LOUVIN BROTHERS, THE					
Charlie and Ira Louvin.					
MGM E-3426	*(M)*	**The Louvin Brothers**	*1956*	**80.00**	**200.00**
Capitol T-769	*(M)*	**Tragic Songs Of Life**	*1956*	**50.00**	**100.00**
Capitol T-825	*(M)*	**Nearer My God To Thee**	*1957*	**40.00**	**100.00**
Capitol T-910	*(M)*	**Ira And Charlie**	*1958*	**40.00**	**100.00**
		— Capitol albums above have turquoise labels.—			
Capitol T-769	*(M)*	**Tragic Songs Of Life**	*195?*	**16.00**	**40.00**
Capitol T-825	*(M)*	**Nearer My God To Thee**	*195?*	**16.00**	**40.00**
Capitol T-910	*(M)*	**Ira And Charlie**	*195?*	**16.00**	**40.00**
Capitol T-1061	*(M)*	**The Family Who Prays**	*1958*	**30.00**	**75.00**
Capitol T-1106	*(M)*	**Country Love Ballads**	*1959*	**30.00**	**75.00**
Capitol T-1277	*(M)*	**Satan Is Real**	*1960*	**30.00**	**75.00**
Capitol T-1385	*(M)*	**My Baby's Gone**	*1960*	**30.00**	**75.00**
Capitol T-1449	*(M)*	**A Tribute To The Delmore Brothers**	*1960*	**30.00**	**75.00**
Capitol T-1547	*(M)*	**Encore**	*1961*	**20.00**	**50.00**
Capitol T-1616	*(M)*	**Country Christmas**	*1961*	**20.00**	**50.00**
Capitol ST-1616	*(S)*	**Country Christmas**	*1961*	**30.00**	**75.00**
		— Capitol albums above have black labels with the logo on the left side.—			
Capitol T-769	*(M)*	**Tragic Songs Of Life**	*196?*	**10.00**	**25.00**
Capitol DT-769	*(E)*	**Tragic Songs Of Life**	*196?*	**8.00**	**20.00**
Capitol T-910	*(M)*	**Ira And Charlie**	*196?*	**10.00**	**25.00**
Capitol T-1061	*(M)*	**The Family Who Prays**	*196?*	**10.00**	**25.00**
Capitol DT-1061	*(E)*	**The Family Who Prays**	*196?*	**8.00**	**20.00**
Capitol T-1106	*(M)*	**Country Love Ballads**	*196?*	**10.00**	**25.00**
Capitol T-1277	*(M)*	**Satan Is Real**	*196?*	**10.00**	**25.00**
Capitol T-1385	*(M)*	**My Baby's Gone**	*196?*	**10.00**	**25.00**
Capitol T-1449	*(M)*	**A Tribute To The Delmore Brothers**	*196?*	**10.00**	**25.00**
Capitol T-1547	*(M)*	**Encore**	*196?*	**20.00**	**50.00**
Capitol T-1616	*(M)*	**Country Christmas**	*196?*	**20.00**	**50.00**
Capitol ST-1616	*(S)*	**Country Christmas**	*196?*	**10.00**	**25.00**
Capitol T-1721	*(M)*	**Weapon Of Prayer**	*1962*	**16.00**	**40.00**
Capitol ST-1721	*(S)*	**Weapon Of Prayer**	*1962*	**20.00**	**50.00**
Capitol T-1834	*(M)*	**Keep Your Eyes On Jesus**	*1963*	**16.00**	**40.00**
Capitol ST-1834	*(S)*	**Keep Your Eyes On Jesus**	*1963*	**20.00**	**50.00**
Capitol T-2091	*(M)*	**The Louvin Brothers Sing And Play Their Current Hits**	*1964*	**12.00**	**30.00**
Capitol ST-2091	*(S)*	**The Louvin Brothers Sing And Play Their Current Hits**	*1964*	**16.00**	**40.00**
Capitol T-2331	*(M)*	**Thank God For My Christian Home**	*1965*	**12.00**	**30.00**
Capitol ST-2331	*(S)*	**Thank God For My Christian Home**	*1965*	**16.00**	**40.00**

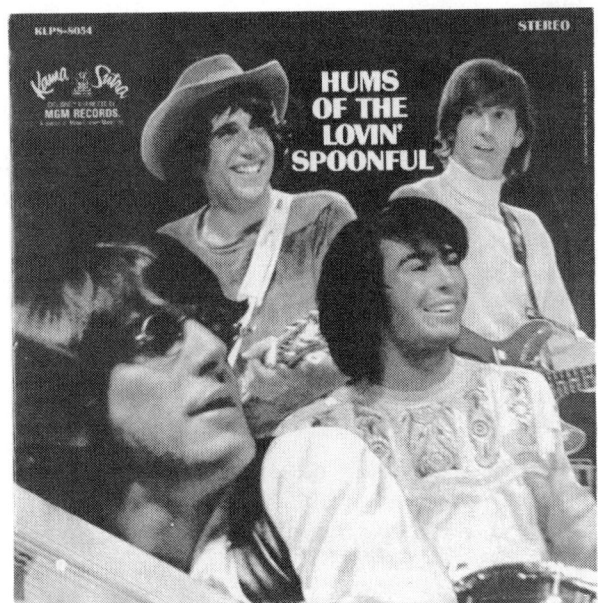

The Lovin' Spoonful was one of the great American bands of the '60s who responded to the British Invasion—especially The Beatles—with a brand of music so American that it could never be mistaken for anything else. Their music combined many elements already common to rock'n roll, including a healthy grounding in folk-blues, and mixed in a little jugband and lunacy. They remain under-appreciated by the critics and the collectors and their LPs are much more difficult to find in nearly mint condition than the values assigned indicate. Do You Believe In Magic and Hums Of The Lovin' Spoonful are the best, the latter a singular display of John Sebastian's prodigious songwriting and singing abilities.

Label & Catalog #		Title	Year	VG+	NM
Capitol T-2827	(M)	The Great Roy Acuff Songs	1967	12.00	30.00
Capitol ST-2827	(S)	The Great Roy Acuff Songs	1967	16.00	40.00
Tower T-5038	(M)	Two Different Worlds	1966	12.00	30.00
Tower DT-5038	(E)	Two Different Worlds	1966	8.00	20.00
Tower DT-5122	(E)	Country Heart And Soul	1968	10.00	25.00

LOVE
Love was the brainchild of Arthur Lee.

Elektra EKL-4001	(M)	Love	1966	20.00	50.00
Elektra EKS-74001	(S)	Love	1966	10.00	25.00
Elektra EKL-4005	(M)	Da Capo	1966	20.00	50.00
Elektra EKS-74005	(S)	Da Capo	1966	10.00	25.00
Elektra EKL-4013	(M)	Forever Changes	1967	30.00	75.00
Elektra EKS-74013	(S)	Forever Changes	1967	10.00	25.00
		— Elektra albums above have brown labels.—			
Elektra EKS-74049	(S)	Four Sail *(White label promo)*	1969	12.00	30.00

LOVE EXCHANGE, THE

Tower ST-5115	(S)	The Love Exchange	1968	10.00	25.00

LOVE IS A HEART-ON

Heavy	(S)	Love Is A Heart-On	1970	100.00	250.00

LOVE, MIKE, & DEAN TORRENCE

Premore PL-1083	(S)	Rock N' Roll Is Here Again	1983	10.00	25.00

LOVE SCULPTURE
Love Sculpture features Dave Edmunds.

Rare Earth RS-505	(S)	Blues Helping	1969	16.00	40.00
Parrot PAS-71035	(S)	Forms And Feeling	1970	10.00	25.00

LOVECRAFT: *Refer to* H.P. LOVECRAFT

LOVIN' SPOONFUL, THE
The original Spoonful were Steve Boone, Joe Butler, John Sebastian and Zal Yanovsky, replaced in 1967 by Jerry Yester, formerly of The Modern Folk Quartet. By 1969 Boone was the only original member left.

Kama Sutra KLP-8050	(M)	Do You Believe In Magic?	1965	10.00	25.00
Kama Sutra KLPS-8050	(S)	Do You Believe In Magic?	1965	12.00	30.00
Kama Sutra ST-90597	(S)	Do You Believe In Magic? *(Capitol Rec. Club)*	1965	12.00	30.00
Kama Sutra KLP-8051	(M)	Daydream	1966	10.00	25.00
Kama Sutra KLPS-8051	(S)	Daydream	1966	12.00	30.00
Kama Sutra KLP-8053	(M)	What's Up, Tiger Lily? *(Soundtrack)*	1966	8.00	20.00
Kama Sutra KLPS-8053	(S)	What's Up, Tiger Lily? *(Soundtrack)*	1966	10.00	25.00
Kama Sutra KLP-8054	(M)	Hums Of The Lovin' Spoonful	1966	10.00	25.00
Kama Sutra KLPS-8054	(S)	Hums Of The Lovin' Spoonful	1966	12.00	30.00
Kama Sutra KLPS-8073	(S)	Revelations: Revolution '69	1969	10.00	25.00

LOWE, JIM

Mercury MG-20246	(M)	The Door Of Fame	1957	60.00	150.00
Dot DLP-3114	(M)	Wicked Women	1958	60.00	150.00
Dot DLP-3681	(M)	Songs They Sing Behind The Green Door	1965	40.00	100.00

LOWE, MUNDELL, & HERB STRAUSS

Riverside RLP-7541	(M)	Folk Music For People Who Hate Folk Music	1963	10.00	25.00
Riverside RS-9541	(S)	Folk Music For People Who Hate Folk Music	1963	12.00	30.00

LOWERY, FRED

Decca DL-8476	(M)	Walking Along Kicking The Leaves	1958	10.00	25.00
Decca DL-8995	(M)	Whistle A Happy Tune	1959	10.00	25.00
Decca DL-78995	(S)	Whistle A Happy Tune	1959	14.00	35.00

LRY

Congress/Crow 8031002	(S)	The LRY Record	1968	40.00	100.00

LUCAS, NICK

Cavalier 5003	(10")	Tiptoe Thru The Tulips	1955	12.00	30.00
Decca DL-8653	(M)	Painting The Clouds With Sunshine	1957	20.00	50.00

Label & Catalog #		Title	Year	VG+	NM

LULU

Parrot PA-61016	(M)	From Lulu With Love	1967	10.00	25.00
Parrot PAS-71016	(S)	From Lulu With Love	1967	12.00	30.00
Epic LN-24339	(M)	To Sir With Love	1967	10.00	25.00
Epic BN-26339	(S)	To Sir With Love	1967	12.00	30.00
		("Morning Dew" and "Let's Pretend" are rechanneled on this album.)			
Atco 33-310	(M)	New Routes (White label promo)	1970	12.00	30.00
Atco 33-330	(M)	Melody Fair (White label promo)	1970	12.00	30.00

LULU BELLE & SCOTTY

Super SR-6201	(M)	Lulu Belle & Scotty	1963	20.00	50.00
Starday SLP-206	(M)	The Sweethearts Of Country Music	1963	16.00	40.00
Starday SLP-285	(M)	Down Memory Lane	1964	16.00	40.00
Starday SLP-351	(M)	Lulu Belle & Scotty	1965	16.00	40.00
		— Starday albums above have yellow labels.—			

LUMAN, BOB

Warner Bros. W-1396	(M)	Let's Think About Livin'	1960	20.00	50.00
Warner Bros. WS-1396	(S)	Let's Think About Livin'	1960	30.00	75.00
Hickory LPM-124	(M)	Livin' Lovin' Sounds	1965	10.00	25.00
Hickory LPS-124	(S)	Livin' Lovin' Sounds	1965	12.00	30.00

LUMBEE

| Radnor 2003 | (S) | Overdose (Includes a bonus game) | 197? | 30.00 | 75.00 |
| Radnor 2003 | (S) | Overdose (Without the game) | 197? | 20.00 | 50.00 |

LUND, GARRETT

| (No label) | (S) | Almost Grown (With insert) | 1975 | 150.00 | 300.00 |

LUNN, ROBERT

| Starday SLP-228 | (M) | The Original Talking Blues Man (Yellow label) | 1962 | 16.00 | 40.00 |

LUNSFORD, BASCOM LAMAR

Bascom Lunsford was an old-time banjo and fiddle player, singer and writer of folk-based music.

Folkways FP-40	(10")	Smoky Mountain Ballads	195?	20.00	50.00
Folkways FA-2040	(10")	Smoky Mountain Ballads	195?	20.00	50.00
Riverside RLP-12-645	(M)	Minstrel Of The Appalachians	195?	12.00	30.00

LUSE, HARLEY: Refer to DECKER, EVA / HARLEY LUSE

LUTCHER, NELLIE

Capitol H-232	(10")	Real Gone	1950	20.00	50.00
Capitol T-232	(M)	Real Gone	1955	16.00	40.00
Epic LN-1108	(10")	Wheel Nellie	1955	20.00	50.00
Liberty LRP-3014	(M)	Our New Nellie	1956	10.00	25.00

LUTHER, FRANK

| Decca DL-5035 | (10") | Get Along, Little Doggies | 1950 | 20.00 | 50.00 |

LUTHER, FRANK, & ZORA LAYMAN

| Decca DL-8093 | (M) | Songs Of The North And South (1961-65) | 1956 | 12.00 | 30.00 |

LYMAN, ARTHUR

Hawaiian born Lyman, a vibraphone and marimba player, originally recorded with Martin Denny's band before launching his own successful career as a maker of "exotic music."

Hifi R-806	(M)	Taboo	1958	8.00	20.00
Hifi SR-806	(S)	Taboo	1958	12.00	30.00
Hifi R-815	(M)	Bahia	1959	8.00	20.00
Hifi SR-815	(S)	Bahia	1959	12.00	30.00
Hifi R-818	(M)	On Broadway	1960	8.00	20.00
Hifi SR-818	(S)	On Broadway	1960	12.00	30.00
Hifi L-1004	(M)	Yellow Bird	1961	8.00	20.00
Hifi SL-1004	(S)	Yellow Bird	1961	12.00	30.00
Hifi L-1005	(M)	The Colorful Percussions Of Arthur Lyman	1962	8.00	20.00
Hifi SL-1005	(S)	The Colorful Percussions Of Arthur Lyman	1962	12.00	30.00
Hifi L-1007	(M)	The Many Moods Of Arthur Lyman	1962	8.00	20.00
Hifi SL-1007	(S)	The Many Moods Of Arthur Lyman	1962	12.00	30.00

Label & Catalog #		Title	Year	VG+	NM
Hifi L-1009	(M)	I Wish You Love	1963	8.00	20.00
Hifi SL-1009	(S)	I Wish You Love	1963	12.00	30.00
Hifi L-1014	(M)	Blowin' In The Wind	1963	8.00	20.00
Hifi SL-1014	(S)	Blowin' In The Wind	1963	12.00	30.00
Hifi L-1018	(M)	Merry Christmas (Mele Kalikimaka)	1963	8.00	20.00
Hifi SL-1018	(S)	Merry Christmas (Mele Kalikimaka)	1963	12.00	30.00
Hifi L-1024	(M)	Midnight Sun	1964	8.00	20.00
Hifi SL-1024	(S)	Midnight Sun	1964	12.00	30.00

LYMON, FRANKIE
Frankie Lymon originally recorded with The Teenagers.

Roulette R-25013	(M)	Frankie Lymon At The London Palladium	1958	150.00	300.00
Roulette R-25036	(M)	Rock 'N Roll!	1958	150.00	300.00
Guest G-1406	(M)	Teen Time Tunes Starring Frankie Lymon	1959	16.00	40.00
Guest GS-1406	(E)	Teen Time Tunes Starring Frankie Lymon	1959	12.00	30.00
		(Guest Star 1406 is actually a various artists compilation.			
		Original covers have full-color photo of Frankie.)			
Guest G-1406	(M)	Rock & Roll Party Starring Frankie Lymon	1959	12.00	30.00
Guest GS-1406	(E)	Rock & Roll Party Starring Frankie Lymon	1959	8.00	20.00
		(Later covers have black & white photo of Frankie.)			

LYNCH, CHRISTOPHER
Columbia ML-2016	(10")	The Minstrel Boy	195?	16.00	40.00

LYNCH, JACK, & THE MIAMI VALLEY BOYS
Jalyn JLP-121	(M)	Bluegrass Music	196?	10.00	25.00

LYNN, BARBARA
Jamie JLP-3023	(M)	You'll Lose A Good Thing	1962	20.00	50.00
Jamie JLPS-3023	(E)	You'll Lose A Good Thing	1962	24.00	60.00
Atlantic 8171	(M)	Here Is Barbara Lynn	1968	20.00	50.00
Atlantic SD-8171	(S)	Here Is Barbara Lynn	1968	20.00	50.00

LYNN, LORETTA
Decca DL-4457	(M)	Loretta Lynn Sings	1963	16.00	40.00
Decca DL-74457	(S)	Loretta Lynn Sings	1963	20.00	50.00
Decca DL-4541	(M)	Before I'm Over You	1964	12.00	30.00
Decca DL-74541	(S)	Before I'm Over You	1964	16.00	40.00
Decca DL-4620	(M)	Songs From My Heart	1965	12.00	30.00
Decca DL-74620	(S)	Songs From My Heart	1965	16.00	40.00
Decca DL-4665	(M)	Blue Kentucky Girl	1965	12.00	30.00
Decca DL-74665	(S)	Blue Kentucky Girl	1965	16.00	40.00
Decca DL-4695	(M)	Hymns	1965	10.00	25.00
Decca DL-74695	(S)	Hymns	1965	12.00	30.00
Decca DL-4744	(M)	I Like 'Em Country	1966	10.00	25.00
Decca DL-74744	(S)	I Like 'Em Country	1966	12.00	30.00
Decca DL-4783	(M)	You Ain't Woman Enough	1966	10.00	25.00
Decca DL-74783	(S)	You Ain't Woman Enough	1966	12.00	30.00
Decca DL-4817	(M)	A Country Christmas	1966	10.00	25.00
Decca DL-74817	(S)	A Country Christmas	1966	12.00	30.00
		— Decca albums above have black labels with "Mfrd. by Decca" beneath the rainbow.—			
Decca DL-75084	(S)	Your Squaw Is On The Warpath	1969	16.00	40.00
		(Decca 75084 was originally issued with "Barney.")			
MCA PRO-1934	(DJ)	Loretta Lynn	1974	16.00	40.00
MCA 35013	(DJ)	Allis-Chambers Presents Loretta Lynn	1978	16.00	40.00
MCA 35018	(DJ)	Crisco Presents Loretta Lynn	1979	16.00	40.00

LYNN, LORETTA, & ERNEST TUBB
Decca DL-4639	(M)	Mr & Mrs Used To Be	1965	10.00	25.00
Decca DL-74639	(S)	Mr & Mrs Used To Be	1965	12.00	30.00

LYNNE, GLORIA: *Refer to* GOLDMINE'S PRICE GUIDE TO COLLECTIBLE JAZZ ALBUMS

LYNYRD SKUNYRD
MCA 1946	(DJ)	One More From The Road *(Blue vinyl)*	1976	20.00	50.00
MCA 1946	(DJ)	One More From The Road *(Gold vinyl)*	1976	20.00	50.00
MCA 1946	(DJ)	One More From The Road *(Purple vinyl)*	1976	20.00	50.00
MCA 1946	(DJ)	One More From The Road *(Red vinyl)*	1976	20.00	50.00

Frankie Lymon left the confines of his group, The Teenagers, where he had recorded one of the definitive group rockers of the '50s, "Why Do Fools Fall In Love," for a shot at solo stardom. Unfortunately, this move did not bring the rewards expected. The man who was bigger than Elvis to black kids all over New York City died at the age of 25, another loss to the insanities of drug abuse and its attendant prohibition.

M

MABON, WILLIE

Chess LP-1439	(M)	**Willie Mabon** (Black label)	1958	200.00	400.00

MAC-KAC

Atlantic 8012	(M)	**Mac-Kac & His French Rock & Roll**	1956	20.00	50.00

MacARTHUR

R. P. C.	(S)	**MacArthur**	1970	200.00	400.00
Bay Music	(S)	**MacArthur II**	1982	50.00	125.00

MacARTHUR, GENERAL JAMES

Atlantic 8095	(M)	**The Life Of General MacArthur**	1964	16.00	40.00

MacARTHUR, MARGARET

Margaret and John MacArthur is a singer and instrumentalist in the traditional American folk vein.

Folkways FH-5314	(M)	**Folksongs Of Vermont**	1960	10.00	25.00

MacBEE, HAMMER

Folklore FRLP-14008	(M)	**Cumberland Moonshiner**	1964	8.00	20.00
Folklore FRST-14008	(S)	**Cumberland Moonshiner**	1964	10.00	25.00

MacCOLL, EWAN

Ewan MacColl is a Scottish singer and writer of music using the traditional lore of Great Britain. Refer to A. L. Lloyd & Ewan MacColl; Peggy Seeger & Ewan MacColl;.

Stinson SLP-79	(10")	**British Industrial Folk Songs**	195?	20.00	50.00
Topic T-26	(10")	**Barrack Room Ballads**	1958	20.00	50.00
Riverside RLP-12-605	(M)	**Scots Drinking Songs**	195?	12.00	30.00
Riverside RLP-12-609	(M)	**Scots Folk Songs**	195?	12.00	30.00
Riverside RLP-12-612	(M)	**Scots Street Songs**	195?	12.00	30.00
Riverside RLP-12-632	(M)	**Bad Lads And Hard Cases**	195?	12.00	30.00
Riverside RLP-12-642	(M)	**Bless 'Em All**	195?	12.00	30.00

MacDONALD, JEANETTE, & NELSON EDDY

RCA Victor LPM-1738	(M)	**Favorites In Hi-Fi**	1958	16.00	40.00
RCA Victor LPV-526	(M)	**Jeanette McDonald And Nelson Eddy**	1965	10.00	25.00

MACEO/MACEO & ALL THE KING'S MEN

Maceo Parker from James Brown's band.

House Of Fox LP-1	(S)	**Doing Their Own Thing**	197?	10.00	25.00
People PE-6601	(S)	**Us** (Produced by James Brown)	1973	10.00	25.00

MACK, LONNIE

Fraternity SF-1014	(M)	**The Wham Of That Memphis Man**	1963	30.00	75.00
Fraternity SSF-1014	(S)	**The Wham Of That Memphis Man**	1963	60.00	150.00

MacKENZIE, GISELE

Vik LX-1055	(M)	**Gisele MacKenzie**	1956	16.00	40.00
Vik LX-1075	(M)	**Mam' Selle Gisele**	1956	16.00	40.00
Vik LX-1099	(M)	**Christmas With Gisele**	1957	16.00	40.00
RCA Victor LPM-1790	(M)	**Gisele**	1958	12.00	30.00
RCA Victor LSP-1790	(S)	**Gisele**	1958	16.00	40.00
RCA Victor LPM-2006	(M)	**Christmas With Gisele**	1959	12.00	30.00
RCA Victor LSP-2006	(S)	**Christmas With Gisele**	1959	16.00	40.00
Everest LPBR-5069	(M)	**In Person At The Empire Room**	1959	8.00	20.00
Everest SDBR-1069	(S)	**In Person At The Empire Room**	1959	10.00	25.00

MACON, UNCLE DAVE

Singer, songwriter and banjo player Dave Macon is a pioneering figure in the history of country music.

Decca DL-4760	(M)	**Uncle Dave Macon**	1966	8.00	20.00
Decca DL-74760	(S)	**Uncle Dave Macon**	1966	10.00	25.00

These two albums collect a number of performances of silly songs that had originally been made available on flexi-discs as freebies in Mad's annuals and other special editions. According to the liner notes, the bulk of the credit for these recordings belong to Jeanne Hayes and The Dellwoods (these LPs were listed under this group in previous editions).

Label & Catalog #		Title	Year	VG+	NM
MacRAE, GORDON					
Refer to Jane Powell.					
Capitol H-231	(10")	**Songs**	1950	16.00	40.00
MGM E-104	(10")	**Prisoner Of Love** (Soundtrack)	1952	20.00	50.00
Capitol L-334	(10")	**Roberta** (Studio Cast)	1952	20.00	50.00
Capitol L-335	(10")	**Merry Widow** (Studio Cast)	1952	20.00	50.00
Capitol L-351	(10")	**Desert Song** (Studio Cast)	1953	24.00	60.00
Capitol L-407	(10")	**Student Prince** (Studio Cast)	1953	20.00	50.00
Capitol H-422	(10")	**By The Light Of The Silvery Moon** (Sdtk)	1953	24.00	60.00
Capitol L-530	(10")	**The Red Mill** (Soundtrack)	1954	20.00	50.00
Capitol T-219	(M)	**New Moon / Vagabond King** (Soundtrack)	1952	16.00	40.00
Capitol T-384	(M)	**The Desert Song / Roberta** (Soundtrack)	1953	16.00	40.00
Capitol T-428	(M)	**Memory Songs** (With Jo Stafford)	1954	16.00	40.00
Capitol T-437	(M)	**Merry Widow /**			
		The Student Prince (Soundtracks)	1954	16.00	40.00
Capitol T-537	(M)	**Romantic Ballads**	1955	14.00	35.00
Capitol T-551	(M)	**The Red Mill /**			
		Naughty Marietta (Soundtracks)	1954	16.00	40.00
Capitol SAO-595	(M)	**Oklahoma** (Soundtrack)	1955	12.00	30.00
Capitol T-681	(M)	**Operetta Favorites**	1956	12.00	30.00
Capitol W-694	(M)	**Carousel** (Soundtrack)	1956	12.00	30.00
Capitol T-765	(M)	**The Best Things In Life Are Free**	1956	12.00	30.00
Capitol T-834	(M)	**Cowboy's Lament**	1957	12.00	30.00
Capitol T-875	(M)	**Motion Picture Soundstage**	1957	12.00	30.00
Capitol T-980	(M)	**Gordon MacRae In Concert**	1958	12.00	30.00
Capitol T-1050	(M)	**This Is Gordon MacRae**	1958	12.00	30.00
MAD DOG					
Fish Head	(S)	**Mad Dog**	1975	16.00	40.00
MAD FABLE					
Magic MAD-101	(S)	**Get Off!**	1977	40.00	100.00
MAD LADS, THE					
Volt 414	(M)	**The Mad Lads In Action**	1966	8.00	20.00
Volt S-414	(S)	**The Mad Lads In Action**	1966	10.00	25.00

MAD MAGAZINE
This collection of pop parodies is from the gang at Mad Magazine and collects material from several flexi-discs that the magazine had previously included as freebies in their annuals. This LP apparently was available for purchase only through the mail. The back cover credits the performances to Jeanne Hayes and Mike Russo backed by The Dellwoods. For more on Mad, refer to Bernie Greene.

Big Top 12-1305	(M)	**Mad "Twists" Rock 'N' Roll**	1961	40.00	100.00
Big Top 12-1306	(M)	**Fink Along With Mad**	1961	40.00	100.00
MAD RIVER					
Capitol ST-2985	(S)	**Mad River**	1968	20.00	50.00
Capitol ST-185	(S)	**Paradise Bar And Grill**	1969	16.00	40.00
		(Counterfeits of 185— perhaps 2985— exist.)			
MADDOX, ROSE					
Columbia CL-1159	(M)	**Precious Memories**	1958	20.00	50.00
Capitol T-1312	(M)	**The One Rose**	1960	16.00	35.00
Capitol ST-1312	(S)	**The One Rose**	1960	20.00	50.00
Capitol T-1437	(M)	**Glorybound Train**	1960	16.00	35.00
Capitol ST-1437	(S)	**Glorybound Train**	1960	20.00	50.00
Capitol T-1548	(M)	**A Big Bouquet Of Roses**	1961	16.00	35.00
Capitol ST-1548	(S)	**A Big Bouquet Of Roses**	1961	20.00	50.00
		— Capitol albums above have black "rainbow" labels with the logo on the right side.—			
Capitol T-1779	(M)	**Rose Maddox Sing Bluegrass**	1962	16.00	35.00
Capitol ST-1779	(S)	**Rose Maddox Sing Bluegrass**	1962	20.00	50.00
Capitol T-1993	(M)	**Alone With You**	1963	12.00	30.00
Capitol ST-1993	(S)	**Alone With You**	1963	16.00	40.00
Starday SSLP-463	(E)	**Rosie**	1970	12.00	30.00

MADDOX BROTHERS, THE, & ROSE
The Maddox brothers are Calvin, Don, Fred and Henry with sister Rose.

King 669	(M)	**A Collection Of Standard Sacred Songs**	1959	80.00	200.00
King 677	(M)	**The Maddox Brothers And Rose**	1960	60.00	150.00

Label & Catalog #		Title	Year	VG+	NM
King 752	(M)	I'll Write Your Name In The Sand	1961	60.00	150.00
Wrangler W-1003	(M)	The Maddox Brothers And Rose	1962	14.00	35.00
Wrangler WS-1003	(S)	The Maddox Brothers And Rose	1962	20.00	50.00
Sears SPS-107	(E)	The Maddox Brothers And Rose			
		Go Honky Tonkin'	196?	20.00	50.00
Piccadilly PIC-3340	(M)	Old Pals Of Yesterday	1980	10.00	25.00

MADIGAN, BETTY: *Refer to* GOLDMINE'S PRICE GUIDE TO COLLECTIBLE JAZZ ALBUMS

MADONNA

Sire 23967	(S)	Madonna	1983	10.00	25.00
		(Original pressings of Sire 23967 have a longer— 4:48			
		versus 3:41— remixed version of "Burning Up.")			
Sire 25157	(DJ)	Like A Virgin (White vinyl)	1984	16.00	40.00

MADRIGAL

(No label)	(S)	Madrigal	196?	200.00	400.00

MAESTRO, JOHNNY

Johnny Maestro was formerly the lead singer for The Crests; The Brooklyn Bridge.

Buddah BDS-5091	(P)	The Johnny Maestro Story (With inserts)	1971	16.00	40.00

MAGI

Uncle Dirty 6102-N13	(S)	Win Or Lose	1975	80.00	200.00

MAGIC

Armadillo 8031	(S)	Enclosed	1970	80.00	200.00

MAGIC

Magic features Jay Ferguson.

Rare Earth 527	(S)	Magic	1971	10.00	25.00

MAGIC FERN, THE

Piccadilly PIC-	(S)	The Magic Fern	1980	20.00	50.00

MAGIC LANTERNS, THE

Atlantic SD-8217	(S)	Shame Shame	1969	10.00	25.00

MAGIC SAM

Delmark DL-615	(S)	West Side Soul	1968	20.00	50.00
Delmark DL-620	(S)	Black Magic	1969	20.00	50.00

MAGNIFICENTS, THE : *Refer to* THE EL DORADOS / THE MAGNIFICENTS

MAGNUS, JOHNNY

Reprise R-6003	(M)	The X-15 & Other Sounds			
		Of Missiles, Rockets & Jets	1961	8.00	20.00
Reprise R9-6003	(S)	The X-15 & Other Sounds			
		Of Missiles, Rockets & Jets	1961	10.00	25.00

MAHOGANY RUSH

Nine 936	(S)	Maxoom	1972	20.00	50.00

MAIDEN, SIDNEY

Bluesville BVLP-1035	(M)	Trouble An' Blues	1961	30.00	75.00
		— Bluesville albums above have bright blue labels with silver print.—			
Bluesville BVLP-1035	(M)	Trouble An' Blues	1964	10.00	25.00
		— Bluesville albums above have blue labels with a trident logo on the right side.—			

MAIN ATTRACTION, THE

Tower ST-5177	(S)	And Now	1968	10.00	25.00

MAINER, J. E., & HIS MOUNTAINEERS

King 666	(M)	Good Ole Mountain Music	1960	40.00	100.00
King 765	(M)	Variety Album	1961	40.00	100.00

MAINER, WADE

King 769	(M)	Soulful Sacred Songs	1961	40.00	100.00

Label & Catalog #		Title	Year	VG+	NM
MAIZE, JOE					
Decca DL-8590	(M)	**Presenting Joe Maize & His Cordsmen**	1958	16.00	40.00
Decca DL-8817	(M)	**Hawaiian Dreams**	1959	12.00	30.00
Decca DL-4555	(M)	**Isle Of Dreams**	1965	8.00	20.00
Decca DL-74555	(S)	**Isle Of Dreams**	1965	10.00	25.00
MAJIC SHIP					
Bel Ami BA-711	(S)	**Majic Ship**	1968	200.00	400.00
MAIYEROS, THE / THE INSTINCTS					
TCS 3952	(S)	**The Loving Sandwich**	1969	200.00	400.00
MAJORS, THE					
Imperial LP-9222	(M)	**Meet The Majors**	1963	60.00	150.00
Imperial LP-12222	(P)	**Meet The Majors**	1963	150.00	300.00
MAKEBA, MIRIAM					
Ms. Makeba also recorded with Harry Belafonte.					
RCA Victor LPM-2267	(M)	**Miriam Makeba**	1960	8.00	20.00
RCA Victor LSP-2267	(S)	**Miriam Makeba**	1960	12.00	30.00
		— RCA mono albums above have "Long Play" on the bottom of the label;			
		stereo albums have "Living Stereo" on the bottom.—			
Kapp KL-1274	(M)	**The Many Voices Of Miriam Makeba**	1962	8.00	20.00
Kapp KS-3274	(S)	**The Many Voices Of Miriam Makeba**	1962	10.00	25.00
RCA Victor LPM-2750	(M)	**The World Of Miriam Makeba**	1963	8.00	20.00
RCA Victor LSP-2750	(S)	**The World Of Miriam Makeba**	1963	10.00	25.00
RCA Victor LPM-2845	(M)	**The Voice Of Africa**	1964	8.00	20.00
RCA Victor LSP-2845	(S)	**The Voice Of Africa**	1964	10.00	25.00
RCA Victor LPM-3321	(M)	**Makeba Sings**	1965	8.00	20.00
RCA Victor LSP-3321	(S)	**Makeba Sings**	1965	10.00	25.00
RCA Victor LPM-3512	(M)	**The Magic Of Makeba**	1966	8.00	20.00
RCA Victor LSP-3512	(S)	**The Magic Of Makeba**	1966	10.00	25.00
		— RCA albums above have black labels.—			
MAKEM, TOMMY					
Tommy Makem, a multi-instrumentalist, singer and songwriter, is closely associated with The Clancy					
Brothers, with whom he performed and recorded for more than a decade.					
Tradition TLP-1044	(M)	**Songs Of Tommy Makem**	1961	10.00	25.00
Tradition TLPS-1044	(S)	**Songs Of Tommy Makem**	1961	12.00	30.00
MALCOLM X					
Douglas SD-795	(S)	**Malcolm X Talks To Young People**	1968	12.00	30.00
Douglas Z-30743	(S)	**By Any Means Neccessary**	1971	10.00	25.00
MALVIN, ARTIE, & THE ROCK 'N ROLL RHYTHM ROCKETS					
Waldorf Music 33-149	(10")	**Rock And Roll**	1955	40.00	100.00
MAMAS & THE PAPAS, THE					
The Mamas were Michelle Phillips and Cass Elliott; the Papas were John Phillips and Denny Doherty, all					
of whom also had solo careers. Refer to Barry McGuire.					
Dunhill D-50006	(M)	**If You Can Believe Your Eyes And Ears**	1966	40.00	100.00
Dunhill DS-50006	(S)	**If You Can Believe Your Eyes And Ears**	1966	60.00	150.00
		(First pressing covers of Dunhill 50006 plainly show the toilet in the			
		lower right corner. On all subsequent pressings a scroll with the			
		titles of the album's hit singles has been placed over the toilet.)			
Dunhill D-50006	(M)	**If You Can Believe Your Eyes And Ears**	1966	8.00	20.00
Dunhill DS-50006	(S)	**If You Can Believe Your Eyes And Ears**	1966	10.00	25.00
		(The toilet on the cover is concealed by a scroll.)			
Dunhill DS-50006	(S)	**If You Can Believe Your Eyes And Ears**	1968	20.00	50.00
		(Some later pressings have a black border on all four sides of			
		the cover, eliminating all but the faces of the four members.			
		The label reads "A Subsidiary of ABC" on the bottom.)			
Dunhill D-50010	(M)	**The Mamas & The Papas**	1966	8.00	20.00
Dunhill DS-50010	(S)	**The Mamas & The Papas**	1966	10.00	25.00
Dunhill D-50014	(M)	**The Mamas & The Papas Deliver**	1967	8.00	20.00
Dunhill DS-50014	(S)	**The Mamas & The Papas Deliver**	1967	10.00	25.00
		— Dunhill albums above read "Dist. by ABC-Paramount" on the bottom of the label.—			

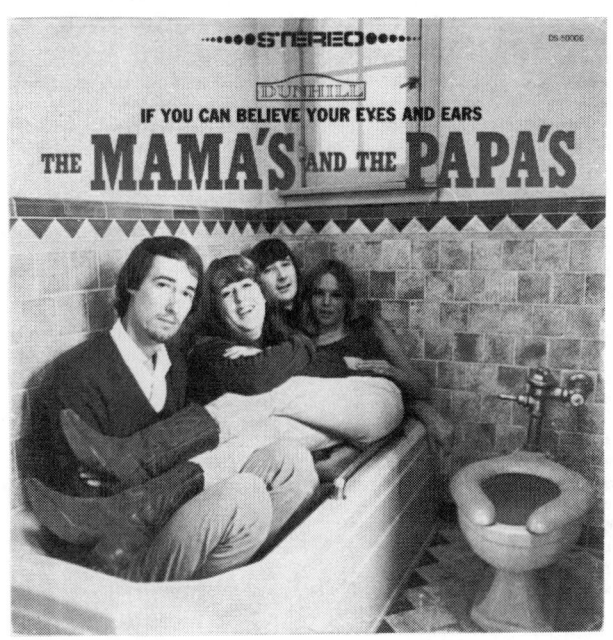

The original pressings of If You Can Believe Your Eyes And Ears *plainly featured a toilet in the lower right corner (above), a normal fixture in most every bathroom in the Western World. For some reason, this was deemed potentially offensive and the cover was pulled and amended (below). The Record Club version (not shown) went even further, placing a generous black border around the front cover, making the whole cover art unnecessary. Their first four albums hit the charts big-time and received RIAA Gold Records.*

Label & Catalog #		Title	Year	VG+	NM

MANCINI, HENRY

Composer-conductor Henry Mancini's vast catalog includes pop, jazz and his legendary television and movie scores. The list below includes only those of a generalized interest.

Label & Catalog #		Title	Year	VG+	NM
Liberty LRP-3121	(M)	The Versatile Henry Mancini	1959	8.00	20.00
Liberty LST-7121	(S)	The Versatile Henry Mancini	1959	12.00	30.00
Warner Bros. W-1312	(M)	March Step In Stereo And Hi-Fi	1959	8.00	20.00
Warner Bros. WS-1312	(S)	March Step In Stereo And Hi-Fi	1959	12.00	30.00
RCA Victor LPM-1956	(M)	The Music From "Peter Gunn"	1959	16.00	40.00
RCA Victor LSP-1956	(S)	The Music From "Peter Gunn"	1959	20.00	50.00
		(First pressings of RCA 1956 feature cover art by Jason Kirby.)			
RCA Victor LPM-1956	(M)	The Music From "Peter Gunn"	1959	8.00	20.00
RCA Victor LSP-1956	(S)	The Music From "Peter Gunn"	1959	10.00	25.00
		(Later pressings feature cover art by Fritz Miller.)			
RCA Victor LPM-2040	(M)	More Music From "Peter Gunn"	1959	8.00	20.00
RCA Victor LSP-2040	(S)	More Music From "Peter Gunn"	1959	10.00	25.00
RCA Victor LPM-2101	(M)	The Mancini Touch	1960	8.00	20.00
RCA Victor LSP-2101	(S)	The Mancini Touch	1960	10.00	25.00
RCA Victor LPM-2147	(M)	The Blues And The Beat	1960	10.00	25.00
RCA Victor LSP-2147	(S)	The Blues And The Beat	1960	12.00	30.00
RCA Victor LPM-2198	(M)	Music From "Mr. Lucky"	1960	10.00	25.00
RCA Victor LSP-2198	(S)	Music From "Mr. Lucky"	1960	12.00	30.00
RCA Victor LPM-2258	(M)	The Original "Peter Gunn"	1961	10.00	25.00
RCA Victor LSP-2258	(S)	The Original "Peter Gunn"	1961	12.00	30.00
RCA Victor LPM-2360	(M)	"Mr. Lucky" Goes Latin	1961	10.00	25.00
RCA Victor LSP-2360	(S)	"Mr. Lucky" Goes Latin	1961	12.00	30.00

— Mono mono albums above have "Long Play" on the bottom of the label; stereo albums have "Living Stereo" on the bottom.—

MANDEL, HARVEY

Label & Catalog #		Title	Year	VG+	NM
Philips PHS-600-281	(S)	Cristo Redentor	1968	10.00	25.00
Philips PHS-600-306	(S)	Righteous	1969	10.00	25.00
Philips PHS-600-325	(S)	Games Guitars Play	1969	10.00	25.00

MANDRAKE MEMORIAL

Label & Catalog #		Title	Year	VG+	NM
Poppy PYS-40,002	(S)	Mandrake Memorial	1968	12.00	30.00
Poppy PYS-40,003	(S)	Medium	1969	12.00	30.00
Poppy PYS-40,006	(S)	Puzzle	1970	12.00	30.00

MANFRED MANN

Label & Catalog #		Title	Year	VG+	NM
Ascot ALM-13015	(M)	The Manfred Mann Album	1964	16.00	40.00
Ascot ALS-16015	(P)	The Manfred Mann Album	1964	20.00	50.00
Ascot ALM-13018	(M)	The Five Faces Of Manfred Mann	1965	16.00	40.00
Ascot ALS-16018	(P)	The Five Faces Of Manfred Mann	1965	20.00	50.00
Ascot ALM-13021	(M)	My Little Red Book Of Winners	1965	16.00	40.00
Ascot ALS-16021	(S)	My Little Red Book Of Winners	1965	20.00	50.00
Ascot ALM-13024	(M)	Mann Made	1966	16.00	40.00
Ascot ALS-16024	(S)	Mann Made	1966	20.00	50.00
United Arts. UAL-94	(DJ)	Manfred Mann Interview	1966	80.00	200.00
		(Promotional interview issued in a plain cardboard jacket.)			
United Arts. UAL-3549	(M)	Pretty Flamingo	1966	12.00	30.00
United Arts. UAS-6549	(P)	Pretty Flamingo	1966	16.00	40.00
United Arts. UAL-3551	(M)	Manfred Mann's Greatest Hits	1966	10.00	25.00
United Arts. UAS-6551	(P)	Manfred Mann's Greatest Hits	1966	12.00	30.00
United Arts. UAS-5177	(S)	Charge Of The Light Brigade *(Soundtrack)*	1968	16.00	40.00

MANHATTAN STRINGS, THE

Label & Catalog #		Title	Year	VG+	NM
Tower T-5067	(M)	Hits Made Famous By The Monkees	1967	8.00	20.00
Tower ST-5067	(S)	Hits Made Famous By The Monkees	1967	10.00	25.00

MANHATTAN TRANSFER, THE

Label & Catalog #		Title	Year	VG+	NM
Mobile Fidelity MFSL-022	(S)	Manhattan Transfer Live	1978	8.00	25.00

MANHATTANS, THE

Label & Catalog #		Title	Year	VG+	NM
Carnival CLP-201	(M)	Dedicated To You	1964	100.00	250.00
Carnival CLPS-201	(S)	Dedicated To You	1964	200.00	400.00
Carnival CLP-202	(M)	For You And Yours	1965	50.00	125.00
Carnival CLPS-202	(S)	For You And Yours	1965	80.00	200.00

Label & Catalog #		Title	Year	VG+	NM
MANN, BARRY					
ABC-Paramount ABC-399	*(M)*	**Who Put The Bomp**	1963	40.00	100.00
ABC-Paramount ABCS-399	*(S)*	**Who Put The Bomp**	1963	60.00	150.00
RCA Victor DJL1-1162	*(DJ)*	**Flo & Eddie Interview Barry Mann**	1973	20.00	50.00
MANN, CARL					
Phillips Inter. PLP-1960	*(M)*	**Like Mann**	1960	300.00	600.00
MANN, REVEREND COLUMBUS					
Tamla T-227	*(M)*	**They Shall Be Mine**	1962		*See below*

(With the sole, miniscule printing of this gospel album distributed solely in Detroit, Tamla 227 may be the rarest of all Motown albums with a suggested Near Mint value of $3,000-6,000.)

MANN, HERBIE: *Refer to* **GOLDMINE'S PRICE GUIDE TO COLLECTIBLE JAZZ ALBUMS**

MANN, SHADOW					
Tomorrow's TPS-69001	*(S)*	**Come Live With Me**	1974	20.00	50.00

MANSFIELD, JAYNE
Refer to Kurt Jensen; Victor Lopez / Enoch Light; Lew Raymond; Henri Rene; The Stradivari Strings.

20th Fox 3049	*(M)*	**Jayne Mansfield Busts Up Las Vegas**	1961	80.00	200.00
MGM E-4204	*(M)*	**Shakespeare, Tchaikovsky And Me**	1964	20.00	50.00
MGM SE-4204	*(S)*	**Shakespeare, Tchaikovsky And Me**	1964	24.00	60.00
MANSON, CHARLES					
ESP-Disk' 2003	*(M)*	**Lie: The Love And Terror Cult**	1970	80.00	200.00

(ESP 2003 was counterfeited on the Awareness label later in '70s. This LP is also hard to find and, given the suitable subject matter, rather collectible with a suggested Near Mint value of $25-50.)

MANTLE, MICKEY					
RCA Victor LPM-1704	*(M)*	**My Favorite Hits... Mickey Mantle**	1958	250.00	500.00

(This is actually a various artists compilation of big band and jazz recordings featuring the Mick on the cover.)

MAPHIS, JOE
Joe Maphis' guitar playing can be heard on many other country'n western albums. Refer to Merle Travis.

Columbia CL-1005	*(M)*	**Fire On The Strings**	1957	30.00	75.00
— *Columbia albums above have six white-on-black "eye" logos around the perimeter of the label.*—					
MacGregor MGR-1205	*(M)*	**King Of The Strings**	196?	30.00	75.00
Kapp KSL-1347	*(M)*	**Hootenanny Star**	1964	8.00	20.00
Kapp KS-3347	*(S)*	**Hootenanny Star**	1964	10.00	25.00
Starday SLP-316	*(M)*	**King Of The Strings**	1966	16.00	40.00
Starday SLP-373	*(M)*	**Country Guitar Goes To The Jimmy Dean Show** *(With book)*	1966	24.00	60.00
		(Issued with a "Joe Maphis Method" book for guitar players.)			
Starday SLP-373	*(M)*	**Country Guitar Goes To The Jimmy Dean Show** *(Without book)*	1966	16.00	40.00
— *Starday albums above have yellow labels.*—					
Mosrite MA-400	*(M)*	**The New Sound Of Joe Maphis**	1967	12.00	30.00
Mosrite MS-400	*(S)*	**The New Sound Of Joe Maphis**	1967	16.00	40.00

MAPHIS, JOE & ROSE LEE
Refer to Badlands; The Blue Ridge Mountain Boys.

Capitol T-1778	*(M)*	**Rose Lee And Joe Maphis With The Blue Ridge Mountain Boys**	1962	12.00	30.00
Capitol ST-1778	*(S)*	**Rose Lee And Joe Maphis With The Blue Ridge Mountain Boys**	1962	16.00	40.00
Starday SLP-286	*(S)*	**Mr. And Mrs. Country Music**	1964	16.00	40.00
Starday SLP-322	*(M)*	**Golden Gospel**	1966	16.00	40.00
— *Starday albums above have yellow labels.*—					

MAPHIS, ROSE LEE					
Columbia CL-1598	*(M)*	**Rose Lee Maphis**	1961	12.00	30.00
Columbia CS-8398	*(S)*	**Rose Lee Maphis**	1961	16.00	40.00
— *Columbia albums above have six white-on-black "eye" logos around the perimeter of the label.*—					

Label & Catalog #		Title	Year	VG+	NM
MAR-KEYS, THE					
Atlantic 8055	(M)	**Last Night**	1961	20.00	50.00
—Atlantic albums above multi-color labels with a white "fan" logo on the right side.—					
Atlantic 8055	(M)	**Last Night**	1962	10.00	25.00
Atlantic SD-8055	(E)	**Last Night**	1966	12.00	30.00
Atlantic 8062	(M)	**Do The Pop-Eye With The Mar-Kays**	1962	16.00	40.00
Atlantic SD-8062	(E)	**Do The Pop-Eye With The Mar-Keys**	1966	12.00	30.00
—Atlantic albums above multi-color labels with a black "fan" logo on the right side.—					
Stax ST-707	(M)	**Great Memphis Sound**	1966	12.00	30.00
Stax STS-707	(E)	**Great Memphis Sound**	1966	8.00	20.00
MAR-KEYS, THE, & BOOKER T. & THE M.G.'S					
Stax ST-720	(M)	**Back To Back**	1967	8.00	20.00
Stax STS-720	(S)	**Back To Back**	1967	10.00	25.00
MARAIS, JOSEPH					
Josef Marais is a classically trained guitar and violin player who specializes in African folk music.					
Decca DL-5014	(10")	**South AfricanVeld**	1949	20.00	50.00
Decca DL-5083	(10")	**Songs From The Veld-Vol. 2**	1950	20.00	50.00
Decca DL-5106	(10")	**Songs Of Many Lands**	1950	20.00	50.00
MARAIS, JOSEPH & MIRANDA					
Joseph and Miranda Marais are singers of traditional folk music of many lands, especially African Bantu and South Africa.					
Decca DL-5268	(10")	**Ballads Of Many Lands**	1950	20.00	50.00
Columbia ML-4894	(M)	**Ballads Of Long Ago**	1951	16.00	40.00
Columbia CL-6225	(10")	**Songs**	1953	20.00	50.00
Columbia CL-6226	(10")	**South African Folk Songs**	1953	20.00	50.00
Decca DL-9026	(M)	**In Person—Recorded At Fullerton Hall, Chicago, Feb. 2, 1955, Vol. 1**	1955	12.00	30.00
Decca DL-9027	(M)	**In Person—Recorded At Fullerton Hall, Chicago, Feb. 2, 1955, Vol. 2**	1955	12.00	30.00
Decca DL-9030	(M)	**Christmas With Marais & Miranda**	1955	12.00	30.00
Decca DL-9047	(M)	**African Suite & Songs Of Spirit And Humor**	1956	12.00	30.00
Decca DL-8711	(M)	**Sundown Songs**	1958	12.00	30.00
MARANATHA					
Members of Maranatha later recorded as The Emmaus Road Band.					
(No label)	(S)	**Soon**	197?	80.00	200.00
MARATHONS, THE					
Arvee A-428	(M)	**Peanut Butter**	1961	60.00	150.00
MARAUDERS, THE					
No label	(M)	**The Marauders Check In**	1964	24.00	60.00
No label	(M)	**Maraudin' '65**	1965	24.00	60.00
MARBLE PHROGG, THE					
Derrick 8868	(S)	**The Marble Phrogg**	1968	300.00	500.00
MARCELS, THE					
Colpix CP-416	(M)	**Blue Moon** (Gold Label)	1961	150.00	400.00
Colpix SCP-416	(S)	**Blue Moon** (Gold Label)	196?		See below
		(Should stereo copies of Colpix 415 exist on the gold label they would have a suggested Near Mint value of $600-800.)			
Colpix CP-416	(M)	**Blue Moon** (Blue Label)	196?	60.00	150.00
Colpix SCP-416	(S)	**Blue Moon** (Blue Label)	196?		See below
		(Should stereo copies of Colpix 415 exist on the blue label they would have a suggested Near Mint value of $200-400.)			
MARCH, JO					
Kapp KL-1079	(M)	**Jo March**	1958	10.00	25.00
MARCH, "LITTLE" PEGGY					
RCA Victor LPM-2732	(M)	**I Will Follow Him**	1963	14.00	35.00
RCA Victor LSP-2732	(S)	**I Will Follow Him**	1963	20.00	50.00
RCA Victor LPM-3883	(M)	**No Foolin'**	1968	20.00	50.00
RCA Victor LSP-3883	(S)	**No Foolin'**	1968	14.00	35.00

In 1963 Margaret Battavio became the youngest female singer to top the charts when the fifteen year old hit with the precocious "I Will Follow Him." (Um, first she became Little Peggy March. . .)

Label & Catalog #		Title	Year	VG+	NM
MARCH, PEGGY, & BENNIE THOMAS					
RCA Victor LPM-3408	(M)	**In Our Fashion**	1965	14.00	35.00
RCA Victor LSP-3408	(S)	**In Our Fashion**	1965	20.00	50.00
		(RCA 3408 features four tracks by each artist with four duets.)			
MARCHAN, BOBBY					
Sphere Sound SR-7004	(M)	**There's Something On Your Mind**	1964	80.00	200.00
Sphere Sound SSR-7004	(S)	**There's Something On Your Mind**	1964	150.00	300.00
MARCUS					
NR 10788	(S)	**From The House Of Trax**	1979	660.00	1,000.00
MARCUS, STEVE: *Refer to* **GOLDMINE'S PRICE GUIDE TO COLLECTIBLE JAZZ ALBUMS**					
MARESCA, ERNIE					
Seville SV-77001	(M)	**Shout! Shout! Knock Yourself Out**	1962	40.00	100.00
Seville SV-87001	(S)	**Shout! Shout! Knock Yourself Out**	1962	60.00	150.00
MARIACHI BRASS, THE: *Refer to* **GOLDMINE'S PRICE GUIDE TO COLLECTIBLE JAZZ ALBUMS**					
MARIANI					
Mariani features Eric Johnson, later of The Electromagnets.					
Sonobeat 1001	(M)	**Perpetuum Mobile** (Issued without a cover)	196?	1,000.00	2,000.00
MARIE, ROSE					
Kapp KFL-4500	(M)	**Songs For Single Girls**	1963	14.00	35.00
MARKETTS, THE/THE MAR-KETTS					
Liberty LRP-3226	(M)	**Surfer's Stomp**	1962	16.00	40.00
Liberty LST-7226	(S)	**Surfer's Stomp**	1962	20.00	50.00
Liberty LRP-3226	(M)	**The Surfing Scene**	1963	12.00	30.00
Liberty LST-7226	(S)	**The Surfing Scene**	1963	16.00	40.00
		("Surfing Scene" is a reissue of "Surfer's Stomp.")			
Warner Bros. W-1509	(M)	**The Marketts Take To Wheels**	1963	16.00	40.00
Warner Bros. WS-1509	(S)	**The Marketts Take To Wheels**	1963	20.00	50.00
Warner Bros. W-1537	(M)	**Out Of Limits**	1964	12.00	30.00
Warner Bros. WS-1537	(S)	**Out Of Limits**	1964	16.00	40.00
Warner Bros. W-1642	(M)	**Batman Theme**	1966	12.00	30.00
Warner Bros. WS-1642	(S)	**Batman Theme**	1966	16.00	40.00
World Pacific WP-1870	(M)	**Sun Power**	1967	8.00	20.00
World Pacific ST-1870	(S)	**Sun Power**	1967	10.00	25.00
MARKLEY					
Forward 1007	(S)	**Markley: A Group**	1969	12.00	30.00
MARKS, J., & SHIPEN LEBZELTER					
Columbia 7193	(S)	**Rock And Other Four Letter Words** (2 LPs)	1968	12.00	30.00
MARLBOROS, THE					
Justice JLP-???	(S)	**The Marlboros**	1969	80.00	200.00
MARLENE: *Refer to* **MARLENE VER PLANCK**					
MARLEY, BOB, & THE WAILERS					
The various albums listed below prior to the Island Records listings care albums that collect Wailers' sides recorded prior to their 1973 signing with Island.For additional listings refer to Johnny Nash.					
Studio One	(M)	**The Wailing Wailers**	196?	80.00	200.00
Island ILPS-9241	(S)	**Catch A Fire**	1973	20.00	50.00
		(Original covers for Island 9241 are shaped like a cigarette lighter with a hinge that allows the top to flip open.)			
Island ILPS-9383	(S)	**Rastaman Vibration**	1976	40.00	100.00
		(Issued promotionally in a burlap box with a press kit.)			
		— Original Island albums above have black labels with an "i" on the bottom.—			
Mango BMSP-100	(S)	**Bob Marley & The Wailers-The Box Set**	1982	40.00	100.00
		(Boxed set of nine Island albuims.)			
MARLO, MICKI					
ABC-Paramount ABC-295	(M)	**Married I Can Always Get**	1959	8.00	20.00
ABC-Paramount ABCS-295	(S)	**Married I Can Always Get**	1959	10.00	25.00

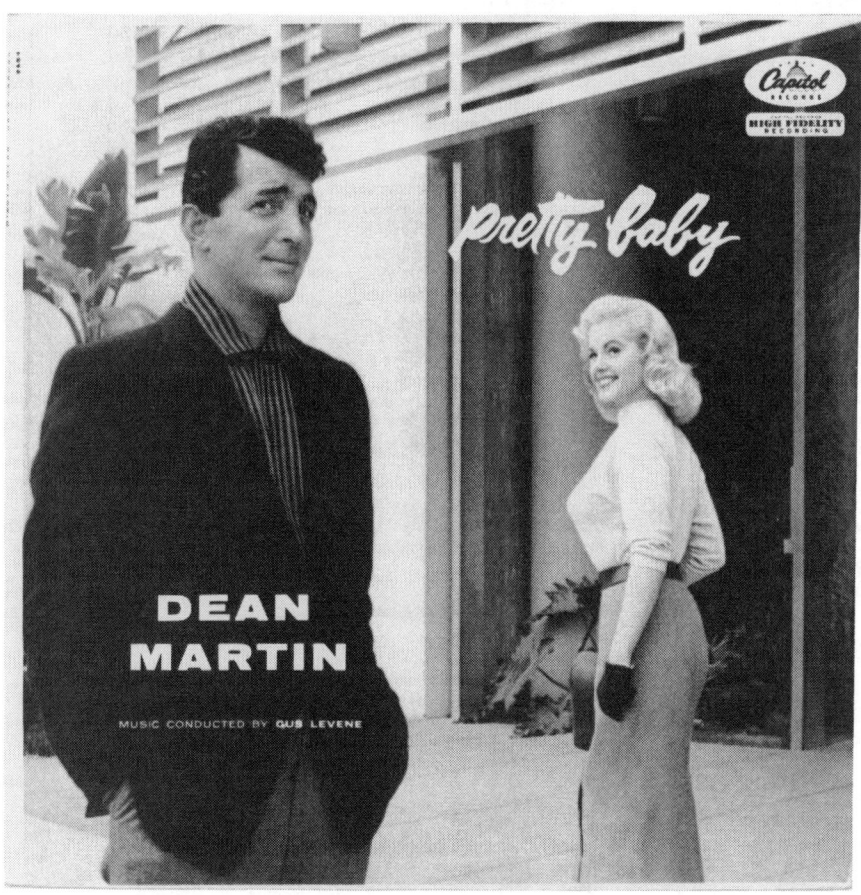

As much as some folks in the field of collecting records would strive to elevate the stature of Dino among other collectors, he remains of little interest to most collectors and his albums, especially the early ones on Capitol, are therefore undervalued. This one is worth placing in any collection just for the great cover, whether you dig Martin's great expression or the obvious cause of this expression.

Label & Catalog #		Title	Year	VG+	NM

MARLOWE, MARION: *Refer to* FESS PARKER

MARLOWE, MEXIE

King 799	(M)	**Meet Mexie Marlowe**	1962	40.00	100.00

MARSHALL, HERTA

Folkways FA-2333	(10")	**To You With Love—**			
		American Folk Songs For Women	1957	20.00	50.00

MARSHALL, JACK, & THE NEWPORT BEACH LITTLE THEATER SURFING GROUP
Guitarist Marshall's discogrpaphy can be found in Goldmine's Price Guide To Collectible Jazz Albums.

Capitol T-1939	(M)	**My Son The Surf Nut**	1963	12.00	30.00
Capitol ST-1939	(S)	**My Son The Surf Nut**	1963	16.00	40.00

MARTHA & THE VANDELLAS

Gordy G-902	(M)	**Come And Get These Memories**	1963	150.00	300.00
Gordy GS-902	(S)	**Come And Get These Memories**	1963	225.00	450.00
Gordy G-907	(M)	**Heat Wave**	1963	60.00	150.00
Gordy G-907	(E)	**Heat Wave**	1963	60.00	150.00
		(Copies of Gordy G-907 issued in covers with "Stereo" on the top are rechanneled stereo.)			
Gordy GS-907	(S)	**Heat Wave**	1963	150.00	400.00
		(Copies of Gordy G-907 issued in mono covers with a black "Stereo" sticker are real stereo.)			
Gordy G-915	(M)	**Dance Party**	1965	12.00	30.00
Gordy GS-915	(S)	**Dance Party**	1965	16.00	40.00
Gordy G-917	(M)	**Martha & The Vandellas' Greatest Hits**	1966	8.00	20.00
Gordy GS-917	(S)	**Martha & The Vandellas' Greatest Hits**	1966	10.00	25.00
Gordy G-920	(M)	**Watchout!**	1967	8.00	20.00
Gordy GS-920	(S)	**Watchout!**	1967	10.00	25.00
Gordy G-925	(M)	**Martha & The Vandellas' Live!**	1967	8.00	20.00
Gordy GS-925	(S)	**Martha & The Vandellas' Live!**	1967	10.00	25.00

MARTIN, BENNY

Starday SLP-131	(M)	**Country Music's**			
		Sensational Entertainer *(Yellow label)*	1961	20.00	50.00

MARTIN, DEAN
Refer to The Reprise Repertory Theatre.

Capitol L-401	(10")	**The Stooge** *(Soundtrack)*	1953	40.00	100.00
Capitol T-401	(M)	**The Stooge** *(Soundtrack)*	1953	24.00	60.00
Capitol T-401	(M)	**Dean Martin Sings**	1954	20.00	50.00
		("Dean Martin Sings" is a repackage of "The Stooge.")			
Capitol T-576	(M)	**Swingin' Down Yonder**	1955	12.00	40.00
Capitol T-849	(M)	**Pretty Baby**	1957	12.00	40.00
Capitol T-1047	(M)	**This Is Martin**	1958	12.00	40.00
		— Original Capitol albums above have turquoise labels —			
Capitol T-1150	(M)	**Sleep Warm**	1959	12.00	30.00
Capitol ST-1150	(S)	**Sleep Warm**	1959	16.00	40.00
		(The orchestra on Capitol 1150 was conducted by Frank Sinatra.)			
Capitol T-1285	(M)	**Winter Romance**	1959	8.00	20.00
Capitol ST-1285	(S)	**Winter Romance**	1959	12.00	30.00
Capitol W-1435	(M)	**Bells Are Ringing** *(Soundtrack)*	1960	14.00	35.00
Capitol SW-1435	(S)	**Bells Are Ringing** *(Soundtrack)*	1960	20.00	50.00
Capitol T-1442	(M)	**This Time I'm Swingin'**	1961	8.00	20.00
Capitol ST-1442	(S)	**This Time I'm Swingin'**	1961	12.00	30.00
Capitol W-1580	(M)	**Dean Martin**	1961	8.00	20.00
Capitol SW-1580	(S)	**Dean Martin**	1961	12.00	30.00
Capitol T-1659	(M)	**Dino**	1962	8.00	20.00
Capitol ST-1659	(S)	**Dino**	1962	12.00	30.00
Capitol T-1702	(M)	**Cha Cha De Amor**	1962	8.00	20.00
Capitol ST-1702	(S)	**Cha Cha De Amor**	1962	12.00	30.00
		— Capitol albums above have black labels with the logo on the left side.—			
Capitol TCL-2815	(M)	**Deluxe Set** *(3 LP box)*	1967	10.00	25.00
Capitol DTCL-2815	(P)	**Deluxe Set** *(3 LP box)*	1967	8.00	20.00
		— Capitol albums above have black labels with the logo on top.—			
Sears SPS-434	(E)	**I'm Yours**	196?	10.00	25.00
Sears SPS-450	(E)	**Just One More Chance**	196?	10.00	25.00
Reprise PRO-246	(DJ)	**Dean Martin Month**	1965	10.00	25.00

Label & Catalog #		Title	Year	VG+	NM

MARTIN, GEORGE

As producer and occasional keyboardist, Mr. George Martin was the "fifth" Beatle, and one of the pivotal figures in the British Invasion of 1963-65. Martin's scores for the "A Hard Day's Night," "Help!" and "Yellow Submarine" soundtracks are listed under The Beatles while "Ferry Cross The Mersey" is under Gerry & The Pacemakers..

United Arts. UAL-3377	(M)	Off The Beatle Track	1964	30.00	75.00
United Arts. UAS-6377	(S)	Off The Beatle Track	1964	40.00	100.00
United Arts. UAL-3420	(M)	George Martin	1965	16.00	40.00
United Arts. UAS-6420	(S)	George Martin	1965	20.00	50.00
United Arts. UAL-3448	(M)	George Martin Plays "Help"	1965	20.00	50.00
United Arts. UAS-6448	(S)	George Martin Plays "Help"	1965	30.00	75.00
United Arts. UAL-3539	(M)	George Martin Salutes The Beatle Girls	1966	20.00	50.00
United Arts. UAS-6539	(S)	George Martin Salutes The Beatle Girls	1966	30.00	75.00
United Arts. UAL-3647	(M)	London By George	1967	12.00	30.00
United Arts. UAS-6647	(S)	London By George	1967	16.00	40.00

MARTIN, GRADY, & HIS SLEW-FOOT FIVE

Decca DL-5566	(10")	Dance-O-Rama #6	1955	200.00	400.00
Decca DL-8181	(M)	Powerhouse Dance Party	1955	16.00	40.00
Decca DL-8292	(M)	Juke Box Jamboree	1956	16.00	40.00
Decca DL-8648	(M)	The Roaring Twenties	1957	16.00	40.00
Decca DL-8883	(M)	Hot Time Tonight	1959	8.00	20.00
Decca DL-78883	(S)	Hot Time Tonight	1959	12.00	30.00
Decca DL-4072	(M)	Big City Lights	1960	8.00	20.00
Decca DL-74072	(S)	Big City Lights	1960	12.00	30.00

MARTIN, JIMMY/JIMMY MARTIN & THE SUNNY MOUNTAIN BOYS

Decca DL-4016	(M)	Good 'N' Country	1960	8.00	20.00
Decca DL-74016	(S)	Good 'N' Country	1960	12.00	30.00
Decca DL-4285	(M)	Country Music Time	1962	8.00	20.00
Decca DL-74285	(S)	Country Music Time	1962	10.00	25.00
Decca DL-4360	(M)	This World Is Not My Home	1963	8.00	20.00
Decca DL-74360	(S)	This World Is Not My Home	1963	10.00	25.00

MARTIN, MAC, & THE DIXIE TRAVELERS

Singer William Colleran aka Mac Martin and The Dixie Travlers are a traditional bluegrass ensemble.

Gateway GLP-2080	(M)	Folk And Bluegrass Favorites	1963	16.00	40.00

MARTIN, MARTY

Marty later recorded as Boxcar Willie.

A.H.M.C. 118	(S)	Marty Martin Sings Country Music	197?	20.00	50.00

MARTIN, MARY

Columbia OL-4180	(M)	South Pacific (Original Cast. Green label)	1949	12.00	30.00
Columbia ML-2061	(10")	Mary Martin Sings For You	1949	20.00	50.00
Columbia ML-2159	(10")	Anything Goes	1950	20.00	50.00
Columbia ML-2160	(10")	Bandwagon	1950	20.00	50.00
Columbia ML-4475	(M)	Girl Crazy	1951	16.00	40.00
Columbia ML-4488	(M)	Babes In Arms	1951	16.00	40.00
Columbia ML-4751	(M)	Anything Goes / Bandwagon	1954	16.00	40.00
		(Columbia 4751 is a reissue of 2159 and 2160.)			
Columbia CL-2582	(10")	Anything Goes	1956	12.00	30.00
		(Columbia 2582 is a reissue of 2159.)			
Columbia CL-2061	(M)	Mary Martin Sings For You	195?	16.00	40.00
Columbia CL-822	(M)	Girl Crazy	1955	10.00	25.00
		(Columbia 822 is a reissue of 4475.)			
Decca DL-8030	(M)	On The Town / Lute Song (Original Cast)	1950	16.00	40.00
Capitol W-913	(M)	Annie Get Your Gun (Original Cast)	1957	10.00	25.00
		— Capitol albums above have turquoise labels.—			
Disneyland WDL-3031	(M)	Mary Martin Sings A Musical Love Story	1958	8.00	20.00
Disneyland STER-3031	(S)	Mary Martin Sings A Musical Love Story	1958	14.00	35.00
Disneyland WDL-4016	(M)	Hi Ho	1958	14.00	35.00
Disneyland WDL-3038	(M)	Hi Ho	1958	10.00	25.00
Disneyland STER-3038	(S)	Hi Ho	1958	20.00	50.00
		(Disneyland 3038 is a reissue of 4016.)			
Disneyland ST-3911	(M)	Story Of Sleeping Beauty	1958	10.00	25.00
Disneyland ST-2002	(M)	Little Lame Lamb	1959	20.00	50.00
Columbia KOL-2020	(M)	Sound Of Music (Orig. Cast. Gatefold cover)	1959	6.00	15.00
Columbia KOS-2020	(S)	Sound Of Music (Orig. Cast. Gatefold cover)	1959	8.00	20.00

Label & Catalog #		Title	Year	VG+	NM
RCA Victor LOC-1019	(M)	**Peter Pan** *(TV Soundtrack.. Green cover)*	1954	16.00	40.00
RCA Victor LOC-1019	(M)	**Peter Pan** *(TV Soundtrack.. White cover)*	1959	10.00	25.00
RCA Victor LSO-1019	(E)	**Peter Pan** *(TV Soundtrack.. White cover)*	1959	6.00	15.00
RCA Victor LPM-1539	(M)	**Mary Martin Sings, Richard Rogers Plays**	1958	10.00	25.00
RCA Victor LPM-2012	(M)	**Cinderella / 3 To Make Music**	1959	10.00	25.00
RCA Victor LSP-2012	(S)	**Cinderella / 3 To Make Music**	1959	16.00	40.00
RCA Victor LOC-1083	(M)	**Jennie** *(Original Cast)*	1963	10.00	25.00
RCA Victor LSO-1083	(S)	**Jennie** *(Original Cast)*	1963	16.00	40.00
RCA Victor LOCD-2007	(M)	**Hello Dolly** *(British Cast)*	1963	6.00	15.00
RCA Victor LSOD-2007	(S)	**Hello Dolly** *(British Cast)*	1963	8.00	20.00
Decca DL-9122	(M)	**One Touch Of Venus** *Original Cast)*	1965	16.00	40.00
Decca DL-79122	(E)	**One Touch Of Venus** *Original Cast)*	1965	10.00	25.00
Disneyland ST-3936	(M)	**Sound Of Music** *(Gatefold cover with book)*	1966	6.00	15.00
Disneyland STER-3936	(S)	**Sound Of Music** *(Gatefold cover with book)*	1966	10.00	25.00
Disneyland ST-3943	(M)	**Mary Martin Sings Walt Disney Favorites** *(Disneyland 3943 is a reissue of 4016.)*	1966	8.00	20.00

MARTIN, MARY, & NOEL COWARD

CBS-TV *(No number)*	(M)	**Together With Music** *(Promotional)*	1955	80.00	200.00

MARTIN, MARY, & ETHEL MERMAN

Decca DL-7027	(10")	**Ford 50th Anniversary TV Show**	1953	60.00	150.00

MARTIN, TONY

RCA Victor LPM-2146	(M)	**Tony Martin At The Desert Inn**	1960	8.00	20.00
RCA Victor LSP-2146	(S)	**Tony Martin At The Desert Inn**	1960	10.00	25.00

MARTIN & NEIL
Vince Martin & Fed Neil.

Elektra EKL-248	(M)	**Tear Down The Walls**	1965	20.00	50.00
Elektra EKS-7248	(S)	**Tear Down The Walls**	1965	30.00	75.00

MARTINEZ, TONY

Del Fi DFLP-1205	(M)	**The Many Sides Of Pepino**	1959	12.00	30.00
Del Fi DFLP-1205S	(S)	**The Many Sides Of Pepino**	1959	16.00	40.00

MARTINO, AL

20th Century SF-3025	(M)	**Al Martino**	1959	10.00	25.00
20th Century SFX-3025	(S)	**Al Martino**	1959	12.00	30.00
20th Century SF-3032	(M)	**Sing Along With Al Martino**	1959	10.00	25.00
20th Century SFX-3032	(S)	**Sing Along With Al Martino**	1959	12.00	30.00
20th Century TF-4168	(M)	**Al Martino Sings**	1962	8.00	20.00
20th Century TFS-4168	(S)	**Al Martino Sings**	1962	10.00	25.00
20th Century TF-5009	(M)	**Love Notes**	1963	8.00	20.00
20th Century TFS-5009	(S)	**Love Notes**	1963	10.00	25.00

MARVELETTES, THE

Tamla T-228	(M)	**Please Mr. Postman** *(White label)*	1961	300.00	600.00
Tamla T-228	(M)	**Please Mr. Postman** *(Yellow label)*	1961	250.00	500.00
Tamla T-229	(M)	**The Marveletts Sing Smash Hits Of '62**	1962		*See below*
		(Original covers for Tamla 229 are white with a large "M" and a "62" inside a circle. The cover reads "The Marveletts Sing Smash Hits Of '62" but the label titles the album "The Marvelettes Sing." Rare with a suggested Near Mint value of $1,000-1,500.)			
Tamla T-229	(M)	**The Marveletts Sing**	1962	250.00	500.00
		(Later covers are black with the titles of the hits inside circles and the group's name mis-spelled. Both the cover and the label title the album "The Marvelettes Sing.")			
Tamla T-231Tamla T-231	(M)	**Playboy** *(Tan label)*	1962	300.00	600.00
	(M)	**Playboy** *(White label)*	1962	250.00	500.00
— *Tamla albums above have a disc over-lapping a globe at the top of the label.* —					
Tamla T-228	(M)	**Please Mr. Postman**	1963	80.00	200.00
Tamla T-229	(M)	**The Marvelettes Sing**	1963	80.00	200.00
Tamla T-231	(M)	**Playboy**	1963	80.00	200.00
Tamla T-237	(M)	**The Marvelous Marvelettes**	1963	80.00	200.00
Tamla T-243	(M)	**Recorded Live On Stage**	1963	30.00	75.00
Tamla T-253	(M)	**The Marvelettes' Greatest Hits**	1966	8.00	20.00
Tamla TS-253	(S)	**The Marvelettes' Greatest Hits**	1966	10.00	25.00

Label & Catalog #		Title	Year	VG+	NM
Tamla T-274	(M)	**The Marvelettes**	1967	8.00	20.00
Tamla TS-274	(S)	**The Marvelettes**	1967	10.00	25.00
Tamla T-286	(M)	**Sophisticated Soul**	1968	12.00	30.00
Tamla TS-286	(S)	**Sophisticated Soul**	1968	8.00	20.00

—Tamla albums above have yellow labels with two side-by-side circles at the top.—

MARVELOWS, THE

ABC-Paramount S-643	(S)	**The Mighty Marvelows**	1968	12.00	30.00

MARVIN & JOHNNY
For additional listings refer to The Isley Brothers / Marvin & Johnny.

Crown CLP-5381	(M)	**Marvin & Johnny**	1963	10.00	25.00
Crown CST-381	(E)	**Marvin & Johnny**	1963	4.00	10.00

MARX, BILL
Harpo's son Bill is a modern jazz pianist; his discography can be found in Goldmine's Price Guide To Collectible Jazz Albums.

Vee Jay LP-3035	(M)	**My Son The Folk Singer**	1963	10.00	25.00
Vee Jay SR-3035	(S)	**My Son The Folk Singer**	1963	10.00	25.00

MARX, GROUCHO

Decca DL-5405	(10")	**Hooray For Captain Spaulding**	1952	100.00	250.00
Columbia OL-5480	(M)	**The Mikado** *(TV Soundtrack)*	1960	12.00	30.00
Columbia OS-2022	(S)	**The Mikado** *(TV Soundtrack)*	1960	20.00	50.00

MARX, HARPO

RCA Victor LPM-27	(10")	**Harp By Harpo**	1951	60.00	150.00
Mercury MG-20232	(M)	**Harpo In Hi-Fi**	1957	20.00	50.00
Mercury MG-20363	(M)	**Harpo At Work**	1959	20.00	50.00
Mercury SR-60016	(S)	**Harpo At Work**	1959	30.00	75.00
RCA Victor LPM-2720	(M)	**Harp By Harpo**	1963	20.00	50.00
RCA Victor LSP-2720	(E)	**Harp By Harpo**	1963	16.00	40.00

(RCA 2720 is a reissue of 27.)

MARY BUTTERWORTH

Custom Fidelity	(M)	**Mary Butterworth**	1968	150.00	300.00

MASON, BARBARA

Arctic ALP-1000	(M)	**Yes, I'm Ready**	1965	12.00	30.00
Arctic ALPS-1000	(S)	**Yes, I'm Ready**	1965	16.00	40.00
Arctic ALPS-1004	(S)	**Oh, How It Hurts**	1968	12.00	30.00
National General 2001	(S)	**If You Knew Him Like I Do**	1970	12.00	30.00

MASON, DAVE
Dave Mason was formerly a member of Traffic.

Blue Thumb BTS-19	(S)	**All Together** *(Pink marbled vinyl)*	1970		See below

(Original copies of BTS-19 were pressed on a pink marbled vinyl with the title on the label erroneoulsy printed as "All Together." As most of these were withdrawn and destroyed, this has a suggested Near Mint value of $100-200.)

Blue Thumb BTS-19	(S)	**Alone Together** *(Brown marbled vinyl)*	1970	6.00	15.00
Blue Thumb BTS-19	(S)	**Alone Together** *(Black vinyl)*	1970	10.00	25.00

MASON, DAVE, & CASS ELLIOT

Blue Thumb BTS-25	(S)	**Dave Mason And Cass Elliot**	1969	12.00	30.00
Blue Thumb BTS-8825	(S)	**Dave Mason And Cass Elliot**	1971	6.00	15.00

(Blue Thumb 8825 is a reissue of 25.)

MASTERSOUNDS, THE: *Refer to* **GOLDMINE'S PRICE GUIDE TO COLLECTIBLE JAZZ ALBUMS**

MATHIS, JOHNNY

Columbia CL-887	(M)	**Johnny Mathis**	1957	20.00	50.00
Columbia CS-8897	(E)	**Johnny Mathis**	1959	8.00	20.00
Columbia CL-1028	(M)	**Wonderful, Wonderful**	1957	14.00	35.00
Columbia CL-1078	(M)	**Warm**	1957	14.00	35.00
Columbia CS-8039	(S)	**Warm**	1959	10.00	25.00
Columbia CL-1090	(M)	**Wild Is The Wind** *(Soundtrack)*	1957	80.00	200.00
Columbia CL-1119	(M)	**Good Night, Dear Lord**	1958	14.00	35.00
Columbia CS-8012	(S)	**Good Night, Dear Lord**	1959	10.00	25.00

Label & Catalog #		Title	Year	VG+	NM
Columbia CL-1133	(M)	**Johnny's Greatest Hits**	1958	14.00	35.00
Columbia CL-1165	(M)	**Swing Softly**	1958	14.00	35.00
Columbia CS-8023	(S)	**Swing Softly**	1959	10.00	25.00
Columbia CL-1194	(M)	**A Certain Smile** (Soundtrack)	1958	60.00	150.00
Columbia CS-8068	(S)	**A Certain Smile** (Soundtrack)	1959	80.00	200.00
Columbia CL-1195	(M)	**Merry Christmas**	1958	14.00	35.00
Columbia CS-8021	(S)	**Merry Christmas**	1959	10.00	25.00
Columbia CL-1270	(M)	**Open Fire, Two Guitars** (With Al Caiola)	1959	14.00	35.00
Columbia CS-8026	(S)	**Open Fire, Two Guitars** (With Al Caiola)	1959	14.00	35.00
Columbia CL-1344	(M)	**More Of Johnny's Greatest Hits**	1959	10.00	25.00
— Original Columbia albums above have three white "eye" logos on each side of the spindle hole.—					
Columbia S.P. 6P-6030	(P)	**The Johnny Mathis Treasury** (6 LPs)	197?	12.00	30.00
Columbia S.P. P5-13109	(P)	**Magic Moments** (5 LPs)	197?	10.00	25.00
Columbia S.P. P6-14628	(P)	**Misty Memories** (6 LPs)	197?	12.00	30.00

MATTHEWS, DAVE

People 3000	(S)	**Grodeck Whipperjenny**	1970	20.00	50.00

MATTHEWS, INEZ

Period SLP-580	(M)	**Spirituals**	195?	12.00	30.00

MAXWELL, DIANE

Challenge CHL-607	(M)	**Almost Seventeen**	1959	10.00	25.00
Challenge CHS-2501	(S)	**Almost Seventeen**	1959	14.00	35.00

MAYALL, JOHN/JOHN MAYALL'S BLUESBREAKERS
Refer to the Groundhogs; Mick Taylor.

London LL-3492	(M)	**Blues Breakers With Eric Clapton**	1966	10.00	25.00
London PS-492	(S)	**Blues Breakers With Eric Clapton**	1966	12.00	30.00
London LL-3502	(M)	**A Hard Road**	1967	10.00	25.00
London PS-502	(S)	**A Hard Road**	1967	8.00	20.00
London LL-3529	(M)	**Crusade**	1967	10.00	25.00
London PS-529	(S)	**Crusade**	1967	8.00	20.00
Mobile Fidelity MFSL-183	(S)	**Blues Breakers With Eric Clapton**	1985	10.00	30.00

MAYER, NATHANIEL

Fortune 8014	(M)	**Going Back To The Village Of Love**	1962	80.00	200.00
		(Original pressings of Fortune 8014 have purple labels on thick vinyl.)			
Fortune 8014	(M)	**Going Back To The Village Of Love**	196?	30.00	75.00
		(Second pressings have yellow labels on thick vinyl.)			

MAYSA

United Arts. UAL-3034	(M)	**The Sound Of Love**	1959	8.00	20.00
United Arts. UAS-6034	(S)	**The Sound Of Love**	1959	10.00	25.00

MAZANTI

Mazanti Music	(S)	**Philosopher**	1979	40.00	100.00

MAZE

M.T.A. 5012	(S)	**Armageddon**	1971	80.00	200.00

MC-5, THE/THE MOTOR CITY FIVE

Elektra EKS-74042	(S)	**Kick Out The Jams** (White label promo)	1969	60.00	150.00
Elektra EKS-74042	(S)	**Kick Out The Jams**	1969	30.00	75.00
		(Original pressings open side one with the anthem, "Kick out the jams, motherfuckers!" and feature liner notes on the back cover.)			
Elektra EKS-74042	(S)	**Kick Out The Jams**	1969	16.00	40.00
		(Later pressings replace the expletive with "Kick out the jams, brothers and sisters" and delete the liner notes.)			
Atlantic SD-8247	(S)	**Back In The U.S.A.**	1970	16.00	40.00
Atlantic SD-8285	(S)	**High Time**	1971	16.00	40.00

McAULIFFE, LEON/LEON McAULIFFE & HIS CIMMARON BOYS
Steel guitar player McAuliffe originally recorded with The Lightcrust Doughboys; Bob Wills.

Dot DLP-3139	(M)	**Take Off**	1958	30.00	75.00
Sesac A-1601	(M)	**Points West**	1960	60.00	150.00
Sesac A-1602	(M)	**Just A Minute**	1960	60.00	150.00
Cimarron CLP-202	(M)	**Swingin' Western Strings**	1960	24.00	60.00

Label & Catalog #		Title	Year	VG+	NM
ABC-Paramount ABC-394	(M)	**Cozy Inn**	1961	20.00	50.00
ABC-Paramount ABCS-394	(S)	**Cozy Inn**	1961	30.00	75.00
Starday SLP-171	(M)	**Mr. Western Swing**	1962	20.00	50.00
Starday SLP-280	(M)	**Swinging West**	1962	20.00	50.00
Starday SLP-309	(M)	**Swingin' Western Strings**	1962	20.00	50.00
		— Starday albums above have yellow labels.—			
Capitol T-2016	(M)	**The Dancin'est Band Around**	1964	12.00	30.00
Capitol ST-2016	(S)	**The Dancin'est Band Around**	1964	16.00	40.00
Capitol T-2148	(M)	**Everybody Dance! Everybody Swing!**	1964	12.00	30.00
Capitol ST-2148	(S)	**Everybody Dance! Everybody Swing!**	1964	16.00	40.00
Dot DLP-3689	(M)	**Golden Country Hits**	1966	24.00	60.00
Dot DLP-25689	(E)	**Golden Country Hits**	1966	20.00	50.00

McCALL, MARY ANN: *Refer to* GOLDMINE'S PRICE GUIDE TO COLLECTIBLE JAZZ ALBUMS

McCALL, TOUSSAINT

Ronn 7527	(M)	**Nothing Can Take The Place Of You**	1967	12.00	30.00
Ronn 7527S	(S)	**Nothing Can Take The Place Of You**	1967	16.00	40.00
		("Nothing Can Take The Place Of You" and "Shimmy" are rechanneled on this album.)			

McCANN, LES: *Refer to* GOLDMINE'S PRICE GUIDE TO COLLECTIBLE JAZZ ALBUMS

McCARTNEY, PAUL/PAUL McCARTNEY & WINGS

Albums may be credited to Paul McCartney, Paul & Linda McCartney, Paul McCartney & Wings, or Wings. Refer to The Beatles; The Crickets; Mary Hopkin; Denny Laine; Percy Thrillington. Note: After the fall of Apple, all of Mac's albums were reissued by Capitol, often with several label variations. When Paul moved to Columbia, he took his catalog with him and all of the Apple and Capitol albums were reissued first on Columbia's regular line (with a "JC" prefix) and then on their budget line ("PC"). Those reissues and variations that have significant value are listed below.

Warner Bros. PRO (10")	(DJ)	**The Family Way** *(Radio spots)*	1967	300.00	500.00
London M-76007	(M)	**The Family Way** *(Soundtrack)*	1967	30.00	75.00
London MS-82007	(S)	**The Family Way** *(Soundtrack)*	1967	40.00	100.00
		(Original covers have front and back slicks adhered to cardboard; labels are flat. Counterfeit covers are printed on posterboard and the labels are glossy.)			
Apple STAO-3363	(S)	**McCartney**	1970	12.00	30.00
		(Original pressings have "Manufactured by Apple" on the bottom of the label and "McCartney" and "Paul McCartney" on two lines at the top. The Apple address on the back cover is in California. Counterfeits have inferior reproduction of the labels and cover.)			
Apple STAO-3363	(S)	**McCartney**	1970	12.00	30.00
		(Later pressings have "Manufactured by Apple" on the bottom of the label and "McCartney" only at the top. The back cover reads "An ABKCO managed company.")			
Apple STAO-3363	(S)	**McCartney**	1970	40.00	100.00
		(Apple label with "A Subsidiary of Capitol" on the bottom.)			
Apple SMAS-3363	(S)	**McCartney**	197?	12.00	30.00
		(Apple label with "Manufactured by Apple" on the bottom)			
Apple SMAS-3363	(S)	**McCartney**	1975	20.00	50.00
		(Apple label with "All Rights Reserved" disclaimer.)			
Apple SPRO-6210	(DJ)	**Brung To Ewe By**	1971	200.00	400.00
		(Radio spots for "Ram." Originals have even spacing between the tracks; counterfeits are uneven.)			
Apple MAS-3375	(M)	**Ram**	1971		See below
		(Mono pressing issued to radio stations in standard stereo cover. Rare with a suggested Near Mint value of $3,000-5,000.)			
Apple SMAS-3375	(S)	**Ram**	1971	10.00	25.00
		(Apple label with "Manufactured by Apple" on the bottom. Apple is unsliced on both sides.)			
Apple SMAS-3375	(S)	**Ram**	1971	20.00	50.00
		(Apple label with "A Subsidiary of Capitol" on the bottom.)			
Apple SMAS-3375	(S)	**Ram**	1975	40.00	100.00
		(Apple label with "All Rights Reserved" disclaimer.)			
Capitol SMAS-3363	(S)	**McCartney**	197?	10.00	25.00
		(Black "Manufactured by McCartney Music" label)			
Capitol SMAS-3375	(S)	**Ram**	197?	10.00	25.00
		(Black label with "Manufactured by McCartney Music" on top.)			

Label & Catalog #		Title	Year	VG+	NM
Capitol SMAS-3375	(S)	**Ram**	197?	16.00	40.00
		(Black label with "Manufactured by Capitol" at the top.)			
Capitol SW-3386	(S)	**Wild Life**	197?	10.00	25.00
		(Black label with "Manufactured by McCartney Music" on top.)			
Capitol SMAL-3409	(S)	**Red Rose Speedway** *(With booklet)*	197?	10.00	25.00
		(Black label with "Manufactured by McCartney Music" on top.)			
Capitol SMAL-3409	(S)	**Red Rose Speedway** *(With booklet)*	197?	16.00	40.00
		(Black label with "Manufactured by MPL" on top			
		and the Capitol logo on the back cover.)			
Capitol PRO-2955/56	(DJ)	**Band On The Run Radio Interview**	1973	500.00	1,000.00
		(White label with a script and two photos in a plain cardboard jacket..			
		Counterfeits have yellow labels.)			
Capitol SO-3415	(S)	**Band On The Run** *(With poster)*	1973	16.00	40.00
		(Black label with "Manufactured by Capitol" at the top.)			
Capitol SO-3415	(S)	**Band On The Run** *(With poster)*	197?	10.00	25.00
		(Custom photo label with "Manufactured by MPL.")			
Capitol SO-3415	(S)	**Band On The Run** *(With poster)*	197?	8.00	20.00
		(Black label with "Manufactured by MPL" at the top.)			
Capitol SEAX-11901	(S)	**Band On The Run** *(Picture disc)*	1975	14.00	35.00
Capitol SW-11525	(DJ)	**Wings At The Speed Of Sound** *(White label)*	1976	150.00	300.00
Capitol SW-11593	(DJ)	**Wings Over America**	1976	10.00	25.00
Capitol SOO-11905	(DJ)	**Wings' Greatest** *((White label)*	1978	150.00	300.00
Columbia C3X-37990	(S)	**Wings Over America**	1976	16.00	40.00
Columbia JC-36482	(S)	**Band On The Run**	1981	20.00	50.00
		(Cover has the "MPL" logo in lower left)			
Columbia HC-46482	(S)	**Band On The Run** *(Half-speed master)*	1981	16.00	50.00
Columbia FC-36057	(DJ)	**Back To The Egg** *(Promo label)*	1979	10.00	25.00
Columbia PC-36057	(S)	**Back To The Egg**	1982	10.00	25.00
Columbia FC-36511	(DJ)	**McCartney II** *(White label)*	1980	12.00	30.00
Columbia PC-36511	(S)	**McCartney II**	1982	20.00	50.00
Columbia AS2-821	(DJ)	**The McCartney Interview** *(2 LP promo)*	1980	12.00	30.00
		(Originals have white labels with black print in a glossy cover.			
		Counterfeits have blank white labels.)			
Columbia TC-37462	(S)	**Tug Of War** *(Cover reads "PC-37462.")*	1980	12.00	30.00
Columbia PC-37990	(S)	**Wings Over America** *(3 LPs)*	1982	16.00	40.00
Capitol C1-94778	(S)	**Tripping The Live Fantastic** *(3 LPs)*	1990	30.00	75.00
Capitol C1-95379	(S)	**Highlight! Tripping The Live Fantastic**	1990	10.00	25.00
		(Capitol Record Club single album sampler.)			
McCOYS, THE					
Bang BLP-212	(M)	**Hang On Sloopy**	1965	12.00	30.00
Bang BLPS-212	(S)	**Hang On Sloopy**	1965	16.00	40.00
		("Hang On Sloopy" is rechanneled on this album.)			
Bang BLP-213	(M)	**You Make Me Feel So Good**	1966	12.00	30.00
Bang BLPS-213	(S)	**You Make Me Feel So Good**	1966	16.00	40.00
McCRACKLIN, JIMMY					
Chess 1464	(M)	**Jimmy McCracklin Sings**	1961	30.00	75.00
Crown CLP-5244	(M)	**Twist With Jimmy McCracklin**	1962	10.00	25.00
Imperial LP-9219	(M)	**I Just Gotta Knowy**	1964	10.00	25.00
Imperial LP-12219	(S)	**I Just Gotta Knowy**	1964	12.00	30.00
Imperial LP-9285	(M)	**Every Night, Every Day**	1965	10.00	25.00
Imperial LP-12285	(S)	**Every Night, Every Day**	1965	12.00	30.00
Imperial LP-9297	(M)	**Think**	1965	10.00	25.00
Imperial LP-12297	(S)	**Think**	1965	12.00	30.00
Imperial LP-9306	(M)	**My Answer**	1966	10.00	25.00
Imperial LP-12306	(S)	**My Answer**	1966	12.00	30.00
Imperial LP-9316	(M)	**New Soul Of Jimmy McCracklin**	1966	10.00	25.00
Imperial LP-12316	(S)	**New Soul Of Jimmy McCracklin**	1966	12.00	30.00
Minit LP-40009	(M)	**The Best Of Jimmy McCracklin**	1967	10.00	25.00
Minit LP-24009	(S)	**The Best Of Jimmy McCracklin**	1967	14.00	35.00
Minit LP-24011	(S)	**Let's Get Together**	1968	14.00	35.00
Minit LP-24017	(S)	**Stinger Man**	1969	14.00	35.00
Stax STS-2047	(S)	**Yesterday Is Gone**	1972	10.00	25.00
McCURDY, ED					
Ed McCurdy is a guitar player, singer and writer of traditional English folk music,.					
Tradition TLP-1003	(M)	**A Ballad Singer's Choice**	195?	12.00	30.00
Tradition TLP-1027	(M)	**Children's Songs** *(With Billy Faier)*	195?	12.00	30.00

As the title tells us, Ms. McDonald was known as "the Body." The cover shows us why. . .

Label & Catalog #		Title	Year	VG+	NM
Tradition TLP-2061	(M)	Songs Of The West	196?	8.00	20.00
Riverside RLP-12-180	(M)	The Legend Of Robin Hood	195?	12.00	30.00
Riverside RLP-12-601	(M)	The Ballad Record	195?	12.00	30.00
Riverside RLP-12-807	(M)	Barroom Ballads			
		(Sung & Declaimed) (With Erik Darling)	195?	12.00	30.00
Riverside RLP-12-810	(M)	The Legend Of Robin Hood	195?	12.00	30.00
Elektra EKL-24	(10")	Sin Songs, Pro And Con	195?	16.00	40.00
Elektra EKL-108	(M)	Blood, Booze 'N Bones	195?	12.00	30.00
Elektra EKL-110	(M)	When Dalliance Was In Flower	195?	12.00	30.00
		(EKL-110 also features Alan Arkin and Erik Darling.)			
Elektra EKL-112	(M)	Songs Of The Old West	195?	12.00	30.00
Elektra EKL-124	(M)	Sin Songs, Pro And Con	195?	12.00	30.00
		(Elektra 124 is a reissue of 24 with four additional tracks.)			
Elektra EKL-140	(M)	When Dalliance Was In Flower, Vol. 2	195?	12.00	30.00
Elektra EKL-170	(M)	Son Of Dalliance	1959	12.00	30.00
Dawn DLP-1127	(M)	The Folk Singer	195?	12.00	30.00
By-Line 1	(10")	Frankie And Johnnie	195?	16.00	40.00
Prestige Int. PRLP-13044	(M)	Lyrical Erotica (Vol. 1)	1961	12.00	30.00
Prestige Int. PRLP-13050	(M)	Lyrical Erotica (Vol. 3)	1962	12.00	30.00

McCURDY, ED / OSCAR BRAND / JACK ELLIOTT

Label & Catalog #		Title	Year	VG+	NM
Elektra EKL-16	(10")	Badmen And Heroes	1955	20.00	50.00

McCURDY, ED / OSCAR BRAND / JACK ELLIOTT / DICK WILDER

Label & Catalog #		Title	Year	VG+	NM
Elektra EKL-129	(M)	Badmen And Heroes And Pirate Songs	195?	12.00	30.00
		(Lelktra 129 is a reissue of 16 with six additional tracks.)			

McDANIELS, GENE

Label & Catalog #		Title	Year	VG+	NM
Liberty LRP-3146	(M)	In Times Like These	1960	14.00	35.00
Liberty LST-7146	(S)	In Times Like These	1960	20.00	50.00
Liberty LST-7146	(S)	In Times Like These (Blue vinyl)	1960	40.00	100.00
Liberty LRP-3175	(M)	Sometimes I'm Happy, Sometimes I'm Blue	1960	14.00	35.00
Liberty LST-7175	(S)	Sometimes I'm Happy, Sometimes I'm Blue	1960	20.00	50.00
Liberty LRP-3191	(M)	100 Lbs. Of Clay	1961	12.00	30.00
Liberty LST-7191	(S)	100 Lbs. Of Clay	1961	16.00	40.00
Liberty LRP-3204	(M)	Gene McDaniels Sings Movie Memories	1962	12.00	30.00
Liberty LST-7204	(S)	Gene McDaniels Sings Movie Memories	1962	16.00	40.00
Liberty LRP-3215	(M)	Tower Of Strength	1962	12.00	30.00
Liberty LST-7215	(S)	Tower Of Strength	1962	16.00	40.00
Liberty LRP-3258	(M)	Hit After Hit	1962	10.00	25.00
Liberty LST-7258	(S)	Hit After Hit	1962	12.00	30.00
Liberty LRP-3275	(M)	Spanish Lace	1963	10.00	25.00
Liberty LST-7275	(S)	Spanish Lace	1963	12.00	30.00
Liberty LRP-3311	(M)	The Wonderful Word Of Gene McDaniels	1963	10.00	25.00
Liberty LST-7311	(S)	The Wonderful Word Of Gene McDaniels	1963	12.00	30.00

McDONALD, "COUNTRY" JOE: Refer to COUNTRY JOE (McDONALD)

McDONALD, KATHY

Label & Catalog #		Title	Year	VG+	NM
Capitol ST-11224	(S)	Insane Asylum	1974	12.00	30.00

McDONALD, MARIE

Label & Catalog #		Title	Year	VG+	NM
RCA Victor LPM-1585	(M)	The Body Sings!	1957	20.00	50.00

McDONALD, SKEETS

Label & Catalog #		Title	Year	VG+	NM
Capitol T-1040	(M)	Goin' Steady With The Blues	1958	30.00	75.00
Capitol T-1179	(M)	The Country's Best	1959	20.00	50.00
Columbia CL-2170	(M)	Call Me Skeets!	1964	12.00	30.00
Columbia CS-8970	(S)	Call Me Skeets!	1964	16.00	40.00
Sears SPS-116	(E)	Skeets	196?	10.00	25.00
Fortune 3001	(S)	Tattooed Lady	1969	16.00	40.00

McDOWELL, "MISSISSIPPI" FRED

Fred McDowell was a blues guitar player and singer.

Label & Catalog #		Title	Year	VG+	NM
Arhoolie F-1021	(M)	Delta Blues	1964	20.00	50.00
Arhoolie F-1027	(M)	Delta Blues, Volume 2	1966	20.00	50.00
Sire SASH 97018	(S)	Mississippi Fred McDowell In London	1970	12.00	30.00
Capitol ST-403	(S)	I Do Not Play No Rock & Roll	1973	10.00	25.00

Label & Catalog #		Title	Year	VG+	NM

McDOWELL, "MISSISSIPPI" FRED / GUITAR JR.

| Capitol ST-403/409 | (DJ) | I Do Not Play No Rock & Roll (Picture disc) | 1973 | 30.00 | 75.00 |

McDUFF, BROTHER JACK: *Refer to* GOLDMINE'S PRICE GUIDE TO COLLECTIBLE JAZZ ALBUMS

McEWEN, RORY, & JIM DINE

| Atlantic MM=-020 | (S) | Songs Poems Prints (With prints) | 1969 | 30.00 | 75.00 |
| | | (Atlantic 020 was issued with a pair of silk-screened prints.) | | | |

McFERRIN, ROBERT

| Riverside RLP-12-812 | (M) | Deep River & Other Classic Negro Spirituals | 195? | 162.00 | 30.00 |

McGEE BROTHERS, THE

Sam, guitar, and Kirk McGee, banjo and fiddle, are legendary old-time country musicians and vocalists. Arthur Smith is a fiddler who played with the McGees in their original group, The Dixieliners. Refer to Uncle Dave Macon.

| Folkways FA-2379 | (M) | The McGee Brothers And Arthur Smith | 1957 | 16.00 | 40.00 |
| Starday SLP-182 | (M) | Opry Old Timers (Yellow label) | 196? | 16.00 | 40.00 |

McGHEE, BROWNIE

Walter Brown McGhee is a blues guitar and piano player, singer and writer of traditional style folk-blues. His entire career is linked with partner Sonny Terry. Refer to Sonny Terry & Brownie McGhee.

Folkways FP-30	(10")	Brownie McGhee Blues	1951	60.00	150.00
Folkways FA-2030	(10")	Brownie McGhee Blues	1951	60.00	150.00
Bluesville BVLP-1042	(M)	Brownie's Blues	1962	30.00	75.00
		— Bluesville albums above have bright blue labels with silver print.—			
Bluesville BVLP-1042	(M)	Brownie's Blues	1964	10.00	25.00
		— Bluesville albums above have blue labels with a trident logo on the right side.—			

McGHEE, STICKS, & JOHN LEE HOOKER

| Audio Lab AL-1520 | (M) | Highway Of Blues | 1959 | 150.00 | 300.00 |

McGUIRE, BARRY

Refer to Barry & Barry; The New Christy Minstrels.

Horizon WP-1636	(M)	The Barry McGuire Album	1963	12.00	30.00
Horizon ST-1636	(S)	The Barry McGuire Album	1963	16.00	40.00
Mira LP-3000	(M)	The Barry McGuire Album	1965	8.00	20.00
Mira LPS-3000	(S)	The Barry McGuire Album	1965	10.00	25.00
		(Mira 3000 is a reissue of Horizon 1636.)			
Surrey S-1003	(M)	Star Folk With Barry McGuire	1965	8.00	20.00
Surrey SS-1003	(S)	Star Folk With Barry McGuire	1965	10.00	25.00
Surrey S-1010	(M)	Star Folk Vol. 2 With Barry McGuire	1966	8.00	20.00
Surrey SS-1010	(S)	Star Folk Vol. 2 With Barry McGuire	1966	10.00	25.00
Surrey S-1022	(M)	Star Folk Vol. 3 With Barry McGuire	1966	8.00	20.00
Surrey SS-1022	(S)	Star Folk Vol. 3 With Barry McGuire	1966	10.00	25.00
Surrey S-1023	(M)	Star Folk Vol. 4	1966	8.00	20.00
Surrey SS-1023	(S)	Star Folk Vol. 4	1966	10.00	25.00
		(The Sureyl albums repackage previous Horizon related material.)			
Dunhill D-50003	(M)	Barry McGuire Featuring Eve Of Destruction	1966	12.00	30.00
Dunhill DS-50003	(S)	Barry McGuire Featuring Eve Of Destruction	1966	16.00	40.00
Dunhill D-50005	(M)	This Precious Time	1966	10.00	25.00
Dunhill DS-50005	(S)	This Precious Time	1966	12.00	30.00
		(Dunhill 50005 features backing vocals by The Mamas & The Papas.)			
Dunhill DS-50033	(S)	The World's Last Private Citizen	1968	10.00	25.00

McGUIRE SISTERS, THE

Coral CRL-56123	(10")	By Request	1955	20.00	50.00
Coral CRL-57097	(M)	Children's Holiday	1956	14.00	35.00
Coral CRL-57026	(M)	Do You Remember When?	1956	14.00	35.00
Coral CRL-57028	(M)	S'Wonderful	1956	14.00	35.00
Coral CRL-57033	(M)	He	1956	14.00	35.00
Coral CRL-57052	(M)	Sincerely	1956	14.00	35.00
Coral CRL-57134	(M)	Teenage Party	1957	14.00	35.00
Coral CRL-57145	(M)	While The Lights Are Low	1957	14.00	35.00
Coral CRL-57180	(M)	Musical Magic	1957	12.00	30.00
Coral CRL-57217	(M)	Sugartime	1958	12.00	30.00
Coral CRL-57225	(M)	Greetings From The McGuire Sisters	1958	12.00	30.00
Coral CRL-57296	(M)	May You Always	1959	8.00	20.00
Coral CRL-757296	(S)	May You Always	1959	12.00	30.00

Label & Catalog #		Title	Year	VG+	NM
Coral CRL-57303	(M)	In Harmony With Him	1959	8.00	20.00
Coral CRL-757303	(S)	In Harmony With Him	1959	12.00	30.00
Coral CRL-57337	(M)	His And Her's	1960	8.00	20.00
Coral CRL-757337	(S)	His And Her's	1960	12.00	30.00
Coral CRL-57349	(M)	Our Golden Favorites	1961	8.00	20.00
Coral CRL-57385	(M)	Just For Old Times Sake	1961	8.00	20.00
Coral CRL-757385	(S)	Just For Old Times Sake	1961	12.00	30.00
		— Coral albums above have maroon & silver labels.—			

McINTYRE, KEN: *Refer to* GOLDMINE'S PRICE GUIDE TO COLLECTIBLE JAZZ ALBUMS

McKAY, SCOTTY

Ace LP-1017	(M)	Tonight In Person	1961	30.00	75.00

McKENZIE, SCOTT
Scott McKenzie formerly recorded as a member of The Journeymen.

Ode Z12-44001	(M)	The Voice Of Scott McKenzie	1967	8.00	20.00
Ode Z12-44002	(S)	The Voice Of Scott McKenzie	1967	10.00	25.00

McKINLEY, WILSON
Wilson McKinley also recorded as a California Poppy Picker.

Voice of Elijah 29005/6	(S)	Heaven's Gonna Be A Blast!	197?	80.00	200.00
Voice of Elijah 29077/8	(S)	Spirit Of Elijah	197?	150.00	300.00
No label	(S)	Wilson McKinley On Stage	197?	80.00	200.00

McKUEN, ROD / JULIE MEREDITH / TAK SHINDO

Imperial LP-9036	(M)	The Yellow Unicorn	1958	16.00	40.00
Imperial LP-12036	(S)	The Yellow Unicorn	1958	20.00	50.00

McKUEN, ROD

Liberty LRP-3011	(M)	Lazy Afternoon	1956	16.00	40.00
Decca DL-8714	(M)	Summer Love (Soundtrack)	1958	50.00	125.00
Decca DL-8882	(M)	Anywhere I Wander	1958	8.00	20.00
Decca DL-78882	(S)	Anywhere I Wander	1958	12.00	30.00
Decca DL-8946	(M)	Alone After Dark	1958	8.00	20.00
Decca DL-78946	(S)	Alone After Dark	1958	12.00	30.00

McLAIN, DENNY
Denny was formerly a member of the Detroit Tigers.

Capitol ST-2881	(S)	Denny McLain At The Organ	1968	12.00	30.00
Capitol ST-204	(S)	Denny McLain In Las Vegas	1969	10.00	25.00

McLUHAN, MARSHALL

Columbia CL-2701	(M)	The Medium Is The Message	1967	10.00	25.00
Columbia CS-9501	(S)	The Medium Is The Message	1967	12.00	30.00

McMAHON, ED

Cameo C-2009	(M)	An Me... I'm Ed McMahon	1963	10.00	25.00
Cameo CS-2009	(S)	An Me... I'm Ed McMahon	1963	12.00	30.00
Camden CAL-1083	(M)	What Do You Want To Be When You Grow Up?	1964	8.00	20.00
Camden CAS-1083	(S)	What Do You Want To Be When You Grow Up?	1964	10.00	25.00

McNEELY, BIG JAY

Federal 295-96	(10")	Big Jay McNeely	1954		See below
		(Near Mint copies have a suggested value of $3,000-6,000.)			
Savoy MG-15045	(10")	A Rhythm And Blues Concert	1955	350.00	700.00
Federal 395-530	(M)	Big Jay McNeely In 3-D	1956	350.00	700.00
King 650	(M)	Big Jay McNeely In 3-D	1959	800.00	200.00
		(King 650 is a reissue of Federal 530.)			
Warner Bros. W-1523	(M)	Big Jay McNeely	1963	20.00	50.00
Warner Bros. WS-1523	(S)	Big Jay McNeely	1963	30.00	75.00

McNEIL, BROWNIE
Brownie McNeil is a guitar player and singer of traditional cowboy and Mexican folk-based songs.

Sonic B-16847-8	(M)	Folksongs	1957	16.00	40.00

Label & Catalog #		Title	Year	VG+	NM

McNULTY FAMILY, THE
Colonial LP-121	(M)	Irish Folk Songs	195?	12.00	30.00
Copley COP-610	(M)	Night In Ireland, Vol. 1	1958	12.00	30.00
Copley COP-611	(M)	Night In Ireland, Vol. 2	1958	12.00	30.00

McPEAKE, CURTIS
| ABC-Paramount ABC-446 | (M) | Bluegrass Hillbillies | 1963 | 8.00 | 20.00 |
| ABC-Paramount ABCS-446 | (S) | Bluegrass Hillbillies | 1963 | 10.00 | 25.00 |

McPHATTER, CLYDE
Clyde was formerly the lead singer for Billy Ward & The Dominoes; The Drifters.
Atlantic 8024	(M)	Love Ballads	1958	200.00	400.00
Atlantic 8031	(M)	Clyde (White "bullseye" label)	1959	300.00	600.00
Atlantic 8031	(M)	Clyde	1959	200.00	400.00
		—Atlantic albums above have black labels.—			
Atlantic 8024	(M)	Love Ballads	1960	80.00	200.00
Atlantic 8031	(M)	Clyde	1960	80.00	200.00
Atlantic 8077	(M)	The Best Of Clyde McPhatter	1963	80.00	200.00
		—Atlantic albums above have orange & purple labels.—			
MGM E-3775	(M)	Let's Start Over Again	1959	60.00	150.00
MGM SE-3775	(S)	Let's Start Over Again	1959	80.00	200.00
MGM E-3866	(M)	Clyde McPhatter's Greatest Hits	1960	30.00	75.00
MGM SE-3866	(S)	Clyde McPhatter's Greatest Hits	1960	40.00	100.00
Mercury MG-20597	(M)	Ta Ta	1960	20.00	50.00
Mercury SR-60262	(S)	Ta Ta	1960	24.00	60.00
Mercury MG-20655	(M)	Golden Blues Hits	1962	20.00	50.00
Mercury SR-60655	(S)	Golden Blues Hits	1962	24.00	60.00
Mercury MG-20711	(M)	Lover Please	1962	20.00	50.00
Mercury SR-60711	(S)	Lover Please	1962	24.00	60.00
Mercury MG-20750	(M)	Rhythm And Soul	1962	20.00	50.00
Mercury SR-60750	(S)	Rhythm And Soul	1962	24.00	60.00
Wing MGW-12224	(M)	May I Sing For You?	1962	12.00	30.00
Wing SRW-16224	(S)	May I Sing For You?	1962	16.00	40.00
Mercury MG-20783	(M)	Clyde McPhatter's Greatest Hits	1963	12.00	30.00
Mercury SR-60783	(S)	Clyde McPhatter's Greatest Hits	1963	16.00	40.00
Mercury MG-20902	(M)	Songs Of The Big City	1964	12.00	30.00
Mercury SR-60902	(S)	Songs Of The Big City	1964	16.00	40.00
Mercury MG-20915	(M)	Live At The Apollo	1964	12.00	30.00
Mercury SR-60915	(S)	Live At The Apollo	1964	16.00	40.00
Decca DL-75231	(S)	Welcome Home	1970	10.00	25.00

McRAE, CARMEN: *Refer to* GOLDMINE'S PRICE GUIDE TO COLLECTIBLE JAZZ ALBUMS

McSHANN, JAY: *Refer to* GOLDMINE'S PRICE GUIDE TO COLLECTIBLE JAZZ ALBUMS

McTELL, "BLIND" WILLIE
Melodeon 7323	(M)	Blind Willie McTell 1940	1956	80.00	200.00
Bluesville BVLP-1040	(M)	Last Session	1962	60.00	150.00
		—Bluesville albums above have bright blue labels with silver print.—			
Bluesville BVLP-1040	(M)	Last Session	1964	20.00	50.00
		—Bluesville albums above have blue labels with a trident logo on the right side.—			

MEADE, GENE: *Refer to* CLARK KESSINGER & GENE MEADE

MEAT LOAF
Refer to Stoney & Meatloaf
Epic AS-409	(DJ)	Live At Father's Place (Black vinyl)	1978	12.00	30.00
		(Counterfeits exist on red vinyl.)			
Epic HE-44974	(S)	Bat Out Of Hell (Half-speed master)	1981	8.00	25.00

MECHAU FAMILY, THE
Puala Mechau and her children Dorik, Duna, Michael and Vanni are singers of American folk songs.
| Stinson SLP-47 | (10") | Folk Songs For Young And Old | 195? | 16.00 | 40.00 |

MECKI MARK MEN, THE
| Limelight LS-86054 | (S) | The Mecki Mark Men | 1968 | 14.00 | 35.00 |
| Limelight LS-86068 | (S) | Running In The Summer Night | 1969 | 14.00 | 35.00 |

Label & Catalog #		Title	Year	VG+	NM
MEDIUM					
Gamma GS-503	(S)	**Medium**	196?	80.00	200.00
MEL & TIM					
Mel Hardin and Tim McPherson.					
Bamboo BMS-8001	(S)	**Good Guys Only Win In The Movies**	1970	10.00	25.00
Stax STS-3007	(S)	**Starting All Over Again**	1972	10.00	25.00
Stax STS-5501	(S)	**Mel And Tim**	1974	10.00	25.00
MELLENCAMP, JOHN COUGAR [JOHN COUGAR]					
MCA 2225	(S)	**Chestnut Street Incident**	1977	10.00	25.00
Riva	(DJ)	**The Kid Inside** *(Picture disc)*	198?	16.00	40.00
MELLO-LARKS, THE: *Refer to* **GOLDMINE'S PRICE GUIDE TO COLLECTIBLE JAZZ ALBUMS**					
MELLO-KINGS, THE					
Herald H-1013	(M)	**Tonight-Tonight**	1960	200.00	500.00
MELVIN, MICHAEL					
Dot DLP-25961	(S)	**The Plastic Cow Goes Mooooooog**	1969	10.00	25.00
MEMPHIS SLIM					
Memphis Slim is a pseudonym for Peter Chapman. Refer to Willie Dixon.					
Vee Jay VJLP-1012	(M)	**Memphis Slim At The Gate Of The Horn**	1959	80.00	200.00
Folkways FG-3254	(M)	**The Real Boogie Woogie**	1960	40.00	100.00
Folkways FG-3536	(M)	**Chicago Blues**	1961	40.00	100.00
Chess LP-1455	(M)	**Memphis Slim** *(Black label)*	1961	80.00	200.00
Chess LP-1510	(M)	**Real Folk Blues**	1966	24.00	60.00
United Arts. UAL-3137	(M)	**Broken Soul Blues**	1961	16.00	40.00
United Arts. UAS-6137	(S)	**Broken Soul Blues**	1961	20.00	50.00
Bluesville BVLP-1018	(M)	**Just Blues**	1961	40.00	100.00
Bluesville BVLP-1031	(M)	**No Strain**	1961	40.00	100.00
Bluesville BVLP-1053	(M)	**All Kinds Of Blues**	1962	40.00	100.00
Bluesville BVLP-1075	(M)	**Steady Rollin' Blues**	1963	40.00	100.00
— Bluesville albums above have bright blue labels with silver print.—					
Bluesville BVLP-1018	(M)	**Just Blues**	1964	12.00	30.00
Bluesville BVLP-1031	(M)	**No Strain**	1964	12.00	30.00
Bluesville BVLP-1053	(M)	**All Kinds Of Blues**	1964	12.00	30.00
Bluesville BVLP-1075	(M)	**Steady Rollin' Blues**	1964	12.00	30.00
— Bluesville albums above have blue labels with a trident logo on the right side.—					
Candid CM-8023	(M)	**Tribute To Big Bill Broonzy**	1961	16.00	40.00
Candid CS-9023	(S)	**Tribute To Big Bill Broonzy**	1961	20.00	50.00
Candid CM-8024	(M)	**Memphis Slim, U.S.A.**	1962	16.00	40.00
Candid CS-9024	(S)	**Memphis Slim, U.S.A.**	1962	20.00	50.00
Battle BM-6118	(M)	**Alone With My Friends**	1963	12.00	30.00
Battle BM-6122	(M)	**Baby Please Come Home**	1963	12.00	30.00
Disc D-105	(M)	**If The Rabbit Had A Gun**	1964	20.00	50.00
King LP-885	(M)	**Memphis Slim**	1964	20.00	50.00
Scepter SM-535	(M)	**Self Portrait**	1966	10.00	25.00
Strand SLS-1046	(S)	**The World's Foremost Blues Singer**	196?	8.00	20.00
MEMPHIS WILLIE B.					
Bluesville BVLP-1034	(M)	**Introducing Memphis Willie B.**	1961	40.00	100.00
Bluesville BVLP-1048	(M)	**Hard Working Man Blues**	1962	40.00	100.00
— Bluesville albums above have bright blue labels with silver print.—					
Bluesville BVLP-1034	(M)	**Introducing Memphis Willie B.**	1964	12.00	30.00
Bluesville BVLP-1048	(M)	**Hard Working Man Blues**	1964	12.00	30.00
— Bluesville albums above have blue labels with a trident logo on the right side.—					
MEN AT WORK					
Epic PAL-37978	(DJ)	**Business As Usual** *(Picture disc)*	1983	16.00	40.00
MERCER, MABEL: *Refer to* **GOLDMINE'S PRICE GUIDE TO COLLECTIBLE JAZZ ALBUMS**					
MEREDITH, BUDDY					
Starday SLP-225	(M)	**Sing Me A Heart Song** *(Yellow label)*	1963	16.00	40.00

Label & Catalog #		Title	Year	VG+	NM
MEREDITH, BURGESS					
Epic LN-3756	(M)	Songs And Stories Of The Gold Rush	1961	10.00	25.00
Epic LBN-590	(S)	Songs And Stories Of The Gold Rush	1961	12.00	30.00
Lively Arts 30004	(M)	Burgess Meredith Reads Ray Bradbury	196?	10.00	25.00
Colpix CP-452	(M)	Burgess Meredith Sings Songs			
		From "How The West Was Won"	1964	10.00	25.00
Colpix SCP-452	(S)	Burgess Meredith Sings Songs			
		From "How The West Was Won"	1964	12.00	30.00
MERKIN					
Windi 1004	(S)	Music From Merkin Manor	1972	200.00	400.00
MERMAIDS, THE					
Chattahoochie CHLP-628	(M)	Resurface!	197?	14.00	35.00
MERMAN, ETHEL					
Refer to Mary Martin & Ethel Merman.					
"X" LVA-1004	(M)	Ethel Merman And Gertrude Nielsen	195?	14.00	35.00
Decca DL-5053	(10")	Songs She Made Famous	1950	12.00	30.00
Decca DL-8035	(M)	Twelve Songs From "Call Me Madam"	1956	10.00	25.00
Decca DL-8178	(M)	Musical Autobiography, Volume 1	1956	10.00	25.00
Decca DL-8179	(M)	Musical Autobiography, Volume 2	1956	10.00	25.00
MERRILL, HELEN: *Refer to* GOLDMINE'S PRICE GUIDE TO COLLECTIBLE JAZZ ALBUMS					
MERRILL, TONI					
Rama RLP-5004	(M)	Songs From The Heart	195?	30.00	75.00
MERRIWEATHER, BIG MACEO, & JOHN LEE HOOKER					
Fortune 3002	(M)	Big Maceo Merriweather & John Lee Hooker	196?	60.00	150.00
MERRY-GO-ROUND, THE					
The Merry-Go-Round features Emitt Rhodes.					
A&M LP-132	(M)	The Merry-Go-Round	1967	16.00	40.00
A&M SP-4132	(S)	The Merry-Go-Round	1967	20.00	50.00
MERSEYBOYS, THE					
Vee Jay VJ-1101	(M)	15 Greatest Songs Of The Beatles	1964	30.00	75.00
Vee Jay VJS-1101	(S)	15 Greatest Songs Of The Beatles	1964	60.00	150.00
MESMERIZING EYE, THE					
Smash MGS-27090	(M)	Psychedelia/A Musical Light Show	1967	8.00	20.00
Smash SRS-67090	(S)	Psychedelia/A Musical Light Show	1967	10.00	25.00
MESSINA, JIM, & HIS JESTERS					
Refer to The Buffalo Springfield; Loggins & Messina.					
Audio Fidelity DFM-3037	(M)	The Dragsters	1964	30.00	75.00
Audio Fidelity DFS-7037	(S)	The Dragsters	1964	40.00	100.00
METERS, THE					
Josie JOS-4010	(S)	The Meters	1969	24.00	60.00
Josie JOS-4011	(S)	Look-Ka Py Py	1970	24.00	60.00
Josie JOS-4012	(S)	Struttin'	1970	24.00	60.00
Reprise MS-2076	(S)	Cabbage Alley	1972	16.00	40.00
Reprise MS-2200	(S)	Rejuvenation	1972	16.00	40.00
Virgo 12002	(S)	Best Of The Meters	1975	16.00	40.00
Island 9250	(S)	Cissy Strut	1975	16.00	40.00
Warner Bros. B-3042	(S)	New Directions	1977	16.00	40.00
METRONOMES, THE					
Strand 3002	(M)	The Standard Hits	196?	12.00	30.00
Strand S-3002	(S)	The Standard Hits	196?	16.00	40.00
METROS, THE					
RCA Victor LPM-3776	(M)	Sweetest One	1967	30.00	75.00
RCA Victor LSP-3776	(S)	Sweetest One	1967	40.00	100.00
METROTONES, THE					
Columbia CL-6341	(10")	Tops In Rock And Roll	1955	100.00	250.00

Label & Catalog #		Title	Year	VG+	NM

MICAH
Sterling World ST-1001	(S)	**I'm Only One Man**	197?	80.00	200.00

MICHAELANGELO
Guinn 1050	(S)	**Michaelangelo**	1975	500.00	800.00

MICHAELS, LEE
Columbia	(DJ)	**Lee Michaels In Hawaii**	1975	10.00	25.00

MICKEY & SYLVIA
Mickey Baker and Sylvia Vanderpool.
Vik LX-1102	(M)	**New Sounds**	1957	150.00	400.00
Camden CAL-863	(M)	**Love Is Strange**	1965	20.00	50.00
Camden CAS-863	(E)	**Love Is Strange**	1965	12.00	30.00
		(Camden 863 contains two tracks from the Vik album.)			

MIDNIGHTERS, THE
The Midnighters, originally The Royals, eventually became Hank Ballard & The Midnighters. Material they recorded under this name appeared on King, who sold the albums more or less as Ballard solo vehicles, which is where they are listed in this book.
Federal 295-90	(10")	**The Midnighters: Their Greatest Hits**	1954		*See below*
		(Federal 90 is rare with suggested values in VG of $1,000-2,000; in VG+ of $3,000-4,000; and in NM of $6,000-10,000.)			
Federal 395-541	(M)	**The Midnighters: Their Greatest Hits**	1955		*See below*
		(Federal 541 is rare with suggested values in VG of $250-500; in VG+ of $800-1,200; and in NM of $2,000-4,000.)			
Federal 395-581	(M)	**The Midnighters, Volume 2**	1955		*See below*
		(Federal 581 is rare with suggested values in VG of $250-500; in VG+ of $800-1,200; and in NM of $2,000-4,000.)			
King 541	(M)	**Their Greatest Jukebox Hits**	1958	300.00	600.00
		(King 541 is a reissue of Federal 541.)			
King 581	(M)	**The Midnighters, Volume 2**	1958	300.00	600.00
		(King 541 and 581 are reissues of Federal 541 and 581.)			

MIGHTY BABY
Head LPS-025	(S)	**Mighty Baby**	1969	24.00	60.00

MIGHTY FAITH INCREASERS, THE
The Mighty Faith Increasers also recorded with Willa Dorsey.
King 814	(M)	**A Festival Of Spiritual Songs**	1962	60.00	150.00

MILBURN, AMOS
Aladdin LP-704	(10")	**Rockin' The Boogie** *(Red vinyl)*	1955		*See below*
		(Red vinyl copies of Aladdin 704 were issued in blue covers and are rare with suggested values in VG of $1,000-2,000; in VG+ of $3,000-4,000; and in NM of $6,000-10,000.)			
Aladdin LP-704	(10")	**Rockin' The Boogie**	1955		*See below*
		(Black vinyl copies of Aladdin 704 were issued in brown covers and are rare with suggested values in VG of $300-600; in VG+ of $1,000-2,000; and in NM of $3,000-5,000.)			
Aladdin LP-810	(M)	**Rockin' The Boogie**	1958		*See below*
		(Contrary to previous listings, this 12" album does not exist.)			
Score LP-4012	(M)	**Let's Have A Party**	1957	250.00	700.00
Score LP-4035	(M)	**Amos Milburn Sings The Blues**	1958		*Unreleased*
Imperial LP-9176	(M)	**Million Sellers**	1962	200.00	400.00
Motown 608	(M)	**The Blues Boss**	1963		*See below*
		(Motown 608 has a suggested Near Mint value of $1,000-2,000.)			

MILBURN, AMOS / WYNONIE HARRIS / CROWN PRINCE WATERFORD
Aladdin LP-703	(10")	**Party After Hours** *(Red vinyl)*	1955		*See below*
		(Red vinyl copies of Aladdin 703 were issued in blue covers and are rare with suggested values in VG of $1,000-2,000; in VG+ of $3,000-4,000; and in NM of $6,000-10,000.)			
Aladdin LP-703	(10")	**Party After Hours**	1955		*See below*
		(Black vinyl copies of Aladdin 703 were issued in brown covers and are rare with suggested values in VG of $300-600; in VG+ of $1,000-2,000; and in NM of $3,000-5,000.)			

MILES, LIZZIE: *Refer to* GOLDMINE'S PRICE GUIDE TO COLLECTIBLE JAZZ ALBUMS

In 1957, Mickey Baker and Sylvia Vanderpool recorded and released their only album for RCA Victor's Vik subsidiary, New Sounds. The cover features a fine photo of the duo on stage. In 1965, RCA's budget subsidiary, Camden, issued Love Is Strange, a collection of 45 sides plus a couple of tracks from the Vik LP. The cover boasts a nice painting based on the photo on the earlier album.

Label & Catalog #		Title	Year	VG+	NM
MILES, LONG GONE					
World Pacific WP-1820	(M)	**Country Born**	1964	10.00	25.00
World Pacific ST-1820	(S)	**Country Born**	1964	12.00	30.00
MILKWOOD					
Paramount PAS-6046	(S)	**How's The Weather?**	1973	12.00	30.00
MILLARD & DYCE					
Kaymar KS-7-265	(S)	**Open**	1973	24.00	60.00
MILLER, CLARENCE "BIG"					
United Arts. UAL-3047	(M)	**Did You Ever Hear The Blues?**	1959	16.00	40.00
United Arts. UAS-6047	(S)	**Did You Ever Hear The Blues?**	1959	20.00	50.00
Columbia CL-1611	(M)	**Revelation And The Blues**	1961	12.00	30.00
Columbia CS-8411	(S)	**Revelation And The Blues**	1961	16.00	40.00
— Columbia albums above have six white-on-black "eye" logo around the perimeter of the label.—					
Columbia CL-1808	(M)	**Big Miller Sings, Twists, Shouts & Preaches**	1962	10.00	25.00
Columbia CS-8608	(S)	**Big Miller Sings, Twists, Shouts & Preaches**	1962	12.00	30.00
— Columbia albums above have "Guaranteed High Fidelity" or "360 Sound Stereo" in black on the label.—					
MILLER, FRANKIE					
Starday SLP-134	(M)	**Country Music's Great New Star**	1961	60.00	150.00
Starday SLP-199	(M)	**The True Country Style Of Frankie Miller**	1962	60.00	150.00
Audio Lab AL-1562	(M)	**The Fine Country Singing Of Frankie Miller**	1963	100.00	250.00
Starday SLP-339	(M)	**Blackland Farmer**	1965	30.00	75.00
— Starday albums above have yellow labels.—					
MILLER, MICKEY					
Folkways FA-2393	(M)	**American Folk Songs**	1959	12.00	30.00
MILLER, NED					
Fabor FLP-1001	(M)	**From A Jack To A King**	1963	20.00	50.00
Fabor FLP-1001	(M)	**From A Jack To A King** *(Multi-colored vinyl)*	1963	60.00	150.00
Capitol T-2330	(M)	**Ned Miller Sings The Songs Of Ned Miller**	1965	8.00	20.00
Capitol ST-2330	(S)	**Ned Miller Sings The Songs Of Ned Miller**	1965	10.00	25.00
MILLER, ROGER					
Refer to Jerry Lee Lewis / Roger Miller / Roy Orbison; Willie Nelson / Roger Miller..					
Starday SLP-318	(M)	**Wild-Child**	1964	20.00	50.00
Starday SLP-318	(M)	**The Country Side Of Roger Miller**	1965	12.00	30.00
		("Country Side" is a repackage of "Wild-Child.")			
		— Starday albums above have yellow labels.—			
Smash MGS-27049	(M)	**Roger And Out**	1964	8.00	20.00
Smash SRS-67049	(S)	**Roger And Out**	1964	10.00	25.00
MILLER, STEVE/THE STEVE MILLER BAND					
Refer to Chuck Berry.					
Capitol SKAO-2920	(S)	**Children Of The Future**	1968	10.00	25.00
Capitol ST-2984	(S)	**Sailor**	1968	10.00	25.00
Capitol STBB-177	(S)	**Children Of The Future / Sailor** *(2 LPs)*	1969	10.00	25.00
Capitol ST-184	(S)	**Brave New World**	1969	10.00	25.00
— Capitol albums above have black rainbow labels.—					
Capitol SOO-11872	(DJ)	**Greatest Hits 1974-78** *(Blue vinyl)*	1978	12.00	30.00
Mobile Fidelity MFSL-021	(S)	**Fly Like An Eagle**	1976	12.00	35.00
MILLER, STEVE / QUICKSILVER MESSENGER SERVICE / THE BAND					
Capitol STCR-288	(S)	**Steve Miller Band / Quicksilver Messenger Service / The Band**	1969	16.00	40.00
		(This boxed set contains green label copies of Miller's "Sailor," "Quicksilver Messenger Service" and "Music From Big Pink.")			
MILLS, ALAN					
Alan Mills is a pseudonym for Canadian Albert Miller's career as a guitar player and singer of traditional folk music. Refer to Helene Baillargeon & Alan Mills.					
Folkways FP-831	(10")	**Folk Songs Of Newfoundland**	1952	20.00	50.00
Folkways FW-6831	(10")	**Folk Songs Of Newfoundland**	1952	20.00	50.00
Folkways FP-29	(10")	**Folk Songs Of French Canada**	1952	20.00	50.00
Folkways FW-6929	(10")	**Folk Songs Of French Canada**	1952	20.00	50.00
Folkways FP-18	(10")	**French Songs For Children Sung In English**	195?	20.00	50.00

Label & Catalog #		Title	Year	VG+	NM
Folkways FC-7018	(10")	French Songs For Children Sung In English	195?	20.00	50.00
Folkways FP-21	(10")	Folk Songs For Young Folk, Vol. 1	195?	20.00	50.00
Folkways FC-7021	(10")	Folk Songs For Young Folk, Vol. 1	195?	20.00	50.00
Folkways FP-22	(10")	Folk Songs For Young Folk, Vol. 2	195?	20.00	50.00
Folkways FC-7022	(10")	Folk Songs For Young Folk, Vol. 2	195?	20.00	50.00
Folkways FP-78	(10")	French Songs For Children	1953	20.00	50.00
Folkways FC-7208	(10")	French Songs For Children	1953	20.00	50.00
Folkways FP-709	(10")	More Songs To Grow On	1953	20.00	50.00
Folkways FC-7209	(10")	More Songs To Grow On	1953	20.00	50.00
Folkways FW-3001	(M)	O, Canada—A History Of Canada In Folk Songs (2 LPs)	1956	20.00	50.00
Folkways FC-7750	(M)	Christmas Songs Of Many Lands	195?	12.00	30.00
Folkways FW-8771	(M)	Folk Songs Of Newfoundland	1959	12.00	30.00
		(Folkways 8771 is a reissue of 6831 with additional tracks.)			
Folkways FA-2312	(M)	Songs Of The Sea (With The Shanty Boys)	195?	12.00	30.00

MILLS, HAYLEY
Refer to Annette & Hayley Mills.

Disneyland ST-1960	(M)	Pollyanna (Soundtrack)	1960	20.00	50.00
Buena Vista BV-3311	(M)	Let's Get Together	1962	14.00	35.00
Buena Vista STER-3311	(S)	Let's Get Together	1962	20.00	50.00
Disneyland ST-3916	(M)	In Search Of The Castaways (Soundtrack)	1962	30.00	75.00
Disneyland ST-3916	(S)	In Search Of The Castaways (Soundtrack)	1962	40.00	100.00
Buena Vista BV-4025	(M)	Summer Magic (Soundtrack)	1963	20.00	50.00
Buena Vista STER-4025	(S)	Summer Magic (Soundtrack)	1963	30.00	75.00
Mainstream 56090	(M)	Gypsy Girl (Soundtrack)	1966	14.00	35.00
Mainstream S-6090	(S)	Gypsy Girl (Soundtrack)	1966	20.00	50.00

MILLS BROTHERS, THE

Decca DL-5050	(10")	Barber Shop Ballads	1950	20.00	50.00
Decca DL-5051	(10")	Barber Shop Ballads	1950	20.00	50.00
Decca DL-5102	(10")	Souvenir Album	1950	20.00	50.00
Decca DL-5337	(10")	Wonderful Words	1951	20.00	50.00
Decca DL-5506	(10")	Meet The Mills Brothers	1954	20.00	50.00
Decca DL-5509	(10")	Louis Armstrong And The Mills Brothers	1954	20.00	50.00
Decca DL-5516	(10")	Four Boys And A Guitar	1954	20.00	50.00
Decca DL-8148	(M)	Souvenir Album	1955	12.00	30.00
Decca DL-8209	(M)	Singin' And Swingin'	1956	12.00	30.00
Decca DL-8219	(M)	Memory Lane	1956	12.00	30.00
Decca DL-8491	(M)	One Dozen Roses	1957	12.00	30.00
Decca DL-8664	(M)	The Mills Brothers In Hi-Fi	1958	12.00	30.00
Decca DL-8827	(M)	Glow With The Mills Brothers	1959	12.00	30.00
Decca DL-8890	(M)	Barber Shop Harmony	1959	12.00	30.00
Decca DL-8892	(M)	Harmonizin' With The Mills Brothers	1959	12.00	30.00
		—Decca albums above have black & silver labels.—			
Dot DLP-3103	(M)	Mmmm, The Mills Brothers	1958	8.00	20.00
Dot DLP-25103	(S)	Mmmm, The Mills Brothers	1958	12.00	30.00
Dot DLP-3157	(M)	The Mills Brothers' Great Hits	1958	8.00	20.00
Dot DLP-25157	(S)	The Mills Brothers' Great Hits	1958	12.00	30.00
Dot DLP-25157	(S)	The Mills Brothers' Great Hits (Blue vinyl)	1958	24.00	60.00
Dot DLP-3208	(M)	Great Barbershop Hits	1959	8.00	20.00
Dot DLP-25208	(S)	Great Barbershop Hits	1959	12.00	30.00
Dot DLP-3232	(M)	Merry Christmas	1959	8.00	20.00
Dot DLP-25232	(S)	Merry Christmas	1959	12.00	30.00
Dot DLP-3237	(M)	The Mills Brothers Sing	1960	8.00	20.00
Dot DLP-25237	(S)	The Mills Brothers Sing	1960	12.00	30.00

MILTON, ROY
Refer to Chuck Higgins / Roy Milton.

Kent KLP-5054	(M)	The Great Roy Milton	1963	20.00	50.00
Kent KST-554	(E)	The Great Roy Milton	1963	12.00	30.00

MILWAUKEE IRON

"KM" 2137	(S)	Milwaukee Iron	1978	10.00	25.00

MIMMS, GARNET, & THE ENCHANTERS

United Arts. UAL-3305	(M)	Cry Baby And 11 Other Hits	1963	20.00	50.00
United Arts. UAS-6305	(S)	Cry Baby And 11 Other Hits	1963	24.00	60.00

Label & Catalog #		Title	Year	VG+	NM
United Arts. UAL-3396	(M)	As Long As I Have You	1964	16.00	40.00
United Arts. UAS-6396	(S)	As Long As I Have You	1964	20.00	50.00
United Arts. UAL-3498	(M)	I'll Take Good Care Of You	1966	16.00	40.00
United Arts. UAS-6498	(S)	I'll Take Good Care Of You	1966	20.00	50.00

MIND EXPANDERS, THE

Dot DLP-3773	(M)	What's Happening	1967	20.00	50.00
Dot DLP-25773	(S)	What's Happening	1967	30.00	75.00

MINDBENDERS, THE
The Mindbenders originally recorded with Wayne Fontana.

Fontana MGF-27554	(M)	A Groovy Kind Of Love	1966	16.00	40.00
Fontana SRF-67554	(E)	A Groovy Kind Of Love	1966	12.00	30.00
		(First pressings of "Groovy" include "Don't Cry No More.")			
Fontana MGF-27554	(M)	A Groovy Kind Of Love	1966	14.00	35.00
Fontana SRF-67554	(E)	A Groovy Kind Of Love	1966	1000	25.00
		(Later pressings include "Ashes To Ashes.")			

MINEO, SAL

Epic LN-3405	(M)	Sal	1958	60.00	150.00

MINNELLI, LIZA
Refer to Judy Garland & Liza Minnelli.

Cadence CE-4012	(M)	Best Foot Forward *(Soundtrack)*	1963	20.00	50.00
Cadence CLP-24012	(S)	Best Foot Forward *(Soundtrack)*	1963	30.00	75.00
Capitol STAO-2295	(S)	Live At The London Palladium	1965	10.00	25.00
RCA Victor LOC-1111	(M)	Flora The Red Menace *(Soundtrack)*	1965	20.00	50.00
RCA Victor LSO-1111	(S)	Flora The Red Menace *(Soundtrack)*	1965	30.00	75.00

MINNIE PEARL
Minnie Pearl is a pseudonym for Sarah Ophelia Cannon.

Starday SLP-224	(M)	Howdee	1963	16.00	40.00
Starday SLP-380	(M)	America's Beloved Minnie Pearl	1965	16.00	40.00
Starday SLP-397	(M)	The Country Music Story	1966	12.00	30.00
		— Starday albums above have yellow labels.—			
Nashville NLP-2043	(M)	Lookin' For A Feller	196?	8.00	20.00
Nashville SNLP-2043	(S)	Lookin' For A Feller	196?	10.00	25.00

MINT TATTOO

Dot DLP-25918	(S)	Mint Tattoo	1969	16.00	40.00

MIRACLES, THE/SMOKEY ROBINSON & THE MIRACLES
Tamla 220-254 simply credit The Miracles; later albums credit Smokey Robinson & The Miracles. Note: The Miracles who recorded for Tamla from 1974 on are a different group.

Tamla 220	(M)	Hi! We're The Miracles	1961	300.00	600.00
Tamla 223	(M)	Cookin' With The Miracles	1962	350.00	700.00
Tamla 230	(M)	I'll Try Something New *(Tan label)*	1962	350.00	700.00
Tamla 230	(M)	I'll Try Something New *(White label)*	1962	300.00	600.00
		— Tamla albums above have a disc over-lapping a globe at the top of the label.—			
Tamla 236	(M)	Christmas With The Miracles	1963	150.00	300.00
Tamla 238	(M)	The Fabulous Miracles	1963	150.00	300.00
Tamla 238	(M)	You've Really Got A Hold On Me	1963	80.00	200.00
		("You've Really. . ." is a repackage of "The Fabulous Miracles.")			
Tamla 241	(M)	Recorded Live On Stage	1963	80.00	200.00
Tamla 245	(M)	The Miracles Doin' Mickey's Monkey	1963	80.00	200.00
Tamla T-245	(S)	The Miracles Doin' Mickey's Monkey	1963	150.00	300.00
Tamla 2-254	(M)	Greatest Hits From The Beginning *(2 LPs)*	1965	20.00	50.00
Tamla T-2-254	(P)	Greatest Hits From The Beginning *(2 LPs)*	1965	14.00	35.00
		(The first disc of 254 is rechanneled; the second is stereo.)			
Tamla 267	(M)	Going To A Go-Go	1965	10.00	25.00
Tamla T-267	(S)	Going To A Go-Go	1965	12.00	30.00
Tamla 271	(M)	Away We A Go-Go	1966	8.00	20.00
Tamla T-271	(S)	Away We A Go-Go	1966	10.00	25.00
Tamla 276	(M)	Make It Happen	1967	10.00	25.00
Tamla T-276	(S)	Make It Happen	1967	12.00	30.00
Tamla T-276	(S)	Tears Of A Clown	1970	10.00	25.00
		("Tears Of A Clown" is a repackage of "Make It Happen.")			
Tamla T-280	(S)	Greatest Hits, Volume 2	1968	10.00	25.00

— Tamla albums above have two side-by-side circles at the top of the label.—

The Miracles first album, Hi! We're The Miracles, *features an almost unbelievably amateurish cover that, along with the bold credit for producer Berry Gordy, Jr., fully captures the ambience of the fledgling Tamla/Motown corporation.*

Label & Catalog #		Title	Year	VG+	NM
MIRTHRANDER					
Mirth Music	(S)	**For You, The Old Woman**	1976	40.00	100.00
MISSIONARY QUINTET, THE					
Folkways FP-824	(10")	**Gospel Songs**	1953	20.00	50.00
Folkways FW-6824	(10")	**Gospel Songs**	1953	20.00	50.00
MR. GASSER & THE WEIRDOS					
Mr. Gasser is a pseudonym for Ed "Big Daddy" Roth. The Weirdos are a creation of Gary Usher & Co.					
Capitol T-2010	(M)	**Hot Rod Hootenanny**	1963	20.00	50.00
Capitol ST-2010	(S)	**Hot Rod Hootenanny**	1963	30.00	75.00
Capitol T-2057	(M)	**Rods N' Ratfinks** *(With ratfink decal)*	1963	30.00	75.00
Capitol ST-2057	(S)	**Rods N' Ratfinks** *(With ratfink decal)*	1963	40.00	100.00
Capitol T-2057	(M)	**Rods N' Ratfinks** *(Without decal)*	1963	20.00	50.00
Capitol ST-2057	(S)	**Rods N' Ratfinks** *(Without decal)*	1963	30.00	75.00
Capitol T-2114	(M)	**Surfink!**	1964	30.00	75.00
Capitol ST-2114	(S)	**Surfink!**	1964	40.00	100.00
		(Includes the a bonus single "Santa Barbara" / "Midnight Run" by The Super Stocks in a special "pocket" on the front cover.			
Capitol T-2114	(M)	**Surfink!** *(Without bonus single)*	1964	20.00	50.00
Capitol ST-2114	(S)	**Surfink!** *(Without bonus single)*	1964	30.00	75.00
MRS. MILLER					
Capitol T-2494	(M)	**Mrs. Miller's Greatest Hits**	1966	8.00	20.00
Capitol ST-2494	(S)	**Mrs. Miller's Greatest Hits**	1966	10.00	25.00
Capitol T-2579	(M)	**Will Success Spoil Mrs. Miller?**	1966	8.00	20.00
Capitol ST-2579	(S)	**Will Success Spoil Mrs. Miller?**	1966	10.00	25.00
Capitol T-2734	(M)	**The Country Soul Of Mrs. Miller**	1967	8.00	20.00
Capitol ST-2734	(S)	**The Country Soul Of Mrs. Miller**	1967	10.00	25.00
Amaret 5000	(S)	**Mrs. Miller Does Her Thing**	1969	10.00	25.00
MITCHELL, GUY					
Columbia CL-6231	(10")	**Songs Of Open Spaces**	1953	30.00	75.00
Columbia CL-6282	(10")	**Red Garters** *(Soundtrack)*	1954	40.00	100.00
Columbia CL-1211	(M)	**A Guy In Love**	1959	16.00	40.00
Columbia CL-1226	(M)	**Guy Mitchell's Greatest Hits**	1959	16.00	40.00
Columbia CL-1552	(M)	**Sunshine Guitar**	1960	12.00	30.00
Columbia CS-8352	(S)	**Sunshine Guitar**	1960	16.00	40.00
— Columbia albums above have three white "eye" logos on each side of the spindle hole.—					
Starday SLP-412	(M)	**Traveling Shoes** *(Yellow label)*	1968	16.00	40.00
MITCHELL, PRISCILLA: *Refer to* **ROY DRUSKY & PRISCILLA MITCHELL**					
MITCHELL, WILLIE					
Hi HL-32010	(M)	**Sunrise Serenade**	1963	12.00	30.00
Hi SHL-32010	(E)	**Sunrise Serenade**	1963	8.00	20.00
Hi HL-32021	(M)	**Hold It**	1964	8.00	20.00
Hi SHL-32021	(S)	**Hold It**	1964	10.00	25.00
Hi HL-32026	(M)	**It's Dance Time**	1965	8.00	20.00
Hi SHL-32026	(S)	**It's Dance Time**	1965	10.00	25.00
Hi HL-32029	(M)	**Driving Beat**	1966	8.00	20.00
Hi SHL-32029	(S)	**Driving Beat**	1966	10.00	25.00
Hi HL-32034	(M)	**Hit Sound Of Willie Mitchell**	1967	8.00	20.00
Hi SHL-32034	(S)	**Hit Sound Of Willie Mitchell**	1967	10.00	25.00
Hi HL-32039	(M)	**Ooh Baby, You Turn Me On**	1967	8.00	20.00
Hi HL-32039	(S)	**Ooh Baby, You Turn Me On**	1967	10.00	25.00
MITCHELL TRIO, CHAD/THE MITCHELL TRIO					

The original CMT, a folk-pop vocal ensemble, was Mike Kobluk, Chad Mitchell and Mike Pugh accompanied on the first two albums by guitar player Jim (Roger) McGuinn. Pugh was replaced by Joe Frazier, and, when Chad left in 1965 (his solo recordings are listed separately above), the group continued as The Mitchell Trio. The Mitchell Trio on "That's The Way It's Gonna Be" and "Violets Of Dawn" are Kobluk and Frazier with John Denver. Frazier left in 1967 and was replaced by David Boise for the Reprise album. Refer to Harry Belafonte.

Kapp KL-1262	(M)	**A Mighty Day On Campus**	1961	10.00	25.00
Kapp KS-3262	(S)	**A Mighty Day On Campus**	1961	12.00	30.00
Kapp KL-1281	(M)	**The Chad Mitchell Trio At The Bitter End**	1962	10.00	25.00
Kapp KS-3281	(S)	**The Chad Mitchell Trio At The Bitter End**	1962	12.00	30.00

Okay, so Mitchum couldn't sing, as this album amply demonstrates. He could act better than just about anyone, so why shouldn't he have an album? Besides, the covers a killer!

Label & Catalog #		Title	Year	VG+	NM
Kapp KL-1313	(M)	**Blowin' In The Wind**	1963	8.00	20.00
Kapp KS-3313	(S)	**Blowin' In The Wind**	1963	10.00	25.00
Kapp KL-1334	(M)	**The Best Of The Chad Mitchell Trio**	1963	8.00	20.00
Kapp KS-3334	(S)	**The Best Of The Chad Mitchell Trio**	1963	10.00	25.00
Kapp KL-1344	(M)	**Hootenanny #3**	1963	10.00	25.00
Kapp KS-3344	(S)	**Hootenanny #3**	1963	12.00	30.00
Colpix CP-411	(M)	**The Chad Mitchell Trio Arrives**	1963	8.00	20.00
Colpix SCP-411	(S)	**The Chad Mitchell Trio Arrives**	1963	12.00	30.00
Colpix CP-463	(M)	**The Chad Mitchell Trio In Concert**	1964	8.00	20.00
Colpix SCP-463	(S)	**The Chad Mitchell Trio In Concert**	1964	12.00	30.00

MITCHUM, ROBERT

Capitol T-853	(M)	**Calypso —Is Like So. . .**	1957	40.00	100.00
Monument MLP-8086	(M)	**That Man, Robert Mitchum, Sings**	1967	8.00	20.00
Monument SLP-18086	(S)	**That Man, Robert Mitchum, Sings**	1967	10.00	25.00

MIXTURES, THE

Linda 3301	(M)	**Stompin' At The Rainbow**	1962	20.00	50.00

MOBY GRAPE

Moby Grape is Alexander "Skip" Spence, Bob Mosley, Jerry Miller, Peter Lewis and Don Stephenson.

Columbia CL-2698	(M)	**Moby Grape**	1967	16.00	40.00
Columbia CS-9498	(S)	**Moby Grape**	1967	20.00	50.00
		(First pressings of "Moby Grape" have "360 Sound" labels. The cover features Don Stephenson "giving the finger" while holdin a washboard. Issued with a poster, priced separately below.)			
Columbia 26/9498		**Moby Grape Bonus Poster #1**	1967	8.00	20.00
		(The poster also features Stephenson "giving the finger.")			
Columbia CL-2698	(M)	**Moby Grape**	1967	8.00	20.00
Columbia CS-9498	(S)	**Moby Grape**	1967	10.00	25.00
		(Second pressings have "360 Sound" labels but Stephenson's offending member has been airbrushed off the cover. Issued with a poster, priced separately below.)			
Columbia 26/9498		**Moby Grape Bonus Poster #2**	1967	4.00	10.00
		(The second poster also has Stephenson's finger airbrushed out.)			
Columbia CS-9613	(S)	**Wow**	1968	10.00	25.00
Columbia MGS-1	(S)	**Grape Jam**	1968	4.00	10.00
		("Grape Jam" was issued as bonus album with "Wow.")			
Columbia CS-9696	(S)	**Moby Grape '69**	1969	10.00	25.00
— Columbia albums above have "360 Sound" on the bottom of the label.—					
San Francisco 04801	(S)	**Moby Grape**	1983	8.00	25.00
San Francisco 04805	(S)	**Wow / Grape Jam** *(2LPs. Half speed master)*	1983	14.00	35.00

MOD & THE ROCKERS

Justice JLP-153	(M)	**Mod & The Rockers Now!**	196?	200.00	400.00

MOD-MODS, THE

The M-Ms feature Morton Downey, Jr.

Rep LP-102	(M)	**Heaven's Door**	196?	12.00	30.00

MODERN FOLK QUARTET, THE

The MFQ features Jerry Yester. Refer to Henske & Yester; The Lovin' Spoonful.

Warner Bros. W-1511	(M)	**Modern Folk Quartet**	1963	12.00	30.00
Warner Bros. WS-1511	(S)	**Modern Folk Quartet**	1963	16.00	40.00
Warner Bros. W-1546	(M)	**Changes**	1964	12.00	30.00
Warner Bros. WS-1546	(S)	**Changes**	1964	16.00	40.00

MODERN LOVERS, THE: *Refer to* JONATHAN RICHMAN & THE MODERN LOVERS

MODLIN, DAN, & DAVE SCOTT

700 West 760715	(S)	**The Train Don't Stop Here Anymore**	1976	60.00	150.00

MODUGNO, DOMENICO

Decca DL-8808	(M)	**Nel Blu Dipinti Blu**	1958	20.00	50.00
Decca DL-4133	(M)	**Viva Italia**	1961	12.00	30.00

MOLLY HATCHET

Epic PJE-35347	(DJ)	**Molly Hatchet** *(Picture disc)*	1979	10.00	25.00
Epic AS-528	(DJ)	**Molly Hatchet Live**	1979	10.00	25.00

Label & Catalog #		Title	Year	VG+	NM
MOLOCH					
Enterprise ENS-1002	(S)	**Moloch**	*1969*	**14.00**	**35.00**
MOMENTS, THE					
Stang ST-1003	(S)	**Not On The Outside,**			
		But On The Inside Strong	*1969*	**12.00**	**30.00**
MONESE, GIANNA					
Vox TVX-425910	(M)	**How To Make Love To A Blond**	*1959*	**8.00**	**20.00**
Vox STVX-425910	(S)	**How To Make Love To A Blond**	*1959*	**10.00**	**25.00**
MONICA, CORBETT					
Dot DLP-3303	(M)	**For Laughs**	*1960*	**12.00**	**30.00**
Dot DLP-25303	(S)	**For Laughs**	*1960*	**16.00**	**40.00**
MONITORS, THE					
Soul SS-714	(S)	**Greetings, We're The Monitors**	*1969*	**10.00**	**25.00**

MONKEES, THE
The Monkees were Michael Nesmith, Micky Dolenz, Peter Tork and Davy Jones. Note: Monkees albums outsold everyone for several years, usually ending up in the hands of fans who played the beecheeses out of 'em! Copies of the earlier album, 101-109, are so common in less than Near Mint condition that they are almost unsalable. A reasonable VG value for these titles might be 25¢ to 50¢, if you're a real horsetrader. I have placed the VG+ values for these below at 1/4 of the Near Mint values as a way of hopefully alerting readers to this situation.

Colgems COM-101	(M)	**The Monkees**	*1966*	**7.50**	**30.00**
Colgems COS-101	(S)	**The Monkees**	*1966*	**10.00**	**40.00**
		(Colgems 101 was originally issued with the cover			
		erroneously listing "Papa Jean's Blues.")			
Colgems COM-101	(M)	**The Monkees**	*1967*	**5.00**	**20.00**
Colgems COS-101	(S)	**The Monkees**	*1967*	**7.50**	**30.00**
		(Later pressings correctly list "Papa Gene's Blues.")			
Colgems COM-102	(M)	**More Of The Monkees**	*1967*	**5.00**	**20.00**
Colgems COS-102	(S)	**More Of The Monkees**	*1967*	**7.50**	**30.00**
Colgems COM-102	(S)	**More Of The Monkees** (Clear vinyl)	*1967*		*See below*
		(Probably a one-of-a-kind clear vinyl album pressed surreptitiously			
		by an employee. Impossible to even hazard an estimated value.)			
Colgems COM-103	(M)	**Headquarters**	*1967*	**5.00**	**20.00**
Colgems COS-103	(S)	**Headquarters**	*1967*	**7.50**	**30.00**
Colgems COM-104	(M)	**Pisces, Aquarius, Capricorn & Jones, Ltd.**	*1967*	**15.00**	**60.00**
Colgems COS-104	(S)	**Pisces, Aquarius, Capricorn & Jones, Ltd.**	*1967*	**5.00**	**20.00**
— *Colgems albums above read "TM of Colgems Records" at the top of the label.* —					
Colgems COM-101	(M)	**The Monkees**	*1968*	**7.50**	**30.00**
Colgems COS-101	(S)	**The Monkees**	*1968*	**4.00**	**16.00**
Colgems COM-102	(M)	**More Of The Monkees**	*1968*	**7.50**	**30.00**
Colgems COS-102	(S)	**More Of The Monkees**	*1968*	**4.00**	**16.00**
Colgems COM-103	(M)	**Headquarters**	*1968*	**7.50**	**30.00**
Colgems COS-103	(S)	**Headquarters**	*1968*	**4.00**	**16.00**
		(The back cover has a photo of Mike, Pete and Mickey with beards.)			
Colgems COM-104	(M)	**Pisces, Aquarius, Capricorn & Jones, Ltd.**	*1968*	**15.00**	**60.00**
Colgems COS-104	(S)	**Pisces, Aquarius, Capricorn & Jones, Ltd.**	*1968*	**4.00**	**16.00**
— *Colgems albums above do not have "TM of Colgems Records" on the label and "RE" on the cover.* —					
Colgems COM-109	(M)	**The Birds, The Bees And The Monkees**	*1968*	**80.00**	**200.00**
Colgems COS-109	(S)	**The Birds, The Bees And The Monkees**	*1968*	**7.50**	**30.00**
Colgems COSO-5008	(S)	**Head**	*1968*	**20.00**	**50.00**
Colgems COS-113	(S)	**Instant Replay**	*1969*	**16.00**	**40.00**
Colgems COS-115	(S)	**The Monkees' Greatest Hits**	*1969*	**12.00**	**30.00**
Colgems COS-117	(S)	**The Monkees Present**	*1969*	**16.00**	**40.00**
Colgems COS-119	(S)	**Changes**	*1970*	**50.00**	**125.00**
Colgems SCOS-1001	(S)	**A Barrel Full Of Monkees** (2 LPs)	*1971*	**40.00**	**100.00**
— *Colgems albums above delete "TM of Colgems Records" from the label.* —					
RCA Victor PRS-329	(S)	**The Monkees' Golden Hits** (RCA Rec. Club)	*1972*	**60.00**	**150.00**
Bell 6081	(S)	**Refocus**	*1973*	**20.00**	**50.00**
Laurie House LH-8009	(P)	**The Monkees** (TV advertised)	*1974*	**10.00**	**25.00**
RCA/Pair DPL2-0188	(S)	**The Monkees** (2 LPs)	*1976*	**14.00**	**35.00**
Rhino RNLP-144	(S)	**The Birds, The Bees And The Monkees**	*1985*	**12.00**	**30.00**
		(Pressings with "RE-1" etched in the trail-off vinyl			
		contain an alternate take of "Valleri.")			

Label & Catalog #		Title	Year	VG+	NM

MONRO, MATT

Label & Catalog #		Title	Year	VG+	NM
London LL-1611	(M)	Blue And Sentimental	1957	12.00	30.00
Warwick W-2045	(M)	My Kind Of Girl	1961	14.00	35.00
Warwick W-2045ST	(S)	My Kind Of Girl	1961	20.00	50.00
Columbia OL-6660	(M)	The Quiller Memorandum (Soundtrack)	1966	40.00	100.00
Columbia OS-3060	(S)	The Quiller Memorandum (Soundtrack)	1966	50.00	125.00
Decca DL-79160	(S)	A Matter Of Innocence (Soundtrack)	1968	20.00	50.00
Colgems COSO-5009	(S)	The Southern Star (Soundtrack)	1969	40.00	100.00
Paramount PAS-5007	(S)	The Italian Job (Soundtrack)	1969	14.00	35.00

MONROE, BILL/BILL MONROE & HIS BLUEGRASS BOYS
Refer to Flatt & Scruggs; The Monroe Brothers.

Label & Catalog #		Title	Year	VG+	NM
Decca DL-8731	(M)	Knee Deep In Bluegrass	1958	20.00	50.00
Decca DL-78731	(S)	Knee Deep In Bluegrass	1958	30.00	75.00
Decca DL-8769	(M)	I Saw The Light	1959	20.00	50.00
Decca DL-78769	(S)	I Saw The Light	1959	30.00	75.00
— Decca albums above have black & silver labels.—					
Decca DL-8731	(M)	Knee Deep In Bluegrass	196?	8.00	20.00
Decca DL-78731	(S)	Knee Deep In Bluegrass	196?	10.00	25.00
Decca DL-8769	(M)	I Saw The Light	196?	8.00	20.00
Decca DL-78769	(S)	I Saw The Light	196?	10.00	25.00
Decca DL-4080	(M)	Mr. Bluegrass	1960	12.00	30.00
Decca DL-74080	(S)	Mr. Bluegrass	1960	16.00	40.00
Decca DL-4266	(M)	Bluegrass Ramble	1962	10.00	25.00
Decca DL-74266	(S)	Bluegrass Ramble	1962	14.00	35.00
Decca DL-4327	(M)	My All Time Country Favorites	1962	10.00	25.00
Decca DL-74327	(S)	My All Time Country Favorites	1962	14.00	35.00
Decca DL-4382	(M)	Bluegrass Special	1963	10.00	25.00
Decca DL-74382	(S)	Bluegrass Special	1963	14.00	35.00
Decca DL-4537	(M)	I'll Meet You In Church Sunday Morning	1964	8.00	20.00
Decca DL-74537	(S)	I'll Meet You In Church Sunday Morning	1964	10.00	25.00
Decca DL-4601	(M)	Bluegrass Instrumentals	1965	8.00	20.00
Decca DL-74601	(S)	Bluegrass Instrumentals	1965	10.00	25.00
Decca DL-4780	(M)	The High Lonesome Sound Of Bill Monroe	1966	8.00	20.00
Decca DL-74780	(S)	The High Lonesome Sound Of Bill Monroe	1966	10.00	25.00
— Decca albums above have black labels with "Mfd by Decca" beneath the rainbow.—					

MONROE, CHARLIE/CHARLIE MONROE & THE KENTUCKY PARDNERS
Refer to The Monroe Brothers.

Label & Catalog #		Title	Year	VG+	NM
Starday SLP-361	(M)	Lord, Build Me A Cabin (Yellow label)	1965	12.00	30.00
Starday SLP-372	(M)	Charlie Monroe Sings Again (Yellow label)	1966	12.00	30.00

MONROE, MARILYN, & JANE RUSSELL

Label & Catalog #		Title	Year	VG+	NM
MGM E-208	(10")	Gentlemen Prefer Blondes (Soundtrack)	1953	80.00	200.00
MGM E-3231	(M)	Gentlemen Prefer Blondes (Soundtrack)	1955	40.00	100.00

MONROE, MARILYN
Note: Any stereo album with Marilyn's vocals are reprocessed except those from "Let's Make Love."

Label & Catalog #		Title	Year	VG+	NM
United Arts. UAL-4030	(M)	Some Like It Hot (Soundtrack)	1959	30.00	75.00
United Arts. UAS-5030	(E)	Some Like It Hot (Soundtrack)	1959	20.00	50.00
Columbia CL-1527	(M)	Let's Make Love (Soundtrack)	1960	14.00	35.00
Columbia CS-8327	(S)	Let's Make Love (Soundtrack)	1960	20.00	50.00
20th Century FXG-5000	(M)	Marilyn	1959	80.00	200.00
(Original pressings of FXG-5000 have custom black labels in an orange cover. This and all subsequent pressings were issued with an 8 x 10" black & white bonus photo, priced separately below.)					
20th Century FXG-5000	(M)	Marilyn	1963	40.00	100.00
20th Century SXG-5000	(E)	Marilyn	1963	60.00	150.00
(Second pressings have custom black labels in black covers.)					
20th Century FXG-5000	(M)	Marilyn	1964	30.00	75.00
20th Century SXG-5000	(E)	Marilyn	1964	40.00	100.00
(Later pressings have blue sky labels in black covers.)					
20th Century 5000		Marilyn Bonus Photo	1959	20.00	50.00
Ascot ALM-13008	(M)	Marilyn Monroe	1964	16.00	40.00
Ascot ALS-16008	(S)	Marilyn Monroe	1964	20.00	50.00
(Ascot 16008 has the three MM tracks from "Some Like It Hot" in rechanneled stereo. The rest of the album is "cheezy instrumental lounge covers" in true stereo.)					

Label & Catalog #		Title	Year	VG+	NM
Ascot US-13500	(M)	**Some Like It Hot** (Soundtrack)	1964	12.00	30.00
Ascot US-16500	(E)	**Some Like It Hot** (Soundtrack)	1964	8.00	20.00
Movietone 1016	(M)	**The Unforgettable Marilyn Monroe**	1967	10.00	25.00
Movietone 72016	(E)	**The Unforgettable Marilyn Monroe**	1967	8.00	20.00
20th Century T-901	(E)	**Remember Marilyn**	1972	10.00	25.00
		(Movietone 1/72016 and 20th Cent. 901 are reissues of Fox 5000.)			

MONROE, VAUGHN

Label & Catalog #		Title	Year	VG+	NM
RCA Victor LPM-1799	(M)	**There I Sing, Swing It Again**	1958	8.00	20.00
RCA Victor LSP-1799	(S)	**There I Sing, Swing It Again**	1958	12.00	30.00

MONROES, THE

Label & Catalog #		Title	Year	VG+	NM
Alpha AAE-15015	(S)	**The Monroes** (EP)	198?	12.00	30.00

MONTANA, PATSY

Label & Catalog #		Title	Year	VG+	NM
Sims LP-122	(M)	**The New Sound Of Patsy Montana**	1964	20.00	50.00

MONTANA SLIM
Montana Slim is a pseudonym for Wilf Carter.

Label & Catalog #		Title	Year	VG+	NM
Camden CAL-527	(M)	**Wilf Carter/Montana Slim**	1958	14.00	35.00
Decca DL-8917	(M)	**I'm Ragged But I'm Right**	1959	20.00	50.00
Decca DL-4092	(M)	**The Dynamite Trail**	1960	16.00	40.00
Decca DL-74092	(S)	**The Dynamite Trail**	1960	20.00	50.00
Starday SLP-300	(M)	**Wilf Carter As Montana Slim**	1964	14.00	35.00
Starday SLP-389	(M)	**Montana Slim / Wilf Carter**	1964	14.00	35.00

MONTENEGRO, HUGO, & HIS ORCHESTRA

Label & Catalog #		Title	Year	VG+	NM
RCA Victor LPM-3475	(M)	**Original Music From "The Man From U.N.C.L.E."**	1966	8.00	20.00
RCA Victor LSP-3475	(S)	**Original Music From "The Man From U.N.C.L.E."**	1966	10.00	25.00
RCA Victor LOC-1133	(M)	**Hurry Sundown** (Soundtrack)	1967	10.00	25.00
RCA Victor LSO-1133	(S)	**Hurry Sundown** (Soundtrack)	1967	12.00	30.00
		— RCA Victor albums above have black labels.—			
RCA Victor LSP-4170	(S)	**Moog Power**	1969	10.00	25.00

MONTEZ, CHRIS
Refer to The Chantels.

Label & Catalog #		Title	Year	VG+	NM
Monogram M-100	(M)	**Let's Dance And Have Some Kinda' Fun!!!**	1963	150.00	400.00
A&M LP-115	(M)	**The More I See You/Call Me**	1966	8.00	20.00
A&M SP-4115	(S)	**The More I See You/Call Me**	1966	10.00	25.00
		("Call Me" is rechanneled on this album.)			

MONTGOMERY, "LITTLE BROTHER"
For the bullk of Little Brother's catalog refer to Goldmine's Price Guide To Collectible Jazz Albums

Label & Catalog #		Title	Year	VG+	NM
Windin' Ball 104	(10")	**Little Brother Montgomery**	1954	30.00	75.00
Bluesville BVLP-1012	(M)	**Tasty Blues**	1961	30.00	75.00
		— Bluesville albums above have bright blue labels with silver print.—			
Bluesville BVLP-1012	(M)	**Tasty Blues**	1964	10.00	25.00
		— Bluesville albums above have blue labels with a trident logo on the right side.—			
Riverside RLP-410	(M)	**Little Brother Montgomery**	1962	12.00	30.00
Riverside RS-9410	(S)	**Little Brother Montgomery**	1962	10.00	25.00
		— Riverside mono albums above have silver on blue labels with a reel & mike logo on top; stereo albums have silver on black labels with a reel & mike logo on top.—			

MONTGOMERY, MARIAN: *Refer to* GOLDMINE'S PRICE GUIDE TO COLLECTIBLE JAZZ ALBUMS

MONTY PYTHON
Monty Python is a group of British comedians: Graham Chapman, John Cleese, Eric Idle, Terry Jones, Michael Palin and artist Terry Gilliam.

Label & Catalog #		Title	Year	VG+	NM
Warner Bros. WBMS-110	(DJ)	**Monty Python Examines The Life Of Brian** (Interview)	1979	12.00	30.00
Universal City Studios	(DJ)	**The Meaning Of Life Audio Press Kit**	1983	30.00	75.00
		(2 LPs interview with press kit.)			

MOODY, CLYDE

Label & Catalog #		Title	Year	VG+	NM
King 891	(M)	**The Best Of Clyde Moody**	1964	20.00	50.00

Label & Catalog #		Title	Year	VG+	NM

MOODY BLUES
The Moodys on the first album are Graeme Edge, Denny Laine, Mike Pinder, Ray Thomas and Clint
Warwick. Laine and Warwick were replaced by Justin Hayward and John Lodge.

Label & Catalog #		Title	Year	VG+	NM
London LL-3428	(M)	**Go Now/Moody Blues #1**	1965	20.00	50.00
London PS-428	(E)	**Go Now/Moody Blues #1**	1965	14.00	35.00
Threshold THX-100	(DJ)	**Special Interview Kit** *(Includes script)*	1971	40.00	100.00
London PS-708	(DJ)	**Octave** *(Blue vinyl)*	1978	10.00	25.00
Mobile Fidelity MFSL-042	(S)	**Days Of Future Passed**	1980	16.00	50.00
Nautilus NR-21	(S)	**On The Threshold Of A Dream**	1981	25.00	75.00
Nautilus NR-21	(S)	**On The Threshold Of A Dream** *(DBX)*	1981	20.00	60.00
Mobile Fidelity MFSL-151	(S)	**Seventh Sojourn**	1984	13.00	40.00

MOOG MACHINE, THE, (FEATURING KEN ASCHER)
Columbia CS=9921	(S)	**Switched-On Rock**	1969	10.00	25.00

MOOLAH
Annuit Septus M-1	(S)	**Whoa, Ye Demons Possessed**	1974	40.00	100.00

MOON, KEITH
Keith Moon was formerly a member of The Who.

MCA 2136	(S)	**Two Sides Of The Moon**	1975	16.00	40.00

MOONDOG
Moondog also recorded with Julie Andrews.

Epic LN-1002	(10")	**Moondog And His Friends**	1954	80.00	200.00
Prestige PRLP-7042	(M)	**Moondog**	1956	40.00	100.00
Prestige PRLP-7069	(M)	**More Moondog**	1956	40.00	100.00
Prestige PRLP-7099	(M)	**The Story Of Moondog**	1957	40.00	100.00
		—*Prestige albums above have yellow labels with a W 50th St, NY, address.*—			
Columbia MS-7335	(S)	**Moondog**	1970	10.00	25.00

MOONEY, JOE: *Refer to* GOLDMINE'S PRICE GUIDE TO COLLECTIBLE JAZZ ALBUMS

MOONEY, RALPH, & JAMES BURTON
Capitol T-2872	(M)	**Corn Pickin' And Slick Slidin'**	1967	16.00	40.00
Capitol ST-2872	(S)	**Corn Pickin' And Slick Slidin'**	1967	20.00	50.00

MOONGLOWS, THE
Refer to The Flamingos / The Moonglows.

Chess LP-1430	(M)	**Look, It's The Moonglows**	1959	200.00	500.00
Chess LP-1471	(M)	**The Best Of Bobby Lester & The Moonglows** *(White label promo)*	1962	350.00	750.00
Chess LP-1471	(M)	**The Best Of Bobby Lester & The Moonglows** *(Black label)*	1962	100.00	300.00
Chess LP-1471	(M)	**The Best Of Bobby Lester & The Moonglows** *(Blue & white label)*	196?	20.00	50.00
Constellation C-2	(M)	**Collectors Showcase: The Moonglows**	1962	40.00	100.00
		(First pressings have a light, "electric" blue lettering on the cover.)			
Constellation C-2	(M)	**Collectors Showcase: The Moonglows**	1962	20.00	50.00
		(Later pressings have a cooler, dark blue lettering on the cover.)			

MOORE, ADA: *Refer to* GOLDMINE'S PRICE GUIDE TO COLLECTIBLE JAZZ ALBUMS

MOORE, BOBBY, & THE RHYTHM ACES
Checker LP-3000	(M)	**Searching For My Love**	1966	12.00	30.00
Checker LPS-3000	(E)	**Searching For My Love**	1966	10.00	25.00

MOORE, BOB, & HIS ORCHESTRA
Monument MLP-4005	(M)	**Mexico And Other Great Hits!**	1961	10.00	25.00
Monument SLP-4005	(M)	**Mexico And Other Great Hits!**	1961	14.00	35.00

MOORE, CHARLIE, & BILL NAPIER
King 828	(M)	**Folk 'N' Hill**	1963	30.00	75.00
King 880	(M)	**The Best Of Charlie Moore And Bill Napier**	1964	30.00	75.00
King 917	(M)	**Country Hymnal**	1964	20.00	50.00
King 936	(M)	**Songs Of The Lonesome Truck Drivers**	1965	14.00	35.00
King KS-936	(S)	**Songs Of The Lonesome Truck Drivers**	1965	20.00	50.00
King 982	(M)	**Country Music Goes To Viet Nam**	1966	14.00	35.00
King KS-982	(S)	**Country Music Goes To Viet Nam**	1966	20.00	50.00

On their first long-player, The Moonglows are apparently mistaking something in the middle of the day as the moon a-glowin' above them. A flying saucer? They were rather common back then. A plane carrying off the Chess brothers and the royalties they weren't going to see otherwise. . .

Label & Catalog #		Title	Year	VG+	NM
King 992	(M)	City Folks Back On The Farm	1966	14.00	35.00
King KS-992	(S)	City Folks Back On The Farm	1966	20.00	50.00
King 1014	(M)	Spectacular Instrumentals	1967	8.00	20.00
King KS-1014	(S)	Spectacular Instrumentals	1967	10.00	25.00
King 1017	(M)	Gospel And Sacred Songs	1967	8.00	20.00
King KS-1017	(S)	Gospel And Sacred Songs	1967	10.00	25.00
King 1021	(M)	Brand New Country & Western Songs	1967	8.00	20.00
King KS-1021	(S)	Brand New Country & Western Songs	1967	10.00	25.00

MOORE, DEBBY: *Refer to* GOLDMINE'S PRICE GUIDE TO COLLECTIBLE JAZZ ALBUMS

MOORE, DUDLEY

Capitol W-1792	(M)	Beyond The Fringe (Original cast)	1962	12.00	30.00
Capitol SW-1792	(S)	Beyond The Fringe (Original cast)	1962	16.00	40.00
Atlantic 1403	(M)	"Beyond The Fringe" And All That Jazz	1962	10.00	25.00

—Atlantic albums above have a white fan logo on the right side.—

London MS-82009	(S)	Bedazzled (Soundtrack)	1968	40.00	100.00
London MS-82010	(S)	30 Is A Dangerous Age, Cynthia (Sdtk.)	1968	12.00	30.00

MOORE, GATEMOUTH

King 684	(M)	Gatemouth Moore Sings The Blues	1960	2,000.00	4,000.00
Audio Fidelity AFLP-1921	(M)	Arrival!	1960	16.00	40.00
Audio Fidelity AFSD-5921	(S)	Arrival!	1960	20.00	50.00

MOORE, GEOFFREY

Judson J-3021	(M)	Songs Of Thomas Moore	195?	12.00	30.00

MOORE, LATTIE

Audio Lab AL-1555	(M)	The Best Of Lattie Moore	1960	80.00	200.00
Audio Lab AL-1573	(M)	Country Side	1962	60.00	150.00
Derbytown 102	(M)	Lattie Moore	196?	16.00	40.00

MOORE, MARILYN: *Refer to* GOLDMINE'S PRICE GUIDE TO COLLECTIBLE JAZZ ALBUMS

MOORE, MARY TYLER: *Refer to* NORMAN LESLIE; LEW RAYMOND

MOORE, SCOTTY
Scotty was formerly a member of Elvis, Scotty & Bill.

Epic LN-24103	(M)	The Guitar That Changed The World	1964	20.00	50.00
Epic BN-26103	(S)	The Guitar That Changed The World	1964	30.00	75.00

MOORE, SHELLY: *Refer to* GOLDMINE'S PRICE GUIDE TO COLLECTIBLE JAZZ ALBUMS

MOOREHEAD, AGNES

Decca DL-6022	(10")	Sorry, Wrong Number	1952	40.00	100.00

MORENO, RITA

Strand 1039	(M)	Rita Moreno Sings	195?	16.00	40.00
Wynne 103	(M)	Warm, Wonderful And Wild	195?	16.00	40.00

MOREY STORE BAND, THE

Sound Machine SMS-49007	(S)	Cry For The Dreamer	197?	40.00	100.00

MORGAN, GEORGE

Columbia CL-1044	(M)	Morgan, By George	1957	16.00	40.00
Columbia CL-1831	(M)	Golden Memories	1961	10.00	25.00
Columbia CS-8431	(S)	Golden Memories	1961	12.00	30.00

— Columbia albums above have six white-on-black "eye" logos around the perimeter of the label.—

Starday SLP-400	(M)	Candy Kisses	1967	12.00	30.00
Starday SLP-410	(M)	Country Hits By Candlelight	1967	12.00	30.00

— Starday albums above have yellow labels.—

MORGAN, JANE

Kapp KL-1066	(M)	Fascination	1957	12.00	30.00
Kapp KS-3017	(S)	Fascination	1959	16.00	40.00
Kapp KS-3066	(S)	Fascination	1962	8.00	20.00
Kapp KL-1080	(M)	All The Way	1958	12.00	30.00
Kapp KL-1089	(M)	Something Old, New, Borrowed, Blue	1958	12.00	30.00
Kapp KL-1089S	(S)	Something Old, New, Borrowed, Blue	1958	16.00	40.00

These two albums by Buddy Morrow, whose trombone is familiar to fans of Johnny Carson's "Tonight Show," are included here for their content: Jazzy big band interpretations of popular televison scores of the late '50s and early '60s.

Label & Catalog #		Title	Year	VG+	NM
Kapp UXL-5006	(M)	Great Songs From			
		The Great Shows Of The Century (2 LPs)	195?	16.00	40.00
Kapp KL-1093	(M)	Jane Morgan	1958	12.00	30.00
Kapp KL-1105	(M)	The Day The Rain Came	1958	12.00	30.00
Kapp KL-1105S	(S)	The Day The Rain Came	1958	12.00	30.00
Kapp KS-3001	(S)	Broadway In Stereo	1959	12.00	30.00
Kapp KL-1129	(M)	Jane In Spain	1959	10.00	25.00
Kapp KS-3014	(S)	Jane In Spain	1959	12.00	30.00
Kapp KL-1170	(M)	Jane Morgan Time	1959	8.00	20.00
Kapp KS-3054	(S)	Jane Morgan Time	1959	10.00	25.00
MORGAN, JAYE P.					
RCA Victor LPM-1155	(M)	Jaye P. Morgan	1955	20.00	50.00
Allegro 4111	(10")	Jaye P. Morgan Sings	1856	20.00	50.00
Rondo-Lette A-13	(M)	Jaye P. Morgan	1958	10.00	25.00
MGM E-3774	(M)	Slow And Easy	1959	12.00	30.00
MGM SE-3774	(S)	Slow And Easy	1959	16.00	40.00
MGM E-3830	(M)	Up North	1960	10.00	25.00
MGM SE-3830	(S)	Up North	1960	12.00	30.00
MGM E-3867	(M)	Down South	1960	10.00	25.00
MGM SE-3867	(S)	Down South	1960	12.00	30.00
MGM E-3940	(M)	That Country Sound	1961	10.00	25.00
MGM SE-3940	(S)	That Country Sound	1961	12.00	30.00
MORGEN, STEVE					
Probe CPLP-4507	(M)	Morgen (With insert)	1969	40.00	100.00
MOREL, TERRY					
Bethlehem 47	(M)	Songs Of A Woman In Love	1955	16.00	40.00
MORLY GREY					
Starshine 69000	(M)	The Only Truth (With poster)	1968	300.00	500.00
MORNING DEW					
Roulette R-41045	(M)	Morning Dew	1967	40.00	100.00
Roulette RS-41045	(S)	Morning Dew	1967	60.00	150.00
MORNING GLORY					
Fontana MGF-27573	(M)	Two Suns Worth	1967	8.00	20.00
Fontana SRF-67573	(S)	Two Suns Worth	1967	10.00	25.00
MORNINGLORY					
Toya STLP-003	(S)	Growing	1972	14.00	35.00

MORRISEY, PAT: *Refer to* GOLDMINE'S PRICE GUIDE TO COLLECTIBLE JAZZ ALBUMS

MORRISON, VAN
Van The Man was formerly lead singer for Them.

Bang BLP-218	(M)	Blowin' Your Mind	1967	12.00	30.00
Bang BLPS-218	(S)	Blowin' Your Mind	1967	16.00	40.00
		(Bang 218 was originally issued with the version of "Brown-Eyed			
		Girl" that includes the line "Making love in the green grass.")			
Bang BLPS-218	(S)	Blowin' Your Mind	1968	10.00	25.00
		(Second pressings contain a censored version of "Brown-Eyed			
		Girl" that deletes the line "Making love in the green grass.")			
		—Bang albums above have red & white labels.—			
Warner Bros. WBMS-102	(DJ)	Live At The Roxy	1978	16.00	40.00
Direct Disk SD-16604	(S)	Moondance	1981	16.00	50.00
MORROW, BUDDY					
RCA Victor LPM-1427	(M)	Night Train	1957	20.00	50.00
RCA Victor LPM-2018	(M)	Big Band Guitar	1959	14.00	35.00
RCA Victor LPM-2018	(S)	Big Band Guitar	1959	20.00	50.00
RCA Victor LPM-2042	(M)	Impact	1959	14.00	35.00
RCA Victor LSP-2042	(S)	Impact	1959	20.00	50.00
RCA Victor LPM-2180	(M)	Double Impact	1960	14.00	35.00
RCA Victor LSP-2180	(S)	Double Impact	1960	20.00	50.00
Mercury MG-20???	(M)	Night Train	195?	14.00	35.00
Mercury SR-60009	(S)	Night Train	1959	20.00	50.00

Label & Catalog #		Title	Year	VG+	NM
Mercury MG-20702	(M)	Night Train Goes To Hollywood	1962	10.00	25.00
Mercury SR-60702	(S)	Night Train Goes To Hollywood	1962	12.00	30.00
Epic LN-24095	(M)	Big Band Beatlemania	1964	8.00	20.00
Epic LN-24095	(S)	Big Band Beatlemania	1964	10.00	25.00

MORSE, ELLA MAE

Capitol H-513	(10")	Barrelhouse Boogie And The Blues	1954	200.00	400.00
Capitol T-513	(M)	Barrelhouse Boogie And The Blues	1955	150.00	300.00
Capitol T-898	(M)	Morse Code	1957	40.00	100.00
Capitol T-1802	(M)	Hits Of Ella Mae Morse And Freddie Slack	1962	16.00	40.00
Capitol ST-1802	(S)	Hits Of Ella Mae Morse And Freddie Slack	1962	20.00	50.00

MORSE, ROBERT, & CHARLES NELSON REILLY

Capitol T-1862	(M)	A Jolly Theatrical Christmas	1963	8.00	20.00
Capitol ST-1862	(S)	A Jolly Theatrical Christmas	1963	10.00	25.00

MORTIMER

Philips PHS-600-267	(S)	Mortimer	1968	10.00	25.00

MOSBY, JOHNNY & JONIE

Starday SLP-328	(M)	The New Sweethearts Of Country Music (Yellow label)	1965	12.00	30.00

MOSER, ARTUS

Artus Monroe Moser is a banjo, dulcimer and guitar player and singer of traditional folk songs.

Folkways FP-40	(10")	North Carolina Ballads	195?	20.00	50.00
Folkways FA-2112	(10")	North Carolina Ballads	195?	20.00	50.00

MOSER, J., & THE HOTS

Moco FIT-003	(S)	For Life	1975	20.00	50.00

MOSS, GENE

RCA Victor LPM-2977	(M)	Dracula's Greatest Hits	1964	12.00	30.00
RCA Victor LSP-2977	(S)	Dracula's Greatest Hits	1964	16.00	40.00

MOTHERS OF INVENTION, THE: *Refer to* FRANK ZAPPA (& THE MOTHERS OF INVENTION)

MOTLEY CRUE

Leathur LR-123	(S)	Too Fast For Love (White letter cover)	1981	60.00	150.00
Leathur LR-123	(S)	Too Fast For Love (Red letter cover)	1981	40.00	100.00
Elektra 60395	(S)	Helter Skelter (Picture disc with poster)	1984	14.00	35.00

MOUNTAIN BUS

Good 101	(S)	Sundance	1971	80.00	200.00

MOUNTAIN RAMBLERS, THE

Atlantic 1347	(M)	Blue Ridge Mountain Music	1962	10.00	25.00
Atlantic SD-1347	(S)	Blue Ridge Mountain Music	1962	14.00	35.00

MOUSEKETEERS, THE

Disneyland T-3918	(M)	How To Be A Mouseketeer	1962	14.00	35.00
Disneyland ST-3918	(S)	How To Be A Mouseketeer	1962	20.00	50.00

MOUZOKIS

British Main 90069	(S)	Magic Tube	1972	40.00	100.00

MOVE, THE

A&M SP-4259	(S)	Shazam	1969	16.00	40.00
Capitol ST-658	(S)	Looking On	1971	10.00	25.00

MOVING SIDEWALKS

The Sidewalks featured Billy Gibbons, later of ZZ Top.

Tantara 6919	(S)	Flash	1968	150.00	300.00

MU

Mu is a creation of Merrell Fankhauser.

CAS 300	(S)	Mu (With insert)	1972	16.00	40.00

Label & Catalog #		Title	Year	VG+	NM

MUDDY WATERS
Muddy Waters is a pseudonym for McKinley Morganfield. Refer to Bo Diddley.

Label & Catalog #		Title	Year	VG+	NM
Chess LP-1427	(M)	**The Best Of Muddy Waters** (White label)	1957		See below
		(White label promos have a suggested NM value of $1,000-1,500.)			
Chess LP-1427	(M)	**The Best Of Muddy Waters**	1957	250.00	500.00
Chess LP-1444	(M)	**Muddy Waters Sings Big Bill** (White label)	1960		See below
		(White label promos have a suggested NM value of $500-1,000.)			
Chess LP-1444	(M)	**Muddy Waters Sings Big Bill**	1960	175.00	350.00
Chess LP-1449	(M)	**Muddy Waters At Newport** (White label)	1963	150.00	300.00
Chess LP-1449	(M)	**Muddy Waters At Newport**	1963	50.00	150.00
Chess LP-1483	(M)	**Folk Singer** (White label promo)	1964	150.00	300.00
Chess LP-1483	(M)	**Folk Singer**	1964	50.00	150.00
		— Chess albums above have black & silver labels.—			
Chess LP-1501	(M)	**The Real Folk Blues Of Muddy Waters**	1965	20.00	50.00
Chess LPS-1501	(S)	**The Real Folk Blues Of Muddy Waters**	1965	30.00	75.00
Chess LP-1507	(M)	**Muddy, Brass And Blues**	1966	14.00	35.00
Chess LPS-1507	(S)	**Muddy, Brass And Blues**	1966	20.00	50.00
Chess LP-1511	(M)	**More Real Folk Blues**	1967	14.00	35.00
Chess LPS-1511	(S)	**More Real Folk Blues**	1967	20.00	50.00
Chess LP-1533	(M)	**Blues From Big Bill's Copacabana**	1968	20.00	50.00
Chess LPS-1533	(S)	**Blues From Big Bill's Copacabana**	1968	16.00	40.00
Cadet Concept 314	(S)	**Electric Mud**	1968	10.00	25.00
Cadet Concept 320	(S)	**After The Rain**	1969	10.00	25.00
Chess LPS-1539	(S)	**Sail On**	1969	10.00	25.00
Chess 2CH-60006	(S)	**McKinley Morganfield A.K.A. Muddy Waters** (2 LPs)	1971	10.00	25.00
		— Chess albums above have blue labels.—			
Chess CH-127	(S)	**Fathers And Sons** (2 LPs)	1975	12.00	30.00
Chess CH6-80002	(M)	**Muddy Waters** (6 LP box)	1989	16.00	40.00

MUELLER, BILL, & THE BRAT

Label & Catalog #		Title	Year	VG+	NM
Brat CT-3301	(S)	**No Place Like Home**	1979	30.00	75.00

MUGWUMPS, THE
The Mugwumps were Cass Elliot, Denny Doherty, Jim Hendricks and Zal Yanovsky.

Label & Catalog #		Title	Year	VG+	NM
Warner Bros. W-1697	(M)	**The Mugwumps**	1967	10.00	25.00
Warner Bros. WS-1697	(S)	**The Mugwumps**	1967	12.00	30.00

MULDAUER, GEOFF

Label & Catalog #		Title	Year	VG+	NM
Folklore FRLP-14004	(M)	**Sleepy Man Blues**	1964	16.00	40.00
Folklore FRST-14004	(S)	**Sleepy Man Blues**	1964	20.00	50.00
Prestige PRST-7727	(S)	**Sleepy Man Blues**	1969	10.00	25.00
		(Prestige 7727 is a reissue of Folklore 14004.)			

MULLICAN, MOON

Label & Catalog #		Title	Year	VG+	NM
Coral CRL-57235	(M)	**Moon Over Mullican**	1958	200.00	500.00
Sterling ST-601	(M)	**I'll Sail My Ship Alone**	1958	80.00	200.00
King 555	(M)	**Moon Mullican Sings His All-Time Greatest Hits**	1958	80.00	200.00
King 628	(M)	**Moon Mullican Sings 16 Of His Favorite Tunes**	1959	80.00	200.00
King 681	(M)	**The Many Moods Of Moon Mullican**	1960	80.00	200.00
King 937	(M)	**Moon Mullican Sings 24 Of His Favorite Tunes**	1965	20.00	50.00
Audio Lab AL-1568	(M)	**Instrumentals**	1962	80.00	200.00
Spar SP-3005	(M)	**Mister Honky Tonk Man**	196?	40.00	100.00
Starday SLP-135	(M)	**Playin' And Singin'**	1963	40.00	100.00
Starday SLP-267	(M)	**Mister Piano Man**	1964	20.00	50.00
Starday SLP-398	(M)	**The Unforgettable Moon Mullican Plays And Sings His Greatest Hits**	1967	16.00	40.00
Kapp KS-3600	(S)	**Showcase**	1968	16.00	40.00
Pickwick/Hilltop JS-6033	(S)	**Good Times Gonna Roll Again**	1966	12.00	30.00

MULLINS, REV. PAUL

Label & Catalog #		Title	Year	VG+	NM
Jalyn JLP-106	(M)	**Hymns From The Hills**	196?	10.00	25.00

MUMY, BILL

Label & Catalog #		Title	Year	VG+	NM
"BB" 103	(S)	**Bill Mumy**	1980	10.00	25.00

Label & Catalog #		Title	Year	VG+	NM

MUNSTERS, THE
Studio musicians recording rock music as The Munsters with a great cover photo from the TV series.

Decca DL-4588	(M)	The Munsters	1964	40.00	100.00
Decca DL-74588	(S)	The Munsters	1964	60.00	150.00

MURAI, JEAN
Jean Murai is a multi-instrumentalist and singer of folk songs favoring Latin-American music.

Stinson SLP-75	(10")	Mama, I Want A Husband	195?	20.00	50.00

MURE, BILLY

RCA Victor LPM-1536	(M)	Supersonic Guitars In Hi-Fi	1957	16.00	40.00
RCA Victor LPM-1694	(M)	Fireworks	1958	12.00	30.00
RCA Victor LSP-1694	(S)	Fireworks	1958	16.00	40.00
RCA Victor LPM-1869	(M)	Supersonic In Flight	1959	12.00	30.00
RCA Victor LSP-1869	(S)	Supersonic In Flight	1959	20.00	50.00
MGM E-3780	(M)	Supersonic Guitars	1959	12.00	30.00
MGM SE-3780	(S)	Supersonic Guitars	1959	20.00	50.00
MGM E-3807	(M)	Supersonic Guitars, Vol. 2	1959	12.00	30.00
MGM SE-3807	(S)	Supersonic Guitars, Vol. 2	1959	20.00	50.00
United Arts. UAL-3031	(M)	Bandstand Record Hop	1959	12.00	30.00
United Arts. UAS-6031	(S)	Bandstand Record Hop	1959	16.00	40.00
Everest LPBR-5067	(M)	String Of Trumpet	1960	8.00	20.00
Everest SDBR-1067	(S)	String Of Trumpet	1960	12.00	30.00
Everest LPBR-5072	(M)	Songs Of Hank Williams	1960	12.00	30.00
Everest SDBR-1072	(S)	Songs Of Hank Williams	1960	16.00	40.00
Everest LPBR-5120	(M)	Strictly Cha-Cha-Cha	1960	8.00	20.00
Everest SDBR-1120	(S)	Strictly Cha-Cha-Cha	1960	12.00	30.00
Kapp KL-1253	(M)	Tough Strings	1961	8.00	20.00
Kapp KS-3253	(S)	Tough Strings	1961	12.00	30.00
MGM E-4131	(M)	Teen Bossa Nova	1963	8.00	20.00
MGM SE-4131	(S)	Teen Bossa Nova	1963	12.00	30.00
MGM E-4406	(M)	Happy Guitars	1966	8.00	20.00
MGM SE-4406	(S)	Happy Guitars	1966	12.00	30.00

MURPHY, MARK: *Refer to* GOLDMINE'S PRICE GUIDE TO COLLECTIBLE JAZZ ALBUMS

MURPHY, ROSE: *Refer to* GOLDMINE'S PRICE GUIDE TO COLLECTIBLE JAZZ ALBUMS

MURRAY, ANNE
Refer to Glen Campbell & Anne Murray.

Capitol ST-11743	(DJ)	Let's Keep It That Way *(Picture disc)*	1978	20.00	50.00

MUSIC COMPANY, THE

Crestview CRS-3057	(S)	Hard & Heavy	196?	10.00	25.00

MUSIC EMPORIUM, THE

Sentinal 69001	(S)	The Music Emporium	1969	2,000.00	3,000.00

MUSIC EXPLOSION, THE

Laurie LLP-2040	(M)	A Little Bit O' Soul	1967	8.00	20.00
Laurie SLLP-2040	(S)	A Little Bit O' Soul	1967	10.00	25.00

MUSIC MACHINE, THE/BONNIWELL'S MUSIC MACHINE
The Music Machine features Sean Bonniwell. Refer to T.S. Bonniwell.

Original Sound 5015	(M)	Turn On The Music Machine	1966	12.00	30.00
Original Sound 8875	(S)	Turn On The Music Machine	1966	20.00	50.00
Warner Bros. W-1732	(M)	Bonniwell's Music Machine	1967	10.00	25.00
Warner Bros. WS-1732	(S)	Bonniwell's Music Machine	1967	16.00	40.00

(Warner Bros. 1732 credits Bonniwell's Music Machine.)

MUSSELWHITE, CHARLIE

Vanguard VRS-9232	(M)	Stand Back! Here Comes Charlie Musselwhite's South Side Band	1966	8.00	20.00
Vanguard VSD-79232	(S)	Stand Back! Here Comes Charlie Musselwhite's South Side Band	1966	10.00	25.00

MUSSO, VIDO: *Refer to* GOLDMINE'S PRICE GUIDE TO COLLECTIBLE JAZZ ALBUMS

Label & Catalog #		Title	Year	VG+	NM

MUSTANGS, THE

| Providence PLP-001 | (M) | **Dartell Stomp** | 1963 | 20.00 | 50.00 |

MUTHA GOOSE

| Alpha Omega 264-01 | (S) | **Mutha Goose I** | 197? | 60.00 | 150.00 |

MYERS, DAVE

Del-Fi DFLP-1239	(M)	**Hangin' Twenty**	1963	16.00	40.00
Del-Fi DFST-1239	(S)	**Hangin' Twenty**	1963	24.00	60.00
		(Del-Fi 1239 is credited to Dave Myers & The Surftones.)			
Carole CAR-8002	(M)	**Greatest Racing Themes**	1966	16.00	40.00
		(Carole 8002 is credited to The Dave Myers Effect.)			

MYSTIC ASTROLOGIC CRYSTAL BAND, THE

Carole 8001	(M)	**Mystic Astrologic Crystal Band**	1967	10.00	25.00
Carole S-8001	(S)	**Mystic Astrologic Crystal Band**	1967	12.00	30.00
Carole S-8003	(S)	**Clip Out, Put On Book**	1968	12.00	30.00

MYSTIC MOODS ORCHESTRA, THE

Mobile Fidelity MFSL-001	(S)	**Emotions**	1979	12.00	35.00
Mobile Fidelity MFSL-002	(S)	**Cosmic Force**	1979	12.00	35.00
Mobile Fidelity MFSL-003	(S)	**Stormy Weekend**	1979	12.00	35.00

MYSTIC NUMBER NATIONAL BANK, THE

| Probe CPLPS-4501 | (S) | **The Mystic Number National Bank** | 1969 | 10.00 | 25.00 |

MYSTIC SIVA

| V.O. 19713 | (S) | **Mystic Siva** | 1970 | 300.00 | 500.00 |

NAPOLEON XIV

Warner Bros. W-1661	(M)	**They're Coming To Take Me Away Ha-Haaa!**	1966	30.00	75.00
Warner Bros. WS-1661	(S)	**They're Coming To Take Me Away Ha-Haaa!**	1966	60.00	150.00

NASH, JOHNNY

ABC-Paramount ABC-244	(M)	**Johnny Nash**	1958	12.00	30.00
ABC-Paramount ABCS-244	(S)	**Johnny Nash**	1958	16.00	40.00
ABC-Paramount ABC-276	(M)	**Quiet Hour**	1959	12.00	30.00
ABC-Paramount ABCS-276	(S)	**Quiet Hour**	1959	16.00	40.00
ABC-Paramount ABC-299	(M)	**I Got Rhythm**	1959	12.00	30.00
ABC-Paramount ABCS-299	(S)	**I Got Rhythm**	1959	16.00	40.00
ABC-Paramount ABC-344	(M)	**Let's Get Lost**	1960	10.00	25.00
ABC-Paramount ABCS-344	(S)	**Let's Get Lost**	1960	12.00	30.00
ABC-Paramount ABC-383	(M)	**Studio Time**	1961	10.00	25.00
ABC-Paramount ABCS-383	(S)	**Studio Time**	1961	12.00	30.00

NASHVILLE ALL-STARS, THE
The All-Stars feature Chet Atkins, Gary Burton and Hank Garland.

RCA Victor LPM-2302	(M)	**After The Riot At Newport**	1960	16.00	40.00
RCA Victor LSP-2302	(S)	**After The Riot At Newport**	1960	20.00	50.00

— RCA mono albums above have "Long Play" on the bottom of the label;
stereo albums have "Living Stereo" on the bottom. —

NASHVILLE BRASS, THE: *Refer to* **DANNY DAVIS & THE NASHVILLE BRASS**

NASHVILLE TEENS, THE

London LL-3407	(M)	**Tobacco Road**	1964	30.00	75.00
London PS-407	(E)	**Tobacco Road**	1964	20.00	50.00

NAVARRO, TONY, & THE SUNDIALERS

Urania UR-900	(M)	**Twist Around The Town**	1961	40.00	100.00

NAZZ, THE
The Nazz features Todd Rundgren.

SGC 5001	(S)	**Nazz**	1968	16.00	40.00
SGC 5002	(S)	**Nazz Nazz** *(Red vinyl)*	1969	16.00	40.00
		(Orange & red label with a blue SGC logo.)			
SGC 5002	(S)	**Nazz Nazz** *(Red vinyl)*	1969	20.00	50.00
		(Orange & red label with a purple SGC logo.)			
SGC 5002	(S)	**Nazz Nazz** *(Black vinyl)*	1970	30.00	75.00
SGC 5004	(S)	**Nazz III**	1971	16.00	40.00
		(Poorly reproduced counterfeits of each of the Nazz albums exist.)			

NEGATIVE SPACE

Evil 1001	(M)	**Hard, Heavy, Mean**	196?	300.00	500.00
		(Heavy cardboard cover with the title in blue print on the front.			
		Counterfeits have flimsy covers with black print.)			

NEIGHB'RHOOD CHILDR'N, THE

Acta 8005	(M)	**The Neighb'rhood Childr'n**	1968	30.00	75.00
Acta 38005	(S)	**The Neighb'rhood Childr'n**	1968	40.00	100.00

NEIL, FRED
Refer to Martin & Neil.

Elektra EKL-293	(M)	**Bleecker And MacDougal**	1965	12.00	30.00
Elektra EKS-7293	(S)	**Bleecker And MacDougal** *(Gold label)*	1965	16.00	40.00
Capitol T-2665	(M)	**Fred Neil**	1966	10.00	25.00
Capitol ST-2665	(S)	**Fred Neil**	1966	12.00	30.00
		(Original covers of Capitol 2665 have a full color photo			
		of Neil on the back .)			

Label & Catalog #		Title	Year	VG+	NM
Capitol T-2862	(M)	**Fred Neil: Sessions**	1967	8.00	20.00
Capitol ST-2862	(S)	**Fred Neil: Sessions**	1967	10.00	25.00
		— Capitol albums above have black "rainbow" labels.—			
NELSON, PORTIA					
New Sound NS-302	(M)	**Let Me Love You**	1956	20.00	50.00
Columbia ML-4722	(M)	**Love Songs For A Late Evening**	195?	12.00	30.00
Dolphin 4	(M)	**Autumn Leaves**	195?	10.00	25.00
NELSON, RICK/RICKY NELSON					
Verve V-2083	(M)	**Teen Time**	1957	100.00	250.00
		(This is actually a various artists album containing Ricky's first three sides for Verve but, as it gets its hefty value from the great shot of Ricky on the cover, it is listed here.)			
Imperial LP-9048	(M)	**Ricky**	1957	40.00	100.00
Imperial LP-9050	(M)	**Ricky Nelson**	1958	40.00	100.00
Imperial LP-9061	(M)	**Ricky Sings Again**	1959	40.00	100.00
Imperial LP-12090	(S)	**Ricky Sings Again**	1962	60.00	150.00
Imperial LP-9082	(M)	**Songs By Ricky**	1959	30.00	75.00
Imperial LP-12030	(S)	**Songs By Ricky**	1959	80.00	200.00
Imperial LP-9122	(M)	**More Songs By Ricky**	1960	30.00	75.00
Imperial LP-12059	(S)	**More Songs By Ricky** *(Blue vinyl)*	1960	660.00	1,000.00
		(Blue vinyl copies of LP-12059 were issued with a fold-open poster, priced separately below.)			
Imperial LP-12059		**More Songs By Ricky Bonus Poster**	1960	80.00	200.00
Imperial LP-12059	(S)	**More Songs By Ricky**	1960	40.00	100.00
Imperial LP-9152	(M)	**Rick Is 21**	1961	16.00	40.00
Imperial LP-12071	(S)	**Rick Is 21**	1961	40.00	100.00
Imperial LP-9167	(M)	**Album Seven By Rick**	1962	16.00	40.00
Imperial LP-12082	(S)	**Album Seven By Rick**	1962	40.00	100.00
Imperial LP-9218	(M)	**Best Sellers**	1963	16.00	40.00
Imperial LP-9223	(M)	**It's Up To You**	1963	16.00	40.00
Imperial LP-9232	(M)	**Million Sellers**	1963	16.00	40.00
Imperial LP-9244	(M)	**A Long Vacation**	1963	16.00	40.00
Imperial LP-9251	(M)	**Rick Nelson Sings For You**	1964	16.00	40.00
Imperial LP-12251	(E)	**Rick Nelson Sings For You**	1964	10.00	25.00
		— Imperial mono albums above have black labels with stars on top; stereo albums have black labels with silver print.—			
Imperial LP-9048	(M)	**Ricky**	1964	10.00	25.00
Imperial LP-9050	(M)	**Ricky Nelson**	1964	10.00	25.00
Imperial LP-9061	(M)	**Ricky Sings Again**	1964	10.00	25.00
Imperial LP-12090	(M)	**Ricky Sings Again**	1964	16.00	40.00
Imperial LP-9082	(M)	**Songs By Ricky**	1964	10.00	25.00
Imperial LP-12030	(S)	**Songs By Ricky**	1964	16.00	40.00
Imperial LP-9122	(M)	**More Songs By Ricky**	1964	10.00	25.00
Imperial LP-12059	(S)	**More Songs By Ricky**	1964	16.00	40.00
Imperial LP-9152	(M)	**Rick Is 21**	1964	10.00	25.00
Imperial LP-12071	(S)	**Rick Is 21**	1964	16.00	40.00
Imperial LP-9167	(M)	**Album Seven By Rick**	1964	10.00	25.00
Imperial LP-12082	(S)	**Album Seven By Rick**	1964	16.00	40.00
Imperial LP-9218	(M)	**Best Sellers**	1964	10.00	25.00
Imperial LP-12218	(E)	**Best Sellers**	1964	6.00	15.00
Imperial LP-9232	(M)	**Million Sellers**	1964	10.00	25.00
Imperial LP-12232	(E)	**Million Sellers**	1964	6.00	15.00
Imperial LP-9244	(M)	**A Long Vacation**	1964	10.00	25.00
Imperial LP-12244	(E)	**A Long Vacation**	1964	6.00	15.00
Imperial LP-9251	(M)	**Rick Nelson Sings For You**	1964	10.00	25.00
Imperial LP-12251	(E)	**Rick Nelson Sings For You**	1964	6.00	15.00
		— Imperial albums above have black, white & pink labels.—			
Decca DL-4419	(M)	**For Your Sweet Love**	1963	12.00	30.00
Decca DL-74419	(S)	**For Your Sweet Love**	1963	16.00	40.00
Decca DL-4479	(M)	**Rick Nelson Sings For You**	1963	12.00	30.00
Decca DL-74479	(S)	**Rick Nelson Sings For You**	1963	16.00	40.00
Decca DL-4559	(M)	**The Very Thought Of You**	1964	12.00	30.00
Decca DL-74559	(S)	**The Very Thought Of You**	1964	16.00	40.00
Decca DL-4608	(M)	**Spotlight On Rick**	1964	12.00	30.00
Decca DL-74608	(S)	**Spotlight On Rick**	1964	16.00	40.00
Decca DL-4660	(M)	**Best Always**	1965	12.00	30.00
Decca DL-74660	(S)	**Best Always**	1965	16.00	40.00

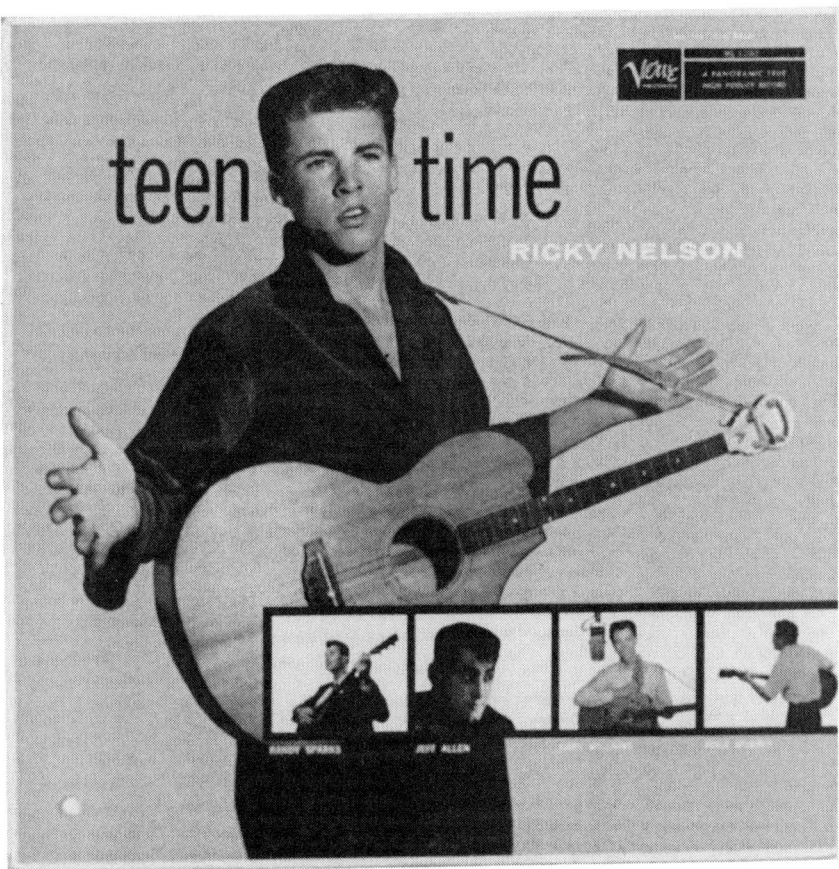

Ricky's first album ain't his album., That is, while almost everyone refers to this as his first, Teen Time is a various artists album that features the kid on the cover (if he's supposed to look appealing, he looks like he's appealing for help) and the three sides he cut for Verve prior to moving to Imperial. Note the shot of Randy Sparks in the box on the extreme left.

Label & Catalog #		Title	Year	VG+	NM
Decca DL-4678	(M)	**Love And Kisses**	1965	**12.00**	**30.00**
Decca DL-74678	(S)	**Love And Kisses**	1965	**16.00**	**40.00**
Decca DL-4779	(M)	**Bright Lights And Country Music**	1966	**12.00**	**30.00**
Decca DL-74779	(S)	**Bright Lights And Country Music**	1966	**16.00**	**40.00**
Decca DL-4827	(M)	**Country Fever**	1967	**12.00**	**30.00**
Decca DL-74827	(S)	**Country Fever**	1967	**16.00**	**40.00**
Decca DL-4836	(M)	**On The Flip Side** *(TV Soundtrack)*	1967	**12.00**	**30.00**
Decca DL-74836	(S)	**On The Flip Side** *(TV Soundtrack)*	1967	**16.00**	**40.00**
		("On The Flip Side" also features Joanie Sommers.)			
		— Decca albums above have black labels with "Mfrd by Decca" beneath the rainbow.—			
Decca DL-4944	(M)	**Another Side Of Rick**	1967	**12.00**	**30.00**
Decca DL-74944	(S)	**Another Side Of Rick**	1967	**16.00**	**40.00**
Decca DL-5014	(M)	**Perspective** *(White label promo)*	1968	**40.00**	**100.00**
Decca DL-75014	(S)	**Perspective**	1968	**16.00**	**40.00**
Decca DL-75236	(S)	**Rick Sings Nelson** *(With poster)*	1970	**10.00**	**25.00**
United Arts. UAS-960	(M)	**Legendary Masters** *(2 LPs. Brown label)*	1971	**10.00**	**25.00**

NELSON, SANDY

Label & Catalog #		Title	Year	VG+	NM
Imperial LP-9105	(M)	**Sandy Nelson Plays Teen Beat**	1960	**12.00**	**30.00**
Imperial LP-12044	(S)	**Sandy Nelson Plays Teen Beat**	1962	**16.00**	**40.00**
Imperial LP-9136	(M)	**He's A Drummer Boy**	1962	**16.00**	**40.00**
Imperial LP-12089	(E)	**He's A Drummer Boy**	1962	**12.00**	**30.00**
Imperial LP-9159	(M)	**Let There Be Drums**	1962	**16.00**	**40.00**
Imperial LP-12080	(E)	**Let There Be Drums**	1962	**12.00**	**30.00**
Imperial LP-9168	(M)	**Drums Are My Beat!**	1962	**8.00**	**20.00**
Imperial LP-12083	(S)	**Drums Are My Beat!**	196?	**12.00**	**30.00**
Imperial LP-9189	(M)	**Drummin' Up A Storm**	1962	**8.00**	**20.00**
Imperial LP-12189	(S)	**Drummin' Up A Storm**	1962	**10.00**	**25.00**
Imperial LP-9202	(M)	**Golden Hits**	1962	**8.00**	**20.00**
Imperial LP-12202	(P)	**Golden Hits**	1962	**10.00**	**25.00**
Imperial LP-9203	(M)	**Country Style**	1962	**10.00**	**25.00**
Imperial LP-12203	(S)	**Country Style**	1962	**12.00**	**30.00**
Imperial LP-9204	(M)	**...And Then There Were Drums**	1962	**8.00**	**20.00**
Imperial LP-12204	(S)	**...And Then There Were Drums**	1962	**10.00**	**25.00**
Imperial LP-9215	(M)	**Teenage House Party**	1962	**8.00**	**20.00**
Imperial LP-12215	(S)	**Teenage House Party**	1962	**10.00**	**25.00**
		— Imperial mono albums above have black labels with stars on top; stereo albums have black labels with silver print.—			

NELSON, TRACY
Ms. Nelson was also a member of Mother Earth.

Label & Catalog #		Title	Year	VG+	NM
Prestige PRLP-7393	(M)	**Deep Are The Roots**	1965	**12.00**	**30.00**
Prestige PRST-7393	(S)	**Deep Are The Roots**	1965	**16.00**	**40.00**

NELSON, WILLIE
Refer to Waylon Jennings & Willie Nelson; The Outlaws.

Label & Catalog #		Title	Year	VG+	NM
Liberty LRP-3238	(M)	**And Then I Wrote**	1962	**16.00**	**40.00**
Liberty LST-7238	(S)	**And Then I Wrote**	1962	**20.00**	**50.00**
Liberty LRP-3308	(M)	**Here's Willie Nelson**	1963	**16.00**	**40.00**
Liberty LST-7308	(S)	**Here's Willie Nelson**	1963	**20.00**	**50.00**
RCA Victor LPM-3418	(M)	**Country Willie: His Own Songs**	1965	**10.00**	**25.00**
RCA Victor LSP-3418	(S)	**Country Willie: His Own Songs**	1965	**12.00**	**30.00**
RCA Victor LPM-3528	(M)	**Country Favorites, Willie Nelson Style**	1966	**10.00**	**25.00**
RCA Victor LSP-3528	(S)	**Country Favorites, Willie Nelson Style**	1966	**12.00**	**30.00**
RCA Victor LPM-3659	(M)	**Live Country Music Concert**	1966	**10.00**	**25.00**
RCA Victor LSP-3659	(S)	**Live Country Music Concert**	1966	**12.00**	**30.00**
RCA Victor LPM-3748	(M)	**Make Way For Willie Nelson**	1967	**12.00**	**30.00**
RCA Victor LSP-3748	(S)	**Make Way For Willie Nelson**	1967	**10.00**	**25.00**
RCA Victor LPM-3858	(M)	**The Party's Over**	1967	**12.00**	**30.00**
RCA Victor LSP-3858	(S)	**The Party's Over**	1967	**10.00**	**25.00**
RCA Victor LPM-3937	(M)	**Texas In My Soul**	1968	**40.00**	**100.00**
RCA Victor LSP-3937	(S)	**Texas In My Soul**	1968	**10.00**	**25.00**
		— RCA Victor albums above have black labels.—			
Columbia HC-43482	(S)	**Red Headed Stranger** *(Half-speed master)*	1982	**10.00**	**30.00**
Columbia PAL-35305	(DJ)	**Stardust** *(Picture disc)*	1978	**12.00**	**30.00**
Columbia HC-45305	(S)	**Stardust** *(Half-speed master)*	1982	**25.00**	**75.00**
Columbia HC-47951	(S)	**Always On My Mind** *(Half-speed master)*	1982	**13.00**	**40.00**
Columbia HC-48248	(S)	**Tougher Than Leather** *(Half-speed master)*	1983	**13.00**	**40.00**
Columbia CX-38258	(DJ)	**Always On My Mind** *(Picture disc)*	1983	**13.00**	**40.00**

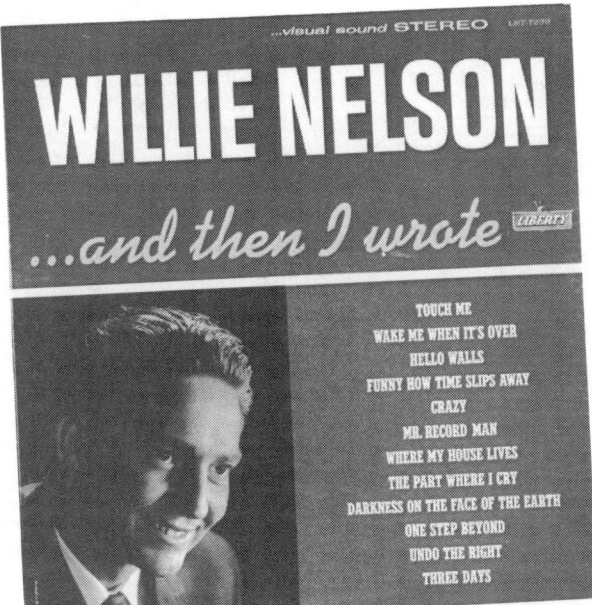

Willie's first pair of LPs way back when no one paid much attention to him as a singer. . .

Label & Catalog #		Title	Year	VG+	NM
NEON PHILHARMONIC					
Warner Bros. WS-1769	(S)	**The Moth Confesses**	1969	10.00	25.00
Warner Bros. WS-1804	(S)	**Neon Philharmonic**	1969	10.00	25.00
NEP-TUNES, THE					
Family FLP-152	(M)	**Surfer's Holiday**	1963	14.00	35.00
Family SFLP-552	(S)	**Surfer's Holiday**	1963	20.00	50.00
NERVOUS KATS, THE					
Emma	(M)	**The Nervous Kats**	196?	40.00	100.00
NESMITH, MICHAEL					
Nesmith was formerly a member of The Monkees. Refer to Wichita Train Whistle.					
Pacific Arts 7-101	(S)	**The Prison** (Box with booklet)	1978	16.00	40.00
Pacific Arts	(DJ)	**The Michael Nesmith Radio Special**	1979	16.00	40.00
NETHERWORLD					
R.E.M. 4441	(S)	**Netherworld**	1981	30.00	75.00
NEVILLE, AARON					
Par-Lo LP-1	(M)	**Tell It Like It Is**	1967	20.00	50.00
Par-Lo LP-1	(S)	**Tell It Like It Is**	1967	60.00	150.00
Minit LP-40007	(M)	**Like It 'Tis**	1967	10.00	25.00
Minit LP-40007	(E)	**Like It 'Tis**	1967	8.00	20.00
NEW COLONY SIX, THE					
Sentar LP-101	(M)	**Breakthrough**	1966	200.00	400.00
Sentar ST-3001	(M)	**Colonization**	1967	12.00	30.00
Sentar SST-3001	(S)	**Colonization**	1967	16.00	40.00
NEW DAWN					
Hoot GR70-4569	(M)	**There's A New Dawn**	1969	300.00	500.00
NEW DIMENSIONS, THE					
Sutton SU-331	(M)	**Deuces And Eights**	1963	14.00	35.00
Sutton SSU-331	(S)	**Deuces And Eights**	1963	20.00	50.00
Sutton SU-332	(M)	**Surf 'N' Bongos**	1963	10.00	25.00
Sutton SSU-332	(S)	**Surf 'N' Bongos**	1963	16.00	40.00
Sutton SU-336	(M)	**Soul Surf**	1964	10.00	25.00
Sutton SSU-336	(S)	**Soul Surf**	1964	16.00	40.00
NEW GOSPEL KEYS, THE					
Bluesville BVLP-1066	(M)	**The New Gospel Keys**	1963	20.00	50.00
		—Bluesville albums above have bright blue labels with silver print.—			
Bluesville BVLP-1066	(M)	**The New Gospel Keys**	1964	10.00	25.00
		—Bluesville albums above have blue labels with a trident logo on the right side.—			
NEW HIGH, A					
Tempo Two T-2	(S)	**Dallas, 1971**	1972	20.00	50.00
NEW LEGION ROCK SPECTACULAR, THE					
Spectacular SPLP-7777	(S)	**Wild Ones!**	197?	30.00	75.00
NEW LOST CITY RAMBLERS, THE					
The New Lost City Ramblers—John Cohen, Mike Seeger and Tom Paley, replaced by Tracy Schwarz in 1962—were a vocal and instrumental trio dedicated to old-time string-band music. Refer to The Putnam String County Band.					
Folkways VC-7064	(M)	**Old Timey Songs For Children**	1959	12.00	30.00
Folkways FH-5263	(M)	**American Moonshine And Prohibition**	1959	12.00	30.00
Folkways FH-5264	(M)	**Songs From The Depression**	1960	12.00	30.00
Folkways FA-2395	(M)	**The New Lost City Ramblers, Volume 1**	1960	12.00	30.00
Folkways FA-2396	(M)	**The New Lost City Ramblers, Volume 2**	1960	12.00	30.00
Folkways FA-2397	(M)	**The New Lost City Ramblers, Volume 3**	1960	12.00	30.00
Folkways FA-2398	(M)	**The New Lost City Ramblers, Volume 4**	1960	12.00	30.00
Folkways FA-2399	(M)	**The New Lost City Ramblers, Volume 5**	1960	12.00	30.00
Folkways FA-2491	(M)	**The New Lost City Ramblers**	1961	10.00	25.00
Folkways FA-2492	(M)	**String Band Instrumentals**	1961	10.00	25.00
Folkways FA-2494	(M)	**Songs Of The New Lost City Ramblers**	1962	10.00	25.00
Folkways FA-2496	(M)	**Rural Delivery No. 1**	1964	10.00	25.00

One of the most interesting of all cover designs is The New Tweedy Brothers, a six-sided "cube" printed with a silver foil finish. This finish and the size of the jacket make the likelihood of finding it in Near Mint condition extremely difficult. A copy such as the one above, with its dog-eared corners, is better than what many collectors have had to settle for to fit this record into their collection.

Label & Catalog #		Title	Year	VG+	NM

NEW ORDER
New Order is made up of surviving members of Joy Division.

Rough Trade FACT-50	(S)	**Movement** *(Purple tinted vinyl)*	1981	16.00	40.00
Rough Trade FACT-50	(S)	**Movement** *(Red tinted vinyl)*	1981	8.00	20.00

NEW RENAISSANCE SOCIETY, THE

HBR HLP-9504	(M)	**Baroque N' Stones**	1966	8.00	20.00
HBR HST-9504	(S)	**Baroque N' Stones**	1966	10.00	25.00

NEW STRANGERS, THE

Folklore FRLP-14027	(M)	**Meet The New Strangers**	1964	8.00	20.00
Folklore FRST-14027	(S)	**Meet The New Strangers**	1964	10.00	25.00

NEW TWEEDY BROTHERS, THE

Ridon 234	(S)	**The New Tweedy Brothers**	1968	1,000.00	2,000.00

(Issued in an oversized, hexagonal cover designed to look like an acid laced sugar cube, only a few of which exist today! Near Mint copies in plain white covers sell for $300-400.)

NEW WORLD SINGERS, THE

Atlantic 8087	(M)	**The New World Singers**	1963	10.00	25.00
Atlantic SD-8087	(S)	**The New World Singers**	1963	14.00	35.00

(Atlantic 8087 features liner notes by Bob Dylan.)

NEW YORK DOLLS, THE
Both Dolls albums were originally issued with custom dolls labels and inner sleeves.

Mercury SRM-1-675	(S)	**New York Dolls**	1973	16.00	40.00
Mercury SRM-1-1001	(S)	**Too Much, Too Soon**	1974	16.00	40.00

—Mercury albums above have custom "doll" labels and inner sleeves.—

NEW YORK METS, THE

Buddah BDS-1969	(S)	**The Amazing Mets**	1969	16.00	40.00

NEWBEATS, THE
Larry Henley, Dean Mathis and Mark Mathis.

Hickory LP-120	(M)	**Bread And Butter**	1964	30.00	75.00
Hickory LPS-120	(E)	**Bread And Butter**	1964	60.00	150.00

("Everything's Alright" and "Pink Dolly Rue" are in stereo.)

Hickory DT-90701	(E)	**Bread And Butter** *(Capitol Record Club)*	1964	60.00	150.00
Hickory ST-90701	(S)	**Bread And Butter** *(Capitol Record Club)*	1964	100.00	250.00
Hickory LP-122	(M)	**Big Beat Sounds By The Newbeats**	1965	20.00	50.00
Hickory LPS-122	(S)	**Big Beat Sounds By The Newbeats**	1965	30.00	75.00
Hickory LP-128	(M)	**Run Baby Run**	1965	20.00	50.00
Hickory LPS-128	(S)	**Run Baby Run**	1965	30.00	75.00

NEWMAN, BOB

Audio Lab AL-1536	(M)	**The Kentucky Colonel**	1961	80.00	200.00

NEWMAN, JIMMY C.

MGM E-3777	(M)	**This Is Jimmy Newman**	1959	10.00	25.00
MGM SE-3777	(S)	**This Is Jimmy Newman**	1959	14.00	35.00

NEWMAN, RANDY

Epic LN-24147	(M)	**Peyton Place** *(TV Soundtrack)*	1965	16.00	40.00
Epic BN-26147	(S)	**Peyton Place** *(TV Soundtrack)*	1965	20.00	50.00
Reprise PRO-484	(DJ)	**Randy Newman Live**	1970	20.00	50.00

NEWTON-JOHN, OLIVIA

RCA Victor LSA-3008	(S)	**Toomorrow** *(UK Soundtrack)*	1971	80.00	200.00
Uni 73117	(S)	**If Not For You**	1971	8.00	25.00
MCA 16011	(S)	**Physical** *(Half-speed master)*	1981	8.00	25.00

NEXT MORNING, THE

Calla SC-2002	(S)	**The Next Morning**	1972	40.00	100.00

NICHOLAS BROTHERS, THE

Mercury MG-20355	(M)	**We Do Sing, Too**	1958	10.00	25.00

Label & Catalog #		Title	Year	VG+	NM
NICHOLS, MIKE, & ELAINE MAY					
Mercury MG-20376	(M)	**Improvisations To Music**	1959	12.00	30.00
Mercury SR-600??	(S)	**Improvisations To Music**	1959	16.00	40.00
Mercury OCM-2200	(M)	**An Evening With Mike Nichols & Elaine May**	1960	12.00	30.00
Mercury OCS-6200	(S)	**An Evening With Mike Nichols & Elaine May**	1960	16.00	40.00
		(Mercury 2/6200 is the original cast album.)			
Mercury MG-20680	(M)	**Mike Nichols & Elaine May Examine Doctors**	1962	10.00	25.00
Mercury SR-60680	(S)	**Mike Nichols & Elaine May Examine Doctors**	1962	12.00	30.00
		— Mercury albums above have black labels with silver print.—			
NICHOLS, NICHELLE					
Ms Nichols was formerly a member of the U.S.S. Enterprise.					
Epic LN-24351	(M)	**Down To Earth**	1968	16.00	40.00
Epic BN-26351	(S)	**Down To Earth**	1968	20.00	50.00
NICKEL BAG, THE					
Kama Sutra KLPS-8066	(S)	**Doing Their Love Thing**	1968	10.00	25.00
NICKS, STEVIE					
Refer to Buckingham/Nicks; Fleetwood Mac.					
Modern PR-2881	(DJ)	**Reflections From The Other Side**			
		Of The Mirror (Interview with script)	1989	16.00	40.00
Mobile Fidelity MFSL-121	(S)	**Bella Donna**	1984	15.00	45.00
NICO					
Nico originally recorded with The Velvet Underground.					
Verve V-5032	(M)	**Chelsea Girl**	1967	12.00	30.00
Verve V6-5032	(S)	**Chelsea Girl**	1967	16.00	40.00
Elektra EKS-74029	(S)	**The Marble Index**	1968	10.00	25.00
Reprise RS-6424	(S)	**Desert Shore**	1970	8.00	20.00
NIGHT OWLS, THE					
Valmor 79	(M)	**Twisting The Oldies**	1962	20.00	50.00
NIGHT SHADOWS, THE					
Spectrum	(S)	**The Square Root Of Two**	1968	660.00	1,000.00
Hottrax 1414	(S)	**The Square Root Of Two**	1968	60.00	150.00
Hottrax 1430	(S)	**Live At The Spot**	1981	10.00	25.00
NIGHTCAPS, THE					
Vandan VRLP-8124	(M)	**Wine, Wine, Wine**	196?	60.00	150.00
NIGHTCRAWLERS, THE					
Kapp KL-1520	(M)	**The Little Black Egg**	1967	30.00	75.00
Kapp KS-3520	(E)	**The Little Black Egg**	1967	20.00	50.00
NIGHTHAWKS, THE					
Aladdin LP-101	(M)	**Rock And Roll** (Thick vinyl)	1974	100.00	250.00
NIELSEN, GERTRUDE					
Decca DL-5138	(10")	**Gertrude Nielsen**	1951	20.00	50.00
NILES, JOHN JACOB					
John Niles, "Dean of American Balladeers," is a multi-instrumentalist, singer and writer of folk music in					
the "high", or artistic, manner.					
Boone Tolliver BTR-22	(10")	**American Folk Love Songs**	195?	20.00	50.00
Boone Tolliver BTR-23	(10")	**Ballads**	195?	20.00	50.00
Tradition TRP-1023	(M)	**I Wonder As I Wander**	1957	12.00	30.00
Camden CAL-219	(M)	**American Folk And Gambling Songs**	195?	10.00	25.00
Camden CAL-245	(M)	**American Folk Songs**	195?	10.00	25.00
Camden CAL-330	(M)	**50th Anniversary Album**	195?	10.00	25.00
NILSSON					
Tower T-5095	(M)	**Spotlight On Nilsson**	1967	8.00	20.00
Tower ST-5095	(S)	**Spotlight On Nilsson**	1967	10.00	25.00
RCA Victor LPM-3874	(M)	**Pandemonium Shadow Show**	1967	16.00	40.00
RCA Victor LSP-3874	(S)	**Pandemonium Shadow Show**	1967	10.00	25.00

Label & Catalog #		Title	Year	VG+	NM
RCA Victor	(DJ)	**The True One**	1967	80.00	200.00
		(Boxed set includes a copy of LPM-3874, two black & white			
		glossy photos, a button, poster, stickers and bios.)			
RCA Victor LPM-3956	(M)	**Aerial Ballet**	1968	40.00	100.00
RCA Victor LSP-3956	(S)	**Aerial Ballet**	1968	10.00	25.00
		—RCA albums above have black labels.—			
RCA Victor LSO-1152	(S)	**Skidoo** *(Soundtrack)*	1968	10.00	25.00
		—RCA albums above have orange labels on non-flexible vinyl—			
RCA SPS-33-567	(DJ)	**Nilssons Scatalogue**	1971	60.00	150.00
		(SPS-567 is a sampler of "song pieces from the Nilsson catalog,			
		creatively sequenced by Rich Paladino." Bootlegs with the same title,			
		"Scatalogue," contain unreleased tracks.)			
RCA Victor CPL1-0570	(S)	**Pussy Cats**	1974	10.00	25.00
RCA Victor APD1-0570	(Q)	**Pussy Cats**	1974	12.00	30.00
		(RCA 0580 was produced by and features 'Arry's buddy,			
		John Lennon, on vocals and etc.)			
Solo Music 165	(S)	**Schmilsson**	197?	20.00	50.00

NIMOY, LEONARD
Mr. Nimoy was formerly a member of the U.S.S. Enterprise.

Dot DLP-3794	(M)	**Mr. Spock's Music From Outer Space**	1967	20.00	50.00
Dot DLP-25794	(S)	**Mr. Spock's Music From Outer Space**	1967	30.00	75.00
Dot DLP-3835	(M)	**Two Sides Of Leonard Nimoy**	1968	16.00	40.00
Dot DLP-25835	(S)	**Two Sides Of Leonard Nimoy**	1968	20.00	50.00
Dot DLP-25883	(S)	**The Way I Feel**	1968	20.00	50.00
Dot DLP-25910	(S)	**The Touch Of Leonard Nimoy**	1969	20.00	50.00
Dot DLP-25966	(S)	**The New World Of Leonard Nimoy**	1969	20.00	50.00
Paramount PAS-1030	(S)	**Outer Space/Inner Mind**	1970	16.00	40.00
Pickwick SPC-3199	(S)	**Space Odyssey**	197?	20.00	50.00
Sears SPS-491	(S)	**Leonard Nimoy** *(Counterfeits exist)*	197?	30.00	75.00
Caedmon TC-1466	(S)	**"The Martian Chronicles"**	1976	12.00	30.00
Caedmon TC-1479	(S)	**"The Illustrated Man"**	1976	12.00	30.00
Caedmon TC-1520	(S)	**"War Of The Worlds"**	1977	12.00	30.00
Caedmon TC-1526	(S)	**"Green Hills Of Earth"**	1977	12.00	30.00

NINA & FREDERIK

Atco 33-119	(M)	**Introducing The Fabulous Nina & Frederik**	1960	10.00	25.00
Atco SD-33-119	(S)	**Introducing The Fabulous Nina & Frederik**	1960	14.00	35.00
		—Atco albums above have yellow "harp" labels.—			
Atco 33-154	(M)	**Where Have All The Flowers Gone?**	1963	8.00	20.00
Atco SD-33-154	(S)	**Where Have All The Flowers Gone?**	1963	10.00	25.00

NIRVANA

Bell 6015	(S)	**The Story Of Simon Simopath**	1968	10.00	25.00
Bell 6024	(S)	**All Of Us**	1969	10.00	25.00
Metromedia 1018	(S)	**Nirvana**	1970	10.00	25.00

NIRVANA SITAR & STRING GROUP, THE

Mr. G G-8001	(M)	**Sitar & Strings**	1968	8.00	20.00
Mr. G GS-9001	(S)	**Sitar & Strings**	1968	12.00	30.00

NITTY GRITTY DIRT BAND, THE/THE DIRT BAND

Liberty LRP-3501	(M)	**The Nitty Gritty Dirt Band**	1967	10.00	25.00
Liberty LST-7501	(S)	**The Nitty Gritty Dirt Band**	1967	12.00	30.00
Liberty LRP-3516	(M)	**Ricochet**	1967	10.00	25.00
Liberty LST-7516	(S)	**Ricochet**	1967	12.00	30.00
Liberty LST-7540	(S)	**Rare Junk**	1968	10.00	25.00
Liberty LST-7611	(S)	**Alive**	1969	8.00	20.00
Liberty LST-7642	(DJ)	**Uncle Charlie & His Dog Teddy Promo Pack**	1970	30.00	75.00
United Arts. LA-469	(DJ)	**A Programmers Guide To Dream**	1975	12.00	30.00

NITZSCHE, JACK

Reprise R-6101	(M)	**The Lonely Surfer**	1963	30.00	75.00
Reprise RS-6101	(S)	**The Lonely Surfer**	1963	60.00	150.00
Reprise R-6115	(M)	**Dance To The Hits Of The Beatles**	1964	16.00	40.00
Reprise RS-6115	(S)	**Dance To The Hits Of The Beatles**	1964	20.00	50.00
Reprise R-6200	(M)	**Chopin '66**	1966	10.00	25.00
Reprise RS-6200	(S)	**Chopin '66**	1966	12.00	30.00
		—Reprise albums above have pink, gold & green labels.—			

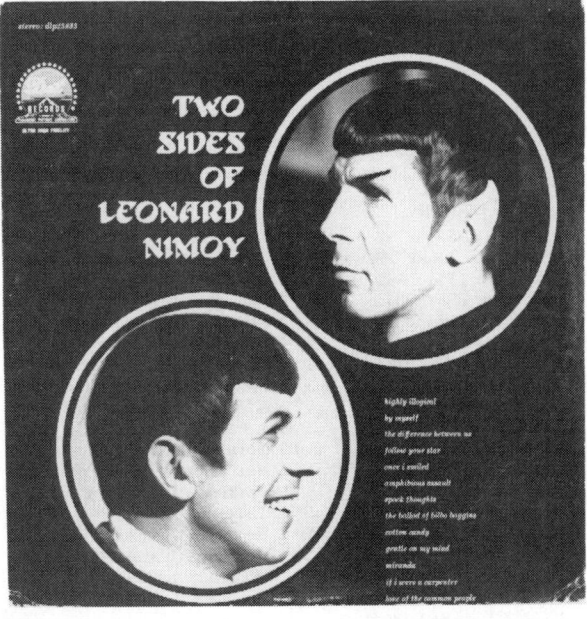

While one could spend pages extolling the merits of Nimoy's contribution to the success of Star Trek the enterprise, not the least of which is the fleshing out of a character that may be one of television's few contributions to American lore, let it be said that his versions of "If I Were A Carpenter" and "Gentle On My Mind" are unparalleled, the product of a set of gilded pipes and a vision of illogical proportions.

Label & Catalog #		Title	Year	VG+	NM
NOBLES, CLIFF, & COMPANY					
Phil L.A. Of Soul 4001	(S)	**The Horse**	1968	20.00	50.00
Moon Shot 601	(S)	**Pony The Horse**	1969	10.00	25.00
NOGUEZ, JACKY					
Jamie JLP-70-3007	(M)	**Chow Chow Bambina**	1959	8.00	20.00
Jamie JS-3007	(S)	**Chow Chow Bambina**	1959	12.00	30.00
Jamie JLP-70-3013	(M)	**Dance Along With Jacky Noguez**	1960	8.00	20.00
Jamie JS-3013	(S)	**Dance Along With Jacky Noguez**	1960	12.00	30.00
NOLAND, TERRY					
Brunswick BL-54041	(M)	**Terry Noland** (With Buddy Holly on guitar)	1958	300.00	600.00
NOMADDS, THE					
Radex MLP-6521	(M)	**The Nomadds**	1965	150.00	300.00
NORDINE, KEN					
Decca DL-8550	(M)	**Concert In The Sky**	1957	30.00	75.00
Dot DLP-3075	(M)	**Word Jazz**	1957	20.00	50.00
Dot DLP-25075	(E)	**Word Jazz**	1958	12.00	30.00
Dot DLP-3096	(M)	**Son Of Word Jazz**	1958	16.00	40.00
Dot DLP-25096	(S)	**Son Of Word Jazz**	1958	20.00	50.00
Dot DLP-3115	(M)	**Love Words**	1958	12.00	30.00
Dot DLP-25115	(S)	**Love Words**	1958	16.00	40.00
RCA Victor SP-33-13	(DJ)	**Sounds In Space**	1958	40.00	100.00
		("Sounds In Space" contains music with narration by KN.)			
Dot DLP-3142	(M)	**My Baby**	1958	12.00	30.00
Dot DLP-25142	(S)	**My Baby**	1958	16.00	40.00
Dot DLP-3196	(M)	**Next!**	1959	12.00	30.00
Dot DLP-25196	(S)	**Next!**	1959	16.00	40.00
Dot DLP-3301	(M)	**Word Jazz, Volume 2**	1960	12.00	30.00
Dot DLP-25301	(S)	**Word Jazz, Volume 2**	1960	16.00	40.00
Hamilton HLP-102	(M)	**The Voice Of Love**	1964	8.00	20.00
Hamilton HLS-102	(S)	**The Voice Of Love**	1964	10.00	25.00
Philips PHM-200-224	(M)	**Colors**	1966	8.00	20.00
Philips PHS-600-224	(S)	**Colors**	1966	10.00	25.00
Philips PHM-200-258	(M)	**Ken Nordine Does Robert Shure's "Twink"**	1967	8.00	20.00
Philips PHS-600-258	(S)	**Ken Nordine Does Robert Shure's "Twink"**	1967	10.00	25.00
NORMA JEAN					
Norma Jean Taylor also recorded with Porter Wagoner.					
RCA Victor LPM-2961	(M)	**Let's Go All The Way**	1964	8.00	20.00
RCA Victor LSP-2961	(S)	**Let's Go All The Way**	1964	10.00	25.00
RCA Victor LPM-3449	(M)	**Pretty Miss Norma Jean**	1965	8.00	20.00
RCA Victor LSP-3449	(S)	**Pretty Miss Norma Jean**	1965	10.00	25.00
RCA Victor LPM-3541	(M)	**Please Don't Hurt Me**	1966	8.00	20.00
RCA Victor LSP-3541	(S)	**Please Don't Hurt Me**	1966	10.00	25.00
RCA Victor LPM-3664	(M)	**A Tribute To Kitty Wells**	1966	8.00	20.00
RCA Victor LSP-3664	(S)	**A Tribute To Kitty Wells**	1966	10.00	25.00
RCA Victor LPM-3700	(M)	**Norma Jean Sings Porter Wagoner**	1967	10.00	25.00
RCA Victor LSP-3700	(S)	**Norma Jean Sings Porter Wagoner**	1967	8.00	20.00
RCA Victor LPM-3836	(M)	**Jackson Ain't A Very Big Town**	1967	10.00	25.00
RCA Victor LSP-3836	(S)	**Jackson Ain't A Very Big Town**	1967	8.00	20.00
RCA Victor LPM-3910	(M)	**Heaven's Just A Prayer Away**	1968	20.00	50.00
RCA Victor LSP-3910	(S)	**Heaven's Just A Prayer Away**	1968	8.00	20.00
		— RCA albums above have black labels.—			
NORMAN, LARRY					
Larry was formerly a member of People.					
Capitol ST-446	(S)	**Upon This Rock**	1969	12.00	30.00
One Way JC-7397	(S)	**Street Level**	1970	12.00	30.00
One Way JC-4847	(S)	**Bootleg** (Gatefold cover)	1971	12.00	30.00
One Way 2JC-900	(S)	**Bootleg** (Regular cover)	1971	10.00	25.00
Verve V6-5092	(S)	**Only Visiting This Planet** (Tri-fold cover)	1972	8.00	20.00
Verve V6-5092	(S)	**Only Visiting This Planet** (Gatefold cover)	1972	10.00	25.00
MGM SE-4942	(S)	**So Long Ago The Garden**	1973	16.00	40.00
NORTH, JAY					
Kem LP-27	(M)	**Look Who's Singing!**	196?	50.00	125.00

Label & Catalog #		Title	Year	VG+	NM
NORTHERN FRONT, THE					
(No label)	(M)	**The Furniture Store**	1975	30.00	75.00
NOSY PARKER					
(No label)	(S)	**Nosy Parker**	1975	80.00	200.00
NOTES FROM THE UNDERGROUND					
Vanguard VSD-6502	(S)	**Notes From The Underground**	1970	12.00	30.00
NOVA LOCAL, THE					
Decca DL-74977	(S)	**Nova 1**	1968	16.00	40.00
NOVAK, KIM: Refer to JOHN CARLTON; MORRIS STOLOFF					
NOVELLS, THE					
Mother's MLPS-73	(S)	**That Did It!**	197?	12.00	30.00
NRBQ					
The New Rhythm & Blues Quintet also recorded with Carl Perkin. Refer to Wildweeds.					
Columbia CS-9858	(S)	**NRBQ** ("360 Sound" label)	1969	10.00	25.00
Kama Sutra KSBS-2045	(S)	**Scraps**	1972	10.00	25.00
Kama Sutra KSBS-2065	(S)	**Workshop**	1973	16.00	40.00
NUTTY SQUIRRELS, THE					
The Nutty Squirrels were a pair of beatnik rodents with their own televised cartoon show in the early '60s. The music on these albums was provided by top notch musicians, including jazz greats Don Elliott, Cannonball Adderely, Bobby Jaspar, Hal McKusick, Sam Most and vocalist Sascha Burland.					
Hanover HML-8014	(M)	**The Nutty Squirrels**	1960	20.00	50.00
Columbia CL-1589	(M)	**Bird Watching**	1961	12.00	30.00
Columbia CS-8389	(S)	**Bird Watching**	1961	16.00	40.00
MGM E-4272	(M)	**A Hard Day's Night**	1964	10.00	25.00
MGM SE-4272	(S)	**A Hard Day's Night**	1964	12.00	30.00
NYE, HERMES					
Hermes Nye is a guitar player and singer of traditional American folk songs.					
Folkways FP-37	(10")	**Anglo-American Folk Songs**	195?	20.00	50.00
Folkways FA-2037	(10")	**Anglo-American Folk Songs**	195?	20.00	50.00
Folkways FP-47	(10")	**Texas Folk Songs**	195?	20.00	50.00
Folkways FA-2128	(10")	**Texas Folk Songs**	195?	20.00	50.00
Folkways FP-48	(10")	**Ballads Of The Civil War**	195?	20.00	50.00
Folkways FA-2187	(10")	**Ballads Of The Civil War, Vol. 1**	195?	20.00	50.00
Folkways FA-2188	(10")	**Ballads Of The Civil War, Vol. 2**	195?	20.00	50.00
Folkways FA-2305	(M)	**Ballads And Reliques (Early English Ballads Of Francis James Child And Thomas Percy)**	195?	12.00	30.00
NYE, LOUIS					
Riverside RLP-842	(M)	**Heigh-Ho, Madison Avenue**	195?	10.00	25.00
NYRO, LAURA					
Verve/Folkways FT-3020	(M)	**More Than A New Discovery**	1967	12.00	30.00
Verve/Folkways FTS-3020	(S)	**More Than A New Discovery**	1967	16.00	40.00
Verve/Frecast FTS-3020	(S)	**The First Songs...**	1968	10.00	25.00
		("First Songs" is a reisue of "Discovery.")			
Capitol ST-93036	(S)	**The First Songs...** (Capitol Record Club)	1968	10.00	25.00
Verve/Frecast FTS-3029	(S)	**Laura Nyro**	1968		Unreleased
Columbia CL-2826	(M)	**Eli And The 13th Confession**	1968	12.00	30.00
Columbia CS-9626	(S)	**Eli And The 13th Confession**	1968	6.00	15.00
		— Columbia albums above have "360 Sound" labels. —			
Columbia JG-34331	(DJ)	**Seasons Of Light** (2 LPs)	1976	20.00	50.00
		(Issued in a plain cardboard jacket. This album was edited down to a single LP for commercial release in 1977.)			

O' BRIAN, HUGH
ABC-Paramount ABC-203 *(M)*   **TV's Wyatt Earp Sings**   *1957*   **30.00**   **75.00**

O' BRYANT, JOAN
Joan O' Bryant is a guitar player and singer of traditional American folk songs.
Folkways FA-2134   *(10")*   **Folksongs And Ballads Of Kansas**   *195?*   **20.00**   **50.00**
Folkways FA-2338   *(M)*   **American Ballads And Folksongs**   *195?*   **12.00**   **30.00**

O' CONNELL, HELEN
Vik LX-1093   *(M)*   **Green Eyes**   *1957*   **16.00**   **40.00**

O' DAY, ANITA: *Refer to* **GOLDMINE'S PRICE GUIDE TO COLLECTIBLE JAZZ ALBUMS**

O' DAY, MOLLY
Starday SLP-367   *(M)*   **The Living Legend**
                            Of Country Music *(Yellow label)*   *1966*   **12.00**   **30.00**

O' DELL, DOYLE
Era EL-20004   *(M)*   **Doyle O' Dell** *(Red vinyl)*   *1956*   **20.00**   **50.00**
Era EL-20004   *(M)*   **Doyle O' Dell**   *1956*   **12.00**   **30.00**
Sage C-36   *(M)*   **Crossroads**   *195?*   **12.00**   **30.00**

O' DELL, MAC
Audio Lab AL-1544   *(M)*   **Hymns For The Country Folk**   *1960*   **80.00**   **200.00**

O' GWYNN, JAMES
Mercury MG-20727   *(M)*   **The Best Of James O' Gwynn**   *1962*   **8.00**   **20.00**
Mercury SR-60727   *(S)*   **The Best Of James O' Gwynn**   *1962*   **10.00**   **25.00**

O' HARA, MARY
Mary O' Hara is an Irish singer of traditional folk music of the British Isles in both English and Gaelic.
Tradition TLP-1024   *(M)*   **Songs Of Ireland**   *1958*   **12.00**   **30.00**
London LL-1572   *(M)*   **Songs Of Erin**   *195?*   **12.00**   **30.00**
London LL-1784   *(M)*   **Love Songs Of Ireland**   *1959*   **12.00**   **30.00**

O' HARA, MAUREEN
RCA Victor LPM-1953   *(M)*   **Love Letters From Maureen**   *1958*   **20.00**   **50.00**
RCA Victor LSP-1953   *(S)*   **Love Letters From Maureen**   *1958*   **30.00**   **75.00**
Columbia CL-1750   *(M)*   **Maureen O' Hara Sings**
                            Her Favorite Irish Songs   *1961*   **16.00**   **40.00**
Columbia CS-8550   *(S)*   **Maureen O' Hara Sings**
                            Her Favorite Irish Songs   *1961*   **20.00**   **50.00**

O' JAYS, THE
Imperial LP-9290   *(M)*   **Comin' Through**   *1965*   **16.00**   **40.00**
Imperial LP-12290   *(S)*   **Comin' Through**   *1965*   **20.00**   **50.00**
Minit LP-40008   *(M)*   **Soul Sounds**   *1967*   **12.00**   **30.00**
Minit LP-24008   *(S)*   **Soul Sounds**   *1967*   **16.00**   **40.00**

O' KAYSIONS, THE
ABC S-664   *(S)*   **Girl Watcher** *("Girl Watcher" is rechanneled)* 1968   **16.00**   **40.00**

OAK RIDGE QUARTET, THE
*Since the debut of the "new" Oak Ridge Quartet in 1956 there have been fourteen singing members, four
of which have achieved enormous success as The Oak Ridge Boys (listed below). Refer to Wally Fowler.*
Cadence CLP-3019   *(M)*   **The Oak Ridge Quartet**   *1959*   **30.00**   **75.00**
Cumberland MGC-29526   *(M)*   **The Oak Ridge Quartet In Concert**   *1963*   **10.00**   **25.00**
Cumberland SRC-69526   *(S)*   **The Oak Ridge Quartet In Concert**   *1963*   **12.00**   **30.00**
Skylite RLP-5974   *(M)*   **The Oak Ridge Quartet Sing And Shout**   *1964*   **8.00**   **20.00**
Skylite SRLP-5974   *(S)*   **The Oak Ridge Quartet Sing And Shout**   *1964*   **10.00**   **25.00**

The albums of actors Hugh O' Brian and Maureen O' Hara fit comfortably into the "personality" field of collectible records. O' Brian gained recognition for his portrayal of Wyatt Earp in the television series during the puberty period of TV when westerns were everywhere. Irish beauty O' Hara has been in countless films, including two John Ford classics, Rio Grande and The Quiet Man, both opposite John Wayne.

Label & Catalog #		Title	Year	VG+	NM

OAK RIDGE BOYS, THE
The ORB on ABC have been Duane Allen, Joe Bonsall, Noel Fox and Richard Sterban.

Label & Catalog #		Title	Year	VG+	NM
Warner Bros. W-1497	(M)	Sounds Of Nashville	1963	10.00	25.00
Warner Bros. WS-1497	(S)	Sounds Of Nashville	1963	12.00	30.00
Warner Bros. W-1521	(M)	Folk-Minded Spirituals			
		For Spiritual-Minded Folks	1963	10.00	25.00
Warner Bros. WS-1521	(S)	Folk-Minded Spirituals			
		For Spiritual-Minded Folks	1963	12.00	30.00
Skylite RLP-6020	(M)	The Oak Ridge Boys Sing For You	1964	8.00	20.00
Skylite SRLP-6020	(S)	The Oak Ridge Boys Sing For You	1964	10.00	25.00
Skylite RLP-6030	(M)	I Wouldn't Take Nothing			
		For My Journey Now	1965	8.00	20.00
Skylite SRLP-6030	(S)	I Wouldn't Take Nothing			
		For My Journey Now	1965	10.00	25.00
Skylite RLP-6040	(M)	The Solid Gospel Sound			
		Of The Oak Ridge Boys	1966	8.00	20.00
Skylite SRLP-6040	(S)	The Solid Gospel Sound			
		Of The Oak Ridge Boys	1966	10.00	25.00
Skylite RLP-6045	(M)	River Of Love	1967	8.00	20.00
Skylite SRLP-6045	(S)	River Of Love	1967	10.00	25.00
Starday SLP-356	(M)	The Sensational Oak Ridge Boys			
		From Nashville, Tennessee	1965	10.00	25.00
United Arts. UAL-3554	(M)	The Oak Ridge Boys At Their Best	1966	8.00	20.00
United Arts. UAS-6554	(S)	The Oak Ridge Boys At Their Best	1966	10.00	25.00

OBJECTS, THE

Label & Catalog #		Title	Year	VG+	NM
(No label)	(S)	Live At The Greatwood Cafe	1980	24.00	60.00

OBOLER, ARCH

Label & Catalog #		Title	Year	VG+	NM
Capitol T-1763	(M)	Drop Dead! An Exercise In Horror	1962	8.00	20.00
Capitol ST-1763	(S)	Drop Dead! An Exercise In Horror	1962	10.00	25.00

OCHS, PHIL
Phil Ochs was a guitar player, singer and writer of topical, folk-based songs. Refer to Sammy Walker.

Label & Catalog #		Title	Year	VG+	NM
Elektra EKL-269	(M)	All The News That's Fit To Sing	1964	10.00	25.00
Elektra EKS-7269	(S)	All The News That's Fit To Sing	1964	12.00	30.00
Elektra EKL-287	(M)	I Ain't Marching Anymore	1965	10.00	25.00
Elektra EKS-7287	(S)	I Ain't Marching Anymore	1965	12.00	30.00
		— Elektra albums above have a guitar player logo on the label.—			
Elektra EKL-310	(M)	Phil Ochs In Concert	1966	10.00	25.00
Elektra EKS-7310	(S)	Phil Ochs In Concert	1966	12.00	30.00
Folkways FB-5321	(M)	Interviews With Phil Ochs	196?	20.00	50.00
		— A&M albums above have brown labels.—			

ODA

Label & Catalog #		Title	Year	VG+	NM
Loud A0011	(S)	Oda	1974	200.00	400.00

ODETTA
Odetta Holmes is a guitar player and singer of traditional and contemporary folk-based music.

Label & Catalog #		Title	Year	VG+	NM
Fantasy 3-15	(10")	Odetta And Larry	1955	20.00	50.00
Fantasy F-3252	(M)	Odetta And Larry (Dark red vinyl)	1957	20.00	50.00
Fantasy F-3252	(M)	Odetta And Larry	1958	12.00	30.00
Tradition TRP-1010	(M)	Odetta Sings Ballads And Blues	1956	12.00	30.00
Tradition TRP-1025	(M)	Odetta At The Gate Of Horn	1957	12.00	30.00
Vanguard VRS-9059	(M)	My Eyes Have Seen	1960	8.00	20.00
Vanguard VSD-2046	(S)	My Eyes Have Seen	1960	10.00	25.00
Vanguard VRS-9066	(M)	Ballads For Americans	1960	8.00	20.00
Vanguard VSD-2057	(S)	Ballads For Americans	1960	10.00	25.00
Vanguard VRS-9076	(M)	Odetta At Carnegie Hall	1961	8.00	20.00
Vanguard VSD-2072	(S)	Odetta At Carnegie Hall	1961	10.00	25.00
Vanguard VRS-9079	(M)	Christmas Spirituals	1961	8.00	20.00
Vanguard VSD-2079	(S)	Christmas Spirituals	1961	10.00	25.00
Vanguard VRS-9103	(M)	Odetta At Town Hall	1962	8.00	20.00
Vanguard VSD-2109	(S)	Odetta At Town Hall	1962	10.00	25.00
Vanguard VRS-9137	(M)	One Grain Of Sand	1963	8.00	20.00
Vanguard VSD-2153	(S)	One Grain Of Sand	1963	10.00	25.00
Vanguard VRS-3003	(M)	Odetta At Carnegie Hall	1964	8.00	20.00
Vanguard VSD-73003	(S)	Odetta At Carnegie Hall	1964	10.00	25.00

Label & Catalog #		Title	Year	VG+	NM
Riverside RLP-417	(M)	**Odetta And The Blues**	1962	10.00	25.00
Riverside RS-9417	(S)	**Odetta And The Blues**	1962	12.00	30.00
RCA Victor LPM-2573	(M)	**Sometimes I Feel Like Crying**	1962	8.00	20.00
RCA Victor LSP-2573	(S)	**Sometimes I Feel Like Crying**	1962	10.00	25.00

— RCA mono albums above have "Long Play" on the bottom of the label;
stereo albums have "Living Stereo" on the bottom.—

ODYSSEY

Organic ORG-1	(M)	**Odyssey**	196?	660.00	1,000.00
Trip T-1000	(S)	**Setting Forth**	198?	10.00	25.00

(Reissue of the original pressing on Organic.)

OHIO EXPRESS, THE

Cameo C-20,000	(M)	**Beg, Borrow And Steal**	1968	12.00	30.00
Cameo CS-20,000	(S)	**Beg, Borrow And Steal**	1968	16.00	40.00

OHIO PLAYERS, THE

Capitol ST-192	(S)	**Observations In Time**	1969	16.00	40.00

OHRLIN, GLENN
Glenn Ohrlin is a guitar player and singer of traditional American folk music.

Campus Folksong Club 301	(M)	**The Hell-Bound Train**	196?	10.00	25.00

OKUN, MILT
Milt Okun is a banjo and guitar player and singer of traditional folk songs.

Stinson SLP-65	(10")	**Every Inch A Sailor-**			
		Fo'c'sle Songs And Shanties	195?	20.00	50.00
Stinson SLP-71	(10")	**I Sing Of Canada**	195?	20.00	50.00
Stinson SLP-82	(10")	**Adirondack Folk Songs And Ballads**	195?	20.00	50.00
Riversdie RLP-12-603	(M)	**Merry Ditties—Folk Songs Of Love And Play**	195?	12.00	30.00
Riversdie RLP-12-634	(M)	**Traditional American Love Songs**	195?	12.00	30.00
Baton BL-1203	(M)	**America's Best Loved Folk Songs**	195?	12.00	30.00

OLAY, RUTH: *Refer to* GOLDMINE'S PRICE GUIDE TO COLLECTIBLE JAZZ ALBUMS

OLD & IN THE WAY
Features Jerry Garcia, David Grisman and Peter Rowan.

Round RX-103	(S)	**Old And In The Way**	1975	10.00	25.00

OLDFIELD, MIKE

Virgin QR13-105	(Q)	**Tubular Bells**	1974	10.00	25.00
Virgin HE-44116	(S)	**Tubular Bells** *(Half-speed master)*	198?	10.00	25.00
Virgin PZQ-33913	(Q)	**Ommadawn**	1975	10.00	25.00

OLDHAM, ANDREW LOOG
As the personal manager of The Rolling Stones (he was responsible for their "we don't wanna hold your hand" image, including the ground-breaking LP covers and their attendant liner notes, swiped with aplomb from Anthony Burgess' "A Clockwork Orange") and producer of said albums through 1966, Andrew Oldham was a man of wealth and taste and pivotal importance to both what many consider "the greatest rock'n roll band in the world" and the early years of the British Invasion. The albums below are Oldham's more or less pop-orchestral arrangements and productions of the period's hits. . .

London LL-3457	(M)	**The Rolling Stones Songbook**	1965	30.00	75.00
London PS-457	(S)	**The Rolling Stones Songbook**	1965	40.00	100.00
Parrot PA-61003	(M)	**East Meets West**	1965	20.00	50.00
Parrot PAS-71003	(S)	**East Meets West**	1965	30.00	75.00

OLENN, JOHNNY

Liberty LRP-3029	(M)	**Just Rollin' With Johnny Olenn**	1957	150.00	300.00

OLIVER & THE TWISTERS

Colpix CP-423	(M)	**Look Who's Twistin' Everybody**	1961	16.00	40.00

OLLIE & THE NIGHTINGALES

Stax STS-2021	(S)	**Ollie And The Nightingales**	1969	20.00	50.00

OLSEN, DOROTHY

RCA Victor LPM-1606	(M)	**I Know Where I'm Going**	1957	12.00	30.00

Label & Catalog #		Title	Year	VG+	NM
OLYMPICS, THE					
Arvee A-423	(M)	**Doin' The Hully Gully**	1960	80.00	200.00
Arvee A-424	(M)	**Dance By The Light Of The Moon**	1961	60.00	150.00
Arvee A-429	(M)	**Party Time**	1961	60.00	150.00
Tri-Disc 1001	(M)	**Do The Bounce**	1963	20.00	50.00
Mirwood M-7003	(M)	**Something Old, Something New**	1966	12.00	30.00
Mirwood MS-7003	(S)	**Something Old, Something New**	1966	16.00	40.00
		(Mirwood 7003 contains rerecorded versions of earlier hits.)			
Post 8000	(E)	**The Olympics Sing**	196?	10.00	25.00
OMNIBUS					
United Arts. UAS-6743	(S)	**Omnibus**	1970	30.00	75.00
ONE					
Village	(S)	**Creation Earth** *(With posters)*	1977	20.00	50.00
ORANG-UTAN					
Bell 6054	(S)	**Orang-Utan**	1971	16.00	40.00
ORANGE COLORED SKY					
Uni 73031	(S)	**Orange Colored Sky**	1968	16.00	40.00
ORANGE WEDGE: *Refer to* WEDGE					
ORBISON, ROY					
For additional listing refer to Jerry Lee Lewis / Johnny Cash / Roy Orbison; The Traveling Wilburys.					
Sun SLP-1260	(M)	**Roy Orbison At The Rockhouse**	1961	300.00	600.00
Monument M-4002	(M)	**Lonely And Blue**	1961	60.00	150.00
Monument SM-14002	(S)	**Lonely And Blue**	1961	300.00	500.00
Monument M-4007	(M)	**Crying**	1962	40.00	100.00
Monument SM-14007	(S)	**Crying**	1962	200.00	400.00
Monument M-4009	(M)	**Roy Orbison's Greatest Hits**	1962	14.00	35.00
Monument SM-14009	(S)	**Roy Orbison's Greatest Hits**	1962	20.00	50.00
		—Monument albums above have copper & white swirl labels.—			
Monument MLP-8000	(M)	**Roy Orbison's Greatest Hits**	1963	12.00	30.00
Monument SLP-18000	(S)	**Roy Orbison's Greatest Hits**	1963	16.00	40.00
Monument MLP-8003	(M)	**In Dreams**	1963	30.00	75.00
Monument SLP-18003	(S)	**In Dreams**	1963	60.00	150.00
		—Monument albums above have rainbow & white swirl labels.—			
Monument MLP-8023	(M)	**Early Orbison**	1964	12.00	30.00
Monument SLP-18023	(S)	**Early Orbison**	1964	20.00	50.00
Monument MLP-8024	(M)	**More Of Roy Orbison's Greatest Hits**	1964	12.00	30.00
Monument SLP-18024	(S)	**More Of Roy Orbison's Greatest Hits**	1964	16.00	40.00
		("It's Over" is in stereo on this album.)			
Monument MLP-8035	(M)	**Orbisongs**	1965	10.00	25.00
Monument SLP-18035	(S)	**Orbisongs**	1965	14.00	35.00
Monument MLP-8045	(M)	**The Very Best Of Roy Orbison**	1966	10.00	25.00
Monument SLP-18045	(S)	**The Very Best Of Roy Orbison**	1966	14.00	35.00
		("It's Over" is rechanneled on this album.)			
		—Monument albums above have green labels with a gold perimeter.—			
Coca Cola TX-??	(DJ)	**Roy Orbison Swings The Jingle**	1965	250.00	500.00
MGM E-4308	(M)	**There Is Only One Roy Orbison**	1965	8.00	20.00
MGM SE-4308	(S)	**There Is Only One Roy Orbison**	1965	10.00	25.00
MGM E-4322	(M)	**The Orbison Way**	1965	8.00	20.00
MGM SE-4322	(S)	**The Orbison Way**	1965	10.00	25.00
MGM E-4379	(M)	**The Classic Roy Orbison**	1966	8.00	20.00
MGM SE-4379	(S)	**The Classic Roy Orbison**	1966	10.00	25.00
MGM E-4424	(M)	**Roy Orbison Sings Don Gibson**	1966	8.00	20.00
MGM SE-4424	(S)	**Roy Orbison Sings Don Gibson**	1966	10.00	25.00
MGM E-4514	(M)	**Cry Softly, Lonely One**	1967	8.00	20.00
MGM SE-4514	(S)	**Cry Softly, Lonely One**	1967	10.00	25.00
MGM SE-4475	(S)	**The Fastest Guitar Alive** *(Soundtrack)*	1968	10.00	25.00
Monument KZG-31484	(S)	**All-Time Greatest Hits** *(2 LPs)*	1972	10.00	25.00
		("It's Over" is rechanneled on this album.)			
Hits Unlimired 233-0	(S)	**My Spell On You**	1982	20.00	50.00
ORCHIDS, THE					
Roulette R-25169	(M)	**Twistin' At The Roundtable**	1962	10.00	25.00
Roulette SR-25169	(S)	**Twistin' At The Roundtable**	1962	12.00	30.00

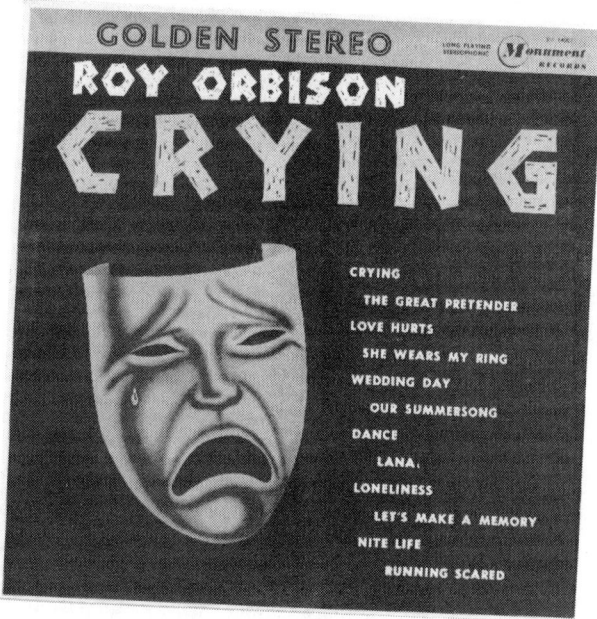

Roy Orbison's early albums for Monument were recorded under more or less ideal conditions for achieving the full effect of the stereo of the day. Produced by Fred Foster with the board in the nimble hands of legendary engineer Bill Porter, these two albums in particular have become cause for celebration among audiophiles in recent years. . . with the attendant rise in values, especially for those few copies in nearly mint condition.

Label & Catalog #		Title	Year	VG+	NM

ORIENT EXPRESS, THE
| Mainstream 6117 | (S) | The Orient Express | 1969 | 16.00 | 40.00 |

ORIGINAL SURFARIS, THE
| Diplomat D-2309 | (M) | Wheels-Shorts-Hot Rods | 1963 | 10.00 | 25.00 |
| Diplomat DS-2309 | (S) | Wheels-Shorts-Hot Rods | 1963 | 14.00 | 35.00 |

ORIGINAL WASHBOARD BAND, THE
| RCA Victor LPM-1958 | (M) | Scrubbin' And Pickin' | 1959 | 8.00 | 20.00 |
| RCA Victor LSP-1958 | (S) | Scrubbin' And Pickin' | 1959 | 12.00 | 30.00 |

ORIGINALS, THE
| Soul SS-716 | (S) | Green Grow The Lilacs | 1969 | 12.00 | 30.00 |

ORIOLES, THE
Refer to The Cadillacs; Sonny Til & The Orioles.
Charley Parker PLP-816	(M)	Modern Sounds Of The Orioles	1962	40.00	100.00
Charley Parker PLP-816S	(S)	Modern Sounds Of The Orioles	196?	10.00	25.00
Big-A LP-2001	(M)	The Orioles' Greatest All Time Hits	1969	10.00	25.00

ORION, P. J., & THE MAGNATES
| Magnate 122459 | (M) | P. J. Orion And The Magnates | 196? | 60.00 | 150.00 |

ORLANDO, TONY
| Epic LN-611 | (M) | Bless You & 11 Other Great Hits | 1961 | 12.00 | 30.00 |
| Epic BN-611 | (S) | Bless You & 11 Other Great Hits | 1961 | 16.00 | 40.00 |

ORLONS, THE
Cameo C-1020	(M)	The Wah Watusi	1962	30.00	75.00
Cameo C-1033	(M)	All The Hits	1962	30.00	75.00
Cameo C-1041	(M)	South Street	1963	30.00	75.00
Cameo C-1054	(M)	Not Me	1963	30.00	75.00
Cameo C-1061	(M)	The Orlons' Biggest Hits	1963	30.00	75.00
Cameo C-1073	(M)	Down Memory Lane	1963	30.00	75.00

ORLONS, THE / THE DOVELLS
| Cameo C-1067 | (M) | Golden Hits Of The Orlons & The Dovells | 1963 | 30.00 | 75.00 |

ORPHAN EGG
| Carole CARS-8004 | (S) | Orphan Egg | 1968 | 16.00 | 40.00 |
| American Inter. ST-A-1033 | (S) | The Cycle Savages *(Soundtrack)* | 1970 | 16.00 | 40.00 |

ORPHANN
| O.M.I. M-70021 | (S) | Up For Adoption | 1977 | 30.00 | 75.00 |

ORPHEUS
MGM E-4524	(M)	Orpheus	1968	8.00	20.00
MGM SE-4524	(S)	Orpheus	1968	10.00	25.00
MGM SE-4569	(S)	Ascending	1968	10.00	25.00
MGM SE-4599	(S)	Joyful	1969	10.00	25.00

OSBORNE, JIMMY
Audio Lab AL-1527	(M)	Singing Songs He Wrote	1959	80.00	200.00
King 730	(M)	The Legendary Jimmy Osborne	1961	30.00	75.00
King 782	(M)	Golden Harvest, Volume 3	1962	30.00	75.00
King 892	(M)	The Very Best Of Jimmy Osborne	1964	20.00	50.00
King 941	(M)	Jimmy Osborne's Golden Harvest	1965	20.00	50.00

OSBORNE, MARY: *Refer to* GOLDMINE'S PRICE GUIDE TO COLLECTIBLE JAZZ ALBUMS

OSBORNE BROTHERS, THE
The brothers Osborne are Bobby and Sonny.
MGM E-3734	(M)	Country Pickin' And Hillside Singin'	1959	20.00	50.00
MGM E-4018	(M)	Blue Grass Music	1961	12.00	30.00
MGM SE-4018	(S)	Blue Grass Music	1961	16.00	40.00
MGM E-4090	(M)	Bluegrass Instrumentals	1962	12.00	30.00
MGMS E-4090	(S)	Bluegrass Instrumentals	1962	16.00	40.00
MGM E-4149	(M)	Cuttin' Grass... Osborne Brothers Style	1963	12.00	30.00
MGM SE-4149	(S)	Cuttin' Grass... Osborne Brothers Style	1963	16.00	40.00

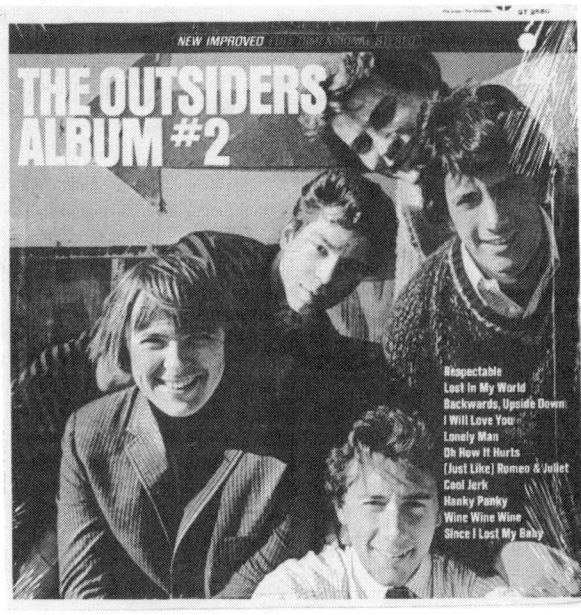

The Outsiders scored a big hit in 1966 with the catchy "Time Won't Let Me." This was followed by three more top 40 hits and commercial oblivion: While these two albums contain three of their hits, only the first one even dented the top 40 album charts. Lead singer Sonny Geraci abandoned his swagger with The Outsiders to adopt a wimpy persona as the lead with Climax, who topped the charts with "Precious And Few" in 1972.

Label & Catalog #		Title	Year	VG+	NM

OSMOND BROTHERS, THE
The Osmonds feature Donny Osmond.

MGM E-4146	(M)	Songs We Sang On The Andy Williams Show	1963	10.00	25.00
MGM SE-4146	(S)	Songs We Sang On The Andy Williams Show	1963	12.00	30.00
MGM PM-7	(DJ)	AC Spark Plug Division			
		Presents The Osmond Brothers	1963	30.00	75.00
		(PM-7 contains six tracks from MGM 4145 on side 1 and the TV			
		soundtrack for "The Travels Of Jaimie McPheeters" on side 2.)			
MGM E-4187	(M)	We Sing You A Merry Christmas	1963	10.00	25.00
MGM SE-4187	(S)	We Sing You A Merry Christmas	1963	12.00	30.00
MGM E-4235	(M)	All-Time Hymn Favorites	1964	8.00	20.00
MGM SE-4235	(S)	All-Time Hymn Favorites	1964	10.00	25.00
MGM E-4291	(M)	The New Sound Of The Osmond Brothers	1965	8.00	20.00
MGM SE-4291	(S)	The New Sound Of The Osmond Brothers	1965	10.00	25.00

OSWALD, BASHFULM BROTHER
Bashful Brother Oswald is a pseudonym for Pete Kirby.

Starday SLP-192	(M)	Bashful Brother Oswald *(Yellow label)*	1962	12.00	30.00

OSWALD, LEE HARVEY
Lee Harvey Oswald, the alleged but unconvicted assassin of President John F. Kennedy, was a the most noted wizard of this century for his uncanny control of the "Magic Bullet."

Truth 22-65	(M)	Lee Harvey Oswald Speaks	1967	40.00	100.00
Inca 1001	(M)	Self Portrait In Red	1967	40.00	100.00

OTHER HALF, THE

"7/2"	(M)	The Other Half	196?	300.00	600.00
		(Original covers open on the left; counterfeits open on the right.			
		Counterfeit's vinyl shows blue when held up to a light.)			

OTHER HALF, THE
The Other Half features Randy Holden, later of Blue Cheer.

Acta 8004	(M)	The Other Half	1968	20.00	50.00
Acta 38004	(S)	The Other Half	1968	30.00	75.00

OTIS, JOHNNY
Refer to Mel Williams.

Dig 104	(M)	Rock And Roll Hit Parade, Volume 1	1957	300.00	600.00
		(Original covers for Dig 104 are gold; counterfeits are yellow.)			
Capitol T-940	(M)	The Johnny Otis Show	1958	80.00	200.00
Kent KST-534	(S)	Cold Shot	1968	10.00	25.00
Epic BN-26524	(S)	Cuttin' Up	1970	10.00	25.00
Epic EG-30473	(S)	Live At Monterey	1971	10.00	25.00

OUTLAW BLUES BAND, THE

BluesWay BLS-6021	(S)	The Outlaw Blues Band	1968	10.00	25.00

OUTLAWS, THE

Direct Disk SD-16617	(S)	Outlaws	198?	8.00	25.00

OUTSIDERS, THE

Capitol T-2501	(M)	Time Won't Let Me	1966	10.00	25.00
Capitol ST-2501	(S)	Time Won't Let Me	1966	12.00	30.00
Capitol T-2568	(M)	Album #2	1966	8.00	20.00
Capitol ST-2568	(S)	Album #2 *("Respectable" is rechanneled)*	1966	10.00	25.00
Capitol T-2636	(M)	In	1967	8.00	20.00
Capitol ST-2636	(S)	In	1967	10.00	25.00
Capitol T-2745	(M)	Happening Live	1967	8.00	20.00
Capitol ST-2745	(S)	Happening Live	1967	10.00	25.00

OWEN, REG

Bally BAL-12006	(M)	Swing Me High	1957	12.00	30.00
RCA Victor LPM-1542	(M)	Best Of Irving Berlin	1957	10.00	25.00
RCA Victor LPM-1580	(M)	Dreaming	1958	10.00	25.00
RCA Victor LPM-1582	(M)	Coffee Break	1958	8.00	20.00
RCA Victor LSP-1582	(S)	Coffee Break	1958	12.00	30.00
RCA Victor LPM-1597	(M)	Holiday Abroad In Dublin	1958	8.00	20.00
RCA Victor LSP-1599	(S)	Holiday Abroad In London	1958	12.00	30.00
RCA Victor LPM-1675	(M)	The British Isles	1958	10.00	25.00

Label & Catalog #		Title	Year	VG+	NM
RCA Victor LPM-1906	(M)	I'll Sing You 1,000 Love Songs	1959	8.00	20.00
RCA Victor LSP-1906	(S)	I'll Sing You 1,000 Love Songs	1959	12.00	30.00
RCA Victor LPM-1907	(M)	Deep In A Dream	1959	10.00	25.00
RCA Victor LPM-1908	(M)	Girls Were Made To Take Care Of Boys	1959	8.00	20.00
RCA Victor LSP-1908	(S)	Girls Were Made To Take Care Of Boys	1959	12.00	30.00
RCA Victor LPM-1914	(M)	Cuddle Up A Little Closer	1959	8.00	20.00
RCA Victor LSP-1914	(S)	Cuddle Up A Little Closer	1959	12.00	30.00
RCA Victor LPM-1915	(M)	You Don't Know Paree	1958	10.00	25.00
Decca DL-8859	(M)	Under Paris Skies	1959	8.00	20.00
Decca DL-78859	(S)	Under Paris Skies	1959	12.00	30.00
Palette 1001	(M)	Manhattan Spritual	1959	12.00	30.00
Palette S-1001	(S)	Manhattan Spritual	1959	16.00	40.00
Palette PZ-1001	(M)	Hypnotic Swing	1960	8.00	20.00
Palette SPZ-31001	(S)	Hypnotic Swing	1960	12.00	30.00
		("Hypnotic Swing" is a repackage of "Manhattan Spritual.")			
Palette PZ-1004	(M)	Get Happy	1960	6.00	15.00
Palette SPZ-31004	(S)	Get Happy	1960	10.00	25.00
Palette PZ-1018	(M)	Fiorello!	1960	6.00	15.00
Palette SPZ-31018	(S)	Fiorello!	1960	10.00	25.00

OWEN-B

C. B. 19210	(S)	Owen-B	197?	24.00	60.00

OWENS, BONNIE/BONNIE OWENS & THE STRANGERS
Refer to Merle Haggard.

Capitol T-2403	(M)	Don't Take Advantage Of Me	1965	10.00	25.00
Capitol ST-2403	(S)	Don't Take Advantage Of Me	1965	12.00	30.00
Capitol T-2660	(M)	All Of Me Belongs To You	1967	10.00	25.00
Capitol ST-2660	(S)	All Of Me Belongs To You	1967	12.00	30.00
Capitol ST-2861	(S)	Somewhere Between	1968	10.00	25.00
Capitol ST-195	(S)	Lead Me On	1969	10.00	25.00
Capitol ST-341	(S)	Hifi To Cry By	1969	10.00	25.00
Capitol ST-557	(S)	Mother's Favorite Hymns	1970	10.00	25.00

OWENS, BUCK/BUCK OWENS & THE BUCKAROOS
Refer to Buddy Alan; The Bakersfield Brass; The Buckaroos; The Hee-Haw Gospel Quartet.

LaBrea 1017	(M)	Buck Owens	1961	40.00	100.00
LaBrea 8017	(S)	Buck Owens	1961	60.00	150.00
Starday SLP-172	(M)	The Fabulous Country Music Sound Of Buck Owens (Yellow label)	1962	20.00	50.00
Starday SLP-324	(M)	The Fabulous Country Music Sound Of Buck Owens (Yellow label)	1965	14.00	35.00
		(Starday 324 is a repackage of 172.)			
Capitol T-1482	(M)	Buck Owens Sings Harlan Howard	1961	16.00	40.00
Capitol ST-1482	(S)	Buck Owens Sings Harlan Howard	1961	20.00	50.00
Capitol T-1489	(M)	Under Your Spell Again	1961	16.00	40.00
Capitol DT-1489	(E)	Under Your Spell Again	1961	10.00	25.00
Capitol T-1777	(M)	You're For Me	1962	16.00	40.00
Capitol ST-1777	(S)	You're For Me	1962	20.00	50.00
Capitol T-1879	(M)	Buck Owens On The Bandstand	1963	16.00	40.00
Capitol ST-1879	(S)	Buck Owens On The Bandstand	1963	20.00	50.00
Capitol T-1989	(M)	Buck Owens Sings Tommy Collins	1963	16.00	40.00
Capitol ST-1989	(S)	Buck Owens Sings Tommy Collins	1963	20.00	50.00
Capitol T-2105	(M)	The Best Of Buck Owens	1964	10.00	25.00
Capitol ST-2105	(S)	The Best Of Buck Owens	1964	12.00	30.00
		(First pressings of Capitol 2105 have black Starline labels.)			
Capitol T-2135	(M)	Together Again/My Heart Skips A Beat	1964	10.00	25.00
Capitol ST-2135	(S)	Together Again/My Heart Skips A Beat	1964	12.00	30.00
Capitol T-2186	(M)	I Don't Care	1964	10.00	25.00
Capitol ST-2186	(S)	I Don't Care	1964	12.00	30.00
Capitol T-2283	(M)	I've Got A Tiger By The Tail	1965	10.00	25.00
Capitol ST-2283	(S)	I've Got A Tiger By The Tail	1965	12.00	30.00
Capitol T-2353	(M)	Before You Go	1965	10.00	25.00
Capitol ST-2353	(S)	Before You Go	1965	12.00	30.00
Capitol T-2367	(M)	The Instrumental Hits Of Buck Owens & The Buckaroos	1965	10.00	25.00
Capitol ST-2367	(S)	The Instrumental Hits Of Buck Owens & The Buckaroos	1965	12.00	30.00

Label & Catalog #		Title	Year	VG+	NM
Capitol T-2396	(M)	Christmas With Buck Owens & The Buckaroos	1965	10.00	25.00
Capitol ST-2396	(S)	Christmas With Buck Owens & The Buckaroos	1965	12.00	30.00
Capitol T-2443	(M)	Roll Out The Red Carpet	1966	10.00	25.00
Capitol ST-2443	(S)	Roll Out The Red Carpet	1966	12.00	30.00
Capitol T-2497	(M)	Dust On Mother's Bible	1966	10.00	25.00
Capitol ST-2497	(S)	Dust On Mother's Bible	1966	12.00	30.00
Capitol T-2556	(M)	Carnegie Hall Concert	1966	10.00	25.00
Capitol ST-2556	(S)	Carnegie Hall Concert	1966	12.00	30.00
Capitol SPRO-2980	(DJ)	Minute Masters (Radio sampler)	1966	20.00	50.00
Capitol T-2640	(M)	Open Up Your Heart	1967	10.00	25.00
Capitol ST-2640	(S)	Open Up Your Heart	1967	12.00	30.00
Capitol T-2715	(M)	Buck Owens & His Buckaroos In Japan	1967	10.00	25.00
Capitol ST-2715	(S)	Buck Owens & His Buckaroos In Japan	1967	12.00	30.00
Capitol T-2760	(M)	Your Tender Loving Care	1967	10.00	25.00
Capitol ST-2760	(S)	Your Tender Loving Care	1967	12.00	30.00
Capitol ST-2841	(S)	It Takes People Like You To Make People Like Me	1968	10.00	25.00
Capitol ST-2897	(S)	The Best Of Buck Owens, Volume 2	1968	10.00	25.00
Capitol ST-2902	(S)	A Night On The Town	1968	10.00	25.00
Capitol ST-2962	(S)	Sweet Rosie Jones	1968	10.00	25.00
Capitol ST-2977	(S)	Christmas Shopping	1968	10.00	25.00
Capitol ST-2994	(S)	Buck Owens, The Guitar Player	1968	10.00	25.00
— Capitol albums above have black labels with the Capitol logo on top.—					
Capitol STBB-486	(S)	A Merry "Hee Haw" Christmas (2 LPs)	1970	10.00	25.00
Capitol STCL-574	(S)	Buck Owens (3 LP box)	1970	16.00	40.00
— Capitol albums above have green labels.—					
Longines Symph. LS-301	(S)	Let The Good Times Roll (5 LPs)	197?	20.00	50.00

OXFORD, VERNON

Label & Catalog #		Title	Year	VG+	NM
RCA Victor LPM-3704	(M)	Woman, Let Me Sing You A Song	1967	8.00	20.00
RCA Victor LSP-3704	(S)	Woman, Let Me Sing You A Song	1967	10.00	25.00

OZ KNOZZ

Label & Catalog #		Title	Year	VG+	NM
Ozone 02-1000	(S)	Ruff Mix	1975	80.00	200.00

OZZIE & HARRIET
Ozzie and Harriet Nelson are the real life (!) and TV parents of Rick Nelson.

Label & Catalog #		Title	Year	VG+	NM
Imperial LP-9049	(M)	The Ozzie And Harriet Show	1957	80.00	200.00
Sunset SUM-1146	(M)	Ozzie And Harriet Sing	1967	16.00	40.00
Sunset SUS-5146	(E)	Ozzie And Harriet Sing	1967	8.00	20.00
		(Sunset 1145 is a reissue of Imperial 9049.)			

P

P. H. PHACTOR					
Piccadilly PIC-3343	(S)	P. H. Factor	*1980*	**24.00**	**60.00**

PACE, JOHNNY: *Refer to* GOLDMINE'S PRICE GUIDE TO COLLECTIBLE JAZZ ALBUMS

PACIFIC DRIFT					
Deram DES-18040	(S)	Feelin' Free	*1970*	**12.00**	**30.00**
PACIFIC, GAS & ELECRIC					
Bright Orange 701	(S)	Get It On	*1968*	**10.00**	**25.00**
PACK, MARSHALL					
Starday SLP-120	(M)	Marshall Pack *(Yellow label)*	*1960*	**16.00**	**40.00**
PAGE, JIMMY					
Refer to Cartoone; Led Zepplin; The Yardbirds.					
Springboard SPB-4038	(S)	Special Early Works	*1972*	**10.00**	**25.00**
PAGE, PATTI					
Mercury MG-25059	(10")	Songs	*1950*	**16.00**	**40.00**
Mercury MG-25101	(10")	Folksong Favorites	*1951*	**16.00**	**40.00**
Mercury MG-25109	(10")	Christmas	*1951*	**16.00**	**40.00**
Mercury MG-25154	(10")	Tennessee Waltz	*1952*	**16.00**	**40.00**
Mercury MG-25185	(10")	Patti Sings For Romance	*1954*	**16.00**	**40.00**
Mercury MG-25187	(10")	Song Souvenirs	*1954*	**16.00**	**40.00**
Mercury MG-25196	(10")	Just Patti	*1954*	**16.00**	**40.00**
Mercury MG-25197	(10")	Patti's Songs	*1954*	**16.00**	**40.00**
Mercury MG-25209	(10")	And I Thought About You	*1954*	**16.00**	**40.00**
Mercury MG-25210	(10")	So Many Memories	*1954*	**16.00**	**40.00**
EmArcy MG-36074	(M)	In The Land Of Hi Fi	*1956*	**20.00**	**50.00**
EmArcy MG-36116	(M)	The East Side	*1957*	**20.00**	**50.00**
EmArcy SR-60014	(S)	The East Side	*1959*	**20.00**	**50.00**
EmArcy MG-36136	(M)	The West Side	*1958*	**20.00**	**50.00**
EmArcy SR-60113	(S)	The West Side	*1959*	**20.00**	**50.00**
Mercury MG-20076	(M)	Romance On The Range	*1955*	**12.00**	**30.00**
Mercury MG-20093	(M)	Christmas With Patti Page	*1956*	**12.00**	**30.00**
Mercury MG-20095	(M)	Page I	*1955*	**12.00**	**30.00**
Mercury MG-20096	(M)	Page II	*1955*	**12.00**	**30.00**
Mercury MG-20097	(M)	Page III	*1955*	**12.00**	**30.00**
Mercury MG-20098	(M)	You Go To My Head	*1955*	**12.00**	**30.00**
Mercury MG-20099	(M)	Music For Two In Love	*1955*	**12.00**	**30.00**
Mercury MG-20100	(M)	The Voices Of Patti Page	*1955*	**12.00**	**30.00**
Mercury MG-20101	(M)	Page IV	*1955*	**12.00**	**30.00**
Mercury MG-20102	(M)	This Is My Song	*1955*	**12.00**	**30.00**
Mercury MG-20226	(M)	Manhattan Tower	*1956*	**12.00**	**30.00**
Mercury MG-20318	(M)	The Waltz Queen	*1957*	**12.00**	**30.00**
Mercury SR-60049	(S)	The Waltz Queen	*1959*	**14.00**	**35.00**
Mercury SR-80000	(S)	In The Land Of Hi-Fi	*1959*	**14.00**	**35.00**
Mercury MG-20387	(M)	Let's Get Away From It All	*1957*	**12.00**	**30.00**
Mercury SR-60010	(S)	Let's Get Away From It All	*1959*	**14.00**	**35.00**
Mercury MG-20388	(M)	I've Heard That Song Before	*1958*	**12.00**	**30.00**
Mercury SR-60011	(S)	I've Heard That Song Before	*1959*	**14.00**	**35.00**
Mercury MG-20398	(M)	Patti Page On Camera	*1959*	**12.00**	**30.00**
Mercury SR-60025	(S)	Patti Page On Camera	*1959*	**14.00**	**35.00**
Mercury MG-20417	(M)	Three Little Words	*1960*	**12.00**	**30.00**
Mercury SR-60037	(S)	Three Little Words	*1960*	**14.00**	**35.00**
Mercury MG-20405	(M)	Indiscretion	*1959*	**12.00**	**30.00**
Mercury SR-60059	(S)	Indiscretion	*1959*	**14.00**	**35.00**
Mercury MG-20406	(M)	I'll Remember April	*1959*	**12.00**	**30.00**
Mercury SR-60081	(S)	I'll Remember April	*1959*	**14.00**	**35.00**

Label & Catalog #		Title	Year	VG+	NM
Mercury MG-20573	(M)	**Just A Closer Walk With Thee**	1960	12.00	30.00
Mercury SR-60233	(S)	**Just A Closer Walk With Thee**	1960	14.00	35.00
Mercury MG-20599	(M)	**Patti Page Sings & Stars In "Elmer Gantry"**	1960	10.00	25.00
Mercury SR-60260	(M)	**Patti Page Sings & Stars In "Elmer Gantry"**	1960	12.00	30.00
		— Mercury albums above have black labels with silver print.—			

PAISLEYS, THE

Audio City 70	(S)	**Cosmic Mind At Play**	196?	80.00	200.00

PALANCE, JACK

Warner Bros. WS-1865	(S)	**Palance**	1970	12.00	30.00

PALEY, TOM

Tom Paley is a banjo and guitar player and singer of traditional folk songs. Refer to The New Lost City Ramblers; Jean Ritchie & Oscar Brand / Tom Paley.

Elektra EKL-12	(10")	**Folk Songs**			
		From The Southern Appalachians	1953	20.00	50.00

PALEY & ALEXANDER

Sounds Int. 005	(M)	**Boston Incest Album**	196?	20.00	50.00

PALMER, EARL

Liberty LRP-3201	(M)	**Drumsville**	1961	8.00	20.00
Liberty LST-7201	(S)	**Drumsville**	1961	10.00	25.00
Liberty LRP-3227	(M)	**Percolator Twist**	1962	8.00	20.00
Liberty LST-7227	(S)	**Percolator Twist**	1962	10.00	25.00

PANDIT, KORLA

Vita VLP-12	(10")	**Musical Gems**	195?	40.00	100.00
Fantasy F-3272	(M)	**Music Of The Exotic Easy** *(Red vinyl)*	1958	20.00	50.00
Fantasy F-3272	(M)	**Music Of The Exotic Easy**	1958	10.00	25.00
Fantasy F-8013	(S)	**Music Of The Exotic Easy** *(Blue vinyl)*	1962	20.00	50.00
Fantasy F-8013	(S)	**Music Of The Exotic Easy**	1962	10.00	25.00
Fantasy F-3284	(M)	**Latin Holiday** *(Red vinyl)*	1959	20.00	50.00
Fantasy F-3284	(M)	**Latin Holiday**	1959	10.00	25.00
Fantasy F-8027	(S)	**Latin Holiday** *(Blue vinyl)*	1962	20.00	50.00
Fantasy F-8027	(S)	**Latin Holiday**	1962	10.00	25.00
Fantasy F-3286	(M)	**Korla Pandit At The Pipe Organ** *(Red vinyl)*	1959	20.00	50.00
Fantasy F-3286	(M)	**Korla Pandit At The Pipe Organ**	1959	10.00	25.00
Fantasy F-3288	(M)	**Tropical Magic** *(Red vinyl)*	1959	20.00	50.00
Fantasy F-3288	(M)	**Tropical Magic**	1959	10.00	25.00
Fantasy F-8034	(S)	**Tropical Magic** *(Blue vinyl)*	1962	20.00	50.00
Fantasy F-8034	(S)	**Tropical Magic**	1962	10.00	25.00
Fantasy F-3293	(M)	**Speak To Me Of Love** *(Red vinyl)*	1959	20.00	50.00
Fantasy F-3293	(M)	**Speak To Me Of Love**	1959	10.00	25.00
Fantasy F-8039	(S)	**Speak To Me Of Love** *(Blue vinyl)*	1962	20.00	50.00
Fantasy F-8039	(S)	**Speak To Me Of Love**	1962	10.00	25.00
Fantasy F-3304	(M)	**Korla Pandit In Concert** *(Red vinyl)*	1960	20.00	50.00
Fantasy F-3304	(M)	**Korla Pandit In Concert**	1960	10.00	25.00
Fantasy F-8049	(S)	**Korla Pandit In Concert** *(Blue vinyl)*	1962	20.00	50.00
Fantasy F-8049	(S)	**Korla Pandit In Concert**	1962	10.00	25.00
Fantasy F-3320	(M)	**Songs Of Mystery And Romance** *(Red vinyl)*	1961	20.00	50.00
Fantasy F-3320	(M)	**Songs Of Mystery And Romance**	1961	10.00	25.00
Fantasy F-8061	(S)	**Songs Of Mystery And Romance** *(Blue vinyl)*	1962	20.00	50.00
Fantasy F-8061	(S)	**Songs Of Mystery And Romance**	1962	10.00	25.00
		— Fantasy albums above are pressed on thick, non-flexible vinyl.			

PANDORA

(No label)	(S)	**Pandora** *(10" flexidisc)*	198?	20.00	50.00

PANICS, THE

Chancellor CHL-5026	(M)	**Panicsville**	1962	8.00	20.00
Chancellor CHLS-5026	(S)	**Panicsville**	1962	10.00	25.00

PARAGONS, THE / THE JESTERS

Jubilee JLP-1098	(M)	**The Paragons**			
		Meet The Jesters *(Multi-color vinyl)*	1959	800.00	1,200.00
Jubilee JLP-1098	(M)	**The Paragons Meet The Jesters**	1959	150.00	300.00
		— Jubilee albums above have glossy blue labels.—			

After the critical acclaim accorded Pet Sounds and both the laurels and the sales for "Good Vibrations," Brian Wilson envisioned a series of albums with themes that transcended anything that had ever been contemplated in rock music. The first album, initially titled Dumb Angel and then Smile, was to incorporate advanced production techniques, hip humor, several Americana themes such as the old West, vocal arrangements so complex as to set new standards in all fields of endeavor, and all this was to be held together by the intentionally opaque lyrics of one van Dyke Parks. In the wake of the disaster that Smile was for Capitol records, Parks was perceived by the company as one of the bad guys and instead of signed, was allowed to escape the lunacy and find refuge with the progressive Warner Bros. label. His first album, Song Cycle, was a brilliant journey to some of the places that Brian had been heading with The Beach Boys. . .

Label & Catalog #		Title	Year	VG+	NM
Jubilee JLP-1098	(M)	The Paragons Meet The Jesters	196?	60.00	150.00
		—Jubilee albums above have flat black labels.—			
Jubilee JLP-1098	(M)	The Paragons Meet The Jesters	196?	30.00	75.00
		—Jubilee albums above have glossy black labels with a multi-color logo.—			
Winley LP-6003	(M)	War! The Jesters Vs. The Paragons	1960	250.00	500.00

PARAGONS, THE / THE HARPTONES

Musicnote M-8001	(M)	The Paragons Vs. The Harptones	1964	14.00	35.00

PARIS, JACKIE: *Refer to* GOLDMINE'S PRICE GUIDE TO COLLECTIBLE JAZZ ALBUMS

PARIS PILOT

Hip 7004	(S)	Paris Pilot	197?	16.00	40.00

PARIS SISTERS, THE

Unifilms 505	(M)	The Paris Sisters Sing Songs From Glass House	1966	10.00	25.00
Unifilms 505	(S)	The Paris Sisters Sing Songs From Glass House	1966	12.00	30.00
Sidewalk T-5906	(M)	The Hits Of The Paris Sisters	1967	20.00	50.00
Sidewalk DT-5906	(E)	The Hits Of The Paris Sisters	1967	14.00	35.00
Reprise R-6259	(M)	Everything Under The Sun	1967	20.00	50.00
Reprise RS-6259	(S)	Everything Under The Sun	1967	30.00	75.00

PARKER, FESS

Columbia CL-576	(M)	TV Sweethearts (With Marion Marlowe)	1955	30.00	75.00
Columbia CL-666	(M)	Davy Crockett (TV Soundtrack)	1955	40.00	100.00
Disneyland WDA-3007	(M)	Three Adventures Of Davy Crockett	195?	20.00	50.00
Disneyland WDA-3602	(M)	Yarns And Songs	196?	20.00	50.00
RCA Victor LPM-2973	(M)	Fess Parker Sings About Daniel Boone, Davy Crockett and Abe Lincoln	1964	12.00	30.00
RCA Victor LSP-2973	(S)	Fess Parker Sings About Daniel Boone, Davy Crockett and Abe Lincoln	1964	16.00	40.00
Disneyland DQS-1336	(M)	Cowboy And Indian Songs	1968	12.00	30.00

PARKER, GRAHAM, & THE RUMOUR

Arista SP-63	(DJ)	Live Sparks	1979	12.00	30.00

PARKER, LITTLE JUNIOR

Duke DLP-72	(S)	Blues Consolidated (With Bobby Bland)	1961	60.00	150.00
		—Duke albums above have purple & yellow labels.—			
Duke DLP-72	(S)	Blues Consolidated (With Bobby Bland)	196?	16.00	40.00
Duke DLP-76	(M)	Driving Wheel	1962	30.00	75.00
Duke DLP-83	(M)	The Best Of Junior Parker	1967	16.00	40.00
Duke DLPS-83	(P)	The Best Of Junior Parker	1967	16.00	40.00
		—Duke albums above have orange labels.—			
Mercury MG-21101	(M)	Like It Is	1967	8.00	20.00
Mercury SR-61101	(S)	Like It Is	1967	10.00	25.00

PARKER, ROBERT

Nola LP-1001	(M)	Barefootin'	1966	16.00	40.00

PARKER FAMILY, THE

Audio Lab AL-1548	(M)	Songs For Salvation	196?	80.00	200.00
Audio Lab AL-1574	(M)	Songs For Salvation, Vol. 2	196?	80.00	200.00
King 932	(M)	Just A Real Nice Family	1965	20.00	50.00

PARKS, VAN DYKE

Warner Bros. WS-1727	(S)	Song Cycle (Gold Label)	1968	10.00	25.00

PARLIAMENT

Parliament, who also recorded as Funkadelic, is the brainchild of George Clinton.

Invictus 7302	(S)	Osmium	1970	50.00	125.00
Casablanca NBLP-9003	(S)	Up For The Down Stroke	1974	16.00	40.00
Casablanca NBLP-7002	(S)	Up For The Down Stroke	1975	12.00	30.00
Casablanca NBLP-7014	(S)	Chocolate City	1975	12.00	30.00
Casablanca NBLP-7022	(S)	Mothership Connection	1976	12.00	30.00
Casablanca NBLP-7034	(S)	The Clones Of Dr. Funkenstein	1976	12.00	30.00
Casablanca NBLP-7053	(S)	Parliament Live/P. Funk Earth Tour	1977	12.00	30.00

Label & Catalog #		Title	Year	VG+	NM
Casablanca NBLP-7084	(S)	Funkentelechy Vs. The Placebo Syndrome	1977	12.00	30.00
Casablanca NBLP-7125	(S)	Motor-Booty Affair	1978	12.00	30.00
Casablanca NBLP-7125	(S)	Motor Booty Affair (Picture disc)	1979	16.00	40.00
Casablanca NBLP-7195	(S)	Gloryhallastoopid	1979	12.00	30.00
Casablanca NBLP-7249	(S)	Trombipulation	1980	12.00	30.00

PARSONS, ALAN/THE ALAN PARSONS PROJECT

Arista SP-68	(DJ)	Audio Guide To The Alan Parsons Project	1979	16.00	40.00
		(Boxed set of four Project albums with a special double-album set of Parson's work with other artists.)			
Arista SP-140	(DJ)	Audio Guide To The Alan Parsons Project	1979	20.00	50.00
		(Boxed set of six Project albums with a special double-album set of Parson's work with other artists.)			
Mobile Fidelity MFSL-084	(S)	I, Robot	1980	8.00	25.00
Mobile Fidelity MFQR-084	(S)	I, Robot (Ultra High Quality Record. in a box)	1982	16.00	50.00

PARTON, DOLLY
Dolly also recorded with Porter Wagoner.

Monument MLP-8085	(M)	Hello, I'm Dolly Parton	1967	12.00	30.00
Monument SLP-18085	(S)	Hello, I'm Dolly Parton	1967	16.00	40.00
RCA Victor LPM-3949	(M)	Just Because I'm A Woman	1968	40.00	100.00
RCA Victor LSP-3949	(S)	Just Because I'm A Woman	1968	12.00	30.00
		— RCA albums above have black labels with Nipper on top.—			

PARTON, DOLLY / GEORGE JONES

Starday LP-429	(P)	Dolly Parton And George Jones	1968	16.00	40.00
		(Dolly's side is in stereo; George's side is rechanneled.)			

PARTON, DOLLY / FAYE TUCKER

Somerset S-9700	(M)	Hits Made Famous By Country Queens	1963	10.00	25.00
Somerset SF-19700	(S)	Hits Made Famous By Country Queens	1963	12.00	30.00

PARTRIDGE FAMILY, THE
The Partridge Family features David Cassidy.

Bell 6050	(S)	Album (With 10" x 10" bonus photo)	1970	12.00	30.00
Bell 6050	(S)	Album (Without the photo)	1970	8.00	20.00
Bell 6059	(S)	Up To Date (With book cover)	1971	12.00	30.00
		(Bell 6059 was issued with a 12" x 20" school book cover.)			
Bell 6059	(S)	Up To Date (Without the ook cover)	1971	8.00	20.00
Bell 6066	(S)	A Christmas Card	1971	10.00	25.00
		(Bell 6066 was issued originally with a Christmas card attached to the front cover.)			
Bell 6066	(S)	A Christmas Card	1972	14.00	35.00
		(Later pressings have the card printed on the cover.)			
Bell 6072	(S)	Shopping Bag (With bonus shopping bag)	1972	14.00	35.00
		(Bell 6072 was issued with a bonus shopping bag.)			
Bell 6072	(S)	Shopping Bag (Without the shopping bag)	1972	8.00	20.00
Bell 1122	(S)	Crossword Puzzle	1973	12.00	30.00
Bell 1137	(S)	Bulletin Board	1973	20.00	50.00
Bell 1319	(S)	The World Of The Partridge Family (2 LPs)	1974	16.00	40.00
Laurie House H-8014	(S)	The Partridge Family (2 LPs)	197?	20.00	50.00

PASTEL SIX, THE

Mark-56 MLP-511	(M)	Bob Eubanks Presents The "42" Dance Party Golden Oldies	1962	40.00	100.00
Zen 1001	(M)	Cinnamon Cinder	1963	24.00	60.00

PATCHEN, KENNETH

Cadence CLP-3004	(M)	Kenneth Patchen With The Chamber Jazz Sextet	1958	150.00	300.00

PATRON SAINTS, THE

(No label)	(M)	Fohhoh Bohob	1969	1,000.00	1,500.00

PATTO
Mike Patto Of Spooky Tooth.

Island SW-9322	(S)	Roll 'Em, Smoke 'Em Put Another Line Out	197?	12.00	30.00

Label & Catalog #		Title	Year	VG+	NM
PATTON, CHARLEY					
Origin Jazz Library 1	(M)	The Immortal Charley Patton No. 1	1962	10.00	25.00
Origin Jazz Library 7	(M)	The Immortal Charley Patton No. 2	1964	10.00	25.00
Yazoo 2001	(M)	King Of The Delta Blues (2 LPs)	197?	12.00	30.00
Yazoo 2010	(M)	Founder Of The Delta Blues (2 LPs)	197?	12.00	30.00
PATTON, JIMMY					
Stereophonic LP-1002	(S)	Take 30 Minutes With Jimmy Patton	196?	50.00	125.00
Sourdough 127	(M)	Blue Darlin'	1965	20.00	50.00
Sims 127	(M)	Blue Darlin'	1965	16.00	40.00
Moon 101	(M)	Make Room For The Blues	1966	20.00	50.00
PAUL, LES, & MARY FORD					
Decca DL-5018	(10")	Hawaiian Paradise	1949	40.00	100.00
Decca DL-5376	(10")	Galloping Guitars	1952	40.00	100.00
Capitol H-226	(10")	New Sound, Volume 1	1950	40.00	100.00
Capitol H-286	(10")	New Sound, Volume 2	1951	40.00	100.00
Capitol H-356	(10")	Bye Bye Blues	1952	40.00	100.00
Capitol H-416	(10")	The Hit Makers	1953	40.00	100.00
Capitol H-577	(10")	Les & Mary	1955	40.00	100.00
Capitol T-226	(M)	New Sound, Volume 1	1955	20.00	50.00
Capitol T-286	(M)	New Sound, Volume 2	1955	20.00	50.00
Capitol T-356	(M)	Bye Bye Blues	1955	20.00	50.00
Capitol T-416	(M)	The Hitmakers	1955	20.00	50.00
Capitol T-577	(M)	Les And Mary	1955	20.00	50.00
Capitol T-802	(M)	Time To Dream	1957	20.00	50.00
— Capitol albums above have turquoise or gray labels.—					
Capitol T-1476	(M)	The Hits Of Les And Mary	1960	10.00	25.00
Capitol DT-1476	(E)	The Hits Of Les And Mary	1960	8.00	20.00
— Capitol albums above have black "rainbow" labels with the logo on the left side.—					
Decca DL-8589	(M)	More Of Les	1958		50.00
Columbia CL-1276	(M)	Lover's Luau	1959	14.00	35.00
Columbia CL-1688	(M)	Warm And Wonderful	1962	10.00	25.00
Columbia CS-8488	(S)	Warm And Wonderful	1962	14.00	35.00
Columbia CL-1821	(M)	Bouquet Of Roses	1962	10.00	25.00
Columbia CS-8621	(S)	Bouquet Of Roses	1962	14.00	35.00
— Columbia albums above have three white "eye" logos on each side of the spindle hole.—					
Columbia CL-1928	(M)	Swingin' South	1963	8.00	20.00
Columbia CS-8728	(S)	Swingin' South	1963	10.00	25.00
PAUL, LOUIS					
Enterprise ENS-1034	(S)	Reflections Of The Way It Really Is	1971	6.00	150.00
PAUL & PAULA					
Phillips PHM-200-078	(M)	Paul And Paula Sing For Young Lovers	1963	12.00	30.00
Phillips PHS-600-078	(S)	Paul And Paula Sing For Young Lovers	1963	16.00	40.00
Phillips PHM-200-089	(M)	We Go Together	1963	12.00	30.00
Phillips PHS-600-089	(S)	We Go Together	1963	16.00	40.00
Phillips PHM-200-101	(M)	Holiday For Teens	1963	12.00	30.00
Phillips PHS-600-101	(S)	Holiday For Teens	1963	16.00	40.00
PAXTON, TOM					
Tom Paxton is a guitar player, singer and writer of contemporary folk-based music.					
Gaslight GV-116	(M)	I'm The Man That Built The Bridges— Recorded Live At The Gaslight Caf In Greenwich Village	1962	30.00	75.00
PAYNE, FREDA					
Impulse A-53	(M)	After The Lights Go Down Low	1963	12.00	30.00
Impulse AS-53	(S)	After The Lights Go Down Low	1963	12.00	30.00
— Impulse albums above have orange & black labels.—					
PAYNE, LEON					
Starday SLP-231	(M)	Leon Payne (Yellow label)	1963	30.00	75.00
Starday SLP-236	(M)	Americana (Yellow label)	1963	20.00	50.00
PEACE, JOE					
(No label)	(S)	Finding Peace Of Mind	1972	40.00	100.00

Label & Catalog #		Title	Year	VG+	NM
PEACHES & HERB					
Date TE-3004	(M)	**Let's Fall In Love**	1967	8.00	20.00
Date TES-4004	(S)	**Let's Fall In Love**	1967	10.00	25.00
Date TE-3005	(M)	**For Your Love**	1967	8.00	20.00
Date TES-4005	(S)	**For Your Love**	1967	10.00	25.00
PEACOCK, KENNETH					
Classically trained Canadian Kenneth Peacock is also a singer of traditional folk songs.					
Folkways FG-3505	(M)	**Songs And Ballads Of Newfoundland**	195?	12.00	30.00
PEANUT BUTTER CONSPIRACY, THE					
The Conspiracy Columbia albums were produced by Gary Usher.					
Columbia CL-2654	(M)	**Peanut Butter Conspiracy Is Spreading**	1967	10.00	25.00
Columbia CS-9495	(S)	**Peanut Butter Conspiracy Is Spreading**	1967	12.00	30.00
Columbia CL-2790	(M)	**The Great Conspiracy**	1968	12.00	30.00
Columbia CS-9590	(S)	**The Great Conspiracy**	1968	12.00	30.00
Challenge 2000	(M)	**For Children Of All Ages**	1969	12.00	30.00
PEARL, MINNIE: *Refer to* **MINNIE PEARL**					
PEARLS BEFORE SWINE					
Pearls features Tom Rapp, formerly of The Yett-Men.					
ESP-Disk' 1054	(M)	**One Nation Under Ground**	1967	20.00	50.00
ESP-Disk' 1054	(S)	**One Nation Under Ground**	1967	20.00	50.00
		(First covers for ESP 1054 are brown with a two white borders.)			
ESP-Disk' 1054	(S)	**One Nation Under Ground**	196?	16.00	40.00
		(Second covers are brown without the border.)			
ESP-Disk' 1054	(S)	**One Nation Under Ground**	196?	16.00	40.00
		(Third covers are black & white.)			
ESP-Disk' 1054	(S)	**One Nation Under Ground**	1968	12.00	30.00
		(Fourth covers are in full color.)			
ESP-Disk' 1075	(S)	**Balaklava**	1968	12.00	30.00
PECK, GREGORY					
Decca DL-8009	(M)	**Lullabye Of Christmas**	1966	8.00	20.00
Decca DL-78009	(S)	**Lullabye Of Christmas**	1966	10.00	25.00
PEDICIN, MIKE					
Apollo LP-484	(M)	**Musical Medicine**	1957	60.00	150.00
PEEL, DAVID & THE LOWER EAST SIDE					
Elektra EKS-74032	(S)	**Have A Marijuana**	1968	12.00	30.00
Elektra EKS-74069	(S)	**The American Revolution**	1970	10.00	25.00
Apple SW-3391	(S)	**The Pope Smokes Dope**	1972	30.00	75.00
		(Apple 3391 produced by John & Yoko.)			
PEELS, THE					
Karate 5402	(M)	**Juanita Banana**	1966	30.00	75.00
PEGRAM, GEORGE, & WALTER PARHAM					
Riverside RLP-12-650	(M)	**Pickin' And Blowin'**	195?	12.00	30.00
PELFREY BROTHERS, THE					
Jalyn JLP-107	(M)	**Songs That Never Grow Old**	196?	10.00	25.00
PENGUINS, THE					
Dootone DTL-204	(M)	**The Best Vocal Groups...**			
		Rhythm And Blues *(Red vinyl)*	1957		*See below*
		(Original pressings of DTL-204 are on red vinyl with flat maroon labels. Actually a various artists album, because all of side one is by The Penguins it is iften referred to as the "first Penguins album." Rare with suggested values in VG of $150-300; in VG+ of $500-750; and in NM, $1,500-2,500.)			
Dootone DTL-204	(M)	**The Best Vocal Groups... Rhythm And Blues**	1959	200.00	400.00
		(Second pressings are on black vinyl with glossy maroon labels. Counterfeits have black & white covers and multi-color labels.)			
Dooto DTL-204	(M)	**The Best Vocal Groups... Rhythm And Blues**	1959	80.00	200.00
		(Later pressings on the Dooto imprint have blue & yellow labels.)			

Label & Catalog #		Title	Year	VG+	NM
Dooto DTL-242	(M)	The Cool Cool Penguins	1959	200.00	600.00
		(Original pressings of DTL-242 have yellow & red labels.)			
Dooto DTL-242	(M)	The Cool Cool Penguins	196?	80.00	200.00
		(Later pressings have multi-color labels. Counterfeits have maroon Dootone labels and black & white covers.)			

PENNY, HANK

Audio Lab AL-1508	(M)	Hank Penny Sings	195?	80.00	200.00

PEOPLE
People features Larry Norman.

Capitol ST-2924	(S)	I Love You	1968	16.00	40.00
Capitol ST-151	(S)	Both Sides Of People	1969	16.00	40.00
Paramount PAS-5013	(S)	There Are People And There Are People	1970	10.00	25.00

PEPPER, JIM

Embryo SD-731	(S)	Pepper's Pow Wow (2 LPs)	196?	24.00	60.00

PEPPERMINT TROLLEY COMPANY, THE

Acta 8007	(M)	The Peppermint Trolley Company	1968	10.00	25.00
Acta 38007	(S)	The Peppermint Trolley Company	1968	14.00	35.00

PERKINS, CARL

Sun SLP-1225	(M)	The Dance Album Of Carl Perkins	1957	400.00	750.00
Sun SLP-1225	(M)	Teen Beat—The Best Of Carl Perkins	1961	300.00	500.00
		("Teen Beat" is a repackage of "Dance Album.")			
Columbia CL-1234	(M)	Whole Lotta Shakin' (White label promo)	1958	400.00	750.00
Columbia CL-1234	(M)	Whole Lotta Shakin'	1958	150.00	300.00
Dollie 4001	(M)	Country Boy's Dream	196?	12.00	30.00
Dollie ST-91428	(S)	Country Boy's Dream (Capitol Record Club)	196?	16.00	40.00

PERKINS, CARL, & NRBQ

Columbia CS-9981	(S)	Boppin' The Blues	1970	10.00	25.00
		— Columbia albums above have "360 Sound Stereo" labels.—			

PERKINS, TONY

Epic LN-3394	(M)	Tony Perkins	1957	20.00	50.00
RCA Victor LPM-1679	(M)	From My Heart	1958	16.00	40.00
RCA Victor LSP-1679	(S)	From My Heart	1958	24.00	60.00
RCA Victor LPM-1853	(M)	On A Rainy Afternoon	1958	16.00	40.00
RCA Victor LSP-1853	(S)	On A Rainy Afternoon	1958	24.00	60.00

PERREY, JEAN-JACQUES
French born Jean-Jacques Perrey is a composer, arranger and performer of "20th Century music," notably utilizing the Ondioline and the Moog synthesizer.

Pickwick PC-3160	(M)	The Happy Moog	196?	8.00	20.00
Pickwick SPC-3160	(S)	The Happy Moog	196?	10.00	25.00
Vanguard VSD-79286	(S)	The Amazing New Electronic Pop Sound Of Jean-Jacques Perrey	1968	14.00	35.00
Vanguard VSD-6549	(S)	Moog Indigo	1969	14.00	35.00

PERREY—KINGSLEY
Jean-Jacques Perrey and Kingsley Kingsley.

Vanguard VRS-9222	(M)	The In Sound From Way Out!	1966	10.00	25.00
Vanguard VSD-79222	(S)	The In Sound From Way Out!	1966	14.00	35.00
Vanguard VSD-6525	(S)	Kaleidoscopic Vibrations— Spotlight On The Moog	1969	10.00	25.00
Vanguard VSD-	(S)	The Best Of Perrey & Kingsley (2 LPs)	197?	10.00	25.00

PERRINE, PEP

Hideout 1003	(M)	Pep Perrine Live And In Person	196?	60.00	150.00

PERSUADERS, THE

Saturn SAT-5000	(M)	Surfer's Nightmare	1963	100.00	250.00
Saturn SATS-5000	(S)	Surfer's Nightmare	1963	175.00	350.00

PERSUASIONS, THE

Catamount CATA-905	(S)	Stardust	197?	20.00	50.00
Straight STS-6394	(S)	Acappella	1970	12.00	30.00

Label & Catalog #		Title	Year	VG+	NM

PETER & GORDON
Peter Asher and Gordon Waller.

Capitol T-2115	(M)	A World Without Love	1964	8.00	20.00
Capitol ST-2115	(S)	A World Without Love	1964	10.00	25.00
Capitol T-2220	(M)	I Don't Want To See You Again	1964	8.00	20.00
Capitol ST-2220	(S)	I Don't Want To See You Again	1964	10.00	25.00
Capitol T-2324	(M)	I Go To Pieces	1965	8.00	20.00
Capitol ST-2324	(S)	I Go To Pieces	1965	10.00	25.00
Capitol T-2368	(M)	True Love Ways	1965	8.00	20.00
Capitol ST-2368	(S)	True Love Ways	1965	10.00	25.00
Capitol T-2430	(M)	Peter & Gordon Sing The Hits Of Nashville	1966	12.00	30.00
Capitol ST-2430	(S)	Peter & Gordon Sing The Hits Of Nashville	1966	16.00	40.00
Capitol T-2477	(M)	Woman	1966	8.00	20.00
Capitol ST-2477	(S)	Woman ("Woman" is rechanneled)	1966	10.00	25.00
Capitol T-2664	(M)	Lady Godiva	1967	8.00	20.00
Capitol ST-2664	(S)	Lady Godiva	1967	10.00	25.00
Capitol T-2729	(M)	A Knight In Rusty Armour	1967	8.00	20.00
Capitol ST-2729	(S)	A Knight In Rusty Armour	1967	10.00	25.00
Capitol T-2747	(M)	In London For Tea	1967	8.00	20.00
Capitol ST-2747	(S)	In London For Tea	1967	10.00	25.00
Capitol T-2882	(M)	Hot, Cold And Custard	1968	10.00	25.00
Capitol ST-2882	(S)	Hot, Cold And Custard	1968	12.00	30.00

PETER, PAUL & MARY
Peter Yarrow, Paul Stookey and Mary Travers are a folk-based vocal and instrumental trio..

Warner Bros. W-1449	(M)	Peter, Paul & Mary	1962	8.00	20.00
Warner Bros. WS-1449	(S)	Peter, Paul & Mary	1962	10.00	25.00
Warner Bros. W-1473	(M)	Moving	1962	8.00	20.00
Warner Bros. WS-1473	(S)	Moving	1962	10.00	25.00
Warner Bros. W-1507	(M)	In The Wind	1963	8.00	20.00
Warner Bros. WS-1507	(S)	In The Wind	1963	10.00	25.00
Warner Bros. W2-1555	(M)	Peter, Paul & Mary In Concert (2 LPs)	1964	8.00	20.00
Warner Bros. W2S-1555	(S)	Peter, Paul & Mary In Concert (2 LPs)	1964	10.00	25.00
Warner Bros. W-1589	(M)	A Song Will Rise	1965	8.00	20.00
Warner Bros. WS-1589	(S)	A Song Will Rise	1965	10.00	25.00
Warner Bros. W-1615	(M)	See What Tomorrow Brings	1965	8.00	20.00
Warner Bros. WS-1615	(S)	See What Tomorrow Brings	1965	10.00	25.00

— *Warner mono albums above have grey labels; stereo albums have gold labels.* —

PETERS, BROCK

United Arts. UAL-3041	(M)	Sing'a Man	1959	10.00	25.00
United Arts. UAS-6041	(S)	Sing'a Man	1959	14.00	35.00
United Arts. UAL-3062	(M)	Brock Peters At The Villlage Gate	1959	10.00	25.00
United Arts. UAS-6062	(S)	Brock Peters At The Villlage Gate	1959	14.00	35.00

PETERSEN, PAUL
Refer to James Darren / Shelly Fabares / Paul Petersen.

Colpix CP-429	(M)	Lollipops And Roses	1962	20.00	50.00
Colpix SCP-429	(S)	Lollipops And Roses	1962	30.00	75.00
Colpix CP-442	(M)	My Dad	1963	20.00	50.00
Colpix SCP-442	(S)	My Dad	1963	30.00	75.00

PETERSON, RAY

RCA Victor LPM-2297	(M)	Tell Laura I Love Her	1960	40.00	100.00
RCA Victor LSP-2297	(S)	Tell Laura I Love Her	1960	60.00	150.00

— *RCA mono albums above have "Long Play" on the bottom of the label;*
stereo albums have "Living Stereo" on the bottom. —

MGM E-4250	(M)	The Very Best Of Ray Peterson	1964	10.00	25.00
MGM SE-4250	(S)	The Very Best Of Ray Peterson	1964	12.00	30.00
MGM E-4277	(M)	The Other Side Of Ray Peterson	1965	10.00	25.00
MGM SE-4277	(S)	The Other Side Of Ray Peterson	1965	12.00	30.00

PETTY, NORMAN
Norman Petty is better known as the producer of Buddy Holly & The Crickets and The Fireballs.

Vik LX-1073	(M)	Corsage	1957	30.00	75.00
Columbia CL-1092	(M)	Moondreams	1958	60.00	150.00

(Columbia 1092 features Buddy Holly on guitar on the title track.)

Top Rank RM-339	(M)	Petty For Your Thoughts	1960	14.00	35.00
Top Rank RS-639	(S)	Petty For Your Thoughts	1960	20.00	50.00

Label & Catalog #		Title	Year	VG+	NM

PETTY, TOM/TOM PETTY & THE HEARTBREAKERS
Refer to The Traveling Wilburys.

Shelter/ABC TP-12677	(DJ)	**Official Live 'Leg**	1976	16.00	40.00
		(One-sided with official letter to DJs. Convincing counterfeits exist.)			

PHANTOM'S DIVINE COMEDY, THE

Capitol ST-11313	(S)	**Part One**	1974	24.00	60.00

PHAPHNER

Dragon LP-101	(S)	**Overdrive**	197?		*See below*
		(Dragon 101 has a suggested Near Mint value of $1,500-2,500.)			

PHELPS, JACKIE

Starday SLP-265	(M)	**The Ten Talented Fingers**			
		Of Jackie Phelps *(Yellow label)*	1963	16.00	40.00

PHILBIN, REGIS

Mercury SR-61169	(S)	**It's Time For Regis**	1968	10.00	25.00

PHILLIPS, "LITTLE ESTHER"

King 622	(M)	**Down Memory Lane With Little Esther**	1959	1,000.00	*See below*
		(King 622 has a suggested Near Mint value of $1,500-2,500.)			
Lenox 227	(M)	**Release Me**	1962	30.00	75.00
Lenox 227	(S)	**Release Me**	1962	60.00	150.00
Atlantic 8102	(M)	**And I Love Him**	1965	12.00	30.00
Atlantic SD-8102	(S)	**And I Love Him**	1965	16.00	40.00
Atlantic 8122	(M)	**Esther**	1966	12.00	30.00
Atlantic SD-8122	(S)	**Esther**	1966	16.00	40.00
Atlantic 8130	(M)	**The Country Side Of Esther Phillips**	1966	12.00	30.00
Atlantic SD-8130	(S)	**The Country Side Of Esther Phillips**	1966	16.00	40.00
		(Atlantic 8130 is a repackage of Lenox 227.)			

PHILLIPS, GENE

Crown CLP-5375	(S)	**Gene Phillips And The Rockers**	1963	10.00	25.00
Crown CST-375	(E)	**Gene Phillips And The Rockers**	1963	4.00	10.00

PHILLIPS, JOHN
Mr. Phillips was formerly a member of The Journeymen; The Mamas & The Papas.

20th Century 4210	(DJ)	**Myra Breckinridge** *(Soundtrack)*	1970	300.00	500.00

PHILLIPS, U. UTAH
Bruce Phillips is a guitar player, singer and writer of topical material with more than a bit of humor.

Prestige Inter. PR-13040	(M)	**No One Knows Me**	1961	12.00	30.00

PHILLIPS, WARREN, & THE ROCKETS
Members of The Rockets later recorded as Foghat.

Parrot PAS-71044	(S)	**Rocked Out**	1970	12.00	30.00

PHILOSOPHERS, THE

Philo Spectrum LP-1001	(S)	**After Sundown**	1970	40.00	100.00

PHIPPS FAMILY, THE

Starday SLP-139	(M)	**The Phipps Family Sings The Most Requested**			
		Sacred Songs Of The Carter Family	1961	16.00	40.00
Starday SLP-195	(M)	**Old Time Pickin' And Singin'**	1962	16.00	40.00
Starday SLP-248	(M)	**Echoes Of The Carter Family**	1963	16.00	40.00
		— Starday albums above have yellow labels.—			

PHLUPH

Verve V-5054	(M)	**Phluph**	1968	10.00	25.00
Verve V6-5054	(S)	**Phluph**	1968	12.00	30.00

PIAF, EDITH

Decca DL-6004	(10")	**Chansons De Cafes De Paris**	1951	30.00	60.00
Columbia ML-4779	(M)	**Chansons**	1951	20.00	50.00
Columbia CL-898	(M)	**La Vie En Rose**	1956	10.00	25.00
Capitol TCL-2953	(M)	**Deluxe Set** *(3 LPs)*	1968	12.00	30.00
Capitol DTCL-2953	(E)	**Deluxe Set** *(3 LPs)*	1968	12.00	30.00

Label & Catalog #		Title	Year	VG+	NM

PIANO RED
Piano Red also recorded as Dr. Feelgood.

Groove LG-1001	(M)	**Jump Man Jump**	1956		*See below*
		("Jump Man Jump" was released only as an EP.)			
Groove LG-1002	(M)	**Piano Red In Concert**	1956	300.00	500.00
Mastersound 1116	(S)	**Dr. Feelgood Goes To College**	196?	20.00	50.00
King KS-1117	(S)	**Happiness Is Piano Red**	1970	8.00	20.00

PICKETT, BOBBY "BORIS", & THE CRYPT KICKERS

Garpax CPX-57001	(M)	**The Monster Mash**	1962	60.00	150.00
Garpax SGP-67001	(S)	**The Monster Mash**	1962	100.00	250.00
Parrott XPAS-71063	(E)	**The Original Monster Mash**	1973	10.00	25.00
		(Parrot 71063 is a reissue of Garpax 67001.)			

PICKETT, WILSON

Double-L DL-2300	(M)	**It's Too Late**	1963	16.00	40.00
Double-L SDL-8300	(S)	**It's Too Late**	1963	20.00	50.00
		("R 'n B Special" is rechanneled on this album.)			
Wand WD-672	(M)	**Great Wilson Pickett Hits**	196?	12.00	30.00
Wand WDS-672	(E)	**Great Wilson Pickett Hits**	196?	10.00	25.00
Atlantic 8114	(M)	**In The Midnight Hour**	1965	16.00	40.00
Atlantic SD-8114	(E)	**In The Midnight Hour**	1965	12.00	30.00
Atlantic 8129	(M)	**The Exciting Wilson Pickett**	1966	16.00	40.00
Atlantic SD-8129	(E)	**The Exciting Wilson Pickett**	1966	12.00	30.00
Atlantic 8138	(M)	**The Wicked Pickett**	1967	16.00	40.00
Atlantic SD-8138	(E)	**The Wicked Pickett**	1967	12.00	30.00
Atlantic 8145	(M)	**The Sound Of Wilson Pickett**	1967	16.00	40.00
Atlantic SD-8145	(P)	**The Sound Of Wilson Pickett**	1967	12.00	30.00
Atlantic 8151	(M)	**The Best Of Wilson Pickett**	1967	10.00	25.00
Atlantic SD-8151	(E)	**The Best Of Wilson Pickett**	1967	8.00	20.00
Wicked 9001	(S)	**Chocolate Mountain**	1976	10.00	25.00

PIERCE, WEBB

Decca DL-5536	(10")	**That Wondering Boy**	1953	40.00	100.00
Decca DL-8129	(M)	**Webb Pierce**	1955	20.00	50.00
Decca DL-8295	(M)	**That Wondering Boy**	1956	20.00	50.00
Decca DL-8728	(M)	**Just Imagination**	1957	16.00	40.00
Decca DL-8889	(M)	**Bound For The Kingdom**	1959	10.00	25.00
Decca DL-78889	(S)	**Bound For The Kingdom**	1959	16.00	40.00
Decca DL-8899	(M)	**Webb!**	1959	10.00	25.00
Decca DL-78899	(S)	**Webb!**	1959	16.00	40.00
		— Decca albums above have black & silver labels.—			
King 648	(M)	**The One And Only Webb Pierce**	1959	20.00	50.00
Decca DL-4015	(M)	**Webb With A Beat**	1960	8.00	20.00
Decca DL-74015	(S)	**Webb With A Beat**	1960	10.00	25.00
Decca DL-4079	(M)	**Walking The Streets**	1960	8.00	20.00
Decca DL-74079	(S)	**Walking The Streets**	1960	10.00	25.00
Decca DXB-181	(M)	**The Webb Pierce Story** *(2 LPs with book)*	1964	10.00	25.00
Decca DXSB-181	(S)	**The Webb Pierce Story** *(2 LPs with book)*	1964	12.00	30.00
Decca DXB-181	(M)	**The Webb Pierce Story** *(2 LPs without book)*	1964	8.00	20.00
Decca DXSB-7181	(S)	**The Webb Pierce Story** *(2 LPs without book)*	1964	10.00	25.00
		— Decca albums above have black labels with "Mfrd by Decca" beneath the rainbow.—			
Sears SPS-103	(E)	**I Saw Your Face In The Moon**	196?	10.00	25.00

PIERCE, WEBB / MARVIN RAINWATER / STUART HAMBLEN

Audio Lab AL-1563	(M)	**Sing For You**	1960	80.00	200.00

PIKE, PETE

Audio Lab AL-1559	(M)	**Pete Pike**	1960	80.00	200.00

PINETOPPERS, THE

Coral CRL-56200	(10")	**Square Dances**	195?	20.00	50.00

PINK FLOYD
Pink Floyd was the brainchild of Syd Barrett, who completed the first album and "retired." The other members are Nick Mason, Roger Waters, Roger Wright and Barrett's replacement, David Gilmour.

Tower T-5093	(M)	**Piper At The Gates Of Dawn** *(White label)*	1967		*See below*
		(Apparently unreleased. Should Tower 5093 exist as a white label promo, it would have a suggested NM value of $300-600.)			

Label & Catalog #		Title	Year	VG+	NM
Tower T-5093	(M)	Piper At The Gates Of Dawn	1967	60.00	150.00
Tower ST-5093	(S)	Piper At The Gates Of Dawn	1967	24.00	60.00
Tower ST-5131	(S)	A Saucerful Of Secrets (White label promo)	1968		See below
		(Apparently unreleased. Should Tower 5131 exist as a white label promo, it would have a suggested NM value of $300-600.)			
Tower ST-5131	(S)	A Saucerful Of Secrets	1968	24.00	60.00
		—Tower albums above have flat orange labels.—			
Tower ST-5093	(S)	Piper At The Gates Of Dawn	1969	20.00	50.00
Tower ST-5131	(S)	A Saucerful Of Secrets	1969	20.00	50.00
Tower ST-5169	(S)	More (Soundtrack. Promo label)	1968	60.00	150.00
Tower ST-5169	(S)	More (Soundtrack.)	1968	20.00	50.00
		—Tower albums above have multi-colored striped labels.—			
Harvest STBB-388	(S)	Ummagumma (2 LPs)	1969	16.00	40.00
		(Original covers of Harvest 388 have a copy of the "Gigi" soundtrack album leaning against the wall in the lower foreground. Later, more common covers, have "Gigi" airbrushed into blankness. . .)			
Harvest STBB-388	(S)	Ummagumma (2 LPs)	1969		See below
		(The cover has a copy of "Ummagumma" leaning against the wall. Contrary to previous listings, there appears to be no foundation to believe the rumors that this album exists.)			
Harvest SMAS-11163	(S)	The Dark Side Of The Moon	1973	10.00	25.00
		(SMAS-11163 originally issued with two posters and two stickers.)			
Capitol SPRO-8116	(DJ)	Pink Floyd Tour '75	1975	30.00	75.00
Capitol SEAX-11902	(S)	The Dark Side Of The Moon (Picture disc)	1978	12.00	30.00
Columbia PCQ-33453	(Q)	Wish You Were Here	1975	16.00	40.00
Columbia JC-34474	(S)	Animals (Promo label with insert)	1977	40.00	100.00
Columbia PCQ-34474	(Q)	Animals	1977	16.00	40.00
Columbia HC-33453	(S)	Wish You Were Here (Half-speed master)	1981	20.00	60.00
Columbia HC-43453	(S)	Wish You Were Here (Half-speed master)	1982	15.00	45.00
Columbia HC2-46183	(S)	The Wall (2 LPs. Half-speed master)	1983	50.00	150.00
Columbia AS-	(DJ)	Off The Wall	1983	30.00	75.00
Columbia HC-47680	(S)	Collection Of Great Dance Songs (Half-speed master)	1983	16.00	50.00
Mobile Fidelity MFSL-017	(S)	The Dark Side Of The Moon	1977	16.00	40.00
Mobile Fidelity MFQR-017	(S)	The Dark Side Of The Moon (UHQR box set)	1982	120.00	360.00
Mobile Fidelity MFSL-197	(S)	Meddle	198?	10.00	30.00
Mobile Fidelity MFSL-202	(S)	Atom Heart Mother	198?	10.00	30.00

PINK GRASS

(No label)	(S)	Rhubarb's Revenge	197?	300.00	500.00

PINK PUZZ: Refer to PAUL REVERE & THE RAIDERS

PIRANHAS, THE

Custom Fidelity 1452	(S)	Somethin' Fishy	1969	60.00	150.00

PISANI, FRANK

Dellwood DLD-56010	(S)	Sky	1977	40.00	100.00

PITNEY, GENE
Gene also recorded with George Jones.

Musicor MM-2001	(M)	The Many Sides Of Gene Pitney	1962	20.00	50.00
Musicor MS-3001	(E)	The Many Sides Of Gene Pitney	1962	16.00	40.00
		—Musicor albums above have brown labels.—			
Musicor MM-2001	(M)	The Many Sides Of Gene Pitney	1962	12.00	30.00
Musicor MS-3001	(E)	The Many Sides Of Gene Pitney	1962	10.00	25.00
Musicor MM-2003	(M)	Only Love Can Break A Heart	1962	12.00	30.00
Musicor MS-3003	(S)	Only Love Can Break A Heart	1962	16.00	40.00
Musicor MM-2004	(M)	Gene Pitney Sings Just For You	1963	12.00	30.00
Musicor MS-3004	(S)	Gene Pitney Sings Just For You	1963	16.00	40.00
Musicor MM-2005	(M)	Gene Pitney Sings World-Wide Winners	1963	12.00	30.00
Musicor MS-3005	(P)	Gene Pitney Sings World-Wide Winners	1963	16.00	40.00
		("Only Love Can Break A Heart," "If I Didn't Have A Dime," "The Man Who Shot Liberty Valance," "Tower Tall" and "Half Heaven-Half Heartache" are in stereo on this album.)			
Musicor MM-2006	(M)	Blue Gene	1963	12.00	30.00
Musicor MS-3006	(S)	Blue Gene	1963	16.00	40.00
Musicor MM-2007	(M)	The Fair Young Ladies Of Folkland	1964	12.00	30.00
Musicor MS-3007	(S)	The Fair Young Ladies Of Folkland	1964	16.00	40.00

Label & Catalog #		Title	Year	VG+	NM
Musicor MM-2008	(M)	Gene Pitney's Big Sixteen	1964	12.00	30.00
Musicor MS-3008	(S)	Gene Pitney's Big Sixteen	1964	16.00	40.00
		("Town Without Pity" and "Take Me Tonight" are rechanneled.)			
		— Musicor albums above have black labels with "Distributed by United Artists." —			
Musicor MM-2015	(M)	Gene Italiano	1964	10.00	25.00
Musicor MS-3015	(S)	Gene Italiano	1964	12.00	30.00
Musicor MM-2019	(M)	It Hurts To Be In Love	1964	10.00	25.00
Musicor MS-3019	(P)	It Hurts To Be In Love	1964	12.00	30.00
Musicor MM-2043	(M)	Gene Pitney's More Big Sixteen, Volume 2	1965	10.00	25.00
Musicor MS-3043	(S)	Gene Pitney's More Big Sixteen, Volume 2	1965	12.00	30.00
		("It Hurts To Be In Love," "Today's Teardrops," "Hello, Mary Lou," "Every Breath I Take" and "I Laughed So Hard I Cried" are re-channeled on this album.)			
Musicor MM-2056	(M)	I Must Be Seeing Things	1965	10.00	25.00
Musicor MS-3056	(S)	I Must Be Seeing Things	1965	12.00	30.00
Musicor MM-2069	(M)	Looking Through The Eyes Of Love	1965	10.00	25.00
Musicor MS-3069	(S)	Looking Through The Eyes Of Love	1965	12.00	30.00
Musicor MM-2072	(M)	Gene Pitney Espanol	1965	10.00	25.00
Musicor MS-3072	(S)	Gene Pitney Espanol	1965	12.00	30.00
Musicor MM-2085	(M)	Gene Pitney's Big Sixteen, Volume 3	1966	8.00	20.00
Musicor MS-3085	(S)	Gene Pitney's Big Sixteen, Volume 3	1966	10.00	25.00
Musicor MM-2095	(M)	Backstage I'm Lonely	1966	8.00	20.00
Musicor MS-3095	(S)	Backstage I'm Lonely	1966	10.00	25.00
Musicor MM-2100	(M)	Messumo Mi Puo Giudicare	1966	8.00	20.00
Musicor MS-3100	(S)	Messumo Mi Puo Giudicare	1966	10.00	25.00
Musicor MM-2101	(M)	The Gene Pitney Show	1966	8.00	20.00
Musicor MS-3101	(S)	The Gene Pitney Show	1966	10.00	25.00
Musicor MM-2102	(M)	Greatest Hits Of All Time	1966	8.00	20.00
Musicor MS-3102	(P)	Greatest Hits Of All Time	1966	10.00	25.00
		("Town Without Pity," "Every Breath I Take" and "It Hurts To Be In Love" are rechanneled this album.)			
Musicor MM-2104	(M)	The Country Side Of Gene Pitney	1966	8.00	20.00
Musicor MS-3104	(S)	The Country Side Of Gene Pitney	1966	10.00	25.00
Musicor MM-2108	(M)	Young And Warm And Wonderful	1966	8.00	20.00
Musicor MS-3108	(S)	Young And Warm And Wonderful	1966	10.00	25.00
Musicor MM-2117	(M)	Just One Smile	1967	8.00	20.00
Musicor MS-3117	(S)	Just One Smile	1967	10.00	25.00
Musicor MM-2134	(M)	Golden Greats	1967	8.00	20.00
Musicor MS-3134	(P)	Golden Greats	1967	10.00	25.00
Musicor M2S-3148	(P)	Gene Pitney Story (2 LPs with photo)	1968	14.00	35.00
Musicor M2S-3148	(P)	Gene Pitney Story (2 LPs without photo)	1968	10.00	25.00
Musicor MS-3161	(S)	Gene Pitney Sings Burt Bacharach	1968	8.00	20.00
Musicor MS-3164	(S)	She's A Heartbreaker	1968	10.00	25.00
Musicor P2S-5025	(P)	This Is Gene Pitney (2 LPs. Record Club)	1968	10.00	25.00
		— Musicor albums above have black labels. —			
PIUTE PETE & HIS COUNTRY COUSINS					
Folkways FP-1	(10")	Square Dances	195?	20.00	50.00
Folkways FA-2001	(10")	Square Dances	195?	20.00	50.00
PIXIES, THE					
Elektra PR-8127	(DJ)	The Pixies Live (One sided)	1989	20.00	50.00
PIXIES THREE, THE					
Mercury MG-20912	(M)	Party With The Pixies Three	1964	40.00	100.00
Mercury SR-60912	(P)	Party With The Pixies Three	1964	60.00	150.00
PLAIN JANE					
Hobbit 5000	(S)	Plain Jane	1969	10.00	25.00
PLASTER CASTERS, THE					
Bluestime BTS-9001	(S)	The Plaster Casters Blues Band	1969	20.00	50.00

PLATTERS, THE

The original Platters feature Tony Williams.

Federal 295-549	(10")	The Platters	1956		See below

(Contrary to the statement in the previous edition of this book, Federal 549 does exist, although it is rare with suggested values in VG of $200-400; in VG+ of 500-600; and in NM of $1,000-1,500.)

Label & Catalog #		Title	Year	VG+	NM
King 395-549	(M)	The Platters	1956		See below
		(King 549 has a suggested Near Mint value of $500-1,000.)			
King 651	(M)	Only You	1959	200.00	500.00
		(King 651 is a reissue of Federal 549.)			
Mercury MG-20146	(M)	The Platters	1956	50.00	100.00
Mercury MG-20216	(M)	The Platters, Volume 2	1956	40.00	100.00
Mercury MG-20298	(M)	Flying Platters	1957	40.00	100.00
Mercury MG-20366	(M)	Flying Platters Around The World	1959	16.00	40.00
Mercury SR-60043	(S)	Flying Platters Around The World	1959	40.00	100.00
Mercury MG-20410	(M)	Remember When?	1959	16.00	40.00
Mercury SR-60087	(S)	Remember When?	1959	40.00	100.00
Mercury MG-20472	(M)	Encore Of Golden Hits	1960	12.00	30.00
Mercury SR-60243	(P)	Encore Of Golden Hits	1960	16.00	40.00
Mercury MG-20481	(M)	Reflections	1960	12.00	30.00
Mercury SR-60160	(S)	Reflections	1960	16.00	40.00
Mercury MG-20589	(M)	Life Is Just A Bowl Of Cherries	1960	12.00	30.00
Mercury SR-60245	(S)	Life Is Just A Bowl Of Cherries	1960	16.00	40.00
Mercury MG-20591	(M)	More Encore Of Golden Hits	1960	12.00	30.00
Mercury SR-60252	(S)	More Encore Of Golden Hits	1960	16.00	40.00
Mercury MG-20613	(M)	Encore Of Broadway Golden Hits	1961	12.00	30.00
Mercury SR-60613	(S)	Encore Of Broadway Golden Hits	1961	16.00	40.00
Mercury MG-20669	(M)	Song For The Lonely	1962	12.00	30.00
Mercury SR-60669	(S)	Song For The Lonely	1962	16.00	40.00
Mercury MG-20759	(M)	Moonlight Memories	1963	12.00	30.00
Mercury SR-60759	(S)	Moonlight Memories	1963	16.00	40.00
Mercury MG-20782	(M)	The Platters Present All-Time Movie Hits	1963	12.00	30.00
Mercury SR-60782	(S)	The Platters Present All-Time Movie Hits	1963	16.00	40.00
Mercury MG-20808	(M)	The Platters Sing Latino	1963	12.00	30.00
Mercury SR-60808	(S)	The Platters Sing Latino	1963	16.00	40.00
Mercury MG-20841	(M)	Christmas With The Platters	1963	12.00	30.00
Mercury SR-60841	(S)	Christmas With The Platters	1963	16.00	40.00
Mercury MG-20893	(M)	Encore Of Golden Hits Of The Groups	1964	12.00	30.00
Mercury SR-60893	(S)	Encore Of Golden Hits Of The Groups	1964	16.00	40.00
Mercury MG-20933	(M)	10th Anniversary Album	1964	10.00	25.00
Mercury SR-60933	(S)	10th Anniversary Album	1964	12.00	30.00
		— Mercury albums above have black & silver labels. —			
Mercury MG-20983	(M)	The New Soul Of The Platters	1965	8.00	20.00
Mercury SR-60983	(S)	The New Soul Of The Platters	1965	10.00	25.00
PLAYBACKS, THE					
Round LP-1111	(M)	Greatest Of The Latest	196?	30.00	75.00
PLAYERS, THE					
Minit 40006	(M)	He'll Be Back	1966	10.00	25.00
Minit 24006	(S)	He'll Be Back	1966	12.00	30.00
PLAYMATES, THE					
Roulette R-25001	(M)	Calypso	1958	8.00	20.00
Roulette SR-25001	(S)	Calypso	1958	10.00	25.00
Roulette R-25043	(M)	At Play With The Playmates	1958	8.00	20.00
Roulette SR-25043	(S)	At Play With The Playmates	1958	10.00	25.00
Roulette R-25059	(M)	Rock And Roll Record Hop	1959	8.00	20.00
Roulette SR-25059	(S)	Rock And Roll Record Hop	1959	10.00	25.00
Roulette R-25068	(M)	Cuttin' Capers	1959	8.00	20.00
Roulette SR-25068	(S)	Cuttin' Capers	1959	10.00	25.00
Roulette R-25084	(M)	Broadway Show Stoppers	1959	8.00	20.00
Roulette SR-25084	(S)	Broadway Show Stoppers	1959	10.00	25.00
PLIMSOULS, THE					
Beat BE-1001	(S)	Zero Hour	1980	10.00	25.00
POINT, THE					
Rad Lab 1045	(S)	The Point *(10" on white vinyl)*	1981	30.00	75.00
POITIER, SIDNEY					
Warner Bros. W-1561	(M)	Poitier Reads Plato	1965	10.00	25.00
Warner Bros. WS-1561	(S)	Poitier Reads Plato	1965	12.00	30.00

Label & Catalog #		Title	Year	VG+	NM
Warner Bros. W-1740	(M)	Journeys Inside The Mind	1968	8.00	20.00
Warner Bros. WS-1740	(S)	Journeys Inside The Mind	1968	10.00	25.00
		(Warner Bros. 1740 is a reissue of 1561.)			
United Art.s UAS-6693	(S)	Sidney Poitier Reads Poetry Of The Black Man	1969	10.00	25.00

POLICE

A&M SP-3735	(S)	Synchronicity (Brown & grey cover)	1983	12.00	30.00
A&M SP-3735	(S)	Synchronicity (Black & white cover)	1983	20.00	50.00
Nautilus NR-40	(S)	Ghost In The Machine	198?	8.00	25.00
Nautilus NR-40	(S)	Ghost In The Machine (DBX)	198?	10.00	30.00

POLK, LUCY ANN: *Refer to* GOLDMINE'S PRICE GUIDE TO COLLECTIBLE JAZZ ALBUMS

POLLUTION
Pollution features Dobie Gray.

Prophecy SD-6051	(S)	Pollution	1971	12.00	30.00
Prophecy SD-6057	(S)	Pollution II	1972	12.00	30.00

PONCE, PONCIE

Warner Bros. W-1453	(M)	Poncie Ponce Sings	1962	8.00	20.00
Warner Bros. WS-1453	(S)	Poncie Ponce Sings	1962	10.00	25.00

PONTY, JEAN LUC

World Pacific WPS-20172	(S)	King Kong/Ponty Plays Zappa	1970	10.00	25.00
		(Although uncredited, Frank Zappa produces and plays guitar.)			

POOBAH

Peppermint	(S)	Let Me In	1969	200.00	400.00
Peppermint	(S)	U.S. Rock	1969	60.00	150.00
Peppermint	(S)	Steamroller	1969	60.00	150.00

POOLE, BILLIE: *Refer to* GOLDMINE'S PRICE GUIDE TO COLLECTIBLE JAZZ ALBUMS

POOLE, BRIAN, & THE TREMELOES

Audio Fidelity AF-2151	(M)	Brian Poole Is Here	1966	12.00	30.00
Audio Fidelity AFS-6151	(E)	Brian Poole Is Here	1966	10.00	25.00
Audio Fidelity AF-2177	(M)	The Tremeloes Are Here	1967	10.00	25.00
Audio Fidelity AFS-6177	(E)	The Tremeloes Are Here	1967	8.00	20.00
		(Audio Fidelity 2177 is a reissue of 2151.)			

POPCORN BLIZZARD, THE

De-Lite DE-2004	(S)	Explode!	1968	14.00	35.00

PORTER, PEPPER

First American FA-7756	(S)	Invasion	197?	10.00	25.00

POWELL, DICK

Decca DL-8837	(S)	Song Book	1958	20.00	50.00
Dot DLP-3421	(M)	Themes From Original TV Soundtracks	1962	12.00	30.00
Dot DLP-25421	(S)	Themes From Original TV Soundtracks	1962	16.00	40.00
Columbia C2L-44	(M)	Dick Powell In Hollywood (2 LPs)	1966	8.00	20.00
Columbia C2S-44	(S)	Dick Powell In Hollywood (2 LPs)	1966	10.00	25.00

POWELL, JANE
Refer to Gordon MacRae; Marilyn Monroe.

Columbia CL-2034	(10")	Romance	1949	40.00	100.00
Columbia CL-2045	(10")	A Date With Jane Powell	1949	40.00	100.00
Columbia ML-4148	(M)	Alice In Wonderland	1950	40.00	100.00
MGM E-508	(10")	Nancy Goes To Rio (Soundtrack)	1950	40.00	100.00
MGM E-530	(10")	Two Weeks With Love (Soundtrack)	1950	40.00	100.00
MGM E-543	(10")	Royal Wedding (Soundtrack)	1951	40.00	100.00
MGM E-86	(10")	Rich, Young And Pretty (Soundtrack)	1951	40.00	100.00
Mercury MG-25202	(M)	Athena (Soundtrack)	1954	80.00	200.00
MGM E-224	(10")	7 Brides For 7 Brothers (Soundtrack)	1954	40.00	100.00
MGM E-3233	(M)	Two Weeks With Love (Soundtrack)	1955	20.00	50.00
MGM E-3236	(M)	Rich, Young And Pretty (Soundtrack)	1955	20.00	50.00
MGM E-3451	(M)	Something Wonderful	1957	16.00	40.00
Verve V-2023	(M)	Can't We Be Friends?	1956	14.00	35.00

Label & Catalog #		Title	Year	VG+	NM

POWER & THE MAJESTY, THE

Mobile Fidelity MFSL-004	(S)	**The Power And The Majesty**	1979	**13.00**	**40.00**
		(Thunder storm and railroad sound effects.)			

PRADO, PREZ

RCA Victor LPM-3108	(10")	**Mambo By The King**	1953	**24.00**	**60.00**
RCA Victor LPM-1075	(M)	**Mambo Mania**	1955	**20.00**	**50.00**
RCA Victor LPM-1101	(M)	**Voodoo Suite (& Six All Time Greats)**	1955	**20.00**	**50.00**
RCA Victor LPM-1196	(M)	**Mambo By The King**	1956	**20.00**	**50.00**
RCA Victor LPM-1257	(M)	**Havana 3 A.M.**	1956	**20.00**	**50.00**
RCA Victor LPM-1459	(M)	**Latin Satin**	1957	**20.00**	**50.00**
RCA Victor LPM-1556	(M)	**Prez**	1958	**12.00**	**30.00**
RCA Victor LPM-1556	(M)	**Prez**	1958	**16.00**	**40.00**
RCA Victor LPM-1883	(M)	**Dilo Ugh!**	1958	**12.00**	**30.00**
RCA Victor LPM-1883	(M)	**Dilo Ugh!**	1958	**16.00**	**40.00**
RCA Victor LPM-2028	(M)	**Pops And Prado**	1959	**12.00**	**30.00**
RCA Victor LPM-2028	(M)	**Pops And Prado**	1959	**16.00**	**40.00**
RCA Victor LPM-2104	(M)	**Big Hits By Prado**	1959	**12.00**	**30.00**
RCA Victor LSP-2104	(P)	**Big Hits By Prado**	1959	**16.00**	**40.00**
RCA Victor LPM-2133	(M)	**A Touch Of Tobasco**	1960	**8.00**	**20.00**
RCA Victor LPM-2133	(S)	**A Touch Of Tobasco**	1960	**12.00**	**30.00**
		(RCA 2133 also features Rosemary Clooney.)			
RCA Victor LPM-2308	(M)	**Rockambo**	1961	**8.00**	**20.00**
RCA Victor LSP-2308	(S)	**Rockambo**	1961	**12.00**	**30.00**
RCA Victor LPM-2379	(M)	**The New Dance La Chunga**	1961	**8.00**	**20.00**
RCA Victor LPM-2379	(S)	**The New Dance La Chunga**	1961	**12.00**	**30.00**
RCA Victor LPM-2524	(M)	**The Twist Goes Latin**	1962	**8.00**	**20.00**
RCA Victor LSP-2524	(S)	**The Twist Goes Latin**	1962	**12.00**	**30.00**
RCA Victor LPM-2571	(M)	**Exotic Suite**	1962	**8.00**	**20.00**
RCA Victor LPM-2571	(S)	**Exotic Suite**	1962	**12.00**	**30.00**
RCA Victor LPM-2610	(M)	**Our Man In Latin America**	1963	**8.00**	**20.00**
RCA Victor LSP-2610	(S)	**Our Man In Latin America**	1963	**12.00**	**30.00**

"RCA mono albums above have "Long Play" on the bottom of the label; stereo albums have "Living Stereo" on the bottom.—

PREMIERS, THE

Warner Bros. W-1565	(M)	**Farmer John**	1964	**16.00**	**40.00**
Warner Bros. WS-1565	(S)	**Farmer John**	1964	**20.00**	**50.00**

PRESLEY, ELVIS

Elvis Aron Presley is the single most collectible artist in all of recorded music. With few exceptions, each of Elvis' albums remained in print through the vinyl era. For this third edition, the listings were expanded for those albums issued prior to 1965 to include each of the mono and stereo label variations for RCA's classic black label with Nipper on top listening to "his master's voice." Beginning with LPM-4088 and continuing through 4445, original pressings have orange labels and were pressed on thick, non-flexible vinyl. These were reissued with identical labels but on flimsy, flexible vinyl in 1971-73.

Similarly, Camden CAS-2304 through 2428 were pressed on the non-flexible vinyl and also reissued on the flexible vinyl. The flexible issues of the RCA and the Camden reissues are worth 50-60% of the non-flexible prices. (Each of the Camden titles were reissued by Pickwick when it took over the line in 1975. These Pickwick reissues have little collector value.)

RCA switched to a babypoo brown label in 1975 and back to a "new" black label, with Nipper in the upper right, in the late '70s. The values for these vary dramatically and are not listed here; for more information on where to acquire data for these records, refer to the main introduction of this book.

Very few records prior to the early 1960s were factory sealed; a shrink-wrapped Presley LP prior to 2231 must be a re-seal. During the 1960s, it was common practice for RCA to have millions of covers printed at once (saving money on a per unit cost) and then using the jackets as the demand arose. Consequently, it's possible that a first pressing jacket could as easily hold a second or third pressing record as a first. So, as a rule of thumb, mono covers prior to 2756 could conceivably hold a first ("Long Play" at the bottom of the label), second ("Mono") or third ("Monaural") pressing album. Any sealed mono album after 2756 must hold a first pressing album with the "Monaural" label.

With stereo albums, there are some first pressing covers that only held original LPs, and there are some stereo jackets that were printed in the mid '60s and used into the 1970s. Albums initially issued from 1969-70 (4088 through 4460) found sealed can be determined by attempting to carefully "bend" the record: If the disc inside is non-flexible, it's an original. But, if the disc is flexible, it may be any number of

Label & Catalog #	Title	Year	VG+	NM

pressings. *Certain Elvis albums that only saw a single pressing with the original prefix (APL1-0283 and APL1-0388) are reasonably safe bets as being original. These "safe bets," both mono and stereo, generally command little more than twice the listed Near Mint value. Otherwise, the wise Elvis investor is better off seeing what he is buying.*

While the listings here are more than adequate for most dealers and collectors to assess their acquisitions, they may be less than so for the completist. For the true Elvis collector, or the dealer who caters to such collectors' needs, I recommend my own A Touch Of Gold: The American Record Collectors Price Guide To Elvis Presley Records & Memorabilia. This book is 8 1/2" x 11" with 350 pages containing nearly 5,000 listings covering singles, EPs, LPs, tapes, compact discs, sheet music and RCA released memorabilia. A Touch Of Gold is available for $20.00 (includes postage and handling) from: White Dragon Press, 33309 Santiago Road, Suite 16, Acton, CA 91350.

Everything Elvis released in the '50s was cut "live" in the studio in mono. (Although during January 1957, when RCA's regular back-up tape machine was inoperative, they used one of their new two-track recorders on Elvis. The binaural results are available on Stereo 57 (Essential Elvis, Volume 2). All other appearances of Elvis' '50s recordings on stereo albums are [hideously] rechanneled. This includes several tracks first issued in the '60s: "Tomorrow Night," "When It Rains, It Really Pours," "Ain't That Loving You, Baby" and "Your Cheatin' Heart."

The following soundtrack songs have not been released in stereo in their original versions:: "In My Way," "Forget Me Never," "I Slipped, I Stumbled, I Fell," and the single versions of "Wild In The Country" and "Lonely Man" (from Wild In The Country, 1960); "Follow That Dream," "What A Wonderful Life," "I'm Not The Marrying Kind," "A Whistling Tune," and "Sound Advice" (from Follow That Dream, 1961); "King Of The Whole Wide World," "This Is Living," "Riding The Rainbow," "Home Is Where The Heart Is," "I Got Lucky," and "A Whistling Tune" (from Kid Galahad, 1961); "Mama" (from Girls, Girls, Girls, 1962): and "Stay Away" and "Stay Away, Joe" (from Stay Away, Joe, 1967).

The sessions held in NBC's Burbank studios in June 1968, used as the basis for the '68 TV Special, were recorded in mono. Aside from the soundtrack from the special (LPM-4088), these astounding recordings have been scattered to the wind on various and sundry compilations, primarily the "Legendary Performer" series.

Section 1. lists those albums issued by RCA Victor. The albums originally issued on the classic RCA black label with Nipper on top are followed through their many black label permutations. Reissues from 1968-1970 first appeared on stiff, non-flexible vinyl; these are worth approximately $25-40. They were then reissued in the early '70s with the same orange label on the flimsily flexible vinyl common to the time; these are worth $15-30. This was followed by a light brown label ($10-20) and, finally, the "new" black label where Nipper is in the upper right ($10-15). These albums often are the staples of used-shops and are not listed, although many are difficult to find for the Presley completist.

Section 2. collects albums were issued promotionally that are entirely Elvis. Any RCA promotional sampler with an Elvis track has some value; several are listed in the Various Artists section of this book. Section 3. lists RCA's Camden budget subsidiary. Section 4. lists albums issued through the RCA Record Club Releases or leased to such mail-order outlets as Reader's Digest and Candlelite Music.

Regarding the musicians that played with Elvis: On his first Sun recordings, he was backed by Scotty Moore on lead guitar and Bill Black on stand-up bass. They were eventually was joined by drummer D.J. Fontana for the later Sun sides. It was this quartet that was the backbone of his recordings for RCA through the '50s, although he also had the occasional services of such luminaries as Chet Atkins, guitar, and pianists Floyd Cramer and Dudley Brooks. For his first sessions of the '60s—that make up Elvis Is Back" and half of "Golden Records, Volume 3," he assembled a veritable supergroup consisting of Moore, Fontana and Cramer along with bassists Hank Garland and Bob Moore, second drummer Buddy Harman, and Boots Randolph on sax. Many other session musicians eventually found their way into Elvis' camp, including Hal Blaine and Barney Kessell in Hollywood and Jerry Kennedy, Billy Strange and Charlie McCoy in Nashville.. From 1969-77, the centerpiece of his band in and out of the studio was guitar player James Burton. And, through all of this, he was most ably backed by the gospel-tinged doo-wopping of The Jordanaires, with whom he recorded through 1966.

In the wake of Elvis' death in August 1977, pressing plant employees working for RCA around the country took it upon themselves to create their own collectibles by squeezing a little colored vinyl into the molds they were tending, producing a limited edition of one or two copies for themselves. Several titles exist on the brown label, the later black label with Nipper in the upper right, and on the Pickwick reissues of the original Camden titles. Exactly which titles—and how many of each were pressed—is unknown (and may, in fact, never be known). But each album on colored vinyl carries a suggested Near Mint value of $400-800 each.

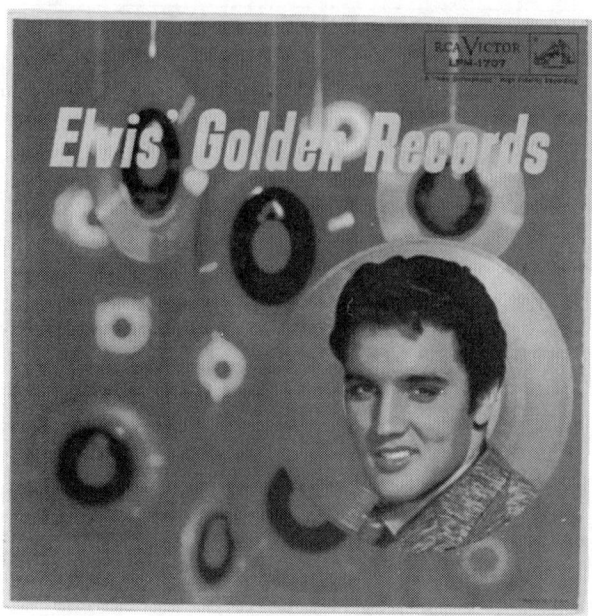

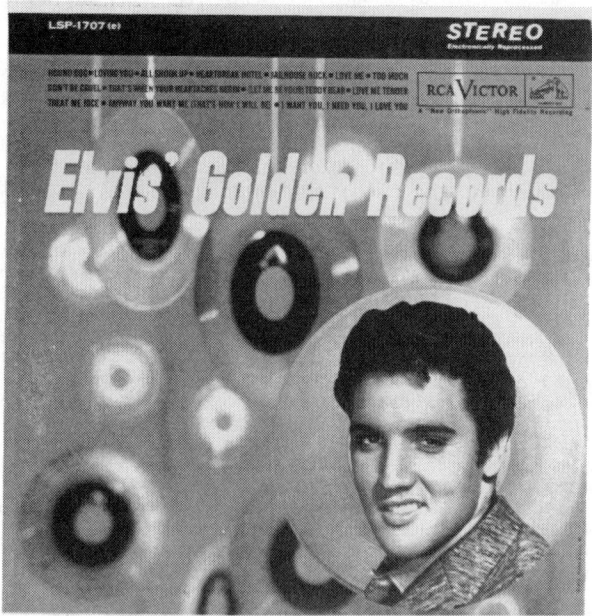

Original pressings of Elvis' Golden Records *from the '50s had the title in light blue print (above); later pressings (below) changed the print to white print and added the song titles in a black border at the cover's top. As for Elvis' golden records, during his career RCA Victor released over 70 catalog albums of studio recording, hit packages (including two boxed sets of four LPs each), soundtracks and live outings plus ten budget compilations. Of these, 75 made the charts and 36 received RIAA Gold Records during his career. An additional eight releases have gone gold since his death.*

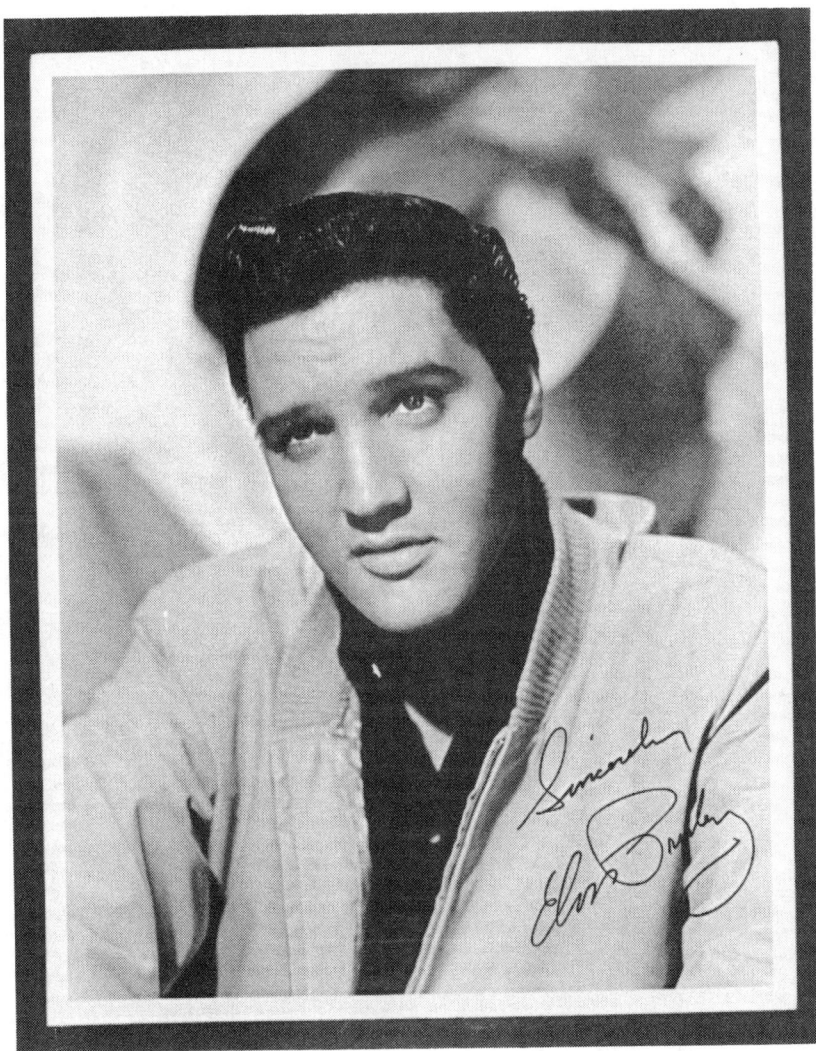

This bonus photo accompanied first pressings of Elvis' Gold Records, Vol. 4 in 1968 and for reasons not known, was printed in dramatically smaller quantities than was usual for the by then common bonus photo scam used by RCA and the Colonel to help boost Presley's sagging '60s sales. In fact, this is so rare that many Elvis fans have never seen one!

Label & Catalog #		Title	Year	VG+	NM

Many of the albums listed as soundtracks contain versions of the movie songs rerecorded for commercial release. Also, many albums were issued with bonus photos; these are listed after the first pressings.

Finally, the Presley completist will often pay extraordinary prices for anything with Elvis on it. Hence, virtually any various artist album with at least one Elvis track will have some value to these collectors. Several of these— those with exceptional value— are noted in the RCA Victor section of the Various Artists chapter at the end of the book.

1. RCA Victor 1955-1977

Label & Catalog #		Title	Year	VG+	NM
RCA Victor LPM-1254	(M)	**Elvis Presley**	1956	100.00	300.00
		(Black label with "Long Play" on the bottom. Original covers for LPM-1254 have "Elvis" on the front cover in pale pink letters.)			
RCA Victor LPM-1254	(M)	**Elvis Presley**	1956	60.00	150.00
		(Black label with "Long Play" on the bottom. On the cover of this and all subsequent pressings, "Elvis" is in dark pink letters.)			
RCA Victor LPM-1254C	(M)	**Elvis Presley**	1956		See below
		(Black label with all silver print, including Nipper on top. "33" is in a triangle on the bottom of the label with "Recco BIEM" in a box on the right side. This was manufactured in the U.S. for export to West Germany, possibly to U.S. military personnel. Rare with a suggested Near Mint value of $300-600.)			
RCA Victor LPM-1254	(M)	**Elvis Presley**	1963	24.00	60.00
		(Black label with "Mono" on the bottom.)			
RCA Victor LPM-1254	(M)	**Elvis Presley**	1965	20.00	50.00
		(Black label with "Monaural" on the bottom.)			
RCA Victor LSP-1254	(E)	**Elvis Presley**	1962	24.00	60.00
		(Black label with a silver "RCA Victor" on top and "Stereo Electronically Reprocessed" on the bottom.)			
RCA Victor LSP-1254	(E)	**Elvis Presley**	1969	12.00	30.00
		(Orange label on non-flexible vinyl.)			
RCA Victor LSP-1254	(E)	**Elvis Presley**	1965	16.00	40.00
		(Black label with a white "RCA Victor" on top and "Stereo Electronically Reprocessed" on the bottom.)			
RCA Victor LPM-1382	(M)	**Elvis**	1956	100.00	250.00
		(Black label with "Long Play" on the bottom. Original covers for LPM-1382 have ads for other albums along the border of the back.)			
RCA Victor LPM-1382	(M)	**Elvis**	1956	80.00	200.00
		(Black label with "Long Play" on the bottom. On this and all subsequent pressings the ads on the back cover have been expunged.)			
RCA Victor LPM-1382	(M)	**Elvis**	1956	300.00	600.00
		(Black label with "Long Play" on the bottom. The label prefixes each track with "Band 1" through "Band 6.")			
RCA Victor LPM-1382	(M)	**Elvis**	195?		See below
		(Black label with "Long Play" on the bottom. Some later pressings contain an alternate take of "Old Shep" in which Elvis sings "he grew old and his eyes were fast growing dim." All other pressings have a version in which Elvis sings "he grew old... his eyes were fast growing dim." Copies with the matrix number in the trail-off vinyl ending with either "15S," "17S" and "19S" have thus far been identified. Rare with a suggested Near Mint value of $1,000-2,000.)			
RCA Victor LPM-1382	(M)	**Elvis**	1963	24.00	60.00
		(Black label with "Mono" on the bottom.)			
RCA Victor LPM-1382	(M)	**Elvis**	1965	20.00	50.00
		(Black label with "Monaural" on the bottom.)			
RCA Victor LSP-1382	(E)	**Elvis**	1962	24.00	60.00
		(Black label with a silver "RCA Victor" on top and "Stereo Electronically Reprocessed" on the bottom.)			
RCA Victor LSP-1382	(E)	**Elvis**	1969	12.00	30.00
		(Orange label on non-flexible vinyl.)			
RCA Victor LSP-1382	(E)	**Elvis**	1965	16.00	40.00
		(Black label with a white "RCA Victor" on top and "Stereo Electronically Reprocessed" on the bottom.)			
RCA Victor LPM-1515	(M)	**Loving You** *(Soundtrack)*	1957	80.00	200.00
		(Black label with "Long Play" on the bottom.)			
RCA Victor LPM-1515	(M)	**Loving You** *(Soundtrack)*	1963	24.00	60.00
		(Black label with "Mono" on the bottom.)			

Label & Catalog #		Title	Year	VG+	NM
RCA Victor LPM-1515	(M)	**Loving You** (Soundtrack)	1965	20.00	50.00
		(Black label with "Monaural" on the bottom.)			
RCA Victor LSP-1515	(E)	**Loving You** (Soundtrack)	1962	24.00	60.00
		(Black label with a silver "RCA Victor" on top and			
		"Stereo Electronically Reprocessed" on the bottom.)			
RCA Victor LSP-1515	(E)	**Loving You** (Soundtrack)	1965	16.00	40.00
		(Black label with a white "RCA Victor" on top and			
		"Stereo Electronically Reprocessed" on the bottom.)			
RCA Victor LSP-1515	(E)	**Loving You** (Soundtrack)	1969	12.00	30.00
		(Orange label on non-flexible vinyl.)			
RCA Victor LOC-1035	(M)	**Elvis' Christmas Album**	1957	800.00	1,200.00
		(Original copies of LOC-1035 was issued a special "gift certificate"			
		sticker. This may have been affixed to the cover or to the loose			
		plastic bag in which some distributors packaged the album.)			
RCA Victor LOC-1035	(M)	**Elvis' Christmas Album**	1957	300.00	600.00
		(Without the "gift certificate" sticker.)			
RCA Victor LPM-1707	(M)	**Elvis' Golden Records**	1958	60.00	150.00
		(Black label with "Long Play" on the bottom. Original covers			
		have the title on the front in light blue print.)			
RCA Victor LPM-1707	(M)	**Elvis' Golden Records**	1959	40.00	100.00
		(Black label with "Long Play" on the bottom. Second covers have the			
		title on the front in light blue print but have "RE" on the back cover.)			
RCA Victor LPM-1707	(M)	**Elvis' Golden Records**	1963	24.00	60.00
		(Black label with "Mono" on the bottom. On this and all subsequent			
		mono and stereo pressings the title on the cover is in white print.)			
RCA Victor LPM-1707	(M)	**Elvis' Golden Records**	1965	20.00	50.00
		(Black label with "Monaural" on the bottom.)			
RCA Victor LSP-1707	(E)	**Elvis' Golden Records**	1962	24.00	60.00
		(Black label with a silver "RCA Victor" on top and			
		"Stereo Electronically Reprocessed" on the bottom.)			
RCA Victor LSP-1707	(E)	**Elvis' Golden Records**	1965	16.00	40.00
		(Black label with a white "RCA Victor" on top and			
		"Stereo Electronically Reprocessed" on the bottom.)			
RCA Victor LSP-1707	(E)	**Elvis' Golden Records**	1969	12.00	30.00
		(Orange label on non-flexible vinyl.)			
RCA Victor LPM-1884	(M)	**King Creole** (Soundtrack)	1958	60.00	150.00
		(Black label with "Long Play" on the bottom.)			
RCA Victor 1884		**King Creole Bonus Photo**	1963	60.00	150.00
RCA Victor LPM-1884	(M)	**King Creole** (Soundtrack)	1963	24.00	60.00
		(Black label with "Mono" on the bottom.)			
RCA Victor LPM-1884	(M)	**King Creole** (Soundtrack)	1965	20.00	50.00
		(Black label with "Monaural" on the bottom.)			
RCA Victor LSP-1884	(E)	**King Creole** (Soundtrack)	1962	24.00	60.00
		(Black label with a silver "RCA Victor" on top and			
		"Stereo Electronically Reprocessed" on the bottom.)			
RCA Victor LSP-1884	(E)	**King Creole** (Soundtrack)	1965	16.00	40.00
		(Black label with a white "RCA Victor" on top and			
		"Stereo Electronically Reprocessed" on the bottom.)			
RCA Victor LSP-1884	(E)	**King Creole** (Soundtrack)	1969	12.00	30.00
		(Orange label on non-flexible vinyl.)			
RCA Victor LPM-1951	(M)	**Elvis' Christmas Album**	1958	40.00	100.00
		(Black label with "Long Play" on the bottom.			
		RCA 1951 is a reissue of 1035.)			
RCA Victor LPM-1951	(M)	**Elvis' Christmas Album**	1963	24.00	60.00
		(Black label with "Mono" on the bottom.)			
RCA Victor LPM-1951	(M)	**Elvis' Christmas Album**	1965	20.00	50.00
		(Black label with "Monaural" on the bottom.)			
RCA Victor LSP-1951	(E)	**Elvis' Christmas Album**	1965	20.00	50.00
		(Black label with a white "RCA Victor" on top and			
		"Stereo Electronically Reprocessed" on the bottom.)			
RCA Victor LSP-1951	(E)	**Elvis' Christmas Album**	1969	20.00	50.00
		(Orange label on non-flexible vinyl.)			
RCA Victor LPM-1990	(M)	**For LP Fans Only**	1959	80.00	200.00
		(Black label with "Long Play" on the bottom. On this and all			
		subsequent mono isues except one noted below, the back			
		cover has a photo of Elvis in uniform.)			

Label & Catalog #		Title	Year	VG+	NM
RCA Victor LPM-1990	(M)	**For LP Fans Only**	1963	**24.00**	**60.00**
		(Black label with "Mono" on the bottom.)			
RCA Victor LPM-1990	(M)	**For LP Fans Only**	1965	**20.00**	**50.00**
		(Black label with "Monaural" on the bottom.)			
RCA Victor LPM-1990	(M)	**For LP Fans Only**	1965	**150.00**	**300.00**
		(Black label with "Monaural" on the bottom. Misprinting with the same photo of Elvis on the back cover as the front.)			
RCA Victor LSP-1990	(E)	**For LP Fans Only**	1965	**20.00**	**50.00**
		(Black label with a white "RCA Victor" on top and "Stereo Electronically Reprocessed" on the bottom. On this and all subsequent stereo issues except one noted below, the back cover has a photo of Elvis in uniform.)			
RCA Victor LSP-1990	(E)	**For LP Fans Only**	1965	**150.00**	**300.00**
		(Black label with a white "RCA Victor" on top and "Stereo Electronically Reprocessed" on the bottom. Misprinting with the same photo of Elvis on the back cover as the front.)			
RCA Victor LSP-1990	(E)	**For LP Fans Only**	1969	**16.00**	**40.00**
		(Orange label on non-flexible vinyl.)			
RCA Victor LPM-2011	(M)	**A Date With Elvis** *(With sticker)*	1959	**150.00**	**300.00**
RCA Victor LPM-2011	(M)	**A Date With Elvis** *(Without sticker)*	1959	**80.00**	**200.00**
		(Black label with "Long Play" on the bottom. LPM-2011 was originally issued in a gatefold jacket without the song titles printed on the front. The back cover has a 1960 calendar. Most copies have a red sticker affixed to the front that reads "Never Before On LP" and lists the ten song titles.)			
RCA Victor LPM-2011	(M)	**A Date With Elvis**	1963	**24.00**	**60.00**
		(Black label with "Mono" on the bottom.)			
RCA Victor LPM-2011	(M)	**A Date With Elvis**	1965	**20.00**	**50.00**
		(Black label with "Monaural" on the bottom.)			
RCA Victor LSP-2011	(E)	**A Date With Elvis**	1965	**16.00**	**40.00**
		(Black label with a white "RCA Victor" on top and "Stereo Electronically Reprocessed" on the bottom.)			
RCA Victor LSP-2011	(E)	**A Date With Elvis**	1969	**16.00**	**40.00**
		(Orange label on non-flexible vinyl.)			
RCA Victor LPM-2075	(M)	**Elvis' Gold Records, Volume 2**	1960	**60.00**	**150.00**
		(Black label with "Long Play" on the bottom.)			
RCA Victor LPM-2075	(M)	**Elvis' Gold Records, Volume 2**	1963	**24.00**	**60.00**
		(Black label with "Mono" on the bottom.)			
RCA Victor LPM-2075	(M)	**Elvis' Gold Records, Volume 2**	1965	**20.00**	**50.00**
		(Black label with "Monaural" on the bottom.)			
RCA Victor LSP-2075	(E)	**Elvis' Gold Records, Volume 2**	1962	**24.00**	**60.00**
		(Black label with a silver "RCA Victor" on top and "Stereo Electronically Reprocessed" on the bottom.)			
RCA Victor LSP-2075	(E)	**Elvis' Gold Records, Volume 2**	1965	**16.00**	**40.00**
		(Black label with a white "RCA Victor" on top and "Stereo Electronically Reprocessed" on the bottom.)			
RCA Victor LSP-2075	(E)	**Elvis' Gold Records, Volume 2**	1969	**12.00**	**30.00**
		(Orange label on non-flexible vinyl.)			
RCA Victor LPM-2231	(M)	**Elvis Is Back!** *(With sticker)*	1960	**60.00**	**150.00**
RCA Victor LPM-2231	(M)	**Elvis Is Back!** *(Without sticker)*	1960	**40.00**	**100.00**
		(Black label with "Long Play" on the bottom. LPM-2231 was originally issued in a gatefold jacket without the song titles printed on the front. Most copies have a yellow sticker affixed to the front that lists the twelve song titles. Both the label and the sticker list the fourth song on the second side as "The Girl Next Door.")			
RCA Victor LPM-2231	(M)	**Elvis Is Back!** *(With sticker)*	1960	**60.00**	**150.00**
RCA Victor LPM-2231	(M)	**Elvis Is Back!** *(Without sticker)*	1960	**40.00**	**100.00**
		(Black label with "Long Play" on the bottom. Second pressings were issued in a gatefold jacket without the song titles printed on the front. Most copies have a yellow sticker affixed to the front that lists the twelve song titles.. On this and all subsequent pressings, the sticker and the label list "The Girl Next Door Went A-Walking.")			
RCA Victor LPM-2231	(M)	**Elvis Is Back!** *(Gatefold cover)*	1960	**40.00**	**100.00**
		(Black label with "Long Play" on the bottom. Third pressings have the song titles printed on the front cover.)			
RCA Victor LPM-2231	(M)	**Elvis Is Back!** *(Gatefold cover)*	1963	**24.00**	**60.00**
		(Black label with "Mono" on the bottom.)			

All of Elvis' films were plugged on the AM airwaves by the issuance of radio "spot announcements" by the movie production company; MGM's Double Trouble from 1967 is pictured here. These spots, generally between a half-minute and a minute in length, featured an announcer alerting the listener that Elvis' latest movie was out and might feature soundtrack bits (a line or two from a scene), sound effects, background music (never the King's), etc., to attract attention. These are all rare and all but impossible to find unplayed but, as they rarely if ever featured even Presley's speaking voice, the demand for them is low, especially given there high market value. Note: These spots were issued in 10" and 12" formats in plain paper or cardboard jackets.

Label & Catalog #		Title	Year	VG+	NM
RCA Victor LPM-2231	(M)	**Elvis Is Back!** *(Gatefold cover)*	1965	20.00	50.00
		(Black label with "Monaural" on the bottom.)			
RCA Victor LSP-2231	(S)	**Elvis Is Back!** *(With sticker)*	1960	80.00	200.00
RCA Victor LSP-2231	(S)	**Elvis Is Back!** *(Without sticker)*	1960	60.00	150.00
		(Black label with "Living Stereo" on the bottom. LSP-2231 was origi-nally issued in a gatefold jacket without the song titles printed on the front. Most copies have a yellow sticker affixed to the front that lists the twelve song titles. Both the label and the sticker list the fourth song on the second side as "The Girl Next Door.")			
RCA Victor LSP-2231	(S)	**Elvis Is Back!** *(With sticker)*	1960	80.00	200.00
RCA Victor LSP-2231	(S)	**Elvis Is Back!** *(Without sticker)*	1960	60.00	150.00
		(Black label with "Living Stereo" on the bottom. Second pressings were issued in a gatefold jacket without the song titles printed on the front. Most copies have a yellow sticker affixed to the front that lists the twelve song titles.. Both the label and the sticker list "The Girl Next Door Went A-Walking.")			
RCA Victor LSP-2231	(S)	**Elvis Is Back!** *(Gatefold cover)*	1960	50.00	125.00
		(Black label with "Living Stereo" on the bottom. Third pressings have the song titles printed on the front cover.)			
RCA Victor LSP-2231	(S)	**Elvis Is Back!** *(Gatefold cover)*	1965	20.00	50.00
		(Black label with "Stereo" on the bottom.)			
RCA Victor LSP-2231	(S)	**Elvis Is Back!** *(Gatefold cover)*	1969	20.00	50.00
		(Orange label on non-flexible vinyl.)			
RCA Victor LPM-2256	(M)	**G.I. Blues** *(Soundtrack with sticker)*	1960	40.00	100.00
RCA Victor LPM-2256	(M)	**G.I. Blues** *(Soundtrack without sticker)*	1960	30.00	75.00
		(Black label with "Long Play" on the bottom. Some copies have a heart-shaped sticker on the cover advertising "Wooden Heart.)			
RCA Victor LPM-2256	(M)	**G.I. Blues** *(Soundtrack)*	1963	24.00	60.00
		(Black label with "Mono" on the bottom.)			
RCA Victor LPM-2256	(M)	**G.I. Blues** *(Soundtrack)*	1965	20.00	50.00
		(Black label with "Monaural" on the bottom.)			
RCA Victor LSP-2256	(S)	**G.I. Blues** *(Soundtrack with sticker)*	1960	50.00	125.00
RCA Victor LSP-2256	(S)	**G.I. Blues** *(Soundtrack without sticker)*	1960	40.00	100.00
		(Black label with "Living Stereo" on the bottom. Some copies have a heart-shaped sticker on the cover advertising "Wooden Heart.)			
RCA Victor LSP-2256	(S)	**G.I. Blues** *(Soundtrack)*	1963	20.00	50.00
		(Black label with "Stereo" on the bottom.)			
RCA Victor LSP-2256	(S)	**G.I. Blues** *(Soundtrack)*	1969	12.00	30.00
		(Orange label on non-flexible vinyl.)			
RCA Victor LPM-2328	(M)	**His Hand In Mine**	1961	30.00	75.00
		(Black label with "Long Play" on the bottom.)			
RCA Victor LPM-2328	(M)	**His Hand In Mine**	1963	20.00	50.00
		(Black label with "Mono" on the bottom.)			
RCA Victor LPM-2328	(M)	**His Hand In Mine**	1965	16.00	40.00
		(Black label with "Monaural" on the bottom.)			
RCA Victor LSP-2328	(S)	**His Hand In Mine**	1961	40.00	100.00
		(Black label with "Living Stereo" on the bottom.)			
RCA Victor LSP-2328	(S)	**His Hand In Mine**	1963	20.00	50.00
		(Black label with "Stereo" on the bottom.)			
RCA Victor LSP-2328	(S)	**His Hand In Mine**	1969	12.00	30.00
		(Orange label on non-flexible vinyl.)			
RCA Victor LPM-2370	(M)	**Something For Everybody**	1961	30.00	75.00
		(Black label with "Long Play" on the bottom. Original covers for LPM-2370 advertise Elvis' Compact-33s on the back.)			
RCA Victor LPM-2370	(M)	**Something For Everybody**	1961	20.00	50.00
		(Black label with "Long Play" on the bottom. The back cover advertises "Viva Las Vegas.".)			
RCA Victor LPM-2370	(M)	**Something For Everybody**	1961	24.00	60.00
		(Black label with "Long Play" on the bottom. Later covers delete the ads for Elvis' Compact-33s on the back.)			
RCA Victor LPM-2370	(M)	**Something For Everybody**	1963	20.00	50.00
		(Black label with "Mono" on the bottom.)			
RCA Victor LPM-2370	(M)	**Something For Everybody**	1965	16.00	40.00
		(Black label with "Monaural" on the bottom.)			
RCA Victor LSP-2370	(S)	**Something For Everybody**	1961	40.00	100.00
		(Black label with "Living Stereo" on the bottom. Original covers for LSP-2370 advertise Elvis' Compact-33s on the back.)			

Label & Catalog #		Title	Year	VG+	NM
RCA Victor LSP-2370	(S)	**Something For Everybody** (Black label with "Living Stereo" on the bottom. The back cover advertises "Viva Las Vegas.".)	1961	30.00	75.00
RCA Victor LSP-2370	(S)	**Something For Everybody** (Black label with "Stereo" on the bottom.)	1963	20.00	50.00
RCA Victor LSP-2370	(S)	**Something For Everybody** (Orange label on non-flexible vinyl. The back cover has ads for Elvis' 1968 NBC-TV Special.)	1969	16.00	40.00
RCA Victor LPM-2426	(M)	**Blue Hawaii** (Soundtrack with sticker)	1961	40.00	100.00
RCA Victor LPM-2426	(M)	**Blue Hawaii** (Soundtrack without sticker) (Black label with "Long Play" on the bottom. Some covers have a red sticker that reads "Contains the Twist Special Rock-A-Hula Baby.")	1961	30.00	75.00
RCA Victor LPM-2426	(M)	**Blue Hawaii** (Soundtrack) (Black label with "Mono" on the bottom.)	1963	20.00	50.00
RCA Victor LPM-2426	(M)	**Blue Hawaii** (Soundtrack) (Black label with "Monaural" on the bottom.)	1965	16.00	40.00
RCA Victor LSP-2426	(S)	**Blue Hawaii** (Soundtrack with sticker)	1961	60.00	150.00
RCA Victor LSP-2426	(S)	**Blue Hawaii** (Soundtrack without sticker) (Black label with "Living Stereo" on bottom. Some covers have a red sticker that reads "Contains the Twist Special Rock-A-Hula Baby.")	1961	40.00	100.00
RCA Victor LSP-2426	(S)	**Blue Hawaii** (Soundtrack) (Black label with "Stereo" on the bottom.)	1963	20.00	50.00
RCA Victor LSP-2426	(S)	**Blue Hawaii** (Soundtrack) (Orange label on non-flexible vinyl.)	1969	12.00	30.00
RCA Victor LPM-2523	(M)	**Pot Luck With Elvis** (Black label with "Long Play" on the bottom.)	1962	30.00	75.00
RCA Victor LPM-2523	(M)	**Pot Luck With Elvis** (Black label with "Mono" on the bottom.)	1963	20.00	50.00
RCA Victor LPM-2523	(M)	**Pot Luck With Elvis** (Black label with "Monaural" on the bottom.)	1965	16.00	40.00
RCA Victor LSP-2523	(S)	**Pot Luck With Elvis** (Black label with "Living Stereo" on the bottom.)	1962	40.00	100.00
RCA Victor LSP-2523	(S)	**Pot Luck With Elvis** (Black label with "Stereo" on the bottom.)	1963	20.00	50.00
RCA Victor LSP-2523	(S)	**Pot Luck With Elvis** (Orange label on non-flexible vinyl.)	1969	16.00	40.00
RCA Victor LPM-2621	(M)	**Girls! Girls! Girls!** (Soundtrack) (Black label with "Long Play" on the bottom.)	1962	24.00	60.00
RCA Victor LPM-2621	(M)	**Girls! Girls! Girls!** (Soundtrack) (Black label with "Mono" on the bottom.)	1963	20.00	50.00
RCA Victor LPM-2621	(M)	**Girls! Girls! Girls!** (Soundtrack) (Black label with "Monaural" on the bottom.)	1965	16.00	40.00
RCA Victor LSP-2621	(S)	**Girls! Girls! Girls!** (Soundtrack) (Black label with "Living Stereo" on the bottom.)	1962	30.00	75.00
RCA Victor LPM/LSP-2621		**Girls! Girls! Girls! Bonus Calendar #1** (1963 calendar with ads for Elvis' EPs and LPs on the back)	1962	60.00	150.00
RCA Victor LPM/LSP-2621		**Girls! Girls! Girls! Bonus Calendar #2** (1963 calendar with ads for Elvis' 45s on the back)	1962	100.00	250.00
RCA Victor LPM/LSP-2621		**Girls! Girls! Girls! Bonus Calendar #3** (1963 calendar with Col. Parker as Santa Claus on the back)	1962	200.00	400.00
RCA Victor LSP-2621	(S)	**Girls! Girls! Girls!** (Soundtrack) (Black label with "Stereo" on the bottom.)	1963	20.00	50.00
RCA Victor LSP-2621	(S)	**Girls! Girls! Girls!** (Soundtrack) (Orange label on non-flexible vinyl.)	1969	12.00	30.00
RCA Victor LPM-2697	(M)	**It Happened At The World's Fair** (Sdtk) (Black label with "Long Play" on the bottom.)	1963	30.00	75.00
RCA Victor LSP-2697	(S)	**It Happened At The World's Fair** (Sdtk) (Black label with "Living Stereo" on the bottom.)	1963	40.00	100.00
RCA Victor 2697		**It Happened At The World's Fair Photo**	1963	80.00	200.00
RCA Victor LPM-2756	(M)	**Fun In Acapulco** (Soundtrack) (Black label with "Mono" on the bottom.)	1963	20.00	50.00
RCA Victor LPM-2756	(M)	**Fun In Acapulco** (Soundtrack) (Black label with "Monaural" on the bottom.)	1965	16.00	40.00
RCA Victor LSP-2756	(S)	**Fun In Acapulco** (Soundtrack) (Black label with "Stereo" on the bottom.)	1963	24.00	60.00
RCA Victor LSP-2756	(S)	**Fun In Acapulco** (Soundtrack) (Orange label on non-flexible vinyl.)	1969	12.00	30.00

Label & Catalog #		Title	Year	VG+	NM
RCA Victor LPM-2765	(M)	**Elvis' Golden Records, Volume 3**	1963	20.00	50.00
		(Black label with "Mono" on the bottom.)			
RCA Victor LPM-2765	(M)	**Elvis' Golden Records, Volume 3**	1963	16.00	40.00
		(Black label with "Monaural" on the bottom.)			
RCA Victor LSP-2765	(S)	**Elvis' Golden Records, Volume 3**	1963	24.00	60.00
		(Black label with "Stereo" on the bottom.)			
RCA Victor LPM/LSP-2765		**Elvis' Golden Records, Volume 3 Bonus Book**	1963	20.00	50.00
		(Elvis Full Color Picture Folio Plus Special Giant Size Pin-Up Picture Inside. Halve the value if the pin-up is pulled out.)			
RCA Victor LSP-2765	(S)	**Elvis' Golden Records, Volume 3**	1969	12.00	30.00
		(Orange label on non-flexible vinyl.)			
RCA Victor LPM-2894	(M)	**Kissin' Cousins** *(Soundtrack)*	1964	20.00	50.00
		(Black label with "Mono" on the bottom. Most front covers have a small black & white photo of the cast inset into the lower right.)			
RCA Victor LPM-2894	(M)	**Kissin' Cousins** *(Soundtrack)*	1964	36.00	90.00
		(Black label with "Mono" on the bottom. Some covers do not have the inset black & white photo on the front .)			
RCA Victor LPM-2894	(M)	**Kissin' Cousins** *(Soundtrack)*	1965	16.00	40.00
		(Black label with "Monaural" on the bottom.)			
RCA Victor LSP-2894	(S)	**Kissin' Cousins** *(Soundtrack)*	1964	24.00	60.00
		(Black label with "Stereo" on the bottom. Most front covers have a small black & white photo of the cast inset into the lower right.)			
RCA Victor LSP-2894	(S)	**Kissin' Cousins** *(Soundtrack)*	1964	40.00	100.00
		(Black label with "Stereo" on the bottom. Some covers do not have the inset black & white photo on the front .)			
RCA Victor LSP-2894	(S)	**Kissin' Cousins** *(Soundtrack)*	1969	16.00	40.00
		(Orange label on non-flexible vinyl.)			
RCA Victor LPM-2999	(M)	**Roustabout** *(Soundtrack)*	1964	20.00	50.00
		(Black label with "Mono" on the bottom.)			
RCA Victor LPM-2999	(M)	**Roustabout** *(Soundtrack)*	1965	16.00	40.00
		(Black label with "Monaural" on the bottom.)			
RCA Victor LSP-2999	(S)	**Roustabout** *(Soundtrack)*	1964	300.00	500.00
		(Original pressings of LSP-2999 have black labels with a silver "RCA Victor" logo on top and "Stereo" on the bottom.)			
RCA Victor LSP-2999	(S)	**Roustabout** *(Soundtrack)*	1965	24.00	60.00
		(Second pressings have black labels with a white "RCA Victor" logo on top and "Stereo" on the bottom.)			
RCA Victor LSP-2999	(S)	**Roustabout** *(Soundtrack)*	1969	12.00	30.00
		(Orange label on non-flexible vinyl.)			
RCA Victor LPM-3338	(M)	**Girl Happy** *(Soundtrack)*	1965	20.00	50.00
RCA Victor LSP-3338	(S)	**Girl Happy** *(Soundtrack)*	1965	24.00	60.00
		(Black label with "Stereo" on the bottom.)			
RCA Victor LSP-3338	(S)	**Girl Happy** *(Soundtrack)*	1969	16.00	40.00
		(Orange label on non-flexible vinyl.)			
RCA Victor LPM-3450	(M)	**Elvis For Everyone**	1965	20.00	50.00
RCA Victor LSP-3450	(P)	**Elvis For Everyone**	1965	16.00	40.00
		(Black label with "Stereo" on the bottom. "Your Cheatin' Heart," "In My Way," "Tomorrow Night," "Forget Me Never," "Sound Advice," and "When It Rains, It Really Pours" are rechanneled .)			
RCA Victor LSP-3450	(P)	**Elvis For Everyone**	1969	12.00	30.00
		(Orange label on non-flexible vinyl.)			
RCA Victor LPM-3468	(M)	**Harum Scarum** *(Soundtrack)*	1965	16.00	40.00
RCA Victor LSP-3468	(S)	**Harum Scarum** *(Soundtrack)*	1965	20.00	50.00
		(Black label with "Stereo" on the bottom.)			
RCA Victor 3468		**Harum Scarum Bonus Photo**	1965	10.00	30.00
RCA Victor LPM-3553	(M)	**Frankie And Johnny** *(Soundtrack)*	1966	16.00	40.00
RCA Victor LSP-3553	(S)	**Frankie And Johnny** *(Soundtrack)*	1966	20.00	50.00
		(Black label with "Stereo" on the bottom.)			
RCA Victor 3553		**Frankie And Johnny Bonus Print**	1966	10.00	30.00
RCA Victor LPM-3643	(M)	**Paradise Hawaiian Style** *(Soundtrack)*	1966	16.00	40.00
RCA Victor LSP-3643	(S)	**Paradise Hawaiian Style** *(Soundtrack)*	1966	20.00	50.00
		(Black label with "Stereo" on the bottom.)			
RCA Victor LSP-3643	(S)	**Paradise Hawaiian Style**	1969	12.00	30.00
		(Orange label on non-flexible vinyl.)			
RCA Victor LPM-3702	(M)	**Spinout** *(Soundtrack)*	1966	16.00	40.00
RCA Victor LSP-3702	(S)	**Spinout** *(Soundtrack)*	1966	20.00	50.00
		(Black label with "Stereo" on the bottom.)			
RCA Victor LSP-3702	(S)	**Spinout Bonus Photo**	1966	10.00	30.00

Label & Catalog #		Title	Year	VG+	NM
RCA Victor LPM-3758	(M)	**How Great Thou Art**	1967	**24.00**	**60.00**
		(Black label with "Mono Dynagroove" on the bottom.)			
RCA Victor LSP-3758	(S)	**How Great Thou Art**	1967	**20.00**	**50.00**
		(Black label with "Stereo Dynagroove" on the bottom. Original covers do not have the RIAA Gold Record Award printed on the front.)			
RCA Victor LSP-3758	(S)	**How Great Thou Art**	1967	**12.00**	**30.00**
		(Black label with "Stereo Dynagroove" on the bottom. Later covers have the RIAA Gold Record Award printed on the upper left corner.)			
RCA Victor LSP-3758	(S)	**How Great Thou Art**	1969	**12.00**	**30.00**
		(Orange label on non-flexible vinyl.)			
RCA Victor LPM-3787	(M)	**Double Trouble** *(Soundtrack)*	1967	**20.00**	**50.00**
RCA Victor LSP-3787	(S)	**Double Trouble** *(Soundtrack)*	1967	**16.00**	**40.00**
		(Black label with "Stereo" on the bottom. Original covers for both mono and stereo pressings have a printed announcement for a bonus photo between the two photos of Elvis.)			
RCA Victor 3787		**Double Trouble Bonus Photo**	1967	**10.00**	**30.00**
RCA Victor LPM-3787	(M)	**Double Trouble** *(Soundtrack)*	1967	**20.00**	**50.00**
RCA Victor LSP-3787	(S)	**Double Trouble** *(Soundtrack)*	1967	**16.00**	**40.00**
		(Black label with "Stereo" on the bottom.)			
RCA Victor LSP-3787	(S)	**Double Trouble** *(Soundtrack)*	1969	**30.00**	**75.00**
		(Orange label on non-flexible vinyl.)			
RCA Victor LPM-3893	(M)	**Clambake** *(Soundtrack)*	1967	**80.00**	**200.00**
RCA Victor LSP-3893	(S)	**Clambake** *(Soundtrack)*	1967	**16.00**	**40.00**
		(Black label with "Stereo" on the bottom.)			
RCA Victor 3893		**Clambake Bonus Photo**	1967	**10.00**	**30.00**
RCA Victor LPM-3921	(M)	**Elvis' Gold Records, Volume 4**	1968	**800.00**	**1,200.00**
RCA Victor LSP-3921	(S)	**Elvis' Gold Records, Volume 4**	1968	**16.00**	**40.00**
		(Black label with "Stereo" on the bottom.)			
RCA Victor 3921		**Elvis' Gold Records, Volume 4 Bonus Photo**	1968	**60.00**	**150.00**
RCA Victor LSP-3921	(S)	**Elvis' Gold Records, Volume 4**	1969	**12.00**	**30.00**
		(Orange label on non-flexible vinyl.)			
RCA Victor LPM-3989	(M)	**Speedway** *(Soundtrack)*	1968	**800.00**	**1,200.00**
RCA Victor LSP-3989	(S)	**Speedway** *(Soundtrack)*	1968	**16.00**	**40.00**
		(Black label with "Stereo" on the bottom. "Speedway" contains one track, "Your Groovy Self," by Nancy Sinatra.)			
RCA Victor 3989		**Speedway Bonus Photo**	1968	**16.00**	**40.00**
RCA Victor LSP-3989	(S)	**Speedway** *(Soundtrack)*	1969	**12.00**	**30.00**
		(Orange label on non-flexible vinyl.)			
RCA Victor LPM-4088	(M)	**Elvis** *(TV Soundtrack)*	1968	**10.00**	**25.00**
		(Original pressings have orange labels on non-flexible vinyl. Approximately half of this album is stereo.)			
RCA Victor PRS-279	(S)	**Singer Presents Elvis**			
		Singing Flaming Star & Others	1968	**10.00**	**25.00**
		(Available through Singer Sewing Centers in the latter quarter of 1968 in preparation for the Singer sponsored NBC TV Special. With the purchase of an album the fan was rewarded with several bonuses, priced separately below. "Tiger Man" is in mono on this album. This album was reissued as Elvis' first Camden budget LP.)			
RCA Victor PRS-279		**Singer Presents Elvis Bonus #1**	1968	**40.00**	**100.00**
		(32 page booklet listing all of the stations carrying the TV Special.)			
RCA Victor PRS-279		**Singer Presents Elvis Bonus #2**	1968	**10.00**	**25.00**
		(Full color photo with Elvis in-print catalog on the back and an ad for the TV Special on the bottom.)			
RCA Victor PRS-279		**Singer Presents Elvis Bonus #3**	1968	**6.00**	**15.00**
		(Full color photo with the catalog on the back but without the ad.)			
RCA Victor PRS-279		**Singer Presents Elvis Bonus #4**	1968	**6.00**	**15.00**
		(A 4" x 6" "ticket" inviting the customer to watch the TV Special.)			
RCA Victor LSP-4155	(S)	**From Elvis In Memphis** *(Without the photo)*	1969	**10.00**	**25.00**
		(Original pressings have orange labels on non-flexible vinyl.)			
RCA Victor 4155		**From Elvis In Memphis Bonus Photo**	1969	**5.00**	**15.00**
RCA Victor LSP-6020	(S)	**From Memphis To Vegas / From Vegas To Memphsi** *(2 LPs)*	1969	**10.00**	**25.00**
		(Original pressings have orange labels on non-flexible vinyl.)			
RCA Victor LSP-6020	(S)	**From Memphis To Vegas / From Vegas To Memphsi Bonus Photo**	1969	**5.00**	**15.00**
		(LSP-6020 was issued with two of four possible bonus photos, each with a value of $15 in Near Mint.)			

Label & Catalog #		Title	Year	VG+	NM
RCA Victor *(No number)*		**International Hotel Presents Elvis, 1969**	*1969*		*See below*
		(This special box was given to those persons who attended Elvis' opening shows in Las Vegas in July 1969. The box includes a copy of LPM-4088; a copy of LSP-4155; three photos; a 1969 Elvis Record Catalog; and a letter of thanks from Elvis and the Colonel. Very rare with a suggested Near Mint value of $2,000-4,000 of which at least 90% is for the box in NM condition alone.)			
RCA Victor *(No number)*		**International Hotel Presents Elvis, 1970**	*1970*		*See below*
		(This special box was given to those persons who attended Elvis' opening shows in Las Vegas in February 1970. The box includes a copy of LSP-6020; a copy of the single "Kentucky Rain;" one photo; an Elvis 1970 Record Catalog; a 1970 wallet calendar; a hotel menu; a photo album; and a letter of thanks from Elvis and the Colonel. Very rare with a suggested Near Mint value of $$2,000-4,000 of which at least 90% is for the box in NM condition alone.)			
RCA Victor LSP-4362	(S)	**On Stage-February, 1970**	1970	10.00	25.00
		(Original pressings have orange labels on non-flexible vinyl.)			
RCA Victor LPM-6401	(M)	**Worldwide 50 Gold Award Hits,**			
		Vol. 1 *(4 LP box with bonus booklet)*	1970	30.00	75.00
RCA Victor LPM-6401	(M)	**Worldwide 50 Gold Award Hits,**			
		Vol. 1 *(4 LP box without the booklet)*	1970	20.00	50.00
		(Original pressings have orange labels on non-flexible vinyl.)			
RCA Victor LSP-4428	(S)	**Elvis In Person At The International Hotel**	1970	10.00	25.00
		(Original pressings have orange labels on non-flexible vinyl.)			
RCA Victor LSP-4429	(S)	**Back In Memphis**	1970	10.00	25.00
		(Original pressings have orange labels on non-flexible vinyl.)			
RCA Victor LSP-4445	(S)	**That's The Way It Is**	1970	10.00	25.00
		(Original pressings have orange labels on non-flexible vinyl.)			
RCA Victor LSP-4460	(S)	**Elvis Country**	1971	10.00	25.00
		(Original pressings have orange labels on non-flexible vinyl.)			
RCA Victor 4460		**Elvis Country Bonus Photo**	1971	5.00	15.00
RCA Victor LSP-4530	(S)	**Love Letters From Elvis**	1971	20.00	50.00
		(Original pressings have orange labels with the RCA logo and catalog number at the top center of the front cover.)			
RCA Victor LSP-4530	(S)	**Love Letters From Elvis**	1971	10.00	25.00
		(Second pressings have orange labels with the RCA logo and catalog number in the lower right corner of the cover.)			
RCA Victor LPM-6402	(M)	**The Other Sides:—Worldwide Gold Award Hits,**			
		Vol. 2 *(4 LP box with 2 bonuses)*	1971	28.00	70.00
RCA Victor LPM-6402	(M)	**The Other Sides:—Worldwide Gold Award Hits,**			
		Vol. 2 *(4 LP box without the bonuses)*	1971	16.00	40.00
		(Original pressings have orange labels with printed ads on the cover for two bonuses: A full color fold-open print of a jumpsuited Elvis and a small envelope with a piece of cloth from Elvis' wardrobe.)			
RCA Victor LSP-4579	(S)	**The Wonderful World Of Christmas**	1971	12.00	30.00
RCA Victor LSP-4579	(S)	**The Wonderful World Of Christmas Bonus Photo**	1971	7.00	20.00
RCA Victor LSP-4671	(S)	**Elvis Now** *(Orange label)*	1972	10.00	25.00
RCA Victor LSP-4690	(S)	**He Touched Me** *(Orange label)*	1972	10.00	25.00
RCA SPS-33-571-1	(DJ)	**Recorded At Madison Square Garden**	1972	150.00	300.00
		(2 LPs banded for air-play and issued in a plain white cover.)			
RCA Victor VPSX-6089	(Q)	**Aloha From Hawaii Via Satellite** *(2 LPs)*	1973		*See below*
		(RCA provided the Van Camp Co., sponsors of Elvis' "Aloha From Hawaii" TV Special, with advance copies of VPSX-6089, to which the company affixed stickers with the mermaid from their "Chicken of the Sea" logo. These copies were distributed among employees only and are rare with a suggested Near Mint value of $2,000-4,000.)			
RCA Victor VPSX-6089	(Q)	**Aloha From Hawaii Via Satellite** *(2 LPs)*	1973	12.00	30.00
		(Original commercial copies of VPSX-6089 have dark orange labels with a dark "Quadradisc" on top and "RCA" on the bottom.)			
RCA Victor APL1-0283	(S)	**Elvis** *(Orange label)*	1973	20.00	50.00
RCA Victor CPL1-0341	(P)	**A Legendary Performer, Volume 1**	1974	10.00	25.00
		(Black label with gold print in a die-cut cover with a bonus book.)			
RCA Victor APL1-0388	(S)	**Raised On Rock/ For Ol' Times Sake** *(Orange label)*	1973	10.00	25.00
RCA Victor CPL1-0475	(S)	**Good Times**	1974	10.00	25.00

Label & Catalog #		Title	Year	VG+	NM
RCA Victor DJL1-0606	(S)	**Elvis Recorded Live**			
		On Stage In Memphis *(White label)*	1974	150.00	300.00
RCA Victor APD1-0606	(Q)	**Elvis Recorded Live**			
		On Stage In Memphis *(Orange label)*	1974	80.00	200.00
Boxcar *(No number)*	(M)	**Having Fun With Elvis On Stage**	1974	80.00	200.00
RCA Victor CPM1-0818	(M)	**Having Fun With Elvis**			
		On Stage *(Orange label)*	1974	10.00	25.00
RCA Victor APL1-0873	(S)	**Promised Land** *(Orange label)*	1975	10.00	25.00
RCA Victor APD1-0873	(Q)	**Promised Land** *(Orange label)*	1975	60.00	150.00
RCA Victor APD1-0873	(Q)	**Promised Land** *(Black label)*	1975	20.00	50.00
RCA Victor APL1-1039	(S)	**Elvis Today** *(Orange label)*	1975	20.00	50.00
RCA Victor APD1-1039	(Q)	**Elvis Today** *(Orange label)*	1975	60.00	150.00
RCA Victor APD1-1039	(Q)	**Elvis Today** *(Black label)*	1975	20.00	50.00
RCA Victor CPL1-1349	(P)	**A Legendary Performer, Volume 2**	1976	10.00	25.00
		(Black label with gold print in a die-cut cover with a bonus book.)			
RCA Victor AFL1-2428	(S)	**Moody Blue** *(Colored vinyl)*	1977		*See below*
		(Copies of AFL1-2428 were pressed on colored vinyl, including gold, green, red, and white vinyl, apparently for experimental purrposes, purposes, and then distributed among RCA employes. These are all rare with a suggested Near Mint value of $1,000-2,000 each.)			
RCA Victor AFL1-2428	(S)	**Moody Blue** *(Multi-colored vinyl)*	1977		*See below*
		(Copies of AFL1-2428 were pressed on multi-colored vinyl with a "splash" effect, including purple-on-white, red-on-white, and yellow-on-white, apparently for experimental purposes, and distributed among RCA employes. These are all rare with a suggested Near Mint value of $2,000-3,000 each.)			
RCA Victor AFL1-2428	(S)	**Moody Blue** *(Black vinyl)*	1977	150.00	300.00
		(RCA had printed 250,000 copies of AFL1-2428 on blue vinyl and had switched to basic black— when Elvis died. All subsequent pressings were on blue vinyl. Hence there are literally millions of blue copies— worth about $5— and very few black.)			
RCA Victor CPL1-3078	(P)	**A Legendary Performer, Volume 3**	1979	10.00	25.00
		(Black label with gold print in a die-cut cover with a bonus book.)			
RCA Victor DJL1-3455	(S)	**Pure Elvis**	1979	150.00	300.00
RCA Victor CPL8-3699	(P)	**Elvis Aron Presley** *(8 LP box with book)*	1980	24.00	60.00
RCA Victor DJL1-3729	(P)	**Elvis Aron Presley In-Store Sampler**	1980	60.00	150.00
RCA Victor DJL1-3780	(P)	**Elvis Aron Presley Radio Station Sampler**	1980	80.00	200.00
RCA Victor CPL1-4848	(P)	**A Legendary Performer, Volume 4**	1980	10.00	25.00
		(Black label with gold print in a die-cut cover with a bonus book.)			
RCA Victor CPM6-5172	(P)	**A Golden Celebration** *(6 LP box with photo)*	1984	12.00	30.00
Mobile Fidelity MFSL-059	(S)	**From Elvis In Memphis**	1980	12.00	35.00

2. Special Promotional Releases

RCA Victor SP-33-461	(M)	**Special Palm Sunday Programming**	1967		*See below*
		(Radio program consisting of previously released album tracks issued without a cover. Rare with a suggested Near Mint value of $1,000-2,000. Counterfeits exist!)			
RCA Victor UNMR-5697	(M)	**Special Christmas Programming**	1967		*See below*
		(Radio program consisting of previously released album tracks issued without a cover. Rare with a suggested Near Mint value of $1,000-2,000. Counterfeits exist!)			
RCA Victor FJ-1981	(M)	**Felton Jarvis Talks About Elvis**	1981	60.00	150.00
		(issued with script sheets in a plain cardboard jacket.)			

3. RCA Camden, 1969-1973

Camden CAS-2304	(S)	**Elvis Sings Flaming Star**	1969	10.00	25.00
Camden CAS-2408	(S)	**Let's Be Friends**	1970	10.00	25.00
Camden CAS-2440	(S)	**Almost In Love**	1970	10.00	25.00
Camden CAL-2428	(M)	**Elvis' Christmas Album**	1970	10.00	25.00
		(The eight songs from LOC-1035 are mono while "If Every Day Was Like Christmas" and "Mama Liked The Roses" are stereo.)			

— Camden albums above have blue labels on non-flexible vinyl. —

Label & Catalog #		Title	Year	VG+	NM
Camden CAS-2595	(S)	**Burning Love & Hits From His Movies, Vol. 2**	1972	10.00	25.00
		(Original pressings of CAS-2595 have a star on the front cover advertising the bonus photo,.)			
Camden CAS-2595	(S)	**Burning Love Bonus Photo**	1972	10.00	25.00

4. RCA Record Club Releases & Miscellaneous Mail Order Releases

Label & Catalog #		Title	Year	VG+	NM
RCA Victor R-213690	(M)	**Worldwide Gold Award Hits, Parts 1 & 2**	1974	14.00	35.00
		(Record Club. 2 LPs with orange labels.)			
RCA Victor DPL2-0056	(E)	**Elvis** *(2 LPs on blue labels)*	1973	12.00	30.00
RCA Victor DPL2-0056	(E)	**Elvis Commemorative Album**	1978	12.00	30.00
		(Gold vinyl reissue of 0056, "Elvis.")			
RCA Victor DPL2-0168	(P)	**Elvis In Hollywood** *(2 LPs on blue labels)*	1976	10.00	25.00
		(Special TV mail-order compilation issued with a bonus book.)			
RCA Victor DML5-0263	(P)	**The Elvis Presley Story** *(5 LPs)*	1977	12.00	30.00
		(Issued with a bonus album, "Elvis-His Songs Of Inspiration," priced separately below.)			
RCA Victor DML1-0264	(P)	**Elvis-His Songs Of Inspiration**	1977	6.00	15.00
RCA Victor DML5-0347	(P)	**Memories Of Elvis** *(5 LPs)*	1978	12.00	30.00
		(Issued with a bonus album, "The Greatest Show On Earth," priced separately below.)			
RCA Victor DML1-0348	(P)	**The Greatest Show On Earth**	1978	6.00	15.00
RCA Victor DML6-0412	(P)	**The Legendary Recordings Of Elvis Presley** *(6 LPs)*	1980	16.00	40.00
		(Issued with a bonus book and print, included in the price, and an album, "Greatest Moments In Music," priced separately below.)			
RCA Victor DML1-0413	(P)	**Greatest Moments In Music**	1980	6.00	15.00
RCA Victor DVL1-0461	(P)	**The Legendary Magic Of Elvis Presley**	1980	6.00	15.00
RCA Victor RD4A-0101	(P)	**Elvis! His Greatest Hits** *(8 LPs)*	1982	150.00	300.00
RCA Victor RD4A-0102	(P)	**Elvis! His Greatest Hits** *(7 LPs)*	1982	20.00	50.00
		(Issued with a bonus book and print, included in the price, and an album, "Inspirational Favorites," priced separately below.)			
RCA Victor RD4A-181	(P)	**Elvis Sings Inspirational Favorites**	1982	6.00	15.00
RCA Victor RB4-191	(P)	**The Legend Lives On** *(7 LPs)*	1984	16.00	40.00
RCA Victor RDA-242D	(P)	**Elvis Sings Country Favorites**	1985	20.00	50.00
		(Issued as a bonus album with Reader's Digest's various artists boxed set "The Great Country Entertainers.")			
RCA Victor DVM1-0704	(M)	**Elvis (One Night With You)**	1985	12.00	30.00
RCA Victor DVM1-0704		**Elvis (One Night With You) Bonus Poster**	1985	4.00	10.00
RCA Victor DJM1-0835	(M)	**An Audio Self Portrait**	1985	20.00	50.00
RCA Victor 6313-1-R	(M)	**Elvis Talks** *(Reissue of DJM1-0835)*	1988	10.00	25.00

5. Miscellaneous Label Albums

Label & Catalog #		Title	Year	VG+	NM
Sun Inter. 1001	(M)	**The Sun Years** *('50s Sun label)*	1977	20.00	50.00
Starday SD-995	(M)	**Interviews With Elvis**	1977	12.00	30.00
Green Valley GV-2001	(M)	**Exclusive Live Press Conference** *(2 LPs)*	1977	10.00	25.00
		(Originally issued in a soft cardboard jacket.)			
Green Valley GV-2002	(M)	**Elvis Speaks To You** *(2 LPs)*	1977	10.00	25.00
		(Originally issued in a gatefold jacket with a bonus photo.)			
Silhouette 1001/2	(M)	**Personally Elvis** *(2 LPs with EP silhouette)*	1979	14.00	35.00
Silhouette 1001/2	(M)	**Personally Elvis** *(2 LPs without silhouette)*	1979	10.00	25.00
Mavenco *(No number)*	(M)	**Elvis, Scotty & Bill** *(Pink vinyl)*	1988	20.00	50.00
		(Includes a copy of Elvis' management contract with Scotty Moore.)			

6. Soundtrack Radio Spots & Interviews

The albums below are either 10" or 12" radio spots prepared and released by the movie's production company. Most contain several spots— the little ads you heard on the radio alerting everyone to Elvis' latest celluloid romp, usually accompanied by uptempo incidental music— per side and were sent to radio stations sans covers. Several interview records were also issued, usually querying a co-star about her or his experience with The King. These are are very rare, hard to find in Near Mint condition but have a relatively small demand. The values listed are conservative estimates..

Label & Catalog #		Title	Year	VG+	NM
20th Century Fox	(M)	**Lover Me Tender**	1956	500.00	1,000.00
Paramount Pictures	(M)	**Loving You**	1957	375.00	750.00

Label & Catalog #		Title	Year	VG+	NM
MGM Studios	(M)	Jailhouse Rock	1957	375.00	750.00
MGM Studios	(M)	Jailhouse Rock Interview (Red vinyl)	1957	500.00	1,000.00
		(Dick Simmons interviews Jerry Leiber and Mike Stoller			
		on working with Elvis. Issued in a plain cardboard jacket.)			
Paramount Pictures	(M)	King Creole	1958	375.00	750.00
Paramount Pictures	(M)	King Creole / Loving You	1959	250.00	500.00
Paramount Pictures	(M)	G. I. Blues	1960	250.00	500.00
20th Century Fox	(M)	Flaming Star	1960	250.00	500.00
20th Century Fox	(M)	Wild In The Country	1961	250.00	500.00
Paramount Pictures	(M)	Blue Hawaii	1961	250.00	500.00
Mirisch Company	(M)	Follow That Dream	1962	250.00	500.00
Mirisch Company	(M)	Kid Galahad	1962	250.00	500.00
Paramount Pictures	(M)	Girls! Girls! Girls!	1962	250.00	500.00
MGM Studios	(M)	It Happened At The World's Fair	1963	150.00	300.00
Paramount Pictures	(M)	Fun In Acapulco	1963	150.00	300.00
MGM Studios	(M)	Kissin' Cousins	1964	150.00	300.00
MGM Studios	(M)	Viva Las Vegas	1964	150.00	300.00
Paramount Pictures	(M)	Roustabout	1965	150.00	300.00
MGM Studios	(M)	Girl Happy	1965	150.00	300.00
Allied Artists	(M)	Tickle Me	1965	150.00	300.00
MGM Studios	(M)	Harum Scarum	1965	150.00	300.00
United Artists	(M)	Frankie And Johnny	1966	150.00	300.00
Paramount Pictures	(M)	Paradise, Hawaiian Style	1965	150.00	300.00
Paramount Pictures	(M)	Fun In Acapulco / Girls! Girls! Girls!	1966	150.00	300.00
MGM Studios	(M)	Spinout	1966	150.00	300.00
MGM Studios	(M)	Spinout Interview With Shelley Fabares,			
		Diane McBain & Deborah Walley	1966	150.00	300.00
Paramount Pictures	(M)	Easy Come, Easy Go	1967	150.00	300.00
MGM Studios	(M)	Double Trouble	1967	150.00	300.00
MGM Studios	(M)	Double Trouble Interview With Annette Day	1967	150.00	300.00
United Artists	(M)	Clambake	1967	150.00	300.00
MGM Studios	(M)	Stay Away, Joe	1968	150.00	300.00
MGM Studios	(M)	Speedway	1968	150.00	300.00
MGM Studios	(M)	Live A Little, Love A Little	1968	150.00	300.00
MGM Studios	(M)	Live A Little, Love A Little Interviews			
		With Rudy Valle & Michelle Carey	1968	150.00	300.00
National General	(M)	Charro	1969	150.00	300.00
National General	(M)	Charro Interview With Ina Balin	1969	150.00	300.00
MGM Studios	(M)	The Trouble With Girls			
		(And How To Get Into It)	1968	150.00	300.00
Universal Studios	(M)	Change Of Habit	1969	150.00	300.00
Universal Studios	(M)	Change Of Habit Interview			
		With Mary Tyler Moore	1969	150.00	300.00
MGM Studios	(M)	That's The Way It Is	1970	250.00	500.00
MGM Studios	(M)	Elvis On Tour	1972	250.00	500.00
MGM Studios	(S)	This Is Elvis	1984	150.00	300.00

PRESLEY, ELVIS / THE SILVER BEATLES

United Dist. UDL-2382	(M)	Lightning Strikes Twice	1981	30.00	75.00
		(Side 1 contains early live Elvis while side two			
		features The Beatles' Decca audition tapes.)			

PRESTON, BILLY
Refer to George Harrison & Friends.

Derby LPM-701	(M)	16 Year Old Soul	1963	60.00	150.00
Vee Jay LP-1123	(M)	The Most Exciting Organ Ever	1965	12.00	30.00
Vee Jay LPS-1123	(S)	The Most Exciting Organ Ever	1965	20.00	50.00
Vee Jay LP-1142	(M)	Billy Preston's Greatest Hits	1965	12.00	30.00
Vee Jay LPS-1142	(S)	Billy Preston's Greatest Hits	1965	20.00	50.00
Exodus EX-304	(M)	Early Hits Of 1965	1965	8.00	20.00
Exodus EX-304	(S)	Early Hits Of 1965	1965	10.00	25.00
Capitol T-2532	(M)	Wildest Organ In Town	1966	8.00	20.00
Capitol ST-2532	(S)	Wildest Organ In Town	1966	10.00	25.00
Apple ST-3359	(S)	That's The Way God Planned It	1969	20.00	50.00
		(Original covers feature a close-up of Mr. Preston's face.			
		Apple label with "A Subsidiary of Capitol" on the bottom.			
		Produced by George Harrison.)			

Label & Catalog #		Title	Year	VG+	NM
Apple ST-3359	(S)	**That's The Way God Planned It**	1969	16.00	40.00
		(*Original covers feature a close-up of Mr. Preston's face.*			
		Apple label with "Manufactured by Apple" on the bottom.)			

PRESTON, JOHNNY
Mercury MG-20592	(M)	**Running Bear**	1960	40.00	100.00
Mercury SR-60250	(P)	**Running Bear**	1960	60.00	150.00
Mercury MG-20609	(M)	**Come Rock With Me**	1961	30.00	75.00
Mercury SR-60609	(P)	**Come Rock With Me**	1961	40.00	100.00

PRETENDERS, THE
| Warner Bros. WBMS-121 | (DJ) | **The Pretenders Live** | 198? | 16.00 | 40.00 |

PRETTY THINGS, THE
Fontana MGF-27544	(M)	**The Pretty Things**	1965	40.00	100.00
Fontana SRF-67544	(P)	**The Pretty Things**	1965	30.00	75.00
Rare Earth RS-506	(S)	**S.F. Sorrow**	1969	20.00	50.00
Rare Earth RS-515	(S)	**Parachute**	1970	10.00	25.00

PRICE, ALAN
Price was formerly a member of the original Animals.
Parrot PA-1018	(M)	**The Price Is Right**	1968	12.00	30.00
Parrot PAS-71018	(S)	**The Price Is Right**	1968	10.00	25.00
		(*"I Put A Spell On You" and "Shame" are rechanneled on this album.*)			

PRICE, LLOYD
Specialty SP-2105	(M)	**Lloyd Price**	1959	60.00	150.00
ABC-Paramount ABC-277	(M)	**The Exciting Lloyd Price**	1959	30.00	75.00
ABC-Paramount ABCS-277	(S)	**The Exciting Lloyd Price**	1959	40.00	100.00
ABC-Paramount ABC-297	(M)	**Mr. Personality**	1959	30.00	75.00
ABC-Paramount ABCS-297	(S)	**Mr. Personality**	1959	40.00	100.00
ABC-Paramount ABC-315	(M)	**Mr. Personality Sings The Blues**	1960	30.00	75.00
ABC-Paramount ABCS-315	(S)	**Mr. Personality Sings The Blues**	1960	40.00	100.00
ABC-Paramount ABC-324	(M)	**Mr. Personality's 15 Hits**	1960	20.00	50.00
ABC-Paramount ABCS-324	(E)	**Mr. Personality's 15 Hits**	1960	14.00	35.00
ABC-Paramount ABC-346	(M)	**The Fantastic Lloyd Price**	1960	20.00	50.00
ABC-Paramount ABCS-346	(E)	**The Fantastic Lloyd Price**	1960	14.00	35.00
ABC-Paramount ABC-366	(M)	**Lloyd Price Sings The Million Sellers**	1961	14.00	35.00
ABC-Paramount ABCS-366	(S)	**Lloyd Price Sings The Million Sellers**	1961	20.00	50.00
ABC-Paramount ABC-382	(M)	**Cookin' With Lloyd Price**	1961	14.00	35.00
ABC-Paramount ABCS-382	(S)	**Cookin' With Lloyd Price**	1961	20.00	50.00
Double-L D-2301	(M)	**The Lloyd Price Orchestra**	1963	10.00	25.00
Double-L SDL-8301	(S)	**The Lloyd Price Orchestra**	1963	14.00	35.00
Double-L D-2303	(M)	**Misty**	1963	10.00	25.00
Double-L SDL-8303	(S)	**Misty**	1963	14.00	35.00
Monument MLP-8032	(M)	**Lloyd Swings For Sammy**	1965	10.00	25.00
Monument SMP-18032	(S)	**Lloyd Swings For Sammy**	1965	14.00	35.00
Jad 1002	(S)	**Lloyd Price Now**	1969	10.00	25.00

PRICE, RAY
Columbia CL-1015	(M)	**Ray Price Sings Heart Songs**	1957	20.00	50.00
Columbia CL-1148	(M)	**Talk To Your Heart**	1958	16.00	40.00
Columbia CL-1494	(M)	**Faith**	1960	12.00	30.00
Columbia CS-8285	(S)	**Faith**	1960	16.00	40.00
Columbia CL-1566	(M)	**Ray Price's Greatest Hits**	1961	12.00	30.00
Columbia CL-1758	(M)	**San Antonio Rose—**			
		A Tribute To The Great Bob Wills	1962	8.00	20.00
Columbia CS-8556	(S)	**San Antonio Rose—**			
		A Tribute To The Great Bob Wills	1962	12.00	30.00
		— Columbia albums above have three white "eye" logos on each side of the spindle hole.—			

PRICE, RUTH: Refer to GOLDMINE'S PRICE GUIDE TO COLLECTIBLE JAZZ ALBUMS

PRICE, VINCENT
Columbia ML-5668	(M)	**America The Beautiful**	1961	10.00	25.00
Dot DLP-3195	(M)	**Gallery**	1962	10.00	25.00
Dot DLP-25195	(S)	**Gallery**	1962	12.00	30.00
Caedmon TC-1059	(M)	**Poems Of Shelley**	1962	10.00	25.00

Label & Catalog #		Title	Year	VG+	NM
Capitol Cust. SGP-6256/7	(S)	**This World Tomorrow** (Blue vinyl)	1965	12.00	30.00
Capitol Cust. SGP-6258/9	(S)	**The World Of The 21st Century** (Blue vinyl)	1965	12.00	30.00
		(Both Capitol Custom albums were made for Guild Publications.)			
Capitol SWBB-342	(S)	**Witchcraft/Magic** (2 LPs)	1969	10.00	25.00

PRIMA, LOUIS

Mercury MG-25142	(10")	**Louis Prima Plays**	1953	30.00	75.00
Capitol T-755	(M)	**The Wildest**	1956	20.00	50.00
Capitol T-836	(M)	**Call Of The Wildest**	1957	20.00	50.00
Capitol T-908	(M)	**The Wildest Show At Tahoe**	1957	20.00	50.00
Capitol T-1010	(M)	**Las Vegas Prima Style**	1958	20.00	50.00
		— Capitol albums above have turquoise labels.—			
Capitol T-1132	(M)	**Strictly Prima**	1959	16.00	40.00
		— Capitol albums above have black "rainbow" labels with the logo on the left.—			
Capitol T-1723	(M)	**The Wildest Comes Home**	1962	10.00	25.00
Capitol ST-1723	(S)	**The Wildest Comes Home**	1962	12.00	30.00
Capitol T-1797	(M)	**Lake Tahoe Prima Style** (With Sam Butera)	1963	8.00	20.00
Capitol ST-1797	(S)	**Lake Tahoe Prima Style** (With Sam Butera)	1963	10.00	25.00
Columba CL-1206	(M)	**Breakin' It Up**	1958	14.00	35.00
Rond-o-lette 8-9	(M)	**Louis Prima In All His Moods**	1959	10.00	25.00
Dot DLP-3262	(M)	**His Greatest Hits**	1960	12.00	30.00
Dot DLP-25262	(S)	**His Greatest Hits**	1960	10.00	25.00
Dot DLP-3264	(M)	**Pretty Music Prima Style**	1960	12.00	30.00
Dot DLP-25264	(S)	**Pretty Music Prima Style**	1960	10.00	25.00
Dot DLP-3352	(M)	**Wonderland By Night**	1961	12.00	30.00
Dot DLP-25352	(S)	**Wonderland By Night**	1961	10.00	25.00
Dot DLP-2385	(M)	**Blue Moon**	1961	12.00	30.00
Dot DLP-25385	(S)	**Blue Moon**	1961	10.00	25.00
Dot DLP-3410	(M)	**Doin' The Twist**	1961	12.00	30.00
Dot DLP-25410	(S)	**Doin' The Twist**	1961	10.00	25.00

PRIMA, LOUIS, & KEELY SMITH

Capitol T-1160	(M)	**Hey Boy, Hey Girl** (Soundtrack)	1959	20.00	50.00
		— Capitol albums above have black "rainbow" labels with the logo on the left.—			
Dot DLP-3210	(M)	**Louis And Keely**	1959	14.00	35.00
Dot DLP-25210	(S)	**Louis And Keely**	1959	16.00	40.00
Dot DLP-3263	(M)	**Together**	1960	10.00	25.00
Dot DLP-25263	(S)	**Together**	1960	12.00	30.00
Dot DLP-3266	(M)	**Louis And Keely On Stage**	1961	10.00	25.00
Dot DLP-25266	(S)	**Louis And Keely On Stage**	1961	12.00	30.00
Dot DLP-3392	(M)	**Return Of The Wildest**	1961	10.00	25.00
Dot DLP-25392	(S)	**Return Of The Wildest**	1961	12.00	30.00
Capitol T-1531	(M)	**The Hits Of Louis And Keely**	1961	10.00	25.00
Capitol ST-1531	(S)	**The Hits Of Louis And Keely**	1961	12.00	30.00

PRIMEVAL

700 West 740105	(S)	**Smokin' Bats At Campton's**	1974	50.00	125.00

PRINCE

Warner Bros. 25110	(DJ)	**Purple Rain** (Purple vinyl)	1984	12.00	30.00
Warner Bros. 25677DJ	(S)	**The Black Album** (2 LPs)	1987		See below
		(Two 45 rpm promos containing the complete unreleased album. Rare with a suggested Near Mint value of $4,000-8,000.)			
Warner Bros. 25677	(S)	**The Black Album**	1987		See below
		(A completed album withdrawn by the artist prior to release. Rare with a suggested Near Mint value of $3,000-6,000.)			

PRINCE BUSTER

RCA Victor LPM-3792	(M)	**Ten Commandments**	1967	10.00	25.00
RCA Victor LSP-3792	(S)	**Ten Commandments**	1967	14.00	35.00

PRONZ, ROSEMARY

Pharos MN-10001	(M)	**TV's "Penny" Sings**	196?	12.00	30.00
Pharos SN-30001	(S)	**TV's "Penny" Sings**	196?	16.00	40.00

PROBE

Eborp SS-21396-01	(S)	**Direction**	197?	150.00	300.00

Label & Catalog #		Title	Year	VG+	NM

PROBY, P.J.

Liberty LRP-3406	(M)	Somewhere/Go Go P. J. Proby	1965	10.00	25.00
Liberty LST-7406	(S)	Somewhere/Go Go P. J. Proby	1965	12.00	30.00
Liberty LRP-3421	(M)	P. J. Proby	1965	10.00	25.00
Liberty LST-7421	(S)	P. J. Proby	1965	12.00	30.00
Liberty LRP-3497	(M)	Enigma	1967	10.00	25.00
Liberty LST-7497	(S)	Enigma	1967	12.00	30.00
Liberty LRP-3515	(M)	Phenomenon	1967	10.00	25.00
Liberty LST-7515	(S)	Phenomenon	1967	10.00	25.00
Liberty LRP-3561	(M)	What's Wrong With My World?	1968	12.00	30.00
Liberty LST-7561	(S)	What's Wrong With My World?	1968	10.00	25.00

PROCOL HARUM

Deram DE-16008	(M)	Procol Harum (With bonus poster)	1967	30.00	75.00
Deram DE-16008	(M)	Procol Harum (Without the poster)	1967	20.00	50.00
Deram DES-18008	(E)	Procol Harum (With bonus poster)	1967	20.00	50.00
Deram DES-18008	(E)	Procol Harum (Without the poster)	1967	10.00	25.00
A&M SP-8503	(DJ)	Procol Harum Lives (Interview)	197?	16.00	40.00
Sweet Thunder 15	(S)	Grand Hotel	198?	13.00	40.00

PROFESSOR LONGHAIR
Professor Longhair is a pseudonym for Henry Roland Byrd.

Atlantic SD-7225	(M)	New Orleans Piano	1972	10.00	25.00

PROFFITT, FRANK
Frank Proffitt was a guitar and banjo player and singer of traditional American folk music.

Folkways FA-2306	(M)	Frank Proffitt Songs Folk Songs	196?	12.00	30.00
Folk/Legacy FSA-1	(M)	Reese, North Carolina	1962	12.00	30.00
Folk/Legacy FSA-36	(M)	Frank Proffitt/A Memorial Album	1962	12.00	30.00

PROOF

Proof Prod.	(S)	Proof	197?	200.00	400.00

PROVINE, DOROTHY

Warner Bros. W-1394	(M)	The Roaring '20's	1961	8.00	20.00
Warner Bros. WS-1394	(S)	The Roaring '20's	1961	10.00	25.00
Warner Bros. W-1419	(M)	The Vamp Of The Roaring '20's	1961	8.00	20.00
Warner Bros. WS-1419	(S)	The Vamp Of The Roaring '20's	1961	10.00	25.00

PRYSOCK, ARTHUR: Refer to GOLDMINE'S PRICE GUIDE TO COLLECTIBLE JAZZ ALBUMS

PRYSOCK, RED

Mercury MG-20088	(M)	Rock 'N' Roll	1955	80.00	200.00
Mercury MG-20211	(M)	Fruit Boots	1957	50.00	125.00
Mercury MG-20512	(M)	Swing Softly Red	1959	16.00	40.00
Mercury SR-60188	(M)	Swing Softly Red	1959	20.00	50.00
Mercury MG-20???	(M)	The Beat	1960	16.00	40.00
Mercury SR-60307	(S)	The Beat	1960	20.00	50.00
Wing MGW-12007	(M)	Fruit Boots	196?	10.00	25.00

PRYSOCK, RED, & SIL AUSTIN

Mercury MG-20???	(M)	Battle Royal	1958	16.00	40.00
Mercury SR-60106	(M)	Battle Royal	1959	20.00	50.00

PUGSLEY MUNION

J&S SLP-0001	(S)	Just Like You	196?	40.00	100.00

PULLEN, WHITEY

Crown CLP-5332	(M)	Whitey Pullen	1963	10.00	25.00
Crown CST-332	(E)	Whitey Pullen	1963	4.00	10.00

PURIFY, JAMES & BOBBY

Bell 6003	(M)	James And Bobby Purify	1967	8.00	20.00
Bell 6003	(S)	James And Bobby Purify	1967	12.00	30.00
Bell 6010	(M)	The Pure Sound Of The Purifys	1967	8.00	20.00
Bell 6010	(S)	The Pure Sound Of The Purifys	1967	12.00	30.00

Label & Catalog #		Title	Year	VG+	NM

PYRAMIDS, THE

Best LPM-1001	(M)	**The Original Penetration**	1964	100.00	250.00
		(Best 1001 includes "Walkin' The Dog.")			
Best BR-16501	(M)	**The Original Penetration**	1964	80.00	200.00
Best BRS-36501	(E)	**The Original Penetration**	1964	60.00	150.00
		(Best 16501 replaces "Walkin' The Dog" with "Road Runnah.")			

QUATTLEBAUM, DOUG

Bluesville BVLP-1065	(M)	**Softee Man Blues**	1963	30.00	75.00
		—Bluesville albums above have bright blue labels with silver print.—			
Bluesville BVLP-1065	(M)	**Softee Man Blues**	1964	10.00	25.00
		—Bluesville albums above have blue labels with a trident logo on the right side.—			

QUEEN

Elektra EKS-75064	(S)	**Queen** *(White label promo)*	1973	20.00	50.00
Elektra EKS-75064	(S)	**Queen** *(Gold embossed on the cover)*	1973	12.00	30.00
Elektra EQ-5064	(Q)	**Queen**	1973	16.00	40.00
Elektra EKS7-5082	(S)	**Queen II** *(White label promo)*	1974	20.00	50.00
Elektra 7E-1026	(S)	**Sheer Heart Attack** *(White label promo)*	1974	20.00	50.00
Elektra 6E-112	(DJ)	**News Of The World**	1977	60.00	150.00
		(White label promo with 13" x 13" cover and press kit)			
Elektra 6E-166	(DJ)	**Jazz** *(Picture disc)*	1978	20.00	50.00
Mobile Fidelity MFSL-067	(S)	**A Night At The Opera**	1980	25.00	75.00

QUEENSRYCHE

"206" R-101	(S)	**Queensryche** *(4 track EP)*	1982	40.00	100.00
EMI ST-17134	(S)	**The Warning** *(Promo on High Quality Vinyl)*	1984	16.00	40.00
EMI SPRO-1436	(DJ)	**Operation Mindcrime** *(Picture disc)*	1988	20.00	50.00
EMI SPRO-9869	(DJ)	**Speak The Word** *(Interview)*	1988	16.00	40.00

QUESTION MARK & THE MYSTERIANS

Cameo C-2004	(M)	**96 Tears**	1966	30.00	75.00
Cameo CS-2004	(E)	**96 Tears**	1966	20.00	50.00
Cameo C-2006	(M)	**Action**	1967	20.00	50.00
Cameo SC-2006	(E)	**Action**	1967	16.00	40.00

QUICKSILVER MESSENGER SERVICE/QUICKSILVER

Original members were John Cippolina, Gary Duncan, Greg Elmore and David Freiberg. Later members include Nicky Hopkins and co-founder Dino Valenti. Refer to Steve Miller / Quicksilver Mesenger Service / The Band; Rocky Sullivan.

Capitol ST-2904	(S)	**Quicksilver Messenger Service**	1968	16.00	40.00
		(ST-2904 is very difficult to find with the glossy black, Rick Griffin cover in Near Mint condition.)			
Capitol ST-120	(S)	**Happy Trails**	1969	12.00	30.00
		—Capitol albums above have black rainbow labels.—			

R

R. E. O. SPEEDWAGON

Epic HE-45082	(S)	**You Can Tune A Piano But You Can't**			
		Tuna Fish (Half-speed master)	1982	8.00	25.00
Epic HE-46844	(S)	**Hi Infidelity** (Half-speed master)	1982	8.00	25.00
Epic HE-48100	(S)	**Good Trouble** (Half-speed master)	1982	8.00	25.00

R. P. S.

Mars/Mid-America	(S)	**R .P .S.**	197?	30.00	75.00

RABBLE, THE

Roulette SR-42010	(S)	**The Rabble**	1968	80.00	200.00

RADHA KRSNA TEMPLE, THE
Produced by George Harrison.

Apple SKAO-3376	(S)	Radha Krsna Temple	1971	10.00	25.00

RAFFERTY, GERRY

Mobile Fidelity MFSL-058	(S)	**City To City**	1978	10.00	30.00

RAIDERS, THE

Liberty LRP-3225	(M)	**Twistin' The Country Classics**	1962	10.00	25.00
Liberty LST-7225	(S)	**Twistin' The Country Classics**	1962	12.00	30.00

RAIN

Whazoo USR-3049	(S)	**Live, Christmas Night** (No cover)	1969	40.00	100.00

RAINBOW PRESS

Mr. G 9003	(S)	**There's A War On**	1968	12.00	30.00
Mr. G 9004	(S)	**Sunday Funnies**	1969	16.00	40.00

RAINBOW PROMISE, THE

New Wine LPS-251-01	(S)	**The Rainbow Promise**	196?	150.00	300.00

RAINBOW RANCH GANG, THE

Cumberland MGC-29531	(M)	**We're Moving On**	1965	10.00	25.00
Cumberland SRC-69531	(S)	**We're Moving On**	1965	12.00	30.00

RAINDROPS, THE
The Raindrops feature Jeff Barry and Ellie Greenwich.

Jubilee J-5023	(M)	**The Raindrops**	1963	60.00	150.00
Jubilee SJ-5023	(S)	**The Raindrops**	1963	150.00	300.00

RAINEY, MA: *Refer to* GOLDMINE'S PRICE GUIDE TO COLLECTIBLE JAZZ ALBUMS

RAINWATER, MARVIN
Refer to Webb Pierce / Marvin Rainwater / Stuart Hamblen.

MGM E-3534	(M)	**Songs By Marvin Rainwater** (Yellow label)	1957	80.00	200.00
MGM E-3721	(M)	**With A Heart, With A Beat** (Yellow label)	1958	60.00	150.00
MGM E-4046	(M)	**Gonna Find Me A Bluebird** (Black label)	1962	30.00	75.00
MGM SE-4046	(E)	**Gonna Find Me A Bluebird** (Black label)	1962	20.00	50.00

RAINY DAZE

Uni 3002	(M)	**That Acapulco Gold**	1967	8.00	20.00
Uni 73002	(S)	**That Acapulco Gold**	1967	10.00	25.00

RAITT, JOHN

Capitol T-583	(M)	**Highlights Of Broadway**	1955	12.00	30.00
Capitol T-714	(M)	**Mediterranean Magic**	1956	12.00	30.00
Capitol T-1058	(M)	**Under Open Skies**	1958	12.00	30.00
Capitol ST-1058	(S)	**Under Open Skies**	1958	16.00	40.00

Label & Catalog #		Title	Year	VG+	NM
RAM, BUCK					
Mercury MG-20392	(M)	The Magic Touch	1960	12.00	30.00
Mercury SR-60067	(S)	The Magic Touch	1960	16.00	40.00
RAMBEAU, EDDIE					
DynoVoice 9001	(M)	Concrete And Clay	1965	8.00	20.00
DynoVoice DS-9001	(S)	Concrete And Clay	1965	10.00	25.00
RAMONES					
Sire SASD-7520	(S)	Ramones	1976	10.00	25.00
Sire SASD-7528	(S)	Ramones Leave Home	1977	12.00	30.00
		(Original pressings of Sire 7528 contain "Carbona Not Glue.")			
Sire SASD-7528	(S)	Ramones Leave Home	1977	10.00	25.00
		(Second pressings replace "Carbona" with "Sheena Is A Punk Rocker.")			
RAMSAY, OBRAY					
Riverside RLP-12-649	(M)	Banjo Songs Of The Blue Ridge And Great Smokies	195?	12.00	30.00
Prestige Inter. PRLP-13009	(M)	Obray Ramsey Sings Jimmie Rodgers Favorites	1960	12.00	30.00
Prestige Inter. PRLP-13020	(M)	Folksongs From The Three Laurels	1961	12.00	30.00
Washington WLP-707	(M)	Blue Ridge Banjo	196?	10.00	25.00
RANDALL, TONY					
Imperial LP-9090	(M)	Tony Randall	1960	12.00	30.00
Imperial LP-12090	(S)	Tony Randall	1960	16.00	40.00
Mercury MG-21108	(M)	Vo, Vo, De, Oh, Doe	1967	8.00	20.00
Mercury SR-61108	(S)	Vo, Vo, De, Oh, Doe	1967	10.00	25.00
Mercury MG-21178	(M)	Warm And Wavery	1967	8.00	20.00
Mercury SR-61178	(S)	Warm And Wavery	1967	10.00	25.00
RANDAZZO, TEDDY					
Randazzo was formerly a member of The Three Chuckles.					
Vik LX-1121	(M)	I'm Confessin'	195?	20.00	50.00
ABC-Paramount 352	(M)	Journey To Love	1961	12.00	30.00
ABC-Paramount S-352	(S)	Journey To Love	1961	16.00	40.00
ABC-Paramount 421	(M)	Teddy Randazzo Twists	1962	12.00	30.00
ABC-Paramount S-421	(S)	Teddy Randazzo Twists	1962	16.00	40.00
Roulette R-25168	(M)	Hey, Let's Twist (Soundtrack)	1962	12.00	30.00
Roulette SR-25168	(S)	Hey, Let's Twist (Soundtrack)	1962	16.00	40.00
Colpix CP-445	(M)	Big Wide World	1963	10.00	25.00
Colpix SCP-445	(S)	Big Wide World	1963	16.00	40.00
RANDOLPH, BOOTS					
Refer to Chet Atkins, Floyd Cramer & Boots Randolph.					
RCA Victor LPM-2165	(M)	Yakety Sax	1960	16.00	40.00
RCA Victor LSP-2165	(S)	Yakety Sax	1960	20.00	50.00
		— RCA mono albums above have black labels with "Long Play" on the bottom; stereo albums have "Living Stereo" on the bottom.—			
Monument MLP-8002	(M)	Yakety Sax	1963	8.00	20.00
Monument SLP-18002	(S)	Yakety Sax	1963	10.00	25.00
		(Monument 8002/18002 was issued with two different covers.)			
RANEY, WAYNE					
King 588	(M)	Songs From The Hills	1958	60.00	150.00
Starday SLP-124	(M)	Wayne Raney And The Raney Family	1960	20.00	50.00
Starday SLP-279	(M)	Don't Try To Be What You Ain't	1962	20.00	50.00
		— Starday albums above have yellow labels.—			
RANGER, ANDY					
Dot DLP-3028	(M)	The Song That Never Ends	1956	30.00	75.00
RARE BIRD					
Rare Bird features Nicky James.					
Probe 24-4514	(S)	Rare Bird	1970	10.00	25.00
RARE EARTH					
Rare Earth 507	(S)	Get Ready (Shape cover)	1969	14.00	35.00

Label & Catalog #		Title	Year	VG+	NM

RACSALS, THE/THE YOUNG RASCALS
The Rascals—The Young Rascals through 1967—were Eddie Brigati, Felix Cavaliere, Gene Cornish and Dino Danelli. Brigati left in 1970 followed by Cornish in 1971; they were replaced by Buzzy Feiten, Robert Popwell and Ann Sutton. Refer to The Critters & The Young Rascals & Lou Christie.

Label & Catalog #		Title	Year	VG+	NM
Atlantic 8123	(M)	The Young Rascals	1966	12.00	30.00
Atlantic SD-8123	(S)	The Young Rascals	1966	14.00	35.00
Atlantic SD-8123	(S)	The Young Rascals	196?	20.00	50.00
		(Some copies of SD-8123 were erroneously pressed with Atco-style purple & brown labels.)			
Atlantic 8134	(M)	Collections	1967	12.00	30.00
Atlantic SD-8134	(S)	Collections	1967	14.00	35.00
Atlantic 8148	(M)	Groovin'	1967	12.00	30.00
Atlantic SD-8148	(S)	Groovin'	1967	14.00	35.00
Atlantic 8169	(M)	Once Upon A Dream	1968	14.00	35.00
Atlantic SD-8169	(S)	Once Upon A Dream	1968	10.00	25.00
Atlantic 8190	(M)	Time Peace/The Rascals' Greatest Hits *(White label promo)*	1968	20.00	50.00
Atlantic SD-8190	(S)	Time Peace/The Rascals' Greatest Hits	1968	10.00	25.00
		—Atlantic stereo albums above have green & blue labels.—			
Atlantic ST-	(DJ)	Freedom Suite Narration *(Interview)*	1969	20.00	50.00
Atlantic ST-137	(DJ)	Freedom Suite *(Sampler)*	1969	16.00	40.00
Atlantic SD-2-901	(S)	Freedom Suite *(2 LPs)*	1969	10.00	25.00
		—Atlantic albums above have green & orange labels with a Broadway address on the bottom.—			

RASPBERRIES, THE
The Raspberries were Jim Bonfanti, Wally Bryson, Eric Carmen and Dave Smalley When Bonfanti and Smalley left in '73, they were replaced by Michael McBride and Scott McCarl. Refer to Dave Smalley.

Label & Catalog #		Title	Year	VG+	NM
Capitol ST-11036	(S)	Raspberries	1972	10.00	25.00
		(Green label with scratch'n sniff cover)			
Capitol SMAS-11220	(S)	Side Three *(Shape cover)*	1973	10.00	25.00

RATHBONE, BASIL
Refer to Errol Flynn.

Label & Catalog #		Title	Year	VG+	NM
Columbia ML-4038	(10")	Peter And The Wolf / Treasure Island	195?	20.00	50.00
Columbia ML-4072	(10")	Sinbad The Sailor / Oliver Twist	195?	20.00	50.00
Columbia ML-4081	(10")	Dicken's Christmas Carol	195?	20.00	50.00
Columbia CL-673	(M)	Treasure Island / Robin Hood	1955	16.00	40.00
Caedmon TC-1028	(M)	Edgar Allen Poe	196?	10.00	25.00
Caedmon TC-1044	(M)	Wilde Fairy Tales	196?	10.00	25.00
Caedmon TC-1115	(M)	Edgar Allen Poe, Vol. 2	196?	10.00	25.00
Caedmon TC-1120	(M)	Stories Of Hawthorne	196?	10.00	25.00
Caedmon TC-1172	(M)	Sherlock Holmes, Vol. 1	196?	10.00	25.00
Caedmon TC-1195	(M)	Edgar Allen Poe, Vol. 3	196?	10.00	25.00
Caedmon TC-1197	(M)	Stories Of Hawthorne, Vol. 2	196?	10.00	25.00
Caedmon TC-1208	(M)	Sherlock Holmes, Vol. 2	196?	10.00	25.00
Co-Star C-107	(M)	Scenes From "The Brothers Karamazov"	196?	8.00	20.00
Co-Star CS-107	(S)	Scenes From "The Brothers Karamazov"	196?	10.00	25.00

RATIONALS, THE

Label & Catalog #		Title	Year	VG+	NM
Crewe CR-1334	(S)	The Rationals	1968	12.00	30.00

RATTLES, THE
Refer to The Searchers / The Rattles.

Label & Catalog #		Title	Year	VG+	NM
Mercury MG-21127	(M)	The Rattles' Greatest Hits	1967	30.00	75.00
Mercury SR-61127	(E)	The Rattles' Greatest Hits	1967	20.00	50.00

RAVEN

Label & Catalog #		Title	Year	VG+	NM
Owl	(M)	Back To Ohio Blues	196?	200.00	400.00

RAVEN

Label & Catalog #		Title	Year	VG+	NM
Discovery 36133	(M)	Live At The Inferno	1967	30.00	75.00

RAVENS, THE

Label & Catalog #		Title	Year	VG+	NM
Regent MG-6062	(M)	Write Me A Letter *(Green label)*	195?	150.00	300.00
Regent MG-6062	(M)	Write Me A Letter *(Red label)*	196?	30.00	75.00

RAW

Label & Catalog #		Title	Year	VG+	NM
Coral CRL7-57515	(S)	Raw Holly	1971	12.00	30.00

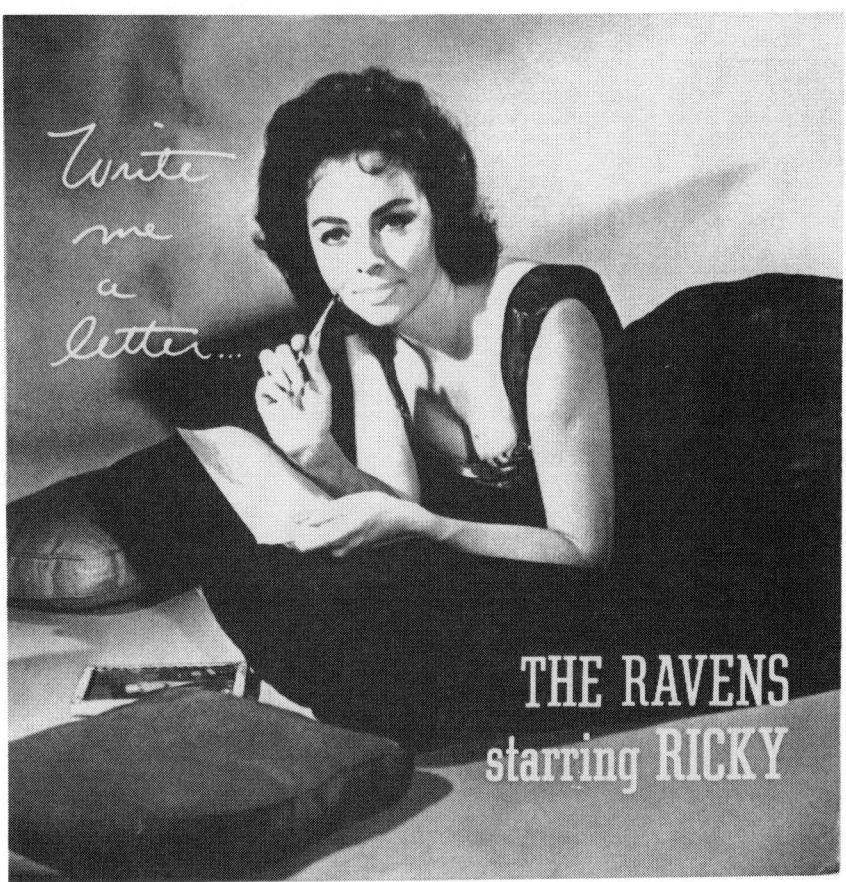

The Ravens were one of the premier rhythm'n blues vocal groups of the late '40s and early '50s. While they featured lead tenor Ollie Jones and, later, Maithe Marshall, it was bass singer Jimmy Ricks that took the lead, popularizing the lead bass for a period that is now all but forgotten. This, their sole LP collection, was not untypical for the time (i.e., the album cover does not feature a picture of the [black] group but that of a lovely young [white] woman.

Label & Catalog #		Title	Year	VG+	NM

RAY, DIANE

Label & Catalog #		Title	Year	VG+	NM
Mercury MG-20903	(M)	The Exciting Years	1964	30.00	75.00
Mercury SR-60903	(S)	The Exciting Years	1964	40.00	100.00

RAY, JAMES

Caprice LP-1002	(M)	If You Gotta Make A Fool Of Somebody	1962	16.00	40.00
Caprice SLP-1002	(S)	If You Gotta Make A Fool Of Somebody	1962	24.00	60.00

RAY, JOHNNIE

Columbia CL-6199	(10")	Johnnie Ray	1951	30.00	75.00
Columbia CL-2510	(10")	I Cry For You	1955	30.00	75.00
Epic LN-1120	(10")	Johnnie Ray	1955	30.00	75.00
Columbia CL-961	(M)	Johnnie Ray Sings The Big Beat	1957	16.00	40.00
Columbia CL-1093	(M)	At The Desert Inn In Las Vegas	1959	16.00	40.00
Columbia CL-1225	(M)	'Til Morning	1959	16.00	40.00
Columbia CL-1227	(M)	Johnnie Ray's Greatest Hits	1959	12.00	30.00
Columbia CL-1385	(M)	On The Trail	1959	16.00	40.00
— Columbia albums above have three white "eye" logos on each side of the spindle hole.—					
Liberty LRP-3221	(M)	Johnnie Ray	1962	8.00	20.00
Liberty LST-7221	(S)	Johnnie Ray	1962	12.00	30.00

RAYBURN, MARGE

Liberty LRP-3126	(M)	Margie	1959	8.00	20.00
Liberty LST-7126	(S)	Margie	1959	12.00	30.00

RAYE, JERRY, & FENWICK

DeVille LP-101	(M)	The Many Sides Of Jerry Raye & Fenwick	1969	40.00	100.00

RAYE, MARTHA
Refer to Carol Burnett & Martha Raye.

Discovery 3010	(10")	Martha Raye Sings	1951	20.00	50.00
Epic LG-3061	(M)	Here's Martha Raye	1954	16.00	40.00

RAYMOND, LEW

Tops L-1583	(M)	For Men Obly (Jayne Mansfield cover)	1958	16.00	40.00
Tops L-1647	(M)	Million Sellers (Mary Tyler Moore cover)	1960	12.00	30.00

RAYNE

(No label)	(S)	Rayne	1979	300.00	500.00

REAGAN, RONALD

"X" LXA-3051	(M)	Tales From The Great Book	1959	12.00	30.00
Key 690	(M)	Rendezvous With Destiny	1964	10.00	25.00
Decca DL-4943	(M)	Freedom's Finest Hour	1867	10.00	25.00
Decca DL-74943	(S)	Freedom's Finest Hour	1867	12.00	30.00

REBS, THE

Fredlo 6830	(M)	1968 A.D. Breakthrough	1968	100.00	250.00

RED CRAYOLA

International Art.	(S)	Parable Of Arable	1968	16.00	40.00
International Art.	(S)	Parable Of Arable	1979	6.00	15.00
International Art.	(S)	God Bless The Crayon	1968	16.00	40.00
International Art.	(S)	God Bless The Crayon	1979	6.00	15.00
(1979 reissues have "Masterfonics" stamped in the trail-off vinyl.)					

REDD, VI: *Refer to* **GOLDMINE'S PRICE GUIDE TO COLLECTIBLE JAZZ ALBUMS**

REDDING, OTIS
Note: As Volt did not record in stereo until 1965, Otis' first two albums above were reissued in minute press runs in electronically rechanneled stereo several years after the initial mono release. As the press runs were small they are quite rare. Refer to Jimi Hendrix / Otis Redding.

Atco 33-161	(M)	Pain In My Heart	1964	80.00	200.00
Atco SD-33-161	(E)	Pain In My Heart	1967	100.00	250.00
Volt 411	(M)	Soul Ballads	1965	30.00	75.00
Volt S-411	(E)	Soul Ballads	1967	40.00	100.00
Volt 412	(M)	Otis Blue/Otis Redding Sings Soul	1965	16.00	40.00
Volt S-412	(S)	Otis Blue/Otis Redding Sings Soul	1965	20.00	50.00
("Respect" and "Old Man Trouble" were rerecorded in stereo.)					

Label & Catalog #		Title	Year	VG+	NM
Volt 413	(M)	The Soul Album	1966	16.00	40.00
Volt S-413	(P)	The Soul Album	1966	20.00	50.00
Volt 415	(M)	Dictionary Of Soul (White label promo)	1966	40.00	100.00
Volt 415	(M)	Dictionary Of Soul	1966	16.00	40.00
Volt S-415	(S)	Dictionary Of Soul	1966	20.00	50.00
Volt 416	(M)	Live In Europe	1967	12.00	30.00
Volt S-416	(S)	Live In Europe	1967	16.00	40.00
Volt 418	(M)	The History Of Otis Redding	1967	12.00	30.00
Volt S-418	(P)	The History Of Otis Redding	1967	16.00	40.00
Volt S-419	(P)	The Dock Of The Bay	1968	12.00	30.00
Atco 33-252	(M)	The Immortal Otis Redding (White label)	1968	20.00	50.00
Atco SD-33-265	(S)	In Person At The Whiskey A Go Go(White label)	1968	20.00	50.00
Atco SD-33-289	(S)	Love Man (White label promo)	1969	20.00	50.00

REDDING, OTIS, & CARLA THOMAS

Stax 716	(M)	King And Queen	1967	16.00	40.00
Stax S-716	(S)	King And Queen	1967	20.00	50.00

REDFORD, ROBERT

Tonsil 003	(S)	The Language And Music Of The Wolves	1971	10.00	25.00

REDPATH, JEAN
Jean Redpath is a Scottish singer of traditional songs.

Prestige Inter. PR-13041	(M)	Skipping Barefoot Through The Heather	1962	12.00	30.00
Elektra EKL-214	(M)	Scottish Ballad Book	1962	8.00	20.00
Elektra EKS-7214	(S)	Scottish Ballad Book	1962	10.00	25.00
Elektra EKL-224	(M)	Songs Of Love, Lilt And Laughter	1962	8.00	20.00
Elektra EKS-7224	(S)	Songs Of Love, Lilt And Laughter	1962	10.00	25.00
Elektra EKL-274	(M)	Laddie Lie Near Me	1964	8.00	20.00
Elektra EKS-7274	(S)	Laddie Lie Near Me	1964	10.00	25.00

REED, DOCK, & VERA HALL

Folkways FP-38	(10")	Spirituals	195?	20.00	50.00
Folkways FA-2038	(10")	Spirituals	195?	20.00	50.00

REED, JIMMY

Vee Jay LP-1004	(M)	I'm Jimmy Reed	1958	60.00	150.00
Vee Jay LP-1008	(M)	Rockin' With Reed	1959	60.00	150.00
Vee Jay LP-1022	(M)	Found Love	1959	60.00	150.00
— Vee Jay albums above have maroon labels with silver print.—					
Vee Jay LP-1004	(M)	I'm Jimmy Reed	196?	20.00	50.00
Vee Jay LP-1008	(M)	Rockin' With Reed	196?	20.00	50.00
Vee Jay LP-1022	(M)	Found Love	1960	20.00	50.00
Vee Jay LP-1025	(M)	Now Appearing	1960	24.00	60.00
Vee Jay 2LP-1035	(M)	Jimmy Reed At Carnegie Hall (2 LPs)	1961	18.00	45.00
Vee Jay 2SR-1035	(P)	Jimmy Reed At Carnegie Hall (2 LPs)	1961	24.00	60.00
Vee Jay LP-1039	(M)	The Best Of Jimmy Reed	1962	10.00	25.00
Vee Jay SR-1039	(P)	The Best Of Jimmy Reed	1962	14.00	35.00
Vee Jay LP-1050	(M)	Just Jimmy Reed	1962	14.00	35.00
Vee Jay LPS-1050	(S)	Just Jimmy Reed	1962	20.00	50.00
Vee Jay LP-1067	(M)	T'Ain't No Big Thing	1963	14.00	35.00
Vee Jay LPS-1067	(S)	T'Ain't No Big Thing	1963	20.00	50.00
Vee Jay LP-1072	(M)	The Best Of The Blues	1963	16.00	40.00
Vee Jay LP-1073	(M)	The 12 String Guitar Blues	1963	16.00	40.00
Vee Jay LP-1080	(M)	More Of The Best Of Jimmy Reed	1964	16.00	40.00
Vee Jay LP-1095	(M)	Jimmy Reed At Soul City	1964	16.00	40.00
Vee Jay VJ-8501	(M)	The Legend, The Man	1965	16.00	40.00
(Should stereo copies of Vee Jay 1073, 1080 or 8501 exist, they would carry a suggested Near Mint value of $75-150.)					
— Vee Jay albums above have black labels with a rainbow border.—					
BluesWay BL-6004	(M)	The New Jimmy Reed Album	1967	8.00	20.00
BluesWay BLS-6004	(S)	The New Jimmy Reed Album	1967	10.00	25.00
BluesWay BL-6009	(M)	Soulin'	1967	8.00	20.00
BluesWay BLS-6009	(S)	Soulin'	1967	10.00	25.00
BluesWay BLS-6013	(S)	Big Boss Man	1968	10.00	25.00
BluesWay BLS-6024	(S)	Down In Virginia	1969	10.00	25.00

Label & Catalog #		Title	Year	VG+	NM

REED, LOU
Lou Reed was formerly a member of The Velvet Underground.

RCA Victor CPL22-1101	(S)	**Metal Machine Music** *(Orange label)*	1975	**20.00**	**50.00**
RCA Victor CPL22-1101	(S)	**Metal Machine Music** *(Brown label)*	1975	**14.00**	**35.00**
RCA Victor APD2-1101	(Q)	**Metal Machine Music**	1975	**60.00**	**150.00**
Direct Disk	(DJ)	**The Bells** *(Test pressing)*	198?	**50.00**	**150.00**

REED, LUCY: Refer to GOLDMINE'S PRICE GUIDE TO COLLECTIBLE JAZZ ALBUMS

REED, LULA
For additional listings refer to Freddie King & Lula Reed.

King 395-604	(M)	**Blue And Moody**	1959	**1,000.00**	*See below*
		(King 604 has a suggested Near Mint value of $2,000-3,000.)			

REED, SUSAN
Susan Reed is an Irish harp player and singer of traditional folk songs.

RCA Victor LXA-3019	(10")	**I Know My Love**	195?	**20.00**	**50.00**
Elektra EKL-26 (10")	(M)	**Old Airs From Ireland, Scotland & England**	195?	**20.00**	**50.00**
Elektra EKL-116	(M)	**Susan Reed/Folk Songs**	195?	**12.00**	**30.00**
Elektra EKL-126	(M)	**Susan Reed Sings Old Airs**	195?	**12.00**	**30.00**
		(Elektra 126 is a reissue of 26 with three additional tracks.)			
Columbia ML-54368	(M)	**Folk Songs**	1958	**12.00**	**30.00**

REESE, DELLA

Jubilee JLP-1026	(M)	**Melancholy Baby**	1957	**12.00**	**30.00**
Jubilee JLP-1071	(M)	**A Date With Della Reese**	1958	**10.00**	**25.00**
Jubilee SDJLP-1071	(S)	**A Date With Della Reese**	1958	**12.00**	**30.00**
Jubilee JLP-1083	(M)	**Amen**	1958	**10.00**	**25.00**
Jubilee SDJLP-1083	(S)	**Amen**	1958	**12.00**	**30.00**
Jubilee JLP-1095	(M)	**The Story Of The Blues**	1958	**10.00**	**25.00**
Jubilee SDJLP-1095	(S)	**The Story Of The Blues**	1958	**12.00**	**30.00**
Jubilee JLP-1109	(M)	**What Do You Know About Love?**	1959	**10.00**	**25.00**
Jubilee SDJLP-1109	(S)	**What Do You Know About Love?**	1959	**12.00**	**30.00**
Jubilee JLP-1116	(M)	**And That Reminds Me**	1959	**10.00**	**25.00**
Jubilee SDJLP-1116	(S)	**And That Reminds Me**	1959	**12.00**	**30.00**
RCA Victor LPM-2157	(M)	**Della**	1960	**10.00**	**25.00**
RCA Victor LSP-2157	(S)	**Della**	1960	**12.00**	**30.00**
RCA Victor LPM-2204	(M)	**Della By Starlight**	1960	**10.00**	**25.00**
RCA Victor LSP-2204	(S)	**Della By Starlight**	1960	**12.00**	**30.00**
RCA Victor LPM-2280	(M)	**Della Della Cha-Cha-Cha**	1961	**10.00**	**25.00**
RCA Victor LSP-2280	(S)	**Della Della Cha-Cha-Cha**	1961	**12.00**	**30.00**
RCA Victor LPM-2391	(M)	**Special Delivery**	1961	**10.00**	**25.00**
RCA Victor LSP-2391	(S)	**Special Delivery**	1961	**12.00**	**30.00**
RCA Victor LPM-2419	(M)	**Classic Della**	1961	**10.00**	**25.00**
RCA Victor LSP-2419	(S)	**Classic Della**	1961	**12.00**	**30.00**
RCA Victor LPM-2568	(M)	**Della Reese On Stage**	1962	**10.00**	**25.00**
RCA Victor LSP-2568	(S)	**Della Reese On Stage**	1962	**12.00**	**30.00**
RCA Victor LPM-2711	(M)	**Waltz With Me**	1963	**8.00**	**20.00**
RCA Victor LSP-2711	(S)	**Waltz With Me**	1963	**10.00**	**25.00**
		— RCA mono albums above have "Long Play" on the bottom of the label;			
		stereo albums have "Living Stereo" on the bottom.—			
RCA Victor LPM-2872	(M)	**Della Reese At Basin Street East**	1964	**8.00**	**20.00**
RCA Victor LSP-2872	(S)	**Della Reese At Basin Street East**	1964	**10.00**	**25.00**

REEVES, JIM/JIM REEVES & THE BLUE BOYS
Refer to The Blue Boys.

Abbott LP-5001	(M)	**Jim Reeves Sings**	1956		*See below*
		(Abbot 5001 has a suggested Near Mint vlaue of $1,000-2,000.)			
RCA Victor LPM-1256	(M)	**Singing Down The Lane**	1956	**150.00**	**300.00**
RCA Victor LPM-1410	(M)	**Bimbo**	1957	**80.00**	**200.00**
		(RCA 1410 is a reissue of Abbott 5001.)			
RCA Victor LPM-1576	(M)	**Jim Reeves**	1957	**30.00**	**75.00**
RCA Victor LPM-1685	(M)	**Girls I Have Known**	1958	**20.00**	**50.00**
RCA Victor LPM-1950	(M)	**God Be With You**	1958	**12.00**	**30.00**
RCA Victor LSP-1950	(S)	**God Be With You**	1958	**20.00**	**50.00**
RCA Victor LPM-2001	(M)	**Songs To Warm Your Heart**	1959	**12.00**	**30.00**
RCA Victor LSP-2001	(S)	**Songs To Warm Your Heart**	1959	**16.00**	**40.00**
RCA Victor LPM-2216	(M)	**The Intimate Jim Reeves**	1960	**8.00**	**20.00**
RCA Victor LSP-2216	(S)	**The Intimate Jim Reeves**	1960	**12.00**	**30.00**

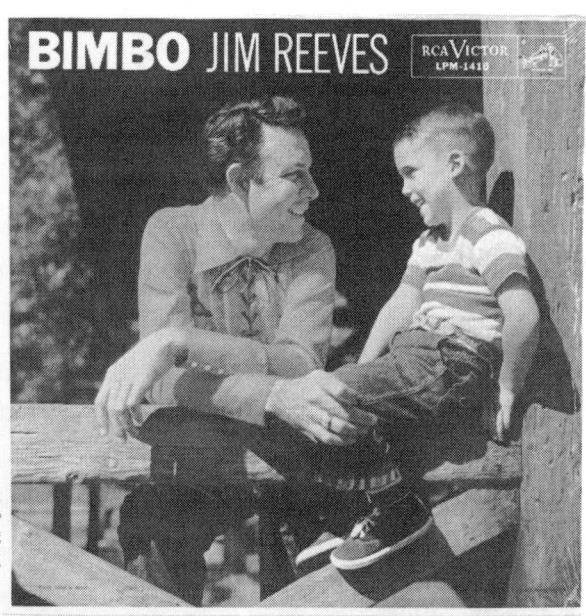

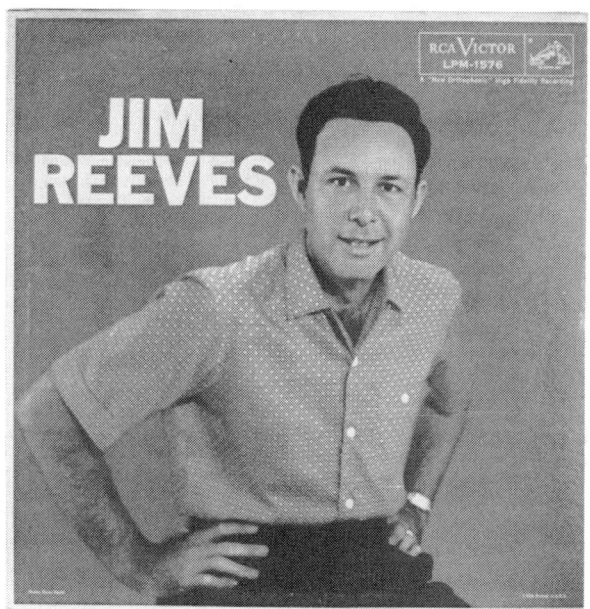

While Jim Reeves Sings on Abbott is a now-legendary country'n western collectible, the majority of Reeves' albums have not achieved high status (i.e., value) with most collectors, his first couple of Victor LPs have passed the three figure mark. Bimbo (top) is a reissue of the Abbott album and a reasonable alternative to having to spend years— and hundreds if not thousands of dollars— searching for the original. His eponymous third RCA album (bottom) is has only beginning to receive attention and is therefore a bargain at any price under three figures (in nearly mint condition, of course).

Label & Catalog #		Title	Year	VG+	NM
RCA Victor LPM-2223	(M)	**He'll Have To Go**	1960	8.00	20.00
RCA Victor LSP-2223	(S)	**He'll Have To Go**	1960	12.00	30.00
RCA Victor LPM-2284	(M)	**Tall Tales And Short Tempers**	1961	8.00	20.00
RCA Victor LSP-2284	(S)	**Tall Tales And Short Tempers**	1961	12.00	30.00
RCA Victor LPM-2339	(M)	**Talkin' To Your Heart**	1961	8.00	20.00
RCA Victor LSP-2339	(S)	**Talkin' To Your Heart**	1961	12.00	30.00
RCA Victor LPM-2487	(M)	**A Touch Of Velvet**	1962	8.00	20.00
RCA Victor LSP-2487	(S)	**A Touch Of Velvet**	1962	12.00	30.00
RCA Victor LPM-2552	(M)	**We Thank Thee**	1962	8.00	20.00
RCA Victor LSP-2552	(S)	**We Thank Thee**	1962	12.00	30.00
RCA Victor LPM-2605	(M)	**Gentleman Jim**	1963	8.00	20.00
RCA Victor LSP-2605	(S)	**Gentleman Jim**	1963	12.00	30.00
RCA Victor LPM-2704	(M)	**The International Jim Reeves**	1963	8.00	20.00
RCA Victor LSP-2704	(S)	**The International Jim Reeves**	1963	12.00	30.00

— RCA mono albums above have "Long Play" on the bottom of the label;
stereo albums have "Living Stereo" on the bottom. —

RCA Victor SP-33-479	(DJ)	**Something Special For Disc Jockeys**	1966	60.00	150.00
RCA Victor LPM-3793	(M)	**The Blue Side Of Lonesome**	1967	10.00	25.00
RCA Victor LSP-3793	(S)	**The Blue Side Of Lonesome**	1967	8.00	20.00
RCA Victor LPM-3903	(M)	**My Cathedral**	1967	10.00	25.00
RCA Victor LSP-3903	(S)	**My Cathedral**	1967	8.00	20.00
RCA Victor LPM-3987	(M)	**A Touch Of Sadness**	1968	20.00	50.00
RCA Victor LSP-3987	(S)	**A Touch Of Sadness**	1968	8.00	20.00

— RCA albums above have black labels. —

REFLECTIONS, THE

Golden World 300	(M)	**(Just Like) Romeo And Juliet**	1964	30.00	75.00

REGENTS, THE

Gee GLP-706	(M)	**Barbara Ann**	1961	60.00	150.00
Gee SGLP-706	(S)	**Barbara Ann**	1961	150.00	300.00

("Barbara Ann" and "I'm So Lonely" are rechanneled on this album.)

Gee SGLP-706	(S)	**Barbara Ann**	197?	10.00	25.00

(Reissue from Publishers Central Bureau licensed through
Roulette Records, as noted on the back cover.)

Capitol KAO-2153	(M)	**Live At The AM/PM Discotheque**	1964	20.00	50.00
Capitol SKAO-2153	(S)	**Live At The AM/PM Discotheque**	1964	30.00	75.00

REID, IRENE: *Refer to* **GOLDMINE'S PRICE GUIDE TO COLLECTIBLE JAZZ ALBUMS**

RELAYER

H.S.R. LSR-1006	(S)	**Relayer**	1979	24.00	60.00

RELATIVELY CLEAN RIVERS

Pacific PC-17601	(S)	**Relatively Clean Rivers**	1976	80.00	200.00

REMAINS, THE

Epic LN-24214	(M)	**The Remains** (White label promo)	1966	200.00	400.00
Epic LN-24214	(M)	**The Remains**	1966	80.00	200.00
Epic BN-26214	(S)	**The Remains**	1966	150.00	300.00

REMINGTON, HERBIE

"D" 7002	(M)	**Herbie Remington Plays The Steel**	195?	40.00	100.00
"D" 7005	(M)	**Aloha Hawaii**	195?	40.00	100.00
United Arts. UAL-3167	(M)	**Steel Guitar Holiday**	1961	20.00	50.00
United Arts. UAS-6167	(E)	**Steel Guitar Holiday**	1961	10.00	25.00

(United Arts. 3/6167 is a repackage of "D" 7002.)

RENAISSANCE

While the original group, which features Keith Relf and Jim McCarty of The Yardbirds, eventually evolved
into the group that recorded "Scheherazade," they have no members in common. . .

Elektra EKS-74068	(S)	**Renaissance** ("Mstic baby' back cover)	1969	10.00	25.00
Mobile Fidelity MFSL-099	(S)	**Scheherezade**	1982	15.00	45.00

RENAY, DIANE

20th Century TF-3133	(M)	**Navy Blue**	1964	30.00	75.00
20th Century TFS-3133	(P)	**Navy Blue**	1964	60.00	150.00

("Man Of Mystery," "Navy Blue," "Sooner Or Later" and
"Unbelievable Guy" are rechanneled on this album.)

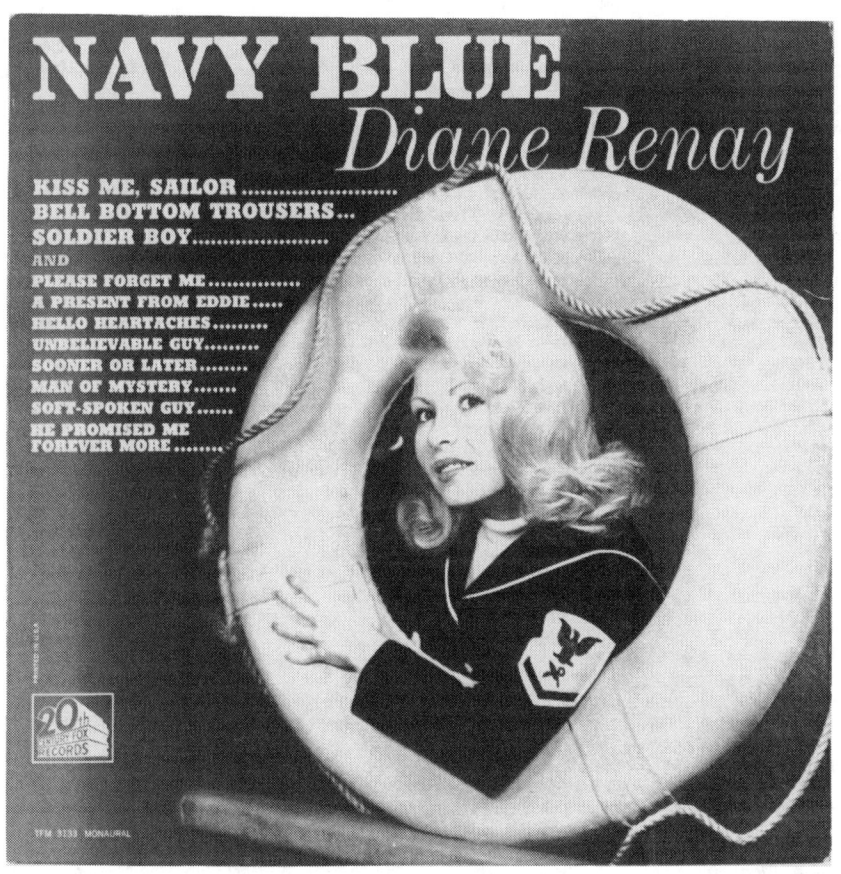

Renee Diane Kushner could boast a top 10 single with "Navy Blue" during the opening salvo of 1964's famed "British Invasion" and followed with another top 30 side in "Kiss Me Sailor." Both of these hits are included on her lone album outing. Pictured here is the more common (sic) mono pressing; stereo versions are much rarer.

Label & Catalog #		Title	Year	VG+	NM

RENE, HENRI

RCA Victor LPM-1033	(M)	Passion In Paint	1955	30.00	75.00
RCA Victor LPM-1046	(M)	Music For Bachelors *(Jayne Mansfield cover)*	1955	40.00	100.00

RENO & HARRELL
Don Reno and Bill Harrell.

Jalyn JLP-108	(M)	Bluegrass Favorites	196?	10.00	25.00
Jalyn JLP-119	(M)	The Most Requested Songs	196?	10.00	25.00
King KSD-1029	(S)	A Variety Of New Scared Gospel songs	1968	10.00	25.00
King KSD-1033	(S)	All The Way To Reno	1968	10.00	25.00
King KSD-1068	(S)	I'm Using My Bible For A Road Map	1969	10.00	25.00

RENO & SMILEY
Don Reno and Red Smiley.

King 550	(M)	Sacred Songs	1958	60.00	150.00
King 552	(M)	Reno & Smiley Instrumentals	1958	60.00	150.00
King 579	(M)	Folk Ballads And Instrumentals	1958	60.00	150.00
King 617	(M)	Someone Will Love Me In Heaven	1959	60.00	150.00
King 621	(M)	Good Old Country Ballads	1959	60.00	150.00
King 646	(M)	A Variety Of Country Songs	1959	60.00	150.00
King 693	(M)	Hymns Sacred And Gospel	1959	60.00	150.00
King 701	(M)	Country Songs	1959	60.00	150.00
King 718	(M)	Wanted	1961	60.00	150.00
King 756	(M)	Folk Songs Of The Civil War	1961	60.00	150.00
King 776	(M)	Country Singing And Instrumentals	1962	40.00	100.00
King 787	(M)	Banjo Special	1962	40.00	100.00
King 816	(M)	Another Day With Reno & Smiley	1962	40.00	100.00
King 853	(M)	The 15 Greatest Hymns Of All Time	1963	40.00	100.00
King 861	(M)	The World's Best 5 String Banjo	1963	40.00	100.00
King 874	(M)	The True Meaning Of Christmas	1963	40.00	100.00
King 911	(M)	On The Road With Reno & Smiley	1964	40.00	100.00
King 914	(M)	A Bluegrass Tribute To Cowboy Copas	1964	40.00	100.00

— King albums above have crownless black or blue labels. The logo on the covers have a crown with "King" in open capitol block letters below.—

King KSD-1044	(E)	I Know You're Married (But I Love You Still)	1969	10.00	25.00
King KSD-1091	(E)	The Best Of Reno & Smiley	1970	10.00	25.00
Dot DLP-3490	(M)	Bluegrass Hits	1963	8.00	20.00
Dot DLP-25490	(S)	Bluegrass Hits	1963	10.00	25.00

REPARATA & THE DELRONS

World Artists WAM-2006	(M)	Whenever A Teenager Cries	1965	16.00	40.00
World Artists WAS-3006	(S)	Whenever A Teenager Cries	1965	20.00	50.00

REPLACEMENTS, THE

Warner Bros. WBMS-148	(DJ)	An Interview With Paul Westerberg	1987	12.00	30.00
Sire/Reprise PRO-4632	(S)	Don't Sell Or Buy... It's Crap *(5 tracks)*	1991	12.00	30.00

REPRISE REPERTORY THEATRE, THE
Rosemary Clooney, Bing Crosby, Sammy Davis, Jr., the Hi-Lo's, Dean Martin, The McGuire Sisters, Debbie Reynolds, Allan Sherman, Dinah Shore, Frank Sinatra, Keely Smith and Jo Stafford.

Reprise F-2015	(M)	Finian's Rainbow *(Gatefold cover)*	1964	16.00	40.00
Reprise FS-2015	(S)	Finian's Rainbow *(Gatefold cover)*	1964	20.00	50.00
Reprise F-2015	(M)	Finian's Rainbow *(Standard cover)*	1964	8.00	20.00
Reprise FS-2015	(S)	Finian's Rainbow *(Standard cover)*	1964	10.00	25.00
Reprise F-2016	(M)	Guys And Dolls *(Gatefold cover)*	1964	20.00	50.00
Reprise FS-2016	(S)	Guys And Dolls *(Gatefold cover)*	1964	24.00	60.00
Reprise F-2016	(M)	Guys And Dolls *(Standard cover)*	1964	10.00	25.00
Reprise FS-2016	(S)	Guys And Dolls *(Standard cover)*	1964	12.00	30.00
Reprise F-2017	(M)	Kiss Me, Kate *(Gatefold cover)*	1964	16.00	40.00
Reprise FS-2017	(S)	Kiss Me, Kate *(Gatefold cover)*	1964	20.00	50.00
Reprise F-2017	(M)	Kiss Me, Kate *(Standard cover)*	1964	8.00	20.00
Reprise FS-2017	(S)	Kiss Me, Kate *(Standard cover)*	1964	10.00	25.00
Reprise F-2018	(M)	South Pacific *(Gatefold cover)*	1964	16.00	40.00
Reprise FS-2018	(S)	South Pacific *(Gatefold cover)*	1964	20.00	50.00
Reprise F-2018	(M)	South Pacific *(Standard cover)*	1964	8.00	20.00
Reprise FS-2018	(S)	South Pacific *(Standard cover)*	1964	10.00	25.00
Reprise F-2019	(M)	The Reprise Repertory Theatre *(4 LP box)*	1964	100.00	250.00
Reprise FS-2019	(S)	The Reprise Repertory Theatre *(4 LP box)*	1964	150.00	300.00

(The boxed sets contain the first album pressings in gatefold covers.)

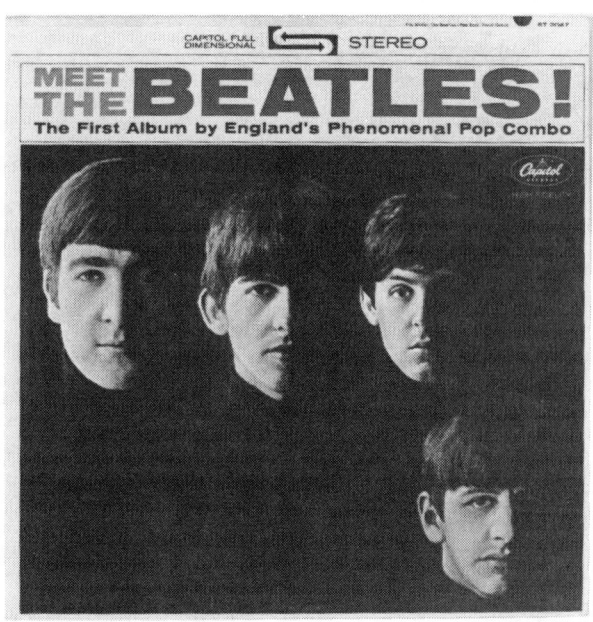

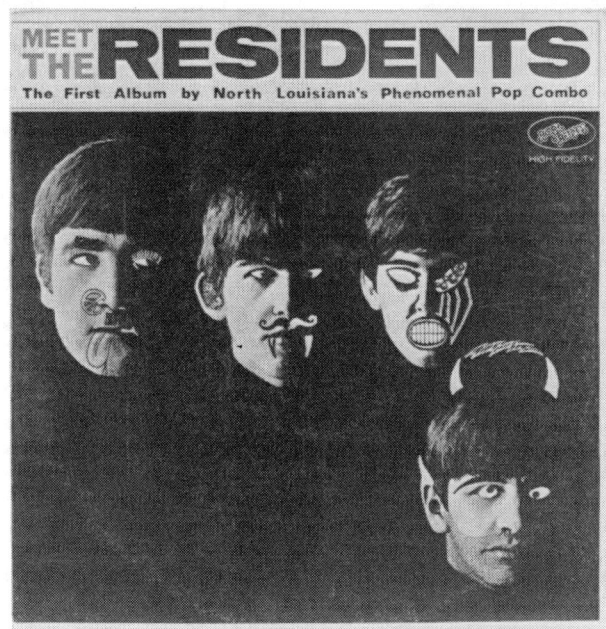

The Bay Area's most well-known unknown group began their lengthy career with a bit of a problem with their first album. It seems that the powers-that-be at Capitol Records took a dim view of the group's icon-oclastic alteration of their client's legendary album cover art and convinced Ralph Records to cease and desist. A new cover was substituted, the record was remixed and sent out to the marketplace. . .

Label & Catalog #		Title	Year	VG+	NM

RESIDENTS, THE

Ralph RR-0274	(M)	Meet The Residents	1974	150.00	300.00
		(Covers of the first 1,000 copies feature a reproduction of Capitol's "Meat The Beatles" only graphically "altered" (i.e., moustaches, teeth, etc are drawn over the Fabs' faces). The back cover reads "First Pressing-1,000 Discs-February, 1974.")			
Ralph RR-0677	(S)	Meet The Residents	1977	10.00	25.00
		(Remixed reissue with new cover art of an alien-like crustacean. There is a split "a" in the Ralph logo on the back cover.)			
Ralph RR-0677	(S)	Meet The Residents (Picture disc)	1987	10.00	25.00
Ralph RR-1075	(S)	Third Reich 'N' Roll	1976	20.00	50.00
		(The covers of the first 1,000 copies have a matte finish and depict Dick Clark in Nazi regalia holding an orange and green hand-colored carrot. Back cover reads "First Pressing-1,000 Copies.")			
Ralph RR-1075	(S)	Third Reich 'N' Roll Collectors Box	1977		See below
		(Limited edition of 25 numbered copies with marbled red vinyl albums with silk-screened labels and box cover. The velvet lined box also contained a set of signed and numbered lithographs. Rare with a suggested Near Mint value of $500-1,500.)			
Ralph RR-1276	(S)	Fingerprince	1976	30.00	75.00
		(The first 1,000 copies have a textured, chocolate-brown cover that states "First Pressing December 1976" on the back)			
Ralph RR-1174	(S)	Not Available (Maroon & purple label)	1978	10.00	25.00
		(The Residents' second album, intentionally made "not available" to the public for four years...)			
Ralph DJ-7901	(DJ)	Please Do Not Steal It!	1979	15.00	75.00
		(Promo compilation of 1,000 copies.)			
Ralph ESK-7906	(S)	Eskimo (10,000 copies pressed on white vinyl)	1980	12.00	30.00
Ralph RZ-8006	(S)	Diskomo	1980	10.00	25.00
Ralph RZ-8052	(S)	Commercial Album (Green vinyl)	1980	20.00	50.00
Ralph RZ-8152	(S)	Mark Of The Mole (Brown vinyl)	1981	20.00	50.00
		(Limited edition of 1,000 in an autographed, silk-screened cover.)			
Ralph RZ-0001	(S)	The Mole Show	1983	12.00	30.00
Ralph RZ-0001	(S)	The Mole Show (Picture disc)	1983	10.00	25.00
Ralph RZ-0001	(S)	The Mole Show (Ralph bootleg)	1983	20.00	50.00
Ralph RZ-8402	(S)	George & James (100 copies on clear vinyl)	1984	12.00	30.00
Ralph RZ-8402	(S)	George & James	1984	12.00	30.00
		(A first pressing of less than 200 copies was erroneously shipped with a matrix number of "RZ-8402-A Re-1" in the trail-off vinyl.)			
Ralph RZ-8452	(S)	Whatever Happened To Vileness Fats?	1984	60.00	150.00
		(100 copies of RZ-8452 were pressed on red vinyl.)			
Episode ED-21	(S)	Census Taker (Soundtrack)	1985	60.00	150.00
		(500 copies of ED-21 were pressed on red vinyl.)			
Episode ED-21	(S)	Census Taker (Soundtrack)	1985	20.00	50.00
Ralph RZ-7707	(S)	Meet The Residents 13th Anniversary Picture Disc	1985	10.00	25.00
Ralph RZ-7707	(S)	Meet The Residents (White vinyl)	1985	20.00	50.00
Ralph RZ-8552	(S)	The Big Bubble/Part Four Of The Mole Trilogy (Marbled pink vinyl)	1985	20.00	50.00

RESTIVO, JOHNNY

RCA Victor LPM-2149	(M)	Oh, Johnny	1959	20.00	50.00
RCA Victor LSP-2149	(S)	Oh, Johnny	1959	30.00	75.00

REVELLS, THE

The Revells are a creation of Gary Usher & Co. Note: There are alternate takes of some tracks between the mono and stereo pressings

Reprise R-6160	(M)	The Go Sound Of The Slots	1965	40.00	100.00
Reprise RS-6160	(S)	The Go Sound Of The Slots	1965	60.00	150.00

REVELS, THE

Impact LPM-1	(M)	Revels On A Rampage	1964	360.00	600.00

REVENGERS, THE

Metro M-565	(M)	Batman And Other Supermen	1966	12.00	30.00
Metro MS-565	(S)	Batman And Other Supermen	1966	16.00	40.00

Label & Catalog #		Title	Year	VG+	NM

REVERE, PAUL, & THE RAIDERS/THE RAIDERS

Revolving around Revere and Mark Lindsay were various Raiders, including the "classic" line-up (1965-67) with Phil Volk, Michael Smith and Drake Levin and later members Jim Valley, Freddy Weller and Keith Allison. By late '67 the albums were recorded mainly by studio musicians under Lindsay's guidance. Refer to Brotherhood; Michael Christian; The Falconaires; Friendsound.

Gardena LP-G1000	(M)	**Like, Long Hair**	1961	200.00	400.00
Sande S-1001	(M)	**Paul Revere & The Raiders**	1963	360.00	600.00
		(Original pressings of Sande 1001 have "Sande" in the trail-off vinyl with no mention of Etiquette Records. Reissues have both "Sande" and "Etiquette" etched in the trail-off vinyl.)			
Jerden JRL-7004	(M)	**In The Beginning**	1966	16.00	40.00
Jerden JRS-7004	(E)	**In The Beginning**	1966	12.00	30.00
		(Jerden 7004 is a repackage of Sande 1001.)			
Jerden T-90709	(M)	**In The Beginning** *(Capitol Record Club)*	1966	20.00	50.00
Jerden ST-90709	(E)	**In The Beginning** *(Capitol Record Club)*	1966	20.00	50.00
Columbia CL-2307	(M)	**Here They Come!**	1965	14.00	35.00
		(Label reads "Guaranteed High Fidelity" on the bottom.)			
Columbia CS-9107	(P)	**Here They Come!**	1965	20.00	50.00
		(Label reads "360 Sound Stereo" in black on the bottom.)			
Columbia Cl-2307	(M)	**Here They Come!**	1965	10.00	25.00
		(Label reads "360 Sound Mono" on the bottom.)			
Columbia CS-9107	(P)	**Here They Come!**	1965	14.00	35.00
		(Label reads "360 Sound Stereo" in white on the bottom.)			
Columbia CL-2451	(M)	**Just Like Us!**	1966	10.00	25.00
Columbia CS-9251	(P)	**Just Like Us!**	1966	12.00	30.00
Columbia CL-2508	(M)	**Midnight Ride**	1966	10.00	25.00
Columbia CS-9308	(P)	**Midnight Ride**	1966	12.00	30.00
		(First pressings for 25/9308 have the songs titles on the front cover in hard-to-read black print.)			
Columbia CL-2508	(M)	**Midnight Ride**	1966	8.00	20.00
Columbia CS-9308	(P)	**Midnight Ride**	1966	10.00	25.00
		(Later pressings have the song titles on the front cover in bold, readable print.)			
Columbia CL-2595	(M)	**The Spirit Of '67**	1966	8.00	20.00
Columbia CS-9395	(P)	**The Spirit Of '67**	1966	10.00	25.00
Columbia 62963	(S)	**Good Thing**	196?		*See below*
		(Recently unearthed, this album has ten of the tracks from "Spirit Of '67" with two older tracks. Its origins are unknown although it has a '60s type label and was manufactured in the U.S.)			
Columbia CS-9753	(S)	**Hard 'N' Heavy (With Marshmallow)**	1969	16.00	40.00
		(CS-9753 was originally issued with a black & white cover.)			
Columbia CS-9753	(S)	**Hard 'N' Heavy (With Marshmallow)**	1969	10.00	25.00
		(L:ater pressings have full-color covers.)			
Columbia *(No number)*	(DJ)	**Pink Puzz**	1969		*See below*
		(In an attempt to gain a portion of the FM market that condemned the group as teenyboppers, Lindsay compiled ten tracks from the group's 1967-68 albums and issued it to stations as an "advance copy" of a new album by a new group, Pink Puzz. Whether this album exists as an acetate or a test pressing is unknown. . .)			
— Columbia albums above have "360 Sound" on the bottom of the label.—					
Sears SPS-493	(E)	**Paul Revere & The Raiders**	1969	20.00	50.00
		(Sears 493 is a repackage of Sande 1001.)			
Realm 2V-8008	(S)	**We Gotta All Get Together** *(2 LPs)*	1976	12.00	30.00
Realm 1V-8009	(S)	**Paul Revere & The Raiders**			
		Featuring Mark Lindsay's "Arizona"	1976	12.00	30.00
		(Both of the Realm albums above were sold through TV offers only.)			

REXROTH, KENNETH, & LAWRENCE FERLINGHETTI

Fantasy 7002	(M)	**Poetry Readings From The Cellar** *(Red vinyl)*	1957	80.00	200.00
Fantasy 7002	(M)	**Poetry Readings From The Cellar**	195?	40.00	100.00

REXROTH, KENNETH

Fantasy 7008	(M)	**Poetry & Jazz At The Blackhawk** *(Red vinyl)*	1958	80.00	200.00
Fantasy 7008	(M)	**Poetry & Jazz At The Blackhawk**	195?	40.00	100.00

REY, ALVINO

Capitol T-808	(M)	**Aloha**	1957	12.00	30.00
Capitol T-1085	(M)	**Swinging Fling**	1958	12.00	30.00
		— *Capitol albums above have turquoise labels.* —			

Label & Catalog #		Title	Year	VG+	NM
Capitol ST-1085	(S)	**Swinging Fling**	1958	12.00	30.00
Capitol T-1262	(M)	**Ping Pong**	1960	8.00	20.00
Capitol ST-1262	(S)	**Ping Pong**	1960	12.00	30.00
Capitol T-1395	(M)	**That Lonely Feeling**	1960	8.00	20.00
Capitol ST-1395	(S)	**That Lonely Feeling**	1960	12.00	30.00

— Capitol albums above have black "rainbow" labels with the logo on the left side.—

REYNOLDS, BURT

Mercury MK-4	(DJ)	**A Burt Reynolds Radio Special**	1973	10.00	25.00

REYNOLDS, DEBBIE
Refer to The Reprise Repertory Theatre.

MGM E-530	(10")	**Two Weeks With Love** *(Soundtrack)*	1950	40.00	100.00
MGM E-113	(10")	**Singing In The Rain** *(Soundtrack)*	1952	40.00	100.00
MGM E-190	(10")	**I Love Melvin** *(Soundtrack)*	1953	40.00	100.00
Mercury MG-25202	(M)	**Athena** *(Soundtrack)*	1954	80.00	200.00
MGM E-3233	(M)	**Two Weeks With Love** *(Soundtrack)*	1955	20.00	50.00
MGM E-3236	(M)	**Singing In The Rain /** **Rich Young And Pretty** *(Soundtracks)*	1955	20.00	50.00
RCA Victor LPM-1339	(M)	**A Bundle Of Joy** *(Soundtrack)*	1956	20.00	50.00
Coral CRL-57159	(M)	**Tammy And The Bachelor** *(Soundtrack)*	1957	80.00	200.00
MGM E-3806	(M)	**From Debbie With Love**	1959	20.00	50.00
Columbia CL-1337	(M)	**Say One For Me** *(Soundtrack)*	1959	16.00	40.00
Columbia CS-8137	(S)	**Say One For Me** *(Soundtrack)*	1959	40.00	100.00
Dot DLP-3191	(M)	**Debbie**	1959	12.00	30.00
Dot DLP-25191	(S)	**Debbie**	1959	16.00	40.00
Dot DLP-3295	(M)	**Am I That Easy To Forget?**	1960	12.00	30.00
Dot DLP-25295	(S)	**Am I That Easy To Forget?**	1960	16.00	40.00
Dot DLP-25295	(S)	**Am I That Easy To Forget?** *(Blue vinyl)*	1960	30.00	75.00
Dot DLP-3298	(M)	**Fine And Dandy**	1960	8.00	20.00
Dot DLP-25298	(S)	**Fine And Dandy**	1960	12.00	30.00
Dot DLP-3492	(M)	**Tammy**	1963	8.00	20.00
Dot DLP-25492	(S)	**Tammy**	1963	12.00	30.00
MGM 1E-5	(M)	**How The West Was Won** *(Soundtrack)*	1963	14.00	35.00
MGM S1E-5	(S)	**How The West Was Won** *(Soundtrack)*	1963	18.00	45.00
MGM 1E-7	(M)	**The Singing Nun** *(Soundtrack)*	1966	8.00	20.00
MGM S1E-7	(S)	**The Singing Nun** *(Soundtrack)*	1966	12.00	30.00
United Arts. UAL-4163	(M)	**Divorce American Style** *(Soundtrack)*	1967	8.00	20.00
United Arts. UAS-5163	(S)	**Divorce American Style** *(Soundtrack)*	1967	12.00	30.00
Columbia KC-32266	(S)	**Irene** *(Soundtrack)*	1973	12.00	30.00

REYS, RITA: *Refer to* **GOLDMINE'S PRICE GUIDE TO COLLECTIBLE JAZZ ALBUMS**

RHODES, EMITT
Emitt Rhodes was the leader of The Merry-Go-Round.

A&M SP-4254	(S)	**American Dream**	1970	14.00	35.00
		(First pressings of SP-4254 have a photo of a shirt-sleeved Rhodes in front of a paint splattered backdrop on the cover and contains the song "You're A Very Lovely Woman.")			
A&M SP-4254	(S)	**American Dream**	1970	10.00	25.00
		(Second pressings have a framed photo of a jacketed Rhodes on the cover and replaces "Lovely Woman" with "Saturday Night.")			

RHODES, RED

Crown CLP-5520	(M)	**Once A Day**	196?	8.00	20.00
Crown CST-520	(S)	**Once A Day**	196?	10.00	25.00
Crown CLP-5528	(M)	**Blue, Blue Day**	196?	8.00	20.00
Crown CST-528	(S)	**Blue, Blue Day**	196?	10.00	25.00
Crown CLP-5555	(M)	**Steel Guitar Rag**	196?	8.00	20.00
Crown CST-555	(S)	**Steel Guitar Rag**	196?	10.00	25.00
Happy Tiger HT-1003	(S)	**Live At The Palomino**	1969	10.00	25.00

RHODES, TODD

King 295-88	(10")	**Todd Rhodes Playing His Greatest Hits**	1954	500.00	1,500.00
King 658	(M)	**Dance Music**	1960	400.00	800.00

RHYTHM MASTERS, THE

Ace LP-1010	(M)	**Hymns And Spirituals**	1961	40.00	100.00

Label & Catalog #		Title	Year	VG+	NM
RHYTHM ROCKERS, THE					
Challenge CHL-617	(M)	Soul Surfin'	1963	30.00	75.00
RICH, CHARLIE					
Philips Inter. PLP-1970	(M)	Lonely Weekends	1960	250.00	500.00
Groove G-1000	(M)	Charlie Rich	1964	60.00	150.00
Groove GS-1000	(S)	Charlie Rich	1964	150.00	300.00
RCA Victor LPM-3352	(M)	That's Rich	1965	16.00	40.00
RCA Victor LSP-3352	(S)	That's Rich	1965	20.00	50.00
RCA Victor LPM-3537	(M)	Big Boss Man	1966	16.00	40.00
RCA Victor LSP-3537	(S)	Big Boss Man	1966	20.00	50.00
Smash MGS-27070	(M)	The Many Sides Of Charlie Rich	1965	10.00	25.00
Smash SRS-67070	(S)	The Many Sides Of Charlie Rich	1965	12.00	30.00
Smash MGS-27078	(M)	The Best Years	1966	10.00	25.00
Smash SRS-67078	(S)	The Best Years	1966	12.00	30.00
Hi HL-32037	(M)	Charlie Rich Sings Country And Western	1967	8.00	20.00
Hi SHL-32037	(S)	Charlie Rich Sings Country And Western	1967	10.00	25.00
Epic AS-50	(DJ)	Charlie Rich (Sampler)	1972	12.00	30.00
RICH, DON, & THE BUCKAROOS: *Refer to* **THE BUCKAROOS**					
RICHARD, CLIFF, & THE SHADOWS					
Refer to The Shadows.					
ABC-Paramount ABC-321	(M)	Cliff Sings	1960	16.00	40.00
ABC-Paramount ABCS-321	(S)	Cliff Sings	1960	20.00	50.00
ABC-Paramount ABC-391	(M)	Listen To Cliff	1961	16.00	40.00
ABC-Paramount ABCS-391	(S)	Listen To Cliff	1961	20.00	50.00
Dot DLP-3474	(M)	Wonderful To Be Young (Soundtrack)	1962	16.00	40.00
Dot DLP-25474	(S)	Wonderful To Be Young (Soundtrack)	1962	20.00	50.00
Epic LN-24063	(M)	Summer Holiday (Soundtrack)	1963	20.00	50.00
Epic BN-26063	(S)	Summer Holiday (Soundtrack)	1963	30.00	75.00
Epic LN-24089	(M)	It's All In The Game	1964	10.00	25.00
Epic BN-26089	(S)	It's All In The Game	1964	12.00	30.00
Epic LN-24115	(M)	Cliff Richard In Spain	1964	10.00	25.00
Epic BN-26115	(S)	Cliff Richard In Spain	1964	12.00	30.00
Epic LN-24145	(M)	Swinger's Paradise (Soundtrack)	1965	12.00	30.00
Epic BN-26145	(S)	Swinger's Paradise (Soundtrack)	1965	16.00	40.00
RICHARD, CLIFF					
Uni (No number)	(S)	Two A Penny (Soundtrack)	1971	20.00	50.00
RICHARD, CYRIL					
Riverside RLP-406	(M)	Alice In Wonderland	1961	12.00	30.00
RICHARDS, ANN					
Capitol T-1087	(M)	I'm Shooting High	1959	16.00	40.00
Capitol ST-1087	(M)	I'm Shooting High	1959	20.00	50.00
Capitol T-1406	(M)	The Many Moods Of Ann Richards	1960	16.00	40.00
Capitol ST-1406	(S)	The Many Moods Of Ann Richards	1960	20.00	50.00
Capitol T-1495	(M)	Two Much (With Stan Kenton)	1961	16.00	40.00
Capitol ST-1495	(S)	Two Much (With Stan Kenton)	1961	20.00	50.00
Atco 33-136	(M)	Ann, Man!	1961	20.00	50.00
Atco SD-33-136	(S)	Ann, Man!	1961	30.00	75.00
Vee Jay LP-1070	(M)	Live... At The Losers	1963	16.00	40.00
Vee Jay SR-1070	(M)	Live... At The Losers	1963	20.00	50.00
RICHARDS, TRUDY					
Capitol T-838	(M)	Crazy In Love	1957	12.00	30.00
RICHARDS, WARREN S.					
Cotillion SD-9013	(S)	Warren S. Richards Jr.	1970	20.00	50.00
RICHARDSON, JIMMY					
Starday SLP-126	(M)	Sweet With A Beat (Yellow label)	1960	16.00	40.00
RICHMAN, JONATHAN, & THE MODERN LOVERS					
Home Of The Hits HH-1910	(S)	The Modern Lovers	1975	20.00	50.00
Beserkley BX-0048	(S)	Jonathan Richman & The Modern Lovers	1976	14.00	35.00
Beserkley BZ-0050	(S)	The Modern Lovers	1976	14.00	35.00

Charlie Rich, one of Sam Phillips' premier proteges in the post-Presley days, issued one album for Phillips International before signing with RCA Victor (the label that had picked up Elvis and another Sun star, Roy Orbison). His first album for his new label was issued on their Groove subsidiary to little fanfare or sales. He then moved to Mercury's Smash label, where success on a large—and deserving—scale, eluded him. Of course, in his later, more mellow years, he would achieve country'n western superstardom with Epic.

Ann Richards first hit the roads with Charlie Barnett followed by a stint with George Redman before touring with, and subsequently marrying, Stan Kenton. She then "retired" from touring although she continued to record on her own and with Kenton for Capitol.

Label & Catalog #		Title	Year	VG+	NM

RICKS, JIMMY
Mr. Ricks was formerly a member of The Ravens.

Label & Catalog #		Title	Year	VG+	NM
Signature 1032	(M)	Jimmy Ricks *(White label promo)*	1961	100.00	200.00
Signature 1032	(M)	Jimmy Ricks	1961	150.00	300.00
Mainstream 56050	(M)	Vibrations	1965	20.00	50.00
Mainstream S-6050	(S)	Vibrations	1965	24.00	60.00
Jubilee JGS-8021	(S)	Tell Her You Love Her	1969	24.00	60.00

RIGHTEOUS BROTHERS, THE
The brothers righteous are Bobby Hatfield and Bill Medley.

Label & Catalog #		Title	Year	VG+	NM
Moonglow MLP-1001	(M)	Right Now!	1963	12.00	30.00
Moonglow MSP-1001	(S)	Right Now!	1963	16.00	40.00
Moonglow MLP-1002	(M)	Some Blue-Eyed Soul	1964	12.00	30.00
Moonglow MSP-1002	(S)	Some Blue-Eyed Soul	1964	16.00	40.00
Moonglow MLP-1003	(M)	This Is New!	1965	12.00	30.00
Moonglow MSP-1003	(S)	This Is New!	1965	16.00	40.00
Moonglow MLP-1004	(M)	The Best Of The Righteous Brothers	1966	10.00	25.00
Moonglow MSP-1004	(S)	The Best Of The Righteous Brothers	1966	12.00	30.00
Philles PHLP-4007	(M)	You've Lost That Loving Feelin' *(White label)*	1965	60.00	150.00
Philles PHLP-4007	(M)	You've Lost That Loving Feelin'	1965	10.00	25.00
Philles PHLP-ST-4007	(P)	You've Lost That Loving Feelin'	1965	16.00	40.00
Philles PHLP-4008	(M)	Just Once In My Life	1965	10.00	25.00
Philles PHLP-ST-4008	(P)	Just Once In My Life	1965	16.00	40.00
Philles PHLP-4009	(M)	Back To Back	1966	8.00	20.00
Philles PHLP-ST-4009	(P)	Back To Back	1966	10.00	25.00
		(Portions of Philles 4007 and 4009 were produced by Phil Spector.)			
Verve V-5001	(M)	Soul And Inspiration	1966	8.00	20.00
Verve V6-5001	(S)	Soul And Inspiration	1966	10.00	25.00
Verve V-5004	(S)	Go Ahead And Cry	1966	8.00	20.00
Verve V6-5004	(S)	Go Ahead And Cry	1966	10.00	25.00
Verve V-5058	(M)	One For The Road	1968	12.00	30.00
Verve V6-5058	(S)	One For The Road	1968	10.00	25.00
		(Original covers of Verve 5058 credit The Blossoms on the back.)			

RILEY, BILLY LEE

Label & Catalog #		Title	Year	VG+	NM
Mercury MG-20958	(M)	The Whiskey A-Go-Go Presents Billy Lee Riley	1963	8.00	20.00
Mercury SR-60958	(S)	The Whiskey A-Go-Go Presents Billy Lee Riley	1963	10.00	25.00
Mercury MG-20965	(M)	Big Harmonica Special	1964	8.00	20.00
Mercury SR-60965	(S)	Big Harmonica Special	1964	10.00	25.00
Mercury MG-20974	(M)	Beatlemania Harmonica	1964	10.00	25.00
Mercury SR-60974	(S)	Beatlemania Harmonica	1964	12.00	30.00
Mojo 1933	(S)	Southern Soul	1967	200.00	500.00

RINCON SURFSIDE BAND, THE
The Rincons are a creation of Steve Barri and Phil Sloan. Refer to The Grass Roots; The Fantastic Baggys.

Label & Catalog #		Title	Year	VG+	NM
Dunhill D-50001	(M)	Surfing Songbook	1965	60.00	150.00
Dunhill DS-50001	(S)	Surfing Songbook	1965	80.00	200.00

RIP CHORDS, THE
The Rip Chords are a creation of Bruce Johnston and Terry Melcher & Co.

Label & Catalog #		Title	Year	VG+	NM
Columbia CL-2151	(M)	Hey, Little Cobra (& Other Hot Rod Hits)	1964	14.00	35.00
Columbia CS-8951	(S)	Hey, Little Cobra (& Other Hot Rod Hits)	1964	20.00	50.00
Columbia CL-2216	(M)	Three Window Coupe	1964	20.00	50.00
Columbia CS-9016	(S)	Three Window Coupe	1964	30.00	75.00
		(CS-9016 was originally issued with a borderless, full view cover.)			

RISERS, THE

Label & Catalog #		Title	Year	VG+	NM
Imperial LP-9269	(M)	She's A Bad Motorcycle	1964	16.00	40.00
Imperial LP-12269	(S)	She's A Bad Motorcycle	1964	20.00	50.00

RISING STORM, THE

Label & Catalog #		Title	Year	VG+	NM
Remnant BBA-3571	(M)	Calm Before The Rising Storm	1968	800.00	1,200.00
Arf Arf 007	(S)	Back In Anover Again	1983	60.00	150.00
		(Limited pressing of 1,000 numbered copies.)			

Label & Catalog #		Title	Year	VG+	NM

RITCHIE, JEAN
Jean Ritchie is a guitar and dulcimer player and singer of Appalachian folk music. Refer to Edna Ritchie.

Label & Catalog #		Title	Year	VG+	NM
Elektra EKL-2	(10")	Jean Ritchie Singing Traditional Songs Of Her Kentucky Mountain Home	1952	20.00	50.00
Elektra EKL-25	(10")	Kentucky Mountain Songs	1954	20.00	50.00
Elektra EKL-125	(M)	Kentucky Mountain Songs	195?	20.00	50.00
		(Elektra 125 is a reissue of 25 with five additional tracks.)			
Westminster WP-6037	(M)	Songs From Kentucky	1956	20.00	50.00
Collector Lim. Ed. 1201	(M)	Field Trip	1956	20.00	50.00
Riverside RLP-12-620	(M)	Saturday Night And Sunday, Too	195?	20.00	50.00
Riverside RLP-12-646	(M)	Songs From Kentucky	195?	20.00	50.00
Riverside RLP-12-653	(M)	Singing Family Of The Cumberlands—Songs & Folktales Of A Famous Mountain Family	195?	20.00	50.00
Folkways FC-754	(M)	Southern Mountain Children's Songs And Games	195?	20.00	50.00
Folkways FC-7054	(M)	Southern Mountain Children's Songs And Games	195?	20.00	50.00
Folkways FA-2316	(M)	The Ritchie Family Of Kentucky	195?	12.00	30.00
Folkways FA-2426	(M)	Jean Ritchie At Folk City *(With Doc Watson)*	195?	12.00	30.00
Folkways FA-2427	(M)	Precious Memories	195?	12.00	30.00
Folkways FI-8352	(M)	The Appalachian Dulcimer	1963	8.00	20.00
Tradition TLP-1031	(M)	Carols Of All Seasons	1959	12.00	30.00
Prestige Int. PRLP-13003	(M)	The Best Of Jean Ritchie	1961	10.00	25.00
Folklore FRLP-14009	(M)	The Best Of Jean Ritchie	1964	10.00	25.00
Folklore FRST-14009	(S)	The Best Of Jean Ritchie	1964	10.00	25.00
		(Folklore 14004 is a reissue of Prestige 13003.)			
Verve/Folkways FVS-9026	(M)	Jean Ritchie At Folk City *(With Doc Watson)*	1965	8.00	20.00
Verve/Folkways FVS-9026	(S)	Jean Ritchie At Folk City *(With Doc Watson)*	1965	10.00	25.00
		(Verve/Folkways 9026 is a reissue of 2426.)			
Warner Bros. W-1592	(M)	A Time For Singing	1965	8.00	20.00
Warner Bros. WS-1592	(S)	A Time For Singing	1965	10.00	25.00

RITCHIE, JEAN, & OSCAR BRAND
Refer to Oscar Brand.

Elektra EKL-22	(10")	Courting Songs	1954	20.00	50.00
Riverside RLP-12-646	(M)	Riddle Me This (Courting And Riddle Songs)	195?	20.00	50.00
Folkways FA-2428	(M)	Folk Song Concert At Town Hall	195?	12.00	30.00

RITCHIE, JEAN, & OSCAR BRAND / TOM PALEY
Refer to Oscar Brand; Tom Paley.

Elektra EKL-122	(M)	Courtin's A Pleasure—Folksongs From The Southern Appalachians	1954	12.00	30.00
		(Elektra 122 reissues portions of 12 and 22.)			

RITCHIE, JEAN, & PAUL CLAYTON
Refer to Paul Clayton.

Tradition TLP-1011	(M)	American Folk Tales And Songs	1958	12.00	30.00

RITCHIE, JEAN, & TONY KRABER

New Records LP-2005	(10")	Ballads In Colonial America	195?	20.00	50.00

RITCHIE, LITTLE JOE
Little Joe Ritchie is a pseudonym for Joe Pesci.

Brunswick BL-54135	(M)	Little Joe Sure Can Sing	1967	80.00	200.00
Brunswick BL-754135	(S)	Little Joe Sure Can Sing	1967	100.00	250.00

RITTER, TEX

Capitol H-4004	(10")	Cowboy Favorites	1949	80.00	200.00
Capitol T-971	(M)	Songs From The Western Screen	1958	30.00	75.00
		— Capitol albums above have turquoise labels.—			
Capitol T-1100	(M)	Psalms	1959	20.00	50.00
Capitol T-1292	(M)	Blood On The Saddle	1960	12.00	30.00
Capitol ST-1292	(S)	Blood On The Saddle	1960	16.00	40.00
Capitol W-1562	(M)	The Lincoln Hymns	1961	12.00	30.00
Capitol SW-1562	(S)	The Lincoln Hymns	1961	16.00	40.00
Capitol T-1623	(M)	Hillbilly Heaven	1961	12.00	30.00
Capitol ST-1623	(S)	Hillbilly Heaven	1961	16.00	40.00
		— Capitol albums above have black labels with the logo on the left side.—			

Label & Catalog #		Title	Year	VG+	NM
LaBrea L-8036	(M)	Jamboree, Nashville Style	1962	12.00	30.00
LaBrea LS-8036	(S)	Jamboree, Nashville Style	1962	16.00	40.00
Capitol T-1757	(M)	Stan Kenton/Tex Ritter	1962	10.00	25.00
Capitol ST-1757	(S)	Stan Kenton/Tex Ritter	1962	12.00	30.00
Capitol T-1910	(M)	Border Affair	1963	8.00	20.00
Capitol ST-1910	(S)	Border Affair	1963	10.00	25.00
Capitol T-2402	(M)	The Friendly Voice Of Tex Ritter	1965	8.00	20.00
Capitol ST-2402	(S)	The Friendly Voice Of Tex Ritter	1965	10.00	25.00
		— Capitol albums above have black labels with the logo on top.—			

RIVERA, LUIS, & DOC BAGBY

King 631	(M)	Battle Of The Organs	1959	40.00	100.00

RIVERS, JERRY

Starday SLP-281	(M)	Fantastic Fiddlin' & Tall Tales (Yellow label)	1964	12.00	30.00

RIVERS, JOHNNY

Capitol T-2161	(M)	The Sensational Johnny Rivers	1964	8.00	20.00
Capitol STT-2161	(S)	The Sensational Johnny Rivers	1964	10.00	25.00
United Arts. UAL-3386	(M)	Go Johnny, Go	1964	8.00	20.00
United Arts. UAS-6386	(S)	Go Johnny, Go	1964	10.00	25.00
United Arts. ST-90813	(S)	Go Johnny, Go (Capitol Record Club)	1966	12.00	30.00
Imperial LP-9264	(M)	Johnny Rivers At The Whiskey A-Go-Go	1964	7.00	35.00
Imperial LP-12264	(S)	Johnny Rivers At The Whiskey A-Go-Go	1964	20.00	50.00
		— Imperial mono albums above have black labels with stars on top; stereo albums have black labels with silver print.			
Imperial LP-9264	(M)	Johnny Rivers At The Whiskey A-Go-Go	1964	8.00	20.00
Imperial LP-12264	(S)	Johnny Rivers At The Whiskey A-Go-Go	1964	10.00	25.00
Imperial LP-9274	(M)	Here We A-Go-Go Again	1964	8.00	20.00
Imperial LP-12274	(S)	Here We A-Go-Go Again	1964	10.00	25.00
Imperial LP-9280	(M)	Johnny Rivers In Action	1965	8.00	20.00
Imperial LP-12280	(S)	Johnny Rivers In Action	1965	10.00	25.00
Imperial LP-9284	(M)	Meanwhile Back At The Whiskey A-Go-Go	1965	8.00	20.00
Imperial LP-12284	(S)	Meanwhile Back At The Whiskey A-Go-Go	1965	10.00	25.00
Imperial LP-9293	(M)	Johnny Rivers Rocks The Folk	1965	8.00	20.00
Imperial LP-12293	(S)	Johnny Rivers Rocks The Folk	1965	10.00	25.00
Imperial LP-9307	(M)	And I Know You Wanna Dance	1966	8.00	20.00
Imperial LP-12307	(S)	And I Know You Wanna Dance	1966	10.00	25.00
		— Imperial albums above have blac, pink & white labels.—			
Sears SPS-417	(S)	Mr. Teenage	1968	10.00	25.00
Sears SPS-487	(S)	Groovin'	1968	12.00	30.00
United Artists LA-020G	(S)	Rockin' Rivers (Canadian)	1974	16.00	40.00

RIVERS, MAVIS: *Refer to* GOLDMINE'S PRICE GUIDE TO COLLECTIBLE JAZZ ALBUMS

RIVIERAS, THE

Riviera 701	(M)	Campus Party	1964	60.00	150.00
U.S.A. 102	(M)	Let's Have A Party	1964	40.00	100.00
Post 2000	(S)	The Rivieras Sing	196?	6.00	15.00

RIVINGTONS, THE

Liberty LRP-3282	(M)	Doin' The Bird	1963	40.00	100.00
Liberty LST-7282	(S)	Doin' The Bird	1963	60.00	150.00

ROAD RUNNERS, THE

The Road Runners are a creation of Gary Usher & Co.

London LL-3381	(M)	The New Mustang (& Other Hot Rod Hits)	1964	60.00	150.00
London PS-381	(S)	The New Mustang (& Other Hot Rod Hits)	1964	80.00	200.00

ROBBINS, MARTY

Marty Robbins is a pseudonym for Martin Robertson. Refer to Carl Smith / Lefty Frizzell / M. Robbins..

Columbia CL-2601	(10")	Rock 'N Roll 'N Robbins	1956	300.00	800.00
Columbia CL-976	(M)	The Song Of Robbins	1957	40.00	100.00
Columbia CL-1087	(M)	Song Of The Islands	1957	60.00	150.00
Columbia CL-1189	(M)	Marty Robbins	1958	30.00	75.00
Columbia CL-1325	(M)	Marty's Greatest Hits	1959	30.00	75.00
Columbia CS-8639	(E)	Marty's Greatest Hits	1962	16.00	40.00
		(CS-8639 has "Ain't I The Lucky One," "The Hanging Tree," and "The Blues Country Style" in stereo.)			

Label & Catalog #		Title	Year	VG+	NM
Columbia CL-1349	(M)	Gunfighter Ballads And Trail Songs	1959	12.00	30.00
Columbia CS-8158	(S)	Gunfighter Ballads And Trail Songs	1959	16.00	40.00
Columbia CL-1481	(M)	More Gunfighter Ballads And Trail Songs	1960	10.00	30.00
Columbia CS-8272	(S)	More Gunfighter Ballads And Trail Songs	1960	16.00	40.00
Columbia CL-1558	(M)	The Alamo (Soundtrack)	1960	10.00	30.00
Columbia CS-8358	(S)	The Alamo (Soundtrack)	1960	16.00	40.00
Columbia CL-1635	(M)	More Greatest Hits	1961	10.00	30.00
Columbia CS-8435	(S)	More Greatest Hits	1961	16.00	40.00
Columbia CL-1666	(M)	Just A Little Sentimental	1961	10.00	30.00
Columbia CS-8466	(S)	Just A Little Sentimental	1961	16.00	40.00
Columbia CL-1801	(M)	Marty After Midnight	1962	20.00	50.00
Columbia CS-8601	(S)	Marty After Midnight	1962	30.00	75.00
— Columbia albums above have six white-on-black "eye" logos around the perimeter of the label.—					
Columbia CL-1855	(M)	Portrait Of Marty (With bonus portrait)	1962	28.00	70.00
Columbia CL-1855	(M)	Portrait Of Marty (Without the portrait)	1962	16.00	40.00
Columbia CS-8655	(S)	Portrait Of Marty (With bonus portrait)	1962	32.00	80.00
Columbia CS-8655	(S)	Portrait Of Marty (Without the portrait)	1962	20.00	50.00
Columbia CL-1918	(M)	Devil Woman	1962	12.00	30.00
Columbia CS-8718	(S)	Devil Woman	1962	16.00	40.00
Columbia CL-2040	(M)	Hawaii's Calling Me	1963	15.00	35.00
Columbia CS-8840	(S)	Hawaii's Calling Me	1963	20.00	50.00
Columbia CL-2072	(M)	Return Of The Gunfighter	1963	10.00	25.00
Columbia CS-8872	(S)	Return Of The Gunfighter	1963	14.00	35.00
Columbia CL-2176	(M)	Island Woman	1964	15.00	35.00
Columbia CS-8976	(S)	Island Woman	1964	20.00	50.00
Columbia CL-2220	(M)	R.F.D. Marty Robbins	1964	12.00	30.00
Columbia CS-9020	(S)	R.F.D. Marty Robbins	1964	16.00	40.00
Columbia CL-2304	(M)	Turn The Lights Down Low	1965	8.00	20.00
Columbia CS-9104	(S)	Turn The Lights Down Low	1965	12.00	30.00
Columbia CL-2448	(M)	What God Has Done	1965	8.00	20.00
Columbia CS-9248	(S)	What God Has Done	1965	10.00	25.00
Columbia CL-2527	(M)	The Drifter	1966	8.00	20.00
Columbia CS-9327	(S)	The Drifter	1966	10.00	25.00
Columbia CL-2621	(M)	The Song Of Robbins	1967	12.00	30.00
Columbia CS-9421	(E)	The Song Of Robbins	1967	8.00	20.00
		(Columbia 26/9421 is a reissue of 976.)			
Columbia CL-2625	(M)	Song Of The Islands	1967	12.00	30.00
Columbia CS-9425	(E)	Song Of The Islands	1967	8.00	20.00
		(Columbia 26/9425 is a reissue of 1087.)			
Columbia CL-2645	(M)	My Kind Of Country	1967	12.00	30.00
Columbia CS-9445	(S)	My Kind Of Country	1967	8.00	20.00
Columbia CL-2725	(M)	Tonight Carmen	1967	12.00	30.00
Columbia CS-9525	(S)	Tonight Carmen	1967	8.00	20.00
Columbia CL-2735	(M)	Christmas With Marty Robbins	1967	20.00	50.00
Columbia CS-9535	(S)	Christmas With Marty Robbins	1967	12.00	30.00
Columbia CL-2817	(M)	By The Time I Get To Phoenix	1968	20.00	50.00
Columbia CS-9617	(S)	By The Time I Get To Phoenix	1968	8.00	20.00
Columbia CS-9811	(S)	It's A Sin	1969	10.00	25.00
— Columbia albums above have "360 Sound" on the bottom of the label.—					
— Columbia Budget Reissues & Special Products Releases—					
Columbia DS-445	(S)	Bend In The River (Columbia Record Club)	1968	20.00	50.00
Columbia ST-2016	(E)	The Heart Of Marty Robbins (2 LPs)	1969	20.00	50.00
Columbia P5S-5812	(S)	Marty (5 LP box)	1972	16.00	40.00
Columbia CSP-13358	(S)	Christmas With Marty Robbins	197?	12.00	30.00

ROBBS, THE

Label & Catalog #		Title	Year	VG+	NM
Mercury MG-21130	(M)	The Robbs	1967	12.00	30.00
Mercury SR-61130	(S)	The Robbs	1967	16.00	40.00

ROBERTS, JOAN

Label & Catalog #		Title	Year	VG+	NM
Quality 719-26	(10")	Joan Roberts Sings	195?	16.00	40.00

ROBERTS, KENNY

Label & Catalog #		Title	Year	VG+	NM
Starday SLP-336	(M)	Indian Love Call	1965	16.00	40.00
Starday SLP-406	(M)	The Incredible Kenny Roberts	1967	16.00	40.00
— Starday albums above have yellow labels.—					

Label & Catalog #		Title	Year	VG+	NM

ROBERTS, PERNELL
Also refer to Lorne Greene & Dan Blocker & Mike Landon & Pernell Roberts.

RCA Victor LPM-2662	(M)	Come All Ye Fair And Tender Ladies	1963	12.00	30.00
RCA Victor LSP-2662	(S)	Come All Ye Fair And Tender Ladies	1963	16.00	40.00

ROBERTS, ROBIN
Robin Roberts is a guitar and dulcimer player and singer of traditional folk songs.

Stinson SLP-63	(10")	Irish Street Songs	195?	20.00	50.00
Stinson SLP-7?	(10")	Folk And Traditional Love Songs	195?	20.00	50.00
Stinson SLP-7?	(M)	Traditional Folk Songs And Ballads	1958	12.00	30.00

ROBERTSON, DALE

RCA Victor LPM-2158	(M)	His Album Of Western Classics	1960	40.00	100.00
RCA Victor LSP-2158	(S)	His Album Of Western Classics	1960	60.00	150.00
Western Americana SR-100	(M)	Quarter Horse (Soundtrack)	1965	30.00	75.00

ROBERTSON, DON

RCA Victor LPM-3348	(M)	Heart On My Sleeve	1965	8.00	20.00
RCA Victor LSP-3348	(S)	Heart On My Sleeve	1965	10.00	25.00

ROBERTSON, JEANNIE
Jeannie Robertson is a Scottish ballad singer.

Riverside RLP-12-633	(M)	Songs Of A Scots Tinker Lady	195?	12.00	30.00
Prestige Inter. PRLP-13006	(M)	The World's Greatest Folksinger	1961	12.00	30.00
Prestige Inter. PRLP-13075	(M)	Scotch Folk Songs	1963	12.00	30.00

ROBERTSON, "TEXAS JIM"

Masterseal	(10")	Eight Top Western Hits	195?	24.00	60.00

ROBERTSON, WALT

Folkways FP-46	(10")	American Northwest Ballads	195?	20.00	50.00
Folkways FA-2046	(10")	American Northwest Ballads	195?	20.00	50.00

ROBESON, PAUL
Paul Robeson was a singer of traditional Black spirituals and folk-based songs.

Columbia ML-2038	(10")	Swing Low, Sweet Chariot	1949	20.00	75.00
Columbia ML-4105	(10")	Spirituals	1949	20.00	75.00
Vanguard VRS-9037	(M)	Spirituals And Folksongs	1959	16.00	40.00

ROBIN & THE FOLKSTRINGERS

SeSac A-1801/2	(M)	Hootenanny	196?	12.00	30.00

ROBINS, THE

Whippet WLP-703	(M)	Rock 'N' Roll With The Robins	1958	150.00	400.00

ROBINSON, BETTY JEAN: *Refer to* CARL BELEW & BETTY JEAN ROBINSON

ROBINSON, CARSON

Columbia CL-6029	(10")	Square Dances	1949	20.00	50.00
MGM E-557	(10")	Square Dances With Calls	195?	20.00	50.00
RCA Victor LPM-1238	(M)	Square Dances	1956	16.00	40.00
MGM E-3594	(M)	Life Get's Tee-jus, Don't It	1958	16.00	40.00

ROBINSON, FLOYD

RCA Victor LPM-2162	(M)	Floyd Robinson	1960	30.00	75.00
RCA Victor LSP-2162	(S)	Floyd Robinson	1960	40.00	100.00

ROBINSON, FREDDIE

Enterprise ENS-1025	(S)	At The Dribe-In	1972	40.00	100.00
Enterprise ENS-1035	(S)	Off The Cuff	1973	40.00	100.00

ROBINSON, SMOKEY, & THE MIRACLES: *Refer to* THE MIRACLES

ROCHE, BETTY: *Refer to* GOLDMINE'S PRICE GUIDE TO COLLECTIBLE JAZZ ALBUMS

ROCK-A-TEENS, THE

Roulette R-25109	(M)	Woo-Hoo	1960	60.00	150.00
Roulette SR-25109	(S)	Woo-Hoo ("Woo-Hoo" is rechanneled)	1960	80.00	200.00

Label & Catalog #		Title	Year	VG+	NM
ROCK, THE					
LeeMo *(No number)*	(M)	**The Rock Shop**	1969	80.00	200.00
ROCKETS, THE					
The Rockets feature Ralph Molina and Danny Talbot, later of Crazy Horse.					
White Whale WWS-7116	(S)	**The Rockets**	1968	16.00	40.00
ROCKIN' REBELS, THE					
Swan SLP-509	(M)	**Wild Weekend**	1963	100.00	250.00
ROCKY FELLERS, THE					
Scepter SP-512	(M)	**Killer Joe**	1963	10.00	25.00
Scepter SPS-512	(S)	**Killer Joe**	1963	20.00	50.00
ROD & THE COBRAS					
Somerset SF-20500	(M)	**Drag Race At Surf City**	1964	10.00	25.00
Somerset SS-20500	(S)	**Drag Race At Surf City**	1964	12.00	30.00
RODGERS, JIMMIE					
Jimmie Rodgers was a guitar player, singer and songwriter known as both the "Singing Brakeman" and the "Father of Country Music," he is one of the single most important figures in the history of both country and American folk music. Refer to Gene Austin & Vernon Dalhart & Jimmie Rodgers.					
RCA Victor LPT-3037	(10")	**Jimmie Rodgers Memorial Album, Volume 1**	1952	200.00	400.00
RCA Victor LPT-3038	(10")	**Jimmie Rodgers Memorial Album, Volume 2**	1952	200.00	400.00
RCA Victor LPT-3039	(10")	**Jimmie RodgersMemorial Album, Volume 3**	1952	200.00	400.00
RCA Victor LPT-3073	(10")	**Travelin' Blues**	1952	200.00	400.00
RCA Victor LPM-1232	(M)	**Never No Mo' Blues— Memorial Album**	1955	60.00	150.00
RCA Victor LPM-1640	(M)	**Train Whistle Blues**	1957	60.00	150.00
RCA Victor LPM-2112	(M)	**My Rough And Rowdy Ways**	1960	20.00	50.00
RCA Victor LPM-2213	(M)	**Jimmie The Kid**	1961	20.00	50.00
RCA Victor LPM-2531	(M)	**Country Music Hall Of Fame**	1962	20.00	50.00
RCA Victor LPM-2634	(M)	**The Short But Brilliant Life Of Jimmie Rodgers**	1963	20.00	50.00
— RCA albums above have "Long Play" on the bottom of the label.—					
RCA Victor LPM-2865	(M)	**My Time Ain't Long**	1964	10.00	25.00
RCA Victor LPM-3315	(M)	**Best Of The Legendary Jimmie Rodgers**	1965	10.00	25.00
RCA Victor LSP-3315	(E)	**Best Of The Legendary Jimmie Rodgers**	1965	6.00	15.00
— RCA albums above have glossy black labels.—					
RODGERS, JIMMIE					
Roulette R-25020	(M)	**Jimmie Rodgers**	1958	20.00	50.00
Roulette R-25026	(M)	**The Long Hot Summer** *(Soundtrack)*	1958	20.00	50.00
Roulette R-25033	(M)	**Number One Ballads**	1958	20.00	50.00
Roulette R-25042	(M)	**Jimmie Rodgers Sings Folk Songs**	1958	20.00	50.00
— Roulette albums above have black labels.—					
Roulette R-25020	(M)	**Jimmie Rodgers**	196?	10.00	25.00
Roulette R-25033	(M)	**Number One Ballads**	196?	10.00	25.00
Roulette R-25042	(M)	**Jimmie Rodgers Sings Folk Songs**	196?	10.00	25.00
Roulette SR-25042	(E)	**Jimmie Rodgers Sings Folk Songs**	196?	10.00	25.00
Roulette R-25057	(M)	**His Golden Year**	1959	20.00	50.00
Roulette R-25071	(M)	**TV Favorites**	1959	12.00	30.00
Roulette SR-25071	(S)	**TV Favorites**	1959	20.00	50.00
Roulette R-25081	(M)	**Twilight On The Trail**	1959	12.00	30.00
Roulette SR-25081	(S)	**Twilight On The Trail**	1959	20.00	50.00
Roulette R-25095	(M)	**It's Christmas Once Again**	1959	12.00	30.00
Roulette SR-25095	(S)	**It's Christmas Once Again**	1959	20.00	50.00
Roulette R-25103	(M)	**When The Spirit Moves You**	1960	12.00	30.00
Roulette SR-25103	(S)	**When The Spirit Moves You**	1960	16.00	40.00
Roulette R-25128	(M)	**At Home With Jimmie Rodgers**	1960	12.00	30.00
Roulette SR-25128	(S)	**At Home With Jimmie Rodgers**	1960	16.00	40.00
Roulette R-25150	(M)	**The Folk Song World Of Jimmie Rodgers**	1961	12.00	30.00
Roulette SR-25150	(S)	**The Folk Song World Of Jimmie Rodgers**	1961	16.00	40.00
Roulette R-25160	(M)	**The Best Of Jimmie Rodgers Folk Songs**	1961	12.00	30.00
Roulette SR-25160	(S)	**The Best Of Jimmie Rodgers Folk Songs** *(Red vinyl)*	1961	100.00	250.00
Roulette SR-25160	(S)	**The Best Of Jimmie Rodgers Folk Songs**	1961	16.00	40.00
Roulette R-25179	(M)	**15 Million Sellers**	1962	10.00	25.00
Roulette SR-25179	(P)	**15 Million Sellers**	1962	12.00	30.00
— Roulette albums above have white labels.—					

Label & Catalog #		Title	Year	VG+	NM
Roulette R-25199	(M)	**Folk Songs**	1963	8.00	20.00
Roulette SR-25199	(S)	**Folk Songs**	1963	10.00	25.00

ROE, TOMMY
Refer to The Four Seasons..

ABC-Paramount ABC-432	(M)	**Sheila**	1962	16.00	40.00
ABC-Paramount ABCS-432	(S)	**Sheila**	1962	20.00	50.00
ABC-Paramount ABC-467	(M)	**Something For Everybody**	1964	12.00	30.00
ABC-Paramount ABCS-467	(E)	**Something For Everybody**	1968	16.00	40.00
		(ABCS-467 was issued in rechanneled stereo briefly in 1968.)			
ABC-Paramount ABC-575	(M)	**Sweet Pea**	1966	10.00	25.00
ABC-Paramount ABCS-575	(S)	**Sweet Pea**	1966	12.00	30.00
ABC-Paramount ABC-594	(M)	**It's Now Winter's Day**	1967	8.00	20.00
ABC-Paramount ABCS-594	(S)	**It's Now Winter's Day**	1967	10.00	25.00

ROGERS, BUDDY

Teem 5006	(M)	**The Greatest Songs Of Jimmy Reed**	196?	12.00	30.00

ROGERS, EILEEN

Columbia CL-1229	(M)	**Blue Swing**	1959	8.00	20.00
Columbia CS-8029	(S)	**Blue Swing**	1959	12.00	30.00

ROGERS, GINGER

Decca DL-5040	(10")	**Alice In Wonderland**	1950	30.00	75.00
Citel CLP-201	(M)	**Hello, Ginger!**	195?	20.00	50.00

ROGERS, KENNY, & THE FIRST EDITION: *Refer to* **THE FIRST EDITION**

ROGERS, KENNY

Jolly Rogers 5001	(S)	**BacKenny Rogersoads** *(Picture disc)*	1975	40.00	100.00
United Artists LA-934	(DJ)	**The Gambler** *(Picture disc)*	1978	20.00	50.00

ROGERS, ROY/ROY ROGERS & DALE EVANS

RCA Victor LPT-3041	(10")	**Roy Rogers Souvenir Album**	1952	80.00	300.00
RCA Victor LPT-3168	(10")	**Hymns Of Faith**	1954	40.00	200.00
RCA Victor LPM-1439	(M)	**Sweet Hour Of Prayer**	1957	20.00	75.00
Golden GRC-6	(M)	**Roy Rogers & Dale Evans' Song Wagon**	1958	30.00	75.00
Golden GRC-7	(M)	**16 Great Songs Of The Old West**	1958	30.00	75.00
RCA Victor LBY-1022	(M)	**Jesus Loves Me**	1959	20.00	50.00
Capitol T-1745	(M)	**The Bible Tells Me So**	1962	16.00	40.00
Capitol ST-1745	(S)	**The Bible Tells Me So**	1962	20.00	50.00
Camden CAL-1022	(M)	**Jesus Loves Me**	1963	10.00	25.00
Camden CAL-1022	(E)	**Jesus Loves Me**	1963	6.00	15.00
Camden CAL-1054	(M)	**Pecos Bill** *(With The Sons Of The Pioneers)*	1964	10.00	25.00
Camden CAL-1054	(E)	**Pecos Bill** *(With The Sons Of The Pioneers)*	1964	6.00	15.00
Camden CAL-1074	(M)	**Lore Of The West (& Favorite Western Songs For Growing Boys And Girls)**	1966	10.00	25.00
Camden CAL-1074	(E)	**Lore Of The West (& Favorite Western Songs For Growing Boys And Girls)**	1966	6.00	15.00
Capitol T-2818	(M)	**Christmas Is Always**	1967	12.00	30.00
Capitol ST-2818	(S)	**Christmas Is Always**	1967	12.00	30.00
Camden CAL-1097	(M)	**Peter Cottontail And His Friends**	1968	10.00	25.00

ROKES, THE

RCA Victor Int. FPM-185	(M)	**Che Mondo Strano**	1968	10.00	25.00

ROLLING STONES, THE
The original recording group consisted of Mick Jagger, Brian Jones, Keith Richards, Charlie Watts and Bill Wyman with unofficial member, keyboardist Ian Stewart. Jones left in 1969 (he died shortly thereafter) and was replaced by Mick Taylor, who left in 1972. Ron Wood took over good in 1976. Refer to Howlin' Wolf; Alexis Korner; Rocket 88. With the [inexplicable] exceptions of "Look What You've Done" on "December's Children," the material on the Stones' first five studio albums have not been issued in stereo in this country. And, excepting singles lifted from albums issued since 1966, all of their non-LP singles through 1966 have only appeared in rechanneled stereo. These recordings were almost certainly done on multi-track equipment.

London LL-3375	(M)	**The Rolling Stones** *(White label promo)* *(White label promos for LL-3375 are rare with a suggested Near Mint value of $1,200-2,000.)*	1964		*See below*

Roy Rogers was Republic's Numero Uno cowboy star way back when western movies, shorts and serials were a part of every red-blooded American kid's Saturday afternoon. That Rogers was a genuine cowboy who could sing only made the box office gate that much more lucrative. After he was paired with actress Dale Evans in an early film, the two fell in love, married, and formed a personal and professional team that lasted the duration of both their lives. As for their recording career, it spanned the gamut of cowboy songs, pop music, hymns, and children's records. It is from this final category that I selected the illustration here. Golden Records was the kiddie label of the '50s and early '60s; their product was made exclusively with children in mind. Consequently, as these records were as much playthings as played things, they are nigh on impossible to find in anything but NW condition (that's Neatly Wrecked to the novice). Plus, many of the albums featured some fine drawing and paintings, as does 16 Great Songs Of The Old West.

Label & Catalog #		Title	Year	VG+	NM
London LL-3375	(M)	**The Rolling Stones**	1964	80.00	200.00
		(In the lower left corber of original covers for LL-3375 is printed an advertisement for a bonus photo, which is priced separately below.)			
London LL-3375		**The Rolling Stones Bonus Photo**	1964	70.00	200.00
London LL-3402	(M)	**12 X 5**	1964	80.00	200.00
London LL-3420	(M)	**The Rolling Stones, Now!**	1965	80.00	200.00
London LL-3429	(M)	**Out Of Our Heads**	1965	80.00	200.00
— London albums above have maroon labels with the London/ffrr" logo and "Made in England by the Decca Group" at the top.—					
London LL-3375	(M)	**The Rolling Stones**	1965	24.00	60.00
London PS-375	(E)	**The Rolling Stones**	1965	10.00	25.00
London LL-3402	(M)	**12 X 5** *(Blue vinyl)*	1965		See below
		(Blue vinyl copies of LL-3402 have a suggested Near Mint value of $5,000-10,000.)			
London LL-3402	(M)	**12 X 5**	1965	24.00	60.00
London PS-402	(E)	**12 X 5**	1965	10.00	25.00
London LL-3420	(M)	**The Rolling Stones, Now!**	1965	24.00	60.00
London PS-420	(E)	**The Rolling Stones, Now!**	1965	10.00	25.00
London LL-3429	(M)	**Out Of Our Heads**	1965	24.00	60.00
London PS-429	(E)	**Out Of Our Heads**	1965	10.00	25.00
London LL-3451	(M)	**December's Children (And Everybody's)**	1965	24.00	60.00
London PS-451	(E)	**December's Children (And Everybody's)**	1965	10.00	25.00
— London mono albums above have maroon labels with a silver "London" on top; stereo albums above have blue labels with a silver "London" on top.—					
I.N.S. Radio 1003	(M)	**It's Here Luv!!**	1965	100.00	250.00
		(Originals of INS 1003 are on thick vinyl with crisp printing on the cover. Counterfeits are on thin vinyl with a poorly reproduced cover.)			
London LL-3375	(M)	**The Rolling Stones**	1965	16.00	40.00
London PS-375	(E)	**The Rolling Stones**	1966	4.00	10.00
London LL-3402	(M)	**12 X 5**	1965	16.00	40.00
London PS-402	(E)	**12 X 5**	1966	4.00	10.00
London LL-3420	(M)	**The Rolling Stones, Now!**	1965	16.00	40.00
London PS-420	(E)	**The Rolling Stones, Now!**	1966	4.00	10.00
London LL-3429	(M)	**Out Of Our Heads**	1965	16.00	40.00
London PS-429	(E)	**Out Of Our Heads**	1966	4.00	10.00
London LL-3451	(M)	**December's Children (And Everybody's)**	1965	16.00	40.00
London PS-451	(E)	**December's Children (And Everybody's)**	1966	4.00	10.00
London NP-1	(M)	**Big Hits (High Tide And Green Grass)**	1966		See below
		(The original cover has "big hits (high tide and green grass)" in lower case letters. These was replaced by the familiar cover, which has BIG HITS (HIGH TIDE & GREEN GRASS) in upper case. Rare with a suggested Near Mint value of $2,000-4,000.)			
London NP-1	(M)	**Big Hits (High Tide And Green Grass)**	1966	16.00	40.00
London NPS-1	(E)	**Big Hits (High Tide And Green Grass)**	1966	4.00	10.00
London LL-3476	(M)	**Aftermath**	1966	16.00	40.00
London PS-476	(S)	**Aftermath**	1966	4.00	10.00
London LL-3493	(M)	**Got Live If You Want It**	1966	16.00	40.00
London PS-493	(P)	**Got Live If You Want It**	1966	4.00	10.00
London LL-3499	(M)	**Between The Buttons**	1967	16.00	40.00
London PS-499	(S)	**Between The Buttons**	1967	4.00	10.00
London LL-3509	(M)	**Flowers**	1967	20.00	50.00
London PS-509	(P)	**Flowers**	1967	4.00	10.00
London NP-2	(M)	**Their Satanic Majesties Request** *(3-D cover)*	1967	80.00	200.00
London NPS-2	(S)	**Their Satanic Majesties Request** *(3-D cover)*	1967	16.00	40.00
— London mono albums above have maroon labels with a "London" on top in a silver box; stereo albums above have deep blue labels with a "London" on top in a silver box.—					
London NPS-3	(DJ)	**Through The Past, Darkly (Big Hits Vol. 2)**	1969		See below
		(Picture disc. London pressed up fifteen prototypes: Seven copies have the front cover of "High Tide & Green Grass" on both sides; the other eight have Ten Years After's "Sssh" on one side. Suggested value in Near Mint of $3,000-5,000.)			
London RSD-1	(DJ)	**The Rolling Stones—The Promotional Album**	1969	800.00	1,200.00
		(Counterfeits with poorly reproduced covers are common.)			
Abkco DVL2-0268	(P)	**The Rolling Stones' Greatest Hits** *(2 LPs.)*	1975	12.00	30.00
Abkco MPD-1	(S)	**Songs Of The Rolling Stones**	1975		See below
		(Orange cover with a shot taken from the "Rock & Roll Circus." Rare with a suggested Near Mint value of $1,000-2,000.)			
Abkco MPD-1	(S)	**Songs Of The Rolling Stones**	1975	150.00	300.00
		(Cover photo has a shot of the group in a field.)			

Two rarities from The Rolling Stones' first greatest hits collection, the classic Big Hits *(High Tide & Green Grass): The illustration on top is of the original cover design with the title on one line and artist's name on one line, all in lower case letters. This version was rejected and the album was issued with the more familiar graphics where the title is on three lines and the artist's credit is on two—a total of five lines versus the original two—and the letters are in upper case. These graphics can be seen (below) on the experimental picture disc made up in 1969 to hype the group's second big hits package,* Through The Past, Darkly.

Label & Catalog #		Title	Year	VG+	NM
Rolling Stones COC 59100	(M)	**Sticky Fingers** *(White label promo)*	1971	**200.00**	**400.00**
Rolling Stones COC 59100	(S)	**Sticky Fingers** *(White label promo)*	1971	**80.00**	**200.00**
Rolling Stones PRB-164	(DJ)	**Mick Jagger Interview With Tom Donahue**	1971	**100.00**	**250.00**
		(White label promo with letter from Tom Donahue. Originals have			
		the matrix numbers in the trail-off vinyl; counterfeits do not.)			
Rolling Stones PRB-164	(DJ)	**Mick Jagger Interview With Tom Donahue**	1971	**60.00**	**150.00**
		(White label promo with letter from Tom Donahue..)			
Rolling Stones COC-39100	(S)	**Jamming With Edward** *(White label promo)*	1972	**20.00**	**50.00**
Rolling Stones COC 39113	(S)	**Still Life** *(Picture disc)*	1982	**16.00**	**40.00**
Mobile Fidelity MFSL-060	(S)	**Sticky Fingers**	1980	**14.00**	**35.00**
Mobile Fidelity MFSL-087	(S)	**Some Girls**	1982	**14.00**	**35.00**
Mobile Fidelity RC-1	(P)	**The Rolling Stones** *(11 LP box)*	1984	**100.00**	**300.00**

ROMEOS, THE

Mark-II 1001	(M)	**Precious Memories**	1967	**10.00**	**25.00**

ROMERO, CESAR

Tops L-1631	(M)	**Songs By A Latin Lover**	195?	**12.00**	**30.00**
Blue Sky LP-101	(M)	**Man's Greatest Story**	196?	**10.00**	**25.00**
Co-Star CS-101	(M)	**Cesar Romero**	196?	**8.00**	**20.00**
Co-Star CSS-101	(S)	**Cesar Romero**	196?	**10.00**	**25.00**

ROMNEY, HUGH
Mr. Romney later claimed fame in the counter-culture as Digger deluxe "Wavy Gravy."

World Pacific WP-1805	(M)	**Third Stream Humor**	1962	**10.00**	**25.00**
World Pacific ST-1805	(S)	**Third Stream Humor**	1962	**14.00**	**35.00**

RONETTES, THE
The Ronettes feature Veronica Bennett, a.k.a. Ronnie Spector. Philles 4006 was produced by Phil Spector.

Colpix CLP-486	(M)	**The Ronettes**			
		Featuring Veronica *(White label promo)*	1965	**150.00**	**300.00**
Colpix CLP-486	(M)	**The Ronettes Featuring Veronica**	1965	**60.00**	**150.00**
Colpix CST-486	(S)	**The Ronettes Featuring Veronica**	1965	**100.00**	**200.00**
		— Colpix albums above have gold labels.—			
Colpix CLP-486	(M)	**The Ronettes Featuring Veronica**	196?	**40.00**	**100.00**
Colpix CST-486	(S)	**The Ronettes Featuring Veronica**	196?	**60.00**	**150.00**
		— Colpix albums above have blue labels.—			
Philles PHLP-4006	(M)	**Presenting The Fabulous Ronettes**	1965	**200.00**	**400.00**
		— Philles albums above have blue labels.—			
Philles PHLP-4006	(M)	**Presenting The Fabulous Ronettes**	1965	**100.00**	**250.00**
Philles PHLPST-4006	(S)	**Presenting The Fabulous Ronettes**	1965	**300.00**	**500.00**
Philles T-90271	(M)	**Presenting The Fabulous Ronettes**	1965	**150.00**	**300.00**
Philles ST-90271	(S)	**Presenting The Fabulous Ronettes**	1965	**200.00**	**400.00**
		— Philles albums above have yellow & red labels.—			

RONNY & THE DAYTONAS

Mala 4001	(M)	**G. T. O.**	1964	**60.00**	**150.00**
Mala 4002	(M)	**Sandy**	1966	**16.00**	**40.00**
Mala 4002S	(S)	**Sandy**	1966	**30.00**	**75.00**

RONNIE & THE POMONA CASUALS

Donna 2112	(M)	**Everybody Jerk**	1965	**12.00**	**30.00**

RONSTADT, LINDA, & THE STONE PONEYS: *Refer to* **THE STONE PONEYS**

RONSTADT, LINDA
Linda Ronstadt originally recorded as a member of The Stone Poneys.

Mobile Fidelity MFSL-158	(S)	**What's New?**	198?	**10.00**	**30.00**
Nautilus NR-26	(S)	**Simple Dreams**	198?	**16.00**	**50.00**

ROOFTOP SINGERS, THE
The Rooftop Singers— Erik Darling, Bill Svanoe and Lynne Taylor— are a contemporary urban folk vocal and instrumental trio.

Vanguard VRS-9136	(M)	**Walk Right In!**	1963	**8.00**	**20.00**
Vanguard VSD-2136	(S)	**Walk Right In!**	1963	**10.00**	**25.00**

ROONEY, MICKEY

RCA Victor LPM-1520	(M)	**Mickey Rooney Sings George M. Cohan**	1957	**30.00**	**75.00**

Roxy Music's first album for Atco, Country Life, *originally featured a pair of lovely models posed nearly naked neath some flood lights and surrounded by a hedge. Deemed unsuitable, the ladies were removed altogether and the album was issued with a cover depicting the shrubbery. . .*

Label & Catalog #		Title	Year	VG+	NM

ROSIE
Rosalie Hamlin of Rosie & The Originals.

Brunswick BL-54102	(M)	Lonely Blue Nights	1961	60.00	150.00
Brunswick BL7-54102	(S)	Lonely Blue Nights	1961	80.00	200.00

ROSS, ANNIE: *Refer to* GOLDMINE'S PRICE GUIDE TO COLLECTIBLE JAZZ ALBUMS

ROSS, BOB

Folkways FA-2334	(M)	To You With Love— American Folk Songs For Men	1957	12.00	30.00

ROSS, DIANA / NEIL DIAMOND

MCA SM-734727	(S)	It's Happening! Diana Ross-Neil Diamond	1972	30.00	75.00

ROSS, DR. ISAIAH

Testament 2206	(M)	Call The Doctor	196?	30.00	75.00

ROSS, JACK

Dot DLP-3429	(M)	Cinderella	1962	8.00	20.00
Dot DLP-25429	(S)	Cinderella	1962	12.00	30.00

ROSS, MISS JACKIE

Chess LP-1489	(M)	In Full Bloom	1966	12.00	30.00
Chess LPS-1489	(S)	In Full Bloom	1966	16.00	40.00

ROSS, JOE E.
Mr. Ross also recorded as Officer Gunther Toody.

Roulette R-25281	(M)	Love Songs From A Cop	1964	10.00	25.00
Roulette SR-25281	(S)	Love Songs From A Cop	1964	12.00	30.00

ROSS, STAN

Del-Fi DFLP-1233	(M)	My Son The Copy Cat	1963	8.00	20.00
Del-Fi DFST-1233	(S)	My Son The Copy Cat	1963	12.00	30.00

ROTH, LILLIAN

Epic LN-3206	(M)	I'll Cry Tomorrow	195?	14.00	35.00
Tops L-1567	(M)	Lillian Roth Sings	1958	10.00	25.00

ROUGH TRADE

True North APHT-5010	(S)	For Those Who Think Young *(Half-speed)*	198?	10.00	30.00

ROUND ROBIN

Domain 101	(M)	Greatest Hits, Slauson Style	1964	10.00	25.00
Challenge LP-620	(M)	Lloyd Thaxton Presents The Land Of 1,000 Dances Featuring Round Robin	1965	10.00	25.00

ROUTERS, THE

Warner Bros. W-1490	(M)	Let's Go With The Routers	1963	10.00	25.00
Warner Bros. WS-1490	(S)	Let's Go With The Routers	1963	12.00	30.00
Warner Bros. W-1524	(M)	1963's Great Instrumental Hits	1964	12.00	30.00
Warner Bros. WS-1524	(S)	1963's Great Instrumental Hits	1964	16.00	40.00
Warner Bros. W-1559	(M)	Charge!	1964	8.00	20.00
Warner Bros. WS-1559	(S)	Charge!	1964	10.00	25.00
Warner Bros. W-1595	(M)	Go Go Go With The Chuck Berry Songbook	1965	8.00	20.00
Warner Bros. WS-1595	(S)	Go Go Go With The Chuck Berry Songbook	1965	10.00	25.00

ROWAN, DAN, & DICK MARTIN

Trey T-901	(M)	Rowan & Martin At Work	1960	10.00	25.00
Epic FXS-15118	(S)	Laugh-In *(TV Soundtrack)*	1969	10.00	25.00
Reprise RS-6335	(S)	Laugh-In '69 *(TV Soundtrack)*	1969	10.00	25.00

ROXX

Sit On It & Spin	(S)	Get Your Roxx Off	1976	20.00	50.00

ROXY MUSIC
The original Roxy Music featured Brian Eno and Brian Ferry.

Reprise MS-2114	(S)	Roxy Music	1972	12.00	30.00
Warner Bros. BS-2969	(S)	For Your Pleasure	1973	12.00	30.00
Atco SD-33-106	(S)	Country Life *(Nearly naked ladies cover)*	1975	10.00	25.00

Label & Catalog #		Title	Year	VG+	NM
ROYAL, BILLY JOE					
Columbia CL-2403	(M)	Down In The Boondocks	1965	8.00	20.00
Columbia CS-9203	(S)	Down In The Boondocks	1965	10.00	25.00
Columbia CL-2781	(M)	Billy Joe Royal	1967	8.00	20.00
Columbia CS-9581	(S)	Billy Joe Royal	1967	10.00	25.00
ROYAL GUARDSMEN, THE					
Laurie LLP-2038	(M)	Snoopy Vs. The Red Baron	1967	10.00	25.00
Laurie SLLP-2038	(S)	Snoopy Vs. The Red Baron	1967	12.00	30.00
Laurie LLP-2039	(M)	The Return Of The Red Baron	1967	10.00	25.00
Laurie SLLP-2039	(S)	The Return Of The Red Baron	1967	12.00	30.00
Laurie LLP-2042	(M)	Snoopy And His Friends	1967	12.00	30.00
Laurie SLLP-2042	(S)	Snoopy And His Friends	1967	16.00	40.00
		(Issued with a "Merry Snoopy's Christmas" tear-off sheet attached to the back cover.)			
Laurie LLP-2042	(M)	Snoopy And His Friends *(Without sheet)*	1967	8.00	20.00
Laurie SLLP-2042	(S)	Snoopy And His Friends *(Without sheet)*	1967	10.00	25.00
Laurie SLLP-2046	(S)	Snoopy For President	1968	10.00	25.00
ROYAL PLAYBOYS, THE					
Waldorf Music Hall 136	(10")	Rock And Roll/New Orleans Blues	195?	200.00	500.00
		(This is actually a various artists albums with six of the eight songs featuring The Royal Playboys.)			
ROYALETTES, THE					
MGM E-4332	(M)	It's Gonna Take A Miracle	1965	8.00	20.00
MGM SE-4332	(S)	It's Gonna Take A Miracle	1965	10.00	25.00
MGM E-4366	(M)	The Elegant Sound Of The Royalettes	1966	8.00	20.00
MGM SE-4366	(S)	The Elegant Sound Of The Royalettes	1966	10.00	25.00
RUBBER BAND, THE					
GRT 10007	(S)	The Jimi Hendrix Songbook	1969	10.00	25.00
GRT 10010	(S)	The Cream Songbook	1969	10.00	25.00
GRT 10015	(S)	The Beatles Songbook	1969	10.00	25.00
RUBBER MEMORY					
R.P.C. 69401	(M)	Welcome	1969		*See below*
		(RPC 69-401 has a suggested Near Mint value of $1,000-2,000.)			
RUBIN, RUTH					
Ruth Rosenbaltt Rubin is a singer of traditional Fewish folk songs.					
Folkways FC-724	(10")	Jewish Children's Songs And Games	195?	20.00	50.00
Folkways FC-7224	(10")	Jewish Children's Songs And Games	195?	20.00	50.00
Oriole Vol. III	(M)	Jewish Folk Songs	1954	12.00	30.00
Riverside RLP-12-647	(M)	Yiddish Love Songs	195?	12.00	30.00
RUBY & THE ROMANTICS					
Kapp KL-1323	(M)	Our Day Will Come	1963	12.00	30.00
Kapp KS-3323	(S)	Our Day Will Come	1963	16.00	40.00
Kapp KL-1341	(M)	Till Then	1963	10.00	25.00
Kapp KS-3341	(S)	Till Then	1963	12.00	30.00
Kapp KL-1458	(M)	Greatest Hits Album	1966	8.00	20.00
Kapp KS-3458	(S)	Greatest Hits Album	1966	10.00	25.00
Kapp KL-1526	(M)	Ruby And The Romantics	1967	8.00	20.00
Kapp KS-3526	(S)	Ruby And The Romantics	1967	10.00	25.00
RUFFIN, JIMMY					
Soul 704	(M)	Jimmy Ruffin Sings Top 10	1967	8.00	20.00
Soul S-704	(S)	Jimmy Ruffin Sings Top 10	1967	10.00	25.00
RUGBYS, THE					
Amazon 1000	(S)	Hot Cargo	1970	10.00	25.00
RUMBLERS, THE					
Downey DLP-1001	(M)	Boss!	1963	60.00	150.00
Downey DLPS-1001	(S)	Boss!	1963	80.00	200.00
Dot DLP-3509	(M)	Boss!	1963	16.00	40.00
Dot DLP-25509	(S)	Boss!	1963	20.00	50.00
		(Dot 3/25509 is a reissue of Downey 1001.)			

Label & Catalog #		Title	Year	VG+	NM

RUNDGREN, TODD
Mr. Rundgren was formerly a member of The Nazz. Todd's nickname, Runt, was also used as the name of his band for the first two albums on Ampex.

Ampex 10105	(S)	**Runt**	1970	30.00	75.00
		(Apparently, original pressings of 10105 include "Say No More.")			
Ampex 10105	(S)	**Runt**	1970	60.00	150.00
		(Some original pressings of 10105 that include "Say No More" also include an alternate take of the medley, a longer intro to "Broke Down And Busted," plus an extra track. Both of these original pressings are identifiable only by track count as the titles of the extra tracks are not listed on the label or cover.)			
Ampex 10105	(S)	**Runt**	1970	12.00	30.00
		(Later pressings delete "Say No More" and all of the other extras.)			
Ampex 10116	(S)	**Ballad Of Todd Rundgren**	1971	20.00	50.00
		(Counterfeits of both Ampex albums are plentiful.)			
Bearsville 2066	(S)	**Something/Anything** *(2 LPs. Colored vinyl)*	1972	200.00	400.00
		(Promo features one record on blue vinyl and one on red vinyl.)			
Bearsville 2066	(S)	**Something/Anything** *(2 LPs. Promo label)*	1972	16.00	40.00
Bearsville PRO-524	(DJ)	**The Todd Rundgren Radio Show**	1972	80.00	200.00
Bearsville 2133	(S)	**A Wizard/A True Star** *(Promo label + insert)*	1973	10.00	25.00
Bearsville PRO-597	(DJ)	**Banded Radio Interview**	1974	60.00	150.00
Bearsville PRO-788	(DJ)	**Back To The Bars—**			
		Todd Rundgren Radio Sampler	1979	20.00	50.00

RUNGE, JOHN

Riverside RLP-12-814	(M)	**A Concert Of English Folk Songs**	195?	12.00	30.00
Stinson SLP-88	(M)	**Traditional English Folk Songs**	1958	12.00	30.00

RUSH

Mercury MK-32	(DJ)	**Everything Your Listener**			
		Ever Wanted To Hear By By Rush	1975	40.00	100.00
Mercury SRP-1300	(S)	**Hemispheres** *(Picture disc)*	1979	10.00	25.00

RUSH, OTIS
Refer to Albert King & Otis Rush.

Blue Horizion BM-4602	(S)	**Blues Masters, Volume 2**	1968	10.00	25.00
Blue Horizion BM-4805	(S)	**Chicago Blues**	1970	10.00	25.00
Cotillion SD-9006	(S)	**Mourning In The Morning**	1969	10.00	25.00

RUSH, TOM
Tom Rush is a guitar player, singer and writer of folk and folk-based pop music.

Folklore FRLP-14003	(M)	**Got A Mind To Ramble**	1963	10.00	25.00
Folklore FRST-14003	(M)	**Got A Mind To Ramble**	1963	12.00	30.00
Prestige PRLP-7374	(M)	**Blues/Songs/Ballads**	1965	10.00	25.00
Prestige PRST-7374	(S)	**Blues/Songs/Ballads**	1965	12.00	30.00

RUSHING, JIMMY: *Refer to* **GOLDMINE'S PRICE GUIDE TO COLLECTIBLE JAZZ ALBUMS**

RUSKIN-SPEAR, ROGER
Ruskin-Spear was formerly a member of The Bonzo Dog Band.

United Arts. LA097	(S)	**Electric Shocks**	1973	10.00	25.00

RUSSELL, CONNIE

United Arts. UAL-3022	(M)	**Don't Smoke In Bed**	1959	12.00	30.00
United Arts. UAS-6022	(S)	**Don't Smoke In Bed**	1959	20.00	50.00

RUSSELL, JANE
Refer to Marilyn Monroe & Jane Russell.

Mercury MG-25182	(10")	**The French Line** *(Soundtrack)*	1954	50.00	125.00
Capitol T-822	(M)	**Magic Of Believing**	1957	20.00	50.00
MGM E-3715	(M)	**Jane Russell**	1959	20.00	50.00
MGM SE-3715	(S)	**Jane Russell**	1959	40.00	100.00

RUTLES, THE
The Rutles feature Neil Innes of The Bonzo Dog Band and Eric Idle.

Warner Bros. PRO-723	(DJ)	**Meet The Rutles** *(Sampler on gold vinyl)*	1978	10.00	25.00
Warner Bros. H-3151	(S)	**Meet The Rutles** *(With booklet)*	1978	10.00	25.00

Label & Catalog #		Title	Year	VG+	NM
RYAN, BUCK, & SMITTY IRVIN					
Monument MLP-8031	(M)	Ballads And Bluegrass	1965	8.00	20.00
Monument SLP-18031	(S)	Ballads And Bluegrass	1965	10.00	25.00
RYAN, CHARLIE					
King 751	(M)	Hot Rod Lincoln	1961	250.00	500.00
Pickwick K-417	(M)	Hot Rod Lincoln	196?	20.00	50.00
Pickwick KS-417	(E)	Hot Rod Lincoln	196?	10.00	25.00
Pickwick/Hilltop JM-6006	(M)	Hot Rod Lincoln Drags Again	1964	20.00	50.00
Pickwick/Hilltop JS-6006	(E)	Hot Rod Lincoln Drags Again	1964	10.00	25.00
RYDELL, BOBBY					
Cameo C-1006	(M)	We Got Love	1959	20.00	50.00
Cameo C-1007	(M)	Bobby Sings	1960	20.00	50.00
Cameo C-1009	(M)	Biggest Hits (Fold-open cover with insert)	1961	20.00	50.00
Cameo C-1010	(M)	Bobby Rydell Salutes The "Great Ones"	1961	20.00	50.00
Cameo SC-1010	(S)	Bobby Rydell Salutes The "Great Ones"	1961	30.00	75.00
Cameo C-1011	(M)	Rydell At The Copa	1961	20.00	50.00
Cameo SC-1011	(S)	Rydell At The Copa	1961	30.00	75.00
Cameo C-1019	(M)	All The Hits	1962	20.00	50.00
Cameo C-1028	(M)	Biggest Hits, Volume 2	1962	20.00	50.00
Cameo C-1040	(M)	All The Hits, Volume 2	1963	20.00	50.00
Cameo SC-1040	(P)	All The Hits, Volume 2	1963	30.00	75.00
Cameo C-1043	(M)	Bye Bye Birdie	1963	12.00	30.00
Cameo C-1055	(M)	Wild (Wood) Days	1963	12.00	30.00
Cameo CS-1055	(S)	Wild (Wood) Days	1963	20.00	50.00
Cameo C-1070	(M)	The Top Hits Of '63	1964	12.00	30.00
Cameo CS-1070	(S)	The Top Hits Of '63	1964	20.00	50.00
Cameo C-1080	(M)	Forget Him	1964	12.00	30.00
Cameo CS-1080	(E)	Forget Him	1964	12.00	30.00
Cameo C-2001	(M)	16 Golden Hits	1965	12.00	30.00
Cameo CS-2001	(E)	16 Golden Hits	1965	12.00	30.00
RYDELL, BOBBY, & CHUBBY CHECKER					
Cameo C-1013	(M)	Bobby Rydell / Chubby Checker	1961	20.00	50.00
Cameo C-1063	(M)	Chubby Checker And Bobby Rydell	1963	12.00	30.00
RYDER, MITCH/MITCH RYDER & THE DETROIT WHEELS					
New Voice 2000	(M)	Take A Ride	1966	10.00	25.00
New Voice S-2000	(S)	Take A Ride	1966	12.00	30.00
New Voice 2002	(M)	Breakout!!!	1966	10.00	25.00
New Voice S-2002	(S)	Breakout!!!	1966	12.00	30.00
		(NV 2002 was originally issued without "Devil With A Blue Dress.")			
New Voice 2002	(M)	Breakout!!!	1966	8.00	20.00
New Voice S-2002	(S)	Breakout!!!	1966	10.00	25.00
		(Later pressings include "Devil With A Blue Dress.")			
New Voice 2003	(M)	Sock It To Me!	1967	10.00	25.00
New Voice S-2003	(S)	Sock It To Me!	1967	12.00	30.00
New Voice 2004	(M)	All Mitch Ryder Hits!	1967	8.00	20.00
New Voice S-2004	(S)	All Mitch Ryder Hits!	1967	10.00	25.00

SABRAS, THE
Tikva 122   (M)   The Sabras   196?   150.00   300.00

SACCO, LOU CHRISTIE: *Refer to* LOU CHRISTIE

SACRED MUSHROOM, THE
Parallax P-4001   (S)   The Sacred Mushroom   1969   40.00   100.00

SAGE & SEER
Stylist SA-600   (S)   Sage & Seer   197?   60.00   150.00

SAGITTARIUS
Sagittarius features Curt Boetcher.
Columbia CS-9644   (S)   Present Tense *(Produced by Gary Usher)*   1968   12.00   30.00
Together STT-1002   (S)   The Blue Marble *(With 2 bonus photos)*   1969   20.00   50.00
Together STT-1002   (S)   The Blue Marble *(Without the photos)*   1969   14.00   35.00

ST. ANTHONY'S FIRE
Zonk   (M)   St. Anthony's Fire   1968   200.00   400.00

ST. CLAIRE, BETTY: *Refer to* GOLDMINE'S PRICE GUIDE TO COLLECTIBLE JAZZ ALBUMS

ST. JOHN GREEN
Flick Disc FLS-45001   (S)   St. John Green   1968   10.00   25.00

ST. LOUIS JIMMY
Bluesville BVLP-1028   (M)   Goin' Down Blues   1961   30.00   75.00
          — Bluesville albums above have bright blue labels with silver print.—
Bluesville BVLP-1028   (M)   Goin' Down Blues   1964   10.00   25.00
          — Bluesville albums above have blue labels with a trident logo on the right side.—

ST. LOUIS HOUNDS, THE
(No label)   (S)   The St. Louis Hounds   197?   60.00   150.00

ST. PETERS, CRISPIAN
Jamie JLPM-3027   (M)   The Pied Piper   1966   16.00   40.00
Jamie JLPS-3027   (E)   The Pied Piper   1966   12.00   30.00

SAKAMOTO, KYU
Capitol Int. T-10349   (M)   Sukiyaki   1963   10.00   25.00
Capitol Int. DT-10349   (E)   Sukiyaki   1963   8.00   20.00

SALES, SOUPY
Reprise R-6010   (M)   The Soupy Sales Show   1961   12.00   30.00
Reprise R-96010   (S)   The Soupy Sales Show   1961   16.00   40.00
Reprise R-6052   (M)   Up In The Air   1962   12.00   30.00
Reprise R-96052   (S)   Up In The Air   1962   16.00   40.00
ABC-Paramount ABC-503   (M)   Spy With A Pie   1965   10.00   25.00
ABC-Paramount ABCS-503 (S)   Spy With A Pie   1965   12.00   30.00
ABC-Paramount ABC-517   (M)   Soupy Sez Do The Mouse   1965   10.00   25.00
ABC-Paramount ABCS-517 (S)   Soupy Sez Do The Mouse   1965   12.00   30.00
Motown MS-686   (S)   A Bag Of Soup   1969   10.00   25.00
???? 5274   (S)   Still Soupy After All These Years   1981   4.00   10.00

SALEM MASS
Salem Mass SM-101   (S)   Witch Burning   1972   80.00   200.00

SALETAN, TONY
Tony Saletan is a multi-instrumentalist, singer and writer of folk music.
Prestige Inter. PR-13036   (M)   I'm A Stranger Here   1962   12.00   30.00

Label & Catalog #		Title	Year	VG+	NM

SALLYANGIE
Sallyangie is Sally and Mike Oldfield.

Warner Bros. WS-1783	(S)	**Children Of The Sun**	1969	10.00	25.00

SALVATION

ABC S-623	(S)	**Salvation**	1968	10.00	25.00
ABC S-653	(S)	**Gypsy Carnival Caravan**	1968	10.00	25.00

SAM & DAVE
Sam Moore and Dave Prater.

Roulette R-25323	(M)	**Sam And Dave**	1966	12.00	30.00
Roulette SR-25323	(P)	**Sam And Dave**	1966	16.00	40.00
		(Half of the tracks on SR-25323 are rechanneled.)			
Stax ST-708	(M)	**Hold On I'm Comin'**	1966	16.00	40.00
Stax STS-708	(S)	**Hold On I'm Comin'**	1966	20.00	50.00
		("I Take What I Want" is rechanneled)			
Stax ST-712	(M)	**Double Dynamite**	1966	12.00	30.00
Stax STS-712	(S)	**Double Dynamite**	1966	16.00	40.00
Stax ST-725	(M)	**Soul Men**	1967	12.00	30.00
Stax STS-725	(S)	**Soul Men**	1967	16.00	40.00
Atlantic SD-8205	(S)	**I Thank You**	1968	10.00	25.00

SAM THE SHAM/SAM THE SHAM & THE PHARAOHS
Sam The Sham is a [mocking] pseudonym for Sam Samudio.

MGM E-4297	(M)	**Wooly Bully**	1965	12.00	30.00
MGM SE-4297	(S)	**Wooly Bully**	1965	16.00	40.00
MGM E-4314	(M)	**Their Second Album**	1965	10.00	25.00
MGM SE-4314	(S)	**Their Second Album**	1965	12.00	30.00
MGM E-4347	(M)	**On Tour**	1966	10.00	25.00
MGM SE-4347	(S)	**On Tour**	1966	12.00	30.00
MGM E-4407	(M)	**Lil' Red Riding Hood**	1966	10.00	25.00
MGM SE-4407	(S)	**Lil' Red Riding Hood**	1966	12.00	30.00
MGM E-4422	(M)	**The Best Of Sam The Sham**	1967	10.00	25.00
MGM SE-4422	(S)	**The Best Of Sam The Sham**	1967	12.00	30.00
MGM E-4479	(M)	**Nefertiti**	1967	8.00	20.00
MGM SE-4479	(S)	**Nefertiti**	1967	10.00	25.00
MGM SE-4526	(S)	**Ten Of Pentacles**	1968	10.00	25.00

SAN REMO STRINGS, THE

RicTic 901	(M)	**Hungry For Love**	1966	10.00	25.00
RicTic 901	(S)	**Hungry For Love**	1966	12.00	30.00
Gordy G-923	(M)	**Hungry For Love**	1967	8.00	20.00
Gordy GS-923	(S)	**Hungry For Love**	1967	10.00	25.00
		(Gordy 923 is a reissue of RicTic 901.)			
Gordy G-928	(M)	**Swing**	1968	8.00	20.00
Gordy GS-928	(S)	**Swing**	1968	10.00	25.00

SANDALS, THE/THE SANDELLS

World Pacific WP-1818	(M)	**Scrambler**	1964	16.00	40.00
World Pacific ST-1818	(S)	**Scrambler**	1964	20.00	50.00
World Pacific ST-1818	(S)	**Scrambler** *(Red vinyl)*	1964	40.00	100.00
		(World Pacific 1818 is credited to The Sandells.)			
World Pacific WP-1832	(M)	**The Endless Summer** *(Soundtrack)*	1966	8.00	20.00
World Pacific ST-1832	(S)	**The Endless Summer** *(Soundtrack)*	1966	10.00	25.00
		(World Pacific 1832 is a repackage of W.P. 1818.)			
World Pacific WPS-21884	(S)	**The Last Of The Ski Bums** *(Soundtrack)*	1969	10.00	25.00
		(Orange cover with three skiers' silhouettes.)			
World Pacific WPS-21884	(S)	**The Last Of The Ski Bums** *(Soundtrack)*	1969	10.00	25.00
		(Blue cover with cartoon skiers in a VW bus.)			

SANDBURG, CARL

Lyrichord LL-4	(10")	**The American Songbag**	195?	20.00	50.00
Lyrichord LL-66	(M)	**Ballads And Songs**	195?	20.00	50.00
Columbia ML-5339	(M)	**Flat Rock Ballads**	1959	10.00	25.00

SANDERS, ED
Mr. Sanders was formerly a member of The Fugs.

Reprise RS-6374	(S)	**Sanders' Truckstop**	1969	12.00	30.00
Reprise MS-2105	(S)	**Beer Cans On The Moon**	1972	8.00	20.00

Label & Catalog #		Title	Year	VG+	NM
SANDERS, FELICIA					
Columbia CL-654	(M)	**Felicia Sanders At The Blue Angel**	1955	14.00	35.00
Columbia CL-713	(M)	**Girl Meets Boy**	1955	14.00	35.00
Decca DL-8762	(M)	**That Certain Feeling**	1958	10.00	25.00
Decca DL-78762	(S)	**That Certain Feeling**	1958	14.00	35.00
SANDERS, GEORGE					
ABC-Paramount ABC-231	(M)	**The George Sanders Touch**	1958	12.00	30.00
ABC-Paramount ABCS-231	(S)	**The George Sanders Touch**	1958	16.00	40.00
SANDERS, JELLY					
Global LP-1001	(M)	**Fiddlin' Country Style**	1960	10.00	25.00
SANDS, TOMMY					

Tommy also recorded a pair of soundtracks with Annette. Refer to Ferlin Husky / Sonny James / Tommy Sands / Gene Vincent..

Capitol T-848	(M)	**Steady Date With Tommy Sands**	1957	30.00	75.00
Capitol T-929	(M)	**Sing Boy Sing** (Soundtrack)	1958	30.00	75.00
		— Capitol albums above turquoise labels.—			
Capitol T-1081	(M)	**Sands Storm**	1959	20.00	50.00
Capitol T-1123	(M)	**This Thing Called Love**	1959	12.00	30.00
Capitol ST-1123	(S)	**This Thing Called Love**	1959	16.00	40.00
Capitol T-1239	(M)	**When I'm Thinking Of You**	1960	12.00	30.00
Capitol ST-1239	(S)	**When I'm Thinking Of You**	1960	16.00	40.00
Capitol T-1364	(M)	**Sands At The Sands**	1960	12.00	30.00
Capitol ST-1364	(S)	**Sands At The Sands**	1960	16.00	40.00
Capitol T-1426	(M)	**Dream With Me**	1961	12.00	30.00
Capitol ST-1426	(S)	**Dream With Me**	1961	16.00	40.00
		— Capitol albums above black "rainbow" labels with the logo on the left.—			

SANDY COAST: *Refer to* **VANITY FARE**

SANELLA, ANDY, & HIS IMPERIAL HAWAIIANS					
SeSac H-101/2	(M)	**Hawaii**	195?	24.00	60.00
SANTANA					

Group named after leader Carlos Santana.

Columbia HC-40130	(S)	**Abraxas** (Half-speed master)	1981	25.00	75.00
Columbia HC-47158	(S)	**Zebop!** (Half-speed master)	1981	12.00	35.00
SANTO & JOHNNY					

Santo and Johnny Farina.

Canad. Am. CALP-1001	(M)	**Santo & Johnny**	1959	30.00	75.00
Canad. Am. SCALP-1001	(S)	**Santo & Johnny**	1959	40.00	100.00
		("All Night Diner," "Sleepwalk" and "Slave Girl" are rechanneled.)			
Canad. Am. CALP-1002	(M)	**Encore**	1960	16.00	40.00
Canad. Am. SCALP-1002	(S)	**Encore**	1960	20.00	50.00
		("Tear Drop" is rechanneled on this album.)			
Canad. Am. CALP-1004	(M)	**Hawaii**	1961	12.00	30.00
Canad. Am. SCALP-1004	(S)	**Hawaii**	1961	16.00	40.00
Canad. Am. CALP-1006	(M)	**Come On In**	1962	12.00	30.00
Canad. Am. SCALP-1006	(S)	**Come On In**	1962	16.00	40.00
Canad. Am. CALP-1008	(M)	**Around The World With Santo & Johnny**	1962	12.00	30.00
Canad. Am. SCALP-1008	(S)	**Around The World With Santo & Johnny**	1962	16.00	40.00
Canad. Am. CALP-1011	(M)	**Off Shore**	1963	12.00	30.00
Canad. Am. SCALP-1011	(S)	**Off Shore**	1963	16.00	40.00
Canad. Am. CALP-1014	(M)	**In The Still Of The Night**	1963	12.00	30.00
Canad. Am. SCALP-1014	(S)	**In The Still Of The Night**	1963	16.00	40.00
		("Sleep Walk" and "Tear Drop" are rechanneled on this album.)			
Canad. Am. CALP-1016	(M)	**Wish You Love**	1964	12.00	30.00
Canad. Am. SCALP-1016	(S)	**Wish You Love**	1964	16.00	40.00
Canad. Am. CALP-1017	(M)	**The Beatles' Greatest Hits**	1964	16.00	40.00
Canad. Am. SCALP-1017	(S)	**The Beatles' Greatest Hits**	1964	20.00	50.00
Canad. Am. CALP-1018	(M)	**Mucho**	1965	12.00	30.00
Canad. Am. SCALP-1018	(S)	**Mucho**	1965	16.00	40.00
SAPPHIRES, THE					
Swan LP-513	(M)	**Who Do You Love**	1964	150.00	300.00

Lawrence Schiller's LSD is a hilarious attempt to capture the horrific mood of an acid trip. The users interviewed sound like stoned junkies, not enlightened trippers. And the authority used by Schiller to play up the dangers is one Dr. Sidney Cohen who, prior to his being co-opted by the anti-drug crusaders, had been a medical pioneer in determining the negative affects of LSD in a broad testing of healthy users. His findings: Under normal conditions, LSD-25 produced demonstrably negative affects in less than two uses per 1,000, making the likelihood of a pleasant acid experience better than 99%. . . Albums such as this one, not in and of themselves remotely psychedelic, are of interest to psych collectors due to their shear exploitative nature.

Label & Catalog #		Title	Year	VG+	NM

SATAN & THE DECIPLES
| Goldband 7750 | (S) | Underground | 1969 | 14.00 | 35.00 |

SATANS, THE
| (No label) | (M) | Raisin' Hell | 1962 | 150.00 | 300.00 |

SATINS FOUR, THE, & THE CINNAMON ANGELS
| B.T. Puppy BTS-1010 | (S) | Mixed Soul | 1970 | 60.00 | 150.00 |

SAUVAGE, KATHERINE
| Epic LN-3489 | (M) | The Songs Of Kurt Weill | 195? | 16.00 | 40.00 |

SAVAGE SONS OF YO HO WA, THE: *Refer to* FATHER YOD

SAVAGES, THE
| Duane 1047 | (M) | Live And Wild | 1966 | 60.00 | 150.00 |

SAVITT, BUDDY
Mr. Savitt has backed all of the Cameo/Parkway artists at one time or another.
| Parkway P-7012 | (M) | The Most Heard Sax In The World | 1962 | 40.00 | 100.00 |

SAXONS, THE
| Mirrosonic AS-1017 | (M) | Love Minus Zero | 1966 | 30.00 | 75.00 |

SCAFFOLD
| Bell 6018 | (M) | Thank U Very Much (White label promo) | 1968 | 20.00 | 50.00 |
| Bell 6018 | (S) | Thank U Very Much | 1968 | 20.00 | 50.00 |

SCAGGS, BOZ
Boz was formerly a member of the Steve Miller Band.
| Columbia A2S-71-4 | (DJ) | KSAN Live Concert (2 LPs) | 1974 | 20.00 | 50.00 |
| | | (Issued in a plain cardboard jacket.) | | | |

SCALLYWAGS, THE
| Justice JLP- | (S) | The Scallywags | 196? | 300.00 | 500.00 |

SCAMPS, THE
| Project 8002 | (M) | Teen Dance And Sing Along Party | 1962 | 16.00 | 40.00 |

SCHILLER, LAWRENCE
These albums are documentaries with Mr. Schiller as the narrator.
Capitol TAO-2574	(M)	LSD	1966	16.00	40.00
Capitol STAO-2574	(S)	LSD	1966	20.00	50.00
Capitol PRO-4153	(DJ)	Open-End Interview With Dr. Sidney Cohen	1966	40.00	100.00
		(An interview with the "expert" quoted in charge of the LSD album.)			
Capitol KAO-2630	(M)	Why Did Lenny Bruce Die?	1967	10.00	25.00
Capitol SKAO-2630	(S)	Why Did Lenny Bruce Die?	1967	12.00	30.00
Capitol KAO-2652	(M)	Homosexuality In The American Male	1967	10.00	25.00
Capitol SKAO-2652	(S)	Homosexuality In The American Male	1967	12.00	30.00

SCHLAMME, MARTHA
Austrian born and classically trained Martha Schlamme is a singer of traditional European folk songs.
Vanguard VRS-7012	(10")	Folk Songs Of Many Lands	195?	20.00	50.00
Folkways FP-843	(10")	German Folk Songs (With Pete Seeger)	1954	20.00	50.00
Folkways FW-6843	(10")	German Folk Songs (With Pete Seeger)	1954	20.00	50.00
Vanguard VRS-9011	(M)	Raisins And Almonds & Other Jewish Folk Songs	195?	12.00	30.00
Vanguard VRS-9019	(M)	Folk Songs Of Many Lands	195?	12.00	30.00
		(Vanguard 9019 is a reissue of 7012 with six additional songs.)			

SCHORY, DICK/DICK SCHORY'S NEW PERCUSSION ENSEMBLE
RCA Victor LPM-1866	(M)	Music For Bang, Barroom And Harp	1958	20.00	50.00
RCA Victor LSP-1866	(S)	Music For Bang, Barroom And Harp	1958	60.00	150.00
RCA Victor LPM-2125	(M)	Music To Break Any Mood	1960	12.00	30.00
RCA Victor LSP-2125	(S)	Music To Break Any Mood	1960	40.00	100.00
RCA Victor LPM-2613	(M)	Supercussion	1963	12.00	30.00
RCA Victor LSP-2613	(S)	Supercussion	1963	20.00	50.00

*— RCA mono albums above have "Long Play" on the bottom of the label;
stereo albums have "Living Stereo" on the bottom.—*

Label & Catalog #		Title	Year	VG+	NM
RCA Victor LPM-2806	(M)	**Dick Schory On Your**	1964	8.00	20.00
RCA Victor LSP-2806	(S)	**Dick Schory On Your**	1964	10.00	25.00
SCORPION					
Tower ST-5171	(S)	**Scorpion**	1969	20.00	50.00
SCOT, PATRICIA					
ABC-Paramount 301	(M)	**Once Around The Clock**	1959	8.00	20.00
ABC-Paramount S-301	(S)	**Once Around The Clock**	1959	12.00	30.00

SCOTT, BOBBY: *Refer to* GOLDMINE'S PRICE GUIDE TO COLLECTIBLE JAZZ ALBUMS

SCOTT, CALVIN					
Stax STS-2046	(S)	**I'm Not Blind. . . I Just Can't See**	1972	40.00	100.00

SCOTT, CLIFORD: *Refer to* GOLDMINE'S PRICE GUIDE TO COLLECTIBLE JAZZ ALBUMS

SCOTT, FREDDIE					
Colpix CP-461	(M)	**Freddie Scott Sings** (Gold label)	1964	20.00	50.00
Colpix SCP-461	(S)	**Freddie Scott Sings** (Gold label)	1964	40.00	100.00
Colpix CP-461	(M)	**Freddie Scott Sings** (Blue label)	1965	12.00	30.00
Colpix SCP-461	(E)	**Freddie Scott Sings** (Blue label)	1965	8.00	20.00

SCOTT, HAZEL: *Refer to* GOLDMINE'S PRICE GUIDE TO COLLECTIBLE JAZZ ALBUMS

SCOTT, JACK					
Carlton LP-12-107	(M)	**Jack Scott**	1959	80.00	200.00
Carlton STLP-12-107	(S)	**Jack Scott**	1959	200.00	400.00
		(The cover has "Stereo" in felt-like letters pasted vertically along the left side. "My True Love" and "Leroy" are rechanneled on this and each subsequent pressing below.)			
Carlton STLP-12-107	(S)	**Jack Scott**	1959	150.00	300.00
		(The cover has "Stereo" in felt-like letters across the top.)			
Carlton STLP-12-107	(S)	**Jack Scott**	1959	100.00	200.00
		(The cover has "Stereo" printed across the top.)			
Carlton LP-12-122	(M)	**What Am I Living For**	1959	60.00	150.00
Carlton STLP-12-122	(S)	**What Am I Living For**	1959	150.00	300.00
		("What Am I Living For" is rechanneled on this album.)			
Top Rank RM-319	(M)	**I Remember Hank Williams**	1960	60.00	150.00
Top Rank RS-619	(S)	**I Remember Hank Williams**	1960	100.00	250.00
Top Rank RM-326	(M)	**What In The World's Come Over You?**	1960	60.00	150.00
Top Rank RS-626	(S)	**What In The World's Come Over You?**	1960	100.00	250.00
Top Rank RM-348	(M)	**The Spirit Moves Me**	1961	60.00	150.00
Top Rank RS-648	(S)	**The Spirit Moves Me**	1961	100.00	250.00
Sesac 4201	(M)	**Soul Stirring**	196?	200.00	400.00
Capitol T-2035	(M)	**Burning Bridges** (Black label)	1964	30.00	75.00
Capitol ST-2035	(S)	**Burning Bridges** (Black label)	1964	80.00	200.00
Capitol ST-2035	(S)	**Burning Bridges** (Green label)	197?	20.00	50.00
SCOTT, LINDA					
Canad. Am. CALP-1005	(M)	**Starlight, Starbright**	1961	20.00	50.00
Canad. Am. SCALP-1005	(S)	**Starlight, Starbright**	1961	40.00	100.00
Canad. Am. CALP-1007	(M)	**Great Scott!! Her Greatest Hits**	1962	20.00	50.00
Canad. Am. SCALP-1007	(S)	**Great Scott!! Her Greatest Hits**	1962	40.00	100.00
Congress 3001	(M)	**Linda**	1962	12.00	30.00
Congress S-3001	(S)	**Linda**	1962	16.00	40.00
Kapp KL-1424	(M)	**Hey, Look At Me Now**	1965	10.00	25.00
Kapp KS-3424	(S)	**Hey, Look At Me Now**	1965	12.00	30.00
SCOTT, LIZABETH					
Vik LXA-1130	(M)	**Lizabeth**	195?	30.00	75.00

SCOTT, TOM

Thomas Jefferson Scott is a banjo, guitar and harmonica player and singer of traditional American folk songs and spirituals.

Coral CRL-56056	(10")	**Sing Of America— Gems Of American Folklore**	1952	20.00	50.00

Label & Catalog #		Title	Year	VG+	NM
SCOTTSVILLE SQUIRREL BARKERS, THE					
The Barkers feature Chris Hillman. Refer to The Hillmen; The Byrds.					
Crown CLP-5346	(M)	**Blue-Grass Favorites**	1963	16.00	40.00
Crown CST-346	(S)	**Blue-Grass Favorites**	1963	20.00	50.00
SCRUGGS, EARL					
Earl Scruggs is a legendary three-finger banjo player. Refer to Flatt & Scruggs.					
Peer International	(S)	**5-String Instruction Album**	1967	10.00	25.00
SEA, JOHNNY					
Philips PHM-200-139	(M)	**World Of A Country Boy**	1964	8.00	20.00
Philips PHS-600-139	(S)	**World Of A Country Boy**	1964	10.00	25.00
Philips PHM-200-194	(M)	**Live At The Bitter End**	1965	8.00	20.00
Philips PHS-600-194	(S)	**Live At The Bitter End**	1965	10.00	25.00
SEALS & CROFTS					
Nautilus NR-10	(S)	**Summer Breeze**	197?	8.00	25.00
SEARCH PARTY					
Century 32013	(S)	**Montgomery Chapel**	197?	660.00	1,000.00
SEARCHERS, THE					
Mercury MG-20914	(M)	**Hear! Hear!**	1964	30.00	75.00
Mercury SR-60914	(E)	**Hear! Hear!**	1964	20.00	50.00
		(Original covers for Mercury 2/60914 merely note the album's title.)			
Mercury MG-20914	(M)	**Hear! Hear!**	1964	20.00	50.00
Mercury SR-60914	(E)	**Hear! Hear!**	1964	16.00	40.00
		(Some original covers have a sticker reading "Live From The Star Club" affixed to the front.)			
Mercury MG-20914	(M)	**Hear! Hear!**	1964	16.00	40.00
Mercury SR-60914	(E)	**Hear! Hear!**	1964	12.00	30.00
		(Later covers have "Live From The Star Club" printed on the front.)			
Kapp KL-1363	(M)	**Meet The Searchers**	1964	20.00	50.00
Kapp KS-3363	(S)	**Meet The Searchers**	1964	30.00	75.00
		— Kapp albums above have black & blue labels.—			
Kapp KL-1363	(M)	**Meet The Searchers**	1964	12.00	30.00
Kapp KS-3363	(S)	**Meet The Searchers**	1964	16.00	40.00
Kapp KL-1409	(M)	**This Is Us**	1964	12.00	30.00
Kapp KS-3409	(S)	**This Is Us**	1964	16.00	40.00
		(Original covers for Kapp 1/3409 have no stickers.)			
Kapp KL-1409	(M)	**This Is Us**	1964	12.00	30.00
Kapp KS-3409	(S)	**This Is Us**	1964	16.00	40.00
		(Later covers have a "Love Potion No. 9" sticker on the cover.)			
Kapp KL-1412	(M)	**The New Searchers LP**	1965	16.00	40.00
Kapp KS-3412	(S)	**The New Searchers LP**	1965	20.00	50.00
		(Original covers for 1/3412 list "Bumble Bee" on the top. "What Have They Done To The Rain" is rechanneled.)			
Kapp KL-1412	(M)	**The New Searchers LP**	1965	12.00	30.00
Kapp KS-3412	(S)	**The New Searchers LP**	1965	16.00	40.00
Kapp KL-1449	(M)	**The Searchers No. 4**	1965	12.00	30.00
Kapp KS-3449	(S)	**The Searchers No. 4**	1965	16.00	40.00
Kapp KL-1477	(M)	**Take Me For What I'm Worth**	1966	12.00	30.00
Kapp KS-3477	(S)	**Take Me For What I'm Worth**	1966	16.00	40.00
		— Kapp albums above have black labels.—			
SEARCHERS, THE / THE RATTLES					
Mercury MG-20994	(M)	**The Searchers Meet The Rattles**	1965	30.00	75.00
Mercury SR-60994	(E)	**The Searchers Meet The Rattles**	1965	20.00	50.00
SEASTONES					
Seastones features Jerry Garcia, Micky Hart and Phil Lesh of The Grateful Dead.					
Round RX-106	(S)	**Seastones**	1975	10.00	25.00
SEDAKA, NEIL					
RCA Victor LPM-2035	(M)	**Neil Sedaka**	1959	30.00	75.00
RCA Victor LSP-2035	(S)	**Neil Sedaka**	1959	40.00	100.00
RCA Victor LPM-2317	(M)	**Circulate**	1960	14.00	35.00
RCA Victor LSP-2317	(S)	**Circulate**	1960	20.00	50.00

Label & Catalog #		Title	Year	VG+	NM
RCA Victor LPM-2421	(M)	**Little Devil And His Other Hits**	1961	14.00	35.00
RCA Victor LSP-2421	(S)	**Little Devil And His Other Hits**	1961	16.00	40.00
RCA Victor LPM-2627	(M)	**Neil Sedaka Sings His Greatest Hits**	1962	14.00	35.00
RCA Victor LSP-2627	(S)	**Neil Sedaka Sings His Greatest Hits**	1962	20.00	50.00

— RCA mono albums above have "black labels with Long Play" on the bottom; stereo albums have have black labels with "Living Stereo" on the bottom. —

RCA Victor LPM-10181	(M)	**Smile** *(Sung in Italian)*	1966	20.00	50.00

SEEDS, THE

Crescendo GNP-2023	(M)	**The Seeds**	1966	12.00	30.00
Crescendo GNPS-2023	(S)	**The Seeds** ("Pushin' Too Hard" is rechanneled)	1966	10.00	25.00
Crescendo GNP-2033	(M)	**A Web Of Sound**	1966	12.00	30.00
Crescendo GNPS-2033	(S)	**A Web Of Sound**	1966	10.00	25.00
Crescendo ST-91224	(S)	**A Web Of Sound** *(Capitol Record Club)*	1969	10.00	25.00
Crescendo GNP-2038	(M)	**Future** *(With three inserts)*	1967	16.00	40.00
Crescendo GNPS-2038	(S)	**Future** *(With three inserts)*	1967	12.00	30.00
Crescendo GNP-2038	(M)	**Future** *(Without inserts)*	1967	12.00	30.00
Crescendo GNPS-2038	(S)	**Future** *(Without inserts)*	1967	10.00	25.00
Crescendo GNP-2040	(M)	**Full Spoon of Seedy Blues**	1967	12.00	30.00
Crescendo GNPS-2040	(S)	**Full Spoon of Seedy Blues**	1967	10.00	25.00
Crescendo GNP-2043	(M)	**Raw And Alive**	1967	12.00	30.00
Crescendo GNPS-2043	(S)	**Raw And Alive**	1967	10.00	25.00

— GNP albums above have red labels. —

SEEGER, PEGGY
Pete's sister Peggy Seeger is a guitar and piano player, singer and writer of topical folk-based music. Refer to Tom Paley; The Seegers.

Folkways FP-49	(10")	**Folk Songs Of Courting And Complaint**	195?	40.00	100.00
Folkways FA-2049	(10")	**Folk Songs Of Courting And Complaint**	195?	40.00	100.00
Folkways FC-7051	(10")	**Animal Folk Songs For Children**	195?	40.00	100.00
Topic T-9	(10")	**Folksongs**	195?	40.00	100.00
Riverside RLP-12-655	(M)	**Peggy Seeger**	195?	12.00	30.00
Tradition TLP-2059	(M)	**Manchester Angel**	195?	12.00	30.00
Prestige Int. PRLP-13005	(M)	**The Best Of Peggy Seeger**	1961	12.00	30.00
Prestige Int. PRLP-13058	(M)	**A Song For You And Me**	1962	12.00	30.00
Folklore FRLP-14016	(M)	**The Best Of Peggy Seeger**	196?	10.00	25.00
Folklore FRST-14016	(E)	**The Best Of Peggy Seeger**	196?	8.00	20.00

(Folklore 1406 is a reissue of Prestige 13005.)

SEEGER, PEGGY, & EWAN MacCOLL
Refer to Ewan MacColl.

Tradition TLP-1015	(M)	**Classic Scotts Ballads**	195?	12.00	30.00
Riverside RLP-12-637	(M)	**Matching Songs Of The British Isles And America**	195?	12.00	30.00
Topic T-13	(10")	**Shuttle And Cage**	1958	20.00	50.00
Prestige Int. PRLP-13061	(M)	**A Lover's Garland**	1962	12.00	30.00

SEEGER, PETE
Peggy's brother Pete Seeger as a guitar player, singer and writer is the most important single figure in folk music between Woody Guthrie and Bob Dylan. Refer to The Almanac Singers; Big Bill Broonzy; Clearwater; Arlo Guthrie & Pete Seeger; The Seegers; The Weavers..

Stinson SLP-52	(10")	**Lincoln Brigade**	1953	40.00	100.00
Stinson SLP-57	(10")	**Pete Seeger Concert** *(2 LPs)*	1953	60.00	150.00
Stinson SLP-90	(M)	**Pete**	195?	20.00	50.00
Folkways FP-3	(10")	**Darling Corey**	1950	40.00	100.00
Folkways FA-2003	(10")	**Darling Corey**	1950	40.00	100.00
Folkways FP-5	(10")	**Seegers**	195?	40.00	100.00
Folkways FA-2005	(10")	**Seegers**	195?	40.00	100.00
Folkways FP-43	(10")	**Pete Seeger Sampler**	195?	40.00	100.00
Folkways FA-2043	(10")	**Pete Seeger Sampler**	195?	40.00	100.00
Folkways FP-45	(10")	**Goofing Off Suite**	1958	40.00	100.00
Folkways FA-2045	(10")	**Goofing Off Suite**	1958	40.00	100.00
Folkways FP-48	(10")	**Frontier Ballads**	1958	40.00	100.00
Folkways FA-2175	(10")	**Frontier Ballads, Vol. 1**	1958	40.00	100.00
Folkways FA-2176	(10")	**Frontier Ballads, Vol. 2**	1958	40.00	100.00
Folkways FP-911	(10")	**Folk Songs Of Four Continents**	195?	40.00	100.00
Folkways FW-6911	(10")	**Folk Songs Of Four Continents**	195?	40.00	100.00
Folkways FP-701	(10")	**American Folk Songs For Children**	1953	40.00	100.00
Folkways FC-7001	(10")	**American Folk Songs For Children**	1953	40.00	100.00

Label & Catalog #		Title	Year	VG+	NM
Folkways FP-710	(10")	Birds, Beasts, Bugs And Little Fishes	195?	40.00	100.00
Folkways FC-7010	(10")	Birds, Beasts, Bugs And Little Fishes	195?	40.00	100.00
Folkways FC-7053	(10")	American Christmas Songs	195?	40.00	100.00
Folkways 85-1	(M)	Talking Union	1955	16.00	40.00
Folkways 85-2	(M)	Peter Seeger Sings	1955	16.00	40.00
Folkways 85-3	(M)	Love Songs	1955	16.00	40.00
Folkways FH-5251	(M)	American Industrial Ballads	195?	12.00	30.00
Folkways FA-2319	(M)	American Ballads	1957	12.00	30.00
Folkways FA-2320	(M)	American Favorite Ballads, Vol. I	1957	12.00	30.00
Folkways FA-2321	(M)	American Favorite Ballads, VoL. II	1958	12.00	30.00
Folkways FA-2351	(M)	Pete Seeger At Carnegie Hall	1958	12.00	30.00
Folkways FA-2412	(M)	Pete Seeger At Carnegie Hall With Sonny Terry	1958	12.00	30.00
Folkways FA-2452	(M)	With Voices Together We Sing	1959	10.00	25.00
Folkways FA-2453	(M)	Love Songs For Friends And Foes	1959	10.00	25.00
Folkways FA-2454	(M)	Rainbow Design	1995	10.00	25.00
Folkways FA-2456	(M)	Broadsides	1959	10.00	25.00
Folkways FN-2501	(M)	Gazette, Vol. 1, No. 1	1958	10.00	25.00
Folkways FN-2512	(M)	Hootenanny At Carnegie Hall	1959	10.00	25.00
Folkways FI-8303	(M)	How To Play The Five String Banjo	196?	10.00	25.00
Columbia CL-1101	(M)	We Shall Overcome	1958	16.00	40.00
Columbia CL-1648	(M)	Story Songs	1961	10.00	25.00
Columbia CS-8448	(S)	Story Songs	1961	12.00	30.00
Columbia CL-1916	(M)	In Person At The Bitter End	1962	10.00	25.00
Columbia CS-8716	(S)	In Person At The Bitter End	1962	12.00	30.00

— Columbia albums above have three white "eye" logos on each side of the spindle hole.—

Label & Catalog #		Title	Year	VG+	NM
Philips PHM-2-300	(M)	The Story Of The Nativity (2 LPs)	1963	8.00	20.00
Philips PHS-2-300	(S)	The Story Of The Nativity (2 LPs)	1963	10.00	25.00
Verve/Folkways FV-9008	(M)	Pete Seeger & Big Bill Broonzy In Concert	1965	8.00	20.00
Verve/Folkways FVS-9008	(S)	Pete Seeger & Big Bill Broonzy In Concert	1965	10.00	25.00
Verve/Folkways FV-9009	(M)	Pete Seeger On Campus	1965	8.00	20.00
Verve/Folkways FVS-9009	(S)	Pete Seeger On Campus	1965	10.00	25.00
Verve/Folkways FV-9013	(M)	Recorded Live At The Village Gate	1965	8.00	20.00
Verve/Folkways FVS-9013	(S)	Recorded Live At The Village Gate	1965	10.00	25.00
Verve/Folkways FV-9020	(M)	Little Boxes And Other Broadsides	1965	8.00	20.00
Verve/Folkways FVS-9020	(S)	Little Boxes And Other Broadsides	1965	10.00	25.00

SEEGERS, THE
Barbara, Michael and Peggy Seeger.

Label & Catalog #		Title	Year	VG+	NM
Folkways FA-2005	(10")	American Folk Songs Sung By The Seegers	195?	20.00	50.00

SEEGERS, THE
Barbara, Peggy and Penny Seeger.

Label & Catalog #		Title	Year	VG+	NM
Folkways FC-7053	(10")	American Folk Songs For Christmas	195?	20.00	50.00

SEEGERS, THE
Michael, Peggy and Pete Seeger.

Label & Catalog #		Title	Year	VG+	NM
Prestige PRLP-7375	(M)	Pete, Peggy & Mike Seeger (2 LPs)	1965	8.00	20.00
Prestige PRST-7375	(S)	Pete, Peggy & Mike Seeger (2 LPs)	1965	10.00	25.00

SEGALL, RICKY

Label & Catalog #		Title	Year	VG+	NM
Bell 1138	(S)	Ricky Segall And The Segalls	1973	10.00	25.00

SEGER, BOB

Label & Catalog #		Title	Year	VG+	NM
Capitol ST-172	(S)	Ramblin' Gamblin' Man	1969	12.00	30.00
Capitol ST-236	(S)	Noah	1969	20.00	50.00
Capitol SKAO-499	(S)	Mongrel (Gatefol cover)	1970	10.00	25.00
Capitol ST-731	(S)	Brand New Morning	1971	20.00	50.00
Palladium P-1006	(S)	Smokin' O.P.'s	1972	12.00	30.00
Reprise/Pallad. MS-2126	(S)	Back In '72	1973	14.00	35.00
Capitol SPRO-8433	(DJ)	"Live" Bullet	1976	16.00	40.00
Capitol ST-11557	(DJ)	Night Moves (Picture disc)	1978	14.00	35.00
Capitol SEAX-11904	(S)	Stranger In Town (Picture disc)	1979	14.00	35.00
Mobile Fidelity MFSL-034	(S)	Night Moves	1980	10.00	30.00
Mobile Fidelity MFSL-127	(S)	Against The Wind	1983	8.00	25.00

SELAH JUBILEE QUARTET, THE

Label & Catalog #		Title	Year	VG+	NM
Remington 1023	(10")	Spirituals	195?	80.00	200.00

On this Angel recording, Mr. Sellers, who had not yet achieved the international stardom we associate with him today, and Miss Loren, who had been a star for years, teamed up to provide "satire without malice in songs and sketches by England's gooniest and Italy's loveliest." The photo on the cover is from the film The Millionaires, in which Loren plays a heiress trying to trap a doctor from India, played by Sellers, as her next husband. So this album has interest to collectors of comedy, collectors of personality records, and movie buffs.

Label & Catalog #		Title	Year	VG+	NM

SELLERS, BROTHER JOHN
BRother John Sellers is a guitar player and singer of traditional folk songs, blues and spirituals.

Vanguard VRS-8005	(10")	**Brother John Sellers**	1954	20.00	50.00
Vanguard VRS-9036	(M)	**Blues And Folk Songs**	195?	12.00	30.00

SELLERS, BROTHER JOHN, & MICKEY BAKER
Refer to Mickey Baker.

Monitor 505	(M)	**Big Beat Up The River**	1959	20.00	50.00

SELLERS, BROTHER JOHN, & SONNY TERRY
Refer to Sonny Terry.

Vanguard VRS-7022	(10")	**Blues And Folk Songs**	195?	40.00	100.00

SELLERS, PETER
For additional listings refer to The Hollies; Ringo Starr & Peter Sellers.

Angel 35884	(M)	**The Best Of Peter Sellers**	1960	12.00	30.00
Angel 35884	(S)	**The Best Of Peter Sellers**	1960	16.00	40.00
Warner Bros. W-1711	(M)	**The Bobo** (Soundtrack)	1967	12.00	30.00
Warner Bros. WS-1711	(S)	**The Bobo** (Soundtrack)	1967	16.00	40.00

SELLERS, PETER, & JOAN COLLINS & ANTHONY NEWLEY

Acapella 1	(M)	**Fool Brittania**	1963	10.00	25.00

SELLERS, PETER, & SOPHIA LOREN

Angel 35910	(M)	**Peter Sellers And Sophia Loren**	1961	12.00	30.00
Angel 35910	(S)	**Peter Sellers And Sophia Loren**	1961	16.00	40.00

SENSATIONS, THE
The Sensations feature Yvonne Baker.

Argo LP-4022	(M)	**Let Me In/Music, Music, Music**	1963	150.00	400.00

SENTINALS, THE

Del-Fi DFLP-1232	(M)	**Big Surf**	1963	14.00	35.00
Del-Fi DFST-1232	(S)	**Big Surf**	1963	20.00	50.00
Del-Fi DFLP-1241	(M)	**Surfer Girl**	1963	14.00	35.00
Del-Fi DFST-1241	(S)	**Surfer Girl**	1963	20.00	50.00
Sutton SU-338	(M)	**Vegas Go-Go**	1964	10.00	25.00
Sutton SSU-338	(S)	**Vegas Go-Go**	1964	14.00	35.00

SERPENT POWER
Serpent Power features David and Tina Meltzer.

Vanguard VRS-9252	(M)	**Serpent Power**	1967	8.00	20.00
Vanguard VSD-79252	(S)	**Serpent Power**	1967	10.00	25.00

SEVILLE, DAVID
David Seville is a pseudonym for Ross Bagdasarian, the creator of The Chipmunks.

Liberty LRP-3073	(M)	**The Music Of David Seville**	1957	30.00	75.00
Liberty LRP-3092	(M)	**The Witch Doctor**	1958	50.00	125.00

SEWARD, ALEC

Bluesville BVLP-1076	(M)	**Creepin' Blues**	1963	16.00	40.00

SHADES OF BLUE, THE

Impact IM-101	(M)	**Happiness Is The Shades Of Blue**	1966	12.00	30.00
Impact IM-1001	(S)	**Happiness Is The Shades Of Blue**	1966	16.00	40.00

SHADOWS, THE
The Shadows also recorded with Cliff Richard.

Atlantic 8089	(M)	**Surfing With The Shadows**	1963	30.00	75.00
Atlantic SD-8089	(S)	**Surfing With The Shadows**	1963	40.00	100.00
Atlantic 8097	(M)	**The Shadows Know**	1964	16.00	40.00
Atlantic SD-8097	(S)	**The Shadows Know**	1964	20.00	50.00

SHADOWS OF KNIGHT, THE

Dunwich 666	(M)	**Gloria**	1966	16.00	40.00
Dunwich S-666	(S)	**Gloria**	1966	20.00	50.00
Dunwich 667	(M)	**Back Door Men**	1966	16.00	40.00
Dunwich S-667	(S)	**Back Door Men**	1966	20.00	50.00
Super-K SKS-6002	(S)	**The Shadows Of Knight**	1969	12.00	30.00

Label & Catalog #		Title	Year	VG+	NM
SHADRACK CHAMELEON					
No label	(S)	Shadrack Chameleon	1972	80.00	200.00
SHAGGS, THE					
MCM 6311	(S)	Wink	1967	150.00	300.00
SHAGGS, THE					
Third World 3001	(S)	Philosophy Of The World	197?		See below
		(T.W. 3001 has a suggested Near Mint value of $1,000-2,000.)			
SHAKERS, THE					
Audio Fidelity 2155	(M)	The Break It All	1966	16.00	40.00
Audio Fidelity S-6155	(S)	The Break It All (Silver label)	1966	20.00	50.00
Audio Fidelity S-6155	(S)	The Break It All (Brown label)	197?	10.00	25.00
SHAKEY JAKE					
Bluesville BVLP-1008	(M)	Good Times	1960	30.00	75.00
Bluesville BVLP-1027	(M)	Mouth Harp Blues	1961	30.00	75.00
		— Bluesville albums above have bright blue labels with silver print.—			
Bluesville BVLP-1008	(M)	Good Times	1964	10.00	25.00
Bluesville BVLP-1027	(M)	Mouth Harp Blues	1964	10.00	25.00
		— Bluesville albums above have blue labels with a trident logo on the right side.—			
SHANGRI-LAS, THE					
Red Bird 20-101	(M)	Leader Of The Pack	1965	60.00	150.00
Red Bird 20-104	(M)	The Shangri-Las '65	1965	60.00	150.00
Red Bird 20-104	(M)	I Can Never Go Home Anymore	1966	30.00	75.00
		("I Can Never Go Home Anymore" is a repackage of "'65"			
		replacing "Sophisticated Boom Boom" with the title hit.)			
Mercury MG-21099	(M)	The Shangri-Las' Golden Hits	1966	16.00	40.00
Mercury SR-61099	(P)	The Shangri-Las' Golden Hits	1966	20.00	50.00
Post 4000	(S)	The Shangri-Las Sing	196?	10.00	25.00
Bac-Trac	(S)	The Best Of The Shangri-Las (Red vinyl)	1985	10.00	25.00
SHANKAR, ANANDA					
Ananda Shankar is Ravi's son.					
Reprise RS-6398	(S)	Ananda Shankar	1970	10.00	25.00
SHANKAR, L.					
Zappa SRZ-1-1602	(S)	Touch Me There (Produced by Frank Zappa)	1979	10.00	25.00
SHANKAR, RAVI					
Ravi Shankar is a master Indian sitar player whose other albums are of a more "classical" nature and not					
included in this volume. Refer to George Harrison & Friends.					
Bluesville BVLP-1078	(M)	The Master Musicians Of India	1964	10.00	25.00
Apple SWAO-3384	(S)	Raga (Sdtk produced by George Harrison)	1971	10.00	25.00
Apple SVBB-3396	(S)	Ravi Shankar In Concert (2 LPs)	1973	16.00	40.00
SHANNON, DEL					
Big Top 12-1303	(M)	Runaway	1961	80.00	200.00
Big Top 12-1303	(S)	Runaway	1961	750.00	1,500.00
Big Top 12-1308	(M)	Little Town Flirt	1963	80.00	200.00
Big Top 12-1308	(S)	Little Town Flirt	1963	600.00	1,200.00
		(Stereo copies are not identified on the cover or label so they must			
		be listened to, although an "S" may be etched in the trail-off vinyl.)			
Amy 8003	(M)	Handy Man	1964	16.00	40.00
Amy S-8003	(S)	Handy Man	1964	20.00	50.00
Amy 8004	(M)	Del Shannon Sings Hank Williams	1965	16.00	40.00
Amy S-8004	(S)	Del Shannon Sings Hank Williams	1965	20.00	50.00
Amy 8006	(M)	1,661 Seconds	1965	20.00	50.00
Amy S-8006	(S)	1,661 Seconds	1965	30.00	75.00
Liberty LRP-3453	(M)	This Is My Bag	1966	12.00	30.00
Liberty LST-7453	(S)	This Is My Bag	1966	16.00	40.00
Liberty LRP-3479	(M)	Total Commitment	1966	12.00	30.00
Liberty LST-7479	(S)	Total Commitment	1966	16.00	40.00
Liberty LRP-3539	(M)	Further Adventures Of Charles Westover	1968	20.00	50.00
Liberty LST-7539	(S)	Further Adventures Of Charles Westover	1968	30.00	75.00
Dot DLP-3824	(M)	The Best Of Del Shannon	1967	16.00	40.00
Dot DLP-25824	(E)	The Best Of Del Shannon	1967	12.00	30.00

Label & Catalog #		Title	Year	VG+	NM
Post 9000	(E)	Del Shannon Sings	196?	12.00	30.00
United Arts. LA151	(S)	Del Shannon Live In England	1973	8.00	20.00
Sire SHAH-3708-2	(P)	The Vintage Years (2 LPs)	1975	10.00	25.00
SHANNON, HUGH					
Atlantic ALS-406	(10")	Hugh Shannon Sings	195?	40.00	100.00
SHANTY BOYS, THE					
Elektra EKL-142	(M)	Off-Beat Folk Songs	1958	12.00	30.00
SHAPIRO, HELEN					
Epic LN-24075	(M)	A Teenager In Love	1963	8.00	20.00
Epic BN-26075	(S)	A Teenager In Love	1963	10.00	25.00
SHARON, RALPH					

SHARON, RALPH
Pianist Ralph Sharon's discography can be found in Goldmine's Price Guide To Collectible Jazz Albums.

Gordy G-903	(M)	Modern Innovations On Country And Western Music	1963	100.00	250.00
SHARP, DEE DEE					
Cameo C-1018	(M)	It's Mashed Potato Time	1962	20.00	50.00
Cameo C-1022	(M)	Songs Of Faith	1962	12.00	30.00
Cameo SC-1022	(S)	Songs Of Faith	1962	24.00	60.00
Cameo C-1027	(M)	All The Hits	1962	20.00	50.00
Cameo SC-1027	(S)	All The Hits	1962	30.00	75.00
Cameo C-1032	(M)	All The Hits, Vol. 2	1962	20.00	50.00
Cameo SC-1032	(S)	All The Hits, Vol. 2	1962	30.00	75.00
Cameo C-1050	(M)	Do The Bird	1963	20.00	50.00
Cameo SC-1050	(S)	Do The Bird	1963	30.00	75.00
Cameo C-1062	(M)	Biggest Hits	1963	20.00	50.00
Cameo C-1074	(M)	Down Memory Lane	1963	20.00	50.00
Cameo C-2002	(M)	18 Golden Hits	1964	20.00	50.00
Cameo SC-2002	(P)	18 Golden Hits	1964	30.00	75.00
SHARP, DEE DEE, & CHUBBY CHECKER					
Cameo C-1029	(M)	Down To Earth	1962	20.00	50.00
Cameo SC-1029	(S)	Down To Earth	1962	30.00	75.00
SHARPE, RAY					
Award LMP-711	(M)	Welcome Back, Linda Lou	1964	60.00	150.00
SHATNER, WILLIAM					

SHATNER, WILLIAM
William Shatner was formerly a member of The U.S.S. Enterprise.

Decca DL-5043	(M)	Transformed Man	1968	16.00	40.00
Decca DL-75043	(S)	Transformed Man	1968	20.00	50.00
Caedmon TC-1509	(M)	William Shatner Reads Henry Kuttner's "Mimsy Were The Borogoves"	1970	12.00	30.00
Caedmon TC-1508	(S)	Isaac Asimov's "Foundation"	1976	12.00	30.00
Lemli 00001	(S)	William Shatner "Live" (With poster)	1977	16.00	40.00
Lemli 00001	(S)	William Shatner "Live" (Without poster)	1977	12.00	30.00
Century-21 2476/7	(DJ)	Interview With The Star Of "Big Bad Mama" (Issued without a cover.)	1974	30.00	75.00
K-Tel NC-494	(S)	Captain Of The Starship (Rare reissue of Lemli 00001 with a new cover.)	1978	20.00	50.00
SHAW, SANDIE					
Reprise R-6166	(M)	Sandi Shaw	1965	16.00	40.00
Reprise RS-6166	(E)	Sandi Shaw	1965	12.00	30.00
Reprise R-6191	(M)	Me	1966	12.00	30.00
Reprise RS-6191	(S)	Me	1966	16.00	40.00
SHAW, SERENA					
Rama	(M)	Cry My Love	195?	300.00	500.00
SHELTON, ROSCOE					
Excello LP-8002	(M)	Roscoe Shelton Sings	1961	200.00	500.00
Sound Stage-7 500	(S)	Music In His Soul, Soul In His Music	196?	20.00	50.00

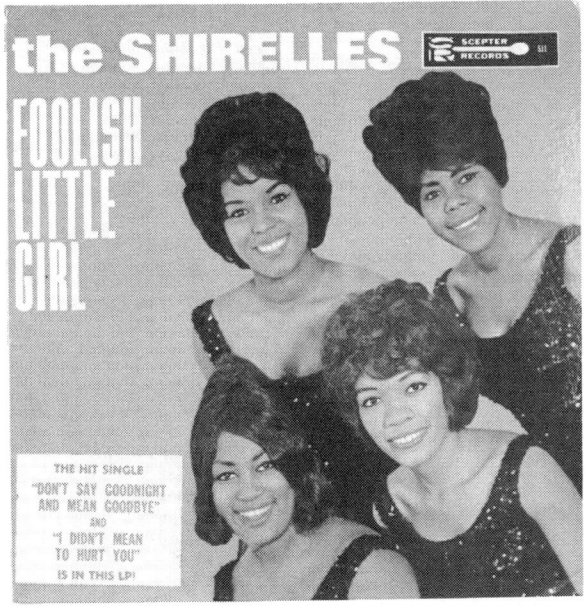

From 1958 through the early '60s, The Shirelles—Shirley Owens with Micki Harris, Doris Kenner and Beverly Lee—were one of the definitive rhythm'n blues based girl groups. They placed more than two-dozen sides, many of them genre classics, on the national charts before losing their audience to the British Invasion (although their recording of inferior material certainly played a part in their demise). The two LPs pictured here, their third and sixth, are the original mono versions. In attempting to cash in on the growing stereo market, Scepter reissued the group's first six albums in stereo in 1965, as much as four years after their initial mono release. These stereos are very rare and just starting to receive real attention from collectors.

Label & Catalog #		Title	Year	VG+	NM

SHEP & THE LIMELITES
James "Shep" Sheppard of The Heartbeats with Limelites Clarence Bassett and Charles Baskerville.
Refer to Refer to The Heartbeats / Shep & The Limelites.

Hull 1001	(M)	**Our Anniversary**	1962	400.00	800.00
Roulette R-25350	(M)	**Our Anniversary**	1967	30.00	75.00
Roulette RS-25350	(E)	**Our Anniversary**	1967	20.00	50.00
		(Roulette 25350 is a reissue of Hull 1001.)			

SHEPARD, JEAN/JEAN SHEPARD & THE SECOND FIDDLES

Capitol T-728	(M)	**Songs Of A Love Affair**	1956	24.00	60.00
		— Capitol albums above have turquoise labels.—			
Capitol T-728	(M)	**Songs Of A Love Affair**	195?	12.00	30.00
Capitol T-1126	(M)	**Lonesome Love**	1959	16.00	40.00
Capitol T-1253	(M)	**This Is Jean Shepard**	1959	16.00	40.00
Capitol T-1525	(M)	**Got You On My Mind**	1961	12.00	30.00
Capitol ST-1525	(S)	**Got You On My Mind**	1961	16.00	40.00
Capitol T-1663	(M)	**Heartaches And Tears**	1962	12.00	30.00
Capitol ST-1663	(S)	**Heartaches And Tears**	1962	16.00	40.00
		— Capitol albums above have black labels with the logo on the left side.—			

SHEPHARD, JEAN

Abbott LP-5003	(M)	**Into The Unknown With Jazz**	1956	60.00	150.00
Elektra EKL-172	(M)	**Jean Shephard And Other Foibles**	195?	20.00	50.00

SHEPPARDS, THE

Constellation C-4	(M)	**Collectors Showcase: The Sheppards**	1964	30.00	75.00
Constellation CS-4	(E)	**Collectors Showcase: The Sheppards**	1964	14.00	35.00

SHERRILL, JOYA: *Refer to* GOLDMINE'S PRICE GUIDE TO COLLECTIBLE JAZZ ALBUMS

SHERRYS, THE

Guyden GLP-503	(M)	**At The Hop With The Sherry's**	1962	80.00	200.00

SHIGETA, JAMES

Choreo A-7	(M)	**We Speak The Same Language**	196?	10.00	25.00
Choreo AS-7	(S)	**We Speak The Same Language**	196?	12.00	30.00

SHILOH
Shiloh features Don Henley, later of The Eagles.

Amos AAS-7015	(S)	**Shiloh**	1969	30.00	75.00

SHIP, THE

Elektra EKS-75036	(S)	**The Ship** (Produced by Gary Usher)	1972	10.00	25.00

SHIRELLES, THE
The original Shireeles were Shirley Owens Alston with Doris Coley, Addie "Micki" Harris and Beverley Lee.

Scepter SRM-501	(M)	**Tonight's The Night**	1961	80.00	200.00
		— Scepter albums above have red labels with a black & silver scroll logo on top.—			
Scepter SRM-501	(M)	**Tonight's The Night**	1961	30.00	75.00
Scepter SPS-501	(S)	**Tonight's The Night**	1965	40.00	100.00
Scepter SRM-502	(M)	**The Shirelles Sing To Trumpets & Strings**	1961	30.00	75.00
Scepter SPS-502	(S)	**The Shirelles Sing To Trumpets & Strings**	1965	40.00	100.00
Scepter SRM-504	(M)	**Baby It's You**	1962	30.00	75.00
Scepter SPS-504	(S)	**Baby It's You**	1965	40.00	100.00
Scepter SRM-505	(M)	**A Twist Party**	1962	30.00	75.00
Scepter SPS-505	(S)	**A Twist Party**	1965	40.00	100.00
		(Scepter 505 also features King Curtis.)			
Scepter SRM-507	(M)	**The Shirelles' Greatest Hits**	1963	16.00	40.00
Scepter SPS-507	(P)	**The Shirelles' Greatest Hits**	1963	20.00	50.00
		("Dedicated To The One I Love" is rechanneled on this album.)			
Scepter SRM-511	(M)	**Foolish Little Girl**	1963	20.00	50.00
Scepter SPS-511	(S)	**Foolish Little Girl**	1965	30.00	75.00
Scepter SRM-514	(M)	**It's A Mad, Mad, Mad, Mad, World**	1963	16.00	40.00
Scepter SPS-514	(S)	**It's A Mad, Mad, Mad, Mad, World**	1963	20.00	50.00
Scepter SRM-516	(M)	**The Shirelles Sing The Golden Oldies**	1964	16.00	40.00
Scepter SPS-516	(S)	**The Shirelles Sing The Golden Oldies**	1964	20.00	50.00
Scepter SRM-560	(M)	**The Shirelles' Greatest Hits, Volume 2**	1967	8.00	20.00
Scepter SPS-560	(S)	**The Shirelles' Greatest Hits, Volume 2**	1967	10.00	25.00
		("Please Be My Boy Friend" is rechanneled on this album.)			

Label & Catalog #		Title	Year	VG+	NM
Scepter SRM-562	(M)	**Spontaneous Combustion**	1967	16.00	40.00
Scepter SPS-562	(S)	**Spontaneous Combustion**	1967	20.00	50.00
		— Scepter albums above have orange labels with a black oval-like center.—			
Coca-Cola TX-??	(DJ)	**The Shirelles Swing The Jingle**	1965	100.00	250.00
Pricewise P-4001	(S)	**Swing The Most**	196?	10.00	25.00
Pricewise P-4002	(S)	**Here And Now**	196?	10.00	25.00

SHIRLEY & LEE
Shirley Goodman and Leonard Lee.

Aladdin LP-807	(M)	**Let The Good Times Roll**	1956	750.00	1,500.00
Score SLP-4023	(M)	**Let The Good Times Roll**	1957	300.00	600.00
Warwick W-2028	(M)	**Let The Good Times Roll**	1961	50.00	125.00
Warwick WST-2028	(S)	**Let The Good Times Roll**	1961	80.00	200.00
		(New recordings with a rerecorded title tune.)			
Imperial LP-9179	(M)	**Let The Good Times Roll**	1962	100.00	250.00
United Arts. LA-026-G	(P)	**Legendary Masters** *(2 LPs. Canadian)*	1974	20.00	50.00

SHIVA'S HEADBAND

Armadillo	(S)	**Coming To A Head**	1969	60.00	150.00
Capitol ST-538	(S)	**Take Me To The Mountains**	1970	20.00	50.00
Ape 1001	(S)	**Psychedelic Yesterday**	1981	10.00	25.00

SHOES, THE

(No label)	(S)	**Un Dans Versailles**	1974	40.00	100.00
Black Vinyl S-51477	(S)	**Black Vinyl Shoes**	1977	15.00	75.00
		(Original covers have the title written on a blackboard background.)			

SHONDELL, TROY

Everest LPBR-5206	(M)	**The Many Sides Of Troy Shondell**	1963	16.00	40.00
Everest SDBR-1206	(S)	**The Many Sides Of Troy Shondell**	1963	20.00	50.00
		(One track, "Na-Ne No," was produced by Phil Spector.)			

SHONDELLS, THE

La Louisiane 109	(M)	**The Shondells At The Saturday Hop**	1964	50.00	125.00

SHORE, DINAH
Refer to The Reprise Repertory Theatre.

Columbia CL-6004	(10")	**Dinah Shore Sings**	1949	20.00	50.00
Columbia CL-6069	(10")	**Reminiscing**	1949	20.00	50.00
Columbia JL-8503	(M)	**Bongo / Land Of The Lost**	1950	16.00	40.00
RCA Victor LOC-1000	(10")	**Call Me Madam**	1950	40.00	100.00
RCA Victor LK-1022	(10")	**The King And I**	1951	20.00	50.00
RCA Victor LPM-39	(10")	**Two Tickets To Broadway**	1951	20.00	50.00
RCA Victor LPM-3006	(10")	**Aaron Slick From Punkin Crick** *(Sdtk)*	1952	40.00	100.00
RCA Victor LPM-3103	(10")	**Dinah Shore Sings The Blues**	1953	14.00	35.00
RCA Victor LPM-3214	(10")	**The Dinah Shore TV Show**	1954	14.00	35.00
RCA Victor LPM-1154	(M)	**Holding Hands At Midnight**	1955	14.00	35.00
RCA Victor LPM-1214	(M)	**Bouquet Of Blues**	1956	10.00	25.00
RCA Victor LPM-1719	(M)	**Moments Like These**	1958	10.00	25.00
		—RCA mono albums above have black labels with "Long Play" on the bottom;			
		stereo albums have have "Living Stereo" on the bottom.—			
Capitol T-1247	(M)	**Dinah, Yes Indeed**	1959	8.00	20.00
Capitol ST-1247	(S)	**Dinah, Yes Indeed**	1959	10.00	25.00
Capitol T-1296	(M)	**Somebody Loves Me**	1959	8.00	20.00
Capitol ST-1296	(S)	**Somebody Loves Me**	1959	10.00	25.00
Capitol T-1354	(M)	**Dinah Sings Some Blues With Red**	1960	8.00	20.00
Capitol ST-1354	(S)	**Dinah Sings Some Blues With Red**	1960	10.00	25.00
		(Capitol 1354 features backing by Red Norvo.)			
Capitol T-1422	(M)	**Dinah Sings/Previn Plays**	1960	8.00	20.00
Capitol ST-1422	(S)	**Dinah Sings/Previn Plays**	1960	10.00	25.00
		(Capitol 1422 features backing by Andre Previn.)			
Capitol T-1655	(M)	**Dinah Down Home**	1962	8.00	20.00
Capitol ST-1655	(S)	**Dinah Down Home**	1962	10.00	25.00
Capitol T-1704	(M)	**Fabulous Hits Newly Recorded**	1962	8.00	20.00
Capitol ST-1704	(S)	**Fabulous Hits Newly Recorded**	1962	10.00	25.00
		— Capitol albums above have black labels with the logo on the left side.—			
S&H Green Stamps SH-1	(M)	**Dinah!** *(TV Soundtrack)*	1962	40.00	100.00
Capitol Custom *(No #)*	(S)	**My Very Best To You**	1964	10.00	25.00

Label & Catalog #		Title	Year	VG+	NM

SHORT, BOBBY: *Refer to* GOLDMINE'S PRICE GUIDE TO COLLECTIBLE JAZZ ALBUMS

SHORT, J. D.: *Refer to* SON HOUSE & J. D. SHORT

SHORT CROSS

Grizzly S16-013	(S)	**Arising**	*197?*	**50.00**	**125.00**

SICKNICKS, THE

Amy 2	(M)	**Sick # 2**	*196?*	**12.00**	**30.00**

SIDEKICKS, THE

RCA Victor LPM-3712	(M)	**Fifi The Flea**	*1966*	**8.00**	**20.00**
RCA Victor LSP-3712	(S)	**Fifi The Flea**	*1966*	**10.00**	**25.00**

SIEGEL-SCHWALL BLUES BAND, THE

Vanguard VRS-9235	(M)	**The Siegel-Schwall Band**	*1966*	**8.00**	**20.00**
Vanguard VSD-79235	(S)	**The Siegel-Schwall Band**	*1966*	**10.00**	**25.00**

SIGLER, BUNNY

Parkway P-50000	(M)	**Let The Good Times Roll**	*1967*	**12.00**	**30.00**
Parkway PS-50000	(S)	**Let The Good Times Roll**	*1967*	**16.00**	**40.00**

SIGNATURES, THE: *Refer to* GOLDMINE'S PRICE GUIDE TO COLLECTIBLE JAZZ ALBUMS

SILHOUETTES, THE

Goodway GLP-100	(M)	**The Silhouettes 1958-1968—Get A Job**	*1968*	**150.00**	**300.00**

SILKIE, THE

Fontana MGF-27548	(M)	**You've Got To Hide Your Love Away**	*1965*	**20.00**	**50.00**
Fontana SRF-67548	(E)	**You've Got To Hide Your Love Away**	*1965*	**16.00**	**40.00**
		(Original covers for Fontana 2/67548 are in full color.)			
Fontana MGF-27548	(M)	**You've Got To Hide Your Love Away**	*1965*	**16.00**	**40.00**
Fontana SRF-67548	(E)	**You've Got To Hide Your Love Away**	*1965*	**12.00**	**30.00**
		(Later covers are black & white with a violet tone.)			

SILLY SURFERS, THE / THE WEIRD-OHS
Issued by the Hawk Model Co., The Surfers and The Weird-Ohs are Gary Usher & Co. projects. The tracks on this album were used by Gary to create individual albums by The Surfers (below) and The Weird-Ohs.

Hairy 101	(DJ)	**The Sounds Of The Silly Surfers /**			
		The Sounds Of The Weird-Ohs	*1964*	**60.00**	**150.00**

SILLY SURFERS, THE

Mercury MG-20977	(M)	**The Sounds Of The Silly Surfers**	*1965*	**20.00**	**50.00**
Mercury SR-60977	(S)	**The Sounds Of The Silly Surfers**	*1965*	**30.00**	**75.00**

SILVER

Grammie Fonics 8322	(S)	**Children Of The Lord**	*1975*	**40.00**	**100.00**

SILVER APPLES

Kapp KS-3562	(S)	**Silver Apples**	*1968*	**20.00**	**50.00**
Kapp KS-3584	(S)	**Contact**	*1969*	**14.00**	**35.00**

SILVER BEATLES, THE: *Refer to* ELVIS PRESLEY / THE SILVER BEATLES

SILVERA, DICK

Stinson SLP-87	(M)	**Folk Songs, Ballads, Blues,**			
		Work Songs *(With Dick Weissman)*	*1958*	**12.00**	**30.00**

SILVERMAN, JERRY
Jerry Silverman is a banjo and guitar player and singer of traditional folk songs and blues.

Audio Video AV-101	(M)	**Folk Blues**	*1958*	**12.00**	**30.00**

SILVERS, PHIL
Refer to Benny Fields.

Columbia CL-1011	(M)	**Phil Silvers And The Swinging Brass**	*1957*	**20.00**	**50.00**
Promenade 2088	(M)	**Bilko Marches** *(With Sgt. Bilko cover)*	*1958*	**30.00**	**75.00**
Harmony HL-7170	(M)	**Phil Silvers Swings Bugle Calls For Big Band**	*196?*	**10.00**	**25.00**
		(Harmony 7170 is a reissue of CL-1011.)			

This little gem was commissioned by the Hawk Model Company, manufacturer of plastic model kits, as a promotional one-shot. Vocals are credited to The Surfers and The Weird-ohs, both accompanied by Shary Richards, with production credit to Jimmie Haskell and Gary Usher. The illustrations above show the front and back cover of the album. Usher took the creations to Mercury where he released one album as the former and recorded an unreleased album as the latter.

Label & Catalog #		Title	Year	VG+	NM

SILVERSTEIN, SHEL
Shel Silverstein is a guitar player, singer and writer of folk and pop music with a wacked sense of humor.

Elektra EKL-176	(M)	**Hairy Jazz**	1959	40.00	100.00
Elektra EKS-7176	(S)	**Hairy Jazz**	1959	60.00	150.00
Atlantic 8072	(M)	**Inside Folk Songs**	1963	14.00	35.00
Atlantic SD-8072	(S)	**Inside Folk Songs**	1963	20.00	50.00
Cadet LP-4052	(M)	**I'm So Good I Don't Have To Brag!**	1965	10.00	25.00
Cadet LPS-4052	(S)	**I'm So Good I Don't Have To Brag!**	1965	12.00	30.00
Cadet LP-4054	(M)	**Drain My Brain**	1966	12.00	30.00
Cadet LPS-4054	(S)	**Drain My Brain**	1966	16.00	40.00
RCA Victor LSP-4192	(S)	**A Boy Named Sue** **(& His Other Country Songs)**	1969	8.00	20.00

— RCA albums above have orange labels on non-flexible vinyl —

SIMMONS, "JUMPIN'" GENE

Hi HL-2018	(M)	**Jumpin' Gene Simmons**	1964	14.00	35.00
Hi SHL-32018	(S)	**Jumpin' Gene Simmons**	1964	20.00	50.00

SIMMONS, GENE: *Refer to* KISS

SIMMONS, JEFF
Mr. Simmons was formerly a member of The Easy Chair.

Straight STS-1057	(S)	**Lucille Has Messed Up My Mind**	1969	20.00	50.00
Reprise STS-1057	(S)	**Lucille Has Messed Up My Mind**	1970	10.00	25.00

SIMON, JOE

Sound Stage-7 5003	(M)	**Pure Soul**	1967	10.00	25.00
Sound Stage-7 15003	(S)	**Pure Soul**	1967	12.00	30.00
Sound Stage-7 15004	(S)	**No Sad Songs**	1968	12.00	30.00
Sound Stage-7 15005	(S)	**Simon Sings**	1969	12.00	30.00
Sound Stage-7 15006	(S)	**The Chokin' Kind**	1969	12.00	30.00
Buddah BDS-7512	(S)	**Joe Simon**	1969	10.00	25.00
Sound Stage 7 15008	(S)	**Better Than Ever**	1969	10.00	25.00

SIMON & GARFUNKEL

Columbia CQ-30995	(Q)	**Bridge Over Troubled Water**	1973	12.00	30.00
Columbia HC-49914	(S)	**Bridge Over Troubled Water** (*Half-speed*)	1982	10.00	25.00
Columbia HC-41350	(S)	**Greatest Hits** (*Half-speed master*)	1982	10.00	25.00
Pickwick SPC-3059	(S)	**The Hit Sounds Of Simon & Garfunkel**	1966	20.00	50.00
		(Compilation of S&G's earlier incarnation as Tom & Jerry.)			
Sears SP-435	(S)	**Simon & Garfunkel**	1969	20.00	50.00
		(Sears 435 is a resissue of Pickwick 3059.)			
Mobile Fidelity MFSL-173	(S)	**Bridge Over Troubled Water**	198?	10.00	30.00

SIMON, PAUL

Crest EBM-7172	(DJ)	**The Early Songs Of Paul Simon**	1972	20.00	50.00
		(Crest 7172 is a collection of publishers demos from the pre-S&G period. Issued with a booklet and sheet music.)			
MCP 9267	(S)	**Paul Simon Plus**	196?	20.00	50.00
Solo Music 166	(S)	**Paul Simon**	196?	20.00	50.00
Columbia CQ-30750	(Q)	**Paul Simon**	1974	8.00	20.00
Columbia CQ-32280	(Q)	**There Goes Rhymin' Simon**	1974	8.00	20.00
Columbia PCQ-33540	(Q)	**Still Crazy After All These Years**	1975	8.00	20.00
Columbia HC-43540	(S)	**Still Crazy After All These Years** (*Half-speed*)	1981	16.00	50.00
Columbia HC-45032	(S)	**Greatest Hits, Etc.** (*Half-speed master*)	1981	16.00	50.00

SIMON SISTERS, THE
Carly and Lucy Simon are singer of folk-based pop music.

Kapp KL-1359	(M)	**Winkin,' Blinkin' And Nod**	1964	14.00	35.00
Kapp KS-3359	(S)	**Winkin,' Blinkin' And Nod**	1964	20.00	50.00
Kapp KL-1397	(M)	**Cuddlebug**	1964	14.00	35.00
Kapp KS-3397	(S)	**Cuddlebug**	1964	20.00	50.00

SIMONE, NINA

Bethlehem BCP-6028	(M)	**Little Girl Blue**	1958	40.00	100.00
Bethlehem SBCP-6028	(S)	**Little Girl Blue**	1958	60.00	150.00
Bethlehem BCP-6028	(M)	**The Original Nina Simone**	1961	16.00	40.00
Bethlehem SBCP-6028	(S)	**The Original Nina Simone**	1961	20.00	50.00

(Reissue of Nina's first album with the same catalogue number.)

Label & Catalog #		Title	Year	VG+	NM
Bethlehem BCP-6041	(M)	Nina Simone And Her Friends	1959	20.00	50.00
Bethlehem SBCP-6041	(S)	Nina Simone And Her Friends	1959	30.00	75.00
Colpix CP-407	(M)	The Amazing Nina Simone	1959	10.00	25.00
Colpix SCP-407	(S)	The Amazing Nina Simone	1959	12.00	30.00
Colpix CP-409	(M)	Nina At Town Hall	1959	10.00	25.00
Colpix SCP-409	(S)	Nina At Town Hall	1959	12.00	30.00
Colpix CP-412	(M)	Nina Simone At Newport	1960	10.00	25.00
Colpix SCP-412	(S)	Nina Simone At Newport	1960	12.00	30.00
Colpix CP-419	(M)	Forbidden Fruit	1961	10.00	25.00
Colpix SCP-419	(S)	Forbidden Fruit	1961	12.00	30.00
Colpix CP-421	(M)	Nina Simone At The Village Gate	1961	10.00	25.00
Colpix SCP-421	(S)	Nina Simone At The Village Gate	1961	12.00	30.00
Colpix CP-425	(M)	Nina Simone Sings Ellington	1962	10.00	25.00
Colpix SCP-425	(S)	Nina Simone Sings Ellington	1962	12.00	30.00
Colpix CP-443	(M)	Nina's Choice	1963	10.00	25.00
Colpix SCP-443	(S)	Nina's Choice	1963	12.00	30.00
Colpix CP-455	(M)	Nina Simone At Carnegie Hall	1963	10.00	25.00
Colpix SCP-455	(S)	Nina Simone At Carnegie Hall	1963	12.00	30.00
Colpix CP-465	(M)	Folksy Nina	1964	10.00	25.00
Colpix SCP-465	(S)	Folksy Nina	1964	12.00	30.00
Colpix CP-496	(M)	Nina With Strings	1966	10.00	25.00
Colpix SCP-496	(S)	Nina With Strings	1966	12.00	30.00

— Colpix albums above have gold labels.—

SIMPSON, CAROLE: *Refer to* GOLDMINE'S PRICE GUIDE TO COLLECTIBLE JAZZ ALBUMS

SIMPSON, FRANK

Audio Lab AL-1552	(M)	Four Star Hits	1960	80.00	200.00

SIMPSON, RED

Portland 1003	(M)	Hello, I'm A Truck	1965	30.00	75.00
Capitol T-2468	(M)	Roll Truck, Roll	1966	8.00	20.00
Capitol ST-2468	(S)	Roll Truck, Roll	1966	10.00	25.00
Capitol T-2569	(M)	The Man Behind The Badge	1966	8.00	20.00
Capitol ST-2569	(S)	The Man Behind The Badge	1966	10.00	25.00
Capitol T-2691	(M)	Truck Drivin' Fool	1967	8.00	20.00
Capitol ST-2691	(S)	Truck Drivin' Fool	1967	10.00	25.00
Capitol T-2829	(M)	A Bakersfield Dozen	1967	8.00	20.00
Capitol ST-2829	(S)	A Bakersfield Dozen	1967	10.00	25.00

— Capitol albums above have black "rainbow" labels.—

SIMS, FRANKIE LEE

Specialty SPS-2124	(M)	Lucy Mae Blues	1969	16.00	40.00

SIN SAY SHUNS, THE

Venett V-940	(M)	I'll Be There	196?	14.00	35.00
Venett VS-940	(S)	I'll Be There	196?	20.00	50.00

SINATRA, FRANK

Frank Sinatra virtually defines a genre, although defining the genre may be difficult. Combining the emotional distance of most [white] pop singers with a crooner's romanticism, a hint of jazz, and the back rooms of too many bars with a sense of timing and phrasing that is the envy of all other singers, Ol' Blue Eyes has created a repertoire that will accompany slow dancing and candlelight for generations. While the values attached to his originals are comparable to other male vocalists of his era, they are dramatically undervalued for an artist of his stature. The listings below are broken up into logical groupings: His early sides with Tommy Dorsey's Orchestra (there are many Dorsey collections with a couple of Sinatra tracks; refer to Goldmine's Price Guide To Collectible Jazz Albums for a more complete listing); his solo career with Columbia; his amazing resurrection with Capitol and Nelson Riddle in the '50s; and his attempts to run his own Reprise Records in the '60s. Refer to Peggy Lee; Dean Martin; The Reprise Repertory Theater.

—1. The Dorsey Years—

RCA Victor LPT-3063	(10")	Fabulous Frankie	1953	20.00	50.00
RCA Victor LPM-1569	(M)	Frankie And Tommy	1957	20.00	50.00
RCA Victor LPM-1569	(M)	Tommy Plays, Frankie Sings	1957	16.00	40.00

("Tommy Plays..." is a repackage of "Frankie And Tommy.")

RCA Victor LPM-1632	(M)	We Three	1957	16.00	40.00

— RCA Victor albums have "Long Play" on the bottom of the label.—

Label & Catalog #		Title	Year	VG+	NM
		—2. The Columbia Recordings 1943-1952—			
Columbia CL-6001	(10")	**The Voice Of Frank Sinatra**	1949	**30.00**	**75.00**
		(CL-6001 was originally issued in a pink paper sleeve.)			
Columbia CL-6001	(10")	**The Voice Of Frank Sinatra**	1950	**20.00**	**50.00**
		(Later pressings have a blue cardboard cover.)			
Columbia CL-6019	(10")	**Christmas Songs By Sinatra**	1950	**24.00**	**60.00**
		(CL-6019 was originally issued with a gingerbread man cover.)			
Columbia CL-6019	(10")	**Christmas Songs By Sinatra**	1951	**20.00**	**50.00**
		(Later pressings have a green cover.)			
Columbia CL-6059	(10")	**Frankly Sentimental**	1951	**24.00**	**60.00**
Columbia CL-6087	(10")	**Songs By Sinatra, Volume 1**	1952	**24.00**	**60.00**
Columbia CL-6096	(10")	**Dedicated To You**	1952	**24.00**	**60.00**
Columbia CL-6143	(10")	**Sing And Dance With Frank Sinatra**	1953	**24.00**	**60.00**
Columbia CL-6290	(10")	**I've Got A Crush On You**	1954	**24.00**	**60.00**
Columbia CL-2521	(10")	**Get Happy**	1955	**20.00**	**50.00**
Columbia CL-2539	(10")	**I've Got A Crush On You**	1955	**20.00**	**50.00**
Columbia CL-2542	(10")	**Christmas With Sinatra**	1955	**20.00**	**50.00**
Columbia ML-4271	(M)	**Frank Sinatra Conducts Music Of Alec Wilder**	1955	**30.00**	**75.00**
Columbia CL-606	(M)	**Frankie** *(Sinatra drawing cover)*	1955	**12.00**	**30.00**
Columbia CL-606	(M)	**Frankie** *(Sinatra & Debbie Reynolds cover)*	1956	**12.00**	**30.00**
		— Original Columbia albums above have labels with "Long LP Playing" on the bottom.—			
Columbia CL-743	(M)	**The Voice**	1955	**10.00**	**25.00**
Columbia CL-884	(M)	**Frank Sinatra Conducts Music Of Alec Wilder**	1956	**20.00**	**50.00**
Columbia CL-902	(M)	**That Old Feeling**	1956	**10.00**	**25.00**
Columbia CL-953	(M)	**Adventures Of The Heart**	1957	**10.00**	**25.00**
Columbia CL-1032	(M)	**Christmas Dreaming**	1957	**12.00**	**30.00**
Columbia C2L-6	(M)	**The Frank Sinatra Story In Music** *(2 LPs)*	1958	**10.00**	**25.00**
Columbia CL-1130	(M)	**The Frank Sinatra Story In Music, Volume 1**	1958	**10.00**	**25.00**
Columbia CL-1131	(M)	**The Frank Sinatra Story In Music, Volume 2**	1958	**10.00**	**25.00**
Columbia CL-1136	(M)	**Put Your Dreams Away**	1958	**10.00**	**25.00**
Columbia CL-1241	(M)	**Love Is A Kick**	1958	**10.00**	**25.00**
Columbia CL-1297	(M)	**The Broadway Kick**	1959	**10.00**	**25.00**
Columbia CL-1359	(M)	**Come Back To Sorrento**	1959	**10.00**	**25.00**
Columbia CL-1448	(M)	**Reflections**	1959	**16.00**	**40.00**
		— Original Columbia albums above have three white "eye" logos on each side of the spindle hole.—			
Columbia C3L-42	(M)	**The Essential Frank Sinatra** *(3 LPs)*	1966	**40.00**	**100.00**
Columbia C3S-42	(E)	**The Essential Frank Sinatra** *(3 LPs)*	1966	**20.00**	**50.00**
Columbia CL-2739	(M)	**The Essential Frank Sinatra, Volume 1**	1967	**12.00**	**30.00**
Columbia CS-9539	(E)	**The Essential Frank Sinatra, Volume 1**	1967	**6.00**	**15.00**
Columbia CL-2740	(M)	**The Essential Frank Sinatra, Volume 2**	1967	**12.00**	**30.00**
Columbia CS-9540	(E)	**The Essential Frank Sinatra, Volume 2**	1967	**6.00**	**15.00**
Columbia CL-2741	(M)	**The Essential Frank Sinatra, Volume 3**	1967	**12.00**	**30.00**
Columbia CS-9541	(E)	**The Essential Frank Sinatra, Volume 3**	1967	**6.00**	**15.00**
Columbia CL-2913	(M)	**Frank Sinatra In Hollywood 1943-1949**	1968	**1400**	**35.00**
		— Original Columbia albums above have "360 Sound" on the bottom of the label.—			
Columbia C6X-40343	(M)	**The Voice:— The Columbia Years 1943-1952** *(6 LPs)*	1986	**20.00**	**50.00**
Columbia CAS-2475	(M)	**The Voice: The Columbia Years** *(Sampler)*	1986	**10.00**	**25.00**
Columbia C2X-40897	(M)	**Hello Young Lovers** *(2 LPs)*	1987	**10.00**	**25.00**
Columbia PC-44236	(M)	**Sinatra Rarities**	1988	**10.00**	**25.00**
		—3. The Capitol Recordings 1953-1962—			
Capitol H-488	(10")	**Songs For Young Lovers**	1954	**20.00**	**50.00**
Capitol H-528	(10")	**Swing Easy**	1954	**20.00**	**50.00**
Capitol H1-581	(10")	**In The Wee Small Hours—Part 1**	1955	**20.00**	**50.00**
Capitol H2-581	(10")	**In The Wee Small Hours—Part 2**	1955	**20.00**	**50.00**
Capitol W-581	(M)	**In The Wee Small Hours**	1955	**12.00**	**30.00**
Capitol W-587	(M)	**Swing Easy / Songs For Young Lovers**	1955	**12.00**	**30.00**
Capitol W-653	(M)	**Songs For Swingin' Lovers**	1956	**16.00**	**40.00**
		(The cover shows Sinatra turned away from the embracing couple.)			
Capitol W-653	(M)	**Songs For Swingin' Lovers**	1956	**12.00**	**30.00**
		(The cover shows Sinatra turned towards the embracing couple.)			
Capitol W-735	(M)	**Frank Sinatra Conducts Tone Poems Of Color** *(Turquoise label)*	1956	**20.00**	**50.00**

On collecting Sinatra: As Ol' Blue Eyes always sold well, his albums are, for the most part, not all that hard to find. The Columbias receive the least attention and are the most obviously undervalued. Most collectors prefer to Capitol albums, original gray or turquoise labels if mono, the black "rainbow" label for the later stereos. The hit albums are still fairly common, given their age. Some of the compilations from the '60s are far rarer than their values would indicate. Most collectors prefer the Reprise titles in mono over stereo, especially on the titles from the early '60s. And, for those who wish to run the Reprise 1000 series—Frank's series—the items to look for are the Reprise Repertory Theatre albums in their original gatefold covers.

Label & Catalog #		Title	Year	VG+	NM
Capitol W-750	(M)	**High Society** (Soundtrack)	1956	12.00	30.00
Capitol T-768	(M)	**This Is Sinatra!** (Turquoise label)	1956	12.00	30.00
Capitol W-789	(M)	**Close To You**	1957	12.00	30.00
Capitol W-803	(M)	**A Swingin' Affair**	1957	12.00	30.00
Capitol W-855	(M)	**Where Are You?**	1957	12.00	30.00
Capitol W-894	(M)	**A Jolly Christmas From Frank Sinatra**	1957	12.00	30.00
Capitol W-912	(M)	**Pal Joey** (Soundtrack)	1958	12.00	30.00
Capitol W-920	(M)	**Come Fly With Me**	1958	12.00	30.00
Capitol W-982	(M)	**This Is Sinatra, Volume 2**	1958	12.00	30.00
Capitol W-1053	(M)	**Frank Sinatra Sings For Only The Lonely**	1958	12.00	30.00
		— Capitol albums above have gray or turquoise labels with "Long Playing" on the bottom.—			
Capitol W-750	(M)	**High Society** (Soundtrack)	1958	8.00	20.00
Capitol SW-750	(S	**High Society** (Soundtrack)	1958	12.00	30.00
Capitol T-768	(M)'	**This Is Sinatra!** (Gold Starline label)	195?	10.00	25.00
Capitol W-855	(M)	**Where Are You?**	1958	8.00	20.00
Capitol SW-855	(S)	**Where Are You?**	1958	12.00	30.00
		(Original stereo pressings are missing "I Cover The Water Front.")			
Capitol SW-855	(S)	**Where Are You?**	1959	10.00	25.00
		(Later stereo pressings contain "I Cover The Water Front.")			
Capitol W-912	(M)	**Pal Joey** (Soundtrack)	1958	8.00	20.00
Capitol SW-912	(S)	**Pal Joey** (Soundtrack)	1958	10.00	25.00
Capitol W-920	(M)	**Come Fly With Me**	1958	8.00	20.00
Capitol SW-920	(S)	**Come Fly With Me**	1958	12.00	30.00
Capitol W-1053	(M)	**Frank Sinatra Sings For Only The Lonely**	1958	8.00	20.00
Capitol SW-1053	(S)	**Frank Sinatra Sings For Only The Lonely**	1958	12.00	30.00
		(Original stereo pressings of SW-1053 do not include It's A Lonesome Old Town" and "Spring Is Here.")			
Capitol SW-1053	(S)	**Frank Sinatra Sings For Only The Lonely**	1959	10.00	25.00
		(Later pressings include "It's A Lonesome Old Town" and "Spring Is Here.")			
Capitol W-1069	(M)	**Come Dance With Me!**	1959	8.00	20.00
Capitol SW-1069	(S)	**Come Dance With Me!**	1959	10.00	25.00
Capitol W-1164	(M)	**Look To Your Heart**	1959	8.00	20.00
Capitol W-1221	(M)	**No One Cares**	1959	8.00	20.00
Capitol SW-1221	(S)	**No One Cares**	1959	10.00	25.00
Capitol W-1301	(M)	**Can-Can** (Soundtrack)	1960	8.00	20.00
Capitol SW-1301	(S)	**Can-Can** (Soundtrack)	1960	12.00	30.00
Capitol W-1417	(M)	**Nice 'N' Easy**	1960	8.00	20.00
Capitol SW-1417	(S)	**Nice 'N' Easy**	1960	10.00	25.00
Capitol W-1429	(M)	**Swing Easy**	1960	8.00	20.00
Capitol W-1432	(M)	**Songs For Young Lovers**	1960	8.00	20.00
Capitol W-1491	(M)	**Sinatra's Swingin' Session!!!**	1961	8.00	20.00
Capitol SW-1491	(S)	**Sinatra's Swingin' Session!!!**	1961	10.00	25.00
Capitol W-1538	(M)	**All The Way**	1961	8.00	20.00
Capitol SW-1538	(S)	**All The Way**	1961	10.00	25.00
Capitol W-1594	(M)	**Come Swing With Me!**	1961	8.00	20.00
Capitol SW-1594	(S)	**Come Swing With Me!**	1961	10.00	25.00
Capitol W-1676	(M)	**Point Of No Return**	1961	8.00	20.00
Capitol SW-1676	(S)	**Point Of No Return**	1961	10.00	25.00
		— Original Capitol albums above have black labels with the logo on the left side.—			
Capitol PRO-2163/4/5/6	(DJ)	**Selections From "Sinatra, The Great Years"** (2 LPs)	1962	12.00	30.00
Capitol WCO-1762	(M)	**Sinatra, The Great Years** (3 LPs)	1962	12.00	30.00
Capitol SWCO-1762	(P)	**Sinatra, The Great Years** (3 LPs)	1962	16.00	40.00
Capitol T-2123	(M)	**Sinatra Sings The Select Harold Arlen**	1964	40.00	100.00
		(Capitol 2123 was only issued in Australia, Canada and the U.K.)			
Capitol PRO-2974/5	(DJ)	**Minute Masters** (20 edited selections)	1965	16.00	40.00
Capitol TFL-2814	(M)	**Deluxe Set** (3 LP box)	1968	16.00	40.00
Capitol STFL-2814	(P)	**Deluxe Set** (3 LP box)	1968	12.00	30.00
Capitol DQBO-91261	(M)	**Songs For The Young At Heart** (2 LPs)	1959	10.00	25.00
		(Capitol Record Club)			
		— Original Capitol albums above have black labels with the logo on top.—			
Capitol LS-308A	(P)	**Sinatra-The Works** (10 LP box)	1972	20.00	50.00
		(This boxed set for the Longines Symphonette was issued with a bonus album, priced separately below.)			
Capitol SYS-5637	(P)	**Sinatra Like Never Before**	1972	10.00	25.00
Capitol DNFR-7630	(P)	**The Sinatra Touch** (6 LP box)	19??	20.00	50.00
Capitol C1-94777	(P)	**The Capitol Years** (5 LP box)	1990	30.00	75.00

Label & Catalog #		Title	Year	VG+	NM

—4. The Reprise Recordings 1960-1982—

Label & Catalog #		Title	Year	VG+	NM
Reprise F-1001	(M)	Ring-A-Ding-Ding!	1961	12.00	30.00
Reprise R9-1001	(S)	Ring-A-Ding-Ding!	1961	10.00	25.00
Reprise F-1002	(M)	Swing Along With Me	1961	12.00	30.00
Reprise R9-1002	(S)	Swing Along With Me	1961	10.00	25.00
Reprise F-1002	(M)	Sinatra Swings	1962	10.00	25.00
Reprise R9-1002	(S)	Sinatra Swings	1962	8.00	20.00
		("Sinatra Swings" is a repackaged version of "Swing Along With Me.")			
Reprise F-1003	(M)	I Remember Tommy	1962	10.00	25.00
Reprise R9-1003	(S)	I Remember Tommy	1962	8.00	20.00
Reprise F-1004	(M)	Sinatra And Strings	1962	10.00	25.00
Reprise R9-1004	(S)	Sinatra And Strings	1962	8.00	20.00
Reprise F-1005	(M)	Sinatra And Swingin' Brass (Gatefold cover)	1962	10.00	25.00
Reprise R9-1005	(S)	Sinatra And Swingin' Brass (Gatefold cover)	1962	8.00	20.00
Reprise F-1007	(M)	All Alone (Gatefold cover)	1962	10.00	25.00
Reprise R9-1007	(S)	All Alone (Gatefold cover)	1962	8.00	20.00
Reprise R-6045	(M)	Sinatra Conducts Music From Pictures And Plays	1962	16.00	40.00
Reprise R9-6045	(S)	Sinatra Conducts Music From Pictures And Plays	1962	12.00	30.00
Reprise R-50001	(M)	Frank Sinatra & His Friends Want You To Have Yourself A Merry Little Christmas (With bag)	1962	20.00	50.00
Reprise R-50001	(M)	Frank Sinatra & His Friends Want You To Have Yourself A Merry Little Christmas (Without bag)	1962	10.00	25.00
		(R-50001 is a promotional various artists compilation with FS on the cover and originally issued in a special vinyl outer bag.)			
Colpix CP-516	(M)	The Victors (Soundtrack)	1963	20.00	50.00
Colpix SCP-516	(S)	The Victors (Soundtrack)	1963	30.00	75.00
Reprise F-1008	(M)	Sinatra-Basie (Gatefold cover)	1963	10.00	25.00
Reprise R9-1008	(S)	Sinatra-Basie (Gatefold cover)	1963	8.00	20.00
Reprise F-1009	(M)	The Concert Sinatra (Gatefold cover)	1963	10.00	25.00
Reprise R9-1009	(S)	The Concert Sinatra (Gatefold cover)	1963	8.00	20.00
Reprise F-1010	(M)	Sinatra's Sinatra (Gatefold cover)	1963	10.00	25.00
Reprise R9-1010	(S)	Sinatra's Sinatra (Gatefold cover)	1963	8.00	20.00
Reprise R-6116	(M)	Greatest Hits From The Greatest Films	1963	12.00	30.00
Reprise R9-6116	(S)	Greatest Hits From The Greatest Films	1963	10.00	25.00
Reprise F-1011	(M)	Days Of Wine And Roses	1964	10.00	25.00
Reprise FS-1011	(S)	Days Of Wine And Roses	1964	8.00	20.00
Reprise F-1012	(M)	It Might As Well Be Swing	1964	10.00	25.00
Reprise FS-1012	(S)	It Might As Well Be Swing	1964	8.00	20.00
Reprise F-1013	(M)	Softly, As I Leave You	1964	10.00	25.00
Reprise FS-1013	(S)	Softly, As I Leave You	1964	8.00	20.00
Reprise R-6167	(M)	Sinatra '65	1965	10.00	25.00
Reprise RS-6167	(S)	Sinatra '65	1965	8.00	20.00
Reprise F-1014	(M)	September Of My Years	1965	10.00	25.00
Reprise FS-1014	(S)	September Of My Years	1965	8.00	20.00
Reprise F-1015	(M)	My Kind Of Broadway	1965	10.00	25.00
Reprise FS-1015	(S)	My Kind Of Broadway	1965	8.00	20.00
Reprise 2F/FS-1016	(M)	A Man & His Music Slipcase (With card)	1965	80.00	200.00
Reprise 2F/FS-1016	(M)	A Man & His Music Slipcase (Without card)	1965	40.00	100.00
		(A limited number of stock copies were issued in a blue slipcase with an embossed silver front, which included a four page booklet. The price above is for the slipcase with the booklet; add the value of the mono or stereo albums below for a value for the complete set. Also, some cases had Sinatra's signed card attached to it.)			
Reprise 2F-1016	(M)	A Man And His Music (2 LPs)	1965	12.00	30.00
Reprise 2FS-1016	(S)	A Man And His Music (2 LPs)	1965	10.00	25.00
Reprise PRO-3004	(DJ)	A Man And His Music, Part II: Frank Sinatra CBS Television Special	1965	60.00	150.00
		(Promotional album for Budweiser's corporate use.)			
Reprise F-1017	(M)	Strangers In The Night	1966	10.00	25.00
Reprise FS-1017	(S)	Strangers In The Night	1966	8.00	20.00
Reprise F-1018	(M)	Moonlight Sinatra	1966	10.00	25.00
Reprise FS-1018	(S)	Moonlight Sinatra	1966	8.00	20.00
Reprise 2F-1019	(M)	Sinatra At The Sands (2 LPs)	1966	12.00	30.00
Reprise 2FS-1019	(S)	Sinatra At The Sands (2 LPs)	1966	10.00	25.00

Label & Catalog #		Title	Year	VG+	NM
Reprise F-1020	(M)	That's Life	1966	10.00	25.00
Reprise FS-1020	(S)	That's Life	1966	8.00	20.00
Reprise F-1021	(M)	Francis Albert Sinatra And Antonio Carlos Jobim	1967	10.00	25.00
Reprise FS-1021	(S)	Francis Albert Sinatra And Antonio Carlos Jobim	1967	8.00	20.00
Reprise F-1022	(M)	The World We Knew	1967	10.00	25.00
Reprise FS-1022	(S)	The World We Knew	1967	8.00	20.00
Reprise FS-1023	(S)	The Frank Sinatra Christmas Album	1967		Unreleased

(Covers for FS-1023 have a suggested Near Mint value of $50-100.)

Reprise F-1024	(M)	Francis A. And Edward K.	1968	10.00	25.00
Reprise FS-1024	(S)	Francis A. And Edward K.	1968	8.00	20.00

— Original Reprise albums have custom Frank Sinatra photo labels.—

Reprise FS-1028	(DJ)	Sinatra Jobim (Test pressing)	1969		See below
Reprise FS-1028	(S)	Sinatra Jobim	1969		See below

(Although FS-1028 was deleted prior to release, a handful of vinyl test pressings and commercial 8-track tapes exist. Suggested Near Mint value for the LP is $2,0000-6,000.)

Reprise FS-41029	(Q)	My Way	1974	10.00	25.00
Reprise FS-1030	(S)	A Man Alone (Gatefold cover)	1970	20.00	50.00
Reprise FS-1031	(S)	Watertown (Gatefold cover with poster)	1970	12.00	30.00
Reprise FS-42155	(Q)	Ol' Blue Eyes Is Back (Gatefold cover)	1973	10.00	25.00
Reprise FS-42195	(Q)	Some Nice Things I've Missed (Gatefold cover)	1974	10.00	25.00
Mobile Fidelity SC-1	(P)	Sinatra (16 LP box)	1984	100.00	300.00

SINATRA, FRANK, & BING CROSBY

Reprise F-2020	(M)	America, I Hear You Singing	1964	12.00	30.00
Reprise FS-2020	(S)	America, I Hear You Singing	1964	10.00	25.00
Reprise F-2021	(M)	Robin And The Seven Hoods	1964	12.00	30.00
Reprise FS-2021	(S)	Robin And The Seven Hoods	1964	10.00	25.00
Reprise F-2022	(M)	Twelve Songs Of Christmas	1964	12.00	30.00
Reprise FS-2022	(S)	Twelve Songs Of Christmas	1964	10.00	25.00

SINATRA, FRANK, & DORIS DAY

Columbia CL-6339	(10")	Young At Heart (Soundtrack)	1954	30.00	75.00

SINATRA, NANCY
Refer to Elvis Presley; Mel Tillis & Nancy Sinatra.

Reprise R-6202	(M)	Boots	1966	10.00	25.00
Reprise RS-6202	(S)	Boots	1966	12.00	30.00
Reprise R-6207	(M)	How Does That Grab You?	1966	8.00	20.00
Reprise RS-6207	(S)	How Does That Grab You?	1966	10.00	25.00
RCA Victor VPS-6078	(S)	This Is Nancy Sinatra (2 LPs)	1972	20.00	50.00
RCA Victor LSP-4774	(S)	Woman	1972	10.00	25.00

SINATRA, NANCY, & LEE HAZLEWOOD
Refer to Lee Hazlewood.

RCA Victor LSP-4645	(S)	Nancy & Lee—Did You Ever?	1972	10.00	25.00

SING A SONG WITH THE BEATLES
While some fab photos of the Fab Four grace this album's gatefold cover, the record contains anonymous "Instrumental Background Re-Creations of Their Big Hits."

Tower KAO-5000	(M)	Sing A Song With The Beatles	1965	40.00	100.00
Tower DKAO-5000	(E)	Sing A Song With The Beatles	1965	60.00	150.00

SIR DOUGLAS QUINTET, THE
Refer to Doug Sahm.

Tribe TR-37001	(M)	The Best Of The Sir Douglas Quintet	1966	20.00	50.00
Tribe TRS-47001	(E)	The Best Of The Sir Douglas Quintet	1966	16.00	40.00
Smash SRS-67108	(S)	Honkey Blues	1968	12.00	30.00
Smash SRS-67115	(S)	Mendocino	1969	10.00	25.00
Smash SRS-67130	(S)	Together After Five	1970	10.00	25.00
Philips PHS-600-344	(S)	1+1+1=4	1970	10.00	25.00
Philips PHS-600-353	(S)	The Return Of Doug Saldana	1971	10.00	25.00
Mercury SRM-1-655	(S)	Rough Edges	1972	12.00	30.00

SIR LANCELOT

Mercury MG-25159	(10")	Calypso	1952	20.00	50.00

Label & Catalog #		Title	Year	VG+	NM
SIR LORD BALTIMORE					
Mercury SR-61328	(S)	Kingdom Come	1970	10.00	25.00
Mercury SRM-1-613	(S)	Sir Lord Baltimore	1971	10.00	25.00
SIRVENT, FERNANDO					
Prestige Inter. PRLP-13077	(M)	Flamenco Fantastico	1963	12.00	30.00
SKELTON, RED					
Liberty LRP-3425	(M)	Red Skelton Conducts	1966	8.00	20.00
Liberty LST-7425	(S)	Red Skelton Conducts	1966	10.00	25.00
Liberty LRP-3477	(M)	Music From The Heart	1966	8.00	20.00
Liberty LST-7477	(S)	Music From The Heart	1966	10.00	25.00
SKINNER, CORNELIA & OTIS					
Camden CAL-190	(M)	Cornelia Skinner With Otis Skinner	195?	10.00	25.00
SKINNER, JIMMIE					
Mercury MG-20352	(M)	Songs That Make The Juke Box Play	1957	30.00	75.00
Decca DL-4132	(M)	Country Singer	1961	12.00	30.00
Decca DL-74132	(S)	Country Singer	1961	16.00	40.00
Mercury MG-20700	(M)	Jimmie Skinner Sings Jimmie Rodgers	1962	12.00	30.00
Mercury SR-60700	(S)	Jimmie Skinner Sings Jimmie Rodgers	1962	16.00	40.00
Starday SLP-240	(M)	The Kentucky Colonel *Yellow label)*	1963	12.00	30.00
SKIP & THE CREATIONS					
Justice JLP-???	(S)	Mobam	196?	200.00	400.00
SKUNKS, THE					
Teen Town TTLP-101	(S)	Gettin' Started	196?	20.00	50.00
SKYLARKS, THE					
Decca DL-8083	(M)	White Christmas *(Soundtrack)*	1950	24.00	60.00
SKYLINERS, THE					
Calico LP-3000	(M)	The Skyliners *(Yellow & blue label)*	1959	200.00	500.00
Calico LP-3000	(M)	The Skyliners *(Blue label)*	196?	60.00	150.00
Original Sound OS-8873	(M)	Since I Don't Have You	1963	14.00	35.00
Original Sound OSS-8873	(S)	Since I Don't Have You	1963	20.00	50.00
		("Since I Don't Have You," "One Night, One Night" and This I Swear" are rechanneled on this album.)			

SLADE: *Refer to* AMBROSE SLADE

Label & Catalog #		Title	Year	VG+	NM
SLEDGE, PERCY					
Atlantic 8125	(M)	When A Man Loves A Woman	1966	16.00	40.00
Atlantic SD-8125	(E)	When A Man Loves A Woman	1966	12.00	30.00
Atlantic 8132	(M)	Warm And Tender Soul	1966	16.00	40.00
Atlantic SD-8132	(E)	Warm And Tender Soul	1966	12.00	30.00
Atlantic 8146	(M)	The Percy Sledge Way	1967	16.00	40.00
Atlantic SD-8146	(S)	The Percy Sledge Way	1967	20.00	50.00
Atlantic SC-8180	(S)	Take Time To Know Her	1968	20.00	50.00
		("I Love Everything About You" is rechanneled on this album.)			
Atlantic SD-8210	(S)	The Best Of Percy Sledge	1969	16.00	40.00
		("When A Man Loves A Woman," "Warm And Tender Love," "Baby Help Me" and "It Tears Me Up" are rechanneled on this album.)			
SLIM HARPO					
Excello LP-8003	(M)	Raining In My Heart	1961	100.00	250.00
		(First pressings of Excello 8003 have a red & white drawing cover.)			
Excello LPS-8003	(M)	Raining In My Heart	1968	30.00	75.00
		(Later "Electronic Stereo" covers contain mono albums.)			
Excello LP-8005	(M)	Baby, Scratch My Back	1966	80.00	200.00
		(First pressings of Excello 8005 have a green & white drawing cover.)			
Excello LPS-8005	(M)	Baby, Scratch My Back	1968	30.00	75.00
		(Later "Electronic Stereo" covers contain mono albums.)			
Excello LPS-8008	(M)	Tip On In	1968	20.00	50.00
Excello LPS-8010	(M)	The Best Of Slim Harpo	1969	16.00	40.00
Excello LPS-8013	(M)	Slim Harpo Knew The Blues	1970	16.00	40.00

Label & Catalog #		Title	Year	VG+	NM
SLIM JIM					
Soma 1225	(M)	**Slim Jim Sings** (Black label)	1958	20.00	50.00
SLOAN, P.F.					
Refer to The Fantastic Baggys; The Grass Roots.					
Dunhill D-50004	(M)	**Songs Of Our Times**	1965	12.00	30.00
Dunhill DS-50004	(S)	**Songs Of Our Times**	1965	16.00	40.00
Dunhill D-50007	(S)	**Twelve More Times**	1966	12.00	30.00
Dunhill DS-50007	(S)	**Twelve More Times**	1966	16.00	40.00
Atco SD-33-268	(S)	**Measure Of Pleasure**	1968	12.00	30.00
Mums KZ-31260	(S)	**Raised On Records**	1972	10.00	25.00

SLOANE, CAROL: *Refer to* GOLDMINE'S PRICE GUIDE TO COLLECTIBLE JAZZ ALBUMS

SLY & THE FAMILY STONE					
Sly is Sylvester Stewart; The Family Stone features Larry Graham, later of Graham Central Station.					
Epic LN-24324	(M)	**A Whole New Thing**	1967	12.00	30.00
Epic BN-26324	(S)	**A Whole New Thing**	1967	16.00	40.00
Epic EQ-30325	(Q)	**Sly & The Family Stone's Greatest Hits**	1973	40.00	100.00
		("Everybody Is A Star," "Hot Fun In The Summertime," and "Thank You" are remixed from the multi-tracks on this album.)			
Epic PEQ-32930	(Q)	**Small Talk**	1974	10.00	25.00
Epic AS-264	(DJ)	**Everything You Always Wanted To Hear From Sly & The Family Stone But Were Afraid To Ask For**	1976	10.00	25.00
Epic PEQ-33835	(Q)	**High On You**	1975	10.00	25.00
SMALL, MILLIE					
Smash MGS-27055	(M)	**My Boy Lollipop**	1964	20.00	50.00
Smash SRS-67055	(E)	**My Boy Lollipop**	1964	16.00	40.00

SMALL FACES, THE/THE FACES					
Features Steve Marriott, Ronnie Lane, Kenny Jones and Ian McLagen. The Warners and Mercury albums include Rod Stewart and Ron Wood.					
Immediate Z12-52-002	(S)	**There Are But Four Small Faces**	1968	20.00	50.00
		(Original covers are full color; counterfeits are green & white.)			
Immediate Z12-52-008	(S)	**Ogden's Nut Gone Flake** (Round cover)	1968	20.00	50.00
Warner Bros. PRO-???	(DJ)	**First Step Box**	1970		See below
		(Box contains a copy of the album, a badge, a sheet of cutouts with a pair of scissors, and a complete press kit with photos, etc. Rare as a plynth with a suggested Near Mint value of $300-500.)			

SMART SET, THE: *Refer to* GOLDMINE'S PRICE GUIDE TO COLLECTIBLE JAZZ ALBUMS

SMECK, ROY					
Smeck also recorded as Prince Kailua. Refer to The Ames Brothers.					
"X" LPX-3012	(10")	**South Of The Border**	195?	60.00	150.00
"X" LPA-3016	(10")	**Christmas In Hawaii**	195?	60.00	150.00
Coral CRL-56013	(10")	**Drifting And Dreaming**	195?	40.00	100.00
Decca DL-5458	(10")	**Memory Lane**	1953	40.00	100.00
Decca DL-5473	(10")	**Songs Of The Range**	1953	40.00	100.00
Decca DL-8674	(M)	**Memories Of You**	1958	12.00	40.00
ABC-Paramount ABC-119	(M)	**South Seas Serenade**	1956	16.00	40.00
ABC-Paramount ABC-174	(M)	**Melodies With Memories**	1957	16.00	40.00
ABC-Paramount ABC-234	(M)	**Hi Fi Paradise**	1958	16.00	40.00
ABC-Paramount ABC-330	(M)	**The Haunting Hawaiian Guitar**	1960	10.00	25.00
ABC-Paramount ABCS-330	(S)	**The Haunting Hawaiian Guitar**	1960	12.00	30.00
ABC-Paramount ABC-379	(M)	**His Singing Guitar & Paradise Serenaders**	1961	10.00	25.00
ABC-Paramount ABCS-379	(S)	**His Singing Guitar & Paradise Serenaders**	1961	12.00	30.00
ABC-Paramount ABC-412	(M)	**Stringing Along**	1962	10.00	25.00
ABC-Paramount ABCS-412	(S)	**Stringing Along**	1962	12.00	30.00
ABC-Paramount ABC-452	(M)	**The Many Guitar Moods Of Roy Smeck**	1963	10.00	25.00
ABC-Paramount ABCS-452	(S)	**The Many Guitar Moods Of Roy Smeck**	1963	12.00	30.00
SMILE					
Pickwick SPC-3288	(S)	**Smile**	1973	12.00	30.00

Label & Catalog #		Title	Year	VG+	NM

SMITH, AL

| Bluesville BVLP-1001 | (M) | Hear My Blues | 1960 | 30.00 | 75.00 |
| Bluesville BVLP-1013 | (M) | Midnight Special | 1961 | 30.00 | 75.00 |

— Bluesville albums above have bright blue labels with silver print.—

Bluesville BVLP-1001	(M)	Hear My Blues	1964	10.00	25.00
Bluesville BVLP-1013	(M)	Midnight Special	1964	10.00	25.00
Bluesville BVLP-1069	(M)	Blues Shout	1964	10.00	25.00

(Bluesville 1069 is a reissue of 1001.)

SMITH, "FIDDLIN'" ARTHUR

Arthur Smith was a fidle and banjo player, singer and writer of folk-based country music. Refer to The McGee Brothers.

| Starday SLP-202 | (M) | Fiddlin' Arthur Smith And The Dixie Liners *(Yellow label)* | 1963 | 16.00 | 40.00 |

SMITH, ARTHUR "GUITAR BOOGIE"/ARTHUR SMITH & HIS CRACKERJACKS

MGM E-236	(10")	Foolish Questions	1954	40.00	100.00
MGM E-533	(10")	Fingers On Fire	1955	40.00	100.00
MGM E-3301	(M)	Specials	1955	30.00	75.00
MGM E-3525	(M)	Fingers On Fire	1957	30.00	75.00

— MGM albums above have yellow labels.—

Starday SLP-173	(M)	Mister Guitar	1962	16.00	40.00
Starday SLP-186	(M)	Arthur Smith And The Crossroads Quartet	1962	16.00	40.00
Starday SLP-216	(M)	Arthur Guitar Boogie Smith Goes To Town	1963	16.00	40.00
Starday SLP-241	(M)	In Person	1963	16.00	40.00
Starday SLP-266	(M)	Down Home	1964	16.00	40.00

— Starday albums above have yellow labels.—

ABC Paramount ABC-441	(M)	Arthur "Guitar" Smith And Voices	1963	8.00	20.00
ABC Paramount ABCS-441	(S)	Arthur "Guitar" Smith And Voices	1963	10.00	25.00
Dot DLP-3600	(M)	Original Guitar Boogie	1964	8.00	20.00
Dot DLP-25600	(S)	Original Guitar Boogie	1964	10.00	25.00

SMITH, BESSIE: *Refer to* GOLDMINE'S PRICE GUIDE TO COLLECTIBLE JAZZ ALBUMS

SMITH, BOB

| Kent KST-551 | (S) | The Visit *(2 LPs with poster)* | 1969 | 30.00 | 75.00 |
| Kent KST-551 | (S) | The Visit *(2 LPs without poster)* | 1969 | 20.00 | 50.00 |

SMITH, CARL

Columbia HL-9023	(10")	Sentimental Songs	195?	30.00	75.00
Columbia HL-9026	(10")	Softly And Tenderly	195?	30.00	75.00
Columbia HL-2579	(10")	Carl Smith	1956	30.00	75.00
Columbia CL-959	(M)	Sunday Down South	1957	20.00	50.00
Columbia CL-1022	(M)	Smith's The Name	1957	20.00	50.00
Columbia CL-1172	(M)	Let's Live A Little	1958	20.00	50.00
Columbia CL-1532	(M)	The Carl Smith Touch	1960	10.00	25.00
Columbia CS-8332	(S)	The Carl Smith Touch	1960	12.00	30.00
Columbia CL-1740	(M)	Easy To Please	1962	10.00	25.00
Columbia CS-8540	(S)	Easy To Please	1962	12.00	30.00

— Columbia albums above have three white-on-black "eye" logos on each side of the spindle hole.—

Columbia CL-1937	(M)	Carl Smith's Greatest Hits	1962	8.00	20.00
Columbia CS-8737	(P)	Carl Smith's Greatest Hits	1962	10.00	25.00
Columbia CL-2091	(M)	Tall, Tall Gentleman	1963	8.00	20.00
Columbia CS-8891	(S)	Tall, Tall Gentleman	1963	10.00	25.00
Columbia CL-2173	(M)	There Stands The Glass	1964	8.00	20.00
Columbia CS-8973	(S)	There Stands The Glass	1964	10.00	25.00
Columbia CL-2293	(M)	I Want To Live And Love	1965	8.00	20.00
Columbia CS-9093	(S)	I Want To Live And Love	1965	10.00	25.00
Columbia CL-2358	(M)	Kisses Don't Lie	1965	8.00	20.00
Columbia CS-9158	(S)	Kisses Don't Lie	1965	10.00	25.00
Columbia CL-2501	(M)	Man With A Plan	1966	8.00	20.00
Columbia CS-9301	(S)	Man With A Plan	1966	10.00	25.00
Columbia CL-2610	(M)	The Country Gentleman	1967	8.00	20.00
Columbia CS-9410	(S)	The Country Gentleman	1967	10.00	25.00
Columbia CL-2687	(M)	The Country Gentleman Sings	1967	8.00	20.00
Columbia CS-9487	(S)	The Country Gentleman Sings	1967	10.00	25.00
Columbia CL-2822	(M)	Deep Water	1968	10.00	25.00
Columbia CS-9622	(S)	Deep Water	1968	6.00	15.00

— Columbia albums above have "360 Sound" on the bottom of the label.—

Label & Catalog #		Title	Year	VG+	NM
SMITH, CARL / LEFTY FRIZZELL / MARTY ROBBINS					
Columbia CL-2544	(10")	Carl, Lefty And Marty	1956	200.00	400.00
SMITH, CONNIE					
RCA Victor LPM-3341	(M)	The Other Side Of Connie Smith	1965	8.00	20.00
RCA Victor LSP-3341	(S)	The Other Side Of Connie Smith	1965	10.00	25.00
RCA Victor LPM-3444	(M)	Cute 'N Country	1965	8.00	20.00
RCA Victor LSP-3444	(S)	Cute 'N Country	1965	10.00	25.00
RCA Victor LPM-3520	(M)	Miss Smith Goes To Nashville	1966	8.00	20.00
RCA Victor LSP-3520	(S)	Miss Smith Goes To Nashville	1966	10.00	25.00
RCA Victor LPM-3589	(M)	Great Sacred Songs	1966	8.00	20.00
RCA Victor LSP-3589	(S)	Great Sacred Songs	1966	10.00	25.00
RCA Victor LPM-3628	(M)	Born To Sing	1966	8.00	20.00
RCA Victor LSP-3628	(S)	Born To Sing	1966	10.00	25.00
RCA Victor LPM-3768	(M)	Connie Smith Sings Bill Anderson	1967	8.00	20.00
RCA Victor LSP-3768	(S)	Connie Smith Sings Bill Anderson	1967	10.00	25.00
RCA Victor LPM-3848	(M)	The Best Of Connie Smith	1967	8.00	20.00
RCA Victor LSP-3848	(S)	The Best Of Connie Smith	1967	10.00	25.00
RCA Victor LPM-3889	(M)	Soul Of Country Music	1968	20.00	50.00
RCA Victor LSP-3889	(S)	Soul Of Country Music	1968	8.00	20.00
		—RCA albums above have black labels with Nipper on top.—			
SMITH, GOLDIE HILL: *Refer to* GOLDIE HILL					
SMITH, HUEY "PIANO"					
Ace LP-1004	(M)	Having A Good Time	1959	150.00	400.00
Ace LP-1015	(M)	For Dancing	1961	125.00	300.00
Ace LP-1027	(M)	Twas The Night Before Christmas	1962	125.00	300.00
Ace LP-2021	(M)	Rock 'N' Roll Revival	1971	12.00	30.00
SMITH, HOWARD K.: *refer to* DWIGHT D. EISENHOWER; JOHN F. KENNEDY					
SMITH, JACK					
Bel Canto BCM-37	(M)	You Asked For It—Jack Smith Sings	196?	10.00	25.00
Bel Canto SR-1015	(S)	You Asked For It—Jack Smith Sings	196?	14.00	35.00
SMITH, JENNIE					
RCA Victor LPM-1523	(M)	Jennie	1957	16.00	40.00
Columbia CL-1242	(M)	Love Among The Young	1958	10.00	25.00
SMITH, KEELY					
Keely Smith also recorded with Louis Prima. Refer to The Reprise Repertory Theatre.					
Capitol W-914	(M)	I Wish You Love	1957	20.00	50.00
		—Capitol albums above have turquoise labels.—			
Capitol W-914	(M)	I Wish You Love	1958	12.00	30.00
Capitol T-1073	(M)	Politely	1958	16.00	40.00
Capitol ST-1073	(S)	Politely	1958	20.00	50.00
Capitol T-1145	(M)	Swingin' Pretty	1959	16.00	40.00
Capitol ST-1145	(S)	Swingin' Pretty	1959	20.00	50.00
		—Capitol albums above have black labels with the logo on the left side.—			
Dot DLP-3241	(M)	Be My Love	1960	10.00	25.00
Dot DLP-25241	(S)	Be My Love	1960	12.00	30.00
Dot DLP-3265	(M)	Swing, You Lovers	1960	10.00	25.00
Dot DLP-25265	(S)	Swing, You Lovers	1960	12.00	30.00
Dot DLP-3387	(M)	Dearly Beloved	1961	10.00	25.00
Dot DLP-25387	(S)	Dearly Beloved	1961	12.00	30.00
Dot DLP-3345	(M)	A Keely Christmas	1961	10.00	25.00
Dot DLP-25345	(S)	A Keely Christmas	1961	12.00	30.00
Dot DLP-3415	(M)	Because You're Mine	1962	10.00	25.00
Dot DLP-25415	(S)	Because You're Mine	1962	12.00	30.00
Dot DLP-3423	(M)	Twist With Keely Smith	1962	10.00	25.00
Dot DLP-25423	(S)	Twist With Keely Smith	1962	12.00	30.00
Dot DLP-3460	(M)	Cherokeely Swings	1962	10.00	25.00
Dot DLP-25460	(S)	Cherokeely Swings	1962	12.00	30.00
Dot DLP-3461	(M)	What Kind Of Fool Am I	1962	10.00	25.00
Dot DLP-25461	(S)	What Kind Of Fool Am I	1962	12.00	30.00
Reprise R-6086	(M)	Little Girl Blue, Little Girl New	1963	10.00	25.00
Reprise R-96086	(S)	Little Girl Blue, Little Girl New	1963	12.00	30.00

Clarence Eugene Snow, the "Singing Ranger," first recorded for Victor in his home, Nova Scotia, in the '30s. He moved to the States and by 1950 was a mainstay on the Grand Ole Opry. Along with Eddy Arnold and Jim Reeves, he gave RCA considerable clout in the country music field of the '50s, a decade in which Hank placed three-dozen sides in the national country top 10. It was his partner in a management company, Tom Parker, who signed the young Elvis Presley, to an exclusive contract, cutting Snow out of what should have been a 50-50 split on the singer. To this day, Hank's fans and Elvis fans alike would like to know how and why the "colonel" was able to pull off the heist of the century. . .

Label & Catalog #		Title	Year	VG+	NM
Reprise R-6132	(M)	The Intimate Keely Smith	1964	10.00	25.00
Reprise RS-6132	(S)	The Intimate Keely Smith	1964	12.00	30.00
Reprise R-6142	(M)	The Lennon-McCartney Songbook	1964	10.00	25.00
Reprise RS-6142	(S)	The Lennon-McCartney Songbook	1964	12.00	30.00
Reprise R-6175	(M)	That Old Black Magic	1965	10.00	25.00
Reprise RS-6175	(S)	That Old Black Magic	1965	12.00	30.00

SMITH, LaVERGNE: *Refer to* GOLDMINE'S PRICE GUIDE TO COLLECTIBLE JAZZ ALBUMS

SMITH, OSBORNE: *Refer to* GOLDMINE'S PRICE GUIDE TO COLLECTIBLE JAZZ ALBUMS

SMITH, RAY

Judd JLPA-701	(M)	Travelin' With Ray	1960	300.00	600.00
"T" 56062	(M)	The Best Of Ray Smith	196?	80.00	200.00
		("T" 56062 is a reissue of Judd 701.)			
Columbia CL-1937	(M)	Ray Smith's Greatest Hits	1963	10.00	25.00
		(The label reads "Guaranteed High Fidelity" on the bottom.)			
Columbia CS-8737	(P)	Ray Smith's Greatest Hits	1963	12.00	30.00
		(The label reads "360 Sound Stereo" in black on the bottom.)			

SMITH, RAY / PAT CUPP

Crown CLP-5364	(M)	Ray Smith And Pat Cupp	1963	12.00	30.00
Crown CST-364	(E)	Ray Smith And Pat Cupp	1963	5.00	12.00

SMITH, ROBERT CURTIS

Bluesville BVLP-1064	(M)	Clarksdale Blues	1963	30.00	75.00
		—Bluesville albums above have bright blue labels with silver print.—			
Bluesville BVLP-1064	(M)	Clarksdale Blues	1964	10.00	25.00
		—Bluesville albums above have blue labels with a trident logo on the right side.—			

SMITH, ROGER

Warner Bros. W-1305	(M)	Beach Romance	1959	14.00	35.00
Warner Bros. WS-1305	(S)	Beach Romance	1959	20.00	50.00

SMITH, TAB

United LP-001	(10")	Music Styled By Tab Smith	1955	80.00	200.00
United LP-003	(10")	Red, Hot And Cool Blues	1955	80.00	200.00
Checker LP-2971	(M)	Tab Smith *(Multi-color vinyl promo)*	1960	250.00	500.00
Checker LP-2971	(M)	Tab Smith *(Black label)*	1960	30.00	75.00

SMITH, WARREN

Liberty LRP-3199	(M)	First Country Collection Of Warren Smith	1961	20.00	50.00
Liberty LST-7199	(S)	First Country Collection Of Warren Smith	1961	30.00	75.00

SMOKE, THE

Sidewalk ST-5912	(S)	The Smoke	1968	16.00	40.00
Tower ST-5912	(S)	The Smoke	1968	16.00	40.00

SMOKEY BABE

Bluesville BVLP-1063	(M)	Hottest Brand Going	1963	30.00	75.00
		—Bluesville albums above have bright blue labels with silver print.—			
Bluesville BVLP-1063	(M)	Hottest Brand Going	1964	10.00	25.00
		—Bluesville albums above have blue labels with a trident logo on the right side.—			

SMOTHERS, SMOKEY

King 779	(M)	The Backporch Blues	1962	250.00	750.00

SNAKEGRINDER

Alligator Shoes 40004	(S)	Snakegrinder & The Shredded Field Mice	1977	50.00	125.00

SNOW

Dynamic RM-1177	(S)	Snow *(10" album)*	1980	20.00	50.00

SNOW, HANK
Refer to Chet Atkins & Hank Snow.

RCA Victor LPT-3026	(10")	Country Classics	1952	80.00	200.00
RCA Victor LPT-3070	(10")	Hank Snow Sings	1952	80.00	200.00
RCA Victor LPT-3131	(10")	Hank Snow Salutes Jimmie Rodgers	1953	80.00	200.00
RCA Victor LPT-3267	(10")	Hank Snow's Country Guitar	1954	80.00	200.00

Label & Catalog #		Title	Year	VG+	NM
RCA Victor LPM-1113	(M)	Just Keep A-Movin'	1955	30.00	75.00
RCA Victor LPM-1156	(M)	Old Doc Brown & Other Narrations	1955	30.00	75.00
RCA Victor LPM-1233	(M)	Country Classics	1955	30.00	75.00
RCA Victor LPM-1419	(M)	Country And Western Jamboree	1957	30.00	75.00
RCA Victor LPM-1435	(M)	Hank Snow's Country Guitar	1957	30.00	75.00
RCA Victor LPM-1638	(M)	Hank Snow Sings Sacred Songs	1958	30.00	75.00
RCA Victor LPM-1861	(M)	When Tragedy Struck	1958	30.00	75.00
School Of Music 1149	(M)	The Guitar (With booklet)	1958	100.00	250.00
School Of Music 1149	(M)	The Guitar (Without booklet)	1958	80.00	200.00
		(School 1149 is a privately pressed ialbum with instruction booklet.)			
RCA Victor LPM-2043	(M)	Hank Snow Sings Jimmie Rodgers Songs	1959	20.00	50.00
RCA Victor LSP-2043	(S)	Hank Snow Sings Jimmie Rodgers Songs	1959	30.00	75.00
RCA Victor LPM-2285	(M)	Souvenirs	1961	12.00	30.00
RCA Victor LSP-2285	(S)	Souvenirs	1961	16.00	40.00
RCA Victor LPM-2458	(M)	Big Country Hits	1961	12.00	30.00
RCA Victor LSP-2458	(S)	Big Country Hits	1961	16.00	40.00
RCA Victor LPM-2675	(M)	I've Been Everywhere	1963	12.00	30.00
RCA Victor LSP-2675	(S)	I've Been Everywhere	1963	16.00	40.00
RCA Victor LPM-2705	(M)	Railroad Man	1963	12.00	30.00
RCA Victor LSP-2705	(S)	Railroad Man	1963	16.00	40.00
		—RCA mono albums above have "black labels with Long Play" on the bottom;			
		stereo albums have have "Living Stereo" on the bottom.—			
RCA Victor LPM-2812	(M)	More Hank Snow Souvenirs	1964	10.00	25.00
RCA Victor LSP-2812	(S)	More Hank Snow Souvenirs	1964	12.00	30.00
RCA Victor LPM-2901	(M)	Songs Of Tragedy	1964	10.00	25.00
RCA Victor LSP-2901	(S)	Songs Of Tragedy	1964	12.00	30.00
RCA Victor LPM-3317	(M)	Your Favorite Country Hits	1965	10.00	25.00
RCA Victor LSP-3317	(S)	Your Favorite Country Hits	1965	12.00	30.00
RCA Victor LPM-3378	(M)	Gloryland March	1965	12.00	30.00
RCA Victor LSP-3378	(S)	Gloryland March	1965	16.00	40.00
RCA Victor LPM-3471	(M)	Heartbreak Trail	1965	10.00	25.00
RCA Victor LSP-3471	(S)	Heartbreak Trail	1965	12.00	30.00
RCA Victor LPM-3478	(M)	The Best Of Hank Snow	1966	8.00	20.00
RCA Victor LSP-3478	(S)	The Best Of Hank Snow	1966	10.00	25.00
RCA Victor LPM-3548	(M)	The Guitar Stylings Of Hank Snow	1966	12.00	30.00
RCA Victor LSP-3548	(S)	The Guitar Stylings Of Hank Snow	1966	16.00	40.00
RCA Victor LPM-3595	(M)	Gospel Train	1966	12.00	30.00
RCA Victor LSP-3595	(S)	Gospel Train	1966	16.00	40.00
RCA Victor LPM-6014	(M)	This Is My Story (2 LPs)	1966	16.00	40.00
RCA Victor LSP-6014	(S)	This Is My Story (2 LPs)	1966	20.00	50.00
RCA Victor LPM-3737	(M)	Snow In Hawaii	1967	16.00	40.00
RCA Victor LSP-3737	(S)	Snow In Hawaii	1967	12.00	30.00
RCA Victor LPM-3826	(M)	Christmas With Hank Snow	1967	16.00	40.00
RCA Victor LSP-3826	(S)	Christmas With Hank Snow	1967	12.00	30.00
RCA Victor LPM-3857	(M)	Spanish Fireball	1967	16.00	40.00
RCA Victor LSP-3857	(S)	Spanish Fireball	1967	12.00	30.00
RCA Victor LPM-3965	(M)	Hits, Hits And More Hits	1968	40.00	100.00
RCA Victor LSP-3965	(S)	Hits, Hits And More Hits	1968	8.00	20.00
RCA Victor LSP-4032	(S)	Tales Of The Yukon	1968	12.00	30.00
		—RCA albums above have black labels.—			
RCA Victor LSP-4122	(S)	Snow In All Seasons	1969	10.00	25.00
		—RCA albums above have orange labels on non-flexible vinyL—			
RCA Victor DPL2-0134	(P)	The Living Legend (2 LPs)	1978	40.00	100.00
RCA Victor RDA-216	(P)	I'm Movin' On	197?	40.00	100.00
		(Reader's Digest 6 LP box with booklet)			

SNOW, HANK, & CHET ATKINS

Label & Catalog #		Title	Year	VG+	NM
RCA Victor LPM-2952	(M)	Reminiscing	1964	10.00	25.00
RCA Victor LSP-2952	(S)	Reminiscing	1964	12.00	30.00
		—RCA albums above have black labels.—			

SNOW, HANK, & ANITA CARTER

Label & Catalog #		Title	Year	VG+	NM
RCA Victor LPM-2580	(M)	Together Again	1962	12.00	30.00
RCA Victor LSP-2580	(S)	Together Again	1962	16.00	40.00
		—RCA mono albums above have "black labels with Long Play" on the bottom;			
		stereo albums have have "Living Stereo" on the bottom.—			

SOFT MACHINE

Label & Catalog #		Title	Year	VG+	NM
Probe 4500	(S)	The Soft Machine (Movable parts cover)	1968	14.00	35.00

Label & Catalog #		Title	Year	VG+	NM
SOMMER, ELKE					
MGM E-4321	(M)	Love In Any Language	1966	8.00	20.00
MGM SE-4321	(S)	Love In Any Language	1966	10.00	25.00
SOMMERS, JOANIE					
Ms. Sommers also appeared with Rick Nelson on the TV soundtrack "On The Flip Side."					
Warner Bros. W-1346	(M)	Positively The Most	1960	14.00	35.00
Warner Bros. WS-1346	(S)	Positively The Most	1960	20.00	50.00
Warner Bros. B-1348	(M)	Behind Closed Doors At			
		A Recording Session (Box with booklet)	1960	60.00	150.00
Warner Bros. W-1412	(M)	Joanie Sommers	1961	12.00	30.00
Warner Bros. WS-1412	(S)	Joanie Sommers	1961	16.00	40.00
Warner Bros. W-1436	(M)	For Those Who Think Young	1962	12.00	30.00
Warner Bros. WS-1436	(S)	For Those Who Think Young	1962	16.00	40.00
Warner Bros. W-1470	(M)	Johnny Get Angry	1962	16.00	40.00
Warner Bros. WS-1470	(S)	Johnny Get Angry	1962	20.00	50.00
Warner Bros. W-1474	(M)	Let's Talk About Love	1962	10.00	25.00
Warner Bros. WS-1474	(S)	Let's Talk About Love	1962	12.00	30.00
Warner Bros. W-1504	(M)	Sommer's Seasons	1964	10.00	25.00
Warner Bros. WS-1504	(S)	Sommer's Seasons	1964	12.00	30.00
Warner Bros. W-1575	(M)	Softly, The Brazilian Sound	1965	10.00	25.00
Warner Bros. WS-1575	(S)	Softly, The Brazilian Sound	1965	12.00	30.00
		— Warner Bros. albums above have grey labels.—			
Columbia CL-2495	(M)	Come Alive	1966	8.00	20.00
Columbia CS-9295	(S)	Come Alive	1966	10.00	25.00
SONICS, THE					
Etiquette ALB-024	(M)	Here Are The Sonics!!!	1965	60.00	150.00
Etiquette LPS-024	(S)	Here Are The Sonics!!!	1965	150.00	300.00
Etiquette ALB-027	(M)	The Sonics Boom	1966	60.00	150.00
Etiquette LPS-027	(E)	The Sonics Boom	1966	40.00	100.00
		— Etiquette albums above have red labels.—			
Etiquette LPS-024	(S)	Here Are The Sonics!!!	197?	16.00	40.00
Etiquette LPS-027	(E)	The Sonics Boom	197?	16.00	40.00
		— Etiquette albums above have purple labels.—			
Jerden JRL-7007	(M)	Introducing The Sonics (White label promo)	1967	150.00	300.00
Jerden JRL-7007	(M)	Introducing The Sonics	1967	60.00	150.00
Jerden JRS-7007	(E)	Introducing The Sonics	1967	40.00	100.00
Buckshot BSR-001	(S)	Explosives	1974	20.00	50.00
SONICS, THE / THE WAILERS / THE GALAXIES					
Etiquette ALB-02	(M)	Merry Christmas	1965	150.00	300.00
SONNY & CHER & FRIENDS					
Reprise R-6177	(M)	Baby Don't Go	1965	12.00	30.00
Reprise RS-6177	(S)	Baby Don't Go	1965	16.00	40.00
		(This LP credits Sonny & Cher & Friends and includes their sides as Caesar & Cleo along with The Blendells, The Lettermen and Bill Medley. "Baby Don't Go," "La-La-La-La-La," "Walkin' The Quetzal," "When" and "Their Hearts Were Full Of Spring" are rechanneled.)			
SONNY & CHER					
Atco 33-177	(M)	Look At Us	1965	8.00	20.00
Atco SD-33-177	(S)	Look At Us	1965	10.00	25.00
SONNY & THE DEMONS					
United Arts. UAL-3316	(M)	Drag Kings	1964	8.00	45.00
United Arts. UAS-6316	(S)	Drag Kings	1964	24.00	60.00

SONNY TERRY & BROWNIE McGHEE: *Refer to* **TERRY, SONNY, & BROWNIE McGHEE**

SONS OF CHAMPLIN					
Capitol SWBB-200	(S)	Loosen Up Naturally (2 LPs)	1969		See below
		("First-state scratch cover." Original black "rainbow" label LPs were issued with several four-letter words as part of the graffiti in the cover art. Capitol recalled the albums and had the offending expletives scratched off by hand! Covers with the foul language intact are very rare with no values known at this time.)			

Label & Catalog #		Title	Year	VG+	NM
Capitol SWBB-200	(S)	Loosen Up Naturally (2 LPs)	1969	20.00	50.00
		("Second-state scratch cover." The foul language scratched off of the cover.)			

SONS OF THE PIONEERS, THE

Label & Catalog #		Title	Year	VG+	NM
RCA Victor LPM-3032	(10")	Cowboy Classics	1952	40.00	100.00
RCA Victor LPM-3095	(10")	Cowboy Hymns And Spirituals	1952	40.00	100.00
RCA Victor LPM-3162	(10")	Western Classics	1953	40.00	100.00
RCA Victor LPM-1130	(M)	Favorite Cowboy Songs	1955	20.00	50.00
RCA Victor LPM-1431	(M)	How Great Thou Art	1957	20.00	50.00
RCA Victor LPM-1483	(M)	One Man's Songs	1957	20.00	50.00
RCA Victor LPM-2118	(M)	Cool Water	1960	8.00	20.00
RCA Victor LSP-2118	(S)	Cool Water	1960	12.00	30.00
RCA Victor LPM-2356	(M)	Lure Of The West	1961	8.00	20.00
RCA Victor LSP-2356	(S)	Lure Of The West	1961	12.00	30.00
RCA Victor PRM-108	(DJ)	Westward Ho!	1961	10.00	25.00
RCA Victor LPM-2456	(M)	Tumbleweed Trails	1962	8.00	20.00
RCA Victor LSP-2456	(S)	Tumbleweed Trails	1962	12.00	30.00
RCA Victor LPM-2603	(M)	Our Men Out West	1963	8.00	20.00
RCA Victor LSP-2603	(S)	Our Men Out West	1963	12.00	30.00
RCA Victor LPM-2652	(M)	Hymns Of The Cowboy	1963	8.00	20.00
RCA Victor LSP-2652	(S)	Hymns Of The Cowboy	1963	12.00	30.00

— RCA mono albums above have black labels with "Long Play" on the bottom; stereo albums have have "Living Stereo" on the bottom.—

Label & Catalog #		Title	Year	VG+	NM
RCA Victor LPM-3714	(M)	Campfire Favorites	1967	10.00	25.00
RCA Victor LSP-3714	(S)	Campfire Favorites	1967	8.00	20.00
RCA Victor LPM-3964	(M)	South Of The Border	1968	15.00	75.00
RCA Victor LSP-3964	(S)	South Of The Border	1968	8.00	20.00

—RCA albums above have black labels.—

SONS OF THE PURPLE SAGE

Label & Catalog #		Title	Year	VG+	NM
Waldorf Music Hall 143	(10")	Songs Of the Golden West	1955	24.00	60.00
Tops L-1588	(M)	Western Favorites	1959	10.00	25.00

SOPHOMORES, THE

Label & Catalog #		Title	Year	VG+	NM
Dawn DLP-1128	(M)	The Sophomores	1958	Unreleased?	
Seeco CELP-451	(M)	The Sophomores	196?	80.00	200.00
		(Seeco 451 is a reissue of the unreleased Dawn 1128. This is not the "doo wop" group of the '50s but an early soul group.)			

SOPWITH CAMEL, THE

Label & Catalog #		Title	Year	VG+	NM
Kama Sutra KLP-8060	(M)	The Sopwith Camel	1967	12.00	30.00
Kama Sutra KLPS-8060	(S)	The Sopwith Camel	1967	14.00	35.00
Kama Sutra KSBS-2063	(S)	The Sopwith Camel In "Hello, Hello"	1973	10.00	25.00
		(Kama Sutra 2063 is a reissue of 8060.)			

SORRELL, FRANK

Label & Catalog #		Title	Year	VG+	NM
Coral CRL-57234	(M)	Frank Sorrell And His Four Guitars	1958	12.00	30.00

SOTHERN, ANN

Label & Catalog #		Title	Year	VG+	NM
RCA Victor LM-1882	(M)	Lady In The Dark (TV Soundtrack)	195?	20.00	50.00
Craftsmen C-8061	(M)	It's Ann Sothern Time!	195?	20.00	50.00
Tops L-1611	(M)	Ann Sothern Sings	1958	10.00	25.00

SOUL, JIMMY
Refer to Bobby Bland / Jimmy Soul.

Label & Catalog #		Title	Year	VG+	NM
S.P.Q.R. E-16001	(M)	If You Wanna Be Happy	1963	30.00	75.00

SOUL CHILDREN, THE

Label & Catalog #		Title	Year	VG+	NM
Stax STS-2018	(S)	Soul Children	1972	20.00	50.00
Stax ST-2043	(M)	The Best Of Two Worlds (Promo)	1972	20.00	50.00
Stax STS-2043	(S)	The Best Of Two Worlds	1972	20.00	50.00
Stax STS-3003	(S)	Genesis	1972	20.00	50.00
Stax STS-5507	(S)	Friction	1974	20.00	50.00

SOUL SISTERS, THE

Label & Catalog #		Title	Year	VG+	NM
Sue LP-1022	(M)	I Can't Stand It (Orange label)	1964	200.00	400.00
Sue STLP-1022	(S)	I Can't Stand It (Orange label)	1964	300.00	600.00

Label & Catalog #		Title	Year	VG+	NM

SOUL STIRRERS, THE
The Stirrers lead singers included Sam Cooke and Johnny Taylor.

Specialty SPS-2106	(M)	**The Soul Stirrers Featuring Sam Cooke**	1959	20.00	50.00

SOUL SURVIVORS, THE

Crimson LP-502	(M)	**When The Whistle Blows Anything Goes**	1967	10.00	25.00
Crimson LP-502	(S)	**When The Whistle Blows Anything Goes**	1967	12.00	30.00
		("Expressway To Your Heart" and "A Change Is Gonna Come"			
		are rechanneled on this album.)			
Atco SD-33-277	(S)	**Take Another Look**	1969	10.00	25.00

SOUND SYMPOSIUM, THE

Dot DLP-25952	(S)	**Bob Dylan Interpreted**	1969	10.00	25.00

SOUP

Arf Arm 1	(S)	**Soup** *(Insert cover)*	1970	40.00	100.00

SOUTH, JOE
Refer to Billy Joe Royal.

Capitol ST-108	(S)	**Introspect**	1968	10.00	25.00
		— Capitol albums above have black "rainbow" labels.—			

SOUTH CENTRAL AVENUE MUNICIPAL BLUES BAND

BluesWay BL-6018	(S)	**The Soul Of Bonnie And Clyde**	1968	10.00	25.00

SOUTH 40

Metrobeat MBS-1000	(S)	**Live At The Someplace Else**	1968	14.00	35.00

SOUTH PAW

Bad Man RHBP-318	(S)	**South Paw**	1980	20.00	50.00

SOUTHERN, JERI: *Refer to* **GOLDMINE'S PRICE GUIDE TO COLLECTIBLE JAZZ ALBUMS**

SOUTHSIDE JOHNNY & THE ASBURY JUKES

Epic AS-275	(DJ)	**Live At The Bottom Line**	1976	10.00	25.00

SOUTHSIDE JOHNNY & RONNIE SPECTOR
Refer to The Ronnie Spector.

Epic AS-362	(DJ)	**A Conversation With**			
		Southside Johnny & Ronnie Spector	1977	10.00	25.00

SOUTHWEST F. O. B.
Southwest F. O. B. feature England Dan and John Ford Coley.

Hip HIS-7001	(S)	**Smell Of Incense**	1969	16.00	40.00

SOVINE, RED
Red Sovine is a pseudonym for Woodrow Wilson Sovine.

MGM E-3465	(M)	**Red Sovine**	1957	30.00	75.00
Starday SLP-132	(M)	**The One And Only Red Sovine**	1961	16.00	40.00
Starday SLP-197	(M)	**The Golden Country Ballads Of The 1960s**	1962	16.00	40.00
Decca DL-4445	(M)	**Red Sovine**	1964	10.00	25.00
Decca DL-74445	(S)	**Red Sovine**	1964	12.00	30.00
Decca DL-4736	(M)	**Country Music Time**	1966	10.00	25.00
Decca DL-74736	(S)	**Country Music Time**	1966	12.00	30.00
Starday SLP-341	(M)	**Little Rosa**	1966	12.00	30.00
Starday SLP-363	(M)	**Giddy-Up Go**	1966	12.00	30.00
Starday SLP-383	(M)	**Town And Country Action**	1966	12.00	30.00
Starday SLP-396	(M)	**The Nashville Sound Of Red Sovine**	1967	12.00	30.00
Starday SLP-405	(M)	**I Didn't Jump The Fence**	1967	12.00	30.00
Starday SLP-414	(M)	**Phantom 309**	1967	12.00	30.00
		— Starday albums above have yellow labels.—			

SOXX, BOBB B., & THE BLUE JEANS

Philles PHLP-4002	(M)	**Zip A Dee Doo Dah** *(White label promo)*	1963	400.00	900.00
Philles PHLP-4002	(M)	**Zip A Dee Doo Dah**	1963	150.00	400.00

SPACE

Hand 5167	(S)	**Space**	1969	10.00	25.00

Label & Catalog #		Title	Year	VG+	NM
SPACEMEN, THE					
Roulette MG-25275	(M)	**Rockin' In The 25th Century**	1964	12.00	30.00
Roulette SR-25275	(S)	**Rockin' In The 25th Century**	1964	16.00	40.00
Roulette MG-25322	(M)	**Music For Batman And Robin**	1966	16.00	40.00
Roulette SR-25322	(S)	**Music For Batman And Robin**	1966	20.00	50.00
SPANIELS, THE					
Vee Jay LP-1002	(M)	**Goodnite, It's Time To Go** *(Maroon label)*	1958	200.00	600.00
Vee Jay LP-1002	(M)	**Goodnite, It's Time To Go** *(Black label)*	1961	100.00	250.00
		(Reproductions exist of Vee Jay 1002 with a black label.)			
SPANN, OTIS					
Otis Spann also recorded with Fleetwood Mac.					
Candid CM-8001	(M)	**Otis Spann Is The Blues**	1960	60.00	150.00
Candid CS-9001	(S)	**Otis Spann Is The Blues**	1960	80.00	200.00
BluesWay BL-6003	(M)	**The Blues Is Where It's At**	1967	10.00	25.00
BluesWay BLS-6003	(S)	**The Blues Is Where It's At**	1967	12.00	30.00
BluesWay BLS-6013	(S)	**The Bottom Of The Blues**	1968	10.00	25.00
London PS-543	(S)	**Raw Blues**	1968	10.00	25.00
London PS-551	(S)	**Cracked Spanner Head**	1969	10.00	25.00
SPARK PLUGS, THE					
Sutton SU-322	(M)	**The Spark Plugs**	1963	10.00	25.00
Sutton SSU-322	(S)	**The Spark Plugs**	1963	12.00	30.00
SPARKS, RANDY					
Randy also recorded with The Back Porch Majority.					
Verve MGV-2103	(M)	**Randy Sparks**	1959	14.00	35.00
Verve MGV-2126	(M)	**Walkin' The Low Road**	1960	14.00	35.00
Verve MGV-2143	(M)	**Randy Sparks Three**	1960	14.00	35.00
		— Verve albums above have "Verve Records, Inc." on the bottom of the label. —			
SPARROWS, THE					
Elkay 3009	(M)	**That Mersey Sound**	1964	16.00	40.00
SPATS					
ABC-Paramount ABC-502	(M)	**Cookin' With The Spats**	1965	8.00	20.00
ABC-Paramount ABCS-502	(S)	**Cookin' With The Spats**	1965	12.00	30.00

SPECTOR, PHIL

The LPs below are various artists compilations produced and compiled by Spector. Refer to The Beatles; Bobb B. Soxx & The Bluejeans; The Checkmates Ltd; The Crystals; George Harrison; John Lennon; Ramones; The Righteous Brothers; The Ronettes; Troy Shondell; The Teddy Bears; Ike & Tina Turner.

Label & Catalog #		Title	Year	VG+	NM
Philles PHLP-4004	(M)	**Today's Hits** *(White label promo)*	1963	400.00	1,000.00
Philles PHLP-4004	(M)	**Today's Hits**	1963	150.00	400.00
Philles PHLP-4005	(M)	**A Christmas Gift For You** *(White label)*	1963	400.00	1,000.00
Philles PHLP-4005	(M)	**A Christmas Gift For You**	1963	80.00	200.00
		— Philles albums above have blue labels. —			
Philles PHLP-4004	(M)	**Today's Hits**	1964	80.00	200.00
Philles PHLP-4005	(M)	**A Christmas Gift For You**	1964	30.00	75.00
		— Philles albums above have red & yellow labels. —			
Apple SW-3400	(M)	**Phil Spector's Christmas Album**	1972	12.00	30.00
		("Phil Spector's Christmas Album" is a reissue of "A Christmas Gift For You." The Apple album bears a stereo prefix but plays mono.)			
Warner/Spector 9104	(M)	**Phil Spector's Greatest Hits** *(2 LPs)*	1977	12.00	30.00
		("Spanish Harlem," "River Deep-Mountain High" and "He's Sure The Boy I Love" are in stereo.)			

SPENCE, ALEXANDER "SKIP"					
Mr. Spence was formerly a member of The Jefferson Airplane; Moby Grape.					
Columbia CS-9831	(S)	**Oar**	1969	20.00	50.00
SPIDER-MAN					
Lifesong 6001	(S)	**Rock Reflections Of A Superhero**	1976	10.00	25.00
SPIDERS, THE					
Imperial LP-9140	(M)	**I Didn't Wanna Do It**	1961	300.00	700.00

Label & Catalog #		Title	Year	VG+	NM
SPIFFYS, THE					
R.I. 2597	(M)	**The Spiffys**	1968	80.00	200.00
SPINNERS, THE					
Time 52092	(M)	**Party-My Pad After Surfin'**	1963	10.00	25.00
Time S-2092	(S)	**Party-My Pad After Surfin'**	1963	12.00	30.00
SPINNERS, THE					
Motown M-639	(M)	**The Original Spinners**	1967	10.00	25.00
Motown MS-639	(S)	**The Original Spinners**	1967	12.00	30.00
		("That's What Girls Are Made For" is rechanneled on this album.)			
V.I.P. 405	(S)	**The Second Time Around**	1970	10.00	25.00
SPIRAL STARECASE, THE					
Correction: The Starecase LP below was produced by Jerry Fuller, not Gary Usher.					
Columbia CS-9852	(S)	**More Today**			
		Than Yesterday ("360 Sound" label)	1969	10.00	25.00
SPIRIT & WORM					
A&M SP-4229	(S)	**Spirit And Worm**	1969	300.00	500.00
SPIVEY, VICTORIA					
Victoria Spivey is a piano player, singer and writer of blues music. Refer to with Lonnie Johnson.					
Spivey LP-1001	(M)	**Basket Of Blues**	1962	10.00	25.00
Spivey LP-1002	(M)	**Victoria And Her Blues**	1963	10.00	25.00
Spivey LP-1004	(M)	**Three Kings And A Queen**	1964	20.00	50.00
		(The three kings on Spivey 1004 and 1010 are Lonnie Johnson, Roosevelt Sykes and Big Joe Williams . Both featurea very young Bob Dylan on harmonica on two tracks.)			
Spivey LP-1004	(M)	**Three Kings And A Queen**	1964	12.00	30.00
		(Later pressings read "Historic Tracks/Bob Dylan appears with Big Joe Williams" on the cover.)			
Spivey LP-1006	(M)	**The Queen And Her Knights**	1964	10.00	25.00
Spivey LP-1008	(M)	**The Bluesmen Of The Muddy Waters Band**	1964	10.00	25.00
Spivey LP-1009	(M)	**Encore For The Chicago Blues**	1964	10.00	25.00
Spivey LP-1010	(M)	**The Bluesmen Of The Muddy Waters Band, Volume Two**	1964	10.00	25.00
Spivey LP-1012	(M)	**Spivey's Blues Parade**	1964	10.00	25.00
Spivey LP-1014	(M)	**Three Kings And A Queen, Volume 2**	1964	12.00	30.00
Spivey LP-2001	(M)	**Recorded Legacy Of The Blues**	196?	10.00	25.00
Spivey LP-1015	(M)	**Spivey's Blues Cavalcade**	196?	10.00	25.00
Spivey LP-1017	(M)	**Spivey's Blues Showcase**	196?	10.00	25.00
SPLIT LEVEL, THE					
Dot DLP-25836	(S)	**The Split Level**	1968	10.00	25.00
SPOELSTRA, MARK					
Mark Spoelstra is a guitar player, singer and writer of contemporary topical folk songs.					
Verve/Folkways FV-9018	(M)	**The Time I've Had**	1965	8.00	20.00
Verve/Folkways FVS-9018	(S)	**The Time I've Had**	1965	10.00	25.00
SPOKESMEN, THE					
Decca DL-4712	(M)	**Dawn Of Correction**	1965	12.00	30.00
Decca DL-74712	(S)	**Dawn Of Correction**	1965	16.00	40.00
SPOOKY TOOTH					
Spooky Tooth features Mike Patto.					
Bell 6019	(S)	**Spooky Tooth**	1968	10.00	25.00
SPRING					
Spring is Marilyn and Diane Rovell of The Honeys. The album boasts Brian Wilson as executive producer.					
United Arts. 5571	(S)	**Spring** (With insert)	1972	10.00	25.00
SPRINGFIELD, DUSTY					
Ms. Springfield was originally a member of The Springfields. Refer to Led Zeppelin / Dusty Springfield.					
Philips PHM-200-133	(M)	**Stay Awhile**	1964	12.00	30.00
Philips PHS-600-133	(P)	**Stay Awhile**	1964	16.00	40.00
Philips PHM-200-156	(M)	**Dusty**	1964	12.00	30.00
Philips PHS-600-156	(P)	**Dusty**	1964	16.00	40.00

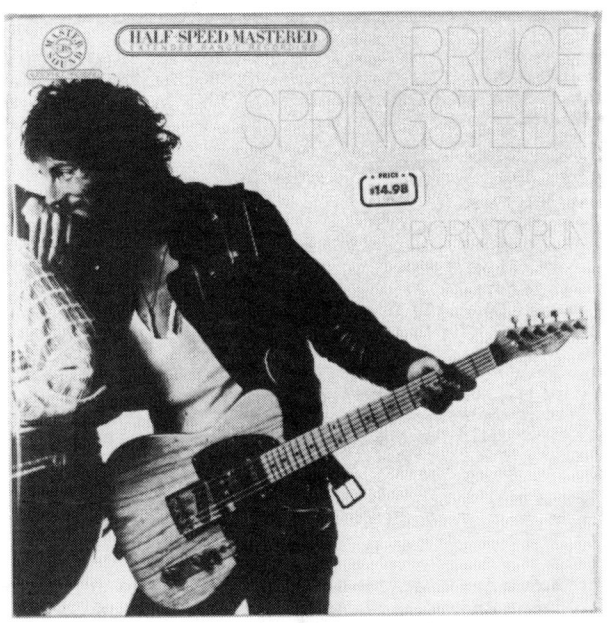

Even Bruce's best, Born To Run *and* Darkness On The Edge Of Town, *could not make the CBS Mastersound Half-Speed mastered series a success with audiophile oriented consumers. Using poor quality vinyl and plating and compromised masters, the discs simply did not live up to the levels of quality that market demanded. . .*

Label & Catalog #		Title	Year	VG+	NM
Philips PHM-200-174	(M)	Ooooo Weeee!!!	1965	16.00	40.00
Philips PHS-600-174	(S)	Ooooo Weeee!!!	1965	20.00	50.00
Philips PHM-200-210	(M)	You Don't Have To Say You Love Me	1966	12.00	30.00
Philips PHS-600-210	(S)	You Don't Have To Say You Love Me	1966	16.00	40.00
Philips PHM-200-220	(M)	Dusty Springfield's Golden Hits	1966	10.00	25.00
Philips PHS-600-220	(P)	Dusty Springfield's Golden Hits	1966	14.00	35.00
		(Philips 220 was originally issued with "Goin' Back.")			
Philips PHM-200-220	(M)	Dusty Springfield's Golden Hits	1967	8.00	20.00
Philips PHS-600-220	(P)	Dusty Springfield's Golden Hits	1967	10.00	25.00
		(Philips 220 was reissued without "Goin' Back.")			
Philips PHM-200-256	(M)	The Look Of Love	1967	10.00	25.00
Philips PHS-600-256	(S)	The Look Of Love	1967	12.00	30.00
Philips PHM-200-303	(M)	Everything's Coming Up Dusty	1967	10.00	25.00
Philips PHS-600-303	(S)	Everything's Coming Up Dusty	1967	12.00	30.00
Colgems COMO-5005	(M)	Casino Royale (Soundtrack)	1967	12.00	30.00
Colgems COSO-5005	(S)	Casino Royale (Soundtrack)	1967	40.00	100.00
United Arts. UAL-4158	(M)	The Corrupt Ones (Soundtrack)	1967	20.00	50.00
United Arts. UAS-5158	(S)	The Corrupt Ones (Soundtrack)	1967	30.00	75.00
Atlantic SD-8214	(S)	Dusty In Memphis (Purple & brown label)	1969	12.00	30.00

SPRINGFIELD RIFLE

Burdette ST-5159	(S)	Springfield Rifle	1968	16.00	40.00

SPRINGFIELDS, THE
Tom and Dusty Springfield.

Philips PHM-200-052	(M)	Silver Threads And Golden Needles	1962	12.00	30.00
Philips PHS-600-052	(S)	Silver Threads And Golden Needles	1962	16.00	40.00
Philips PHM-200-076	(M)	Folksongs From The Hills	1963	12.00	30.00
Philips PHS-600-076	(S)	Folksongs From The Hills	1963	16.00	40.00

SPRINGSTEEN, BRUCE/BRUCE SPRINGSTEEN & THE E STREET BAND

Columbia PC-33795	(DJ)	Born To Run (Test pressing)	1975		See below
		(Advance copy with the title in script print on the cover and issued in a special mailing envelope with a letter of introduction from CBS and an orange patch, which are included in the price. The complete set has a suggested Near Mint value of 800-1,2000. The value for incomplete sets drops dramatically. . .)			
Columbia PC-33795	(S)	Born To Run (White label promo)	1975	20.00	50.00
Columbia PC-33795	(S)	Born To Run	1975	10.00	25.00
		(Jon Landau's name is misspelled as "John" on the back cover.)			
Columbia PAL-35318	(DJ)	Darkness On The Edge Of Town (Picture disc)	1978	40.00	100.00
Columbia JC-35318	(S)	Darkness On The Edge Of Town (White label promo)	1978	20.00	50.00
Columbia HC-33795	(S)	Born To Run (Half-speed master)	1980	13.00	40.00
Columbia HC-43795	(S)	Born To Run (Half-speed master)	1981	10.00	30.00
Columbia HC-45318	(S)	Darkness On The Edge Of Town (Half-speed master)	1981	13.00	40.00
Columbia AS-978	(DJ)	As Requested Around The World	1981	20.00	50.00
Columbia FC-36854	(DJ)	The River (2 LPs. White label with letter)	1984	20.00	50.00
Columbia FC-36854	(DJ)	The River (2 LPs. White label without letter)	1984	14.00	35.00
Columbia AS-1957	(DJ)	Born In The U.S.A. (5 song mini-LP)	1985	14.00	35.00
Columbia AS-1957	(DJ)	Born In The U.S.A. (5 song mini-LP)	1987	10.00	25.00
		(Second pressings of AS-1957 note so on the label.)			

SPUR

Cinema CSLP-1500	(M)	Spur Of The Moment	1969	30.00	75.00

SPYRO GYRA

Nautilus NR-9	(S)	Morning Dance	197?	10.00	30.00

SRC

Capitol ST-2991	(S)	SRC	1968	16.00	40.00
Capitol ST-134	(S)	Milestones	1969	12.00	30.00
Capitol SKAO-273	(S)	Travellers Tale	1970	12.00	30.00

STACK

Charisma CRS-303	(S)	Above All	1966	660.00	1,000.00

Label & Catalog #		Title	Year	VG+	NM

STAFFORD, JO
Refer to Gordon MacRae; Frank Sinatra; The Reprise Repertory Theatre.

Label & Catalog #		Title	Year	VG+	NM
Capitol H-75	(10")	**American Folk Songs**	1950	30.00	75.00
Capitol H-157	(10")	**Kiss Me Kate** *(Studio Cast)*	1950	30.00	75.00
Capitol H-9014	(10")	**Songs Of Faith**	1950	30.00	75.00
Capitol H-197	(10")	**Autumn In New York**	1950	30.00	75.00
Capitol H-247	(10")	**Songs For Sunday Evening**	1950	30.00	75.00
Capitol H-435	(10")	**Starring Jo Stafford**	1953	30.00	75.00
Capitol T-197	(M)	**Autumn In New York**	1954	24.00	60.00
Capitol T-435	(M)	**Starring Jo Stafford**	1955	24.00	60.00
		— Capitol albums above have turquoise labels.—			
Capitol T-197	(M)	**Autumn In New York**	195?	12.00	30.00
Capitol T-435	(M)	**Starring Jo Stafford**	195?	12.00	30.00
		— Capitol albums above have black "rainbow" labels with the logo on the left side.—			
Columbia CL-6210	(10")	**As You Desire Me**	1952	24.00	60.00
Columbia CL-6238	(10")	**Broadway's Best**	1953	24.00	60.00
Columbia CL-6274	(10")	**My Heart's In The Highland**	1954	24.00	60.00
Columbia CL-6286	(10")	**Garden Of Prayer**	1954	24.00	60.00
Columbia CL-578	(M)	**New Orleans**	1954	20.00	50.00
		(Columbia 578 is a reissue of 6268 plus four tracks.)			
Columbia CL-584	(M)	**Broadway's Best**	1954	20.00	50.00
		(Columbia 584 is a reissue of 6238 plus four tracks.)			
		— Columbia albums above have "Long Playing" on the bottom of the label.—			
Columbia CL-2501	(10")	**Soft And Sentimental**	1955	20.00	50.00
Columbia CL-2591	(10")	**A Gal Named Jo**	1956	20.00	50.00
Columbia CL-2597	(10")	**My Fair Lady** *(Studio Cast)*	1956	30.00	75.00
Columbia CL-578	(M)	**New Orleans**	195?	12.00	30.00
Columbia CL-584	(M)	**Broadway's Best**	195?	12.00	30.00
Columbia CL-691	(M)	**Happy Holiday**	1955	20.00	50.00
Columbia CL-910	(M)	**Ski Trails**	1956	16.00	40.00
Columbia CL-968	(M)	**Once Over Lightly**	1957	16.00	40.00
Columbia CL-1043	(M)	**Songs Of Scotland**	1957	16.00	40.00
Columbia CL-1124	(M)	**Swingin' Down Broadway**	1958	16.00	40.00
Columbia CL-1228	(M)	**Jo Stafford's Greatest Hits**	1959	12.00	30.00
Columbia CL-1280	(M)	**I'll Be Seeing You**	1959	12.00	30.00
Columbia CS-8080	(S)	**I'll Be Seeing You**	1959	16.00	40.00
Columbia CL-1339	(M)	**Ballad Of The Blues**	1959	12.00	30.00
Columbia CS-8139	(S)	**Ballad Of The Blues**	1959	16.00	40.00
Columbia CL-1561	(M)	**Jo + Jazz**	1960	16.00	40.00
Columbia CS-8361	(S)	**Jo + Jazz**	1960	20.00	50.00
		— Columbia albums above have three white "eye" logos on each side of the spindle hole.—			
Capitol T-1653	(M)	**American Folk Songs**	1962	8.00	20.00
Capitol ST-1653	(S)	**American Folk Songs**	1962	10.00	25.00
Capitol T-1921	(M)	**The Hits Of Jo Stafford**	1963	8.00	20.00
Capitol ST-1921	(S)	**The Hits Of Jo Stafford**	1963	10.00	25.00
Capitol T-2069	(M)	**Sweet Hour Of Prayer**	1964	8.00	20.00
Capitol ST-2069	(S)	**Sweet Hour Of Prayer**	1964	10.00	25.00
Capitol T-2166	(M)	**Joyful Season**	1964	8.00	20.00
Capitol ST-2166	(S)	**Joyful Season**	1964	10.00	25.00
Reprise R-6090	(M)	**Getting Sentimental Over Tommy Dorsey**	1963	8.00	20.00
Reprise R-96090	(S)	**Getting Sentimental Over Tommy Dorsey**	1963	10.00	25.00
Dot DLP-3673	(M)	**Do I Hear A Waltz?**	1966	8.00	20.00
Dot DLP-25673	(S)	**Do I Hear A Waltz?**	1966	10.00	25.00
Dot DLP-3745	(M)	**This Is Jo Stafford**	1966	8.00	20.00
Dot DLP-25745	(S)	**This Is Jo Stafford**	1966	10.00	25.00

STAFFORD, JO, & FRANKIE LAINE

Label & Catalog #		Title	Year	VG+	NM
Columbia CL-2567	(10")	**Guys And Dolls** *(Soundtrack)*	1955	40.00	100.00
Columbia CL-2598	(10")	**Mosy Happy Fella**	1956	20.00	50.00

STAFFORD, JO, & GORDON MacRAE

Label & Catalog #		Title	Year	VG+	NM
Capitol T-423	(M)	**Memory Songs**	1955	24.00	60.00
		— Capitol albums above have turquoise labels.—			
Capitol T-423	(M)	**Memory Songs**	195?	12.00	30.00
		— Capitol albums above have black "rainbow" labels with the logo on the left side.—			
Capitol T-1696	(M)	**Whispering Hope**	1962	8.00	20.00
Capitol ST-1696	(S)	**Whispering Hope**	1962	10.00	25.00
Capitol T-1916	(M)	**Peace In The Valley**	1963	8.00	20.00
Capitol ST-1916	(S)	**Peace In The Valley**	1963	10.00	25.00

Label & Catalog #		Title	Year	VG+	NM

STAFFORD, TERRY

Crusader CLP-1001	(M)	Suspicion!	1964	16.00	40.00
Crusader CLP-1001S	(P)	Suspicion!	1964	20.00	50.00

STAIRSTEPS, THE: *Refer to* THE FIVE STAIRSTEPS

STANDELLS, THE
The Standells feature Dick Dodd.

Liberty LRP-3384	(M)	The Standells In Person At P.J.'s	1964	20.00	50.00
Liberty LST-7384	(S)	The Standells In Person At P.J.'s	1964	30.00	75.00
Sunset SUM-1136	(M)	Live And Out Of Sight	1966	10.00	25.00
Sunset SUS-5136	(S)	Live And Out Of Sight	1966	12.00	30.00
		(The Sunset album is a reissue of the Liberty album.)			
Tower T-5027	(M)	Dirty Water	1966	16.00	40.00
Tower ST-5027	(P)	Dirty Water	1966	20.00	50.00
Tower T-5044	(M)	Why Pick On Me	1966	16.00	40.00
Tower ST-5044	(S)	Why Pick On Me	1966	20.00	50.00
Tower T-5049	(M)	Hot Ones	1966	16.00	40.00
Tower ST-5049	(S)	Hot Ones	1966	20.00	50.00
Tower T-5098	(M)	Try It	1967	16.00	40.00
Tower ST-5098	(S)	Try It	1967	20.00	50.00

STANDLEY, JOHNNY

Capitol T-732	(M)	Comedy Caravan	1956	10.00	25.00

STANLEY, PAUL: *Refer to* KISS

STANLEY, RALPH
Refer to Lee Allen.

Jalyn JLP-118	(M)	Old Time Music	196?	10.00	25.00
Jalyn JLP-120	(M)	The Bluegrass Sound Of Ralph Stanley	196?	10.00	25.00
Jalyn JLP-129	(M)	And The Clinch Mountain Boys	196?	10.00	25.00

STANLEY BROTHERS, THE
Carter and Ralph Stanley are a vocal and instrumental bluegrass duo.

Mercury MG-20349	(M)	Country Pickin' And Singin'	1958	30.00	75.00
Mercury MG-20884	(M)	Hard Times	1963	10.00	25.00
Mercury SR-60884	(S)	Hard Times	1963	12.00	30.00
Starday SLP-106	(M)	Mountain Song Favorites	1959	20.00	50.00
Starday SLP-122	(M)	Sacred Songs From The Hills	1960	20.00	50.00
Starday SLP-201	(M)	The Mountain Music Sound			
		Of The Stanley Brothers	1962	16.00	40.00
Starday SLP-384	(M)	Jacob's Vision	1966	16.00	40.00
		— Starday albums above have yellow labels.—			
King 615	(M)	The Stanley Brothers	1959	60.00	150.00
King 645	(M)	Hymns And Sacred Songs	1960	40.00	100.00
King 690	(M)	Everybody's Country Favorites	1961	40.00	100.00
King KS-690	(S)	Everybody's Country Favorites	1961	60.00	150.00
King 698	(M)	For The Good People	1961	40.00	100.00
King 719	(M)	The Stanleys In Person	1961	40.00	100.00
King KS-719	(S)	The Stanleys In Person	1961	60.00	150.00
King 750	(M)	Old Time Camp Meeting	1961	40.00	100.00
King 772	(M)	The Stanley Brothers And The Clinch Mountain			
		Boys Sing The Songs They Like Best	1961	40.00	100.00
King 791	(M)	Award Winners	1962	40.00	100.00
King KS-791	(S)	Award Winners	1962	60.00	150.00
King 805	(M)	Good Old Camp Meeting Songs	1962	40.00	100.00
King KS-805	(S)	Good Old Camp Meeting Songs	1962	60.00	150.00
King 834	(M)	Just Because	1963	30.00	75.00
King 864	(M)	Country Folk Music Spotlight	1963	30.00	75.00
King 872	(M)	Five String Banjo Hootenanny	1963	30.00	75.00
King 918	(M)	Hymns Of The Cross	1964	30.00	75.00
King 924	(M)	The Remarkable Stanley Brothers			
		Play And Sing Bluegrass Songs For You	1964	30.00	75.00
King 953	(M)	The Best Of The Stanley Brothers	1966	16.00	40.00
King 963	(M)	A Collection Of Gospel And Sacred Songs	1966	16.00	40.00

— King mono albums above have crownless black labels; stereo albums have crownless blue labels.
The logo on the covers have a crown with "King" in open capital block letters below.—

Kay Starr (born Katherine Starks) was a teenage singing star with Joe Venuti's orchestra in the late '30s, singing with Glenn Miller, Charlie Barnet and Bob Crosby's orchestras before opting for a career as a solo. As a pop singer capitalizing on the rock'n roll fad (sic) of the '50s, she scored a major #1 hit with 1956's "Rock And Roll Waltz," which, needless to say, had nothing to do with rock and roll. Her early albums on Capitol and RCA attract the most interest from collectors, both for the material and the lovely period covers.

Label & Catalog #		Title	Year	VG+	NM
King 1013	(M)	The Stanley Brothers Sing			
		The Best Loved Songs Of The Carter Family	1967	12.00	30.00
King KSD-1013	(S)	The Stanley Brothers Sing			
		The Best Loved Songs Of The Carter Family	1967	20.00	50.00
King KSD-1028	(S)	Brand New Country Songs By Ralph Stanley	1968	20.00	50.00
King KSD-1032	(S)	Over The Sunset Hill	1968	12.00	30.00
King KSD-1046	(S)	How Far To Little Rock?	1969	12.00	30.00
King KSD-1069	(S)	The Hills Of Home	1969	12.00	30.00

— King mono albums above have black labels with a crown on top; stereo albums have blue or red labels with a crown on top. The covers have a crown with "King" in open capital block letters.—

Vintage Collectors ZK-002	(M)	Live At Antioch College	1961	20.00	50.00
Cabin Creek LP-203	(M)	Bluegrass Gospel Favorites	1966	16.00	40.00

STAPLE SINGERS, THE
Refer to Albert King & Steve Cropper & Pop Staples.

Vee Jay LP-5000	(M)	Uncloudy Day	1959	14.00	35.00
Vee Jay LPS-5000	(S)	Uncloudy Day	1959	20.00	50.00
Vee Jay LP-5008	(M)	Will The Circle Be Unbroken	196?	14.00	35.00
Vee Jay LPS-5008	(S)	Will The Circle Be Unbroken	196?	20.00	50.00
Vee Jay LP-5014	(M)	Swing Low	196?	14.00	35.00
Vee Jay LPS-5014	(S)	Swing Low	196?	20.00	50.00
Vee Jay LP-5019	(M)	The Best Of The Staples	196?	12.00	30.00
Vee Jay LPS-5019	(S)	The Best Of The Staples	196?	16.00	40.00
Vee Jay LP-5030	(M)	Swing Low, Sweet Chariot	196?	12.00	30.00
Vee Jay LPS-5030	(S)	Swing Low, Sweet Chariot	196?	16.00	40.00
Epic LN-24132	(M)	Amen	1967	12.00	30.00
Epic LN-26132	(S)	Amen	1967	16.00	40.00
Epic LN-24196	(M)	Why	1967	12.00	30.00
Epic LN-26196	(S)	Why	1967	16.00	40.00
Epic LN-24332	(M)	For What It's Worth	1967	10.00	25.00
Epic BN-26332	(S)	For What It's Worth	1967	12.00	30.00
Stax STS-2004	(S)	Soul Folk In Action	1968	12.00	30.00
Stax STS-2016	(S)	We"ll Get Over	1971	12.00	30.00
Stax STS-2034	(S)	Staple Swingers	1971	12.00	30.00

STARCHER, BUDDY

Starday SLP-211	(M)	Buddy Starcher And His Mountain Guitar	1962	14.00	35.00
Starday SLP-382	(M)	History Repeats Itself	1966	12.00	30.00

— Starday albums above have yellow labels.—

STARFIRE

Crimson S-4476/7	(S)	Starfire	1974	100.00	250.00

STARFIRES, THE

Ohio Recording Serv. 34	(M)	The Starfires Play	1964	20.00	50.00
La Brea LS-8018	(M)	Teenbeat A-Go-Go	1965	20.00	50.00

STARK NAKED

RCA Victor LSP-4592	(S)	Stark Naked	1971	10.00	25.00

STARLITES, THE: Refer to THE KODAKS / THE STARLITES

STARR, KAY

Capitol H-211	(10")	Songs By Starr	1950	30.00	75.00
Capitol H-363	(10")	Kay Starr Style	1953	30.00	75.00
Capitol H-415	(10")	The Hits Of Kay Starr	1953	30.00	75.00
Capitol T-211	(M)	Songs By Starr	1955	24.00	60.00
Capitol T-363	(M)	Kay Starr Style	1955	24.00	60.00
Capitol T-415	(M)	The Hits Of Kay Starr	1955	24.00	60.00
Capitol T-580	(M)	In A Blue Mood	1955	24.00	60.00

— Capitol albums above have turquoise labels.—

Capitol T-211	(M)	Songs By Starr	195?	12.00	30.00
Capitol T-363	(M)	Kay Starr Style	195?	12.00	30.00
Capitol T-415	(M)	The Hits Of Kay Starr	195?	12.00	30.00
Capitol T-580	(M)	In A Blue Mood	195?	12.00	30.00
Capitol T-1254	(M)	Movin'	1959	12.00	30.00
Capitol ST-1254	(S)	Movin'	1959	16.00	40.00
Capitol T-1303	(M)	Losers, Weepers	1960	12.00	30.00
Capitol ST-1303	(S)	Losers, Weepers	1960	16.00	40.00

Label & Catalog #		Title	Year	VG+	NM
Capitol T-1358	(M)	One More Time	1960	12.00	30.00
Capitol ST-1358	(S)	One More Time	1960	16.00	40.00
Capitol T-1374	(M)	Movin' On Broadway	1960	12.00	30.00
Capitol ST-1374	(S)	Movin' On Broadway	1960	16.00	40.00
Capitol T-1438	(M)	Jazz Singer	1960	12.00	30.00
Capitol ST-1438	(S)	Jazz Singer	1960	16.00	40.00
Capitol T-1468	(M)	All Starr Hits	1961	10.00	25.00
Capitol ST-1468	(S)	All Starr Hits	1961	12.00	30.00
Capitol T-1681	(M)	I Cry By Night	1962	10.00	25.00
Capitol ST-1681	(S)	I Cry By Night	1962	12.00	30.00

— *Capitol albums above have black labels with the logo on the left side.*—

Liberty LRP-9001	(M)	Swingin' With The Starr	1956	24.00	60.00
RCA Victor LPM-1149	(M)	The One And Only Kay Starr	1955	24.00	60.00
RCA Victor LPM-1549	(M)	Blue Starr	1957	24.00	60.00
RCA Victor LPM-1720	(M)	Rockin' With Kay	1958	30.00	75.00
RCA Victor LPM-2055	(M)	I Hear The Word	1959	16.00	40.00
RCA Victor LSP-2055	(S)	I Hear The Word	1959	20.00	50.00

— *RCA mono albums above have "black labels with Long Play" on the bottom;*
stereo albums have have "Living Stereo" on the bottom.—

STARR, KAY / ERROLL GARNER

Modern MLP-1203	(M)	Singin' Kay Starr, Swingin' Erroll Garner	1956	30.00	75.00
Crown CLP-5003	(M)	Singin' Kay Starr, Swingin' Erroll Garner	1957	12.00	30.00
		(Crown 5003 is a reissue of Modern 9001. Original pressings			
		have ten tracks; later pressings have eight.)			

STARR, RINGO & PETER SELLERS & TERRY SOUTHERN

Commonwealth Un. 1761	(DJ)	"The Magic Christian" Interview	1969	80.00	200.00
		(One-sided, open-end interview with script.)			

STARR, RINGO

Refer to Badfinger; TheBeatles; Leon Russell; Doris Troy.

Apple SWAL-3413	(S)	Ringo	1973	10.00	25.00
		(First pressings covers erroneously identify "Hold On"			
		as "Have You Seen My Baby.")			
Apple SWAL-3413	(S)	Ringo	1973	200.00	400.00
		(Some early pressings, usually with a cut-out hole in the cover,			
		contain a longer, 5:26 version of "Six O' Clock." Unfortunately,			
		this must be listened to for identification)			
Atlantic SD-18193	(DJ)	Ringo's Rotogravure	1978	16.00	40.00
		(Standard copy with "DJ only" etched in trail-off vinyl.)			
Atlantic SD-19108	(S)	Ringo The 4th	1978	10.00	25.00
		(Standard copy with "DJ only" etched in trail-off vinyl.)			
Portrait JR-35378	(S)	Bad Boy	1978	30.00	75.00
		(White label with "Advance Promotion" issued in a plain white cover.)			
Portrait JR-35378	(S)	Bad Boy	1978	10.00	25.00
		(White label with "Demonstration" issued in regular cover.)			
Capitol SW-3365	(S)	Sentimental Journey (Purple label)	1978	16.00	40.00
Capitol SN-16218	(S)	Sentimental Journey (Green label)	1978	10.00	25.00
RCA Victor DXL1-3233	(S)	Old Wave (Canadian)	1983	14.00	35.00
		(This album was also released in Japan and West Germany.)			
Rykodisc RALP-0190	(S)	Ringo & His All-Star Band (Clear vinyl)	1990	10.00	25.00
		(Limited live edition sequentially numbered through #5000.)			

STARZ

Capitol SPRO-8857/58	(DJ)	Live In Louisville	1978	12.00	30.00

STATLER BROTHERS, THE

The Statler Brothers are Harold and Don Reid with Lew DeWitt and Phil Balsley.

Columbia CL-2449	(M)	Flowers On The Wall	1966	10.00	25.00
Columbia CS-9249	(S)	Flowers On The Wall	1966	12.00	30.00
Columbia CL-2719	(M)	The Statler Brothers Sing The Big Hits	1967	8.00	20.00
Columbia CS-9519	(S)	The Statler Brothers Sing The Big Hits	1967	10.00	25.00

— *Columbia albums above have red labels with "360 Sound" on the bottom.*—

STATON, CANDI

Fame 1800	(S)	Candi Staton	1972	10.00	25.00
Fame 4201	(S)	I'm Just A Prisoner	1972	10.00	25.00

Label & Catalog #		Title	Year	VG+	NM

STATON, DAKOTA: *Refer to* GOLDMINE'S PRICE GUIDE TO COLLECTIBLE JAZZ ALBUMS

STATUS QUO, THE

Cadet Concept LPS-315	(E)	**Messages From The Status Quo**	1968	20.00	50.00

STEELE, PETE

Folkways FS-3828	(M)	**Banjo Tunes And Songs**	1958	12.00	30.00

STEELE, TOMMY

London LL-1770	(M)	**Rock Around The World**	1957	20.00	50.00

STEELEYE SPAN

Steeleye Span plays traditional British folk material on electric instruments with Fairport Convention's Ashley Hutchings as a founding member.

Big Tree BTS-2004	(S)	**Please To See The King**	1971	12.00	30.00
		(*Original pressings of BTS-2004 have the matrix number stamped in the trail-off viny. Counterfeits have those numbers hand-etched.*)			
Mobile Fidelity MFSL-027	(S)	**All Around My Hat**	1979	10.00	30.00

STEELY DAN

Mobile Fidelity MFSL-007	(S)	**Katy Lied**	1979	25.00	75.00
Mobile Fidelity MFSL-033	(S)	**Aja**	1980	13.00	40.00
MCA 16009	(S)	**Gaucho** (*Half-speed master*)	1981	16.00	40.00

STEIN, MARK, & THE PIGEONS

Wand WDS-687	(S)	**While The World Was Eating Vanilla Fudge**	1968	10.00	25.00

STEKERT, ELLEN

Ellen Stekert is a banjo, guitar, harmonica and mandolin player and singer of traditional folk songs.

Stinson SLP-49	(10")	**Ozark Mounatin Folk Songs**	195?	20.00	50.00
Folkways FA-2354	(M)	**Songs Of A New Yorl Lumberjack**	195?	12.00	30.00

STEPHEN & THE FARM BAND: *Refer to* THE FARM BAND

STEPHENS, LEIGH

Stevens was formerly a member of Blue Cheer.

Phillips PHS-600-294	(S)	**Red Weather**	1969	30.00	75.00

STEPPENWOLF

Dunhill D-50029	(M)	**Steppenwolf**	1968	60.00	150.00
Dunhill DS-50029	(S)	**Steppenwolf**	1968	10.00	25.00
		— *Dunhill albums above read "A Subsidiary of ABC Records" on the bottom of the label.* —			
Dunhill D-50037	(M)	**The Second**	1968	80.00	200.00
Dunhill DS-50037	(S)	**The Second** (*Chrome border cover*)	1968	10.00	25.00
Dunhill DS-50037	(S)	**The Second** (*White border cover*)	196?	12.00	30.00
		— *Dunhill albums above have black labels with "Dunhill/ABC" on top and "Dunhill Records is a subsidiary" on the bottom.* —			
Nautilus NR-53	(S)	**Wolftracks**	198?	10.00	30.00
		(*Nautilus 53 credits John Kay & Steppenwolf.*)			

STEVENS, APRIL

Refer to Nino Tempo & April Stevens.

Audio Lab AL-1534	(M)	**Torrid Tunes**	1959	100.00	250.00
Imperial LP-9118	(M)	**Teach Me Tiger**	1960	24.00	60.00
Imperial LP-12055	(P)	**Teach Me Tiger**	1960	40.00	100.00

STEVENS, BOBBY: *Refer to* THE CHECKMATES LTD.

STEVENS, CAROL

Atlantic 1256	(M)	**That Satin Doll** (*Black label*)	1957	20.00	50.00

STEVENS, CAT

Deram DE-18005	(M)	**Matthew And Son**	1967	8.00	20.00
Deram DES-18005	(P)	**Matthew And Son**	1967	10.00	25.00
Deram DES-18010	(S)	**New Masters**	1968	10.00	25.00
A&M QU-54280	(Q)	**Tea For The Tillerman**	1974	10.00	25.00
A&M QU-54313	(Q)	**Teaser And The Firecat**	1974	10.00	25.00
A&M QU-54365	(Q)	**Catch Bull At Four**	1974	10.00	25.00
A&M QU-54391	(Q)	**Foreigner**	1974	10.00	25.00

Label & Catalog #		Title	Year	VG+	NM
A&M QU-53623	(Q)	Buddha And The Chocolate Box	1974	10.00	25.00
A&M QU-54519	(Q)	Greatest Hits	1975	10.00	25.00
Mobile Fidelity MFSL-035	(S)	Tea For The Tillerman	1979	10.00	30.00
Mobile Fidelity MFQR-035	(S)	Tea For The Tillerman	1984	35.00	105.00
		(Ultra High Quality Recording in a box.)			

STEVENS, CONNIE

Warner Bros. W-1208	(M)	Conchetta	1958	16.00	40.00
Warner Bros. WS-1208	(S)	Conchetta	1958	20.00	50.00
Warner Bros. W-1382	(M)	Connie Stevens From "Hawaiian Eye"	1960	12.00	30.00
Warner Bros. WS-1382	(S)	Connie Stevens From "Hawaiian Eye"	1960	16.00	40.00
Warner Bros. W-1431	(M)	From Me To You	1962	12.00	30.00
Warner Bros. WS-1431	(S)	From Me To You	1962	16.00	40.00
Warner Bros. W-1432	(M)	Connie	1962	12.00	30.00
Warner Bros. WS-1432	(S)	Connie	1962	16.00	40.00
Warner Bros. W-1460	(M)	The Hank Williams Songbook	1962	12.00	30.00
Warner Bros. WS-1460	(S)	The Hank Williams Songbook	1962	16.00	40.00
Warner Bros. W-1519	(M)	Palm Springs Weekend *(Soundtrack)*	1963	20.00	50.00
Warner Bros. WS-1519	(S)	Palm Springs Weekend *(Soundtrack)*	1963	30.00	75.00
		— Warner albums above have grey labels.—			

STEVENS, DODIE

Dot DLP-3212	(M)	Dodie Stevens	1960	14.00	35.00
Dot DLP-25212	(S)	Dodie Stevens	1960	20.00	50.00
Dot DLP-3323	(M)	Over The Rainbow	1960	14.00	35.00
Dot DLP-25323	(S)	Over The Rainbow	1960	20.00	50.00
Dot DLP-3371	(M)	Pink Shoelaces	1961	14.00	35.00
Dot DLP-25371	(S)	Pink Shoelaces	1961	20.00	50.00

STEVENS, RAY
Ray also recorded as Baby Ray.

Mercury MG-20732	(M)	1,837 Seconds Of Humor/Ahab The Arab	1962	16.00	40.00
Mercury SR-60732	(S)	1,837 Seconds Of Humor/Ahab The Arab	1962	20.00	50.00
Mercury MG-20828	(M)	This Is Ray Stevens	1963	10.00	25.00
Mercury SR-60828	(S)	This Is Ray Stevens	1963	12.00	30.00

STEWARD, ALEC

Bluesville BVLP-1076	(M)	Creepin' Blues	1963	30.00	75.00
		— Bluesville albums above have bright blue labels with silver print.—			
Bluesville BVLP-1076	(M)	Creepin' Blues	1964	10.00	25.00
		— Bluesville albums above have blue labels with a trident logo on the right side.—			

STEWART, AL

Arista SP-40	(DJ)	The Live Radio Concert	1980	16.00	40.00
Mobile Fidelity MFSL-009	(S)	Year Of The Cat	1979	10.00	30.00
Mobile Fidelity MFSL-082	(S)	Time Passages	1981	8.00	25.00

STEWART, ALEK: *Refer to* GUTHRIE, WOODY / SONNY TERRY / ALEK STEWART

STEWART, BILLY

Chess LP-1496	(M)	I Do Love You	1965	20.00	50.00
Chess LPS-1496	(S)	I Do Love You	1965	30.00	75.00
		(Original covers for Chess 1496 are red with a black wheel design.)			
Chess LP-1496	(M)	I Do Love You	1965	16.00	40.00
Chess LPS-1496	(S)	I Do Love You	1965	20.00	50.00
		(Later pressings have a green cover with a woman at the bottom.)			
Chess LP-1499	(M)	Unbelievable	1965	16.00	40.00
Chess LPS-1499	(S)	Unbelievable	1965	20.00	50.00
Chess LP-1513	(M)	Billy Stewart Teaches Old Standards New Tricks	1967	12.00	30.00
Chess LPS-1513	(S)	Billy Stewart Teaches Old Standards New Tricks	1967	16.00	40.00
Chess LPS-1547	(S)	Billy Stewart Remembered	1968	12.00	30.00

STEWART, JOHN
Refer to The Cumberland Three; The Kingston Trio.

Capitol T-2975	(M)	Signals Through The Glass	1968	12.00	30.00
Capitol ST-2975	(S)	Signals Through The Glass	1968	8.00	20.00
		— Capitol albums above have black "rainbow" labels labels.—			

Label & Catalog #		Title	Year	VG+	NM
STEWART, REDD					
Audio Lab AL-1528	(M)	**Redd Stewart Sings Favorite Old Songs**	1959	80.00	200.00
STEWART, ROD					
Refer to Steampacket; The Jeff Beck Group; The Small Faces.					
Mercury SR-61237	(S)	**The Rod Stewart Album**	1969	10.00	25.00
		(Original covers for Mercury 61237 are gold without a black border.)			
STEWART, WYNN/WYNN STEWART & THE TOURISTS					
Wrangler W-1006	(M)	**Wynn Stewart**	1962	12.00	30.00
Wrangler WS-1006	(S)	**Wynn Stewart**	1962	16.00	40.00
Forum G-506	(M)	**Wynn Stewart**	196?	10.00	25.00
Forum GS-506	(S)	**Wynn Stewart**	196?	12.00	30.00
Capitol T-2332	(M)	**The Songs Of Wynn Stewart**	1965	10.00	25.00
Capitol ST-2332	(S)	**The Songs Of Wynn Stewart**	1965	12.00	30.00
Capitol T-2737	(M)	**It's Such A Pretty World Today**	1967	8.00	20.00
Capitol ST-2737	(S)	**It's Such A Pretty World Today**	1967	10.00	25.00
Capitol T-2849	(M)	**Love's Gonna Happen To Me**	1968	12.00	30.00
Capitol ST-2849	(S)	**Love's Gonna Happen To Me**	1968	8.00	20.00
		— *Capitol albums above have black "rainbow" labels.* —			
STEWART, WYNN, & JAN HOWARD					
Challenge CHL-611	(M)	**Sweethearts Of Country Music**	1961	24.00	60.00
Starday SLP-421	(S)	**Wynn Stewart & Jan Howard Sing Their Hits**	1968	10.00	25.00
STEWART FAMILY, THE					
King 687	(M)	**Country Sacred Songs**	1969	16.00	40.00
King 695	(M)	**Golden Country Favorites**	1969	16.00	40.00
STIDHAM, ARBEE					
Bluesville BVLP-1021	(M)	**Tired Of Wandering**	1961	40.00	100.00
		— *Bluesville albums above have bright blue labels with silver print.* —			
Bluesville BVLP-1021	(M)	**Tired Of Wandering**	1964	12.00	30.00
		— *Bluesville albums above have blue labels with a trident logo on the right side.* —			
STILLER, JERRY: *Refer to* **ANNE MEARA & JERRY STILLER**					
STITES, GARY					
Carlton LP-120	(M)	**Lonely For You**	1960	30.00	75.00
Carlton STLP-120	(S)	**Lonely For You**	1960	50.00	125.00
STOLOFF, MORRIS					
Decca DL-8574	(M)	**This Is Kim** *(With Kim Novak cover)*	1957	30.00	75.00
STONE, CLIFFIE/CLIFFIE STONE'S HOMBRES					
Cliffie Stone is a pseudonym for Clifford Snyder.					
Capitol H-400)	(10")	**Square Dances**	195?	30.00)	75.00
Capitol T-1080	(M)	**The Party's On Me**	1958	20.00	50.00
Capitol T-1230	(M)	**Cool Cowboy**	1959	14.00	35.00
Capitol ST-1230	(S)	**Cool Cowboy**	1959	20.00	50.00
Capitol T-1286	(M)	**Square Dance Promenade**	1960	14.00	35.00
Capitol ST-1286	(S)	**Square Dance Promenade**	1960	20.00	50.00
Capitol KAO-1555	(M)	**Original Cowboy Sing-A-Long**	1961	14.00	35.00
Capitol SKAO-1555	(S)	**Original Cowboy Sing-A-Long**	1961	20.00	50.00
		— *Capitol albums above have black labels with the logo on the left side.* —			
Tower T-5073	(M)	**Together Again**	1967	8.00	20.00
Tower ST-5073	(S)	**Together Again**	1967	10.00	25.00
STONE, ROLAND					
Ace LP-1018	(M)	**Just A Moment**	1961	60.00	150.00
STONE COUNTRY					
RCA Victor LSP-3958	(S)	**Stone Country**	1968	20.00	50.00
STONE HARBOUR					
Stone Harbour 398	(S)	**Stone Harbour Emerges**	1974	360.00	600.00

The original Stone Poneys were Bob Kimmel and Ken Edwards backing vocalist Linda Ronstadt. This threesome added temporary members for each of their albums—they had five other musicians assisting their debut, from which came their hit, a nice reading of Michael Nesmith's "Different Drum," in which Miss Ronstadt turns the lyric's gender around. The title of this, their third album, could confuse anyone: Is it a Linda Ronstadt album titled Stone Poneys And Friends Vol. III? *Or is it a Stone Poneys album titled* Linda Ronstadt Vol. III? *Or maybe* Linda Ronstadt/Stone Poneys And Friends Vol. III? *The most difficult of their three to find, it boasts this atmospheric photo of the oh so lovely Linda just before she broke the bonds and went solo.*

Label & Catalog #		Title	Year	VG+	NM
STONE PONEYS, THE/LINDA RONSTADT & THE STONE PONEYS					
Lead singer Linda Ronstadt went on to a successful solo career.					
Capitol T-2666	(M)	The Stone Poneys	1967	12.00	30.00
Capitol ST-2666	(S)	The Stone Poneys	1967	16.00	40.00
Capitol T-2763	(M)	Evergreen, Volume II	1967	10.00	25.00
Capitol ST-2763	(S)	Evergreen, Volume II	1967	12.00	30.00
Capitol ST-2863	(S)	Linda Ronstadt, Stone Poneys & Friends	1968	16.00	40.00
STONEGROUND					
Stoneground features Sal Valentino of The Beau Brummels.					
Warner Bros. 2ZS-1956	(S)	Family Album *(2 LPs)*	1971	10.00	25.00
STONEHILL, RANDY					
One Way JC-31252	(S)	Born Twice	1972	20.00	50.00
STONEMANS, THE/THE STONEMAN FAMILY					
Refer to Jimmy Dean / The Stoneman Family.					
Folkways FA-2315	(M)	American Banjo Tunes And Songs	196?	12.00	30.00
World Pacific WP-1828	(M)	Big Ball In Monterey	1964	12.00	30.00
World Pacific ST-1828	(S)	Big Ball In Monterey	1964	16.00	40.00
Starday SLP-393	(M)	White Lightning *(Yellow label)*	1965	16.00	40.00
MGM E-4363	(M)	Those Singin,' Swingin,' Stompin,' Sensational Stonemans	1966	8.00	20.00
MGM SE-4363	(S)	Those Singin,' Swingin,' Stompin,' Sensational Stonemans	1966	10.00	25.00
MGM E-4453	(M)	Stoneman's Country	1967	8.00	20.00
MGM SE-4453	(S)	Stoneman's Country	1967	10.00	25.00
MGM E-4511	(M)	All In The Family	1967	8.00	20.00
MGM SE-4511	(S)	All In The Family	1967	10.00	25.00
MGM E-4578	(M)	The Great Stonemans	1968	10.00	25.00
STONEY & MEAT LOAF					
Rare Earth R-528	(S)	Stoney And Meatloaf	1971	10.00	25.00
STOOGES, THE					
The Stooges feature Iggy Pop.					
Elektra EKS-74051	(S)	The Stooges *(White label promo)*	1969	60.00	150.00
Elektra EKS-74051	(S)	The Stooges	1969	20.00	50.00
Elektra EKS-74101	(S)	Fun House *(White label promo)*	1970	60.00	150.00
Elektra EKS-74101	(S)	Fun House	1970	20.00	50.00
		— Elektra albums above have red labels.—			
Columbia KC-32111	(S)	Raw Power *(White label promo)*	1973	60.00	150.00
Columbia KC-32111	(S)	Raw Power *(With inner sleeve)*	1973	20.00	50.00
STORIES					
The original album features Michael Brown of The Left Banke.					
Kama Sutra KSBS-2068	(S)	About Us	1973	16.00	40.00
		(Original promo and stock pressings of KS 2068 do not contain "Brother Louie" and were issued in a glossy, fold-open jacket.)			
STORCH, LARRY					
Prestige PRST-7683	(S)	Phillip Roth's "Epstein"	1968	10.00	25.00
STORM, BILLY					
Buena Vista BV-3315	(M)	Billy Storm	1963	60.00	150.00
Buena Vista STER-3315	(S)	Billy Storm	1963	150.00	400.00
STORM, BILLY, & THE VALIANTS					
Famous F-504	(M)	This Is The Night	1969	150.00	300.00
		(Famous 504 contains Storm's early vocal group recordings.)			
STORM, GALE					
Dot DLP-3011	(M)	Gale Storm	1956	30.00	50.00
Dot DLP-3017	(M)	Sentimental Me	1956	30.00	50.00
Dot DLP-3098	(M)	Gale Storm Hits	1958	16.00	40.00
Dot DLP-3197	(M)	Softly And Tenderly	1959	12.00	30.00
Dot DLP-25197	(S)	Softly And Tenderly	1959	16.00	40.00
Dot DLP-3209	(M)	Gale Storm Sings	1959	12.00	30.00
Dot DLP-25209	(S)	Gale Storm Sings	1959	16.00	40.00

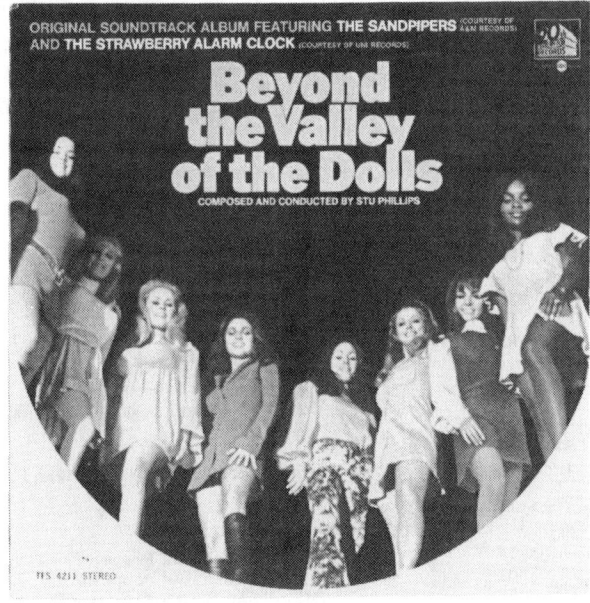

Pictured here are The Strawberry Alarm Clock's two most valuable albums: Their stereo pressing of their first, Incense And Peppermints, *containing their big bubble gummed up bit of flower-power (and a cover that's as wonderfully silly as the single), and the soundtrack to the cult classic movie,* Beyond The Valley Of The Dolls, *that lampoons every aspect of the original film,* The Valley Of The Dolls, *and the then burgeoning underground dope scene.*

Label & Catalog #		Title	Year	VG+	NM
STORY, CARL					
Refer to The Lewis Family.					
Mercury MG-20323	(M)	**Gospel Quartet Favorites**	1958	16.00	40.00
Starday SLP-107	(M)	**America's Favorite Country Gospel Artist**	1959	20.00	50.00
Mercury MG-20584	(M)	**More Gospel Quartet Favorites**	1961	12.00	30.00
Mercury SR-60584	(S)	**More Gospel Quartet Favorites**	1961	16.00	40.00
Starday SLP-127	(M)	**Gospel Revival**	1961	16.00	40.00
Starday SLP-137	(M)	**All Day Singing With Dinner On The Ground**	1961	16.00	40.00
Starday SLP-152	(M)	**Get Religion**	1961	16.00	40.00
Starday SLP-219	(M)	**Mighty Close To Heaven**	1963	16.00	40.00
Starday SLP-278	(M)	**All Day Sacred Singing**	1964	16.00	40.00
Starday SLP-315	(M)	**Sacred Songs Of Life And The Hereafter**	1965	16.00	40.00
Starday SLP-348	(M)	**There's Nothing On Earth** **(That Heaven Can't Cure)**	1965	16.00	40.00
Starday SLP-411	(M)	**My Lord Keeps A Record**	1968	12.00	30.00
		— Starday albums above have yellow labels.—			
STOWAWAYS, THE					
Justice SLP-???	(S)	**The Stowaways**	196?	200.00	400.00
STRACKE, WIN					
Win Stracke is a guitar player, singer and writer of traditional-style folk music.					
Bally BAL-12013	(M)	**Americana** *(With Richard Pick)*	1957	16.00	40.00
Golden GLP-31	(M)	**Golden Treasury Of Songs America Sings**	1958	16.00	40.00
STRADAVARI STRINGS, THE					
Spin-O-Rama 590	(M)	**String Along With Me**	196?	12.00	30.00
Spin-O-Rama S-590	(S)	**String Along With Me**	196?	16.00	40.00
		(S-O-R 590 features a Jayne Mansfield cover)			
STRANGE/TERRY BROOKS & STRANGE					
Outer Galaxie 1000	(S)	**Translucent World**	1973	12.00	30.00
Outer Galaxie 1001	(S)	**Raw Power**	1976	20.00	50.00
Star People 0005	(S)	**To Earth With Love** *(Green vinyl)*	1980	12.00	30.00
STRANGE, BILLY					
Refer to Glen Campbell / Billy Strange / Howard Roberts.					
Coliseum CM-1001	(M)	**Limbo Rock**	1962	20.00	50.00
Tower ST-5170	(S)	**De Sade** *(Soundtrack)*	1969	16.00	40.00
STRANGELOVES, THE					
Bang BLP-211	(M)	**I Want Candy**	1965	30.00	75.00
Bang BLPS-211	(S)	**I Want Candy**	1965	40.00	100.00
STRANGERS, THE					
The Strangers are Merle Haggard's backing band.					
Capitol ST-169	(S)	**The Instrumental Sound Of The Strangers**	1969	10.00	25.00
		— Capitol albums above have black "rainbow" labels.—			
STRAUSS, HERB					
Judson J-3033	(M)	**Folk Music For People Who Hate Folk Music**	195?	12.00	30.00
STRAWBERRY ALARM CLOCK, THE					
Refer to The Who / The Strawberry Alarm Clock.					
Uni 3014	(M)	**Incense And Peppermints**	1967	14.00	35.00
Uni 73014	(S)	**Incense And Peppermints**	1967	20.00	50.00
Uni 3025	(M)	**Wake Up It's Tomorrow**	1967	12.00	30.00
Uni 73025	(S)	**Wake Up It's Tomorrow**	1967	16.00	40.00
Uni 73035	(S)	**The World In A Sea Shell**	1968	16.00	40.00
Uni 73054	(S)	**Good Morning Starshine**	1969	16.00	40.00
Uni 73074	(S)	**The Best Of The Strawberry Alarm Clock**	1970	10.00	25.00
20th Century TFS-4211	(S)	**Beyond The Valley Of The Dolls** *(Sdtk)*	1970	20.00	50.00
Vocalion VL-73915	(S)	**Changes**	1971	10.00	25.00
STRAY					
Transatlantic TRA-216	(S)	**Stray**	197?	12.00	30.00
STRAYWINDS					
Shamyn-Alexus 413504	(S)	**Straywinds**	1973	30.00	75.00

Label & Catalog #		Title	Year	VG+	NM
STREISAND, BARBRA					
Columbia KOL-5780	(M)	**I Can Get It For You Wholesale** (White label)	1962	40.00	100.00
Columbia KOL-5780	(M)	**I Can Get It For You Wholesale** (Soundtrack)	1962	10.00	25.00
Columbia KOS-2180	(S)	**I Can Get It For You Wholesale** (White label)	1962	60.00	150.00
Columbia KOS-2180	(S)	**I Can Get It For You Wholesale** (Soundtrack)	1962	12.00	30.00
Columbia OL-5810	(M)	**Pins And Needles** (White label promo)	1962	40.00	100.00
Columbia OL-5810	(M)	**Pins And Needles** (Soundtrack)	1962	10.00	25.00
Columbia OS-2210	(S)	**Pins And Needles** (White label promo)	1962	60.00	150.00
Columbia OS-2210	(S)	**Pins And Needles** (Soundtrack)	1962	12.00	30.00
Columbia CL-2007	(M)	**The Barbra Streisand Album** (White label)	1963	30.00	75.00
Columbia CS-8807	(S)	**The Barbra Streisand Album** (White label)	1963	40.00	100.00
		(Long standing rumors that Columbia 20/8807 was released promotionally on purple vinyl appear to be just rumors. . .)			
Columbia CL-2054	(M)	**The Second Barbra Streisand Album** (White label promo on blue vinyl)	1963	50.00	125.00
Columbia CL-2054	(M)	**The Second Barbra Streisand Album** (White label promo)	1963	16.00	40.00
Columbia CS-8854	(S)	**The Second Barbra Streisand Album** (White label promo on blue vinyl)	1963	80.00	200.00
Columbia CS-8854	(S)	**The Second Barbra Streisand Album** (White label promo)	1963	24.00	60.00
Columbia CL-2154	(M)	**The Third Barbra Streisand Album** (White label promo)	1964	16.00	40.00
Columbia CS-8954	(S)	**The Third Barbra Streisand Album** (White label promo)	1964	24.00	60.00
Capitol No number	(DJ)	**Funny Girl** (Soundtrack radio spots)	1964	60.00	150.00
Capitol VAS-2059	(M)	**Funny Girl** (Soundtrack)	1964	8.00	20.00
Capitol SVAS-2059	(S)	**Funny Girl** (Soundtrack)	1964	10.00	25.00
Columbia CL-2215	(M)	**People** (White label promo)	1964	16.00	40.00
Columbia CS-9015	(S)	**People** (White label promo)	1964	24.00	60.00
Columbia CL-2336	(M)	**My Name Is Barbra** (White label promo)	1965	16.00	40.00
Columbia CS-9136	(S)	**My Name Is Barbra** (White label promo)	1965	24.00	60.00
		— Columbia mono labels above read "Guaranteed High Fidelity" on the bottom; stereo albums read "360 Sound Stereo" in black .—			
Columbia CL-2409	(M)	**My Name Is Barbra, Two...** (White label)	1965	16.00	40.00
Columbia CS-9209	(S)	**My Name Is Barbra, Two...** (White label)	1965	24.00	60.00
Columbia CL-2478	(DJ)	**Color Me Barbra** (White label on red vinyl)	1966	40.00	100.00
Columbia CL-2478	(DJ)	**Color Me Barbra** (White label promo)	1966	16.00	40.00
Columbia CS-9278	(DJ)	**Color Me Barbra** (White label on red vinyl)	1966	60.00	150.00
Columbia CS-9278	(DJ)	**Color Me Barbra** (White label promo)	1966	24.00	60.00
		— Columbia albums above have "360 Sound" in white on the bottom of the label.—			
Columbia PCQ-30378	(Q)	**Stoney End**	1974	10.00	25.00
Columbia PCQ-30792	(Q)	**Barbra Joan Streisand**	1974	10.00	25.00
Columbia SQ-30992	(Q)	**Funny Girl** (Soundtrack)	1974	10.00	25.00
Columbia PCQ-31760	(Q)	**Live In Concert At The Forum**	1974	10.00	25.00
Columbia PCQ-32801	(Q)	**The Way We Were And All In Love Is Fair**	1974	10.00	25.00
Columbia HC-42801	(S)	**The Way We Were And All In Love Is Fair** (Half-speed master)	1982	20.00	60.00
Columbia PCQ-33005	(Q)	**Butterfly**	1974	10.00	25.00
Arista AQ-9004	(Q)	**Funny Lady** (Soundtrack)	1975	10.00	25.00
Columbia PCQ-33815	(Q)	**Lazy Afternoon**	1975	10.00	25.00
Columbia HC-45679	(S)	**Barbra Streisand's Greatest Hits, Volume 2** (Half-speed master)	1982	10.00	30.00
Columbia HC-46750	(S)	**Guilty** (Half-speed master)	1982	10.00	25.00
Columbia HC-47678	(S)	**Memories** (Half-speed master)	1982	20.00	60.00
Columbia AS-1779	(DJ)	**The Legend Of Barbra Streisand** (2 LPs)	1983	12.00	30.00
		(Columbia 1779 is an interview with music promoting "Yentl.")			
STRING-A-LONGS, THE					
Warwick W-2036	(M)	**Pick-A-Hit Featuring "Wheels"**	1961	20.00	50.00
Warwick W-2036ST	(S)	**Pick-A-Hit Featuring "Wheels"**	1961	40.00	100.00
STRINGBEAN					
Stringbean is a pseudonym for David Akerman.					
Starday SLP-142	(M)	**Old Time Pickin' And Singin'**	1961	20.00	50.00
Starday SLP-179	(M)	**Stringbean**	1962	16.00	40.00
Starday SLP-215	(M)	**A Salute To Uncle Dave Macon**	1963	16.00	40.00
Starday SLP-260	(M)	**Way Back In The Hills Of Old Kentucky**	1964	16.00	40.00
		— Starday albums above have yellow labels.—			

Label & Catalog #		Title	Year	VG+	NM
STROKE BAND, THE					
Abacus 78-095	(S)	**Green And Yellow**	1978	60.00	150.00
STRONG, NOLAN, & THE DIABLOS					
Fortune LP-8010	(M)	**Fortune Of Hits**	1961	80.00	200.00
Fortune LP-8012	(M)	**Fortune Of Hits, Volume 2**	1962	80.00	200.00
Fortune LP-8015	(M)	**Mind Over Matter**	1963	100.00	250.00
		— Fortune albums above have purple labels on thick vinyl.—			
Fortune LP-8010	(M)	**Fortune Of Hits**	196?	20.00	50.00
Fortune LP-8012	(M)	**Fortune Of Hits, Volume 2**	196?	20.00	50.00
Fortune LP-8015	(M)	**Mind Over Matter**	196?	30.00	75.00
		— Fortune albums above have yellow labels on thick vinyl.—			
STRYPER					
Enigma E-1064	(S)	**The Yellow And Black Attack** *(Yellow vinyl)*	1984	16.00	40.00
STYX					
A&M SP-8431	(DJ)	**The Styx Radio Special** *(2 LPs)*	1977	10.00	25.00
A&M SP-17053	(DJ)	**The Styx Radio Special** *(3 LP box)*	1978	16.00	40.00
A&M SP-17222	(DJ)	**The Styx Radio Sampler** *(2 LPs)*	1978	10.00	25.00
A&M SP-3711	(S)	**Cornerstone** *(Chrome-plated fan club issue)*	1979	20.00	50.00
Mobile Fidelity MFSL-026	(S)	**The Grand Illusion**	1978	8.00	25.00
SUB-ZERO BAND, THE					
Sub-Zero 1172	(S)	**The Sub-Zero Band**	197?	100.00	250.00
SUGAR BEARS, THE					
The Bears feature Kim Carnes.					
Big Tree BTS-2009	(S)	**Introducing The Sugar Bears**	1971	10.00	25.00
SUGARLOAF					
Sugarloaf features Jerry Corbetta, later of The Four Seasons.					
Liberty LST-7640	(S)	**Sugarloaf**	1970	10.00	25.00
Claridge CL-1000	(S)	**Don't Call Us**	1975	10.00	25.00
SULLIVAN, MAXINE: *Refer to* **GOLDMINE'S PRICE GUIDE TO COLLECTIBLE JAZZ ALBUMS**					
SULLIVAN, ROCKY					
Both albums feature John Cippolina on guitar. Refer to Quicksilver Messenger Service.					
Jupiter 2006	(S)	**Illegal Entry**	1980	10.00	25.00
SUMAC, YMA					
Coral CRL-56058	(10")	**Presenting Yma Sumac/Early Recordings**	1952	60.00	150.00
Capitol H-244	(10")	**Voice Of Xtabay**	1950	40.00	100.00
Capitol S-284	(10")	**Flahooey** *(Original Cast)*	1951	60.00	150.00
Capitol H-299	(10")	**Legend Of The Sun Virgin**	1951	40.00	100.00
Capitol L-423	(10")	**Inca Taqui**	1953	40.00	100.00
Capitol L-564	(10")	**Mambo!**	1954	30.00	75.00
Capitol T-299	(M)	**Legend Of The Sun Virgin**	1954	20.00	50.00
Capitol T-564	(M)	**Mambo!**	1954	20.00	50.00
Capitol W-684	(M)	**Voice Of The Ixtabay And Inca Tacqui**	1956	20.00	50.00
		(Capitol 684 is a repackage of 244 and 423.)			
Capitol T-770	(M)	**Legend Of The Jivaro**	1957	20.00	50.00
Capitol T-1169	(M)	**Fuego Del Andes**	1959	12.00	30.00
Capitol ST-1169	(S)	**Fuego Del Andes**	1959	20.00	50.00
London XPS-608	(S)	**Miracles**	1972	30.00	75.00
SUMMER SOUNDS					
Laurel 90973	(S)	**Up And Down**	196?	500.00	800.00
SUMMERS, ANDREW ROWAN					
Andrew Rown Summers is a dulcimer player and singer of traditional folk songs.					
Folkways FA-2002	(10")	**Christmas Carols**	195?	20.00	50.00
Folkways FP-21	(10")	**Seeds Of Love**	195?	20.00	50.00
Folkways FA-2021	(10")	**Seeds Of Love**	195?	20.00	50.00
Folkways FP-41	(10")	**The Lady Gay**	195?	20.00	50.00
Folkways FA-2041	(10")	**The Lady Gay**	195?	20.00	50.00
Folkways FP-44	(10")	**The False Ladye**	195?	20.00	50.00
Folkways FA-2044	(10")	**The False Ladye**	195?	20.00	50.00

Label & Catalog #		Title	Year	VG+	NM
Folkways FA-2348	(M)	Andrew Rowan Summers Sings Ballads	195?	12.00	30.00
Folkways FP-61	(M)	Hymnns And Carols—			
		Early American Folksongs	195?	12.00	30.00
Folkways FA-2361	(M)	Hymnns And Carols—			
		Early American Folksongs	195?	12.00	30.00
Folkways FP-64	(M)	The Unqueit Grave—			
		American Tragic Ballds	195?	12.00	30.00
Folkways FA-2364	(M)	The Unqueit Grave—			
		American Tragic Ballds	195?	12.00	30.00
SUNDOG SUMMIT					
(No label)	(S)	**On Summit Hill**	1976	40.00	100.00
SUNDOWNERS, THE					
Liberty LRP-3269	(M)	**Folk Songs For The Rich**	1962	8.00	20.00
Liberty LST-7269	(S)	**Folk Songs For The Rich**	1962	10.00	25.00
SUNGLOWS, THE					
Sunglow SLP-103	(M)	**The Original Peanuts**	1965	40.00	100.00
SUNNY & THE SUNLINERS					
Tear Drop 2000	(M)	**Talk To Me/Rags To Riches**	1963	40.00	100.00
Tear Drop 2019	(M)	**All Night Worker**	1964	30.00	75.00
Key-Loc KL-3003	(M)	**Sunny & The Sunliners Live In Hollywood**	196?	16.00	40.00
SUNNYLAND SLIM					
Bluesville BVLP-1016	(M)	**Slim's Shout**	1961	40.00	100.00
		— Bluesville albums above have bright blue labels with silver print.—			
Bluesville BVLP-1016	(M)	**Slim's Shout**	1964	12.00	30.00
		— Bluesville albums above have blue labels with a trident logo on the right side.—			
SUNRAYS, THE					
Tower T-5017	(M)	**Andrea**	1966	14.00	35.00
Tower ST-5017	(S)	**Andrea**	1966	20.00	50.00
SUNSET DRAGSTERS, THE					
Palace M-775	(M)	**Hot Rod Rally**	196?	20.00	50.00
Palace PST-775	(S)	**Hot Rod Rally**	196?	30.00	75.00
SUNSETS, THE					
Palace M-752	(M)	**Surfing With The Sunsets**	1963	8.00	20.00
Palace PST-752	(S)	**Surfing With The Sunsets**	1963	10.00	25.00
SUNSHINE BOYS, THE					
Dot DLP-3189	(M)	**Sing Unto Him**	1959	12.00	30.00
Dot DLP-25189	(S)	**Sing Unto Him**	1959	16.00	40.00
Starday SLP-113	(M)	**America's Number One Gospel Group**	1960	16.00	40.00
Starday SLP-166	(M)	**More Country Music Sing-Along**	1962	16.00	40.00
Starday SLP-349	(M)	**A Happy Home Up There**	1965	16.00	40.00
		— Starday albums above have yellow labels.—			
SUNSHINE COMPANY, THE					
Imperial LP-9359	(M)	**Happy Is The Sunshine Company**	1967	8.00	20.00
Imperial LP-12359	(S)	**Happy Is The Sunshine Company**	1967	10.00	25.00
Imperial LP-9368	(M)	**The Sunshine Company**	1968	8.00	20.00
Imperial LP-12368	(S)	**The Sunshine Company**	1968	10.00	25.00
Imperial LP-12399	(S)	**Sunshine And Shadows**	1968	10.00	25.00
SUPERFINE DANDELION					
Mainstream 56102	(M)	**Superfine Dandelion**	1967	8.00	20.00
Mainstream S-6102	(S)	**Superfine Dandelion**	1967	10.00	25.00
SUPERSTOCKS, THE					
The Superstocks are a creation of Gary Usher & Co.					
Capitol T-1997	(M)	**Hot Rod Rally**	1963	20.00	50.00
Capitol ST-1997	(S)	**Hot Rod Rally**	1963	30.00	75.00
		(While this is actually a various artists compilation, half of the album consists of The Superstocks' earliest recordings.)			

Label & Catalog #		Title	Year	VG+	NM
Capitol T-2060	(M)	**Thunder Road**	1964	60.00	150.00
Capitol ST-2060	(S)	**Thunder Road**	1964	80.00	200.00
		(Capitol 2060 was issued with a poster of a drawing of a hot rod, priced separately below.)			
Capitol 2060		**Thunder Road Poster**	1964	10.00	30.00
Capitol T-2113	(M)	**Surf Route 101**	1964	50.00	125.00
Capitol ST-2113	(S)	**Surf Route 101**	1964	60.00	150.00
		(Issued with a bonus single by Mr. Gasser & The Weirdos in a special "pocket" on the cover.)			
Capitol T-2113	(M)	**Surf Route 101** *(Without the single)*	1964	40.00	100.00
Capitol ST-2113	(S)	**Surf Route 101** *(Without the single)*	1964	50.00	125.00
Capitol T-2190	(M)	**School Is A Drag**	1964	50.00	125.00
Capitol ST-2190	(S)	**School Is A Drag**	1964	60.00	150.00

SUPERTRAMP

Label & Catalog #		Title	Year	VG+	NM
Mobile Fidelity MFSL-005	(S)	**Crime Of The Century**	1979	13.00	40.00
Mobile Fidelity MFSL-045	(S)	**Breakfast In America**	1980	8.00	25.00
Mobile Fidelity MFQR-005	(S)	**Crime Of The Century**	1983	35.00	100.00
		(Ultra High Quality Recording in a box.)			
Sweet Thunder 5	(S)	**Even In The Quietest Moments**	198?	12.00	35.00

SUPREMES, THE/DIANA ROSS & THE SUPREMES
Original members include Florence Ballard, Diana Ross and Mary Wilson.

Label & Catalog #		Title	Year	VG+	NM
Motown M-606	(M)	**Meet The Supremes**	1963	300.00	500.00
		(Original covers for the first mono pressing of Motown 606 feature a photo of Flo, Di and Mary seated on stools.)			
Motown M-606	(M)	**Meet The Supremes**	1964	10.00	25.00
Motown MS-606	(S)	**Meet The Supremes**	1964	12.00	30.00
		(Later covers feature a close-up of the group.)			
Motown M-621	(M)	**Where Did Our Love Go**	1964	10.00	25.00
Motown MS-621	(S)	**Where Did Our Love Go**	1964	12.00	30.00
Motown M-623	(M)	**A Bit Of Liverpool**	1964	16.00	40.00
Motown MS-623	(S)	**A Bit Of Liverpool**	1964	20.00	50.00
Motown M-625	(M)	**Country, Western And Pop**	1965	12.00	30.00
Motown MS-625	(S)	**Country, Western And Pop**	1965	16.00	40.00
Motown M-627	(M)	**More Hits By The Supremes**	1965	10.00	25.00
Motown MS-627	(S)	**More Hits By The Supremes**	1965	12.00	30.00
Motown M-629	(M)	**We Remember Sam Cooke**	1965	12.00	30.00
Motown MS-629	(S)	**We Remember Sam Cooke**	1965	16.00	40.00
Motown M-636	(M)	**The Supremes At The Copa**	1965	10.00	25.00
Motown MS-636	(S)	**The Supremes At The Copa**	1965	12.00	30.00
Motown M-638	(M)	**Merry Christmas**	1965	12.00	30.00
Motown MS-638	(S)	**Merry Christmas**	1965	16.00	40.00
Motown M-643	(M)	**I Hear A Symphony**	1966	10.00	25.00
Motown MS-643	(S)	**I Hear A Symphony**	1966	12.00	30.00
Motown M-649	(M)	**Supremes A' Go-Go**	1966	10.00	25.00
Motown MS-649	(S)	**Supremes A' Go-Go**	1966	12.00	30.00
Motown M-650	(M)	**Holland-Dozier-Holland**	1967	10.00	25.00
Motown MS-650	(S)	**Holland-Dozier-Holland**	1967	12.00	30.00
Motown M-659	(M)	**The Supremes Sing Rodgers And Hart**	1967	10.00	25.00
Motown MS-659	(S)	**The Supremes Sing Rodgers And Hart**	1967	12.00	30.00
Motown M-663	(M)	**The Supremes' Greatest Hits** *(2 LPs with poster)*	1967	14.00	35.00
Motown M-663	(M)	**The Supremes' Greatest Hits** *(2 LPs without poster)*	1967	10.00	25.00
Motown MS-663	(S)	**The Supremes' Greatest Hits** *(2 LPs with poster)*	1967	14.00	35.00
Motown MS-663	(S)	**The Supremes' Greatest Hits** *(2 LPs without poster)*	1967	10.00	25.00
Motown M-665	(M)	**Reflections**	1968	12.00	30.00
Motown MS-665	(S)	**Reflections**	1968	6.00	15.00
Motown M-670	(M)	**Love Child**	1968	12.00	30.00
Motown MS-670	(S)	**Love Child**	1968	6.00	15.00
Motown M-672	(M)	**Funny Girl**	1968	12.00	30.00
Motown MS-672	(S)	**Funny Girl**	1968	6.00	15.00
Motown M-676	(M)	**Live At London's Talk Of The Town** *(Promo)*	1968	12.00	30.00
Motown MS-676	(S)	**Live At London's Talk Of The Town**	1968	6.00	15.00

—Motown albums above have the company's Detroit, MI, address on the bottom of the label.—

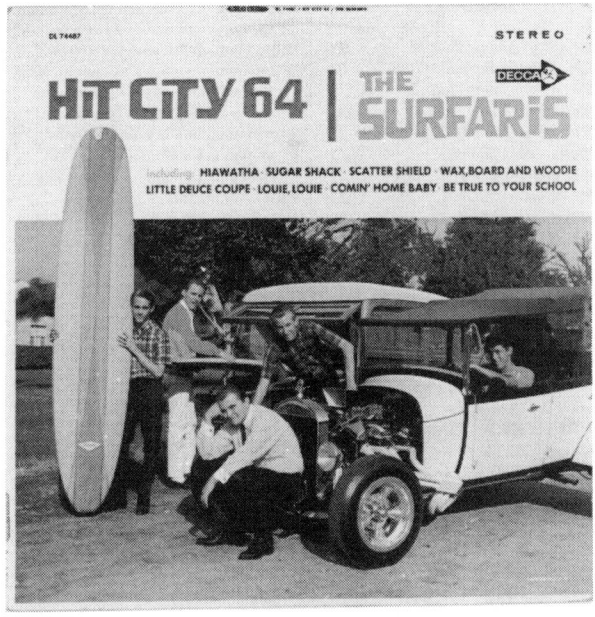

The original Surfaris consisted of Bob Berryhill, Pat Connolly, Jim Fuller, Jim Pash and Ron Wilson; their recordings appear on the Dot album. After signing with Decca in 1963 they found themselves basically a touring band while "their" albums were recorded by Gary Usher and crew, often using Wilson as the vocalist. The covers of these two albums capture the mood of the period's West Coast [white] youth— rods, boards, woodies and bikes. (Hey, where are the honeys?)

Label & Catalog #		Title	Year	VG+	NM
Doral	(S)	**Doral Presents Diana Ross & The Supremes**	1971	20.00	50.00
		(Promotional compilation of previously released material.)			
Motown PR-102	(DJ)	**Touch Interview**	1971	10.00	25.00
Motown MS-794	(DJ)	**Anthology 1962-1969** *(3 LPs)*	1974	16.00	40.00

SUPREMES, THE, & THE TEMPTATIONS

Motown M-679	(M)	**Diana Ross & The Supremes Join The Temptations**	1968	12.00	30.00
Motown MS-679	(S)	**Diana Ross & The Supremes Join The Temptations**	1968	6.00	15.00

SURF SIDE FIVE, THE

Intermountain 153	(M)	**Recorded Live**	196?	60.00	150.00

SURF STOMPERS, THE

Del-Fi DFLP-1236	(M)	**The Original Surfer Stomp**	1963	30.00	75.00
Del-Fi DFST-1236	(S)	**The Original Surfer Stomp**	1963	40.00	100.00
		(This is a reissue of The Bruce Johnston Surfing Band album.)			

SURF TEENS, THE

Sutton SU-339	(M)	**Surf Mania**	196?	12.00	30.00
Sutton SSU-339	(S)	**Surf Mania**	196?	16.00	40.00

SURFARIS, THE

On the Dot album only "Wipe Out" and "Surfer Joe" are by The Surfaris; the other tracks were cut by The Challengers. The final two Decca albums are essentially Gary Usher & Co. with vocalist Ron Wilson.

Dot DLP-3535	(M)	**Wipe Out**	1963	20.00	50.00
Dot DLP-25535	(P)	**Wipe Out**	1963	30.00	75.00
		(First pressings of Dot 3/25535 have a photo of the group with five members on the back cover.)			
Dot DLP-3535	(M)	**Wipe Out**	1963	16.00	40.00
Dot DLP-25535	(P)	**Wipe Out**	1963	20.00	50.00
		(Second pressings have a photo of the group with four members.)			
Dot DLP-3535	(M)	**Wipe Out**	196?	12.00	30.00
Dot DLP-25535	(P)	**Wipe Out**	196?	16.00	40.00
		(Later pressings deletes the photo of the group entirely.)			
Decca DL-4470	(M)	**The Surfaris Play Wipe Out**	1963	16.00	40.00
Decca DL-74470	(S)	**The Surfaris Play Wipe Out**	1963	20.00	50.00
Decca DL-4487	(M)	**Hit City '64**	1964	16.00	40.00
Decca DL-74487	(S)	**Hit City '64**	1964	20.00	50.00
Decca DL-4560	(M)	**Fun City, U.S.A.**	1964	20.00	50.00
Decca DL-74560	(S)	**Fun City, U.S.A.**	1964	30.00	75.00
Decca DL-4614	(M)	**Hit City '65**	1965	20.00	50.00
Decca DL-74614	(S)	**Hit City '65**	1965	30.00	75.00
Decca DL-4683	(M)	**It Ain't Me, Babe**	1965	16.00	40.00
Decca DL-74683	(S)	**It Ain't Me, Babe**	1965	20.00	50.00

SURFRIDERS, THE

Vault LP-105	(M)	**Surfbeat, Volume 2**	1963	12.00	30.00
Vault VS-105	(S)	**Surfbeat, Volume 2**	1963	16.00	40.00

SURFSIDERS, THE

Design DLP-208	(M)	**The Beach Boy's Songbook**	1965	10.00	25.00
Design DLPS-208	(S)	**The Beach Boy's Songbook**	1965	12.00	30.00

SURPRISE

(No label)	(S)	**Assault On Merryland** *(With booklet)*	197?	40.00	100.00

SURPRISE PACKAGE

L.H.I. S-12005	(S)	**Free Up**	1968	10.00	25.00

SURRATT, CECIL, & SMITTY SMITH

Audio Lab AL-1565	(M)	**Songs Everybody Knows**	1961	80.00	200.00
King 860	(M)	**Country Music From The Heart Of The Country**	1963	30.00	75.00
King 966	(M)	**Good Country Singin' And Pickin'**	1966	20.00	50.00

Label & Catalog #		Title	Year	VG+	NM
SUZUKI, PAT					
Vik LX-1127	(M)	The Many Sides Of Pat Suzuki	1958	10.00	25.00
Vik LX-1147	(M)	Pat Suzuki	1958	10.00	25.00
SWAGMEN, THE					
Parkway P-7015	(M)	Meet The Swagmen	1962	20.00	50.00
SWAMP DOGG					
Canyon LP-7706	(S)	Total Destruction To Your Mind	1970	12.00	30.00
SWANN, BETTYE					
Money 1103	(M)	Make Me Yours	1967	8.00	20.00
Money S-1103	(S)	Make Me Yours	1967	10.00	25.00
SWEET, THE					
Bell ST-1124	(S)	Sweet	1973	10.00	25.00
Capitol SPRO-8371/3	(DJ)	Sweet For A.O.R. Radio Only (Sampler)	1976	10.00	25.00
Capitol SPRO-8849	(DJ)	Short And Sweet	1978	12.00	30.00
Capitol PRO-11929	(DJ)	Cut Above The Rest	1979	20.00	50.00

(Box contains LP, cassette, 8-track, photo and biography.)

SWEET ADELINES, THE: *Refer to the Cadence listings in the* **VARIOUS ARTISTS** Section

SWEET INSPIRATIONS, THE					
Atlantic 8155	(M)	The Sweet Inspirations	1968	12.00	30.00
Atlantic SD-8155	(S)	The Sweet Inspirations	1968	8.00	20.00
SWEET PANTS					
Barkley LP-1141	(S)	Fat Peter Presents Sweet Pants	1972	80.00	200.00

SWEET SUE & HER SOCIETY SYNCOPATERS
The Society Syncopaters were the group featuring Marilyn Monroe from the film "Some Like It Hot."

United Arts. UAL-3029	(M)	Some Like It Hot (Soundtrack material)	1959	40.00	100.00
United Arts. UAS-6029	(S)	Some Like It Hot (Soundtrack material)	1959	60.00	150.00
SWEET TOOTHE					
Dominion NR-7360	(S)	Testing	1974	80.00	200.00
SWINGIN' MEDALLIONS, THE					
Smash MGS-27083	(M)	Double Shot	1966	16.00	40.00
Smash SRS-67083	(S)	Double Shot	1966	20.00	50.00

(Original pressings include an unedited version of "Double Shot.")

Smash MGS-27083	(M)	Double Shot	1966	12.00	30.00
Smash SRS-67083	(S)	Double Shot	1966	16.00	40.00

(Later pressings include the edited, single version of "Double Shot.")

SWINGING BLUE JEANS, THE					
Imperial LP-9261	(M)	Hippy Hippy Shake	1964	30.00	75.00
Imperial LP-12261	(E)	Hippy Hippy Shake	1964	30.00	75.00
SYKES, PAUL					
Crown CLP-5057	(M)	Great American Folk Songs (Black label)	195?	20.00	50.00

SYKES, ROOSEVELT
Refer to Victoria Spivey.

Bluesville BVLP-1006	(M)	The Return Of Roosevelt Sykes	1960	40.00	100.00
Bluesville BVLP-1014	(M)	The Honeydripper	1961	40.00	100.00

—Bluesville albums above have bright blue labels with silver print.—

Bluesville BVLP-1006	(M)	The Return Of Roosevelt Sykes	1964	12.00	30.00
Bluesville BVLP-1014	(M)	The Honeydripper	1964	12.00	30.00

—Bluesville albums above have blue labels with a trident logo on the right side.—

Delmark DL-607	(S)	The Hard Driving Blues Of Roosevelt Sykes	1963	12.00	30.00
SYNDICATE OF SOUND, THE					
Bell LP-6001	(M)	Little Girl	1966	14.00	35.00
Bell SLP-6001	(S)	Little Girl	1966	20.00	50.00

SYMS, SYLVIA: *Refer to* **GOLDMINE'S PRICE GUIDE TO COLLECTIBLE JAZZ ALBUMS**

T

T-BONES, THE

Liberty LRP-3346	(M)	Boss Drag	1963	20.00	50.00
Liberty LST-7346	(S)	Boss Drag	1963	30.00	75.00
Liberty LRP-3363	(M)	Boss Drag At The Beach	1964	20.00	50.00
Liberty LST-7363	(S)	Boss Drag At The Beach	1964	30.00	75.00
Liberty LRP-3404	(M)	Doin' The Jerk	1965	10.00	25.00
Liberty LST-7404	(S)	Doin' The Jerk	1965	12.00	30.00
Liberty LRP-3439	(M)	No Matter What Shape	1966	8.00	20.00
Liberty LST-7439	(S)	No Matter What Shape	1966	10.00	25.00
Liberty LRP-3446	(M)	Sippin' And Chippin'	1966	8.00	20.00
Liberty LST-7446	(S)	Sippin' And Chippin'	1966	10.00	25.00
Liberty LRP-3471	(M)	Everyone's Gone To The Moon	1966	8.00	20.00
Liberty LST-7471	(S)	Everyone's Gone To The Moon	1966	10.00	25.00

T. C. ATLANTIC

Dove LP-4459	(M)	T. C. Atlantic	1966	50.00	125.00

T. I. M. E.

T.I.M.E. means Trust In Men Everywhere.

Liberty LST-7558	(S)	T. I. M. E.	1968	10.00	25.00
Liberty LST-7605	(S)	Smooth Ball	1969	10.00	25.00

T-REX/TYRANNOSAURUS REX

T-Rex features Marc Bolan.

Blue Thumb BTS-7	(S)	Unicorn	1969	10.00	25.00
Blue Thumb BTS-18	(S)	A Beard Of Stars	1970	10.00	25.00
Reprise PRO-511	(DJ)	An Interview With Marc Bolan	1971	60.00	150.00
MFP 5274	(S)	Ride A White Swan	1974	10.00	25.00

(Manufactured by Capitol for export only.)

T. V. & THE TRIBESMEN

HBR HLP-9507	(M)	Barefootin'	1966	10.00	25.00
HBR HST-9507	(S)	Barefootin'	1966	12.00	30.00

TALISMEN, THE

Blue Star M-6323	(M)	Treasury Of American Railroad Songs And Ballads	1964	8.00	20.00
Blue Star MS-6323	(S)	Treasury Of American Railroad Songs And Ballads	1964	10.00	25.00
Prestige PRLP-7406	(M)	Folk Swingers Extraordinaire	1965	10.00	25.00
Prestige PRST-7406	(S)	Folk Swingers Extraordinaire	1965	12.00	30.00

TALKING HEADS, THE

Warner Bros. WBMS-104	(DJ)	Live At The Roxy (Counterfeits exist)	1979	16.00	40.00
Sire 23771	(S)	Speaking In Tongues (Clear vinyl)	1983	12.00	30.00

(Limited edition of Sire 23771 issued in a clear plastic box with artwork by Robert Rauschenberg.)

TAMPA RED

Bluesville BVLP-1030	(M)	Don't Tampa With The Blues	1961	50.00	125.00
Bluesville BVLP-1043	(M)	Don't Jive Me	1962	50.00	125.00

—Bluesville albums above have bright blue labels with silver print.—

Bluesville BVLP-1030	(M)	Don't Tampa With The Blues	1964	14.00	35.00
Bluesville BVLP-1043	(M)	Don't Jive Me	1964	14.00	35.00

—Bluesville albums above have blue labels with a trident logo on the right side.—

TAMS, THE

ABC-Paramount ABC-481	(M)	Presenting The Tams	1964	16.00	40.00
ABC-Paramount ABCS-481	(E)	Presenting The Tams	1964	12.00	30.00
ABC-Paramount ABC-499	(M)	Hey Girl, Don't Bother Me	1964	12.00	30.00
ABC-Paramount ABCS-499	(S)	Hey Girl, Don't Bother Me	1964	16.00	40.00

Norma Tanega had a good sized hit with the folk-bluesy "Walkin' My Cat Named Dog" for New Voice in 1966. The company followed the obvious course and issued an album titled after the hit. As was the norm, mono copies were pressed and distributed first. In the case of Ms. Tanega's album, apparently the sales were very slow and the stereo pressing (pictured here) was miniscule and has been a sought-after stereo album for years.

Label & Catalog #		Title	Year	VG+	NM
ABC 596	(M)	Time For The Tams	1967	10.00	25.00
ABC S-596	(S)	Time For The Tams	1967	12.00	30.00
ABC S-627	(S)	A Little More Soul	1968	10.00	25.00
ABC S-673	(S)	A Portrait Of The Tams	1969	10.00	25.00

TANEGA, NORMA
| New Voice NV-2001 | (M) | Walkin' My Cat Named Dog | 1966 | 12.00 | 30.00 |
| New Voice NVS-2001 | (S) | Walkin' My Cat Named Dog | 1966 | 20.00 | 50.00 |

TANGERINE
| Stephen Prod. SPST-001 | (S) | The Peeling Of Tangerine | 197? | 40.00 | 100.00 |

TANGERINE ZOO
| Mainstream S-6107 | (S) | Tangerine Zoo | 1968 | 20.00 | 50.00 |
| Mainstream S-6116 | (S) | Outside Looking In | 1968 | 20.00 | 50.00 |

TAR BABY
| New South NR-4500 | (S) | February *(Issued without a cover)* | 197? | 70.00 | 175.00 |

TARGAL, JEM
| Sheavy | (M) | Lucky Guy | 196? | 50.00 | 125.00 |

TARRIERS, THE
Original members were Alan Arkin, Erik Darling and Bob Carey. Arkin left in 1958 and was replaced by Clarence Cooper. By 1962 the group was Carey and Cooper with Eric Weissberg and Marshall Brickman.
Glory PG-1200	(M)	The Tarriers	1958	20.00	50.00
United Arts. UAL-4033	(M)	Hard Travelin'	1959	14.00	35.00
United Arts. UAS-5033	(S)	Hard Travelin'	1959	20.00	50.00
Atlantic 8042	(M)	Tell The World	1960	14.00	35.00
Atlantic SD-8042	(S)	Tell The World	1960	20.00	50.00

— Atlantic albums above have multi-color labels with a white "fan" logo on the right side.—
Decca DL-4342	(M)	The Tarriers	1962	10.00	25.00
Decca DL-74342	(S)	The Tarriers	1962	12.00	30.00
Kapp KL-1349	(M)	The Original Tarriers	1963	10.00	25.00
Kapp KS-3349	(S)	The Original Tarriers	1963	12.00	30.00
Decca DL-4538	(M)	Gather 'Round	1964	10.00	25.00
Decca DL-74538	(S)	Gather 'Round	1964	12.00	30.00

TASTE
Taste features Rory Gallagher.
| Atco SD-33-296 | (S) | Taste | 1969 | 10.00 | 25.00 |
| Atco SD-33-322 | (S) | On The Boards | 1970 | 10.00 | 25.00 |

TATE, BABY
| Bluesville BVLP-1072 | (M) | The What You Done | 1963 | 30.00 | 75.00 |

— Bluesville albums above have bright blue labels with silver print.—
| Bluesville BVLP-1072 | (M) | The What You Done | 1964 | 10.00 | 25.00 |

— Bluesville albums above have blue labels with a trident logo on the right side.—

TAYLOR, BOBBY, & THE VANCOUVERS
Gordy G-930	(M)	Bobby Taylor & The Vancouvers *(White label)*	1968	16.00	40.00
Gordy GS-930	(S)	Bobby Taylor & The Vancouvers	1968	10.00	25.00
Gordy GS-942	(S)	Taylor Made Soul	1968	10.00	25.00

TAYLOR, CREED
Creed Taylor is best known as a jazz producer and founder of such labels as Impulse! and CTI.
ABC-Paramount ABC-259	(M)	Shock Music In Hi-Fi	1958	14.00	35.00
ABC-Paramount ABCS-259	(S)	Shock Music In Hi-Fi	1958	20.00	50.00
ABC-Paramount ABC-???	(M)	Panic: Son Of Shock	1959	14.00	35.00
ABC-Paramount ABCS-???	(S)	Panic: Son Of Shock	1959	20.00	50.00

TAYLOR, EARL/EARL TAYLOR & THE STONEY MOUNTAIN BOYS
United Arts. UAL-3049	(M)	Folk Songs From The Bluegrass	1960	14.00	35.00
United Arts. UAS-6049	(S)	Folk Songs From The Bluegrass	1960	20.00	50.00
Capitol T-2090	(M)	Bluegrass Taylor Made	1963	14.00	35.00
Capitol ST-2090	(S)	Bluegrass Taylor Made	1963	20.00	50.00

TAYLOR, EDDIE: *Refer to* ELMORE JAMES & EDDIE TAYLOR

Label & Catalog #		Title	Year	VG+	NM

TAYLOR, JAMES

Apple SKAO-3352	(S)	**James Taylor**	1969	14.00	35.00
		(First pressings have the title on the cover in black print.)			
Apple SKAO-3352	(S)	**James Taylor**	1971	10.00	25.00
		(Later pressings have the title on the cover in orange print.)			
Columbia HC-47009	(S)	**Dad Loves His Work** *(Half-speed master)*	1983	13.00	40.00
Nautilus NR-29	(S)	**Gorilla**	1981	8.00	25.00

TAYLOR, "LITTLE" JOHNNY

Galaxy 203	(M)	**Little Johnny Taylor**	1963	12.00	30.00
Galaxy 8203	(S)	**Little Johnny Taylor**	1963	16.00	40.00
Galaxy 207	(M)	**Little Johnny Taylor's Greatest Hits**	1964	12.00	30.00
Galaxy 8207	(S)	**Little Johnny Taylor's Greatest Hits**	1964	16.00	40.00

TAYLOR, JOHNNIE
Johnnie Taylor originally recorded with The Soul Stirrers.

Stax ST-715	(M)	**Wanted: One Soul Singer**	1967	12.00	30.00
Stax STS-715	(S)	**Wanted: One Soul Singer**	1967	16.00	40.00
Stax STS-2005	(S)	**Who's Making Love?**	1968	12.00	30.00
Stax STS-2008	(S)	**Raw Blues**	1969	10.00	25.00
Stax STS-2012	(S)	**Rare Stamps**	1969	10.00	25.00
		("I Had A Dream" is rechanneled on this album.)			
Stax STS-2023	(S)	**The Philosophy Continues**	1969	10.00	25.00
Stax STS-2030	(S)	**One Step Beyond**	1970	10.00	25.00

TAYLOR, KINGSIZE, & THE DOMINOS

Midnight HLP-2101	(M)	**Real Gonk Man**	196?	12.00	30.00
Midnight HST-2101	(S)	**Real Gonk Man**	196?	14.00	35.00

TAYLOR, KOKO

Chess LPS-1532	(S)	**Koko Taylor**	1968	14.00	35.00
Chess CHS-50018	(S)	**Basic Soul**	1972	10.00	25.00

TAYLOR, MEL, & THE MAGICS

Warner Bros. W-1624	(M)	**Mel Taylor In Action**	1966	8.00	20.00
Warner Bros. WS-1624	(S)	**Mel Taylor In Action**	1966	10.00	25.00

TAYLOR, TED
Refer to Little Johnny Taylor & Ted Taylor.

OKeh OKM-12104	(M)	**Be Ever Wonderful**	1963	10.00	25.00
OKeh OKS-14104	(S)	**Be Ever Wonderful**	1963	14.00	35.00
OKeh OKM-12109	(M)	**Blues And Soul**	1965	10.00	25.00
OKeh OKS-14109	(S)	**Blues And Soul**	1965	14.00	35.00
OKeh OKM-12113	(M)	**Ted Taylor's Greatest Hits**	1966	8.00	20.00
OKeh OKS-14113	(S)	**Ted Taylor's Greatest Hits**	1966	10.00	25.00

TAYLOR, TUT, & THE FOLKSWINGERS

World Pacific WP-1816	(M)	**12 String Dobro**	1964	10.00	25.00
World Pacific ST-1816	(S)	**12 String Dobro** *(Red vinyl)*	1964	30.00	75.00
World Pacific ST-1816	(S)	**12 String Dobro**	1964	12.00	30.00

TAYLOR, TUT, WITH CLARENCE & ROLAND WHITE

World Pacific WP-1829	(M)	**Dobro Country**	1964	10.00	25.00
World Pacific ST-1829	(S)	**Dobro Country**	1964	12.00	30.00

TEA COMPANY, THE

Smash SRS-67105	(S)	**Come And Have Some Tea**	1968	12.00	30.00

TEDDY & THE PANDAS

Tower ST-5125	(S)	**Basic Magnetism**	1968	10.00	25.00

TEDDY BEARS, THE

Imperial LP-9067	(M)	**The Teddy Bears Sing!**	1959	150.00	300.00
Imperial LPS-12010	(S)	**The Teddy Bears Sing!**	1959	500.00	1,000.00

TEEMATES, THE

Audio Fidelity AFLP-3042	(M)	**Jet Set Dance Discotheque**	1964	6.00	15.00
Audio Fidelity AFSD-7042	(S)	**Jet Set Dance Discotheque**	1964	10.00	25.00

Label & Catalog #		Title	Year	VG+	NM

TEEN QUEENS, THE

Label & Catalog #		Title	Year	VG+	NM
RPM LRP-3007	(M)	Eddie, My Love	1956		See below
		(RPM 3007 was not released.)			
Crown CLP-5022	(M)	Eddie, My Love	1956	80.00	200.00
		(Crown 5022 is a reissue of the unreleased RPM 3007.)			
Crown CLP-5373	(M)	The Teen Queens	1963	20.00	50.00
Crown CST-373	(E)	The Teen Queens	1963	8.00	20.00

TEENAGERS, THE/THE TEENAGERS FEATURING FRANKIE LYMON

Label & Catalog #		Title	Year	VG+	NM
Gee GLP-701	(M)	The Teenagers Featuring Frankie Lymon	1957	600.00	1,200.00
		(White label promo on thick vinyl.)			
Gee GLP-701	(M)	The Teenagers Featuring Frankie Lymon	1957	200.00	400.00
		(First pressings of Gee 701 have red labels on non-flexible vinyl.)			
Gee GLP-701	(M)	The Teenagers Featuring Frankie Lymon	1961	60.00	150.00
Gee GLPS-701	(E)	The Teenagers Featuring Frankie Lymon	1961	80.00	200.00
		(Second pressings have grey labels on non-flexible vinyl.)			
Gee GLP-701	(M)	The Teenagers Featuring Frankie Lymon	1978	4.00	10.00
		(Third pressings have a white label on thin, flexible vinyl.)			

TELEVISION

Television features Tom Verlaine and Richard Lloyd, who later recorded as Richerd Hell.

Label & Catalog #		Title	Year	VG+	NM
Elektra 7E-1098	(S)	Marquee Moon	1977	10.00	25.00
Elektra 6E-133	(S)	Adventure	1978	10.00	25.00

TEMPEST

Label & Catalog #		Title	Year	VG+	NM
Earth 0378	(S)	Tempest	1976	40.00	100.00

TEMPLE, PICK

Lafayette Parker Temple is a guitar player and singer of traditional American folk songs.

Label & Catalog #		Title	Year	VG+	NM
"X" LXA-3022	(10")	Folk Songs Of The People	195?	20.00	50.00

TEMPLE, SHIRLEY

Label & Catalog #		Title	Year	VG+	NM
20th Century TFM-3006	(M)	Shirley Temple Hits	1959	20.00	50.00
		(Original covers of TFM-3006 picture Miss Temple as an adult.)			
20th Century TFM-3006	(M)	Shirley Temple Hits	1961	20.00	50.00
		(Later pressings show Miss Temple as a child on the cover.)			
20th Century TCF-103	(M)	Complete Shirley Temple Songbook (2 LPs)	1961	16.00	40.00
20th Century TFM-3045	(M)	More Little Miss Wonderful	1962	16.00	40.00
20th Century TFM-3102	(M)	The Best Of Shirley Temple	1963	10.00	25.00
		(TFM-3102 is an abridged reissue of 3006.)			

TEMPO, NINO

Label & Catalog #		Title	Year	VG+	NM
Liberty LRP-3023	(M)	Rock 'N Roll Beach Party	1958	30.00	75.00

TEMPO, NINO, & APRIL STEVENS

Label & Catalog #		Title	Year	VG+	NM
Atco 33-156	(M)	Deep Purple	1963	16.00	40.00
Atco SD-33-156	(S)	Deep Purple	1963	20.00	50.00
Atco 33-162	(M)	Nino Tempo & April Stevens Sing The Great Songs	1964	12.00	30.00
Atco SD-33-162	(S)	Nino Tempo & April Stevens Sing The Great Songs	1964	16.00	40.00
Atco 33-180	(M)	Hey Baby	1966	12.00	30.00
Atco SD-33-180	(S)	Hey Baby	1966	16.00	40.00
White Whale WW-113	(M)	All Strung Out	1967	8.00	20.00
White Whale WWS-7113	(S)	All Strung Out	1967	12.00	30.00

TEMPOS, THE

Label & Catalog #		Title	Year	VG+	NM
Justice JLP-104	(M)	Speaking Of The Tempos	1966	250.00	500.00

TEMPREES, THE

Label & Catalog #		Title	Year	VG+	NM
WeProduce 1901	(S)	Love Men	1972	30.00	75.00
WeProduce 1903	(S)	Love Maze	1974	30.00	75.00
WeProduce 1905	(S)	Temprees 3	1974	30.00	75.00

TEMPTATIONS, THE

Label & Catalog #		Title	Year	VG+	NM
Gordy G-911	(M)	Meet The Temptations	1964	12.00	30.00
Gordy GS-911	(S)	Meet The Temptations	1964	16.00	40.00
Gordy G-912	(M)	The Temptations Sing Smokey	1965	12.00	30.00
Gordy GS-912	(S)	The Temptations Sing Smokey	1965	16.00	40.00

The Teen Queen were sisters Betty and Rosie Collins, whose older brother, Aaron, was the lead singer for the rhythm'n blues group The Cadets, who also recorded as The Jacks. Their sole hit on the national pop charts was the "Eddie, My Love," also a smash on the R&B charts. An album was scheduled for release by RPM and then cancelled. The masters ended up with Crown, then a fledgling label wetting its feet with rhythm'n blues albums. Pictured here is the first album, Eddie, My Love, sports an all too typical teen scene on the cover, although its unlikely that many black teenagers would identify with the image. The second album, The Teen Queens, featuring a fabulous Fazzio cover, is an abridged (ten tracks versus twelve) reissue of the earlier title.

Label & Catalog #		Title	Year	VG+	NM
Gordy G-914	(M)	Temptin' Temptations	1965	8.00	20.00
Gordy GS-914	(S)	Temptin' Temptations	1965	10.00	25.00
		("Since I Lost My Baby" is rechanneled on this album.)			
Gordy G-918	(M)	Gettin' Ready	1966	8.00	20.00
Gordy GS-918	(S)	Gettin' Ready	1966	10.00	25.00
Gordy G-919	(M)	The Temptations' Greatest Hits	1966	8.00	20.00
Gordy GS-919	(S)	The Temptations' Greatest Hits	1966	10.00	25.00
		("Since I Lost My Baby" is rechanneled on this album.)			
Gordy G-921	(M)	The Temptations Live	1967	8.00	20.00
Gordy GS-921	(S)	The Temptations Live	1967	10.00	25.00
Gordy G-922	(M)	With A Lot O' Soul	1967	8.00	20.00
Gordy GS-922	(S)	With A Lot O' Soul	1967	10.00	25.00
		— Gordy albums above have "Gordy" in yellow script at the top of the label.—			
Gordy G-924	(M)	In A Mellow Mood	1967	8.00	20.00
Gordy GS-924	(S)	In A Mellow Mood	1967	10.00	25.00
Gordy G-927	(M)	The Temptations Wish It Would Rain	1968	16.00	40.00
		(White label promo)			
Gordy GS-927	(S)	The Temptations Wish It Would Rain	1968	8.00	20.00
Gordy GS-951	(S)	The Temptations' Christmas Card	1969	10.00	25.00

TEMPTATIONS, THE / STEVIE WONDER

Gordy PR-101	(DJ)	The Sky's The Limit / Where I'm Coming From (Sampler)	1971	10.00	25.00

TENNESSEE FARM BAND, THE: Refer to THE FARM BAND

TERRELL, TAMMI
Ms. Terrell also recorded with Marvin Gaye; Chuck Jackson.

Motown MS-652	(S)	Irresistible Tammi	1969	16.00	40.00

TERRY, DON

Columbia CL-6288	(10")	Teen-Age Dance Session	1955	20.00	50.00

TERRY, SONNY
Saunders Terrell aka Sonny Terry was a harmonica player and singer of traditional folk/blues songs. Refer to Big Bill Broonzy; Woody Guthrie / Sonny Terry; Lightnin' Hopkins; Leadbelly / Josh White / Sonny Terry; Pete Seeger; Brother John Sellers & Sonny Terry.

Elektra EKL-14	(10")	Folk Blues	1954	80.00	200.00
Elektra EKL-15	(10")	City Blues (With Alec Stewart)	1954	80.00	200.00
Folkways FP-6	(10")	Sonny Terry's Washboard Band	1950	80.00	200.00
Folkways FA-2006	(10")	Sonny Terry's Washboard Band	1950	80.00	200.00
Folkways FP-35	(10")	Harmonica And Vocal Solos	1952	80.00	200.00
Folkways FA-2035	(10")	Harmonica And Vocal Solos	1952	80.00	200.00
Stinson SLP-55	(10")	Sonny Terry And His Mouth Harp	1950	80.00	200.00
Riverside RLP-644	(M)	Sonny Terry And His Mouth Harp	195?	30.00	75.00
Bluesville BVLP-1025	(M)	Sonny's Story	1961	30.00	75.00
Bluesville BVLP-1059	(M)	Sonny Is King	1963	30.00	75.00
		— Bluesville albums above have bright blue labels with silver print.—			
Bluesville BVLP-1025	(M)	Sonny's Story	1964	10.00	25.00
Bluesville BVLP-1059	(M)	Sonny Is King	1964	10.00	25.00
		— Bluesville albums above have blue labels with a trident logo on the right side.—			

TERRY, SONNY, & BROWNIE McGHEE
The albums below may credit Sonny Terry or Brownie McGhee or both..

Sharp 2003	(M)	Down Home Blues	195?	60.00	150.00
Columbia OL-5240	(M)	Simply Heavenly (Soundtrack)	1957	50.00	100.00
Topic T-29	(M)	Songs	1958	20.00	50.00
Roulette R-25074	(M)	The Folk Songs Of Sonny & Brownie	1959	20.00	50.00
Roulette SR-25074	(S)	The Folk Songs Of Sonny & Brownie	1959	24.00	60.00
World Pacific WP-1294	(M)	Blues Is A Story	1960	14.00	35.00
World Pacific ST-1294	(S)	Blues Is A Story	1960	20.00	50.00
World Pacific WP-1296	(M)	Way Down South Summit Meetin'	1960	14.00	35.00
World Pacific ST-1296	(S)	Way Down South Summit Meetin'	1960	20.00	50.00
Bluesville BVLP-1002	(M)	Down Home Blues	1960	30.00	75.00
Bluesville BVLP-1005	(M)	Blues And Folk	1960	30.00	75.00
Bluesville BVLP-1020	(M)	Blues All Around My Head	1961	30.00	75.00
Bluesville BVLP-1033	(M)	Blues In My Soul	1961	30.00	75.00
Bluesville BVLP-1058	(M)	Live At The Second Fret	1962	30.00	75.00
		— Bluesville albums above have bright blue labels with silver print.—			

Label & Catalog #		Title	Year	VG+	NM
Bluesville BVLP-1002	(M)	**Down Home Blues**	1964	10.00	25.00
Bluesville BVLP-1005	(M)	**Blues And Folk**	1964	10.00	25.00
Bluesville BVLP-1020	(M)	**Blues All Around My Head**	1964	10.00	25.00
Bluesville BVLP-1033	(M)	**Blues In My Soul**	1964	10.00	25.00
Bluesville BVLP-1058	(M)	**Live At The Second Fret**	1964	10.00	25.00
		—Bluesville albums above have blue labels with a trident logo on the right side.—			
Folkways FA-2327	(M)	**Blues And Folksongs**	1960	12.00	30.00
Folkways F-2421	(M)	**Traditional Blues, Volume 1**	1961	12.00	30.00
Folkways FS-2421	(S)	**Traditional Blues, Volume 1**	1961	16.00	40.00
Folkways F-2422	(M)	**Traditional Blues, Volume 2**	1961	12.00	30.00
Folkways FS-2422	(S)	**Traditional Blues, Volume 2**	1961	16.00	40.00
Verve MGV-3008	(M)	**Blues Is My Companion**	1961	30.00	75.00
Washington W-702	(M)	**Talkin' 'Bout The Blues**	1961	20.00	50.00
Fantasy F-3254	(M)	**Sonny Terry & Brownie McGhee** *(Red vinyl)*	1961	40.00	100.00
Fantasy F-3254	(M)	**Sonny Terry & Brownie McGhee**	1961	16.00	40.00
Fantasy F-3296	(M)	**Just A Closer Walk With Thee** *(Red vinyl)*	1962	40.00	100.00
Fantasy F-3296	(M)	**Just A Closer Walk With Thee**	1962	16.00	40.00
Fantasy F-3317	(M)	**Blues & Shouts** *(Red vinyl)*	1962	40.00	100.00
Fantasy F-3317	(M)	**Blues & Shouts**	1962	16.00	40.00
Fantasy F-3340	(M)	**Sonny & Brownie At Sugar Hill** *(Red vinyl)*	1962	40.00	100.00
Fantasy F-3340	(M)	**Sonny & Brownie At Sugar Hill**	196?	16.00	40.00
Fantasy FS-8091	(S)	**Sonny & Brownie At Sugar Hill** *(Blue vinyl)*	1962	60.00	150.00
Fantasy FS-8091	(S)	**Sonny & Brownie At Sugar Hill**	1962	20.00	50.00
Folklore FRLP-14013	(M)	**Down Home Blues**	1964	16.00	40.00
Folklore FRST-14013	(S)	**Down Home Blues**	1964	20.00	50.00
		(Folklore 14013 is a reissue of Bluesville 1002.)			
Verve/Folkways FV-9010	(M)	**Get Together**	1965	10.00	25.00
Verve/Folkways FVS-9010	(S)	**Get Together**	1965	12.00	30.00
Verve/Folkways FV-9019	(M)	**Guitar Highway**	1965	10.00	25.00
Verve/Folkways FVS-9019	(S)	**Guitar Highway**	1965	12.00	30.00
Smash MGS-27067	(M)	**Brownie McGhee At The Bunkhouse**	1965	12.00	30.00
Smash SRS-67067	(S)	**Brownie McGhee At The Bunkhouse**	1965	16.00	40.00
Mainstream M-6049	(M)	**Hometown Blues**	1965	8.00	20.00
Mainstream MS-6049	(S)	**Hometown Blues**	1965	10.00	25.00
Everest 206	(S)	**Sonny Terry**	1968	10.00	25.00
Everest 242	(S)	**Brownie McGhee & Sonny Terry**	1969	10.00	25.00
Fontana SGF-67599	(S)	**Where The Blues Begin**	1969	10.00	25.00

TERRY-THOMAS

London LL-5764	(M)	**Strictly It**	1963	10.00	25.00
Warner Bros. W-1558	(M)	**Terry-Thomas Disovers America**	1964	8.00	20.00
Warner Bros. WS-1558	(S)	**Terry-Thomas Disovers America**	1964	10.00	25.00

TEX, JOE

Checker LP-2993	(M)	**Hold On**	1964	60.00	150.00
King 935	(M)	**The Best Of Joe Tex**	1965	40.00	100.00
King KS-935	(E)	**The Best Of Joe Tex**	1965	30.00	75.00
		—King mono albums above have crownless black labels; stereo albums have crownless blue labels.			
		The logo on the covers have a crown with "King" in open capital block letters below.—			
Parrot PA-61002	(M)	**The Best Of Joe Tex**	1965	20.00	50.00
Parrot PAS-71002	(E)	**The Best Of Joe Tex**	1965	14.00	35.00
Atlantic 8106	(S)	**Hold On To What You've Got**	1965	20.00	50.00
Atlantic SD-8106	(S)	**Hold On To What You've Got**	1965	24.00	60.00
		("Hold On To What You've Got" is rechanneled on this album.)			
Atlantic 8115	(M)	**The New Boss**	1965	20.00	50.00
Atlantic SD-8115	(S)	**The New Boss**	1965	24.00	60.00
Atlantic 8124	(M)	**The Love You Save**	1966	20.00	50.00
Atlantic SD-8124	(S)	**The Love You Save**	1966	24.00	60.00
Atlantic 8133	(M)	**I've Got To Do A Little Better**	1966	20.00	50.00
Atlantic SD-8133	(S)	**I've Got To Do A Little Better**	1966	24.00	60.00
Atlantic 8144	(M)	**The Best Of Joe Tex**	1967	8.00	20.00
Atlantic SD-8144	(S)	**The Best Of Joe Tex**	1967	10.00	25.00
		("Hold On To What You've Got" is rechanneled on this album.)			

TEXAS RUBY

Ms. Ruby also recorded with Curly Fox.

King 840	(M)	**Favorite Songs Of Texas Ruby**	1964	20.00	50.00

Label & Catalog #		Title	Year	VG+	NM
TEXAS TROUBADORS, THE					
The Texas Troubadors are Ernest Tubb's backing group.					
Decca DL-4459	(M)	**The Texas Troubadors**	*1964*	12.00	30.00
Decca DL-74459	(S)	**The Texas Troubadors**	*1964*	16.00	40.00
Decca DL-4644	(M)	**Country Dance Time**	*1965*	12.00	30.00
Decca DL-74644	(S)	**Country Dance Time**	*1965*	16.00	40.00
Decca DL-4745	(M)	**Ernest Tubb's Fabulous Texas Troubadors**	*1966*	10.00	25.00
Decca DL-74745	(S)	**Ernest Tubb's Fabulous Texas Troubadors**	*1966*	12.00	30.00
Decca DL-75017	(S)	**The Terrific Texas Troubadors**	*1968*	10.00	25.00
THAXTON, LLOYD					
Decca DL-4594	(M)	**Lloyd Thaxton Presents**	*1964*	8.00	20.00
Decca DL-74594	(S)	**Lloyd Thaxton Presents**	*1964*	10.00	25.00
THEE MIDNIGHTERS					
Chattahoochee C-1001	(M)	**Thee Midniters**	*1965*	30.00	75.00
Whittier WS-1001	(S)	**Thee Midniters**	*1966*	20.00	50.00
		(Whittier 1001 is a reissue of Chattahoochie 1001.)			
Whittier WS-5000	(S)	**Bring You Love Special Delivery**	*1966*	20.00	50.00
Whittier WS-5001	(S)	**Unlimited**	*1966*	20.00	50.00
Whittier WS-5002	(S)	**Giants**	*1967*	20.00	50.00
THEE MUFFINS					
(No label)	(M)	**Thee Muffins Pop Up!** *(Fan club issue)*	*1967*	80.00	200.00
THEM					
The Parrot recordings feature vocalist Van Morrison.					
Parrot PA-61005	(M)	**Them**	*1965*	30.00	75.00
Parrot PAS-71005	(E)	**Them**	*1965*	24.00	60.00
		(Original covers read "Them Featuring Here Comes The Night.")			
Parrot PA-61005	(M)	**Them**	*1965*	20.00	50.00
Parrot PAS-71005	(E)	**Them**	*1965*	16.00	40.00
		(Later covers read "Them Featuring Gloria.")			
Parrot PA-61008	(M)	**Them Again**	*1966*	20.00	50.00
Parrot PAS-71008	(E)	**Them Again**	*1966*	16.00	40.00
Tower T-5104	(M)	**Now And Them**	*1968*	20.00	50.00
Tower ST-5104	(S)	**Now And Them**	*1968*	24.00	60.00
Tower T-5116	(M)	**Time Out! Time In For Them**	*1968*	24.00	60.00
Tower ST-5116	(S)	**Time Out! Time In For Them**	*1968*	30.00	75.00
Happy Tiger 1004	(S)	**Them**	*1969*	20.00	50.00
Happy Tiger 1012	(S)	**Them In Reality**	*1971*	40.00	100.00
THEODORE					
Coral CRL-757322	(S)	**Coral Records Presents Theodore In Stereo**	*195?*	40.00	100.00
THIN LIZZY					
Thin Lizzy features Phil Lynott.					
London PS-594	(S)	**Thin Lizzy**	*1971*	16.00	40.00
London PS-636	(S)	**Vagabonds Of The Western World**	*1973*	12.00	30.00
THINGS TO COME					
Century 45333	(S)	**Things To Come** *(Recorded in the late '60s)*	*1978*	660.00	1,000.00
THIRD ESTATE, THE					
3rd Estate PPE-LP1000	(S)	**Years Before The Wine**	*197?*	150.00	300.00
THIRD POWER, THE					
Vanguard VSD-6554	(S)	**The Third Power Believe**	*1970*	14.00	35.00
THIRD QUADRANT, THE					
Rock Cottage	(S)	**Seeing Yourself As You Really Are**	*1989*	60.00	150.00
		(Issued in a paper sleeve with a lyric sheet.)			
THIRD RAIL, THE					
Epic LN-24327	(M)	**Id Music**	*1967*	12.00	30.00
Epic BN-26327	(S)	**Id Music**	*1967*	16.00	40.00

Label & Catalog #		Title	Year	VG+	NM

THIRTEENTH FLOOR ELEVATORS, THE
The Elevators feature Roky Erikson.

International Art. 1	(M)	**Psychedelic Sounds**	1967	100.00	250.00
		— Original Int. Art. album above has green & yellow labels.—			
International Art. 1	(M)	**Psychedelic Sounds**	1967	40.00	100.00
International Art. 1	(S)	**Psychedelic Sounds**	1967	30.00	75.00
		("You're Gonna Miss Me" is rechanneled on this album.)			
International Art. 5	(M)	**Easter Everywhere** *(White label promo)*	1967	200.00	400.00
International Art. 5	(M)	**Easter Everywhere**	1967	50.00	125.00
International Art. 5	(S)	**Easter Everywhere**	1967	30.00	75.00
International Art. 8	(S)	**Thirteenth Floor Elevators Live**	1968	30.00	75.00
International Art. 9	(S)	**Bull Of The Woods**	1968	30.00	75.00
		— Original Int. Art. albums above copies were pressed on thick vinyl.—			

31 FLAVORS, THE

Crown CST-592	(S)	**Hair**	1968	20.00	50.00

31ST OF FEBRUARY, THE

Vanguard VSD-6503	(S)	**The 31st Of February**	1969	10.00	25.00

THOMAS, B. J.

Pacemaker PLP-3001	(M)	**B. J. Thomas & The Triumphs**	1965	20.00	50.00
Hickory LPM-133	(M)	**The Very Best Of B. J. Thomas**	1966	10.00	25.00
Hickory LPS-133	(S)	**The Very Best Of B. J. Thomas**	1966	12.00	30.00
Scepter SRM-535	(M)	**I'm So Lonesome I Could Cry**	1966	8.00	20.00
Scepter SPS-535	(S)	**I'm So Lonesome I Could Cry**	1966	10.00	25.00

THOMAS, BENNIE: *Refer to* PEGGY MARCH & BENNIE THOMAS

THOMAS, CARLA
Ms. Thomas also recorded with Otis Redding; Rufus Thomas.

Atlantic 8057	(M)	**Gee Whiz**	1961	40.00	100.00
Atlantic SD-8057	(S)	**Gee Whiz**	1961	60.00	150.00
		—Atlantic albums above have multi-color labels with a white "fan" logo on the right side.—			
Atlantic 8057	(M)	**Gee Whiz**	1961	10.00	25.00
Atlantic SD-8057	(S)	**Gee Whiz**	1961	14.00	35.00
		—Atlantic albums above have multi-color labels with a black "fan" logo on the right side.—			
Atlantic SD-8232	(P)	**The Best Of Carla Thomas**	1969	10.00	25.00
Stax ST-706	(M)	**Comfort Me**	1966	14.00	35.00
Stax STS-706	(S)	**Comfort Me**	1966	20.00	50.00
		("Comfort Me" and "No Time To Lose" are rechanneled on this LP.)			
Stax ST-709	(M)	**Carla**	1966	14.00	35.00
Stax STS-709	(S)	**Carla**	1966	20.00	50.00
Stax ST-718	(M)	**The Queen Alone**	1967	14.00	35.00
Stax STS-718	(S)	**The Queen Alone**	1967	20.00	50.00
Stax STS-2019	(S)	**Memphis Queen**	1969	12.00	30.00
Stax STS-2044	(S)	**Love Means Carla Thomas**	1971	12.00	30.00

THOMAS, IRMA

Imperial LP-9266	(M)	**Wish Someone Would Care**	1964	20.00	50.00
Imperial LP-12266	(S)	**Wish Someone Would Care**	1964	24.00	60.00
Imperial 9302	(M)	**Take A Look**	1966	20.00	50.00
Imperial LP-12302	(S)	**Take A Look**	1966	24.00	60.00
Fungus FB-25150	(S)	**In Between Tears**	1973	14.00	35.00

THOMAS, JEANNE: *Refer to* GOLDMINE'S PRICE GUIDE TO COLLECTIBLE JAZZ ALBUMS

THOMAS, JOE, & BILL ELLIOTT

Sue SLP-1025	(S)	**Speak Your Piece**	1964	20.00	50.00

THOMAS, JON

ABC-Paramount ABC-351	(M)	**Heartbreak**	1960	10.00	25.00
ABC-Paramount ABCS-351	(S)	**Heartbreak**	1960	14.00	35.00
		("Heartbreak" and "Buffalo Blues" are rechanneled on this album.)			

THOMAS, RAY
Thomas is a member of The Moody Blues.

Threshold THSX-102	(DJ)	**Ray Thomas Discusses The Recording Of His First Solo Album**	1975	16.00	40.00

Label & Catalog #		Title	Year	VG+	NM

THOMAS, RUFUS

Stax ST-704	(M)	Walking The Dog	1963	40.00	100.00
Stax STS-2028	(S)	Do The Funky Chicken	1970	10.00	25.00
Stax STS-2039	(S)	Doing The Push And Pull Live At P.J.'s	1971	10.00	25.00
Stax STS-3004	(S)	Did You Heard Me	1972	10.00	25.00
Stax STS-3008	(S)	Crown Prince Of Dance	1973	10.00	25.00

THOMPSON, HANK/HANK THOMPSON & THE BRAZOS VALLEY BOYS
Refer to The Brazos Valley Boys.

Capitol H-418	(10")	Songs Of The Brazos Valley	1953	60.00	150.00
Capitol H-618	(10")	North Of The Rio Grande	1953	60.00	150.00
Capitol H-729	(10")	New Recordings Of Hank's All-Time Hits	1953	60.00	150.00
Capitol H-911	(10")	Hank Thompson Favorites	1953	60.00	150.00
Capitol T-418	(M)	Songs Of The Brazos Valley	1956	40.00	100.00
Capitol T-618	(M)	North Of The Rio Grande	1956	40.00	100.00
Capitol T-729	(M)	New Recordings Of Hank's All-Time Hits	1956	40.00	100.00
Capitol T-826	(M)	Hank!	1957	40.00	100.00
Capitol T-911	(M)	Hank Thompson Favorites	1957	40.00	100.00
Capitol T-975	(M)	Hank Thompson's Dance Ranch	1958	40.00	100.00
		— Capitol albums above have turquoise labels.—			
Capitol T-1111	(M)	Favorite Waltzes	1959	30.00	75.00
Capitol T-1246	(M)	Songs For Rounders	1959	14.00	35.00
Capitol ST-1246	(S)	Songs For Rounders	1959	20.00	50.00
Capitol T-1360	(M)	Most Of All	1960	14.00	30.00
Capitol ST-1360	(S)	Most Of All	1960	20.00	40.00
Capitol T-1469	(M)	This Broken Heart Of Mine	1960	12.00	30.00
Capitol ST-1469	(S)	This Broken Heart Of Mine	1960	16.00	40.00
Capitol T-1544	(M)	An Old Love Affair	1961	10.00	25.00
Capitol ST-1544	(S)	An Old Love Affair	1961	12.00	30.00
Capitol T-1632	(M)	Hank Thompson At The Golden Nugget	1961	10.00	25.00
Capitol ST-1632	(S)	Hank Thompson At The Golden Nugget	1961	12.00	30.00
Capitol T-1741	(M)	The #1 Country & Western Band	1962	12.00	30.00
Capitol DT-1741	(E)	The #1 Country & Western Band	1962	8.00	20.00
		— Capitol albums above have black labels with the logo on the left side.—			
Capitol T-1775	(M)	Cheyenne Frontier Days	1962	8.00	20.00
Capitol ST-1775	(S)	Cheyenne Frontier Days	1962	10.00	25.00
Capitol T-1878	(M)	The Best Of Hank Thompson	1963	8.00	20.00
Capitol ST-1878	(P)	The Best Of Hank Thompson	1963	10.00	25.00
Capitol T-1955	(M)	Hank Thompson At The State Fair Of Texas	1963	10.00	25.00
Capitol DT-1955	(E)	Hank Thompson At The State Fair Of Texas	1963	6.00	15.00
Capitol T-2089	(M)	Golden Country Hits	1964	8.00	20.00
Capitol ST-2089	(S)	Golden Country Hits	1964	10.00	25.00
Capitol T-2154	(M)	It's Christmas Time	1964	8.00	20.00
Capitol ST-2154	(S)	It's Christmas Time	1964	10.00	25.00
Capitol T-2274	(M)	Breakin' In Another Heart	1965	8.00	20.00
Capitol ST-2274	(S)	Breakin' In Another Heart	1965	10.00	25.00
Capitol T-2342	(M)	The Luckiest Heartache In Town	1965	8.00	20.00
Capitol ST-2342	(S)	The Luckiest Heartache In Town	1965	10.00	25.00
Capitol T-2460	(M)	A Six Pack To Go	1966	10.00	25.00
Capitol DT-2460	(E)	A Six Pack To Go	1966	8.00	20.00
Capitol T-2575	(M)	Breakin' The Rules	1966	8.00	20.00
Capitol ST-2575	(S)	Breakin' The Rules	1966	10.00	25.00
Capitol T-2661	(M)	The Best Of Hank Thompson, Volume 2	1967	8.00	20.00
Capitol ST-2661	(S)	The Best Of Hank Thompson, Volume 2	1967	10.00	25.00
Capitol T-2826	(M)	Just An Old Flame	1967	8.00	20.00
Capitol ST-2826	(S)	Just An Old Flame	1967	10.00	25.00
		— Capitol albums above have black labels with the logo on top.—			

THOMPSON, HAYDEN

| Kapp KL-1507 | (M) | Here's Hayden Thompson | 1966 | 14.00 | 35.00 |
| Kapp KS-3507 | (S) | Here's Hayden Thompson | 1966 | 20.00 | 50.00 |

THOMPSON, KAY

| MGM E-3146 | (M) | Kay Thompson | 1954 | 14.00 | 35.00 |
| Signature SM-1017 | (M) | Let's Talk About Russia | 1959 | 10.00 | 25.00 |

THOMPSON, MAYO

| Texas Revolution | (S) | Corky's Debt To His Father | 1969 | 40.00 | 100.00 |

Label & Catalog #		Title	Year	VG+	NM

THOMPSON, SONNY
For additional listings refer to Freddie King & Lula Reed & Sonny Thompson.

King 568	(M)	**Moody Blues**	1956	150.00	400.00
King 655	(M)	**Mellow Blues For The Late Hours**	1959	80.00	200.00

THOMPSON, SUE
Refer to Don Gibson & Sue Thompson.

Hickory LPM-104	(M)	**Meet Sue Thompson**	1962	12.00	30.00
Hickory LPS-104	(S)	**Meet Sue Thompson**	1962	16.00	40.00
Hickory LPM-107	(M)	**Two Of A Kind**	1962	12.00	30.00
Hickory LPS-107	(S)	**Two Of A Kind**	1962	16.00	40.00
Hickory LPM-111	(M)	**Sue Thompson's Golden Hits**	1963	12.00	30.00
Hickory LPS-111	(S)	**Sue Thompson's Golden Hits**	1963	16.00	40.00
Wing MGW-12317	(M)	**The Country Side Of Sue Thompson**	1965	8.00	20.00
Wing SRW-16317	(S)	**The Country Side Of Sue Thompson**	1965	12.00	30.00
Hickory LPM-121	(M)	**Paper Tiger**	1965	8.00	20.00
Hickory LPS-121	(S)	**Paper Tiger**	1965	12.00	30.00
Hickory LPM-130	(M)	**Sue Thompson With Strings Attached**	1966	8.00	20.00
Hickory LPS-130	(S)	**Sue Thompson With Strings Attached**	1966	12.00	30.00
Hickory LPS-148	(S)	**This Is Sue Thompson**	1969	10.00	25.00

THORINSHIELD

Philips PHS-600-251	(S)	**Thorinshield**	1968	10.00	25.00

THORNTON, TERI: *Refer to GOLDMINE'S PRICE GUIDE TO COLLECTIBLE JAZZ ALBUMS*

THREE CHUCKLES, THE
The Three Chuckles feature Teddy Randazzo.

Vik LX-1067	(M)	**The Three Chuckles**	1956	80.00	200.00

THREE DEGREES, THE

Roulette SR-42050	(S)	**Maybe**	1970	16.00	40.00

THREE DOG NIGHT
Three Dog Night features Danny Hutton, Cory Wells and Chuck Negron.

Dunhill DS-50078	(S)	**It Ain't Easy**	1970	50.00	125.00
		(Original covers have the group posing in the buff.)			
Dunhill DSD-50168	(S)	**Hard Labor**	1974	20.00	50.00
		("First-state delivery cover." Original covers depict a hospital delivery with a female creature giving birth to a record album.)			

THREE FLAMES, THE

Mercury MG-20239	(M)	**At The Bon Soir**	1957	20.00	50.00

THREE MAN ARMY

Kama Sutra SKBS-2044	(S)	**A Third Of A Lifetime** *(Gatefold cover)*	1971	12.00	30.00
Reprise MS-2150	(S)	**Three Man Army**	1973	10.00	25.00
Reprise MS-2182	(S)	**Three Man Army Two**	1974	10.00	25.00

THREE SOUNDS, THE: *Refer to GOLDMINE'S PRICE GUIDE TO COLLECTIBLE JAZZ ALBUMS*

THREE STOOGES, THE
The Stooges are Moe, Larry, Curly, Shemp and Curly Joe. Refer to Francis Langford .

Coral CRL-57289	(M)	**The Nonsense Songbook**	1959	40.00	100.00
Coral CRL-757289	(S)	**The Nonsense Songbook**	1959	60.00	150.00
Golden GLP-43	(M)	**Madcap Musical Nonsense**	1959	40.00	100.00
Columbia CL-1650	(M)	**Snow White & The Three Stooges** *(Sdtk)*	1961	20.00	50.00
Columbia CS-8450	(S)	**Snow White & The Three Stooges** *(Sdtk)*	1961	30.00	75.00
Vocalion VL-73823	(S)	**The Three Stooges Sing For Kids**	1968	10.00	25.00
		(Vocalion 73823 is a repackage of Coral 757289.)			

THREE SUNS, THE

Varsity VLP-6001	(10")	**Twilight Time**	1950	20.00	50.00
Varsity VLP-6048	(10")	**Midnight Time**	1950	20.00	50.00
Royale 1	(10")	**Twilight Time**	1951	20.00	50.00
Royale 29	(10")	**Midnight Time**	1951	20.00	50.00
RCA Victor LPM-3	(10")	**Three-Quarter Time**	1951	20.00	50.00
RCA Victor LPM-20	(10")	**Hands Across The Table**	1951	20.00	50.00
RCA Victor LPM-52	(10")	**Christmas Favorites**	1951	20.00	50.00

Label & Catalog #		Title	Year	VG+	NM
RCA Victor LPM-3012	(10")	Twilight Moods	1952	20.00	50.00
RCA Victor LPM-3034	(10")	The Three Suns Present	1952	20.00	50.00
RCA Victor LPM-3040	(10")	Busy Fingers	1952	20.00	50.00
RCA Victor LPM-3056	(10")	Christmas Party	1952	20.00	50.00
RCA Victor LPM-3075	(10")	Slumbertime	1952	20.00	50.00
RCA Victor LPM-3113	(10")	Pop Concert Favorites	1953	20.00	50.00
RCA Victor LPM-3125	(10")	Mods	1953	20.00	50.00
RCA Victor LPM-3130	(10")	Top Pops	1953	20.00	50.00
RCA Victor LPM-3146	(10")	Polka Time	1953	20.00	50.00
RCA Victor LPM-3174	(10")	Sacred Hymns	1953	20.00	50.00
RCA Victor LPM-1041	(M)	Soft And Sweet	1955	12.00	30.00
RCA Victor LPM-1132	(M)	Sounds Of Christmas	1955	12.00	30.00
RCA Victor LPM-1171	(M)	Twilight Time	1956	12.00	30.00
RCA Victor LPM-1173	(M)	My Reverie	1956	12.00	30.00
RCA Victor LPM-1219	(M)	Slumber Time	1956	12.00	30.00
RCA Victor LPM-1220	(M)	Malaguena	1956	12.00	30.00
RCA Victor LPM-1249	(M)	High Fi And Wide	1956	12.00	30.00
RCA Victor LPM-1316	(M)	Easy Listening	1956	12.00	30.00
RCA Victor LPM-1333	(M)	Midnight For Two	1957	12.00	30.00
RCA Victor LPM-1543	(M)	The Things In Love In Hi-Fi	1958	8.00	20.00
RCA Victor LSP-1543	(S)	The Things In Love In Hi-Fi	1958	12.00	30.00
RCA Victor LPM-1578	(M)	Let's Dance With The Three Suns	1958	8.00	20.00
RCA Victor LSP-1578	(S)	Let's Dance With The Three Suns	1958	12.00	30.00
RCA Victor LPM-1669	(M)	Love In The Afternoon	1959	8.00	20.00
RCA Victor LSP-1669	(S)	Love In The Afternoon	1959	12.00	30.00
RCA Victor LPM-1734	(M)	Having A Ball With The Three Suns	1959	8.00	20.00
RCA Victor LSP-1734	(S)	Having A Ball With The Three Suns	1959	12.00	30.00
RCA Victor LPM-1964	(M)	Swingin' On A Star	1959	8.00	20.00
RCA Victor LSP-1964	(S)	Swingin' On A Star	1959	12.00	30.00
RCA Victor LPM-2054	(M)	A Ding Dong Daddy Christmas	1959	8.00	20.00
RCA Victor LSP-2054	(S)	A Ding Dong Daddy Christmas	1959	12.00	30.00
RCA Victor LPM-2120	(M)	Twilight Memories	1960	8.00	20.00
RCA Victor LSP-2120	(S)	Twilight Memories	1960	10.00	25.00
RCA Victor LPM-2235	(M)	On A Magic Carpet	1960	8.00	20.00
RCA Victor LSP-2235	(S)	On A Magic Carpet	1960	10.00	25.00
RCA Victor LPM-2307	(M)	Dancing On A Cloud	1961	8.00	20.00
RCA Victor LSP-2307	(S)	Dancing On A Cloud	1961	10.00	25.00
RCA Victor LPM-2310	(M)	Fever And Smoke	1961	8.00	20.00
RCA Victor LSP-2310	(S)	Fever And Smoke	1961	10.00	25.00
RCA Victor LPM-2437	(M)	Fun In The Sun	1961	8.00	20.00
RCA Victor LSP-2437	(S)	Fun In The Sun	1961	10.00	25.00
RCA Victor LPM-2532	(M)	Movin' 'N' Groovin'	1962	8.00	20.00
RCA Victor LPM-2532	(S)	Movin' 'N' Groovin'	1962	10.00	25.00
RCA Victor LPM-2617	(M)	Warm And Tender	1962	8.00	20.00
RCA Victor LPM-2617	(S)	Warm And Tender	1962	10.00	25.00

— RCA mono albums above have "Long Play" on the bottom of the label;
stereo albums have "Living Stereo" on the bottom.—

THRILLINGTON, PERCY "THRILLS"
Thrills Thrillington is a pseudonym for Paul McCartney.

Capitol ST-11642	(S)	Thrillington	1977	60.00	150.00

THUNDER, JOHNNY

Diamond D-5001	(M)	Loop De Loop	1963	30.00	75.00
Diamond SD-5001	(S)	Loop De Loop	1963	50.00	125.00

THUNDERBIRDS, THE

Red Feather TH-1	(M)	Meet The Fabulous Thunderbirds	196?	80.00	200.00

THUNDERCLAP NEWMAN: *Refer to* PETE TOWNSHEND

THUNDERPUSSY

M.R.T. RL-31748	(S)	Document Of Captivity	1973	60.00	150.00

TIDE, THE

Mouth 7237	(S)	Almost Live	196?	20.00	50.00

Two albums pictured here are two releases from Mainstream, Tangerine Zoo's Outside Looking In, *and The Tiffany Shade's eponymous album, both examples of major label albums that were laughed at a few years ago but have collectors rethinking their positions on "mainstream" psych albums.*

Label & Catalog #		Title	Year	VG+	NM
TIDES, THE					
Wing MGW-12265	(M)	**Surf City And Other Surfin' Favorites**	1963	10.00	25.00
Wing SRW-16265	(S)	**Surf City And Other Surfin' Favorites**	1963	12.00	30.00
TIEKIN, FREDDIE, & THE ROCKERS					
I.T. 2301	(M)	**By Popular Demand**	1957	20.00	50.00
I.T. 2304	(M)	**Freddie Tieken & The Rockers**	1958	20.00	50.00
TIFFANY SHADE					
Mainstream 56105	(S)	**Tiffany Shade**	1969	20.00	50.00
TIKIS, THE					
Minaret TLP-7001	(M)	**The Tikis**	196?	20.00	50.00
Philips PHM-200-043	(M)	**The Tikis**	1962	10.00	25.00
Philips PHS-600-043	(S)	**The Tikis**	1962	14.00	35.00
TILLIS, MEL/MEL TILLIS & THE STATESIDERS					
Columbia CL-1724	(M)	**Heart Over Mind (& Other Big Country Hits)**	1962	12.00	30.00
Columbia CS-8524	(S)	**Heart Over Mind (& Other Big Country Hits)**	1962	16.00	40.00
— Columbia albums above have six white-on-black "eye" logos around the perimeter of the label.—					
TILLMAN, FLOYD					
RCA Victor LPM-1686	(M)	**Floyd Tillman's Best**	1958	30.00	75.00
Sims LP-110	(M)	**Slippin' Around**	196?	30.00	75.00
Cimarron C-2003	(M)	**Let's Make Memories**	1962	30.00	75.00
Harmony HL-7316	(M)	**Floyd Tillman's Best**	1964	10.00	25.00
Starday SLP-310	(M)	**Let's Make Memories** *(Yellow label)*	1965	16.00	40.00
		(Starday 310 is a reissue of Cimarron 2003.)			
Musicor MM-2136	(M)	**Floyd Tillman's Country**	1967	8.00	20.00
Musicor MS-3136	(S)	**Floyd Tillman's Country**	1967	10.00	25.00
Musicor MS-3157	(S)	**Dream On**	1968	8.00	20.00
Harmony HS-11297	(S)	**I'll Still Be Loving You**	1969	10.00	25.00
TILLOTSON, JOHNNY					
Cadence CLP-3052	(M)	**Johnny Tillotson's Best**	1961	14.00	35.00
Cadence CLP-25052	(S)	**Johnny Tillotson's Best**	1961	20.00	50.00
		("Dreamy Eyes," "True, True Happiness," and "Without You"			
		are rechanneled on this album.)			
Cadence CLP-3058	(M)	**It Keeps Right On A-Hurtin'**	1962	14.00	35.00
Cadence CLP-25058	(S)	**It Keeps Right On A-Hurtin'**	1962	20.00	50.00
Cadence CLP-3067	(M)	**You Can Never Stop Me Loving You**	1963	12.00	30.00
Cadence CLP-25067	(S)	**You Can Never Stop Me Loving You**	1963	16.00	40.00
		("Lonesome Town," "Donna," "I Got A Feelin'," "Where Is She?,"			
		"Venus" and "Come Softly To Me" are rechanneled on this album.)			
MGM E-4188	(M)	**Talk Back Trembling Lips**	1964	8.00	20.00
MGM SE-4188	(S)	**Talk Back Trembling Lips**	1964	10.00	25.00
MGM E-4224	(M)	**The Tillotson Touch**	1964	8.00	20.00
MGM SE-4224	(S)	**The Tillotson Touch**	1964	10.00	25.00
MGM E-4270	(M)	**She Understands Me**	1964	8.00	20.00
MGM SE-4270	(S)	**She Understands Me**	1964	10.00	25.00
MGM E-4302	(M)	**That's My Style**	1965	8.00	20.00
MGM SE-4302	(S)	**That's My Style**	1965	10.00	25.00
MGM E-4328	(M)	**Our World**	1965	8.00	20.00
MGM SE-4328	(S)	**Our World**	1965	10.00	25.00
MGM E-4395	(M)	**No Love At All**	1966	8.00	20.00
MGM SE-4395	(S)	**No Love At All**	1966	10.00	25.00
MGM E-4402	(M)	**The Christmas Touch**	1966	8.00	20.00
MGM SE-4402	(S)	**The Christmas Touch**	1966	10.00	25.00
MGM E-4452	(M)	**Here I Am**	1967	8.00	20.00
MGM SE-4452	(S)	**Here I Am**	1967	10.00	25.00
		— MGM albums above have black labels.—			
TIMBER CREEK					
Renegade JAH-95014	(S)	**Hellbound Highway**	1975	60.00	150.00
TIMOTHY					
Pear	(S)	**Strange But True**	1972	80.00	200.00

The original Tokens of the mid '50s were a white doo wop group featuring Hank Medress and a pre-Julliard Neil Sedaka. By 1961 the group consisted of Medress with Jay Siegel and the Margo brothers, Mitch and Phil. "The Lion Sleeps Tonight," was a highly stylized pop arrangement of a traditional South African chant of the Zulu tribe previously a favorite in the folkie community. The Wheels album (below) is highly sought-after by collectors of vocal car songs, automotive buffs and, of course, The Tokens' fans. . .

Label & Catalog #		Title	Year	VG+	NM
TINO & THE REVLONS					
Dearborn 1004	(M)	**By Request At The Sway-Zee**	1966	150.00	300.00
TIPTON, CARL					
Sims LP-143	(M)	**The Carl Tipton Show**	196?	20.00	50.00
TITANS, THE					
MGM E-3992	(M)	**Today's Teen Beat**	1961	12.00	30.00
MGM SE-3992	(S)	**Today's Teen Beat**	1961	16.00	40.00
TITUS OATES					
(No label)	(S)	**Jungle Lady**	197?	60.00	150.00
TOAD					
Hallelujah	(S)	**Toad**	1968	150.00	300.00
TOAD HALL					
Liberty LST-7580	(S)	**Toad Hall**	1968	10.00	25.00
TOADS, THE					
Wiggins 64021	(M)	**The Toads**	1964	150.00	300.00
TOADS, THE					
Rite	(M)	**The Toads**	196?	60.00	150.00
TODD, DYLAN					
Judson J-3010	(M)	**Love Songs, Old And New**	195?	12.00	30.00
TOKENS, THE					
Refer to Neil Sedaka & The Tokens.					
RCA Victor LPM-2514	(M)	**The Lion Sleeps Tonight**	1961	30.00	75.00
RCA Victor LSP-2514	(S)	**The Lion Sleeps Tonight**	1961	60.00	150.00
RCA Victor LPM-2631	(M)	**We, The Tokens, Sing Folk**	1962	16.00	40.00
RCA Victor LSP-2631	(S)	**We, The Tokens, Sing Folk**	1962	20.00	50.00
		— RCA mono albums above have "Long Play" on the bottom of the label; stereo albums have "Living Stereo" on the bottom.—			
RCA Victor LPM-2886	(M)	**Wheels**	1964	30.00	75.00
RCA Victor LST-2886	(S)	**Wheels**	1964	40.00	100.00
RCA Victor LPM-3685	(M)	**The Tokens Again**	1966	12.00	30.00
RCA Victor LSP-3685	(S)	**The Tokens Again**	1966	16.00	40.00
Diplomat D-2308	(M)	**Kings Of The Hot Rods**	196?	10.00	25.00
Diplomat DS-2308	(S)	**Kings Of The Hot Rods**	196?	12.00	30.00
Warner Bros. W-1685	(M)	**It's A Happening World**	1966	8.00	20.00
Warner Bros. WS-1685	(S)	**It's A Happening World**	1966	10.00	25.00
B.T. Puppy BTP-1000	(M)	**I Hear Trumpets Blow**	1966	8.00	20.00
B.T. Puppy BTPS-1000	(P)	**I Hear Trumpets Blow**	1966	10.00	25.00
B.T. Puppy BTPS-1006	(S)	**Tokens Of Gold**	1969	14.00	35.00
B.T. Puppy BTPS-1012	(S)	**Greatest Moments**	1970	14.00	35.00
B.T. Puppy BTPS-1014	(S)	**December 5th**	1971	14.00	35.00
B.T. Puppy BTPS-10??	(S)	**Intercourse**	1971		*See below*
		("Intercourse" is so rare that it bares a suggestive value of $1,000-2,000 in virtually any playable condition!)			
TOLBERT, ISRAEL					
Warren STS-2038	(S)	**Popper Stopper**	1971	16.00	40.00
TOM & JERRY					
Charlie Tomlinson and Jerry Kennedy. Refer to Tomlinson & Baker.					
Mercury MG-20626	(M)	**Guitar's Greatest Hits**	1961	8.00	20.00
Mercury SR-60626	(S)	**Guitar's Greatest Hits**	1961	12.00	30.00
Mercury MG-20671	(M)	**Guitars Play The Sound Of Ray Charles**	1962	8.00	20.00
Mercury SR-60671	(S)	**Guitars Play The Sound Of Ray Charles**	1962	12.00	30.00
Mercury MG-20756	(M)	**Guitar's Greatest Hits, Volume 2**	1962	8.00	20.00
Mercury SR-60756	(S)	**Guitar's Greatest Hits, Volume 2**	1962	12.00	30.00
Mercury MG-20842	(M)	**Surfin' Hootenanny**	1963	12.00	30.00
Mercury SR-60842	(S)	**Surfin' Hootenanny**	1963	16.00	40.00

Label & Catalog #		Title	Year	VG+	NM
TOMMY & THE TWISTERS					
Regent MG-6104	(M)	**Let's All Do The Twist**	1961	12.00	30.00
TOMORROW					
Tomorrow features Steve Howe and Twink.					
Sire SES-97912	(S)	**Tomorrow**	1968	16.00	40.00
		("My White Bicycle" and "Revolution" are rechanneled.)			
TONEY, OSCAR, JR.					
Bell 6006	(M)	**For Your Precious Love**	1967	10.00	25.00
Bell S-6006	(S)	**For Your Precious Love**	1967	12.00	30.00
TONGUE					
Hemisphere HIS-101	(S)	**Tongue**	197?	30.00	75.00
TONGUE & GROOVE					
Fontana SRF-67593	(S)	**Tongue & Groove Featuring Lynn Hughes**	1968	12.00	30.00
TONTO'S EXPANDING HEAD BAND					
Embryo SD-732	(S)	**Zero Time**	1971	12.00	30.00
TOP DRAWER					
Wish Bone 721207	(S)	**Solid Oak**	197?	200.00	400.00
TOPSIDERS, THE					
Josie J-4000	(M)	**Rock Goes Folk**	1963	8.00	20.00
Josie JS-4000	(S)	**Rock Goes Folk**	1963	10.00	25.00
TORAK, MITCHELL					
Guyden T-502	(M)	**Caribbean**	1960	10.00	25.00
Guyden ST-502	(S)	**Caribbean**	1960	12.00	30.00
Reprise R-6223	(M)	**Guitar Course** *(Instructional album)*	1966	8.00	20.00
Reprise RS-6223	(S)	**Guitar Course** *(Instructional album)*	1966	10.00	25.00
TORME, MEL: *Refer to* GOLDMINE'S PRICE GUIDE TO COLLECTIBLE JAZZ ALBUMS					
TORMENTORS, THE					
Royal RLP-111	(M)	**Hanging Around**	196?	80.00	200.00
TORNADOES, THE					
This Tornadoes also recorded 45s as The Hollywood Tornadoes.					
Josie J-4005	(M)	**Bustin' Surfboards**	1963	60.00	150.00
Josie JS-4005	(S)	**Bustin' Surfboards**	1963	80.00	200.00
TORNADOS, THE					
London LL-3279	(M)	**Telstar**	1962	60.00	150.00
London LL-3293	(M)	**The Sounds Of The Tornados**	1963	80.00	200.00
		(London 3293 is a repackage of 3279 with two additional tracks.)			
TORQUES, THE					
Wiggins 64010	(M)	**Zoom!**	1967	80.00	200.00
Lemco 604	(M)	**The Torques Live**	1968	60.00	150.00
TOSSI, AARON					
Prestige Int. PRLP-13027	(M)	**Folk Songs And Ballads**	1962	12.00	30.00
TOTTY					
Our First BT-205	(S)	**Totty**	197?	50.00	125.00
Our First OFRO-2	(S)	**Totty Too**	1981	12.00	30.00
TOUCH					
Mainline PS-70-116-7	(S)	**Street Suite**	197?	660.00	1,000.00
TOUCHSTONE					
Touchstone features Tom Constanten of The Grateful Dead.					
United Arts. UAS-5563	(S)	**Tarot**	1972	12.00	30.00

Label & Catalog #		Title	Year	VG+	NM
TOUCHSTONE					
(No label)	(S)	**Touchstone**	1979	150.00	300.00
TOUSSAINT, ALLEN					
RCA Victor LPM-1767	(M)	**The Wild Sound Of New Orleans**	1958	80.00	200.00
TOWER, THE					
Other World OUR-1001	(S)	**The Tower**	1975	16.00	40.00
TOWER OF POWER					
San Francisco 204	(S)	**East Bay Grease**	1971	20.00	50.00
TOWNSEND, ED					
Capitol T-1140	(M)	**New In Town**	1959	8.00	20.00
Capitol ST-1140	(S)	**New In Town**	1959	10.00	25.00
Capitol T-1214	(M)	**Glad To Be Here**	1959	8.00	20.00
Capitol ST-1214	(S)	**Glad To Be Here**	1959	10.00	25.00
TOWNSEND, HENRY					
Bluesville BVLP-1041	(M)	**Tired Bein' Mistreated**	1962	30.00	75.00
		—Bluesville albums above have bright blue labels with silver print.—			
Bluesville BVLP-1041	(M)	**Tired Bein' Mistreated**	1964	10.00	25.00
		—Bluesville albums above have blue labels with a trident logo on the right side.—			
TOWNSHEND, PETE					
Townshend is a member of The Who. Refer to Thunderclap Newman.					
Track PR-A-160	(DJ)	**Pete Townshend Talks To**			
		& About Thunderclap Newman (One-sided)1970		30.00	75.00
Track 79189	(S)	**Who Came First** (With poster)	1972	10.00	25.00
Track 79189	(S)	**Who Came First** (Without poster)	1972	6.00	15.00
TOYS, THE					
DynoVoice 9002	(M)	**A Lovers Concerto/Attack**	1966	16.00	40.00
DynoVoice 9002-S	(S)	**A Lovers Concerto/Attack**	1966	20.00	50.00
		("A Lover's Concerto," "Attack," "I Got A Man" and "This Night" are rechanneled.)			
TRADEWINDS, THE					
The Tradewinds were Pete Anders and Vinnie Poncia.					
Kama Sutra KLP-8057	(M)	**Excursions**	1967	10.00	25.00
Kama Sutra KLPS-8057	(S)	**Excursions**	1967	12.00	30.00
TRAFFIC					
Traffic was origianlly Steve Winwood with Jim Capaldi, Dave Mason and Chris Wood.					
United Arts. UAS-6651	(S)	**Heaven Is In Your Mind**	1969	20.00	50.00
United Arts. UAS-6651	(S)	**Mr. Fantasy**	1969	14.00	35.00
		("Mr. Fantasy" is a reissue of "Heaven Is In Your Mind." First pressing reissues have the original back covers with "Heaven Is In Your Mind" across the top.)			
United Arts. UAS-6651	(S)	**Mr. Fantasy**	1969	10.00	25.00
		(Second pressing reissues have a green strip across the top of the back cover listing the album's songs.)			
		—United Arts. albums above have black labels.—			
TRAILER, REX, & THE PLAYBOYS					
Crown CLP-5158	(M)	**Country & Western**	196?	10.00	25.00
TRAMLINE					
A&M SP-4208	(S)	**Somewhere Down The Line**	197?	10.00	25.00
TRAMMELL, BOBBY LEE					
Atlanta 1503	(M)	**Arkansas Twist** (Black label)	1962	350.00	800.00
TRANSIENTS, THE					
Horizon T-1633	(M)	**Funky Twelve String**	1963	8.00	20.00
Horizon ST-1633	(S)	**Funky Twelve String**	1963	10.00	25.00

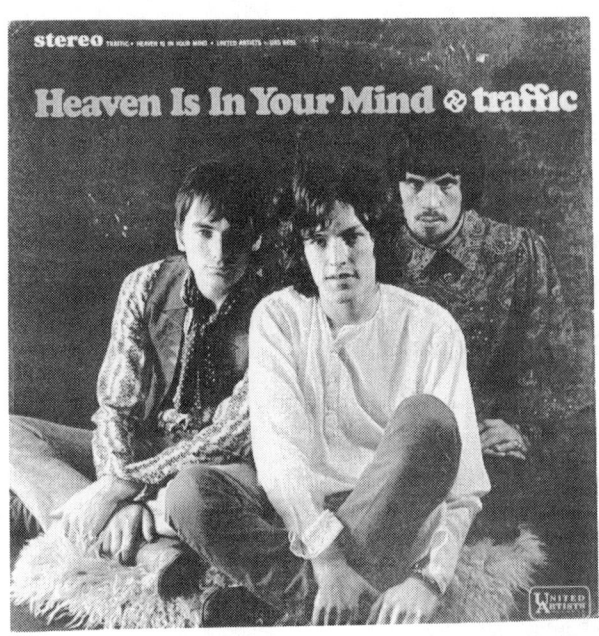

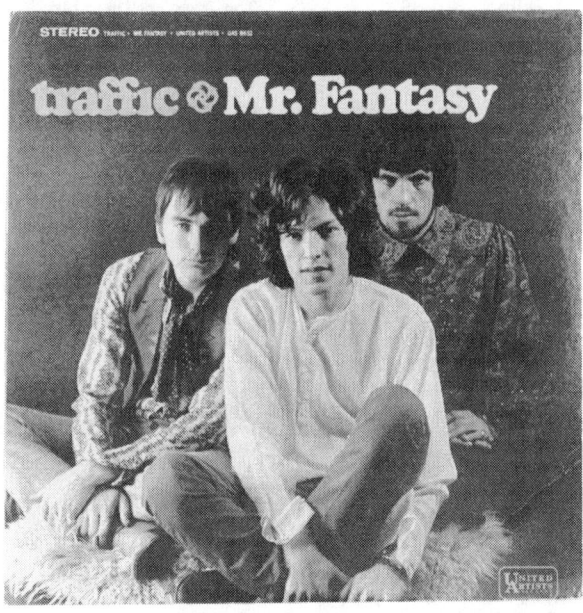

Pictured here is the first pressing for Traffic's first album, initially titled Heaven Is In Your Mind, *after its original UK counterpart, and its more popular incarnation as* Mr. Fantasy.

Label & Catalog #		Title	Year	VG+	NM
TRASHMEN, THE					
Garrett GA-200	(M)	**Surfin' Bird**	1964	80.00	200.00
Garrett GAS-200	(E)	**Surfin' Bird**	1964	150.00	300.00
TRASK, DIANA					
Columbia CL-1601	(M)	**Diana Trask**	1961	10.00	25.00
Columbia CS-8401	(S)	**Diana Trask**	1961	14.00	35.00
Columbia CL-1705	(M)	**Diana Trask On TV**	1961	10.00	25.00
Columbia CS-8505	(S)	**Diana Trask On TV**	1961	14.00	35.00
— *Columbia albums above have six white-on-black "eye" logos around the perimeter of the label.* —					
TRAUBEL, HELEN					
Columbia ML-4221	(M)	**Negro Spirituals And Ballads**	195?	12.00	30.00
TRAVEL AGENCY, THE					
Viva V-36017	(S)	**Viva**	1969	10.00	25.00
TRAVELLERS, THE					
Kapp KL-1051	(M)	**Journey With The Travellers**	1960	10.00	25.00
Kapp KS-3051	(S)	**Journey With The Travellers**	1960	2.00	30.00
TRAVELERS THREE, THE					
The Travelers Three are a vocal and instrumental folk-based pop group.					
Elektra EKL-216	(M)	**The Travelers Three**	1962	8.00	20.00
Elektra EKS-7216	(S)	**The Travelers Three**	1962	10.00	25.00
Elektra EKL-226	(M)	**Open House**	1962	8.00	20.00
Elektra EKS-7226	(S)	**Open House**	1962	10.00	25.00
Elektra EKL-236	(M)	**The Travelers Three Live, Live, Live**	1963	8.00	20.00
Elektra EKS-7236	(S)	**The Travelers Three Live, Live, Live**	1963	10.00	25.00
TRAVIS, MERLE					
Refer to Chet Atkins; Badlands.					
Capitol T-650	(M)	**The Merle Travis Guitar** *(Turquoise label)*	1956	40.00	100.00
Capitol T-891	(M)	**Back Home** *(Gray label)*	1957	30.00	75.00
Capitol T-1391	(M)	**Walkin' The Strings**	1960	30.00	75.00
Capitol T-1664	(M)	**Travis**	1962	14.00	35.00
Capitol ST-1664	(S)	**Travis**	1962	20.00	50.00
— *Capitol albums above have black labels with the logo on the left side.* —					
Capitol T-1956	(M)	**Songs Of The Coal Mines**	1963	12.00	30.00
Capitol ST-1956	(S)	**Songs Of The Coal Mines**	1963	16.00	40.00
Capitol T-2662	(M)	**The Best Of Merle Travis**	1967	10.00	25.00
Capitol ST-2662	(P)	**The Best Of Merle Travis**	1967	12.00	30.00
Capitol ST-2938	(S)	**Strictly Guitar**	1969	12.00	30.00
— *Capitol albums above have black labels with the logo on top.* —					
TRAVIS, MERLE, & JOE MAPHIS					
Refer to Joe Maphis.					
Capitol T-2102	(M)	**Merle Travis And Joe Maphis**	1964	16.00	40.00
Capitol ST-2102	(S)	**Merle Travis And Joe Maphis**	1964	20.00	50.00
TREES, THE					
Pomegranate TR-751	(S)	**The Christ Tree**	1975	20.00	50.00
TREMELOES, THE					
Refer to Brian Poole & the Tremeloes.					
Epic LN-24310	(M)	**Here Comes My Baby**	1967	12.00	30.00
Epic BN-26310	(E)	**Here Comes My Baby**	1967	8.00	20.00
Epic LN-24326	(M)	**Even The Bad Times Are Good**	1967	8.00	20.00
Epic BN-26326	(P)	**Even The Bad Times Are Good**	1967	12.00	30.00
Epic LN-24363	(M)	**Suddenly You Love Me**	1968	12.00	30.00
Epic BN-26363	(E)	**Suddenly You Love Me**	1968	8.00	20.00
Epic BN-26388	(S)	**World Explosion '58/'68**	1968	12.00	30.00
TRENIERS, THE					
Epic LG-3125	(M)	**The Treniers On TV**	1955	60.00	150.00
Dot DLP-3257	(M)	**Souvenir Album**	1960	40.00	100.00
Hermitage H-1002	(M)	**After Hours**	196?	20.00	50.00
Hermitage HS-1002	(S)	**After Hours**	196?	30.00	75.00

Diana Trask's first album above bears a silver sticker on the cover with a star that reads "A New Star On Columbia Records." This was affixed copies of debut albums used promotionally (the label may be white or be a stock red with a sticker) for several years. While this generally has little affect on the record's value for most artists, it can place a premium on some, such as Dylan's first. Her second album teams her with producer and then hot television host Mitch Miller's singers (and features a much more flattering photo of the singer).

Label & Catalog #		Title	Year	VG+	NM

TREVOR, JEANNIE: *Refer to* GOLDMINE'S PRICE GUIDE TO COLLECTIBLE JAZZ ALBUMS

TRIGGER, VIC
| Sanctuary 12103 | (S) | Electronic Wizzard | 1977 | 40.00 | 100.00 |

TRIMBLE, BOBB
| Vengeance BT-8458 | (S) | Iron Curtain Dream | 1980 | 660.00 | 1,000.00 |
| (No label) | (S) | Harvest Of Dreams | 1982 | 60.00 | 150.00 |

TRIPSICHORD MUSIC BOX, THE
| Janus JLS-3016 | (S) | The Tripsichord Music Box | 1971 | 60.00 | 150.00 |

TRIZO-50
| Cavern Custom 740142 | (S) | Cavern-50 | 197? | 150.00 | 300.00 |

TROGGS, THE
Atco 33-193	(M)	Wild Thing	1966	20.00	50.00
Atco SD-33-193	(E)	Wild Thing	1966	16.00	40.00
Fontana MGF-27556	(M)	The Troggs	1966	16.00	40.00
Fontana SRF-67556	(E)	The Troggs	1966	12.00	30.00
		(Atco 193 and Fontana 2/57556 are the same album.)			
Fontana SRF-67576	(E)	Love Ia All Around	1968	10.00	25.00

TROLL
| Smash SRS-67114 | (S) | Animated Music | 1969 | 10.00 | 25.00 |

TROUP, BOBBY: *Refer to* GOLDMINE'S PRICE GUIDE TO COLLECTIBLE JAZZ ALBUMS

TROY, BO
| Diplomat D-2304 | (M) | Wild Hot Rod Wails | 196? | 8.00 | 20.00 |
| Diplomat DS-2304 | (S) | Wild Hot Rod Wails | 196? | 10.00 | 25.00 |

TROY, DORIS
Atlantic 8088	(M)	Just One Look	1964	14.00	35.00
Atlantic SD-8088	(S)	Just One Look	1964	20.00	50.00
		("Just One Look" is rechanneled)			
Apple ST-3371	(S)	Doris Troy	1970	10.00	25.00
		(Features George Harrison on guitar and Ringo Starr on drums.)			

TRUE ENDEAVOR JUG BAND, THE
| Folklore FRLP-14022 | (M) | The Art Of The Jug Band | 1964 | 8.00 | 20.00 |
| Folklore FRST-14022 | (S) | The Art Of The Jug Band | 1964 | 10.00 | 25.00 |

TRUMAN, MARGARET
| RCA Victor LPM-57 | (10") | American Songs | 1951 | 20.00 | 50.00 |

TRUMPETEERS, THE
| Score SLP-4021 | (M) | Milky White Way | 1956 | 150.00 | 300.00 |
| Grand 7701 | (M) | The Last Supper | 195? | 40.00 | 100.00 |

TRUTH & JANEY
| Montrose | (S) | No Rest For The Wicked | 197? | 30.00 | 75.00 |
| Bee Bee 711X98 | (S) | Just A Little Bit Of Magic | 197? | 16.00 | 40.00 |

T2
| London PS-583 | (S) | It'll All Work Out In Boomland | 1971 | 20.00 | 50.00 |

TUBB, ERNEST/ERNEST TUBB & THE TEXAS TROUBADORS
Refer to Red Foley; The Texas Troubadors..
Decca DL-5301	(10")	Ernest Tubb Favorites	1951	60.00	150.00
Decca DL-5334	(10")	Old Rugged Cross	1951	60.00	150.00
Decca DL-5336	(10")	Jimmie Rodgers Songs	1951	60.00	150.00
Decca DL-5497	(10")	Sing A Song Of Christmas	1954	60.00	150.00
Decca DL-8291	(M)	Ernest Tubb Favorites	1956	30.00	75.00
Decca DL-8553	(M)	The Daddy Of 'Em All	1956	30.00	75.00
Decca DL-8834	(M)	The Importance Of Being Ernest	1959	20.00	50.00
Decca DL-78834	(S)	The Importance Of Being Ernest	1959	30.00	75.00
		— Decca albums above have black & silver labels.—			

Label & Catalog #		Title	Year	VG+	NM
Decca DL-4042	(M)	**Record Shop**	1960	14.00	35.00
Decca DL-74042	(S)	**Record Shop**	1960	20.00	50.00
Decca DL-4046	(M)	**All Time Hits**	1961	12.00	30.00
Decca DL-74046	(S)	**All Time Hits**	1961	16.00	40.00
Decca DL-4118	(M)	**Ernest Tubb's Golden Favorites**	1961	12.00	30.00
Decca DL-74118	(S)	**Ernest Tubb's Golden Favorites**	1961	16.00	40.00
Decca DL-4321	(M)	**On Tour**	1962	12.00	30.00
Decca DL-74321	(S)	**On Tour**	1962	16.00	40.00
Decca DL-4385	(M)	**Just Call Me Lonesome**	1963	12.00	30.00
Decca DL-74385	(S)	**Just Call Me Lonesome**	1963	16.00	40.00
Decca DL-4397	(M)	**The Family Bible**	1964	10.00	25.00
Decca DL-74397	(S)	**The Family Bible**	1964	12.00	30.00
Decca DL-4514	(M)	**Thanks A Lot**	1964	10.00	25.00
Decca DL-74514	(S)	**Thanks A Lot**	1964	12.00	30.00
Decca DL-4518	(M)	**Blue Christmas**	1964	10.00	25.00
Decca DL-74518	(S)	**Blue Christmas**	1964	12.00	30.00
Decca DL-4640	(M)	**My Pick Of The Hits**	1965	8.00	20.00
Decca DL-74640	(S)	**My Pick Of The Hits**	1965	10.00	25.00
Decca DL-4681	(M)	**Hittin' The Road**	1965	8.00	20.00
Decca DL-74681	(S)	**Hittin' The Road**	1965	10.00	25.00
Decca DXA-159	(M)	**Ernest Tubb Story** (2 LPs with bonus book)	1965	16.00	40.00
Decca DXSA-7159	(E)	**Ernest Tubb Story** (2 LPs with bonus book)	1965	12.00	30.00
Decca DXA-159	(M)	**Ernest Tubb Story** (2 LPs without book)	1965	12.00	30.00
Decca DXSA-7159	(E)	**Ernest Tubb Story** (2 LPs without book)	1965	8.00	20.00
Decca DL-4746	(M)	**By Request**	1966	8.00	20.00
Decca DL-74746	(S)	**By Request**	1966	10.00	25.00
Decca DL-4772	(M)	**Country Hits, Old And New**	1966	8.00	20.00
Decca DL-74772	(S)	**Country Hits, Old And New**	1966	10.00	25.00

— *Decca albums above have black labels with "Mfrd by Decca" beneath the rainbow.*—

First Generation LP-0002	(S)	**The Legend And The Legacy** (2 LPs)	1979	20.00	50.00

(Original covers are approximately 1/2" shorter than regulation size and have no ads on the back.)

First Generation LP-0002	(S)	**The Legend And The Legacy** (2 LPs)	1979	16.00	40.00

(Second pressings are regulation size and have ads on the back for Tubb's Record Shop in Nashville.)

First Generation TV-1033	(S)	**The Legend And The Legacy** (2 LPs)	1979	10.00	25.00

(This later pressing was avaialbe exclusively through TV mail-order.)

TUBB, ERNEST, & LORETTA LYNN

Decca DL-4639	(M)	**Mr. And Mrs. Used To Be**	1965	8.00	20.00
Decca DL-74639	(S)	**Mr. And Mrs. Used To Be**	1965	10.00	25.00

— *Decca albums above have black labels with "Mfrd by Decca" beneath the rainbow.*—

TUBB, JUSTIN

Decca DL-8644	(M)	**Country Boy In Love** (Black & silver label)	1957	30.00	75.00
Starday SLP-160	(M)	**Star Of The Grand Ole Opry**	1962	20.00	50.00
Starday SLP-198	(M)	**The Modern Country Music Sound**	1962	20.00	50.00
Starday SLP-334	(M)	**The Best Of Justin Tubb**	1965	12.00	30.00

— *Starday albums above have yellow labels.*—

RCA Victor LPM-3339	(M)	**Where You're Concerned**	1965	8.00	20.00
RCA Victor LSP-3339	(S)	**Where You're Concerned**	1965	10.00	25.00

TUBB, JUSTIN, & LORENE MANN

RCA Victor LPM-3591	(M)	**Together And Alone**	1966	8.00	20.00
RCA Victor LSP-3591	(S)	**Together And Alone**	1966	10.00	25.00

TUCKER, FAYE

Time S-2108	(M)	**Country & Western Soul**	1963	8.00	20.00
Time ST-2108	(S)	**Country & Western Soul**	1963	12.00	30.00

TUCKER, TOMMY

Checker LP-2990	(M)	**Hi Heel Sneakers**	1964	150.00	300.00

TUNETOPPERS, THE

Amy A-1	(M)	**At The Madison Dance Party**	1960	14.00	35.00
Amy AS-1	(S)	**At The Madison Dance Party**	1960	20.00	50.00

("The Madison" is rechanneled on this album.)

Label & Catalog #		Title	Year	VG+	NM

TURNER, IKE

| Crown CLP-5367 | (M) | Ike Turner Rocks The Blues | 1963 | 80.00 | 200.00 |
| Crown CST-367 | (E) | Ike Turner Rocks The Blues | 1963 | 40.00 | 100.00 |

TURNER, IKE & TINA

Sue LP-2001	(M)	The Soul Of Ike And Tina Turner	1961	100.00	350.00
Sue LP-2003	(M)	Ike & Tina Turner's Kings Of Rhythm Dance	1962	100.00	350.00
Sue LP-2004	(M)	Dynamite	1963	100.00	350.00
Sue LP-2005	(M)	Don't Play Me Cheap	1963	100.00	350.00
Sue LP-2007	(M)	It's Gonna Work Out Fine	1963	100.00	350.00
Sue LP-1038	(M)	Ike And Tina Turner's Greatest Hits	1965	80.00	250.00

(Note: Truly Mint copies of the six Sue albums above re worth twice the listed Near Mint value.)

Kent K-5014	(M)	The Ike And Tina Turner Revue Live	1964	12.00	30.00
Kent KST-514	(S)	The Ike And Tina Turner Revue Live	1964	16.00	40.00
Kent K-5019	(M)	The Soul Of Ike And Tina	1966	12.00	30.00
Kent KST-519	(S)	The Soul Of Ike And Tina	1966	16.00	40.00
Kent KST-538	(S)	Festival Of Live Performances	1969	12.00	30.00
Kent KST-550	(S)	Please Please Please	1971	12.00	30.00
Warner Bros. W-1579	(M)	The Ike And Tina Turner Show Live	1965	12.00	30.00
Warner Bros. WS-1579	(S)	The Ike And Tina Turner Show Live	1965	16.00	40.00
Warner Bros. WS-1810	(S)	Ike And Tina Turner's Greatest Hits	1969	10.00	25.00
Loma 5904	(M)	Live/The Ike And Tina Show	1966	12.00	30.00
Loma 5904	(S)	Live/The Ike And Tina Show	1966	16.00	40.00
Philles PHLP-4011	(M)	River Deep-Mountain High	1966		See below

(Philles 4011, more or less produced by Phil Spector, was manufactured and pressed in minute quantities, most of which were then destroyed by Mr. Spector shortly afterward. No covers are known to have been completed. Ravenoulsy rare with a suggested Near Mint value for the record alone of $5,000-15,000.)

Minit 24018	(S)	Ike And Tina Turner In Person	1968	10.00	25.00
Pompeii SD-6000	(S)	So Fine	1968	10.00	25.00
Pompeii SD-6004	(S)	Cussin,' Cryin' And Carryin' On	1969	10.00	25.00
Pompeii SD-6006	(S)	Get It Together	1969	10.00	25.00
A&M SP-4178	(S)	River Deep-Mountain High *(Brown label)*	1969	10.00	25.00

(A&M 4178 is the official release of Philles 4011.)

TURNER, "BIG" JOE

Refer to Wynonie Harris / Joe Turner.

Decca DL-8044	(M)	Joe Turner Sings Kansas City Jazz	1953	100.00	250.00
Atlantic 1234	(M)	The Boss Of The Blues	1956	50.00	125.00
Atlantic SD-1234	(S)	The Boss Of The Blues	1959	70.00	175.00
Atlantic 8005	(M)	Joe Turner	1957	50.00	125.00
Atlantic 8023	(M)	Rockin' The Blues	1958	60.00	150.00
Atlantic 8033	(M)	Big Joe Is Here *(White "bullseye" label)*	1959	100.00	250.00
Atlantic 8033	(M)	Big Joe Is Here	1959	60.00	150.00

— Atlantic mono albums above have black labels; stereo albums have green labels.—

Atlantic 1234	(M)	The Boss Of The Blues	196?	16.00	40.00
Atlantic SD-1234	(S)	The Boss Of The Blues	196?	20.00	50.00
Atlantic 8005	(M)	Joe Turner	1960	16.00	40.00
Atlantic 8023	(M)	Rockin' The Blues	1960	16.00	40.00
Atlantic 8033	(M)	Big Joe Is Here	1960	16.00	40.00
Atlantic 1332	(M)	Big Joe Rides Again	1960	30.00	75.00
Atlantic SD-1332	(M)	Big Joe Rides Again	1960	40.00	100.00

— Atlantic albums above have multi-colored labels with a white "fan" logo.—

| Atlantic 8081 | (M) | The Best Of Joe Turner | 1963 | 20.00 | 50.00 |

— Atlantic albums above have multi-colored labels with a black "fan" logo.—

Savoy MG-14012	(M)	Joe Turner And The Blues	1958	50.00	125.00
Savoy MG-14106	(M)	Careless Love	1963	30.00	75.00
BluesWay BL-6006	(M)	Singing The Blues	1967	8.00	20.00
BluesWay BLS-6006	(S)	Singing The Blues	1967	10.00	25.00

TURNER, "BIG" JOE, & PETE JOHNSON

| EmArcy MG-36014 | (M) | Joe Turner And Pete Johnson | 1955 | 60.00 | 150.00 |

TURNER, MARY LOU,: *Refer to* BILL ANDERSON & MARY LOU TURNER

Label & Catalog #		Title	Year	VG+	NM
TURNER, MICKEY					
Edmar E-1040	(M)	The Mickey Turner Show	1966	10.00	25.00
TURNER, SAMMY					
Big Top 12-1301	(M)	Lavender Blue Mods	1960	150.00	300.00
Big Top S-12-1301	(S)	Lavender Blue Mods	1960	1,000.00	1,500.00
TURNER, SPYDER					
MGM E-4450	(M)	Stand By Me	1967	8.00	20.00
MGM SE-4450	(S)	Stand By Me	1967	10.00	25.00
TURNER, TITUS					
Jamie JLP-70-3018	(M)	Sound Off	1961	8.00	20.00
Jamie JLP-3018	(S)	Sound Off	1961	10.00	25.00
TURNER, ZEB					
Audio Lab AL-1537	(M)	Country Music In The Turner Style	195?	80.00	200.00
TURNQUIST REMEDY					
Pentegram PE-10004	(S)	Turnquist Remedy	1970	10.00	25.00
TURTLES, THE					
The Turtles feature Howard Kaylan and Mark Volman, who also recorded as Flo & Eddie.					
White Whale WW-111	(M)	It Ain't Me Babe	1965	12.00	30.00
White Whale WWS-7111	(S)	It Ain't Me Babe	1965	16.00	40.00
White Whale WW-112	(M)	You Baby	1966	12.00	30.00
White Whale WWS-7112	(S)	You Baby	1966	16.00	40.00
White Whale WW-114	(M)	Happy Together	1967	8.00	20.00
White Whale WWS-7114	(S)	Happy Together	1967	10.00	25.00
White Whale WWS-7133	(S)	Wooden Head	1971	12.00	30.00
Sire SASH-3703	(S)	Happy Together Again *(2 LPs)*	1974	10.00	25.00
TUSKEGEE INSTITUTE CHOIR, THE					
Westminster XWN-18080	(M)	Spirituals	195?	20.00	50.00
TWEETY PIE					
Bugs and most of the other WB characters were done by Mel Blanc.					
Capitol J-3261	(M)	Tweety Pie And Other Favorites	1962	20.00	50.00
20TH CENTURY ZOO					
Vault LPS-122	(S)	Thunder On A Clear Day	1968	16.00	40.00
$27 SNAP ON FACE					
Heterodyne 0001	(S)	$27 Snap On Face *(Blue vinyl + lyric sheet)*	1977	40.00	100.00
TWINK					
Refer to The Pretty Things; Tomorrow.					
Sire SES-97022	(S)	Think Pink	1970	30.00	75.00
TWINS, THE					
RCA Victor LPM-1708	(M)	Teenagers Love The Twins	1958	20.00	50.00
TWISTERS, THE					
Treasure TLP-890	(M)	Doin' The Twist	1962	12.00	30.00
TWISTIN' KINGS, THE					
Motown MLP-601	(M)	Twistin' The World Around	1960	100.00	250.00
TWITTY, CONWAY					
Conway Twitty is a pseudonym for Harold Jenkins.					
MGM E-3744	(M)	Conway Twitty Sings	1959	40.00	100.00
MGM SE-3744	(S)	Conway Twitty Sings	1959	60.00	150.00
MGM E-3786	(M)	Saturday Night With Conway Twitty	1959	40.00	100.00
MGM SE-3786	(S)	Saturday Night With Conway Twitty	1959	60.00	150.00
MGM E-3818	(M)	Lonely Blue Boy	1960	40.00	100.00
MGM SE-3818	(S)	Lonely Blue Boy	1960	60.00	150.00
		— MGM albums above have yellow labels—			

Label & Catalog #		Title	Year	VG+	NM
MGM E-3744	(M)	Conway Twitty Sings	196?	16.00	40.00
MGM SE-3744	(S)	Conway Twitty Sings	196?	20.00	50.00
MGM E-3786	(M)	Saturday Night With Conway Twitty	196?	16.00	40.00
MGM SE-3786	(S)	Saturday Night With Conway Twitty	196?	20.00	50.00
MGM E-3818	(M)	Lonely Blue Boy	196?	16.00	40.00
MGM SE-3818	(S)	Lonely Blue Boy	196?	20.00	50.00
MGM E-3849	(M)	Conway Twitty's Greatest Hits (With fold-open poster)	1960	26.00	65.00
MGM E-3849	(M)	Conway Twitty's Greatest Hits (Without the poster)	1960	16.00	40.00
MGM SE-3849	(P)	Conway Twitty's Greatest Hits (With fold-open poster)	1960	30.00	75.00
MGM SE-3849	(P)	Conway Twitty's Greatest Hits (Without the poster)	1960	20.00	50.00
MGM E-3907	(M)	The Rock And Roll Story	1961	20.00	50.00
MGM SE-3907	(S)	The Rock And Roll Story	1961	40.00	100.00
MGM E-3943	(M)	The Conway Twitty Touch	1961	20.00	50.00
MGM SE-3943	(S)	The Conway Twitty Touch	1961	40.00	100.00
MGM E-4019	(M)	Portrait Of A Fool And Others	1962	16.00	40.00
MGM SE-4019	(S)	Portrait Of A Fool And Others	1962	20.00	50.00
MGM E-4089	(M)	R&B '63	1963	16.00	40.00
MGM SE-4089	(S)	R&B '63	1963	20.00	50.00
MGM E-4217	(M)	Hit The Road	1964	10.00	25.00
MGM SE-4217	(S)	Hit The Road	1964	12.00	30.00
		—MGM albums above have black labels—			
Decca DL-4724	(M)	Conway Twitty Sings	1966	8.00	20.00
Decca DL-74724	(S)	Conway Twitty Sings	1966	10.00	25.00
Decca DL-4828	(M)	Look Into My Teardrops	1966	8.00	20.00
Decca DL-74828	(S)	Look Into My Teardrops	1966	10.00	25.00
		—Decca albums above have black labels with "Mfrd. by Decca" beneath the rainbow.—			

TYLER, ALVIN "RED," & THE GYROS

Ace LP-1006	(M)	Rockin' And Rollin'	1960	60.00	150.00
Ace LP-1021	(M)	Twistin' With Mr. Sax	1961	60.00	150.00

TYLER, T. TEXAS
T. Tyler Texas is a pseudonym for David Myrick.

Sound 607	(M)	Deck Of Cards	1958	40.00	100.00
King 664	(M)	T. Texas Tyler	1959	60.00	150.00
King 689	(M)	The Great Texan	1960	60.00	150.00
King 721	(M)	T. Texas Tyler	1961	40.00	100.00
King 734	(M)	Songs Along The Way	1961	40.00	100.00
Wrangler W-1002	(M)	T. Tyler Texas	1962	14.00	35.00
Wrangler WS-1002	(S)	T. Tyler Texas	1962	20.00	50.00
Capitol T-1662	(M)	Salvation	1962	10.00	25.00
Capitol ST-1662	(S)	Salvation	1962	14.00	35.00
Capitol T-2344	(M)	The Hits Of T. Texas Tyler	1965	10.00	25.00
Capitol ST-2344	(S)	The Hits Of T. Texas Tyler	1965	12.00	30.00
Starday SLP-379	(M)	The Man With A Million Friends (Yellow label)	1966	12.00	30.00

TYLER, WILLIE & LESTER

Tamla T-265	(M)	Hello Dummy	1965	80.00	200.00
Tamla TS-265	(S)	Hello Dummy	1965	80.00	200.00

TYMES, THE

Parkway P-7032	(M)	So Much In Love (Group cover)	1963	80.00	200.00
Parkway P-7032	(M)	So Much In Love (Title cover)	1963	20.00	50.00
Parkway P-7038	(M)	The Sound Of Wonderful Tymes	1963	20.00	50.00
Parkway P-7039	(M)	Somewhere	1964	20.00	50.00
Parkway P-7048	(M)	18 Greatest Hits	1964	20.00	50.00

U

U. F. O.

Rare Earth RS-524	(S)	UFO 1	1971	10.00	25.00

ULTIMATE SPINACH

MGM E-4518	(M)	Ultimate Spinach	1968	8.00	20.00
MGM SE-4518	(S)	Ultimate Spinach	1968	10.00	25.00
MGM SE-4570	(S)	Behold And See	1968	10.00	25.00
MGM SE-4600	(S)	Ultimate Spinach	1969	10.00	25.00

UNBEATABLES, THE

Fawn LP-5050	(M)	Live At Palisades Park	1964	60.00	150.00

UNCLE JOSH & COUSIN JAKE

Cotton Town 101	(M)	Just Joshing	196?	30.00	75.00

UNDERGROUND SUNSHINE

Intrepid IT-74003	(S)	Let There Be Light	1969	12.00	30.00

UNDERGROUNDS, THE

Mercury MG-16337	(M)	Psychedelic Visions	1967	12.00	30.00
Mercury SR-16337	(S)	Psychedelic Visions	1967	16.00	40.00

UNDISPUTED TRUTH

Gorty G-955L	(S)	Undisputed Truth	1971	10.00	25.00

UNFOLDING, THE

Audio Fidelity AFLP-2184	(M)	How To Blow Your Mind And Have A Freakout Party	1967	20.00	50.00
Audio Fidelity AFSD-6184	(S)	How To Blow Your Mind And Have A Freakout Party	1967	30.00	75.00

UNIQUES, THE

The Uniques feature Joe Stampley.

Paula LP-2190	(M)	Uniquely Yours	1966	10.00	25.00
Paula LPS-2190	(P)	Uniquely Yours	1966	12.00	30.00
Paula LP-2194	(M)	Happening Now	1967	10.00	25.00
Paula LPS-2194	(S)	Happening Now	1967	12.00	30.00
Paula LP-2199	(M)	Playtime	1968	10.00	25.00
Paula LPS-2199	(S)	Playtime	1968	10.00	25.00
Paula LPS-2204	(S)	The Uniques	1969	10.00	25.00
Paula LPS-2208	(P)	Golden Hits	1970	10.00	25.00

UNIT 4 + 2

London LL-3427	(M)	Unit 4 + 2 #1	1965	16.00	40.00
London PS-427	(P)	Unit 4 + 2 #1	1965	20.00	50.00

(Half of this album is rechanneled including "Concrete And Clay.")

UNITED STATES DOUBLE QUARTET, THE

The U.S.D.Q. is The Tokens with The Kirby Stone Four.

B.T. Puppy BTS-1005	(S)	Life Is Groovy	1969	20.00	50.00

UNITED STATES OF AMERICA, THE

Columbia CS-9614	(S)	The United States Of America (With bag)	1968	24.00	60.00
Columbia CS-9614	(S)	The United States Of America (Without bag)	1968	16.00	40.00

(CS-9614 was originally issued in a special bag.)

UNUSUAL WE

Pulsar 10608	(S)	Unusual We	1969	10.00	25.00

Label & Catalog #		Title	Year	VG+	NM

UPCHURCH, PHIL

Boyd B-398	(M)	**You Can't Sit Down**	1961	20.00	50.00
Boyd BS-398	(S)	**You Can't Sit Down**	1961	30.00	75.00
United Arts. UAL-3162	(M)	**You Can't Sit Down, Part 2**	1961	10.00	25.00
United Arts. UAS-6162	(S)	**You Can't Sit Down, Part 2**	1961	12.00	30.00
United Arts. UAL-3175	(M)	**Big Hits Dances**	1962	10.00	25.00
United Arts. UAS-6175	(S)	**Big Hits Dances**	1962	12.00	30.00

URSA MAJOR

RCA Victor LSP-4777	(S)	**Ursa Major**	1972	10.00	25.00

USHER, GARY

Gary Usher was one of the most creative producers of the '60s. For his work as a producer refer to Keith Allison; The Beatles; Curt Boetcher; The Byrds; Chad & Jeremy; Danny Cox; Andy Goldmark; Bruce Johnston; Millenium; The Peanut Butter Conspiracy; Sagittarius; Ship; and Alan Watts. He also recorded and produced albums under a variety of pseudonyms. For these "Gary Usher Creations" refer to The Competitors; The Ghouls; The Hondells; The Kickstands; The Knights; Mr. Gasser; The Revells; The Road Runners; The Silly Surfers; The Super Stocks; The Surfaris; and The Weird-Ohs.

U2

Warner Bros. WBMS-117	(DJ)	**Two Sides Live** (Black vinyl)	1981	40.00	100.00
		(Counterfeits on clear vinyl exist.)			

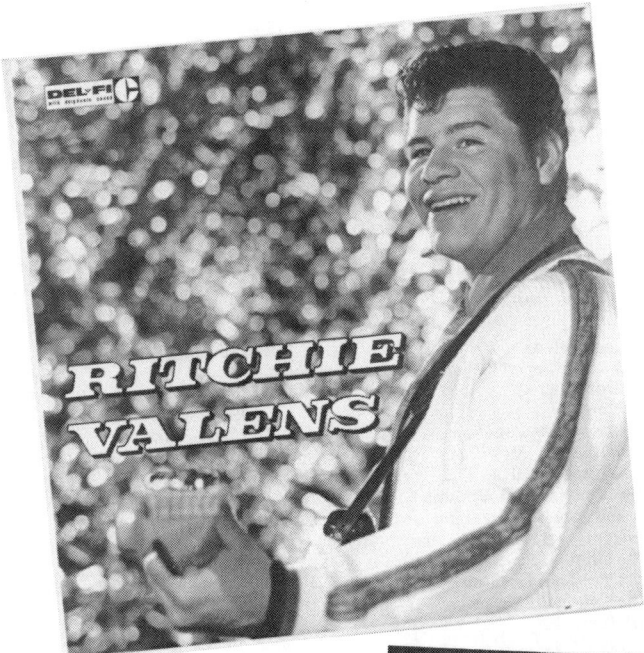

Ritchie Valens (born Richard Valenzuela) was able to fuse Latino rhythms and folk tunes to the rock n roll beat and produce a couple of memorable hits, "La Bamba" being the most noteworthy. His emergence and acceptance on top 40 radio was recognized by the Hispanic communities in the States as a cultural breakthrough. Unfortunately, Ritchie's career, and the potential it envisioned, were cut short when, along with Buddy Holly and the Big Bopper, he was killed in an airplane crash on February 3, 1959, immortalized on vinyl by Don McLean as "the day the music died."

V

VALE, RICKY, & HIS SURFERS

Strand SL-1104	(M)	Everybody's Surfin'	1963	10.00	25.00
Strand SLS-1104	(S)	Everybody's Surfin'	1963	14.00	35.00

VALENS, RITCHIE

Del Fi DFLP-1201	(M)	Ritchie Valens	1959	100.00	300.00

— Del Fi albums above have blue labels with a black border.—

Del Fi DFLP-1201	(M)	Ritchie Valens	1959	80.00	200.00
Del Fi DFLP-1206	(M)	Ritchie	1959	80.00	200.00
Del Fi DFLP-1214	(M)	In Concert At Pacoima Jr. High	1960	100.00	250.00
Del Fi DFLP-1225	(M)	His Greatest Hits (Black cover)	1963	100.00	250.00
Del Fi DFLP-1225	(M)	His Greatest Hits (White cover)	1963	40.00	100.00
Del Fi DFLP-1247	(M)	His Greatest Hits, Volume 2	1965	40.00	100.00

— Del Fi albums above have black labels with a blue/gold diamonds around the perimeter—

Guest Star GS-1469	(M)	The Original Ritchie Valens	1963	12.00	30.00
Guest Star GSS-1469	(E)	The Original Ritchie Valens	1963	6.00	15.00
Guest Star GS-1484	(M)	The Original La Bamba	1963	12.00	30.00
Guest Star GSS-1484	(E)	The Original La Bamba	1963	6.00	15.00
MGM GAS-117	(E)	Ritchie Valens	1970	12.00	30.00

VALENS, RITCHIE / JERRY KOLE
Jerry Kole alos recorded as both Cole and Kole.

Crown CLP-5336	(M)	Ritchie Valens And Jerry Kole	1963	12.00	30.00
Crown CST-336	(E)	Ritchie Valens And Jerry Kole	1963	6.00	15.00

VALENTE, CATERINA

Decca DL-8203	(M)	The Hi-Fi Nightingale	1956	10.00	25.00
Decca DL-8436	(M)	Ole Catarina	1957	10.00	25.00
Decca DL-8440	(M)	Plenty Valente!	1957	10.00	25.00
Decca DL-8755	(M)	A Toast To The Girls	1958	10.00	25.00
Decca DL-8852	(M)	Schlager Parade	1959	8.00	20.00
Decca DL-78852	(S)	Schlager Parade	1959	10.00	25.00
Decca DL-4035	(M)	More Schlager Parade	1959	8.00	20.00
Decca DL-74035	(S)	More Schlager Parade	1959	10.00	25.00
Decca DL-4050	(M)	Catarina A La Carte	1960	8.00	20.00
Decca DL-74050	(S)	Catarina A La Carte	1960	10.00	25.00
Decca DL-4051	(M)	Ariba	1960	8.00	20.00
Decca DL-74051	(S)	Ariba	1960	10.00	25.00
Decca DL-4052	(M)	Catarina	1961	8.00	20.00
Decca DL-74052	(S)	Catarina	1961	10.00	25.00
RCA Victor LPM-2119	(M)	Classics With A Chaser	1960	8.00	20.00
RCA Victor LSP-2119	(S)	Classics With A Chaser	1960	10.00	25.00
RCA Victor LPM-2241	(M)	Superfonics	1961	8.00	20.00
RCA Victor LSP-2241	(S)	Superfonics	1961	10.00	25.00

— RCA mono albums above have "Long Play" on the bottom of the label;
stereo albums have "Living Stereo" on the bottom.—

VALENTE, DINO
Dino Valenti co-founded Quicksilver Messenger Service, got busted prior and then rejoined in 1971.

Epic LN-24335	(M)	Dino Valente	1967	8.00	20.00
Epic BN-26335	(S)	Dino Valente	1967	10.00	25.00

VALENTINE, HILTON
Valentine was formerly a member of The Animals.

Capitol ST-330	(S)	All In Your Head	1969	12.00	30.00

VALENTINO, MARK

Swan LP-508	(M)	Mark Valentino	1963	20.00	50.00

Folk singer Dave Van Ronk has been a bit of a legend since the '60s, especially among his peers. His early work is firmly grounded in folk and folk-blues traditions; the two albums here, recorded for Prestige's short-lived Folklore label, capture him aptly during this period. As the decade moved ahead, so did Ronk, adapting bit and pieces of the contemporary rock'n roll scene so that, by the time he had recorded Dave Van Ronk And The Hudson Dusters for Verve's Forecast subsidiary, he could be comfortably fit by critics in that category-that-cannot-be-described-in-words reserved for such idiosyncratic visionaries as The Fugs and Captain Beefheart.

Label & Catalog #		Title	Year	VG+	NM
VALLEE, RUDY					
RCA Victor LPM-2507	(M)	**Young Rudy Vallee**	1961	12.00	30.00
RCA Victor LSP-2507	(E)	**Young Rudy Vallee**	1961	8.00	20.00
VALLEY, JIM					
Valley was formerly a member of Paul Revere's Raiders.					
Panorama 104	(M)	**Harpo** *(With Don & The Goodtimes)*	1968	16.00	40.00
Panorama 104-S	(S)	**Harpo** *(With Don & The Goodtimes)*	1968	20.00	50.00
VALLEY RAMBLERS, THE					
Jalyn JLP-116	(M)	**Strictly Bluegrass**	196?	10.00	25.00
Jalyn JLP-125	(M)	**Pickin' And Singin' Solid Bluegrass**	196?	10.00	25.00
VALLI, FRANKI					
Refer to The Four Lovers; The Four Seasons.					
Phillips PHM-200-247	(M)	**Frankie Valli Solo**	1967	8.00	20.00
Phillips PHS-600-247	(S)	**Frankie Valli Solo**	1967	10.00	25.00
Phillips PHS-600-274	(S)	**Timeless**	1968	10.00	25.00
VAMPIRES, THE					
United Arts. UAL-3378	(M)	**At The Monster Ball**	1964	10.00	25.00
United Arts. UAS-6378	(S)	**At The Monster Ball**	1964	14.00	35.00
VAN DYKE, DICK					
Command R-860	(M)	**Songs I Like**	1963	10.00	25.00
Command RS-860SD	(S)	**Songs I Like**	1963	12.00	30.00
VAN DYKE, DICK / IRENE DUNNE					
Guideposts GP-114	(M)	**Christmas Stories From Guideposts**	1967	12.00	30.00
VAN DYKE, EARL					
Motown M-631	(M)	**The Motown Sound**	1965	8.00	20.00
Motown MS-631	(S)	**The Motown Sound**	1965	10.00	25.00
VAN DYKE, LeROY					
Mercury MG-20682	(M)	**Walk On By**	1962	8.00	20.00
Mercury SR-60682	(S)	**Walk On By**	1962	10.00	25.00
Mercury MG-20716	(M)	**Movin' Van Dyke**	1963	8.00	20.00
Mercury SR-60716	(S)	**Movin' Van Dyke**	1963	10.00	25.00
Mercury MG-20802	(M)	**Great Hits Of LeRoy Van Dyke**	1963	8.00	20.00
Mercury SR-60802	(S)	**Great Hits Of LeRoy Van Dyke**	1963	10.00	25.00
Mercury MG-20825	(M)	**The Great Hits Of LeRoy Van Dyke**	1964	8.00	20.00
Mercury SR-60825	(S)	**The Great Hits Of LeRoy Van Dyke**	1964	10.00	25.00
Mercury MG-20922	(M)	**Songs For Mon And Dad**	1964	8.00	20.00
Mercury SR-60922	(S)	**Songs For Mon And Dad**	1964	10.00	25.00
Mercury MG-20950	(M)	**LeRoy Van Dyke At The Trade Winds**	1964	8.00	20.00
Mercury SR-60950	(S)	**LeRoy Van Dyke At The Trade Winds**	1964	10.00	25.00
MGM E-4506	(M)	**What Am I Bid?** *(Soundtrack)*	1967	8.00	20.00
MGM SE-4506	(S)	**What Am I Bid?** *(Soundtrack)*	1967	10.00	25.00
VAN DYKES, THE					
The Van Dykes are Charlie Tomlinson and Billy Baker, under whose names this album was also released.					
Sutton SU-307	(M)	**A Hootin' Hootenanny**	196?	8.00	20.00
Sutton SSU-307	(S)	**A Hootin' Hootenanny**	196?	10.00	25.00
VAN DYKES, THE					
Bell 6004	(M)	**Tellin' It Like It Is**	1967	20.00	50.00
Bell 6004	(S)	**Tellin' It Like It Is**	1967	24.00	60.00
VAN HALEN					
Although Eddie Van Halen is the lead guitar player, the group's name is Van Halen.					
Warner Bros. PRO-705	(DJ)	**Looney Tunes** *(Promo EP on red vinyl)*	1978	20.00	50.00
VAN RONK, DAVE					
Dave Van Ronk is a guitar player, singer and writer of folk and blues-based music.					
Folkways FA-2383	(M)	**Dave Van Ronk Sings**	1961	16.00	40.00
Folkways FA-3818	(M)	**Ballads, Blues & Spirituals**	196?	16.00	40.00
Folkways FT-31020	(M)	**Black Mountain Blues**	196?	10.00	25.00
Folkways FTS-31020	(S)	**Black Mountain Blues**	196?	12.00	30.00

Label & Catalog #		Title	Year	VG+	NM
Folklore FRLP-14001	(M)	In The Tradition	1963	12.00	30.00
Folklore FRST-14001	(S)	In The Tradition	1963	16.00	40.00
Folklore FRLP-14012	(M)	Dave Van Ronk, Folksinger	1963	12.00	30.00
Folklore FRST-14012	(S)	Dave Van Ronk, Folksinger	1963	16.00	40.00
Folklore FRLP-14025	(M)	Inside Dave Van Ronk	1964	12.00	30.00
Folklore FRST-14025	(S)	Inside Dave Van Ronk	1964	16.00	40.00
Mercury MG-20908	(M)	Just Dave Van Ronk	1964	10.00	25.00
Mercury SR-60908	(S)	Just Dave Van Ronk	1964	12.00	30.00
Verve/Folkways FV-9006	(M)	Dave Van Ronk Sings The Blues	1965	10.00	25.00
Verve/Folkways FVS-9006	(S)	Dave Van Ronk Sings The Blues	1965	12.00	30.00
Verve/Folkways FV-9017	(M)	Gambler's Blues	1965	10.00	25.00
Verve/Folkways FVS-9017	(S)	Gambler's Blues	1965	12.00	30.00
Verve/Folkways FT-3009	(M)	No Dirty Names	1966	10.00	25.00
Verve/Folkways FTS-3009	(S)	No Dirty Names	1966	12.00	30.00
Verve/Forecast FVS-3041	(S)	Dave Van Ronk & The Hudson Dusters	1968	10.00	25.00

VAN WEY, ADELAIDE
Classically trained Adelaide Van Wey is also a singer of traditional folk songs.

Folkways FP-9	(10")	All Day Singin'—			
		Louisiana And Smoky Mountain Ballads	195?	20.00	50.00
Folkways FA-2009	(10")	All Day Singin'—			
		Louisiana And Smoky Mountain Ballads	195?	20.00	50.00
Folkways FP-602	(10")	Creole Songs & Street Cries Of New Orleans	195?	20.00	50.00
Folkways FA-2202	(10")	Creole Songs & Street Cries Of New Orleans	195?	20.00	50.00

VAN ZANDT, TOWNES

Poppy PYS-40001	(S)	For The Sake Of A Song	1968	10.00	25.00

VANGELIS

RCA Victor DJL1-1849	(DJ)	The Vangelis Radio Special	1976	80.00	200.00

(Issued in a jacket for RCA LPL1-5110, "Heaven And Hell" with a sticker that reads "Radio Special Self-Portrait.)

VANILLA FUDGE
Vanilla Fudge is Carmine Appice, Tim Bogert, Vince Martell and Mark Stein. Refer to Beck, Bogert & Appice; Cream / Vanilla Fudge.

Atco 33-224	(M)	Vanilla Fudge	1967	10.00	25.00
Atco SD-33-224	(S)	Vanilla Fudge	1967	8.00	20.00

— Atco stereo albums above have purple & brown labels.—

VANITY FARE

Page One 2502	(S)	Early In The Morning	1970	30.00	75.00

(Mispressing plays one side from the unreleased Sandy Coast album. Mispressed albums have less tracks than the label credits.)

Page One 2502	(S)	Early In The Morning	1970	8.00	20.00

VAUGHAN, SARAH: *Refer to* GOLDMINE'S PRICE GUIDE TO COLLECTIBLE JAZZ ALBUMS

VAUGHN, BILLY, & HIS ORCHESTRA/THE BILLY VAUGHN SINGERS
Billy Vaughn was originally a member of The Hilltoppers.

Dot DLP-3001	(M)	Sweet Music And Memories	1955	10.00	25.00

(Original covers of Dot 3001 feature a painting of a lovely young woman holding a rose.)

Dot DLP-3016	(M)	The Golden Instrumentals	1956	10.00	25.00

— Dot albums above have maroon labels.—

VAUGHN, ROBERT

MGM E-4488	(M)	Readings From Hamlet	1962	10.00	25.00
MGM SE-4488	(S)	Readings From Hamlet	1962	12.00	30.00

VAUGHT, BOB, & THE RENEGAIDS

Crescendo GNP-83	(M)	Surf Crazy	1963	10.00	25.00
Crescendo GNPS-83	(S)	Surf Crazy	1963	10.00	25.00

VEE, BOBBY

Liberty LRP-3165	(M)	Bobby Vee Sings Your Favorites	1960	18.00	45.00
Liberty LST-7165	(S)	Bobby Vee Sings Your Favorites	1960	24.00	60.00
Liberty LRP-3181	(M)	Bobby Vee	1961	14.00	35.00
Liberty LST-7181	(S)	Bobby Vee	1961	20.00	50.00

Label & Catalog #		Title	Year	VG+	NM
Liberty LRP-3186	(M)	**Bobby Vee With Strings And Things**	*1961*	**14.00**	**35.00**
Liberty LST-7186	(S)	**Bobby Vee With Strings And Things**	*1961*	**20.00**	**50.00**
Liberty LRP-3205	(M)	**Bobby Vee Sings Hits Of The Rockin' 50's**	*1961*	**14.00**	**35.00**
Liberty LST-7205	(S)	**Bobby Vee Sings Hits Of The Rockin' 50's**	*1961*	**20.00**	**50.00**
Liberty LRP-3211	(M)	**Take Good Care Of My Baby**	*1961*	**14.00**	**35.00**
Liberty LST-7211	(S)	**Take Good Care Of My Baby**	*1961*	**20.00**	**50.00**
Liberty LRP-3228	(M)	**Bobby Vee Meets The Crickets**	*1962*	**18.00**	**45.00**
Liberty LST-7228	(S)	**Bobby Vee Meets The Crickets**	*1962*	**24.00**	**60.00**
Liberty LRP-3232	(M)	**A Bobby Vee Recording Session**	*1962*	**12.00**	**30.00**
Liberty LST-7232	(S)	**A Bobby Vee Recording Session**	*1962*	**16.00**	**40.00**
Liberty LRP-3245	(M)	**Bobby Vee's Golden Greats**	*1962*	**12.00**	**30.00**
Liberty LST-7245	(S)	**Bobby Vee's Golden Greats**	*1962*	**16.00**	**40.00**
		("Suzie Baby" is rechanneled on this album.)			
Liberty LRP-3267	(M)	**Merry Christmas From Bobby Vee**	*1962*	**12.00**	**30.00**
Liberty LST-7267	(S)	**Merry Christmas From Bobby Vee**	*1962*	**16.00**	**40.00**
Liberty LRP-3285	(M)	**The Night Has A Thousand Eyes**	*1963*	**12.00**	**30.00**
Liberty LST-7285	(S)	**The Night Has A Thousand Eyes**	*1963*	**16.00**	**40.00**
Liberty LRP-3289	(M)	**Bobby Vee Meets The Ventures**	*1963*	**12.00**	**30.00**
Liberty LST-7289	(S)	**Bobby Vee Meets The Ventures**	*1963*	**16.00**	**40.00**
Liberty LRP-3336	(M)	**I Remember Buddy Holly**	*1963*	**16.00**	**40.00**
Liberty LST-7336	(S)	**I Remember Buddy Holly**	*1963*	**20.00**	**50.00**
Liberty LRP-3352	(M)	**The New Sound From England!**	*1964*	**10.00**	**25.00**
Liberty LST-7352	(S)	**The New Sound From England!**	*1964*	**12.00**	**30.00**
Liberty LRP-3385	(M)	**30 Big Hits From The 60's**	*1964*	**10.00**	**25.00**
Liberty LST-7385	(S)	**30 Big Hits From The 60's**	*1964*	**12.00**	**30.00**
Liberty LRP-3393	(M)	**Bobby Vee Live On Tour**	*1965*	**10.00**	**25.00**
Liberty LST-7393	(S)	**Bobby Vee Live On Tour**	*1965*	**12.00**	**30.00**
Liberty LRP-3448	(M)	**30 Big Hits From The 60's, Volume 2**	*1966*	**10.00**	**25.00**
Liberty LST-7448	(S)	**30 Big Hits From The 60's, Volume 2**	*1966*	**12.00**	**30.00**
		— Liberty albums above have black labels with a gold logo on the left side.—			
Liberty LRP-3464	(M)	**Bobby Vee's Golden Greats, Volume 2**	*1966*	**8.00**	**20.00**
Liberty LST-7464	(S)	**Bobby Vee's Golden Greats, Volume 2**	*1966*	**10.00**	**25.00**
Liberty LRP-3480	(M)	**Look At Me Girl**	*1966*	**8.00**	**20.00**
Liberty LST-7480	(S)	**Look At Me Girl**	*1966*	**10.00**	**25.00**
United Arts. LA025	(S)	**Legendary Masters** (2 LPs)	*1973*	**12.00**	**30.00**
		("Suzie Baby" is rechanneled on this album.)			

VEGAS, PAT & LOLLY

Label & Catalog #		Title	Year	VG+	NM
Mercury MG-21059	(M)	**At The Haunted House**	*1966*	**12.00**	**30.00**
Mercury SR-61059	(S)	**At The Haunted House**	*1966*	**16.00**	**40.00**

VELEZ, MARTHA

Label & Catalog #		Title	Year	VG+	NM
Sire SES-97008	(S)	**Fiends And Angels** (Features Jimi Hendrix)	*1969*	**12.00**	**30.00**

VELVET UNDERGROUND, THE

The VU was Lou Reed, Sterling Morrison, Maureen Tucker and John Cale, replaced by Doug Yule in 1968.

Label & Catalog #		Title	Year	VG+	NM
Verve V-5008	(M)	**The Velvet Underground & Nico**	*1967*	**150.00**	**300.00**
Verve V6-5008	(S)	**The Velvet Underground & Nico**	*1967*	**80.00**	**200.00**
		(First pressing: the cover has a yellow, peel-off banana over the pink banana printed on the cover. The photo of the group on the back cover is framed by a male torso. The price here is for copies with the banana sticker completely intact on the cover! The value of these albums with the banana peeled off is up to the discretion of the seller and the buyer.)			
Verve V-5008	(M)	**The Velvet Underground & Nico**	*1967*	**150.00**	**300.00**
Verve V6-5008	(S)	**The Velvet Underground & Nico**	*1967*	**80.00**	**200.00**
		(Second pressing covers have the yellow, peel-off banana over the pink banana but the photo on the back is covered with a sticker, hiding the torso. The price here is for copies with the banana sticker completely intact on the cover! The value of these albums with the banana peeled off is up to the discretion of the seller and the buyer.)			
Verve V-5008	(M)	**The Velvet Underground & Nico**	*1967*	**80.00**	**200.00**
Verve V6-5008	(S)	**The Velvet Underground & Nico**	*1967*	**60.00**	**150.00**
		(Third pressing covers have the yellow, peel-off banana over the pink banana but the torso on the back has been air-brushed out. The price here is for copies with the banana sticker completely intact intact on the cover! The value of these albums with the banana peeled off is up to the discretion of both the seller and the buyer.)			

Label & Catalog #		Title	Year	VG+	NM
Verve V6-5008	(S)	The Velvet Underground & Nico	196?	40.00	100.00
		(Later pressings have the un-peeled banana printed on the cover.)			
Verve V-5046	(M)	White Light/White Heat (White label promo)	1967	100.00	250.00
Verve V-5046	(M)	White Light/White Heat	1967	40.00	100.00
Verve V6-5046	(S)	White Light/White Heat (Yellow label promo)	1967	80.00	200.00
Verve V6-5046	(S)	White Light/White Heat	1967	20.00	50.00
		(A black-on-black skull is visible in the lower left corner of the cover when viewed at an angle. Counterfeits have lumpy, pitted labels.)			
MGM SE-4617	(S)	The Velvet Underground (Yellow label)	1969	60.00	150.00
MGM SE-4617	(S)	The Velvet Underground	1969	20.00	50.00
MGM GAS-131	(S)	The Velvet Underground	1970	10.00	25.00
Cotillion SD-9034	(S)	Loaded (White label promo)	1970	20.00	50.00
Cotillion SD-9500	(S)	Live At Max's Kansas City (White label)	1972	20.00	50.00
Mercury SRM-2-7504	(M)	Live 1969 (Gatefold cover. White label)	1972	20.00	50.00

VENTURA, CAROL: *Refer to* GOLDMINES PRICE GUIDE TO COLLECTIBLE JAZZ ALBUMS

VENTURA, RAY

Atlantic 8011	(M)	Hi-Fi Music For Young Parisisans	1956	20.00	50.00
		—Atlantic albums above have black labels.—			
Dot DLP-3120	(M)	La Belle Bardot (Bridget Bardot cover)	1958	20.00	50.00
Dot DLP-25120	(S)	La Belle Bardot (Bridget Bardot cover)	1958	30.00	75.00

VENTURAS, THE

Drum Boy DBM-1003	(M)	Here They Are	1964	30.00	75.00
Drum Boy DFS-1003	(S)	Here They Are	1964	50.00	125.00

VENTURES, THE
The Ventures also recorded with Trini Lopez; Bobby Vee.

Dolton BLP-2003	(M)	Walk, Don't Run	1960	16.00	40.00
Dolton BST-8003	(S)	Walk, Don't Run	1960	20.00	50.00
		("Home" and "Walk, Don't Run" are rechanneled on this album.)			
Dolton BLP-2004	(M)	The Ventures	1961	16.00	40.00
Dolton BST-8004	(S)	The Ventures	1961	20.00	50.00
Dolton BLP-2006	(M)	Another Smash!!!	1961	16.00	40.00
Dolton BST-8006	(S)	Another Smash!!!	1961	20.00	50.00
Dolton BLP-2008	(M)	The Colorful Ventures	1961	16.00	40.00
Dolton BST-8008	(S)	The Colorful Ventures	1961	20.00	50.00
Dolton BLP-2010	(M)	Twist With The Ventures	1962	16.00	40.00
Dolton BST-8010	(S)	Twist With The Ventures	1962	20.00	50.00
Dolton BLP-2014	(M)	The Ventures' Twist Party	1962	16.00	40.00
Dolton BST-8014	(S)	The Ventures' Twist Party	1962	20.00	50.00
		—Dolton albums above have light blue labels with the fish logo above the spindle hole.—			
Dolton BLP-2003	(M)	Walk-Don't Run	1963	10.00	25.00
Dolton BST-8003	(S)	Walk-Don't Run	1963	12.00	30.00
Dolton BLP-2004	(M)	The Ventures	1963	10.00	25.00
Dolton BST-8004	(S)	The Ventures	1963	12.00	30.00
Dolton BLP-2006	(M)	Another Smash!!!	1963	10.00	25.00
Dolton BST-8006	(S)	Another Smash!!!	1963	12.00	30.00
Dolton BLP-2008	(M)	The Colorful Ventures	1963	10.00	25.00
Dolton BST-8008	(S)	The Colorful Ventures	1963	12.00	30.00
Dolton BLP-2010	(M)	Dance!	1963	10.00	25.00
Dolton BST-8010	(S)	Dance!	1963	12.00	30.00
		("Dance!" is a repackage of "Twist With The Ventures.")			
Dolton BLP-2014	(M)	Dance With The Ventures	1963	10.00	25.00
Dolton BST-8014	(S)	Dance With The Ventures	1963	12.00	30.00
		("Dance With The Ventures" is a repackage of "Twist Party.")			
Dolton BLP-2016	(M)	Mashed Potatoes And Gravy	1962	12.00	30.00
Dolton BST-8016	(S)	Mashed Potatoes And Gravy	1962	16.00	40.00
Dolton BLP-2017	(M)	Going To The Ventures' Dance Party!	1962	12.00	30.00
Dolton BST-8017	(S)	Going To The Ventures' Dance Party!	1962	16.00	40.00
		—Dolton albums above have dark green or light blue labels with a Sunset Blvd. address on the bottom.—			
Dolton BLP-2016	(M)	Beach Party	196?	10.00	25.00
Dolton BST-8016	(S)	Beach Party	196?	12.00	30.00
		("Beach Party" is a repackage of "Mashed Potatoes.")			
Dolton BLP-2019	(M)	Telstar, The Lonely Bull	1963	12.00	30.00
Dolton BST-8019	(S)	Telstar, The Lonely Bull	1963	16.00	40.00
Dolton BLP-2022	(M)	Surfing	1963	12.00	30.00
Dolton BST-8022	(S)	Surfing	1963	16.00	40.00

Label & Catalog #		Title	Year	VG+	NM
Dolton BLP-2023	(M)	Ventures Play The Country Classics	1963	12.00	30.00
Dolton BST-8023	(S)	Ventures Play The Country Classics	1963	14.00	35.00
Dolton BLP-2024	(M)	Let's Go!	1963	12.00	30.00
Dolton BST-8024	(S)	Let's Go!	1963	14.00	35.00
Dolton BLP-2027	(M)	(The) Ventures In Space	1964	14.00	35.00
Dolton BST-8027	(S)	(The) Ventures In Space	1964	20.00	50.00
Dolton BLP-2029	(M)	The Fabulous Ventures	1964	12.00	30.00
Dolton BST-8029	(S)	The Fabulous Ventures	1964	14.00	35.00
Dolton BLP-2031	(M)	Walk, Don't Run, Volume 2	1964	12.00	30.00
Dolton BST-8031	(S)	Walk, Don't Run, Volume 2	1964	14.00	35.00
Dolton BLP-2033	(M)	The Ventures Knock Me Out!	1965	12.00	30.00
Dolton BST-8033	(S)	The Ventures Knock Me Out!	1965	14.00	35.00
Dolton BLP-2035	(M)	The Ventures On Stage	1965	12.00	30.00
Dolton BST-8035	(S)	The Ventures On Stage	1965	14.00	35.00
Dolton BLP-16501	(M)	Play Guitar With The Ventures	1965	10.00	25.00
Dolton BST·17501	(S)	Play Guitar With The Ventures	1965	12.00	30.00
Dolton BLP-16502	(M)	Play Guitar With The Ventures, Volume 2	1965	10.00	25.00
Dolton BST-17502	(S)	Play Guitar With The Ventures, Volume 2	1965	12.00	30.00
Dolton BLP-16503	(M)	Play Guitar With The Ventures, Volume 3	1965	10.00	25.00
Dolton BST-17503	(S)	Play Guitar With The Ventures, Volume 3	1965	12.00	30.00
Dolton BLP-16504	(M)	Play Guitar With The Ventures, Volume 4	1965	10.00	25.00
Dolton BST-17504	(S)	Play Guitar With The Ventures, Volume 4	1965	12.00	30.00
Dolton BLP-2037	(M)	The Ventures A Go-Go	1965	10.00	25.00
Dolton BST-8037	(S)	The Ventures A Go-Go	1965	12.00	30.00
Dolton BLP-2038	(M)	The Ventures' Christmas Album	1965	12.00	30.00
Dolton BST-8038	(S)	The Ventures' Christmas Album	1965	14.00	35.00
Dolton BLP-2040	(M)	Where The Action Is!	1966	10.00	25.00
Dolton BST-8040	(S)	Where The Action Is!	1966	12.00	30.00
Dolton BLP-2042	(M)	Batman Theme	1966	14.00	35.00
Dolton BST-8042	(S)	Batman Theme	1966	20.00	50.00
— Dolton albums above have dark blue/green labels with "A Division of Liberty."—					
Dolton BLP-2045	(M)	Go With The Ventures!	1966	10.00	25.00
Dolton BST-8045	(S)	Go With The Ventures!	1966	12.00	30.00
Dolton BLP-2047	(M)	Wild Things!	1966	10.00	25.00
Dolton BST-8047	(S)	Wild Things!	1966	12.00	30.00
Dolton BLP-2050	(M)	Guitar Freakout	1967	10.00	25.00
Dolton BST-8050	(S)	Guitar Freakout	1967	12.00	30.00
— Dolton albums above have black labels with "A Division of Liberty."—					
Liberty LST-8031	(S)	Walk-Don't Run, Volume 2	1970	10.00	25.00
(Liberty 8003 is a reissue of Dolton 8003 with new covers.)					
Liberty LST-8050	(S)	Revolving Sounds	1970	14.00	35.00
("Revolving Sounds" is a rare repackage of "Guitar Freakout.")					
Liberty LRP-2052	(M)	Super Psychedelics	1967	8.00	20.00
Liberty LST-8052	(S)	Super Psychedelics	1967	10.00	25.00
Liberty LST-8052	(S)	Changing Times	1967	16.00	40.00
("Changing Times" is a rare repackage of "Super Psychedelics.")					
Liberty BG-101	(DJ)	The Ventures	196?	60.00	150.00
(Promo compilation of 22 early tracks.)					
United Arts. LA717	(S)	TV Themes	1977	10.00	25.00

VER PLANCK, MARLENE/MARLENE

Savoy MG-12058	(M)	I Think Of You With Every Breath I Take	1956	30.00	75.00
Mounted 108	(M)	A Breath Of Fresh Air	1963	12.00	30.00
Mounted 108	(S)	A Breath Of Fresh Air	1963	16.00	40.00

VERA, BILLY
Refer to Judy Clay & Billy Vera.

Atlantic SD-8197	(S)	With Pen In Hand	1968	10.00	25.00

VERDON, GWEN

RCA Victor LPM-1152	(M)	The Girl I Left Home For	1956	16.00	40.00

VERNE, LARRY

Era 104	(M)	Mister Larry Verne	196?	20.00	50.00

VERNON, MILLI: Refer to GOLDMINE'S PRICE GUIDE TO COLLECTIBLE JAZZ ALBUMS

VERSATONES, THE

RCA Victor LPM-1538	(M)	The Versatones	1957	60.00	150.00

Label & Catalog #		Title	Year	VG+	NM
VESTICH BROTHERS, THE					
Eclipse W11779VB	(S)	Live At Woofendale's	1979	30.00	75.00
VETTES, THE					
The Vettes feature Bruce Johnston.					
MGM E-4193	(M)	Rev-Up	1963	30.00	75.00
MGM SE-4193	(S)	Rev-Up	1963	50.00	125.00
VIBRATIONS, THE					
Checker LP-2978	(M)	Watusi	1961	60.00	150.00
OKeh OKM-4111	(M)	Shout	1965	14.00	35.00
OKeh OKS-14111	(S)	Shout	1965	20.00	50.00
OKeh OKM-4112	(M)	Misty	1966	12.00	30.00
OKeh OKS-14112	(S)	Misty	1966	16.00	40.00
OKeh OKM-4114	(M)	The New Vibrations	1966	12.00	30.00
OKeh OKS-14114	(S)	The New Vibrations	1966	16.00	40.00
OKeh OKS-14129	(S)	The Vibrations' Greatest Hits	1969	12.00	30.00
Mandate 3006	(S)	Taking A New Step	1972	10.00	25.00
VICEROYS, THE					
Bolo BLP-8000	(M)	The Viceroys At Granny's Pad	1963	20.00	50.00
VICTIMS OF CHANCE, THE					
Crestview CRS-3052	(S)	The Victims Of Chance	197?	24.00	60.00
VINCENT, GENE					
Refer to Ferlin Husky / Sonny James / Tommy Sands / Gene Vincent..					
Capitol T-764	(M)	Bluejean Bop!	1957	100.00	300.00
Capitol T-811	(M)	Gene Vincent & The Blue Caps	1957	100.00	300.00
Capitol T-970	(M)	Gene Vincent Rocks! & The Blue Caps Roll	1958	100.00	300.00
Capitol T-1059	(M)	A Gene Vincent Record Date	1958	100.00	300.00
Capitol T-1207	(M)	Sounds Like Gene Vincent	1959	100.00	300.00
Capitol T-1342	(M)	Crazy Times	1960	100.00	300.00
Capitol ST-1342	(S)	Crazy Times	1960	250.00	500.00
Capitol DKAO-380	(E)	Gene Vincent's Greatest (Green label)	1969	12.00	30.00
Dandelion 9-102	(S)	I'm Back And I'm Proud	1970	10.00	25.00
Kama Sutra 2019	(S)	Gene Vincent	1970	10.00	25.00
Kama Sutra 2027	(S)	The Day The World Turned Blue	1971	10.00	25.00
VINCENT, JENNY WELLS					
Ms. Vincent is a singer of folk songs in many languages, specializing in Spanish-American music.					
Amerecord ALP-102	(10")	Spanish-American Children's Songs	1957	20.00	50.00
VINSON, EDDIE "CLEANHEAD"					
Refer to Roy Brown; Jimmy Witherspoon.					
Bethlehem BCP-5005	(M)	Cleanhead's Back In Town	1957	20.00	50.00
Aamco 312	(M)	Cleanhead's Back In Town	196?	12.00	30.00
		(Aamco 312 is a reissue of Bethlehem 5005.)			
Riverside RLP-502	(M)	Back Door Blues	1965	16.00	40.00
Riverside RLS-9502	(S)	Back Door Blues	1965	16.00	40.00
BluesWay BL-6007	(M)	Cherry Red	1967	8.00	20.00
BluesWay BLS-6007	(S)	Cherry Red	1967	10.00	25.00
King KS-1087	(M)	Cherry Red	1969	10.00	25.00
VINTON, BOBBY					
Epic BN-3727	(M)	Dancing At The Hop	1961	14.00	35.00
Epic LN-579	(S)	Dancing At The Hop	1961	20.00	50.00
Epic BN-3780	(M)	Young Man With A Big Band	1961	14.00	35.00
Epic LN-597	(S)	Young Man With A Big Band	1961	20.00	50.00
Epic LN-24020	(M)	Roses Are Red	1962	10.00	25.00
Epic BN-26020	(S)	Roses Are Red	1962	14.00	35.00
Epic LN-24035	(M)	Bobby Vinton Sings The Big Ones	1963	10.00	25.00
Epic BN-26035	(S)	Bobby Vinton Sings The Big Ones	1963	14.00	35.00
Epic LN-24049	(M)	The Greatest Hits Of The Greatest Groups	1963	10.00	25.00
Epic BN-26049	(S)	The Greatest Hits Of The Greatest Groups	1963	14.00	35.00
— Epic albums above have yellow labels with the Epic logo along the perimeter.—					
Epic LN-24068	(M)	Blue On Blue (Blue vinyl promo)	1963	60.00	150.00
Epic LN-24068	(M)	Blue On Blue	1963	8.00	20.00
Epic BN-26068	(S)	Blue On Blue	1963	10.00	25.00

Label & Catalog #		Title	Year	VG+	NM
Epic LN-24068	(M)	**Blue Velvet**	1963	8.00	20.00
Epic BN-26068	(S)	**Blue Velvet**	1963	10.00	25.00
		("Blue Velvet" is a repackage of "Blue On Blue.")			
Epic LN-24081	(M)	**There! I've Said It Again**	1964	8.00	20.00
Epic BN-26081	(S)	**There! I've Said It Again**	1964	10.00	25.00
		— Epic albums above have yellow labels with Epic on top. —			

VIOLINAIRES, THE

Checker 2CK-10065	(M)	**Please Answer This Prayer** (2 LPs)	197?	10.00	25.00

VIRGIN INSANITY

Funky 71411	(S)	**Illusions Of The Maintenance Man**	1970	80.00	200.00

VIRGINIANS, THE

United Arts. UAL-3293	(M)	**The Wonderful World Of Bluegrass Music**	1963	8.00	20.00
United Arts. UAS-6293	(S)	**The Wonderful World Of Bluegrass Music**	1963	10.00	25.00
Monument MLP-8031	(M)	**Ballads And Bluegrass**	1965	8.00	20.00
Monument SLP-18031	(S)	**Ballads And Bluegrass**	1965	10.00	25.00

VIRTUE, FRANK, & THE VIRTUES

Wynne WLP-111	(M)	**Guitar Boogie Shuffle**	1960	40.00	100.00
Wynne WLP-711	(S)	**Guitar Boogie Shuffle**	1960	60.00	150.00
Strand L-1061	(M)	**Guitar Boogie Shuffle**	1960	14.00	35.00
Strand SL-1061	(S)	**Guitar Boogie Shuffle**	1960	20.00	50.00
CMI 122	(M)	**Guitar Boogie Shuffle**	196?	14.00	35.00
Fayette 1816	(M)	**Frank Virtue & The Virtues** (Blue cover)	196?	30.00	75.00
Fayette 1816	(M)	**Frank Virtue & The Virtues** (White cover)	196?	20.00	50.00

VISCOUNTS, THE

Madison 1001	(M)	**The Viscounts**	1960	60.00	150.00
Amy 8008	(M)	**Harlem Nocturne**	1965	12.00	30.00
Amy S-8008	(S)	**Harlem Nocturne**	1965	16.00	40.00
		("Harlem Nocturne" is rechanneled on this album.)			

VOGUES, THE

Co&Ce 1229	(M)	**Meet The Vogues**	1965	16.00	40.00
Co&Ce 1229	(S)	**Meet The Vogues**	1965	24.00	60.00
Co&Ce 1230	(M)	**Five O' Clock World**	1966	16.00	40.00
Co&Ce 1230	(S)	**Five O' Clock World**	1966	24.00	60.00

VON SCHMIDT, ERIC

Folklore FRLP-14005	(M)	**Folk Blues**	1964	12.00	30.00
Folklore FRST-14005	(S)	**Folk Blues**	1964	16.00	40.00
Prestige PRLP-7384	(M)	**Eric Sings Von Schmidt**	1966	8.00	20.00
Prestige PRST-7384	(S)	**Eric Sings Von Schmidt**	1966	10.00	25.00

VULCAN

13th Records	(S)	**Vulcan**	1985	80.00	200.00

WABASH RESURRECTION, THE

Pepperland 76294	(S)	Get It Off!	197?	50.00	125.00

WADE, ADAM

Coed LPC-902	(M)	And Then Came Adam	1960	16.00	40.00
Coed LPCS-902	(S)	And Then Came Adam	1960	24.00	60.00
Coed LPC-903	(M)	Adam And Evening	1961	16.00	40.00
Coed LPCS-903	(S)	Adam And Evening	1961	24.00	60.00
Epic LN-24019	(M)	Adam Wade's Greatest Hits	1962	8.00	20.00
Epic BN-26019	(S)	Adam Wade's Greatest Hits	1962	10.00	25.00
Epic LN-24026	(M)	One Is A Lonely Number	1962	8.00	20.00
Epic BN-26026	(S)	One Is A Lonely Number	1962	10.00	25.00
Epic LN-24044	(M)	What Kind Of Fool Am I?	1963	8.00	20.00
Epic BN-26044	(S)	What Kind Of Fool Am I?	1963	10.00	25.00
Epic LN-24056	(M)	A Very Good Year For Girls	1963	8.00	20.00
Epic BN-26056	(S)	A Very Good Year For Girls	1963	10.00	25.00

— Epic albums above have yellow labels.—

WAGNER, ROGER

Capitol P-8324	(M)	Folk Songs Of The New World	195?	12.00	30.00
Capitol P-8332	(M)	Folk Songs Of The Frontier	195?	12.00	30.00

WAGONER, PORTER, & THE WAGONMASTERS

Refer to Hank Snow / Hank Lochlin / Porter Wagoner.

RCA Victor LPM-1358	(M)	A Satisfied Mind	1956	100.00	250.00
RCA Victor LPM-2447	(M)	A Slice Of Life-Songs Happy 'N' Sad	1962	12.00	30.00
RCA Victor LSP-2447	(S)	A Slice Of Life-Songs Happy 'N' Sad	1962	16.00	40.00
RCA Victor LPM-2650	(M)	The Porter Wagoner Show	1963	12.00	30.00
RCA Victor LSP-2650	(S)	The Porter Wagoner Show	1963	16.00	40.00
RCA Victor LPM-2706	(M)	Y'All Come	1963	12.00	30.00
RCA Victor LSP-2706	(S)	Y'All Come	1963	16.00	40.00

— RCA mono albums above have "Long Play" on the bottom of the label;
stereo albums have "Living Stereo" on the bottom.—

RCA Victor LPM-2960	(M)	The Bluegrass Story	1964	10.00	25.00
RCA Victor LSP-2960	(S)	The Bluegrass Story	1964	12.00	30.00
RCA Victor LPM-3389	(M)	The Thin Man From West Plains	1965	10.00	25.00
RCA Victor LSP-3389	(S)	The Thin Man From West Plains	1965	12.00	30.00
RCA Victor LPM-3488	(M)	Grand Old Gospel	1966	10.00	25.00
RCA Victor LSP-3488	(S)	Grand Old Gospel	1966	12.00	30.00
RCA Victor LPM-3560	(M)	The Best Of Porter Wagoner	1966	10.00	25.00
RCA Victor LSP-3560	(S)	The Best Of Porter Wagoner	1966	12.00	30.00
RCA Victor LPM-3593	(M)	Confessions Of A Broken Man	1966	10.00	25.00
RCA Victor LSP-3593	(S)	Confessions Of A Broken Man	1966	12.00	30.00
RCA Victor LPM-3683	(M)	Soul Of A Convict	1967	12.00	30.00
RCA Victor LSP-3683	(S)	Soul Of A Convict	1967	10.00	25.00
RCA Victor LPM-3797	(M)	The Cold Hard Facts Of Life	1967	12.00	30.00
RCA Victor LSP-3797	(S)	The Cold Hard Facts Of Life	1967	10.00	25.00
RCA Victor LPM-3855	(M)	More Grand Old Gospel	1967	12.00	30.00
RCA Victor LSP-3855	(S)	More Grand Old Gospel	1967	10.00	25.00
RCA Victor LPM-3968	(M)	The Bottom Of The Bottle	1968	40.00	100.00
RCA Victor LSP-3968	(S)	The Bottom Of The Bottle	1968	10.00	25.00
RCA Victor LSP-4034	(S)	Gospel Country	1968	10.00	25.00

— RCA albums above have black labels with Nipper on top.—

WAGONER, PORTER, & SKEETER DAVIS

RCA Victor LPM-2529	(M)	Porter Wagoner And Skeeter Davis Sings Duets	1962	12.00	30.00
RCA Victor LSP-2529	(S)	Porter Wagoner And Skeeter Davis Sings Duets	1962	16.00	40.00

— RCA mono albums above have "Long Play" on the bottom of the label;
stereo albums have "Living Stereo" on the bottom.—

Label & Catalog #		Title	Year	VG+	NM
WAGONER, PORTER, & NORMA JEAN					
RCA Victor LPM-2840	(M)	Porter Wagoner And Norma Jean In Person	1964	10.00	25.00
RCA Victor LSP-2840	(S)	Porter Wagoner And Norma Jean In Person	1964	12.00	30.00
RCA Victor LPM-3509	(M)	Live On The Road	1966	10.00	25.00
RCA Victor LSP-3509	(S)	Live On The Road	1966	12.00	30.00
		— RCA albums above have black labels with Nipper on top.—			
WAGONER, PORTER, & DOLLY PARTON					
RCA Victor LPM-3926	(M)	Just Between You And Me	1968	40.00	100.00
RCA Victor LSP-3926	(S)	Just Between You And Me	1968	10.00	25.00
		— RCA albums above have black labels with Nipper on top.—			
WAGONERS, THE					
Folkways FP-730	(10")	Folk Songs For Camp	195?	20.00	50.00
Folkways FC-7030	(10")	Folk Songs For Camp	195?	20.00	50.00
WAILERS, THE					
Refer to The Sonics.					
Golden Crest CR-3075	(M)	Fabulous Wailers	1959	80.00	200.00
		(Original pressings of CR-3075 have the cover photo in full color.)			
Golden Crest CR-3075	(M)	Fabulous Wailers	196?	30.00	75.00
		(Second pressings have a black & white cover with the title in blue.)			
Golden Crest CR-3075	(M)	Fabulous Wailers	196?	20.00	50.00
		(Later pressings replace the photo with a title cover.)			
Etiquette ALB-01	(M)	Wailers At The Castle	1962	20.00	50.00
Etiquette ALB-022	(M)	Wailers & Company	1963	20.00	50.00
Imperial LP-9262	(M)	Tall Cool One	1964	20.00	50.00
Imperial LP-12262	(S)	Tall Cool One	1964	24.00	60.00
Etiquette ALB-023	(M)	Wailers, Wailers, Everywhere	1965	30.00	75.00
Etiquette ALB-026	(M)	Out Of Our Tree	1966	30.00	75.00
Etiquette ALBS-026	(E)	Out Of Our Tree	1966	16.00	40.00
United Arts. UAL-3557	(M)	Outburst!	1966	14.00	35.00
United Arts. UAS-6557	(S)	Outburst!	1966	20.00	50.00
		("Out Of Our Tree" is rechanneled and "It's You Alone" is mono.)			
WAILERS, THE: Refer to BOB MARLEY & THE WAILERS					
WAKELY, JIMMY					
Wakely was formerly a member of Gene Autry's traveling band.					
Capitol H-9004	(10")	Christmas On The Range	1950	60.00	150.00
Capitol H-4008	(10")	Songs Of The West	1950	60.00	150.00
Decca DL-8409	(M)	Santa Fe Trail	1956	30.00	75.00
Decca DL-8680	(M)	Enter And Rest And Pray	1957	30.00	75.00
		— Decca albums above have black & silver labels.—			
Tops L-1601	(M)	A Cowboy Serenade	1959	10.00	25.00
Dot DLP-3711	(M)	Slippin' Around	1966	8.00	20.00
Dot DLP-25711	(S)	Slippin' Around	1966	10.00	25.00
Dot DLP-3754	(M)	Christmas With Jimmy Wakely	1966	8.00	20.00
Dot DLP-25754	(S)	Christmas With Jimmy Wakely	1966	10.00	25.00
WAKEMAN, RICK					
Wakeman was formerly a member of Yes.					
A&M QU-54361	(Q)	The Six Wives Of Henry The VIII	1973	10.00	25.00
A&M QU-53621	(Q)	Journey To The Center Of The Earth	1975	10.00	25.00
A&M QU-54515	(Q)	Myths And Legends Of King Arthur	1975	10.00	25.00
Sweet Thunder 1	(S)	Journey To The Center Of The Earth	1981	15.00	45.00
WALKER, BILLY					
Columbia CL-1624	(M)	Everybody's Hits But Mine	1961	8.00	20.00
Columbia CS-8424	(S)	Everybody's Hits But Mine	1961	12.00	30.00
		— Columbia albums above have three white "eye" logos on each side of the spindle hole.—			
WALKER, CHARLIE					
Columbia CL-1691	(M)	Charlie Walker's Greatest Hits	1961	8.00	20.00
Columbia CS-8491	(S)	Charlie Walker's Greatest Hits	1961	12.00	30.00
		— Columbia album above has three white "eye" logos on each side of the spindle hole.—			

Label & Catalog #		Title	Year	VG+	NM
WALKER, CINDY					
Monument MLP-8020	(M)	**Words And Music By Cindy Walker**	1964	10.00	25.00
Monument SLP-18020	(S)	**Words And Music By Cindy Walker**	1964	14.00	35.00
WALKER, CLINT					
Warner Bros. W-1343	(M)	**Inspiration**	1959	14.00	35.00
Warner Bros. WS-1343	(S)	**Inspiration**	1959	20.00	50.00

WALKER, JERRY JEFF
Jerry Jeff is a guitar player, singer and writer of folk and country-based pop music. Refer to Circus Maximus.

Atco SD-33-297	(S)	**Five Years Gone**	1969	12.00	30.00

WALKER, JUNIOR/JUNIOR WALKER & THE ALL STARS					
Soul 701	(M)	**Shotgun**	1965	20.00	50.00
Soul 702	(M)	**Soul Session**	1965	20.00	50.00
		— Soul albums above have purple & white labels.—			
Soul 701	(M)	**Shotgun**	1965	8.00	20.00
Soul SS-701	(S)	**Shotgun**	1965	12.00	30.00

WALKER, LOU					
Sims LP-114	(M)	**Swing Western Style**	1964	30.00	75.00
Sims LPS-114	(S)	**Swing Western Style**	1964	40.00	100.00

WALKER, LUCILLE					
Checker LP-1428	(M)	**The Best Of Lucille Walker**	1957		*See below*
		("The Best Of Lucille Walker" was erroneously listed in the previous edition; apparently it does not exist.)			

WALKER, T-BONE
T-Bone Walker is a pseudonym for Aaron Walker.

Capitol H-370	(10")	**Classics In Jazz**	1953	250.00	500.00
Capitol T-370	(M)	**Classics In Jazz**	1953	150.00	300.00
Atlantic 8020	(M)	**T-Bone Blues** *(Black label)*	1959	60.00	150.00
Atlantic 8020	(M)	**T-Bone Blues** *(Purple & orange label)*	196?	20.00	50.00
Atlantic SD-8256	(S)	**T-Bone Blues**	1970	8.00	20.00
		(Atlantic 8256 is a reissue of 8020.)			
Imperial LP-9098	(M)	**Sings The Blues**	1959	80.00	200.00
Imperial LP-9116	(M)	**Singing The Blues**	1960	80.00	200.00
Imperial LP-9146	(M)	**I Get So Weary**	1961	150.00	300.00
Capitol T-1958	(M)	**T-Bone Walker**	1963		*See below*
		(The existence of T-1958 as an original on Capitol's black "rainbow" label remains an unverified possibility. Should one exist, it would be a very rare record indeed with a suggested Near Mint value of, oh, let's say $1,000-5,000. . .)			
Capitol T-1958	(M)	**T-Bone Walker** *(Black "Starline" label)*	1963	40.00	100.00
Delmark D-633	(M)	**I Want A Little Girl**	1967	10.00	25.00
Delmark DS-633	(S)	**I Want A Little Girl**	1967	12.00	30.00
Wet Soul 1002	(M)	**Stormy Monday Blues**	1967	10.00	25.00
Wet Soul 1002	(S)	**Stormy Monday Blues**	1967	12.00	30.00
Brunswick BL-754126	(S)	**The Truth**	1968	10.00	25.00
BluesWay BLS-6008	(S)	**Stormy Monday Blues**	1968	10.00	25.00
BluesWay BLS-6014	(S)	**Funky Town**	1968	10.00	25.00

WALKER BROTHERS, THE
Features Scott Engel, Gary Leeds and John Maus a.k.a. John Stewart as Scott, Gary and John Walker.

Smash MGS-27076	(M)	**Introducing The Walker Brothers**	1966	20.00	50.00
Smash SRS-67076	(E)	**Introducing The Walker Brothers**	1966	16.00	40.00
Smash MGS-27082	(M)	**The Sun Ain't Gonna Shine Anymore**	1967	16.00	40.00
Smash SRS-67082	(S)	**The Sun Ain't Gonna Shine Anymore**	1967	20.00	50.00
		("The Sun Ain't Gonna Shine (Anymore)" and "After The Lights Go Out" are rechanneled.)			

WALLACE, JERRY					
Challenge CHL-606	(M)	**Just Jerry**	1959	30.00	75.00
Challenge CHL-612	(M)	**There She Goes**	1961	14.00	35.00
Challenge CHS-612	(S)	**There She Goes**	1961	18.00	45.00
Challenge CHL-616	(M)	**Shutters And Boards**	1962	14.00	35.00
Challenge CHS-616	(S)	**Shutters And Boards**	1962	18.00	45.00

Label & Catalog #		Title	Year	VG+	NM
Challenge CHL-619	(M)	In The Misty Moonlight	1964	10.00	25.00
Challenge CHS-619	(S)	In The Misty Moonlight	1964	12.00	30.00

WALLACE BROTHERS, THE

Sims LP-128	(M)	Soul, Soul And More Soul	1965	40.00	100.00
Sims LPS-128	(S)	Soul, Soul And More Soul	1965	60.00	150.00

WALLER, JIM, & THE DELTAS

Arvee A-432	(M)	Surfin' Wild	1963	20.00	50.00
Arvee AS-432	(S)	Surfin' Wild	1963	30.00	75.00

WALNUT BAND, THE

Appaloosa CSL452	(S)	The Walnut Band Goes Nuts!	197?	50.00	125.00

WALSTON, RAY

Vee Jay LP-1110	(M)	My Favorite Songs From "Mary Poppins" & Other Songs To Delight	1965	12.00	30.00
Vee Jay VJS-1110	(S)	My Favorite Songs From "Mary Poppins" & Other Songs To Delight	1965	16.00	40.00

WALTON, MERCY DEE

Bluesville BVLP-1039	(M)	Pity And A Shame	1962	30.00	75.00

— *Bluesville albums above have bright blue labels with silver print.* —

Bluesville BVLP-1039	(M)	Pity And A Shame	1964	10.00	25.00

— *Bluesville albums above have blue labels with a trident logo on the right side.* —

WALTON, WADE

Bluesville BVLP-1060	(M)	Shake 'Em On Down	1963	30.00	75.00

— *Bluesville albums above have bright blue labels with silver print.* —

Bluesville BVLP-1060	(M)	Shake 'Em On Down	1964	10.00	25.00

— *Bluesville albums above have blue labels with a trident logo on the right side.* —

WARD, BILLY, & THE DOMINOES

Federal 295-94	(10")	Billy Ward & His Dominoes	1955		See below
		(Federal 94 is rare with suggested values in VG of $500-1,000; in VG+ of $3,000-6,000 and in NM of $15,000 or more....)			
Federal 395-548	(M)	Billy Ward & His Dominoes	1956	750.00	1,500.00
Federal 395-559	(M)	Clyde McPhatter With Billy Ward & His Dominoes *(Yellow cover)*	1957	750.00	1,500.00
King LP-548	(M)	Billy Ward & His Dominoes	1958		See below
		(King 548 was not released.)			
King LP-559	(M)	Clyde McPhatter With Billy Ward & His Dominoes *(Pink cover)*	195?	250.00	500.00
King LP-733	(M)	Billy Ward & His Dominoes Featuring Clyde McPhatter And Jackie Wilson	1960	300.00	600.00
Decca DL-8621	(M)	Billy Ward & His Dominoes	1958	80.00	200.00
Liberty LRP-3056	(M)	Sea Of Glass	1957	30.00	75.00
Liberty LST-7056	(S)	Sea Of Glass	1957	40.00	100.00
Liberty LRP-3083	(M)	Yours Forever	1958	30.00	75.00
Liberty LST-7083	(S)	Yours Forever	1958	40.00	100.00
Liberty LRP-3113	(M)	Pagan Love Song	1959	30.00	75.00
Liberty LST-7113	(S)	Pagan Love Song	1959	40.00	100.00
King LP-952	(M)	Twenty Four Songs	1966	20.00	50.00

WARD, HELEN: *Refer to* GOLDMINE'S PRICE GUIDE TO COLLECTIBLE JAZZ ALBUMS

WARD, ROBIN

Robin also recorded with Wink Martindale.

Dot DLP-3555	(M)	Wonderful Summer	1963	80.00	200.00
Dot DLP-25555	(S)	Wonderful Summer	1963	150.00	300.00

WARD, WADE

Refer to Roscoe Holcomb & Wade Ward.

Folkways FA-2380	(10")	Memorial To Wade Ward, Banjo Picker	195?	20.00	50.00

WARFIELD, WILLIAM

Columbia AAL-232	(10")	Deep River	195?	20.00	50.00
Columbia ML-2206	(10")	Old American Songs & Five Sea Chanties	195?	20.00	50.00

After changing the face of popular rhythm'n blues vocal music with his early groups, Billy Ward signed with Liberty and received decent national exposure on retail racks for the first time. Unfortunately, the music he was making was rather undistinguished—especially when compared to that he made with Clyde McPhatter and Jackie Wilson—and the albums did not capture either a large black or white audience. While they have never set the hearts of collectors afire, in recent years they have appreciated in value. Finally, the cover for Pagan Love Song is a kitsch classic and would not be out of place on any of the "exotic music" masters of the time.

Label & Catalog #		Title	Year	VG+	NM

WARNER, FRANK
Frank Warner is a banjo player and singer of traditional American folk music.

| Elektra EKL-3 | (10") | **American Folk Songs And Ballads** | 195? | 20.00 | 50.00 |
| Elektra EKL-13 | (10") | **Songs And Ballads Of America's Wars** | 1954 | 20.00 | 50.00 |

WARREN, BEVERLY: Refer to ANDREA CARROLL / BEVERLY WARREN

WARREN, FRAN

RCA Victor LM-61	(10")	**Mr. Imperium** (Soundtrack)	1951	40.00	100.00
MGM E-3394	(M)	**Mood Indigo** (Yellow label)	1956	20.00	50.00
Venise 7019	(M)	**Come Rain Or Come Shine**	195?	8.00	20.00
Venise 10019	(S)	**Come Rain Or Come Shine**	195?	12.00	30.00
Warwick W-2012	(M)	**Something's Coming**	1960	8.00	20.00
Warwick W-2012ST	(S)	**Something's Coming**	1960	12.00	30.00

WARREN, RUSTY

Jubilee JGM-2024	(M)	**Songs For Sinners**	196?	10.00	25.00
Jubilee JGM-2029	(M)	**Knockers Up!**	196?	10.00	25.00
Jubilee JGM-2034	(M)	**The Sensational Rusty Warren**	196?	10.00	25.00
Jubilee JGM-2039	(M)	**Rusty Warren Bounces Back**	196?	10.00	25.00
Jubilee JGM-2044	(M)	**Rusty Warren In Orbit**	196?	10.00	25.00
Jubilee JGM-2049	(M)	**Banned In Boston**	196?	10.00	25.00
Jubilee JGM-2054	(M)	**Sex-X-Ponent**	1964	10.00	25.00
Jubilee JGM-5025	(M)	**Rusty Warren Sings A Portrait On Life**	1964	10.00	25.00
Jubilee JGM-2059	(M)	**More Knockers Up!**	1967	10.00	25.00
Jubilee JGM-2064	(M)	**Rusty Rides Again**	1967	10.00	25.00
Jubilee JGS-2069	(S)	**Bottoms Up**	1969	10.00	25.00

WARWICK, DEE DEE

Mercury MG-21100	(M)	**I Want To Be With You**	1967	10.00	25.00
Mercury SR-61100	(S)	**I Want To Be With You**	1967	12.00	30.00
		("I Want To Be With You" is rechanneled on this album.)			
Mercury SR-61221	(S)	**Foolish Fool** ("Alfie" is rechanneled)	1969	10.00	25.00
Atco SD-33-337	(S)	**Turnin' Around**	1970	10.00	25.00

WARWICK, DIONNE

| Mobile Fidelity MFSL-098 | (S) | **Hot! Live And Otherwise** (2 LPs) | 1980 | 8.00 | 25.00 |
| Everest 4103 | (S) | **Dionne Warwick** | 1981 | .80 | 4.00 |

WASHBOARD SAM
Washboard Sam is a pseudonym for Robert Brown.

| RCA Victor LPV-577 | (M) | **Feeling Lowdown** | 1965 | 10.00 | 25.00 |

WASHINGTON, BABY

Sue LP-1014	(M)	**That's How Heartaches Are Made**	1963	50.00	125.00
Sue LP-1042	(M)	**Only Those In Love**	1965	40.00	100.00
Sue LPS-1042	(S)	**Only Those In Love**	1965	60.00	150.00
Veep VPS-16528	(S)	**With You In Mind**	1968	10.00	25.00

WASHINGTON, DINAH
Refer to Brook Benton; Sarah Vaughan.

Mercury MG-25060	(10")	**Dinah Washington Songs**	1950	60.00	150.00
Mercury MG-25138	(10")	**Dynamic Dinah**	1951	50.00	125.00
Mercury MG-25140	(10")	**Blazing Ballads**	1951	50.00	125.00
EmArcy MG-26032	(10")	**After Hours With Miss D**	1954	50.00	125.00
EmArcy MG-36000	(M)	**Dinah Jams**	1954	20.00	50.00
EmArcy MG-36011	(M)	**For Those In Love**	1955	20.00	50.00
EmArcy MG-36028	(M)	**After Hours With Miss D**	1955	20.00	50.00
EmArcy MG-36065	(M)	**Dinah**	1956	20.00	50.00
EmArcy MG-36073	(M)	**In The Land Of Hi Fi**	1956	20.00	50.00
EmArcy MG-36104	(M)	**The Swingin' Miss D**	1956	20.00	50.00
EmArcy MG-36119	(M)	**Dinah Washington Sings Fats Waller**	1957	20.00	50.00
EmArcy MG-36130	(M)	**Dinah Washington Sings Bessie Smith**	1958	20.00	50.00
EmArcy MG-36141	(M)	**Newport '58**	1958	20.00	50.00
Mercury MG-20119	(M)	**Music For A First Love**	1957	16.00	50.00
Mercury MG-20120	(M)	**Music For Late Hours**	1957	16.00	50.00
Mercury MG-20247	(M)	**The Best In Blues**	1957	16.00	50.00
Mercury MG-20439	(M)	**The Queen**	1959	12.00	30.00
Mercury SR-60111	(S)	**The Queen**	1959	16.00	40.00

Dinah Washington kicked off her career with Lionel Hampton in 1943, cutting her first sides by the end of the year with members of the band. By 1946 she had established herself in both the jazz and the R&B fields before moving into a more mainstream style that included standards and pop tunes. Unfortunately, while her eclecticism may have sold a few more records, it ultimately diluted her strength, which was not as a jazz singer but as an R&B diva.

Label & Catalog #		Title	Year	VG+	NM
Mercury MG-20479	(M)	What A Diff'rence A Day Makes	1959	12.00	30.00
Mercury SR-60158	(S)	What A Diff'rence A Day Makes	1959	16.00	40.00
Mercury MG-20523	(M)	Newport '58	1959	12.00	30.00
Mercury SR-60200	(S)	Newport '58	1959	16.00	40.00
Mercury MG-20525	(M)	Dinah Washington Sings Fats Waller	1959	12.00	30.00
Mercury SR-60202	(S)	Dinah Washington Sings Fats Waller	1959	16.00	40.00
Mercury MG-20572	(M)	Unforgettable	1960	10.00	25.00
Mercury SR-60232	(S)	Unforgettable	1960	12.00	30.00
Mercury MG-20604	(M)	I Concentrate On You	1961	10.00	25.00
Mercury SR-60604	(S)	I Concentrate On You	1961	12.00	30.00
Mercury MG-20614	(M)	For Lonely Lovers	1961	10.00	25.00
Mercury SR-60614	(S)	For Lonely Lovers	1961	12.00	30.00
Mercury MG-20638	(M)	September In The Rain	1961	10.00	25.00
Mercury SR-60638	(S)	September In The Rain	1961	12.00	30.00
Mercury MG-20661	(M)	Tears And Laughter	1962	10.00	25.00
Mercury SR-60661	(S)	Tears And Laughter	1962	12.00	30.00
Mercury MG-20729	(M)	I Wanna Be Loved	1962	10.00	25.00
Mercury SR-60729	(S)	I Wanna Be Loved	1962	12.00	30.00
Mercury MG-20788	(M)	This Is My Story, Volume 1	1963	10.00	25.00
Mercury SR-60788	(S)	This Is My Story, Volume 1	1963	12.00	30.00
Mercury MG-20789	(M)	This Is My Story, Volume 2	1963	10.00	25.00
Mercury SR-60789	(S)	This Is My Story, Volume 2	1963	12.00	30.00
Mercury MG-20829	(M)	The Good Old Days	1963	10.00	25.00
Mercury SR-60829	(E)	The Good Old Days	1963	6.00	15.00
		—Mercury albums above have black labels with silver print.—			
Grand Award GA-33-318	(M)	Dinah Washington Sings The Blues	1955	30.00	75.00
		(G.A. 321 was issued with a removable "second" cover of a David Stone Martin Painting that could be peeled off and framed.)			
Grand Award GA-33-318	(M)	Dinah Washington Sings The Blues	1955	20.00	50.00
		(The price here is for the album without the removable second cover.)			
Roulette R-25170	(M)	Dinah '62	1962	10.00	25.00
Roulette SR-25170	(S)	Dinah '62	1962	12.00	30.00
		— Roulette albums above have white labels.—			
Roulette R-25170	(M)	Dinah '62	1962	8.00	20.00
Roulette SR-25170	(S)	Dinah '62	1962	10.00	25.00
Roulette R-25180	(M)	In Love	1962	8.00	20.00
Roulette SR-25180	(S)	In Love	1962	10.00	25.00
Roulette R-25183	(M)	Drinking Again	1962	8.00	20.00
Roulette SR-25183	(S)	Drinking Again	1962	10.00	25.00
Roulette R-25189	(M)	Back To The Blues	1962	8.00	20.00
Roulette SR-25189	(S)	Back To The Blues	1962	10.00	25.00
Roulette R-25220	(M)	Dinah '63	1963	8.00	20.00
Roulette SR-25220	(S)	Dinah '63	1963	10.00	25.00
		— Roulette albums above have orange & pink labels.—			

WASHINGTON, GINO

Label & Catalog #		Title	Year	VG+	NM
Atac AT-2743	(M)	Gino Washington's Golden Hits	196?	12.00	30.00
Kapp KL-1415	(M)	Ram Jam Band	1965	8.00	20.00
Kapp KS-3415	(S)	Ram Jam Band	1965	10.00	25.00

WATERFORD, CROWN PRINCE: *Refer to* AMOS MILBURN

WATERS, ETHEL: *Refer to* GOLDMINE'S PRICE GUIDE TO COLLECTIBLE JAZZ ALBUMS

WATSON, DOC/DOC & MERLE WATSON
Arthel "Doc" Watson is a guitar and banjo player and singer of traditional folk music. Merle is Doc's son. Refer to Tom Ashley; Chet Atkins; Flatt & Scruggs; Jean Ritchie.

Label & Catalog #		Title	Year	VG+	NM
Folkways FA-2366	(M)	Doc Watson And Family	1963	10.00	25.00
Folkways FA-2370	(M)	Progressive Bluegrass And Other Instrumentals *(With Roger Sprung)*	1963	10.00	25.00
Vanguard VRS-9152	(M)	Doc Watson	1964	8.00	20.00
Vanguard VSD-79152	(S)	Doc Watson	1964	10.00	25.00
Vanguard VRS-9170	(M)	Doc Watson & Son	1965	8.00	20.00
Vanguard VSD-79170	(S)	Doc Watson & Son	1965	10.00	25.00

WATSON, JOHNNY "GUITAR"
Refer to Bobby Bland / Jimmy Soul / Johnny Watson.

Label & Catalog #		Title	Year	VG+	NM
King 857	(M)	Johnny Guitar Watson	1963	200.00	400.00
		— King albums above have crownless labels.—			

Label & Catalog #		Title	Year	VG+	NM
Chess LP-1490	(M)	**Blues Soul**	1965	20.00	50.00
Chess LPS-1490	(S)	**Blues Soul**	1965	30.00	75.00
OKeh OKM-12118	(M)	**Bad**	1967	10.00	25.00
OKeh OKS-14118	(S)	**Bad**	1967	14.00	35.00
OKeh OKM-12124	(M)	**In The Fats Bag**	1967	10.00	25.00
OKeh OKS-14124	(S)	**In The Fats Bag**	1967	12.00	30.00
Cadet LP-4056	(M)	**I Cried For You**	1967	10.00	25.00
Cadet LPS-4056	(S)	**I Cried For You**	1967	12.00	30.00

WATSON, JOHNNY "GUITAR", & LARRY WILLIAMS

OKeh OKM-12122	(M)	**Two For The Price Of One**	1967	16.00	40.00
OKeh OKS-14122	(S)	**Two For The Price Of One**	1967	20.00	50.00

WATTS, ALAN

MEA LP-1001	(M)	**Haiku**	1962	20.00	50.00
MEA LP-1002	(M)	**Zen And Senryu**	1962	20.00	50.00
MEA LP-1007	(M)	**This Is It**	1962	30.00	75.00
Warner Bros. W-1923	(M)	**Sounds Of Hinduism**	1968	10.00	25.00
Ascension	(S)	**Dhyana: Of The Art Of Meditation, Vol. 2**	1970	12.00	30.00
		(Both "Dhyana" albums were produced by Gary Usher.)			
Electronic Universe '73	(S)	**The Essential Alan Watts**	1974	50.00	125.00

WAVECRESTS, THE

Viking VKS-6606	(M)	**Surftime U.S.A.**	1963	12.00	30.00

WAYFARERS, THE

RCA Victor LPM-1213	(M)	**The Wayfarers**	1956	20.00	50.00

WAYFARERS, THE
This version of The Wayfarers features Sean Bonniwell.

RCA Victor LPM-2666	(M)	**Come Along With The Wayfarers**	1963	12.00	30.00
RCA Victor LSP-2666	(S)	**Come Along With The Wayfarers**	1963	16.00	40.00
RCA Victor LPM-2735	(M)	**The Wayfarers At The Hungry i**	1963	12.00	30.00
RCA Victor LSP-2735	(S)	**The Wayfarers At The Hungry i**	1963	16.00	40.00
		— RCA mono albums above have "Long Play" on the bottom of the label;			
		stereo albums have "Living Stereo" on the bottom.—			
RCA Victor LPM-2946	(M)	**The Wayfarers At The World's Fair**	1964	16.00	40.00
RCA Victor LSP-2946	(S)	**The Wayfarers At The World's Fair**	1964	20.00	50.00

WAYFARERS TRIO, THE
The Wayfarers Trio features Mason Williams.

Mercury MG-20634	(M)	**Songs Of The Blue And Grey**	1961	8.00	20.00
Mercury SR-60634	(S)	**Songs Of The Blue And Grey**	1961	10.00	25.00

WAYNE, FRANCES: Refer to GOLDMINE'S PRICE GUIDE TO COLLECTIBLE JAZZ ALBUMS

WAYNE, "WEE" WILLIE

Imperial LP-9144	(M)	**Travelin' Mood**	1961	150.00	400.00

WEASELS, THE

Wing MGW-12282	(M)	**The Liverpool Beat**	1964	10.00	25.00
Wing SRW-16282	(S)	**The Liverpool Beat**	1964	12.00	30.00

WEAVERS, THE
The Weavers— Fred Hellerman, Ronnie Gilber, Lee Hays and Pete Seeger— were a vocal and instrumental group that plays traditional folk music and are probably the single most important folk group in history. After Seeger left in 1958, later members included Erik Darling, Frank Hamilton and Bernie Krause. Refer to The Almanac Singers.

Decca DL-5285	(10")	**Folk Songs Of America And Other Lands**	1951	40.00	100.00
Decca DL-5373	(10")	**We Wish You A Merry Christmas**	1952	40.00	100.00
Decca DL-8893	(M)	**The Best Of The Weavers**	1959	16.00	40.00
Decca DL-8909	(M)	**Folk Songs Around The World**	1959	16.00	40.00
		— Decca albums above have black labels with silver print.—			
Decca DXB-173	(M)	**Best Of The Weavers** (2 LPs)	1965	12.00	30.00
Decca DXSB-7173	(E)	**Best Of The Weavers** (2 LPs)	1965	8.00	20.00
Vanguard VRS-9010	(M)	**The Weavers At Carnegie Hall**	1957	16.00	40.00
Vanguard VRS-9013	(M)	**The Weavers On Tour**	1957	16.00	40.00
Vanguard VRS-9022	(M)	**Travelling On With The Weavers**	1959	16.00	40.00

Label & Catalog #		Title	Year	VG+	NM
Vanguard VRS-9024	(M)	The Weavers At Home	1958	12.00	30.00
Vanguard VSD-2030	(S)	The Weavers At Home	1960	16.00	40.00
Vanguard VRS-9043	(M)	The Weavers Travelling On	1959	12.00	30.00
Vanguard VSD-2022	(S)	The Weavers Travelling On	1960	16.00	40.00
Vanguard VRS-9075	(M)	The Weavers At Carnegie Hall, Volume 2	1962	10.00	25.00
Vanguard VSD-2069	(S)	The Weavers At Carnegie Hall, Volume 2	1962	12.00	30.00
Vanguard VRS-9100	(M)	Almanac	1963	10.00	25.00
Vanguard VSD-2102	(S)	Almanac	1963	12.00	30.00

— Vanguard mono albums above maroon labels with silver print; stereo albums have black labels with silver print.—

Vanguard VRS-9130	(M)	Reunion At Carnegie Hall—Part 1	1964	8.00	20.00
Vanguard VSD-2150	(S)	Reunion At Carnegie Hall—Part 1	1964	10.00	25.00
Vanguard VRS-9161	(M)	Reunion At Carnegie Hall—Part 2	1965	8.00	20.00
Vanguard VSD-79161	(S)	Reunion At Carnegie Hall—Part 2	1965	10.00	25.00
Vanguard SRV-3001	(M)	The Weavers Song Bag (2 LPs)	1967	8.00	20.00
Vanguard SRV-73001	(S)	The Weavers Song Bag (2 LPs)	1967	10.00	25.00

WEB, THE

Deram DES-18018	(S)	Fully Interlocking	1968	10.00	25.00

WEBB, JACK

RCA Victor LPM-3199	(10")	Dragnet—The Christmas Story	1954	60.00	150.00
RCA Victor LPM-1126	(M)	Pete Kelly's Blues (Soundtrack)	1955	20.00	50.00
Warner Bros. W-1207	(M)	You're My Girl	1958	12.00	30.00
Warner Bros. WS-1207	(S)	You're My Girl	1958	16.00	40.00

WEBB, PAT: *Refer to* CHARLOTTE DANIELS & PAT WEBB

WEDGE/ORANGE WEDGE

(No label)	(S)	Wedge	1974	100.00	250.00
Wedge	(S)	No One But Me	1975	80.00	200.00

("No One But Me" credits Orange Wedge.)

WEDGES, THE

Time T-2090	(M)	Hang Ten (For Surfers Only)	1963	10.00	25.00
Time ST-2090	(S)	Hang Ten (For Surfers Only)	1963	14.00	35.00

WEIR, BOB

Refer to Bobby & The Midnites; The Grateful Dead.

Warner Bros. BS-2627	(S)	Ace (Color photo on the back cover)	1972	16.00	40.00
Warner Bros. BS-2627	(S)	Ace (Black & white photo on the back cover)	1972	12.00	30.00

WEIRD-OHS, THE

The Wierd-Ohs are a creation of Gary Usher & Co. Refer to The Silly Surfers / The Weird-Ohs.

Mercury MG-20976	(M)	The Sounds Of The Weird-Ohs	1964	30.00	75.00
Mercury SR-60976	(S)	The Sounds Of The Weird-Ohs	1964	40.00	100.00

WEIRZ, THE

Bonsall W2-2622	(S)	The Weirz	1975	12.00	30.00
Parallel JBX-272	(S)	The Weirz	1979	12.00	30.00

WEISSBERG, ERIC, & MARSHALL BRICKMAN

Elektra EKL-238	(M)	New Dimensions In Banjo And Bluegrass	1963	8.00	20.00
Elektra EKS-7238	(S)	New Dimensions In Banjo And Bluegrass	1963	10.00	25.00

WEISSMAN, DICK, & BILLY FAIER & ERIC WEISSBERG

Jusdon J-3017	(M)	Banjos, Banjos, And More Banjos!	195?	20.00	50.00

WELCH, LENNY

Cadence CLP-5068	(M)	Since I Fell For You	1963	14.00	35.00
Cadence CLP-25068	(S)	Since I Fell For You	1963	20.00	50.00
Columbia CL-2430	(M)	Since I Fell For You ("360 Sound" label)	1965	8.00	20.00
Columbia CS-9230	(S)	Since I Fell For You ("360 Sound" label)	1965	12.00	30.00

(Columbia 24/9230 is a reissue of the Cadence 25068.)

WELLS, JUNIOR

Delmark DL-612	(M)	Hoodoo Man Blues	1966	12.00	30.00
Delmark DS-612	(S)	Hoodoo Man Blues	1966	16.00	40.00

Kitty Wells (born Muriel Deason) is the forerunner of the modern "Queens of Country" (she was the first to be prominently gifted with that title) and the model after which many fine singers patterned themselves, notably Patsy Cline. She first topped the national country charts in 1952 and preceded to place another eighty sides on the charts both as a solo but also duetting , primarily with Red Foley.

Label & Catalog #		Title	Year	VG+	NM
Vanguard VRS-9231	(M)	It's My Life Baby	1966	12.00	30.00
Vanguard VSD-79231	(S)	It's My Life Baby	1966	16.00	40.00
Delmark DLS-628	(S)	Southside Blues Jam	1967	12.00	30.00
Vanguard VSD-79262	(S)	Comin' At You	1968	12.00	30.00
Blue Rock 64002	(S)	You're Tuff Enough	1968	12.00	30.00
Blue Rock 64003	(S)	Live At The Golden Bear	1969	16.00	40.00
Delmark DLS-640	(S)	Blues Hit Big Town	1969	10.00	25.00

WELLS, KITTY

Decca DL-8293	(M)	Country Hit Parade	1956	30.00	75.00
Decca DL-8552	(M)	Winner Of Your Heart	1957	30.00	75.00
Decca DL-8732	(M)	Lonely Street	1958	30.00	75.00
Decca DL-8858	(M)	Dust On The Bible	1959	30.00	75.00
Decca DL-8888	(M)	After Dark	1959	30.00	75.00
Decca DL-8979	(M)	Kitty's Choice	1960	20.00	50.00
Decca DL-78979	(S)	Kitty's Choice	1960	30.00	75.00

— Decca albums above have black & silver labels.—

Decca DL-8293	(M)	Country Hit Parade	196?	12.00	30.00
Decca DL-78293	(E)	Country Hit Parade	196?	8.00	20.00
Decca DL-8552	(M)	Winner Of Your Heart	196?	12.00	30.00
Decca DL-78552	(E)	Winner Of Your Heart	196?	8.00	20.00
Decca DL-8732	(M)	Lonely Street	196?	12.00	30.00
Decca DL-78732	(E)	Lonely Street	196?	8.00	20.00
Decca DL-8858	(M)	Dust On The Bible	196?	12.00	30.00
Decca DL-78858	(E)	Dust On The Bible	196?	8.00	20.00
Decca DL-8888	(M)	After Dark	196?	12.00	30.00
Decca DL-78888	(E)	After Dark	196?	8.00	20.00
Decca DL-8979	(M)	Kitty's Choice	196?	10.00	25.00
Decca DL-78979	(S)	Kitty's Choice	196?	12.00	30.00
Decca DL-4075	(M)	Seasons Of My Heart	1960	12.00	30.00
Decca DL-74075	(S)	Seasons Of My Heart	1960	16.00	40.00
Decca DL-4108	(M)	Kitty Wells' Golden Favorites	1961	12.00	30.00
Decca DL-74108	(E)	Kitty Wells' Golden Favorites	1961	8.00	20.00
Decca DL-4141	(M)	Heartbreak U.S.A.	1961	12.00	30.00
Decca DL-74141	(S)	Heartbreak U.S.A.	1961	16.00	40.00
Decca DL-4197	(M)	Queen Of Country Music	1962	12.00	30.00
Decca DL-74197	(S)	Queen Of Country Music	1962	16.00	40.00
Decca DL-4270	(M)	Singing On Sunday	1962	12.00	30.00
Decca DL-74270	(S)	Singing On Sunday	1962	16.00	40.00
Decca DL-4349	(M)	Christmas With Kitty Wells	1962	12.00	30.00
Decca DL-74349	(S)	Christmas With Kitty Wells	1962	16.00	40.00
Decca DXB-174	(M)	The Kitty Wells Story (2 LPs)	1963	8.00	20.00
Decca DXSB-7174	(P)	The Kitty Wells Story (2 LPs)	1963	10.00	25.00
Decca DL-4493	(M)	Especially For You	1964	8.00	20.00
Decca DL-74493	(S)	Especially For You	1964	10.00	25.00
Decca DL-4554	(M)	Country Music Time	1964	8.00	20.00
Decca DL-74554	(S)	Country Music Time	1964	10.00	25.00
Decca DL-4612	(M)	Burning Memories	1965	8.00	20.00
Decca DL-74612	(S)	Burning Memories	1965	10.00	25.00
Decca DL-4658	(M)	Lonesome, Sad And Blue	1965	8.00	20.00
Decca DL-74658	(S)	Lonesome, Sad And Blue	1965	10.00	25.00
Decca DL-4679	(M)	Family Gospel Sing	1965	8.00	20.00
Decca DL-74679	(S)	Family Gospel Sing	1965	10.00	25.00
Decca DL-4741	(M)	Songs Made Famous By Jim Reeves	1966	8.00	20.00
Decca DL-74741	(S)	Songs Made Famous By Jim Reeves	1966	10.00	25.00
Decca DL-4776	(M)	Country All The Way	1966	8.00	20.00
Decca DL-74776	(S)	Country All The Way	1966	10.00	25.00
Decca DL-4831	(M)	The Kitty Wells Show	1966	8.00	20.00
Decca DL-74831	(S)	The Kitty Wells Show	1966	10.00	25.00

— Decca albums above have black labels with "Mfrd by Decca" beneath the rainbow.—

WELLS, KITTY, & RED FOLEY

Decca DL-4109	(M)	Golden Favorites	1961	10.00	25.00
Decca DL-74109	(S)	Golden Favorites	1961	12.00	30.00

— Decca albums above have black labels with "Mfrd by Decca" beneath the rainbow.—

Label & Catalog #		Title	Year	VG+	NM

WELLS, MARY

Label & Catalog #		Title	Year	VG+	NM
Motown M-600	(M)	Bye Bye Baby, I Don't Want To Take A Chance	1961	150.00	300.00
		—Motown albums above have white labels.—			
Motown M-600	(M)	Bye Bye Baby, I Don't Want To Take A Chance	1961	60.00	150.00
Motown M-605	(M)	The One Who Really Loves You	1962	60.00	150.00
Motown M-607	(M)	Two Lovers	1963	40.00	100.00
Motown M-611	(M)	Recorded Live On Stage	1963	30.00	75.00
		—Motown albums above have the company address above the spindle hole on the label.—			
Motown M-612	(M)	Second Time Around	1963		*Unreleased*
Motown M-616	(M)	Mary Wells' Greatest Hits	1964	10.00	25.00
Motown MS-616	(S)	Mary Wells' Greatest Hits	1964	12.00	30.00
Motown M-617	(M)	My Guy	1964	20.00	50.00
Motown M-653	(M)	Vintage Stock	1966	12.00	30.00
Motown MS-653	(S)	Vintage Stock	1966	16.00	40.00
20th Century TFM-3171	(M)	Mary Wells	1965	16.00	40.00
20th Century TFS-4171	(S)	Mary Wells	1965	20.00	50.00
20th Century TFM-3178	(M)	Love Songs To The Beatles	1965	20.00	50.00
20th Century TFS-4178	(S)	Love Songs To The Beatles	1965	30.00	75.00
Movietone 71010	(M)	Ooh	1966	10.00	25.00
Movietone 72010	(S)	Ooh	1966	12.00	30.00
Atco 33-199	(M)	Two Sides Of Mary Wells	1966	10.00	25.00
Atco SD-33-199	(S)	Two Sides Of Mary Wells	1966	12.00	30.00
Jubilee JGS-8018	(S)	Servin' Up Some Soul	1968	10.00	25.00

WELLS, MARY, & MARVIN GAYE

Label & Catalog #		Title	Year	VG+	NM
Motown M-613	(M)	Together	1964	20.00	50.00

WENDY & BONNIE

Label & Catalog #		Title	Year	VG+	NM
Skye SK-1006D	(S)	Genesis	197?	20.00	50.00

WEST, ADAM, & BURT WARD: *Refer to NELSON RIDDLE*

WEST, DOTTIE

Refer to Jimmy Dean & Dottie West.

Label & Catalog #		Title	Year	VG+	NM
Starday SLP-302	(M)	Country Girl Singing Sensation *(Yellow label)*	1964	16.00	40.00
RCA Victor LPM-3368	(M)	Here Comes My Baby	1965	10.00	25.00
RCA Victor LSP-3368	(S)	Here Comes My Baby	1965	12.00	30.00
RCA Victor LPM-3490	(M)	Dottie West Sings	1966	10.00	25.00
RCA Victor LSP-3490	(S)	Dottie West Sings	1966	12.00	30.00
RCA Victor LPM-3587	(M)	Suffer Time	1966	10.00	25.00
RCA Victor LSP-3587	(S)	Suffer Time	1966	12.00	30.00
RCA Victor LPM-3693	(M)	With All My Heart And Soul	1967	12.00	30.00
RCA Victor LSP-3693	(S)	With All My Heart And Soul	1967	10.00	25.00
RCA Victor LPM-3784	(M)	Dottie West Sings Sacred Ballads	1967	12.00	30.00
RCA Victor LSP-3784	(S)	Dottie West Sings Sacred Ballads	1967	10.00	25.00
RCA Victor LPM-3830	(M)	I'll Help You Forget Her	1967	12.00	30.00
RCA Victor LSP-3830	(S)	I'll Help You Forget Her	1967	10.00	25.00
RCA Victor LPM-3932	(M)	What I'm Cut Out To Be	1968	20.00	50.00
RCA Victor LSP-3932	(S)	What I'm Cut Out To Be	1968	10.00	25.00
RCA Victor LSP-4004	(S)	Country Girl	1968	10.00	25.00
		—RCA albums above have black labels with Nipper on top.—			

WEST, DOTTIE / MELBA MONTGOMERY

Label & Catalog #		Title	Year	VG+	NM
Starday SLP-352	(M)	Queens Of Country Music *(Yellow label)*	1965	16.00	40.00

WEST, HARRY & JEANNIE

Harry and Jeannie West are banjo, guitar and mandolin players and singers of traditional folk songs.

Label & Catalog #		Title	Year	VG+	NM
Stinson SLP-36	(10")	Southern Mountain Folk Songs	195?	20.00	50.00
Stinson SLP-74	(10")	More Southern Mountain Folk Songs	195?	20.00	50.00
Folkways FA-2352	(10")	Songs Of The Southland	195?	20.00	50.00
Folkways FA-2357	(10")	Gospel Songs	195?	20.00	50.00
Esoteric ES-538	(M)	Shivaree!	195?	12.00	30.00
Esoteric ES-545	(M)	Smoky Mountain Ballads	195?	12.00	30.00
Prestige Inter. PRLP-13038	(M)	Roamin' The Blue Ridge	1960	12.00	30.00
Prestige Inter. PRLP-13049	(M)	Country Music In A Bluegrass Style	1960	12.00	30.00

Label & Catalog #		Title	Year	VG+	NM

WEST, HEDY
Hedy West is a guitar and banjo player, singer and writer of traditional American folk music.

Vanguard VRS-9124	(M)	**Hedy West Accompanying Herself On The 5-String Banjo**	1963	8.00	20.00
Vanguard VSD-2124	(S)	**Hedy West Accompanying Herself On The 5-String Banjo**	1963	10.00	25.00
Vanguard VRS-9126	(M)	**Hedy West, Volume II**	1963	8.00	20.00
Vanguard VSD-2126	(S)	**Hedy West, Volume II**	1963	10.00	25.00

WEST, JEAN

Prestige Int. PRLP-13038	(M)	**Roamin' The Blue Ridge**	1962	12.00	30.00
Prestige Int. PRLP-13049	(M)	**Country Bluegrass**	1962	12.00	30.00

WEST, LUCRETIA

Westminster WP-6063	(M)	**Spirituals**	1957	16.00	40.00

WEST, MAE
Refer to W.C. Fields & Mae West.

Mezzotone 1	(10")	**Album Of Mae West Songs**	195?	40.00	100.00
Decca DL-9016	(M)	**The Fabulous Mae West**	1955	30.00	75.00
		— Decca albums above have black & silver labels.—			
Decca DL-9016	(M)	**The Fabulous Mae West**	196?	10.00	25.00
Decca DL-79016	(E)	**The Fabulous Mae West**	196?	6.00	15.00
		— Decca albums above have black rainbow labels.—			
Tower T-5028	(M)	**Way Out West**	1966	12.00	30.00
Tower ST-5028	(S)	**Way Out West**	1966	16.00	40.00

WEST, SPEEDY, & JIMMY BRYANT

Capitol H-520	(10")	**Two Guitars Country Style**	1954	100.00	250.00
Capitol T-520	(M)	**Two Guitars Country Style**	1956	60.00	150.00

WEST, SPEEDY

Capitol T-956	(M)	**West Of Hawaii**	1958	40.00	100.00
Capitol T-1341	(M)	**Steel Guitar**	1960	20.00	50.00
Capitol ST-1341	(S)	**Steel Guitar**	1960	30.00	75.00
Capitol T-1835	(M)	**Guitar Spectacular**	1962	16.00	40.00
Capitol ST-1835	(S)	**Guitar Spectacular**	1962	20.00	50.00

WEST COAST POP ART EXPERIMENTAL BAND, THE
The WCPAEB features Dan Harris, Shaun Harris and Bob Markley.

Fifo M101	(M)	**West Coast Pop Art Experimental Band**	1966	1,400.00	2,000.00
		(The price includes a regular cover.)			
Fifo M101	(M)	**West Coast Pop Art Experimental Band**	1966	300.00	500.00
		(The price is for the album in a plain cardboard jacket.)			
Razzberry Sawfly 800	(M)	**West Coast Pop Art Experimental Band**	1980	50.00	125.00
		(Razzberry Sawfly 800 is a reissue of Fifo 101.)			
Reprise R-6247	(M)	**Part One**	1967	14.00	35.00
Reprise RS-6247	(S)	**Part One**	1967	20.00	50.00
Reprise R-6270	(M)	**Volume 2**	1967	14.00	35.00
Reprise RS-6270	(S)	**Volume 2**	1967	20.00	50.00
Reprise RS-6298	(S)	**A Child's Guide To Good And Evil**	1968	12.00	30.00
Amos AAS-7004	(S)	**Where's My Daddy**	1969	16.00	40.00

WESTERN, JOHNNY

Columbia CL-1788	(M)	**Have Gun, Will Travel**	1962	8.00	20.00
Columbia CS-8588	(S)	**Have Gun, Will Travel**	1962	10.00	25.00

WESTFAUSTER

Nasco 9008	(S)	**In A King's Dream**	1971	24.00	60.00

WESTON, KIM
Ms. Weston also recorded with Marvin Gaye.

MGM E-4477	(M)	**For The First Time**	1967	12.00	30.00
MGM SE-4477	(S)	**For The First Time**	1967	16.00	40.00
MGM SE-4561	(S)	**This Is America**	1968	14.00	35.00
Volt VO-6014	(M)	**Kim Kim Kim** *(White label promo)*	1971	14.00	35.00
Volt VOS-6014	(S)	**Kim Kim Kim**	1971	10.00	25.00

Label & Catalog #		Title	Year	VG+	NM
WHALE FEATHERS					
Nasco 9003	(S)	Whalefeathers Declare	1969	20.00	50.00
Nasco 9005	(S)	Whalefeathers	1970	20.00	50.00
WHEELER, BILLY EDD					
Monitor MF-354	(M)	Billy Edd	1961	12.00	30.00
Monitor MF-367	(M)	Billy Edd And Bluegrass	1962	12.00	30.00
WHEELS, BURT, & THE SPEEDSTERS					
Coronet CX-216	(M)	Sounds Of The Big Racers	196?	10.00	25.00
Coronet CXS-216	(S)	Sounds Of The Big Racers	196?	14.00	35.00
WHEELS, THE					
Montgomery Ward 10	(S)	Sounds Of The Hot Rods	196?	30.00	75.00
WHISPERS, THE					
Soul Clock 22001	(S)	Planets Of Life	197?	40.00	100.00
Janus JLS-3041	(S)	The Whispers' Love Story	197?	20.00	50.00

WHISKEYHILL SINGERS, THE: *Refer to* **DAVE GUARD & THE WHISKEYHILL SINGERS.**

WHITCOMB, IAN					
Tower T-5004	(M)	You Turn Me On	1965	12.00	30.00
Tower DT-5004	(E)	You Turn Me On	1965	10.00	25.00
Tower T-5042	(M)	Mod, Mod, Music Hall	1966	8.00	20.00
Tower ST-5042	(S)	Mod, Mod, Music Hall	1966	10.00	25.00
Tower T-5071	(M)	Yellow Underground	1967	8.00	20.00
Tower ST-5071	(S)	Yellow Underground	1967	10.00	25.00
Tower ST-5100	(S)	Sock Me Some Rock	1968	10.00	25.00

WHITE, JOSH
Josh White was a guitar player, singer and writer of folk-blues. Refer to Big Bill Broonzy; Leadbelly.

Mercury MG-25014	(10")	Josh White Sings Blues	1949	80.00	200.00
Decca DL-5082	(10")	Ballads And Blues	1949	80.00	200.00
Stinson SLP-14	(10")	Josh White Sings The Blues	1950	60.00	150.00
Stinson SLP-15	(10")	Josh White Sings	1950	60.00	150.00
London LPB-338	(10")	A Josh White Program	1951	60.00	150.00
Decca DL-5247	(10")	Ballads, Volume 2	1952	60.00	150.00
EmArcy MG-26010	(10")	Strange Fruit	1954	60.00	150.00
London LL-1147	(M)	A Josh White Program	1956	24.00	60.00
		(London 1147 is a reissue of 338.)			
London LL-1341	(M)	A Josh White Program, Vol. 2	1956	24.00	60.00
Period SLP-1115	(10")	Josh White Comes A-Visiting	1956	30.00	75.00
ABC-Paramount ABC-124	(M)	The Josh White Stories, Vol. 1	1956	30.00	75.00
ABC-Paramount ABC-166	(M)	The Josh White Stories, Vol. 2	1957	30.00	75.00
Elektra EKL-102	(M)	Josh At Midnight	1956	20.00	50.00
Elektra EKL-114	(M)	Josh Sings Blues	1957	20.00	50.00
Elektra EKL-123	(M)	25th Anniversary Album	1957	20.00	50.00
Elektra EKL-158	(M)	Chain Gang Songs	1958		*See below*
		(Each track on "Chain Gang Songs" features vocal backing by The Four Fellows, with White functioning as the lead singer of a five piece vocal group. This little known aspect of the recording should make the album of interest to rhythm'n blues group collectors leaving us with a suggested NM value of $100-300.)			
Elektra EKL-701	(M)	The Story Of John Henry / Ballads, Blues & Other Songs *(2 LPs)*	195?	24.00	60.00
ABC-Paramount ABC-407	(M)	Josh White - Live!	1962	12.00	30.00
Mercury MG-20203	(M)	Josh White's Blues	1957	30.00	75.00
Decca DL-8665	(M)	Josh White/Ballads And Blues	1958	24.00	60.00
ABC-Paramount ABCS-407	(S)	Josh White - Live!	1962	16.00	40.00
Mercury MG-20821	(M)	The Beginning	1963	12.00	30.00
Mercury SR-60821	(E)	The Beginning	1963	8.00	20.00

WHITE, KITTY: *Refer to* **GOLDMINE'S PRICE GUIDE TO COLLECTIBLE JAZZ ALBUMS**

WHITE BOY & THE AVERAGE RAT BAND					
Tradewind MM-11761	(S)	White Boy & The Average Rat Band	1975	50.00	125.00

Label & Catalog #		Title	Year	VG+	NM
WHITE LIGHT					
Century 39955	(S)	**White Light** (With "Heartbreak Hotel")	1968	50.00	125.00
Century 39955	(S)	**White Light** (Without "Heartbreak Hotel")	1969	60.00	150.00
WHITE SUMMER					
(No label)	(S)	**White Summer**	197?	80.00	200.00
WHITING, MARGARET					
Ms. Whiting also recorded with Mel Torme.					
Capitol H-163	(10")	**South Pacific**	1950	20.00	50.00
Capitol H-209	(10")	**Margaret Whiting Sings Rodgers & Hart**	1950	20.00	50.00
Capitol H-234	(10")	**Songs**	1950	20.00	50.00
Capitol T-410	(M)	**Love Songs**	1955	14.00	35.00
Capitol T-685	(M)	**For The Starry-Eyed**	1955	14.00	35.00
Dot DLP-3072	(M)	**Goin' Places**	1957	10.00	25.00
Dot DLP-25072	(S)	**Goin' Places**	1958	10.00	25.00
Dot DLP-3113	(M)	**Margaret**	1958	8.00	20.00
Dot DLP-25113	(S)	**Margaret**	1958	10.00	25.00
Dot DLP-3176	(M)	**Margaret Whiting Great Hits**	1959	8.00	20.00
Dot DLP-25176	(S)	**Margaret Whiting Great Hits**	1959	10.00	25.00
Dot DLP-3235	(M)	**Ten Top Hits**	1960	8.00	20.00
Dot DLP-25235	(S)	**Ten Top Hits**	1960	10.00	25.00
Dot DLP-3337	(M)	**Just A Dream**	1960	8.00	20.00
Dot DLP-25337	(S)	**Just A Dream**	1960	10.00	25.00
Verve V-4038	(M)	**Margaret Whiting Sings The Jerome Kern Song Book**	1961	8.00	20.00
Verve V6-4038	(S)	**Margaret Whiting Sings The Jerome Kern Song Book**	1961	10.00	25.00
WHITMAN, SLIM					
RCA Victor LPM-3217	(10")	**Slim Whitman Sings And Yodels**	1954	150.00	300.00
Imperial LP-3004	(10")	**America's Favorite Folk Artist**	1954	200.00	400.00
Imperial LP-9003	(M)	**Favorites**	1956	20.00	50.00
Imperial LP-9026	(M)	**Slim Whitman Sings**	1957	20.00	50.00
		— Imperial albums above have maroon labels.—			
Imperial LP-9003	(M)	**Favorites**	1958	12.00	30.00
Imperial LP-9026	(M)	**Slim Whitman Sings**	1958	12.00	30.00
Imperial LP-9056	(M)	**Slim Whitman Sings**	1958	12.00	30.00
Imperial LP-9064	(M)	**Slim Whitman Sings**	1959	12.00	30.00
Imperial LP-9077	(M)	**Annie Laurie**	1959	12.00	30.00
Imperial LP-9088	(M)	**I'll Walk With God**	1960	12.00	30.00
Imperial LP-12032	(E)	**I'll Walk With God**	1960	6.00	15.00
Imperial LP-9100	(M)	**Country Hits, Volume 1**	1960	10.00	25.00
Imperial LP-9101	(M)	**Million Record Hits**	1960	10.00	25.00
Imperial LP-9104	(M)	**Country Hits, Volume 2**	1960	10.00	25.00
Imperial LP-9105	(M)	**My Best To You**	1960	10.00	25.00
Imperial LP-9106	(M)	**Country Favorites**	1960	10.00	25.00
Imperial LP-9135	(M)	**First Visit To Britain**	1961	10.00	25.00
Imperial LP-9137	(M)	**Just Call Me Lonesome**	1961	10.00	25.00
Imperial LP-9156	(M)	**Once In A Lifetime**	1961	10.00	25.00
Imperial LP-9171	(M)	**Forever**	1962	10.00	25.00
Imperial LP-9194	(M)	**Slim Whitman Sings**	1962	10.00	25.00
Imperial LP-12194	(S)	**Slim Whitman Sings**	1962	12.00	30.00
Imperial LP-9209	(M)	**Heart Songs And Love Songs**	1962	10.00	25.00
Imperial LP-9226	(M)	**I'm A Lonely Wanderer**	1963	10.00	25.00
Imperial LP-9235	(M)	**Yodeling**	1963	10.00	25.00
Imperial LP-9245	(M)	**Irish Songs, The Whitman Way**	1963	10.00	25.00
Imperial LP-9252	(M)	**All Time Favorites**	1963	10.00	25.00
		— Imperial mono albums above have black labels with colored stars on top; stereo albums have blac labels with silver print.—			
WHITNEY, MARVA					
King KS-1053	(S)	**I Sing Soul**	1969	12.00	30.00
King KS-1062	(S)	**It's My Thing**	1969	12.00	30.00
King KS-1079	(S)	**Live And Lowdown At The Apollo**	1969	24.00	60.00
		(King 1053, 1062 and 1079 were produced by James Brown.)			

Label & Catalog #		Title	Year	VG+	NM

WHO, THE

The Who are Roger Daltrey, John Entwhistle, Keith Moon and Pete Townshend. Moon died in 1978 and was replaced by Kenny Jones of The Faces.

Label & Catalog #		Title	Year	VG+	NM
Decca DL-4664	(M)	The Who Sing My Generation (White label)	1966	80.00	200.00
Decca DL-4664	(M)	The Who Sing My Generation	1966	50.00	125.00
Decca DL-74664	(E)	The Who Sing My Generation (White label)	1966	50.00	125.00
Decca DL-74664	(E)	The Who Sing My Generation	1966	24.00	60.00
Life DL-74664	(E)	The Who Sing My Generation	1967	80.00	200.00
		(The Life album is a reissue on a little-known subsidiary of Decca.)			
Decca DL-4892	(M)	Happy Jack (White label promo)	1967	60.00	150.00
Decca DL-4892	(M)	Happy Jack	1967	20.00	50.00
Decca DL-74892	(S)	Happy Jack (White label promo)	1967	50.00	125.00
Decca DL-74892	(S)	Happy Jack	1967	20.00	50.00
		("Happy Jack" and "Don't Look Away" are rechanneled.)			
Decca DL-4950	(M)	The Who Sell Out (White label promo)	1967	100.00	250.00
		(On some mono promos of DL-4950, side 1 is specially banded for air-play with a different song order and all of the "commercials" are placed on one side.)			
Decca DL-4950	(M)	The Who Sell Out (White label promo)	1967	50.00	125.00
		(The playing order is the same as the commercial release.)			
Decca DL-4950	(M)	The Who Sell Out	1967	40.00	100.00
Decca DL-74950	(S)	The Who Sell Out (White label promo)	1967	60.00	150.00
Decca DL-74950	(S)	The Who Sell Out	1967	12.00	30.00
Decca DL-5064	(M)	Magic Bus/The Who On Tour (White label)	1968	70.00	175.00
Decca DL-75064	(E)	Magic Bus/The Who On Tour (White label)	1968	50.00	125.00
Decca DL-75064	(E)	Magic Bus/The Who On Tour	1968	20.00	50.00
		("Magic Bus," "I Can't Reach You" and "Tatoo" are stereo on this LP.)			
Decca DXW-7205	(M)	Tommy (White label promo)	1969		See below
		(Mono promos have a suggested Near Mint value of $500-1,000.)			
Decca DXSW-7205	(S)	Tommy (White label promo)	1969	60.00	150.00
Decca DXSW-7205	(S)	Tommy (2 LPs with booklet)	1969	16.00	40.00
Decca DL-79175	(S)	Live At Leeds	1970	16.00	40.00
		(Fold-open jacket includes twelve different inserts and photos including reproductions of old contracts.)			
Decca DL-79182	(S)	Who's Next	1971	10.00	25.00
Track 2408-102	(S)	Who's Next	1971	60.00	150.00
		(Black Track label reads "Made in USA" on the bottom. Manufactured for export and issued in a regular UK cover.)			
Decca DL-79184	(S)	Meaty Beaty Big & Bouncy (With poster)	1971	14.00	35.00
Decca DL-79184	(S)	Meaty Beaty Big & Bouncy (Without poster)	1971	10.00	25.00
		("I Can't Explain," "Anyway, Anyhow, Anywhere," "Substitute," "My Generation," "Pictures Of Lily" and an alternate take of "Magic Bus" are rechanneled on this album. Originally issued with a brown & white, 10" x 20" poster with photos and notes.)			
MCA 2044	(E)	The Who Sing My Generation	1974	16.00	40.00
MCA 2045	(P)	Happy Jack	1974	16.00	40.00
MCA 3050	(DJ)	Who Are You (White label promo)	1978	10.00	25.00
		(Promos judiciously edit "Who the fuck are you" out of the title tune.)			
Warner Bros. WBMS-116	(DJ)	Filling In The Gaps (2 LP interview)	1981	30.00	75.00
		(WBMS-116 was originally issued with a special drawing cover.)			
Warner Bros. WBMS-116	(DJ)	Filling In The Gaps (2 LP interview)	1981	20.00	50.00
		(Later pressings have a red omnibus Warner Bros. cover.)			
Warner Bros. 23731	(S)	It's Hard (Promo on Quiex II vinyl)	1982	8.00	25.00
Direct Disc SD-16610	(S)	Who Are You	1979	8.00	25.00

WHO, THE / THE STRAWBERRY ALARM CLOCK

Label & Catalog #		Title	Year	VG+	NM
Decca DL-734568	(S)	The Who / The Strawberry Alarm Clock	1969	60.00	150.00
		(Available briefly in 1969 through Philco Electronics stores.)			

WICHITA TRAIN WHISTLE, THE

The Whistle features Michael Nesmith.

Label & Catalog #		Title	Year	VG+	NM
Dot DLP-25861	(S)	The Wichita Train Whistle Sings	1968	16.00	40.00

WIGGINS, LITTLE ROY

Label & Catalog #		Title	Year	VG+	NM
Starday SLP-188	(M)	Mister Steel Guitar	1962	16.00	40.00
Starday SLP-259	(M)	The Fabulous Steel Guitar Artistry	1963	16.00	40.00
Starday SLP-392	(M)	Nashville Steel Guitar	1965	16.00	40.00
		— Starday albums above have yellow labels.—			

Label & Catalog #		Title	Year	VG+	NM
WILBURN BROTHERS, THE					
Decca DL-8576	(M)	The Wilburn Brothers	1957	20.00	50.00
Decca DL-8774	(M)	Side By Side	1958	20.00	50.00
Decca DL-78774	(S)	Side By Side	1958	30.00	75.00
Decca DL-8959	(M)	Livin' In God's Country	1959	20.00	50.00
Decca DL-78959	(S)	Livin' In God's Country	1959	30.00	75.00
		— Decca albums above have black & silver labels.—			
Decca DL-4058	(M)	The Big Heartbreak	1960	12.00	30.00
Decca DL-74058	(S)	The Big Heartbreak	1960	16.00	40.00
Decca DL-4142	(M)	The Wilburn Brothers Sing	1961	12.00	30.00
Decca DL-74142	(S)	The Wilburn Brothers Sing	1961	16.00	40.00
Decca DL-4211	(M)	City Limits	1961	12.00	30.00
Decca DL-74211	(S)	City Limits	1961	16.00	40.00
King 746	(M)	The Wonderful Wilburn Brothers	1961	40.00	100.00
Decca DL-4225	(M)	Folk Songs	1962	8.00	20.00
Decca DL-74225	(S)	Folk Songs	1962	12.00	30.00
Decca DL-4391	(M)	Trouble's Back In Town	1963	8.00	20.00
Decca DL-74391	(S)	Trouble's Back In Town	1963	10.00	25.00
Decca DL-4464	(M)	Take Up Thy Cross	1964	8.00	20.00
Decca DL-74464	(S)	Take Up Thy Cross	1964	10.00	25.00
Decca DL-4544	(M)	Never Alone	1964	8.00	20.00
Decca DL-74544	(S)	Never Alone	1964	10.00	25.00
Decca DL-4615	(M)	Country Gold	1965	8.00	20.00
Decca DL-74615	(S)	Country Gold	1965	10.00	25.00
Decca DL-4645	(M)	I'm Gonna Tie One On Tonight	1965	8.00	20.00
Decca DL-74645	(S)	I'm Gonna Tie One On Tonight	1965	10.00	25.00
Decca DL-4721	(M)	The Wilburn Brothers Show	1966	14.00	35.00
Decca DL-74721	(S)	The Wilburn Brothers Show	1966	16.00	40.00
Decca DL-4764	(M)	Let's Go Country	1966	8.00	20.00
Decca DL-74764	(S)	Let's Go Country	1966	10.00	25.00
Decca DL-4824	(M)	Two For The Show	1967	8.00	20.00
Decca DL-74824	(S)	Two For The Show	1967	10.00	25.00
		— Decca albums above have black "rainbow" labels that read "Mfrd. by Decca Records."—			
WILD COUNTRY: *Refer to* **ALABAMA**					
WILD, JACK					
Capitol SKAO-545	(S)	The Jack Wild Album	1970	10.00	25.00
Buddah BDS-5083	(S)	Everything's Coming Up Roses	1971	10.00	25.00
Buddah BDS-5110	(S)	A Beautiful World	1972	10.00	25.00
WILD ONES, THE					
United Arts. UAL-6450	(M)	The Arthur Sound	1965	10.00	25.00
United Arts. UAS-6450	(S)	The Arthur Sound	1965	12.00	30.00
WILDCATS, THE					
United Arts. UAL-3031	(M)	Bandstand Record Hop	1958	20.00	50.00
WILDE, MARTY					
Epic LN-3686	(M)	Bad Boy	1960	30.00	75.00
Epic LN-3711	(M)	Wilde About Marty	1960	30.00	75.00
Epic BN-575	(S)	Wilde About Marty	1960	40.00	100.00

WILDER, DICK
Dick Wilder is a guitar player and singer of traditional folk songs. Refer to Ed McCurdy / Oscar Brand / Jack Elliott / Dick Wilder.

Elektra EKL-18	(10")	Pirate Songs And Ballads	195?	20.00	50.00

WILDWEEDS, THE
Wildweeds features Al Anderson, later of NRBQ.

Vanguard VSD-6552	(S)	Wildweeds	1970	16.00	40.00

WILEY, LEE: *Refer to* **GOLDMINE'S PRICE GUIDE TO COLLECTIBLE JAZZ ALBUMS**

WILLETT, SLIM

Audio Lab AL-1542	(M)	Slim Willett	195?	80.00	200.00

Label & Catalog #		Title	Year	VG+	NM

WILLIAMS, ANDY

Cadence CLP-1018	(M)	Andy Williams Sings... Steve Allen	1957	20.00	50.00
Cadence CLP-3002	(M)	Andy Williams	1958	20.00	50.00
		(Original covers for CLP-002 have a shot of a standing AW.)			
Cadence CLP-3002	(M)	Andy Williams	1960	8.00	20.00
		(Later covers depict a reclining AW.)			
Cadence CLP-3005	(M)	Andy Williams Sings Rodgers & Hammerstein	1959	16.00	40.00
		(Original covers for CLP-3005 featuree a cafe scene.)			
Cadence CLP-3005	(M)	Andy Williams Sings Rodgers & Hammerstein	1960	8.00	20.00
		(Later covers have a close-up of AW's face.)			
Cadence CLP-3026	(M)	Two Time Winners	1960	8.00	20.00
Cadence CLP-25026	(S)	Two Time Winners	1960	12.00	30.00
Cadence CLP-3027	(M)	Andy Williams Sings Steve Allen	1960	8.00	20.00
Cadence CLP-25027	(E)	Andy Williams Sings Steve Allen	1960	6.00	15.00
		(Cadence 3/25027 is a reissue of 1018.)			
Cadence CLP-3029	(M)	To You Sweetheart, Aloha	1960	8.00	20.00
Cadence CLP-25029	(S)	To You Sweetheart, Aloha	1960	12.00	30.00
Cadence CLP-3030	(M)	Lonely Street	1960	8.00	20.00
Cadence CLP-25030	(S)	Lonely Street	1960	12.00	30.00
Cadence CLP-3038	(M)	The Village Of St. Bernadette	1960	8.00	20.00
Cadence CLP-25038	(S)	The Village Of St. Bernadette	1960	12.00	30.00
Cadence CLP-3047	(M)	Under Paris Skies	1961	8.00	20.00
Cadence CLP-25047	(S)	Under Paris Skies	1961	12.00	30.00
Cadence CLP-3054	(M)	Andy Williams' Best	1962	8.00	20.00
Cadence CLP-25054	(S)	Andy Williams' Best	1962	10.00	25.00
— Cadence albums above have burgundy & silver labels. —					
Cadence CLP-3061	(M)	Million Seller Songs	1963	8.00	20.00
Cadence CLP-25061	(S)	Million Seller Songs	1963	10.00	25.00
— Cadence albums above have red & black labels. —					

WILLIAMS, BETTY VAIDEN

Betty Vaiden Williams is a autoharp, dulcimer and guitar player and singer of traditional folk songs.

Vanguard VRS-9028	(M)	Folk Songs And Ballads Of North Carolina	195?	12.00	30.00

WILLIAMS, BILLY

Mr. Williams was formerly a member of The Charioteers.

Coral CRL-57184	(M)	Billy Williams	1957	20.00	50.00
MGM E-3400	(M)	The Billy Williams Quartet	1957	20.00	50.00
Mercury MG-20317	(M)	Billy Williams Singing "Oh Yeah"	1958	20.00	50.00
Wing MGW-12131	(M)	Vote For Billy Williams	1959	16.00	40.00
Coral CRL-57251	(M)	Half Sweet, Half Beat	1959	20.00	50.00
Coral CRL-757251	(S)	Half Sweet, Half Beat	1959	30.00	75.00
Coral CRL-57343	(M)	The Billy Williams Revue	1960	20.00	50.00
Coral CRL-757343	(S)	The Billy Williams Revue	1960	30.00	75.00

WILLIAMS, BILLY DEE

Lively Arts LA-30001	(M)	Let's Misbehave	196?	14.00	35.00

WILLIAMS, CAMILLA

MGM E-156	(10")	Spirituals	1952	40.00	100.00

WILLIAMS, DENIECE

Columbia HC-47952	(S)	Niecy (Half-speed master)	198?	12.00	35.00

WILLIAMS, HANK

Hank Williams also recorded as Luke The Drifter; these Luke albums are included here. On several albums, MGM addded strings and choruses to the original recordings; in some cases the mono albums do not have the sweetening but the stereos do. On the "Hank With Strings" albums, the sweetening is on both the mono and stereo versions; the stereo albums have Hank's original mono tracks with the sweetening in stereo. Most albums with the strings are avoided by all but the completist. Refer to The Drifting Cowboys.

MGM E-107	(10")	Hank Williams Sings	1952	200.00	400.00
MGM E-168	(10")	Moanin' The Blues	1952	200.00	400.00
MGM E-202	(10")	Hank Williams Memorial Album	1953	200.00	400.00
MGM E-203	(10")	Hank Williams As Luke The Drifter	1953	200.00	400.00
MGM E-242	(10")	Honky Tonkin'	1954	200.00	400.00
MGM E-243	(10")	I Saw The Light	1954	200.00	400.00

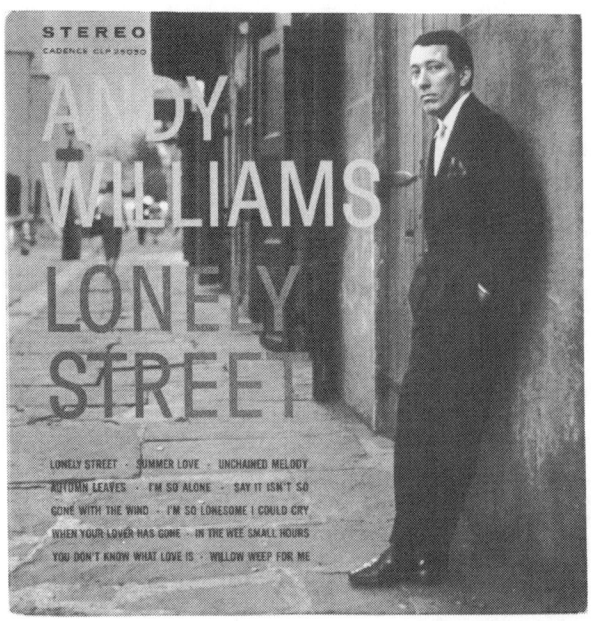

Andy Williams was gifted with a smooth, truly beautiful voice and perfect, if passionless, pitch. While his career led to his own television series, movie deals, and very wise investments, most collectors place less than nominal value on his Columbia catalog, searching instead for his early Cadence releases, two of which are pictured here.

Hank Williams is the progenitor of modern country music and an obvious primary influence on the development of rock'n roll through his influence on such early masters as Elvis, Chuck and Jerry Lee, among a host of others. His third long-playing album was released in the wake of his death at the age of 29 in January of 1953. Pictured above is the 10" version of the Memorial Album containing eight of his eight of his biggest hits. Below that is the 12" reissue, fleshed out to twelve tracks.

Label & Catalog #		Title	Year	VG+	NM
MGM E-291	(10")	Ramblin' Man	1954	200.00	400.00
MGM E-3219	(M)	Ramblin' Man	1955	50.00	125.00
MGM E-3267	(M)	Hank Williams As Luke The Drifter	1955	50.00	125.00
MGM E-3272	(M)	Hank Williams Memorial Album	1955	50.00	125.00
MGM E-3330	(M)	Moanin' The Blues	1956	50.00	125.00
MGM E-3331	(M)	I Saw The Light (Green cover)	1956	70.00	175.00
MGM E-3331	(M)	I Saw The Light (Church cover)	1959	50.00	125.00
MGM E-3412	(M)	Honky Tonkin'	1957	50.00	125.00
MGM E-3560	(M)	Sing Me A Blue Song	1957	50.00	125.00
MGM E-3605	(M)	The Immortal Hank Williams	1958	50.00	125.00
MGM 3E-2	(M)	36 Of Hank Williams' Greatest Hits (3 LPs)	195?	80.00	200.00
MGM 3E-4	(M)	36 More Greatest Hits (3 LPs)	195?	80.00	200.00
MGM E-3733	(M)	The Unforgettable Hank Williams	1959	50.00	125.00
		—MGM albums above have yellow labels.—			
MGM E-3219	(M)	Ramblin' Man	1960	16.00	40.00
MGM E-3267	(M)	Hank Williams As Luke The Drifter	1960	16.00	40.00
MGM E-3272	(M)	Hank Williams Memorial Album	1960	16.00	40.00
MGM SE-3272	(E)	Hank Williams Memorial Album	196?	8.00	20.00
MGM E-3330	(M)	Moanin' The Blues	1960	16.00	40.00
MGM E-3331	(M)	I Saw The Light	1960	16.00	40.00
MGM SE-3331	(E)	I Saw The Light	196?	8.00	20.00
MGM E-3412	(M)	Honky Tonkin'	1960	16.00	40.00
MGM E-3560	(M)	Sing Me A Blue Song	1960	16.00	40.00
MGM E-3605	(M)	The Immortal Hank Williams	1960	16.00	40.00
MGM E-3733	(M)	The Unforgettable Hank Williams	1960	16.00	40.00
MGM SE-3733	(E)	The Unforgettable Hank Williams	196?	8.00	20.00
MGM 3E-2	(M)	36 Of Hank Williams' Greatest Hits (3 LPs)	1960	40.00	100.00
MGM 3SE-2	(E)	36 Of Hank Williams' Greatest Hits (3 LPs)	1960	20.00	50.00
MGM 3E-4	(M)	36 More Greatest Hits (3 LPs)	1960	40.00	100.00
MGM 3SE-4	(E)	36 More Greatest Hits (3 LPs)	1960	20.00	50.00
MGM E-3803	(M)	The Lonesome Sound Of Hank Williams	1960	16.00	40.00
MGM SE-3803	(E)	The Lonesome Sound Of Hank Williams	196?	8.00	20.00
MGM E-3850	(M)	Wait For The Light To Shine	1960	16.00	40.00
MGM SE-3850	(E)	Wait For The Light To Shine	196?	8.00	20.00
MGM E-3918	(M)	Hank Williams' Greatest Hits	1961	16.00	40.00
MGM SE-3918	(E)	Hank Williams' Greatest Hits	196?	8.00	20.00
MGM E-3923	(M)	Hank Williams Lives Again	1961	16.00	40.00
MGM SE-3923	(E)	Hank Williams Lives Again	196?	8.00	20.00
MGM E-3924	(M)	Sing Me A Blue Song	1961	16.00	40.00
MGM SE-3924	(E)	Sing Me A Blue Song	196?	8.00	20.00
MGM E-3925	(M)	Wanderin' Around	1961	16.00	40.00
MGM SE-3925	(E)	Wanderin' Around	196?	8.00	20.00
MGM E-3926	(M)	I'm Blue Inside	1961	16.00	40.00
MGM SE-3926	(E)	I'm Blue Inside	196?	8.00	20.00
MGM E-3927	(M)	Luke The Drifter	1961	16.00	40.00
MGM SE-3927	(E)	Luke The Drifter	196?	8.00	20.00
MGM E-3928	(M)	First, Last And Always, Hank Williams	1961	16.00	40.00
MGM SE-3928	(E)	First, Last And Always, Hank Williams	196?	8.00	20.00
		(MGM 3928 is a repackage of MGM 3605.)			
MGM E-3955	(M)	The Spirit Of Hank Williams	1961	16.00	40.00
MGM SE-3955	(E)	The Spirit Of Hank Williams	196?	8.00	20.00
MGM E-3999	(M)	On Stage! Hank Williams Recorded Live	1962	24.00	60.00
		(First pressings of MGM 3999 were titled "On Stage!")			
MGM E-3999	(M)	On Stage Recorded Live (Yellow label)	1962	20.00	50.00
MGM E-3999	(M)	On Stage Recorded Live (Black label)	1962	16.00	40.00
MGM SE-3999	(E)	Hank Williams On Stage Recorded Live	1962	8.00	20.00
MGM E-4040	(M)	14 More Greatest Hits, Volume 2	1962	16.00	40.00
MGM SE-4040	(E)	14 More Greatest Hits, Volume 2	196?	8.00	20.00
MGM E-4109	(M)	Hank Williams On Stage, Volume 2	1963	16.00	40.00
MGM SE-4109	(E)	Hank Williams On Stage, Volume 2	1963	8.00	20.00
MGM E-4138	(M)	Beyond The Sunset	1963	16.00	40.00
MGM SE-4138	(E)	Beyond The Sunset	196?	8.00	20.00
MGM E-4140	(M)	14 More Greatest Hits, Volume 3	1963	12.00	30.00
MGM SE-4140	(E)	14 More Greatest Hits, Volume 3	196?	6.00	15.00
MGM E-4168	(M)	The Very Best Of Hank Williams	1963	12.00	30.00
MGM SE-4168	(E)	The Very Best Of Hank Williams	1963	6.00	15.00
MGM E-4227	(M)	The Very Best Of Hank Williams, Volume 2	1964	12.00	30.00
MGM SE-4227	(E)	The Very Best Of Hank Williams, Volume 2	1964	6.00	15.00

Label & Catalog #		Title	Year	VG+	NM
MGM E-4254	(M)	Lost Highway (& Other Folk Ballads)	1964	16.00	40.00
MGM SE-4254	(E)	Lost Highway (& Other Folk Ballads)	196?	8.00	20.00
MGM E-4267	(M)	The Hank Williams Story (4 LP box.)	1965	20.00	50.00
MGM SE-4267	(E)	The Hank Williams Story (4 LP box.)	1965	10.00	25.00
MGM E-4300	(M)	Kaw-Liga And Other Humorous Songs	1965	12.00	30.00
MGM SE-4300	(E)	Kaw-Liga And Other Humorous Songs	1965	6.00	15.00
MGM E-4377	(M)	The Legend Lives Anew—	1966	8.00	20.00
		Hank Williams With Strings			
MGM SE-4377	(S)	The Legend Lives Anew—	1966	10.00	25.00
		Hank Williams With Strings			
MGM E-4380	(M)	Luke The Drifter	1966	12.00	30.00
MGM SE-4380	(E)	Luke The Drifter	1966	6.00	15.00
MGM E-4429	(M)	More Hank Williams And Strings	1966	8.00	20.00
MGM SE-4429	(S)	More Hank Williams And Strings	1966	10.00	25.00
MGM E-4481	(M)	I Won't Be Home No More	1967	12.00	30.00
MGM SE-4481	(E)	I Won't Be Home No More	1967	6.00	15.00
		— MGM albums above have black labels.—			
MGM E-4529	(M)	Hank Williams And Strings, Volume 3	1968	12.00	30.00
MGM SE-4529	(E)	Hank Williams And Strings, Volume 3	1968	6.00	15.00
MGM E-4576	(M)	Hank Williams In The Beginning	1968	12.00	30.00
MGM SE-4576	(E)	Hank Williams In The Beginning	1968	6.00	15.00
MGM SE-240	(E)	24 Karat Hits (2 LPs)	1970	10.00	25.00
MGM 1SE-33ST	(E)	The Last Picture Show (Soundtrack)	1971	12.00	30.00
		— MGM albums above have blue & gold labels.—			
MGM PRO-912	(DJ)	Reflections Of Those Who Loved Him	1975	80.00	200.00
		(Promotional 3 LP boxed set of various artists eulogizing Hank.)			
Columbia P4S-5616	(E)	The Hank Williams Treasury (4 LP box)	197?	12.00	30.00

WILLIAMS, HANK, & HANK WILLIAMS, JR.

MGM E-4276	(M)	Hank Williams, Sr., & Hank Williams. Jr.	1965	8.00	20.00
MGM SE-4276	(S)	Hank Williams, Sr., & Hank Williams. Jr.	1965	10.00	25.00
MGM E-4378	(M)	Again	1966	8.00	20.00
MGM SE-4378	(S)	Again	1966	10.00	25.00
		— MGM albums above have black labels.—			

WILLIAMS, HANK, JR./HANK WILLIAMS JR & THE CHEATIN' HEARTS
Hank Jr. also recorded with Connie Francis.

MGM E-4213	(M)	Songs Of Hank Williams	1963	8.00	20.00
MGM SE-4213	(S)	Songs Of Hank Williams	1963	10.00	25.00
MGM E-4260	(M)	Your Cheatin' Heart (Soundtrack)	1964	8.00	20.00
MGM SE-4260	(S)	Your Cheatin' Heart (Soundtrack)	1964	10.00	25.00
MGM E-4316	(M)	Ballads Of The Hills And Plains	1965	8.00	20.00
MGM SE-4316	(S)	Ballads Of The Hills And Plains	1965	10.00	25.00
MGM E-4344	(M)	Blue's My Name	1966	8.00	20.00
MGM SE-4344	(S)	Blue's My Name	1966	10.00	25.00
MGM E-4391	(M)	Country Shadows	1966	8.00	20.00
MGM SE-4391	(S)	Country Shadows	1966	10.00	25.00
MGM E-4428	(M)	In My Own Way	1967	8.00	20.00
MGM SE-4428	(S)	In My Own Way	1967	10.00	25.00
		— MGM albums above have black labels.—			

WILLIAMS, JOE: Refer to GOLDMINE'S PRICE GUIDE TO COLLECTIBLE JAZZ ALBUMS

WILLIAMS, "BIG" JOE
Joe Williams is a guitar player and singer of country blues. Refer to Victoria Spivey.

Folkways F-3820	(M)	Mississippi's Big Joe Williams	1962	12.00	30.00
Folkways FS-3820	(S)	Mississippi's Big Joe Williams	1962	16.00	40.00
Delmark DL-604	(M)	Blues On Highway 49	1962	16.00	40.00
Bluesville BVLP-1056	(M)	Blues For 9 Strings	1962	30.00	75.00
Bluesville BVLP-1067	(M)	Big Joe Williams At Folk City	1963	30.00	75.00
Bluesville BVLP-1083	(M)	Studio Blues	1964	30.00	75.00
		— Bluesville albums above have bright blue labels with silver print.—			
Bluesville BVLP-1056	(M)	Blues For 9 Strings	1964	10.00	25.00
Bluesville BVLP-1067	(M)	Big Joe Williams At Folk City	1964	10.00	25.00
Bluesville BVLP-1083	(M)	Studio Blues	1964	10.00	25.00
		— Bluesville albums above have blue labels with a trident logo on the right side.—			
Delmark DL-609	(M)	Starvin' Chain Blues	1966	10.00	25.00
Milestone 3001	(M)	Classic Delta Blues	1966	10.00	25.00
Folkways 31004	(M)	Hell Bound And Heaven Sent	1967	10.00	25.00

Label & Catalog #		Title	Year	VG+	NM

WILLIAMS, LARRY
Larry also recorded with Johnny Watson.

Specialty SP-2109	(M)	Here's Larry Williams *(Black & gold label)*	1959	100.00	250.00
Chess LP-1457	(M)	Larry Williams	1961	60.00	150.00
OKeh OKM-12123	(M)	Larry Williams' Greatest Hits	1967	10.00	25.00
OKeh OKS-14123	(S)	Larry Williams' Greatest Hits	1967	12.00	30.00

WILLIAMS, MASON
Mason Williams is a guitar player, singer and writer of pop music. Refer to The Wayfarers Trio.

Vee Jay LP-1103	(M)	Them Poems	1965	14.00	35.00
Vee Jay LPS-1103	(S)	Them Poems	1965	20.00	50.00

WILLIAMS, MAURICE, & THE ZODIACS

Herald HLP-1014	(M)	Stay	1961	200.00	400.00
Sphere Sound SR-7007	(M)	Stay	1965	40.00	100.00
Sphere Sound SSR-7007	(E)	Stay	1965	20.00	50.00
		(Sphere Sound 7007 is a reissue of Herald 1014.)			
Snyder 5586	(M)	At The Beach	196?	30.00	75.00

WILLIAMS, MEL, & JOHNNY OTIS

Dig 103	(M)	All Through The Night	1955	250.00	600.00

WILLIAMS, OTIS, & THE CHARMS

Deluxe 750	(M)	Otis Williams & The Charms—Their All Time Hits	1957	500.00	1,000.00
King 570	(M)	Otis Williams & The Charms—Their All Time Hits	1957	250.00	500.00
King 614	(M)	This Is Otis Williams & The Charms	1959	100.00	300.00

WILLIAMS, OTIS, & THE MIDNIGHT COWBOYS

Stop STLP-1022	(S)	Otis Williams & The Midnight Cowboys	1971	10.00	25.00

WILLIAMS, ROBERT PETE

Folk/Lyric FL-109	(M)	Prison Blues	1960	40.00	100.00
Bluesville BVLP-1026	(M)	Free Again	1961	40.00	100.00
		—Bluesville albums above have bright blue labels with silver print.—			
Bluesville BVLP-1026	(M)	Free Again	1964	12.00	30.00
		—Bluesville albums above have blue labels with a trident logo on the right side.—			

WILLIAMS, TEX

Decca DL-5565	(10")	Dance-O-Rama #5	1955	200.00	400.00
Camden CAL-363	(M)	Tex Williams' Best	1958	10.00	25.00
Capitol T-1463	(M)	Smoke! Smoke! Smoke!	1960	12.00	30.00
Capitol ST-1463	(S)	Smoke! Smoke! Smoke!	1960	16.00	40.00
Decca DL-4295	(M)	Country Music Time	1962	8.00	20.00
Decca DL-74295	(S)	Country Music Time	1962	12.00	30.00
Liberty LRP-3304	(M)	Tex Williams In Las Vegas	1963	8.00	20.00
Liberty LST-7304	(S)	Tex Williams In Las Vegas	1963	12.00	30.00

WILLIAMS, TONY
Tony Williams was formerly the lead singer for The Platters.

Mercury MG-20454	(M)	A Girl Is A Girl Is A Girl	1959	14.00	35.00
Mercury SR-60138	(S)	A Girl Is A Girl Is A Girl	1959	20.00	50.00
Reprise R-6006	(M)	Tony Williams—His Greatest Hits	1961	10.00	25.00
Reprise R-96006	(S)	Tony Williams—His Greatest Hits	1961	12.00	30.00
Phillips PHM-200-051	(M)	Magic Touch Of Tony	1962	10.00	25.00
Phillips PHS-600-051	(S)	Magic Touch Of Tony	1962	12.00	30.00

WILLIAMSON, "SONNY BOY" #2
Sonny Boy Williamson was later the pseudonym for Alec Rice Williamson.

Checker LP-1437	(M)	Down And Out Blues *(White label promo)*	1959	500.00	1,000.00
Checker LP-1437	(M)	Down And Out Blues	1959	150.00	350.00
		(Rumors exist that "Down And Out Blues" was also issued as Chess LP-1437. Should such an album exist, it would hav a suggested Near Mint value of $750-1,500.)			
Checker LP-1503	(M)	The Real Folk Blues	196?	30.00	75.00
Checker LP-1509	(M)	More Real Folk Blues	196?	30.00	75.00
		—Checker albums above have black labels.—			
Chess LPS-1536	(S)	Bummer Road	1969	10.00	25.00

Maurice Williams had originally led The Gladiolas, but changed the group's name to The Zodiacs in 1959. He then replaced the original members with a new line-up and, billed as Maurice Williams & The Zodiacs, topped the pop charts during the 1960 Christmas season with "Stay." Pictured here is his first—and only—album on Herald, a rare record indeed. This was later reissued ob Sphere Sound in both mono and electronically rechanneled stereo. All Through The Night (bottom) features the smooth rhythm'n blues-based vocalist Mel Williams backed by the redoubtable Johnny Otis and his orchestra.

Label & Catalog #		Title	Year	VG+	NM
WILLIAMSON, "SONNY BOY" #2, & THE YARDBIRDS					
Mercury MG-21071	(M)	**Sonny Boy Williamson & The Yardbirds**	1966	24.00	60.00
Mercury SR-61071	(E)	**Sonny Boy Williamson & The Yardbirds**	1966	16.00	40.00
WILLING, FOY, & THE RIDERS OF THE PURPLE SAGE					
Varsity VLP-6032	(10")	**Riders Of The Purple Sage**	1950	30.00	75.00
Royale 6032	(10")	**Riders Of The Purple Sage**	1952	30.00	75.00
Roulette R-25035	(M)	**Cowboy**	1958	16.00	40.00
Jubilee JL-5028	(M)	**The New Sound Of American Folk**	1962	8.00	20.00
Jubilee JLS-5028	(S)	**The New Sound Of American Folk**	1962	10.00	25.00
WILLIS, CHUCK					
Epic LN-3425	(M)	**Chuck Willis Wails The Blues**	1958	250.00	500.00
Epic LN-3728	(M)	**A Tribute To Chuck Willis**	1960	150.00	300.00
Atlantic 8018	(M)	**The King Of The Stroll**	1958	150.00	300.00
		— Atlantic albums above have black labels.—			
Atlantic 8018	(M)	**The King Of The Stroll**	1960	40.00	100.00
Atlantic 8079	(M)	**I Remember Chuck Willis**	1963	40.00	100.00
Atlantic SD-8079	(P)	**I Remember Chuck Willis**	1963	60.00	150.00
		—Atlantic albums above have orange & purple labels.—			
WILLS, BOB/BOB WILLS & HIS TEXAS PLAYBOYS					
Refer to Asleep At The Wheel & Bob Wills.					
Columbia HL-9003	(10")	**Bob Wills Round-Up**	1949	200.00	400.00
Antones LP-6000	(10")	**Old Time Favorites** *(Fan club issue)*	195?	250.00	500.00
Antones LP-6010	(10")	**Old Time Favorites** *(Fan club issue)*	195?	250.00	500.00
MGM E-91	(10")	**Ranch House Favorites**	1951	200.00	400.00
Decca DL-5562	(10")	**Dance-O-Rama #2**	1955	200.00	400.00
MGM E-3352	(M)	**Ranch House Favorites** *(Yellow label)*	1956	80.00	200.00
Decca DL-8727	(M)	**Bob Wills And His Texas Playboys**	1957	40.00	100.00
		— Decca albums above have black labels with silver print.—			
Harmony HL-7036	(M)	**Bob Wills Special** *(Maroon label)*	1957	14.00	35.00
Harmony HL-7304	(M)	**The Best Of Bob Wills** *(Blue label)*	1963	10.00	25.00
Harmony HL-7345	(M)	**The Great Bob Wills** *(Blue label)*	1965	8.00	20.00
Liberty LRP-3182	(M)	**Living Legend**	1961	14.00	35.00
Liberty LST-7182	(S)	**Living Legend**	1961	20.00	50.00
Liberty LRP-3194	(M)	**Mr. Words And Music**	1961	14.00	35.00
Liberty LST-7194	(S)	**Mr. Words And Music**	1961	20.00	50.00
Liberty LRP-3303	(M)	**Bob Wills Sings And Plays**	1963	14.00	35.00
Liberty LST-7303	(S)	**Bob Wills Sings And Plays**	1963	20.00	50.00
Starday SLP-375	(M)	**San Antonio Rose** *(Yellow label)*	1965	20.00	50.00
Longhorn LP-001	(M)	**Keepsake Album #1**	1965	20.00	50.00
WILLS, BOB, & TOMMY DUNCAN					
Liberty LRP-3173	(M)	**Together Again**	1960	14.00	35.00
Liberty LST-7173	(S)	**Together Again**	1960	20.00	50.00
WILLS, JOHNNY LEE					
Sims LP-101	(M)	**Where There's A Wills, There's A Way**	1962	20.00	50.00
Sims LPS-101	(S)	**Where There's A Wills, There's A Way**	1962	30.00	75.00
Sims LP-108	(M)	**Johnny Lee Wills At The Tulsa Stampede**	1963	20.00	50.00
Sims LPS-108	(S)	**Johnny Lee Wills At The Tulsa Stampede**	1963	30.00	75.00
WILMER & THE DUKES					
Aphrodisiac 6001	(S)	**Wilmer And The Dukes**	1969	10.00	25.00
WILSON, AL					
Soul City SCS-92006	(S)	**Searching For The Dolphins**	1969	10.00	25.00
WILSON, BRIAN					
Brian Wilson was The Beach Boys. . . in the '60s. Refer to Spring.					
Crawdaddy	(DJ)	**The Crawdaddy Brian Wilson Interview**	1977	60.00	150.00
WILSON, DENNIS					
Dennis Wilson was a member of The Beach Boys.					
Caribou PZ-34354	(S)	**Pacific Ocean Blue** *(White label promo)*	1977	100.00	250.00
		(Special advance copies of PZ-34354 were issued with a letter from			
		DW printed on the cover and each copy signed in felt-tip pen by DW.)			
Caribou PZ-34354	(S)	**Pacific Ocean Blue**	1977	10.00	25.00

Label & Catalog #		Title	Year	VG+	NM

WILSON, J. FRANK, & THE CAVALIERS

Josie JM-4006	(M)	Last Kiss	1964	20.00	50.00
Josie JS-4006	(S)	Last Kiss	1964	30.00	75.00

WILSON, JACKIE
Mr. Wilson was formerly the lead singer for Billy Ward & The Dominoes.

Brunswick BL-54042	(M)	He's So Fine	1959	60.00	150.00
Brunswick BL-54045	(M)	Lonely Teardrops	1959	60.00	150.00
Sesac 160?	(M)	Jackie Wilson	1960	250.00	500.00
Brunswick BL-54050	(M)	So Much	1960	30.00	75.00
Brunswick BL-754050	(S)	So Much	1960	60.00	150.00
Brunswick BL-54055	(M)	Jackie Sings The Blues	1960	30.00	75.00
Brunswick BL-754055	(S)	Jackie Sings The Blues	1960	60.00	150.00
Brunswick BL-54058	(M)	My Golden Favorites	1960	20.00	50.00
Brunswick BL-54059	(M)	A Woman, A Lover, A Friend	1961	16.00	40.00
Brunswick BL-754059	(S)	A Woman, A Lover, A Friend	1961	20.00	50.00
Brunswick BL-54100	(M)	You Ain't Heard Nothin' Yet	1961	16.00	40.00
Brunswick BL-754100	(S)	You Ain't Heard Nothin' Yet	1961	20.00	50.00
Brunswick BL-54101	(M)	By Special Request	1961	16.00	40.00
Brunswick BL-754101	(S)	By Special Request	1961	20.00	50.00
Brunswick BL-54105	(M)	Body And Soul	1962	16.00	40.00
Brunswick BL-754105	(S)	Body And Soul	1962	20.00	50.00
Brunswick BL-54106	(M)	The World's Greatest Melodies	1962	16.00	40.00
Brunswick BL-754106	(S)	The World's Greatest Melodies	1962	20.00	50.00
Brunswick BL-54108	(M)	Jackie Wilson At The Copa	1962	16.00	40.00
Brunswick BL-754108	(S)	Jackie Wilson At The Copa	1962	20.00	50.00
		— Brunswick albums above have black & silver labels.—			
Brunswick BL-54110	(M)	Baby Workout	1963	12.00	30.00
Brunswick BL-754110	(S)	Baby Workout	1963	16.00	40.00
Brunswick BL-54112	(M)	Merry Christmas From Jackie Wilson	1963	12.00	30.00
Brunswick BL-754112	(S)	Merry Christmas From Jackie Wilson	1963	16.00	40.00
Brunswick BL-54113	(M)	Shake A Hand *(With Linda Hopkins)*	1963	10.00	25.00
Brunswick BL-754113	(S)	Shake A Hand *(With Linda Hopkins)*	1963	12.00	30.00
Brunswick BL-54115	(M)	My Golden Favorites, Volume 2	1964	10.00	25.00
Brunswick BL-754115	(S)	My Golden Favorites, Volume 2	1964	12.00	30.00
Brunswick BL-54117	(M)	Somethin' Else	1964	10.00	25.00
Brunswick BL-754117	(S)	Somethin' Else	1964	12.00	30.00
Brunswick BL-54118	(M)	Soul Time	1965	10.00	25.00
Brunswick BL-754118	(S)	Soul Time	1965	12.00	30.00
Brunswick BL-54119	(M)	Spotlight On Jackie Wilson	1965	10.00	25.00
Brunswick BL-754119	(S)	Spotlight On Jackie Wilson	1965	12.00	30.00
Brunswick BL-54120	(M)	Soul Galore	1966	10.00	25.00
Brunswick BL-754120	(S)	Soul Galore	1966	12.00	30.00
Brunswick BL-54112	(M)	Whispers	1967	8.00	20.00
Brunswick BL-754112	(S)	Whispers	1967	10.00	25.00
Brunswick BL-54130	(M)	Higher And Higher	1967	8.00	20.00
Brunswick BL-754130	(S)	Higher And Higher	1967	10.00	25.00
		— Brunswick albums above have black labels with a "Division of Decca Records" on the left side.—			

WILSON, JULIE

Dolphin 6	(M)	Love	1956	20.00	50.00
Vik LX-1095	(M)	My Old Flame	1957	12.00	30.00
Vik LX-1118	(M)	Julie Wilson At The St. Regis	1958	12.00	30.00
Cameo C-1021	(M)	Meet Julie Wilson	1962	10.00	25.00
Cameo SC-1021	(S)	Meet Julie Wilson	1962	16.00	40.00
Arden 101	(S)	Julie Wilson At The Brothers, Vol. 1	1976	20.00	50.00
Arden 102	(S)	Julie Wilson At The Brothers, Vol. 2	1976	8.00	20.00

WILSON, MURRY
The father of Brian, Dennis and Carl Wilson of The Beach Boys. Refer to The Sunrays.

Capitol T-2819	(M)	The Many Moods Of Murry Wilson	1967	10.00	25.00
Capitol ST-2819	(S)	The Many Moods Of Murry Wilson	1967	12.00	30.00

WILSON, NANCY

Capitol T-1319	(M)	Like In Love	1959	8.00	20.00
Capitol ST-1319	(S)	Like In Love	1959	10.00	25.00
Capitol T-1440	(M)	Something Wonderful	1960	8.00	20.00
Capitol ST-1440	(S)	Something Wonderful	1960	10.00	25.00

Label & Catalog #		Title	Year	VG+	NM
Capitol T-1524	(M)	**Swingin's Mutual**	1961	8.00	20.00
Capitol ST-1524	(S)	**Swingin's Mutual**	1961	10.00	25.00
Capitol T-1657	(M)	**Nancy Wilson/Cannonball Adderley**	1962	8.00	20.00
Capitol ST-1657	(S)	**Nancy Wilson/Cannonball Adderley**	1962	10.00	25.00

— *Capitol albums above have black "rainbow" labels with the logo on the left side.*—

WILSON, STAN
Stan Wilson is a singer of blues, calypso and folk-based music.

Cavalier CAV-5505	(10")	**Wanderin' With Stan Wilson**	195?	30.00	75.00
Cavalier CAV-6002	(10")	**Wanderin' With Stan Wilson**	195?	20.00	50.00
Cavalier CAV-6003	(10")	**Leisure Time**	195?	20.00	50.00
Clef MGC-163	(10")	**An Evening With Stan Wilson**	1954	40.00	100.00
Clef MGC-672	(M)	**A Stan Wilson Recital**	1955	30.00	75.00
Verve MGV-2019	(M)	**Ballads And Calypso**	1956	16.00	40.00
		(Verve 2019 is a reissue of Clef 672.)			
Verve MGV-2051	(M)	**Calypso**	1957	16.00	40.00
Verve MGV-2076	(M)	**Folk Songs**	1957	16.00	40.00
Verve MGV-2122	(M)	**Stan Wilson At The Ash Grove**	1959	16.00	40.00
Verve MGV-2139	(M)	**Stan Wilson**	1960	16.00	40.00
Verve MGV-2140	(M)	**Leisure Time**	1960	16.00	40.00

— *Verve albums above have "Verve Records, Inc." on the bottom of the label.*—

WINCHESTER, JESSE

Bearsville PRO-693	(DJ)	**Live At The Bijou Cafe Plus A Live Interview At Media College In Montreal** *(2 LPs)*	1975	30.00	75.00

WIND IN THE WILLOWS, THE
W.I.T.W. features Debbie Harry, later of Blondie.

Capitol SKAO-2956	(S)	**The Wind In The Willows**	1968	20.00	50.00

WINGFIELD, DICK: *Refer to* **WILL GREER & DICK WINGFIELD**

WINGS: *Refer to* **PAUL McCARTNEY (& WINGS)**

WINNERS, THE

Crown CLP-5394	(M)	**Checkered Flag**	1963	10.00	25.00
Crown CST-394	(S)	**Checkered Flag**	1963	12.00	30.00

WINSTONS, THE

Metromedia MD-1010	(S)	**Color Him Father**	1969	30.00	75.00

WINTER, EDGAR/EDGAR WINTER & WHITE TRASH

Blue Sky ASZ-242	(DJ)	**Johnny And Edger Discuss "Together"**	1976	10.00	25.00

WINTER, JOHNNY

Sonobeat RS-1002	(DJ)	**Progressive Blues Experiment**	1968	200.00	400.00
		(Issued in a plain cardboard jacket.)			
Imperial LP-12431	(S)	**Progressive Blues Experiment**	1969	14.00	35.00
		(Imperial 12431 is a reissue of Sonobeat 1002.)			
Columbia CS-9947	(S)	**Second Winter** *(2 LPs)*	1969	10.00	25.00

— *Columbia albums above have "360 Sound Stereo" on the bottom of the label.*—

WINTERS, JONATHAN

Verve MGV-15009	(M)	**The Wonderful World Of Jonathan Winters**	1960	8.00	20.00
Verve MGVS-6099	(S)	**The Wonderful World Of Jonathan Winters**	1960	10.00	25.00
Verve MGV-15011	(M)	**Down To Earth**	1960	8.00	20.00
Verve MGVS-6155	(S)	**Down To Earth**	1960	10.00	25.00
Verve MGV-15025	(M)	**Here's Jonathan (In Concert)**	1961	10.00	25.00
Verve MGV-15027	(M)	**A Personal Appearance**	1961	10.00	25.00

— *Verve albums above have "Verve Records, Inc." on the bottom.*—

WINTERS, JONATHAN / SHELLY BERMAN / MORT SAHL

Verve MGV-15022	(M)	**The Wit Of America** *(3 LPs)*	195?	16.00	40.00

— *Verve labums above have "Verve Records, Inc." on the bottom.*—

WISE, CHUBBY

Starday SLP-154	(M)	**The Tennessee Fiddler** *(Yellow label)*	1961	16.00	40.00

Label & Catalog #		Title	Year	VG+	NM

WISEMAN, MAC
Mac Wiseman is a guitar player and singer of bluegrass music. Refer to Lester Flatt.

Label & Catalog #		Title	Year	VG+	NM
Dot DLP-3084	(M)	Tis Sweet To Be Remembered	1958	24.00	60.00
Dot DLP-25084	(E)	Tis Sweet To Be Remembered	196?	8.00	20.00
Dot DLP-3135	(M)	Beside The Still Waters	1959	16.00	40.00
Dot DLP-25135	(S)	Beside The Still Waters	1959	20.00	50.00
Dot DLP-3213	(M)	Great Folk Ballads	1959	16.00	40.00
Dot DLP-25213	(S)	Great Folk Ballads	1959	20.00	50.00
Dot DLP-3313	(M)	12 Great Hits	1960	16.00	40.00
Dot DLP-25313	(S)	12 Great Hits	1960	20.00	50.00
Dot DLP-3336	(M)	Keep On The Sunnyside	1960	16.00	40.00
Dot DLP-25336	(E)	Keep On The Sunnyside	196?	6.00	15.00
Dot DLP-3373	(M)	Best Loved Gospel Hymns	1961	8.00	20.00
Dot DLP-25373	(S)	Best Loved Gospel Hymns	1961	12.00	30.00
Dot DLP-3408	(M)	Fireball Mail	1961	12.00	30.00
Dot DLP-25408	(E)	Fireball Mail	196?	6.00	15.00
Capitol T-1800	(M)	Bluegrass Favorites	1962	12.00	30.00
Capitol ST-1800	(S)	Bluegrass Favorites	1962	16.00	40.00
Hamilton HLP-12130	(M)	Sincerely	1964	8.00	20.00
Hamilton HLP-12167	(M)	Songs Of The Dear Old Days	1966	8.00	20.00
Dot DLP-3697	(M)	This Is Mac Wiseman	1966	8.00	20.00
Dot DLP-25697	(S)	This Is Mac Wiseman	1966	10.00	25.00
Dot DLP-3730	(M)	A Master At Work	1966	8.00	20.00
Dot DLP-25730	(S)	A Master At Work	1966	10.00	25.00
Dot DLP-3731	(M)	Bluegrass	1966	8.00	20.00
Dot DLP-25731	(S)	Bluegrass	1966	10.00	25.00
Dot DLP-25896	(S)	Golden Hits Of Mac Wiseman	1968	8.00	20.00

WISHBONE ASH

Label & Catalog #		Title	Year	VG+	NM
Decca DL-71919	(DJ)	An Evening Program With Wishbone Ash	1972	12.00	30.00
MCA L33-1922	(DJ)	Live From Memphis	1974	20.00	50.00

WITHERSPOON, JIMMY
Jimmy Witherspoon also recorded with Eric Burdon. Refer to Ray Charles / Jimmy Witherspoon.

Label & Catalog #		Title	Year	VG+	NM
RCA Victor LPM-1639	(M)	Goin' To Kansas City Blues	1957	40.00	100.00
Hifi J-421	(M)	At The Monterey Jazz Festival	1959	40.00	100.00
Hifi J-422	(M)	Feelin' The Spirit	1959	40.00	100.00
Hifi J-426	(M)	Jimmy Witherspoon At The Renaissance	1959	40.00	100.00
World Pacific WP-1267	(M)	Singin' The Blues	1959	30.00	75.00
World Pacific WP-1402	(M)	There's Good Rockin' Tonight	1961	24.00	60.00
		(W.P. 1402 is a reissue of 1267.)			
Crown CLP-5156	(M)	Jimmy Witherspoon	1959	20.00	50.00
Crown CLP-5192	(M)	Jimmy Witherspoon Sings The Blues	1960	20.00	50.00
Crown CST-215	(E)	Jimmy Witherspoon			
		Sings The Blues *(Red vinyl)*	1960	30.00	75.00
Crown CST-215	(E)	Jimmy Witherspoon Sings The Blues	1960	10.00	25.00
Reprise R-2008	(M)	Spoon	1961	16.00	40.00
Reprise R9-2008	(S)	Spoon	1961	20.00	50.00
Reprise R-6012	(M)	Hey, Mrs. Jones	1962	16.00	40.00
Reprise R9-6012	(S)	Hey, Mrs. Jones	1962	20.00	50.00
Reprise R-6059	(M)	Roots	1962	12.00	30.00
Reprise R9-6059	(S)	Roots	1962	16.00	40.00
Prestige PRLP-7290	(M)	Baby, Baby, Baby	1963	16.00	40.00
Prestige PRST-7290	(S)	Baby, Baby, Baby	1963	16.00	40.00
Prestige PRLP-7300	(M)	Evenin' Blues	1964	16.00	40.00
Prestige PRST-7300	(S)	Evenin' Blues	1964	16.00	40.00
Prestige PRLP-7314	(M)	Goin' To Chicago Blues	1964	16.00	40.00
Prestige PRST-7314	(S)	Goin' To Chicago Blues	1964	16.00	40.00
Prestige PRLP-7327	(M)	Blue Spoon	1964	16.00	40.00
Prestige PRST-7327	(S)	Blue Spoon	1964	16.00	40.00

— Prestige mono albums above have yellow labels with a Bergenfield, NJ, address; stereo albums have silver labels. —

Label & Catalog #		Title	Year	VG+	NM
Prestige PRLP-7356	(M)	Some Of My Best Friends Are The Blues	1964	8.00	20.00
Prestige PRST-7356	(S)	Some Of My Best Friends Are The Blues	1964	10.00	25.00
Prestige PR-7418	(M)	Spoon In London	1965	8.00	20.00
Prestige PRS-7418	(S)	Spoon In London	1965	10.00	25.00
Prestige PRLP-7475	(M)	Blues For Easy Livers	1967	8.00	20.00
Prestige PRST-7475	(S)	Blues For Easy Livers	1967	10.00	25.00

— Prestige albums above have blue labels with a trident logo on the right side. —

Label & Catalog #		Title	Year	VG+	NM
Constellation CM-1422	(M)	**Take This Hammer**	1964	**12.00**	**30.00**
Constellation CMS1422	(E)	**Take This Hammer**	1964	**6.00**	**15.00**
Surrey S-1106	(M)	**Blues For Spoon And Groove**	1965	**10.00**	**25.00**
Surrey SS-1106	(S)	**Blues For Spoon And Groove**	1965	**12.00**	**30.00**
		(Surrey 1106 also features Groove Holmes.)			
Verve V-5007	(M)	**Blue Point Of View**	1967	**8.00**	**20.00**
Verve V6-5007	(S)	**Blue Point Of View**	1967	**10.00**	**25.00**
Verve V-5030	(SM	**The Blues Is Now** (With Jack McDuff)	1967	**8.00**	**20.00**
Verve V6-5030	(S)	**The Blues Is Now** (With Jack McDuff)	1967	**10.00**	**25.00**
Verve V6-5050	(S)	**A Spoonful Of Soul**	1968	**10.00**	**25.00**

WITHERSPOON, JIMMY / EDDIE VINSON

King 634	(M)	**Battle Of The Blues, Volume 3**	1959		See below
		(King 634 is rare with a suggested Near Mint value of $1,000-1,500.)			

WIZARD

Peon 1069	(S)	**Original Wizard**	1971	**60.00**	**150.00**

WIZARDS FROM KANSAS, THE

Mercury SR-61309	(S)	**The Wizards From Kansas**	1970	**30.00**	**75.00**

WOMACK, BOBBY

Minit LP-24014	(S)	**Fly Me To The Moon**	1968	**10.00**	**25.00**
Minit LP-24027	(S)	**My Prescription**	1969	**10.00**	**25.00**

WOMB

Dot DLP-25933	(S)	**Womb**	1969	**10.00**	**25.00**
Dot DLP-25959	(S)	**Overdub**	1969	**10.00**	**25.00**

WONDER, "LITTLE" STEVIE

For additional listings refer to The Temptations / Stevie Wonder.

Tamla T-232	(M)	**A Tribute To Uncle Ray**	1963	**80.00**	**200.00**
Tamla T-233	(M)	**The Jazz Soul Of Stevie Wonder**	1963	**80.00**	**200.00**
		—*Tamla albums above have a disc over-lapping a globe at the top of the label.*—			
Tamla T-240	(M)	**Recorded Live-The 12 Year Old Genius**	1963	**40.00**	**100.00**
Tamla T-250	(M)	**With A Song In My Heart**	1963	**20.00**	**50.00**
Tamla T-255	(M)	**Stevie At The Beach**	1964	**16.00**	**40.00**
Tamla T-268	(M)	**Up-Tight (Everything's Alright)**	1966	**10.00**	**25.00**
Tamla TS-268	(S)	**Up-Tight (Everything's Alright)**	1966	**12.00**	**30.00**
Tamla T-272	(M)	**Down To Earth**	1966	**8.00**	**20.00**
Tamla TS-272	(S)	**Down To Earth**	1966	**10.00**	**25.00**
Tamla T-279	(M)	**I Was Made To Love Her**	1967	**8.00**	**20.00**
Tamla TS-279	(S)	**I Was Made To Love Her**	1967	**10.00**	**25.00**
		(Original pressings have the album title on two lines.)			
Tamla TS-279	(S)	**I Was Made To Love Her**	1968	**8.00**	**20.00**
		(Later pressings have the album title on three lines.)			
Tamla T-281	(M)	**Someday At Christmas**	1967	**12.00**	**30.00**
Tamla TS-281	(S)	**Someday At Christmas**	1967	**14.00**	**35.00**
Tamla T-282	(M)	**Stevie Wonder's Greatest Hits**	1968	**12.00**	**30.00**
Tamla TS-282	(P)	**Stevie Wonder's Greatest Hits**	1968	**6.00**	**15.00**
Motown PR-77	(DJ)	**Hotter Than July**	1980	**12.00**	**30.00**

WOOD, BRENTON

Brent 5100	(M)	**Introducing Brenton Wood! Boogaloo**	196?	**14.00**	**35.00**
Brent S-100	(S)	**Introducing Brenton Wood! Boogaloo**	196?	**20.00**	**50.00**
		(The Brent album is a various artists compilation with only four tracks by Wood and the rest by David Bryant, The Golden Boys, and Clarence Hill.)			
Double Shot 1002	(M)	**Oogum Boogum**	1967	**10.00**	**25.00**
Double Shot 5002	(S)	**Oogum Boogum**	1967	**12.00**	**30.00**
Double Shot 1003	(M)	**Baby You Got It**	1967	**10.00**	**25.00**
Double Shot 5003	(S)	**Baby You Got It**	1967	**12.00**	**30.00**
Double Shot 5003	(S)	**Baby You Got It** (Multi-color vinyl)	1967	**80.00**	**200.00**

WOOD, HALLY

Hally Wood is a guitar player and singer of traditional folk music .

Elektra EKL-10	(10")	**American Folksongs Of Sadness And Melancholy**	1953	**20.00**	**50.00**
Stinson SLP-73	(10")	**Texas Folk Songs**	195?	**20.00**	**50.00**

Label & Catalog #		Title	Year	VG+	NM

WOOD, ROY
Roy Wood is a founding member of both The Move and Electric Light Orchestra.

| United Arts. LA168 | (S) | **Boulder Folder** | 1973 | 16.00 | 40.00 |

(Promotional package with the LP in a 13" x 13" gatefold cover with press kit and postcards.)

WOODHULL'S OLD-TYME MASTERS

| Camden CAL-220 | (M) | **Square Dances** | 195? | 10.00 | 25.00 |

WOODS, BILL

| Country Town CTR-24803 | (M) | **Bill Woods From Bakersfield** | 196? | 40.00 | 100.00 |

WOODY'S TRUCK STOP

| Smash SRS-67111 | (S) | **Woody's Truck Stop** | 1969 | 12.00 | 30.00 |

WOOFERS, THE

| Wyncote W-9011 | (M) | **Dragsville** | 1964 | 16.00 | 40.00 |
| Wyncote SW-9001 | (S) | **Dragsville** | 1964 | 20.00 | 50.00 |

WOOLEY, SHEB
Shelby "Sheb" Wooley also recorded as Ben Colder.

| MGM E-3299 | (M) | **Sheb Wooley** | 1956 | 60.00 | 150.00 |

— MGM albums above have yellow labels. —

MGM E-3904	(M)	**Songs From The Days Of Rawhide**	1961	16.00	40.00
MGM SE-3904	(S)	**Songs From The Days Of Rawhide**	1961	24.00	60.00
MGM E-4026	(M)	**That's My Ma And That's My Pa**	1962	12.00	30.00
MGM SE-4026	(S)	**That's My Ma And That's My Pa**	1962	16.00	40.00
MGM E-4136	(M)	**Tales Of How The West Was Won**	1963	12.00	30.00
MGM SE-4136	(S)	**Tales Of How The West Was Won**	1963	16.00	40.00
MGM E-4275	(M)	**The Very Best Of Sheb Wooley**	1965	10.00	25.00
MGM SE-4275	(S)	**The Very Best Of Sheb Wooley**	1965	12.00	30.00
MGM E-4325	(M)	**It's A Big Land**	1965	10.00	25.00
MGM SE-4325	(S)	**It's A Big Land**	1965	12.00	30.00

— MGM albums above have black labels. —

WOOLIES, THE

| Spirit 9645-2001 | (S) | **Basic Rock** | 1970 | 16.00 | 40.00 |
| Spirit 9645-2005 | (S) | **Live At Lizards** | 1973 | 12.00 | 30.00 |

WOOLY BEAR

| Stereo Lab Sound NR-5057 | (S) | **Wouldya?** | 1974 | 24.00 | 60.00 |

WORLD OF OZ, THE

| Deram DES-18022 | (S) | **The World Of Oz** | 1969 | 12.00 | 30.00 |

WRAY, LINK/LINK WRAY & HIS WRAYMEN

Epic LN-3661	(M)	**Link Wray And The Wraymen**	1960	80.00	200.00
Swan SLP-510	(M)	**Jack The Ripper**	1963	80.00	200.00
Vermillion 1924	(M)	**Great Guitar Hits**	1963	60.00	150.00
Vermillion 1925	(M)	**Link Wray Sings And Plays Guitar**	1964	60.00	150.00
Record Factory 1929	(S)	**Yesterday And Today**	1969	40.00	100.00

WRAY, VERNON

| Vermillion 1972 | (S) | **Wasted** *(With Link Wray)* | 196? | 40.00 | 100.00 |

WRIGHT, BETTY

| Atco SD-33-260 | (S) | **My First Time Around** | 1968 | 10.00 | 25.00 |

WRIGHT, NAT: *Refer to* GOLDMINE'S PRICE GUIDE TO COLLECTIBLE JAZZ ALBUMS

WRIGHT, O. V.

Back Beat 61	(M)	**If It's Only For Tonight**	1965	40.00	100.00
Back Beat 61	(S)	**If It's Only For Tonight**	1965	40.00	100.00
Back Beat 66	(S)	**8 Men And 4 Women**	1968	30.00	75.00
Back Beat 67	(S)	**Nucleus Of Soul**	1969	30.00	75.00
Back Beat 70	(S)	**A Nickle And A Nail And Ace Of Spades**	1972	24.00	60.00
Back Beat 72	(S)	**Memphis Unlimited**	1973	20.00	50.00
Hi 6008	(S)	**Bottom Line**	1978	10.00	25.00
Hi 6011	(S)	**We're Still Together**	1979	10.00	25.00

Label & Catalog #		Title	Year	VG+	NM

WU, BOB LIN
| RCA Victor LPM-1936 | (M) | **Music For A Chinese Dinner At Home** | 1959 | 16.00 | 40.00 |

WYLER, GRETCHEN
| Jubilee JLP-1100 | (M) | **Wild, Wyler, Wildest** | 1959 | 10.00 | 25.00 |
| Jubilee SDJLP-1100 | (S) | **Wild, Wyler, Wildest** | 1959 | 16.00 | 40.00 |

WYMAN, BILL
Mr. Wyman is a member of The Rolling Stones. Refer to The End; John Hammond; Sons Of Heroes.
Roll. Stones QD-79100	(Q)	**Monkey Grip**	1974	10.00	25.00
Roll. Stones QD-79103	(Q)	**Stone Alone**	1976	10.00	25.00
Ripple *(No number)*	(S)	**Digital Dreams** *(Soundtrack)*	1983	80.00	200.00
		(Promo given away at a screening of the film.)			

WYNN, ED
| Riverside RLP-1417 | (M) | **Grandpa Magic's Sports Car Race** | 195? | 16.00 | 40.00 |

X

XXX
No label
| | (S) | **Live First Legal Bootleg Album** | 1973 | 30.00 | 75.00 |

Y

Y KANT TORI READ
YKTR features Tori Amos.
| Atlantic ???? | (S) | **Y Kant Tori Raad** | 1990 | 30.00 | 75.00 |

YAMA & THE KARMA DUSTERS
| Manhole 1 | (S) | **Up From The Sewers** *(With insert)* | 197? | 40.00 | 100.00 |

YANCEY, JIMMY: *Refer to* GOLDMINE'S PRICE GUIDE TO COLLECTIBLE JAZZ ALBUMS

YANCEY, MAMA, & ART RODES
| Verve/Folkways FV-9015 | (M) | **Blues** | 1965 | 8.00 | 20.00 |
| Verve/Folkways FVS-9015 | (S) | **Blues** | 1965 | 10.00 | 25.00 |

YANCY DERRINGER
| Hemisphere H-15104 | (S) | **Openers** | 1975 | 24.00 | 60.00 |

YANKEE DOLLAR, THE
| Dot DLP-3874 | (M) | **The Yankee Dollar** | 1968 | 30.00 | 75.00 |
| Dot DLP-25874 | (S) | **The Yankee Dollar** | 1968 | 40.00 | 100.00 |

YANOVSKY, ZALMAN
Zallie was formerly a member of The Mugwumps; The Lovin' Spoonful.
| Buddah BDS-5019 | (S) | **Alive And Well In Argentina** | 1968 | 12.00 | 30.00 |
| Kama Sutra KSBS-2030 | (S) | **Alive And Well In Argentina** | 1971 | 8.00 | 20.00 |

Label & Catalog #		Title	Year	VG+	NM

YARBROUGH, GLENN
Former Limeliter Glenn Yarbrough is a guitar player and singer of folk-based music.

Tradition TLP-1019	(M)	**Come And Sit By My Side**	1957	20.00	50.00
Elektra EKL-135	(M)	**Here We Go, Baby**	1957	20.00	50.00

YARBROUGH, GELNN, & MARILYN CHILD

Elektra EKL-143	(M)	**English And American Folk Songs**	1957	16.00	40.00

YARDBIRDS, THE
Members were Chris Dreja, Jim McCarty, Keith Relf, Paul Samwell-Smith and Eric Clapton. Later members were Jeff Beck and Jimmy Page. Refer to Armageddon; Philamore Lincoln; Renaissance; Sonny Boy Williamson. Note: Cheesy counterfeits of the first thres stereo albums— 26167, 26177 and 26210— with obviously photocopied covers, etc., are common.

Epic LN-24167	(M)	**For Your Love** (White label promo)	1965	150.00	300.00
Epic LN-24167	(M)	**For Your Love**	1965	30.00	75.00
Epic BN-26167	(S)	**For Your Love**	1965	30.00	75.00
		("Sweet Music" is rechanneled)			
Epic LN-24177	(M)	**Having A Rave Up** (White label promo)	1965	150.00	300.00
Epic LN-24177	(M)	**Having A Rave Up**	1965	30.00	75.00
Epic BN-26177	(E)	**Having A Rave Up**	1965	20.00	50.00
Epic LN-24210	(M)	**Over Under Sideways Down** (White label)	1966	150.00	300.00
Epic LN-24210	(M)	**Over Under Sideways Down**	1966	24.00	60.00
Epic BN-26210	(S)	**Over Under Sideways Down**	1966	30.00	75.00
		("Over Under Sideways Down" is rechanneled)			
Epic LN-24246	(M)	**The Yardbirds' Greatest Hits** (White label)	1966	80.00	200.00
Epic LN-24246	(M)	**The Yardbirds' Greatest Hits**	1966	20.00	50.00
Epic BN-26246	(E)	**The Yardbirds' Greatest Hits**	1966	12.00	30.00
MGM E-4447	(M)	**Blow-Up** (Soundtrack)	1967	12.00	30.00
MGM SE-4447	(S)	**Blow-Up** (Soundtrack)	1967	16.00	40.00
Epic LN-24313	(M)	**Little Games** (White label promo)	1967	80.00	200.00
Epic LN-24313	(M)	**Little Games**	1967	30.00	75.00
Epic BN-26313	(S)	**Little Games**	1967	30.00	75.00
Epic EG-30135	(P)	**The Yardbirds** (2 LPs)	1970	20.00	50.00
Epic KE-30615	(S)	**Live Yardbirds Featuring Jimmy Page**	1972	30.00	75.00
		(Original copies of KE-30615 have full-color covers and have been counterfeited: The matrix numbers are blurred and the label is slightly off-color. All copies with black & white covers are boots.)			
Columbia P-13311	(S)	**Live Yardbirds Featuring Jimmy Page**	1972	24.00	60.00
Epic HE-38455	(S)	**The Yardbirds** (Half-speed master)	1983	30.00	90.00
		(Epic 33455 is a reissue of 26210 plus two extra tracks.)			

YARKONI, YAFFA

Prestige Int. PRLP-13067	(M)	**International Songs**	1963	12.00	30.00

YEAR ONE

(No label)	(S)	**Year One** (2 LPs)	197?	20.00	50.00

YELLO

Ralph YL-8059	(S)	**Solid Pleasure**	198?	12.00	30.00
Ralph YL-8159	(S)	**Claro Que Se**	198?	8.00	20.00

YELLOW BALLOON, THE

Canterbury CLPM-1502	(M)	**The Yellow Balloon**	1967	12.00	30.00
Canterbury CLPS-1502	(S)	**The Yellow Balloon**	1967	16.00	40.00

YELLOW PAYGES, THE

Uni 73045	(S)	**The Yellow Payges, Volume 1**	1969	10.00	25.00

YES
Jon Anderson, Bill Bruford, Steve Howe, Tony Kaye, Chris Squire and Rick Wakeman.

Atlantic 2-908	(DJ)	**Tales From Topographic Oceans** (2 LPs)	1974	14.00	35.00
		(Promo copies are banded for air play.)			
Atlantic PR-260	(DJ)	**Yes Solos LP Sampler** (Plain white jacket)	1976	16.00	40.00
Atlantic PR-285	(DJ)	**Yes Music: An Evening With Jon Anderson**	1977	20.00	50.00
Mobile Fidelity MFSL-077	(S)	**Close To The Edge**	1982	15.00	45.00

YESTERDAY'S CHILDREN

Map 3012	(S)	**Yesterday's Children**	196?	10.00	25.00

Label & Catalog #		Title	Year	VG+	NM

YESTERDAY'S FOLK
| Buddah BDS-5035 | (S) | U.S. 69 | 1969 | 10.00 | 25.00 |

YETTI-MEN, THE / THE UPPA-TRIO
The Yetti-Men feature Tom Rapp, later of Perals Before Swine.
| Kal KB-4348 | (S) | The Yetti-Men / The Uppa-Trio | 1967 | 300.00 | 600.00 |

YORK BROTHERS, THE
King 581	(M)	The York Brothers	1958	60.00	150.00
King 586	(M)	The York Brothers, Volume 2	1958	60.00	150.00
King 820	(M)	16 Great Country & Western Hits	1963	40.00	100.00

YOU KNOW WHO GROUP, THE
| Inter. Allied 420 | (M) | The You Know Who Group | 1965 | 20.00 | 50.00 |

YOUNG, CATHY
| Mainstream S-6121 | (S) | A Spoonful Of Cathy Young | 1968 | 16.00 | 40.00 |

YOUNG, KATHY, & THE INNOCENTS
The Innocents recorded independently of Ms. Young.
| Indigo 504 | (M) | The Sound Of Kathy Young | 1961 | 150.00 | 300.00 |

YOUNG, FARON
Capitol T-778	(M)	Sweethearts Or Strangers	1957	24.00	60.00
Capitol T-1004	(M)	The Object Of My Affection	1958	24.00	60.00
Capitol T-1096	(M)	This Is Faron Young	1959	24.00	60.00
— Capitol albums above have turquoise labels.—					
Capitol T-778	(M)	Sweethearts Or Strangers	196?	10.00	25.00
Capitol T-1004	(M)	The Object Of My Affection	196?	10.00	25.00
Capitol T-1096	(M)	This Is Faron Young	196?	10.00	25.00
Capitol T-1185	(M)	My Garden Of Prayer	1959	20.00	50.00
Capitol T-1245	(M)	Talk About Hits	1959	16.00	40.00
Capitol ST-1245	(S)	Talk About Hits	1959	20.00	50.00
Capitol T-1450	(M)	The Best Of Faron Young	1960	12.00	30.00
Capitol ST-1450	(P)	The Best Of Faron Young	1960	16.00	40.00
Capitol T-1528	(M)	Hello, Walls	1961	12.00	30.00
Capitol ST-1528	(S)	Hello, Walls	1961	16.00	40.00
Capitol T-1634	(M)	The Young Approach	1961	12.00	30.00
Capitol ST-1634	(S)	The Young Approach	1961	16.00	40.00
— Capitol albums above have black labels with the logo on the left side.—					
Capitol T-1876	(M)	The All-Time Great Hits of Faron Young	1963	8.00	20.00
Capitol ST-1876	(P)	The All-Time Great Hits of Faron Young	1963	10.00	25.00
SeSac	(M)	Church Songs	196?	40.00	100.00
Mary Carter 1000	(DJ)	On Stage For Mary Carter Paints	196?	20.00	50.00
Mercury MG-20785	(M)	This Is Faron	1963	8.00	20.00
Mercury SR-60785	(S)	This Is Faron	1963	10.00	25.00
Mercury MG-20840	(M)	Faron Young Aims At The West	1963	8.00	20.00
Mercury SR-60840	(S)	Faron Young Aims At The West	1963	10.00	25.00
Mercury MG-20896	(M)	Story Songs For Country Fans	1964	8.00	20.00
Mercury SR-60896	(S)	Story Songs For Country Fans	1964	10.00	25.00
—Mercury albums above have black labels with a Mercury-head logo on top.—					

YOUNG, JESSE COLIN
Jesse Colin Young is a pseudonym for Perry Miller. Both Capitol and Mercury reissued JCY's early solo albums in an attempt to capitalize on the popularity of his group, The Youngbloods, even though the group does not appear on either of the albums.
Capitol T-2070	(M)	Soul Of A City Boy	1964	20.00	50.00
Capitol T-2070	(M)	Jesse Colin Young & The Youngbloods	1967	12.00	30.00
Capitol ST-2070	(E)	Jesse Colin Young & The Youngbloods	1967	8.00	20.00
("JCY & The Youngbloods" is a repackage of "Soul Of A City Boy.")					
Mercury MG-21005	(M)	Young Blood (With John Sebastian)	1965	12.00	30.00
Mercury SR-61005	(S)	Young Blood (With John Sebastian)	1965	16.00	40.00
Mercury SR-61005	(S)	Jesse Colin Young & The Youngbloods	1969	8.00	20.00
("JCY & The Youngbloods" is a repackage of "Young Blood.")					

YOUNG, JOHNNY
| Arhoolie F-1029 | (S) | Johnny Young And His Chicago Blues Band | 1965 | 10.00 | 25.00 |
| Arhoolie 1037 | (S) | Chicago Blues (With Big Walter) | 1966 | 10.00 | 25.00 |

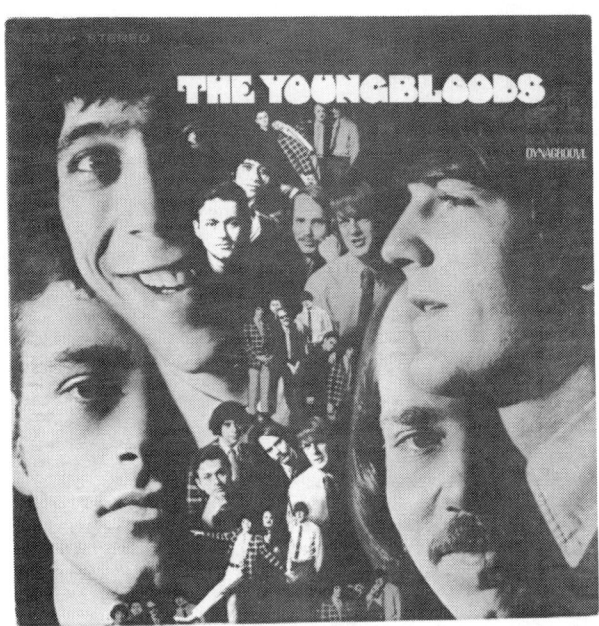

After his solo career as a folk artist stalled. Jesse Colin Young formed The Youngbloods with Banana (born Lyle Levinger), Joe Bauer, Jerry Corbitt. Signing with RCA Victor as their second big Rock act (Jefferson Airplane was first), they produced a marvelous first album that produced the seminal '60s classic, "Get Together," which was a minor hit in '67, rereleased a year later to no avail, and then a major hit in '69 as the theme song for the National Council For Christians And Jews. At which point the album was reissued with a new cover and a new title, Get Together— naturally. Their second album, Earth Music, followed the upbeat folk-rock of the first and led many fans and critics to assume great offings from the talented quartet. . . a potential that was, sadly, never realized.

Label & Catalog #		Title	Year	VG+	NM

YOUNG, NEIL/NEIL YOUNG & CRAZY HORSE
Crazy Horse backs Neil on 6349, 2221, 2242. Refer to The Buffalo Springfield; Crazy Horse; Crosby, Stills, Nash & Young; The Stills-Young Band.

Label & Catalog #		Title	Year	VG+	NM
Reprise RS-6317	(S)	**Neil Young** (White label promo)	1968	60.00	150.00
Reprise RS-6317	(S)	**Neil Young** (Brown & orange label)	1968	40.00	100.00
		(First promo and stock pressings of RS-6317 do not have Neil Young at the top of the portrait of Neil on the front cover.)			
Reprise RS-6317	(S)	**Neil Young**	1969	20.00	50.00
		(Second pressings with four remixed tracks have brown & orange labels and "RE 1" is etched in the trail-off vinyl. Young's name does not appear on the front cover.)			
Reprise RS-6349	(S)	**Everybody Knows This Is Nowhere** (White label promo)	1969	20.00	50.00
Reprise RS-6383	(S)	**After The Gold Rush** (White label promo)	1970	20.00	50.00
Reprise RS-6383	(S)	**After The Gold Rush** (White label promo)	1970	16.00	40.00
Reprise RS-6383	(S)	**After The Gold Rush** (With lyric sheet)	1970	12.00	30.00
		(Brown & orange label. A photo of Marc Bolan was erroneously printed on the inside cover.)			
Reprise RS-6383	(S)	**After The Gold Rush** (With lyric sheet)	1970	12.00	30.00
		(Brown & orange label. A photo of Neil was erroneously printed upside down on the inside cover.)			
Reprise RS-6383	(S)	**After The Gold Rush** (With lyric sheet)	1978	12.00	30.00
		(Includes a remixed, extended version of "When You Dance I Can Really Love." Brown label with RE 2" is etched in the trail-off vinyl and the title on the cover is in red print.)			
Reprise 2XS-6480	(S)	**Journey Through The Past** (2 LPs. White label promo)	1972	16.00	40.00
		(The cover bears a sticker that reads "Album must be played prior to airing; this album may contain words offensive to the public.")			
Reprise M-2151	(M)	**Time Fades Away** (White label promo)	1973	20.00	50.00
Reprise MS-2151	(S)	**Time Fades Away** (White label promo)	1973	10.00	25.00
Reprise MS-2221	(S)	**Tonight's The Night** (Promo label)	1975	16.00	40.00
Reprise MS-2242	(S)	**Zuma** (With lyric sheet)	1975	10.00	25.00
Reprise 3RS-2257	(DJ)	**Decade** (3 LPs. Test pressing)	1976	200.00	400.00
		("Campaigner" contains a verse deleted from the official version.)			
Reprise MSK-2266	(DJ)	**Give To The Wind**	1978		See below
		(MSK-2266 was originally titled "Give To The Wind" and eventually released as "Comes A Time." Issued in a plain jacket with inserts. Rare with a suggested Near Mint value of $500-1,000.)			
Reprise MSK-2266	(S)	**Comes A Time**	1978	20.00	50.00
		(Original pressings of MSK-2266 play "Lotta Love" as the last song on the first side. The back cover, which also lists "Lotta Love," is rather common, being used to package later pressings.)			
Warner Bros. WBMS-107	(DJ)	**The Warner Bros. Music Show** (Interview)	1979	16.00	40.00
Nautilus NR-44	(S)	**Harvest**	1982	40.00	120.00

YOUNG RASCALS, THE: *Refer to* **THE RASCALS**

YOUNGBLOODS, THE
Original members were Lowell "Banana" Levinger, Joe Bauer, Jerry Corbitt and Jesse Colin Young.

Label & Catalog #		Title	Year	VG+	NM
RCA Victor LPM-3724	(M)	**The Youngbloods**	1967	12.00	30.00
RCA Victor LSP-3724	(S)	**The Youngbloods**	1967	10.00	25.00
RCA Victor LPM-3865	(M)	**Earth Music**	1968	20.00	50.00
RCA Victor LSP-3865	(S)	**Earth Music**	1968	10.00	25.00
		— RCA albums above have black labels with Nipper on top.—			
Mercury SR-61273	(S)	**Two Trips** (Gold bordered cover)	1970	12.00	30.00
Mercury SR-61273	(S)	**Two Trips** (Red bordered cover)	1970	10.00	25.00
		(Mercury 61273 contains The Youngbloods' pre-RCA recordings with the best of Jesse Colin Young's "Young Blood" album.)			

YOUNGMAN, HENNY

Label & Catalog #		Title	Year	VG+	NM
Urania UR-9014	(M)	**The Horse And Auto Race Game**	195?	16.00	40.00

YURO, TIMI

Label & Catalog #		Title	Year	VG+	NM
Liberty LRP-3208	(M)	**Hurt**	1961	12.00	30.00
Liberty LST-7208	(S)	**Hurt**	1961	16.00	40.00
Liberty LRP-3212	(M)	**Soul**	1962	10.00	25.00
Liberty LST-7212	(S)	**Soul**	1962	12.00	30.00

Z

ZABACH, FLORIAN

Decca DL-5367	(10")	The Hot Canary	1951	20.00	50.00

ZACHERLE, JOHN

Elektra EKL-7190	(M)	Spook Along With Zacherle	1960	20.00	50.00
Elektra EKS-7190	(S)	Spook Along With Zacherle	1960	30.00	75.00
Parkway P-7018	(M)	Monster Mash	1962	20.00	50.00
Parkway P-7023	(M)	Scary Tales	1963	20.00	50.00
Crestview CR-803	(M)	Zacherle's Monster Gallery	1963	14.00	35.00
Crestview CRS7-803	(S)	Zacherle's Monster Gallery	1963	20.00	50.00

ZANIES, THE

Dore 321	(S)	The Zanies	1969	10.00	25.00

ZAPPA, FRANK/FRANK ZAPPA & THE MOTHERS OF INVENTION

While Zappa is always in charge, the Verve albums and an occasional later album credit The Mothers Of Invention or simply The Mothers. The original group (1964-1969) was Zappa with Jimmy Carl Black, Ray Collins, Roy Estrada and Elliott Ingber. The second group (1970-72), consists of Zappa and Underwood with George Duke, Aynsley Dunbar, Jim Pons and former Turtles Howard Kaylan and Mark Volman. Refer to The Animals; Captain Beefheart; Wild Man Fischer; G.T.O.'s; Sandy Hurvitz; Jean Luc Ponty; Ruben & The Jets; and L. Shankar.

Verve V-5005-2	(M)	Freak Out! (2 LPs. White label promo)	1966	200.00	400.00
Verve V-5005-2	(M)	Freak Out! (2 LPs)	1966	80.00	200.00
Verve V6-5005-2	(S)	Freak Out! (2 LPs. Yellow label promo)	1966	100.00	250.00
Verve V6-5005-2	(S)	Freak Out! (2 LPs)	1966	30.00	75.00
		(Original covers for Verve 5005 had a blurb on the inside advertising the availability of the mail-order map of "freak out hot spots" in L.A., which is listed separately below.)			
Verve 5005		Freak Out! Spots In L.A. Map	1966		See below
		(The "bonus" map has a suggested Near Mint value of $150-300.)			
Verve V-5005-2	(M)	Freak Out! (2 LPs)	1966	60.00	150.00
Verve V6-5005-2	(S)	Freak Out! (2 LPs)	1966	20.00	50.00
		(Second pressing covers delete the blurb for the "hot spots" map.)			
Verve V6-5013	(M)	Absolutely Free (White label promo)	1967	100.00	250.00
Verve V-5013	(M)	Absolutely Free	1967	60.00	150.00
Verve V6-5013	(S)	Absolutely Free	1967	20.00	50.00
Verve V6-5045	(M)	We're Only In It For The Money (White label)	1968	80.00	200.00
Verve V-5045	(M)	We're Only In It For The Money	1968	40.00	100.00
Verve V6-5045	(S)	We're Only In It For The Money	1968	30.00	75.00
		(Original pressings have "V6 5045 MGS 1250-REV-F" scratched in the trail off-vinyl. Issued with a sheet of Sgt Pepper-ish cut-outs.)			
Verve V6-5045	(S)	We're Only In It For The Money	1968	80.00	200.00
		(Later edited version: In the song "Who Needs The Peace Corps?" the line "I will love the police as they kick the shit out of me" has been deleted. Similarly, in the song "Let's Make The Water Turn Black" the line "And I still remember Mama with her apron and her pad feeding all the boys at Ed's Cafe" has also been erased. The trail off reads "V6 5045 MGS 1250-REV.")			
Verve V6-8741	(S)	Lumpy Gravy (Yellow label promo)	1968	80.00	200.00
Verve V6-8741	(S)	Lumpy Gravy	1968	20.00	50.00
Verve V6-5055	(S)	Cruising With Ruben & The Jets (Yellow label promo)	1968	80.00	200.00
Verve V6-5055	(S)	Cruising With Ruben & The Jets	1968	30.00	75.00
		(Supposedly, a set of three "bonus' paper inserts is associated with this album. They include "The Story Of Ruben & The Jets," "How To Comb & Set A Jellyroll," and a guide on how to do the "bop." These may have been included with early pressings of the album— unlikely given their extreme scarcity— or as part of a mail-order/promotional package. Since I know of no one who knows of anyone who has ever seen these gems,there is no way to suggest any sotra value.)			

Label & Catalog #		Title	Year	VG+	NM
Verve V6-5068	(S)	**Mothermania** *(Yellow label promo)*	1969	60.00	150.00
Verve V6-5068	(S)	**Mothermania**	1969	30.00	75.00
Verve V6-5074	(S)	**The XXXX Of The Mothers** **Of Invention** *(Yellow label promo)*	1969	60.00	150.00
Verve V6-5074	(S)	**The XXXX Of The Mothers Of Invention**	1969	20.00	50.00
MGM GAS-112	(S)	**The Mothers Of Invention** *(Yellow label)*	1970	40.00	100.00
MGM GAS-112	(S)	**The Mothers Of Invention**	1970	20.00	50.00
MGM SE-4754	(S)	**The Worst Of The Mothers** *(Yellow label)*	1971	60.00	150.00
MGM SE-4754	(S)	**The Worst Of The Mothers**	1971	20.00	50.00
Warner Bros. PRO-368	(DJ)	**Zapped** *(Collage cover)*	1969	20.00	50.00
Warner Bros. PRO-368	(DJ)	**Zapped** *(Zappa cover)*	1969	10.00	25.00
		(Various artists sampler for Zappa's Bizarre/Straight labels.)			
Bizarre MS-2024	(S)	**Uncle Meat** *(2 LPs with booklet)*	1969	16.00	40.00
Bizarre RS-6356	(S)	**Hot Rats**	1969	10.00	25.00
Bizarre RS-6370	(S)	**Burnt Weenie Sandwich** *(With booklet)*	1969	10.00	25.00
Bizarre MS-2028	(S)	**Weasels Ripped My Flesh**	1970	10.00	25.00
Bizarre MS-2030	(S)	**Chunga's Revenge**	1970	10.00	25.00
Bizarre MS-2042	(S)	**Fillmore East, June 1971**	1971	10.00	25.00
United Arts. UAS-9956	(S)	**200 Motels** *(2 LPs. Soundtrack)*	1971	16.00	40.00
Bizarre MS-2075	(S)	**Just Another Band From L.A.**	1972	10.00	25.00
Bizarre MS-2093	(S)	**The Grand Wazoo**	1972	10.00	25.00
Bizarre MS-2094	(S)	**Waka/Jawaka**	1972	10.00	25.00
		— Bizarre albums above have blue labels.—			
DiscReet MS4-2149	(Q)	**Over-Nite Sensation**	1973	16.00	40.00
DiscReet DS-2175	(S)	**Apostrophe** *(White label promo)*	1974	16.00	40.00
DiscReet DS4-2175	(Q)	**Apostrophe**	1974	14.00	35.00
DiscReet 2D-2290	(DJ)	**Zappa In New York Cover** *(2 LPs)* *(Test pressing with "Punky's Whips.")*	1978	200.00	400.00
DiscReet 2D-2290	(S)	**Zappa In New York Cover** *(2 LPs)*	1978	100.00	250.00
		(Original covers erroneously list the deleted "Punky's Whips.")			
Zappa	(DJ)	**Lather** *(4 LP test pressing)*	1978		See below
		(Rare with a suggested Near Mint value $500-1,000.)			

ZENITHS, THE

Atlantic 8043	(M)	**Makin' The Scene**	1960	40.00	100.00
Atlantic SD-8043	(S)	**Makin' The Scene**	1960	60.00	150.00

ZEPHYR

Probe CPLP-4510	(S)	**Zephyr**	1969	16.00	40.00
Warner Bros. BS-1897	(S)	**Going Back To Colorado**	1971	10.00	25.00
Warner Bros. BS-2603	(S)	**Sunset Ride**	1972	10.00	25.00

ZERFAS

700 West 730710	(S)	**Zerfas**	1973	660.00	1,000.00

ZIG ZAG PEOPLE, THE

Decca DL-75110	(S)	**The Zig Zag People** **Take Bubble Gum Music Underground**	1969	10.00	25.00

ZIP CODES

Liberty LRP-3367	(M)	**Mustang**	1964	40.00	100.00
Liberty LST-7367	(S)	**Mustang**	1964	60.00	150.00

ZIPPER

Whizeagle	(S)	**Zipper**	1975	16.00	40.00

ZOMBIES

Features Rod Argent and Colin Blunstone.

Parrot PAR-61001	(M)	**The Zombies**	1965	20.00	50.00
Parrot PAS-71001	(E)	**The Zombies**	1965	16.00	40.00
RCA Victor LOC-1115	(M)	**Bunny Lake Is Missing** *(Soundtrack)*	1965	30.00	75.00
RCA Victor LSO-1115	(S)	**Bunny Lake Is Missing** *(Soundtrack)*	1965	40.00	100.00
Date TES-4013	(S)	**Odessey And Oracle**	1968	12.00	30.00
		(First pressing covers make no mention of "Time Of The Season." "This Will Be Our Year" is rechanneled on this album.)			

ZOO

Sunburst 7500	(S)	**The Zoo Presents The Chocolate Mousse**	1968	20.00	50.00

Label & Catalog #		Title	Year	VG+	NM
ZVI, RUTH BEN					
Prestige Int. PRLP-13070	*(M)*	**Israeli Percussion**	*1963*	**12.00**	**30.00**
ZZ TOP					
London PS-X-1001	*(DJ)*	**Takin' Texas to The People**	*1976*	**20.00**	**50.00**

Cartoon Characters On Record
(& Kindred Kiddie Kollectibles)

This section collects over one hundred albums that feature, more or less, cartoon characters from the television series of the '50s and '60s. That is, these albums feature [often delightful] drawn or painted cartoon covers with stories, jokes and/or music told through the "voices" of the familiar characters. (Note: Many of these albums are showcases for the extraordinary vocal abilities of Mel Blanc, who also has a few titles listed under his own name in the main body of this volume.) While these are, in their way, sorta soundtrack related, they nonetheless appeal to a different market. Oddly, many of the hardest rocking collectors have an inordinate soft spot for this type of material.

Should the values assigned seem high to the newcomer, one must remember that, on release, these records were sold almost exclusively to pre-pubescents (or, at least, the parents of these nascent consumers) and suffered long and hard at their hands. To find many of these albums today in anything resembling acceptable collectible condition is an Herculean task (it's probably easier finding R&B albums from the same era in better condition). While this list does cover most of the important releases by the three labels commonly associated with this type of release— Colpix, Golden and Hanna Barbera, or HBR— it is far from complete.

There are other albums that fall into this genre, such as soundtracks to television shows of the nature of *The Addams Family*, *The Munsters* and *Star Trek*. There are albums that relate the voyages of the U.S,.S. Enterprise, primarily on the Power label, but these have as yet to attract an audience to place their value above the $10-15 range. During the '70s, several labels issued comic book related albums, often accompanying them with actual comic books. Golden's set featured reproductions of early Marvel Comics; another series commissioned legendary EC Comics artist Wally Wood to design the packaging and do the cover artwork. Fort the time being, these have not been included. Collectors or dealers interested in seeing this line of data expanded should contact me. . .

I intend to address the missing numbers from these labels— especially the many Golden records, which includes just about anything one can associate with a child's appetite, the kiddy stuff on Capitol's hard-to-find "J" series, etc.— in future guides. Collectors of such artifacts are eagerly invited to offer corrections, additions and suggestions via phone, mail or in-person. . .

"A.A." AA-60	(M)	**Huckleberry Hound For President**	1960	60.00	150.00
Big Tree BTS-2009	(S)	**Presenting The Sugar Bears**	197?	10.00	25.00
Camden CAL-1075	(M)	**Rodger Ramjet & The American Eagles**	1966	30.00	75.00
Camden CAS-1075	(S)	**Rodger Ramjet & The American Eagles** *(TV Soundtrack)*	1966	40.00	100.00
Capitol JAO-3251	(M)	**Woody Woodpecker And His Talent Show**	1961	20.00	50.00
Capitol J-3254	(M)	**Sparky's Magic Piano**	1961	20.00	50.00
Capitol J-3255	(M)	**Rusty In Orchestraville**	1961	20.00	50.00
Capitol J-3257	(M)	**Bugs Bunny And His Friends**	1961	20.00	50.00
Capitol JAO-3259	(M)	**Bozo At The Circus**	1961	20.00	50.00
Capitol J-3263	(M)	**Woody Woodpecker's Picnic**	1962	20.00	50.00
Capitol J-3264	(M)	**Mickey Mouse's Birthday Party**	1962	20.00	50.00
Capitol J-3266	(M)	**Bugs Bunny In Storyland**	1963	20.00	50.00
Colpix CP-201	(M)	**Ruff And Ready**	1959	100.00	250.00
Colpix CP-202	(M)	**Huckleberry Hound: The Great Kellogg's TV Show**	1959	80.00	200.00
Colpix CP-203	(M)	**Quickdraw McGraw**	1960	40.00	100.00
Colpix CP-204	(M)	**The Misadventures Of Dennis The Menace**	1961	100.00	250.00
Colpix CP-205	(M)	**Yogi Bear And Boo Boo**	1961	60.00	150.00
Colpix CP-207	(M)	**Here Comes Huckleberry Hound**	1961	80.00	200.00
Colpix CP-208	(M)	**Mr. Jinx, Pixie And Dixie**	1961	50.00	125.00
Colpix CP-209	(M)	**Mr. Ed, The Talking Horse**	1961	100.00	250.00
Colpix CP-210	(M)	**Huckleberry Hound And The Ghost Ship**	1962	40.00	100.00

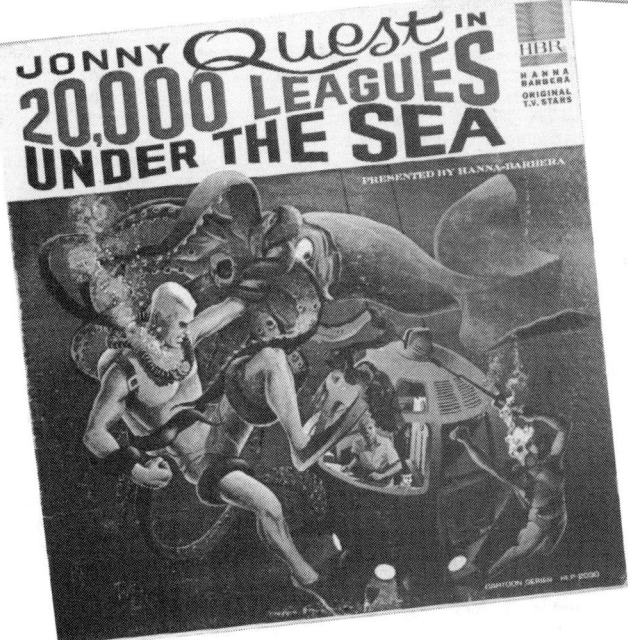

Two examples of "kiddie record" that are highly collectible due to their also being television related. Mister Ed, The Talking Horse is a straight original TV soundtrack with a shot of Ed and Wilbur framed on the cover by a TV screen. The Johnny Quest album is sought after both by collectors of television related albums (the cover notes that the characters are "Original T.V. Stars") and by those interested in the comic book aspects of the Quest and his friends. Like many kiddie records, these were sold almost exclusively to children and handled in, shall we say, less than audiophile standards. Hence, they are rare as hen's fillings in collectible condition.

Label & Catalog #		Title	Year	VG+	NM
Colpix CP-211	(M)	Quick Draw McGraw:			
		The Treasure Of Sarah's Mattress	1962	50.00	125.00
Colpix CP-212	(M)	Top Cat	1963	100.00	250.00
Colpix CP-213	(M)	The Jetsons	1963	100.00	250.00
Colpix CP-302	(M)	The Flintstones	1961	80.00	200.00
Colpix CP-410	(M)	Mr. Magoo: 1,001 Arabian Nights *(TV Sdtk)*	1959	20.00	50.00
Colpix SCP-410	(S)	Mr. Magoo: 1,001 Arabian Nights *(TV Sdtk)*	1959	80.00	200.00
Colpix CP-453	(M)	Yogi Bear: Wake Up America!	1964	12.00	30.00
Colpix SCP-453	(S)	Yogi Bear: Wake Up America!	1964	20.00	50.00
Colpix CP-472	(M)	Hey There, It's Yogi Bear *(Soundtrack)*	1964	30.00	75.00
Colpix SCP-472	(S)	Hey There, It's Yogi Bear *(Soundtrack)*	1964	40.00	100.00
Cricket CR-17	(M)	Woody Woodpecker & His Friends	1958	20.00	50.00
Cricket CR-28	(M)	Felix The Cat	1958	50.00	125.00
Decca DL-8659	(M)	Woody Woodpecker's Family Album	1958	60.00	150.00
Diplomat D-5017	(M)	Popeye The Sailor Man	196?	30.00	75.00
Diplomat DS-5017	(E)	Popeye The Sailor Man	196?	30.00	75.00
Epic LN-24231	(M)	Original TV Adventures Of King Kong	1966	10.00	25.00
Epic BN-26231	(M)	Original TV Adventures Of King Kong	1966	12.00	30.00
Forward STF-1018	(S)	Cattanooga Cats	1969	20.00	50.00
Golden GLP-27	(M)	Top TV Jamboree	1958	30.00	75.00
Golden GLP-51	(M)	Quick Draw McGraw			
		And Huckleberry Hound	1959	60.00	150.00
Golden GLP-55	(M)	Howl Along With			
		Huckleberry Bound And Yogi Bear	1959	60.00	150.00
Golden GLP-56	(M)	Popeye The Sailor Man And His Friends	1960	30.00	75.00
Golden GLP-59	(M)	Dennis The Menace Songs	1960	30.00	75.00
Golden GLP-60	(M)	Huckleberry Hound For President	1960	40.00	100.00
		— Golden albums above have black labels.—			
Golden GLP-64	(M)	Rocky And His Friends	1961	80.00	200.00
Golden GLP-66	(M)	Songs Of The Flintstones	1961	100.00	250.00
Golden GLP-70	(M)	Songs Of Yogi Bear And His Pals	1961	30.00	75.00
Golden GLP-71	(M)	Bugs Bunny Songfest	1961	30.00	75.00
Golden GLP-73	(M)	Popeye Songs About			
		Health, Safety, Friendship	1961	30.00	75.00
		— Golden albums above have gold labels.—			
Golden GLP-88	(M)	Mr. Ed: Straight From The Horses Mouth	1962	80.00	200.00
Golden GLP-90	(M)	Yogi Bear:			
		How To Be A Better Than Average Child	1962	30.00	75.00
Golden GLP-91	(M)	Officer Gunther Toody Tells Toody Tales	1963	20.00	50.00
Golden GLP-96	(M)	Dream Along With Bozo	1963	16.00	40.00
Golden GLP-98	(M)	The Jetsons	1963	80.00	200.00
		(Original covers are red cover with Rosie the Robot in foreground.)			
Golden GLP-98	(M)	The Jetsons	1964	25.00	125.00
		(Later covers are blue cover with Rosie the Ribot in background.)			
Golden GLP-109	(M)	Mighty Hercules	1963	80.00	200.00
Golden GLP-112	(M)	Woody Woodpecker	1963	20.00	50.00
Golden GLP-113	(M)	Casper And His Friends	1964	16.00	40.00
Golden GLP-120	(M)	Magilla Gorilla And His Pals	1964	20.00	50.00
Golden GLP-124	(M)	Hey There, It's Yogi Bear	1964	16.00	40.00
Golden GLP-139	(M)	At Home With The Minsters	1965	100.00	250.00
Golden GLP-151	(M)	King Kong	1965	14.00	35.00
		— Golden albums above have yellow or red labels.—			
HBR A-101	(DJ)	Drop-Ins, Volume 1	1965	100.00	250.00
		(HBR 101 is a compilation of short character "drop-ins")			
HBR HLP-2020	(M)	Super Snooper And Blabber Mouse:			
		Monster Shindig	1965	40.00	100.00
HBR HLP-2021	(M)	The Flintstones' Flip Fables: Goldi-rocks			
		& The Three Bearosauruses	1965	40.00	100.00
HBR HLP-2022	(M)	Huckleberry Hound Tells			
		Stories Of Uncle Remus	1965	40.00	100.00

Label & Catalog #		Title	Year	VG+	NM
HBR HLP-2023	(M)	Yogi Bear And Boo Boo Tell Stories Of Little Red Riding Hood And Jack & The Beanstalk	1965	40.00	100.00
HBR HLP-2024	(M)	Magilla Gorilla Tells Ogee The Story Alice In Wonderland	1965	40.00	100.00
HBR HLP-2025	(M)	Pixie And Dixie With Mr. Jinx Tell The Story Of Cinderella	1965	40.00	100.00
HBR HLP-2026	(M)	Snaggle Puss Tells The Story Of Wizard Of Oz	1965	40.00	100.00
HBR HLP-2027	(M)	Wilma Flintstone Tells The Story Of Bambi	1965	40.00	100.00
HBR HLP-2028	(M)	Doggy Daddy Tells Augie Doggy: The Story Of Pinocchio	1965	40.00	100.00
HBR HLP-2029	(M)	Touche Turtle & Dum Dum: The Reluctant Dragon	1965	40.00	100.00
HBR HLP-2030	(M)	Johnny Quest In 20,000 Leagues Under The Sea	1965	60.00	150.00
HBR HLP-2031	(M)	Robin Hood Starring Top Cat	1965	40.00	100.00
HBR HLP-2032	(M)	Merry Christmas	1965	40.00	100.00
HBR HLP-2033	(M)	Pebbles And Bamm-Bamm Sing Songs Of Christmas	1965	40.00	100.00
HBR HLP-2035	(M)	Fred Flintstone & Barney Rubble In Sings From Mary Poppins	1965	40.00	100.00
HBR HLP-2036	(M)	James Bomb Starring Super Snooper And Blabber Mouse	1965	40.00	100.00
HBR HLP-2037	(M)	The Jetsons: 1st Family On The Moon	1965	60.00	150.00
HBR HLP-2038	(M)	Hansel & Gretel Starring The Flintstones	1965	40.00	100.00
HBR HLP-2039	(M)	Sinbad Jr.: Treasure Island	1965	50.00	125.00
HBR HLP-2040	(M)	On The Good Ship Lollipop Starring Pebbles & Bamm-Bamm	1965	40.00	100.00
HBR HLP-2041	(M)	Atom Ant: Muscle Magic	1966	80.00	200.00
HBR HLP-2042	(M)	Winsome Witch: It's Magic	1966	60.00	150.00
HBR HLP-2043	(M)	Squiddley Diddley: Surfin' Safari	1966	60.00	150.00
HBR HLP-2044	(M)	The Hillbilly Bears: Hillbilly Shindig	1966	60.00	150.00
HBR HLP-2045	(M)	Precious Pupp: Hot Rod Granny	1966	60.00	150.00
HBR HLP-2046	(M)	Secret Squirrel & Morocca Mole: Super Spy	1966	60.00	150.00
HBR HLP-2047	(M)	The Flintstones: S.A.S.F.A.T.P.O.G.O.B.S.O.A.L.T.	1966	40.00	100.00
HBR HLP-2048	(M)	Golden Cartoons In Song, Volume 1	1966	60.00	150.00
HBR HLP-2049	(M)	Golden Cartoons In Song, Volume 2	1966	60.00	150.00
HBR HLP-2050	(M)	Yogi Bear & The Three Stooges: Mad Mad Dr. No No	1966	40.00	100.00
HBR HLP-2051	(M)	New Adventures Of Alice In Wonderland	1966	40.00	100.00
HBR HLP-2052	(M)	The Flintstones & Jose Jimenez: Time Machine	1966	40.00	100.00
HBR HLP-2053	(M)	Golden Cartoons In Song, Volume 3	1966	60.00	150.00
HBR HLP-2054	(M)	Golden Cartoons In Song, Volume 4	1966	60.00	150.00
HBR HLP-2055	(M)	A Man Called Flintstone (Soundtrack)	1966	60.00	150.00
HBR HLP-2057	(M)	Stories Of G. I. Joe	1966	100.00	250.00
Leo CH-1002	(M)	Mighty Mouse To The Rescue	196?	30.00	75.00
Leo CH-1019	(M)	The Official Adventures Of Batman & Robin	1966	12.00	30.00
Leo CH-1027	(M)	More Official Adventures Of Batman & Robin	1966	12.00	30.00
Leo CH-1022	(M)	Official Adventures Of Superman	1966	20.00	50.00
MGM E-????	(M)	Terrytoon's Mighty Mouse TV Playhouse	195?	40.00	100.00
MGM CH-100	(M)	TV Storytime With Tom & Jerry	196?	40.00	100.00
MGM CH-106	(M)	More TV Storytime With Tom & Jerry	196?	40.00	100.00
MGM E-901	(M)	How The Grinch Stole Christmas (TV Sdtk)	1966	14.00	35.00
MGM SE-901	(S)	How The Grinch Stole Christmas (TV Sdtk)	1966	20.00	50.00
Peter Pan 8018	(M)	Laurel & Hardy: This Is Your Laff	196?	20.00	50.00
Peter Pan 8049	(S)	Children's Treasury Of Batman Musical Stories	196?	10.00	25.00
Peter Pan 8105	(M)	The Flintstones	1972	12.00	30.00
Peter Pan 8137	(M)	Holly-Daze	1974	10.00	25.00
Peter Pan 8154	(S)	U.S. Of Archie	1972	10.00	25.00
Power 8155	(M)	Batman	1975	10.00	25.00
Power 8158	(M)	Star Trek	1975	10.00	25.00

Label & Catalog #		Title	Year	VG+	NM
Power 8167	(M)	Batman	1975	10.00	25.00
Power 8168	(M)	Star Trek	1975	10.00	25.00
Power 512	(M)	Batman	1976	10.00	25.00
RCA Victor LBY-1018	(M)	Popeye's Favorite Sea Shanties	1959	30.00	75.00
RCA Victor LPM-1362	(M)	Mr. MaGoo In Hi Fi	1956	20.00	50.00
Simon Says M-32	(M)	Courageous Cat	1962	30.00	75.00
Star-Bright HLP-101	(M)	Walter Lantz' Woody Woodpecker Presents	195?	30.00	75.00
Wonderland WLP-318	(S)	Mr. Magoo	1978	10.00	25.00

"Various Artists"
Compilations & Soundtracks

A complete list of various artists compilations would take up another whole volume. I have listed those titles that are rare and those most sought after by collectors. Even for its stated goals, this list far from complete. Most of these albums have a nominal value, especially given their age and the fact that as a genre these albums didn't sell in overwhelming numbers. The presence of any collectible artist on an otherwise mediocre compilation will affect its value somewhat; a track by a major artist can dramatically increase a value. For instance, Clarion 609, *Discoteque In Astrosound*, an otherwise nondescript comp, is sought-after by Beatles collectors because it contains one of The Beat Brothers sides.

RCA Victor issued samplers to radio stations throughout the '50s and '60s, often con-taining an Elvis track; each of these fetches three figure prices, even though the Elvis material is available elsewhere. To a lesser extent comps with tracks by The Beach Boys, Bowie, Dylan and The Stones also attract a premium from completists. It is simply not possible in this book to list each of the collectible artists who appear on the albums below, although a few special items have been singled out. (I *have* listed several of thes aforementioned Elvis items in a section following the regular RCA titles.) Finally, several albums that are, in fact, various artists compilations have been listed under individual artists for technical reasons; a note refers the reader to the artist. . .

(No label)	(DJ)	**Carnival Rock** (Soundtrack on red vinyl)	1955		See below
		("Carnival Rock" was issued without a cover and has a suggested Near Mint value of $2,000-4,000.)			
(No label)	(DJ)	**Rock, Rock, Rock** (Soundtrack)	1955		See below
		("Rock, Rock, Rock" is a publisher's demo, most of which were issued without a cover, and has a suggested Near Mint value of $2,000-4,000. Copies with a cover are even rarer with a suggested Near Mint value of $3,000-5,000.)			
(No label)	(DJ)	**Go, Johnny, Go** (Soundtrack)	1959		See below
		("Go, Johnny, Go" has a suggested NM value of $1,500-2,500.)			
(No label)	(S)	**Unite**	1970	**60.00**	**150.00**
		(Semi-legal benefit album supporting the San Jose State Student Strike Committe. Included was a copy of the underground paper, "San Jose Red Eye," dated May 21-June 3, 1970 .)			
(No label)	(M)	**Psychedelic Patchwork, Vol. 1**	198?	**12.00**	**30.00**
A-Bet LP-401	(M)	**Records Galore**	196?	**12.00**	**30.00**
A&M SP-8022	(DJ)	**The A&M Bootleg Album** (2 LPs with letter)	1973	**10.00**	**25.00**
A&M PR-4876	(DJ)	**Propaganda** (Picture disc)	1980	**16.00**	**40.00**
A Go-Go	(M)	**Chosen Few, Volume 1**	198?	**16.00**	**40.00**
ABC-Paramount ABC-216	(M)	**A Million Or More**	1958	**20.00**	**50.00**
		(Original pressing covers and labels credit the last track as Tommy Roe's "Sheila" while the disc plays Paul Anka's "Diana.")			
ABC-Paramount ABC-504	(M)	**Shindig!**	1964	**10.00**	**25.00**
ABC-Paramount ABCS-504	(S)	**Shindig!**	1964	**12.00**	**30.00**
ABC 2151	(DJ)	**Zachariah: A Special One-Hour Open-End Radio Show** (With script)	1970	**20.00**	**50.00**
Ace 1012	(M)	**Greatest 15 Hits**	1960	**40.00**	**100.00**
Ace 1019	(M)	**Let's Have A Dance Party**	1961	**40.00**	**100.00**
Ace 1020	(M)	**For Twisters Only**	1962	**40.00**	**100.00**
Acid 1	(M)	**Chocolate Soup, Volume 2**	198?	**12.00**	**30.00**

Label & Catalog #		Title	Year	VG+	NM
AGNC 100	(M)	**Nightmares From The Underworld, Vol. 1**	198?	**40.00**	**100.00**
Aladdin LP-710	(M)	**Rock & Roll With Rhythm & Blues**	195?	**1,000.00**	*See below*
		(LP-710 is a 12" album that carries an Aladdin 700 series catalog			
		number designating a 10" album. One of the rarest various artists			
		compilations with a suggested Near Mint value of $2,000-3,000.)			
Allegro 1704	(M)	**Let's Rock And Roll**	1956	**40.00**	**100.00**
Allegro Royale 1594	(M)	**Cowboy Song Favorites**	195?	**16.00**	**40.00**
All God's Delerium	(M)	**Good Roots**	198?	**30.00**	**75.00**
Almo/Irving *(No number)*	(P)	**East Memphis Music-**			
		The Hits From The Stax Era *(5 LP box)*	1982	**24.00**	**60.00**
Almo/Irving EM-50009	(P)	**East Memphis Music-**			
		The Hits From The Stax Era *(2 LPs)*	1982	**10.00**	**25.00**
Almor A-103	(M)	**Golden Souvenirs**	1963	**10.00**	**25.00**
Almor AS-103	(S	**Golden Souvenirs**	1963	**10.00**	**25.00**
Almor A-105	(M)	**Teen Bandstand**	1963	**10.00**	**25.00**
Almor AS-105	(S)	**Teen Bandstand**	1963	**10.00**	**25.00**
Almor A-108	(M)	**The World Of Surfin'**	1963	**16.00**	**40.00**
Almor AS-108	(S)	**The World Of Surfin'**	1963	**20.00**	**50.00**
Almor A-109	(M)	**Hot Rod Drag Races**	1963	**20.00**	**50.00**
Almor AS-109	(S)	**Hot Rod Drag Races**	1963	**24.00**	**60.00**
Amazon 1007	(M)	**Greatest Rhythm & Blues Hits**	195?	**20.00**	**50.00**
Amazon 1008	(M)	**Greatest Rhythm & Blues Hits, Volume 2**	195?	**20.00**	**50.00**
Amos AAS-8002	(S)	**Vanishing Point** *(Soundtrack)*	1971	**10.00**	**25.00**
Angel 65016	(M)	**Irish Festival Singers/Album 1**	195?	**10.00**	**25.00**
Angel 65025	(M)	**Irish Festival Singers/Album 2**	195?	**10.00**	**25.00**
Apollo LP-477	(M)	**Saxomaniac**	1956	**40.00**	**100.00**
Apollo LP-490	(M)	**Jackpot Of Hits**	1957	**60.00**	**150.00**
Apple SW-3377	(S)	**Come Together** *(Soundtrack)*	1971	**10.00**	**25.00**
Apple STCX-3385	(S)	**Concert For Bangla Desh:** *Refer to* George Harrison & Friends			
Apple SW-3400	(M)	**Phil Spector's Christmas Album:** *Refer to* Phil Spector			
Argo LP-649	(DJ)	**Remember The Oldies** *(Multi-color vinyl)*	1963	**60.00**	**150.00**
Argo LP-649	(M)	**Remember The Oldies**	1963	**20.00**	**50.00**
Argo LP-656	(M)	**Fanfare Of Hits**	1963	**10.00**	**25.00**
Argo LP-4026	(M)	**The Blues, Volume 1**	1963	**10.00**	**25.00**
Argo LPS-4026	(S)	**The Blues, Volume 1**	1963	**10.00**	**25.00**
Argo LP-4027	(M)	**The Blues, Volume 2**	1963	**10.00**	**25.00**
Argo LPS-4027	(S)	**The Blues, Volume 2**	1963	**10.00**	**25.00**
Argo LP-4031	(M)	**Folk Festival Of The Blues**	1964	**20.00**	**50.00**
Argo LPS-4031	(S)	**Folk Festival Of The Blues**	1964	**20.00**	**50.00**
Argo LP-4041	(M)	**The Blues, Volume 3**	1965	**10.00**	**25.00**
Argo LPS-4041	(S)	**The Blues, Volume 3**	1965	**10.00**	**25.00**
Argo LP-4042	(M)	**The Blues, Volume 4**	1965	**10.00**	**25.00**
Argo LPS-4042	(S)	**The Blues, Volume 4**	1965	**10.00**	**25.00**
Arrawak 100	(M)	**A Night Train Of Oldies**	195?	**16.00**	**40.00**
Arvee 433	(M)	**Golden Echoes**	1962	**10.00**	**25.00**
Ascot ALM-13007	(M)	**All Girl Million Sellers**	1962	**14.00**	**35.00**
Ascot ALS-16007	(P)	**All Girl Million Sellers**	1962	**14.00**	**35.00**
Astra 1001	(M)	**Terry Lee Presents For Lovers Only**	1964	**20.00**	**50.00**
Atco 33-103	(M)	**Rockin' Together**	1958	**50.00**	**125.00**
Atco 33-118	(M)	**The Good Old '50's**	1960	**30.00**	**75.00**
Atco 33-143	(M)	**The Great Group Goodies**	1962	**30.00**	**75.00**

The cover for Audio Fidelity's How To Blow Your Mind And Have A Freak-Out Party also reads "Mind Tripping Sound. Hallucinations. Journey Into Your Mind. Electric Buddhas. Love Supreme Deal. Play Your Game. Acid Rock. I've A Zebra. She Can Fly" and "Electric Mind Sound by Unfolding." The collage cover art also hints at the psychedelicisms within. Albums of this sort, exploiting the phenomenon of the late '60s and early '70s where people were using chemicals for other than recreational purposes, are far less common than the casual observer might think. But the recorded medium was as slow to recognize the potentials of the psychedelic era as the moving picture medium, which is even more bereft of anything resembling a serious consideration of the consciousness expansion movement. Neither medium would miss out on subsequent "fads," such as disco or new age-isms.

Label & Catalog #		Title	Year	VG+	NM
Atco 33-159	(M)	Apollo Saturday Night	1964	16.00	40.00
Atco SD-33-159	(S)	Apollo Saturday Night	1964	30.00	75.00
Atco 33-169		Ain't She Sweet: *Refer to* The Beatles			
Atco 33-245	(M)	The Savage Seven (*Soundtrack. White label*)	1968	20.00	50.00
Atco SD-33-245	(S)	The Savage Seven (*Soundtrack*)	1968	10.00	25.00
Atco D-33-269	(S)	Soul Christmas	1968	10.00	25.00
Atlantic 1239	(M)	Rock & Roll Forever	1956	80.00	200.00
		— Original Atlantic albums above have black labels.—			
Atlantic 1346	(M)	Sounds Of The South	1960	10.00	25.00
Atlantic SD-1346	(S)	Sounds Of The South	1960	16.00	40.00
Atlantic 1347	(M)	Blue Ridge Mountain Music	1960	10.00	25.00
Atlantic SD-1347	(S)	Blue Ridge Mountain Music	1960	16.00	40.00
Atlantic 1348	(M)	Roots Of The Blues	1960	10.00	25.00
Atlantic SD-1348	(S)	Roots Of The Blues	1960	16.00	40.00
Atlantic 1349	(M)	White Spirituals	1960	10.00	25.00
Atlantic SD-1349	(S)	White Spirituals	1960	16.00	40.00
Atlantic 1350	(M)	American Folk Songs For Children	1960	10.00	25.00
Atlantic SD-1350	(S)	American Folk Songs For Children	1960	16.00	40.00
Atlantic 1351	(M)	Negro Church Music	1960	10.00	25.00
Atlantic SD-1351	(S)	Negro Church Music	1960	16.00	40.00
Atlantic 1352	(M)	The Blues Roll On	1960	10.00	25.00
Atlantic SD-1352	(S)	The Blues Roll On	1960	16.00	40.00
		— Atlantic albums above have multi-color labels with a white "fan" logo on the right side.—			
Atlantic 8001	(M)	The Greatest Rock & Roll·	1956	60.00	150.00
Atlantic 8010	(M)	Rock & Roll Forever, Volume 1	1956	40.00	100.00
Atlantic 8013	(M)	Dance The Rock & Roll	1957	40.00	100.00
Atlantic 8021	(M)	Rock & Roll Forever, Volume 2	1957	40.00	100.00
Atlantic 8037	(M)	The Rockin' '50's	1959	40.00	100.00
		— Original Atlantic albums above have black labels.—			
Atlantic 8001	(M)	The Greatest Rock & Roll	196?	20.00	50.00
Atlantic 8010	(M)	Rock & Roll Forever, Volume 1	196?	20.00	50.00
Atlantic 8013	(M)	Dance The Rock & Roll	196?	20.00	50.00
Atlantic 8021	(M)	Rock & Roll Forever, Volume 2	196?	20.00	50.00
Atlantic 8037	(M)	The Rockin' '50's	196?	20.00	50.00
Atlantic 8058	(M)	The Greatest Twist Hits	1962	20.00	50.00
		— Atlantic albums above have multi-color labels with a white "fan" logo on the right side.—			
Atlantic 8001	(M)	The Greatest Rock & Roll	196?	10.00	25.00
Atlantic 8010	(M)	Rock & Roll Forever, Volume 1	196?	10.00	25.00
Atlantic 8013	(M)	Dance The Rock & Roll	196?	10.00	25.00
Atlantic 8021	(M)	Rock & Roll Forever, Volume 2	196?	10.00	25.00
Atlantic 8037	(M)	The Rockin' '50's	196?	10.00	25.00
Atlantic 8058	(M)	The Greatest Twist Hits	1962	10.00	25.00
Atlantic 8065	(M)	The Solid Gold Groups	1962	20.00	50.00
Atlantic 8068	(M)	Hound Dog's Old Gold	1962	20.00	50.00
Atlantic 8098	(M)	Jamaica Ska	1963	8.00	20.00
Atlantic SD-8098	(S)	Jamaica Ska	1963	10.00	25.00
Atlantic 8100	(M)	Porky's Golden Dusties	1964	8.00	20.00
Atlantic SD-8100	(S)	Porky's Golden Dusties	1964	10.00	25.00
Atlantic 8101	(M)	Saturday Night At The Uptown	1964	10.00	25.00
Atlantic SD-8101	(S)	Saturday Night At The Uptown	1964	14.00	35.00
Atlantic 8108	(M)	Killer Joe's International Disco	1965	8.00	20.00
Atlantic SD-8108	(S)	Killer Joe's International Disco	1965	12.00	30.00
Atlantic AT-1	(M)	Atlantic/Atco All Star Showcase	1965	12.00	30.00
Atlantic ATSD-1	(S)	Atlantic/Atco All Star Showcase	1965	12.00	30.00
		— Atlantic albums above have multi-color labels with a black "fan" logo on the right side.—			
Audio Fidelity AFLP-2168	(M)	Where It's At (Live At The Cheetah)	1966	30.00	75.00
Audio Lab LP-1520	(M)	Highway Of Blues	1959	60.00	150.00
Audio Lab AL-1546	(M)	Swing Billies	1959	60.00	150.00
Audio Lab AL-1566	(M)	Swing Billies, Volume 2	1960	60.00	150.00
Audio-Lab AL-1567	(M)	A Little Rock And Roll For Everybody (*Blue label*)	1960	100.00	250.00
August 100	(M)	Money Music	1967	300.00	500.00

Label & Catalog #		Title	Year	VG+	NM
Authentic DTL-501	(M)	**Rhythm & Blues Hit Vocal Groups**	197?	10.00	25.00
		(Authentic 501 is a reissue of Dooto 501.)			
Autumn 101	(M)	**KYA's Memories Of The Cow Palace**	1963	40.00	100.00
B. F. 20183	(M)	**Son Of The Gathering Of The Tribe**	198?	20.00	50.00
B.F.D. 5016	(M)	**Pebbles, Volume 1** *(Original cover)*	198?	40.00	100.00
Bang LP-215	(M)	**Golden Hits From The Gang At Bang**	1966	8.00	20.00
Bang LPS-215	(P)	**Golden Hits From The Gang At Bang**	1966	10.00	25.00
Bell 6030	(S)	**Dial A Hit**	1969	10.00	25.00
Bell 6035	(S)	**Summer Souvenirs**	1969	10.00	25.00
Beta 1414S	(M)	**Gathering At The Depot**	196?	16.00	40.00
Belvedere TY 8-7100	(M)	**Michigan Brand Nuggets** *(2 LPs)*	198?	16.00	40.00
Bethlehem BLP-6071	(M)	**Blues 'N' Folk**	195?	40.00	100.00
Blast 6803	(M)	**Blasts From The Past With Clay Cole**	196?	20.00	50.00
Blast 6805	(M)	**16 Goodies: Blasts From The Past**	196?	20.00	50.00
Bluesville BVLP-1009	(M)	**Soul Jazz, Volume 1**	1960	20.00	50.00
Bluesville BVLP-1010	(M)	**Soul Jazz, Volume 2**	1960	20.00	50.00
Bluesville BVLP-1052	(M)	**Blues We Taught Your Mother**	1962	20.00	50.00
Bluesville BVLP-1055	(M)	**Bawdy Blues**	1962	20.00	50.00
		—Bluesville albums above have bright blue labels with silver print.—			
Bluesville BVLP-1009	(M)	**Soul Jazz, Volume 1**	1964	10.00	25.00
Bluesville BVLP-1010	(M)	**Soul Jazz, Volume 2**	1964	10.00	25.00
Bluesville BVLP-1052	(M)	**Blues We Taught Your Mother**	1964	10.00	25.00
Bluesville BVLP-1055	(M)	**Bawdy Blues**	1964	10.00	25.00
		—Bluesville albums above have blue labels with a trident logo on the right side.—			
Bolo 8002	(M)	**Bolo Bash**	1964	16.00	40.00
Bona Fide 5913-330001	(M)	**Gathering Of The Tribe**	198?	20.00	50.00
Bona Fide BFR-16274-66	(M)	**Return Of The Young Pennsylvanians**	198?	16.00	40.00
Bona Fide BFR-NJ 6601	(M)	**Attack Of The Jersey Teens**	198?	16.00	40.00
Bonded 777	(M)	**20 Original R&B Goodies**	196?	20.00	50.00
Bone 101	(M)	**Oil Stanes, Volume 2**	198?	20.00	50.00
Broadside BR-301	(S)	**Broadside Ballads, Volume 1** *(With booklet)*	1964	12.00	30.00
Broadside BR-3??	(S)	**Broadside Ballads, Volume 2** *(With booklet)*	1964	10.00	25.00
Broadside BR-3??	(S)	**Broadside Ballads, Volume 3** *(With booklet)*	1964	10.00	25.00
Broadside BR-3??	(S)	**Broadside Ballads, Volume 4** *(With booklet)*	1964	10.00	25.00
Broadside BR-3??	(S)	**Broadside Ballads, Volume 5** *(With booklet)*	1964	10.00	25.00
Broadside BR-315	(S)	**Broadside Ballads, Volume 6** *(With booklet)*	1964	10.00	25.00
		—Original Broadside albums above have cream colored labels.—			
Brooklyn 301	(M)	**Murray The K's Greatest Holiday Show**	196?	10.00	25.00
Brooklyn S-301	(S)	**Murray The K's Greatest Holiday Show**	196?	10.00	25.00
Brooklyn 302	(M)	**Murray The K Presents**	196?	10.00	25.00
Brooklyn S-302	(S)	**Murray The K Presents**	196?	10.00	25.00
Brunswick 59000	(10")	**Mountain Frolic**	195?	30.00	75.00
Brunswick 54001	(10")	**Listen To Our Story**	1958	30.00	75.00
Bud Jet 301	(M)	**Country Western Hits (Volume 1)**	1968	12.00	30.00
Bud Jet 302	(M)	**Country Western Hits (Volume 2)**	1968	12.00	30.00
Bud Jet 303	(M)	**Country Western Hits (Volume 3)**	1968	12.00	30.00
Bud Jet 311	(M)	**Top Teen Bands (Volume 1)**	1968	20.00	50.00
Bud Jet 312	(M)	**Top Teen Bands (Volume 2)**	1968	20.00	50.00
Bud Jet 313	(M)	**Top Teen Bands (Volume 3)**	1968	24.00	60.00

Label & Catalog #		Title	Year	VG+	NM
Buddah Vol. 1 No. 1	(P)	Current Audio Magazine	1972	10.00	25.00
Buena Vista BV-3313	(M)	Teen Street	1962	12.00	30.00
Buena Vista STER-3313	(S)	Teen Street	1962	20.00	50.00
Cadence CLP-3009	(M)	The Sweet Adelines	1958	20.00	50.00
		(Cadence 3009 collects performances by the first through fifth place winners of the 1957 "Queens of Harmony" competition of the national female, four-part harmony singing organization, The Sweet Adelines Inc.)			
Cadence CLP-3041	(M)	Rock-A-Ballads	1960	20.00	50.00
Cadence CLP-3042	(M)	Rock-A-Hits	1960	20.00	50.00
Cadence CLP-3043	(M)	Golden Encores	1960	20.00	50.00
Cadet LP-4051	(M)	The Blues, Volume 5	1966	10.00	25.00
Cadet LPS-4051	(S)	The Blues, Volume 5	1966	10.00	25.00
		(This is a continuation of the series begun by Argo, Cadet's former corporate identity.)			
Calico PSY-101	(M)	Psychedelic Unknowns	198?	10.00	25.00
California Recording 101	(M)	Battle Of The Beat (Yellow label)	1964	150.00	300.00
Camay C-3001	(M)	Country & Western Bonanza	1962	6.00	15.00
Camay CS-3001	(S)	Country & Western Bonanza	1962	10.00	25.00
Camden CAL-318	(M)	The Biggest Hits Of '56	1957	8.00	20.00
Camden CAL-781	(M)	The Greatest Stars And Songs	195?	8.00	20.00
Camden CAL-371	(M)	Rhythm & Blues	195?	20.00	50.00
Camden CAL-435	(M)	RCA Camden Rockers	195?	20.00	50.00
Camden CAL-740	(M)	Original Rhythm & Blues Hits By Rhythm & Blues Stars	1963	20.00	50.00
Camden CAS-740	(E)	Original Rhythm & Blues Hits By Rhythm & Blues Stars	1963	10.00	25.00
Camden CAL-820	(M)	Special Delivery	1964	10.00	25.00
Camden CAS-820e	(E)	Special Delivery	1964	6.00	15.00
Capitol T-9030	(M)	Merry Christmas To You	1955	20.00	50.00
Capitol H-9101	(M)	Today's Top Hits, Volume 1	1955	12.00	30.00
Capitol H-9102	(M)	Today's Top Hits, Volume 2	1955	12.00	30.00
Capitol H-9103	(M)	Today's Top Hits, Volume 3	1955	12.00	30.00
Capitol H-9104	(M)	Today's Top Hits, Volume 4	1955	12.00	30.00
Capitol H-9105	(M)	Today's Top Hits, Volume 5	1955	12.00	30.00
Capitol H-9106	(M)	Today's Top Hits, Volume 6	1955	12.00	30.00
Capitol H-9107	(M)	Today's Top Hits, Volume 7	1955	12.00	30.00
Capitol H-9108	(M)	Today's Top Hits, Volume 8	1955	12.00	30.00
Capitol H-9109	(M)	Today's Top Hits, Volume 9	1955	12.00	30.00
Capitol H-9110	(M)	Today's Top Hits, Volume 10	1955	12.00	30.00
Capitol H-9116	(M)	Today's Top Hits, Volume 11	1955	12.00	30.00
Capitol L-9117	(M)	Top Hits Of '54, Volume 1	1955	12.00	30.00
Capitol L-9119	(M)	Top Hits Of '54, Volume 2	1955	12.00	30.00
Capitol T-9124	(M)	Today's Top Hits, Volume 12	1955	12.00	30.00
Capitol T-9127	(M)	Today's Top Hits, Volume 13	1955	12.00	30.00
Capitol T-9130	(M)	Today's Top Hits, Volume 14	1955	12.00	30.00
Capitol T-732	(M)	Comedy Caravan	1951	20.00	50.00
Capitol T-308	(M)	Top Banana	1951	20.00	50.00
Capitol T-830	(M)	Gold Record	1957	20.00	50.00
Capitol T-1009	(M)	Teenage Rock	1958	20.00	50.00
Capitol T-1025	(M)	Everybody Rocks	1958	20.00	50.00
		— Capitol albums above have turquoise or gray labels.—			
Capitol SW-1062	(S)	Stars In Stereo	1958	10.00	25.00
Capitol T-1179	(S)	The Country's Best	1959	12.00	30.00
Capitol T-1414	(M)	Those Good Old Memories	1959	20.00	50.00
Capitol KAO-1555	(M)	The Original Country Sing-A-Long	1961	8.00	20.00
Capitol SKAO-1555	(S)	The Original Country Sing-A-Long	1961	10.00	25.00
Capitol T-1561	(M)	Golden Gassers	1961	10.00	25.00
Capitol ST-1561	(S)	Golden Gassers	1961	12.00	30.00

Capitol was the major label for '60s surf music. Aside from Brian Wilson's Beach Boys, they had Dick "King of the Surf Guitar" Dale and Gary Usher. Big Surfing Sounds is a promo sampler shipped to radio stations for air-play while My Son The Surf Nut plays on both the surfing phenomenon and the successful shtick of comedian Allan Sherman. Note that the latter includes a cartoon cover of "Murf the Surf" from the pen of the late, great Rick Griffin.

Label & Catalog #		Title	Year	VG+	NM
Capitol TBO-1572	(M)	Shake It And Break It *(2 LPs)*	1961	12.00	30.00
Capitol STBO-1572	(S)	Shake It And Break It *(2 LPs)*	1961	14.00	35.00
— *Capitol albums above have black "rainbow" labels with the logo on the left side.—*					
Capitol T-1918	(M)	Shut Down	1963	12.00	30.00
Capitol ST-1918	(P)	Shut Down	1963	16.00	40.00
Capitol T-1939	(M)	My Son, The Surf Nut	1963	24.00	60.00
Capitol ST-1939	(S)	My Son, The Surf Nut	1963	30.00	75.00
Capitol T/ST-1997		Hot Rod Rally: *Refer to* The Superstocks			
Capitol T-2006	(M)	Chartbusters, Volume 3	1963	10.00	25.00
Capitol DT-2006	(E)	Chartbusters, Volume 3	1963	10.00	25.00
Capitol T-2009	(M)	Country Music Hootenanny	1963	12.00	30.00
Capitol ST-2009	(S)	Country Music Hootenanny	1963	16.00	40.00
Capitol T-2024	(M)	Big Hit Rod Hits	1963	16.00	40.00
Capitol ST-2024	(P)	Big Hit Rod Hits	1963	20.00	50.00
Capitol T-2094	(M)	Chartbusters, Volume 4	1964	20.00	50.00
Capitol ST-2094	(P)	Chartbusters, Volume 4	1964	30.00	75.00
Capitol T-2125	(M)	The Big Hits From England & U.S.A.	1964	16.00	40.00
Capitol DT-2125	(E)	The Big Hits From England & U.S.A.	1964	12.00	30.00
Capitol T-2544	(M)	Liverpool Today	1966	8.00	20.00
Capitol ST-2544	(S)	Liverpool Today	1966	12.00	30.00
— *Special/Promotional Albums—*					
Capitol PRO-289/90/91/92	(M)	Saleman's Double Demo Record *(2 LPs)*	1956	40.00	100.00
Capitol PRO-201/2	(M)	Special Christmas LP For Disc Jockeys	1954	20.00	50.00
Capitol PRO-215/6	(10")	Ground Breaking Ceremony For The New Capitol Tower Building	1954	40.00	100.00
Capitol PRO-246/7	(M)	New Album Preview, March 1956	1956	10.00	25.00
Capitol PRO-272/3/4/5	(M)	New Album Preview, Aug./Sept. 1956	1956	14.00	35.00
Capitol PRO-301/2	(M)	New Album Preview, Nov. 1956	1956	10.00	25.00
Capitol PRO-311/2/3/4	(M)	New Album Preview, Feb. 1957 *(2 LPs)*	1957	14.00	35.00
Capitol PRO-325/6	(M)	New Album Preview *(2 LPs)*	1957	80.00	200.00
Capitol PRO-329	(M)	Merchandising Campaign *(2 LPs)*	1957	40.00	100.00
Capitol PRO-339/40/1/2	(M)	New Album Preview, May 1957 *(2 LPs)*	1957	14.00	35.00
Capitol PRO-391/2/3/4	(M)	New Album Preview, Sept. 1957 *(2 LPs)*	1957	14.00	35.00
Capitol PRO-398/400/1/2	(M)	New Album Preview, Oct. 1957 *(2 LPs)*	1957	14.00	35.00
Capitol PRO-424/5	(M)	Christmas Around The World	1957	10.00	25.00
Capitol PRO-443/4/5/6	(M)	I Love Music *(2 LPs)*	1958	20.00	50.00
		(Contains two selections by Frank Sinatra with an otherwise unavailable spoken intro by FS.)			
Capitol PRO-564/5/6/7	(M)	Salesman's Demo Record, April 1958 *(2 LPs)*	1958	14.00	35.00
Capitol PRO-568/9	(M)	High Fiesta	1958	10.00	25.00
Capitol SPRO-639/40	(S)	Capitol Stereo Demo Record	1958	20.00	50.00
Capitol PRO-696/70	(M)	New Album Preview, Sept. 1958	1958	10.00	25.00
Capitol PRO-727/8/9/30	(M)	New Album Preview, Dec. 1958 *(2 LPs)*	1958	14.00	35.00
Capitol PRO-846/7	(S)	The Stereo Disc Sampler	1959	10.00	25.00
Capitol PRO-1166/7/8/9	(M)	Kaleidoscope *(2 LPs)*	1959	12.00	30.00
Capitol PRO-1390/1	(M)	I Feel A Song Comin' On	1960	10.00	25.00
Capitol PRO-1539/40	(M)	Reach For A Star	1960	8.00	20.00
Capitol PRO-2375/6	(M)	Balanced For Broadcast	1963	16.00	40.00
Capitol PRO-2377/8	(M)	Salesman's Demonstration Record	1963	20.00	50.00
Capitol PRO-239/66	(M)	Big Surfin' Sounds	1963	30.00	75.00
Capitol PRO-2463/4	(M)	Salesman's Demonstration Record	1963	20.00	50.00
Capitol PRO-2479/80	(M)	Hot Rod Music On Capitol	1963	80.00	200.00
Capitol PRO-2493/4	(M)	Salesman's Demonstration Record	1963	20.00	50.00
Capitol PRO-2537/8	(M)	Great New Releases From The Sound Capitol Of The World	1964	40.00	100.00
Capitol PRO-2555/6	(M)	Balanced For Broadcast	1963	20.00	50.00
Capitol PRO-2657/8	(M)	Big Surfin' Sounds	1964	30.00	75.00
Capitol PRO-2685/6	(M)	Balanced For Broadcast	1964	20.00	50.00
Capitol PRO-2743/4	(M)	Programming Aids From Capitol	1964	150.00	300.00
		(Capitol 2743/2744 contains The Beach Boys' "Auld Lang Syne" without a voice-over.)			
Capitol PRO-3123/4	(M)	Silver Platter Service From Hollywood	1965	150.00	300.00
		(Capitol 3123/3124 features Brian Wilson introducing selections from The Hollyridge Strings' "Beach Boys Songbook.")			
Capitol PRO-3265/6	(M)	Silver Platter Service	1967	150.00	300.00
		(Capitol 3265/3266 features Brian Wilson briefly discussing the scrapping of "Smile.")			

Chess' Oldies In Hi-Fi features a daring cover for the time: A white model and a black model, relaxed and apparently digging the cool sounds emanating from the less than high-fidelity player. Like many various artists collections, this sold modestly, leading to a relatively small supply in today's collectors market, but the demand is rather tepid, as most collectors tend to avoid compilations (unless they're cheap). Note: This particular title was issued promotionally on multi-colored vinyl.

Label & Catalog #		Title	Year	VG+	NM
Capitol PRO-4411/2	(M)	Capitol's 25th Anniversary Celebration	1967	12.00	30.00
Capitol SPRO-4673	(M)	Capitol Disc Jockey Album	1969	12.00	30.00
Capitol SPRO-4724	(M)	Capitol Hits Through The Years	1969	16.00	40.00
Capitol SPRO-5003	(M)	Listen In Good Health	1970	12.00	30.00
Capitol SPRO-8511	(M)	The Greatest Music Ever Sold	1976	12.00	30.00
Capitol SPRO-98303/4/5/6	(P)	Christmas In Store Sampler (2 LPs)	1968	8.00	20.00
Carlton 121	(M)	One Dozen Goldies	1958	20.00	50.00
CBS Songs	(DJ)	Radio's Million Performance Songs	1984	20.00	50.00
Celebrity 1000	(M)	World Famous Rhythm And Blues	195?	600.00	1,800.00
Century 23214	(M)	Milwaukee Sentinal: Young America Rock 'n' Roll Songs	1966	150.00	300.00
Chainsaw Sound CSR-001	(M)	Everywhere Chainsaw Sound	198?	30.00	75.00
Chainsaw Sound CSR-002	(M)	Everywhere Interferences	198?	30.00	75.00
Chancellor CHL-50??	(M)	Wild, Wild Twist Recorded Live!	1961	10.00	25.00
Chancellor CHLS-50??	(S)	Wild, Wild Twist Recorded Live!	1961	20.00	50.00
Chancellor CHL-5009	(M)	The Hit Makers	1961	10.00	25.00
Chancellor CHL-5017	(M)	Wild Wildwood	1961	10.00	25.00
Chancellor CHS-5017	(S)	Wild Wildwood	1961	20.00	50.00
Chancellor CHL-5028	(M)	Dance On The Wild Side	1962	10.00	25.00
Checker LP-2973	(M)	Love Those Goodies	1959	300.00	600.00
		(White label promo on multi-colored vinyl)			
Checker LP-2973	(M)	Love Those Goodies	1959	50.00	125.00
Checker LP-2975	(M)	Hits That Jumped	1959	50.00	125.00
Checker LP-2998	(M)	Sing A Song Of Soul	196?	20.00	100.00
Chess LP-1425	(M)	Rock, Rock, Rock (Soundtrack)	1958	80.00	200.00
Chess LP-1439	(M)	Oldies In Hi Fi	1959	300.00	600.00
		(White label promo on multi-colored vinyl)			
Chess LP-1439	(M)	Oldies In Hi Fi	1959	50.00	125.00
Chess LP-1441	(M)	Bunch Of Goodies	1960	300.00	600.00
		(White label promo on multi-colored vinyl)			
Chess LP-1441	(M)	Bunch Of Goodies	1960	50.00	125.00
Chess LP-1446	(M)	Walking By Mtself	1960	20.00	50.00
Chess LP-145?	(M)	Murray The K's Golden Gassers	1960	20.00	50.00
Chess LP-1458	(M)	Golden Gassers Across The U.S.A.	1960	50.00	125.00
Chess LP-1458	(M)	Murray The K's Golden Gassers	1960	50.00	125.00
Chess LP-1458	(M)	KYA's Golden Gate Greats	1961	50.00	125.00
		(Chess 1458 was given various titles for distruiibution to regional markets, although the contents remained the same.)			
Chess LP-1461	(M)	Murray The K's Blasts From The Past	1961	20.00	50.00
Chess LP-1470	(M)	Murray The K's Gassers For Submarine Race Watchers	1963	16.00	40.00
Chess LP-1474	(M)	Treasure Tunes From The Vault	1963	12.00	30.00
Chess LP-1476	(M)	Dance Tunes From The Vault	1964	12.00	30.00
Chess LP-1478	(M)	Group Of Goodies	1964	20.00	50.00
Chess LP-1491	(M)	Group Of Goodies, Vol. 2	1966	20.00	50.00
— Original Chess albums above have black labels with silver print.—					
Chess LP-1520	(M)	Petal Pushers	1967	10.00	25.00
Chess LPS-1520	(S)	Petal Pushers	1967	10.00	25.00
Chess LP-1522	(M)	Heavy Heads	1967	10.00	25.00
Chess LPS-1522	(P)	Heavy Heads	1967	10.00	25.00
Chess LPS-1533	(P)	Blues From Big Bill's Copa Cabana	1969	12.00	30.00
Chess LPS-1544	(P)	Pop Origins	1969	10.00	25.00
Chess LPS-1546	(P)	Souled Out	1969	20.00	50.00
Chess 2CH-50030	(M)	Golden Age Of Rhythm & Blues (2 LPs)	1972	12.00	30.00
Chicago Inter. CRC-1	(10")	Folk Favorites, Vol. 1	195?	16.00	40.00
Chicago Inter. CRC-2	(10")	Frozen Logger	195?	16.00	40.00
Chicago Inter. CRC-4	(10")	Folk Favorites, Vol. 3	195?	16.00	40.00
Chicago Inter. CRC-4	(10")	Folk Favorites, Vol. 3	195?	16.00	40.00

Label & Catalog #		Title	Year	VG+	NM
Clarion 609	(M)	Discoteque In Astrosound	1966	50.00	125.00
Clarion SD-609	(S)	Discoteque In Astrosound	1966	80.00	200.00
Class 5004	(M)	Gone But Not Forgotten	1959	40.00	100.00
		(Class 5004 was reissued as Rendezvous 1314.)			
Collectables 1/2-2500	(P)	History Of Rock & Roll *(2 LP picture disc)*	1982	12.00	30.00
Collector's Edition 505	(P)	All-Time Christmas Favorites *(5 LP box)*	1978	80.00	200.00
Colpix CP/SCP-444		Teenage Triangle: *Refer to* James Darren / S. Fabares / P. Petersen			
Colpix CP-454	(M)	Bye Bye Birdie	1964	20.00	50.00
Colpix SCP-454	(S)	Bye Bye Birdie	1964	30.00	75.00
Colpix CP-466	(M)	Groovy Goodies	1964	30.00	75.00
Colpix SCP-466	(P)	Groovy Goodies	1964	40.00	100.00
Colpix CP/SCP-468		More Teenage Triangle: *Refer to* James Darren / S. Fabares / P. Petersen			
Colpix 712	(S)	Mann & Weill: Solid Gold	196?	20.00	50.00
Colstar S-5001	(S)	San Francisco International Pop Festival, Volume 1	1968	40.00	100.00
Columbia CL-6057	(10")	Popular Favorites	1949	20.00	50.00
Columbia CL-6119	(10")	Popular Favorites, Vol. 2	1953	20.00	50.00
Columbia CL-6150	(10")	Popular Favorites, Vol. 3	1953	20.00	50.00
Columbia CL-6212	(10")	This Is My Best	1953	20.00	50.00
Columbia CL-6254	(10")	Requested By You	1953	20.00	50.00
Columbia CL-2530	(10")	Boys And Girls Together	1955	16.00	40.00
Columbia HL-9008	(10")	Current Country Hits #1	195?	20.00	50.00
Columbia HL-9009	(10")	Swing Your Partner	195?	20.00	50.00
Columbia HL-9011	(10")	Current Country Hits #2	195?	20.00	50.00
Columbia HL-9016	(10")	Current Country Hits #3	195?	20.00	50.00
Columbia CL-2600	(10")	Hall Of Fame	1955	16.00	40.00
Columbia SL-211	(M)	The Columbia Library Of Folk And Primitive Music, Vol. VIII: Canadian Folk Songs	195?	10.00	25.00
Columbia CL-541	(M)	Late Music, Vol. I	1955	10.00	25.00
Columbia CL-599	(M)	Saturday Night Mood	1955	10.00	25.00
Columbia CL-607	(M)	Requested By You	1955	10.00	25.00
Columbia CL-611	(M)	Ballroom Bandstand	195?	10.00	25.00
Columbia CL-613	(M)	Treasure Chest Of Song Hits	195?	10.00	25.00
Columbia CL-713	(M)	Girl Meets Boy	195?	10.00	25.00
Columbia CL-728	(M)	All Star Pops	195?	10.00	25.00
Columbia CL-894	(M)	Country Spectacular	1957	12.00	30.00
Columbia CL-937	(M)	Top 12	195?	10.00	25.00
Columbia CL-944	(M)	Top 12, Vol. II	195?	10.00	25.00
Columbia CL-967	(M)	Dance, Be Happy	195?	10.00	25.00
Columbia CL-1017	(M)	Top 12, Vol. III	1957	10.00	25.00
Columbia CL-1057	(M)	Top 12, Vol. IV	1957	10.00	25.00
Columbia CL-1048	(M)	Phillip Morris Country Music Show	1958	10.00	25.00
Columbia CL-1072	(M)	Town Hall Party	1958	20.00	50.00
Columbia XLP-42371	(DJ)	Going Places On Columbia	1958	40.00	100.00
Columbia CL-1239	(M)	Pop Hit Party	1959	10.00	25.00
Columbia CL-1257	(M)	Greatest Western Hits	1959	10.00	25.00
Columbia CL-1408	(M)	The Greatest Western Hits	195?	10.00	25.00
Columbia CL-1583	(M)	Evolution Of The Blues Song	1960	10.00	25.00
Columbia CS-8383	(E)	Evolution Of The Blues Song	1960	6.00	15.00

— *Original Columbia albums above have three white "eye" logos on each side of the spindle hole.*—

— *Special/Promotional Albums*—

Columbia *(No number)*	(S)	Great Folk Ballads, Country & Western	1962	10.00	25.00
		(4 LP box prepared for Zenith.)			
Columbia D-155	(M)	Disco Teen '66	1966	4.00	10.00
Columbia DS-155	(S)	Disco Teen '66	1966	20.00	50.00
		(Includes an alternate stereo mix of Dylan's "Positively 4th Street.")			
Columbia A2S-174	(DJ)	The Heavyweights *(2 LPs)*	1975	16.00	40.00
Columbia A2S-890	(DJ)	Hitline '80 *(2 LPs)*	1980	12.00	30.00
Columbia AS-902	(S)	Highlights From CBS Mastersound	1981	20.00	50.00
		(Issued with a booklet.)			

Label & Catalog #		Title	Year	VG+	NM
Constellation C-1	(M)	**Collectors Showcase, Volume 1**	1962	20.00	50.00
Constellation CS-1	(E)	**Collectors Showcase, Volume 1**	1962	10.00	25.00
Constellation C-5	(M)	**Collectors Showcase, Groups Three**	1964	20.00	50.00
Constellation CS-5	(E)	**Collectors Showcase, Groups Three**	1964	10.00	25.00
Constellation C-7	(M)	**Aces 3**	1964	20.00	50.00
Constellation CS-7	(E)	**Aces 3**	1964	10.00	25.00
Coral CRL-59001	(10")	**Listen To The Story (American Ballads)**	195?	16.00	40.00
Coral CRL-57269	(M)	**Hitsville**	1959	30.00	75.00
Coral CRL-757269	(S)	**Hitsville**	1959	40.00	100.00
Coral CRL-57310	(M)	**Million Airs**	1959	12.00	30.00
Coral CRL-757310	(S)	**Million Airs**	1959	20.00	50.00
Coral CRL-57431	(M)	**Teenage Goodies**	1963	12.00	30.00
Coral CRL-757431	(S)	**Teenage Goodies**	1963	20.00	50.00
Cotillion CT3-500	(S)	**Woodstock** *(3 LPs. Soundtrack)*	1970	10.00	25.00
Cotillion CT2-400	(S)	**Woodstock, Volume 2** *(2 LPs)*	1971	10.00	25.00
		— Original Cotillion albums above have grey labels with an 1841 Broadway address.—			
Crescendo GNP-84	(M)	**Original Surfin' Hits** *(With bonus photos)*	1963	12.00	30.00
Crescendo GNP-84S	(P)	**Original Surfin' Hits** *(With bonus photos)*	1963	14.00	35.00
Crescendo GNP-84	(M)	**Original Surfin' Hits** *(Without the photos)*	1963	8.00	20.00
Crescendo GNP-84S	(P)	**Original Surfin' Hits** *(Without the photos)*	1963	10.00	25.00
Crescendo GNP-85	(M)	**Winners Of The 18 Band Surf Battle**	1963	8.00	20.00
Crescendo GNP-85S	(S)	**Winners Of The 18 Band Surf Battle**	1963	10.00	25.00
Crown CLP-5001	(M)	**Rock & Roll Dance Party**	1958	60.00	150.00
Crown CLP-5011	(M)	**Hollywood Rock 'N Roll Record Hop**	1958	60.00	150.00
Crown CLP-5013	(M)	**Gigantic Stars Of Rock & Roll**	1958	60.00	150.00
Crown CLP-5144	(M)	**The Best Of Oldies And Goodies**	1960	20.00	50.00
Crown CLP-5202	(M)	**More Of The Oldies And Goodies**	1961	20.00	50.00
Crown CLP-5238	(M)	**Blues Oldies And Goodies**	1961	20.00	50.00
Crown CLP-5241	(M)	**Oldies And Goodies**	1961	20.00	50.00
		— Crown albums above have black labels.—			
Crypt RR-66	(M)	**Back From The Grave, Vol. 1** *(First edition)*	198?	12.00	30.00
"DB" 101	(M)	**Oil Stains**	198?	16.00	40.00
"DB" 102	(M)	**Relics**	198?	16.00	40.00
Dawn DLP-1i19	(M)	**Rock And Roll Spectacular**	195?	40.00	100.00
Decca DL-5054	(10")	**Lonesome Train: A Musical Legend About**			
		The Martyrdom Of Abraham Lincoln	195?	10.00	25.00
Decca DL-38008	(DJ)	**Fill The Air With Music**	195?	40.00	100.00
Decca DL-738241	(DJ)	**Admiral Stereophonic Demo**	195?	40.00	100.00
Decca DL-70??	(10")	**Curtain Call**	195?	16.00	40.00
Decca DL-7019	(10")	**Curtain Call, Volume 2**	195?	16.00	40.00
Decca DL-8012	(M)	**American Square Dance Group:**			
		Running Set And Long-Ways Dances	195?	10.00	25.00
Decca DL-8349	(M)	**The Wild One**	1958	20.00	50.00
Decca DL-8429	(M)	**Rock, Pretty Baby** *(Soundtrack)*	1956	100.00	250.00
		(Decca 8429 has three cover variation with the title on the cover in either blue, red or yellow print. At this time there is no difference in value between the three. A 10" promotional radio transcription of this soundtrack was issued by Universal International Pictures and can be found listed under that label.)			
Decca DL-8655	(M)	**Let's Have A Party**	1958	40.00	100.00
Decca DL-8860	(M)	**Top Pops**	1959	16.00	40.00
		— Original Decca albums above have black labels with silver print.—			
Decca DL-4004	(M)	**The Early Fifties**	1960	20.00	50.00
Decca DL-4005	(M)	**The Late Fifties**	1960	20.00	50.00
Decca DL-4009	(M)	**The Fifties**	1960	20.00	50.00
Decca DL-4011	(M)	**Rhythm, Blues & Boogie Woogie**	1960	20.00	50.00
Decca DL-4036	(M)	**Golden Oldies**	1960	20.00	50.00
Decca DL-4045	(M)	**Midnight Jamboree**	1960	12.00	30.00
Decca DL-74045	(S)	**Midnight Jamboree**	1960	16.00	40.00

Label & Catalog #		Title	Year	VG+	NM
Decca DL-4057	(M)	**Country Music Time**	1960	12.00	30.00
Decca DL-74057	(S)	**Country Music Time**	1960	16.00	40.00
Decca DL-4172	(M)	**Country Jubilee**	1962	10.00	25.00
Decca DL-74172	(S)	**Country Jubilee**	1962	12.00	30.00
Decca DL-4434	(M)	**Out Came The Blues**	1964	16.00	40.00
Decca DL-74434	(E)	**Out Came The Blues**	1964	12.00	30.00
Decca DL-4699	(M)	**Wild, Wild Winter** (Soundtrack)	1966	8.00	20.00
Decca DL-74699	(S)	**Wild, Wild Winter** (Soundtrack)	1966	12.00	30.00
Decca DL-4751	(M)	**Out Of Sight** (Soundtrack)	1966	12.00	30.00
Decca DL-74751	(S)	**Out Of Sight** (Soundtrack)	1966	16.00	40.00
Decca DL-9119	(M)	**The Lively Set** (Soundtrack)	1964	20.00	50.00
Decca DL-79119	(S)	**The Lively Set** (Soundtrack)	1964	30.00	75.00
Decca DL-9157	(M)	**Playback '66**	1964	30.00	75.00
Decca DL-79157	(S)	**Playback '66**	1964	40.00	100.00
Del-Fi (No number)	(DJ)	**Del-Fi Album Sampler** (Green vinyl)	1959	200.00	400.00
Del-Fi DFLP-1210	(M)	**Del-Fi Record Hop**	1960	30.00	75.00
Del-Fi DFLP-1219	(M)	**Barrel Of Oldies**	1961	20.00	50.00
Del-Fi DFLP-1227	(M)	**Very Best Of The Oldies**	1963	20.00	50.00
Del-Fi DFLP-1235	(M)	**KYA's Battle Of The Surfing Bands**	1964	20.00	50.00
Del-Fi DFST-1235	(S)	**KYA's Battle Of The Surfing Bands**	1964	30.00	75.00
Del-Fi DFLP-1249	(M)	**Big Surf Hits**	1964	20.00	50.00
Del-Fi DFST-1249	(S)	**Big Surf Hits**	1964	30.00	75.00
Design DLP-187	(M)	**Soundsville!**	196?	8.00	20.00
Design SDLP-187	(S)	**Soundsville!**	196?	10.00	25.00
		(Design 187 includes tracks by The Beachnuts and The Roughnecks, both featuring Lou Reed.)			
Design DLP-611	(M)	**Tennessee**	1963	12.00	30.00
Design SDLP-611	(E)	**Tennessee**	1963	8.00	20.00
Domain 102	(M)	**Rosko's Evergreens**	1963	20.00	50.00
Dooto DTL-501	(M)	**Rhythm & Blues Hit Vocal Groups**	195?	60.00	150.00
		(Dooto 501 was reissued as Authentic 501.)			
Dooto DTL-203	(M)	**Rock & Roll Vs. Rhythm & Blues**	1957	40.00	100.00
Dooto DTL-204	(M)	**Best In Rhythm 'N Blues:** Refer to The Penguins			
Dooto LP-224	(M)	**Best Vocal Groups In Rhythm & Blues**	1958	40.00	100.00
Dot DLP-3049	(M)	**Great Hits On Dot**	1957	20.00	50.00
Dot DLP-3181	(M)	**The Great Millions**	1959	20.00	50.00
Dot DLP-3183	(M)	**Young Love**	1959	30.00	75.00
Double-L DL-2302	(M)	**Washington Committee**	1963	20.00	50.00
Double-L DDS-2302	(P)	**Washington Committee**	1963	30.00	75.00
Duke DLP-73	(M)	**Like 'Em Red Hot** (Yellow & purple label)	1965	60.00	150.00
Dunhill DS-50063	(S)	**Easy Rider** (Soundtrack)	1969	12.00	30.00
Economic Consultants	(M)	**Country & Western Classics 1955***	1973	12.00	30.00
Economic Consultants	(M)	**Country & Western Classics 1957***	1973	12.00	30.00
Economic Consultants	(M)	**Country & Western Classics 1958***	1973	12.00	30.00
Economic Consultants	(M)	**A Journey Into Yesterday 1956***	1973	12.00	30.00
Economic Consultants	(M)	**A Journey Into Yesterday 1969***	1973	12.00	30.00
Economic Consultants	(M)	**Old & Heavy Gold 1956***	1973	12.00	30.00
Economic Consultants	(M)	**Old & Heavy Gold 1957***	1973	12.00	30.00
Economic Consultants	(M)	**Old & Heavy Gold 1958***	1973	12.00	30.00
Economic Consultants	(M)	**Old & Heavy Gold 1960***	1973	12.00	30.00
Economic Consultants	(M)	**Old & Heavy Gold 1961***	1973	12.00	30.00
Economic Consultants	(M)	**Old & Heavy Gold 1962***	1973	12.00	30.00

— Economic Consultant titles above marked with an asterisk conatin at least one track by Elvis Presley. The volumes in this series without an Elvis track are worth $10-20 each.—

Elektra EKL-5	(10")	**Voices Of Haiti**	195?	16.00	40.00
Elektra EKL-23	(10")	**Nova Scotia Folk Music From Cape Breton**			
Elektra EKL-151	(M)	**Our Singing Heritage, Vol. I**	1958	10.00	25.00
Elektra EKL-152	(M)	**Our Singing Heritage, Vol. II**	1958	10.00	25.00

Label & Catalog #		Title	Year	VG+	NM
Elektra EKL-153	(M)	Our Singing Heritage, Vol. III	1958	10.00	25.00
Elektra EKL-SMP2	(M)	Elektra New Folk Sampler	1956	10.00	25.00
Elektra EKL-264	(M)	The Blues Project	1964	8.00	20.00
Elektra EKLS-7264	(S)	The Blues Project	1964	12.00	30.00
Elektra EKL-299	(M)	Singer Songwriter Project	1965	8.00	20.00
Elektra EKS-7299	(S)	Singer Songwriter Project	1965	12.00	30.00
Elektra EKL-4002	(M)	What's Shakin' (With booklet)	1966	16.00	40.00
Elektra EKS-74002	(S)	What's Shakin' (With booklet)	1966	18.00	45.00
Elektra EKL-4002	(M)	What's Shakin' (Without booklet)	1966	10.00	25.00
Elektra EKS-74002	(S)	What's Shakin' (Without booklet)	1966	12.00	30.00
Elektra 7E-2006	(P)	Nuggets (2 LPs)	1972	12.00	30.00
Ember 500	(M)	Carload O' His	1959		Unreleased?
		(Reissued as Muse 500.)			
EMR Ent. RH-8	(DJ)	The Age Of Rock	1969	60.00	150.00
End LP-302	(M)	Having A Ball (Groups cover)	1959	300.00	600.00
End LP-302	(M)	Rock & Roll Jamboree (Puppet cover)	1959	50.00	125.00
End LP-305	(M)	Battle Of The Groups	1960	30.00	75.00
End LP-309	(M)	Battle Of The Groups, Volume 2	1960	30.00	75.00
End LP-310	(M)	12 + 3 + 15 Hits	1960	30.00	75.00
End LP-313	(M)	Alan Freed's Golden Picks	1961	16.00	40.00
End LP-314	(M)	Alan Freed's Top 15	1962	16.00	40.00
End LP-315	(M)	Alan Freed's Top 15	1962	16.00	40.00
— Original End albums above have grey labels with dogs on top.—					
Epic LN-3701	(M)	Cream Of The Crop	1959	20.00	50.00
Epic LN-3702	(M)	Please Say You Want Me	1959	20.00	50.00
Epic LN-24040	(M)	Great Golden Grooves	1963	12.00	30.00
Era 1	(DJ)	Golden Era Series, Volume 1	1962	40.00	100.00
Esoteric ES-538	(M)	Shivaree! A New Presentation Of Folk Music	195?	10.00	25.00
ESP-Disk' 1023	(M)	The ESP Sampler	1966	40.00	100.00
ESP-Disk' 1034	(M)	East Village Other: Electric Newspaper	1967	40.00	100.00
ESP-Disk' 1071	(M)	The ESP Sampler	1967	12.00	30.00
Etiquette ETLB-028	(P)	The Northwest Collection (6 LP box)	197?	60.00	150.00
Evatone 106811	(M)	The Magic Cube	198?	30.00	75.00
		(10" flexidisc with cardboard "magic cube")			
Everlast 201	(M)	Our Best To You	196?	80.00	200.00
Excello 8001	(M)	Tunes To Be Remembered	1960	60.00	150.00
Excello 8011	(M)	The Real Blues	1969	10.00	25.00
Excello 8021	(M)	Blues Live In Baton Rouge	1971	10.00	25.00
Excello 8025	(M)	The Excello Story (2 LPs)	1972	10.00	25.00
Famous 501	(M)	Rockin' Slumber Party	196?	12.00	30.00
Fanfare FM-101	(M)	Memories Of Garner State Park	196?	14.00	35.00
Felsted 7503	(M)	Night At The Boulevard	196?	20.00	50.00
Fifth Pipe Dream 11680	(S)	San Francisco Sound (Black & white cover)	1969	60.00	150.00
Fifth Pipe Dream 11680	(S)	San Francisco Sound (Color cover)	1969	40.00	100.00
Fillmore 31390	(S)	The Last Days Of The Fillmore	1972	14.00	35.00
		(2 LP box with poster, booklet and bonus single.)			
Fire FLP-100	(M)	Here Are The Hits	196?	150.00	300.00
		(White & red label with a cover photo of dancing teenagers.)			
Fire FLP-100	(M)	Memory Lane Hits By The Original Groups	1960	100.00	200.00
		(Red & black label with a red & green cover.)			

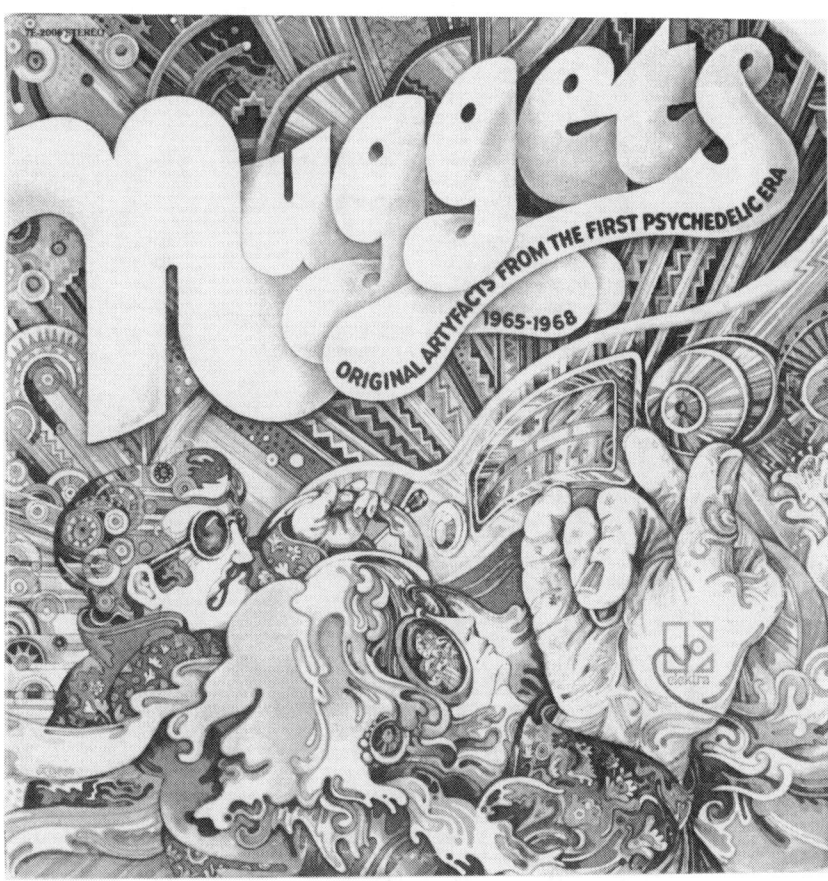

Elektra commissioned Andy Kaye to assemble a collection of "artyfacts from the first psychedelic era"
and compile them into a reasonable same album. Nuggets is more of a hodge-podge than its reputation
generally acknowledges but a fun-filled treasure nonetheless. Its resurrection by Sire several years later—
and its subsequent flooding of cut-out bins throughout the latter '70s and early '80s—did lead more than
a few collectors towards the joys of this era's music, no small accomplishment indeed.

Label & Catalog #		Title	Year	VG+	NM
Flanders Ballad Coll. *(No #)*	*(M)*	**British-American Ballads**			
		Of New England *(With notes)*	*1953*	**16.00**	**40.00**
Flashback 1001	*(M)*	**Flashback, Vol. 1**	*198?*	**30.00**	**75.00**
Flashback 1002	*(M)*	**Flashback, Vol. 2**	*198?*	**30.00**	**75.00**
Flashback 1003	*(M)*	**Flashback, Vol. 3**	*198?*	**30.00**	**75.00**
Flashback 1004	*(M)*	**Flashback, Vol. 4: Fuzz Tone**	*198?*	**30.00**	**75.00**
Flashback 1005	*(M)*	**Great Texas Flashbacks (Vol. 5)**	*198?*	**30.00**	**75.00**
Flashback 1006	*(M)*	**Great Texas Flashbacks (Vol. 6)**	*198?*	**30.00**	**75.00**
		(Original copies of Flashback 1001-6 have "Limited number of 200 copies" printed on the back cover.)			
Flip 1001	*(M)*	**Twelve Flip Hits**	*196?*	**150.00**	**350.00**
Flip 1002	*(M)*	**Original Recordings**			
		By The Artists Who Made Them Hits	*196?*	**250.00**	**500.00**
FM 309	*(M)*	**Hootenanny Live At The Bitter End**	*1965*	**10.00**	**25.00**
Folklore FRLP-14020	*(M)*	**Hootenanny**	*1964*	**8.00**	**20.00**
Folklore FRST-14020	*(S)*	**Hootenanny**	*1964*	**10.00**	**25.00**
Folklore FRLP-14023	*(M)*	**Folklore Jamboree**	*1964*	**8.00**	**20.00**
Folklore FRST-14023	*(S)*	**Folklore Jamboree**	*1964*	**10.00**	**25.00**
Folklore FRLP-14030	*(M)*	**Old Time Fiddlin' At Union Grove, NC**	*1964*	**8.00**	**20.00**
Folklore FRST-14030	*(S)*	**Old Time Fiddlin' At Union Grove, NC**	*1964*	**10.00**	**25.00**
Folkways FA-2010	*(10")*	**Lonesome Valley**	*195?*	**20.00**	**50.00**
Folkways FP-601	*(10")*	**Country Dance Music, Washboard Band**	*195?*	**20.00**	**50.00**
Folkways FA-2201	*(10")*	**Country Dance Music, Washboard Band**	*195?*	**20.00**	**50.00**
Folkways FA-2314	*(M)*	**American Banjo Tunes And Songs**			
		In The Scruggs Style, 3 Finger	*1957*	**16.00**	**40.00**
Folkways FA-2314	*(M)*	**American Banjo Three-**			
		Finger And Scruggs Style	*1960*	**10.00**	**25.00**
Folkways FA-2318	*(M)*	**Mountain Music, Bluegrass Style**	*1957*	**10.00**	**25.00**
Folkways FA-2356	*(M)*	**Old Harp Singers**	*195?*	**10.00**	**25.00**
Folkways FP-251	*(M)*	**Anthology Of American**			
		Folk Music: Ballads *(2 LPs)*	*195?*	**20.00**	**50.00**
Folkways FA-2951	*(M)*	**Anthology Of American**			
		Folk Music: Ballads *(2 LPs)*	*195?*	**20.00**	**50.00**
Folkways FP-252	*(M)*	**Anthology Of American Folk Music—**			
		Secular & Religious *(2 LPs)*	*195?*	**20.00**	**50.00**
Folkways FA-2952	*(M)*	**Anthology Of American Folk Music—**			
		Secular & Religious *(2 LPs)*	*195?*	**20.00**	**50.00**
Folkways FA-2953	*(M)*	**Anthology Of American Folk Music—**			
		American Ballads *(2 LPs)*	*195?*	**20.00**	**50.00**
Folkways FP-253	*(M)*	**Anthology Of American Folk Music—**			
		American Ballads *(2 LPs)*	*195?*	**20.00**	**50.00**
Folkways P-951	*(10")*	**Songs And Dances Of Quebec**	*195?*	**20.00**	**50.00**
Folkways FW-6951	*(10")*	**Songs And Dances Of Quebec**	*195?*	**20.00**	**50.00**
Folkways FP-20	*(10")*	**Songs To Grow On (School Days)**	*195?*	**20.00**	**50.00**
Folkways FC-7020	*(10")*	**Songs To Grow On (School Days)**	*195?*	**20.00**	**50.00**
Folkways FP-27	*(10")*	**Songs To Grow On (This Is My Land. Vol. 3)**	*195?*	**20.00**	**50.00**
Folkways FC-7027	*(10")*	**Songs To Grow On (This Is My Land. Vol. 3)**	*195?*	**20.00**	**50.00**
Folkways FP-714	*(10")*	**Children's Game Songs Of French Canada**	*195?*	**20.00**	**50.00**
Folkways FC-7214	*(10")*	**Children's Game Songs Of French Canada**	*195?*	**20.00**	**50.00**
Folkways P-417	*(M)*	**Negro Music Of Alabama, Vol. I**	*1951*	**10.00**	**25.00**
Folkways FE-4417	*(M)*	**Negro Music Of Alabama, Vol. I**	*1951*	**10.00**	**25.00**
Folkways P-418	*(M)*	**Negro Music Of Alabama, Vol. II**	*1951*	**10.00**	**25.00**
Folkways FE-4418	*(M)*	**Negro Music Of Alabama, Vol. II**	*1951*	**10.00**	**25.00**
Folkways P-426	*(M)*	**Spanish And Mexican Folk Music**			
		Of New Mexico	*1951*	**10.00**	**25.00**
Folkways FE-4426	*(M)*	**Spanish And Mexican Folk Music**			
		Of New Mexico	*1951*	**10.00**	**25.00**
Folkways FP-438	*(M)*	**Cajun Songs From Louisiana**	*1951*	**10.00**	**25.00**
Folkways FE-4438	*(M)*	**Cajun Songs From Louisiana**	*1951*	**10.00**	**25.00**
Folkways P-450	*(M)*	**Songs From Cape Breton Island**	*1955*	**10.00**	**25.00**
Folkways FE-4450	*(M)*	**Songs From Cape Breton Island**	*1955*	**10.00**	**25.00**
Folkways P-471	*(M)*	**Negro Music Of Alabama, Vol. III**	*1951*	**10.00**	**25.00**
Folkways FE-4471	*(M)*	**Negro Music Of Alabama, Vol. III**	*1951*	**10.00**	**25.00**

Label & Catalog #		Title	Year	VG+	NM
Folkways P-472	(M)	Negro Music Of Alabama, Vol. IV	1951	10.00	25.00
Folkways FE-4472	(M)	Negro Music Of Alabama, Vol. IV	1951	10.00	25.00
Folkways P-473	(M)	Negro Music Of Alabama, Vol. V	1951	10.00	25.00
Folkways FE-4473	(M)	Negro Music Of Alabama, Vol. V	1951	10.00	25.00
Folkways P-474	(M)	Negro Music Of Alabama, Vol. VI	1951	10.00	25.00
Folkways FE-4474	(M)	Negro Music Of Alabama, Vol. VI	1951	10.00	25.00
Folkways P-475	(M)	Negro Prison Camp Work Songs	1951	10.00	25.00
Folkways FE-4475	(M)	Negro Prison Camp Work Songs	1951	10.00	25.00
Folkways P-482	(M)	Songs Of French Canada	195?	10.00	25.00
Folkways FE-4482	(M)	Songs Of French Canada	195?	10.00	25.00
Folkways FP-1001	(M)	Wolf River Song	1956	10.00	25.00
Folkways FW-4001	(M)	Wolf River Song	1956	10.00	25.00
Folkways FP-1006	(M)	Folk Music From Nova Scotia	1956	10.00	25.00
Folkways FM-4006	(M)	Folk Music From Nova Scotia	1956	10.00	25.00
Folkways FP-1009	(M)	Lithuanian Folk Songs			
		In The United States (1936-1950)	195?	10.00	25.00
Folkways FM-4009	(M)	Lithuanian Folk Songs			
		In The United States (1936-1950)	195?	10.00	25.00
Fontana MGF-27560	(M)	England's Greatest Hits (With poster)	1967	20.00	50.00
Fontana MGF-27560	(M)	England's Greatest Hits (Without poster)	1967	16.00	40.00
Fontana SRF-67560	(E)	England's Greatest Hits (With poster)	1967	14.00	35.00
Fontana SRF-67560	(E)	England's Greatest Hits (Without poster)	1967	10.00	25.00
		(Fontana 2/67560 was issued with a Union Jack poster.)			
Fontana MGF-27569	(M)	To Sir With Love (Soundtrack)	1967	8.00	20.00
Fontana SRF-67569	(S)	To Sir With Love (Soundtrack)	1967	10.00	25.00
Fortune 8011	(M)	Treasure Chest Of Musty Dusties, Vol. 1	1961	30.00	75.00
Fortune 8016	(M)	From The Beginning To Now	1963	30.00	75.00
Fortune 8017	(M)	Treasure Chest Of Musty Dusties, Vol. 2	1963	30.00	75.00
		— Fortune albums above have purple labels on thick vinyl. —			
Frantic 555/777	(M)	Psychedelic Disaster Whirl	198?	10.00	25.00
Frog Death GLP-101	(M)	Open Up Your Door, Volume 1	198?	10.00	25.00
Frog Death GLP-1012	(M)	Open Up Your Door, Volume 2	198?	10.00	25.00
G.S.P. 6901	(M)	Beach Party	196?	40.00	100.00
Garrett 1243	(M)	Top Teen Bands	1968	30.00	75.00
Gateway 9004	(M)	1964 In Review	1965	16.00	40.00
Gee GLP-702	(M)	Teenage Party (Red label)	1958	40.00	100.00
Gee GLP-702	(M)	Teenage Party (Gray label)	196?	10.00	25.00
Golden A198-17	(M)	The Fireside Treasury Of Folk Songs	1957	10.00	25.00
Golden Era 123	(M)	Golden Era (3 LPs)	196?	20.00	50.00
Goodman Group PRO-1	(DJ)	Just Let Me Hear Some			
		Of That Rock 'N' Roll Muic	1979	16.00	40.00
Goodman Group PRO-?	(DJ)	Let It Rock (4 LPs)	1985	16.00	40.00
Gott 3	(M)	Valley Of The Son Of Gathering Of The Tribe	198?	16.00	40.00
Grand Prix K-431	(M)	The Greatest R&B Singing Groups	196?	10.00	25.00
Grand Prix KS-431	(E)	The Greatest R&B Singing Groups	196?	8.00	20.00
Grant GLP-3001	(M)	Original 13 Hits, Volume 1	196?	12.00	30.00
		(Grant 3001 is a collection of Dot material			
		distributed through W.T. Grant stores.)			
Groovemaster BR-140	(M)	Beat Battle Of The World (Canadian)	1964	16.00	40.00
Groovemaster GR-140	(E)	Beat Battle Of The World (Canadian)	1964	10.00	25.00
Happy Tiger 1017	(P)	Early Chicago	1969	20.00	50.00

Label & Catalog #		Title	Year	VG+	NM
Harmony HS-30023	(S)	Chartbusters	1981	20.00	50.00
		(Includes both sides of Neil Diamond's first single, "Clown Town" and "I've Never Been The Same.")			
HBR HLP-8500	(M)	A Swingin' Summer *(Soundtrack)*	1966	12.00	30.00
HBR HST-8500	(S)	A Swingin' Summer *(Soundtrack)*	1966	16.00	40.00
Herald HLP-1010	(M)	Herald Of The Beat	1960	60.00	150.00
Herald HLP-1015	(M)	Pot Of Golden Goodies	1960	60.00	150.00
Hickory LP-154	(M)	Treasure Album	196?	10.00	25.00
Hickory LPS-154	(S)	Treasure Album	196?	20.00	50.00
		(LPS-154 contains several songs in stereo that are otherwise hard to find, including The Newbeats' "Bread And Butter.")			
Hideout	(M)	Best Of The Hideouts	1969	100.00	250.00
Hitbound HR-1001	(S)	Rock 'N Roll City	1983	30.00	75.00
Hollywood 30	(M)	Rhythm & Blues In The Night	1957	250.00	500.00
Hollywood 31	(M)	18 Rock "N' Roll Hits	1957	150.00	300.00
Hollywood 40	(M)	Red, Hot & Cool	1958	150.00	300.00
Hollywood 501	(M)	Merry Christmas, Baby	196?	150.00	300.00
Hollywood 503	(M)	R&B Hits	196?	80.00	200.00
House of Bryant HB-1001	(M)	Country Standards From The House Of Bryant	196?	12.00	30.00
House of Bryant HB-1002	(M)	Country Standards From The House Of Bryant, Volume 2	196?	12.00	30.00
Hull 1002	(M)	Your Favorite Singing Groups	195?	500.00	1,000.00
I.G.L. 103	(M)	Roof Garden Jamboree	1967	40.00	200.00
Impact LP-2	(M)	Shake, Shout And Soul	196?	40.00	200.00
Imperial FD-102	(10")	American Folk Dance	195?	16.00	40.00
Imperial DJLP-1 (10")	(DJ)	Imperial Sampler	195?	40.00	100.00
Imperial LP-9021	(M)	A Tribute To James Dean *(Maroon label)*	1957	40.00	100.00
Imperial LP-9021	(M)	A Tribute To James Dean *(Black label)*	1957	20.00	50.00
Imperial LP-9084	(M)	Hitsville U.S.A., Volume 1	1960	16.00	40.00
Imperial LP-9099	(M)	Hitsville U.S.A., Volume 2	1960	16.00	40.00
Imperial LP-9210	(M)	A World Of Blues	1963	16.00	40.00
Imperial LP-9214	(M)	Hillbilly House Party	1963	8.00	20.00
Imperial LP-9230	(M)	Solid Gold Hits	1964	10.00	25.00
Imperial LP-9257	(M)	Best Of The Blues, Volume 1	1964	10.00	25.00
Imperial LP-12257	(E)	Best Of The Blues, Volume 1	1964	8.00	20.00
Imperial LP-9259	(M)	Best Of The Blues, Volume 2	1964	10.00	25.00
Imperial LP-12259	(E)	Best Of The Blues, Volume 2	1964	8.00	20.00
Imperial LP-9260	(M)	New Orleans, Our Home Town	1964	10.00	25.00
Imperial LP-12260	(E)	New Orleans, Our Home Town	1964	8.00	20.00
Imperial LP-9271	(M)	Giant Instrumental R&B Hits	1964	10.00	25.00
Imperial LP-12271	(E)	Giant Instrumental R&B Hits	1964	8.00	20.00
		— Original Imperial mono albums above have black labels with stars on top; stereo albums have black labels with silver print.—			
Imperial MM-423	(DJ)	Special Programmer Selection From 1965	1965	10.00	25.00
Increase	(DJ)	Cruisin' *(Radio sampler)*	1973	12.00	30.00
Instant 71000	(M)	All These Things	196?	16.00	40.00
International Art. 13	(S)	Epitaph For A Legend *(2 LPs)*	1979	20.00	50.00
Jamie JLPM-3017	(M)	The Sounds Of Success	1961	10.00	25.00
Jamie JLPS-3017	(S)	The Sounds Of Success	1961	12.00	30.00
Jamie JLPM-3031	(M)	Old 'N Golden	1964	10.00	25.00
Jamie JLPS-3031	(E)	Old 'N Golden	1964	8.00	20.00

Label & Catalog #		Title	Year	VG+	NM
JAS JAS-5001	(P)	**San Francisco Roots** (Photo cover)	1976	16.00	40.00
JAS JAS-5001	(P)	**San Francisco Roots** (Titles cover)	1976	10.00	25.00
		(JAS 5001 is a reissue of Vault 119.)			
Jerden JRL-7001	(M)	**Original Great Northwest Hits, Volume 1**	1965	20.00	50.00
Jerden JRL-7002	(M)	**Original Great Northwest Hits, Volume 2**	1965	20.00	50.00
Jerden JRL-7005	(M)	**Hitmakers**	1966	20.00	50.00
Jin 4002	(M)	**Rockin' Date**			
		With The South Louisiana Stars	196?	16.00	40.00
Jin 4002	(M)	**South Louisiana Juke Box Hits**	196?	16.00	40.00
Jin 9001	(M)	**Golden Dozen Hits**	196?	16.00	40.00
Jobete PRO-1	(DJ)	**The Top 10 Story In Sound** (2 LPs)	1972	16.00	40.00
Jobete PRO-2	(DJ)	**The Songs Of Smokey Robinson**	1972	12.00	30.00
Jobete PRO-3	(DJ)	**The Songs Of Ashford & Simpson**	1974	12.00	30.00
Jobete PRO-4	(DJ)	**The Songs Of Holland-Dozier-Holland**	1974	12.00	30.00
Jobete PRO-5	(DJ)	**The Songs Of Stevie Wonder**	1974	12.00	30.00
Jobete PRO-6	(DJ)	**The Songs Of Marvin Gaye**	1974	12.00	30.00
Jobete PRO-7	(DJ)	**The Songs Of Norman Whitfield**	1976	12.00	30.00
Jobete PRO-8	(DJ)	**The Songs Of Johnny Bristol / Frank Wilson /**			
		Mickey Stevenson / Freddie Perren	1977	12.00	30.00
Jobete PRO-9	(DJ)	**Holland-Dozier-Holland:**			
		Yesterday, Today & Forever (3 LPs)	1977	16.00	40.00
Jobete PRO-9	(DJ)	**Pure Magic: The Songs**			
		Of Pam Sawyer & Marilyn McLeod	1978	12.00	30.00
		(Each of the Jobete albums above are publisher's demo			
		with snippets of recordings of the writers' material.)			
Josie JOZ-4002	(M)	**Original Goldies**			
		From The Fabulous '50's, Volume 1	1962	30.00	75.00
Josie JOZ-4003	(M)	**Original Goldies**			
		From The Fabulous '50's, Volume 2	1962	30.00	75.00
Jubilee J-1014	(M)	**The Best of Rhythm And Blues** (Red vinyl)	1957	200.00	400.00
Jubilee J-1014	(M)	**The Best of Rhythm And Blues**	1957	80.00	200.00
		—Jubilee albums above have blue labels.—			
Jubilee J-1014	(M)	**The Best of Rhythm And Blues**	1957	50.00	125.00
Jubilee J-1107	(M)	**Surprise Party (Vol. 1)**	196?	60.00	150.00
Jubilee J-1114	(M)	**Rumble**	1960	60.00	150.00
Jubilee J-1118	(M)	**Boppin'**	1960	60.00	150.00
Jubilee J-1119	(M)	**Whoppers**	1960	60.00	150.00
		—Jubilee albums above have flat black labels.—			
Jubilee J-8019	(S)	**Super Golden Hits**	1968	50.00	125.00
Killdozer KILL-001	(M)	**Scum Of The Earth, Part 1**	198?	30.00	75.00
Killdozer KILL-002	(M)	**Scum Of The Earth, Part 2**	198?	30.00	75.00
King 395-513	(M)	**All Star Rock And Roll Revue**	1958	150.00	350.00
King 395-528	(M)	**After Hours**	1958	200.00	500.00
King 395-536	(M)	**Rock & Roll Dance Party**	1958	150.00	350.00
King 395-537	(M)	**All Time Country & Western Hits**	1958	60.00	150.00
King 395-540	(M)	**Piano Variations**	1958	60.00	150.00
King 395-556	(M)	**Sacred Songs**	1958	60.00	150.00
King 395-562	(M)	**Square Dance Music**	1958	60.00	150.00
King 395-576	(M)	**Spirituals, Volume 5**	1958	60.00	150.00
King 395-638	(M)	**Rock & Roll Revue**	1959	80.00	200.00
		(King 638 is a reissue of 513.)			
King 654	(M)	**Rock & Roll Revue, Volume 2**	1959	80.00	200.00
King 680	(M)	**Merry Christmas**	1959	80.00	200.00
King 697	(M)	**Country & Western Jamboree**	1960	40.00	100.00
King 710	(M)	**All Time Country & Western Hits**	1960	40.00	100.00
King 725	(M)	**25 Years Of Rhythm And Blues Hits**	1960	40.00	100.00
King 726	(M)	**Homespun Humor**	1960	40.00	100.00
King 737	(M)	**Hit Makers And Record Breakers**	1960	40.00	100.00
King 745	(M)	**Solo Spotlights**	1961	40.00	100.00
King 749	(M)	**25 Years Of R&B Hits**	1961	40.00	100.00
King 753	(M)	**Bumper Crop Of All Stars**	1961	40.00	100.00

Label & Catalog #		Title	Year	VG+	NM
King 753	(M)	Bumper Crop Of All Stars	1961	40.00	100.00
King 792	(M)	Forgotten Million Sellers	1962	40.00	100.00
King 807	(M)	All Star Country & Western	1962	40.00	100.00
King 811	(M)	Country Christmas	1962	40.00	100.00
King 813	(M)	Nashville Bandstand	1962	40.00	100.00
King 819	(M)	A Carnival Of Songs	1963	40.00	100.00
King 837	(M)	Organ Jazz Giants	1963	60.00	150.00
King 847	(M)	Nashville Bandstand, Volume 2	1963	30.00	75.00
King 855	(M)	Surfin' On Wave Nine	1963	30.00	75.00
King 859	(M)	Turning Back The Clock Blue	1963	30.00	75.00
King 862	(M)	Hootenanny	1963	30.00	75.00
King 866	(M)	Truck Driver Songs	1963	30.00	75.00
King 869	(M)	Railroad Songs	1963	30.00	75.00
King 871	(M)	Songs Of Rivers, Oceans And Seas	1963	30.00	75.00
King 875	(M)	Everybody's Favorite Blues	1964	30.00	75.00
King 876	(M)	Western Swing	1964	30.00	75.00
King 882	(M)	Look Who's Surfin' Now	1964	60.00	150.00
King 884	(M)	Top R&B Artists Sing Country	1964	30.00	75.00
King 890	(M)	14 Great All Time C&W Waltzes	1964	30.00	75.00
King 893	(M)	14 Hit Flashbacks From The Group Era	1964	30.00	75.00
King K-951	(M)	Spirituals (Re-issue of #576)	1966	20.00	50.00
King K-965	(M)	24 Scared Songs	1966	20.00	50.00

—King mono albums above have crownless black labels; stereo albums have crownless blue labels. The logo on the covers have a crown with "King" in open capital block letters below.—

King K-994	(M)	5 String Banjo Pickin' And Singin'	1966	16.00	40.00
King K-1004	(M)	25 Years Of R&B Hits	1966	16.00	40.00
King K-1006	(M)	25 Years Of C&W	1966	12.00	30.00
King K-1008	(M)	25 Years Of Popular Music	1966	12.00	30.00
King KS-1023	(M)	All Time Sacred Hits	1968	12.00	30.00
King KS-1026	(M)	18 All Time R&B Hits	1968	16.00	40.00
King KS-1027	(M)	18 All Time C&W Hits	1968	12.00	30.00
King KS-1050	(E)	Radar Blues	1969	12.00	30.00

—King mono albums above have black labels with a crown on top; stereo albums have blue or red labels with a crown on top. The covers have a crown with "King" in open capital block letters.—

Kramden 101	(M)	Hipsville 29 B.C.	198?	20.00	50.00
Laurie LLP-2010	(M)	Great Groups Great Records	1961	10.00	25.00
Laurie LLP-2041	(M)	Laurie Golden Goodies	1967	6.00	15.00
Laurie SLLP-2041	(P)	Laurie Golden Goodies	1967	10.00	25.00
Liberty LST-101	(DJ)	This Is Stereo (Sampler on red vinyl)	1960	60.00	150.00
Liberty LRP-5503	(M)	Teensville	1962	16.00	40.00
Liberty LRP-5505	(M)	Golden Teen Hits	1962	16.00	40.00
Liberty MM-412	(DJ)	Explosive!	1962	20.00	50.00
Liberty MM-417	(DJ)	Spin Time With Liberty	1962	20.00	50.00
Liberty LRP-3048	(M)	Hot Rod Rumble	1957	14.00	35.00
Liberty LRP-3178	(M)	Original Hits, Volume 1	1961	8.00	20.00
Liberty LST-7178	(P)	Original Hits, Volume 1	1961	10.00	25.00
Liberty LRP-3180	(M)	Original Hits, Volume 2	1961	8.00	20.00
Liberty LST-7180	(P)	Original Hits, Volume 2	1961	10.00	25.00
Liberty LRP-3187	(M)	Original Hits, Volume 3	1961	8.00	20.00
Liberty LST-7187	(P)	Original Hits, Volume 3	1961	10.00	25.00
Liberty LRP-3200	(M)	Original Hits, Volume 4	1962	8.00	20.00
Liberty LST-7200	(P)	Original Hits, Volume 4	1962	10.00	25.00
Liberty LRP-3235	(M)	Original Hits, Volume 5	1962	8.00	20.00
Liberty LST-7235	(P)	Original Hits, Volume 5	1962	10.00	25.00
Liberty LRP-3366	(M)	Shut Downs And Hill Climbs	1964	16.00	40.00
Liberty LST-7366	(P)	Shut Downs And Hill Climbs	1964	20.00	50.00
Liberty LRP-3381	(M)	Original Rhythm & Blues Hits, Vol. 1	1964	8.00	20.00
Liberty LST-7381	(P)	Original Rhythm & Blues Hits, Vol. 1	1964	10.00	25.00
Lion 70108	(M)	Celebrities	1960	10.00	25.00
London LL-3430	(M)	England's Greatest Hitmakers	1964	12.00	30.00
London PS-430	(E)	England's Greatest Hitmakers	1964	8.00	20.00
Lost-Nite LP-10?	(M)	Jerry Blavat Presents For Lovers Only, Vol. 1	1965	8.00	20.00

Label & Catalog #		Title	Year	VG+	NM
Lost-Nite LP-107	(M)	Jerry Blavat Presents For Lovers Only, Vol. 2	1965	8.00	20.00
Lost-Nite LPS-107	(S)	Jerry Blavat Presents For Lovers Only, Vol. 2	1965	10.00	25.00
Lost-Nite LP-114	(M)	Gary Stevens' 22 Good Guy Oldies	1965	10.00	25.00
Lost-Nite LP-119	(M)	Gary Stevens, Volume 2	1965	10.00	25.00
Lost-Nite LP-130	(M)	WIXY's Super Oldie Hits Of The Past, Vol. 1	1965	10.00	25.00
Magistral 2000	(M)	Changes	198?	20.00	50.00
Magna 71014	(M)	Northland Battle Of The Bands	1967	360.00	600.00
Mainstream 56100	(M)	A Pot Of Flowers	1967	10.00	25.00
Mainstream S-6100	(S)	A Pot Of Flowers	1967	12.00	30.00
Mark-56 MLP-510	(M)	Mr. Faruki's Suzuki	196?	20.00	50.00
Mark-56 MLP-511	(M)	Golden Oldies	196?	20.00	50.00
MCA	(DJ)	More American Graffiti (Picture disc)	1976	10.00	25.00
Memphis (No number)	(M)	Rebirth Of Beale Street	1984	16.00	40.00
Mercury MG-25164	(10")	Hit Parade	195?	20.00	50.00
Mercury MG-25166	(10")	Hit Parade	195?	20.00	50.00
Mercury MG-25205	(10")	Hit Parade	195?	20.00	50.00
Mercury MG-20213	(M)	A Collection Of Golden Hits	195?	20.00	50.00
Mercury MG-20262	(M)	Authentic Square Dances	195?	20.00	50.00
Mercury MG-20282	(M)	Hillbilly Hit Parade, Volume 1	1958	20.00	50.00
Mercury MG-20293	(M)	Rock All Night (Soundtrack)	1958	100.00	250.00
Mercury MG-20328	(M)	Hillbilly Hit Parade, Volume 2	1958	16.00	40.00
Mercury MG-20350	(M)	Opry Stars Jamboree	1958	16.00	40.00
Mercury MG-20360	(M)	A Night At The Louisiana Hayride	1958	16.00	40.00
Mercury MG-20493	(M)	14 Newies But Goodies	1960	10.00	25.00
Mercury SR-60172	(S)	14 Newies But Goodies	1960	12.00	30.00
Mercury MG-20511	(M)	Golden Goodies	1960	10.00	25.00
Mercury SR-60217	(S)	Golden Goodies	1960	12.00	30.00
Mercury MG-20581	(M)	14 More Newies But Goodies	1960	10.00	25.00
Mercury SR-60???	(S)	14 More Newies But Goodies	1960	12.00	30.00
Mercury MG-20583	(M)	More Golden Goodies	1960	10.00	25.00
Mercury SR-60???	(S)	More Golden Goodies	1960	12.00	30.00
Mercury MG-20651	(M)	Chart Winners	1962	10.00	25.00
Mercury SR-60651	(S)	Chart Winners	1962	12.00	30.00
Mercury MG-20687	(M)	Twist With The Stars	1962	10.00	25.00
Mercury SR-60687	(S)	Twist With The Stars	1962	12.00	30.00
Mercury MG-20809	(M)	Original Golden Hits Of The Great Groups	1963	12.00	30.00
Mercury SR-60809	(S)	Original Golden Hits Of The Great Groups	1963	12.00	30.00
Mercury MG-20826	(M)	The Great Blues Singers	1964	10.00	25.00
Mercury SR-60826	(S)	The Great Blues Singers	1964	12.00	30.00
Mercury MG-20857	(M)	Hootenanny Bluegrass Style	1964	8.00	20.00
Mercury SR-60857	(S)	Hootenanny Bluegrass Style	1964	10.00	25.00
Mercury SRD-2-29	(S)	Zig Zag Festival	1970	16.00	40.00
Mercury MK2-2-121	(DJ)	The Ultimate Radio Bootleg, Vol. 3	1976	10.00	25.00
Metro M/MS-563		This Is Where It Started: Refer to The Beatles			
MGM DJ-5	(DJ)	MGM Sounds Of 1959	1959	20.00	50.00
MGM E-3814	(M)	MGM Top Hits	1963	8.00	20.00
MGM SE-3814	(P)	MGM Top Hits	1963	10.00	25.00
MGM E-3826	(M)	MGM Hits With A Beat	1963	8.00	20.00
MGM SE-3826	(P)	MGM Hits With A Beat	1963	10.00	25.00
MGM E-3912	(M)	We Wrote 'Em And We Sing 'Em	1964	8.00	20.00
MGM SE-3912	(S)	We Wrote 'Em And We Sing 'Em	1964	12.00	30.00
MGM E-4078	(M)	MGM Parade Of Hits	1964	8.00	20.00
MGM SE-4078	(P)	MGM Parade Of Hits	1964	10.00	25.00
MGM E-4334	(M)	When The Boys Meet The Girls (Sdtk)	1965	8.00	20.00
MGM SE-4334	(S)	When The Boys Meet The Girls (Sdtk)	1965	10.00	25.00
MGM ADV-1	(DJ)	MGM-Verve-Verve/Forecast Radio Spots	1967	300.00	600.00
		(Promo with radio spots for The Mothers Of zInvention, Tim Hardin, Nico, Sam The Sham and others issued without a cover.)			
MGM SE-4668	(S)	Zabriskie Point (Soundtrack)	1968	12.00	30.00

Label & Catalog #		Title	Year	VG+	NM
Minit LP-0001	(M)	New Orleans: Home Of The Blues	1961	20.00	50.00
Minit LP-0003	(M)	We Sing The Blues	1962	20.00	50.00
Minit LP-0004	(M)	New Orleans: Home Of The Blues, Volume 2	1962	20.00	50.00
Mobile Fidelity MFSL-200	(S)	Woodstock (5 LP box)	198?	50.00	150.00
Modern 2001	(10")	Modern Records, Volume 1	1951	250.00	600.00
Modern 2002	(10")	Modern Records, Volume 2	1951	250.00	600.00
Modern 2003	(10")	Modern Records, Volume 3	1951	250.00	600.00
Modern LMP-1210	(M)	Rock & Roll Dance Party	195?	80.00	200.00
Modern LMP-1211	(M)	Rock & Roll Record Hop	195?	80.00	200.00
Monsters 1002	(M)	Monsters Of The Midwest, Volume 2	198?	10.00	25.00
Monsters 1003	(M)	Monsters Of The Midwest, Volume 3	198?	10.00	25.00
Monsters 1004	(M)	Monsters Of The Midwest, Volume 4	198?	10.00	25.00
Monument MLP-8010	(M)	Demand Performances	1963	10.00	25.00
Monument SLP-18010	(S)	Demand Performances	1963	12.00	30.00
Motown MLP-603	(M)	Motown Hits, Volume 1	1962	30.00	75.00
Motown MLP-609	(M)	Recorded Live At The Apollo:			
		The Motortown Revue, Volume 1	1963	30.00	75.00
Motown MLP-614	(M)	A Package Of 16 Big Hits	1963	40.00	100.00
		(Original covers have a postal package motif.)			
Motown MLP-614	(M)	16 Original Big Hits, Volume 1	1967	8.00	20.00
Motown MS-614	(P)	16 Original Big Hits, Volume 1	1967	12.00	30.00
		(Later pressings have the standard "Big Hits" style cover.)			
Motown MLP-615	(M)	Recorded Live: The Motortown Revue, Vol. 2	1964	12.00	30.00
Motown MLP-624	(M)	16 Original Big Hits, Volume 3	1964	8.00	20.00
Motown MS-624	(S)	16 Original Big Hits, Volume 3	1964	10.00	25.00
Motown MLP-630	(M)	Nothing But A Man (Soundtrack)	1965	20.00	50.00
Motown MS-630	(S)	Nothing But A Man (Soundtrack)	1965	30.00	75.00
Motown MLP-633	(M)	16 Original Big Hits, Volume 4	1965	8.00	20.00
Motown MS-633	(S)	16 Original Big Hits, Volume 4	1965	10.00	25.00
Motown M-642	(M)	In Loving Memory	1968	80.00	200.00
Motown MS-642	(S)	In Loving Memory	1968	80.00	200.00
		(Original pressings do not list the song titles on the cover.)			
Motown M-642	(M)	In Loving Memory	1968	60.00	150.00
Motown MS-642	(S)	In Loving Memory	1968	60.00	150.00
		(Second pressings list the song titles on the cover.)			
Motown M-642	(DJ)	In Loving Memory	1969	See below	
		(This special edition has a custom label for the Loucye Gordy Wake- field Scholarship Fund with a silver gatefold cover. This was given to attendees of the October 4, 1969 Sterling Ball at Gordy Manor. Very rare with no transactions from which to suggest a value.)			
Motown M-651	(M)	16 Original Big Hits, Volume 5	1967	12.00	30.00
Motown MS-651	(S)	16 Original Big Hits, Volume 5	1967	6.00	15.00
Motown M-655	(M)	16 Original Big Hits, Volume 6	1967	12.00	30.00
Motown MS-655	(S)	16 Original Big Hits, Volume 6	1967	6.00	15.00
Motown M-661	(M)	16 Original Big Hits, Volume 7	1967	12.00	30.00
Motown MS-661	(S)	16 Original Big Hits, Volume 7	1967	6.00	15.00
Motown M-666	(M)	16 Original Big Hits, Volume 8	1967	12.00	30.00
Motown MS-666	(S)	16 Original Big Hits, Volume 8	1967	6.00	15.00
Motown M-668	(M)	16 Original Big Hits, Volume 9	1968	16.00	40.00
Motown MS-668	(S)	16 Original Big Hits, Volume 9	1968	6.00	15.00
Motown MS-681	(M)	Merry Christmas From Motown	1968	12.00	30.00
Motown MS-684	(S)	16 Original Big Hits, Volume 10	1969	6.00	15.00
Motown MS-688	(S)	The Motortown Revue Recorded Live!	1969	10.00	25.00
— Motown albums above have a Detroit, MI, address on the label.—					
Motown MS-5-726	(S)	The Motown Story (5 LPs)	1971	10.00	25.00
Motown M-739L	(DJ)	1971 Sterling Ball Benefit	1971	100.00	250.00
		(Issued in a custom silver gatefold cover.)			
Motown PR-121	(DJ)	The Motown Story (Boxed set)	1983	100.00	250.00
		(Motown 122 is a promotional boxed set of seven white label albums designated PR-121 A/B, C/D, E/F, G/H, I/J, K/L/ and M/N.)			
Motown PR-122	(DJ)	Moments Of Motown	1983	20.00	50.00

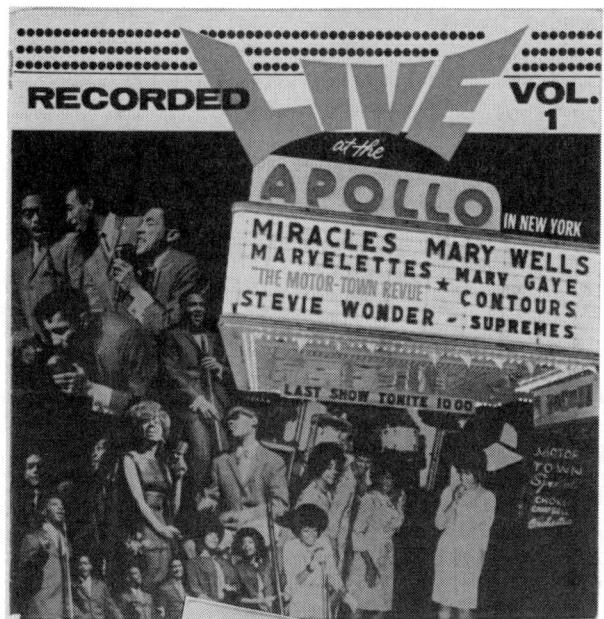

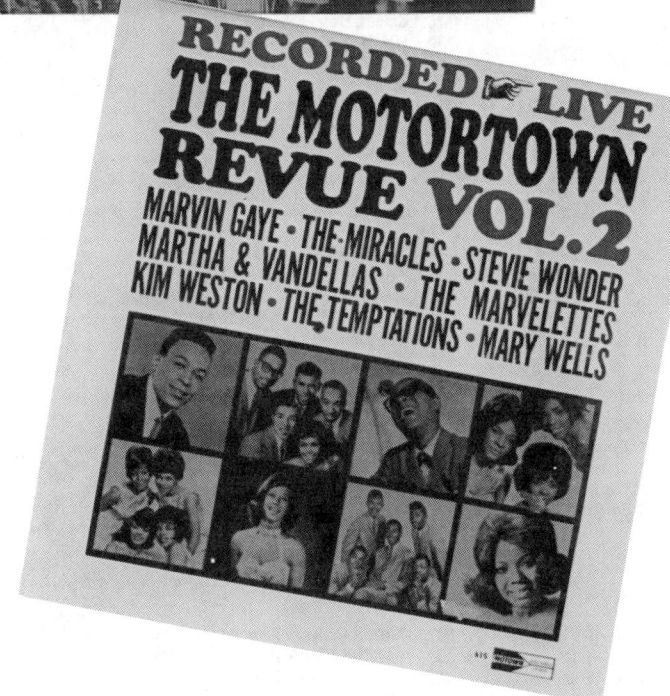

Note the vast differences in the cover designs between the two volumes of these early Motown sets: The first volume, subtitled Recorded Live At The Apollo, *is a rather hectic collage that captures some of the excitement that a rhythm 'n blues show was expected to have (especially at the Apollo). Volume two has a staid, almost sedate, layout, perhaps reflecting the direction that Berry Gordy was grooming his stars towards by its 1964 release.*

Label & Catalog #		Title	Year	VG+	NM
Moulty MLP-101	(M)	New England Teen Scene	198?	20.00	50.00
Moulty MLP-103	(M)	New England Teen Scene, Vol. 2	198?	8.00	20.00
Mt. Vernon MUM-109	(M)	Hitsville	196?	12.00	30.00
Mt. Vernon MUM-183	(M)	All Star Country & Western And Bluegrass, Volume 2	196?	12.00	30.00
Muse 500	(M)	Carload Of Hits	196?	80.00	200.00
Muziek Expres ME-66	(M)	Searching In The Wilderness	198?	10.00	25.00
New World 207	(P)	Country Music In The Modern Era	1976	60.00	150.00
		(Originals have a small border along the bottom front cover.)			
New World 207	(P)	Country Music In The Modern Era	1978	20.00	50.00
		(Later pressings have a wider border along the bottom front cover.)			
Northridge NM-101	(M)	Surf's Up! At Banzai Pipeline	1963	40.00	100.00
Ode SP-99001	(DJ)	Tommy (2 LP boxed soundtrack)	1970	20.00	50.00
Ode SQ-99001	(Q)	Tommy (2 LP boxed soundtrack)	1970	20.00	50.00
Old Town LP-101	(M)	Your Old Favorites On The Old Town	1962	40.00	100.00
		(Old Town 101 was reissued as Cotillion 9032.)			
Oldies-33 OL-8001	(M)	Oldies Dance Party, Volume 1	1963	8.00	20.00
Oldies-33 OL-8002	(M)	Oldies Dance Party, Volume 2	1964	8.00	20.00
Oldies-33 OL-8003	(M)	Oldies Dance Party, Volume 3	1964	10.00	25.00
Oldies-33 OL-8004	(M)	Great Boy Oldies	1964	10.00	25.00
Oldies-33 OL-8005	(M)	Soulful Oldies	1964	10.00	25.00
Oldies-33 OL-8007	(M)	D'oes Crazy Oldies	1964	10.00	25.00
Omega Sales	(M)	Country Super Sounds 1955*	1973	12.00	30.00
Omega Sales	(M)	Country Super Sounds 1956*	1973	12.00	30.00
Omega Sales	(M)	Country Super Sounds 1957*	1973	12.00	30.00
Omega Sales	(M)	Country Super Sounds 1958*	1973	12.00	30.00
		—Omega Sales titles above marked with an asterisk conatin at least one track by Elvis Presley. The volumes in this series without an Elvis track are worth $10-20 each.—			
Original Sound LPM-5001	(M)	Oldies But Goodies	1959	16.00	60.00
Original Sound LPM-5002	(M)	Oldies But Goodies, Volume 2	1960	16.00	40.00
Original Sound LPM-5003	(M)	Oldies But Goodies, Volume 3	196?	16.00	40.00
Original Sound LPM-5004	(M)	Oldies But Goodies, Volume 4	196?	12.00	30.00
Original Sound LPM-5005	(M)	Oldies But Goodies, Volume 5	196?	12.00	30.00
Original Sound LPM-5006	(M)	Oldies But Goodies, Volume 6	196?	12.00	30.00
Original Sound LPM-5007	(M)	Oldies But Goodies, Volume 7	196?	10.00	25.00
Original Sound LPM-5008	(M)	Oldies But Goodies, Volume 8	196?	10.00	25.00
Original Sound LPM-5009	(M)	Oldies But Goodies, Volume 9	196?	10.00	25.00
Original Sound LPM-5010	(M)	Oldies But Goodies, Volume 10	196?	10.00	25.00
		(Originals advertise the next volume only on the back cover.)			
Original Sound OSR-11	(S)	Rock Rock Rock	1972	20.00	50.00
Original Sound OSR-11	(M)	All Star Rock, Volume 2	1972	16.00	40.00
		("All Star Rock" is a reissue of "Rock Rock Rock.")			
Panorama 103	(S)	Battle Of The Bands	1966	12.00	30.00
Panorama 108	(S)	Battle Of The Bands, Volume 2	1966	12.00	30.00
Parkway P-7011	(M)	Don't Knock The Twist (Soundtrack)	1962	12.00	30.00
Parkway P-7013	(M)	All The Hits By All The Stars	1962	12.00	30.00
Parkway P-7028	(M)	Million Seller Dance Hits	1963	10.00	25.00
Parkway P-7031	(M)	12 Greatest Golden Oldies In The Whole World Ever	1963	10.00	25.00
Parkway P-7033	(M)	All The Stars-Biggest Hits	1963	14.00	35.00
Parkway P-7034	(M)	All The Stars-Biggest Hits, Volume 2	1963	14.00	35.00
		(Both Parkway 7033 and 7034 were issued with "Pull Off Pix" of the six artists on the album. The price is for the record and the jacket with the pix intact.)			
Parkway P-7035	(M)	Everybody's Goin' Surfin'	1963	12.00	30.00
Parkway P-7037	(M)	Oldies By The Dozen	1963	12.00	30.00

Label & Catalog #		Title	Year	VG+	NM
Passport PB-3604	(S)	Phil Spector's Christmas Album: *Refer to* Phil Spector			
Pavillion PZ-37686	(S)	Phil Spector's Christmas Album: *Refer to* Phil Spector			
Paul Winley Prod. 1001	(M)	New York City's Greatest Oldies	196?	40.00	100.00
Pepsi Cola PC-51668	(M)	Youth Market Radio	1968	30.00	75.00
		(One-sided promo features radio spots by Wilson Pickett, The Stone Poneys, and The Union Gap.)			
Phantom PRS-1001	(M)	A Journey To Tyme, Vol. 1	198?	14.00	35.00
Phantom PRS-1002	(M)	A Journey To Tyme, Vol. 2	198?	14.00	35.00
Phantom PRS-1003	(M)	A Journey To Tyme, Vol. 3	198?	14.00	35.00
Phantom PLP-1004	(M)	Sound Of The 60s: San Francisco, Part 1	198?	14.00	35.00
Phantom PLP-1005	(M)	Sound Of The 60s: San Francisco, Part 2	198?	14.00	35.00
Phantom PRS-1006	(M)	A Journey To Tyme, Vol. 4	198?	14.00	35.00
Phantom PRS-1007	(M)	A Journey To Tyme, Vol. 5	198?	14.00	35.00
Philles PHLP-4004	(M)	Today's Hits: *Refer to* Phil Spector			
Philles PHLP-4005	(M)	A Christmas Gift For You: *Refer to* Phil Spector			
Pickwick CL-001	(S)	Moving Ahead With Music	197?	12.00	30.00
Playboy 7473	(S)	The Playboy Music Hall Of Fame Winners	1978	20.00	50.00
Prestige PR-7539	(S)	Take A Trip With Psychedelic Hits	196?	20.00	50.00
Prestige Int. PRLP-25001	(M)	Southern Journey Series, Volume 1	1961	10.00	25.00
Prestige Int. PRLP-25002	(M)	Southern Journey Series, Volume II	1961	10.00	25.00
Prestige Int. PRLP-25003	(M)	Southern Journey Series, Volume III	1961	10.00	25.00
Prestige Int. PRLP-25004	(M)	Southern Journey Series, Volume IV	1961	10.00	25.00
Prestige Int. PRLP-25005	(M)	Southern Journey Series, Volume V	1961	10.00	25.00
Prestige Int. PRLP-25006	(M)	Southern Journey Series, Volume VI	1961	10.00	25.00
Prestige Int. PRLP-25007	(M)	Southern Journey Series, Volume VII	1961	10.00	25.00
Prestige Int. PRLP-25008	(M)	Southern Journey Series, Volume VIII	1961	10.00	25.00
Prestige Int. PRLP-25009	(M)	Southern Journey Series, Volume IX	1961	10.00	25.00
Prestige Int. PRLP-25010	(M)	Southern Journey Series, Volume X	1961	10.00	25.00
Prestige Int. PRLP-25011	(M)	Southern Journey Series, Volume XI	1961	10.00	25.00
Prestige Int. PRLP-25012	(M)	Southern Journey Series, Volume XII	1961	10.00	25.00
Prestige Int. PRLP-13073	(M)	Folk Songs For Children	1963	10.00	25.00
Prestige Int. PRLP-13079	(M)	East Of Athens	1963	10.00	25.00
Prestige Int. PRLP-13080	(M)	The Artistry Of Greece	1963	10.00	25.00
Pricewise 4004	(M)	Best Of The Girl Groups	196?	10.00	25.00
Prism 1966	(M)	WONE-The Dayton Scene	1966	150.00	300.00
Psycho 1	(M)	Endless Journey *(Numbered edition)*	1980	24.00	60.00
Psychotic Moose PMS-101	(M)	Psychotic Moose & The Soul Searchers	198?	20.00	50.00
Ralph 8205	(DJ)	10th Anniversary Radio Special *(2 LPs. 1,000 pressed)*	1981	12.00	30.00
Ralph 8205D	(DJ)	10 Years In 20 Minutes *(Clear vinyl)*	1981	20.00	50.00
Rampart LP-3303	(M)	East Side Revue	196?	40.00	100.00
Rampart LP-3305	(M)	East Side Revue, Volume 2 *(With poster)*	196?	50.00	125.00
Rampart LP-3305	(M)	East Side Revue, Volume 2 *(Without poster)*	1969	40.00	100.00
		(Both the Rampart albums are on multi-colored vinyl.)			
RCA Victor LPM-3182	(10")	The Honor Roll Of Hits 1940-41	1954	20.00	50.00
RCA Victor LPM-3183	(10")	The Honor Roll Of Hits 1942-43	1954	20.00	50.00
RCA Victor LPM-3184	(10")	The Honor Roll Of Hits 1944-45	1954	20.00	50.00
RCA Victor LPM-3192	(10")	Tennessee Jamboree	1954	30.00	75.00
RCA Victor LPM-3220	(10")	Country And Western Caravan	1954	30.00	75.00
RCA Victor LPM-3282	(10")	Top Pops	1954	30.00	75.00
RCA Victor SPL-1213	(M)	Pop Shopper	1955	10.00	25.00
RCA Victor LPM-1540	(M)	Teenagers Dance	1957	14.00	35.00

Label & Catalog #		Title	Year	VG+	NM
RCA Victor LPM-1540	(M)	**Teenagers Dance**	1957	14.00	35.00
RCA Victor (No #)	(10")	**Ballad Of Oklahoma**	1957	40.00	100.00
		(A Limited Gold Seal Edition distributed by the Red Plains Trading Post in celebration of Oregon's fiftieth anniversary of its statehood.)			
RCA Victor LPM-1813	(M)	**TV Record Hop**	1958	20.00	50.00
RCA Victor LPM-2210	(M)	**Goodies For LP Fans**	1960	8.00	20.00
RCA Victor LSP-2210	(P)	**Goodies For LP Fans**	1960	10.00	25.00
RCA Victor LPM-2332	(M)	**Twelve Big Ones**	1960	8.00	20.00
RCA Victor LSP-2332	(P)	**Twelve Big Ones**	1960	10.00	25.00
		— RCA mono albums above have black labels with "Long Play" on the bottom; stereo albums have "Living Stereo" on the bottom.—			
RCA Victor LPM-2740	(M)	**Old 'n' Golden Goodies**	1963	8.00	20.00
RCA Victor LSP-2740	(P)	**Old 'n' Golden Goodies**	1963	12.00	30.00
RCA Victor LPM-3441	(M)	**Wild On The Beach** *(Soundtrack)*	1965	8.00	20.00
RCA Victor LSP-3441	(S)	**Wild On The Beach** *(Soundtrack)*	1965	12.00	30.00
RCA Victor LPM-3632	(M)	**The Best Of The Best Of**	1966	8.00	20.00
RCA Victor LSP-3632	(P)	**The Best Of The Best Of**	1966	10.00	25.00
RCA Victor LPM-3641	(M)	**Old 'n' Golden Goodies, Volume 2**	1966	8.00	20.00
RCA Victor LSP-3641	(P)	**Old 'n' Golden Goodies, Volume 2**	1966	12.00	30.00
RCA Victor LPM-6015	(M)	**Stars Of The Grand Ole Opry** *(2 LP box)*	1967	16.00	40.00
		— RCA albums above have black labels.—			
RCA Victor LPM-6070	(M)	**How The West Was One** *(2 LPs)*	195?	12.00	30.00
RCA Victor LPV-507	(M)	**Smoky Mountain Ballads**	1965	8.00	20.00
RCA Victor LPV-518	(M)	**Bluebird Blues**	1965	10.00	25.00
RCA Victor LPV-532	(M)	**The Railroad In Folksong**	1965	8.00	20.00
RCA Victor LPV-534	(M)	**Women In Blues**	1965	10.00	25.00
		— RCA Promotional Albums issued in plain cardboard jackets . Note: Those catalog numbers markerd with an asterisk indicate the presence of at least one track by Elvis Presley on the album.—			
RCA Victor F70P-9681*	(M)	**E-Z Pop Programming #5**	1955	360.00	600.00
RCA Victor G70L-0108*	(M)	**E-Z Country Programming #2**	1955	360.00	600.00
RCA Victor G70L-0197*	(M)	**E-Z Pop Programming #6**	1956	300.00	500.00
RCA Victor G70L-0199*	(M)	**E-Z Country Programming #3**	1956	300.00	500.00
RCA Victor SPL-12-13	(M)	**Pop Shopper**	1955	10.00	25.00
RCA Victor SPL-12-29	(M)	**Pop Showcase In Sound** *(Paper pic. sleeve)*	1955	10.00	25.00
RCA Victor SP-33-4*	(M)	**"Untitled Sampler"**	1956	300.00	500.00
RCA Victor SP-33-10P*	(M)	**"Untitled Sampler"**	1958	150.00	300.00
RCA Victor SP-33-50-7	(M)	**Breck Introduces The New Golden Age Od Sound Albums**	1959	10.00	25.00
RCA Victor SP-33-59-7*	(M)	**February Sampler 59-7**	1959	150.00	300.00
RCA Victor SP-33-66*	(M)	**Christmas Programming From RCA Victor**	1959	300.00	500.00
		(Issued in a paper sleeve, priced separately below.)			
RCA Victor SP-33-66*	(M)	**Christmas Programming From RCA Victor**	1959		*See below*
		(White paper sleeve with a full-color cartoon of Santa and photos of the artists. Rare with a suggested Near Mint value of $1,500-2,500. Counterfeits are obvious black & white photocopies.)			
RCA Victor SP-33-27*	(M)	**August '59 Sampler**	1959	150.00	300.00
RCA Victor SP-33-54*	(M)	**October Christmas Sampler**	1959	150.00	300.00
RCA Victor SPS-33-96*	(S)	**October '60 Popular Stereo Sampler**	1963	60.00	150.00
RCA Victor SPS-33-141*	(S)	**October '61 Pop Sampler**	1963	60.00	150.00
RCA Victor SPS-33-162	(S)	**Sweetheart Soap Presents RCA Victor's Great Songs Of Romance**	1962	10.00	25.00
RCA Victor SPS-33-191*	(S)	**October '63 Pop Sampler**	1963	60.00	150.00
RCA Victor SPS-33-247*	(S)	**December '63 Pop Sampler**	1963	60.00	150.00
RCA Victor SPS-33-248	(S)	**December '63 Pop Sampler**	1963	10.00	25.00
RCA Victor SPS-33-272*	(S)	**April '64 Pop Sampler**	1965	60.00	150.00
RCA Victor SPS-33-331*	(S)	**April '65 Pop Sampler**	1965	60.00	150.00
RCA Victor SPS-33-347*	(S)	**August '65 Pop Sampler**	1965	60.00	150.00
RCA Victor SPS-33-403*	(S)	**April '66 Pop Sampler**	1966	60.00	150.00
RCA Victor SPS-33-525	(S)	**The Groupquake**	1968	10.00	25.00
RCA Victor RWS-0001*	(P)	**Robert W. Sarnoff-25 Years Of Leadership**	1973	80.00	200.00
RCA Victor (No number)*	(S)	**WRCA Plays The Hits For Your Customers**	1976	60.00	150.00
		— Each promo album above features at least one song by Elvis Presley.—			
Red Bird RB-20-102	(M)	**Red Bird Goldies**	196?	16.00	40.00
Regent MG-6015	(M)	**Rock & Roll**	195?	16.00	40.00
Regent MG-6042	(M)	**Rock & Roll Party**	195?	16.00	40.00

These two volumes of RCA Victor's Old 'N' Golden Goodies *deserve mention if only in the fact that the stereo information provided the customer by the record company is in error. While both albums carry the little "(e)" after their catalog number, RCA's way of indicating "electronically reprocessed stereo," several of the singles on both albums are, in fact, in true stereo.*

Label & Catalog #		Title	Year	VG+	NM
Relics CSFD-3	(M)	Chocolate Soup, Volume 3	198?	16.00	40.00
Relics LSD-1	(M)	Chocolate Soup, Volume 1	198?	16.00	40.00
Ren-Vell 317	(M)	Battle Of The Bands, Volume 1	1967	150.00	300.00
Rendezvous M-1314	(M)	Gone But Not Forgotten	196?	10.00	25.00
		(Rendezvous 1314 is a reissue of Class 5004.)			
Reprise RD-1	(DJ)	Beginning A New Tradition *(One-sided)*	1961	16.00	40.00
Reprise RD-3	(DJ)	Are You Ready? (Swing Along With Reprise)	1962	16.00	40.00
Reprise RD-4	(DJ)	A Special Gift To A Longtime Friend	1962	16.00	40.00
Reprise RD-5	(DJ)	The Most—			
		Look Who's Coming To Your House	1962	16.00	40.00
Reprise RD-7	(DJ)	$74,000,000 Talent Bonanza	1962	16.00	40.00
Reprise RD-9	(DJ)	Look Who's Coming To Your House	1962	16.00	40.00
Reprise PRO-112	(DJ)	A Salute To Nat King Cole	196?	40.00	100.00
Reprise R-6028	(M)	Reprise All-Star Spectacular	1962	10.00	25.00
Reprise R-96028	(S)	Reprise All-Star Spectacular	1962	8.00	20.00
Reprise R-6094	(M)	Surf's Up At Banzai Pipeline	1963	14.00	35.00
Reprise RS-6094	(P)	Surf's Up At Banzai Pipeline	1963	20.00	50.00
Reprise R-6116	(M)	The Great Hits From The Greatest Films	1963	8.00	20.00
Reprise R9-6116	(S)	The Great Hits From The Greatest Films	1963	10.00	25.00
Reprise 2MS-2031	(DJ)	The Strawberry Statement *(2 LPs. Sdtk)*	1970	30.00	75.00
		(Issued in a plain jacket with a "Rush release" sticker.)			
Riverside RLP-12-610	(M)	Banjo Songs Of The Southern Mountains	195?	10.00	25.00
Riverside RLP-12-617	(M)	Southern Mountain Folksongs And Ballads	195?	10.00	25.00
Riverside RLP-12-641	(M)	Chicago Mob Scene—			
		A Folk Song Jam Session	195?	10.00	25.00
Riverside S-2	(M)	Riverside Folksong Sampler	1956	10.00	25.00
Riviera R-0052	(M)	Blues In My Heart	1959	40.00	100.00
Roadside RBF-20	(M)	Roots: Rhythm & Blues	196?	12.00	30.00
Ronco LP-1001	(P)	Do It Now! *(Yellow label)*	1970	12.00	30.00
Roulette R-25021	(M)	Pajama Party *(Black label)*	195?	16.00	40.00
Roulette R-25059	(M)	Rock & Roll Record Hop	1959	12.00	30.00
Roulette R-25093	(M)	Rock & Roll Bandstand	1959	12.00	30.00
Roulette R-25106	(M)	Original Hit Records	1962	10.00	25.00
Roulette SR-25106	(S)	Original Hit Records	1962	12.00	30.00
Roulette R-25159	(M)	Murray The K's Sing Along			
		With The Original Golden Gassers	1962	8.00	20.00
Roulette SR-25159	(S)	Murray The K's Sing Along			
		With The Original Golden Gassers	1962	10.00	25.00
Roulette R-25191	(M)	Murray & Jockey The K's Golden Gassers	1963	8.00	20.00
Roulette SR-25191	(S)	Murray & Jockey The K's Golden Gassers	1963	10.00	25.00
Roulette R-25192	(M)	Murray & Jockey The K's			
		Golden Gassers For A Dance Party	1962	8.00	20.00
Roulette SR-25192	(S)	Murray & Jockey The K's			
		Golden Gassers For A Dance Party	1962	10.00	25.00
Roulette R-25304	(M)	20 Big Boss Favorites	1963	8.00	20.00
Roulette SR-25304	(S)	20 Big Boss Favorites	1963	10.00	25.00
Roxey	(M)	Acid Dreams	198?	16.00	40.00
Royale 1439	(M)	An Hour Of Irish Ballads	195?	10.00	25.00
RPM 3001	(M)	Rock & Roll Dance Party	195?	250.00	500.00
San Fran. Sound 11680	(S)	Fifth Pipe Dream *(Black & white cover)*	1968	60.00	150.00
San Fran. Sound 11680	(S)	Fifth Pipe Dream *(Color cover)*	1968	40.00	100.00
Satan SR-666	(M)	Signed D. C.	198?	10.00	25.00
Satan SR-1003	(M)	Riot City	198?	10.00	25.00
Savoy MG-15008	(10")	Rhythm & Blues	195?	80.00	200.00

Label & Catalog #		Title	Year	VG+	NM
Scepter SP-510	(M)	Murray The K's 1962 Golden Gassers	1963	8.00	20.00
Scepter SPS-510	(P)	Murray The K's 1962 Golden Gassers	1963	10.00	25.00
Scepter SP-518	(M)	The Group's Are The Greatest	1963	8.00	20.00
Scepter SPS-518	(P)	The Group's Are The Greatest	1963	10.00	25.00
Scepter SP-524	(M)	The Fifth Beatle			
		Gives You Their Golden Gassers	1964	8.00	20.00
Scepter SPS-524	(P)	The Fifth Beatle			
		Gives You Their Golden Gassers	1964	10.00	25.00
Score LP-4002	(M)	I Dig Rock & Roll	1957	100.00	250.00
Score LP-4018	(M)	Rock & Roll Sock Hop	1958	100.00	250.00
Screen Gems/Colgems	(DJ)	212 Hits (2 LPs)	196?	10.00	25.00
Screen Gems/Colgems	(DJ)	More Solid Gold Programming (2 LPs)	196?	12.00	30.00
Screen Gems/Columbia	(DJ)	Solid Gold-Gerry Goffin & Carole King	196?	20.00	50.00
Shelby Singleton Music 1	(DJ)	Songs For The Seventies (2 LPs)	1969	60.00	150.00
Shepherd 1300	(M)	Surf War	1963	14.00	35.00
Sidewalk T-5901	(M)	Freakout U.S.A.	1967	12.00	30.00
Sidewalk ST-5901	(E)	Freakout U.S.A.	1967	8.00	20.00
Sidewalk T-5911	(M)	Mary Jane (Soundtrack)	1968	12.00	30.00
Sidewalk DT-5911	(P)	Mary Jane (Soundtrack)	1968	8.00	20.00
Sidewalk ST-5913	(S)	Psych-Out (Soundtrack)	1968	16.00	40.00
Smash MGS-27018	(M)	Smash Hits	1963	8.00	20.00
Smash SRS-67018	(P)	Smash Hits	1963	10.00	25.00
Smash MGS-27038	(M)	Group Oldies But Goodies	1964	12.00	30.00
Smash SRS-67038	(P)	Group Oldies But Goodies	1964	16.00	40.00
Smash MGS-27052	(M)	All Time Smash Hits	1964	8.00	20.00
Smash SRS-67052	(P)	All Time Smash Hits	1964	10.00	25.00
Solar S-1000	(M)	Echoes In Time, Vol. 1	198?	14.00	35.00
Solar S-2000	(M)	Echoes In Time, Vol. 2	198?	14.00	35.00
Soma MG-1245	(M)	Big Hits Of Mid America	1968	30.00	75.00
Soma MG-1246	(M)	Big Hits Of Mid America, Volume 2	1968	30.00	75.00
Somerset P-1300	(M)	Rock 'N' Roll Dance Party	1954	30.00	75.00
Sounds Of Hawaii 5014	(M)	Waikiki Surf Battle, Volume 1	1964	80.00	200.00
Sounds Of Hawaii 5014	(M)	Waikiki Surf Battle, Volume 2	1964	80.00	200.00
Specialty SP-2112	(M)	Our Significant Hits (Black & gold label)	1963	30.00	75.00
Spivey LP-1015	(M)	Spivey's Blue Cavalcade	196?	16.00	40.00
Star SRM-101	(M)	Battle Of The Bands	1964	60.00	150.00
Starday SLP-115	(M)	The Bluegrass Special	196?	16.00	40.00
Starday SLP-138	(M)	Nashville Steel Guitar	1961	20.00	50.00
Starday SLP-164	(M)	Country Music Hall Of fame	1962	16.00	40.00
Starday SLP-176	(M)	Tennessee Guitar	1962	16.00	40.00
Starday SLP-233	(M)	Steel Guitar Hall Of Fame	1963	16.00	40.00
Starday SLP-250	(M)	Diesel Smoke, Dangerous Curves & Others	1963	10.00	25.00
Starday SLP-277	(M)	Unforgettable Country Instrumentals	1963	12.00	30.00
Starday SLP-293	(M)	Steel Guitar And Dobro Spectacular	1964	10.00	35.00
Starday SLP-306	(M)	Let's Hit The Road	1964	10.00	25.00
Starday SLP-324	(M)	Country Hitmaker #1	1964	16.00	40.00
Starday SLP-345	(M)	Spectacular C&W Instrumentals	1965	12.00	30.00
Starday SLP-346	(S)	Gone But Not Forgotten	1965	16.00	40.00
Starday SLP-350	(M)	Stars Of The Steel Guitar	1965	14.00	35.00
Starday SLP-357	(M)	That's Truck Drivin'	1965	10.00	25.00
Starday SLP-352	(M)	Queens Of Country Music	1965	16.00	40.00
		— Starday albums above have yellow labels.—			
Starla LPM-1960	(M)	Art Laboe's Memories Of El Monte	1960	30.00	75.00

Label & Catalog #		Title	Year	VG+	NM
Stax ST-702	(M)	Hits From The South	1962		See below
Stax STS-702	(S)	Hits From The South	1962		See below
		(This album has the same catalog number as Gus Cannon's "Walk Right In" album and may not have been released.)			
Stax ST-703	(M)	Treasure Chest Goodies	1962	16.00	40.00
Stax STS-703	(S)	Treasure Chest Goodies	1962	16.00	40.00
		(Stax 703 is a reissue of 702 above.)			
Stax/Volt 11	(DJ)	Stay In School, Don't Be A Dropout	1967	300.00	600.00
Stax ST-721	(M)	The Stax/Volt Revue: Live In London, Vol. 1	1967	8.00	20.00
Stax STS-721	(S)	The Stax/Volt Revue: Live In London, Vol. 1	1967	12.00	30.00
Stax ST-722	(M)	The Stax/Volt Revue: Live In London, Vol. 2	1967	8.00	20.00
Stax STS-722	(S)	The Stax/Volt Revue: Live In London, Vol. 2	1967	12.00	30.00
Stax ST-726	(M)	Memphis Gold, Volume 2	1967	12.00	30.00
Stax STS-726	(S)	Memphis Gold, Volume 2	1967	10.00	25.00
Stax ST-2-2007	(M)	Soul Explosion (2 LPs)	1969	10.00	25.00
Stax ST-2-2024	(M)	Boy Meets Girl (2 LPs. White label promo)	1969	10.00	25.00
Stax	(DJ)	Stax... Once You've Been There You Know You're Home (2 LPs)	197?	16.00	40.00
Stax SLE-0373	(DJ)	Dave Clark Thru '72	1972	20.00	50.00
		(Staz 0373 consists of promo man Dave Clark reminiscing about the early days of the business.)			
Stinson SLP-5	(10")	Folksay, Volume I	195?	16.00	40.00
Stinson SLP-6	(10")	Folksay, Volume II	195?	16.00	40.00
Stinson SLP-9	(10")	Folksay, Volume III	195?	16.00	40.00
Stinson SLP-11	(10")	Folksay, Volume IV	195?	16.00	40.00
Stinson SLP-12	(10")	Folksay, Volume V	195?	16.00	40.00
Stinson SLP-13	(10")	Folksay, Volume VI	195?	16.00	40.00
Stinson SLP-54	(M)	Southern Mountain Hoedowns	195?	10.00	25.00
Straight STS-1056	(S)	Naked Angels (Soundtrack)	1969	20.00	50.00
Sue LP-1021	(M)	The Sue Story (Black cover)	196?	40.00	100.00
Sue LP-1021	(M)	The Sue Story (Orange cover)	196?	30.00	75.00
Sue LP-1021	(M)	Old Goodies	196?	30.00	75.00
Sun LP-1250	(M)	Sun's Gold Hits	1961	40.00	100.00
Sutton SU-321	(M)	Jumpin'	1961	16.00	40.00
Sutton SSU-321	(S)	Jumpin'	1961	20.00	50.00
Sutton SU-323	(M)	Current Craze	1961	16.00	40.00
Sutton SSU-323	(S)	Current Craze	1961	20.00	50.00
Sutton SU-325	(M)	Great Popular Oldies, Volume 2	1961	16.00	40.00
Sutton SSU-325	(S)	Great Popular Oldies, Volume 2	1961	20.00	50.00
Swan LP-501	(M)	Treasure Chest Of Hits	1960	30.00	75.00
Swan LP-506	(M)	Twistin' All Night Long	1961	14.00	35.00
Swan LP-512	(M)	Hits I Forgot To Buy	1963	20.00	50.00
T.V.A.A.	(M)	The Magic Carpet Ride	198?	20.00	50.00
Tamla T-224	(M)	Tamla Special #1	1962	30.00	75.00
		("Tamla Special #1" was issued with several different covers. . .)			
Tamla T-244	(M)	Recorded Live At The Regal	1963		Unreleased
Tamla T-256	(M)	A Collection Of 16 Original Big Hits, Vol. 2	1964	8.00	20.00
Tamla TS-256	(S)	A Collection Of 16 Original Big Hits, Vol. 2	1967	16.00	40.00
Tamla T-264	(M)	Recorded Live The Motortown Revue In Paris	1965	10.00	25.00
Tamla TS-264	(S)	Recorded Live The Motortown Revue In Paris	1965	12.00	30.00
Teem 5002	(M)	Guaranteed To Please	196?	12.00	30.00
Teem 5003	(M)	Greatest Teenage Hits Of All Time	196?	14.00	35.00
Teem 5004	(M)	Approved By 10,000,000	196?	14.00	35.00
Teem 5005	(M)	Kings Sing The Blues	196?	12.00	30.00
Tempo Two T-2	(M)	A New High (With poster)	196?	40.00	100.00
Time T-10000	(M)	Goodies Old And New	1961	12.00	30.00
Time ST-70000	(S)	Goodies Old And New	1961	12.00	30.00

Label & Catalog #		Title	Year	VG+	NM
Time T-10006	(M)	**Riot In Blues**	1961	**30.00**	**75.00**
Time ST-70006	(S)	**Riot In Blues**	1961	**40.00**	**100.00**
Time 52082	(M)	**Original Goodies**	196?	**12.00**	**30.00**
Time S-2082	(S)	**Original Goodies**	196?	**12.00**	**30.00**
Time Tunnel 12174-25	(M)	**Pennsylvania Unknowns**	198?	**20.00**	**50.00**
Together ST-1014	(S)	**Early L.A.**	1971	**12.00**	**30.00**
Tops LP-941	(10")	**Western Favorites**	195?	**20.00**	**50.00**
Tower T-5007	(M)	**Three At The Top**	1965	**10.00**	**25.00**
Tower DT-5007	(E)	**Three At The Top**	1965	**8.00**	**20.00**
Tower T-5065	(M)	**Riot On Sunset Strip** (Soundtrack)	1967	**16.00**	**40.00**
Tower DT-5065	(E)	**Riot On Sunset Strip** (Soundtrack)	1967	**12.00**	**30.00**
Tower DT-5148	(E)	**Best Of The Soundtracks**	1969	**10.00**	**25.00**
Tower DT-5157	(P)	**Instant Replay**	1969	**12.00**	**30.00**
Tower PRO-4409/10	(M)	**Tower Sept. 1967 Album Releases**	1967	**80.00**	**200.00**
		(Tower 4409/10 was issued with a 12" x 12" booklet of cover slicks, priced separately below.)			
Tower PRO-4409/10	(M)	**Tower Sept. 1967 Album Releases Booklet**	1967	**40.00**	**100.00**
Tradition TLP-1007	(M)	**Instrumental Music Of The Southern Appalachians**	1957	**12.00**	**30.00**
Tradition TLP-1020	(M)	**Negro Prison Songs From The Mississippi State Penitentiary**	195?	**12.00**	**30.00**
Tradition TLP-1029	(M)	**Texas Folk Songs**	1958	**12.00**	**30.00**
Trash 0001	(M)	**Ear Piercing Punk**	198?	**20.00**	**50.00**
Trousdale Music Pub.	(S)	**What's Going On Here?**	1966	**60.00**	**150.00**
		(Publishers demo features unreleased Sloan & Barri material.)			
20th Century TFM-3131	(M)	**Surf Party** (Soundtrack)	1964	**12.00**	**30.00**
20th Century TFS-4131	(S)	**Surf Party** (Soundtrack)	1964	**16.00**	**40.00**
Underworld 1205	(M)	**Nightmares From The Underworld, Vol. 2**	198?	**16.00**	**40.00**
Unique LP-109	(M)	**Music James Dean Lived By**	196?	**14.00**	**35.00**
United Arts. UAL-4027	(M)	**Blues In The Mississippi Night**	1959	**10.00**	**25.00**
United Arts. UAS-5027	(S)	**Blues In The Mississippi Night**	1959	**10.00**	**25.00**
United Arts. SP-70	(DJ)	**N. A. P. R. A. 72 Vote**	1972	**16.00**	**40.00**
Universal Unlimited Pict.	(DJ)	**Rock, Pretty Baby** (10" on red vinyl)	1956		See below
		(This radio transcription from the film of the same name issued by the movie production company has a suggested Near Mint value of $2,000-4,000. The soundtrack was issued commercially as Decca DL-8429 and can be found in the Various Artists listings for Decca.)			
Unlimited Prod LP-003	(M)	**Dirty Water**	198?	**10.00**	**25.00**
Unlimited Prod. LP-1001	(M)	**Midwest Vs. The Rest**	198?	**16.00**	**40.00**
Unlimited Prod. LP-1002	(M)	**Midwest Vs. Canada**	198?	**16.00**	**40.00**
USA LP-100	(M)	**The KAAY Silver Dollar Special, Vol. i**	196?	**20.00**	**50.00**
Vanguard SRV-125	(M)	**The Sound Of Folk Music**	196?	**8.00**	**20.00**
Vanguard SRV-125SD	(S)	**The Sound Of Folk Music**	196?	**10.00**	**25.00**
Vanguard SRV-140	(M)	**The Sound Of Folk Music, Vol. 2**	196?	**8.00**	**20.00**
Vanguard SRV-140SD	(S)	**The Sound Of Folk Music, Vol. 2**	196?	**10.00**	**25.00**
Vanguard VRS-9144	(M)	**Newport Broadside**	1964	**10.00**	**25.00**
Vanguard VSD-79144	(E)	**Newport Broadside**	1964	**8.00**	**20.00**
Vanguard VRS-9145	(M)	**Blues At Newport**	1964	**8.00**	**20.00**
Vanguard VSD-79145	(S)	**Blues At Newport**	1964	**10.00**	**25.00**
Vanguard VRS-9148	(M)	**Evening Concerts At Newport, Volume 1**	1964	**10.00**	**25.00**
Vanguard VSD-79148	(E)	**Evening Concerts At Newport, Volume 1**	1964	**8.00**	**20.00**
Vanguard VRS-9149	(M)	**Evening Concerts At Newport, Volume 2**	1964	**10.00**	**25.00**
Vanguard VSD-79149	(E)	**Evening Concerts At Newport, Volume 2**	1964	**8.00**	**20.00**

Label & Catalog #		Title	Year	VG+	NM
Vanguard VRS-9216	(M)	Chicago/The Blues/Today! (Vol. 1)	1965	8.00	20.00
Vanguard VSD-79216	(S)	Chicago/The Blues/Today! (Vol. 1)	1965	10.00	25.00
Vanguard VRS-9217	(M)	Chicago/The Blues/Today! (Vol. 2)	1965	8.00	20.00
Vanguard VSD-79217	(S)	Chicago/The Blues/Today! (Vol. 2)	1965	10.00	25.00
Vanguard VRS-9218	(M)	Chicago/The Blues/Today! (Vol. 3)	1965	8.00	20.00
Vanguard VSD-79218	(S)	Chicago/The Blues/Today! (Vol. 3)	1965	10.00	25.00
Vanguard VRS-9225	(M)	The Newport Folk Festival, 1965	1965	8.00	20.00
Vanguard VSD-79225	(S)	The Newport Folk Festival, 1965	1965	10.00	25.00
Vault LP-103	(M)	Oldies, Goodies And Woodies	1964	16.00	40.00
Vault VS-103	(S)	Oldies, Goodies And Woodies	1964	20.00	50.00
Vault LP-104	(M)	Hot Rod City	1964	20.00	50.00
Vault VS-104	(S)	Hot Rod City	1964	30.00	75.00
Vault LP-113	(M)	West Coast Love-In	1967	12.00	30.00
Vault SLP-113	(S)	West Coast Love-In	1967	16.00	40.00
Vault VS-119	(P)	San Francisco Roots	1968	20.00	50.00
		(Vault 119 was reissued as JAS 5001.)			
Vee Jay LP-100	(M)	Kat's Karavan	1957	20.00	50.00
Vee Jay LP-1020	(M)	The Blues	1962	16.00	40.00
Vee Jay LP-1021	(M)	Teen Delights	1962	16.00	40.00
Vee Jay LP-1036	(M)	Teen Delights, Volume 2	1962	16.00	40.00
Vee Jay LP-1042	(M)	Tomorrow's Hits	1962	16.00	40.00
Vee Jay LP-1051	(M)	Unavailable	1962	16.00	40.00
Vee Jay LP-1074	(M)	Soul Meeting Saturday Night Hootenanny Style	1964	12.00	30.00
Vee Jay VJS-1074	(S)	Soul Meeting Saturday Night Hootenanny Style	1964	20.00	50.00
Vee Jay LP-1084	(M)	The Original Nitty Gritty	1964	12.00	30.00
Vee Jay VJS-1084	(S)	The Original Nitty Gritty	1964	20.00	50.00
Vee Jay LP-1112	(M)	Great Hits Of 1964	1964	12.00	30.00
Vee Jay SR-1112	(P)	Great Hits Of 1964	1964	20.00	50.00
Vee Jay LP-1136	(M)	More Great Hits Of 1964 & Other Golden Goodies	1965	12.00	30.00
Vee Jay SR-1136	(P)	More Great Hits Of 1964 & Other Golden Goodies	1965	20.00	50.00
Veritas XTV-62202	(M)	Folksingers 'Round Harvard Square	1959	100.00	300.00
		("Folksinger..." features Joan Baez's first appearance on an album.)			
Vernon 521	(M)	Chart Busters	196?	16.00	40.00
Verve V-2083	(M)	Teen Time: Refer to Ricky Nelson			
Verve V6-653	(M)	24 Karat Gold From The Underground (2 LPs)	1968	10.00	25.00
Verve/Folkways FT-3011	(M)	Blues Box (3 LPs)	1966	10.00	25.00
Verve/Folkways FTS-3011	(S)	Blues Box (3 LPs)	1966	12.00	30.00
Wand WDM-651	(M)	Rocket To The Stars	1961	20.00	50.00
Wand WDM-652	(M)	Show Stoppers	1961	16.00	40.00
Wand WDM-660	(M)	The Greatest Sing Their Soul Favorites	1964	16.00	40.00
Wand WDM-671	(M)	How To Stuff A Wild Bikini (Soundtrack)	1965	8.00	20.00
Wand WDS-671	(S)	How To Stuff A Wild Bikini (Soundtrack)	1965	12.00	30.00
Wand WDM-677	(M)	Greatest Hits From The Soul Of Texas	1966	12.00	30.00
Wand WDS-677	(S)	Greatest Hits From The Soul Of Texas	1966	16.00	40.00
Warner Bros. (No #)	(DJ)	Jamboree (Soundtrack)	1955		See below
		("Jamboree" is rare with suggested values in VG of $300-500; in VG+ of $600-1,000; and in NM of $1,500-3,000.)			
Warner Bros. X-1307	(M)	You Ain't Heard Nothin' Yet!	1959	12.00	30.00
Warner Bros. SX-1307	(S)	You Ain't Heard Nothin' Yet!	1959	16.00	40.00
Warner Bros. W-1337	(M)	We Wish You A Merry Christmas	1960	10.00	25.00
Warner Bros. WS-1337	(S)	We Wish You A Merry Christmas	1960	12.00	30.00
Warner Bros. W-1448	(M)	Hits Of The Hops	1962	8.00	20.00
Warner Bros. WS-1448	(M)	Hits Of The Hops	1962	10.00	25.00
Warner Bros. W-1511	(M)	Hoot Tonight	1963	8.00	20.00
Warner Bros. WS-1511	(S)	Hoot Tonight	1963	10.00	25.00

Label & Catalog #		Title	Year	VG+	NM
Warner Bros. W-1519	(M)	**Palm Springs Weekend** *(Soundtrack)*	1963	10.00	25.00
Warner Bros. WS-1519	(S)	**Palm Springs Weekend** *(Soundtrack)*	1963	14.00	35.00
Warner Bros. BS-1846	(S)	**Performance** *(Soundtrack)*	1970	10.00	25.00
		—Special/Promotional Releases—			
Warner Bros. 8467/8	(M)	**Christmas Hits From Warner Bros.**	1959	20.00	50.00
		(W.B. 8467 is a compilation of Christmas singles.)			
Warner/Reprise PRO-368	(S)	**Zapped** *(Collage cover)*	1969	16.00	40.00
		(Original covers feature a black & white collage.)			
Warner/Reprise PRO-368	(S)	**Zapped** *(Photo cover)*	1969	10.00	25.00
		(Later covers have a black & white photo of Frank Zappa.)			
Warner/Reprise (10")	(S)	**Woodstock** *(Radio spots)*	1970	200.00	400.00
Warner/Reprise PRO-534	(S)	**Voter Registration Spots**	1972	20.00	50.00
Warner/Reprise PRO-604	(S)	**Burbank's Finest—**			
		100% All Meat *(2 LPs on brown vinyl)*	1975	20.00	50.00
Warner/Reprise PRO-3328	(S)	**Winter Warnerland**	1988	10.00	25.00
		(2 LPs on colored vinyl)			
Warner/Spector 9103	(S)	**Phil Spector's Christmas Album:** *Refer to* Phil Spector			
Warner/Spector 9104	(P)	**Phil Spector's 20 Greatest Hits:** *Refer to* Phil Spector			
Warwick W-2008	(M)	**Gold Hits**	1960	24.00	60.00
Warwick W-2025	(M)	**Best Of The R&B Groups**	1961	30.00	75.00
Warwick W-2026	(M)	**Best Of Rhythm And Blues**	1961	24.00	60.00
Warwick W-2044	(M)	**More Gold Hits, Volume 2**	1961	24.00	60.00
Warwick W-2048	(M)	**Still More Gold Hits, Volume 3**	1962	24.00	60.00
Welk Music *(No number)*	(M)	**Blue Christmas**	1984	20.00	50.00
Wellington 1004	(M)	**Glimpses, Vol. 4**	198?	8.00	20.00
Wellington 201085	(M)	**Glimpses, Vol. 1**	198?	20.00	50.00
Wellington 201086	(M)	**Glimpses, Vol. 2**	198?	14.00	35.00
Wellington 201087	(M)	**Glimpses, Vol. 3**	198?	14.00	35.00
Westchester 1005	(M)	**Friday At The Cage A Go Go**	196?	50.00	125.00
Westminster WF-12008	(M)	**World Festival Of Folk Song And Folk Dance**	1953	10.00	25.00
Westminster WF-12009	(M)	**Folk Music Festivals: The**			
		International Musical Eisteddfod *(2 LPs)*	1953	12.00	30.00
Westminster WP-6026	(M)	**American Children Sing Christmas Carols**	1956	10.00	25.00
White Rabbit LP-001	(M)	**Mind Blowers**	198?	20.00	50.00
White Whale WWS-7125	(S)	**Footprints In Time**	1970	10.00	25.00
White Whale WWS-7129	(S)	**Super Groups From Holland**	1970	10.00	25.00
White Whale WWS-7130	(S)	**Dutch Explosion**	1970	12.00	30.00
Winley 6001	(M)	**Everybody Digs The Boss Record Hop**	195?	150.00	300.00
World Pacific WP-1254	(M)	**Saturday Night At The Coffee House**	1958	12.00	30.00
World Pacific WPS-21898	(S)	**Bluegrass Special**	196?	12.00	30.00
Wreckord Wrack 1025	(M)	**Off The Wall, Vol. 1**	198?	30.00	75.00
Wreckord Wrack 1301	(M)	**Off The Wall, Vol. 2**	198?	30.00	75.00
Zephyr ZP-12010H	(M)	**Premiere**	195?	12.00	30.00

And A Few Late Additions

After the bulk of the innards of this volume was completed and paginated (i.e., more or less ready for the camera), I received two lists from long-time contributors and buds Stephen Braitman and Charlie Ess-meier. As is their wont, both gentle men not only listed items they felt imperative for inclusion, they also added a sort of running commentary on why each item hadda be in the book. I have enjoyed both of their pithy remarks in the past and figured that a nice way to spice up this section was to include snippets of their views. So, listings below accompanied by a a quotation are either followed by a "SB" for Steve's remarks or a "CE" for Charlie's. Snide remarks regarding the state of collecting and the many twits this biz seems to attract have been prudently pruned by Ye Olde Editor. Finally, the list of Record Club releases below was provided by George Bigelow. . .

APPLE PIE MOTHERHOOD BAND, THE
"Neglected hard psych rock. . ." — SB

Atlantic SD-8189	(S)	The Apple Pie Motherhood Band	1968	12.00	30.00
Atlantic SD-8233	(S)	Apple Pie	1969	12.00	30.00

BEATLES, THE

United Arts. UAS-6366	(S)	A Hard Day's Night *(Pink vinyl)*	197?		*See below*

(A copy of this soundtrack was recently found with the later pink & black label pressed on pink vinyl;. Apparently a surreptitious pressing by an employee. A one-of-a-kind Beatles item with no professional transactions from which to derive a value but you know it's gonna go for thousands. . .)

BLACKFOOT, J. D.

Bison B-44	(S)	Live In St. Louis, July 16, 1982	1982	20.00	50.00

BLUES IMAGE

Atco SD-33-300	(S)	Blues Image	1969	10.00	25.00

("Contains their hit but surprisingly hard to find." — CE)

BRASELLE, KEEFE

RKO ULP-126	(M)	The Modern Minstrel	1957	16.00	40.00

BROCKETT, JAIME

Capitol ST-678	(S)	Remember The Wind And The Rain	1969	14.00	35.00

BROWN, ELAINE
"A neglected, revolutionary funk album in The Last Poets vein by a member of the Black Panthers." — SB

Vault VS-131	(S)	Seize The Time	1969	20.00	50.00

BUSH, KATE: *Refer to* **JIMI HENDRIX**

CAMP, HAMILTON

Elektra EKL-278	(M)	Paths Of Victory	1965	12.00	30.00
Elektra EKS-7278	(S)	Paths Of Victory	1965	16.00	40.00

("Though his Warner Bros. album includes his hit, this is the one to have, particularly for its many Dylan songs." — SB)

CAMPER VAN BEETHOVEN
"One of the more significant bands of the past decade. . ." — SB

Independent Proj. IP-016	(S)	Telephone Free Landslide Victory	1985	60.00	150.00

(Original pressing of approximately 1,000 copies issued in hand-made covers with letterpress design with inserts in a stickered shrinkwrap.)

Independent Proj. IP-016	(S)	Telephone Free Landslide Victory	1985	20.00	50.00

(Second pressing of 1,175 copies in regular covers.)

CASH, JOHNNY

Sun T-90668	(M)	Johnny Cash Sings The Songs That Made Him Famous *(Capitol Record Club)*	196?	20.00	50.00
Sun DT-90668	(E)	Johnny Cash Sings The Songs That Made Him Famous *(Capitol Record Club)*	196?	20.00	50.00

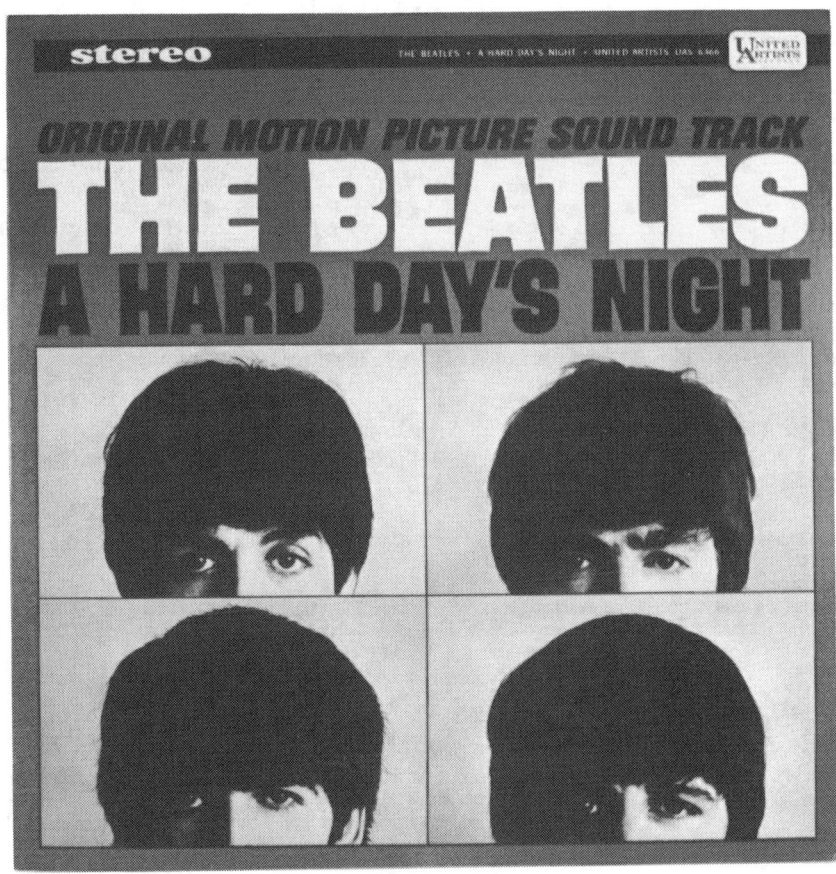

As familiar as this album cover is to collectors everywhere— copies can be found in collectors conventions and stores, at your local swap meet or thrift shop, and it is seemingly ubiquitous at yard and garage sales everywhere— it is also a lesson to the wise to always— always— check what's between the front and back covers. A collector at a yard sale in southern California browsing through a collection of old albums, most of them having seen better days years before, came upon, yes, another copy of A Hard Day's Night. Girding himself for yet another overdone copy, he was astounded to see a nearly mint original stereo pressing slip from the jacket into his hands. And the damned thing was on pink vinyl! For 50¢, yet. As I write this, he has supposedly accepted the first payment of a $10,000 offer for this one-of-a-kind album.

Label & Catalog #		Title	Year	VG+	NM
Columbia D-363	(M)	**Legends & Love Songs** (*Columbia Record Club*)	196?	**8.00**	**20.00**
Columbia DS-363	(S)	**Legends & Love Songs** (*Columbia Record Club*)	196?	**10.00**	**25.00**

CHARLES, RAY

ABC-Para. T-90625	(M)	**Crying Time** (*Capitol Record Club*)	196?	**8.00**	**20.00**
ABC-Para. ST-90625	(S)	**Crying Time** (*Capitol Record Club*)	196?	**10.00**	**25.00**

CHER

Casablanca NBPIX-7133	(S)	**Take Me Home** (*Picture disc*)	1979	**16.00**	**40.00**

("*Last time I advertised one for $40, I had five calls. Even the stores here in SLC charge $25 for it!*" — CE)

CHROME

"*The first albums by this influential punk electronic experimental band.*" — SB

Siren (No number)	(S)	**The Visitation**	1976	**100.00**	**250.00**

(*Original pressing of 25 copies issued in white jackets with spray-painted titles plus colored photocopies as inserts.*)

Siren (No number)	(S)	**The Visitation** (*Standard cover*)	1976	**40.00**	**100.00**
Siren (No number)	(S)	**Alien Soundtracks**	1977	**40.00**	**100.00**

(*With inserts and foil sticker on shrinkwrap.*)

Siren (No number)	(S)	**Half Machine Lip Moves** (*With poster*)	1978	**20.00**	**50.00**

CHRYSALIS

"*A good psych album often overlooked. Not part of MGM's "Bosstown" hype.*" — SB

MGM E-4547	(M)	**Definition**	1968	**10.00**	**25.00**
MGM SE-4547	(S)	**Definition**	1968	**12.00**	**30.00**

COLLINS, SHIRLEY & DOROTHY

"*Moody English folksingers. Very collectable in England though a bit unknown in the U.S.*" — SB

Harvest SKAO-370	(S)	**Anthems In Eden**	1969	**20.00**	**50.00**

DION

Laurie DT-91577	(E)	**Abraham, Martin & John** (*Capitol Rec. Club*)	1968	**10.00**	**25.00**

DIRE STRAITS

Warner Bros. WB-23738	(S)	**Love Over Gold** (*Promo on Quiex II vinyl*)	1982	**20.00**	**50.00**
Warner Bros. WB-27085	(S)	**Alchemy** (*2 LPs. Promo on Quiex II vinyl*)	1984	**20.00**	**50.00**
Warner Bros. WB-25264	(S)	**Brothers In Arms** (*Promo on Quiex II vinyl*)	1985	**20.00**	**50.00**

DON & THE GOODTIMES

Wand WDM-679	(M)	**Where The Action Is**	1968	**12.00**	**30.00**

DYLAN, BOB

Columbia CS-8786	(S)	**The Freewheelin' Bob Dylan** (*Red vinyl*)	197?		*See below*
Columbia CS-8993	(S)	**Another Side Of Bob Dylan** (*Blue vinyl*)	197?		*See below*

(*Two one-of-a-kind colored vinyl pressings on the red & gold label made surreptitiously by a CBS employee. There are no transactions from which to even hazard an estimated value.*)

EDDY, DUANE

Jamie T-90682	(M)	**Have "Twangy" Guitar, Will Travel**	196?	**20.00**	**50.00**
Jamie ST-90682	(P)	**Have "Twangy" Guitar, Will Travel**	196?	**30.00**	**75.00**

(*Capitol Record Club*)

ELLIE POP

Mainstream S-6115	(S)	**Ellie Pop**	1968	**20.00**	**50.00**

FAHEY, JOHN

"*John Fahey deserves mention, particularly his early self-released albums on his own label, Takoma. The problem is the discographical accuracy for Takoma is difficult, given that he kept the albums in print and there are many label and cover variations.*" — SB

Takoma C-1002	(M)	**Blind Joe Death**	196?	**16.00**	**40.00**
Takoma C-1003	(S)	**John Fahey—Guitar**	1964	**16.00**	**40.00**
Takoma C-1004	(S)	**Dance Of Death** (**& Other Plantation Favorites**)	1965	**16.00**	**40.00**
Takoma C-1008	(S)	**The Great San Bernadino Birthday Party**	1966	**10.00**	**25.00**

— *Takoma albums above have black & silver labels.*—

Riverboat RB-1	(M)	**The Transfiguration** **Of Blind Joe Death** (*With booklet*)	1966	**30.00**	**75.00**

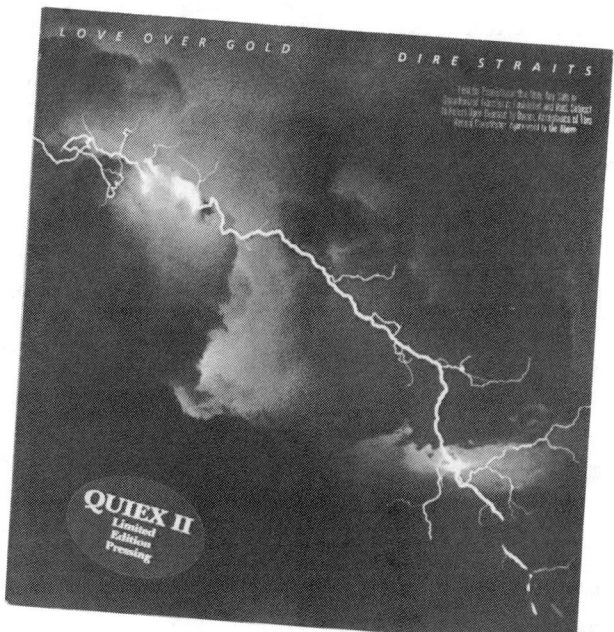

There two by Dire Straits, along with Alchemy, were issued promotionally on "Quiex II" vinyl and are very hot with audiophiles. Charlie Essmeier, whose name appears in this book more than mine, exclaims "I get $50 each for the Quiex IIs. I'm not twisting arms. I advertise them and they sell. . . Quickly."

Label & Catalog #		Title	Year	VG+	NM
Takoma C-1014	(S)	**Days Have Gone By**	1967	10.00	25.00
Vanguard VRS-9259	(M)	**Requia**	1967	8.00	20.00
Vanguard VSD-79259	(S)	**Requia**	1967	10.00	25.00
Vanguard VSD-79293	(S)	**The Yellow Princess**	1968	10.00	25.00
Takoma C-1019	(S)	**The Voice Of The Turtle** (Gatefold jacket + book)	1968	12.00	30.00
Takoma C-1020	(S)	**The New Possibility** (Gatefold jacket + book)	1971	10.00	25.00
Takoma C-1030	(S)	**America** (Gatefold jacket + book)	1971	10.00	25.00

FAITHFUL, MARIANNE

London LL-3452	(M)	**Go Away From My World**	1965	8.00	20.00
London PS-452	(S)	**Go Away From My World**	1965	10.00	25.00

("There are two versions: One credits "Executive Producer: Andrew Loog Oldham," the other leaves this off. Which came first?" — SB)

FLEETWOOD MAC

Epic LN-24416	(M)	**English Rose** (White label promo)	1969	40.00	100.00

FOLEY, RED

Decca DL-38068	(M)	**Gratefully**	1958	40.00	100.00

(DL-38068 was manufactured for Dickies Work & Casual Clothes)

FOUR GIRLS, THE

The Four Girls are Jane Russell, Rhonda Fleming, Connie Haines, Beryl Davis and Della Russell. I know; that's five, but that's what the cover says. . .

Coral CRL-57158	(M)	**Make A Joyful Noise Unto The Lord**	1957	30.00	75.00

FREEMAN, EVELYN, & THE EXCITING VOICES

Bel Canto SR-1010	(M)	**Evelyn Freeman & The Exciting Voices**	196?		See below

(Group vocal setting. Gold foil cover with a blue vinyl record. Rare with a suggested NM value of $50-150.)

Bel Canto SR-1010	(M)	**Evelyn Freeman & The Exciting Voices**	196?		See below

(Photo cover on blue vinyl. Rare with a suggested NM value of $50-150.)

GAME THEORY

"Along with True West, the leaders of the "Davis scene." This first LP was packaged in a big plastic bag with a cover sheet pasted on plus inserts." — SB

Rational ION-003	(S)	**Blaze Of Glory**	1982	30.00	75.00

GILLESPIE, DANA

"English art pop produced by Mike Vickers with lots of connections." — SB

London PS-540	(S)	**Foolish Seasons**	1968	12.00	30.00

HEAD OVER HEELS

"Like Granicus and SRC, another increasingly rare excellent hard rock album." — SB

Capitol ST-797	(S)	**Head Over Heels**	1970	24.00	60.00

HENDRIX, JIMI

Reprise R-6261	(M)	**Are You Experienced** (Brown & orange label)	1968		See below
Reprise R-6281	(M)	**Axis: Bold As Love** (Brown & orange label)	1968		See below

("Believe it or not, R-6281 exists in mono on the brown & orange label. Substantially rarer than the original, even if it is a later pressing."— CE. Since the second album exists this way, I have also listed the first with both having a suggested Near Mint value of $500-1,000.)

EMI America 17171	(DJ)	**Band Of Gypsys 2**	198?		See below

(Prototype pressings used to test colored vinyl for Kate Bush's "Hounds Of Love." Labels credit Ms. Bush's album, although the discs play one side of BOG 2 on both sides.)

HENRY TREE

Mainstream S-6129	(S)	**Electric Holy Man**	1968	20.00	50.00

HONDELLS, THE

Mercury MG-20940	(M)	**Go Little Honda**	1964		See below
Mercury SR-60940	(S)	**Go Little Honda**	1964		See below

(The Hondells first album has two labels, red with the Mercury logo in blue, and red with the logo in white? Is one a later pressing?)

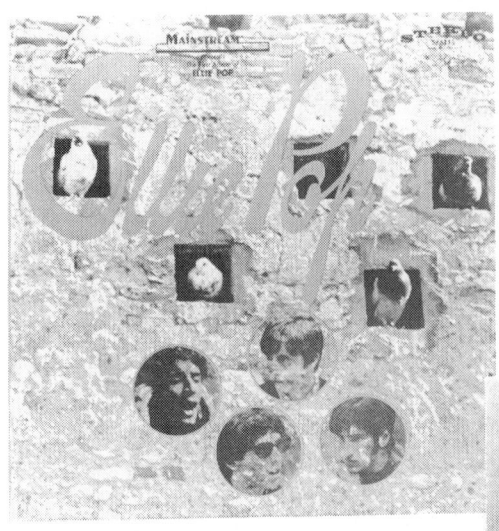

Speaking for these albums here, one each by Ellie Pop, Henry Tree, and Lacewing, is Mr. Stephen Braitman: "These three albums are just a sampling of the garage/psychedelia on the Mainstream label, which are all becoming more and more collectible as people realize that there are gems in the dustbin, so to speak." — SB

Label & Catalog #		Title	Year	VG+	NM
HUMBLEBUMS, THE					
With Gerry Rafferty and Billy Connolly.					
Liberty LST-7636	(S)	**The Humblebums**	*1968*	**14.00**	**35.00**
Liberty LST-7656	(S)	**Open Up The Door**	*1969*	**14.00**	**35.00**
IMPRESSIONS, THE					
ABC-Para. T-90520	(M)	**One By One** *(Capitol Record Club)*	*1965*	**10.00**	**25.00**
ABC-Para. ST-90520	(S)	**One By One** *(Capitol Record Club)*	*1965*	**12.00**	**30.00**
IT'S A BEAUTIFUL DAY					
Columbia CS-9768	(S)	**It's A Beautiful Day** *(Red & gold label)*	*1970*	**10.00**	**25.00**
JACKSON, MAHALIA					
Apollo LP-474	(M)	**In The Upper Room**	*195?*		*See below*
Apollo LP-482	(M)	**No Matter How You Pray**	*195?*		*See below*
Apollo LP-486	(M)	**Mahalia**	*195?*		*See below*

(The Apollo albums above feature Ms. Jackson in a group setting with uncredited backing vocal by The Larks. This little known aspect of the recording should make the album of interest to rhythm'n blues group vocal collectors leaving us with a suggested NM value of $150-300 for 474 and $100-200 for 482 and 486.)

Label & Catalog #		Title	Year	VG+	NM
JAMES, ETTA					
Crown CLP-5234	(M)	**The Best Of Etta James**	*1962*	**16.00**	**40.00**
Crown CLP-5360	(M)	**Etta James**	*1963*	**12.00**	**30.00**
Crown CST-360	(E)	**Etta James**	*1963*	**6.00**	**15.00**
JONES, GEORGE					
Starday T-90080	(M)	**George Jones Sings His Greatest Hits**	*196?*	**20.00**	**50.00**
Starday ST-90080	(E)	**George Jones Sings His Greatest Hits** *(Capitol Record Club)*	*196?*	**20.00**	**50.00**
Columbia P2M-5094	(M)	**Country Heart** *(2 LPs. Columbia Record Club)*	*196?*	**10.00**	**25.00**
Columbia P2S-5094	(S)	**Country Heart** *(2 LPs. Columbia Record Club)*	*196?*	**12.00**	**30.00**
KINGSMEN, THE					
Wand ST-91011	(S)	**Up And Away** *(Capitol Record Club)*	*196?*	**12.00**	**30.00**

LA LUPE
"Oddball release by the Queen of Latin Soul . . . has her crooning hits of the day like "Touch Me" and "Down On Me" in her heavy "Spanglish" accent. Endearing, particularly to the Martin Denny crowd." — SB

Roulette SR-42024	(S)	**The Queen Does Her Own Thing**	*1968*	**12.00**	**30.00**
LACEWING					
Mainstream S-6132	(S)	**Lacewing**	*1968*	**20.00**	**50.00**
LED ZEPPELIN					
Atlantic SD-8216	(S)	**Led Zeppelin** *(Laminated cover)*	*197?*	**80.00**	**200.00**
Atlantic SD-8236	(S)	**Led Zeppelin II** *(Laminated cover)*	*197?*	**80.00**	**200.00**
Atlantic SD-7021	(S)	**Led Zeppelin III** *(Laminated cover)*	*197?*	**80.00**	**200.00**

(Atlantic 8216, 8236 and 7021 above have green & orange labels with "GEMA" on the side in a specially laminated cover. These were manufactured in the U.S. for export to W. Germany.)

Atlantic SD-7208	(DJ)	**Led Zeppelin IV**	*1971*	**200.00**	**400.00**

(Advance white label promos issued in plain white jackets with "New Led Zeppelin LP" rubber-stamped.)

LEOPARDS, THE
"Transcendent Kinks-style rock. Extremely rare independent release." — SB

Moon 300	(S)	**Kansas City Slickers**	*1977*	**60.00**	**150.00**

LITTLE BILL & THE BLUE NOTES

Camelot J-102	(M)	**The Fiesta Club Presents Little Bill & The Blue Notes**	*196?*		*See below*

("Only 1,000 copies were made and [Little] Bill Englehart claims some were sold at the club . . . the rest might have been destroyed." — GB)

These two Etta James albums on Crown nicely illustrate the deft work of the increasingly collectible artist Fazzio: The LP on top, The Best Of Etta James from 1962, features a nice photo of Ms. James. The album below, Etta James from 1963, features a painting by Fazzio using the earlier photo as his guide. As the painting takes up more room, Fazzio graciously added the top of a gown to Etta's figure. He has also, inexplicably, crowned the singer with a white bouffant. . .

Label & Catalog #		Title	Year	VG+	NM

MADONNA

| Sire 25442 | (S) | **True Blue** (Clear vinyl) | 197? | | See below |
| Sire 25442 | (S) | **True Blue** (Picture disc) | 197? | | See below |

(These two pressings of Sire 25442 are confusing: While they feature a U.S. jacket, it was photocopied by the Asian manufacturers.)

| Sire PRO-A-2892 | (DJ) | **You Can Dance** (Single edits of LP remixes) | 198? | 16.00 | 40.00 |
| Sire PRO-A-5904 | (DJ) | **Erotica** (2 LPs. 1,500 made) | 198? | 20.00 | 50.00 |

MARTIN, ROBERTA/THE ROBERTA MARTIN SINGERS

| Apollo LP-480 | (M) | **The Roberta Martin Singers** | 195? | | See below |

(This gospel outing features rhythm'n blues style vocal backing. Rare with a suggested Near Mint value of $75-150.)

McDOWELL, MISSISSIPPI FRED

| Milestone MLP-3003 | (M) | **Long Way From Home** | 1966 | 12.00 | 30.00 |
| Milestone MLS-93003 | (S) | **Long Way From Home** | 1966 | 16.00 | 40.00 |

MIX, THE

"When singer/guitarist Stu Daye was dropped by Columbia, he teamed up with Felix Pappalardi to produce this great pop rock independent album, released used for promotional purposes only." — SB

| Word of Mouth 1011 | (S) | **American Glue** | 1980 | 40.00 | 100.00 |

MOBERLYS, THE

"Major Seattle punk pop band with Jim Basnight." — SB

| Safety First (No number) | (S) | **The Moberlys** | 1979 | 20.00 | 50.00 |

MOODY BLUES

| Deram DE-16102 | (M) | **Days Of Future Passed** | 1968 | | See below |

(DE-16102 has a suggested NM value of $150-300.)

MOON, THE

"Excellent psych pop with Matthew Moore with supposed David Marks involvement." — SB

| Imperial LP-12381 | (S) | **Without Earth** | 1968 | 16.00 | 40.00 |
| Imperial LP-12444 | (S) | **The Moon** | 1969 | 16.00 | 40.00 |

MURPHY, ROSE

Ms. Murphy's discography can be found in Goldmine's Price Guide To Collectible Jazz Albums.

| Royale 1835 | (10") | **Rose Murphy And Quartette** | 195? | | See below |

(Royale 1835 features Rose Murphy with group vocal backing. Rare with a suggested Near Mint value of $100-200.)

NEWTON-JOHN, OLIVIA

| RCA | (S) | **Toomorrow** (UK Soundtrack) | 1971 | 150.00 | 300.00 |

("Last one I had was VG+; sold it with a phone call for $200." — CE)

| MCA 3067 | (S) | **Totally Hot** (Picture disc) | 1979 | 40.00 | 100.00 |

("Not a U.S. release. I sold the last two I had for $85 each." — CE)

ORBISON, ROY

MGM T-90631	(M)	**The Orbison Way**	1966	10.00	25.00
MGM ST-90631	(S)	**The Orbison Way**	1966	12.00	30.00
MGM T-90928	(M)	**The Classic Roy Orbison**	1966	10.00	25.00
MGM ST-90928	(S)	**The Classic Roy Orbison**	1966	12.00	30.00
MGM T-91173	(M)	**Roy Orbison Sings Don Gibson**	1966	10.00	25.00
MGM ST-91173	(S)	**Roy Orbison Sings Don Gibson**	1966	12.00	30.00

(MGM 90000s above are Capitol Record Club issues.)

PARIS, PRISCILLA

Priscilla Paris is one of The Paris Sisters.

York 4005	(M)	**Priscilla Sings Herself**	1967	10.00	25.00
York 4005	(S)	**Priscilla Sings Herself**	1967	12.00	30.00
Happy Tiger HT-1002	(M)	**Priscilla Loves Billy**	1968	12.00	30.00

PINK FLOYD

| Columbia PC-33453 | (DJ) | **Wish You Were Here** | 1975 | 100.00 | 250.00 |

(Advance promos for PC-33453 were banded for air-play and sent out in plain white covers with the title rubber-stamped on the front.)

Albeth, Priscilla and Sherrell Paris, known professionally as The Paris Sisters, scored big in 1961 with "I Love How You Love Me," produced by Phil Spector and a classic early girl group record. While the trio placed four more sides on the national charts, that was the end of their big hits. Later, Priscilla tried her hand at a solo career with these two albums. The sketches of the singer adorning Priscilla Sings Herself on York do her beauty little justice, as the close-up on Priscilla Loves Billy makes evident.

Label & Catalog #		Title	Year	VG+	NM
Columbia PC-33453	(DJ)	**Wish You Were Here**	1975	**150.00**	**300.00**
		(Advance copies for PC-33453 have a blue cover with the photo and title printed on the jacket.)			
Columbia PC-33453	(S)	**Wish You Were Here**	1975	**10.00**	**25.00**
		(Original pressings of PC-33453 were issued in a blue shrinkwrap with a photo & title sticker affixed to the wrap.)			
Columbia AP-1	(DJ)	**Animals**	1977	**60.00**	**150.00**
		(Advance promo with the word "fuck" edited out of "Pigs." Issued in a plain white jacket with the title rubber-stamped on the front.)			

PLUGZ, THE

Plugz RR-101	(S)	**Electrify Me**	1978	**20.00**	**50.00**
		(Originals have textured covers on thick cardboard.)			
Plugz RR-101	(S)	**Electrify Me**	1978	**10.00**	**25.00**
		(Later covers are non-textured on normal cardboard.)			
Fatima FTM-80	(S)	**Better Luck**	1981	**10.00**	**25.00**

POLICE, THE

A&M SP-3730	(DJ)	**Ghost In The Machine** (Picture disc)	1981		See below
		(Prototype picture disc that lights up when placed on the turntable! A copy sold for $200 ten years ago. Rare— less than ten were made— with a suggested NM value of $500-1,000.)			

PORTER, JERRY
"Rare radical folk produced by the notorious Armand P. Schaubroeck." — SB

Mirror SWB-123	(M)	**Don't Bother Me!**	1966	**40.00**	**100.00**

PRICE, RAY

Columbia D-157	(M)	**The Same Old Me** (Columbia Record Club)	196?	**8.00**	**20.00**
Columbia DS-157	(S)	**The Same Old Me** (Columbia Record Club)	196?	**10.00**	**25.00**

PRINCE

Warner Bros. 25677	(S)	**The Black Album**	1987		See below
		(Counterfeits of foreign pressings are currently making the rounds.)			

REBECCA & THE SUNNYBROOK FARMERS
Members of this band later became Chunky, Novi & Ernie.

Musicor MS-3176	(S)	**Rebecca & The Sunnybrook Farmers** (With bonus photo)	1969	**20.00**	**50.00**
Musicor MS-3176	(S)	**Rebecca & The Sunnybrook Farmers** (Without the photo)	1969	**14.00**	**35.00**

RIFT, ZOOG
"With a strong Zappa/Beefheart influence, Zoog Rift's Micro Mastodons issued this cult, independent, new-wave album." — SB

Snout ZRSI-20062	(S)	**Idiots On The Miniature Golf Course**	1979	**30.00**	**75.00**

RIGHTEOUS BROTHERS, THE

Philles T-90692	(M)	**You've Lost That Loving Feelin'**	196?	**12.00**	**30.00**
Philles ST-90692	(S)	**You've Lost That Loving Feelin'** (Capitol Record Club)	196?	**16.00**	**40.00**

SATRIANI, JOE

Rubina ???	(S)	**Joe Satriani**	1984	**100.00**	**250.00**
		(Five track EP privately pressed. Four of the five made their way onto Joe's "Time Machine" album. . .)			

SEVENTH SONS, THE
Buzzy Linhart's first album. . .

ESP-Disk' 1078	(S)	**The Seventh Sons**	1967	**40.00**	**100.00**

SHEPHERD, CYBILL

Paramount PAS-1018	(S)	**Cybill Does It... ...To Cole Porter** (With poster)	1972	**12.00**	**30.00**

SIDEWINDERS, THE
"Great proto-power pop album with Andy Paley." — SB

RCA Victor LSP-4696	(S)	**The Sidewinders**	1972	**14.00**	**35.00**

Once again, I acquiesce to Mr. Essmeier's literate observations: "This album, Cybill Does It. . . . . .To Cole Porter, was issued with a large poster of a rather attractive Ms. Shepherd, which accounts for about 99% of the demand for this album, which, on the whole, isn't very good. Of course, that didn't stop MCA from reissuing it during "Moonlighting's" success." It should be noted that, aside from the bonus poster, the original pressing on Paramount has a fold-open cover. The MCA pressings have neither the gatefold cover nor the poster. Consequently, they are used record staples.

Label & Catalog #		Title	Year	VG+	NM

SKIP-JACKS, THE

Label & Catalog #		Title	Year	VG+	NM
RCA Victor LPM-2060	(M)	Let's Get Away From It All	1959	12.00	30.00
RCA Victor LSP-2060	(S)	Let's Get Away From It All	1959	16.00	40.00
RCA Victor LPM-2200	(M)	Sweet, Hot And Blue	1960	12.00	30.00
RCA Victor LSP-2200	(S)	Sweet, Hot And Blue	1960	16.00	40.00

SNEAKERS, THE

"A significant record as this is the beginning of the whole scene revolving around the db's and Let's Active in the Southeast." — SB

Car CRR-3	(S)	In The Read	1978	30.00	75.00

SPERM BANK BABIES THE (FEATURING AL "LORENZO" DRAKE)

"Independent live release by Boston's premier punk bank, Willie Alexander & The Boom Boom Band, issued by local label Varulven masquerading as Varage in numbered, plain white covers with rubber-stamped titles and pseudononymous autographs by the band members plus a bonus insert!" — SB

Varage NR-8893	(S)	Come Come Now/Talkin' To Baretta Loretta	1977	40.00	100.00

STOGNER, DAVE

Decca DL-8705	(M)	Western Dance In Hi Fi	1957	24.00	60.00

STUFFY

Water Street EST-1002	(S)	Stuffy's Frozen Parachute Band	1974	30.00	75.00

(Very rare independent promo in plain white jacket marked "Advance Reviewer Copy Confidential." — SB)

Paramount PAS-6070	(S)	Stuffy & His Frozen Parachute Band	1974	10.00	25.00

(Major label reissue with slight title change.)

SUICIDE COMMANDOS, THE

"The first and most important new wave band from Minneapolis before The Replacements." — SB

Blank 002	(S)	The Suicide commandos Make A Record	1978	10.00	25.00

(Now getting rare, the only other release by Mercury's "New Wave" label, Pere Ubu's "Modern Dance" being the other.)

Twin Tone TTR-7906	(S)	The Commandos Commit Suicide Dance Concert	1979	30.00	75.00

(Their second and last album, a numbered, limited edition of 1,000.)

SUPERTRAMP

A&M SP-3730	(DJ)	Breakfast In America *(Picture disc)*	1979		See below

(This picdisc was issued in miniscule quantities to A&M employees. Each disc features a photo of the intended recipient posing with the model who appeared on the album cover. Each disc is unique." — CE. Suggested NM value of $300-600.)

TEAGRDEN, JACK

Jack Teagarden's discography can be found in Goldmine's price Guide To Collectible Jazz Albums.

Capitol T-T-820	(M)	Swing Low, Sweet Spiritual	1957		See below

(Teagarden's jazz renditions of gospel music are accompanied by The Five Keys, who hum and provide other vocal effects. Rare with a suggested Near Mint value of $100-300.)

10,000 MANIACS

Christian Burial P-2010	(S)	Human Conflict #5 *(EP)*	1983	24.00	60.00
Christian Burial P- 3001	(S)	Secrets Of The I Ching	1984	40.00	100.00

THOMAS, B. J.

Hickory ST-90956	(S)	The Very Best Of B. J. Thomas *(Capitol Record Club)*	196?	12.00	30.00

TRAFFIC

United Arts. UAL-3651	(M)	Heaven Is In Your Mind	1967	30.00	75.00

VAUGHAN, STEVIE RAY

Epic 39609	(S)	Couldn't Stand The Weather *(Picture disc)*	1984	30.00	75.00

("Copies of this album, were ubiquitous— and poor sellers at $10— until Mr. Vaughan's passing. I never see them anymore and people I know who have had them have been selling them quickly at $85." — CE)

Dionne Warwick has been so much a part of the cross-over pop scene for so long that it is sometimes difficult to remember what a truly talented singer— and a gifted stylist— she is. In my haste to prepare this book, I inadvertently dumped her discography from my files, even though her early albums have reached a level where they certainly belong in a book on collectible albums. Her third album, Make Way For Dionne Warwick, presents the lovely singer in three poses that quite nicely fir the sensuous mood of her best performances. March Is Dionne Warwick Month is basically a greatest hits sampler compiled for radio play.

Label & Catalog #		Title	Year	VG+	NM

VARIOUS ARTISTS

Kenwood LP-481	(M)	**Spiritual Moods**	196?		*See below*
		(Group vocal settings. Rare with a suggested NM value of $150-300.)			
Vanguard VRS-9006	(M)	**A Night At The Apollo**	1959		*See below*
		(A comedy album, this also features the first live performance of the rhythm'n blues vocal group, The Heartbreakers. Rare with a suggested Near Mint value of $200-400.)			
Vanguard VRS-90903	(M)	**Comedy Night At The Apollo**	1961		*See below*
		(VRS-9093 is a reissue of 9006 with a new cover. Rare with a suggested Near Mint value of $100-200.)			

WARWICK, DIONNE

Scepter SP-508	(M)	**Presenting Dionne Warwick**	1963	10.00	25.00
Scepter SPS-508	(S)	**Presenting Dionne Warwick**	1963	14.00	35.00
Scepter SP-517	(M)	**Anyone Who Had A Heart**	1964	10.00	25.00
Scepter SPS-517	(S)	**Anyone Who Had A Heart**	1964	14.00	35.00
Scepter SP-523	(M)	**Make Way For Dionne Warwick**	1964	8.00	20.00
Scepter SPS-523	(S)	**Make Way For Dionne Warwick**	1964	12.00	30.00
Scepter SP-528	(M)	**The Sensitive Sound Of Dionne Warwick**	1965	8.00	20.00
Scepter SPS-528	(S)	**The Sensitive Sound Of Dionne Warwick**	1965	12.00	30.00
Scepter RDW-200	(DJ)	**March Is Dionne Warwick Month**	1967	12.00	30.00

WHO, THE

Life DL-74664	(E)	**The Who Sing My Generation**	1967	60.00	150.00
		(The Life album is a reissue on a little-known subsidiary of Decca.)			

WOOLEY, SHEB

MGM T-90528	(M)	**The Very Best Of Sheb Wooley**	1965	12.00	30.00
MGM ST-90528	(S)	**The Very Best Of Sheb Wooley**	1965	12.00	30.00
		(Capitol Record Club)			

YARDBIRDS, THE

Epic BN-26177	(S)	**Having A Raveup With The Yardbirds**	1965	12.00	30.00
		("Hard as it might be to believe, this LP actually exists on Epic's early '70s orange label. Rare but not highly sought after." — CE)			

Selling Your Albums

By Perry Cox

Collectors and dealers all over the world keep a watchful eye on current market trends to see how their investments are doing, as well as what they can expect to pay for items that remain on their want lists. The burning questions, then, are: "How does one realistically go about selling their records? Sure, the guide says it's worth X dollar amount, but how do I market my item(s) anywhere near its value estimate?" There are several answers, all of which depend on the seller's situation and needs.

The "set-sale" method is probably the only way to achieve near, at, or above market value in a relatively short period of time. At the point you wish to market your item(s), the sale may take no longer than a phone call to complete. Of course, this method involves plenty of prior invested time and interaction with others. As a collector among collectors, it is ideal to socialize, share one's finds, interact for feedback and advice, and keep on the lookout for other collectors' wants. By acquiring a current list of items your friends and colleagues are looking for, you will be better able to determine what you can sell and for how much.

This is not only an ideal way to obtain maximum return from collectibles you have to sell, but this also allows you a keen advantage in terms of trading for items to fill your own collection. As well, many will appreciate your servicing their wants. The longer you are involved, the larger your customer/friendship base grows. This is, *if* you have kept the required high standards of dealing ethics which is absolutely essential in building a solid relationship with other collectors.

Ethics between buyer and seller *must* be given preference over all other factors. Your records and money mean little if your code of conduct allows for dissatisfaction with the other party, especially if you do not promptly remedy the problem to their satisfaction. Universal dealing principals equate to honestly and fairly grading the items. Since most prospective buyers are unable to personally inspect the items prior to the sale, it is good policy to institute a full "money back, satisfaction guarantee" coupled with a reasonable time limit for recourse (usually a couple of weeks is sufficient).

It is very important to formulate your selling prices *before* you contact prospective buyers. It is not wise to gauge your pricing on the customers level of desire or by pitting one customer against another. These tactics spawn little more than frustration and discontent for everyone. If you agree to a set price, do not raise that price if you later realize another party expresses interest in it. (As well, if you agree to buy an item for a certain price, nit picking at minor, flaws in hopes of getting a discount is not wise.) In short, each must live by his own set of standards and always give great respect to another's valid concerns. Remember, if you get in the habit of making undesirable transaction, many will learn not to contact you the next time you have records to sell or trade.

Set Sale & Auctions In Trade Publications

The term "set sale" means to list your items at fixed prices; i.e., the items *are not* being auctioned. The advantage with this method is that your market potential is far greater due to the mass attention your items receive. The *actual* level of exposure depends on what publications you choose. If you have several "high ticket" items or a large amount of quality merchandise to sell, ads in several publications at once is certainly a viable option. This method is a bit more time consuming: ad preparation, distribution of the publication, and mail transactions involve time.

Preparing your ad needs special planning and considerations; you will need to figure the total number of lines each typewritten page gives you (normally between 50 and 60), the cost per ad, then the cost per line. Collectors tend to gravitate to the excellent condition items, so concentrate on listing in-demand items in quality shape. If you list thirty $10 items that take up half your full page ad space, you have only covered your ad cost, *if you sell them all.*

Keep in mind that a full page ad in these types of publications usually run about $300. Smaller space ads are considerably cheaper. The "Showcase" ad section in the back of *Goldmine* is very effective in presenting select items. The inexpensive rates include typesetting and placement among other eye appealing ads. This is often the first section viewed by readers.

When preparing your ad, by all means grade your items very conservatively (refer to the article on grading in this book.) Conservative, accurate grading provides a healthy, happy collecting environment for everyone. Also, you must be prepared to pack your items well with proper, snug packing and padding (2-3" of padding around the item is a good minimum). Always insure the items you are mailing; it is well worth the extra expense.

When dealing with mail-order, the buyers may notify you of their intent to reserve any particular item(s) they are interested in. Normally this is done by telephone (many buyers prefer to talk to the people they are dealing with, since it gives an added sense of security and provides an immediate response as to the availability of the item) or mail. The response you may receive from this type of advertising is an excellent way to broaden your list of other collectors.

If one has the time, this method has the potential of being the most rewarding in terms of highest yield plus it is a good way to learn just how much customers are willing to spend at any given time on any given item. With the mail-order auction, the seller sets a bid deadline; normally an auction runs for one month from the beginning of the issue's publication date. At the deadline all bids are evaluated and the highest bidders then notified.

In some cases, auctions have yielded sales substantially over the going set value; in other cases the results can be most disappointing. The factors involved in determining the final results are far too numerous to detail but the general spending mood of the public is probably the most important factor. When a given artist is focused on in the media, sales tend to surge accordingly. The death of a major star such as Elvis Presley or John Lennon is one example; the hoopla surrounding Madonna's or The Stones' big tours is another.

Reputable auction establishments such as Sothebys, Christies and Phillips are alternative auction methods. They can, however, take the longest time in that they only hold their auctions a few times a year. Exposure to collectors is also limited but the spending frenzy sometimes associated with these houses can often play a favorable role for the seller. One thing is certain: auctions do take the longest period of time on average to sell your items. From start to completion, a mail-order auction consumes an average of two months. This is not the way to go if one wishes to liquidate in a hurry.

Selling Your Items To A Dealer

The quickest manner to sell your items once you have exhausted retail sales to personal contacts is to sell them wholesale to a dealer. If you need cash and you need it right away, selling this way can be quite convenient. Your first responsibility is to contact a *reputable* dealer who is interested in mutual satisfaction between his interests and your own. One must keep in mind that a dealer is not in a position to pay top market dollar for your items. Like any commodity, the record dealer has to buy at a modest percentage of full value in order to make enough profit to stay in business.

As a rule, it is safe to say that the more significantly rare and valuable your item is, the more the dealer will be probably willing to pay, especially if they have a ready buyer. Although the dealer takes into consideration many factors when evaluating, the bottom line is usually this: "How long will one have to keep his money tied up before one actually sells the goods and recovers their money?" Some very rare and valuable items have been known to fetch as much as 60-65% of market retail. A good average for slow movers is about 30-40% of the dealer's opinion of the market value. If the period is lengthy or if the dealer has several copies of the item you are trying to sell, he'll be less generous in his offer or may not express any interest at all! If you intend to solicit offers from various dealers, please advise each dealer of this prior to negotiations to avoid hard feelings. This eliminates the impression the dealer may have in thinking he has an exclusive on your items.

Some dealers will agree to place items obtained from the owner on consignment. That is, he will not pay the owner until the item sells. Usually this method is not entertained unless the dealer feels the item is significant enough to yield a handsome return within a reasonable time. The retail value is mutually agreed upon, while the dealer assumes responsibility for the custody and sale of the item. The final say in retail value usually goes to the dealer who knows his area and market potential best. The average consignment fee is anywhere from 15% to 30% to the dealer, certainly better than the 40-50% usually obtained in a straight sale to the dealer. Compared with some of the others, this selling method can be quite time consuming without guaranteed sales, a factor that must be considered before locking your item(s) in a consignment agreement (which is, in effect, a contract).

Mr. Cox is one of the most well-known collectors and dealers in Beatles records in the country. He is also the co-author of The Beatles Price Guide For American Records, from which this [abridged] article was taken.

The Uncommon Stereo Beatles

By John Christensen

Ever wonder why "I Want To Hold Your Hand" sounded so lousy on *Meet The Beatles?* Or why "I Feel Fine" sounded like it was recorded in a trash can? Or the crummy sound of every Beatles track on United Artists' *A Hard Day's Night?* Fact is, they were presented in rechanneled, or fake, stereo. If the record company didn't have the stereo version by release date, they simply used whatever version they could get their hands on. If it sounded awful. . . so what? Who'd ever know?

Which brings me to the purpose of this article: helping you, the Fab Four fanatic, find those uncommon stereo versions of all too many Beatles songs long neglected and difficult to find on American vinyl. I can guarantee the accuracy of the listings below; I personally listened to all of them. Many of these tracks *are* fairly common outside the U.S., but this article was intended for the American collector and is based on domestic releases. Every source that I have listed below is an American vinyl LP and many, though certainly not all, have been reissued in stereo on CD.

By the way, even though Capitol supplied U.S. Beatle fans with *most* songs in stereo, on earlier LPs they often remixed the original multi-tracks, adding reverb, echo and other obnoxious post-production alterations. A good example is *The Beatles' Second Album.* Both the Parlophone and Mobile Fidelity reissues and some later Capitol compilations (such as the remixed *Rock 'n' Roll Music)* offer much better stereo mixes for many of the more common tracks. In 1987 Capitol finally issued these Parlophone albums, but the first four titles— *Please Please Me, With The Beatles, A Hard Day's Night* and *Beatles For Sale—* were in mono (in both their vinyl and CD incarnations).

Now, a few quick notes on how to use this article: Each song listed below is followed by the title of a domestically issued album (in bold print) where that track can be found in stereo. Titles followed by an asterisk (*) indicate the original EMI/Parlophone version of the album. These were reissued by Mobile Fidelity as part of their "Original Master Recording" series in their stereo format. Therefore, an asterisk refers the reader to either the import version or the "OMR."

These tracks are followed by notes of explanation leading the reader to other sources where possible. Six tracks— both sides of two early singles, "Love Me Do" / "P. S. I Love You" and "She Loves You" / "I'll Get You," along with two latter day recordings, "You Know My Name (Look Up The Number)" and "Only A Northern Song"— apparently cannot be found in stereo on any album anywhere!

9-62	Love Me Do	*Unavailable in stereo*
9-62	P. S. I Love You	*Unavailable in stereo*

"Love Me Do" / "P. S. I Love You" was released as *The Beatles'* first single. They appeared on the first version of Introducing The Beatles *(Vee Jay SR-1062)* in mono, although they are rechanneled on the Parlophone/Mobile Fidelity Please Please Me.

2-63	Misery	**Please, Please Me*; Introducing The Beatles; The Beatles Rarities**
2-63	There's A Place	**Please, Please Me*; Introducing The Beatles; The Beatles Rarities**

Although "Misery" and "There's A Place" did appear in stereo on Introducing The Beatles, as stereo copies of this album are as rare as hen's teeth, they are included here.

3-63	From Me To You	**The Beatles 1962-1966**
3-63	Thank You Girl	**The Beatles' Second Album**

"From Me To You" and "Thank You Girl" are available on Past Masters, *but in mono.*

7-63	She Loves You	*Unavailable in stereo*
7-63	I'll Get You	*Unavailable in stereo*

*"She Loves You" / "I'll Get You" was released as the group's fourth Parlophone single
and their third US single, this time on on Swan.*

10-63	I Want To Hold Your Hand	**20 Greatest Hits; Past Masters**

*"I Want To Hold Your Hand" made its American stereo debut in 1964 on the Capitol
various artists compilation* Chartbusters, Volume 4.

10-63	This Boy	**Past Masters**
1-64	Komm, Gib Mir Deine Hand	**Something New; The Beatles "Rarities"**•
1-64	Sie Liebt Dich	**The Beatles "Rarities"**•

*"Sie Liebt Dich" was issued by Capitol on the album of the same title (SN-12009) but was
withdrawn prior to general release. Note: This was not released by Mobile Fidelity.*

2-64	Can't Buy Me Love	**A Hard Day's Night**•; **Hey Jude; The Beatles 1962-1966**
2-64	You Can't Do That	**A Hard Day's Night**•; **Rock 'n' Roll Music**
4-64	A Hard Day's Night	**A Hard Day's Night**•; **Rock 'n' Roll Music**
4-64	I Should Have Known Better	**A Hard Day's Night**•; **Hey Jude**
10-64	I Feel Fine	**20 Greatest Hits; Past Masters**
10-64	She's A Woman	**Past Masters**
2-65	Ticket To Ride	**Help!**•; **Reel Music**
2-65	Yes It Is	**Past Masters**
6-66	I'm Only Sleeping	**Revolver**•
6-66	Dr. Robert	**Revolver**•
6-66	And Your Bird Can Sing	**Revolver**•
12-66	Penny Lane	**20 Greatest Hits**
12-66	Penny Lane *(Alternate version with trumpet ending)*	**The Beatles Rarities**
?-67	You Know My Name (Look Up The Number)	*Unavailable in stereo*

*"You Know My Name (Look Up The Number)" was recorded in 1967 but first appeared
in 1970 as the B-side of "Let It Be" and eventually showed up on* Rarities *in mono.*

5-67	Baby, You're A Rich Man	*See below*

*The original stereo mix of "Baby, You're A Rich Man" is unavailable in the U.S. although
this track can be found on copies of* Magical Mystery Tour *from Germany (both the Hor Zu
original and the Apple reissue) and France (Apple). The CD of* Magical Mystery Tour *does
contain this song in stereo, but it has been drastically remixed.*

6-67	All You Need Is Love	**Yellow Submarine; The Beatles 1967-1970; 20 Greatest Hits**
2-68	The Inner Light	**Past Masters**
2-68	Only A Northern Song	*Unavailable in stereo*

"Only A Northern Song" appears in rechanneled stereo on all known pressings of
Yellow Submarine. *One can only assume that the multi-tracks have been misplaced. . .*

The following is a list of Beatles albums as originally released by Vee
Jay, Capitol and United Artists in the United States. All tracks should be assumed stereo except for the specific notations accompanying each title. On the
1963 version of *Introducing The Beatles* both "Love Me Do" and "P. S. I Love You"
are in mono. The 1964 reissue of this album with "Please Please Me" and "Ask Me
Why" is entirely in stereo. Similarly, both "From Me To You" and "Thank You Girl"
appear in mono on *The Beatles & Frank Ifield On Stage* (LPS-1085).

The group's first album for Capitol, *Meet The Beatles* (ST-2047) contains
both sides of their fifth Parlophone single, "I Want To Hold Your Hand" and "This
Boy," in rechanneled stereo. On *The Beatles' Second Album* (ST-2080) both sides
of their fourth Parlophone single, "I'll Get You" and "She Loves You," along with
"You Can't Do That," are rechanneled.

When the Mop Tops recorded the material for their first feature length
motion picture, a total of seven new songs were included. They also cut an additional four during these sessions. These eleven new recordings were combined
with both sides of their previous single and issued as their third Parlophone
album, *A Hard Day's Night.*

In the States, these tracks were used to compile two completely different albums. . . United Artists held the rights to the soundtrack and subsequently issued an album of the eight songs that appeared in the film along with four tracks of incidental music from the George Martin Orchestra.

The problem with the United Artists release of *A Hard Day's Night* (UAS-6366) is that all the Beatles tracks— "A Hard Day's Night," "Tell Me Why," "I'll Cry Instead," "I'm Happy Just To Dance With You," "I Should Have Known Better," "If I Fell," "And I Love Her" and "Can't Buy Me Love"— are rechanneled, although the incidental music by George Martin is stereo. Note that "I'll Cry Instead" at 2:06 is the longest released version (others clock in at 1:45) and "And I Love Her" features a single track lead vocal instead of the normal double-tracked lead.

Since Capitol *also* had the rights to the material, they followed the U.A. soundtrack with a new album in a matter of weeks. *Something New* (ST-2108) is completely in stereo and includes "Tell Me Why," "I'm Happy Just To Dance With You," "If I Fell" and the the double-tracked lead vocal version of "And I Love Her" along with the 1:45 version of "I'll Cry Instead." (The four other songs from the soundtrack sessions are also gathered on this album.)

Beatles '65 (ST-2228) contains rechanneled versions of both sides of the group's latest hit, "I Feel Fine" and "She's A Woman." *Beatles VI* (ST-2358) features a rechanneled "Yes It Is," originally issued as the B-side of "Ticket To Ride." In between these, Capitol reissued the Vee Jay material as *The Early Beatles* (ST-2309), rechannelling "Love Me Do" and "P. S. I Love You."

For the Fabs' second film, Capitol handled the soundtrack and followed U.A.'s lead by compiling a selection of seven tracks from the film along with five pieces by George Martin. *Help!* (SMAS-2386) contains the hit "Ticket To Ride" in rechanneled stereo. Outside of the fifty States, EMI issued the seven movie songs with seven new recordings, all in stereo. It is this version of *Help!* that Mobile Fidelity released as an "Original Master Recording."

Both *Rubber Soul* (ST-2442) and *Revolver* (ST-2576) are in stereo, although the LP line-ups issued here are dramatically different from the Parlophone versions. Four of *Rubber Soul's* fourteen tracks were dropped and replaced by a couple of *Help!* left-overs while *Revolver* features only eleven of the Parlophone fourteen. The other three tracks make up one of the more fascinating anecdotes of the Beatles' recording career. . .

Capitol used the remaining tracks from Parlophone's *Help!* and *Rubber Soul* as the basis for *"Yesterday" ...And Today* (ST-2553). They also scooped their UK counterparts when Lennon's not-quite-completed masters for "I'm Only Sleeping," "Dr. Robert," and "And Your Bird Can Sing" were inadvertently *(sic)* shipped to Capitol. As only the mono tapes were sent, Cap's engineers were forced to Duophonticate them into rechanneled stereo. The Parlophone *Revolver*, where these songs were intended, features all the tracks in stereo; it is from these tapes that the Mobile Fidelity "Original Master Recording" was taken.

Capitol issued two albums in 1967: *Sgt. Pepper's Lonely Hearts Club Band* (SMAS-2653) was identical in content to the Parlophone album (except for the missing tag at the end of the second side known as the "Sgt. Pepper inner groove," which was finally issued domestically on Capitol's *Rarities*). *Magical*

Mystery Tour was issued in the UK as a double-EP. From this, Capitol compiled an album by adding five previous single sides. *Magical Mystery Tour* (SMAL-2835) presented the American listener with rechanneled versions of "Penny Lane," "Baby, You're A Rich Man," and "All You Need Is Love."

The stereo version of "Strawberry Fields Forever" on this album is burdened with echo, lack of separation, etc. The version on the later German and French *Magical Mystery Tour* is dramatically different, being a much cleaner representation. Unfortunately, the Parlophone and Mobile Fidelity issues used the Capitol tapes and are subsequently flawed. The CD version is all stereo, although the mixes on most tracks are different (and, in at least some quarters, considered noticeably inferior).

With the formation of their own Apple Records label, the group issued their new album in time for the 1968 Christmas season. *The Beatles* (SWBO-101) was identical in content to the Parlophone release (and all stereo). This was followed two months later with the *Yellow Submarine* compilation (SW-153), featuring the newly recorded "Only A Northern Song" in rechanneled stereo and the first stereo appearance of "All You Need Is Love." All issues of *Yellow Submarine* were taken from the same master tape.

The Beatles' final two studio albums, *Let It Be* (AR-34001, recorded in January 1969) and *Abbey Road* (SO-383) were in stereo. The 1970 American-only *Hey Jude* compilation (SO-385), featured the American stereo debuts of "Can't Buy Me Love" and "I Should Have Known Better." 1970 also saw the fan-club only release of *The Beatles Christmas Album* (SBC-100) gathering the seven recorded messages the group sent out to fan club members in their original mono. Of interest is the fact that none other than Tiny Tim appears as a guest singing "Nowhere Man" on the '68 message.

When a series of bogus hits packages surfaced in ads in 1973, Apple compiled a pair of two-record sets over-viewing the group's career: *The Beatles 1962-1966* (Apple SKBO-3403) features "She Loves You," "A Hard Day's Night," "I Feel Fine" and "Ticket To Ride" in mono while "Love Me Do" and "I Want To Hold Your Hand" are rechanneled. The rest of the album is stereo including "Can't Buy Me Love" and the American stereo debut of "From Me To You." *The Beatles 1967-1970* (SKBO-3404) contains mono versions of "Hello Goodbye" and "Penny Lane" while the rest of the album is stereo, including "All You Need Is Love."

1976 witnessed the release *Rock 'n' Roll Music* (Capitol SKBO-11537) a double-album collection of uptempo tracks. All four sides are in stereo, several remixed, including the American stereo debut of "You Can't Do That." This was followed in 1977 by yet another double compilation: *Love Songs* (SKBL-11711) containing rechanneled versions of "P. S. I Love You" and "Yes It Is." All other tracks are stereo including "And I Love Her" and "If I Fell."

The Beatles "Rarities" (SN-12009) was included as a bonus with the boxed set *The Beatles Collection*. This box offered the American public its first chance to purchase the original Parlophone versions of the albums (as the group intended them to be heard) in a limited edition, heavily hyped package. This *"Rarities"* included "Sie Liebt Dich" in stereo for the first time on an American LP.

The original mix of "Across The Universe" appears here in stereo; it had previously been available on the import-only *No One's Gonna Change Our World* (EMI Star Line SRS-5013) various artists compilation for the World Wildlife Fund. After someone with their head out of the sand determined that most of the tracks on this album were not "rare" by U.S./Capitol standards, it was pulled from proposed release and eventually replaced by. . .

The Beatles Rarities (SHAL-12080) includes alternate mono takes of "Love Me Do," "Help," "Helter Skelter" and "Don't Pass Me By" along with "The Inner Light" and "You Know My Name (Look Up The Number)" in mono. "Misery," "There's A Place," the trumpet-ending version of "Penny Lane" and the original mix of "Across The Universe" appear here in stereo.

Later vinyl releases from Capitol include *Reel Music* (SV-12199) which includes stereo versions of "A Hard Day's Night" and "Ticket To Ride." On *20 Greatest Hits* (SV-12245) "She Loves You" and "Love Me Do" are rechanneled; the rest of the album is stereo including "I Want To Hold Your Hand," "I Feel Fine," "All You Need Is Love" and "Penny Lane."

Capitol's double-album, *Past Masters, Volumes One & Two* (C1-91135), collects those tracks—mostly single sides—that did not appear on the original EMI albums. It contains stereo versions of "I Want To Hold Your Hand" and "I Feel Fine," plus the U.S. stereo debuts of "This Boy," "She's A Woman," "Yes It Is," and "The Inner Light."

Except for *Magical Mystery Tour* (taken from Capitol tapes), the Mobile Fidelity "Original Master Recordings" are taken from the Parlophone masters and share the same stereo content. All tracks on these audiophile pressings are stereo except "Love Me Do" and "P. S. I Love You," rechanneled on *Please, Please Me*, and "Only A Northern Song," rechanneled on *Yellow Submarine*.

Mr. Christensen is a collector specializing in pop, '60s hits in stereo, soundtracks, and audiophile pressings. He is also the photographer responsible for most of the photos in this book. Additions, correction or suggestions should be addressed to John Christensen, Box 40116, Bellevue, WA 98015.

Acetates & Test Pressings

By Christopher Chatman

Many times I have been asked "What *are* acetates and test pressings?" followed closely by "Why do they cost so much?" Record collectors are continually in search of the "rarest records," the "best pressings." This has much to do with the demand for promotional records: they are usually much rarer than the stock copies and, because of their limited press runs, better sounding. However, promotional copies— and even test pressings— pale in comparison to acetates, both in terms of sound quality and particularly in rarity.

Acetates are the first step in the transfer of music from an electronic signal to the actual pressed record. They allow the musicians and producers to hear what the finished record will sound like without going through the time and expense of the plating and pressing. After all, they may decide that they don't like a particular version of a song and change it *or* not release it at all.

Acetates, also known as masters or reference discs, are usually black and 7" to 12" in diameter. While most records are made of vinyl, acetates are made out of aluminum coated with cellulose acetate. Thus, while they look like records, they weigh approximately five times as much. The cellulose acetate for these lacquers is made at a very high level of quality control. Acetates are very expensive to manufacture, therefore record companies normally make only five copies of any one record. Recently, with the sharp reduction of vinyl records, the number of acetates made has dropped dramatically.

After a recording has been taped, edited and equalized, an uncut acetate, or "blank," is sent to the mastering lab where it is placed on the turntable of an electronic lathe system. The master tape is played through a lathe system and electronically transmitted to the cutting needle so that the music literally cuts microscopic wiggles analogous to the sound waves that they represent directly into the acetate coating. Because of this direct cutting from the master tape and the high quality of the cellulose, the sound is substantially better than a record.

An acetate which has received approval is called a master lacquer. After a lacquer has been cut it is sent to a factory to be electroplated with nickel. A label from either the mastering lab or the record company is usually glued to the disc; reference discs *may* have no label at all and master lacquers rarely do. Although acetates are normally packaged in plain paper sleeves, in recent years many are shipped in special boxes with covers; this extra packaging tends to enhance the desirability of the acetate. After the music on a reference disc has been reviewed and the record pressed, the acetate is then discarded.

Acetates should be treated even more carefully than records. Due to the brittleness of the cellulose, the action of playing an acetate with a phonograph needle is quite damaging to the disc's surface. After five plays, the needle begins to cut away at the finer microscopic grooves which produce the high frequencies. It is therefore advisable top play an acetate *once*, record it on tape, and then carefully store it away. Also, acetates chip easily; handle with care.

The nickel plating is then peeled away, which results in a negative metal print of the lacquer commonly referred to as a "mother." The first pressings to be run off the mother are test pressings; the final stop before the record is actually manufactured for mass consumption. Test pressings are vinyl facsimiles of the actual album; that is, they are 12" records pressed in extremely limited runs, usually at a plant that specializes in test pressings. It is not feasible for the large companies to turn on their enormous machines to print a handful of records.

These records allow the people involved to actually hear what the record will sound like as an LP. They may have special labels or they may be blank. Test pressings are checked for sound quality and technical defects; if they are satisfactory, then promotional copies are pressed, generally for distribution to radio stations. Finally, the commercial, or stock, copies are pressed for sale in your favorite endangered record store.

Since the value of an acetate depends primarily on the collectibility of the artist, they range in value from a few dollars to thousands of dollars. Acetates of released material are lowest on the value pyramid. Next are takes of released tracks prior to any sweetening being added, such as strings, horns, and background singers. Above that would be alternate takes of released material; unreleased live material would probably settle in between this level and the previous. The most valuable acetates are obviously those of unreleased material, regardless of the material's aesthetic qualities.

Acetates of albums by Elvis Presley and The Beatles have regularly sold for $500 and more; those by artists who are not quite as collectible have still sold for comparable prices. Hot new artists such as Depeche Mode and The Smiths are attracting serious bids when offered in auction. It is for this reason that some acetates have been bootlegged; be *sure* to check the reputation of the seller before spending heavy money on an acetate. It is important to note that the value increases dramatically when the material on the acetate is different from the released version of the record. However, whether or not the material is different, acetates are extremely rare and highly prized by collectors interested in owning the supposedly unattainable.

Test pressings are always worth several times the listed value of the stock copy. The most desirable are those of either unreleased albums such as Fats Domino's second album for Reprise, *Fats,* scheduled for release in 1971 and then withdrawn, or test pressings with different versions or mixes than the released album, such as the original version of Bob Dylan's *Blood On The Tracks.* Recorded with Eric Weisberg's group, Dylan pulled five of the tracks after hearing the test pressing and recorded them with another group of musicians to change the record's total mood. While the *Fats* album sells for three figures, *Blood On The Tracks* is one of the most valuable albums in the hobby.

A recent variation to the usual type of acetate is the direct metal master, or DMM. Instead of being made of aluminum coated with cellulose acetate, they are made of stainless steel coated with polished copper. The signal from the master tape is cut directly into the copper. This technology, designed to improve the sound quality of records, was designed just as the dominance of compact discs was forcing records into relative obscurity. This, combined with the fact that DMM is very expensive to convert has resulted in few mastering labs investing in this new method. Therefore, DMM acetates are very rare and, because of their beauty, highly prized by collectors.

Collecting Gold & Platinum Record Awards

A Primer By Christopher Chatman

Collecting gold and platinum record awards has progressed and evolved into a specialized field of music memorabilia. Aside from the collectors, there are now investors, museums— even restaurants— contributing to the rising popularity and escalating prices for key awards. Unfortunately, this increased interest and demand has also caused increased incidents of fraud *along* with a broad based abuse of the system by which the awards themselves are ordered. Still, gold and platinum awards *are* great investments if you spend your money on an artist who will maintain collectors' interest over the years. A wise purchase in the present has the potential to grow into a healthy investment for the future. Besides giving the reader a general introduction to this field, this article will serve as an update on the current market scene as well as include tips on avoiding bad purchases, which, needless to say, can be very expensive.

The *primary* purpose of this article is to give the reader a general acquaintance with the terms and descriptions commonly used and the different types, or formats, of the various awards. This is best achieved by providing an illustration, examine it section by section, and define each term. Our example will be a nearly mint white matte RIAA Gold Record Award to Mick Jagger for The Rolling Stones' album *Through The Past, Darkly*. There are seven basic aspects that are crucial in determining the collectibility, or value, of a given award: 1) the artist, 2) the record's title, 3) the organization recognizing the sales achievement, 4) the award designation, 5) the formatting of the award, 6) the individual or group to whom the award was presented, and, finally, 7) the condition of the award.

1) Artist. The artist is probably the most important factor in determining the value of an award. A recent award for a Beatles record would probably sell quicker and for a much higher value than a vintage award for an Isaac Hayes title, simply because they are so much more collectible. Current trends indicate even greater interest and emphasis is being placed on major artists. Nevertheless, since virtually all artists are collected to one extent or another, it is important to state that the tastes of the individual collector gauge desirability.

2) Title. The title of the record greatly affects the desirability of an award. Recently an original RIAA Gold Record for *Sgt. Pepper's Lonely Heart's Club Band* presented to The Beatles sold for more than $20,000 at auction. Yet a few months later in an auction from the same house, an original RIAA Gold Record for *Rubber Soul* presented to The Beatles fetched under $10,000. While part of the reason for the staggering difference in the prices was condition (the *Pepper* award was graded higher), another was title, as *Sgt. Pepper* is one of the classic titles to own.

While different collectors will have differing opinions on what *is* "classic" and therefore desirable, certain constants do exist, such as an artist's first gold record, which most collectors place a certain premium on. The individual's personal preference is a good thought to keep in mind as you read on, as this is a report on general trends, not absolute facts.

3) Organization Recognizing the Sales Achievement. Most collectors in the United States prefer awards certified by the Record Industry Association of America, or RIAA, the membership of which includes most, but not all, of the major labels in the country. Formed in 1952 as a trade organization representing the interests of the country's major record manufacturers, the organization introduced its "official" Gold Record Award in January 1958 primarily to standardize the recognition of sales.[1] Record companies could, at their own expense, open their books to an independent auditor who would then verify the sales figures and authenticate the award later presented, often with some degree of formality, by the RIAA to the artist and the company. Of course, companies did not have to join nor open their books; subsequently, many major sellers have never been certified as gold records, notably the Motown hits of the '60s.

The RIAA has many other functions but the main one which concerns us here is that it acts as *an unbiased accounting firm to verify the actual number of units sold.* It is for this reason that many award collectors give RIAA certification so much importance. However, it is important to note that there are awards certified by the record company itself with outside certification by an umbrella organization. These are commonly referred to as "in-house" awards. These awards are produced by major record companies that belong to the RIAA *as well* as labels that do not. Major labels will often make in-house awards to avoid having to pay the RIAA their accounting and certification fee.

Or a label may choose an in-house award to create an award or plaque with design specifications that do not include the RIAA seal, making some in-house awards far more attractive than the regulation RIAA design. In certain situations, these awards were made for records that were never RIAA certified. In-house awards are increasing in collectibility, the most obvious example being early awards from Berry Gordy's aforementioned Motown conglomeration. . .

Gold record awards from other countries are also collected, with awards from the United Kingdom and Japan highly prized. The official organization certifying sales achievement in the U.K. is British Phonographics Industry, or BPI. Because of the blue, red and black felt backgrounds of these awards they are particularly nice to add to a collection. And, while awards from Japan tend to be in-house, they, too, are especially beautiful.

4) RIAA Award Designation. Qualification for RIAA awards have varied over the years. The original standards were based on one million as gold: 1,000,000 copies of a single and $1,000,000 at the manufacturer's wholesale price for an album, which generally meant *at least* 500,000 copies.[2] Extended Play albums (EPs), which generally consisted of two tracks per side, required half of a single's sales, 500,000 units, to qualify.

---

[1] *Recognizing outstanding sales levels as "Gold" had been a part of the industry for decades. While a variety of presentations had been made, one of the first of the awards today recognized as a Gold Record was made to Glenn Miller in 1942 for sales in excess of 1,000,000 copies of "Chattanooga Choo Choo." Unfortunately, as the promotional impact of such an award became apparent, companies began awarding them willy nilly. By the mid '50s, the accuracy of the awards were held in contempt even by the industry itself. — Ye Olde Editor*

[2] *By 1974 the increased cost of albums at the wholesale level had made it possible to qualify with approximately 450,000 sales. In 1975 the rules were altered so that an LP must sell both the $1,000,000 and the half-million units to qualify. This was followed in 1976 with the establishment of the RIAA Platinum Record Award: 2,000,000 for a single and 1,000,000 copies (i.e., $2,000,000) for an LP. The redundant (and self-explanatory) Multi-Platinum Award was introduced in 1984. — Ye Olde Editor*

In 1970 the sales of tapes were included in the tallies for an album's certification. While the sales of reel-to-reels were negligible, the inclusion of the then popular eight-tracks had a noticeable affect on sales levels, similar to what would follow when the cassette was introduced as the industry standard years later. The chart below illustrates the other changes:

1958-1974

45	Gold Award	1,000,000 unit sales
EP	Gold Award	500,000 unit sales
LP	Gold Award	$1,000,000

1975-1988

45	Gold Award	1,000,000 unit sales
45	Platinum Award	2,000,000 unit sales
EP	Gold Award	500,000 unit sales
EP	Platinum Award	1,000,000 unit sales
LP	Gold Award	$1,000,000 (at least 500,000 unit sales)
LP	Platinum Award	$2,000,000 (at least 1,000,000 unit sales)

1989-1993

45	Gold Award	500,000 unit sales
45	Platinum Award	1,000,000 unit sales
EP	Gold Award	250,000 unit sales
EP	Platinum Award	500,000 unit sales
LP	Gold Award	$1,000,000 (at least 500,000 unit sales)
LP	Platinum Award	$2,000,000 (at least 1,000,000 unit sales)

The recent change in levels of unit sales in order to attain gold or platinum status reflect changing levels of difficulty in accruing these sales amounts.[3] Dates are worth knowing as the minimum requirement for RIAA certification is useful in spotting fakes. It is important to remember that platinum status was recognized by individual record companies years before "official" recognition by the RIAA. Therefore, platinum in-house awards prior to 1976 can be just as valid as an RIAA gold award presented at the same time.

5) Award Format. Over the years the RIAA has varied the formats, or style, in which the award is presented. Through 1989, the RIAA kept very strict control over the specifications that were used to construct each award. These standards are helpful in identifying the different formats as the rigid standards can make visual differences slight.

---

[3]*With the sales of vinyl dropping to all but non-existent and the industries decision to phase out vinyl, Gold Record Awards to singles plummeted: in 1980 there were 42 Gold Awards for singles; by 1986 it was seven. The introduction of the cassette single (or cassingle) in 1987 didn't help much so the RIAA made a radical amendment to its standards: Beginning in 1989, the level of sales for qualification for a single would be halved from 1,000,000 and 500,000 to qualify for Gold and from 2,000,000 to 1,000,000 for Platinum. And, in a complete reversal of previous policies, the standards applied retroactively. . . opening a Pandora's box of possibilities—and complications.*

Gold singles surged to 72, which included thirty older titles that hadn't qualified under the levels extant at the time of their release. For the now historical August 16, 1992 presentation of Gold and Platinum Records to the estate of Elvis Presley, the king of rock 'n roll received 21 retroactive Gold Records for singles and an additional 14 Awards for EPs that did not sell the amount required for those awards during his life. The presentation, which combined Gold, Platinum and Multi-Platinum certifications, totaled over 100 "new" awards, raising Elvis' total to 180 RIAA Awards. It was certainly an attention-getter and will comfortably place Presley way ahead of the pack in the next Guinness Book Of Records. — Ye Olde Editor

A. *White matte (1964-1975)*. Manufactured exclusively by New York Picture & Frame Company, the plaque was an off-white linen material in an unpainted, finished wood frame. This linen material will often turn a reddish-brown with age. The dedication on the plate was engraved with the RIAA seal usually etched in. In the case of LPs, the mini-cover was mounted separately from the plate. Because of their unique looks and the difficulty in counterfeiting them, white matte awards are the most desirable and collectible style (as recent sales trends and auction results bear out). Many collectors pursue this style alone.

B. *Floater (1975-1981)*. The award's background was dark, usually black, enclosed in a wood frame painted either gold or white. The disc and plate appear to be "floating" between the background and the plexiglas. In the case of LPs, the mini-cover (also floating) was mounted separately from the plate.

C. *Strip-plate (1982-1984)*. The award's background was dark. Unlike previous awards, for LPs the plate containing the dedication and the mini-cover appeared on the same strip of metal. This was also the first format to include a gold or silver plated cassette, acknowledging the ever increasing contribution of the tapes to unit sales. These cassettes were located either directly beneath the album disc or resting atop the lower LP lip.

D. *Hologram (1984-1989)*. The award's background is dark. In the case of LPs, the dedication and the mini-cover appear on the same strip of metal. The RIAA logo on the plate is in a rainbow-like hologram to avoid unauthorized duplication. Most, if not all, of these awards have a gold or silver plated cassette's top shell beneath the album disc or resting atop the lower LP lip. Some include a gold or silver plated compact disc.

E. *'R'-Hologram (1980 to present)*. For this new format the traditional RIAA logo was replaced with a large 'R' in a hologram pattern. All size and style restrictions were relaxed, giving the record companies more freedom in choosing a design for a particular award. Thus one can see a multitude of styles during these years with only the 'R'-hologram logo remaining constant. (Both the hologram and the 'R'-hologram award can be found in a new "format," the compact disc award. These feature either a gold or silver plated compact disc with the dedication plate with or without the picture from the CD's jewel box.)

6. Recipient. Presentation has become increasingly important in the last few years. . . and with good reason. The more closely identifiable an award is with the artist, the more desirable the award. In descending order, the desirability of an award based on the recipient is a) the artist who recorded the record, b) the record company who released the record, c) either an individual or organization closely connected with the production of the record, such as anyone listed on the album's credits, d) the production company, e) a radio station, or, finally, f) a record company executive otherwise unknown in the collecting community.

Because of the increased popularity of collecting awards, many award recipients and record company executives have acquired extra awards to sell to the collectors market, either duplicates of presented awards or new (sic) awards signifying a higher level of sales achievement. There is presently a practice running rampant across the country called "ordering," when a licensed manufacturer accepts orders from anyone other than a record company executive to have an RIAA certified award made. This has led to an explosion of hologram and 'R' hologram awards being produced that threaten the collectibility, value and, most importantly, the merit of these two formats.

This unfortunate turn of events has led to the gradual lessening of the prestige of owning awards in general with the latter two hologram styles taking the biggest fall in popularity. While many dealers defend ordering awards as a practice, it devalues the awards. I therefore recommend that, when purchasing an award, the prospective buyer should ask the seller if the award was ordered for the purpose of resale or was it obtained from a "legitimate" recipient. You should always deal with a seller who *will* tell you the truth as there is virtually no difference between the ordered awards and the presented awards *because they were made in the same place!*

The RIAA is presently taking steps to reduce illegitimate orders: Soon all RIAA hologram awards will carry a serial number which will assist in keeping track of all awards made in the future. In the meantime, they have assigned a representative to assist both sellers and buyers in determining whether or not a given award *was certified* at a certain level. Interested parties can write Angela Corio at 1020 Nineteenth Street, Suite 200, Washington, D.C. 20036 or phone 202-775-0101. Keep in mind that she is only able to assist in verifying certification, *not authenticity.* For that you must turn to a knowledgeable, and trusted, expert. . .

7. Condition. The condition of the award is vital: *Everybody* wants *everything* mint and award collectors are no exception. White matte collectors are particularly fussy, sometimes wanting only items that have never been repaired, even if the matte is yellowing. Personally, I would rather have an item that has been restored and looks beautiful than one that is original but looks terrible. (It is best *not* to attempt to repair an award unless you are qualified.)

When buying any award be sure the award is the original format (i.e., the style of the award offered for sale is consistent with the style of the period in which it was presented). The original format containing the original label of the record being certified will usually be the most collectible. Another point to remember is that record companies have been known to reframe awards in a style other than the prevailing format. This was often done to replace damaged frames or the requisite frame was unavailable at the time. Before 1989, when formats were still under strict control, this practice was not met with favor by the RIAA and generally discouraged.

From a collecting point of view it is better to buy an award in its original frame whenever possible. When white mattes are found with different frames the diligent collector will often replace the frame with an original from that period, especially if it is a highly desirable title. As a matter of fact, serious collectors have been known to use parts of a white matte of a less desirable artist to restore an award of an artist of greater value.

There *are* framed gold records that do not indicate any type of music organization recognizing the sales achievement. These are not awards produced by any framing store, trophy and plaque shop, or RIAA certified manufacturers. They are made by specialist establishments for one purpose, resale. The popularity of award collecting and the desire to own a trophy has caused the manufacture of these wall-hangings to escalate. These gold records are usually identifiable by the lack of any music industry seal on the plaque. The most widely distributed of these are the [admittedly beautiful] plaques produced by California Gold Records, now located in New Jersey. This company has produced a gold record for almost every title in The Beatles' catalog. However, as of this writing the company has discontinued all framed gold records of Beatles' records with the exception of a numbered "collectible" for John Lennon's "Imagine" single.

As the hobby develops, new and unusual awards are uncovered. Recently discovered was an award produced by a band and presented to the radio station disc jockey responsible for "breaking" their first certified gold single. Since this item is neither RIAA nor in-house, it represents a new classification where the "organization" recognizing the sales achievement is the artist itself!

Finally, when purchasing an award, compare prices which may vary widely. Consider all the factors mentioned above and be certain to consider the seller's reputation. A good price is a bad buy if you receive a bogus award (or, worse, no award at all). Currently, awards sell for as little as $10 to as much as $20,000. Remember, white mattes appear to be the best investment; while later awards can be enjoyable to own, because of the large amounts legitimately ordered and manufactured it is still uncertain as to the investment potential of awards since the strip plate format. My parting advice is to purchase the best awards you can afford but don't forget that collecting is *supposed* to be fun. Sometimes the best thing to own is simply the title you like the most. . .

Genuine, Pirate & Fake RIAA Awards: What Is Real And What Is A Fake

By Christopher Chatman

[Editor's Note: It is recommended that before you read this article that you first read "Collecting Gold & Platinum Record Awards" in this book. To avoid confusion, when Mr. Chatman refers to a genuine award the word is capitalized as "Award;" when referring to the others, it is not.]

The proliferation of the sale of pirate and fake RIAA gold and platinum record "awards" has become epidemic in the last eighteen months. Fueled by an ever increasing demand and a short supply of genuine awards, the marketplace for RIAA Awards has become flooded with frauds. The combined number of pirate and fake RIAA awards offered for sale now probably equals or exceeds the number of genuine RIAA Awards available in the collectors' marketplace in any given month. In the last year, every RIAA format, including the coveted white matte format, has been either pirated or fraudulently manufactured.

The business of dealing in pirate and fake RIAA awards has become a high profit industry, with the cost of manufacturing these frauds between $50 and $100 and then being offered for sale in the $300-500 range. A fake white matte may be offered for $600 to $2,000 or more! To further the distribution of accurate consumer information, the following guidelines and definitions are being offered in the hope of stemming the tide of these frauds as well as preserving the values of genuine RIAA Record Awards.

Genuine RIAA Records Awards

In order to truly understand what pirate and fake RIAA Awards are, let us first examine the process by which genuine RIAA Awards come into existence. The word "genuine" is described in *Webster's' New 20th Century Dictionary* as "really being what it is said to be; actually coming from the alleged source or origin; real; true; not counterfeit or artificial." A genuine RIAA Award is an award for a record or CD that has been certified by the RIAA, originates from a licensed RIAA Award manufacturer, *and has been distributed in accordance with the regulations specified in the license granted by the RIAA to the manufacturer.*

The first step a record company must take in order to have a record or CD certified by the RIAA is for the company to request that an audit be conducted by the RIAA of the company's sales records to determine that a record or CD has reached RIAA gold, platinum or multi-platinum status. Once the record company has received official RIAA status, the company then has the authorization to order an RIAA certified award from an RIAA licensed award manufacturer. One or more record executives at any given record company may be authorized to order RIAA Awards from an RIAA licensed award manufacturer.A licensing fee is paid by each RIAA licensed manufacturer on a yearly basis.

RIAA licensed award manufacturers are required to keep records of how many RIAA Awards they make. An additional fee is paid by the manufacturer for each award affixed with the [current] RIAA logo. (As of September 1994, that is the logo that looks like the letter 'R' in a hologram pattern.) The award is made according to the specifications spelled out by the record company with the presentation made out to whomever those specifications indicate. The finished award is then usually sent back to the record company, in care of the record company executive who ordered it, who may retain or delegate the responsibility of seeing to it that the award is delivered to whomever the award is presented.

As of September 1994, that is how *genuine* RIAA Awards are legitimately manufactured and distributed. Unless given specific permission to do otherwise by an authorized record company executive, *RIAA licensed award manufacturers may sell RIAA Awards only to the record companies who order them.* The record company is then the sole legal "distributor."

"Pirate" RIAA Record & CD Awards

Webster's defines the word "pirate" as a verb meaning "to publish or use in violation of a copyright or patent." A pirate award is one that has been manufactured or distributed in violation of the license agreement between the RIAA and the RIAA licensed manufacturer. Awards that have been sold by a licensed RIAA manufacturer "out the back door," to various individuals or organizations for resale to the marketplace are pirate awards.

For the past few years, the massive influx of pirate awards from licensed RIAA manufacturers into the collectors' market has adversely affected the value of genuine RIAA Awards. With the sudden, dramatic rise in popularity of award collecting in the late '80s, many collectors and dealers alike were frustrated by the scarcity of genuine RIAA Record Awards. The response of many dealers was to appeal to record company executives and have that executive order extra awards which the dealer would then purchase. In some cases, the executives actually contacted record dealers offering RIAA Awards for sale, probably ab abuse of their position as record company executives. But these RIAA Awards at least went through the established channels as required by the RIAA license granted to the RIAA Award makers.

Unfortunately, other record dealers decided to go directly to the RIAA licensed award makers and seduce them into manufacturing pirate awards for whatever artists they wished. Some dealers have reported licensed RIAA manufacturers offering them *any* award they want and in *any* quantity for which they are willing to pay.

At first, licensed RIAA Award makers that succumbed to the lure of greatly increased sales would only pirate RIAA Awards presented to fictitious persons or radio stations. However, as the demand for better presentations increased, the RIAA Award manufacturers began to pirate RIAA awards made out to the record company and, eventually, to the artist. These pirates can be identical in every way to genuine RIAA Awards, *but most do not have the manufacture's tag on the back,* because the award maker will usually try to avoid having the pirate award traced back to his company. (This situation may have changed recently and pirate awards may indeed have the manufacturer's tag on the back.)

Since, in the case of Hologram and 'R'-Hologram format awards in particular there may be no physical difference between genuine and pirate awards, dealers selling pirate awards have asked me "What is the difference?" The difference between genuine and pirate awards is the difference between reality and illusion; between legitimacy and fraud; between owning a rare promotional treasure and owning something that purports to be promotional, but is actually just a wall hanging than anyone with money can buy.

Pirate awards are "ordered" and marketed to the public with the explanation that they are overruns of genuine awards, meaning that a licensed RIAA manufacturer made too many awards and sold the extras to the record dealer, who offers them for sale. According to Angela Corio − − − her position?− − of the RIAA, this method of disposing of extra awards is totally illegal. In the rare event that a licensed RIAA Award manufacturer does happen to make too many of a given award, the manufacturer is required to either sell the extras to the record company or to destroy them. The selling of these overruns to record dealers who then sell them to the public violates the distribution guidelines in the licensing agreement between the RIAA and manufacturers and makes overruns the same as a pirate award.

"Fake" RIAA Record & CD Awards

The word "fake" is defined in *Webster's* as "fraudulent; not genuine; sham; false." A fake RIAA record or CD award is exactly what the term implies; that is, a totally fraudulent imitation of an RIAA Award. In the last two years, it has become increasingly important to collectors and investors that RIAA Awards be in their original format. Also, with record prices being fetched for certain white matte awards, the demand for this format has skyrocketed.

Corrupt salespersons and award makers responded by the creation of fake RIAA awards, which are total fabrications of every format of genuine awards, including the white mattes. There are even reports that some of these fakes are being manufactured by licensed RIAA manufacturers, claiming that they have the right to reissue *(sic)* old formats of RIAA Awards. However, according to Ms. Corio, the RIAA has *never* licensed the use of the older RIAA trademarks in any recently constructed award, nor do they plan to in the future. Therefore, *any* old format awards recently constructed by anyone, *licensed or not,* are totally fraudulent! They are fakes being sold to soak unsuspecting consumers for large sums of money.

This current wave of fakes being dumped on the market are made of components that resemble those of genuine RIAA Awards enough so that they cannot be easily identified by studying a photograph of the item. and personal examination by an expert may be required. Fakes of older format RIAA Awards may be identified by the use of new construction materials. In other words, they look brand new. These fakes may be identified by the lack of a manufacturers' tag on the back. If there is a tag, it will also look brand new. In the case of white mattes, fakes can be rather obvious, since the last real white matte RIAA Award was presented twenty years ago. . .

Fakes of older format RIAA Awards may also have laser photocopies of the record labels. Laser photocopies weren't used until the mid to late '80s, so the use of them in a white matte, floater or strip-plate RIAA Award is a dead giveaway that the award has either recently undergone major reconstruction due to damage or is a fake.

This surge of new and improved fakes has had a deleterious effect on the market for all genuine RIAA Awards. Since museum quality photographs on quality paper of genuine RIAA Awards in each format have not yet been made available, the opportunity for fraud is great. Extreme caution in the purchase of older format fakes of awards is strongly recommended.

The large number of fake and pirate awards infesting the marketplace is both criminal and tragic. Unsuspecting and uninformed collectors and investors are being cheated because earnest people pay for something which they do not receive. Measures *are being taken* to alleviate this unfortunate state of affairs. In the meantime, each purchaser of a proposed RIAA Award should insist on a written guarantee from the seller that the award they are receiving is genuine and that it is not a pirate or a fake. This will provide additional documentation for legal recourse should the item they receive from *any* seller prove to be less than genuine.

Christopher Chatman is the proprietor of Beyond Records, where, aside from rare records, he has been a pioneer in the investigation of such music memorabilia as acetates, test pressings, RIAA Gold and Platinum Record Awards, original cover art and their four-color transparencies.

An Author's Bio

Born to a modest family of registered Democrats in Wilkes-Barre General Hospital in 1951 (Virgo by birth, radical by inclination), I can honestly count Marcel Duchamp and burning culm-banks as pivotal influences on my developing psyche. While my baby-book, long since lost in the Great Flood of '72, claimed my favorite song in my pre-literate years was "Sh-Boom," I remember "Hound Dog". . . Growing up, Wilkes-Barre seemed more a part of the past than the present: I can recall going to the movies on a Saturday afternoon for 15¢ with my brother Charles and good bud Donny Flynn, spending hours absorbing such seminal works of art as *Earth Vs The Flying Saucers* and *The Atomic Submarine, The Mask* and *Dementia 13, The Delicate Delinquent* and *Abbott & Costello Meet The Wolfman,* and the other staples of '50s and '60s matinees.

Way back then, comic books were 32 pages for a dime, 16 oz. RC Colas were 13¢, Tastycakes were, er, tasty, and I whiled many a day away readin' and sippin' in awe of The Fantastic Four, Batman, and especially Steve Ditko's Dr. Strange and Spiderman. By twelve I had passed through dinosaurs (a phase I joyfully find my six-year old daughter, Ananda, locked in today— she wants to be a Tyranosauus Rex for Halloween), the Civil War, military aircraft of the War To End All Wars (ho ho), and baseball cards. I was ready for something new. . .

I discovered the magic of the "elpee" in 1964 when I found that the big-record-with-the-little-hole played several songs before I had to get up and turn it over. Wow! My record collecting career began with the atrocious "electronically reprocessed stereo" reissues of *Elvis' Golden Records 1* and *2* and greatest hits collections of Chuck Berry, Little Richard, Fats Domino, Jerry Lee Lewis, and The Platters. As Northeastern Pennsylvania was a dumping grounds for cut-outs (all most of us could afford), I was able to pick up anything deleted, which is where my exposure to jazz came from.

Over the course of the next few years my nascent collection grew in rather odd directions: As both my brother, Charles, and my Aunt Judy were members of mail order record clubs, through cast-offs and trades I acquired such essentials as Gary Lewis & The Playboys' *Golden Grass* (still a favorite; Jerry's kid may not have had the world's greatest pipes but he had some of this planet's finest talents supporting him), The Dave Clark Five's *Coast To Coast* (which poses the burning question "Can an LP be less than twelve minutes per side and still be worth the money?" and leaves it unanswered) and Nancy "Yeah, Frank's m'dad but I love 'im anyway" Sinatra's *How Does That Grab You, Darlin'?*

I gradually learned to love an awfully broad spectrum of rock and pop music. (Although, as a pseudo-intellectual acne-ed white teenager I could not for the life of me figure out what alla those black people were moanin' n' groanin', wailin' n' railin', screechin' n' beseechin' about. Like *real* country music, that took a little maturation to make sense. . .) When the British Invasion hit I somehow managed to avoid the charm of The Beatles and The Stones. Don't ask me how; I was, how shall I put it, oh, headstrong? While my contemporaries were wearing the grooves out of The Beatles and The Stones— and, let's never forget Herman's Hermits— I stuck to the "old" stuff:

In 1965 The Byrds' "Mr. Tambourine Man" turned my entire perception of pop music inside out and I spent the next fifteen years or so listening exclusively to the Rock-With-A-Capital-R of the '60s: I became an avid reader of Paul Williams' *Crawdaddy*, which, more than anything else, helped shape my opinions on Rock-with-a-capitol-R. I had discovered *Pet Sounds*, the album that has remained #1 in my heart for more than two decades, and such generally overlooked gems as the debut albums of Buffalo Springfield, the Byrds, Captain Beefheart, Dylan, Jefferson Airplane, Love, the Spoonful, Van Dyke Parks, and the Youngbloods remain favorites decades later. Still I religiously purchased each new [cheesy] Elvis soundtrack, but the necessity of taking home *Frankie And Johnnie* and *Spinout* in brown paper bags eventually woke up even this slow learner.

At a Christmas party in 1967 some noise blurted out of the speakers that had me entranced: "Why don't we sing this song all together, open our heads let the pictures come. . ." I figured it might be time for me to renege on my vow never to buy a record with Mick Jagger on it. Through the past two decades I have grown rather detached from the merchandising aspect of the biz, constantly reminding myself that it was to get away from alla the Mad Ave bullschidt that allowed rock 'n roll to occur. Still, albums such as *Born To Run*, *Armed Forces*, *Remain In Light*, *Dream Of Life* and *Skylarking* keep my hopes up.

Current non-musical obsessions include but are not limited to hiking the mountains of the Pacific Northwest; dreaming of pizza from Arcaro & Jenell's in Old Forge, PA; old movies with Fred Astaire, Jean Arthur, Carol Lombard and particularly Cary Grant; tall women who work out; books on mind-manifesting agents; rereading all of James Clavell's novels and the complete *Cerebus The Aardvark*; and ranting at the lunatic behavior of the owners of Major League Baseball teams.

As for my origins as record collecting's "pricing guru," well. . . In 1983 I was drafted out of art classes for duty on the O' Sullivan Woodside line of record collectors price guides. This was caused by the the departure of the former editor and the need for someone who knew the field in a broad sense; was capable of doing the necessary work; and, most importantly, was readily available! I authored the controversial and iconoclastic *1985-86 Rock Records Album Price Guide* and the *1985-86 Elvis Presley Record Price Guide* before that company's premature demise. In 1985 I inaugurated the *Goldmine* line of price guides for record collectors: *Goldmine's Price Guide To Collectible Record Album*, *Goldmine 45RPM Rock'n Roll Record Price Guide*, and this jazz book you are holding (with more in the future).

I am also associated with White Dragon Press, for whom I produced *A Touch Of Gold: The Elvis Presley Record & Memorabilia Price Guide* and for whom I am completing *Rhythm & Blues: A Discography & Price Guide 1949-1959*, due in the summer of 1994, and, in the not too distant future, *Movie Music: A Discography & Price Guide To Soundtrack Albums*, which will also cover television and original cast recordings. . .